CW00690051

Oxf

Phrasal Verbs

Dictionary

for learners of English

OXFORD
UNIVERSITY PRESS

UNIVERSITY PRESS

Great Clarendon Street, Oxford OX2 6DP

Oxford University Press is a department of the University of Oxford.
It furthers the University's objective of excellence in research, scholarship,
and education by publishing worldwide in

Oxford New York

Auckland Bangkok Buenos Aires Cape Town Chennai Dar es Salaam Delhi
Hong Kong Istanbul Karachi Kolkata Kuala Lumpur Madrid Melbourne
Mexico City Mumbai Nairobi São Paulo Shanghai Taipei Tokyo Toronto

OXFORD and OXFORD ENGLISH are registered trade marks of
Oxford University Press in the UK and in certain other countries

© Oxford University Press 2006
Database right Oxford University Press (maker)

First published 2001
Second edition 2006
2010 2009 2008 2007 2006
10 9 8 7 6 5 4 3 2 1

Photocopying

ISBN-13: 978 0 19 431721 4
ISBN-10: 0 19 431721 8

Text capture and typesetting by Oxford University Press
Printed in China

ACKNOWLEDGEMENTS

Edited by: Colin McIntosh

Contents

Labels used in the dictionary

disapproving   verbs show that you feel disapproval or contempt, for example *dumb sth down, flash sth about.*

figurative   a figurative example is one in which language is used in a non-literal or metaphorical way, as in *His anger blazed up* (= suddenly became very strong) *uncontrollably.*

formal   verbs are usually only used in serious or official language and would not be appropriate in normal everyday conversation. Examples are *abide by sth, embark on/upon sth, vie for sth.*

humorous   expressions are intended to be funny, for example *toddle off.*

informal   verbs are used between friends or in a relaxed or unofficial situation. They are not appropriate for formal situations. Examples are *bang on about sth, kick back, tuck into sth.*

ironic   language uses words to mean the opposite of the meaning that they seem to have, as in *I tried to mend my watch, but only succeeded in breaking it.*

less formal   synonyms are verbs that have a similar meaning to the main phrasal verb, but are used in less official situations or are more common in normal everyday conversation.

less frequent   verbs or grammar patterns are not used as often as the main phrasal verb or the other grammar patterns given.

literary   verbs are used mainly in literature and imaginative writing. Examples are *yearn for sb/sth, eke out sth.*

more formal   verbs have a similar meaning to the main phrasal verb, but are usually used in more serious or official situations, or in a less casual way.

old-fashioned   verbs are passing out of current use, for example *buck up, gad about/around, run along.*

rare   verbs or grammar patterns are not commonly used.

slang   is very informal language, mainly used in speaking and sometimes restricted to a particular group of people, for example people of the same age or those who have similar interests or do the same job. Examples are *knock sb off, shoot up.*

taboo   verbs and expressions are likely to be thought by many people to be obscene or shocking. You should avoid using them. They are indicated by this symbol in the dictionary: ⚠.

Key to the dictionary entries

Main parts of a phrasal verb entry

Information in the dictionary is given in entries, arranged in the alphabetical order of the verbs and then in the alphabetical order of the particles.

Head verb, with pronunciation ——

Phrasal verb, showing the main forms and stress (see page 394), followed by the definition

Examples, showing how the phrasal verb is used in context, with common phrases in **bold type**

Irregular forms of the verb, with variants

Using the phrasal verb

The dictionary gives further information to help you use the phrasal verb correctly and appropriately.

Key symbol, showing that this is an important phrasal verb

Synonyms and **opposites**, given in alphabetical order

---

bask /bɑːsk/

ˈ**bask in sth** to enjoy the good feelings that you have when other people praise or admire you, or when they give you a lot of attention: *He had always basked in his parents' attention.* ◇ *I never minded **basking in** my wife's **reflected glory*** (= enjoying the praise, attention, etc. she got).
♦ v + prep

---

dive /daɪv/ (**dived**, **dived**, *AmE also* **dove** /dəʊv/; *AmE* doʊv/, **dived**)

ˌ**dive ˈin**; ˌ**dive ˈinto sth 1** (*informal*) to start doing sth with enthusiasm and without stopping to think: *She dived in with a question before I had finished speaking.* ◇ *They had dived into the new business without thinking it through.*

ˌ**blow ˈup 1** to explode; to be destroyed by an explosion: *The bomb blew up as experts tried to defuse it.* ◇ *The car blew up when it hit the wall.*
SYN **explode** (*more formal*) ➲ note on page 22
2 to start suddenly and with force: *A storm blew up just after the ship left port.* ◇ *A row has blown up over the leaking of information to the press.*
OPP **die down 3** (**at sb**) (*informal*) to become very angry: *My mum blew up at my dad for keeping me up so late.* ◇ *His attitude annoyed me and I blew up.*

Geographical label, showing where the phrasal verb is used

Register label, showing whether the phrasal verb is formal, informal, etc.

,rock 'up (*BrE*, *AustralE*, *informal*) to arrive, especially in a relaxed way or without giving advance warning: *You can't just rock up to that kind of restaurant without booking—they're very selective.*
SYN **roll up** (*informal*)
• v + adv

Collocations, showing frequent subjects and objects, given in order of frequency

Grammar patterns, showing how the verb is used (see page xi)

,lock 'onto sth (*also* ,lock 'in on sth) if a weapon that is sent through the air **locks onto** sth or **is locked onto** sth that it is aimed at, it finds it and follows it: *The missile can lock onto a target from a kilometre away.* ◇ *The missile was locked onto the target.* **SUBJ** **missile** **OBJ** **target**
• v + prep • v + adv + prep

Building your vocabulary

The dictionary also contains a lot of information that will help you increase your vocabulary and use the language productively.

Note, giving further information about grammar and usage

Idioms section, showing idiomatic phrases in which the phrasal verb is used

Derivatives section, showing nouns or adjectives which come from the phrasal verb

,lie 'down to be or move into a horizontal position on a bed, etc. in order to sleep or rest: *Go and lie down for a while.* ◇ *He lay down on the sofa and went to sleep.* ◇ *The coughing is worse when he's lying down.* ◇ *She was lying down on the bed.*
NOTE Do not confuse this sense of **lie down** with **lay sth down**, which must always have an object: *I'm going to lie down for a while* (not *I'm going to lay down for a while*). ◇ *They were told to lay their guns down* (not *They were told to lie their guns down*).
• v + adv
IDM **lie down on the 'job** to not do sth that you are responsible for doing or expected to do: *Someone at City Hall is obviously lying down on the job, or this would be done by now.* **take sth lying 'down** to accept an insult, a criticism, a violent attack, etc. without protesting or reacting to it: *He has been accused of bribery, but he won't take this lying down.*
▶ ,lie-'down *n* [sing.] (*BrE*, *informal*) a short rest, especially in bed: *to have a lie-down*

Synonym notes

These notes, printed against a blue background, compare phrasal verbs and single-word verbs which have a similar meaning, helping you to choose the verb which is most appropriate.

fall down

Heading, listing the verbs which are being compared

cave in ◆ collapse ◆ **fall down** ◆ **fall over** ◆ **topple over**

These verbs are all used to talk about buildings and other structures falling to the ground.

General meaning, showing what all the verbs have in common

cave in (of a roof, wall, etc.) to fall down and towards the centre: *The ceiling suddenly caved in on top of them.*

Definition of each verb

collapse (of a building, etc.) to fall down or fall in suddenly, often after breaking apart: *The roof collapsed under the weight of snow.*

fall down to suddenly stop standing: *The house looked as if it was about to fall down.*

fall over to become unsteady and fall down: *I thought I was going to fall over.* ◇ *The chair had fallen over.*

topple over to become unsteady and fall down: *The pile of books toppled over.*

WHICH WORD?

Which word? **section**, outlining some of the important differences between the verbs

Only **fall down** and **collapse** can be used to talk about whole buildings. **Cave in** is used with parts of buildings, and **fall over** and **topple over** are used to talk about other structures.

PATTERNS AND COLLOCATIONS

Patterns and collocations, showing the most important words and grammar patterns used with each verb

- a **building/house** falls down/collapses
- a **roof/wall/ceiling** collapses/caves in
- to **completely/suddenly** collapse
- to **be about to** fall down/fall over/collapse/cave in/topple over

Guide to using the dictionary

Finding verbs in the dictionary

1 What is in the dictionary?

In this dictionary we include several different types of verbs that are used with adverbs or prepositions (often called *particles*).

a Idiomatic verb + particle combinations. Sometimes when you meet combinations of verb and particle, it is impossible to guess the meaning in the context from the meaning of the verb and the meaning of the particle. Examples of these are **fall through** (meaning 'not happen') and **put up with somebody** (meaning 'accept somebody who is annoying without complaining'). There is often a single-word verb with the same meaning. Single-word verbs, however, may be more formal than the phrasal verb, or used in slightly different contexts.

b Verbs which are always followed by a particular particle. Examples of these are **rely on**, **crop up**, **abide by**. These cannot be used without the particle.

c Verbs that are followed by a particle in a particular meaning. These verbs can be used on their own without a particle, but have a different meaning when they are used with one. **Brush sth up** is an example of a verb like this. **Brush sth** can be used on its own meaning 'clean, polish or make sth smooth'. **Brush sth up** means 'study or practise sth to get back the skill or knowledge that you had in the past': *You should brush up your French before you go to France.* Other examples are **nod/nod off**, **grow/grow up**, **walk/walk out**.

Many very common verbs fall into this group. **Look**, for example, can be used with several different particles, and it has a special meaning with each one that is different from **look** on its own.

Some more formal verbs also fall into this group. For example you can *furnish a room*, that is, put furniture in it, but if you *furnish somebody with something* you are giving them some useful information.

d Verbs with a particle, where the particle adds to, but does not change, the basic meaning of the verb. The particle often adds something to the meaning, such as completeness. For example, **finish off**, as opposed to **finish**, emphasizes that you are completing your work. Other examples are **spread/spread out**, **fade/fade away**, **slave/slave away**. You will find more information about the meaning of the particles in the *Guide to the Particles* on page 380.

e Verbs plus particles where each has their normal meaning.
Phone back (meaning 'telephone sb again') is an example of a verb
like this. The meaning of **phone back** can be worked out from the
meaning of **phone** and **back**. Verbs of this type have been included
in the dictionary where the combination of verb and particle are
very common, or where there is something unusual or interesting
about the verb. For example, **phone back** can mean two slightly
different things ('telephone somebody who has called you', or
'telephone sb for a second time').

2 Particles

These are the particles used with phrasal verbs in this dictionary.
You will find more information about the most common particles
in the *Guide to the Particles* on page 380.

aback	along	back	forward	out	towards
about	among	before	from	out of	under
above	apart	behind	in	over	up
across	around	between	into	past	upon
after	as	by	of	round	with
against	aside	down	off	through	without
ahead	at	for	on	to	
ahead of	away	forth	onto	together	

3 Finding the verb you want

The phrasal verbs are arranged in the dictionary under their head
verbs (for example **give**, **move**, **sit**) and then in alphabetical order of
the particles. Within each particle you will first find the verb +
particle, with no object. Then there are meanings of the verb that
can be used both without an object and with an object. After that,
there are meanings of the verb used only with an object, first verbs
with people as objects (sb), then verbs that can have people or things
(sb/sth) and then verbs with only things as objects (sth). Verbs with
itself, *yourself*, etc. come at the end of those, and verbs that are only
used in passive forms will be last. For example:

give up; give sth up	break in	put sb out
give sb up	break sb/sth in	put sth out
give sth up	break sth in	put yourself out
give yourself up	break into sth	be put out

Using phrasal verbs

1 The phrasal verb

The arrangement of the verbs in the dictionary will tell you whether they can be used without an object (*intransitive*), with an object (*transitive*), or both with and without an object. Look at the the the entry for **break down**. It shows you that in this meaning **break down** is an intransitive verb, used without an object (*My car broke down on the way to work this morning*).

> **ᵧ break 'down 1** if a vehicle, etc. **breaks down**, it stops working because of a fault: *The washing machine has broken down again.* ◇ *We* (= our car) *broke down twice on the way home.*

There are two forms of the verb at **burn down**. This shows you that you can use burn down as a transitive and an intransitive verb in this meaning.

> **ᵧ burn 'down; burn sth 'down** if a building **burns down**, or sb **burns it down**, it is destroyed by fire: *The palace burnt down in the 19th century.* ◇ *She threatened to burn the house down.*

Look at the entry for **freshen up**. This tells you that you can use it as an intransitive verb with an object (*I'd like to freshen up*) or with **yourself** (*I'd like to freshen myself up*).

> **freshen 'up; freshen yourself 'up** to wash and make yourself look clean and tidy after a journey, before a meeting, etc.: *I'll just freshen* (*myself*) *up before dinner.*

At **keep out**, the entry tells you that in this meaning you can use the verb on its own (*Danger! Keep out!*) or as a transitive verb with the adverb + preposition **out of**, followed by a noun or pronoun (*Keep out of my way!*).

> **ᵧ keep 'out; keep 'out of sth** to not enter a place; to remain outside: *There was a sign saying 'Keep out!'.* ◇ *Please keep out of the office while I'm working.*

The entry for **rush into** tells you that the verb can also be used with an *-ing* form of a verb that follows it (*Don't rush into leaving your course*).

> **rush 'into sth; rush 'into doing sth; rush sb 'into doing sth** to do or decide sth quickly without thinking about it carefully; to make sb do this: *Don't go rushing into anything.*

2 Synonyms and opposites.

When there are helpful synonyms or opposites, these are given in alphabetical order. As the contexts that the synonyms are used in may not always be exactly the same as the original phrasal verb, it is worth looking them up in the dictionary to be sure that you understand how they are used. For example, while **knock down** can be used instead of **break down** in the examples given there, **break down** cannot always be used instead of **knock down**.

3 Grammar patterns of phrasal verbs

To help you use the verbs correctly, a simple system of grammar patterns is given after each one. These show you how the verb combines with an adverb, a preposition, a noun or a pronoun, an infinitive, etc. and the order in which these words can occur. These are the short forms which are used:

adv	=	adverb
inf	=	infinitive (without 'to' e.g. *do*)
-ing	=	a verb form ending in -ing (e.g. *doing*)
n	=	noun
n/pron	=	noun or pronoun
prep	=	preposition
pron	=	pronoun
to inf	=	infinitive with 'to' (e.g. *to do*)
v	=	verb

The following are the most common types of verb patterns used in the dictionary.

v + adv	Intransitive verbs, for example:	
	break down	*My car broke down this morning.*
	sit down	*Come in and sit down.*
v + prep	These are verbs followed by a preposition. For example:	
	rely on sb/sth	*You can rely on me.*
	call for sb	*I'll call for you at eight.*
v + adv + prep	These verbs are followed by an adverb and a preposition:	
	put up with sb/sth	*How do you put up with him?*
	keep out of sth	*Keep out of the kitchen.*

These last two groups are sometimes called *inseparable verbs* as the object always follows the particle.

v + n/pron + adv v + adv + n v + pron + adv	These three patterns are all used with transitive verbs. The patterns show you where to put the object. The most frequent patterns come first. **tear sth up** *She tore the letter up. She tore up the letter. She tore it up.*
v + n/pron + adv v + adv + n	Verbs that can be used with these patterns, where the object can go either between the verb and the particle or after the particle, are sometimes called *separable verbs*. For example: **tear sth up** *She tore the letter up. She tore up the letter. She tore it up.* When the object is a long phrase, it usually comes after the particle: *She tore up all the letters he had sent her.* When the object is a pronoun, it must come between the verb and the particle: *She tore them up.*
v + adv + n v + pron + adv	With some phrasal verbs the object can only come between the verb and the particle when it is a pronoun. A noun must follow the particle. **fight back sth** *I tried to fight back my tears. I wanted to scream but fought it back.*
v + n/pron + adv	There are a few phrasal verbs in which the two parts of the verb must be separated by the object. **mess sb about/around** *They changed the flight time and messed the passengers around.*
v + n/pron + prep	**drill sth into sb** *The teacher drilled grammar into us.*
be/get + v + adv be/get + v + prep	A few phrasal verbs are only used in the passive. For example, **be/get carried away** has the pattern **be/get + v + adv**, and **be/get stuck with sth** has the pattern **be/get + v + prep**. Often a note will tell you if a phrasal verb is commonly used in the passive.

A a

abide /əˈbaɪd/

a'bide by sth (*formal*) to accept a rule, a law, an agreement, a decision, etc. and obey it: *Members must abide by the rules of the club.*
[OBJ] **rules, decision, the law** [SYN] **comply (with sth)**
◆ v + prep

abound /əˈbaʊnd/

a'bound in/with sth to have a lot of sth; to contain a lot of sth: *The rivers there abound in/ with fish.*
◆ v + prep

abstain /əbˈsteɪn/

ab'stain from sth; ab'stain from doing sth to decide not to do or have sth, especially sth that you like or enjoy, because it is bad for your health or considered morally wrong: *Pregnant women are advised to abstain from alcohol.*
[OBJ] **alcohol, sex, drugs**
◆ v + prep

accede /əkˈsiːd/

ac'cede to sth (*formal*) to agree to or allow sth that sb has asked for, often after you have opposed it for a while: *The government acceded to public pressure to review the tax.* ◇ *Have all our requests been acceded to?*
[OBJ] **request, demands, pressure**
↻ note at AGREE TO STH
◆ v + prep

account /əˈkaʊnt/

ac'count for sb/sth to know where sb/sth is or what has happened to them, especially after an accident or a natural disaster: *All the people who were working in the building have now been accounted for.* ◇ *There are three files that I can't account for.*
[NOTE] Often used in the passive.
◆ v + prep

ac'count for sth **1** to explain how or why sth happened; to be the explanation for sth: *How do you* ***account for the fact that*** *the box has disappeared?* ◇ *Poor hygiene may have accounted for the spread of the disease.* **2** to be a particular part of sth; to be a particular amount: *Car crime accounted for 28% of all reported offences.* ◇ *Wages account for less than half of the budget.* [SYN] **make up sth; represent sth 3** to keep a record of how the money in your care will be spent or has been spent: *Every penny of the funds is accounted for.* **4** to consider particular facts or circumstances when you are making a decision about sth, especially when you are calculating the cost of sth: *The cost of the film was accounted for in the calculation of the cost of the service.* [SYN] **take sth into account**
◆ v + prep

[IDM] there's no ac'counting for 'taste used to say that it is impossible to know why sb likes sb/ sth that you do not like: (*humorous*) 'She seems to like you.' 'Well—there's no accounting for taste!'

accustom /əˈkʌstəm/

ac'custom sb/yourself to sth; ac'custom sb/yourself to doing sth (*formal*) to make sb/yourself familiar with sth; to become used to sth: *It took a while for her eyes to accustom themselves to the dark.* ◇ *It shouldn't take long to accustom your students to working in groups.*
◆ v + n/pron + prep

ace /eɪs/

ace sb 'out (*AmE, informal*) to defeat sb in order to obtain an important position or rank: *The company aced out its biggest rival to win the contract.*
◆ v + adv + n ◆ v + n/pron + adv

ache /eɪk/

'ache for sb/sth to have a strong desire for sb/ sth or to do sth: *I was aching for home.*
[SYN] **long for sb/sth**
◆ v + prep

acquaint /əˈkweɪnt/

ac'quaint sb/yourself with sth (*formal*) to make sb/yourself familiar with or aware of sth: *He decided to take his son along and acquaint him with the business.*
◆ v + n/pron + prep

act /ækt/

'act as sth to perform a particular role or function: *Will you act as interpreter for us?* ◇ *Large fines act as a deterrent to motorists.*
[OBJ] **agent, consultant, intermediary, go-between, deterrent** [SYN] **serve as sth**
◆ v + prep

'act for sb (*also* ,act on be'half of sb, ,act on sb's be'half) if sb acts for you or acts on behalf of you, they deal with your affairs for you, for example by representing you in court, or by doing your duty when you are not able to: *Do you have a solicitor acting for you?* ◇ *The Prince was acting on behalf of the Queen.* ◇ *The Prince was acting on the Queen's behalf.*
[OBJ] **client**
◆ v + prep

'act on sth (*also* 'act upon sth *more formal*) **1** to do sth as a result of advice, information, instructions, etc. that you have received: *The police were acting on information from a member of the public.* ◇ *I was just acting on instructions.*

◇ *If my advice had been acted upon, this would never have happened.* [OBJ] **advice**, **information**, **instructions 2** to have an effect on sth: *The drug acts on the central nervous system.*
◆ v + prep

act on be'half of sb; **act on sb's be'half** → ACT FOR SB

act sth 'out 1 to perform a story or events that have happened or might happen, as if you are performing a play: *The teacher read a story and the children acted it out.* ◇ *She acted out her fantasies of pop stardom in front of her bedroom mirror.* ◇ (*figurative*) *The whole nation was following the drama being acted out on the football field.* [OBJ] **story**, **fantasy 2** to act a part in real life: *I found myself acting out the role of good, brave patient.* **3** (*technical*) to express your thoughts and feelings in your behaviour, often without being aware of it
◆ v + adv + n ◆ v + n/pron + adv

act 'up (*informal*) **1** to make sb annoyed by behaving badly, trying to get attention, etc.: *The kids have been acting up all day.* **2** if a machine or part of the body **acts up**, it does not work as it should: *The car's acting up again.* ◇ *My ankle is acting up* (= is painful and causing problems).
[SYN] **play up**
[NOTE] Act up is often used in the progressive tenses.
◆ v + adv

act upon sth → ACT ON STH

---

add up to sth

add up to sth ◆ **amount to sth** ◆ **be sth** ◆ **number sth** ◆ **total sth**
These verbs all mean to reach a particular number or amount when all numbers/amounts have been added together.

add up to sth to make a total amount or number of sth: *The numbers add up to exactly 100.* ◇ *Their earnings were £250, £300 and £420, adding up to a total of £970.*

amount to sth (*business*) to reach a particular number or amount when added together: *His earnings amount to £300 000 per annum.*

be sth to be equal to sth: *Three and three is six.* ◇ *How much is a thousand pounds in euros?*

number sth to make a particular number when added together: *The crowd numbered more than a thousand.* ◇ *We numbered 20* (= there were 20 of us in the group).

total sth (*especially business*) to reach a particular number or amount when added

together: *Imports totalled $1.5 billion last year.* ◇ *In 2005–6, college enrolments totalled some 5 400.*

WHICH WORD?

Add up to and **number** can be used to emphasize the process of calculating a total; **total** and **amount to sth** focus more on the number/amount rather than the process of arriving at the result. **Total** and **amount to** are used especially in business writing when describing the performance of a company, etc. **Number** usually has people as the subject of the sentence; **total** is the only other verb that can be used like this: *The crew totalled/numbered sixteen.*

PATTERNS AND COLLOCATIONS

■ to be/total/add up to/amount to/number **50, 2 million**, etc.
■ to be/total/add up to/amount to **$250/75%**
■ **profits/scores** total/add up to/amount to…
■ a **group/crowd** totals/numbers…

---

add /æd/

add sth 'in to include sth with sth else; to put sth into sth else or between two things: *Send me the new figures when the additional costs have been added in.* ◇ *I've added in two extra paragraphs.*
[NOTE] Add can also be used on its own: *I've added a couple of extra paragraphs.*
◆ v + n/pron + adv

add 'on; **add 'on to sth** (*AmE*) to build an extra room or rooms on to a house or other building: *They decided to add on rather than move.*
◆ v + adv ◆ v + adv + prep

add sth 'on; **add sth 'on to sth** to include sth or attach sth extra: *He added £2 on to the bill.*
[NOTE] Add (**to sth**) can also be used with this meaning: *He added £2 to the bill.*
◆ v + n/pron + adv ◆ v + adv + n
◆ v + n/pron + adv + prep

▶ **'add-on** *n* a thing that is added to or included with sth else: *The catalogue advertised add-ons such as extra memory and software.* ◇ *add-on products/pockets/units*

add to sth to increase the size, amount, number, etc. of sth: *Taking the children with us would only add to our problems.* ◇ *Music playing in the background added to the atmosphere.* ◇ (*BrE*) *The house has been added to over the years.* ◇ *The food at the hotel is of a very high standard. Add to this the quality of the rooms*

and the service and it is clear why this is such a popular hotel.
[OBJ] **problems**, **number**, **knowledge**, **enjoyment**
♦ v + prep

,add to'gether; ,add sth to'gether to come together to produce sth; to join two or more things, numbers, etc. together to produce sth: *The games, the dancing and the good food all added together to make a memorable occasion.* ◊ *When all the different factors are added together, I can understand her decision.* ◊ *Add the two numbers together and divide by three.*
[OBJ] **factors**, **numbers**, **costs**
♦ v + adv ♦ v + adv + n ♦ v + n/pron + adv

,add 'up (*informal*) **1** to seem reasonable; to make sense; to have all the different parts agreeing with each other: *There are things in her story that just don't add up.* ◊ *Now that I know where she was last night, it's all beginning to add up.* [NOTE] Add up with this meaning is used especially in negative sentences. **2** to increase gradually to make a large number or amount: *Save a small amount each month; it'll soon add up.* **3** if two or more numbers **add up**, they come to the total that they should or that you would expect: *These figures just don't add up.*
♦ v + adv

🔒,add 'up (*especially BrE*); ,add sth 'up to calculate the total of two or more numbers or amounts: *I never could add up.* ◊ *She's very good at adding up in her head.* ◊ *She added the figures up in no time.* ◊ *I needed to use a calculator to add up the bill.*
[OBJ] **numbers**, **figures**, **score**, **cost**
♦ v + adv ♦ v + adv + n ♦ v + n/pron + adv

,add 'up to sth **1** if two or more numbers or figures **add up to** sth, they make a total of sth when they are added together: *Can you arrange the numbers in groups that add up to 10?* ◊ *The cost of all the equipment you need for a baby adds up to a considerable sum.* **2** (*informal*) to show sth; to have a particular meaning or result: *His evidence didn't really **add up to much** (= gave us very little information).* ◊ *All in all, it adds up to a pretty desperate situation.*
[SYN] **amount to sth**
♦ v + adv + prep

address /ə'dres/

ad'dress yourself to sth (*formal*) to think about a problem or a situation and decide how you are going to deal with it: *We must address ourselves to the problem of traffic pollution.*
♦ v + pron + prep

adhere /əd'hɪə(r)/

ad'here to sth (*formal*) to act in the way that a particular law, rule or set of instructions says that you should; to follow or support a particular opinion or set of beliefs: *They have adhered strictly to the terms of the treaty.* ◊ *He found the diet very difficult to adhere to.* ◊ *How many people actually adhere to this view?* ◊ *All safety requirements must be adhered to.*
[OBJ] **principles**, **rules**, **guidelines** [SYN] **keep to sth** (*less formal*); **stick to sth** (*less formal*)
♦ v + prep

admit /əd'mɪt/ (-tt-)

ad'mit of sth (*formal*) to show that sth such as an explanation or an answer is possible; to

---

admit to sth

admit to sth ♦ **confess to sth** ♦ **fess up (to sth)** ♦ **own up (to sth)**

These verbs all mean to say that you have done sth wrong.

admit to sth to say that you have done sth wrong or illegal: *He admitted to taking the money.* ◊ *He admitted to having taken the money.* [NOTE] Admit can be used on its own: *He admitted taking the money.*

confess to sth to admit, especially formally or to the police, that you have done sth wrong or illegal: *She confessed to the murder.* ◊ *She confessed to killing him.*

fess up (to sth) (*especially AmE*) to admit that you have done sth wrong: *No one has fessed up to eating my chocolates.*

own up (to sth) to admit that you are responsible for sth bad or wrong: *I'm still*

waiting for someone to own up to the breakages.

WHICH WORD?

Own up and **fess up** are used for actions that are not very serious; **confess** is usually used for serious crimes. **Admit** is often used when the person is under pressure to tell the truth. **Admit** and **confess** can also be used to mention a fact that you feel embarrassed or ashamed about: *I must admit I quite like her new look.* ◊ *I confess I have no experience of this.*

PATTERNS AND COLLOCATIONS

- to **freely/openly** confess/admit to sth
- to **readily/frankly** admit to sth
- to be **prepared/ashamed/embarrassed** to admit/confess
- to be **afraid/reluctant** to admit/own up

allow sth to happen: *The situation admits of only one explanation.*

OBJ **explanation, answer** **SYN** **allow of sth**

♦ v + prep

ad'mit to sth; ad'mit to doing sth 1 to say that you have done sth wrong or illegal: *He admits to the other charges.* ◇ *She admitted to having stolen the car.* **2** to agree, often unwillingly, that sth is true: *She admits to being strict with her children.* ➔ note on page 3

♦ v + prep

age /eɪdʒ/

ˌage 'out **(of sth)** (*AmE*) to become older than the age limit stated in a law or in the rules of a system: *How many children aged out of foster care in 2006?*

♦ v + adv

▶ ˌaged-'out *adj* [only before noun] (*AmE*): *aged-out minors*

agree /əˈɡriː/

a'gree to sth to say yes; to say that you will do what sb wants or that you will allow sth to happen: *Do you think he'll agree to their proposal?*

♦ v + prep

a'gree with sb **1** (**about/on sth**) to have the same opinion as sb: *He agreed with them about the need for change.* **2** to make sb feel happy or healthy: *You look great! Marriage obviously agrees with you.* ◇ *Mushrooms don't agree with me* (= they make me feel ill/sick).

♦ v + prep

a'gree with sth (*grammar*) to match a word or phrase in number (= being singular or plural), gender (= being masculine, feminine, etc.), or person (= whether the subject is I, you, etc.): *In French, adjectives agree with their nouns.*

♦ v + prep

a'gree with sth; a'gree with doing sth to approve of sth, especially a policy or a belief: *I don't agree with capital punishment.*

OPP **disagree with sth, etc.**

♦ v + prep

aim /eɪm/

'aim at sb/sth; 'aim sth at sb/sth to point or direct a weapon, a shot, a kick, etc. at sb/sth: *The gun was aimed at his head.* ◇ *The Rovers youngster aimed a shot at the net* (= in football/soccer).

OBJ **ball, gun, shot**

♦ v + prep ♦ v + n/pron + prep

'aim at sth; 'aim at doing sth to try to achieve sth; to have sth as your aim: *She's aiming at a sports scholarship.* ◇ *We need to aim at increasing exports.*

NOTE **Aim to do sth** is also used with the same meaning: *What do you aim to achieve?*

♦ v + prep

'aim sth at sb/sth if you **aim sth at** a particular person or group, you do or say sth that you intend to have an effect on them: *The advertising campaign is aimed primarily at young people.* ◇ *I was not aiming my remarks at you.*

OBJ **remarks, criticism, campaign**

NOTE Often used in the passive.

♦ v + n/pron + prep

be 'aimed at sth; be 'aimed at doing sth to have sth as an aim or purpose: *The new scheme is aimed at reducing unemployment.*

♦ be + v + prep

alight /əˈlaɪt/

a'light on/upon sb/sth (*formal*) to notice sb/sth suddenly; to find or think of sth by chance: *My eye alighted on an old book.* ◇ *He finally alighted on a solution.*

SYN **light on/upon sb/sth**

♦ v + prep

SYNONYMS

agree to sth

accede to sth ♦ **agree to sth** ♦ **consent to sth** ♦ **go along with sb/sth**

These verbs all mean to say that you will do what sb wants or allow sth to happen.

accede to sth (*formal*) to agree to a request or demand: *He acceded to demands for his resignation.*

agree to sth to say that you will do what sb wants or that you will allow sth to happen: *Do you think he'll agree to their proposal?*

consent (to sth) (*formal*) to agree to sth or give your permission for sth: *He consented to his daughter's marriage.*

go along with sb/sth to agree to sth that sb else has decided: *She just goes along with everything he suggests.*

PATTERNS AND COLLOCATIONS

■ to agree to/go along with/consent to a **plan/ scheme/proposal**

■ to agree to/go along with a **decision**

■ to agree to a **suggestion**

■ to agree to/accede to a **request/demand**

■ to be **prepared/willing/forced** to go along with sb/consent to sth

align /əˈlaɪn/

aˈlign yourself with sb/sth to publicly support a person, a group of people or a set of opinions: *The senator aligned himself with the critics of the proposed reforms.*
* v + pron + prep

allow /əˈlaʊ/

alˈlow for sth to include sth when you are calculating sth or planning sth: *Add an extra ten minutes to your journey time to allow for the traffic.* ◇ *I've bought a large size to allow for the fact that it may shrink in the wash.* ◇ *This had not been allowed for in the budget.*
OBJ the possibility, the fact that…, differences
* v + prep

alˈlow of sth (*formal*) to show that sth, such as an explanation or an answer, is possible; to make sth possible: *The facts allow of only one explanation.*
SYN admit of sth
* v + prep

allude /əˈluːd/

alˈlude to sb/sth (*formal*) to mention sb/sth indirectly or in a few words: *He hated his mother's way of alluding to Jean but never actually saying her name.* ◇ *Do you know the person who was alluded to in the report?* ➔ note at REFER TO SB/STH
* v + prep

amount /əˈmaʊnt/

aˈmount to sth (*not used in the progressive tenses*) **1** to add up to sth; to result in a final total of sth: *The cost of the trip amounted to well over £500.* ◇ *The money I pay in tax amounts to about 40% of my salary.* **SYN** come to sth ➔ note at ADD UP TO STH **2** to be equal to or the same as sth: *What they did amounted to a breach of contract.* ◇ *It doesn't matter who pays—it amounts to the same thing in the end.* ◇ *It all amounts to a lot of hard work.* **SYN** come to sth **3** if you say that sb/sth **doesn't amount to much**, you mean that he/she/it is not very important: *He'll never amount to anything.* ◇ *The information we have doesn't amount to much.*
SYN add up to sth
* v + prep

amp /æmp/

ˌamp sth ˈup (*slang*) to make sth louder or stronger: *The crowd amped up their approval when he started to sing.* ◇ *an amped-up rock band*
* v + n/pron + adv * v + adv + n

angle /ˈæŋgl/

ˈangle for sth (*often used in the progressive tenses*) to try to obtain sth without asking for it directly: *She's angling for an invitation.*

SYN fish for sth
* v + prep

answer /ˈɑːnsə(r); *AmE* ˈæn-/

ˌanswer ˈback to defend yourself against sth bad that sb has said about you: *It's not fair to criticize without giving her the chance to answer back.*
* v + adv

ˌanswer ˈback; ˌanswer sb ˈback if a child **answers back** or **answers you back**, they reply rudely: *Don't answer back!* ◇ *He's a rude little boy, always answering his mother back.*
* v + adv * v + n/pron + adv

ˈanswer for sb to speak on behalf of sb and say what they will do or what they think: *I can't answer for my colleagues, but I can manage a meeting next week.*
SYN speak for sb
NOTE Answer for sb is usually used in negative sentences.
* v + prep

ˈanswer for sth 1 to be responsible for sth bad; to accept the blame for sth: *She has a lot to answer for.* ◇ *He's old enough to answer for his own actions.* ◇ *When it comes to violence among young people, television has a great deal to answer for.* **OBJ** the consequences, sb's actions **2** to say that you are certain that sb has a particular quality or can be trusted or relied on: *I can answer for her honesty.* **SYN** vouch for sth
* v + prep

ˈanswer to sb (**for sth**) to have to explain your actions to sb; to show that your actions are right or reasonable: *You will answer to me for any damage to the car.* ◇ *If anything happens to her, you'll have me to answer to.*
* v + prep

ˈanswer to sth to be called sth; to recognize a name as your own: *I answer to either Susan or Sue.* ◇ *I'm afraid there's no one here answering to that name.* ◇ *She has a cat answering to the name of Dagobert.*
OBJ name, Susan, Sue, etc.
* v + prep

ante /ˈænti/

ˌante ˈup; ˌante ˈup sth 1 (in poker) to put forward a bet before the cards are dealt **2** (*AmE*) to pay a share of an amount of money that a group of people owe: *The check arrived and we all anted up.* ◇ *Some parents ante up big bucks to send their kids to prep school.*
NOTE Ante up is not used with a pronoun object.
* v + adv * v + adv + n

appeal /əˈpiːl/

apˈpeal for sth/sb; apˈpeal for sb to do sth to make a serious and urgent request for sth/sb or for sb to do sth: *The government has* appealed for calm. ◊ The police appealed for witnesses to come forward. ◊ The victim's family has appealed for help in tracking down the killer.

OBJ **witnesses**, **help**, **information**, **calm**, **funds**
➲ note at ASK FOR STH
◆ v + prep ◆ v + prep + n/pron + **to**+inf

ap'peal to sb if sth **appeals to** you, you like it or find it interesting and attractive: The 'Harry Potter' books appeal to readers of all ages. ◊ The prospect of camping didn't appeal to me.
◆ v + prep

ap'peal to sth to try to persuade sb to do sth by reminding them that it is a good, reasonable thing to do: Maybe if you **appeal to** her **better nature** (= her kindness), you can get her to help.
OBJ **sb's better nature**, **sb's sense of justice**
◆ v + prep

appertain /ˌæpəˈteɪn; AmE -pərˈt-/

apper'tain to sth (formal) to belong to sth; to be connected with sth: the duties appertaining to the post
◆ v + prep

apply /əˈplaɪ/ (**applies**, **applying**, **applied**)

ap'ply for sth to make a formal request, usually in writing, for sth such as a job or a place at college, university, etc.: I applied for a new passport. ◊ My son has applied for a place at Warwick University. ➲ note at ASK FOR STH
◆ v + prep

ap'ply to sb/sth to concern or relate to sb/sth: The word 'unexciting' could never be applied to her novels.
◆ v + prep

apprise /əˈpraɪz/

ap'prise sb of sth (formal) to inform sb of sth: We were fully apprised of the situation.
◆ v + n/pron + prep

argue /ˈɑːgjuː; AmE ˈɑːrg-/

ˌargue sb 'into sth; **ˌargue sb 'into doing sth** to persuade sb to do sth by giving them a large number of reasons why they should do it: I managed to argue him into going back home to talk to his parents.
OPP **argue sb out of sth**, **argue sb out of doing sth**
◆ v + n/pron + prep

ˌargue sth 'out to discuss all the details of an idea, a plan, etc., often in an excited or angry way, until you reach a decision: I'm sure they'll manage to argue out any differences that arise. ◊ I'm too tired to **argue it out** with you now. ◊ The issues have all been argued out at great length.
◆ v + adv + n ◆ v + n/pron + adv

ˌargue sb 'out of sth; **ˌargue sb 'out of doing sth** to persuade sb not to do sth by giving them a large number of reasons why they

should not do it: I argued her out of her crazy idea.
OPP **argue sb into sth**, **argue sb into doing sth**
◆ v + n/pron + adv + prep

'argue with sb/sth to disagree with what sb says; to say or show that sth is not right: 'It's cold today, isn't it?' 'I can't argue with you there!' (= I agree with you) ◊ It's a lovely jacket—and you couldn't argue with the price.
NOTE Argue with sb/sth is often used with can't or another negative.
◆ v + prep

armour /ˈɑːmə(r); AmE ˈɑːrmər/ (BrE) (AmE armor)

ˌarmour sth 'up (AmE ˌarmor sth 'up) (especially AmE) to attach extra protection to a military vehicle, so that it is better protected from bombs, bullets, etc.: The Pentagon realized it needed more money to armor up its trucks.
◆ v + n/pron + adv ◆ v + adv + n
▶ **up-'armour** (AmE **up-'armor**) vt (especially AmE) to armour up a vehicle
▶ **up-'armoured** (AmE **up-'armored**) adj [usually before noun] (especially AmE): up-armored Humvees

arrive /əˈraɪv/

ar'rive at sth to agree on sth or to find sth after discussing and thinking about it: They had both arrived at the same conclusion. ◊ It didn't take long to arrive at a decision.
OBJ **conclusion**, **decision**, **agreement**
SYN **reach sth**
◆ v + prep

arse /ɑːs; AmE ɑːrs/

ˌarse aˈbout/aˈround (BrE, △, slang) to behave in a silly or annoying way and waste time instead of doing what you are supposed to be doing: Stop arsing about and give me my bag.
NOTE Mess around and play around are more polite verbs to use to express this.
◆ v + adv

ascribe /əˈskraɪb/

aˈscribe sth to sb to consider that sth has been written, painted, spoken or created by a particular person: This play is usually ascribed to Shakespeare.
SYN **attribute sth to sb**
◆ v + n/pron + prep

aˈscribe sth to sb/sth (formal) **1** to consider that sth is caused by a particular person or thing: He ascribed his exhaustion to the heat. **2** to consider that a person or a thing has a particular quality: I am reluctant to ascribe supernatural powers to a fortune-teller. ◊ The government ascribes great importance to these policies.

SYN **attribute sth to sb/sth**
◆ v + n/pron + prep

ask /ɑːsk; *AmE* æsk/

'ask **after sb** to ask for news about sb and how they are, etc.: *Did she ask after me in her letter?*
SYN **enquire after sb** (*formal*)
◆ v + prep

,ask sb a'long to ask sb if they would like to go with you to an event or activity: *Jane and Ed are going out tonight, and they've asked me along.*
SYN **invite sb along** (*more formal*)
◆ v + n/pron + adv ◆ v + adv + n (*rare*)

,ask a'round to ask a number of different people in order to find out sth: *I don't know if there's any work, but I'll ask around for you.*
◆ v + adv

,ask sb a'round (*AmE*) → ASK SB OVER/ROUND

,ask sb 'back (**to sth**) (*especially BrE*) to invite sb to come back to your house with you for a drink, etc. when you are both out together: *I asked him back for a coffee.*
SYN **have sb back**; **invite sb back** (**to sth**) (*more formal*)
◆ v + n/pron + adv

'ask **for sb** to say that you want to see or speak to sb: *There's somebody at the door asking for Pete.*
◆ v + prep

'ask **for sth** 1 (*also* 'ask **sb for sth**) to say that you want sb to give you sth: *Jodie asked for a guitar for her birthday.* ◇ *Don't hesitate to ask for help.* ◇ *I asked the waiter for the bill.* ◇ *We couldn't have asked for better weather.* ◇ *A beautiful house, husband and children.* **What more could you ask for?** **SYN** **request sth**

(*formal*) 2 (*informal*) if sb is **asking for trouble** or **asking for it**, they are behaving in a way that is likely to cause sth bad to happen to them: *You're asking for trouble walking home alone at night.* ◇ *'You asked for it!* (= you deserve what I am going to do to you)' *she said.* **OBJ** **trouble**, **it**

3 to say that you want to speak to sb or be directed to a place: *When you arrive, go to reception and ask for George.* ◇ *Ask for the station if you get lost.*
◆ v + prep

,ask sb 'in/'up to invite sb to come into the room or building that you are in, especially your home: *Aren't you going to ask me in? It's cold out here.* ◇ *She asked me into her office for a chat.* ◇ *We must ask the neighbours in for coffee.*
SYN **invite sb in/up** (*more formal*)
◆ v + n/pron + adv

,ask sb 'out to invite sb to go out with you, especially when you would like a romantic relationship with them: *Has he asked you out yet?*
SYN **invite sb out** (*more formal*)
◆ v + n/pron + adv

,ask sb 'over/'round (*BrE*) (*AmE* ,ask sb a'round) to invite sb to come and visit you in your home: *She's asked me round for dinner.*
SYN **invite sb over/round** (*more formal*)
◆ v + n/pron + adv

,ask sb 'up → ASK SB IN/UP

aspire /əˈspaɪə(r)/

a'spire **to sth** to have a strong desire to gain or achieve sth: *He's never really aspired to great wealth.*
◆ v + prep

---

ask for sth

appeal for sth ◆ apply for sth ◆ ask for sth ◆ call for sth ◆ request sth

These verbs all mean to tell sb that you would like them to do sth or give you sth, or that you would like sth to happen.

appeal for sth to make a serious and urgent request for sth: *Nationalist leaders have appealed for calm.* ◇ *Police are appealing for witnesses to come forward.*

apply for sth to make a formal request, usually in writing, for sth such as a job or a place at a university: *to apply for a job/passport/grant*

ask for sth to tell sb that you would like them to do or give you sth, or that you would like sth to happen: *I went up to the bar and asked*

for a beer. ◇ *He asked me for a job again yesterday.*

call for sth (*used especially in newspapers*) to ask publicly for sth to happen: *The group called for the immediate release of the hostages.* ◇ *The opposition is calling for the Prime Minister to resign.*

request sth (*formal*) to ask for sth or ask sb to do sth in a polite or formal way: *You can request a free copy of the leaflet.*

PATTERNS AND COLLOCATIONS

■ to ask for/call for/appeal for sth **from** sb
■ to **formally** ask for/call for/request/apply for sth
■ to **repeatedly** ask for/call for/request/appeal for sth

associate /əˈsəʊʃieɪt; AmE əˈsoʊ-/

asˈsociate with sb to be involved with or spend a lot of time with sb or with a group of people, especially people that sb else does not approve of: *I don't like the people you associate with.*
♦ v + prep

asˈsociate yourself with sb/sth (*formal*) to say that you agree with sb/sth: *They do not want to associate themselves with spending cuts and tax increases.*
OPP dissociate yourself from sb/sth
♦ v + pron + prep

attend /əˈtend/

atˈtend to sb/sth (*formal*) to deal with or take responsibility for sth; to give practical help to sb who needs it: *I have some urgent business to attend to.* ◊ (*BrE*) *Are you being attended to?*
OBJ business, needs, customer **SYN** look after sb; look after sth; see to sb/sth (*less formal*)
⊃ note at CARE FOR SB
♦ v + prep

attribute /əˈtrɪbjuːt/

atˈtribute sth to sb to consider that sth has been written, painted, spoken or created by a particular person: *This painting is usually attributed to Goya.*
SYN ascribe sth to sb
♦ v + n/pron + prep

atˈtribute sth to sb/sth to consider that sth is caused by a particular person or thing: *His success can be attributed largely to hard work.* ◊ *She said she was not going to attribute blame or seek revenge for what had happened.*
SYN ascribe sth to sb/sth; put sth down to sth (*less formal*)
♦ v + n/pron + prep

auction /ˈɔːkʃn; BrE also ˈɒk-/

NOTE An **auction** is a public event at which things are sold to the person who offers the most money for them.

ˌauction sth ˈoff to sell sth at an auction, especially sth that sb no longer needs or wants: *The house and all its contents will be auctioned off next week.*
⊃ note at SELL STH OFF
♦ v + adv + n ♦ v + n/pron + adv

avail /əˈveɪl/

aˈvail yourself of sth (*formal*) to make use of sth; to take advantage of sth, usually to improve your situation: *Guests are encouraged to avail themselves of all the hotel's facilities.* ◊ *I'd like to avail myself of this opportunity to thank you all for your support.*
OBJ facilities, opportunity
♦ v + pron + prep

average /ˈævərɪdʒ/

ˌaverage ˈout to result in a fair or equal amount over a period of time: *Sometimes I do the cooking and sometimes my flatmate does. It averages out over a month.*
♦ v + adv

ˌaverage sth ˈout (at sth) to calculate the average of sth: *If you average it out, there's one car stolen every three minutes.* ◊ *The tax authorities averaged out his profit at £10 000 a year over five years.*
♦ v + adv + n ♦ v + n/pron + adv

ˌaverage ˈout at sth to have a particular amount as the average over a period of time: *The time she spends practising the piano averages out at about an hour a day.*
♦ v + adv + prep

awake /əˈweɪk/ (awoke /əˈwəʊk; AmE əˈwoʊk/, awoken /əˈwəʊkən; AmE əˈwoʊkən/)

aˈwake to sth (*formal*) to become aware of sth and its possible results; to realize or understand sth: *They finally awoke to the full extent of the problem.* ◊ *I suddenly awoke to the fact that I had the answer in front of me.*
→ see also AWAKEN TO STH, AWAKEN SB TO STH
♦ v + prep

awaken /əˈweɪkən/

aˈwaken to sth; aˈwaken sb to sth (*formal*) to become aware of sth, or to make sb become aware of sth, and its possible results: *People are gradually awakening to their rights.* ◊ *The public has been awakened to the full horror of the situation.*
→ see also AWAKE TO STH
♦ v + prep ♦ v + n/pron + prep

B b

back /bæk/

ˌback aˈway (from sth) to move backwards away from sb/sth frightening or unpleasant: *He stepped forward and she backed away in alarm.* ◊ *The child backed away from the dog nervously.*
SYN retreat (from sb/sth) (*more formal*)
→ see also BACK OFF 2
♦ v + adv ♦ v + adv + prep

ˌback aˈway from sth; ˌback aˈway from doing sth to avoid doing sth unpleasant or difficult; to show that you no longer support an action or an idea: *We will not back away from tough measures.* ◊ *The union has backed away from calling a strike.*
♦ v + adv + prep

ˌback ˈdown (on/from sth) to take back a claim or a demand that you have made, or sth that you have said, usually because sb forces you to: *Neither of them will back down on this issue.* ◇ *His critics were forced to back down.*

SYN **climb down (over sth)**; **give in (to sb/sth)**
→ see also BACK OFF (FROM STH/FROM DOING STH), BACK OFF STH
♦ v + adv

,**back** '**off 1** (*informal*) to stop threatening or annoying sb: *Back off and let me make my own decisions.* ◇ *The press have agreed to back off and leave the couple alone.* **2** to move away from sb/sth frightening or unpleasant: *As the head teacher approached, the children backed off.* **SYN** **retreat (from sb/sth)** → see also BACK AWAY, BACK AWAY FROM SB/STH
♦ v + adv

,**back** '**off (from sth/ from doing sth)**, ,**back** '**off sth** (*especially AmE*) to decide not to continue to do sth or support an idea, in order to avoid a difficult or unpleasant situation: *The government backed off in the face of strong opposition.* ◇ *He refused to back off from his earlier statement.* ◇ *The rebels backed off their demand for meeting with the President.*
→ see also BACK DOWN (ON/FROM STH)
♦ v + adv ♦ v + prep

,**back** '**onto sth** (*BrE*) if a building **backs onto** sth, it has sth behind it: *The hotel backs onto the golf course.*
♦ v + prep

,**back** '**out**; ,**back** '**out of sth**; ,**back** '**out of doing sth** to decide not to do sth that you had agreed or promised to do: *Everything's arranged. It's too late to back out now.* ◇ *There's still time to back out of selling the house.*
SYN **pull out, pull out of sth, pull out of doing sth**; **withdraw (from sth)** (*more formal*)
♦ v + adv ♦ v + adv + prep

,**back** '**up**; ,**back sb/sth** '**up** to move backwards a short distance, especially in a vehicle; to make sb/sth move backwards a short distance: *The truck in front is going to have to back up.* ◇ *You can back up another two metres or so.* ◇ *Jeff backed the van up and drove off quickly.* ◇ *The woman was backed up against the wall.*
SYN **reverse, reverse sth** (*more formal*)
♦ v + adv ♦ v + n/pron + adv ♦ v + adv + n

,**back** '**up**; ,**back sth** '**up** if traffic **backs up** or **is backed up**, it cannot move and forms a long line: *Two lanes were closed by the accident, causing cars to back up for miles.* ◇ *The traffic is backed up to the traffic lights.*
NOTE Nearly always used in the passive.
♦ v + adv ♦ v + n/pron + adv ♦ v + adv + n

back sb/sth up

back sb/sth up ♦ **bear sb/sth out** ♦ **confirm sth** ♦ **corroborate sth** ♦ **substantiate sth**

These verbs all mean to support what sb says by stating or showing that it is definitely true or correct.

back sb/sth up to support what sb says; to say that what sb says is true: *I'll back you up if they don't believe you.* ◇ *The writer doesn't back up his opinions with examples.*

bear sb/sth out (*especially BrE*) to support a claim, a theory or what sb says: *The other witnesses will bear me out.* ◇ *The other witnesses will bear out what I say.*

confirm sth to state or show that sth is definitely true or correct, especially by providing evidence: *Rumours of job losses were later confirmed.* ◇ *His guilty expression confirmed my suspicions.*

corroborate sth (*often passive*) (*formal*) to provide evidence that proves or supports a claim, theory or other evidence: *The evidence was corroborated by two independent witnesses.* ▶ **corroboration** *n* [U]

substantiate sth (*often passive*) (*formal*) to provide evidence that proves or supports a claim or sth that sb has said: *They made accusations which could not be substantiated.* ▶ **substantiation** *n* [U]

WHICH WORD?

Substantiate and **corroborate** have similar meanings but they tend to be used with different words. Both go with *claim* but **substantiate** is also used with *criticism, remark* and *point*; **corroborate** is commonly used with *findings, theory, results* and *evidence*. **Back sb/sth up** has a similar meaning to **substantiate sth**, but **substantiate** is more formal; **substantiate** cannot have a person as its object. **Back sb/sth up** and **substantiate** imply that you are providing information to prove sth; **bear sb/sth out** and **confirm sth** imply that the facts are already there.

PATTERNS AND COLLOCATIONS

- to confirm/bear out **that/what...**
- it was confirmed **that...**
- to confirm **whether...**
- to confirm/substantiate/back up/corroborate/ bear out a **claim/statement/story/theory**

,**back sb/sth** '**up 1** to say or show that what sb says is true: *If I tell my parents I was with you, will you back me up?* ◇ *His version of events is not backed up by the evidence.* [OBJ] **statement, claim 2** to support or help sb/sth: *Melissa complained that her husband never backed her up when it came to dealing with the children.* ◇ *Backing her up* (= playing music to support her) *was the band 'Midnight Express'.* [SYN] **support sb/sth**

◆ v + n/pron + adv ◆ v + adv + n (*less frequent*)

▸ '**backup** *n* [C, U] (*AmE, music*) (*usually used as an adjective*) music that supports the main singer or player in popular music: *a backup singer for Stevie Wonder* ◇ *She once sang backup for Madonna.*

,**back sth** '**up 1** (*computing*) to make a copy of a file, a program, etc. that can be used if the original one is lost or damaged: *We back up all the files every night.* [OBJ] **file, document 2** to add sth extra to sth, especially as a support: *The lectures will be backed up by practical work.* ◇ *They backed up their demands with threats.*

◆ v + n/pron + adv ◆ v + adv + n

▸ '**backup** *n* **1** [C] (*computing*) a copy of a file, program, etc. for use in case the original is lost or damaged: *Have you kept a backup of this file?* ◇ *a backup disk* **2** [U] support or help that you can use in order to do sth: *military backup* ◇ *They have a huge backup team.* **3** [C] a second piece of equipment, person, etc. that can replace another if necessary: *He's our backup if another player isn't available.* ◇ *the backup plan*

bag /bæg/ (-gg-)

,**bag sth** '**up** to put sth, usually large amounts of sth, into a bag or bags: *The vegetables are bagged up on the farm and then sent out to the market.* [NOTE] **Bag sth** can also be used on its own with this meaning.

◆ v + adv + n ◆ v + n/pron + adv

bail /beɪl/

,**bail** '**out**; ,**bail** '**out of sth 1** (*BrE also* ,**bale** '**out**, ,**bale** '**out of sth**) to jump out of a plane that is going to crash, using a parachute (= a large piece of cloth that opens out like an umbrella and makes people fall slowly and safely): *The crew just had time to bail out.* **2** to escape from a situation that you no longer want to be involved in: *The actor who was supposed to be playing the part bailed out.* → see also BACK OUT

◆ v + adv + prep

,**bail** '**out**; ,**bail sth** '**out** (*BrE also* ,**bale** '**out**, ,**bale sth** '**out**) to throw water out of a boat with a container or with your hands: *The boat will sink unless we bail out.* ◇ *They started bailing the boat out.*

[OBJ] **boat, water**

◆ v + adv ◆ v + n/pron + adv ◆ v + adv + n

,**bail sb** '**out** (*law*) to pay sb's bail (= the money that sb accused of a crime has to pay if they do not appear at their trial) for them, so that they can be set free until their trial

◆ v + n/pron + adv ◆ v + adv + n

,**bail sb/sth** '**out**; ,**bail sb/sth** '**out of sth** (*BrE also* ,**bale sb/sth** '**out**, ,**bale sb/sth** '**out of sth**) (*informal*) to rescue sb/sth from difficulties, especially financial difficulties: *The government has refused to bail the company out again.*

◆ v + n/pron + adv ◆ v + adv + n

◆ v + n/pron + adv + prep

▸ '**bailout** *n* (*especially AmE, finance*) an act of giving financial help to a company, economy, etc. to save it from failing: *government/bank bailouts* ◇ *a bailout package*

balance /'bæləns/

'**balance A against B** to compare the value or importance of one plan, argument, etc. against another: *You must balance the high salary against the long working hours.*

[SYN] **set sth against sth**

◆ v + n/pron + prep

,**balance** '**out**; ,**balance sth** '**out** if things that are very different or have opposite effects **balance out** or you **balance them out**, they become equal in amount or value: *If you eat a variety of food, protein and carbohydrate will balance out over a week.* ◇ *We need to invite three more girls to balance out the numbers* (= so that there are equal numbers of boys and girls).

◆ v + adv ◆ v + adv + n ◆ v + n/pron + adv

bale /beɪl/

,**bale** '**out** (*BrE*) → BALE OUT, ETC.

balk /bɔːk/

'**balk at sth**; '**balk at doing sth** (*especially AmE*) → BAULK AT STH, ETC.

ball /bɔːl/

,**ball sth** '**up** (*AmE*) to make sth that is usually flat into the shape of a ball: *She balled up the paper and tossed it in the garbage.* [SYN] **crumple sth up; scrunch sth up; wad sth up** (*especially AmE*)

◆ v + adv + n ◆ v + n/pron + adv

balls /bɔːlz/

,**balls sth** '**up** (*BrE*, △, *slang*) to spoil sth; to do sth very badly

[NOTE] A more polite, informal way of saying this is **mess sth up**.

◆ v + n/pron + adv ◆ v + adv + n

▸ '**balls-up** *n* (△, *slang, especially BrE*) sth that has been done very badly: *I made a real balls-up of my exams.*

[NOTE] A more polite, informal way of saying this is **mess**.

band /bænd/

,band to'gether to form a group and act together in order to achieve sth, etc.: *We need to band together to fight these reforms.*
♦ v + adv

bandage /'bændɪdʒ/

,bandage sb/sth 'up to wrap a bandage around a part of the body that is injured: *Joe bandaged me up until the doctor came.* ◇ *I didn't see the burns because her fingers were all bandaged up.*
[OBJ] **wound, sb's leg/arm, etc.**
[NOTE] Often used in the passive. ♦ **Bandage sb/sth** is also used on its own.
♦ v + n/pron + adv ♦ v + adv + n

bandy /'bændi/ (bandies, bandying, bandied)

,bandy sth a'bout (*also* ,bandy sth a'round *especially BrE*) if a word, a name, etc. **is bandied about**, it is mentioned or talked about by many people, often in a careless way: *The stories being bandied about are completely false.* ◇ *He's not paid anything like the £4 000 a week figure being bandied around.*
[OBJ] **story, figures, word/term**
[NOTE] Usually used in the passive.
♦ v + adv + n ♦ v + n/pron + adv

bang /bæŋ/

,bang a'round (*also* ,bang a'bout *especially BrE*) to move around noisily: *We could hear them banging about upstairs, moving things.*
♦ v + adv

,bang a'way **1** (*informal*) to hit sth repeatedly with a lot of force or energy: *She picked up the hammer and began banging away.* **2** if sth such as your heart **bangs away**, it makes very loud regular sounds: *My heart was banging away like a drum.*
♦ v + adv

,bang a'way at sth (*informal, especially AmE*) to work very hard at sth: *She banged away all day at her assignment.*
[SYN] **bash away (at sth)** (*BrE*)
♦ v + adv + prep

,bang sth 'down to put sth down quickly and with a lot of force so that it makes a loud noise: *He banged his fist down on the table.* ◇ *She banged the phone down* (= ended the telephone conversation) *before I could explain.*
♦ v + n/pron + adv ♦ v + adv + n

,bang 'into sb/sth to crash into or hit sb/sth violently, usually by mistake: *He ran around the corner and banged into an old lady who was coming the other way.*
♦ v + prep

,bang 'on about sb/sth (*BrE, informal*) to talk or write a lot or in a boring way about sth: *Pat is always banging on about politics.* ◇ *She keeps banging on about how wonderful her son is.*
[SYN] **go on (about sb/sth)**
♦ v + adv + prep

,bang 'out sth (*informal*) **1** to play music very loudly: *He banged out the tune on the piano.* **2** to write sth very quickly and without taking much care: *She bangs out four novels a year.* [SYN] **bash sth out** (*BrE*); **churn sth out**
[NOTE] When the object of **bang out** is a noun, it comes after **out**, but when the object is a pronoun, it comes between **bang** and **out**: *She bangs them out regularly.*
♦ v + adv + n ♦ v + pron + adv

,bang sb/sth 'up (*AmE, informal*) to damage or injure sb/sth, especially by hitting sth else: *I banged up my knee when I fell off the bike.*
♦ v + adv + n ♦ v + n/pron + adv

be/get ,banged 'up (*BrE, informal*) to be locked up or put in prison: *He was banged up in a Singapore jail for six months.*
♦ be/get + v + adv

bank /bæŋk/

'bank on sb/sth; 'bank on doing sth; 'bank on sb/sth doing sth to rely on sb/sth; to be confident that sth will happen: *I'm banking on your help.* ◇ *I'm really banking on you to help me.* ◇ *I'd banked on getting a cup of coffee at the station, but everything was closed.* ◇ *He was banking on the train being on time.* ◇ *She might already have cleaned up the mess, but I wouldn't bank on it.*
[SYN] **count on sb/sth, etc.; reckon on sb/sth, etc.**
♦ v + prep ♦ v + prep + n/pron + **to**+inf

,bank 'up; ,bank sth 'up (*BrE*) to form into a large pile; to make sth form a large pile: *The snow had banked up on either side of the road.*
♦ v + adv ♦ v + n/pron + adv ♦ v + adv + n

bargain /'bɑːgən; AmE 'bɑːrgən/

,bargain sth a'way (*rare*) to give away sth valuable or important in exchange for sth less valuable or important: *The leaders refused to bargain away the freedom of their people.*
♦ v + adv + n ♦ v + pron + adv
♦ v + n + adv (*less frequent*)

'bargain for/on sth; 'bargain for/on doing sth; 'bargain for/on sb/sth doing sth to expect or be prepared to do sth; to expect sth to happen or sb to do sth: *We hadn't bargained for such bad weather.* ◇ *I hadn't bargained on taking the kids with us.* ◇ *I didn't bargain for Jake being at the party.* ◇ *When he tried to argue with Kate, he got more than he had bargained for.* ◇ *What I hadn't bargained for was that very few people would speak English.*
[SYN] **reckon on sb/sth, etc.**

NOTE These phrasal verbs are usually used in negative sentences.
* v + prep

barge /bɑːdʒ; *AmE* bɑːrdʒ/

,barge 'in (on sb/sth), ,barge 'into sth (*informal*) **1** to enter a place or join a group of people quickly and rudely, without being asked: *Sorry to barge in, but…* ◇ *She barged in on our meeting without knocking.* ◇ *He just barged (his way) into the room.* **2** to interrupt what sb is doing or saying, especially when you have not been invited to join in: *As soon as I paused for breath, Bart barged in.* ◇ *You can't just come barging into our conversation!*
* v + adv * v + prep

bark /bɑːk; *AmE* bɑːrk/

,bark sth 'out to shout sth loudly: *She barked out instructions to her secretary.*
OBJ orders, instructions **SYN** rap sth out
NOTE Bark sth can also be used on its own with the same meaning: *He barked orders at Tim.*
* v + adv + n * v + n/pron + adv * v + adv + speech

barricade /ˌbærɪˈkeɪd/

barri,cade yourself/sb 'in; barri,cade yourself/sb 'in/'into/in'side sth to put up a line of objects at the entrance to a room or building, so that nobody can get in or out, usually to protect or defend yourself or sb else: *The police were called when he went mad and barricaded himself in.* ◇ *They barricaded themselves inside their house.* ◇ *Families had to be barricaded inside a restaurant while students protested outside.*
OBJ room, house
* v + n/pron + adv * v + n/pron + prep

base /beɪs/

'base sth on sth (*also* 'base sth upon sth *more formal*) to use or have an idea, an experience, etc. as the point from which sth can be developed: *The novel is based on a true story.* ◇ *She is basing the prosecution case on the evidence of two witnesses.* ◇ *What's the design based on?* ◇ *The report has been based upon inaccurate information.* ◇ *Sue's knowledge of Japan was based only on what she had read in books.*
OBJ decision, theory, design, opinion, etc.
NOTE Often used in the passive.
* v + n/pron + prep

bash /bæʃ/

,bash sb/sth a'bout (*BrE, informal, informal*) to hit or strike sb/sth and treat them/it in a rough way: *The mugger had bashed her about.*
* v + n/pron + adv

,bash a'way (at sth) (*BrE, informal*) to work very hard at sth for a period of time: *I bashed away at the article without a break from 11 until 6.*
* v + adv

,bash sth 'down (*informal, especially BrE*) to destroy sth and make it fall by hitting it violently: *The firefighters had to bash the door down.*
OBJ door **SYN** break sth down (*more formal*); knock sth down (*more formal*)
* v + n/pron + adv * v + adv + n

,bash sth 'in (*informal, especially BrE*) to break or destroy sth by hitting it violently: *The window had been bashed in.*
OBJ window, head, skull, nose **SYN** smash sth in
NOTE Often used in the passive.
* v + n/pron + adv * v + adv + n
IDM ,bash sb's 'head/'brains in (*informal, especially BrE*) to hit sb very hard: *Shut up or I'll bash your brains in!*

,bash 'on (with sth) (*BrE, informal*) to continue working hard at sth: *Let's bash on.* ◇ *I'd better bash on with my work.*
SYN get on (with sth) (*more formal*)
* v + adv

,bash sth 'out (*BrE, informal*) to write sth very quickly, without taking much care: *I don't do drafts of articles. I just bash them out.*
SYN bang out sth
* v + adv + n * v + n/pron + adv

,bash sb 'up (*BrE, informal*) to attack sb violently
SYN beat sb up (*more formal*)
NOTE Beat sb up is more frequent.
* v + n/pron + adv * v + adv + n

bask /bɑːsk/

'bask in sth to enjoy the good feelings that you have when other people praise or admire you, or when they give you a lot of attention: *He had always basked in his parents' attention.* ◇ *I never minded basking in my wife's reflected glory* (= enjoying the praise, attention, etc. she got).
* v + prep

bat /bæt/ (-tt-)

,bat sth a'round (*informal*) to talk about or discuss plans or ideas, etc. before you decide what to do: *We're just batting some ideas around.*
OBJ ideas, figures
* v + n/pron + adv * v + adv + n

batten /ˈbætn/

,batten sth 'down to fasten sth firmly in order to prevent damage by storms or winds: *They managed to batten down the shutters and doors before the hurricane hit.*
* v + adv + n * v + n/pron + adv
IDM ,batten down the 'hatches to prepare for difficult times ahead: *Businesses are battening*

down the hatches and preparing for a difficult year.

batter /'bætə(r)/

,batter sth 'down to hit sth repeatedly until it breaks and falls down: *The only way to get in was to batter the door down.*

OBJ door SYN break sth down; beat sth down

• v + n/pron + adv • v + adv + n

baulk (*especially BrE*) (*AmE usually* **balk**) /bɔ:k/

'baulk at sth; 'baulk at doing sth to be unwilling to do sth or to get involved in sth because it is difficult, dangerous, expensive, etc.: *He baulked at the idea of telling his parents where he was going.*

OBJ idea, expense

• v + prep

bawl /bɔ:l/

,bawl sb 'out (*informal*) to speak angrily to sb because they have done sth wrong: *My boss bawled me out for being late.*

SYN tell sb off

• v + n/pron + adv • v + adv + n

▶ ,bawling-'out *n* [usually sing.] (*informal*) an act of speaking angrily to sb because they have done sth wrong

,bawl sth 'out (*informal, especially BrE*) to say or sing sth very loudly or in an angry voice: *She doesn't give you an order. She bawls it out.* ◇ *The children bawled out the songs.*

• v + adv + n • v + pron + adv • v + n + adv (*rare*)
• v + adv + speech

be /bi; strong form bi:/ (**am/is/are, being, was/were, been**)

be 'after sth to be trying to get or obtain sth: *Several people in the office are after the same job.* ◇ *She's being too nice. I wonder what she's after.* ⊃ note at LOOK FOR SB/STH

• v + prep

be 'at sb (*informal, especially BrE*) → BE/GO/KEEP ON AT SB

be 'at sth to be busy doing sth: *He's been at his essay all night.* ◇ *I'll **be at it** all day tomorrow.*

• v + prep

IDM be 'at it (*informal*) **1** to behave badly; to argue or fight: *The kids are at it again.* **2** to have sex

be a'way to not be at home, especially when you are on holiday/vacation or on a business trip: *We'll be away for the month of August.* ◇ *He's away on business at the moment.*

• v + adv

be be'fore sb → BE UP BEFORE SB

be be'hind sb to give sb your support: *Don't forget that we're behind you all the way.*

• v + prep

be be'hind with sth to be late doing sth, such as paying a bill, your rent, etc.: *We're behind with the mortgage repayments.* ◇ *I'm behind with my college assignments.*

• v + adv + prep

be 'down if a computer system **is down**, it is not working: *Surely your computer isn't down again?*

• v + adv

be 'down on sb to treat sb severely or unfairly: *He's been really down on me lately.*

• v + adv + prep

be 'down to sb **1** to be the responsibility of sb: *It's down to you to help them now.* SYN be up to sb **2** to be sb's fault: *All this trouble is down to Matt.*

• v + adv + prep

be 'down to sth to have only a little money left: *I'm down to my last dollar.*

• v + adv + prep

be/go 'down with sth to have or catch an illness: *Gill's down with flu.*

• v + adv + prep

be 'in **1** to be in fashion: *Miniskirts are in this season.* **2** to be elected to a political position: *The Democrats are in for another term.*

• v + adv

be 'in for sth (*informal*) to be going to experience sth soon, especially sth unpleasant: *She's in for a shock.* ◇ *It looks like we're in for a storm.*

• v + adv + prep

be/get 'in on sth (*informal*) to have a share in or knowledge of sth; to be or become involved in sth: *Are you in on the secret?* ◇ *I'd like to be in on the deal.*

• v + adv + prep

be (well) 'in with sb to be (very) friendly with sb and likely to get an advantage from the friendship

• v + adv + prep

be 'into sth to have a taste for or an interest in sth: *Are you into jazz?* ◇ *He's been into trains since he was a small boy.*

• v + prep

be 'off **1** to leave; to go, especially in a hurry: *I must be off.* **2** to have gone bad and not be fit to eat or drink: *This milk is off.* **3** if a dish in a restaurant **is off**, it is not available: *I'm afraid the liver is off today.*

• v + adv

be 'off sb/sth **1** to have no interest in sb/sth; to have stopped liking sb/sth: *She can't be well. She's been off her food all week.* ◇ *That's it. I'm off men for life.* **2** to have finished speaking on the telephone: *Isn't he off the phone yet?*

• v + prep

be 'off for sth (*informal*) to have a particular amount of sth: *How are we off for coffee* (= how much have we got)?

• v + adv + prep

be 'on **1** (of an event, a show, a performance, etc.) to be happening; to take place: *Is the party still on?* **2** (of a performer) to be on the stage; to perform: *Who's on next?* ◇ *We're on after the* *band.* **3** (of food) to be cooking: *Are the pota-toes on?*

♦ v + adv

IDM **you're 'on** (*informal*) used when you are accepting a bet or a challenge

be 'on sb if sth such as drinks, food, tickets, etc. **are on** sb, they are paid for by that person: *The drinks are on me tonight.*

♦ v + prep

be 'on sth 1 to be taking medicine, a drug, etc.: *She's been on the pill for ten years.* ◊ *I'm on strong painkillers.* **2** to be talking to sb on the telephone: *She's been on the phone for hours.* **3** to be eating or drinking sth: *I'm on my third coffee already this morning.*

♦ v + prep

IDM **what are you 'on?** (*informal*) used when you are very surprised at sb's behaviour and are suggesting that they are acting in a similar way to sb using drugs

be 'on about sth (*informal, especially BrE*) to talk about sth, often in a boring way; to mean sth: *He's always on about how much money he earns.* ◊ *What are you on about?* (= I don't understand)

♦ v + adv + prep

be/go/keep 'on at sb (*also* **be 'at sb**) (*informal, especially BrE*) to try to persuade sb to do sth by talking about it very often and in an annoying way: *I've been on at my husband to go to the doctor, but he won't.*

SYN nag sb

♦ v + adv + prep ♦ v + prep

be 'onto sb (*informal*) **1** to become aware that sb has done sth wrong or illegal and be trying to catch them: *The police aren't onto us yet.* **2** to talk to sb about sth, especially to complain about sth or ask them to do sth: *I've been onto the council about the noise.*

♦ v + prep

be 'onto sth to have found or discovered sth that could have very good results for you or for sb else: *She could be onto something* (= she might have discovered sth that will prove important).

♦ v + prep

be 'out 1 to have stopped work as a protest and be on strike: *The postal workers are still out.* **2** to be no longer in prison: *I've heard Smith's out now.* **3** if a jury (= a group of people who decide the results of a competition or whether or not sb is guilty of a crime) **is out**, they are still trying to make a decision **4** to be no longer in fashion: *Black is out this year.* ◊ *Politeness seems to* **be out of fashion** *these days* (= no one is polite any more). **5** if an action, for example, **is out**, it is not possible or is not allowed: *Shall we get together one evening next week? Monday's out—I've got a French class.*

♦ v + adv

IDM **the jury is** (**still**) **'out on sth** used when you are saying that sth is still not certain: *The jury is still out on whether wine can be good for you.*

be 'out for sth; **be 'out to do sth** to be trying very hard to do sth or to get sth: *He's out for revenge.* ◊ *Everyone's just out for what they can get these days* (= they are trying to get things for themselves). ◊ *The German team want to win this game, but Brazil are out to stop them.*

♦ v + adv + prep ♦ v + adv + **to**+inf

be 'out of sth to have used up a supply of sth and have nothing left: *We're out of sugar.*

♦ v + adv + prep

be 'over sb to have returned to your usual state of happiness after the end of a relationship: *It was hard at first, but I'm over him now.*

♦ v + prep

be 'over sth to have returned to health after an illness: *He's over the flu now.*

♦ v + prep

be 'past it (*informal*) used to show that you think sb is so old that they can no longer do anything useful or interesting: *The children laughed at him and said he was past it.*

♦ v + prep + it

be 'through (**to sb**) to be connected to sb on the telephone: *You're through now.* ◊ *You're through to the manager now.*

♦ v + adv

be 'through (**with sb/sth**) (*especially AmE*) to have finished using or doing sth; to have finished a relationship with sb: *Aren't you through yet? You've been ages!* ◊ *He promised he was through with drugs.* ◊ *Keith and I are through.*

♦ v + adv

be 'up 1 to be awake: *You're up early.* ◊ *I've been up all night.* **2** (of the wind, the sea, etc.) to have increased in strength or become violent: *In the morning the wind was up and we got ready for a day's sailing.* **3** (*informal*) (of a drink, a meal, etc.) to be ready: *Tea's up! Come and get it.* **4** (**with sb**) used to say that sth is happening, especially sth unusual or unpleasant: *You look terrible! What's up?* ◊ *I couldn't understand* **what was up with** *George.*

♦ v + adv

IDM **what's 'up?** (*informal*) used to say hello to sb

be 'up against sb to be playing against sb in a game, competition, etc.: *We're up against some tough competition this year.*

♦ v + adv + prep

be 'up against sth to be facing problems or difficulties: *With three players injured, they were really* **up against it** (= in a difficult situation). ◊ *Do you realize what you're up against?*

♦ v + adv + prep

be up

be amiss ◆ be up ◆ be wrong

These verbs all describe sth that causes problems or difficulties or that is not as it should be.

be amiss (*formal*) to be wrong; to be not as it should be: *She sensed there was something amiss and called the police.*

be up (*informal*) used to say that sth is happening, especially sth unusual or unpleasant: *What's up? Are you OK? ◇ I could tell something was up by the look on his face.*

be wrong to cause problems or difficulties; to be not as it should be: *Is anything wrong? You look worried. ◇ 'What's wrong?' 'Oh, nothing.' ◇ There's something wrong with the printer.*

PATTERNS AND COLLOCATIONS

■ there is sth wrong/up/amiss **with** sb/sth
■ to be **seriously** wrong/amiss
■ to be **badly** wrong
■ **is anything** wrong/up?
■ **what's** wrong/up?

be 'up before sb (*also* **be be'fore sb**) to appear in court or before a judge: *He's up before the judge tomorrow.*
◆ v + adv + prep ◆ v + prep

be 'up for sth 1 to be considered for sth, especially as a candidate for a job, in an election, etc.: *She's up for promotion. ◇ (informal) There are 50 tickets up for grabs* (= available for people who ask quickly). **2** to be for sb to buy: *I see your house is up for sale. ◇ A Picasso is up for auction.* **3** (*informal*) to be ready to take part in an activity: *The new job will be a challenge, but I'm up for it.*
◆ v + adv + prep

be 'up to sb 1 to be sb's responsibility or duty: *It's up to you to make sure the house is kept tidy.* **SYN** **be down to sb 2** to be left to sb to decide: *'Shall we go out?' 'I don't know. It's up to you.'*

be 'up to sth (*informal*) **1** to be busy doing sth, especially sth bad: *What have you been up to lately? ◇ The kids are quiet—I'm sure they're up to no good* (= they are doing sth bad). **2** to be as good as people expect: *Was your meal up to standard?*
◆ v + adv + prep

be u'pon sb (*formal*) to be going to happen very soon: *The election is almost upon us.*
◆ v + prep

beam /biːm/

beam sb 'up/'down (in science fiction) to transport sb from one place to another using a special machine which can separate the atoms in their body and then put them back together again: *This party is so boring! Beam me up, Scotty!* (= used to say that you wish you were somewhere else)
◆ v + adv + n ◆ v + n/pron + adv

bear /beə(r); AmE ber/ (bore /bɔː(r)/, borne /bɔːn; AmE bɔːrn/)

bear 'down on sb/sth (*also* **bear 'down upon sb/sth** *more formal*) **1** (*especially BrE*) to move towards sb/sth in a determined or threatening way: *A crowd of journalists bore down on the minister. ◇ A hurricane is bearing down on Central America.* **2** (*especially AmE*) if a problem or a difficult situation **bears down on** you, it makes you feel very worried and has a severe effect on you: *The drought is bearing down very hard on farmers.* **3** (*especially AmE*) to press or push on sb/sth: *(figurative) The government has announced it will bear down on* (= deal strictly with) *inflation.*
◆ v + adv + prep

bear on/upon sb/sth (*formal*) to be connected with sb/sth; to have an effect on sb/sth: *This decision bears directly on our everyday lives.*
SYN **affect sb/sth**
◆ v + prep

bear sb/sth 'out (*especially BrE*) to show that sth is true or that what sb says is true; to support sb/sth: *I always said she'd do well. John will bear me out on this. ◇ John will bear out what I say. ◇ This theory is not borne out by the facts.* ➔ note at BACK SB/STH UP
◆ v + n/pron + adv ◆ v + adv + n

bear 'up (**under sth**) to remain cheerful and in control in a difficult situation: *'How is your mother?' 'She's bearing up very well.' ◇ 'How are you?' 'Oh, bearing up.'*
◆ v + adv

bear upon sb/sth → BEAR ON/UPON SB/STH

bear with sb to be patient with sb: *If you'll just bear with me for a moment, I'll try to find her. ◇ She's under a lot of strain. Just bear with her.* **NOTE** **Bear with sb** is usually used in the present tense or to ask sb to be patient.
◆ v + prep

beat /biːt/ (beat, beaten /'biːtn/)

beat sb 'back to make sb move backwards away from sth: *She was beaten back by the flames. ◇ They tried to beat the enemy back.* **NOTE** Usually used in the passive.
◆ v + n/pron + adv ◆ v + adv + n

beat 'down (**on/upon sb/sth**) **1** if the sun **beats down**, it shines with great heat: *The sun beat down all afternoon from a clear sky.* **2** if rain

beats down, it falls with great force: *The rain was beating down on them.*

♦ v + adv

,**beat sb 'down** (*AmE, slang*) (of a group of people) to severely injure sb by hitting and kicking them: *We saw pictures on the news of a bunch of kids beating down an older guy.* **SYN bash sb up** (*informal, less frequent*); **beat sb up**

♦ v + n/pron + adv ♦ v + adv + n

▶ **'beat-down** *n* (*AmE, slang*) **1** an occasion when several people severely injure sb by hitting and kicking them **2** (*sport*) an occasion when one team defeats another by a large number of points

,**beat sb/sth 'down** (**to sth**) to persuade sb to reduce the price of sth; to get sb to accept a lower price for sth: *Chris tried to beat them down to a lower price.* **SYN knock sb/sth down**

♦ v + n/pron + adv ♦ v + adv + n (*less frequent*)

,**beat sth 'down 1** to hit sth hard, often many times, until it falls down: *The police had to beat the door down.* ◇ *People are hardly **beating the door down** to get her latest book* (= they are not rushing to buy it). **OBJ door SYN break sth down**; **batter sth down 2** to make sth flatter or lower by hitting it hard, usually with sth flat: *I used a spade to beat down the mud.* ◇ *Two women tried to beat down the flames.* **OBJ flames**

♦ v + n/pron + adv ♦ v + adv + n

,**beat sb/sth 'off 1** to drive sb/sth back or away by fighting: *They beat off an attack by the rebel army.* ◇ *He tried to beat the thugs off with a stick.* **OBJ attack, attacker 2** to defeat sb/sth in a competition or in business: *The company has beaten off very strong competition from abroad.* **OBJ challenge, competition**

♦ v + adv + n ♦ v + n/pron + adv

'**beat on sb** (*AmE, informal*) to hit or kick sb repeatedly

→ see also BEAT SB UP; BEAT UP ON SB

♦ v + prep

,**beat sth 'out 1** to produce a rhythm by hitting sth such as a drum repeatedly **OBJ rhythm 2** to put out a fire by hitting it with sth such as a brush, a jacket, etc.: *He used his jacket to beat out the flames.* **OBJ flames, fire 3** to make a piece of metal flat by hitting it with a hammer, etc.: *Pure gold can be beaten out to form very thin sheets.* **OBJ gold/iron, dent**

♦ v + adv + n ♦ v + pron + adv
♦ v + n + adv (*less frequent*)

,**beat sb 'out of sth** (*AmE, informal*) to get sth from sb by cheating or taking full advantage of a situation: *He beat me out of $500.*

♦ v + n/pron + adv + prep

'**beat sb to sth**; ,**beat sb 'to it** to achieve sth or reach a place before sb else: *Beckham beat*

everyone else to the ball. ◇ *Book now before somebody else beats you to it!*

♦ v + n/pron + prep

,**beat sb 'up** to hit or kick sb repeatedly: *Her husband used to beat her up.* ◇ *The gang went round beating up old ladies.* **SYN bash sb up** (*informal, less frequent*); **beat sb down** (*slang*)

→ see also BEAT UP ON SB

♦ v + n/pron + adv ♦ v + adv + n

▶ ,**beat-'up** (*especially AmE*) (*BrE usually* ,**beaten-'up**) *adj* [usually before noun] (*informal*) old or damaged: *He drives a beat-up old van.*

,**beat yourself 'up** (**about/over sth**) (*informal*) to blame yourself too much for sth; to criticize yourself: *Look, there's no need to beat yourself up over this.*

♦ v + pron + adv

,**beat 'up on sb** (*AmE, informal*) to attack sb physically or with words: *Of course it's not OK to beat up on your wife.* ◇ *He was accused of beating up on the President in the press.*

→ see also BEAT ON SB

♦ v + adv + prep

beaver /'biːvə(r)/

,**beaver a'way** (**at sth**) (*BrE, informal*) to work very hard at sth: *She's been beavering away at her homework for hours.*

♦ v + adv

become /bɪ'kʌm/ (**became** /bɪ'keɪm/, **become**)

be'**come of sb/sth** (*formal*) to happen to sb/ sth: *I wonder what became of the people who lived next door.* ◇ *What will become of us if I lose my job?*

NOTE Become of sb/sth is usually used in a question with *what*.

♦ v + prep

bed /bed/ (-**dd**-)

,**bed 'down 1** to lie down to go to sleep somewhere you do not normally sleep: *Young people bedded down in doorways.* **SYN doss down** (*BrE, less formal*) **2** (*also* ,**bed 'in**) if sth/sb new **beds down**, it/he/she becomes settled and starts to work well: *It'll take a while for the new system to bed down.* ◇ *The new players have bedded down well in the team.*

♦ v + adv

beef /biːf/

,**beef 'up sth** (*informal*) to make sth bigger, stronger, more interesting, etc.: *Security has been beefed up.* ◇ *The company has been trying to beef up its image.*

NOTE When the object of **beef up** is a noun, it comes after **up**, but when the object is a pronoun, it comes between **beef** and **up**: *Try to beef it up a little.*

◆ v + adv + n ◆ v + pron + adv

▶ **'beefed-up** *adj* [only before noun] improved; made bigger, stronger, more interesting, etc.: *beefed-up security*

beg /beg/ (**-gg-**)

,beg 'off; ,beg 'off sth; ,beg 'off doing sth to ask to be excused from sth; to say that you cannot do sth that you are expected or have promised to do: *She was asked to work the weekend shift but she tried to beg off.* ◊ *He begged off visiting his grandparents.*

SYN pull out, pull out of sth, etc.

→ see also CRY OFF, ETC.

◆ v + adv ◆ v + prep

believe /bɪˈliːv/

be'lieve in sb/sth **1** to feel sure that sb/sth exists: *Do you believe in ghosts?* ◊ *I believe in God.* ◊ *I don't believe in aliens.* → see also DISBELIEVE IN SB/STH; DEPEND ON SB/STH **2** to have confidence in sb/sth, to feel sure that they/ it will be successful or achieve sth: *My parents always believed in me.* ◊ *I have to believe in a product before I can sell it.*

◆ v + prep

be'lieve in sth; be'lieve in doing sth to feel that sth is right or valuable; to approve of sth: *Do you believe in capital punishment?* ◊ *She doesn't believe in running risks.* ◊ *I've always believed in giving people a second chance.*

◆ v + prep

be'lieve sth of sb to accept that sb is capable of a particular action, etc., especially a bad or immoral one: *Taking drugs? I can't **believe that of** Lucy!* ◊ *If I hadn't seen him doing it, I would never have **believed it of** him.* ◊ *She is determined to **believe the worst of me** (= think I am capable of doing, and likely to do, sth very bad).*

◆ v + n/pron + prep

belong /bɪˈlɒŋ; AmE -ˈlɔːŋ/

be'long to sb (*not used in the progressive tenses*) **1** to be the property of sb; to be owned by sb: *The house belonged to my cousin.* ◊ *That land belongs to the golf club.* ◊ *Who does the van belong to?* **2** if a time or an event **belongs to** a team, a group of people, etc., they are the most successful, popular or important: *Britain did well in the competition, but the day belonged to Norway.* ◊ *The second half of the 20th century belonged to the young.* **3** if a job, a duty, etc. **belongs to** you, it is your responsibility: *The job of disciplining a child belongs to the parents.* ◊ *The credit for our success belongs to the staff* (= they made us successful).

◆ v + prep

be'long to sth **1** to be a member of sth, for example a club, an organization or a family: *I don't belong to any political party.* ◊ *Latvia already belongs to the European Union.*

OBJ (**trade**) **union**, **club**, (**political**) **party 2** to be part of a particular group or system: *Rattlesnakes belong to the viper family.* ◊ *These three turtles all belong to one species.* **OBJ** **species**, **class**, **group**, **category 3** to be part of sth or connected with a particular time or place: *These things belong to the past.* ◊ *Writers like him belong to a different generation.* **OBJ** **the past**, **generation**

◆ v + prep

belt /belt/

,belt sth 'down (*AmE*, *informal*) to drink sth quickly: *He belted down his beer.*

SYN knock sth back

◆ v + adv + n ◆ v + n/pron + adv

,belt 'out sth (*informal*) if you **belt out** a song or a piece of music, you sing or play it very loudly: *Nobody can belt out a tune like she can.* ◊ *A radio belted out pop music.*

NOTE When the object of **belt out** is a noun, it comes after **out**, but when the object is a pronoun, it comes between **belt** and **out**: *She can belt it out with the best of them.*

◆ v + adv + n ◆ v + pron + adv

,belt 'up (*BrE*) **1** (*informal*) used to tell sb not very politely to be quiet: *Belt up, will you?* **SYN** shut up (*informal*) **2** to fasten the belt that you wear in a car to keep you in your seat if there is an accident (a **seat belt**) **SYN** buckle up

◆ v + adv

bend /bend/ (**bent**, **bent** /bent/)

,bend 'down to lean down: *He bent down and kissed her on the cheek.*

◆ v + adv

,bend 'over; ,bend 'over sth to lean over; to bend from the waist: *Bend over and touch your toes.* ◊ *He was bending over his desk, writing in his diary.*

◆ v + adv ◆ v + prep

IDM bend over 'backwards (**to do sth**) to do everything you can or make a great effort to do sth, especially to help sb: *We bend over backwards to be fair to all the children.*

bet /bet/ (**betting**, **bet**, **bet** or, less frequent, **betting**, **betted**, **betted**)

'bet on sth to rely on sth or on sb doing sth and expect it to happen: *'Do you think she'll come?' 'I wouldn't bet on it* (= I don't think it is very likely).' ◊ *Don't bet on me still being here when you get back!*

SYN count on sb/sth, etc.

◆ v + prep

big /bɪg/ (**-gg-**)

,**big sb/sth ˈup** (*BrE*, *slang*) to praise or recommend sb/sth strongly: *He's been bigging up the CD on his radio show.*
SYN **plug sth** (*more formal*); **promote sth** (*more formal*)
◆ v + n/pron + adv ◆ v + adv + n

,**big it ˈup** (**for sb/sth**) (*BrE*, *slang*) to show enthusiasm and support for sb/sth, especially by clapping, shouting, etc.: *Big it up for the boys in the band!*
◆ v + it + adv

bill /bɪl/

ˈ**bill sb/sth as sth** to describe sb/sth in a particular way; to advertise sb/sth as sth: *Some patients are receiving what has been billed as a revolutionary treatment.* ◇ *The concert was billed as 'A Night of Magic'.*
◆ v + n/pron + prep

bind /baɪnd/ (**bound, bound** /baʊnd/)

,**bind sb ˈover** (*law*) to warn sb that they will have to appear in court if they break the law again: *He was bound over to keep the peace.*
NOTE Usually used in the passive.
◆ v + n/pron + adv ◆ v + adv + n

ˈ**bind sb to sth** (*formal*) to force sb to do sth by making them promise to do it or making it part of a legal document: *The company directors are **bound to secrecy** (= they have promised not to say anything) about the future of the company.* ◇ *The band found they were bound to the contract.*
NOTE Usually used in the passive.
◆ v + n/pron + prep

,**bind sth ˈup** (**with sth**) to tie a long thin piece of material around sth to protect it: *She bound up his wounds with bandages.*
◆ v + adv + n ◆ v + n/pron + adv

IDM **be bound ˈup in sth** to be very busy with sth; to be very interested or involved in sth: *He's too bound up in his work to have much time for his children.* **be bound ˈup with sth** to be closely connected with sth: *The history of the mill is closely bound up with the history of the Wilkins family.*

bitch /bɪtʃ/

,**bitch sb ˈout** (*AmE*, *slang*) to criticize sb angrily: *The teacher bitched me out for being late.*
◆ v + n/pron + adv ◆ v + adv + n

bite /baɪt/ (**bit** /bɪt/, **bitten** /ˈbɪtn/)

ˈ**bite at sth** to try to bite sth: *The dog bit at the boy's hand.*
◆ v + prep

,**bite ˈback** (**at sb/sth**) to react when sb has harmed you and try to harm or criticize them: *If you criticize him, he'll bite back.*

SYN **hit back** (**at sb/sth**)
◆ v + adv

,**bite sth ˈback** to stop yourself from saying sth or from showing how you feel: *She struggled to bite back the tears of disappointment.* ◇ *Mike bit back his anger.* ◇ *The word 'idiot' came into her head, but she bit it back.*
OBJ **words, anger, retort, tears** **SYN** **suppress sth**
NOTE Not used in the passive.
◆ v + adv + n ◆ v + pron + adv ◆ v + n + adv (*rare*)

,**bite ˈinto sth** **1** to cut or press into the surface of sth: *The collar bit into his neck.* **SYN** **cut into sth** **2** to have an unpleasant effect on sth, especially by making it smaller: *The recession is biting into our profits.*
◆ v + prep

,**bite sth ˈoff** to cut sth off by biting it: *She bit off a piece of chocolate.* ◇ *His finger had been bitten off by a dog.*
◆ v + adv + n ◆ v + n/pron + adv

IDM **bite sb's ˈhead off** (*informal*) to shout at sb or speak to them angrily, often for no good reason: *I only asked him when the work would be finished and he almost bit my head off.* **bite off more than you can ˈchew** (*informal*) to try to do too much or sth that is too difficult for you: *This time he's bitten off more than he can chew.* **I, etc. could have bitten my, etc. ˈtongue off/out** used to say that you wish you had not said sth that you have just said: *Sam looked hurt and Maria could have bitten her tongue off.*

black /blæk/

,**black ˈout** to become unconscious or lose your memory for a short time: *The pain hit him and he blacked out.*
◆ v + adv
▸ ˈ**blackout** *n*: *When did you start having these blackouts?*

,**black sth ˈout** to turn out lights completely or cover windows, etc. so that light cannot be seen from outside: *blacked-out windows/houses* ◇ *The city was often blacked out by power cuts.*
OBJ **window, city**
NOTE Often used in the passive.
◆ v + adv + n ◆ v + pron + adv ◆ v + n + adv (*rare*)
▸ ˈ**blackout** *n* **1** (*especially BrE*) (in the past) a period of time during a war when the streets and buildings were kept as dark as possible so that the enemy could not see what to bomb **2** [usually pl.] (*BrE*) a covering for windows that stops light from outside coming in, or that stops bright light being seen from outside: *blackout material* **3** (*also* ˈ**outage** *AmE*) a period of time when the electricity supply to a place stops completely **4** a situation when the government or the police prevent a radio or television programme from being broadcast, or do not allow some news or information to be given to

the public: *The government have been accused of maintaining a news blackout over election fraud.*

blank /blæŋk/

,blank 'out (*AmE, informal*) if you **blank out** or your mind **blanks out**, you cannot remember anything or you become confused: *I hope I don't blank out in the exam.*

NOTE Blank on its own has the same meaning.
 ♦ v + adv

,blank sth 'out **1** to deliberately forget sth unpleasant: *Your childhood may have been difficult but you can't just blank it out.* **2** to cover sth written or printed, for example, with black ink so that it cannot be read: *All the names in the report had been blanked out.*
 ♦ v + adv + n ♦ v + pron + adv ♦ v + n + adv (*rare*)

blare /bleə(r); *AmE* bler/

,blare 'out; ,blare sth 'out if music **blares out**, or a radio, etc. **blares out** music, it is produced or played very loudly: *Music was blaring out from somewhere.* ◇ *The radio was blaring out rock music.*

SYN blast out, blast sth out (*less frequent*)
 ♦ v + adv ♦ v + adv + n ♦ v + n/pron + adv

blast /blɑːst; *AmE* blæst/

,blast a'way (at sb/sth) if a gun or sb using a gun **blasts away**, the gun fires loudly and continuously: *The machine guns blasted away all night.*
 ♦ v + adv

,blast sb/sth a'way (*less frequent*) to kill sb or remove sth or break it apart violently, for example with a gun, bombs, etc.: *They have blasted away the side of this beautiful valley to make a road.* ◇ (*figurative*) *This theory has been blasted away by the new evidence.*

SYN blow sb/sth away
 ♦ v + adv + n ♦ v + n/pron + adv (*rare*)

,blast 'off when a spacecraft **blasts off**, it leaves the ground and goes up into space: *The rocket blasted off at 7.28 p.m.*

SYN lift off
 ♦ v + adv

 ▶ 'blast-off *n* [U] the moment when a spacecraft leaves the ground: *Blast-off will be in 30 seconds.*

,blast 'out; ,blast sth 'out if music **blasts out** or a radio, etc. **blasts out** music, it is produced or played very loudly: *A Beatles song was blasting out at full volume.* ◇ *The radio was blasting out heavy rock music.*

SYN blare out, blare sth out
 ♦ v + adv ♦ v + adv + n ♦ v + n/pron + adv

blaze /bleɪz/

,blaze a'way **1** (at sb/sth) if guns or people **blaze away**, the guns fire continuously: *The guns kept blazing away at the enemy.* **2** if a fire **blazes away**, it burns brightly

NOTE Blaze is used on its own with the same meanings.
 ♦ v + adv

,blaze 'up if a fire **blazes up**, it suddenly starts burning more strongly: (*figurative*) *His anger blazed up uncontrollably.*
 ♦ v + adv

bleep /bliːp/

,bleep sth/sb 'out to remove an offensive word that sb says on television, etc. and replace it with a short high electronic sound: *His obscenities had to be bleeped out.*
 ♦ v + n/pron + adv ♦ v + adv + n

blend /blend/

,blend 'in **1** (with sth) if sth **blends in** with sth else or with its surroundings, it looks similar to it/them or matches well: *The curtains blend in perfectly with the carpet.* ◇ *The new office block doesn't blend in well with its traditional surroundings.* **2** (with sb) if sb **blends in** with other people, they become similar to the people around them: *He should try to blend in with the locals a bit more.*

→ see also BLEND INTO STH; MERGE IN (WITH STH), MERGE INTO STH
 ♦ v + adv

,blend sth 'in **1** (in cooking) to add another substance to sth and mix them together: *Heat the butter gently and then blend in a little flour.*

SYN mix sth in **2** to make a substance mix with another so that you cannot see where one ends and the other starts: *Blend the eyeshadow in with your fingers.* ◇ *He blended in the charcoal lines to make the picture look softer.*
 ♦ v + adv + n ♦ v + pron + adv
 ♦ v + n + adv (*less frequent*)

,blend 'into sth to look or sound so similar to sth that it is difficult for anyone to see or hear it: *The animals can blend into the long grass.* ◇ *The new development should blend into its surroundings.*

OBJ background, surroundings
→ see also BLEND IN; MERGE IN, ETC.
 ♦ v + prep

blimp /blɪmp/

,blimp 'out/'up (*AmE, informal*) to become fat; to gain weight
 ♦ v + adv

blink /blɪŋk/

,blink sth a'way to clear sth from the eyes by blinking (= closing and opening your eyes quickly): *He blinked away a tear.*

OBJ tear(s)
 ♦ v + adv + n ♦ v + n/pron + adv

,blink sth 'back to try to control your tears: *I found myself blinking back tears during his speech.*

bliss

OBJ only **tear(s)**
♦ v + adv + n ♦ v + n/pron + adv

bliss /blɪs/

,bliss 'out; ,bliss sb 'out (*informal*) to feel very happy and relaxed; to make sb feel this: *I was blissing out over my scrambled eggs.* ◇ *Those old black and white movies bliss me out.*
♦ v + adv ♦ v + n/pron + adv
♦ v + adv + n (*less frequent*)
▸ ,blissed 'out *adj* feeling very happy and relaxed: *The regulars at the yoga class looked completely blissed out.*

block /blɒk; *AmE* blɑːk/

,block sb/sth 'in to stop a vehicle from being driven away by parking too close to it: *You're blocking that Mini in.* ◇ *Somebody had parked in front of me, blocking me in.* ◇ *I was blocked in by two lorries so I had to leave the car and walk.*
♦ v + n/pron + adv ♦ v + adv + n (*less frequent*)

,block sth 'off 1 to close a road or another place by placing a barrier across it to stop sb/sth going in or coming out: *The police blocked the street off.* ◇ *The pipe had been blocked off to prevent leaks.* OBJ **street**, **road**, **area**, **entrance** SYN **close sth off (to sth/sb) 2** (*especially AmE*) to reserve a period of time for a particular activity: *Thursday afternoons are blocked off for sports.*
♦ v + n/pron + adv ♦ v + adv + n

,block sth 'out to stop light or noise from coming in; to cover or hide sth: *The trees blocked out much of the sunlight.* ◇ (*figurative*) *I'm so used to the traffic noise now I just block it out* (= I don't hear it).
OBJ **light**, **sun**, **sound**
♦ v + adv + n ♦ v + pron + adv
♦ v + n + adv (*less frequent*)

,block sb/sth 'out; ,block sb/sth 'out of sth to avoid remembering sb/sth or thinking about sb/sth, especially sth unpleasant: *He tried to block the incident out of his mind.*
SYN **blot sb/sth out**, etc.; **shut sth out**, **shut sth out of sth**; **suppress sth**
♦ v + n/pron + adv ♦ v + adv + n
♦ v + n/pron + adv + prep

,block sth 'up to fill sth such as a hole completely so that nothing can get through it: *All the windows had been blocked up.*
OBJ **window**, **door**, **hole**, **fireplace**
♦ v + n/pron + adv ♦ v + adv + n
▸ ,blocked 'up *adj* completely full; not clear: *I've got a blocked-up nose.*

blot /blɒt; *AmE* blɑːt/ (-tt-)

,blot sb/sth 'out; ,blot sb/sth 'out of sth to avoid remembering sb/sth or thinking about sb/sth, especially sth unpleasant: *He wanted to blot out the memory.*

OBJ **memories**, **thoughts** SYN **block sb/sth out**, etc.; **shut sth out**, **shut sth out of sth**
♦ v + n/pron + adv ♦ v + adv + n
♦ v + n/pron + adv + prep

,blot sth 'out to stop light or noise coming in; to cover or hide sth: *Dark clouds were blotting out the sun.*
OBJ **light**, **sun**, **stars**, **sound** SYN **block sth out**
♦ v + adv + n ♦ v + n/pron + adv

blow /bləʊ; *AmE* bloʊ/ (**blew** /bluː/, **blown** /bləʊn; *AmE* bloʊn/)

,blow a'way; ,blow sth a'way to be moved or carried away by the force of the wind or by sb's breath; to move in this way: *It was so windy the tent nearly blew away!* ◇ *A sudden breeze blew his newspaper away.* ◇ *She blew away the dust on the lid.*
♦ v + adv ♦ v + n/pron + adv ♦ v + adv + n

,blow sb a'way 1 (*informal*) to impress sb a lot; to surprise or please sb: *I saw her performance on Broadway last year and it just blew me away.* SYN **bowl sb over**; **knock sb out** (*informal*) 2 (*AmE*, *informal*, *sport*) to defeat sb easily: *Mitchell blew away the other runners.*
♦ v + n/pron + adv ♦ v + adv + n

,blow sb/sth a'way to kill sb or remove or destroy sth with bombs or with a gun: *He threatened to blow us away.* ◇ *They blew his kneecaps away* (= by shooting them).
SYN **blast sb/sth away** ➔ note at SHOOT SB/STH DOWN
♦ v + n/pron + adv ♦ v + adv + n

,blow 'down; ,blow sth 'down if sth **blows down**, or the wind **blows it down**, it falls to the ground because of the force of the wind: *An old oak tree had blown down in the storm.* ◇ *Hundreds of trees have been blown down this winter.*
♦ v + adv ♦ v + n/pron + adv ♦ v + adv + n

,blow 'in; ,blow 'into sth (*informal*) to arrive somewhere where you are not expected: *Look who's just blown in!* ◇ *Have you heard who's just blown into town?*
♦ v + adv ♦ v + adv + prep

,blow 'off (*BrE*, *informal*) to let air from the body escape through your bottom: *Who just blew off?* SYN **break wind** (*more formal*); **fart** (*slang*)
♦ v + adv

,blow 'off; ,blow sth 'off; ,blow sth 'off sth 1 if sth **blows off**, or the wind **blows it off**, it is removed by the force of the wind: *My hat blew off.* ◇ *A gust of wind blew her cap off.* ◇ *The roof was blown off the Greens' house.* 2 if sth **blows off** in an explosion, or an explosion **blows sth off**, it is violently removed: *The door blew off in the explosion.* ◇ *The explosion blew the roof off* (*the house*).
♦ v + adv ♦ v + n/pron + adv ♦ v + adv + n
♦ v + n/pron + adv + prep

IDM **blow off 'steam** (*AmE*) → LET OFF STEAM at LET STH OFF **blow/knock sb's 'socks off** to impress or surprise sb very much: *When I first heard the song, it blew my socks off.* **blow the 'lid off sth** (*BrE also* **blow the 'lid on sth**) to reveal information that was previously kept secret, especially in a dramatic way: *The article blew the lid off the secret scandals inside the previous administration.*

,**blow 'off sth** (*AmE, informal*) to decide not to do sth you should do or were planning to do: *Jessica blew off her classes on Friday afternoon to go shopping.*

NOTE When the object of **blow off** is a noun, it comes after **off**, but when the object is a pronoun, it comes between **blow** and **off**: *I debated going to Joe's, but I blew it off.*

✦ v + adv + n ✦ v + pron + adv

,**blow sb 'off** (*AmE, informal*) **1** to disappoint sb by not meeting them as arranged: *We were supposed to go out yesterday, but he blew me off.* **SYN** **stand sb up** **2** to tell sb that you do not want to have a relationship with them: *I told her I liked her, but she blew me off.*

✦ v + n/pron + adv ✦ v + adv + n

,**blow 'out** **1** if a tyre **blows out**, it bursts suddenly: *One of the front tyres blew out.* **SYN** **burst** **2** if an oil or gas well **blows out**, it suddenly sends out gas with great force

✦ v + adv

▶ '**blowout** *n* **1** an occasion when a tyre bursts on a vehicle while it is being driven **2** an occasion when oil or gas suddenly escapes from an oil well **3** (*BrE, informal*) a large meal at which people eat too much **4** (*AmE, informal*) a large party or social occasion

,**blow 'out**; ,**blow sth 'out** **1** if a flame **blows out** or sb/sth **blows it out**, it is put out by the wind or some air: *There was a sudden gust of wind and the candle blew out.* ◇ *She took a deep breath and blew out all the candles.* ➔ note at PUT STH OUT **2** if a window **blows out**, or an explosion, etc. **blows it out**, the force makes it fall out: *All the windows blew out in the blast.* ◇ *The explosion blew out the windows in the building.* **3** (in surfing) if the waves **blow out** or the wind **blows out** the waves, they become too low for surfing in a particular place

✦ v + adv ✦ v + adv + n ✦ v + n/pron + adv

,**blow sb 'out** **1** (**for sb**) (*BrE, slang*) to tell sb that you do not want to have a relationship with them: *He blew me out for Chris, but I still fancy him.* **2** (*AmE, informal, sport*) to defeat sb easily: *The home team blew out the Suns by 30 points.*

✦ v + n/pron + adv ✦ v + adv + n

▶ '**blowout** *n* (*AmE, informal, sport*) an easy victory

,**blow sth 'out** **1** to breathe sth out from your mouth: *She inhaled and then blew the smoke out.* **SYN** **exhale sth** **2** to fill sth, especially your cheeks, with air: *She blew out her cheeks in exasperation.* **OBJ** **cheeks** **3** (*especially AmE*) to use a machine that blows hot air (a **hairdryer**)

and a brush to make your/sb's hair straight: *Blowing your hair out every day can damage it.* **OBJ** **hair** **4** (*AmE*) to badly injure a part of your body, especially a joint such as a knee or elbow: *He blew out his knee playing basketball.*

✦ v + n/pron + adv ✦ v + adv + n

IDM **blow your/sb's 'brains out** (*informal*) to kill yourself/sb by shooting yourself/them in the head

▶ '**blowout** *n* (*especially AmE*) the act of blowing your hair out

,**blow itself 'out** if a storm **blows itself out**, it loses its force and stops: *By morning the storm had blown itself out.*

✦ v + pron + adv

,**blow 'over** **1** if a storm **blows over**, it becomes less strong and stops: *We sheltered in a barn until the storm blew over.* **SYN** **die down**; **subside** **2** if an argument **blows over**, it becomes less important and is forgotten: *Don't come back to work until the argument has blown over.* **SYN** **subside**

✦ v + adv

,**blow 'over**; ,**blow sb/sth 'over** if sb/sth **blows over** or the wind **blows sb/sth over**, he/she/it falls to the ground because of the force of the wind: *One of the trees had blown over in the storm.* ◇ *The fence had been blown over in a storm.*

NOTE Often used in the passive.

✦ v + adv ✦ v + n/pron + adv

,**blow 'up** **1** to explode; to be destroyed by an explosion: *The bomb blew up as experts tried to defuse it.* ◇ *The car blew up when it hit the wall.* **SYN** **explode** (*more formal*) ➔ note on page 22 **2** to start suddenly and with force: *A storm blew up just after the ship left port.* ◇ *A row has blown up over the leaking of information to the press.* **OPP** **die down** **3** (**at sb**) (*informal*) to become very angry: *My mum blew up at my dad for keeping me up so late.* ◇ *His attitude annoyed me and I blew up.* **4** (*slang*) to become very successful or popular: *Right now Miss Kirstee is totally blowing up. She's in her prime.*

✦ v + adv

IDM **blow up in sb's 'face** if a plan, a deal or a situation **blows up in your face**, it goes very badly wrong and causes you harm or embarrassment

▶ '**blow-up** *n* **1** (*especially AmE*) an explosion **2** (*AmE*) an occasion when sb becomes very angry; an argument: *The tensions between them ended in a big blow-up.*

,**blow sb/sth 'up** to kill sb or destroy sth with a bomb or an explosion: *The hijackers threatened to blow the plane up.* ◇ *A judge in Italy was blown up by a car bomb last week.*

NOTE Often used in the passive.

➔ note on page 22

✦ v + n/pron + adv ✦ v + adv + n

blow (sth) up

blow (sth) up ◆ **burst (sth)** ◆ **explode (sth)** ◆ **go off**

These are all verbs that can be used when sth bursts apart violently, causing damage or injury.

blow (sth) up to be destroyed by an explosion; to destroy sth by an explosion: *A police officer was killed when his car blew up.* ◇ *They were trying to blow up the bridge.*

burst (sth) to break open or apart, especially because of pressure from inside; to make sth break in this way: *That balloon will burst if you blow it up any more.* ◇ *The dam burst under the weight of water.*

explode (sth) to burst loudly and violently, causing damage; to make sth burst in this way: *The jet smashed into a hillside and exploded.* ◇ *Bomb disposal experts exploded the device under controlled conditions.* ▶ explosion *n*: *There were two loud explosions.*

go off (of a bomb) to explode; (of a gun) to be fired: *The bomb went off in a crowded street.* **NOTE** When used about guns, **go off** can suggest that the gun was fired by accident, or that the person who fired it was not really responsible: *A gun went off during the search of his home.*

WHICH WORD?

Blow up has a similar meaning to **explode**, but **explode** is more formal. It is possible to say that a bomb **blows up**, but it is more common to say that it **explodes** or **goes off**.

PATTERNS AND COLLOCATIONS

■ a **bomb** explodes/goes off/bursts
■ a **car/plane/vehicle** explodes/blows up
■ a **firework/rocket** explodes/goes off
■ a **shell** explodes/bursts

blow sth ˈup 1 to fill sth with air or gas: *You need to blow up the tyres on your bike.* OBJ **balloon, tyre** SYN **inflate sth** (*more formal*) OPP **let sth down 2** to make sth larger: *What a lovely photo! Why don't you have it blown up?* OBJ **photo** SYN **enlarge sth** (*more formal*) **3** to make sth seem more important, better or worse than it really is: *The whole affair has been **blown up out of all proportion**.* SYN **exaggerate sth** (*more formal*)
◆ v + n/pron + adv ◆ v + adv + n
▶ ˈblow-up *n* a larger picture made from a photo or picture: *The blow-up showed a scar on the attacker's cheek.*
▶ ˈblow-up *adj* [only before noun] that you can fill with air or gas

bluff /blʌf/

bluff sb ˈout (*old-fashioned, informal, especially AmE*) to lie and pretend in order to trick sb
◆ v + n/pron + adv ◆ v + adv + n

bluff it ˈout (*especially BrE*) to lie to sb in order to get out of a difficult situation, especially when they suspect you are not being honest: *If he asks any difficult questions, you'll have to bluff it out.* ◇ *I know everything so there's no point trying to bluff it out.*
◆ v + it + adv

bluff sb ˈout of sth (*old-fashioned, AmE*) to trick sb in order to get sth from them
SYN **cheat sb of sth, cheat sb out of sth**
◆ v + n/pron + adv + prep

blunder /ˈblʌndə(r)/

blunder aˈround; **blunder aˈround sth** (*also* ˌblunder aˈbout/ˈround, ˌblunder aˈbout/ˈround sth *especially BrE*) to move about a place in an awkward or uncertain way, knocking into things: *He blundered about in the dark, feeling for the light switch.* ◇ *I blundered around the flat, trying to be quiet.*
◆ v + adv ◆ v + prep

blunder ˈinto sth 1 to walk into sb/sth because you are awkward or unable to see: *She blundered into a tree.* **2** to accidentally find yourself in a difficult or dangerous place or situation: *She blundered into a dangerous area of the city after losing her way.* ◇ *He had innocently blundered into a private dispute.*
◆ v + prep

blurt /blɜːt; AmE blɜːrt/

blurt sth ˈout to say sth suddenly and without thinking carefully: *'There's been an accident,' she blurted out.* ◇ *He found himself blurting out the whole story to her.*
◆ v + adv + speech ◆ v + adv + n ◆ v + n/pron + adv

board /bɔːd; AmE bɔːrd/

board sth ˈup to cover a window or a door with boards: *All the windows had been boarded up.*
OBJ **window, house, shop/store**
NOTE Often used in the passive.
◆ v + n/pron + adv ◆ v + adv + n

bob /bɒb; *AmE* bɑːb/ (**-bb-**)

ˌbob 'up **1** to come to the surface quickly: *She dived in and bobbed up a few seconds later in the middle of the pool.* **2** to appear suddenly: *She bobbed up from behind the fence.* SYN **pop up**
♦ v + adv

bog /bɒg; *AmE* bɔːg/ (**-gg-**)

ˌbog 'down (*AmE*) to be unable to make progress: *The bill bogged down after being passed by Congress.*
♦ v + adv

be/get ˌbogged 'down (in sth) **1** to be/get stuck in mud or wet ground; to become stuck in sth and unable to make progress: *The car got bogged down in the mud.* **2** to be unable to make progress in an activity: *Don't get bogged down in details.* ◇ *I'm rather bogged down (with work) at the moment.*
♦ be/get + v + adv

ˌbog 'off (*BrE, slang*) used to tell sb rudely to go away: *Bog off, I'm trying to sleep!* SYN **clear off** (*informal*)
♦ v + adv

boil /bɔɪl/

ˌboil a'way if a liquid **boils away**, it boils until there is nothing left: *The water in the saucepan had all boiled away.* SYN **evaporate** (*more formal*)
♦ v + adv

ˌboil sth 'down **1** to make a liquid less in quantity by boiling it SYN **reduce sth** (*more formal*) **2** (**to sth**) to make sth smaller by removing unimportant parts and leaving only the essential things: *Boil the report down to the key points.* SYN **condense sth** (*more formal*)
♦ v + n/pron + adv ♦ v + adv + n

ˌboil 'down to sth (*not used in the progressive tenses*) if a situation, an issue, etc. **boils down to sth**, it has that as its main point: *It all boils down to money in the end.*
♦ v + adv + prep

ˌboil 'over **1** if a liquid in a pan, etc. **boils over**, it boils and flows over the side of the pan: *Don't let the milk boil over.* **2** (**into sth**) (*informal*) if anger, an argument, etc. **boils over**, it changes and becomes very violent and difficult to control: *The unrest could boil over into civil war.* ◇ *She interrupted swiftly before his temper could boil over again.* SYN **explode**
♦ v + adv

ˌboil 'up if anger, an argument, etc. **boils up**, it starts to become stronger or more violent
♦ v + adv

ˌboil sth 'up (*BrE*) to heat a liquid or some food until it boils: *I'll boil the kettle up again and we'll have a cup of tea.*
NOTE **Boil sth** can be used on its own with the same meaning.
♦ v + n/pron + adv ♦ v + adv + n

bollix /'bɒlɪks; *AmE* 'bɑːl-/

ˌbollix sth 'up (*AmE, slang*) to confuse or change sth; to spoil sth
SYN **mess sth up** (*informal*); **screw sth up** (*slang*)
♦ v + n/pron + adv ♦ v + adv + n

bolster /'bəʊlstə(r); *AmE* 'boʊl-/

ˌbolster sb/sth 'up to support or encourage sb; to make sth better or stronger: *He tried to bolster up their morale.* ◇ *The high interest rates helped to bolster up the economy.*
OBJ **confidence**, **morale**
NOTE **Bolster sb/sth** on its own is more frequent.
♦ v + n/pron + adv ♦ v + adv + n

bolt /bəʊlt; *AmE* boʊlt/

ˌbolt sth 'down (*informal*) to eat sth very quickly: *I had to bolt down my breakfast.*
OBJ **food**
NOTE **Bolt sth** is also used on its own.
♦ v + n/pron + adv ♦ v + adv + n

ˌbolt sth 'on (**to sth**) to add sth to sth else at a later stage: *Statistics should be an integral part of the course and not just bolted on afterwards.*
NOTE Often used in the passive.
♦ v + n/pron + adv ♦ v + adv + n
▶ 'bolt-on *adj* [only before noun]

bomb /bɒm; *AmE* bɑːm/

ˌbomb 'out (*informal, especially AmE*) to fail very badly: *The movie bombed out at the box office.*
NOTE **Bomb** is also used on its own: *The movie bombed at the box office.*
♦ v + adv

be/get ˌbombed 'out; be/get ˌbombed 'out of sth if a person is **bombed out**, their home is destroyed by bombs; if a building is **bombed out**, it is destroyed by bombs: *My mother was bombed out of her house in 1942.* ◇ *They got bombed out.*
♦ be/get + v + adv ♦ be/get + v + adv + prep

bone /bəʊn; *AmE* boʊn/

ˌbone 'up on sth (*informal*) to study sth; to look again at sth you already know: *I must bone up on my French before we go to Paris.*
♦ v + adv + prep

book /bʊk/

ˌbook 'in (**at sth**), ˌbook 'into sth (*BrE*) to arrive at a hotel and arrange to have a room: *They booked in (at the hotel) using a false name.* ◇ *She booked into a hotel in the centre of Boston.*
SYN **check in** (**at sth**); **check into sth** OPP **check out**, **check out of sth**
♦ v + adv ♦ v + prep

ˌbook sb/yourself 'in (**at sth**), ˌbook sb/yourself 'into sth (*BrE*) to reserve a room at a hotel, etc. for sb: *I've booked us in at the Plaza.*

◇ *The hotel I was booked into was awful.* ◇ *He's booked himself into a rehabilitation clinic.*

OBJ hotel

♦ v + n/pron + adv ♦ v + n/pron + prep

ˌbook ˈup (for sth) (*especially BrE*) to reserve a place, for example on a trip or a course: *I booked up for the course months in advance.*

NOTE Book (for sth) can be used with the same meaning.

♦ v + adv

be ˌbooked ˈup **1** if a plane, restaurant, theatre, etc. **is booked up**, there are no seats, tables, etc. available: *All the flights are booked up.* **NOTE** Be fully booked is often used with the same meaning. **2** (*informal*) if a person **is booked up**, they have no time available: *He can't see you tomorrow, he's booked up.*

♦ be + v + adv

boom /buːm/

ˌboom ˈout if a sound or sb's voice **booms out**, it makes a loud, deep noise: *His voice boomed out, announcing the winners.*

♦ v + adv

ˌboom ˈout sth to say sth in a loud deep voice: *The trainer boomed out instructions through a loud hailer.* ◇ *A voice boomed out: 'Nobody move!'*

♦ v + adv + n ♦ v + adv + speech

boot /buːt/

ˌboot sb ˈout; ˌboot sb ˈout of sth (*informal, especially BrE*) to force sb to leave a place, job, school, club, etc.: *I'll have to boot you out soon—I want to lock up.* ◇ *The manager booted him out of the team.* ◇ *He was booted out of the house by his father.*

SYN kick sb out, etc. (*informal*); throw sb out, etc.

NOTE Often used in the passive.

♦ v + n/pron + adv ♦ v + adv + n
♦ v + n/pron + adv + prep

ˌboot ˈup; ˌboot sth ˈup (*computing*) if a computer **boots up**, or sb **boots it up**, it is turned on and becomes ready to use: *My machine isn't booting up properly.* ◇ *When you boot up, a menu will appear on the screen.* ◇ *Boot the computer up and enter your password.*

OBJ computer

♦ v + adv ♦ v + n/pron + adv ♦ v + adv + n

border /ˈbɔːdə(r); AmE ˈbɔːrd-/

ˈborder on sth (*also* ˈborder upon sth *more formal*) **1** to share a border with another country or region; to be next to a place: *Many states formerly bordering on the EU have now joined.* ◇ *Slovenia borders on Italy, Austria, Hungary and Croatia.* **2** to come close to being sth: *Her self-confidence borders on arrogance.* ◇ *Our task borders on the impossible.* **SYN** verge on sth

♦ v + prep

bore /bɔː(r)/

ˌbore ˈinto sb/sth (*literary*) if sb's eyes **bore into** sb/sth, they stare in a way that makes sb feel uncomfortable: *His blue eyes seemed to bore into her.*

♦ v + prep

boss /bɒs; AmE bɔːs/

ˌboss sb aˈround (*also* ˌboss sb aˈbout *especially BrE*) (*informal*) to tell sb what to do in a determined or unpleasant way: *He's always bossing his wife around.*

SYN order sb around

♦ v + n/pron + adv

botch /bɒtʃ; AmE bɑːtʃ/

ˌbotch sth ˈup (*informal*) to spoil sth by doing it badly; to do sth badly: *Instead of fixing my computer, he's botched it up completely.*

SYN mess sth up

NOTE Botch sth is used more frequently on its own: *botched attempts at DIY.*

♦ v + n/pron + adv ♦ v + adv + n

▶ ˈbotch-up (*also* **botch**) *n* (*informal, especially BrE*) a piece of work that is badly done

bottle /ˈbɒtl; AmE ˈbɑːtl/

ˌbottle ˈout; ˌbottle ˈout of sth; ˌbottle ˈout of doing sth (*BrE, informal*) to suddenly decide not to do sth because you are too frightened: *I bottled out of phoning him at the last minute.*

SYN chicken out, etc.

♦ v + adv ♦ v + adv + prep

ˌbottle sth ˈup to keep your feelings, especially sadness or anger, hidden and not tell other people how you are feeling: *Tell someone how you're feeling, instead of bottling it all up.*

OBJ emotions, feelings

♦ v + n/pron + adv ♦ v + adv + n

bottom /ˈbɒtəm; AmE ˈbɑːtəm/

ˌbottom ˈout if markets, prices or bad situations **bottom out**, they reach their lowest point and then stop getting worse: *The recession has finally bottomed out.*

♦ v + adv

bounce /baʊns/

ˌbounce aˈround (*AmE, informal*) to live or work in many different places without developing a routine: *He bounced around for a few years, living in friends' basements.*

♦ v + adv

ˌbounce sth aˈround (*informal, especially AmE*) to discuss sth with other people: *We're bouncing some new ideas around.*

OBJ ideas

♦ v + n/pron + adv ♦ v + adv + n

ˌbounce ˈback (from sth) (*AmE also* ˌsnap ˈback (into sth)) (*informal*) to recover well after you have been ill/sick or had a difficult time: *No* matter what happens, she always bounces back very quickly.

SYN recover (**from sth**) (*more formal*)

◆ v + adv

‚bounce 'back; ‚bounce sth 'back if an email **bounces back**, or the system **bounces it back**, it returns to the person who sent it because the system cannot deliver it

◆ v + adv ◆ v + adv + n ◆ v + n/pron + adv

‚bounce sb 'into sth; ‚bounce sb 'into doing sth (*especially BrE*) to make or force sb to do sth quickly without giving them time to think about it: *I felt I'd been bounced into supporting a proposal I didn't really agree with.*

NOTE Often used in the passive.

◆ v + n/pron + prep

‚bounce sth 'off sb (*informal*) to tell sb else your ideas to find out what they think about them: *We were able to share problems and bounce ideas off each other.*

OBJ ideas

◆ v + n/pron + prep

bow /baʊ/

‚bow 'down 1 (**to/before sb/sth**) to move your head or the top part of your body forwards or downwards as a sign of respect: *He refused to bow down before the king.* 2 (**to sb/sth**) to do what sb tells you to do without trying to resist: *We refuse to just bow down and let the government do whatever it wants.*

◆ v + adv

‚bow 'out; ‚bow 'out of sth to stop doing an activity or a job that you have been doing successfully, often for a long time: *After thirty years in politics, he feels it is time to bow out.* ◇ *Smith will bow out of professional football at the end of the season.*

◆ v + adv ◆ v + adv + prep

'bow to sth to agree unwillingly to do sth or to accept sth that sb else wants you to: *The government eventually bowed to public pressure.*

OBJ pressure, the inevitable **SYN** give in (**to sb/sth**)

◆ v + prep

bowl /bəʊl; AmE boʊl/

‚bowl sb 'out (in cricket) to make the person who is hitting the ball (the **batsman**) or his/her team have to leave the field by throwing a ball that hits the three sticks behind the batsman (the **wicket**): *He bowled Fleming out with the first ball.*

◆ v + n/pron + adv ◆ v + adv + n

‚bowl sb 'over 1 to run into sb and knock them down: *The explosion bowled us all over.* **SYN** knock sb down; knock sb over 2 to surprise or impress sb a lot; to affect sb deeply: *We were bowled over by the news.* ◇ *Philip bowled us all over by deciding to go into advertising.*

SYN blow sb away (*informal*); knock sb out (*informal*) **NOTE** Often used in the passive.

◆ v + n/pron + adv ◆ v + adv + n

box /bɒks; AmE bɑːks/

‚box sb 'in to prevent sb from doing what they want, especially by creating rules or other difficulties: *The President was unable to act because the Democrats were boxing him in.* ◇ *She was boxed in by rules and regulations.*

NOTE Often used in the passive.

◆ v + n/pron + adv

‚box sb/sth 'in to prevent a person or a vehicle from moving by surrounding them/it with other people or vehicles: *You can't park here—you're boxing that car in!* ◇ *He couldn't overtake the leader because he was boxed in by the other runners.*

NOTE Often used in the passive.

◆ v + n/pron + adv ◆ v + adv + n

‚box 'out; ‚box sb 'out (*AmE*) (in basketball) to put yourself between the basket and an opposing player in order to catch a ball which has hit the basket but not gone in: *If we don't start boxing out, we'll lose every game! ◇ We tried to box him out every time he went up for a shot.*

◆ v + adv ◆ v + n/pron + adv ◆ v + adv + n

▸ 'boxout n (*AmE*): *She wasn't shooting well, and she was missing boxouts.*

‚box sb 'out (**of sth**) (*AmE*) to force sb into a situation in which they can no longer take part in an activity, business, etc.: *The Senator accused them of trying to box him out of the Republican convention.*

◆ v + n/pron + adv ◆ v + adv + n

‚box sth 'up to put sth in a box or boxes: *She boxed up all the old baby clothes to send to her niece.*

◆ v + n/pron + adv ◆ v + adv + n

branch /brɑːntʃ; AmE bræntʃ/

‚branch 'off 1 if a road or path **branches off**, it leaves a larger one and goes in a different direction: *She followed the path until it branched off.* ◇ *Over the bridge a road branches off to the right.* 2 if a person **branches off**, they leave a road or path and travel in a different direction: *Go past the farm and branch off towards the trees.*

◆ v + adv

‚branch 'out (**into sth**) to begin to do a new job or an activity that you do not usually do: *The company is branching out into Europe.* ◇ *She's leaving the company to branch out on her own.*

◆ v + adv

brazen /'breɪzn/

‚brazen 'out sth; brazen it 'out to behave in a confident way as if you are not ashamed or embarrassed about sth you have done, even

break down

break down ♦ **crash** ♦ **go down** ♦ **go wrong**

These are all verbs that can be used when a machine stops working because of a fault.

break down (of a machine or vehicle) to stop working because of a fault: *The washing machine has broken down again.* ◊ *We* (= our car) *broke down on the motorway.*

NOTE **Break** can be used on its own, but is not used to talk about vehicles: *My watch has broken.* ▸ **breakdown** *n*: *a breakdown on the motorway*

crash (of a computer or computer system) to stop working suddenly: *Files can be lost if the system suddenly crashes.*

go down (of a computer system) to stop working temporarily: *The system is going down in ten minutes.*

go wrong to stop working correctly: *The new television set will contain fewer components to go wrong.*

WHICH WORD?

Machines, devices and parts inside machines and vehicles can **go wrong**; whole vehicles cannot. If sth **goes wrong**, it may not stop working completely, as it does if it **breaks** or **breaks down**. When computers or computer systems **crash**, this is always sudden and unexpected; when a system **goes down**, it may have been turned off deliberately while work is carried out on it.

PATTERNS AND COLLOCATIONS

- the TV/the DVD player/my watch has broken/gone wrong
- the washing machine has broken down/gone wrong
- my car has broken down
- my computer has gone wrong/crashed
- the computer system has crashed/gone down

though you should be: *The senator **brazened it out** as the list of scandals grew.*
NOTE When the object of **brazen out** is a noun, it comes after **out**, but when the object is the pronoun **it**, it comes between **brazen** and **out**.
♦ v + it + adv ♦ v + adv + n

break /breɪk/ (**broke** /brəʊk; *AmE* broʊk/, **broken** /ˈbrəʊkən; *AmE* ˈbroʊkən/)
ˌbreak aˈway **1** (**from sth**) if an object **breaks away** from sth that is holding it in place, it becomes separated from it: *The boat had broken away from its moorings.* **2** (**from sb**) to escape suddenly from sb who is holding you or keeping you prisoner: *The prisoner broke away from the guards.* **3** (**from sb/sth**) to leave a group or an organization, such as a political party or a state, because of a disagreement, usually in order to form a new one: *Several MPs broke away to form a new party.* ◊ *Two states broke away from the federation.* **4** (**from sb/sth**) to move away from a group of people or a crowd: *She managed to break away from the pack* (= in a race) *and establish a lead.* ◊ *He broke away from the group and came over to talk to us.* **5** (**from sb/sth**) to reject a tradition or the usual way of doing things and do sth new and different: *The company is trying to break away from its traditional image.*
♦ v + adv

▸ ˈbreakaway *adj* [only before noun] a **breakaway** group, political party or part of a country is one that leaves a larger group: *a breakaway faction/movement/republic*

▸ ˈbreakaway *n* [sing.] an act of separating from a larger group/state, etc.

⚷ break ˈdown **1** if a vehicle, etc. **breaks down**, it stops working because of a fault: *The washing machine has broken down again.* ◊ *We* (= our car) *broke down twice on the way home.* **2** if talks, a marriage, etc. **break down**, they fail: *Negotiations between the two sides have broken down.* ◊ *Their marriage broke down after three years.* **3** to lose control of your feelings and start crying: *As she drove away, I just broke down and wept.* **4** if your health **breaks down**, it becomes very bad: *Her health broke down as a result of the strain.* **5** (**into sth**) to be divided into parts so that it is easier to discuss, to analyse or to deal with: *My weekly budget breaks down as follows: 50% for rent, 20% for food, 10% for travel, and 20% for everything else.* ◊ *The job breaks down into seven parts.* → see also BREAK STH DOWN 3 **6** (**into sth**) if a substance **breaks down**, it separates into different parts or changes into sth else in a chemical process: *Some pesticides break down safely in water.* → see also BREAK STH DOWN 4
♦ v + adv

▸ ˈbreakdown *n* **1** [C] an occasion when a vehicle or a machine stops working: *We had a breakdown on the way home.* ◊ *a breakdown truck* **2** [C, U] a failure of talks, a marriage, law and order, etc.: *a breakdown in communication* ◊ *They were both responsible for the breakdown of their marriage.* **3** [C] a period of mental illness when sb becomes tired, depressed and unable to lead a normal life: *He had a **nervous***

breakdown last year. **4** [C, usually sing.] detailed information or figures that are the results of dividing sth into its parts to explain it more clearly: *Get me a breakdown of how the money was spent.* **5** [U] the act of dividing a substance into its parts in a chemical process
▶ ,broken-'down *adj* [only before noun] **1** (of a vehicle or a machine) not working: *a broken-down car* **2** in a poor condition: *a broken-down wall*

,break down 'down **1** to make sth fall down or open by hitting it hard: *They had to get the police to break the door down.* [OBJ] **door** SYN **knock sth down 2** to destroy or remove sth, especially a problem or an attitude or opinion that sb has: *Our aim is to break down barriers that exist between teachers and parents.* [OBJ] **barriers 3** (**into sth**) to separate sth into smaller parts in order to analyse it or deal with it more easily: *I've broken down the costs by country.* ◇ *The company was broken down into smaller units.* ◇ *The question can be broken down into two parts.* → see also BREAK DOWN 5 **4** (**into sth**) to make a substance separate into its parts or change in a chemical process: *Enzymes in the mouth and stomach break the food down.* → see also BREAK DOWN 6
◆ v + n/pron + adv ◆ v + adv + n

⚡,break 'in **1** to enter a building illegally or by force: *Somebody broke in last night and stole the PC and video.* ◇ *The firefighters had to break in to rescue them.* → see also BREAK INTO STH 1 **2** (**on sth**) to interrupt sb when they are speaking or doing sth: *He apologized for breaking in on their conversation.* ◇ *Mary broke in: 'It's not her fault!'*
◆ **1** v + adv
◆ **2** v + adv ◆ v + adv + speech
▶ 'break-in *n* an entry into a building using force, usually illegally: *There has been a series of break-ins in the area.*

,break sb/sth 'in to train a person so that they get used to a new job or situation; to train a horse so that you can ride it: *We try to break newcomers in gently.* ◇ *The horses hadn't been broken in.*
◆ v + n/pron + adv ◆ v + adv + n

,break sth 'in **1** if you **break in** new shoes or boots, you wear them until they become comfortable: *It took me weeks to break in these new boots.* [OBJ] **boots, shoes** SYN **wear sth in 2** (*AmE*) (in the past) to prepare the engine of a new car for normal use by driving it slowly and carefully [OBJ] **car** SYN **run sth in** (*BrE*)
◆ v + adv + n ◆ v + n/pron + adv

⚡,break 'into sth **1** to enter a building, open a car, etc. illegally and by force: *A thief can break into a car in under ten seconds.* ◇ *These houses in our street have been broken into this week.* [OBJ] **house, car 2** to suddenly begin to do sth such as laugh, shout, run, etc.: *He broke into a run when he saw the police.* ◇ *Her face broke into*

a huge smile. ◇ *The audience broke into applause.* [OBJ] **a smile/grin, a run/trot, song, laughter 3** (*BrE*) to use a note/bill of high value to buy sth costing less: *I didn't want to break into a twenty-pound note.* **4** to interrupt sb's thoughts: *Her mother's voice broke into her thoughts.* [OBJ] **thoughts disturb sth 5** to start to get involved in an activity and to be successful at it, especially when this is difficult: *The company is having difficulty breaking into new markets.* ◇ *She is trying to break into journalism.* [OBJ] **market 6** to open and use sth that you have been saving for an emergency or a special occasion: *I had to break into my savings to pay for the trip.*
◆ v + prep

⚡,break 'off; ,break sth 'off **1** (*also* ,break sth 'off sth) to separate sth from sth else, using force; to become separated from sth in this way: *The leg of the table just broke off.* ◇ *A corner of her tooth had broken off.* ◇ *He broke off a piece of chocolate and gave it to me.* **2** to stop speaking or stop doing sth suddenly before you have finished: *He broke off abruptly in the middle of a sentence.* ◇ *We had to break off our holiday and return home immediately.* ◇ *They broke off their conversation as I approached.*
◆ **1** v + adv ◆ v + adv + n ◆ v + n/pron + adv
◆ v + n/pron + prep
◆ **2** v + adv ◆ v + adv + n ◆ v + pron + adv
◆ v + n + adv (*rare*)

SYNONYMS

break (sth) off

break (sth) off ◆ **chip (sth) off** ◆ **snap (sth) off**
These verbs all refer to a piece of sth becoming separated from the rest as a result of force or damage.

break (sth) off to become separated from sth as a result of force; to separate a piece of sth in this way: *The back section of the plane had broken off.* ◇ *She broke off a piece of chocolate and gave it to me.*

chip (sth) off to damage sth by breaking a small piece off it; to become damaged in this way: *The plaster had chipped off and no repairs had been done.*

snap (sth) off to break off suddenly with a sharp noise; to break sth off in this way: *The branch she was standing on must have snapped off.* ◇ *He snapped a twig off a bush.*

WHICH WORD?

Chip off is used for materials like glass, paint or bone; **snap off** is used for objects which tend to break easily under pressure. **Break off** is the most general of these verbs.

,break sth 'off to end sth such as a relationship: *They've broken off their engagement.* ◇ *Britain threatened to break off diplomatic relations.* ◇ *They were having an affair but she **broke it off**.* ⊙BJ **diplomatic relations, engagement, talks/ negotiations, affair** SYN **terminate** (*formal*)
♦ v + adv + n ♦ v + pron + adv ♦ v + n + adv (*rare*)

,break 'out 1 if sth unpleasant such as a fire, a war, etc. **breaks out**, it starts suddenly: *They would have got married in 1939 if war had not broken out.* ◇ *A fire broke out on a ferry yesterday.* SUBJ **war, fire, fighting, row, violence 2** (*also* ,break 'out of sth) to escape from a place or from a situation: *Two terrorists have broken out of Blackwill Prison.* ◇ *She longed to break out of the daily routine.* **3** if sth **breaks out** on your skin, your skin becomes covered in sth: *Sweat broke out all over his body.* ◇ (*AmE*) *I keep breaking out* (= I keep getting lots of spots).
♦ v + adv **2** also v + adv + prep
▸ 'breakout n **1** an escape from prison **2** (*especially AmE*) an occasion when you get spots on the face, etc.: *I'm prone to breakouts on my forehead.*
▸ 'outbreak n the start of sth or the sudden appearance of sth unpleasant or violent: *the outbreak of war* ◇ *an outbreak of food poisoning* ◇ *outbreaks of rain*

,break sth 'out 1 to get sth ready to be used, eaten, drunk, etc.: *That's wonderful news! Let's break out the champagne!* ⊙BJ **champagne 2** (**by sth**) (*AmE*) to separate information into categories in order to study it more closely: *The survey does not break data out by race.* ◇ *It is useful to break out results by state.* ⊙BJ **data**
♦ v + adv + n ♦ v + pron + adv ♦ v + n + adv
▸ 'breakout n the separation of information into categories in order to study it more closely: *Breakouts are organized into ten regions.*

,break 'out in/into sth to suddenly become covered in sth such as sweat: *He broke out in a cold sweat at the thought of the trial.* ◇ *My skin has broken out in an itchy rash.* ⊙BJ **sweat, rash**
♦ v + adv + prep

,break 'through (*especially AmE*) to achieve your first important success in sth; to make an important or new discovery: *Scarlett Johansson broke through as a star with 'Lost in Translation'.* ◇ *Scientists believe they have broken through in their fight against the disease.* NOTE The phrase **to make a breakthrough** is used more often than **to break through**: *Scientists have made a major breakthrough in their fight against AIDS.*
♦ v + adv
▸ 'breakthrough n an important discovery or development; sb's first important success in sth: *an important breakthrough in the negotiations*

◇ *Jo was only 19 when he got his breakthrough as a DJ.*

,break 'through; ,break 'through sth 1 to make a way through a barrier using force: *He ran towards the barrier in an attempt to break through.* ◇ *Demonstrators tried to break through the police cordon.* ⊙BJ **barrier 2** (of the sun or moon) to appear from behind sth: *The sun finally broke through in the afternoon.* ◇ *It stopped raining and the sun broke through the clouds.*
→ see also BREAK THROUGH STH
♦ v + adv ♦ v + prep

,break 'through sth 1 to become greater in size or quantity than a particular level: *Unemployment figures have broken through the three million barrier.* **2** to succeed in dealing with a problem, such as an attitude that sb has: *I tried hard to break through his silent mood.* ◇ *Women are starting to break through the barriers that keep them out of top management.* SYN **overcome sth** (*more formal*)
→ see also BREAK THROUGH, BREAK THROUGH STH
♦ v + prep

,break 'up 1 (*especially BrE*) if a school or the children in it **break up**, school closes for the holidays at the end of a period of the school year (a **term**): *We break up for Christmas next week.* ◇ *Have the schools broken up yet?* **2** (of a relationship, a band, etc.) to come to an end; to stop working together: *Their marriage broke up after ten years.* ◇ *There are rumours that the band is breaking up.* SUBJ **marriage 3** (*usually used in the progressive tenses*) if the connection between two telephones, or two radios that are used for sending and receiving messages, is **breaking up**, the people speaking can no longer hear each other clearly: *The signal was breaking up.* ◇ *I'm sorry—what did you say?* ***You're breaking up.***
▸ 'break-up n [C, U] the ending of a marriage or a relationship: *He moved away after the break-up of his marriage.* ◇ *marriage break-up*
♦ v + adv

,break 'up (**with sb**), ,break sb 'up to end a relationship with sb: *Rob and I broke up last week.* ◇ *She's just broken up with her boyfriend.* ◇ *I can't believe my best friend is really trying to break us up!*
SYN **split up** (**with/from sb**), **split sb up**
♦ v + adv ♦ v + n/pron + adv ♦ v + adv + n

,break 'up; ,break sb/sth 'up (**into sth**) if a group of people or a family **breaks up**, or sb **breaks it up**, the members separate and do not stay together: *The conference broke up into discussion groups.* ◇ *She had never intended to break up his family.* ◇ *The Soviet Union began to break up in 1991.* SYN **split up** (**into sth**), **split sb/sth up** (**into sth**) **2** if a group of people who are gathered together **break up**, or sb **breaks**

break (sth) up

break (sth) up ◆ **shatter (sth)** ◆ **smash sth up**
◆ **splinter (sth)**

These verbs all refer to sth breaking into lots of small pieces.

break (sth) up to separate, or make sth separate, into smaller pieces, either carefully or violently: *Break up the chocolate and place it in a bowl.* ◇ *The ship broke up on the rocks.*

shatter (sth) to suddenly break into small pieces; to make sth do this: *The explosion shattered all the windows in the building.*

smash sth up to destroy sth deliberately: *Youths had broken in and smashed the place up.* NOTE *Smash* can be used on its own, but is not used to talk about buildings, etc.: *She flew into one of her rages and started smashing crockery.*

splinter (sth) (of wood, glass, stone or bone) to break into long, thin, sharp pieces; to

make sth break in this way: *The mirror cracked but did not splinter.*

WHICH WORD?

People **smash** things deliberately; things **shatter** or get **shattered** as a result of explosions, flying bullets, stones, etc.: *The thief smashed a window to get into her car.* ◇ *Windows were shattered in the blast.*

PATTERNS AND COLLOCATIONS

- the **glass/mirror** smashed/shattered/splintered
- to smash/shatter a **glass/mirror/window/windscreen**
- his smashed/shattered/splintered **bones/skull/wrist**
- to smash/smash sth up/shatter/break (sth) up **into** small/a thousand **pieces**

---

them up, they go away in different directions: *The meeting broke up after two hours.* ◇ *Police broke up the demonstration.* ◇ *I don't want to* **break up the party** (= I don't want to make everyone else leave), *but I have to go.*
◆ v + adv ◆ v + pron + adv ◆ v + n + adv (*less frequent*)
▸ **'break-up** n [C, U] the division of a company, a country, an organization or a group of people into smaller parts: *the break-up of the Soviet Union* ◇ *family break-up*

break 'up (into sth), **break sth 'up (into sth)** if sth **breaks up**, or sb/sth **breaks it up**, it becomes separated into smaller pieces: *The ship broke up on the rocks.* ◇ *Break the chocolate up into small pieces.* ◇ *Sentences can be broken up into clauses.*
◆ v + adv ◆ v + n/pron + adv ◆ v + adv + n

break sb 'up (*old-fashioned, AmE*) to make sb laugh a lot: *Watching my grandson blow bubbles just broke me up.*
SYN **crack sb up** (*informal*)
◆ v + n/pron + adv ◆ v + adv + n

break sth 'up to make sth that is rather boring, such as a period of time or a pattern, more interesting by adding sth different to it: *I break up my day by going for a walk in the afternoon.* ◇ *Drawings were used to break up the page.*
OBJ **day, monotony**
◆ v + adv + n ◆ v + pron + adv
◆ v + n + adv (*less frequent*)

break with sb/sth (*formal*) to end your connection or relationship with sb/sth because you no longer agree with them: *Nick broke with his father to set up his own firm.*
◆ v + prep

break with sth (*formal*) to reject sth such as a tradition or the past and decide to do sth different: *The prince broke with tradition by going to study abroad.* ◇ *The new directors are eager to break with the past.*
OBJ **tradition, the past**
◆ v + prep

breathe /briːð/

breathe 'in to take air into your lungs through your nose or mouth: *Breathe in through your nose as you stretch up.* ◇ *He breathed in deeply and then spoke.*
SYN **inhale** (*more formal*) OPP **breathe out**
◆ v + adv

breathe sth 'in to take air, smoke, a smell, etc. in through your nose or mouth: *We walked along the beach, breathing in the sea air.*
OBJ **air, smoke** SYN **inhale sth** (*more formal*)
OPP **breathe sth out**
◆ v + adv + n ◆ v + n/pron + adv

breathe sth 'into sth to fill sth with life, energy or enthusiasm: *She has **breathed fresh life into** the movie industry.*
OBJ **life**
◆ v + n/pron + prep

breathe 'out to send air out of your lungs through your nose or mouth: *Breathe out slowly through your mouth as you stand up.*
SYN **exhale** (*more formal*) OPP **breathe in**
◆ v + adv

breathe sth 'out to send air, smoke, etc. out through your nose or mouth: *Breathe the air out slowly and steadily.*

OBJ **air**, **smoke** SYN **exhale sth** (*more formal*)
OPP **breathe sth in**
◆ v + adv + n ◆ v + n/pron + adv

breeze /briːz/

,breeze 'in; ,breeze 'into sth (*informal*) to arrive somewhere or enter a place in a relaxed, cheerful and confident way: *She breezed in and greeted everyone with a smile.* ◇ *He breezed into the office and announced he was leaving.*
◆ v + adv ◆ v + prep

,breeze 'through sth (*informal*) to succeed in doing sth very easily: *She breezed through the first exam.*
◆ v + prep

brew /bruː/

,brew 'up; ,brew sth 'up (*BrE, informal*) to prepare a hot drink of tea or coffee: *Come into the kitchen while I brew up.* ◇ *I'll brew up a fresh pot of tea when they arrive.*
OBJ **tea**
◆ v + adv ◆ v + adv + n ◆ v + pron + adv
◆ v + n + adv (*rare*)
▶ 'brew-up *n* (*BrE, informal*) an act of making a drink of tea; the drink that you make

brick /brɪk/

,brick sth 'in/'up to fill in or block an opening with bricks: *The fireplace had been bricked in some years before.* ◇ *Somebody had bricked up all the doors and windows.*
OBJ **window**, **fireplace**, **door**
NOTE Often used in the passive.
◆ v + adv + n ◆ v + n/pron + adv

brief /briːf/

,brief a'gainst sb to give information about sb, especially a politician, that is intended to damage their reputation: *The minister accused her office of briefing against her.*
◆ v + prep

brighten /'braɪtn/

,brighten 'up 1 if the weather **brightens up**, it becomes clearer and brighter: *After a dull start, it should brighten up later.* SYN **clear up 2** if a person **brightens up**, they become happier and more cheerful: *He brightened up when they said he could go with them.* SYN **cheer up** ⊃ note at CHEER UP
◆ v + adv

,brighten sth 'up to make sth more interesting, exciting or attractive: *I've brought some flowers to brighten the place up a bit.* ◇ *Brighten up your bedroom with a few posters.*
OBJ **place**, **room** SYN **cheer sth up**
◆ v + n/pron + adv ◆ v + adv + n

brim /brɪm/ (-mm-)

,brim 'over (**with sth**) (*usually used in the progressive tenses*) if a cup or a container is **brimming over** with a liquid, it is so full that the liquid flows over the edge: *He filled my glass so full it was brimming over!* ◇ *Her eyes were brimming over with tears.*
SYN **overflow** (**with sth**) (*more formal*)
◆ v + adv

,brim 'over with sth (*usually used in the progressive tenses*) if sb is **brimming over with** sth, they show a lot of a particular quality: *She's brimming over with confidence and enthusiasm.*
OBJ **confidence**, **excitement**
◆ v + adv + prep

bring /brɪŋ/ (**brought**, **brought** /brɔːt/)

,bring sth a'bout to make sth happen: *What has brought about this change?* ◇ *His nervous breakdown was brought about by stress.*
OBJ **change**, **the end/collapse of sth**
SYN **cause sth**
◆ v + adv + n ◆ v + n/pron + adv

,bring sb a'long (*AmE*) → BRING SB ON
,bring sb/sth a'long to bring sb/sth somewhere with you: *Can I bring my sister along to the party?* ◇ *She brought some CDs along.*
◆ v + n/pron + adv ◆ v + adv + n

,bring sb a'round, etc. (*AmE*) → BRING SB ROUND, ETC.

,bring sb 'back (**to sth**) **1** to return sb to a place; to take sb home: *I'll bring you back again after the party.* ◇ *She tried to bring him back* (= to make him return) *to the matter in hand.* ◇ *Putting the driver of the car in prison won't bring my sister back* (= return her to life). **2** to put sb back in their old job or position: *United have brought back their old manager.*
◆ v + n/pron + adv ◆ v + adv + n

,bring sth 'back **1** (**to sth**) to return sth to the place it came from: *If the dress doesn't fit, bring it back to the shop and we'll change it for you.* **2** to make you remember sth or think about it again: *Talking about his death* **brought it all back** *to me.* ◇ *The photos brought back happy memories.* OBJ **memories 3** to make sth that existed or was done before be used or done again: *Are you in favour of bringing back the death penalty?* SYN **restore sth; reintroduce sth** (*more formal*) **4** to return with sth for sb: *What shall I bring back for the children from Paris?* NOTE In informal language **bring sb back sth** and, less often, **bring sb sth back** are also used: *I brought the kids back some books.* ◇ *Can you bring me something back?*
◆ v + adv + n ◆ v + n/pron + adv

'bring sb/sth before sb/sth (*law*) to present sb for judgement; to present sth to sb/sth for discussion or a decision: *Children should not be* brought before a court. ◇ The case was brought before the judge.

[OBJ] case [SYN] haul sb before sb/sth, etc. (informal)
[NOTE] Usually used in the passive.
◆ v + n/pron + prep

,bring sb 'down (informal) to depress sb; to make sb unhappy: Spending New Year alone brought me right down.
[SYN] get sb down; depress sb (more formal)
◆ v + n/pron + adv

,bring sb/sth 'down 1 to take sb/sth from a higher to a lower level: They brought all the boxes down from the attic. 2 to make sb/sth fall to the ground: He was brought down in the penalty area. ◇ Their plane was brought down by a violent storm. ◇ When she fell, she brought him down with her. ◇ He brought down the bird with a single shot. 3 to make a government, a leader, etc. lose power or be defeated: The scandal brought the government down. [OBJ] government
◆ v + n/pron + adv ◆ v + adv + n
[IDM] bring down the 'curtain on sth; bring the 'curtain down on sth to finish or mark the end of sth: Her decision to retire brought down the curtain on a glittering 30-year career.

ᵀ,bring sth 'down 1 to make sth smaller in size or amount: We are determined to bring down inflation. ◇ The price war is bringing the cost of flights down. [OBJ] inflation, price [SYN] lower sth (more formal) 2 to make an aircraft land: The

pilot brought the plane down safely. [OBJ] plane [SYN] land sth
◆ v + n/pron + adv ◆ v + adv + n
[IDM] bring the 'house down to make an audience laugh or clap in an enthusiastic way: Her performance brought the house down.

,bring sth 'down on/upon sb (formal) to make sth unpleasant happen to sb as a result of your actions: He had brought nothing but trouble down on the family.
◆ v + n/pron + adv + prep ◆ v + adv + n + prep

,bring sb 'forth (old-fashioned, formal, rare) to give birth to sb: She brought forth a son.
[OBJ] child
◆ v + adv + n ◆ v + pron + adv
◆ v + n + adv (less frequent)

,bring sth 'forth (formal) to produce sth; to make sth happen: Her remarks brought forth a harsh response.
◆ v + adv + n ◆ v + pron + adv
◆ v + n + adv (less frequent)

,bring sth 'forward 1 to move sth to an earlier date or time: We'll have to bring the date of the final game forward. [OBJ] meeting, date [SYN] put sth forward [OPP] put sth back 2 to suggest a subject, an idea, etc. for discussion: She brought forward proposals for a new school building.
[OBJ] proposal [SYN] put sth forward 3 (finance) to move a total from the bottom of one page or column of numbers to the top of the next page [OBJ] balance [SYN] carry sth forward [NOTE] Often used in the passive.
◆ v + n/pron + adv ◆ v + adv + n

bring sth down

bring sth down ◆ **decrease sth** ◆ **lower sth** ◆ **minimize sth** ◆ **reduce sth**

These verbs all mean to make sth smaller or less in size, amount or degree. See also **go down, cut back**.

bring sth down to reduce the price, number or level of sth: We aim to bring down prices on all our computers. ◇ The economic recovery will bring down unemployment.

decrease sth (formal) to reduce the amount or level of sth: People should decrease the amount of fat they eat.

lower sth to reduce the level of sth: The company may be forced to lower prices in order to stay competitive.

minimize sth (BrE also **minimise**) to reduce sth, especially sth bad, to the lowest possible level: Good hygiene helps to minimize the risk of infection. ◇ They worked at night in order to minimize the disruption.

reduce sth to make sth less or smaller in size, amount, number or level: The number of

employees was reduced from 40 to 25. ◇ Giving up smoking reduces the risk of heart disease.

WHICH WORD?

Decrease is more formal and less frequent than **increase**; it is used especially in the contexts of health and medicine. The more usual opposite of **increase** is **reduce**. **Lower** is used especially in the contexts of health and finance: to lower blood pressure/cholesterol levels. **Reduce** can also be used in these cases.

PATTERNS AND COLLOCATIONS

■ to reduce sth/lower sth/bring sth down **from.../to.../by...**
■ to reduce/lower/minimize/decrease/bring down the **number/amount/level/cost** of sth
■ to reduce/lower/minimize/decrease the **risk/chance/rate** of sth
■ to reduce/lower/decrease/bring down the **price** of sth

,bring 'in sth; ,bring sb 'in sth to make or earn money for sb: *How much is she bringing in every month?* ◇ *His job only brought him in a small income.*
◆ v + adv + n ◆ v + n/pron + adv + n

,bring sb 'in **1** (**on sth**) to get sb involved in sth, especially to advise or help, etc.: *Can we deal with this without bringing the police in?* ◇ *I'd like to bring Inspector Lacey in on this investigation.* ◇ *Experts were brought in to advise the government.* OBJ **experts**, **police**, **troops 2** if the police **bring sb in**, they take them to a police station to question them or arrest them: *Two men have been brought in for questioning.* OBJ **suspect**
◆ v + adv + n ◆ v + n/pron + adv

ʰ,bring sb/sth 'in **1** to take sb/sth into a room, a house, an office, etc.: *Could you bring in another chair?* ◇ *Bring him in!* NOTE In informal language **bring sb in sth** and, less often, **bring sb sth in** are also used: *Could you bring me in another chair?* ◇ *Could you bring us some tea in?* **2** to attract sb/sth to a place or a business: *The visitor centre is bringing in more and more people.* OBJ **business, customers, tourism**
→ see also BRING SB/STH INTO STH
◆ v + adv + n ◆ v + n/pron + adv

,bring sth 'in **1** to introduce a new law: *A new law was brought in to improve road safety.* ◇ *New controls were brought in to limit spending and borrowing.* OBJ **legislation, law** SYN **introduce sth** (*more formal*) NOTE Often used in the passive. **2** (*law*) to give a decision in a court: *The jury brought in a verdict of guilty.* OBJ only **verdict, decision 3** to mention or include sth: *She brought in other evidence to support her argument.* **4** to pick or cut and collect crops to be stored: *Farmers haven't been able to bring the harvest in because of the weather.*
◆ v + adv + n ◆ v + n/pron + adv

ʰ,bring sb/sth 'into sth **1** to take sb/sth into a place: *Bring that chair into the dining room.* **2** to include or mention sb/sth in a discussion, conversation, etc.: *Why do you always have to bring Pete into it* (= mention Pete when we are discussing sth)*?* ◇ *I knew you'd manage to bring football into the conversation!* **3** to attract sb/sth to a place or business: *The advertising campaign should bring more people into the bookshops.*
→ see also BRING SB/STH IN
◆ v + n/pron + prep

,bring sth 'off (*informal*) to manage to do sth difficult successfully: *England were close to victory, but they couldn't quite **bring it off**.* ◇ *Thompson, the new goalkeeper, brought off a superb save.*
SYN **pull sth off**
◆ v + n/pron + adv ◆ v + adv + n ◆ v + n + adv

,bring sb 'on (*BrE*) (*AmE* ,bring sb a'long) to help sb to develop or improve when they are learning to do sth: *We need to bring on the*

young players quickly. ◇ *There's no time to bring employees along gradually.*
◆ v + adv + n ◆ v + n/pron + adv

,bring sth 'on to make sth unpleasant happen: *The heart attack was brought on by stress.* ◇ *It's not like you to get so upset. What's brought this on* (= has made you so upset)*?*
OBJ **heart attack, depression** SYN **cause sth** (*more formal*)
◆ v + n/pron + adv ◆ v + adv + n

IDM **bring it 'on!** (*informal*) used to say that you are happy that a difficult or challenging situation is coming because you are sure that you can overcome it

'bring sth on sb/yourself (*also* ,bring sth u'pon sb/yourself *more formal*) to be responsible for sth unpleasant that happens to sb/yourself: *You've brought shame on the whole family!* ◇ *Don't blame me! You've brought this on yourself.*
OBJ **shame, disgrace**
◆ v + n/pron + prep

,bring sb 'out to help sb to be more confident and less shy: *He's good at bringing out nervous interviewees.* ◇ *A year at college has really **brought her out of herself**.* ◇ *I hoped that university would **bring him out of his shell**.*
◆ v + adv + n ◆ v + n/pron + adv

,bring sth 'out **1** (*also* ,bring sth 'out of sth) to take sth out of sth; to remove sth from sth: *He brought a card out of his wallet and gave it to her.* SYN **take sth out, take sth out of sth 2** to produce or publish sth: *They're bringing out a new sports car this year.* ◇ *How many albums have the band brought out?* ◇ *The publishers are bringing out a new edition of the dictionary next spring.* **3** to make a particular quality easier to see, taste, or notice: *That dress brings out the colour of your eyes.* OBJ **colour, flavour** SYN **emphasize sth** (*more formal*) **4** to make sth appear that is usually hidden: *She always brings out the worst in me!* ◇ *The situation brought out the viciousness in him.* OBJ **the best, the worst**
◆ v + n/pron + adv
◆ v + adv + n **1** also v + n/pron + adv + prep

,bring sb 'out in sth (*BrE*) to make sb's skin be covered in sth such as sweat or spots: *Tomatoes bring me out in a rash.*
◆ v + n/pron + adv + prep

,bring sb/sth 'over to take or bring sb/sth to a particular place, especially sb's home: *When your sister gets back from New York, bring her over to see us.* ◇ *Bring your chair over and sit with us!*
◆ v + n/pron + adv ◆ v + adv + n

,bring sb/sth 'round (*BrE*) (*AmE* ,bring sb a'round) **1** (*also* ,bring sb 'to) to make sb conscious again: *She gently slapped his face to bring him round.* **2** (**to sth**) to persuade sb to agree with you, or to do what you want: *I brought him round to my*

way of thinking in the end. SYN **win sb over (to sth)**
♦ v + n/pron + adv

bring sb/sth 'round (*especially BrE*) (*AmE usually* **bring sb/sth a'round**) to bring sb/sth to sb's home: *I'll bring the papers round to your house this evening.*
♦ v + n/pron + adv ♦ v + adv + n

bring sth 'round to sth (*BrE*) (*also* **bring sth a'round to sth** *AmE, BrE*) to direct a conversation, a discussion, etc. so that you are talking about the subject you want to talk about: *He always brings the conversation round to football.*
OBJ **conversation**, **discussion**
♦ v + n/pron + adv + prep

bring sb 'through; **bring sb 'through sth** (*AmE*) to help sb to survive a difficult or unpleasant experience or period in their life: *My aunt helped to bring me through the period after my parents died.*
SYN **get sb through, get sb through sth**
♦ v + n/pron + adv ♦ v + n/pron + prep

bring sb 'to → BRING SB ROUND 1

bring A and B to'gether 1 to help two people or groups to end an argument; to unite two people or groups: *The crisis brought the family closer together.* **2** to introduce two people who have never met; to help two people come together socially: *It was me who brought them together.* SYN **get A and B together**
♦ v + n/pron + adv ♦ v + adv + n

bring sb/sth to'gether to collect a group of people or objects together in one place: *This exhibition brings together many artists' work.*
♦ v + n/pron + adv ♦ v + adv + n

bring sb 'up 1 to care for a child until he/she is grown up; to teach a child a particular way to behave, etc.: *She was brought up by her aunt.* ◊ *I was brought up* (= I grew up) *on a farm.* ◊ *They brought their children up very strictly.* ◊ *We were brought up to be polite and do what we were told.* ◊ *a well-brought-up child* OBJ **children, family, daughter, son** SYN **raise sb** (*especially AmE*) NOTE Bring up a child does not mean the same as **look after** a child. **2** (*law*) to make sb appear for trial in court
NOTE Often used in the passive.
♦ v + n/pron + adv ♦ v + adv + n
▶ **'upbringing** *n* [sing., U] the way in which a child is cared for and taught, especially by parents, while he/she is growing up

bring sb/sth 'up (**to sth**) to move sb/sth to a higher place, especially up the stairs: *Breakfast was brought up to our room.* ◊ *Callum is downstairs. Shall I bring him up?* ◊ *She brought her hand up and slapped him.* ◊ *I brought the cup up to my lips and took a sip of coffee.*
♦ v + n/pron + adv ♦ v + adv + n

bring sth 'up 1 to move sth from a lower to a higher position: *She brought up her hand to protect her face.* **2** to mention a subject and start to talk about it: *Every time I bring the matter up, he changes the subject.* OBJ **subject, matter** SYN **raise sth** (*more formal*) **3** (**to sth**) to increase a total, a price, a number, etc. to a higher level or amount: *This donation brings the total up to $6 000.* ◊ *Owen got another goal, bringing the score up to 4-0.* OBJ **total** SYN **raise sth** (*more formal*) **4** to bring food from the stomach back out through the mouth: *The baby's just brought up her breakfast.* SYN **throw sth up** (*informal*);

bring sb up

bring sb up ♦ **educate sb** ♦ **raise sb** ♦ **rear sb**
These verbs all refer to how a child grows up and is cared for.

bring sb up (*often passive*) to care for a child, teaching him/her how to behave, until he/she is grown up: *She brought up five children.* ◊ *He was brought up by his aunt.*

educate sb (*often passive*) to teach sb over a period of time at a school or university: *She was educated in the US.*

raise sb (*often passive*) (*especially AmE*) to care for a child or young animal until it is grown up: *They were both raised in the South.*

rear sb (*often passive*) to care for young animals or children until they are grown up: *She reared a family of five on her own.* ◊ *Lions usually manage to rear about half the number of cubs born to them.*

WHICH WORD?

Raise is more often used to talk about children; **rear** is more often used to talk about animals. When **raise** is used in British English to talk about caring for a child, it is slightly more formal than **bring up**.

PATTERNS AND COLLOCATIONS

- to bring up/raise/rear/educate a **child**
- to bring up/raise/rear a **family/daughter/son**
- to raise/rear **young/animals/sheep/chickens**
- to be brought up/raised/reared **in** Scotland, Oxford, etc.
- to be brought up/raised/reared **on** Indian food, Hollywood movies, etc.

vomit sth up (*more formal*) **5** to make sth appear on a computer screen: *Can you bring that file up on screen?*

♦ v + n/pron + adv ♦ v + adv + n

,**bring sb 'up against sth** to make sb realize sth or face sth and deal with it: *This case brings us up against the problem of punishment in schools.*

♦ v + n/pron + adv + prep

,**bring sb/sth 'up to sth** to help sb/sth to reach an acceptable level or standard: *They have now brought the football ground up to the required safety standards.*

♦ v + n/pron + adv + prep

,**bring sth u'pon sb/yourself** → BRING STH ON SB/YOURSELF

bristle /'brɪsl/

'**bristle with sth** to be covered in sth; to have or contain a large number or amount of sth: *a roof bristling with TV aerials* ◇ *The staff bristle with efficiency.*

♦ v + prep

broaden /'brɔːdn/

,**broaden 'out** if a river, a road, etc. **broadens out**, it becomes wider

NOTE **Broaden** is also used on its own, but less often.

♦ v + adv

,**broaden 'out**; ,**broaden sth 'out** (*especially BrE*) if sth **broadens out**, or you **broaden it out**, it becomes more general or includes a larger number of people or things: *Let's broaden out the discussion to talk about education as a whole.*

NOTE **Broaden** is also used on its own.

♦ v + adv ♦ v + adv + n ♦ v + n/pron + adv

brown /braʊn/

,**brown sth 'out** (*especially AmE*) to reduce the amount of electrical power, water, etc. that is supplied to a particular machine, area, etc.: *Servers were browned out by the increase in Internet traffic.*

♦ v + adv ♦ v + adv + n ♦ v + pron + adv (*rare*)

▶ '**brown-out** n (*especially AmE*): *Recurrent brown-outs brought the city to a standstill.*

browse /braʊz/

,**browse 'through sth** to look through a book, a magazine, etc. without paying close attention or reading everything: *She browsed through the newspaper while she waited.*

OBJ **book**, **newspaper**

♦ v + prep

brush /brʌʃ/

,**brush a'gainst/'by/'past sb/sth** to touch sb/ sth lightly when you move close to them/it: *The*

cat brushed against Alison's leg. ◇ *He brushed by/ past me and ran out.*

♦ v + prep

,**brush sb/sth a'side 1** to push sb/sth to one side: *She brushed a strand of hair aside.* **2** to refuse to listen to sb/sth or treat them/it as important: *He brushed my protests aside and paid the bill.* ◇ *Every time I try to explain, you brush me aside.* SYN **wave sth aside/away**; **dismiss sb/sth** → see also BRUSH SB OFF 1, BRUSH STH OFF 2

♦ v + n/pron + adv ♦ v + adv + n

,**brush sth a'way** (**from sth**) **1** to remove sth from a surface with a brush, your hand, etc.: *She brushed a stray hair away from her face.* OBJ **tears**, **hair**, **dust 2** to ignore an idea, a thought, etc. because you do not want to think about it or you think it is not important: *She quickly brushed the idea away.* SYN **dismiss sth**

♦ v + n/pron + adv ♦ v + adv + n

,**brush 'by sb/sth** → BRUSH AGAINST/BY/PAST SB/STH

,**brush sb/yourself 'down** (*especially BrE*) to clean sb/yourself by brushing their/your clothes with your hand, especially after they/you have fallen: *She stood up and brushed herself down.* → see also BRUSH SB/YOURSELF OFF

♦ v + n/pron + adv

,**brush sth 'down** (*especially BrE*) to clean sth by brushing it thoroughly: *Brush your coat down to get the mud off.* ◇ *The children were taught how to brush down their ponies.* OBJ **coat**, **skirt**, etc.

→ see also BRUSH STH OFF 1

♦ v + n/pron + adv ♦ v + adv + n

,**brush 'off**; ,**brush sth 'off** if mud, dust, etc. **brushes off**, or you **brush it off**, it is removed by brushing: *Don't worry about the mud—it'll brush off easily when it's dry.* ◇ *We were able to brush the dirt off quite easily.*

♦ v + adv ♦ v + n/pron + adv ♦ v + adv + n

,**brush sb 'off** (*informal*) **1** to refuse to listen to sb; to ignore sb in a rude or unkind way: *He tried to explain to her, but she brushed him off impatiently.* SYN **rebuff sb** (*formal*) → see also BRUSH SB/STH ASIDE 2 **2** to get rid of sb: *She couldn't brush Roger off after the party.*

♦ v + n/pron + adv ♦ v + adv + n

▶ '**brush-off** n [sing.] (*informal*) rude or unkind behaviour that shows you do not want to be friendly: *They're just trying to **give me the brush-off**.*

,**brush sb/yourself 'off** to clean sb/yourself by brushing their/your clothes quickly with your hand

→ see also BRUSH SB/YOURSELF DOWN

♦ v + n/pron + adv ♦ v + adv + n

,**brush sth 'off 1** to clean sth quickly by brushing it: *He picked up his hat and brushed it off quickly.* → see also BRUSH STH DOWN **2** to refuse to listen to, discuss or accept sth: *Roberts*

brushed off allegations of corruption. ◇ She brushed off offers of help from her friends.
→ see also BRUSH SB/STH ASIDE 2
◆ v + n/pron + adv ◆ v + adv + n

,brush sth 'out 1 to brush sth, especially hair, thoroughly to remove knots or to make it straighter: She brushed out her hair, washed her face and got into bed. OBJ hair 2 (also ,brush sth 'out of sth) to remove knots, etc. from your hair by brushing: It took half an hour to brush out all the tangles in his hair. OBJ tangles, knots
◆ v + adv + n
◆ v + n/pron + adv 2 also v + n/pron + adv + prep

,brush 'past sb/sth → BRUSH AGAINST/BY/PAST SB/STH

,brush sth 'up; ,brush 'up on sth (especially BrE) to study or practise sth in order to get back the skill or knowledge that you had in the past but have not used for some time: I need to brush up my computer skills. ◇ You should brush up on your French before you go to France.
OBJ skills, French/English, etc. SYN polish sth up; review sth (especially AmE); revise sth (BrE) NOTE Not used in the passive.
◆ v + adv + n ◆ v + pron + adv
◆ v + n + adv (less frequent) ◆ v + adv + prep

bubble /'bʌbl/

,bubble 'over (with sth) to be full of excitement, enthusiasm, ideas, etc.: They were bubbling over with excitement.
◆ v + adv

,bubble 'under; ,bubble 'under sth if sth is bubbling under, it is already fairly successful but is not yet as successful as other things of the same kind, although it is likely to be so soon: This is our list of songs bubbling under.
◆ v + adv ◆ v + prep

,bubble 'up 1 if a liquid bubbles up from the ground, etc., it rises up in the form of bubbles or making the sound of bubbles: Water bubbled up from the pool. ◇ (figurative) Clouds will bubble up (= start to form) later this afternoon. 2 if an emotion, etc. bubbles up, it becomes stronger and starts to be heard or seen: I could feel the anger bubbling up inside me. ◇ Laughter came bubbling up.
◆ v + adv

buck /bʌk/

'buck for sth (AmE) to try in a determined way to win or gain sth you want very much, especially an important position: He was bucking for a Cabinet post in the Nixon administration.
◆ v + prep

,buck 'up (old-fashioned, BrE, informal) used to tell sb to hurry up: Buck up! We'll be late.
SYN hurry up
◆ v + adv

,buck 'up; ,buck sb 'up (old-fashioned, BrE, informal) to become, or to make sb, more cheerful: Buck up! There's no school tomorrow! ◇ He bucked up when I said he could go. ◇ A day out will buck you up.
SYN cheer up, cheer sb/yourself up
◆ v + adv ◆ v + n/pron + adv

IDM buck your i'deas up (BrE, informal) to start behaving in a more acceptable way, so that work gets done better, etc.

bucket /'bʌkɪt/

'bucket down (BrE, informal) to rain heavily: It bucketed down all day.
◆ v + adv

buckle /'bʌkl/

,buckle 'down (to sth) (informal) to start working or doing sth in a serious or determined way: He tried to buckle down to some study.
SYN knuckle down (to sth)
◆ v + adv

,buckle 'up (especially AmE) to fasten the belt that you wear in a car, etc. to keep you in your seat if there is an accident (a seat belt): Buckle up, kids.
SYN belt up (BrE)
◆ v + adv

buddy /'bʌdi/ (buddies, buddying, buddied)

,buddy 'up to/with sb/sth; be/get ,buddied 'up to/with sb/sth (AmE, informal) to become friendly with sb or work closely with another person: She buddied up to Julie, hoping to get to know her brother. ◇ I asked to get buddied up with an experienced diver.
◆ v + adv + prep ◆ be/get + v + adv + prep

budge /bʌdʒ/

,budge 'up (BrE, informal) to move up; to make more room for sb else: Budge up a bit! I'd like to sit down too.
SYN move up
◆ v + adv

budget /'bʌdʒɪt/

'budget for sth to plan to save or provide an amount of money for a particular purpose: Don't forget to budget for the cost of textbooks. ◇ These extra costs have not been budgeted for.
◆ v + prep

buff /bʌf/

,buff 'up (informal) to make yourself look fit and attractive: You'll need to spend some time in the gym if you want to buff up for your summer holiday.
◆ v + adv

,buff sth 'up 1 to polish sth with a soft cloth: Wax isn't as durable as a varnish and it needs

buffing up occasionally. **2** to improve sth: *They're trying to buff up the company's image.*
* v + n + adv * v + pron + adv * v + adv + n

bug /bʌg/ (**-gg-**)

,bug 'off (*AmE, informal*) used to tell sb to stop bothering you: *Should I tell him to bug off, or try to help?*
* v + adv

,bug 'out (*AmE, informal*) **1** if your eyes **bug out**, they suddenly open fully because you are surprised or excited: *They just sat there with their eyes bugging out as if they'd never seen a woman yell at a man before.* **2** (especially of a group of soldiers, etc.) to leave a place quickly, especially to avoid duty or injury: *When the radio went down, a couple of units bugged out.* ◇ *I picked up my pay and then bugged out.* **3** (**about/over sth**) to become very upset or angry: *He came over to my house, bugging out about something.* **SYN** freak out (*informal*)
* v + adv

bugger /'bʌgə(r)/

,bugger a'bout/a'round (**with sth**) (*BrE, △, slang*) to waste time doing stupid or unimportant things; to behave in a silly way: *Stop buggering about and let's get on with it.*
NOTE Mess around or, in British English, **mess about** is a more polite informal way to say this.
* v + adv

,bugger sb a'bout/a'round (*BrE, △, slang*) to treat sb badly or in a way that wastes their time: *I'm sick of being buggered about by my boss.*
NOTE Mess sb around or, in British English, **mess sb about** is a more polite informal way to say this.
* v + n/pron + adv

,bugger 'off (*BrE, △, slang*) to go away: *Bugger off and leave me alone.* ◇ *Clive's buggered off to the pub with Julie.*
NOTE Clear off is a more polite informal way to say this.
* v + adv

,bugger sth 'up (*BrE, △, slang*) to spoil sth; to do sth badly: *I'm not going to let her bugger things up for me.*
NOTE Mess sth up is a more polite informal way to say this.
* v + n/pron + adv * v + adv + n

build /bɪld/ (**built, built** /bɪlt/)

,build sth a'round sth (*BrE also* ,build sth 'round sth) to create sth, basing it on a particular thing, person, idea, etc.: *The story is built around the adventures of twelve knights.*
NOTE Often used in the passive.
* v + n/pron + prep

,build sth 'in; ,build sth 'into sth **1** to make sth a fixed and permanent part of a system, a plan, etc.: *Safeguards against fraud are built into*

the system. **2** to make sth a fixed and permanent part of sth larger: *The flash is built into the camera.* ◇ *This dishwasher can be built in.*
NOTE Often used in the passive.
* v + n/pron + adv * v + adv + n * v + n/pron + prep

▶ ,built-'in (*also* ,in-'built *less frequent*) *adj* [only before noun] forming a fixed part of a larger structure: *a built-in cupboard* ◇ *The camera has a built-in flash.*

▶ 'inbuilt *adj* [only before noun] existing as an essential part of sth/sb: *the inbuilt survival instinct of animals*

'build on sth (*also* 'build upon sth *more formal*) to develop further from sth that you have already achieved: *We need to build on last year's success.* ◇ *This course builds on existing skills.*
OBJ success, skills, strengths, achievements
* v + prep

,build sth 'on; ,build sth 'onto sth to add sth such as an extra room to an existing building: (*BrE*) *They had built on a large extension at the back of the house.* ◇ (*AmE*) *It is often better to build on an addition rather than removing walls.*
OBJ addition, extension
* v + adv + n * v + n/pron + adv * v + n/pron + prep

'build sth on sth (*also* 'build sth upon sth *more formal*) to base sth on sth; to use sth as the basis or foundation for sth: *Our company has built its reputation on the quality of its products.*
* v + n/pron + prep

,build sth 'out (*especially AmE*) **1** to finish a building, house, room, etc. which already exists in a basic form, to suit the needs of the people who will be using it: *Building several offices at a time costs 10% to 20% less than building out a single suite.* **2** to develop or expand a new system, business or computer network: *Our strategy is to build out the network in over 200 cities statewide.*
* v + n/pron + adv * v + adv + n

▶ 'buildout *n* [U, C] (*especially AmE*) **1** the act of building out a house, etc.: *The buildout will take about two weeks.* **2** the act of building out a new system, business or computer network: *the Internet buildout*

,build sth 'round sth (*BrE*) → BUILD STH AROUND STH

,build 'up to become greater, stronger or larger in number: *Queues of traffic are building up after the accident.* ◇ *I could feel the anger building up inside me.*
SYN accumulate (*more formal*)
* v + adv

▶ 'build-up *n* [sing., U] an increase in the amount, strength or number of sth: *a build-up of carbon dioxide in the atmosphere*

,build 'up (**to sth**), ,build yourself 'up (**to sth**) to gradually prepare yourself for sth such as a race or competition: *Start gently and build up to the more strenuous exercises.* ◇ *Build up slowly*

until you can jog for 30 minutes. ◇ *Build yourself up to the day of the performance.*
◆ v + adv ◆ v + pron + adv

▶ **'build-up (to sth)** *n* [C, usually sing.] the time before an important event when people are gradually preparing for it: *the build-up to the Olympics*

build sb/yourself 'up to make sb healthier or stronger: *She gave me lots of vitamins and minerals to build me up.*

NOTE Not used in the passive.
◆ v + n/pron + adv

build sb/sth 'up to speak about sb/sth with great enthusiasm, often praising them more than they deserve: *He has been built up to be the answer to the nation's problems.*

NOTE Often used in the passive.
◆ v + n/pron + adv ◆ v + adv + n

▶ **'build-up** *n* [C, usually sing.] a very enthusiastic description, especially of a performance, that is intended to make people excited about it and want to see it: *The reviewers gave the play a big build-up.*

⚑**build sth 'up 1** to collect or create sth, often gradually over a period of time: *She has built up an impressive collection of paintings.* OBJ **collection, library 2** to develop sth: *The manager had built up a good relationship with his staff.* ◇ *My father built the business up from scratch.* ◇ *Harriet has built up quite a reputation for herself as a reporter.* ◇ *We are gradually building up a picture of what happened.* OBJ **business, reputation, picture 3** to increase sth or make sth stronger: *After an accident, most drivers need to build up their confidence again.* OBJ **confidence, trust, strength 4** to cover sth so that it is higher or stronger than before
◆ v + adv + n ◆ v + n/pron + adv

▶ **built-'up** *adj* [usually before noun] **1** covered with many houses or buildings: *The speed limit is lower in built-up areas.* **2 built-up** shoes, boots, or heels have extra height added

build yourself 'up → BUILD SB/YOURSELF UP

build upon sth, 'build sth upon sth, etc. → BUILD ON STH, 'BUILD STH ON STH, ETC.

bulk /bʌlk/

bulk 'out/'up; bulk sb/sth 'out/'up (*especially AmE*) to increase in size or weight; to make sb/sth increase in size or weight: *Van Gisbergen had bulked up for this match.* ◇ *Local businesses are helping to bulk up school computer labs* (= provide more computers).
◆ v + adv ◆ v + adv + n ◆ v + pron + adv
◆ v + n + adv (*rare*)

bully /'bʊli/ (**bullies, bullying, bullied**)

bully sb 'into sth; bully sb 'into doing sth to force sb to do sth by frightening them or

threatening them: *You can't bully me into saying anything!*
◆ v + n/pron + prep

bum /bʌm/ (-mm-)

bum a'round (*BrE also* **bum 'round**) (*informal*) to travel around or to spend your time doing nothing in particular
◆ v + adv

bum a'round/'round sth (*BrE, informal*) to travel somewhere with no particular plans: *After I left school, I bummed around the world for a year.*
OBJ **the world, Europe, Asia, etc.**
◆ v + prep

bum sb 'out (*AmE, informal*) to annoy sb: *I was really bummed out that there were no tickets left.*
◆ v + n/pron + adv

bum 'round, etc. (*BrE*) → BUM AROUND, ETC.

bumble /'bʌmbl/

bumble a'round; bumble a'round sth (*BrE also* **bumble a'bout, bumble a'bout sth**) to move around in an awkward and noisy way: *I could hear my father bumbling about downstairs.*
◆ v + adv ◆ v + prep

bump /bʌmp/

bump a'long to continue in the same way as before, without making any progress or improvement: *United are still bumping along in the Third Division.*
◆ v + adv

bump 'into sb (*informal*) to meet sb by chance: *I bumped into an old friend in town today.*
SYN **run into sb**
◆ v + prep

bump 'into sb/sth to hit sb/sth by accident: *In the dark I bumped into a chair.*
SYN **collide with sb/sth**
◆ v + prep

bump sb 'off (*informal*) to murder sb: *He admitted bumping off Baines.*
◆ v + n/pron + adv ◆ v + adv + n

bump sb 'off; bump sb 'off sth 1 to not allow sb to have the seat on a plane that they have booked, because too many tickets have been sold: *With more people flying these days, there is a greater chance of getting bumped off your flight.* ◇ *bumped-off travellers* NOTE **Bump sb** can also be used on its own: *We were late arriving at the airport and the airline bumped us.* **2** (*especially AmE, computing*) to break a connection with the Internet, so that it can no longer be used: *Some users couldn't log in, others kept getting bumped off.* ◇ *to be bumped off the Internet* OBJ **the Internet, server, website** SYN **kick sb off, kick sb off sth; disconnect sb (from sth)** (*more formal*)

NOTE Usually used in the passive: *I was worried about being bumped off the flight.*
♦ v + n/pron + adv ♦ v + n/pron + prep

,bump sb 'up (to sth) (*informal*) to move sb to a more expensive seat in a plane without charging them extra, because there are not enough seats at the price they have paid: *I got bumped up to business class.*
NOTE Often used in the passive.
♦ v + n/pron + adv

,bump sth 'up (*informal*) to increase or raise sth: *The company bumped their prices up by 10%.*
OBJ prices
♦ v + n/pron + adv ♦ v + adv + n

bunch /bʌntʃ/

,bunch 'up; ,bunch sth 'up if material **bunches up**, or you **bunch it up**, it forms tight folds: *The sheets bunched up under him every time he moved.* ◇ *She bunched her skirt up and jumped.*
NOTE Often used in the passive.
♦ v + adv ♦ v + n/pron + adv ♦ v + adv + n

,bunch 'up/to'gether; ,bunch sb/sth 'up/to'gether to move closer together to make a tight group; to make sb/sth do this: *The children bunched together in little groups in the playground.* ◇ *All the runners were bunched up behind the leader.*
NOTE Often used in the passive.
♦ v + adv ♦ v + n/pron + adv ♦ v + adv + n

bundle /'bʌndl/

,bundle sb 'off (to sth…) to send sb somewhere in a hurry or when they do not want to go: *She bundled her son off to school.*
SYN pack sb off (to…)
♦ v + n/pron + adv ♦ v + adv + n

,bundle 'up (in sth) (*AmE*) to dress in warm clothes: *Bundle up! It's freezing outside!*
SYN wrap up (in sth), etc.
♦ v + adv

,bundle sb 'up (in sth) to make sb feel warmer by putting warm clothes on them or covering them with blankets: *I bundled Lucy up in a blanket and made her a cup of tea.*
NOTE Often used in the passive.
♦ v + adv ♦ v + n/pron + adv

,bundle sth 'up/to'gether to put or tie things together in a pile: *She bundled up her clothes and pushed them into a cupboard.* ◇ *The papers were all bundled together, ready to be thrown away.*
♦ v + n/pron + adv ♦ v + adv + n

bung /bʌŋ/

,bung sth 'up (with sth) (*BrE, informal*) to stop sth from moving or flowing through sth by putting sth in or across it: *She's bunged the sink up with tea leaves.*
SYN block sth up (*more formal*)
♦ v + n/pron + adv ♦ v + adv + n

▶ ,bunged 'up *adj* blocked; not clear: *My nose is all bunged up this morning.* ◇ *I'm* (= my nose is) *all bunged up.*

bunk /bʌŋk/

,bunk 'down (*especially AmE*) to lie down to sleep somewhere, especially somewhere uncomfortable or for only one night: *We bunked down in an old barn for the night.*
SYN doss down (*BrE, informal*)
♦ v + adv

,bunk 'off; ,bunk 'off sth (*BrE, informal*) to stay away from school or work when you ought to be there; to leave school or work early, especially without permission: *Let's bunk off this afternoon and go shopping.*
OBJ school, work **SYN** skive off, etc. (*BrE*)
♦ v + adv ♦ v + prep

,bunk 'up (with sb) (*BrE, informal*) to share a bed with sb; to have sex with sb: *I'm afraid you two will have to bunk up together tonight.*
♦ v + adv

▶ 'bunk-up *n* (*BrE, informal*) an act of having sex with sb; a person to have sex with: *lads out looking for a bunk-up*

buoy /bɔɪ; *AmE also* 'buːi/

,buoy sb/sth 'up **1** to make or keep sb cheerful and confident: *Winning the match buoyed the team up.* ◇ *The party did little to buoy up her spirits.* ◇ *She was buoyed up by her father's praise.* **2** to keep sb/sth floating; to stop sb/sth from sinking: *I relaxed, letting the salt water buoy me up.*
NOTE Often used in the passive. ♦ **Buoy sb/sth** can also be used on its own: *Buoyed by their recent victory, the team are convinced they can win the final.*
♦ v + n/pron + adv ♦ v + adv + n

,buoy sth 'up (*finance*) to make or keep prices at a high or acceptable level: *Share prices were buoyed up by the news.* ◇ *to buoy up the economy*
OBJ prices
NOTE Often used in the passive. ♦ **Buoy sth** is also used on its own.
♦ v + n/pron + adv ♦ v + adv + n

burn /bɜːn; *AmE* bɜːrn/ (**burnt, burnt** /bɜːnt; *AmE* bɜːrnt/ or **burned, burned** /bɜːnd; *AmE* bɜːrnd/)

,burn a'way; ,burn sth a'way to disappear as a result of burning; to make sth do this: *Half the candle had burnt away.* ◇ *The fire had burned away part of the roof.*
♦ v + adv ♦ v + adv + n ♦ v + pron + adv
♦ v + n + adv (*less frequent*)

,burn 'down if a fire **burns down**, it becomes less strong and burns with smaller flames: *They sat by the fire, watching it slowly burn down.*
OPP burn up
♦ v + adv

burn 'down; **burn sth 'down** if a building **burns down**, or sb **burns it down**, it is destroyed by fire: *The palace burnt down in the 19th century.* ◇ *She threatened to burn the house down.*

NOTE Often used in the passive.

♦ v + adv ♦ v + n/pron + adv ♦ v + adv + n

burn sth 'off 1 to remove sth by burning: *Burn the old paint off before repainting the door.* **2** (*also* **burn sth 'up**) to use energy by exercising: *Walking briskly can burn off a lot of calories.*

OBJ **calories**, **fat**

♦ v + adv + n ♦ v + n/pron + adv

burn 'out; **burn sth 'out** if a machine or part of a machine **burns out** or sb/sth **burns it out**, it stops working because it has been used too much or has got too hot: *The clutch has burnt out.* ◇ *I burnt out the motor in the first car I had.*

♦ v + adv ♦ v + n/pron + adv ♦ v + adv + n

burn 'out; **burn itself 'out** to stop burning because there is no more fuel: *Blow out the candles before they burn out.* ◇ *By the time the fire brigade arrived the fire had burnt (itself) out.*

↻ note at GO OUT; → see also BURN STH OUT

♦ v + adv ♦ v + pron + adv

▸ **'burnout** *n* [C, U] the point at which a spacecraft has used all of its fuel and has no more power

burn 'out; **burn yourself 'out** to become very tired or sick and unable to continue your work because you have worked too hard over a period of time: *It's a high-pressure job and many people burn out at a young age.* ◇ *If he carries on working so hard, he'll burn himself out.*

→ see also BURN SB OUT, BURN SB OUT OF STH

♦ v + adv ♦ v + pron + adv

▸ **'burnout** *n* [C, U] the state of being very tired or sick because you have worked too hard: *Burnout is common among teachers.* **2** [C] a person who is very tired or sick because they have worked too hard

▸ **burnt-'out** (*especially BrE*) (*AmE usually* **burned-'out**) *adj* very tired or sick because you have worked too hard: *burnt-out rock singers*

burn sb 'out; **burn sb 'out of sth** to force sb to leave a building by setting fire to it: *A gang has tried to burn a woman out of her home.*

→ see also BURN OUT, BURN YOURSELF OUT

♦ v + n/pron + adv ♦ v + adv + n

♦ v + n/pron + adv + prep

burn sth 'out to destroy sth completely by fire, so that only the outside or the frame is left: *Two cars were burnt out in the crash.*

NOTE Usually used in the passive.

→ see also BURN OUT, BURN ITSELF OUT

♦ v + n/pron + adv ♦ v + adv + n

▸ **burnt-'out** (*especially BrE*) (*AmE usually* **burned-'out**) *adj* [only before noun] completely destroyed or badly damaged by fire: *burnt-out buses* ◇ *burned-out houses*

burn 'up 1 to be destroyed by heat: *The spacecraft burned up as it entered the earth's atmosphere.* **2** (*usually used in the progressive tenses*) to have a fever or a high temperature: *She's burning up—she needs a doctor.* **3** if a fire **burns up**, it gets stronger and has larger flames

OPP **burn down**

♦ v + adv

burn sb 'up (*AmE*, *informal*) to make sb very angry: *The way he treats me really burns me up.*

♦ v + n/pron + adv

burn sth 'up 1 to get rid of sth completely by burning: *I'm going to burn up all the rubbish/ trash.* **2** → BURN STH OFF 2

♦ v + adv + n ♦ v + n/pron + adv

burrow /'bʌrəʊ; *AmE* 'bɜːroʊ/

'burrow in sth to search for sth among things in a container: *She burrowed in her pocket and eventually found a few coins.*

♦ v + prep

burst /bɜːst; *AmE* bɜːrst/ (**burst**, **burst**)

burst 'in (**on sb/sth**), **burst 'into sth** to enter a room, a building, etc. suddenly and noisily, interrupting the people who are in it: *He apologized for bursting in on our meeting.* ◇ *The door suddenly flew open and Mia burst in.* ◇ *She ran down the stairs and burst into the kitchen.*

→ see also BURST INTO STH

♦ v + adv ♦ v + prep

'burst into sth to start producing or doing sth suddenly and with great force: *The aircraft **burst into flames** (= suddenly started to burn).* ◇ *I was so relieved I **burst into tears** (= suddenly started to cry).* ◇ *The cab's engine **burst into life** (= suddenly started to work).* ◇ *As the curtain fell, the audience burst into applause (= suddenly started to clap).*

OBJ **tears**, **flames**, **laughter**, **life**

→ see also BURST IN (ON SB/STH), BURST INTO STH

♦ v + prep

'burst on/onto sth (*also* **'burst upon sth** *more formal*) to appear somewhere suddenly in a dramatic or unusual way: *A major new talent has burst on/onto the tennis scene.*

OBJ **scene**

♦ v + prep

burst 'out to say sth suddenly, loudly and with strong feeling: *'I hate you!' she burst out.*

SYN **exclaim** (*formal*)

→ see also BURST OUT DOING STH

♦ v + adv + speech

▸ **'outburst** *n* a sudden strong expression of an emotion; a sudden increase in an attitude or an activity: *an outburst of anger/laughter* ◇ *sporadic outbursts of violence* ◇ *She apologized for her outburst.*

burst 'out; **burst 'out of sth** to leave a room, a building, etc. suddenly and noisily: *The door* opened suddenly and a man burst out of the house.

♦ v + adv ♦ v + adv + prep

,burst 'out doing sth to begin doing sth suddenly: *We looked at one another and burst out laughing.*

[OBJ] **laughing, crying**

♦ v + adv + -ing

,burst 'through; ,burst 'through sth to move suddenly through a door, a barrier, etc. with great force: *The car drove fast up to the road block and burst through.* ◇ *She burst through the door pursued by two men.* ◇ *The sun burst through the clouds.*

♦ v + adv ♦ v + prep

'burst upon sth → BURST ON/ONTO STH

bury /'beri/ (**buries, burying, buried**)

'bury yourself in sth **1** to go to or be in a place where you will not meet many people: *He buried himself in the country to write a book.* **2** to involve yourself in sth completely; to spend all your time thinking about or doing sth and ignore everything else: *She buried herself in her work in an attempt to forget.* [OBJ] **work, book**

♦ v + pron + prep

bust /bʌst/ (**bust, bust** or **busted, busted**)

[NOTE] **Bust** is an informal way of saying **break**.

,bust 'out; ,bust 'out of sth; ,bust sb 'out; ,bust sb 'out of sth (*informal*) to escape from somewhere, usually prison; to help sb do this: *His last movie was about a guy busting out of Alcatraz.* ◇ *His friends busted him out of jail.* [SYN] **break out, break out of sth** (*more formal*)

♦ v + adv ♦ v + adv + prep ♦ v + n/pron + adv

♦ v + n/pron + adv + prep

▶ 'bust-out *n* (*informal*): *a prison bust-out*

,bust 'up (**with sb**) (*BrE, informal*) if a couple or two friends **bust up**, they have an argument and separate: *They bust up after five years together.* ◇ *I bust up with Tim a while ago.* [SYN] **break up (with sb); split up (with/from sb)**

♦ v + adv

▶ 'bust-up *n* (*BrE, informal*) **1** (**with sb**) an argument: *We had a huge bust-up and now we're not talking.* **2** the end of a relationship

,bust sth 'up (*informal*) **1** to end sth such as a meeting or a relationship by disturbing or ruining it: *The police busted up the meeting.* [SYN] **break sth up** (*more formal*) **2** (*AmE*) to injure, damage or break sth: *He busted up his knee in the accident.* **3** (*AmE*) to break a company or a larger organization into smaller parts [OBJ] **company** [SYN] **break sth up** (*more formal*)

♦ v + adv + n ♦ v + n/pron + adv

bustle /'bʌsl/

,bustle a'bout/a'round; ,bustle a'bout/a'round sth (*especially BrE*) to move about

somewhere in a busy or hurried way: *She was already bustling about, getting dinner ready for the family.*

♦ v + adv ♦ v + prep

butt /bʌt/

,butt 'in (*informal*) **1** (**on sb/sth**) to rudely interrupt sb when they are speaking: *He apologized for butting in on our conversation.* ◇ *'His name's Terry, actually,' she butted in.* [SYN] **interrupt (sb/sth)** (*more formal*) **2** to become involved in a situation that does not concern you: *Stop butting in. It's nothing to do with you.* [SYN] **interfere (with sth)** (*more formal*)

♦ v + adv **1** also v + adv + speech

,butt 'out (*informal, especially AmE*) used to tell sb rudely to go away or not try to influence matters which do not concern them: *Butt out! It's none of your business.*

♦ v + adv

butter /'bʌtə(r)/

,butter sb 'up (*informal*) to say nice things about sb because you want them to do sth for you or give you sth: *We'd better butter him up a bit before we ask for his help.* [SYN] **soften sb up**

♦ v + n/pron + adv ♦ v + adv + n

button /'bʌtn/

,button 'up (*AmE, informal*) to stop talking suddenly, often because you have said too much already: *She was giggling with her friends, when the teacher told them to button up.*

♦ v + adv

,button 'up; ,button sb/sth 'up to be fastened with buttons; to fasten sth with buttons: *He buttoned up his coat.* [OBJ] **coat, jacket, etc.** [SYN] **do up, do sth up** [OPP] **unbutton, unbutton sth** [NOTE] **Button** and **button sth** are also used on their own.

♦ v + n/pron + adv ♦ v + adv + n

▶ 'button-up *n* (*AmE, informal*) a shirt that closes using buttons

▶ ,buttoned-'up *adj* **1** [usually before noun] not showing or expressing your feelings openly; not very friendly: *his buttoned-up calmness* **2** (*AmE*) very formal in appearance; traditional rather than new or exciting

,button sth 'up (*AmE, informal*) to finish dealing with the final parts or details of sth complicated: *She went home for the funeral and to button up her father's financial affairs.*

♦ v + n/pron + adv ♦ v + adv + n

buy /baɪ/ (**bought, bought** /bɔːt/)

,buy sth 'back if sb **buys sth back**, they buy again sth that they have sold earlier to sb else: *The bank will supply and buy back foreign* currency. ◊ *He sold the car in 1949 for £400. To buy it back last year cost £31 000.*

◆ v + adv + n ◆ v + n/pron + adv

▶ '**buy-back** *n* **1** the action of buying again sth that you have sold earlier: *a book/an equipment buy-back* (= when a shop/store or company buys back sth you have finished using) **2** (*business*) a form of borrowing money in which a company sells its shares with an agreement that it will buy them again at a later date: *a share buy-back* ◊ *a share buy-back programme*

,**buy 'in** (in poker) to pay money for pieces of plastic which represent a particular value (called **chips**) in order to enter a game: *Is anyone else buying in?*

◆ v + adv

▶ '**buy-in** *n* **1** (in poker) the amount paid to buy in: *a $50 buy-in* **2** the fact of accepting an idea or product after being convinced by others that it is good: *It is important to get total Congressional buy-in from the beginning.* → see also BUY INTO STH **3** (*business*) a situation where a group of people from outside a company buy more than 50% of its shares because they want to take over the management of the company → see also BUY INTO STH **4** (*business*) a situation where a company buys its shares back from the people who own them: *The buy-in was part of the company's strategy to protect itself against a hostile takeover.* → see also BUY INTO STH

,**buy sth 'in** (*BrE*) to buy sth or a large amount of sth for a special occasion or in order to have a supply for the future: *I'll have to buy in extra food if they're coming to stay for a while.*

OBJ **food**

◆ v + adv + n ◆ v + n/pron + adv

,**buy 'into sth 1** (*business*) to buy shares in a company, especially to gain control over it: *They are looking to buy into another insurance company.* OBJ **company, business** → see also BUY-IN at BUY IN **2** (*business*) to invest in sth: *The broker advised its clients to buy into the stock.* **3** to accept sth that many other people believe: *We don't buy into the myth that money is the answer to everything.* → see also BUY-IN at BUY IN

◆ v + prep

,**buy sb 'off** to pay sb to stop them acting against you, causing trouble for you, etc.: *They had to buy Brennan off to stop him from talking.*

◆ v + n/pron + adv ◆ v + adv + n

,**buy sb/yourself 'out**; ,**buy sb/yourself 'out of sth** (*BrE*) to pay money so that sb/you can leave an organization, especially the armed forces, before the time agreed: *After four years in the navy I bought myself out.*

◆ v + n/pron + adv ◆ v + n/pron + adv + prep

,**buy sb/sth 'out** to buy part of a company, business, etc. from sb else so that you own all of it and control it: *I want to buy her out and have the house to myself.* ◊ *The company was bought out by two German businessmen.*

OBJ **partner, company**

◆ v + n/pron + adv ◆ v + adv + n

▶ '**buyout** *n* (*finance*) a situation when sb buys enough shares in a company to gain control of it

,**buy 'round** (*informal*, *business*) to buy goods directly from the manufacturer

◆ v + adv

,**buy sth 'up** to buy quickly all of sth or as much as you can: *They've bought up all the land in the area.*

OBJ **company, land, property**

◆ v + adv + n ◆ v + pron + adv ◆ v + n + adv (*rare*)

buzz /bʌz/

,**buzz a'round**; ,**buzz a'round sth** (*also* ,**buzz a'bout/'round**, ,**buzz a'bout/'round sth** *especially BrE*) to move around quickly and actively: *She buzzed round (the kitchen).* ◊ *The photographer buzzed around, checking the light.* ◊ *Questions buzzed round inside my head.*

◆ v + adv ◆ v + prep

,**buzz sb 'down** (*informal*) to cut sb's hair very short using an electric tool (**clippers**): *I asked the barber to buzz me down to zero.*

◆ v + adv + n ◆ v + n/pron + adv

,**buzz sb 'in, 'up, etc.** (*informal*) to let sb enter a building by opening the door using an electronic device: *It's Craig—can you buzz me in?*

◆ v + adv + n ◆ v + n/pron + adv

,**buzz 'off** (*informal*) used to tell sb, not very politely, to go away: *Buzz off, I'm trying to work!* ◊ *I wish he'd buzz off!*

SYN **clear off**; **go away** (*more formal*)

◆ v + adv

,**buzz 'round, etc.** (*especially BrE*) → BUZZ AROUND, ETC.

Cc

calculate /'kælkjuleɪt/

'**calculate on sth**; '**calculate on doing sth** (*especially AmE*) to depend or rely on sth happening or being true, especially as part of a plan: *The developers are calculating on consumers' desire for better and better technology.*

SYN **bank on sb/sth, etc.**; **count on sb/sth, etc.**; **reckon on sb/sth, etc.** ⊃ note at DEPEND ON SB/STH

◆ v + prep

call /kɔːl/

NOTE **To call** is the most common way to say 'to telephone' in American English. It is also used in British English, but **to phone** and **to ring** are more common.

,**call a'round**; ,**call a'round sb/sth** (*AmE*) to telephone a number of different people, usually

to try to get information: *He's been calling around trying to get the best price on a computer.* ◇ *I called around the neighbourhood to get support for my campaign.*
♦ v + adv ♦ v + prep

,call sb a'way to ask sb to stop doing what they are doing and go somewhere else to deal with sth: *He was called away to the phone.* ◇ *She was called away from the meeting to deal with an emergency.*
NOTE Almost always used in the passive.
♦ v + n/pron + adv

,call 'back (*BrE*) to visit sb again: *I'll call back later when your wife's at home.*
♦ v + adv

,call 'back; ,call sb 'back to telephone sb again or to telephone sb who telephoned you earlier: *Call back in an hour—he'll be here then.* ◇ *Kate phoned. Can you call her back?* ◇ *I'll call you back with the details later.*
♦ v + adv ♦ v + n/pron + adv

▶ 'callback *n* **1** a device in a telephone that automatically calls again a number that was busy when you first called it: *a callback facility* **2** a telephone call that you make to sb who has called you earlier

,call sb 'back **1** to shout to sb to turn around and come back to a place they have just left: *I ran off, but he called me back.* ◇ *We started to walk off but were called back by the police officer.* **2** to ask sb who is applying for a job, etc. to return so that you can talk to them again: *Three people were called back for a second interview.*
♦ v + n/pron + adv

,call 'by (*informal, especially BrE*) to visit a place or a person for a short time, usually when you are going somewhere else: *Could you call by on your way home?* ◇ *Jan called by to bring your gift.*
SYN drop by ↻ note at VISIT WITH SB
♦ v + adv

,call sb 'down to shout to sb to ask them to come down from a place which is higher than you: *I've called him down* (= to come downstairs) *to breakfast already.*
♦ v + n/pron + adv

,call sth 'down (on/upon sb) (*literary*) to ask God, etc. to make sth unpleasant happen to sb because of sth bad they have done to you; to make sb bad happen to sb: *He called down curses on them.*
OBJ curses, wrath
♦ v + adv + n ♦ v + n/pron + adv

'call for sb (*BrE*) to go to sb's home, for example, and take them or go with them somewhere: *Shall I call for you at eight?*
♦ v + prep

'call for sth **1** if a situation **calls for** a particular action or quality, it needs or requires it: *This calls for a celebration!* ◇ *What she's doing calls for great skill and courage.* ◇ *Tougher action by the government is called for.* **2** (*AmE*) (of a

weather forecast) to predict a particular type of weather: *The forecast today calls for mostly sunny conditions with a light wind.*
♦ v + prep

▶ un'called for *adj* (of remarks or behaviour) not fair or necessary in the circumstances: *I shall ignore that uncalled-for remark.*

'call for sth; 'call for sb/sth to do sth to demand publicly that sth should be done: *The group has called for a boycott of the elections.* ◇ *The other directors have called for him to resign.* ◇ *A total ban on nuclear weapons has been called for.* ↻ note at ASK FOR STH
♦ v + prep ♦ v + prep + n/pron + **to**+inf

,call sth 'forth (*formal*) to produce a particular reaction: *Her remarks have called forth harsh criticism in the media.*
♦ v + adv + n ♦ v + pron + adv ♦ v + n + adv (*rare*)

,call 'in **1** [+ adv/prep] (*especially BrE*) to visit a place or a person for a short time, usually when you are going somewhere else: *He called in at the office before he left for London.* ◇ *She often calls in for a chat.* **SYN** drop in (on sb/at…) (*informal*) **2** to telephone the place where you work: *She called in sick this morning* (= telephoned to say that she was ill/sick and would not be coming to work). **3** to make a telephone call to a radio or television programme: *Many listeners called in to complain.*
♦ v + adv

▶ 'call-in *n* (*AmE*) a television or radio show in which people can phone to talk to people on the show, ask questions, give their opinions, etc.: *a call-in show*

,call sb 'in to ask sb to come and help, give advice, repair sth, etc.: *He's threatened to call in the police.* ◇ *You'll have to call a plumber in to look at this.* ◇ *Bomb disposal experts were called in to get rid of the device.*
OBJ police, expert **SYN** send for sb
♦ v + adv + n ♦ v + n/pron + adv

,call sth 'in (*BrE*) **1** to order or request the return of a product that has a fault: *The manufacturers have called in the faulty goods.* **SYN** recall sth (*more formal*) **2** to request the return of sth that you have given or lent to sb: *The bank called in the loan* (= asked for the money to be paid back immediately). ◇ *It was the first time Brad had called in a favour* (= asked sb for a favour whom he had previously helped). **OBJ** loan, favour
♦ v + adv + n ♦ v + n/pron + adv

,call sb/sth 'off to order soldiers, dogs, etc. to stop attacking sb, searching for sb/sth, etc.: *Please call your dog off.*
OBJ dog
♦ v + n/pron + adv ♦ v + adv + n

,call sth 'off to cancel or abandon sth that has been planned or that has already started: *The meeting was called off at the last minute.* ◇ *They've called off their engagement* (= they have decided not to get married). ◊ *Police called off the search for the climbers at dusk.*

OBJ match/game, engagement/wedding, deal, search, strike

♦ v + adv + n ♦ v + n/pron + adv

'call on sb **1** (*especially BrE*) to visit sb for a short time: *On our way back, we called on grandma.* **SYN** drop in (on sb/at …) **2** (*AmE*) to ask sb in a class, etc. to answer a question or give their opinion: *The math teacher always calls on the boys.*

♦ v + prep

'call on/upon sth (*formal*) to use your strength, courage, etc. in order to achieve sth or deal with a problem: *She had to call on all her reserves of courage to face the ordeal.*

OBJ strength, courage

♦ v + prep

'call on/upon sb to do sth (*formal*) **1** to make a serious or urgent request to sb to do sth: *I'm available in case I'm called on to help.* ◊ *We call upon all parties to respect the results of the election.* **2** to formally invite or request sb to speak, etc.: *I now call upon Mr Spring to give the vote of thanks.*

NOTE Call on/upon sb to do sth can be used in the passive: *I was called on to make a speech.*

♦ v + prep + n/pron + **to**+inf

call 'out (*AmE*) to telephone to say that you are ill/sick and will not be coming to work: *If you always call out on Mondays it looks suspicious.*

♦ v + adv

call 'out (to sb), call sth 'out (to sb) to shout or say sth loudly in order to get sb's attention or help: *He called out to her, but she carried on walking.* ◊ *He woke in the night, calling out her name.* ◊ *They called out the numbers of the winning tickets.*

OBJ name **SYN** shout out (to sb), shout sth out (to sb)

NOTE Call and call sth can be used on their own with a similar meaning, but call out/call sth out suggests sth louder or more urgent.

♦ v + adv ♦ v + n/pron + adv ♦ v + adv + n
♦ v + adv + speech

call sb 'out **1** to ask sb to come to help you, when there is an emergency: *I've never had to call the doctor out at night before.* ◊ *We had to call out an electrician.* ◊ *Troops were called out to deal with the riot.* **OBJ** doctor, fire brigade, electrician **2** to order or ask workers to stop work as a protest: *Miners were called out on strike by union leaders.* **3** (for sth) (*AmE*) to criticize sb's actions: *Critics are calling the company out for releasing such shabby software.*

♦ v + n/pron + adv ♦ v + adv + n

SYNONYMS

call sb up

call (sb) up ♦ **give sb a call** ♦ **give sb a ring** ♦ **phone (sb) up** ♦ **ring (sb) up** ♦ **telephone (sb)**

These verbs all mean to make a telephone call to sb.

call (sb) up (*especially AmE*) to make a telephone call to sb: *I called him up and asked him how he was doing.* **NOTE** Call can be used on its own: *My brother called me from Germany last night.*

give sb a call (*not formal*) to make a telephone call to sb: *If you need any help, please give me a call.*

give sb a ring (*BrE, informal*) to make a telephone call to sb: *I'll give you a ring tomorrow.*

phone (sb) up (*BrE, not formal*) to make a telephone call to sb: *I was just phoning up for a chat.* **NOTE** Phone can be used on its own: *My brother phoned me from Germany last night.*

ring (sb) up (*BrE, not formal*) to make a telephone call to sb: *She rang me up to say she'd be late.* **NOTE** Ring can be used on its own: *I'll ring you later.*

telephone (sb) (*especially BrE, formal*) to make a telephone call to sb: *Please write or* telephone for details. ◊ *I was about to telephone the police.*

WHICH WORD?

Ring and **phone** are the most frequent verbs in this group in spoken British English, but they are not used in American English. **Call** is usually preferred when asking sb/sth to come to a place: *to call the police/fire brigade.* You can **call**, **ring** or **phone** a person, place or institution, but you must **call** or **ring/phone** for a cab/a taxi/an ambulance. **Give sb a call/ring** is used most frequently when you are telling people to telephone you, or saying that you will telephone them. **Call up**, **ring up**, etc. are never used with this meaning.

PATTERNS AND COLLOCATIONS

■ to call sb (up)/ring sb (up)/phone sb (up)/telephone sb **about** sth
■ to call/ring/phone/telephone **for** a taxi/an ambulance/a doctor
■ to call/ring/phone/telephone the **doctor/fire brigade/police**
■ to call (up)/ring (up)/phone (up)/telephone for **details/information**

▶ **'call-out** *n* (*BrE*) an occasion when you ask sb to come to help you in an emergency: *ambulance call-outs* ◇ *How much is the plumber's call-out charge?*
NOTE The noun **call** is also used.

,**call 'out for sth** (*AmE*) to telephone a shop/store, restaurant, etc. to ask them to deliver food to you at home or at work: *Let's call out for pizza.*
SYN **send out for sth**
♦ v + adv + prep

,**call sb 'over** to call sb to come over to where you are, because you want to speak to them, give or show them sth, etc.: *Call the waiter over.*
♦ v + n/pron + adv ♦ v + adv + n (*rare*)

,**call 'round** (*BrE*) to visit sb at their home for a short time: *I just called round to say hello.*
SYN **drop round**
♦ v + adv

,**call 'up**; ,**call sb/sth 'up** (*especially AmE*) to make a phone call to a person or a place: *Call up and make a reservation for eight o'clock.* ◇ *She called him up from the bus station.* ◇ *Call up the office and ask for Mr Morgan.*
NOTE **Call** and **call sb** are also frequently used on their own with this meaning. **Call up** and **call sb up** are very common in spoken English.
➔ note on page 43
♦ v + adv ♦ v + n/pron + adv ♦ v + adv + n

,**call sb 'up 1** to officially ask sb to go to do training in the army, navy or air force or to fight in a war: *When the war began, he was too old to be called up.* **SYN** **conscript sb** (*especially BrE*); **draft sb** (*AmE*) **2** (*especially BrE*) to ask sb to join sth or take part in sth; to choose sb to play in a team: *He's been called up for next week's match.* **3** (*AmE*) (in baseball) to bring a player from a minor league team onto a major league team: *They called him up last Tuesday, and he'll be on the mound tonight.*
NOTE Often used in the passive.
♦ v + n/pron + adv ♦ v + adv + n
▶ **'call-up** *n* **1** an official order to join the army, navy or air force: *call-up papers/camps* **2** (*especially BrE*, *sport*) an official invitation to play in a team or in a particular game

,**call sth 'up 1** (*computing*) to obtain information that is stored on a computer: *She called up all the files he had worked on.* **OBJ** **file, information 2** to bring sth back to your mind; to make you remember and think about sth: *The sound of their laughter called up memories of his own childhood.* **OBJ** **memory** **SYN** **recall sth** (*formal*) **3** to use a quality that you have: *He called up all his reserves of courage.* **OBJ** **reserves**
♦ v + adv + n ♦ v + n/pron + adv

'**call upon sth, etc.** → CALL ON/UPON STH, ETC.

calm /kɑːm/

,**calm 'down**; ,**calm sb/yourself 'down** if sb **calms down**, or you **calm them down**, they stop being angry or excited and become calm: *Calm down! I've said I'm sorry.* ◇ *There was nothing we could do to calm her down.* ◇ *He went for a walk to calm himself down.* ◇ *Jack was so shocked that he had to be calmed down by his wife and son.*
♦ v + adv ♦ v + n/pron + adv ♦ v + adv + n

,**calm 'down**; ,**calm sth 'down** to become calmer; to make a situation calmer: *The whole fuss will have calmed down by tomorrow.* ◇ *I've spoken to them to try to calm things down a bit.*
NOTE Not used in the passive.
♦ v + adv ♦ v + n/pron + adv ♦ v + adv + n

camp /kæmp/

,**camp 'out** (*informal*) to sleep outside, usually in a tent; to sleep on the floor somewhere for a short time: *If there is nowhere to stay, we'll have to camp out.* ◇ *People camped out in the school hall to escape the floodwater.*
♦ v + adv
▶ **'campout** *n* (*AmE*) a time when people sleep outside in a tent

,**camp it 'up** (*BrE*, *informal*) to behave in a very exaggerated manner, especially to attract attention to yourself or to make people laugh: *He enjoys camping it up.* ◇ *I really camped it up in the final scene.*
♦ v + it + adv

cancel /'kænsl/ (-ll-, *AmE* -l-)

,**cancel 'out**; ,**cancel sth 'out** if two or more things **cancel out** or one **cancels out** the other, they are equally important, but have an opposite effect on a situation so that the situation does not change: *The gains and losses are expected to cancel out.* ◇ *Our expenditure and profits* **cancel each other out**. ◇ *The job is hard work, but this is cancelled out by the fact that the people are so nice.* ➔ note at MAKE UP FOR STH
♦ v + adv ♦ v + n/pron + adv ♦ v + adv + n

cannon /'kænən/

,**cannon 'into sb/sth** (of a moving person, vehicle, etc.) to hit sb/sth by accident and with great force: *She stopped suddenly and I almost cannoned into her.*
♦ v + prep

,**cannon 'off sth** if sth moving **cannons off** sb/sth, it hits them/it by accident and with great force and then goes off in a different direction: *The ball cannoned off his leg into the goal.*
♦ v + prep

capitalize (*BrE also* **capitalise**) /'kæpɪtəlaɪz/

'**capitalize on sth** (*also* '**capitalize upon sth** *less frequent*, *more formal*) to use sth to gain further advantage for yourself: *They capitalized on their success by raising prices.* ◇ *The opposition tried to capitalize on popular discontent over the new law.*

OBJ success, opportunity, potential **SYN** take advantage of sth
♦ v + prep

care /keə(r); AmE ker/

'**care for sb** to like or love sb: *I care deeply for you.* ◇ *I just want to be loved and cared for by somebody.*
♦ v + prep

IDM **would you care for …** (*formal*) used to ask sb if they would like sth to eat or drink: *Would you care for a cup of tea?*

'**care for sb/sth 1** to take care of and be responsible for sb who is very young, old or sick, etc. or for sth that is in danger or could be damaged: *The nurses give advice to the patients and those who care for them.* ◇ *She cares for several children with special needs.* ◇ *The company is committed to caring for the environment.* ◇ *The children were all clean and well cared for.* **OBJ** **children, the sick, the elderly** → see also LOOK AFTER SB/STH/YOURSELF; LOOK AFTER STH **2** not care for sb/sth (*formal*) to not like sb/sth very much: *I don't care for opera.*
♦ v + prep
▶ **un'cared for** *adj* not looked after: *The children looked dirty and uncared for.* ◇ *uncared-for gardens*

carry /'kæri/ (**carries, carrying, carried**)

,**carry sth a'round** (*also* ,**carry sth a'bout/ 'round** *especially BrE*) (**with you**) to take sth from one place to another; to take sth everywhere with you: *I don't want to carry this bag about with me all day.* ◇ *The MP3 player is light enough to carry around in your pocket.*
♦ v + n/pron + adv ♦ v + adv + n

,**carry sb/sth a'long** to take or move sb/sth forward: *His body had been carried along by the river.* ◇ *The crowd was so thick that she was carried along with it.* ◇ (*figurative*) *His immense enthusiasm carried us all along.*
♦ v + n/pron + adv

,**carry sb/sth a'way/'off** to support the weight of sb/sth and take them/it away: *A strong current carried the dinghy away.*
♦ v + n/pron + adv ♦ v + adv + n

be/get ,carried a'way to be so excited and enthusiastic about sth that you lose control of your feelings and may behave in a silly way or without thinking: *I got so carried away with shopping that I completely forgot the time.* ◇ *Don't get carried away—it's not that exciting.*
♦ be/get + v + adv

,**carry sb 'back** (**to sth**) to remind sb of sth that happened in the past: *The song carried her back to her childhood.*
SYN take sb back (to sth)
♦ v + n/pron + adv

---

care for sb

attend to sb/sth ♦ **care for sb** ♦ **look after sb/ yourself** ♦ **take care of sb** ♦ **tend to sb**

These verbs all mean to be responsible for sb's health or safety, especially by giving them everything they need.

attend to sb/sth (*formal*) to look after sb/sth and make sure they have everything they need: *A nurse attended to his needs constantly.*

care for sb to look after sb because they are seriously ill, injured or very old, and to make sure they have what they need: *He gave up work to care for his wife.*

look after sb/yourself (*especially BrE*) to be responsible for sb's general health and happiness, especially because they are ill, injured, very young or old: *Who's going to look after the children while you're away?* ◇ *Don't worry about me—I can look after myself.*

take care of sb to look after sb: *Who's taking care of the children while you're away?*

tend to sb to look after ill or injured people: *Ambulance crews were tending to the injured.*

NOTE Tend can be used on its own, and is also used for animals and plants: *Doctors and nurses tended the injured.* ◇ *They helped the farmers tend their cattle.*

WHICH WORD?

People often **look after sb** for a short time, while they are ill, or while the person who usually takes care of them is away. **Take care of sb** can be used in the same way, and in American English it is more frequent than **look after sb**. Both of these, but especially **take care of sb**, can suggest a feeling of love and care for the person, not just a position of responsibility. **Caring for sb** is more often a long-term, full-time occupation.

PATTERNS AND COLLOCATIONS

■ to look after/take care of/care for/tend (to) **the sick**
■ to look after/take care of/care for **the children/the elderly/an elderly relative**
■ to look after/take care of **yourself**
■ to tend/attend to **a wound**

,**carry sth** ˈ**forward 1** (*also* ,**carry sth** ˈ**over**) (*finance*) to move a total sum of money, or a total amount, from one page or column to the next, or from one week or year to the next: *The figures were carried forward from the previous page.* **SYN** **bring sth forward** **NOTE** Often used in the passive. **2** to help sth to make progress or succeed: *She will carry the project forward after I leave.*
◆ v + n/pron + adv ◆ v + adv + n

,**carry sb** ˈ**off 1** if a disease **carries sb off**, they die as a result of it: *She was carried off by the epidemic.* **2** to capture sb: *The enemy carried off many prisoners.*
◆ v + n/pron + adv ◆ v + adv + n

,**carry sb/sth** ˈ**off** → CARRY SB/STH AWAY/OFF

,**carry sth** ˈ**off 1** to win sth: *She carried off most of the prizes.* **2** to succeed in doing sth difficult; to deal with a difficult situation successfully: *She's the only person I know who can wear a dress like that and carry it off!*
◆ **1** v + adv + n ◆ v + pron + adv
◆ v + n + adv (*less frequent*)
◆ **2** v + n/pron + adv ◆ v + adv + n

,**carry** ˈ**on 1** (**with sth**) (*also* ,**carry** ˈ**on doing sth**) (*especially BrE*) to continue doing sth or moving in a particular direction, without stopping: *Carry on working/with your work while I'm away.* ◇ *If she carries on shoplifting, she'll end up in jail.* ◇ *She ignored me and carried on writing.* ◇ *I called out to him, but he carried on down the road.* **SYN** **go on**, **go on doing sth** → see also CARRY ON ON 1 **2** to manage to continue living or working in your usual way in spite of difficult or unpleasant circumstances: *Life carried on as usual after the fire.* ◇ *We're all going to carry on as if nothing has happened.* **SYN** **go on**; **continue 3** (**with sth**) to continue speaking or doing sth after a short pause: *'Well', she carried on, 'then I realized where I'd met him before!'* ◇ *Ted looked up briefly, then carried on with what he was doing.* **SYN** **go on** (**with sth**) **4** to last for a particular time: *How long can this situation carry on?* **SYN** **go on**; **last 5** (**at sb**) (**about sth**) (*informal*) to argue or complain noisily: *Stop carrying on about how hard your life is.* ◇ *How long are they going to be shouting and carrying on like that?* **SYN** **go on** (**at sb**) (**about sth**) **6** (**with sb**) (*old-fashioned*, *informal*) to have a sexual relationship with sb: *She's carrying on with her boss.*
◆ v + adv **1** also v + adv + -ing
◆ **3** also v + adv + speech

▸ ˈ**carry-on** *n* **1** [usually sing.] (*BrE*, *informal*) excited or noisy behaviour over sth that is not important **2** (*AmE*) a small bag or case that you carry onto a plane with you: *I'm travelling light—I just have a carry-on.* ◇ *Do you have any carry-on luggage?*

,**carry sth** ˈ**on 1** to continue sth, especially sth that sb else has begun: *Our children will carry*

this tradition on after us. → see also CARRY ON ON 1 **2** ,**carry** ˈ**on sth** to do the activity mentioned: *We're trying to carry on a very important conversation!* ◇ *They carried on a correspondence for over forty years.* ◇ *to carry on a business/trade* **OBJ** **conversation**, **correspondence**, **business** **SYN** **conduct sth** **NOTE** When the object of **carry on** is a noun, it comes after **on**, but when the object is a pronoun, it comes between **carry** and **on**: *It's hard to carry it on when your heart's no longer in it.*
◆ **1** v + adv + n ◆ v + n/pron + adv
◆ **2** v + adv + n ◆ v + pron + adv

,**carry sth** ˈ**out 1** to do sth that you said you would do or that you have been asked to do: *to carry out a plan/a promise/an order* ◇ *He had no intention of carrying out his threats.* ◇ *She had carried out all his instructions.* **OBJ** **threat**, **promise**, **order 2** to do and complete a task: *to carry out a survey/an investigation* ◇ *to carry out repairs/checks/tests* ◇ *to carry out research* ◇ *It is not yet clear who carried out the attack.*
◆ v + adv + n ◆ v + pron + adv
◆ v + n + adv (*less frequent*)

▸ ˈ**carry-out** *n* **1** (*AmE*, *ScotE*) a meal that you buy cooked from a restaurant and take away to eat somewhere else: *Let's get a carry-out.* **2** (*ScotE*) alcohol that you buy at a pub and take away to drink somewhere else

,**carry sth** ˈ**over 1** to delay sth until a later time: *The game had to be carried over until Wednesday.* ◇ *You can carry over 4 days' leave to next year.* **SYN** **postpone sth 2** to keep sth from one situation and use or deal with it in a new situation: *You should carry over what you learn in school into your everyday life.* **3** → CARRY STH FORWARD 1
◆ v + adv + n ◆ v + n/pron + adv

▸ ˈ**carry-over** *n* **1** (*finance*) a total sum of money or an amount that is moved to the next column/page/year, etc. **2** sth that is kept from one situation or time and used in another

,**carry sth** ˈ**round** (**with you**) (*especially BrE*) → CARRY STH AROUND (WITH YOU)

,**carry** ˈ**through** (**on/with sth**) (*AmE*) to do and finish what you have promised, agreed or arranged to do: *He convinced us that he would carry through with/on his promise.*
◆ v + adv

,**carry sb** ˈ**through**; ,**carry sb** ˈ**through sth** to help sb to deal with a difficult period: *Her determination carried her through.* ◇ *His courage helped to carry them through the difficult times.*
◆ v + n/pron + adv ◆ v + n/pron + prep

,**carry sth** ˈ**through** to finish a task, a plan, etc. successfully: *She was determined to carry through her plans.* ◇ *Once Helen has started a task, she'll carry it through to the end.*
OBJ **plan**, **proposal**, **decision**, **reforms**
◆ v + adv + n ◆ v + n/pron + adv

cart /kɑːt; *AmE* kɑːrt/

ˌcart sth aˈround (*also* ˌ**cart sth aˈbout/ˈround** *especially BrE*) (**with you**) (*informal*) used to talk about carrying sth large, awkward or unimportant from one place to another or everywhere you go: *I had to cart my shopping around with me all day.* ◇ *He carts all sorts of useless stuff about.*
SYN **carry sth around** (**with you**) (*more formal*); **lug sth around** (**with you**)
◆ v + n/pron + adv ◆ v + adv + n

ˌcart sb/sth aˈway/ˈoff (*informal*) to take sb/sth away with some difficulty: *Two players were carted off to hospital.* ◇ *The police arrived and carted 40 rioters off to jail.*
SYN **take sb/sth away** (*more formal*)
NOTE Often used in the passive.
◆ v + adv + n ◆ v + n/pron + adv

carve /kɑːv; *AmE* kɑːrv/

ˌcarve sth ˈout 1 (*also* ˌ**carve sth ˈout of sth**) (*geology*) to make a physical feature in the earth's surface over a long period of time through the action of water, ice, weather, etc.: *The valley was carved out by glaciers.* **NOTE** Often used in the passive. **2** (**for yourself**) to build a successful career, a good reputation, etc., often with difficulty or hard work: *She carved out a unique niche for herself in the music business.* ◇ *He's carved out a successful career in the building industry.* **OBJ** **career**, **name**, **niche**
◆ v + adv + n
◆ v + n/pron + adv **1** also v + n/pron + adv + prep

ˌcarve sb/sth ˈup (*BrE*, *informal*) **1** to wound sb or their face badly with a knife: *He got carved up outside the pub last night.* **2** to go past a moving vehicle ahead of you and then suddenly move in front of it in a dangerous way: *I was carved up by a lunatic in a Porsche.* ◇ *We saw the van carve up several cars, before turning left.* **OBJ** **person**, **car** **SYN** **cut sb/sth up** (*BrE*)
◆ v + n/pron + adv ◆ v + adv + n

ˌcarve sth ˈup to divide a company, an area of land, etc. into parts and share them out: *They carved the territory up into three provinces.* ◇ *The thieves hurriedly carved up the loot.*
◆ v + adv + n ◆ v + n/pron + adv
▸ **ˈcarve-up** *n* [sing.] (*BrE*, *informal*) the act of dividing sth up into parts and sharing them out

cash /kæʃ/

ˌcash ˈin (**on sth**) (*informal*) to gain an advantage from a situation in a way that people think is wrong or dishonest: *Many businesses cashed in on the massive public interest in her death.* ◇ *The new law means video pirates can no longer cash in by selling illegal copies.*
◆ v + adv

ˌcash sth ˈin to exchange sth for money: *Cash in any remaining travellers' cheques when you*
return. ◇ *You will lose money if you cash your policy in early.*
OBJ **shares**, **policy**
◆ v + adv + n ◆ v + n/pron + adv

ˌcash ˈout (*AmE*) **1** to exchange sth such as an insurance policy, property or shares for money, often before you are supposed to do this: *With house prices still rising, many people are tempted to cash out while they can.* **2** (in poker, roulette, etc.) to stop taking part in a game and exchange pieces of plastic which represent a particular value (called **chips**) for money: *I actually won at the roulette table, so I cashed out and went home.* **3** → CASH UP
◆ v + adv
▸ **ˈcash-out** *n* (*AmE*) the act of cashing out an insurance policy, property, etc.: *cash-out refinancing mortgages*

ˌcash ˈup (*BrE*) (*AmE* ˌ**cash ˈout**) to count the money that has been taken in a shop/store, restaurant, etc. at the end of the day: *We cash up at five o'clock.*
◆ v + adv

cast /kɑːst; *AmE* kæst/ (**cast**, **cast**)

ˌcast aˈround (*BrE also* ˌ**cast aˈbout**) (**for sth**) (*formal*) to look around you to try to find sth; to try very hard to think of sth: *He cast about for an escape route.* ◇ *He was desperately casting around for an excuse.* ◇ *The company is having to cast around feverishly for ways to cut its costs.*
◆ v + adv

ˌcast sb/sth aˈside (*formal*) to get rid of or give no attention to sb/sth that you no longer want or need: *She just cast him aside when she got bored.* ◇ *She has been able to cast aside* (= stop using) *her wheelchair.*
SYN **discard sb/sth**
◆ v + adv + n ◆ v + n/pron + adv

ˌcast sth aˈside (*formal*) **1** to throw sth to one side: *He cast aside the newspaper impatiently.* **2** to get rid of feelings, attitudes, etc. that are bad or negative, or that stop you achieving sth: *He cast aside all his inhibitions.* ◇ *The speakers cast modesty aside and talked about their success.*
SYN **throw sth aside**; **toss sth aside** (*less formal*)
◆ v + adv + n ◆ v + n/pron + adv

be ˌcast aˈway (**on sth**) to be left somewhere after your ship has been destroyed at sea: *What would you do if you were cast away on a desert island?*
◆ be + v + adv
▸ **ˈcastaway** *n* a person whose ship has been destroyed and who has managed to swim to an island, etc.

ˌcast sth ˈback (**to sb/sth**) to make yourself think about a particular time, a situation in the past, etc.: *I cast my mind back to our first meeting all those years ago.*
OBJ only **your mind**
◆ v + n + adv

,cast sth 'down (*literary*) if you **cast** your eyes **down**, you look down: *She cast her eyes down modestly while Jack was talking about her.* [OBJ] only **eyes** [SYN] **lower sth** (*less formal*)
♦ v + n/pron + adv ♦ v + adv + n
▶ 'downcast (*also* ,cast 'down *less frequent*) *adj* (*literary*) **downcast** eyes are looking down

be ,cast 'down (by sth) (*formal*) to be sad or unhappy about sth: *He is not easily cast down.*
♦ be + v + adv
▶ 'downcast (*also* ,cast 'down *less frequent*) *adj* (*literary*) sad or unhappy: *a downcast expression*
◇ *He looked so downcast I took pity on him.*

,cast 'off; ,cast sth 'off **1** to undo the ropes that are holding a boat in position so that it can start to move **2** (in knitting) to remove a row from the needle in a way that will make a finished edge: *When the scarf is the right length, cast off.* [OBJ] **stitches** [OPP] **cast on, cast sth on**
♦ v + adv ♦ v + adv + n ♦ v + pron + adv
♦ v + n + adv (*rare*)

,cast sth 'off (*formal*) **1** to take off a piece of clothing and throw it to one side: *They cast off their clothes and jumped in the pool.* [OBJ] **jacket, shoes, clothes** [SYN] **take sth off** (*less formal*) **2** to get rid of sth bad or sth that you do not like: *She tried to cast off her upbringing.* ◇ *It's time to cast off those winter blues and burst into spring!*
♦ v + adv + n ♦ v + pron + adv ♦ v + n + adv (*rare*)
▶ 'cast-off (*especially BrE*) (*AmE usually* 'hand-me-down) *n* [usually pl.] a piece of clothing that the original owner no longer wants to wear: *She's fed up with wearing her sister's cast-offs.*
▶ 'cast-off *adj* [only before noun] that the original owner no longer wants to wear or use: *cast-off clothing* ◇ *cast-off plastic bags*

,cast 'on; ,cast sth 'on (in knitting) to make the first row on a needle: *Cast on and knit 10 rows.* [SUBJ] **stitches** [OPP] **cast off, cast sth off**
♦ v + adv ♦ v + adv + n ♦ v + pron + adv
♦ v + n + adv (*rare*)

,cast sb/sth 'out; ,cast sb/sth 'out of sth (*formal*) to drive sb away; to get rid of sb/sth, especially by using force: *She was cast out by society.* ◇ *He claimed to be able to cast out demons.* ◇ *The villagers had been cast out of their homes.*
[NOTE] Often used in the passive.
♦ v + adv + n ♦ v + n/pron + adv
♦ v + n/pron + adv + prep
▶ 'outcast *n* a person who is not accepted by other people and who sometimes has to leave their home and friends: *She felt like a social outcast.* ◇ *He was treated like an outcast by the other children.*
▶ 'outcast *adj* [only before noun] ignored or not accepted by other people: *outcast members of society*

,cast sb/sth 'up (on sth) (*literary*) **1** if the sea **casts** sb/sth **up** on the land, it carries them/it in and leaves them/it there: *A whale bone was cast up on the beach.* [SYN] **wash up, wash sth up** (*less formal*) [NOTE] Often used in the passive. **2** if you **cast** your eyes **up**, you look up: *She cast her eyes up to the ceiling and sighed.* [OBJ] only **eyes**
♦ v + n/pron + adv ♦ v + adv + n

catch /kætʃ/ (**caught, caught** /kɔːt/)

'catch at sth/sb to try to get hold of sth quickly: *She tried to catch at a branch but couldn't reach.* [OBJ] **sb's hand/arm/sleeve** [SYN] **clutch at sb/ sth; grasp at sth/sb**
♦ v + prep

,catch 'on (*informal*) **1** (to sth) to understand sth; to realize the truth of sth: *He's very quick to catch on.* ◇ *The students soon caught on to the idea that phrasal verbs are not really difficult.* ◇ *People are catching on to the fact that he's a fraud.* [SYN] **cotton on** (**to sth**) **2** (**with sb**) to become popular or fashionable: *It's a good idea, but it'll never catch on.* ◇ *Paying by credit card has only caught on recently here.* ◇ *3-D films never caught on with a mass audience.*
♦ v + adv

,catch sb 'out **1** to trick sb into making a mistake or doing sth wrong; to discover that sb does not know much or is doing sth wrong: *The test isn't designed to catch you out. It's to see how much you've learnt.* ◇ *The interviewer may try to catch you out with trick questions.* ◇ *She reacted like a child caught out in a lie.* **2** (*especially BrE*) if a situation, bad weather, etc. **catches sb out**, it surprises them and puts them into a difficult situation: *The snow catches us out every year* (= we are not prepared for it). ◇ *Many investors were caught out by the collapse of the company.* [NOTE] Often used in the passive.
♦ v + n/pron + adv ♦ v + adv + n (*less frequent*)

,catch 'up (with sb/sth) (*BrE also* ,catch sb/sth 'up) **1** to reach sb/sth ahead of you by going faster than them/it: *She was walking so fast I had to run to catch up (with her).* ◇ *The police car finally caught up with the van at the junction.* **2** to reach the same level or standard as sb/sth else that was better or more advanced: *We need to catch up with our competitors in Europe.* ◇ *You'll have to work hard to catch up with the rest of the class.* ◇ *When I went back to school I found I **had a lot of catching up to do**.*
♦ v + adv ♦ v + n/pron + adv ♦ v + adv + n (*rare*)
▶ 'catch-up *n* [U] the act of trying to reach the same level or standard as sb who is ahead of you: *catch-up history classes* ◇ *After our bad start to the season we were always **playing catch-up** (= trying to reach the same level as others).*

,catch 'up (with sth) **1** to spend extra time doing all the work, tasks, etc. that you should have done earlier: *I'm so behind with my paperwork, it's going to take me a week to catch up.* **2** to find out about things that have happened: *Come and*

catch up (with sb/sth)

catch up (with sb/sth) ◆ **draw level (with sb/ sth)** ◆ **get to sth** ◆ **reach sb/sth**

These verbs all mean to arrive at a particular place or point.

catch up (with sb/sth) to reach sb/sth that is ahead of you by going faster: *You go on ahead. I'll catch up with you.* ◇ *The car behind us was catching up.* **NOTE** Catch sb up can also be used in British English: *I eventually caught her up and managed to talk to her.*

draw level (with sb/sth) to reach the same level as sb and move forward at the same speed: *She drew level with the police car.*

get to sth to arrive at a particular place or point after travelling there: *We got to San Diego at 7 o'clock.*

reach sb/sth to arrive at a place after travelling to it: *We didn't reach the border until after dark.* ◇ *I hope this letter reaches you.*

PATTERNS AND COLLOCATIONS

- to **eventually/finally** get to/reach/catch up with/draw level with sb/sth
- to **soon/quickly** get to/reach/catch up with (sth)
- to get to/reach your **destination**

---

stay for a few days, so that we have a chance to catch up. ◇ *I want to catch up with all your news.* ◇ *We've **got a lot of catching up to do** after all this time.* → see also CATCH UP ON STH
◆ v + adv

,**catch sb 'up** (**on sth**) (*AmE*) to tell sb about things that have happened: *You can catch me up on the news later.*
◆ v + n/pron + adv

⚓,**catch sb/sth 'up** (*BrE*) **1** → CATCH UP (WITH SB/ STH) 1: *You go ahead. I'll catch you up.* ◇ *She caught the leader up and then overtook her.* **2** → CATCH UP (WITH SB/STH) 2: *This company is the most likely to catch up the market leader.* ◇ *She's training hard to catch her sister up.*

be/get ,caught 'up in sth 1 to become involved in an unpleasant event or situation that you cannot escape from: *A number of tourists got caught up in the riots.* ◇ *children caught up in crime* ◇ *Sorry I'm late—I got caught up in a traffic jam.* OBJ **violence, war, events, traffic 2** to be completely absorbed in an activity, your own feelings, etc.: *She got caught up in the excitement and drama of the auction.* ◇ *I didn't hear you come in; I was so caught up in this book.* OBJ **excitement, book**
◆ be/get + v + adv + prep

,**catch 'up on sb** → CATCH UP WITH SB 2: *Old age is catching up on me.*

,**catch 'up on sth 1** to spend extra time doing all the work, tasks, etc. that you should have done earlier: *I've got a lot of work to catch up on.* ◇ *I spent the weekend catching up on lost sleep.* OBJ **work, sleep 2** to find out about things that have happened: *It was good to see Patsy and catch up on all the gossip.*
→ see also CATCH UP (WITH STH)
◆ v + adv + prep

,**catch 'up with sb 1** if the police or people in authority **catch up with** sb, they finally find out that he/she has done sth wrong and punish him/her: *They were involved in burglary for years before the police caught up with them.* **2** (*also* ,**catch 'up on sb** *less frequent*) if sth you have done or sth that has been happening to you **catches up with** you, it starts to cause you problems that you have so far managed to avoid: *His past is finally catching up with him.* ◇ *The late nights were beginning to catch up with her.* **3** (*informal*) to meet sb you have not seen for a while and hear their news: *He just wants to rest and catch up with old friends.* ◇ *Catch up with you later!* ◇ *We've **got a lot of catching up to do** after all this time!* OBJ **friends**
◆ v + adv + prep

cater /ˈkeɪtə(r)/

'**cater for sb/sth** to provide everything that sb, a group of people or a situation needs or wants: *The careers service caters for the needs of young people and adults.* ◇ *The resort also caters for winter sports.* ◇ *All age groups are well catered for.*
OBJ **needs, children, interests**
◆ v + prep

'**cater to sb/sth** to provide sth that satisfies what a particular type of person wants: *Endless media coverage catered to the public's interest in the scandal.* ◇ *Their every need was catered to.*
◆ v + prep

cave /keɪv/

,**cave 'in 1** (**on sb/sth**) if a roof, wall, etc. **caves in**, it falls down and towards the centre: *The roof of the tunnel caved in on the workmen.* SUBJ **roof, wall** ⊃ note at FALL DOWN **2** (**to sth**) to finally do what sb wants you to do after you have resisted for a long time: *The management refused to cave in to their demands.* ◇ *Under his fierce questioning she caved in and told him the truth.* OBJ **demands, pressure**
◆ v + adv

▸ '**cave-in** *n* **1** the fact of a roof, wall, etc. caving in: *For the people inside the tunnel there was a serious risk of flooding or a cave-in.* **2** an instance of agreeing under pressure to do sth you do not want to do

centre (BrE) (AmE center) /'sentə(r)/

'centre around sb/sth; 'centre sth around sb/sth (BrE also 'centre round sb/sth, 'centre sth round sb/sth) to be, or make sb/sth, the most important person or thing around which most activity takes place: *The debate centres around the question of power.* ◇ *The case centred around the couple's adopted children.* ◇ *Her life was centred entirely around her family.* ◇ *The nightlife of the town is largely centred around the hotels.*
NOTE Often used in the passive.
◆ v + prep ◆ v + n/pron + prep

'centre on sb/sth; 'centre sth on sb/sth (also 'centre upon sb/sth, 'centre sth upon sb/sth *more formal*) to give a lot of attention or thought to one particular activity, idea or person, etc.: *The discussions centred on the hostage issue.* ◇ *Public attention centred largely on the team's stars.* ◇ *The group has centred its attention on the need for reform.* ◇ *His research is centred on the effects of unemployment.*
NOTE Often used in the passive.
◆ v + prep ◆ v + n/pron + prep

chain /tʃeɪn/

,chain sb/sth 'up (to sth) to fasten sb/sth to sth else with chains to stop them escaping or being stolen: *I'd chain your bike up to the fence just in case.* ◇ *The prisoners were chained up in a dark cell.*
NOTE Chain sb/sth (to sth) can also be used with this meaning.
◆ v + n/pron + adv ◆ v + adv + n

chalk /tʃɔːk/

,chalk 'up sth (*informal*) to achieve a success, a victory, a score in a game, etc.: *The team has chalked up its fifth win in a row.* ◇ *This week Dee Brothers chalked up 100 years of business in this town.*
OBJ success, victory, win
NOTE When the object of **chalk up** is a noun, it comes after **up**, but when the object is a pronoun, it comes between **chalk** and **up**: *She keeps on chalking them up.*
◆ v + adv + n ◆ v + pron + adv

IDM chalk one 'up for sb (*AmE*) used to show admiration or praise because sb has won sth: *Chalk one up for the little guy. The city agreed today to pay 25 homeless people $80 000 to settle a lawsuit alleging police harassment.*

,chalk sth 'up to sth (*informal*) to think that sth happens as a result of sth else: *We can chalk our recent victories up to a lot of luck.* ◇ *When the goal was disallowed they **chalked it up to** a bad referee decision.*
SYN attribute sth to sth (*formal*); put sth down to sth
◆ v + n/pron + adv + prep

IDM chalk it up to ex'perience (*informal, especially AmE*) used to say that you can learn from sth bad that has happened to you

chance /tʃɑːns; AmE tʃæns/

'chance on/upon sb/sth (*formal*) to meet sb or find sth when you do not expect to: *I chanced on an old school friend in town.* ◇ *He chanced upon a volume of Japanese poetry in a bookshop.*
◆ v + prep

change /tʃeɪndʒ/

,change sb/sth a'round (*especially AmE*)
→ CHANGE SB/STH ROUND

,change 'back **1** (into sth) to take off your clothes and put on what you were wearing earlier: *I'll just change back into my tracksuit.* **2** (into/to sth) to return to an earlier state or form: *When you double click on SELECT, the screen changes back to the main design screen.* ◇ *Slowly the angry animal changed back into its normal calm self.*
◆ v + adv

,change sth 'back (into/to sth) to exchange an amount of money into the system of money (**currency**) that it was in before: *Can I change these dollars back into sterling?*
◆ v + n/pron + adv ◆ v + adv + n (*less frequent*)

,change 'down (into/to sth) (*BrE*) to control the speed of a vehicle by changing to a lower gear: *Change down into second as you approach the corner.*
OPP change up (into/to sth)
◆ v + adv

,change 'into sth to put on different clothes: *We quickly changed into our swimsuits.* ◇ *I didn't bring anything to change into.*
◆ v + prep

,change 'into sth; ,change sb/sth 'into sth to change, or to make sb/sth change, into sth different: *The castle has changed into a hotel.* ◇ *The handsome prince was changed into a frog.*
SYN turn into sth, turn sb/sth into sth
◆ v + prep ◆ v + n/pron + prep

,change 'out of sth to take off the clothes you are wearing and put on different ones: *I must change out of these wet clothes before I get a chill.* ◇ *She changed out of her suit as soon as she came home.*
◆ v + adv + prep

,change 'over **1** (from sth) (to sth) to stop using one system or thing and start using another: *The magazine changed over from pink paper to white in 1917.* ◇ *We're changing over to a new computer system.* **SYN** switch over (from sth) (to sth) **2** (to sth) (*BrE*) to change from watching one television channel to watching another: *I changed over to BBC1 to see the football.* ◇ *Can we change over?* **SYN** switch over (from sth) (to sth); turn over (to sth)
◆ v + adv

▶ **'changeover** *n* a change from one system or thing to another: *The changeover to the new system will take place gradually.* ◇ *a changeover period*

change 'over/'round (*BrE*) if two people **change over/round**, they move to where the other person was before or do what the other person was doing: *Can you and Phil change round? You're too tall to stand in the front row.* ◇ *When you get tired of driving we can change over.*

SYN **swap around/over/round** (*informal, especially BrE*)

◆ v + adv

change sb/sth 'round (*especially BrE*) (*AmE usually* **change sb/sth a'round**) to move objects, such as furniture, or people into different positions: *Who's changed the desks around?* ◇ *You're always changing this room round!* (= making it look different by moving the furniture, etc.) ◇ *The Yankees keep changing their players around.*

OBJ **room, furniture** **SYN** **swap sb/sth around/over/round** (*especially BrE*)

◆ v + n/pron + adv ◆ v + adv + n (*less frequent*)

change 'up (**into/to sth**) (*BrE*) to control the speed of a vehicle by changing to a higher gear: *Change up into fourth gear now.*

OPP **change down** (**into/to sth**)

◆ v + adv

charge /tʃɑːdʒ; *AmE* tʃɑːrdʒ/

charge sth 'up; charge 'up to pass electricity through sth so that it is stored there; to take in electricity and store it: *This charger will charge up most makes of phone.* ◇ *It takes about two hours for the phone to charge up completely.*

◆ v + n/pron + adv ◆ v + adv + n ◆ v + adv

'charge sb with sth; 'charge sb with doing sth (*formal*) to give sb a duty, responsibility or task: *A solicitor was charged with administering the estate.*

NOTE Often used in the passive.

◆ v + n/pron + prep

charm /tʃɑːm; *AmE* tʃɑːrm/

charm sth 'out of sb if you **charm** money or information **out of** sb, you obtain it by using your power to please or attract people: *She managed to charm £20 out of him.*

◆ v + n/pron + adv + prep

chase /tʃeɪs/

chase 'after sb (*informal*) to try to persuade sb to have a romantic or sexual relationship with you: *He's always chasing after younger women.*

◆ v + prep

chase 'after sb/sth to run, drive, etc. to try to catch sb/sth: *They chased after the thief but he got away.*

◆ v + prep

chase a'round (*BrE also* **chase a'bout/'round**) to be very busy, rushing from one place to another: *I've been chasing around all morning trying to find a gift for my sister.*

◆ v + adv

chase sb/sth a'way/'off/'out to force sb/sth to run away by running after them or threatening them: *He chased the attackers away by firing shots into the air.*

◆ v + n/pron + adv ◆ v + adv + n

chase sb/sth 'down (*AmE, informal*) to try hard to get sth or find sb/sth that you need or want: *I've been trying to chase Sam down all day!*

SYN **seek sb/sth out** (*more formal*); **track sb/sth down**

◆ v + n/pron + adv ◆ v + adv + n

chase sb/sth 'off, 'out, etc. → CHASE SB/STH AWAY/OFF/OUT, ETC.

chase 'round (*BrE*) → CHASE AROUND

chase sb/sth 'up (*informal*) **1** to contact sb and remind them to do sth they have said they would do or that they ought to do: *I'll chase him up and find out what's going on.* ◇ *It is his job to chase up clients with outstanding debts.* ◇ *Could you chase up those late replies* (= remind people to reply). **2** to try to find sb/sth that you need; to try to get more information about sb/sth: *We're chasing up two other people who were at the party.* ◇ *I'll chase up references to the battle in the library.*

◆ v + n/pron + adv ◆ v + adv + n

chat /tʃæt/ (-tt-)

chat sb 'up (*informal*) **1** (*BrE*) to talk in a friendly way to sb because you are sexually attracted to them: *Who was that girl you were chatting up last night?* **2** (*especially AmE*) to talk to sb in a friendly way because you want them to do sth for you or to give you sth: *You'll have to chat the boss up if you want some days off.*

◆ v + n/pron + adv ◆ v + adv + n

▶ **'chat-up** *n* (*BrE, informal*) an attempt to talk in a friendly way to sb you are sexually attracted to: *He was trying some old chat-up lines.*

cheat /tʃiːt/

'cheat sb of sth (*also* **cheat sb 'out of sth**) to prevent sb from having sth, especially in an unfair or dishonest way: *He had cheated the taxman of £60 000.* ◇ *He was cheated out of his rightful inheritance.*

◆ v + n/pron + prep ◆ v + n/pron + adv + prep

'cheat on sb to secretly have sex with sb who is not your regular partner: *He was the last to know that she had been cheating on him.*

OBJ **wife, partner, etc.**

⊃ note on page 52

◆ v + prep

cheat sb 'out of sth → CHEAT SB OF STH

cheat on sb

betray sb ◆ be unfaithful to sb ◆ cheat on sb ◆ commit adultery ◆ play around

These verbs all mean to have a sexual relationship with sb who is not your usual partner.

betray sb (*literary, disapproving*) (of sb who is married or who has a regular sexual partner) to have a secret relationship with sb else: *She could not believe that Sergio had betrayed her.*

be unfaithful to sb (of sb who is married or who has a regular sexual partner) to have a secret relationship with sb else: *Have you ever been unfaithful to him?*

cheat on sb (*not formal, disapproving*) (of sb who is married or who has a regular sexual partner) to have a secret relationship with sb else: *He's cheating on his wife.*

commit adultery (*formal*) to have sex with sb who is not your husband or wife: *She was accused of committing adultery.*

play around (*informal*) to have a sexual relationship with sb who is not your usual partner: *Her husband is always playing around with other women.*

WHICH WORD?

Cheat on sb is slightly less formal than **be unfaithful to sb**. If you use **be unfaithful to sb**, you are not making any obvious moral judgement about a person's actions; using **cheat on sb** suggests that you find such an action dishonest and unacceptable. **Play around** is more often used to talk about men than women; it is often used about a man who has sexual relationships with more than one other woman.

PATTERNS AND COLLOCATIONS

■ to cheat on/be unfaithful to your **girlfriend/ boyfriend/partner**

■ to cheat on/be unfaithful to/betray your **husband/wife/lover**

check /tʃek/

ⓘ,check ˈin 1 (at sth) to go to an official desk at a hotel, an airport, etc. and tell sb that you have arrived: *After checking in, we went out for a meal.* ◇ *Check in at desk 25 an hour before take-off.* → see also CHECK INTO STH 1 2 (with sb) (*especially AmE*) to contact sb to let them know where you are or what you are doing: *I have to check in with my boss every three hours.* ⓢⓨⓝ report in (to sb/sth)
◆ v + adv

▶ ˈcheck-in *n* 1 [U] the act of telling an official at an airport that you have arrived, showing them your ticket, etc.: *the check-in desk* 2 [C, U] the place at an airport where you go to say you have arrived, show your ticket, etc.: *There were long queues at the check-in.*

ⓘ,check sb ˈin to take sb's name when they arrive at a hotel or an airport, look at their ticket, etc.: *Write all the names of the guests in this book as they are checked in.* ◇ *All the passengers have been checked in.*
ⓞⓑⒿ guests, passengers
◆ v + n/pron + adv ◆ v + adv + n

ⓘ,check sth ˈin to leave or accept bags, cases, etc. to be put on a plane or a train: *When we arrived at the airport we checked our bags in straight away.*
ⓞⓑⒿ luggage, bags
◆ v + n/pron + adv ◆ v + adv + n

ⓘ,check ˈinto sth 1 to arrive at a hotel, private hospital, etc. to begin your stay there: *I arrived in Boston and checked into my hotel.* ◇ *She's checked into a private clinic for drug rehabilitation.* ⓞⓑⒿ hotel, motel, clinic ⓢⓨⓝ book into sth ⓞⓟⓟ check out of sth → see also CHECK IN 1 2 to try to find out more about sth or discover the true facts about sth: *The police are checking into the cause of the crash.* ⓢⓨⓝ look into sth
◆ v + prep

,check sth ˈoff 1 to put a mark beside items on a list to show that they are correct, present or have been dealt with: *I've checked off all the furniture on the list.* ◇ *He checked everyone's name off as they arrived.* ⓢⓨⓝ tick sth off 2 (*especially AmE*) to put a mark in a box on a document to give an answer to a question, choose sb/sth, patient 2 to find out if sth is true or instead of checking off the candidates listed. ⓝⓞⓣⓔ Check sth on its own is more usual.
◆ v + adv + n ◆ v + n/pron + adv

ˈcheck on sb/sth 1 to make sure that sb is safe, happy, etc. or that sth is progressing as it should be: *I'll just check on dinner.* ◇ *The doctor visited every day to check on my progress.* ⓞⓑⒿ progress, children, patient 2 to find out if sth is true or correct, especially sth that sb has said about themselves: *Do you always check on future employees?* ◇ *Will you check on his address?* → see also CHECK UP

ⓝⓞⓣⓔ Check on sb/sth can be used in the passive: *The children were put to bed and then not checked on again.* ◆ Check sth can also be used on its own with these meanings.
◆ v + prep

check 'out if facts, etc. **check out,** they can be shown to be correct or true: *His story doesn't check out.* [SUBJ] **story, reference**

check 'out; check 'out of sth 1 to leave a hotel, a hospital, etc. where you have been staying: *She checked out this morning.* ◇ *He decided to check out of the hospital and go home.* [OBJ] **hotel, motel, hospital** [OPP] **check in; check into sth 2** (*AmE, informal*) to leave a place or finish an activity: *The climb was too difficult so I checked out early.* ◇ *He can't just check out on us like that!* ◇ *Let's check out of here.*

♦ v + adv ♦ v + adv + prep

▸ **'checkout** *n* [U] (*AmE*) the act or time of leaving a hotel at the end of your stay: *Checkout is 10 a.m.* ◇ *checkout time*

check 'out; check sb 'out (*AmE*) if you **check out** in a shop/store, or sb **checks you out,** you find out how much you have to pay and give sb the money: *You can check out at aisle eight.* ◇ *The girl who checked me out looked at me strangely.*

♦ v + adv ♦ v + n/pron + adv

▸ **'checkout** *n* the place where you pay for the goods you are buying in a supermarket: *There were huge queues at the checkout.* ◇ *a supermarket checkout*

check sb/sth 'out 1 (*especially AmE*) to find out if sth is true or correct or if sb is honest, works hard, etc.: *Check him out before you give him the job.* ◇ *Police have checked out his story.* ◇ *We need to check out whether the company is reliable.* [OBJ] **story, claim, company 2** (*informal*) to look at sb/sth because they/it seem interesting or attractive: *Check out our new fashion range!* ◇ *It's worth checking out that new restaurant.* ◇ *Check out that gorgeous guy over there!* ⊃ note at LOOK AT SB/STH

♦ v + adv + n ♦ v + n/pron + adv

check sth 'out (*AmE*) to borrow sth such as a book or a video from a library: *I checked out three books from the library.* [OBJ] **book, video**

♦ v + n/pron + adv ♦ v + adv + n

check sb/sth 'over to examine a person or an animal to make sure that they are healthy; to examine a machine, etc. to make sure it is working correctly: *The doctor would like to check you over.* ◇ *I got the car checked over before the trip.* [SYN] **look sb/sth over; examine sb/sth** (*more formal*)

♦ v + n/pron + adv ♦ v + adv + n

check sth 'over (*also* **check 'through sth**) to examine sth written or printed carefully to

SYNONYMS

check sb/sth over

check sb/sth over ♦ **check through sth** ♦ **examine sb/sth** ♦ **go over sth** ♦ **look sb/sth over**

These verbs all mean to look at sb/sth closely to make sure that everything is correct, in good condition, or acceptable.

check sb/sth over to check sb/sth carefully to make sure that everything is correct, in good condition, or satisfactory: *We checked over the house, looking for damp or rot.* ◇ *The doctor checked him over and said he was fit and healthy.* [NOTE] **Check** can be used on its own, but cannot be used for people: *Check the container for cracks or leaks.*

check through sth to examine all parts of sth closely to make sure that everything is correct or satisfactory, or in order to find sth: *The hospital have checked through their records but can find no reference to it.*

examine sb/sth to look at sb/sth closely to see if there is anything wrong or to find the cause of a problem: *The goods were examined for damage on arrival.* ◇ *The doctor examined her but could find nothing wrong.*

go over sth to check sth carefully for mistakes, damage or anything dangerous: *Go*

over your work for spelling mistakes before you hand it in. ◇ *The Health and Safety Officer went over the whole school, checking every fire door.*

look sb/sth over to look at sb/sth closely to see if they are/it is satisfactory: *We looked over the house again before we decided to rent it.* ◇ *The sergeant looked him over and told him to polish his shoes.*

WHICH WORD?

All of these verbs can be used when you are looking for possible problems, but only **check (over/through)** is used for possible mistakes: *Check your work (over) before handing it in.* **Examine** is used more often to describe what a professional person does: *The surveyor examined the walls for signs of damp.*

PATTERNS AND COLLOCATIONS

■ to check (over/through)/examine sth **to see if/ whether…**
■ to check (over/through)/examine/go over/look over sth **carefully**
■ to check (over/through)/examine/go over sth **thoroughly**
■ to check (over)/examine **closely/regularly/ daily**

make sure that it is correct: *I've got to check over my work for spelling before I hand it in.* ◇ *You should get someone to check the letter over for you.*

◆ v + adv + n ◆ v + pron + adv
◆ v + n + adv (*less frequent*)

,check 'through sth (*also* ,check it, them, etc. 'through *less frequent*) → CHECK STH OVER: *Check through your notes carefully.* ◇ *There were 23 files to look at, and Tim spent half his day checking through them all.*

NOTE When the object of **check through** is a noun, it comes after **through**, but when the object is a pronoun, it can come before or after **through**: *Check it through before you hand it in.* ◇ *Check through it before you hand it in.*

↪ note at CHECK SB/STH OVER

◆ v + prep ◆ v + pron + adv (*less frequent*)
◆ v + prep

,check 'up (*especially BrE*) **1** (**on sb**) to make sure that sb is doing what they should be doing, or that what they have said about themselves is true: *They always check up on prospective employees.* ◇ *I won't have you checking up on me like that!* ◇ *I'd better check up to see the kids are OK.* **2** (**on sth**) to find out if sth is true or correct; to find out what is happening: *I think the train's at ten o'clock, but I'll phone the station to check up.* ◇ *I went to the library to check up on a few things.*

NOTE **Check** and **check sth** can also be used on their own with these meanings.

→ see also CHECK ON SB/STH

◆ v + adv

▶ 'check-up *n* an examination by your doctor to see how healthy you are: *to go for a check-up* ◇ *a routine check-up*

cheer /tʃɪə(r); *AmE* tʃɪr/

,cheer sb 'on to encourage sb, especially sb in a race or competition, by shouting: *The crowd cheered the runners on.*

◆ v + n/pron + adv ◆ v + adv + n

,cheer 'up; ,cheer sb/yourself 'up to become, or to make sb/yourself, happier or more cheerful: *She seems to have cheered up since Saturday.* ◇ *Cheer up!* ◇ *Nothing could cheer him up.* ◇ *She bought some chocolates to cheer herself up.*

SYN brighten up; liven up, liven sb/sth up

◆ v + adv ◆ v + n/pron + adv ◆ v + adv + n

,cheer sth 'up to make a room, etc. brighter and more cheerful: *Flowers always cheer up a room.*

OBJ room SYN brighten sth up; liven sth up

◆ v + adv + n ◆ v + n/pron + adv

cheese /tʃiːz/

,cheese sb 'off (*BrE, informal*) to make sb annoyed or bored: *Mike's car got vandalized, which cheesed him off no end.*

NOTE **Cheesed off** (*BrE*) is often used as an adjective: *I was really cheesed off with him.* ◇ *We were feeling a bit cheesed off and didn't know what to do with ourselves.*

◆ v + n/pron + adv ◆ v + adv + n

chew /tʃuː/

'chew on sth **1** (*also* 'chew at sth) to bite sth continuously, especially because you are nervous or to test your teeth: *He chewed on his bottom lip as he considered the question.* **2** → CHEW STH OVER: *Why don't we chew on it for a while?*

◆ v + prep

,chew sb 'out (*AmE, informal*) to tell sb angrily that they have done sth wrong: *He got chewed out by his teacher for being late.*

SYNONYMS

cheer sb on

cheer sb on ◆ root for sb ◆ urge sb on

These verbs all mean to give sb encouragement or support.

cheer sb on to give sb shouts of encouragement in a race or competition: *The spectators cheered the runners on.* NOTE **Cheer** can be used on its own: *We all cheered the team as they came onto the field.* **Cheering sb on** implies giving encouragement to achieve sth in particular.

root for sb (*informal*) if you are **rooting for sb/sth**, you support or encourage them in a sports competition or when they are in a difficult situation: *We're rooting for the Bulls.*

urge sb on to encourage sb to do sth or support them so that they do it better, by shouting or just speaking words of encouragement: *She could hear him urging her on as she ran past.*

WHICH WORD?

Cheering sb on always means shouting and is nearly always done at a sports competition; **urging sb on** need not involve shouting and can be done in other situations. **Rooting for sb** may include shouting, but it mainly involves mental support. You can be **rooting for sb** even if you are not there: *Good luck with your audition tomorrow—I'll be rooting for you.*

cheer (sb) up

brighten up ◆ **cheer (sb) up** ◆ **lift** ◆ **perk up** ◆ **take heart**

These verbs all mean to become more cheerful or make sb feel more cheerful.

brighten up (of people, their eyes, faces or feelings) to look or feel happier: *She brightened up visibly at their words of encouragement.* NOTE **Brighten** can be used on its own: *My spirits brightened at the thought of Chris coming to stay.*

cheer (sb) up (often used in orders) (of a person) to become more cheerful; to make sb feel more cheerful: *Cheer up—things aren't that bad.* ◇ *I tried to cheer her up.*

lift (of sb's heart, spirits or mood) to become more cheerful: *His heart lifted at the sight of her.* ◇ *As the sky began to brighten, my mood lifted.*

perk up (*informal*) (of people, their situation or feelings) to become more cheerful or lively, especially after you have been ill/sick

or sad: *She's been depressed but she seemed to perk up last week.*

take heart (*used especially in newspapers*) to feel more positive about sth, especially when you thought you had no chance of achieving it: *The government can take heart from the latest opinion polls.*

WHICH WORD?

Cheer up, **lift** and **perk up** are used to talk about about how you feel; **brighten up** is more about how you look. It is not used in orders. If you **take heart**, you feel encouraged as well as happier.

PATTERNS AND COLLOCATIONS

- to brighten (up)/cheer up/take heart/lift/perk up **at** sth
- to take heart **from** sth
- his **spirits/mood** brightened/lifted

SYN **tell sb off** (for sth/for doing sth); **reprimand sb** (*formal*)

◆ v + n/pron + adv ◆ v + adv + n

chew sth 'over (*also* **'chew on sth**) to think about or discuss sth carefully and in detail: *He spent the weekend chewing over the problem.*

OBJ **problem, idea**

⊃ note at THINK STH OVER

◆ v + adv + n ◆ v + n/pron + adv

chew sb 'up to make sb less confident, happy or successful; to end sb's career: *The company has chewed up numerous chief executives over the years.* ◇ *The media just **chews** celebrities **up and spits them out**.*

◆ v + n/pron + adv ◆ v + adv + n

chew sth 'up 1 to bite sth until it is completely soft or destroyed: *The baby chewed the cookie up and swallowed it.* **2** if a machine **chews** sth **up**, it damages or destroys it: *The cassette player's chewed the tape up again.*

◆ v + n/pron + adv ◆ v + adv + n

chicken /'tʃɪkɪn/

chicken 'out; chicken 'out of sth; chicken 'out of doing sth (*informal*) to decide not to do sth because you are afraid: *If I don't fight him, everyone will say that I chickened out.* ◇ *She chickened out of telling him the truth.*

SYN **bottle out, bottle out of sth, bottle out of doing sth**

◆ v + adv ◆ v + adv + prep

chill /tʃɪl/

chill 'out (*informal*) to relax completely and not get upset or excited about anything: *Chill out! We'll get there on time!*

NOTE **Chill** is also used on its own: *We went home and chilled in front of the TV.*

◆ v + adv

▶ **'chillout** *adj* [only before noun] that helps you to relax or makes you feel relaxed: *chillout music* ◇ *a chillout room* (= a place at a club, etc. where you can relax when you do not want to dance)

chime /tʃaɪm/

chime 'in (**with sth**) to join in a conversation suddenly or interrupt sb: *'Absolutely!' she chimed in eagerly.* ◇ *He kept chiming in with his own opinions.*

◆ v + adv ◆ v + adv + speech

chime 'in with sth; 'chime with sth to agree with sth; to be similar to sth: *His policies chimed in with the national mood at the time.*

SYN **fit in with sth**

◆ v + adv + prep ◆ v + prep

chip /tʃɪp/ (-**pp**-)

chip a'way at sth (*used especially in the progressive tenses*) to make sth smaller or weaker by continuously breaking small pieces off it: *He was chipping away at the rocks, looking for fossils.* ◇ (*figurative*) *The government seems to be chipping away at people's rights.*

◆ v + adv + prep

,chip sth a'way/'off; ,chip sth 'off sth to remove sth by continuously breaking off small pieces: *She used a hammer to chip away the stone.* ◇ *I chipped the rust off the box with a knife.* ➔ note at BREAK OFF, BREAK STH OFF
  ◆ v + adv + n ◆ v + n/pron + adv ◆ v + n/pron + prep

,chip 'in (with sth) (*informal*) **1** to join in or interrupt a conversation; to add sth to a conversation: *Feel free to chip in if I've forgotten to mention anything.* ◇ *She chipped in with some interesting remarks.* **2** (*also* ,chip 'in sth) to give some money so that a group of people can buy sth together: *Has everyone chipped in for the present?* ◇ *The company has chipped in with a \$200 donation.* ◇ *Let's all chip in five dollars.*
  SYN club together (to do sth)
  ◆ v + adv **2** also v + adv + n

,chip 'off; ,chip 'off sth if paint or a surface **chips off**, it comes off in small pieces: *The varnish is chipping off.* ◇ *Most of the paint had chipped off the gate.*
  ◆ v + adv ◆ v + prep

,chip sth 'off, etc. → CHIP STH AWAY/OFF, ETC.

chivvy /'tʃɪvi/ (chivvies, chivvying, chivvied)

,chivvy sb a'long (*BrE, informal*) to try to make sb move faster or do sth more quickly: *The teacher chivvied the children along.*
  SYN hurry sb/sth along
  ◆ v + n/pron + adv ◆ v + adv + n

choke /tʃəʊk; *AmE* tʃoʊk/

,choke sth 'back to try to stop yourself from showing a strong emotion, or saying sth that might upset sb: *He choked back his tears.* ◇ *A protest rose to her lips, but she choked it back.*
  OBJ tears, sob(s)
  NOTE Not used in the passive.
  ◆ v + adv + n ◆ v + n/pron + adv

,choke sth 'off **1** to prevent or stop sth: *High interest rates have choked off investment.*
  OBJ demand, investment **2** to stop or interrupt sth: *His words were choked off by the sudden screams.*
  ◆ v + adv + n ◆ v + n/pron + adv

,choke 'up; ,choke sb 'up (*informal*) to become, or to make sb, so upset that you/they are unable to speak: *That song really chokes me up.* ◇ *He gets choked up just remembering the day she left.*
  NOTE Usually used in the passive.
  ◆ v + adv ◆ v + n/pron + adv

chop /tʃɒp; *AmE* tʃɑːp/ (-pp-)

'chop at sth; ,chop a'way at sth to aim blows at sth with a sharp heavy tool: *They chopped at the undergrowth with their machetes.*
  ◆ v + prep ◆ v + adv + prep

,chop sth 'down to make sth such as a tree fall down by cutting it at the base with a sharp tool:

They're chopping down thousands of trees every year.
  OBJ tree **SYN** cut sth down
  ◆ v + adv + n ◆ v + n/pron + adv

,chop sth 'off; ,chop sth 'off sth to remove sth by cutting it with a sharp heavy tool: *The king had his head chopped off.* ◇ *She chopped a branch off the tree.*
  SYN cut sth off, cut sth off sth
  ◆ v + n/pron + adv ◆ v + adv + n ◆ v + n/pron + prep

,chop sth 'up to cut sth into small pieces with a knife or a sharp tool: *Shall we chop these logs up for firewood?* ◇ *I have to chop her food up small for her.* ◇ *Chop up the onion into small pieces.*
  SYN cut sth up
  → see also HACK STH UP
  ◆ v + n/pron + adv ◆ v + adv + n

chow /tʃaʊ/

,chow 'down (on sth) (*AmE, informal*) to eat a lot of food: *We chowed down on fried chicken and salad.*
  ◆ v + adv

chuck /tʃʌk/

NOTE Chuck is an informal way of saying **throw**.

,chuck sth a'way (*BrE, informal*) **1** to not make good use of sth; to waste sth: *She's chucking all her money away on presents for him.* ◇ *It's too good an opportunity to chuck away.* **2** (*also* ,chuck sth 'out) to throw sth away because you no longer want or need it: *We chucked the old sofa away.* ◇ *Don't chuck yesterday's paper out. I still haven't done the crossword.*
  SYN throw sth away
  ◆ v + n/pron + adv ◆ v + adv + n

'chuck it down (*also* ,chuck down, 'chuck down sth *less frequent*) (*BrE, informal*) to rain very heavily: *It was chucking it down outside.*
  SYN pour down (*BrE*)
  NOTE Chuck it down and chuck down are always used with the subject it.
  ◆ v + it + adv ◆ v + adv + n ◆ v + adv + n

,chuck sth 'in (*BrE, informal*) to include sth extra with what you are selling or offering without increasing the price: *If you buy the freezer and the fridge we'll chuck in a toaster.*
  SYN throw sth in
  ◆ v + adv + n ◆ v + n/pron + adv

,chuck sth 'in/'up (*BrE, informal*) to decide to stop doing sth such as a job or a course of study: *What made you decide to chuck in your course?* ◇ *I feel like chucking it all in and going back to Africa.*
  OBJ job, course **SYN** jack sth in (*BrE*); pack sth in (*BrE*); give sth up
  NOTE Not used in the passive.
  ◆ v + adv + n ◆ v + n/pron + adv

,chuck sb 'out; ,chuck sb 'out of sth (*informal*) to force sb to leave a place, a job, etc.: *Her parents chucked her out when she got pregnant.* ◊ *She failed her exams and was chucked out of college.* ◊ (*BrE*) *There's always trouble at **chucking-out time** (= the time when pubs, etc. close).*

SYN throw sb out, etc.; turn sb out, etc.

♦ v + n/pron + adv ♦ v + adv + n
♦ v + n/pron + adv + prep

,chuck sth 'out **1** to reject a plan, a proposal, etc.: *The committee chucked my proposal out.* **2** → CHUCK STH AWAY 2

SYN throw sth out

♦ v + n/pron + adv ♦ v + adv + n

,chuck 'up; ,chuck sth 'up (*BrE, informal*) to bring food you have eaten back out of your mouth: *The smell made me want to chuck up.*

SYN bring sth up; throw up; vomit, vomit sth (up)

♦ v + adv ♦ v + adv + n ♦ v + n/pron + adv

▶ 'upchuck *vt, vi* (*informal*) to bring food you have eaten back out of your mouth: *I almost upchucked my dinner.*

,chuck sth 'up (*BrE*) → CHUCK STH IN/UP

chug /tʃʌg/ (-gg-)

,chug a'long (*informal*) to make steady but slow progress: *'Hi! How are things?' 'Oh, fine, just chugging along.'*

♦ v + adv

churn /tʃɜːn; *AmE* tʃɜːrn/

,churn sth 'out (*informal*) to produce sth quickly in large amounts: *She churns out trashy romantic novels.* ◊ *They churn out 3 000 identical toy trains every day.*

♦ v + adv + n ♦ v + n/pron + adv

,churn sb 'up (*informal*) to make sb feel very upset, worried, frightened or angry: *When I drove away from the house for the last time, I was churned up inside.*

♦ v + n/pron + adv ♦ v + adv + n

,churn sth 'up to move sth such as mud or water around and damage or disturb the surface: *Cars and motorbikes had churned up the field.* ◊ *seas churned up by the storm* ◊ (*figurative*) *His visit churned up bitter memories.*

OBJ earth/ground, mud, water

♦ v + adv + n ♦ v + n/pron + adv

claim /kleɪm/

,claim sth 'back to ask for sth to be returned to you: *Claim your expenses back from the company.*

OBJ tax, money

♦ v + n/pron + adv ♦ v + adv + n

clam / klæm/ (-mm-)

,clam 'up (on sb) (*informal*) to refuse to speak about sth because you are afraid, or want to keep it secret: *He always clams up when we ask about his family.*

♦ v + adv

clamp /klæmp/

,clamp 'down; ,clamp 'down on sb/sth (*informal*) to become strict about sth in order to prevent sth happening, especially a crime, a protest, etc.: *The government intends to clamp down on drug smuggling.*

SYN crack down, crack down on sb/sth

♦ v + adv ♦ v + adv + prep

▶ 'clampdown (on sb/sth) *n* sudden action that is taken by a government or other authority to stop a crime, a protest, etc.

,clamp sth 'on; 'clamp sth on sb/sth (*especially AmE*) to force sb to accept sth unpleasant: *The army clamped on a curfew after the riots.* ◊ *The army clamped a curfew on the refugee camps.*

♦ v + n/pron + adv ♦ v + adv + n ♦ v + n/pron + prep

class /klɑːs; *AmE* klæs/

,class sb/sth 'up (*informal, especially AmE*) to make sb/sth better in quality, or look more expensive or more fashionable: *They've classed up the magazine, using better paper and a cleaner design.*

♦ v + n/pron + adv ♦ v + adv + n

claw /klɔː/

NOTE Claws are sharp curved nails on the end of an animal's foot.

'claw at sb/sth to try to catch sb/sth or scratch or tear sb/sth with claws or with your nails: *The cat was clawing at the door.* ◊ *She tried to claw at his face.*

♦ v + prep

,claw sth 'back (*especially BrE*) **1** to work hard to get sth back that you have lost: *They're trying to claw back their share of the market.* **2** if a government **claws back** money it has paid to people, it gets it back, usually by taxing them: *The government are clawing back age allowances in tax.*

♦ v + adv + n ♦ v + n/pron + adv

▶ 'clawback *n* (*BrE, business*) the act of a government getting back in tax the money it has paid to people; the money that is paid back

clean /kliːn/

,clean sth 'down (*BrE*) to clean sth thoroughly by rubbing it with a cloth, etc. or brushing it: *Clean down all the walls before repainting them.*

♦ v + adv + n ♦ v + n/pron + adv

,clean sth 'off; ,clean sth 'off sth to remove sth from the surface of sth by brushing, rubbing, etc.: *She couldn't be bothered to clean her make-up off.* ◊ *How can I clean red wine off the carpet?*

♦ v + n/pron + adv ♦ v + adv + n ♦ v + n/pron + prep

,clean sb/sth 'out; ,clean sb/sth 'out of sth (*informal*) to use up or take all sb's money; to take or buy the whole supply of sth that sb has: *Buying drinks for everyone cleaned me out.* ◊ *It's been a great year for sales. We're completely cleaned out* (= we've sold all our supply). ◊ *The stall was cleaned out of newspapers by 8.00 a.m.* ◊ *Burglars had cleaned the place out* (= had stolen everything).

◆ v + n/pron + adv ◆ v + n/pron + adv + prep

ˌclean sth 'out to clean the inside of sth thoroughly: *We clean the stables out every day.*

◆ v + n/pron + adv ◆ v + n/pron + adv + n

▸ 'clean-out *n* [usually sing.] (*especially BrE*) an occasion when you clean a room, house, cupboard, etc. thoroughly; the activity of cleaning a room, house, cupboard, etc. thoroughly

ˌclean 'up (*informal*) to be very successful; to win a lot of money or prizes: *The movie cleaned up at the awards ceremony.*

◆ v + adv

ˌclean 'up; ˌclean yourself 'up to wash yourself or make yourself clean: *I'll just clean up before dinner.* ◊ *They cleaned themselves up and put on their best clothes.* ◊ *It's time you got cleaned up and ready for the evening.*

◆ v + adv ◆ v + pron + adv

ˌclean 'up; ˌclean sth 'up to remove dirt, etc. from a place and make it clean: *I've got to clean up before my parents get home.* ◊ *Who's going to clean up after* you (= clean the mess that you made)? ◊ *How often is the trash and litter cleaned up?*

OBJ **mess**, **house**, **environment**

◆ v + adv ◆ v + adv + n ◆ v + n/pron + adv

▸ 'clean-up *n* [usually sing.] the act of removing dirt, etc. from a place to clean it

ˌclean sb 'up to clean sb thoroughly: *Dad cleaned me up after I fell over in the mud.*

◆ v + n/pron + adv ◆ v + adv + n

ˌclean sth 'up to remove criminals, crime or immoral behaviour from a place or an organization: *The mayor is determined to clean up the city and make it a safer place to live.* ◊ *The company is trying to clean up its image.*

OBJ **city**, **image**

◆ v + adv + n ◆ v + n/pron + adv

IDM clean up your 'act to start behaving in a responsible way

▸ 'clean-up *n* [usually sing.] the act of removing crime or immoral behaviour from a place or an organization

clear /klɪə(r); *AmE* klɪr/

ˌclear a'way; ˌclear sth a'way (*especially BrE*) to remove things that you have been using and no longer need in order to clear a space: *I'll help you to clear away after tea.* ◊ *to clear away the dishes* ◊ *Can you clear your books away?*

◆ v + adv ◆ v + n/pron + adv ◆ v + adv + n

ˌclear sb a'way (*AmE*) to make sb leave a place: *The police cleared the demonstrators away.*

◆ v + n/pron + adv ◆ v + adv + n

ˌclear 'off (*informal, especially BrE*) to go or run away: *You've no right to be here. Clear off!* ◊ *He*

cleared off as soon as he heard the police car. ◊ *I asked if I could play with them, but they told me to clear off home.* ➔ note at GO AWAY

◆ v + adv

ˌclear 'out; ˌclear 'out of sth (*informal*) to leave a place quickly: *Would it be better for you if I just cleared out and went back to London?* ◊ *I told him to clear out of the house by Monday.*

SYN **get out**; **get out of sth** ➔ note at GO AWAY

◆ v + adv ◆ v + adv + prep

ˌclear sth 'out to make sth empty and clean by removing what you do not want: *I cleared out all the cupboards.*

SYN **tidy sth out** (*BrE*)

◆ v + adv + n ◆ v + n/pron + adv

▸ 'clear-out *n* [usually sing.] (*informal, especially BrE*) the act of throwing away all the things you no longer want or need or of getting rid of people you no longer want: *a clear-out of staff to reduce the wages bill*

ˌclear 'up if the weather **clears up**, it becomes brighter and rain, etc. moves away: *For a week, it rained all day and cleared up in the evening.*

SYN **brighten up**

◆ v + adv

ˌclear 'up; ˌclear sth 'up **1** to make sth clean and neat: *I'll help you clear up.* ◊ *Clear up the mess in here before you go.* OBJ **mess** SYN **tidy up**, **tidy sth up** (*especially BrE*) ➔ note at TIDY UP **2** if an illness, infection, etc. **clears up** or sth **clears it up**, it disappears: *The rash cleared up very quickly.* ◊ *The antibiotics should clear up the infection.* OBJ **rash**, **infection**

◆ v + adv ◆ v + n/pron + adv ◆ v + adv + n

ˌclear sth 'up to solve a problem; to find an explanation for sth: *to clear up a mystery* ◊ *I'm glad we've cleared that misunderstanding up.*

OBJ **confusion**, **matter**, **problem**, **mystery** ➔ note at WORK STH OUT

◆ v + adv + n ◆ v + n/pron + adv

click /klɪk/

ˌclick 'through (**to sth**) to visit a website by clicking on a link or advertisement on another web page: *You can only get that information by clicking through from the home page.*

◆ v + adv

▸ 'click-through *n* [C, U] the number of people who follow a link on the Internet to a particular web page: *Our banner ads have a 2% click-through.* ◊ *poor click-through rates*

climb /klaɪm/

ˌclimb 'down (**over sth**) (*informal*) to admit that you are wrong or have made a mistake; to change your position in an argument: *The president was forced to climb down and issue an apology.*

SYN **back down** (**on/from sth**); **give in** (**to sb/ sth**)

◆ v + adv

▶ **'climbdown** (**over sth**) *n* an act of admitting that you are wrong or have made a mistake; an act of changing your position in an argument

cling /klɪŋ/ (**clung, clung** /klʌŋ/)

,cling 'on (**to sth/sb**), **'cling to sth** to hold sth/sb tightly; to not let go of sth/sb: *She **clung on** for dear life.* ◇ *I clung to the side so as not to fall.*

SYN hang on ⊃ note at HOLD ON
♦ v + adv ♦ v + prep ♦ v + adv + prep

'cling to sth; ,**cling 'on to sth** to be unwilling to stop doing, believing or thinking about sth; to be unwilling to get rid of sth: *I still cling to the hope that he's alive.* ◇ *She's clinging on to the past.*

OBJ past, power, tradition
♦ v + prep ♦ v + adv + prep

clock /klɒk; AmE klɑːk/

,clock 'in/'on; ,clock sb 'in/'on (*BrE*) to record the time that you arrive at work, especially by putting a card into a machine; to do this for sb or check the time they arrive at work: *We arrived and clocked on for the night shift.*

SYN punch in, punch sb in (*AmE*) **OPP** clock off/out, clock sb off/out
♦ v + adv ♦ v + n/pron + adv

,clock 'in at sth to last or take a particular amount of time; to cost a particular amount of money: *The fastest runner clocked in at 3 minutes 40 seconds.*
♦ v + adv + prep

,clock 'off/'out; ,clock sb 'off/'out (*BrE*) to record the time that you leave work, especially by putting a card into a machine; to do this for sb: *Don't forget to clock off when you leave.*

SYN punch out, punch sb out (*AmE*) **OPP** clock in/on, clock sb in/on
♦ v + adv ♦ v + n/pron + adv

,clock 'on, etc. (*BrE*) → CLOCK IN/ON, ETC.

,clock 'out, etc. (*BrE*) → CLOCK OFF/OUT, ETC.

,clock sth 'up (*informal*) to win or achieve a particular number or amount: *We've clocked up 500 miles* (= we've travelled 500 miles) *today.* ◇ *The company has clocked up record exports this year.*

OBJ miles, years **SYN** notch sth up
♦ v + adv + n ♦ v + n/pron + adv (*rare*)

clog /klɒg; AmE klɑːg/ (-**gg-**)

,clog 'up (**with sth**), ,clog sth 'up (**with sth**) to become, or to make sth, blocked so that nothing can move: *The pipe had clogged up* (*with mud*). ◇ *The roads were clogged up with traffic.*

OBJ roads, pipes **SYN** block up, block sth up
NOTE Clog and clog sth are used on their own with a similar meaning.
♦ v + adv ♦ v + adv + n ♦ v + n/pron + adv

close /kləʊz; AmE kloʊz/

,close 'down; ,close sth 'down if a shop/store, business, etc. **closes down**, or sb **closes it down**, it stops operating as a business, usually permanently: *Many businesses have closed down because of the recession.* ◇ *The government has closed down most of the mines.* ◇ *The hospital closed down last year.*

SYN shut down, shut sth down **OPP** open up, open sth up
NOTE Close and close sth are also used on their own: *The factory was closed last year.*
♦ v + adv ♦ v + adv + n ♦ v + n/pron + adv

▶ **'close-down** *n* [U, sing.] the stopping of work, especially permanently, in an office, factory, etc.

,close 'in **1** (**on sb/sth**) to come nearer to and surround sb/sth in a frightening way or in order to attack them: *The enemy is closing in.* ◇ *The fog was closing in on us.* **2** (*especially BrE*) when the days **close in**, they gradually become shorter: *The days/nights are closing in now that autumn/fall is here.* ◇ *The evenings are closing in fast.*

SYN draw in (*BrE*)
♦ v + adv

,close sth 'off (**to sb/sth**) to put sth across the entrance to a road, a room, etc. so that people cannot go in: *Police have closed the area off to traffic.* ◇ (*figurative*) *We don't want to close off any options.*
♦ v + n/pron + adv ♦ v + adv + n

'close on sb/sth (*BrE*) to make the distance between you and sb/sth else smaller, for example in a race: *I was slowly closing on the runner ahead of me.*
♦ v + prep

'close on/over sth to surround sth, covering it or holding it tightly: *His fingers closed over the money.*
♦ v + prep

,close 'out (*AmE*) if a shop/store **closes out**, it sells everything very cheaply before it stops operating as a business: *The store is closing out on Monday with discounts of up to 75%.*
♦ v + adv

▶ **'closeout** *n* (*AmE*) an occasion when a shop/store sells all remaining goods very cheaply before it stops operating: *a closeout sale*
NOTE In British English, this is called a **closing-down sale**.

,close sth 'out **1** to prevent light, sound, etc. from entering a place: *We need a curtain up there to close out the light.* **OBJ** light, noise **SYN** shut sth out **2** (*AmE, informal*) to bring sth to an end: *The vote closed out the three-day debate.* **3** (*AmE*) if you **close out** a bank account, you stop keeping money in it: *I'd like to close out my savings account.* **OBJ** only **account**
NOTE Close sth is also used on its own: *I'd like to close my savings account.*
♦ v + adv + n ♦ v + n/pron + adv

,close 'over sth → CLOSE ON/OVER STH

,close 'up **1** to close completely: *His eye had swollen and closed up.* ◊ *The cut took a long time to close up* (= to heal). **OPP** **open up 2** to hide your thoughts and feelings: *She closed up when I mentioned her father.* **OPP** **open up 3** if people or vehicles **close up**, they move nearer to each other: *Traffic was heavy and cars were closing up behind each other.*
   ◆ v + adv

,close 'up; ,close sth ,up to shut and lock a building completely for a period of time: *You go on home. I'll close up* (= shut the shop/store). ◊ *He closes the shop up at 5.30.* ◊ *They closed the house up and rented an apartment in the city.*
   OPP **open up, open sth up**
   ◆ v + adv ◆ v + n/pron + adv ◆ v + adv + n
   IDM **close up 'shop** (*AmE*) (of a business) to stop operating: *After only six months in business we were forced to close up shop.*

cloud /klaʊd/

,cloud 'over **1** (*AmE also* ,cloud 'up) if the sky or the weather **clouds over**, clouds cover the sky and the sun disappears: *It's starting to cloud over.* **SUBJ** **it, the sky 2** if your face, expression, etc. **clouds over**, you start to look sad, worried or angry: *His face clouded over when she walked into the room.* **SUBJ** **face, expression, eyes**
   ◆ v + adv

,cloud 'up (*AmE*) **1** → CLOUD OVER 1: *After lunch the sky clouded up, and we went home.* **2** if your glasses **cloud up**, they become covered with very small drops of water so that you cannot see through them: *It was cold out and my glasses clouded up when I came inside.*
   ◆ v + adv

clown /klaʊn/

,clown a'round (*BrE also* ,clown a'bout) to behave in a silly way to make other people laugh
   SYN **mess around** (*informal*)
   ◆ v + adv

club /klʌb/ (-bb-)

,club to'gether (**to do sth**) if people **club together**, they each give an amount of money so that the total can be used for a particular purpose: *They clubbed together to buy their teacher a present.*
   SYN **chip in** (**with sth**)
   ◆ v + adv

clue /kluː/

,clue sb 'in (**on/about sth**) (*AmE, informal*) to give sb information about sth: *Can you clue me in on the facts of the case?*
   ◆ v + n/pron + adv
   ▶ ,clued-'in (**on/about sth**) *adj* having a lot of information about sth

NOTE **Clued-up** is used in British English with this meaning.

cluster /'klʌstə(r)/

,cluster a'round sb/sth (*BrE also* ,cluster a'bout/'round sb/sth) to form a group around sb/sth: *People clustered around the market stalls.*
   ◆ v + prep

,cluster to'gether to come together in a small group: *The children clustered together in a corner of the room.*
   ◆ v + adv

clutch /klʌtʃ/

'clutch at sth/sb to try to get hold of sb/sth suddenly: *She clutched at her stomach, obviously in pain.*
   SYN **catch at sth/sb; grasp at sth**
   ◆ v + prep
   IDM **clutch at 'straws** to try every possible way to escape from a difficult situation, even though there seems to be little hope of doing so

clutter /'klʌtə(r)/

,clutter sth 'up (**with sth**) to fill or cover sth with lots of things so that it looks very untidy: *I'm sick of all these books cluttering up my office.*
   NOTE **Clutter sth** is used on its own with a similar meaning.
   ⊃ note at MESS STH UP
   ◆ v + adv + n ◆ v + n/pron + adv

coax /kəʊks; *AmE* koʊks/

,coax sb 'into sth; 'coax sb into doing sth to persuade sb to do sth by talking to them gently: *Can we coax you into singing for us?*
   ◆ v + n/pron + prep

,coax sb 'out of sth; ,coax sb 'out of doing sth to persuade sb not to do sth by talking to them gently: *Try to coax him out of resigning.*
   ◆ v + n/pron + adv + prep

'coax sth out of sb; 'coax sth from sb to persuade sb to do sth or to give you sth by talking gently: *She coaxed a smile from the baby.*
   ◆ v + n/pron + adv + prep ◆ v + n/pron + prep

cobble /'kɒbl; *AmE* 'kɑːbl/

,cobble sth to'gether (*informal*) to put sth together or to make sth quickly or carelessly, with whatever time and materials you have available: (*figurative*) *The government seems to have cobbled together these proposals.*
   ◆ v + adv + n ◆ v + n/pron + adv

cock /kɒk; *AmE* kɑːk/

,cock 'up; ,cock sth 'up (*slang, especially BrE*) to spoil or ruin sth by doing it badly or by making a mistake: *You've really cocked up this time.* ◊ *The travel agency completely cocked up the arrangements.* ◊ *Don't cock things up again!*

SYN **mess up**, etc.; **bungle sth** (*informal*)
♦ v + adv ♦ v + n/pron + adv
▶ '**cock-up** *n* (*slang, especially BrE*) a mistake that spoils or ruins plans or arrangements; sth that has been spoilt because it has been badly done: *She's made a complete cock-up of the arrangements.*

coil /kɔɪl/

NOTE A **coil** is a series of circles formed by winding rope, etc.

ˌcoil '**up**; ˌcoil sth '**up** to wind into coils; to make sth do this: *The snake coiled up in the sunshine.* ◇ *He coiled the rope up neatly.*
OBJ **rope**, **string**
♦ v + adv ♦ v + n/pron + adv ♦ v + adv + n

collect /kə'lekt/

colˌlect sth '**up** to bring together things that are no longer being used: *Would somebody collect up all the dirty glasses?*
♦ v + n/pron + adv ♦ v + adv + n

colour (*BrE*) (*AmE* color) /'kʌlə(r)/

ˌcolour sth '**in** to fill a shape, an area, etc. with colour, using pencils or pens: *Why don't you colour the pictures in?*
OBJ **picture**, **drawing**
♦ v + n/pron + adv ♦ v + adv + n

comb /kəʊm; *AmE* koʊm/

NOTE A **comb** is a flat piece of plastic, etc. with a row of thin teeth along one side, used for making your hair neat.

ˌcomb sth '**out 1** to use a comb to remove knots from your hair or to make it neat: *My hair's so long that it takes me ages to comb it out.*
OBJ **hair 2** (*also* ˌcomb sth '**out of sth**) to remove dirt, knots, etc. from hair or fur with a comb: *She brushed her hair and then combed out the tangles.* **OBJ** **knots**, **tangles**
♦ v + n/pron + adv
♦ v + adv + n **2** also v + n/pron + adv + prep
ˌcomb sth '**over** to arrange your hair to hide a place on your head where there is no hair
OBJ **hair**
♦ v + n/pron + adv ♦ v + adv + n
▶ '**comb-over** *n*: *He sported a terrible comb-over worthy of a football manager.*

come /kʌm/ (**came** /keɪm/, **come**)

ˌcome a'**bout** to happen: *It's hard to understand how the accident came about.* ◇ *Can you tell us how* **it came about that** *you decided to strike?*
SYN **happen**
♦ v + adv
ˌcome a'**cross** (*also* ˌcome '**over**) **1** (*also* ˌcome '**through**) [+adv/prep] (of an idea, an opinion or a feeling) to be expressed clearly and understood easily: *Do you think the film's*

message comes across clearly? ◇ *These themes come across very strongly in the novel.* ◇ *I could tell she was frightened. It came over in her voice.* ◇ *The feeling of solidarity among the people really came through.* **2** (*AmE also* ˌcome '**off** *informal*) [+ **adv/prep**] (**as sth**) to make a particular impression on people: *She comes across well in interviews.* ◇ *At the press conference, he came over as cool and confident.*
♦ v + adv
ˌcome a'**cross** (**with sth**) (*informal*) to provide or supply sth that sb asks for, especially money: *They eventually came across with another $250 000.* ◇ *We still hope the company will come across for us.*
♦ v + adv
ˌcome a'**cross**; '**come across sth** to cross a room, a road, a river, etc. towards the place where the speaker is: *When you've done your homework, come across to my house and we'll listen to some music.* ◇ *She waved and came across the room to talk to me.*
♦ v + adv ♦ v + prep
ˌcome **across sb/sth** to meet or find sb/sth by chance, without having planned or thought about it: *He's the most unpleasant man I've ever come across.* ◇ *She came across a pile of old photographs while she was clearing the attic.*
SYN **encounter sb/sth** (*formal*)
♦ v + prep
ˌcome '**after sb/sth** to chase or follow a person or an animal to try to catch them: *The farmer came after them, threatening to call the police.*
♦ v + prep
ˌcome a'**long 1** to arrive or appear somewhere; to start to exist, happen or be available: *It's lucky you came along when you did or I'd have been stranded at the bus stop for an hour!* ◇ *When the right opportunity comes along, he'll take it.* ◇ *There are new designs coming along.*
SYN **turn up 2** (*AmE also* ˌcome '**with** *informal*) to go somewhere with sb: *We're going to the pub. Do you want to come along?* ◇ *You'd better come along with me to the police station.* **3** → COME ON 4 **4** (*especially BrE*) → COME ON 1
♦ v + adv
ˌcome a'**long**; ˌcome a'**long sth** to move forward or from one end of sth to the other, towards the speaker: *I waited for ages for a bus, then three came along together!* ◇ *The lorry was coming along the road at great speed.*
OBJ **road**
♦ v + adv ♦ v + prep
ˌcome a'**part** to break or fall into pieces: *The teapot just came apart in my hands.* ◇ (*figurative*) *After the first act, the play begins to* **come apart at the seams** (= have a lot of problems).
SYN **fall apart**
♦ v + adv
ˌcome a'**round, etc.** (*especially AmE*) → COME ROUND, ETC.

,**come a'round sth** (BrE also ,**come 'round sth**) to move or travel around a corner: *The bus came round the bend too fast.*
OBJ only **corner**, **bend**
◆ v + prep

'**come at sb** to move towards sb as if you are going to attack them: *She came at me with a knife.* ◇ (*figurative*) *The questions came at me so fast that I didn't have time to think about them.*
◆ v + prep

'**come at sth** to approach, think about or try to deal with a question, problem, etc. in a particular way: *We're getting nowhere. Let's try coming at the problem from a different angle.*
OBJ **problem**
◆ v + prep

,**come a'way**; ,**come a'way from sth 1** to leave a place or a person: *Come away, now. There's nothing to see.* ◇ *Jane came away from the meeting feeling angry and upset.* **2** to become separated from sth: *He pulled at the door handle until it came away in his hands.* ◇ *The plaster had started to come away from the wall.*
◆ v + adv ◆ v + adv + prep

,**come a'way with sth** to leave a place with a particular feeling, impression or result: *She came away from the championship with three medals.* ◇ *We came away with the impression that something was wrong.*
◆ v + adv + prep

↻,**come 'back 1** to return to the place where the speaker is: *Come back here at once!* ◇ *Did she say when she was coming back?* ◇ *Why don't you come back to my place for a coffee?* ◇ *They came back from the trip relaxed and happy.* ◇ *She went into the kitchen and came back with two glasses of milk.* ◇ *We'll come back for the car tomorrow.* ◇ (*figurative*) *Liverpool came back from being 2-0 down to win the game.* SYN **return** (*more formal*) **2** to begin to exist or happen again: *My headache has come back again.* ◇ *Her confidence is starting to come back slowly.* SYN **return** OPP **go away 3** to return to school or work after a break: *Do you know when Bill is coming back to work?* **4** to become popular, successful or fashionable again: *80s hairstyles are coming back into fashion.* ◇ *80s hairstyles are coming back in.* ◇ *Do you think trams will come back?* **5** (of a message or a reply) to be given in answer to a message, letter, etc. that you have sent or a question that you have asked: *I sent her an email and a message came back that she was away.* **6** (**to sb**) to return to your memory, often suddenly: *It's all coming back to me now.* **7** (**at sb**) (**with sth**) to reply to sb quickly, strongly or angrily: *She came back at the speaker with some questions.* ◇ *He came back straight away, telling me what he thought of me.*
◆ v + adv
▸ '**comeback** n **1** [usually sing.] if a person **makes a comeback**, they return to performing

---

come back

come back ◆ get back ◆ go back ◆ return ◆ turn back

These verbs all mean to come or go back from one place to another.

come back to return: *He came back home years later, a changed man.*

get back to arrive back somewhere, especially at your home or the place where you are staying: *What time did you get back last night?* ◇ *When I finally get back home, I'm going to have a big party!*

go back to return to the place you recently or originally came from or that you have been to before: *She went back into the kitchen.*

return to come or go back from one place to another: *She's returning to Australia tomorrow after a year in Europe.* ◇ *I returned from work to find the house empty.* ◇ *The Prime Minister recently returned from a summit at Camp David.*

turn back to return the way that you came, especially because sth stops you from continuing: *The weather got so bad that we had*

to turn back. ◇ *I think we're lost—we'll have to turn back.*

WHICH WORD?

Return is slightly more formal than the other verbs in this group, and is used more often in writing or formal speech. **Come back** is usually used from the point of view of the person or place that sb returns to; **go back** is usually used from the point of view of the person who is returning: *Come back and visit again soon!* ◇ *Do you ever want to go back to China?*

PATTERNS AND COLLOCATIONS

▪ to return/come back/go back/get back **to/ from/with** sth
▪ to come back/go back/get back **outside/ upstairs/down**, etc.
▪ to return/come back/go back/get back/turn back **again**
▪ to return/come back/go back/get back **home/ to work**
▪ to return/come back/get back **safely**

or to public life after a long time, or they become popular again: *The band's trying to make/stage a comeback.* **2** if sth **makes a comeback**, it becomes popular or fashionable again: *Cartoons seem to be making a comeback.* **3** a way of getting payment or a reward for sth unfair or wrong that has been done to you: *Will I have no comeback if the contract falls through?* **4** a quick reply that is often angry, insulting, clever or humorous: *For once in her life, she had no sharp comeback.*

,come 'back to sth to return to a particular subject, an idea, etc. and start to talk about it or think about it: *I'll come back to that point in a moment.* ◇ *It always seems to come back to the question of money.*
SYN **return to sth** (*more formal*)
♦ v + adv + prep

,come be'fore sb/sth (*formal*) (of a legal case, a proposal or an issue) to be presented to sb/sth so that they can discuss it or make a decision or a judgement about it: *The case comes before the court next week.* ◇ *The bill came before parliament last month.*
OBJ **court, committee, judge, parliament**
♦ v + prep

,come be'tween sb and sb; ,come be'tween sb and sth to harm or disturb a relationship between two people; to prevent sb from doing, enjoying or having sth: *Nobody will ever come between them.* ◇ *I don't want to come between her and her work.*
♦ v + prep

,come 'by; ,come 'by sth **1** to pass sb/sth without stopping: *Some kids on bikes came by, but they didn't notice me.* **2** (*especially AmE*) to come to visit sb for a short time in a relaxed or informal way: *Thanks for coming by yesterday.* ◇ *Come by on your way home from work.* ◇ *If you come by the office tomorrow, I'll have it ready for you.* **SYN** **drop by; stop by, stop by sth**
♦ v + adv ♦ v + prep

'come by sth to manage to get sth; to receive sth by chance: *Jobs are hard to come by these days.* ◇ *Information about the company was not easy to come by.* ◇ *How did you come by that cut on your hand?* ◇ *Old postcards are fairly easily come by.*
SYN **get sth; obtain sth** (*more formal*)
♦ v + prep

come 'down **1** (from…) (to…) to travel from one place to another, especially from the north of a country to the south: *When are you going to come down and see us?* **2** if a price, a level or an amount **comes down**, it becomes lower or less than before: *Oil is coming down in price.* ◇ *Inflation has come down twice in the last month.* **SYN** **decrease** (*more formal*); **drop; fall** **OPP** **go up 3** to break and fall to the ground: *Part of the ceiling had come down.* **SYN** **collapse 4** (of a plane, etc.) to fall from the sky; to be brought

---

SYNONYMS

come down

alight ◆ come down ◆ land ◆ settle ◆ touch down

All these words mean to come down through the air and onto the ground or another surface.

alight (*formal*) (of a bird or insect) to land on or in sth after flying to it: *A butterfly fluttered by and alighted on a rose.*

come down (of an aircraft) to land or fall from the sky: *The passenger plane came down somewhere east of Moscow.*

land to come down through the air onto the ground or another surface: *The space shuttle landed safely at 12.45 p.m.* ◇ *A fly landed on the dog's nose.*

settle to come down from the air, land on sth and stay there for some time: *Dust had settled on everything.* ◇ *Two birds settled on the fence.*

touch down (of a plane or spacecraft) to land: *The shuttle will touch down at 6 a.m. GMT.*

PATTERNS AND COLLOCATIONS

■ to land/settle/come down/touch down/alight **safely**
■ to be **due/scheduled to** land/come down/ touch down
■ to be **forced to** land/come down

---

down to the ground: *The pilot was forced to come down in a field.* **5** (of rain, snow, etc.) to fall: *The rain was coming down harder now.* **SUBJ** only **the rain, the snow** **SYN** **fall 6** [+ adv/prep] to decide that you support or oppose sb/sth and say so publicly: *I knew my parents would come down on my sister's side.* ◇ *The committee came down against the proposal.* ◇ *Voters came down firmly in favour of reform.* **7** when the curtain in a theatre **comes down**, it is the end of the performance: *When the curtain came down, we all rushed for the exits.* **OPP** **go up 8** [+adv/ prep] to reach down to a particular point: *My mother's hair comes down to her waist.* **9** (**from sth**) (*informal*) to stop having the pleasant feelings and excitement that sth such as an enjoyable experience or a drug produces: *The party was so good I haven't really come down yet.* ◇ *He still hasn't come down from the caffeine.* **10** (**from sth**) (**to sth**) (of a person selling sth) to suggest or agree to a lower price: *I wasn't prepared to pay £1 500, but they eventually came down to £1 350.* ◇ *Can you come down another $30?* **11** (**from sth**) (*BrE, formal*) to leave a university (especially Oxford or Cambridge) after finishing your studies: *When did you come down (from Oxford)?* OPP **come up (to sth)**

♦ v + adv **10** also v + adv + n

IDM **come (back) down to 'earth (with a 'bang/ 'bump)** to return to the reality of normal life after a period of great excitement or a time when you have been living in a way that is not very practical: *He came (back) down to earth with a bang when he discovered that all his money had run out.*

▸ **'comedown** n [usually sing.] (*informal*) **1** a situation which is not as good, important or interesting as one you have experienced previously: *It's a bit of a comedown after her previous job.* **2** a bad feeling which you get after the pleasant effects of a drug have disappeared

come 'down; **come 'down sth** to move from a higher place or position to a lower one, or from a place that is far away towards the speaker: *Come down from that tree!* ◇ *The car was coming down the road towards us.* ◇ *Jack came down the stairs two at a time.*

OPP **come up, come up sth**

♦ v + adv ♦ v + prep

come 'down on sb (*informal*) to punish sb or criticize sb severely: *The courts are coming down heavily on drug dealers.* ◇ *Don't come down too hard on him—he's young.*

NOTE **Come down on sb** is always used with an adverb such as *hard* or a phrase with a similar meaning: *If it happens again, we'll come down on you so hard that you'll wish you'd never been born.* ◇ *He came down on me like a ton of bricks.*

♦ v + adv + prep

come 'down to sb (from sb/sth) to be passed to sb from sb who lived in the past: *The family estate came down to her from her grandfather.*

SUBJ **story**, **name**, **tradition**

♦ v + adv + prep

come 'down to sth to be able to be explained as one simple, important question or point: *It all comes down to a matter of priorities in the end.* ◇ *When it comes down to it* (= the most important fact is)*, we can't afford to go.* ◇ *What it comes down to is a choice between money or happiness.*

♦ v + adv + prep

come 'down with sth to get an illness, often not a very serious one: *I came down with a bad cold.* ◇ *I think I'm coming down with something.*

OBJ **flu**, **a cold** SYN **go down with sth**; **catch sth**; **get sth** ↪ note at SUFFER FROM STH

♦ v + adv + prep

come for sb/sth 1 to come to sb's home, or to the place where sb/sth is in order to take them/ it somewhere: *The police came for him this morning.* ◇ *Have you come for the parcel?* **2** to attack sb/sth: *Sam came for me with his fists.*

♦ v + prep

come 'forth (*literary*) to appear or be produced: *He struck the rock and water came forth.*

♦ v + adv

▸ **forth'coming** adj **1** [only before noun] about to happen or appear very soon: *Who is in charge of promoting the band's forthcoming album?* **2** [not before noun] ready or made available when you need it: *Unfortunately money for the project has not been forthcoming.* **3** [not before noun] (of a person) ready to give information when they are asked: *He's not very forthcoming about his love life.*

come 'forward (with sth) to offer to give help, information, etc.: *Police have asked witnesses to come forward.* ◇ *We're hoping that a sponsor will come forward with the extra money.* ◇ *No one came forward to claim the reward.*

♦ v + adv

come from ... (*not used in the progressive tenses*) to be born in or live in a particular place: *Where do you come from?* ◇ *She comes from London.*

♦ v + prep

come from sth to start in a particular place or be made from a particular thing: *Most of the wines that we sell come from France.* ◇ *Does your information come from a reliable source?* ◇ *I'm lazy? That's rich, coming from you!* (= you are lazy too) ◇ *He comes from a wealthy family.* ◇ *Where's that terrible noise coming from?* ◇ *93% of our energy comes from fossil fuels.*

♦ v + prep

IDM **where sb is 'coming from** (*informal*) a person's situation, attitude, ideas, etc. that make them say what they have said: *I know exactly where you're coming from.*

come from sth; **come from doing sth**
→ COME OF STH, COME OF DOING STH

come 'in 1 when the sea **comes in**, it moves towards the land: *The tide was coming in fast.* OPP **go out 2** to finish a race in a particular position: *Which horse came in first?* **3** to arrive; to be received: *News is coming in of a train crash in Scotland.* ◇ *We've got more work coming in than we can handle.* ◇ *I met all the trains that came in from London.* ◇ *We've got just enough money coming in each month to pay the bills.* **4** to become available: *English strawberries usually come in in June.* ◇ *New jobs are coming in all the time.* **5** if a law or a rule **comes in**, it is introduced and begins to take effect: *New legislation coming in next month will tackle low pay.* **6** to take part in a discussion or agreement: *I'd like to come in here.* ◇ *I wish he wouldn't keep coming in with his stupid suggestions.* ◇ *If you want to come in on the deal, you need to decide now.*

♦ v + adv

IDM **come in 'handy/'useful** to be useful: *These boxes will come in handy when we move house.*

▸ **'income** n money that you receive regularly, especially as payment for work

▶ **'incoming** *adj* [only before noun] **1** travelling towards a place and arriving there: *incoming flights/passengers* **2** (of the sea) coming towards the land **3** (of a phone call, letter or message) sent to you or received by you: *This phone only takes incoming calls.* **4** recently appointed or elected: *the incoming Socialist government*

come 'in; ,**come 'in sth;** ,**come 'into sth** to enter a room or a building; to pass through sth such as a hole, a window, etc.: *I knocked and heard her say 'Come in'.* ◊ *The rain's coming in through that hole.* ◊ *I'll ask him to call you as soon as he comes in* (= arrives home or at work). ◊ *The sun was coming in at the windows.* ◊ *When you come in the door, you'll find Reception on your left.* ◊ *She came into the room crying.* ⟳ note at GO IN, GO IN STH
♦ v + adv ♦ v + prep

,**come 'in;** ,**come 'into sth 1** to go to an office or the place where you work, in order to do some work: *Are you coming into the office tomorrow?* ⌜OBJ⌝ **the office, work 2** to have a part to play in sth; to play a useful role: *I like the plan, but where do I come in* (= what is my role)? **3** to become fashionable; to start to be worn or used: *When did platform heels come in?* ◊ *Trolleybuses first came in in 1923.* ◊ *Punk clothes seem to be **coming into fashion** again.* ⌜OPP⌝ **go out 4** to go to a hospital to receive treatment, tests, etc.: *Can you come in for the X-rays on Friday?*
♦ v + adv ♦ v + prep

,**come 'in for sth** to receive sth, especially sth unpleasant: *The government has come in for severe criticism from all sides.* ◊ *The company came in for a lot of stick* (= a lot of criticism) *with their advertising campaign.*
⌜OBJ⌝ **(severe) criticism**
♦ v + adv + prep

,**come 'in with sb** (**on sth**), ,**come 'in** (**with sb**) **on sth** if sb **comes in with** you, they join you in a particular project, activity, business, etc.: *Do you want to come in with me on Joe's present?* ◊ *My brother hoped I would come in with him when he started his own business.* ◊ *Do you want to come in on the deal?*
♦ v + adv ♦ v + prep

,**come 'into sth 1** to begin to exist, happen, etc.: *The cherry trees are **coming into blossom**.* ◊ *The band only **came into being** in 2005.* ◊ *When do the new regulations **come into force/effect**?* ◊ *When did the Labour party come into office?* ◊ *A variety of factors **come into play** when choosing an employee.* **2** to receive a large sum of money when sb dies: *She came into a fortune when her cousin died.* ⌜OBJ⌝ **a fortune, money 3** to be important in a particular situation: *I got the job because I was the best. My looks didn't **come into it**.* ◊ *He took the job because he liked the work. Money didn't come into the equation.* ⌜OBJ⌝ **it, the equation**
♦ v + prep

⌜IDM⌝ **come into 'line (with sb/sth)** to behave in the way other people behave, or in the way you should behave **come into your/its 'own** to have the opportunity to show your/its qualities or abilities: *After two poor games, he finally came into his own in the game against Germany.* ◊ *This bike comes into its own on rough ground.*

'come of sth; ,**'come of doing sth** (*also* **'come from sth, 'come from doing sth**) to happen as a result of sth: *I told him no good would **come of it**.* ◊ *He promised to help, but I don't think anything will **come of it**.* ◊ *That's what comes of not listening to my advice!* ◊ *I had the feeling of satisfaction that comes from doing a difficult job well.*
♦ v + prep

,**come 'off 1** to be able to be removed: *Does this knob come off?* **2** (*informal*) to take place; to happen: *Did your trip to New York ever come off?* **3** (*informal*) if a plan, etc. **comes off**, it is successful or it has the result that you intend: *Her attempt to break the world record nearly came off.* **4** [**+ adv**] (*informal*) if sb **comes off** well or badly in a fight, a contest, etc., they finish the fight in a good or a bad condition: *He always comes off worst in fights.* **5** (*AmE, informal*) → COME ACROSS 2
♦ v + adv

,**come 'off;** ,**come 'off sth 1** to become separated from sth: *The handle came off in my hand.* ◊ *A button has come off my coat.* **2** to fall from sth: *My glasses came off when I tripped.* ◊ *She braked sharply and came off her bike.* ⌜OBJ⌝ **bicycle, horse 3** to move away from sth large or important and go in a different direction: *A narrow road comes off on the left.* **4** to leave the stage, the sports field, etc. during a play or a game: *Two players came off just before half time.* **5** to leave sth such as a vehicle or a road: *She looked tired as she came off the plane.* ◊ *Come off (the motorway) at junction five.* **6** if an amount of money **comes off** a price, the price becomes lower by that amount: *Two pence a litre is coming off the price of petrol.*
♦ v + adv ♦ v + prep

,**come 'off sth 1** to stop using sth; to stop taking a drug, medicine, alcohol, etc.: *It's time she tried to come off sleeping pills.* **2** (of heat, a smell, the wind, etc.) to start from a particular place or thing: *There was a mist coming off the sea.* **3** (*AmE, informal*) to have just completed a very successful period of time or returned to normal after a bad period: *Farmers are coming off another tough year.*
♦ v + prep

⌜IDM⌝ ,**come 'off it!** used to tell sb that you think or know that what they have said is not true or that you disagree with it: *Come off it! England will never win!*

🔑 **,come 'on 1** (*also* **,come a'long** *especially BrE, less frequent*) used to encourage sb to do sth, for example, to hurry: *Come on, we'll be late.* ◇ *Come on, things can't be that bad!* **2** used to show that you do not believe what sb has said or that you disagree with them: *Come on! You don't really expect me to believe that, do you?* **3** (of a light, the electricity, etc.) to begin working; to be switched on: *Does the heating come on automatically?* ◇ *I've set the oven to come on at five.* ⓈⓊⒷⒿ **lights** ⓄⓅⓅ **go off 4** (*also* **,come a'long**) to make progress; to improve or develop in the way that you want: *Your French is really coming on.* ◇ *Tim's come on well with the guitar.* ◇ *How's dinner coming along?* **5** (of an actor or a performer) to walk onto the stage and start to perform: *When are McFly coming on?* **6** (*sport*) (of a player) to join a team instead of another player during a game: *Robson came on in place of Wilkins.* **7** (of a television programme, etc.) to start to be shown: *What time does the news come on?* **8** (*especially BrE*) (of a season, a period of time, an illness, etc.) to begin: *It's getting colder. Winter's coming on.* ◇ *I think I've got a cold coming on.* ◇ *It came on to rain.* ⓃⓄⓉⒺ Usually used in the progressive tenses. **9** [+ **adv**] to go to a place: *Come on in and make yourself at home.* ◇ *My wife's coming on later.* **10** (*BrE, informal*) (of a woman) to start your period
◆ v + adv

ⒾⒹⓂ **,come on 'strong** to speak or behave in a very determined way, especially in a way that shows sb you want to have a sexual relationship with them
▶ **'oncoming** *adj* [only before noun] advancing towards you; approaching you

,come 'on; **,come 'on sth** to begin speaking to sb on the telephone: *I had a long talk with my mother, then my dad came on.* ◇ *Sue came on the line for a chat.*
◆ v + adv ◆ v + prep

'come on/upon sb/sth (*formal*) to meet or find sb/sth by chance: *I came upon this beautiful vase in the attic.*
◆ v + prep

,come 'on to sb (*informal*) to behave in a way that clearly shows sb that you want to have a sexual relationship with them
◆ v + adv + prep
▶ **'come-on** *n* [usually sing.] (*informal*) a remark or action that is intended to attract sb

,come 'on to sth to start talking about or discussing a topic: *I'll come on to the subject of exams in a minute.*
ⓄⒷⒿ **question**, **topic**, **subject**
◆ v + adv + prep

🔑 **,come 'out 1** when the sun, moon or stars **come out**, they appear in the sky: *The sun came out in the afternoon.* ⓈⓎⓃ **appear 2** when flowers **come out**, they open: *The daffodils came out late this year.* **3** to be published or produced: *Her new novel's just come out.* ◇ *When do the exam results come out?* ⓈⓎⓃ **appear 4** (of news, the truth, etc.) to become known after a time when it has been secret: *The truth finally came out.* ◇ **It came out that** *she'd made the whole thing up.* **5** to be shown clearly: *His arrogance comes out in every speech he makes.* **6** (**with sb**) to go somewhere with sb for a social event: *Will you come out to dinner with me tonight?* **7** if a photograph **comes out**, the picture can be seen clearly: *My photos didn't come out very well because there wasn't enough light.* **8** when words **come out**, they are spoken: *I opened my mouth to apologize, but the words wouldn't come out.* ◇ *He tried to pay her a compliment but it came out all wrong.* **9** [+ **prep**] to state publicly that you do or do not support sth: *Members of the committee have come out in opposition to the proposal.* **10 come out and do sth** to be brave enough to say or do sth that other people might find it hard to say or do: *Has she actually come out and admitted it yet?* ◇ *Only one member of staff came out and said that the working conditions were unsatisfactory.* **11** (*BrE*) to stop work and go on strike: *The miners have* **come out on strike**. **12** to say openly that you are a homosexual (= a person who is sexually attracted to people of the same sex) **13** when a young girl **came out** in the past, she was formally introduced into society
◆ v + adv

🔑 **,come 'out**; **,come 'out of sth 1** to leave a place or appear from inside a place: *Come out! I know you're in there!* ◇ *I'll speak to her as soon as she comes out of the meeting.* **2** if an object **comes out** of sth, it is removed from the place where it is fixed or becomes separated from sth: *Her tooth came out when she bit into the apple.* ◇ *All the pages have come out of this book.* ◇ *This screw won't come out of the wall.* **3** if a mark or some dirt **comes out**, it is removed from sth by washing or cleaning: *The bloodstains won't come out of my shirt.* ◇ *It was a very expensive skirt, but most of the colour came out when I washed it.* **4** [+ **adv/prep/adj**] to finish sth in a particular state; to have a particular result: *She came out on top in the exams.* ◇ *His reputation came out undamaged.* ◇ *The family didn't come out of the affair very well.* ⓃⓄⓉⒺ In this meaning, **come out** and **come out of sth** are always used either with an adverb, an adjective or a phrase beginning with a preposition.
◆ v + adv ◆ v + adv + prep

ⒾⒹⓂ **,come 'out of yourself** to relax and become more confident and friendly with other people

,**come 'out at sth** to add up to a particular cost or sum: *The total bill comes out at over a thousand pounds.*
◆ v + adv + prep

,**come 'out in sth** if a person **comes out in** sth such as spots, their skin becomes covered in them: *The cream made her face come out in a rash.*
[OBJ] **spots, rash, lumps** SYN **break out in sth**
◆ v + adv + prep

,**come 'out of sth 1** to return to normal after a difficult time: *The country is slowly coming out of recession.* **2** to result or develop from a process or an event: *At least some good came out of all our hard work.* ◇ *The book came out of her travels in Japan.* **3** to be taken away from a total amount: *The money will have to come out of your wages.*
◆ v + adv + prep

,**come 'out with sth** (*informal*) to say sth, especially sth surprising or not polite: *I can't believe the things he comes out with!* ◇ *When I asked her why she was late, she just came out with a load of nonsense.*
◆ v + adv + prep

,**come 'over 1** (**to sb/sth**) to move across a room, a road, an ocean, etc. towards where the speaker is: *Come over and meet my husband.* ◇ *When are you coming over to England again?* ◇ *Lots of people are coming over from America for the wedding.* **2** (**to sth**) to visit sb for a short time, usually at their home: *Her son only comes over to see her occasionally.* ◇ *Our new neighbours came over to our house last night.* **3** [+ adj] (*BrE, informal*) to suddenly start feeling sth: *to come over funny/dizzy/faint* ◇ *I come over all shy whenever I see her.* **4** → COME ACROSS
◆ v + adv

,**come 'over sb/sth** (of a feeling, a mood, etc.) to affect sb/sth: *I'm sorry—I don't know what came over me* (= I don't know what made me behave in that way). ◇ *A remarkable change has come over the group since he left.*
◆ v + prep

,**come 'over to sb/sth** to leave one group of people in order to join a competing group; to change from one opinion to another: *Some of their members have come over to our side.*
◆ v + adv + prep

,**come 'past**; ,**come 'past sb/sth** to pass in front of the speaker or the place where the speaker is: *Charlie came past on his bike.* ◇ *I'll bring the book round on my way to school—I've got to come past your house.*
◆ v + adv ◆ v + prep

,**come 'round** (*BrE*) (*also* ,**come a'round** *AmE, BrE*) **1** (**to sth**) to visit sb or a place; to come to sb's home to see them for a short time: *Come round and see us sometime.* ◇ *Do you want to come round for lunch?* → see also COME OVER 2 **2** (of a regular event) to arrive; to happen at the usual time: *I can't believe Christmas has come round again!* **3** to move among a group of people in order to give them sth: *The waiters came round with drinks.* **4** (**to sth**) (*informal*) to agree to sth that you were against before; to change your opinion about sth: *She'll never come round to our way of thinking.* ◇ *Don't push him; he'll come round in time.*
◆ v + adv

,**come 'round** (*BrE*) (*AmE* ,**come a'round**) (*also* ,**come 'to** *BrE, AmE*) to become conscious again: *When she came round, her sister was sitting beside her bed.* ◇ *He hasn't yet come round after the anaesthetic.*
◆ v + adv

SYNONYMS

come round

come round ◆ **come to** ◆ **regain consciousness** ◆ **wake up**

These verbs all mean to become conscious again.

come round (*BrE*) to become conscious after being unconscious: *She hasn't come round from the anaesthetic yet.* NOTE **Come around** is used in American English.

come to to become conscious after being unconscious: *When she came to, the room was in darkness.*

regain consciousness (*formal*) to become conscious after being unconscious: *She never regained consciousness and died three days later.*

wake up to become conscious after being unconscious, especially after an operation:

I felt really terrible when I woke up after the operation.

WHICH WORD?

With **come to** the emphasis is more on the moment of becoming conscious, less on the process. With **come round/around** the emphasis is more on the process of becoming conscious, less on the moment. All of these expressions can be used for becoming conscious after an operation.

PATTERNS AND COLLOCATIONS

- to wake up/come to/come round/come around **from** sth
- to wake up/come to **suddenly**
- to come to/come round/come around **slowly**

→ see also PASS OUT
♦ v + adv

come 'round; **come 'round sth** (*BrE*) (*also* **come a'round**, **come a'round sth** *AmE, BrE*) **1** (of a letter or a document) to be passed from one person to another: *The card came round for everyone to sign.* **2** to travel to where the speaker is by a longer route than usual, especially around the outside of sth: *The road was blocked so we had to come round by the fields.*
♦ v + adv ♦ v + prep

come 'round sth (*BrE*) → COME AROUND STH

come 'through 1 (**to sth**) (*informal*) used especially to ask sb to enter a room or a building, or move from one room to another: *Come through to my office.* ◇ *Mr Dole can see you now. Will you come through?* **2** (of news, a message, a document, etc.) to be received by telephone, radio, etc. or in an official way: *I've got an international call coming through for you.* ◇ *We're going to buy a new car when the insurance money comes through.* ◇ *He's still waiting for his divorce to come through.* **3** (**with sth**) to provide or do sth that people expect or that you have promised: *The insurance company has finally come through with the money.* **4** → COME ACROSS 1
♦ v + adv

come 'through; **come 'through sth 1** to enter and cross a room, an area of land, a town, a country, etc.; to pass through sth: *Put sth over the hole to stop the rain coming through.* **2** to get better after a serious illness; to avoid serious injury or damage: *He's very ill but his doctors expect him to come through the operation.* **3** to start to appear from under or behind sth: *The baby's front teeth were coming through.* ◇ *The sun's coming through the clouds at last.* **SYN** emerge (*more formal*) **4** to pass from one stage of a competition to the next; to be successful in a test or an exam: *Chris did well to come through the qualifying rounds of the tournament* (= for example in tennis). ◇ *Most of the students came through (the exam) with flying colours* (= were very successful).
♦ v + adv ♦ v + prep

come 'to → COME ROUND; ⟳ note at COME ROUND

'come to sb 1 if an idea **comes to** you, it suddenly enters your mind: *The idea came to me in the middle of the night.* ◇ *It suddenly came to her that she had been wrong.* **2** (*especially BrE*) (of money, property, etc.) to pass to sb else when sb dies: *All my money will come to you when I die.*
♦ v + prep

come to your'self (*old-fashioned*) to return to your normal state: *It took her a while to come to herself again.*
♦ v + prep + pron

'come to sth 1 to add up to sth; to be equal to sth: *The bill came to $50.* **2** to reach a particular

state or condition; to arrive at sth: *We both came to the same conclusion.* ◇ *I don't know what the world's coming to* (= I think things are getting very bad and unpleasant). ◇ *All her dreams had come to nothing.* **OBJ** this, that, nothing **NOTE** In this meaning, **come to sth** is often used with *this* or *that*: *The doctors will operate if necessary, but it may not come to that.*
♦ v + prep

IDM **when it comes to sth/to doing sth** when it is a case, matter or question of sth/of doing sth: *When it comes to cooking, he's better than I am!*

come to'gether if two or more people or things **come together**, they form one group or one piece: *Several local groups came together to fight the proposed housing development.* ◇ *During the last three days of rehearsals, everything came together.*
♦ v + adv

come 'under sth 1 to be included within a particular group or collection of things: *Several different types of schools come under the heading of 'private schools'.* **OBJ** heading, banner, category **2** to be managed, controlled or owned by a particular group or organization: *The prisons now come under central government control.* **OBJ** control, authority, wing **3** if you **come under** attack, criticism, etc., sb attacks, criticizes, etc. you: *The government has come under attack over the new bill.* ◇ *She's come under intense pressure to change her mind.* **OBJ** attack, pressure, fire, scrutiny, criticism
♦ v + prep

come 'up 1 (**to …**) (**from …**) to travel from one place to another, usually from a smaller place to a larger one, or from the south of a country to the north: *They've come up from Texas.* ◇ *We thought we'd go up to London for a weekend in the big city.* **2** (**to sb/sth**) to go towards a person in order to talk to them: *A guy came up to me in the street and asked me for money.* ◇ *The group leader came up to the reception desk.* **3** (of plants) to appear above the ground: *The first snowdrops are just coming up.* **SYN** appear **4** when the sun or moon **comes up**, it rises in the sky: *We sat and watched the sun coming up behind the hills.* **SUBJ** only the sun, the moon **SYN** rise **OPP** go down **5** to rise to the surface of water or another liquid: *I came up gasping for air.* ◇ *Bubbles were coming up to the surface.* **6** to happen, especially when you do not expect it: *Something urgent has come up; I have to go.* ◇ *Opportunities like this don't come up every day.* **SYN** crop up **7** be coming up (*always used in the progressive tenses*) (of an event or a time) to be going to happen very soon: *Our exams are coming up soon.* ◇ *Coming up next is the news.* **8** to be talked about or discussed: *The subject didn't come up in conversation last night.* ◇ *Mary's name keeps coming up.* **SUBJ** name, question, subject **9** to be dealt with by a court: *Her case*

comes up next month. **10** if your name, number or ticket **comes up** in a betting game, it is chosen and you are one of the winners: *My numbers came up and I won a million pounds!* **11** (*informal*) (*usually used in the progressive tenses*) to be ready soon; to be coming soon: '*A cup of tea please.*' '*Coming up!*' **12** (of information) to appear on a computer screen or a board, for example in an airport: *Her flight has just come up on the arrivals board.* **13** [+ **adj/adv**] (*BrE*) (of an object or a substance) to appear in a particular way at the end of a period of time or when sth has been done to it: *When the wool is washed, it comes up beautifully soft.* ◇ *I've given it a good clean and it's **come up like new**.* **14** (of lights in a cinema, a theatre, etc.) to become brighter after the film/movie, play, etc. has finished: *The lights came up to loud applause.* **15** (**to sth**) (*BrE*, *formal*) to begin your studies at a university (especially Oxford or Cambridge): *She came up (to Oxford) in 1982.* OPP **come down** (**from sth**) **16** (**to sth**) to reach as far as a particular point or level: *The water came up to my chin.* ◇ *My sister hardly comes up to my shoulder.* ◇ *His scarf came up over his eyes.* SYN **reach sth 17** (**on sth**) to start to feel the effects of a drug
◆ v + adv

IDM **be coming up 'roses** (*informal*) (of a situation) to be developing in a successful way: *Everything's coming up roses!* **come up 'empty/empty-'handed** (*AmE*) to be unsuccessful in achieving a goal or finding sth you are looking for: *The women's volleyball team came up empty in all three matches Friday.* ◇ *Police are still coming up empty-handed in the search for the missing girl.* **come 'up in the world** to become more important in society or more successful in your career: *She's really come up in the world since she left school.* **come up/turn up 'trumps** to do more than people expect and so make a situation very successful: *The team's new player came up trumps and scored three goals.* ◇ *That was a wonderful meal! You've come up trumps again.*

▶ ,up-and-'coming *adj* [only before noun] (*informal*) making good progress and likely to be successful in the future: *an up-and-coming young actor*

▶ 'upcoming *adj* [only before noun] (*especially AmE*) about to happen soon: *the upcoming presidential election*

,come 'up; ,come 'up sth to move from a lower place or position to a higher one, or upstairs in a building, especially with the speaker or towards the place where the speaker is: *Who wants to come up to the top of the hill with me?* ◇ *My apartment is on the third floor. Are you coming up?* ◇ *I can hear somebody coming up the stairs.*

OBJ **road, stairs** OPP **come down, come down sth**
◆ v + adv ◆ v + prep

,come 'up against sb/sth if you **come up against sb/sth**, you have to face sb/sth that is difficult: *We expect to come up against a lot of opposition to the scheme.* ◇ *You'll come up against the reigning champion in the next round.*
◆ v + adv + prep

,come 'up for sth **1** to come to the time when sth must be done: *He's coming up for retirement soon.* ◇ *She comes up for re-election next year.* ◇ *When does your contract come up for renewal?* OBJ **renewal 2** to become available for a particular purpose: *That house you like has come up for sale.* OBJ **sale, auction**
◆ v + adv + prep

,come 'up on sth (*AmE*) to be almost a particular time or age: *It's coming up on your bedtime.*
◆ v + adv + prep

,come 'up to sth **1** to approach a particular place, an age or a period of time: *You're coming up to a busy road now.* ◇ *It's just coming up to half past twelve.* **2** to reach an acceptable level or standard: *The performance didn't come up to our expectations.* ◇ *You may lose your job if you don't **come up to scratch**.* OBJ **standard, expectations** NOTE In this meaning **come up to sth** is usually used in the negative. ⊃ note at MEASURE UP
◆ v + adv + prep

,come 'up with sth **1** to think of an idea, an answer to a question or a solution to a problem: *She came up with a great idea for increasing sales.* OBJ **idea, answer, suggestion, explanation** ⊃ note at THINK STH UP **2** to find or produce sth that sb needs: *If you want to buy my car, you must come up with the money.* ◇ *He always **comes up with the goods** (= does what he is expected to do) on the day.*
◆ v + adv + prep

'come upon sb/sth → COME ON/UPON SB/STH

,come 'with (*AmE*, *informal*) → COME ALONG: *We're going to the bars. Want to come with?*

'come with sth to be included with or as part of sth: *A new car comes with the job.*
◆ v + prep

commune /kə'mjuːn; *AmE* 'kɑːm-/

com'mune with sth (*formal*) if you **commune with** sth such as nature, you spend time thinking deeply about it and so feel close to it OBJ **nature**
◆ v + prep

complain /kəm'pleɪn/

com'plain of sth to say that you feel ill/sick or are suffering from a pain: *Several children complained of severe stomach pains.*

OBJ **pain**, **headache**, **symptoms**
♦ v + prep

conceive /kənˈsiːv/

con'ceive of sth to form an idea, a plan, etc. in your mind; to imagine sth: *I cannot conceive of any situation in which your plan would work.*
➲ note at THINK STH UP
♦ v + prep

concentrate /ˈkɒnsntreɪt; *AmE* ˈkɑːn-/

'concentrate on sth to spend more time doing one particular thing than others: *In this lecture I shall concentrate on the early years of Charles's reign.*
♦ v + prep

condemn /kənˈdem/

con'demn sb to sth 1 to say what sb's punishment will be: *to be condemned to death/hard labour* 2 to force sb to accept a difficult or unpleasant situation: *They were condemned to a life of hardship.* **SYN** doom sb (**to sth**)
NOTE Usually used in the passive.
♦ v + n/pron + prep

cone /kəʊn; *AmE* koʊn/

NOTE A **cone** is a coloured plastic object that has a round base and a point at the top, used on roads to show where vehicles are not allowed to go.

,cone sth 'off to close a road or part of a road with cones: *Part of the road was coned off while repairs were done.*
NOTE Usually used in the passive.
♦ v + adv + n ♦ v + n/pron + adv

confess /kənˈfes/

con'fess to sth; con'fess to doing sth sth 1 to admit, especially formally or to the police, that you have done sth wrong or illegal: *She confessed to the murder.* ➲ note at ADMIT TO STH 2 to admit sth that you feel ashamed or embarrassed about: *I must confess to knowing nothing about computers.*
♦ v + prep

confide /kənˈfaɪd/

con'fide in sb to tell sb a secret or a piece of information that you would not tell other people: *Can I confide in you?* ◇ *Do you have a friend that you can confide in?*
OBJ **mother**, **friend**
♦ v + prep

confine /kənˈfaɪn/

con'fine sb/sth to sth; con'fine yourself to sth to keep sb/sth/yourself inside the limits of a particular activity, subject, area, etc.: *The work will not be confined to the Glasgow area.*

◇ *I will **confine myself** to looking at the period from 1900 to 1916.*
SYN limit sth to sb/sth; restrict sb/sth/yourself (**to sth**)
NOTE Often used in the passive.
♦ v + n/pron + prep

be con'fined to sth 1 if a person or an animal is confined to a place, they are kept in a small or closed space and not allowed to go out: *The children were confined to their rooms for the evening.* ◇ *The soldiers concerned were **confined to barracks** (= had to stay in the barracks, as a punishment).* 2 if a person is confined to bed, etc., they have to stay in bed, etc. because they are ill/sick or injured: *She was **confined to bed** with the flu.* ◇ *He was **confined to a wheelchair** after the car accident.*
♦ be + v + prep

confront /kənˈfrʌnt/

con'front sb with sth to make sb face or deal with an unpleasant or difficult person or situation: *He confronted her with a choice between her career or their relationship.*
♦ v + n/pron + prep

be con'fronted with sth to have sth in front of you that you have to deal with or react to: *Most people when confronted with a horse will pat it.*
♦ be + v + prep

conjure /ˈkʌndʒə(r)/

,conjure sb/sth 'up to make sb/sth appear suddenly or unexpectedly, as if by magic: *She conjured up a three-course meal in half an hour!*
♦ v + adv + n ♦ v + pron + adv
♦ v + n + adv (*less frequent*)

,conjure sth 'up 1 to make a picture, a memory, etc. appear in your mind: *The word 'birthday' conjures up images of presents and parties.* ◇ *The song conjured up memories of warm summer evenings.* **OBJ** **image**, **picture**, **visions**, **memories** **SYN** evoke sth (*more formal*) ➲ note at REMIND SB OF SB/STH 2 to ask the spirit of a dead person to appear, by using a magic ceremony
♦ v + adv + n ♦ v + pron + adv
♦ v + n + adv (*less frequent*)

conk /kɒŋk; *AmE* kɑːŋk, kɔːŋk/

,conk 'out (*informal* or *humorous*) 1 if a vehicle or a machine conks out, it stops working: *Our car conked out 5 miles from home.* 2 if a person conks out, they fall asleep because they are very tired: *She was so tired she came home and conked out at eight o'clock.* 3 (*old-fashioned*, *BrE*) (of a person) to collapse or become unconscious 4 (*AmE*) to die: *The old guy looks as if he's going to conk out any minute.*
♦ v + adv

connect /kə'nekt/

con,nect sth 'up (to sth), con,nect 'up (to sth) to join sth to a supply of electricity, gas, water, etc. or to another piece of equipment; to be joined to sth in this way: *Connect the computer up (to the power supply).* ◇ *Many canals connected up to major ports.*
OPP disconnect sth (from sth), disconnect (from sth)
NOTE Connect sth and connect are often used on their own with the same meaning.
♦ v + n/pron + adv ♦ v + adv + n ♦ v + adv

connive /kə'naɪv/

con'nive at/in sth (*formal*) to ignore or seem to allow sth that you know is wrong: *The general is accused of conniving in a plot to topple the government.* ◇ *Her brother is believed to have connived at her murder.*
♦ v + prep

consent /kən'sent/

con'sent to sth (*formal*) to agree to sth or give your permission for sth: *He reluctantly consented to their marriage.* ➔ note at AGREE TO STH
♦ v + prep

consign /kən'saɪn/

con'sign sb/sth to sth (*formal*) **1** to get rid of or put somewhere sb/sth that you do not want: *She consigned his letter to the waste basket.* ◇ (*figurative*) *They can't just consign me to the scrap heap because I'm over fifty!* **2** to put sb/sth in an unpleasant situation: *Orphaned children were consigned to institutions.*
NOTE Often used in the passive: *The report was consigned to the dustbin.*
♦ v + n/pron + prep

consist /kən'sɪst/

con'sist in sth; con'sist in doing sth (*formal*) (*not used in the progressive tenses*) to have sth as the main or only feature: *A home does not consist in its architecture and decoration.*
♦ v + prep

con'sist of sth/sb; con'sist of doing sth (*not used in the progressive tenses*) to be formed from the things or people mentioned: *The exam consists of two parts: a written test and an oral.* ◇ *The group consists of senior people from education and business.* ◇ *His job consists of answering the phone and making coffee.*
SYN be made up of sth; comprise sth (*formal*)
♦ v + prep

consort /kən'sɔːt; *AmE* kɑːn'sɔːrt/

con'sort with sb (*formal* or *humorous*) to spend time with sb, especially sb that other people do

---

consist of sth/sb

be composed of sth/sb ♦ comprise sth ♦ consist of sth/sb ♦ constitute sth ♦ make up sth

These verbs all mean to be formed from the things or people mentioned, or to be the parts that form sth.

be composed of sth/sb to be formed from the things or people mentioned: *Our inspection teams are composed of the most qualified and experienced experts available.* ◇ *Around 15% of our diet is composed of protein.*

comprise sth to be formed from the things or people mentioned: *The collection comprises 327 paintings.* **NOTE** The form be comprised of can often be heard: *The committee is comprised of representatives from both the public and private sectors.* Many people consider that this is not correct.

consist of sth/sb to be formed from the things, people or activities mentioned: *Their diet consists largely of vegetables.* ◇ *Most of the fieldwork consisted of making tape recordings.*

constitute sth to be the parts or people that form sth: *People under the age of 40 constitute the majority of the labour force.*

make up sth to be the parts or people that form sth: *Women make up 56% of the student numbers.* ◇ *She wore a necklace made up of hundreds of coloured glass beads.*

WHICH WORD?

Consist of sb/sth is the most general of these verbs and the only one that can be used for activities with the *-ing* form of a verb: *My life consisted of feeding the baby and washing nappies.* Be composed of sth/sb, comprise sth and constitute sth are the most formal of these verbs. None of these verbs is used in the progressive tenses.

PATTERNS AND COLLOCATIONS

■ **The group** consists of/comprises/is made up of/is composed of **ten people**.
■ **Ten people** make up/constitute/comprise/compose **the group**.

not approve of: *The nurses are instructed not to consort with their patients.*
- v + prep

contend /kən'tend/

con'tend with sb/sth to have to deal with a difficult person or situation: *If we leave at eight, we'll have to contend with the rush-hour traffic.* ◇ *Anyone who criticizes her will have me to contend with!* ◇ *He's had a lot of serious problems to contend with.*
[OBJ] **problems**
- v + prep

content /kən'tent/

con'tent yourself with sth to accept and be satisfied with sth and not try to have or do sth better: *Martina contented herself with a single glass of wine.* ◇ *The crowd contented themselves with shouting insults.*
[SYN] **make do with sth**
- v + pron + prep

contract /kən'trækt/

con,tract 'in; con,tract 'into sth (*BrE*) to choose to become involved in and formally agree to a system, plan, etc.: *Employees can contract into the company pension scheme.*
[OBJ] (**pension**) **scheme** [OPP] **contract out, etc.**
- v + adv - v + prep

con,tract 'out; con,tract 'out of sth (*BrE*) to choose and formally state that you do not want to be involved in a system, plan, etc.: *Only a few employees have contracted out (of the pension scheme) so far.*
[OBJ] (**pension**) **scheme** [OPP] **contract in, etc.**
- v + adv - v + adv + prep

con,tract sth 'out (**to sb**) to arrange for work to be done by another company rather than your own: *The company contracts the printing out to an outside firm.*
[OBJ] **work**
- v + n/pron + adv - v + adv + n

contribute /kən'trɪbjuːt; *BrE also* 'kɒntrɪbjuːt/

con'tribute to sth to help to cause sth: *The stress of losing his job contributed to his death.* ◇ *The Prime Minister contributed to his own downfall by failing to control his government.*
[OBJ] **death, decline, downfall**
- v + prep

convert /kən'vɜːt; *AmE* -'vɜːrt/

con'vert into/to sth; con'vert sth into/to sth to be able to be changed from one form, purpose or system to another; to make sth do this: *a sofa that converts into a bed*
[SYN] **turn into sth, turn sb/sth into sth**
- v + prep - v + n/pron + prep

cook /kʊk/

cook sth 'up 1 to cook sth, especially very quickly: *In half an hour she had managed to cook up some delicious chilli.* [OBJ] **meal 2** (*informal*) to invent a story, an excuse or a plan, especially a very clever or dishonest one: *She cooked the plan up while he was away.* ◇ *They cooked up the story between the two of them.* [OBJ] **plan, story, scheme** [SYN] **concoct sth** (*more formal*)
- v + adv + n - v + n/pron + adv

cool /kuːl/

cool 'down; cool sb 'down 1 (*also* **cool 'off, cool sb 'off**) to become, or to make sb become cool or cooler: *I'm going for a swim to cool down.* ◇ *A shower will cool you down.* **2** to become, or to make sb become, less angry or excited: *She's very angry. Give her some time to cool down.* ◇ *He tried to cool her down but she carried on shouting.*
- v + adv - v + n/pron + adv

cool 'down; cool sth 'down to become, or to make sth become, cooler: *He waited for the soup to cool down a bit.* ◇ *Once it had cooled down outside, we went for a walk.* ◇ *Cool the soup down by stirring it.* ◇ *The rain had cooled everything down.*
[NOTE] **Cool** and **cool sth** are also used on their own, but less often.
- v + adv - v + n/pron + adv - v + adv + n (*rare*)

cool 'off 1 to become less interested or enthusiastic: *Our relationship was going well, but then Laura seemed to cool off.* **2** to become less angry or excited: *When I'm angry, I go for a walk to cool off.* **3** if sth hot **cools off**, it becomes cooler: *Leave the engine to cool off before you touch it.*
- v + adv

▸ **cooling-'off period** *n* **1** a period of time in which two sides in a disagreement try to come to an agreement before taking any further action: *There is to be a six-month cooling-off period before divorce proceedings begin.* ◇ *The union and the employers failed to reach an agreement within the cooling-off period.* **2** a period of time when you can change your mind about buying sth, such as an insurance plan, that you have agreed to buy: *Customers have a 14-day cooling-off period in which to cancel the agreement.*

cool 'off, cool sb 'off → COOL DOWN, COOL SB DOWN 1

coop /kuːp/

be ,cooped 'up (**in sth**) if a person or an animal **is cooped up**, they/it are kept in a small place or inside a building: *We've been cooped up (indoors) for hours because of the rain.*
- be + v + adv

count

cop /kɒp; *AmE* kɑːp/ (**-pp-**)

,cop 'off (**with sb**) (*BrE, slang*) to meet sb and start a sexual relationship with them
• v + adv

,cop 'out; ,cop 'out of sth (*informal*) to avoid or not do sth that you should be doing, because you are afraid, shy, lazy, etc.: *Lots of people said they'd help but they've all copped out.* ◇ *You can't just cop out of difficult decisions.*
• v + adv • v + adv + prep

▸ 'cop-out *n* (*informal, disapproving*) a way of, or an excuse for, avoiding sth you should be doing: *You're not too busy to come! That's just a cop-out.*

cope /kəʊp; *AmE* koʊp/

'cope with sth to deal successfully with sth difficult: *He wasn't able to cope with the stresses and strains of the job.* ◇ *Desert plants are adapted to cope with extreme heat.*
SYN deal with sth
• v + prep

copy /'kɒpi; *AmE* 'kɑːpi/ (**copies, copying, copied**)

,copy sth 'down to write sth exactly as it is written somewhere else: *If I don't copy the phone number down, I'll forget it!* ◇ *We copied down what the teacher had written on the blackboard.*
SYN write sth down
• v + n/pron + adv • v + adv + n

,copy sb 'in (**on sth**) to make sure that sb receives a copy of a letter, an email, etc. that you are sending to sb else: *Please copy me in on all correspondence.*
• v + n/pron + adv • v + adv + n (*rare*)

,copy sth 'out to write sth out again; to make a copy of sth that is already written or printed: *She copied out a recipe she found in a library book.*
SYN write sth out
• v + adv + n • v + n/pron + adv

cordon /'kɔːdn; *AmE* 'kɔːrdn/

,cordon sth 'off to stop people going into an area by forming a line or ring around it with police, soldiers, objects, etc.: *Police cordoned off the area until the bomb was defused.* ◇ *The roads were cordoned off.*
OBJ area, street **SYN** close sth off (**to sb/sth**)
NOTE Often used in the passive.
• v + adv + n • v + n/pron + adv

cost /kɒst; *AmE* kɔːst/

,cost sth 'out to estimate how much money will be needed for sth: *We'll have to cost the work out before we make a decision.* ◇ *Have you costed out how much it will be to hire another member of staff?*
NOTE Cost sth on its own is more usual.
• v + n/pron + adv • v + adv + n

cosy (*BrE*) (*AmE* cozy) /'kəʊzi; *AmE* 'koʊzi/ (**cosies, cosying, cosied**)

,cosy 'up to sb (*informal, especially AmE*) to try to become friendly with sb, especially in order to gain an advantage for yourself: *She's only cosying up to him because she needs his help.*
• v + adv + prep

cotton /'kɒtn; *AmE* 'kɑːtn/

,cotton 'on (**to sth**) (*informal*) to come to understand or realize sth without being told directly: *She cottons on very quickly.* ◇ *It took him a while to cotton on to what I was trying to say.*
SYN catch on (**to sth**)
• v + adv

'cotton to sb/sth (*old-fashioned, AmE, informal*) to begin to like or approve of sb/sth: *I didn't much cotton to the idea at first.*
NOTE Cotton to sb is often used in negative sentences.
• v + prep

cough /kɒf; *AmE* kɔːf/

,cough 'up; ,cough sth 'up (*informal*) **1** (*especially BrE*) to pay for sth or give sb money unwillingly: *You owe me £20. Come on, cough up!* ◇ *Don't cough up the money until the job's finished.* **SYN** pay up ⊃ note at PAY OUT, PAY STH OUT **2** (*BrE*) to admit sth or give sb information unwillingly: *Come on, cough up: where have you been?* **SYN** own up (**to sth/to doing sth**); confess (**to sth/to doing sth**) (*more formal*)
• v + adv • v + adv + n • v + n/pron + adv

,cough sth 'up to force sth out of the throat or lungs by coughing: *He's been coughing up blood.*
OBJ blood
• v + adv + n • v + n/pron + adv

count /kaʊnt/

,count a'gainst sb to be a disadvantage to sb: *I'm sure that being late for the interview counted against me.*
SYN weigh against sb (*formal*)
• v + prep

,count a'mong sb/sth; ,count sb/sth a'mong sth to be considered, or to consider sb/sth to be part of the group mentioned: *She counts among the top ten marathon runners in the country.* ◇ *The band count John Lennon among their influences.* ◇ *I no longer counted myself among his friends.*
NOTE Count sb/sth among sb/sth is more frequent than count among sb/sth: *Egypt was counted among the most powerful countries in the world.*
• v + prep • v + n/pron + prep

,count 'down (**to sth**), ,count sth 'down to be waiting for an important or exciting day, event, etc. and be counting the number of days, minutes, etc. there are before it: *The whole world was counting down to the new millennium.* ◊ *I'm counting down the days until my trip to South America.*

♦ v + adv ♦ v + adv + n ♦ v + n/pron + adv (*rare*)

▶ 'countdown (**to sth**) *n* **1** the act of counting backwards to zero, for example before a spacecraft is sent into space **2** the period immediately before sth important happens

‚count sb 'in to include sb in a group or an activity: *If you're going to the theatre, you can count me in.*

SYN deal sb in (*less formal*) **OPP** count sb out

♦ v + n/pron + adv

‚count 'off (*AmE*) if people **count off**, they say loudly in order the numbers they have been given: *He made everyone count off.*

♦ v + adv

⚥‚count on sb/sth; 'count on doing sth; 'count on sb/sth doing sth (*also* 'count upon sb/sth, etc. *more formal*) to rely on sb to do sth; to expect sth to happen and make plans in an appropriate way: *You can count on me!* ◊ *'I'm sure he'll help us.' 'Don't count on it.'* ◊ *She hadn't counted on going swimming when she packed.* ◊ *I'm counting on your support.* ◊ *I'm counting on you to support me.* ◊ *She can be counted upon to contribute good ideas.*

SYN bank on sb/sth, etc.; calculate on sb/sth, etc. (*especially AmE*); reckon on sb/sth, etc.
⟳ note at DEPEND ON SB/STH

♦ v + prep ♦ v + prep + n/pron + **to**+inf

‚count sb 'out; ‚count sb 'out of sth (*informal*) to not include sb in a group or an activity: *You may enjoy those games, but you can count me out.*

SYN deal sb out, deal sb out of sth **OPP** count sb in

♦ v + n/pron + adv ♦ v + n/pron + adv + prep

‚count sth 'out to count coins, etc. one by one and put them somewhere: *He counted out the exact money (on the counter).*

OBJ money, change, notes/coins

♦ v + adv + n ♦ v + n/pron + adv

‚count to'wards sth (*also* ‚count to'ward sth *especially AmE*) to be included as part of sth you hope to obtain or achieve: *Marks from this test count towards your final grade.* ◊ *These sales will not count toward meeting the target.*

♦ v + prep

‚count sb/sth 'up to add together the number of things or people in a group: *Count up the number of times you've been abroad.*

OBJ number

NOTE Count sb/sth is used on its own with the same meaning.

♦ v + adv + n ♦ v + n/pron + adv

'count upon sb/sth, etc. → COUNT ON SB/STH, ETC.

couple /ˈkʌpl/

'couple sb/sth with sb/sth to link one person, thing or situation with another: *The large number of new graduates, coupled with high unemployment, means that there is fierce competition for jobs.*

NOTE Usually used in the passive.

♦ v + n/pron + prep

cover /ˈkʌvə(r)/

‚cover sth 'over (**with sth**) to cover sth completely, especially to hide or protect it: *Put the bulbs in a bowl and cover them over with soil.* ◊ *The shopping mall is covered over with an enormous glass roof.*

NOTE Cover sth (**with sth**) is used more often with this meaning.

♦ v + n/pron + adv ♦ v + adv + n

‚cover 'up; ‚cover yourself 'up (**with sth**) to put on more clothes: *Make sure you cover up before going out in the sun.* ◊ *Cover yourself up. It's cold.*

♦ v + adv ♦ v + pron + adv

‚cover 'up (**for sb/sth**), ‚cover sth 'up to try hard to stop people finding out about a mistake, a crime, etc.; to hide the truth about sth: *He's always covering up for her.* ◊ *The government's attempts to cover up the scandal failed.*

OBJ scandal, mistake, truth **SYN** conceal sth (*more formal*); hide sth

♦ v + adv ♦ v + adv + n ♦ v + pron + adv
♦ v + n/pron + adv (*less frequent*)

▶ 'cover-up *n* [usually sing.] an act of hiding a mistake, a crime, etc.: *The opposition accused the government of a cover-up.*

⚥‚cover sb/sth 'up to put sth over sb/sth in order to hide or protect them/it: *You can cover up ugly pipes with wooden boxes.* ◊ *There was something on the table covered up with a cloth.*

♦ v + adv + n ♦ v + n/pron + adv

cozy /ˈkəʊzi; *AmE* ˈkoʊzi/ (**cozies**, **cozying**, **cozied**)

‚cozy 'up to sb (*AmE*) → COSY UP TO SB

crack /kræk/

‚crack 'down; ‚crack 'down on sb/sth to try harder to prevent people breaking a rule, using sth harmful, committing a crime, etc. and deal severely with those who do: *Police are cracking down hard on drug dealers.* ◊ *The government is cracking down on misleading food labelling.*

SYN clamp down, clamp down on sb/sth

♦ v + adv ♦ v + adv + prep

▶ 'crackdown (**on sb/sth**) *n* severe action that is taken to prevent people committing a crime, opposing the government, etc.: *a police crackdown on car crime*

‚crack 'on (**with sth**) (*BrE, informal*) to work hard and do sth quickly: *We'd better crack on with the painting before it gets dark.*

SYN **get on** (**with sth**)

♦ v + adv

,crack 'up (*informal*) to become physically or mentally ill because you are under pressure: *She's cracking up under the strain.*

♦ v + adv

▶ **'crack-up** *n* (*AmE, informal*) **1** a period of mental illness caused by pressure: *She was never the same again after her crack-up.* **2** a person who is mentally ill: *endless articles about Hollywood crack-ups* **3** a situation in which a system or organization stops functioning well or stops being well organized: *the crack-up of the conservative movement in the US*

,crack 'up; **,crack sb 'up** (*informal*) to start laughing a lot; to make sb laugh a lot: *Everybody cracked up when he fell over.* ◇ *She's so funny—she cracks me up!*

SYN **crease up**, **crease sb up** (*BrE*)

NOTE Not used in the passive.

♦ v + adv ♦ v + n/pron + adv

IDM **be ,cracked 'up to be sth** (*informal*) to be as good, clever, exciting, etc. as people think or say sb/sth is: *Stardom is not all it's cracked up to be.* ◇ *She's not as good as she's cracked up to be.*

▶ **'crack-up** *n* (*AmE, informal*) a person who is good at making other people laugh: *She was always the class crack-up.*

cram /kræm/ (-mm-)

,cram 'into sth; **,cram sb/sth 'in**; **,cram sb/ sth 'in/'into sth** to go into a place or space that is too small for everyone/everything; to push or force sb/sth into a place or space that is too small: *Six of us crammed into Rob's Mini.* ◇ *I only had three days in New York, but I*

crammed in as much sightseeing as I could. ◇ *He crammed all the sweets into his mouth.* ◇ *You can't cram eight children into the car!*

♦ v + prep ♦ v + n/pron + adv ♦ v + adv + n
♦ v + n/pron + prep

crank /kræŋk/

,crank sth 'out (*informal, especially AmE*) to produce sth quickly and in large amounts: *The plant can crank out about 63 cars an hour.*

SYN **churn sth out**; **turn sth out**

♦ v + adv + n ♦ v + n/pron + adv

,crank sth 'up (*informal*) **1** to make a machine start working or work better: *It's time to crank up the air conditioning.* **2** to make music, etc. louder: *They cranked the music up when the party started.* **OBJ** **music**, **volume** **SYN** **turn sth up** (*more formal*)

♦ v + n/pron + adv ♦ v + adv + n

crash /kræʃ/

,crash a'round (*also* **,crash a'bout/'round** *especially BrE*) (*informal*) to move around making a lot of noise: *I heard her crashing about in the bathroom.*

♦ v + adv

,crash 'down to fall with a very loud noise: *Passengers had a lucky escape when a huge tree crashed down onto a bus.* ◇ *John's hand came crashing down on the table* (= he hit the table hard with his hand). ◇ (*figurative*) *All my dreams came crashing down around me* (= I completely failed in what I wanted to do).

NOTE **Crash down** is usually followed by a phrase beginning with a preposition.

♦ v + adv

SYNONYMS

crash (into sth)

collide (with sth/sb) ♦ **crash** (into sth) ♦ **plough into sth** ♦ **slam into/against sb/sth** ♦ **smash into sth**

These are all verbs that can be used when sth, especially a vehicle, hits sth else very hard.

collide (**with sth/sb**) (of a vehicle or person) to crash into sb/sth else: *The car collided with the van in thick fog.* ◇ *As he fell, his head collided with the table.*

crash (**into sth**) to hit an object or another vehicle, causing damage: *He crashed into a tree.*

plough into sth (*BrE*) (*AmE* **plow into sth**) (especially of a vehicle or its driver) to crash into sth with a lot of force, especially because you are driving too fast or not paying enough attention: *A truck ploughed into the back of the bus.*

slam into/against sb/sth to crash against sb/ sth with a lot of force: *The car skidded and slammed into a tree.*

smash into sth to crash into sth with a lot of force: *The car smashed into a tree.*

WHICH WORD?

Crash is used particularly for vehicles and can be used without a preposition: *We're going to crash, aren't we?* In this meaning **slam**, **smash** and **plough** always take a preposition. **Slam** and **smash** are used for a much wider range of things than just vehicles.

PATTERNS AND COLLOCATIONS

- **two vehicles** crash/collide
- **two vehicles** crash/slam/smash/plough **into each other**
- to crash/collide **head-on**

,crash 'into sb/sth (of a vehicle or a driver) to hit sb/sth, causing damage: *The car crashed into a wall.* ◇ *I crashed into the back of the car in front.*
◆ v + prep

,crash 'out (*informal, especially BrE*) to go to sleep because you are very tired: *I was so tired I crashed out in an armchair.*
SYN **flake out** (*BrE*)
◆ v + adv

,crash 'out of sth (*sport*) to lose a game very badly and so not be able to continue to take part in a competition: *England crashed out of the World Cup.*
NOTE This phrasal verb is used especially in newspapers.
◆ v + adv + prep

,crash 'round (*especially BrE*) → CRASH AROUND

crawl /krɔːl/

'crawl with sb/sth (*usually used in the progressive tenses*) to be full of moving people, animals, insects, etc. in an unpleasant way: *The place is crawling with cops!*
OBJ **police**, **insects**
◆ v + prep

cream /kriːm/

,cream sb/sth 'off to take away the best people or things in a group or an amount of money, usually for your own advantage: *The best pupils are creamed off into special classes.* ◇ *The company's directors are creaming off the profits.*
◆ v + adv + n ◆ v + n/pron + adv

crease /kriːs/

,crease 'up; ,crease sb 'up (*BrE, informal*) to start laughing; to make sb start laughing: *We all creased up when we saw her hat!* ◇ *His programme always creases me up.*
SYN **crack up**, **crack sb up**
◆ v + adv ◆ v + n/pron + adv

credit /'kredɪt/

'credit A with B; 'credit B to A **1** to believe that sb/sth is responsible for sth or for doing sth, especially sth good: *Bach is credited with performing the first solo on a piano.* ◇ *She credits her good looks and intelligence to her father's side of the family.* **2** to consider that sb/sth has a particular good quality or characteristic: *I had credited him with more sense.* ◇ *Numerous health benefits are credited to this natural oil.*
NOTE Often used in the passive. ◆ You can also use the pattern **credit sb/sth as sth**, especially in the passive: *The cheetah is generally credited as the world's fastest animal.*
◆ v + n/pron + prep

creep /kriːp/ (**crept**, **crept** /krept/)

,creep 'in; ,creep 'into sth to start happening or affecting sb/sth gradually: *I thought I'd decided, but then doubts started to creep in.* ◇ *A hint of sarcasm crept into his voice.* ◇ *More and more foreign words are creeping into the language.*
◆ v + adv ◆ v + prep

,creep sb 'out (*AmE, informal*) to make sb feel frightened and not safe: *The way that man was watching us really creeped me out.* ◇ *I was a little creeped out by their first video.*
NOTE **Creeped** is used as the past tense and past participle of this verb.
◆ v + n/pron + adv

,creep 'over sb/sth if a feeling **creeps over** you, or an expression **creeps over** your face, it gradually affects you: *A feeling of tiredness began to creep over her.* ◇ *A sly smile crept over her lips.*
SYN **steal over sb/sth**
◆ v + prep

,creep 'up **1** if a price, an amount, etc. **creeps up**, it rises very gradually: *House prices are starting to creep up.* **2** (**on sb**) to move nearer to sb/sth slowly and quietly without being seen or heard: *Don't creep up on me like that!* ◇ *Jack crept up behind me.*
SYN **steal up** (**on sb**)
◆ v + adv

,creep 'up on sb **1** if an event, a date, etc. **creeps up on** you, it arrives before you are really ready for it: *The exams just seemed to creep up on me.* **2** if a feeling, etc. **creeps up on** you, it starts to affect you before you realize it: *Anorexia can creep up on young girls when they least expect it.*
◆ v + adv + prep

crop /krɒp; AmE krɑːp/ (-**pp**-)

,crop 'up (*informal*) to appear, happen, etc. when it is not expected: *I can't make it tonight—something's cropped up.* ◇ *Her name keeps cropping up everywhere.*
SYN **come up**
◆ v + adv

cross /krɒs; AmE krɔːs/

,cross sb/sth 'off; ,cross sb/sth 'off sth to remove sb's name or an item from a list by drawing a line through it because you have dealt with them/it or they are/it is no longer involved: *Cross off any items we've already got.* ◇ *Jane won't be coming, so we can cross her off the list.*
SYN **delete sth** (*more formal*)
◆ v + n/pron + adv ◆ v + adv + n ◆ v + n/pron + prep

,cross sth 'out/'through to remove words from a text by drawing a line through them, usually because they are wrong: *I crossed his name out and wrote mine instead.* ◇ *You've spelt it wrong. Cross it out and try again.*

OBJ **word, name** SYN **delete sth** (*more formal*); **x sth out** (*AmE, informal*)
♦ v + n/pron + adv ♦ v + adv + n

,cross 'over 1 (*also* ,cross 'over sth) (*especially BrE*) to go from one side of sth, for example a road/street, a room, etc. to the other: *Let's cross over to the other side.* ◇ *She crossed over the road.* OBJ **road, bridge 2** (*also*) to move from one style or type of music, culture, politics, etc. to another; to combine parts of different styles or types: *They're a blues band who have succeeded in crossing over to jazz.*
♦ **1** v + adv ♦ v + prep
♦ **2** v + adv
▶ 'crossover *n* a successful combination of different styles of music, etc.; a successful change from one style to another: *an exciting rock-dance crossover* ◇ *a crossover artist* ◇ *She's made the crossover from modelling into pop.*

,cross sth 'through → CROSS STH OUT/THROUGH

crouch /kraʊtʃ/

'crouch over sb/sth to bend over sb/sth so you are near them/it: *She crouched over the injured man, checking his wounds.*
♦ v + prep

crowd /kraʊd/

,crowd a'round, etc. (*especially AmE*) → CROWD ROUND, ETC.

,crowd 'in; ,crowd 'into sth to move in large numbers into a small place: *As soon as the doors opened people began to crowd in.* ◇ *We all crowded into the lift.* ◇ (*figurative*) *Memories she would rather forget came crowding in.* ◇ (*figurative*) *Doubts crowded into my mind.*
SYN **pile in, pile into sth**
♦ v + adv ♦ v + prep

,crowd sb/sth 'in; ,crowd sb/sth 'into/'onto sth to put a large number of people or things into a small space: *I doubt if we can crowd any more people in—the place is packed already.* ◇ *We were all crowded into a small area behind the goal.*
SYN **cram sb/sth in, etc.; pack sb/sth in, etc.**
♦ v + n/pron + adv ♦ v + adv + n ♦ v + n/pron + prep

,crowd 'in (on sb) if high buildings, mountains, etc. **crowd in,** they seem to surround you and threaten you or have a strong effect on you: *The high walls seemed to crowd in (on her).* ◇ (*figurative*) *He tried to resist the fears that were crowding in on him.*
♦ v + adv + prep

,crowd sb/sth 'onto sth → CROWD SB/STH IN, ETC.

,crowd sb/sth 'out (of sth) if a number of people or things **crowd out** other people or things, they are present in such large numbers that there is no room for anyone or anything else: *Tourists are crowding the regular customers out of the bar.* ◇ (*figurative*) *Small shops are increasingly being crowded out by the big supermarkets.*
SYN **squeeze sb/sth out, etc.**
♦ v + n/pron + adv ♦ v + adv + n
♦ v + n/pron + adv + prep

,crowd 'round; ,crowd 'round sb/sth (*especially BrE*) (*AmE usually* ,crowd a'round, ,crowd a'round sb/sth) to gather in large numbers around sb/sth: *People were crowding around to see what was going on.* ◇ *Fans crowded round him to ask for his autograph.*
♦ v + adv ♦ v + prep

crumple /'krʌmpl/

,crumple sth 'up to crush sth, especially a piece of paper, into a ball: *She crumpled his letter up without even looking at it.*
OBJ **paper** SYN **ball sth up** (*AmE*); **scrunch sth up; wad sth up** (*especially AmE*)
♦ v + n/pron + adv ♦ v + adv + n

cry /kraɪ/ (cries, crying, cried)

'cry for sth to ask for or demand sth in a determined or urgent way: *The families of the victims are crying for justice.* ◇ *Listen! That sounds like somebody crying* (= calling) *for help.*
OBJ **help, mercy**
♦ v + prep

,cry 'off; ,cry 'off sth; ,cry 'off doing sth (*BrE*) to decide not to do sth you have promised or agreed to do: *We'd arranged to go together but Luiz cried off at the last moment.* ◇ *Why did you cry off training last night?*
SYN **pull out, pull out of sth, etc.**
→ see also BEG OFF, BEG OFF STH, ETC.
♦ v + adv ♦ v + prep

,cry 'out to make a loud sound without words because you are hurt, afraid, surprised, etc.: *She cried out in/with pain.*
⊃ note on page 78
♦ v + adv

,cry 'out sth to shout sth loudly: *He suddenly cried out, 'Stop at once!'* ◇ *She could hear a voice crying out her name.*
♦ v + adv + speech ♦ v + adv + n

,cry 'out against sth to protest strongly about sth: *People have been crying out against this abuse for years.*
♦ v + adv + prep
▶ 'outcry (**against/at/over sth**) *n* [C, U] a public reaction of strong protest against sth: *There is sure to be a massive outcry against the proposals.*

,cry 'out for sth (*usually used in the progressive tenses*) to clearly need sth very quickly: *The group is crying out for new members.* ◇ *The whole system was crying out for a radical review.*
♦ v + adv + prep

cry out

cry out ✦ scream out ✦ screech ✦ shriek ✦ wail

These verbs all mean to give a loud high cry, or to make a loud high noise.

cry out to make a loud sound without words because you are hurt, afraid, surprised, etc.: *She tried to stop herself from crying out.* ◇ *He cried out in fear.* ▶ cry *n*: *He gave a loud cry of despair.*

scream out to give a loud, high cry, because you are hurt, frightened, excited, etc.: *He covered her mouth to stop her from screaming out.* **NOTE** Scream can be used on its own: *The kids were screaming with excitement.* ▶ scream *n*: *She let out a scream of pain.*

screech to make a loud, high, unpleasant sound: *He screeched with pain.* ▶ screech *n*: *She suddenly let out a screech.*

shriek to give a loud, high cry, for example when you are excited, frightened or in pain: *She shrieked in fright.* ◇ *The audience was shrieking with laughter.* ▶ shriek *n*: *She let out a piercing shriek.*

wail to make a long, loud cry, especially because you are sad or in pain: *The little girl was wailing miserably.* ▶ wail *n*: *He let out a wail of anguish.*

WHICH WORD?

A wail is longer than a scream, but less strong and extreme; it can be high or low in pitch, but a scream is always high, and is used particularly for women. Of these words, only scream, screech and wail can be used to talk about a noise made by things: *Lights flashed and sirens screamed.* ◇ *The car screeched to a halt.* ◇ *Sirens wailed in the distance.* All of these verbs can be used with speech: *'It's broken!' she wailed.*

PATTERNS AND COLLOCATIONS

- to scream (out)/cry out/screech/wail/shriek **at** sb
- to scream (out)/cry (out)/screech/wail/shriek **in/with** pain, terror, etc.
- to scream (out)/cry (out)/screech **helplessly/ shrilly/loudly**
- **brakes/tyres** scream/screech/shriek
- to screech/shriek **to a halt**

cuddle /ˈkʌdl/

ˌcuddle ˈup (to/against sb), ˌcuddle ˈup together if children, pets, etc. cuddle up, they sit or lie close to each other or sb else, because they need warmth or comfort, or want to show affection: *Jack cuddled up to his mother.* ◇ *The cubs cuddle up together for warmth.* **SYN** snuggle up (to/against sb/sth)
♦ v + adv ♦ v + adv + adv

culminate /ˈkʌlmɪneɪt/

ˈculminate in sth (also ˈculminate with sth *less frequent*) (*formal*) to end with a particular result or conclusion, or at a particular point: *The negotiations culminated in an agreement acceptable to all sides.*
♦ v + prep

curl /kɜːl; AmE kɜːrl/

ˌcurl ˈup; be ˌcurled ˈup 1 to lie down or sit down with your back curved and your knees and arms close to your body: *I love curling up in an armchair with a good book.* ◇ *The cat was curled up asleep under the bush.* 2 if the edges of pages, leaves, etc. curl up, they bend towards the middle: *The pages had all curled up at the corners.*
♦ v + adv ♦ be + v + adv
ˌcurl sth ˈup; ˌcurl yourself ˈup to bend sth/ yourself into a tight curved shape: *She curled her legs up under her on the sofa.* ◇ *He curled himself up under the covers and went to sleep.*
♦ v + n/pron + adv

curse /kɜːs; AmE kɜːrs/

ˌcurse sb ˈout (also ˌcuss sb ˈout) (AmE, informal) to swear at sb because you are angry with them: *She came up to me after school and just started cussing me out.*
♦ v + n/pron + adv ♦ v + adv + n

be ˈcursed with sth to have or suffer from sth bad: *He was cursed with poor health from childhood.* ◇ *I've always been cursed with bad luck.*
♦ be + v + prep

curtain /ˈkɜːtn; AmE ˈkɜːrtn/

ˌcurtain sth ˈoff (from sth) to separate part of a room with a curtain or curtains: *A corner of the room was curtained off.*
♦ v + n/pron + adv ♦ v + adv + n

cuss /kʌs/

ˌcuss sb ˈout (AmE, informal) → CURSE SB OUT

cut /kʌt/ (cutting, cut, cut)

ˌcut aˈcross sth 1 (also ˌcut ˈthrough sth) to take a short route (a short cut) across a place instead of going around it: *We'll get there quicker if we cut across the fields.* 2 to affect or be true for people in different groups that usually remain separate: *Opposition to the proposal cuts across party boundaries.* ⓞⒷⒿ **boundary**, **division**

ˌcut a'way if a television programme or a film/movie **cuts away**, it shows sth different from what was shown before: *We cut away to a building site, where Carter is searching through the rubble.*

◆ v + adv

▸ 'cutaway *n*: *There was a cutaway to Jackson's guest on the podium.*

ˌcut sth a'way (**from sth**) to remove sth by cutting with a knife or a sharp tool: *Cut away any dead branches.*

◆ v + adv + n ◆ v + n/pron + adv

▸ 'cutaway *n* a model or diagram with some outside parts left out, in order to show what the inside looks like

ˌcut 'back (**on sth**) **1** to reduce sth such as the amount sb spends or produces: *The recession means that everyone is cutting back.* ◇ *We've had to cut back on staff to save money.* **2** (*especially AmE*) to eat, drink or use less of a particular thing, usually for your health: *I smoke too much. I must cut back.* ◇ *The doctor's told me to cut*

back on red meat. → see also CUT STH BACK 1; CUT DOWN

◆ v + adv

▸ 'cutback (**in sth**) *n* [*usually* pl.] a reduction in sth: *cutbacks in public spending*

ˌcut sth 'back **1** to reduce sth a lot: *Government funding is being cut back.* ◇ *We have agreed to cut back CFC emissions by 2020.* ⓞⒷⒿ **production**, **spending**, **pollution** ⓢⓎⓝ **pare sth down** (**to sth**), **pare sth back** (**to sth**) ⓝⓞⓣⒺ Often used in the passive. **2** to reduce the size of a plant, a bush, etc. by cutting parts off: *That rose bush needs cutting back a lot.* ⓞⒷⒿ **bush**, **tree** ⓢⓎⓝ **prune sth**

◆ v + adv + n ◆ v + pron + adv
◆ v + n + adv (*less frequent*)

ˌcut 'down (**on sth**) **1** to reduce the amount or quantity of sth: *Recycling cuts down on waste.* ◇ *I've spent too much already this month—I'll have to cut down a bit* (= spend less money). **2** to use or buy less of sth: *The doctor's told me to cut down on fatty foods.* ◇ *I haven't stopped smoking, but I've cut down to five a day.* → see also CUT STH DOWN 1; CUT BACK

◆ v + adv

ˌcut sb 'down (*formal*, *BrE*) to kill sb: *He was cut down by pneumonia at an early age.*

cut sth back

axe sth ◆ **cut sth back** ◆ **cut sth down** ◆ **scale sth back** ◆ **scale sth down** ◆ **slash sth**

These verbs all mean to reduce sth, especially an amount of money or the size of a business. *See also* **bring sth down**.

axe sth (*BrE*) (*AmE* usually **ax**) (*often passive*) (*used especially in newspapers*) to get rid of a service, jobs, etc. in order to save money: *Unprofitable services are to be axed next year.* ◇ *250 staff were axed as part of the shake-up.*

cut sth back to reduce sth, especially an amount of money or business: *We'll have to cut back production.* ⓝⓞⓣⒺ **Cut** can be used on its own: *His salary has been cut by 10%.* It is also possible to use **cut back on sth**: *We are trying to cut back on spending.* ▸ **cutback** *n* [usually pl.]: *cutbacks in public spending*

cut sth down to reduce the size, amount or number of sth: *We need to cut the article down to 1 000 words.* ⓝⓞⓣⒺ It is also possible to use **cut down on sth**: *The doctor told him to cut down on his drinking.*

scale sth back (*especially AmE* or *business*) to reduce sth, especially an amount of money or the size of a business: *The IMF has scaled back its growth forecasts.*

scale sth down to reduce the number, size or extent of sth: *We are thinking of scaling down our training programmes next year.*

slash sth (*often passive*) (*used especially in newspapers*) to reduce sth by a large amount: *The workforce has been slashed.*

WHICH WORD?

Cut is the most general of these verbs. **Cut back** and **scale back** are both used especially to talk about money or business. **Cut down** and **scale down** are both more general and are used more for talking about things other than money or business.

PATTERNS AND COLLOCATIONS

- to cut sth/cut sth back/cut sth down/scale sth down **from…/to…/by…**
- to cut sth (back)/cut sth down/scale sth down **considerably/significantly/drastically**
- to cut/slash/cut back on/cut down on/scale back **spending/production**
- to cut/slash/cut back/axe **jobs**
- to cut/slash **costs/prices/taxes/the budget**

NOTE Often used in the passive.
◆ v + n/pron + adv ◆ v + adv + n

,cut sb/sth 'down (*AmE, informal*) to make sb feel or look stupid, especially in front of other people: *He always cuts her down in front of his friends.* ◇ *She's always cutting down my lifestyle.* **SYN** put sb down
◆ v + n/pron + adv ◆ v + adv + n
IDM cut sb down to 'size to show sb that they are not as important as they think they are
▶ 'cutdown (*AmE*) (*BrE* 'put-down) *n* (*informal*) a remark or criticism that is intended to make sb feel or look stupid

,cut sth 'down 1 to reduce the amount or quantity of sth: *Measures were introduced to cut down the number of road accidents involving children.* ◇ *The policy aims at cutting down exhaust emissions.* **OBJ** number, costs, amount **SYN** reduce sth (*more formal*) **NOTE** Cut sth can also be used on its own. **Cut sth**, not **cut sth down** is used for reducing the cost or the price of sth: *Petrol/gas prices have been **cut**.* → see also CUT DOWN; CUT STH BACK 1; ↻ note at CUT STH BACK 2 to make a tree, etc. fall down by cutting it at the base: *Every time we cut a tree down, we plant a new one.* **OBJ** tree **SYN** chop sth down; fell sth (*more formal*) 3 to reduce the length of sth: *Please cut your article down to 1000 words.* **SYN** shorten sth (*more formal*) **NOTE** Cut sth can also be used on its own with this meaning.
◆ v + adv + n ◆ v + n/pron + adv

,cut 'in 1 (on sb/sth) to interrupt sb/sth: *'Listen to me!' she cut in impatiently.* **SYN** interrupt (sb/sth) → see also CUT INTO STH 2 2 (on sb/sth) (of a vehicle or a driver) to move suddenly in front of another vehicle in a dangerous way, leaving little space between the two vehicles: *The lorry cut in (on me) suddenly and I had to brake sharply.* 3 (of an engine, a motor or a piece of equipment) to start working automatically, especially after another source of power has failed: *If the power fails, the generator will cut in.* **SYN** kick in 4 (*AmE, informal*) to push in front of people who have been waiting in a line: *Someone tried to cut in in front of us.* ◇ *She saw some friends in line and cut in with them.* **SYN** push in (*BrE*) 5 to interrupt a couple who are dancing to start dancing with one of them yourself: *May I cut in?*
◆ v + adv ◆ also v + adv + speech

,cut sb 'in (on sth) (*informal*) to include sb in a deal and give them a share of the profits: *Do you think we can cut Harris in on the deal?*
◆ v + n/pron + adv

,cut 'into sth 1 to make a mark, an opening or a wound in sth with a knife or a sharp object: *Make some pencil guidelines before you cut into the wood.* ◇ *The rope was cutting into her wrists* (= because it was very tight). **OBJ** cake, meat, etc. 2 to interrupt sth: *His voice cut into her*

thoughts. **OBJ** thoughts 3 to begin to use part or too much of sb's time, sth that belongs to sb else, etc.: *My work's cutting into my free time at the moment.* ◇ *The independent stations are cutting into our audience.* **OBJ** time **SYN** encroach on/upon sth (*more formal*)
◆ v + prep

,cut sb 'off 1 to interrupt a telephone conversation by breaking the connection: *Operator, I've just been cut off.* **NOTE** Usually used in the passive. 2 to refuse to let sb have any of your money or property after you die: *He cut his son off without a penny.* **OBJ** son, daughter **SYN** disinherit sb (*more formal*) → see also CUT SB OUT, CUT SB OUT OF STH 3 to end a relationship with sb because you do not want to see or talk to them any more: *His family have cut him off since he told them what he'd done.*
◆ 1 v + n/pron + adv
◆ 2,3 v + n/pron + adv ◆ v + adv + n (*less frequent*)
IDM be cut off in your 'prime to die suddenly when you are still young, strong and successful

,cut sb/sth 'off 1 (*also* ,cut yourself 'off) (from sb/sth) to separate sb/sth/yourself physically or socially from other people or things: *His deafness cut him off from his family and friends.* ◇ *She cut herself off from music after her marriage.* ◇ *Why has he **cut off all contact** with his family?* ◇ *The farm was completely cut off in the snowstorm.* ◇ (*figurative*) *Politicians are cut off from the reality of poverty.* **SYN** isolate sb/sth/yourself (from sb/sth) **NOTE** Often used in the passive. 2 to interrupt sb when they are speaking: *He cut me off in mid-sentence.* ◇ *My explanation was abruptly cut off.* 3 to stop the supply of gas, water or electricity to sb's home: *The gas company threatened to cut them off if they didn't pay the bill.* ◇ *The water supply had been cut off.* 4 (*AmE*) → CUT SB/STH UP: *A sports car cut me off as I turned into the road.* 5 to prevent sb from reaching or leaving a place; to stop sb: *Try to cut him off at the traffic lights.*
◆ v + n/pron + adv ◆ v + adv + n
▶ 'cut-off *n* an act of stopping sth

,cut sth 'off to block or get in the way of sth, etc.: *The police cut off all their escape routes.* ◇ *The new hotel cuts off our view of the sea.*
OBJ route, aid, supplies
◆ v + adv + n ◆ v + n/pron + adv
▶ 'cut-off *n* a point or a limit when you stop sth: *a cut-off in aid* ◇ *What is the cut-off date for registration?*

,cut sth 'off; ,cut sth 'off sth to remove sth by cutting it with a knife or a sharp tool: *He cut off a metre of cloth from the roll.* ◇ *Mind you don't cut your fingers off!* ◇ *She's **had** all her hair **cut off**.* ◇ *If the photo is too large for the frame, cut a bit off the top.* ◇ (*figurative*) *Five seconds has been cut off the world record.*
SYN chop sth off, chop sth off sth
◆ v + n/pron + adv ◆ v + adv + n ◆ v + n/pron + prep

▶ **'cut-offs** n [pl.] trousers/pants that have been made shorter by cutting off part of the legs

▶ **'cut-off** adj [only before noun]   **cut-off** trousers/pants have been made shorter by cutting off part of the legs

▶ **'offcut** n (*especially BrE*) a piece of wood, paper, etc. that remains after the main piece has been cut

,**cut yourself 'off** (**from sb/sth**) → CUT SB OFF 1

,**cut 'out** if an engine or a motor **cuts out**, it suddenly stops working: *One of the aircraft's engines cut out.*
◆ v + adv

▶ **'cut-out** n (*especially BrE*) a safety device that stops an electric current from flowing through sth: *A cut-out stops the kettle boiling dry.*

,**cut 'out**; ,**cut 'out of sth** (*AmE*) **1** (of a vehicle or a driver) to move suddenly sideways out of a line of traffic: *Did you see the way the car in front cut out?* **2** (*old-fashioned, slang*) to leave: *I'm cutting out (of here). See you later.*
◆ v + adv ◆ v + adv + prep

,**cut sb 'out**; ,**cut sb 'out of sth** to not allow sb to be involved in sth: *If we deliver the goods ourselves, we can cut out the middleman.* ◊ *Don't cut your parents out of your lives!* ◊ *She cut me out of her will* (= refused to let me have any of her money or property after she died).
→ see also CUT SB OFF 1
◆ v + adv + n ◆ v + n/pron + adv
◆ v + n/pron + adv + prep

,**cut sth 'out 1** to make sth unnecessary: *Cut out some of the administration by computerizing your records.* ◊ *The new fast train service cuts out the need for a long bus journey.* OBJ **need** **2** (*informal*) to stop doing, using or eating sth: *I've cut out sweets to try to lose weight.* OBJ **smoking**, **drink**, **sweets 3** (*informal*) to block light or sound: *That tree in front of the window cuts out the light.* OBJ **light**, **noise** SYN **block sth out 4** (*informal*) used to tell sb to stop doing or saying sth that is annoying you: *I'm sick of you two arguing—just* ***cut it out!*** ◊ *Now cut out the jokes and pay attention!* OBJ **it**, **that 5** to make sth by cutting: *They managed to cut out a path through the jungle.*
◆ v + n/pron + adv ◆ v + adv + n

,**cut sth 'out**; ,**cut sth 'out of sth 1** to remove sth you want from sth larger by cutting; to cut the shape of sth from a piece of material, paper, etc.: *Simply cut out and return the coupon.* ◊ *She cut the article out of the newspaper.* ◊ *The children enjoy cutting shapes out of coloured paper.* OBJ **article**, **picture 2** to remove sth bad from sth by cutting: *I cut out the bad parts of the apple.* **3** (*informal*) to leave sth out of a piece of writing, etc.: *You can cut out the unimportant details.* SYN **omit sth**
◆ v + n/pron + adv + n ◆ v + adv + n
◆ v + n/pron + adv + prep

IDM **have your 'work cut out** (**for you**) (*formal*) to face a difficult task or situation: *You'll have your work cut out to beat him.*

▶ **'cut-out** n a shape cut out of paper, wood, etc.: *a cardboard cut-out*

be ,cut 'out for sth; be ,cut 'out to do/be sth (*informal*) to have the qualities and abilities needed for sth: *I don't think I'm cut out for country life.* ◊ *He's not cut out to be a politician.* NOTE This phrasal verb is usually used in negative sentences.
◆ be + v + adv + prep ◆ be + v + adv + **to**+inf

,**cut 'through sth 1** → CUT ACROSS STH 1: *The path cuts through the wood.* ◊ *It should be quicker if we cut through town.* **2** to pass through sth by cutting: *Will this saw cut through metal?* ◊ (*figurative*) *The sharp wind cut through his shirt.* ◊ (*figurative*) *The pain cut through him like a knife.* **3** to overcome a difficulty that is preventing you from making progress: *Once you cut through the technical language the report is easy to understand.* ◊ *The yacht cut smoothly through the waves.* **4** to interrupt sth: *His voice cut through her thoughts.*
◆ v + prep

,**cut sth 'through sth** to make a path or passage through sth by cutting: *They had to use their knives to cut a path through the undergrowth.*
OBJ **path**
◆ v + n/pron + prep

,**cut 'up** (*AmE, informal*) to behave in a noisy, silly way, especially to try and make people laugh: *He cut up in class.*
◆ v + adv

▶ **'cutup** n (*AmE, informal*) a person who jokes a lot or behaves in a silly way to make people laugh or to get attention

,**cut sb 'up** (*informal*) **1** to injure sb by cutting them with a knife, a piece of glass, etc.: *He was very badly cut up in the fight.* **2** to make sb very emotionally upset: *She's still very cut up about the divorce.* NOTE Usually used in the passive.
◆ **1** v + n/pron + adv ◆ v + adv + n
◆ **2** v + n/pron + adv

,**cut sb/sth 'up** (*BrE*) (*AmE* ,**cut sb/sth 'off**) (of a vehicle or a driver) to suddenly drive in front of another vehicle in a dangerous way: *Did you see how he cut me up?*
SYN **carve sb/sth up** (*BrE*)
◆ v + n/pron + adv ◆ v + adv + n

⚲,**cut sth 'up** to divide sth into small pieces with a knife or a sharp tool: *Who's going to cut up the vegetables?*
SYN **chop sth up**
◆ v + n/pron + adv ◆ v + adv + n

D d

dab /dæb/ (-bb-)

'dab at sth (**with sth**) to touch sth, especially your face, several times, quickly and lightly: *She was crying and dabbing at her eyes with a handkerchief.* ◇ *He gently dabbed at his cuts with a piece of cotton wool.*
[OBJ] **my, your, etc. eyes**
[NOTE] **Dab sth** can be used on its own with the same meaning: *She dabbed her eyes with a handkerchief.*
♦ v + prep

,dab sth 'off to remove sth such as a mark caused by a liquid with quick, light movements: *Dab the coffee off with your handkerchief.*
♦ v + n/pron + adv ♦ v + adv + n

,dab sth 'on (**with sth**) to put sth on a surface with quick, light movements: *Dab the paint on with a sponge.* ◇ *She dabbed on a little perfume.*
♦ v + n/pron + adv ♦ v + adv + n

dabble /'dæbl/

'dabble in sth to take part in an activity or a sport, but not very seriously: *She swims twice a week and has been dabbling in weight training.*
♦ v + prep

dally /'dæli/ (**dallies, dallying, dallied**)

'dally with sth/sb (*old-fashioned*) to think about sth, do sth or treat sb in a way that is not serious enough: *They've been dallying with the idea for years.*
[OBJ] **idea, thought** [SYN] **toy with sth**
♦ v + prep

dam /dæm/ (-mm-)

[NOTE] A **dam** is a barrier built across a river to stop the water from flowing.

,dam sth 'up to stop the water flowing in a river by building a dam across it: *The stream was dammed up to form ornamental lakes.* ◇ (*figurative*) *I tried to dam up my tears.*
♦ v + adv + n ♦ v + n/pron + adv

damp /dæmp/ (*also* **dampen** /'dæmpən/)

,damp sth 'down 1 to make a fire burn more slowly or stop burning: *Firefighters were damping down the embers hours later.* ◇ *He put sand on the fire to try to damp it down.* ◇ *The fire had been damped down but not extinguished.*
[OBJ] **fire 2** if sb/sth **damps down** an emotion or a feeling, it becomes less strong: *She tried to damp down her feelings of despair.* [OBJ] **emotions 3** if sb/sth **damps down** a situation or an activity, it becomes slower or weaker: *The latest increase in interest rates has damped down*

activity in the housing market. **4** (*rare*) to make a surface slightly wet by spraying a small amount of water over it
♦ v + adv + n ♦ v + pron + adv ♦ v + n + adv (*rare*)

dangle /'dæŋgl/

,dangle sth be'fore sb/sth to offer sb sth very attractive to try to persuade them to do sth: *It's the biggest financial incentive ever dangled before British footballers.*
[NOTE] **In front of** can be used instead of **before**.
♦ v + n/pron + prep

dash /dæʃ/

,dash a'bout (*especially BrE*) → DASH AROUND

,dash a'gainst sth (of rain, waves, the sea, etc.) to beat violently against a surface
♦ v + prep

,dash a'round (*also* **,dash a'bout/'round** *especially BrE*) to move very quickly from place to place, being very busy: *I've been dashing around all day!* ◇ *At the scene of the accident, people were **dashing about all over the place**.*
[SYN] **rush around**
♦ v + adv

,dash a'way/'off to go away from a place in a hurry: *He dashes off every day at four o'clock.*
♦ v + adv

,dash sth a'way if you **dash** tears **away**, you remove them quickly from your face: *He dashed away the tears welling up in his eyes with an impatient hand.*
♦ v + n/pron + adv ♦ v + adv + n

,dash 'off → DASH AWAY/OFF

,dash sth 'off to write or draw sth very quickly: *I dashed off a quick letter to my brother.*
[SYN] **scribble sth**
♦ v + adv + n ♦ v + pron + adv ♦ v + n + adv (*rare*)

,dash 'round (*especially BrE*) → DASH AROUND

date /deɪt/

,date 'back ... (*also* **,date 'back to sth**) to have existed since a particular time in the past or for the length of time mentioned: *It's a tradition that dates back at least a thousand years.* ◇ *Her problems date back to her childhood.* ◇ *The town dates back to Roman times.*
♦ v + adv ♦ v + adv + prep

'date from sth to have existed since a particular time in the past: *It is a beautiful vase dating from about 1715.* ◇ *The strike was the latest stage in a dispute which dated from 2004.*
♦ v + prep

dawn /dɔːn/

'dawn on sb (*also* **'dawn upon sb** *more formal*) if an idea, the truth or a fact **dawns on** you, you realize it for the first time: *It suddenly dawned on us that we were lost.* ◇ *The answer finally dawned on me.*

SYN strike sb

♦ v + prep

deal /diːl/ (**dealt, dealt** /delt/)

deal in sth **1** to do business; to make money by buying and selling a particular product or kind of goods: *He made a fortune dealing in stocks and shares.* ◇ *They deal exclusively in Chinese art.* ◇ *The company deals in computer software.* **OBJ** **shares, art** **2** to make money by buying and selling goods illegally, especially drugs: *They're rumoured to be dealing in stolen goods.* **OBJ** **drugs, arms** **3** to be concerned with or involved in sth: *This newspaper doesn't deal in gossip, only in facts.* ◇ *She's not the type to deal in rumours.*

♦ v + prep

deal sb 'in (*informal, especially AmE*) to include sb in an activity: *It sounds like a great plan! Deal me in!*

SYN count sb in **OPP** deal sb out, deal sb out of sth

♦ v + n/pron + adv

deal sb 'out; deal sb 'out of sth (*AmE, informal*) to not include sb in an activity: *You can deal me out of this. I don't want to get involved in anything illegal.*

SYN count sb out, count sb out of sth **OPP** deal sb in

♦ v + n/pron + adv ♦ v + n/pron + adv + prep

deal sth 'out (**to sb**) **1** to share sth among a number of people, groups of people or organizations: *We'll deal out the proceeds to several charities.* ◇ *The profits were dealt out among the investors.* **SYN** distribute sth (*more formal*) **2** (in a game of cards) to give cards to each player: *She dealt out seven cards to each player.* **NOTE** Deal sth can also be used on its own with this meaning. **3** to give sb a particular punishment; to say what punishment sb should have: *She dealt out the same punishment to all the children.* ◇ *Severe penalties are dealt out to persistent offenders.* **OBJ** **punishment** **SYN** administer sth (*formal*)

♦ **1,2** v + adv + n ♦ v + n/pron + adv
♦ **3** v + adv + n ♦ v + pron + adv

deal with sb **1** to look after, talk to or control people in an appropriate way, especially as part of your job: *Her job involves dealing with young offenders.* ◇ *They're very difficult people to deal with.* **SYN** handle sb **2** to take appropriate action in a particular situation or according to who you are talking to, etc.: *Can you deal with this customer?* ◇ *We have to deal with students and handle a load of paperwork as well.* ◇ *Most patients are dealt with within four weeks.* **3** to take appropriate action to punish sb who has done sth wrong: *Your father will deal with you when he gets home.* ◇ *Athletes found guilty*

of taking drugs were swiftly dealt with. **SYN** sort sb out

♦ v + prep

deal with sb/sth **1** to do business regularly with a person, an organization, a government, etc.: *We prefer to deal only with reputable companies.* ◇ *It is best to deal directly with foreign suppliers.* **OBJ** **business, company** **2** to talk to sb, an organization, a government, etc. in order to reach an agreement or settle a disagreement: *I prefer to deal with somebody in authority.* ◇ *It would help if I knew exactly who I'm dealing with.*

♦ v + prep

deal with sth **1** to solve a problem, carry out a task, etc.: *to deal with enquiries/issues/complaints* ◇ *The police dealt with the incident very efficiently.* ◇ *There's some urgent correspondence here that hasn't been dealt with.* **OBJ** **problems, matter, situation, crisis** **2** (of a book, poem, article, etc.) to be about sth: *The next programme deals with the subject of divorce.* **OBJ** **subject, question, issue** **SYN** cover sth **3** if you **deal with** an emotion such as anger or sadness, you learn to control it or become less affected by it: *He is beginning to deal with his anger in a constructive way.* ◇ *'You've got to try and forget her and get on with your life.' 'I'm dealing with it!'* ◇ *She's good at dealing with pressure.* **OBJ** **anger, grief, loss** **SYN** cope (**with sth**)

♦ v + prep

debar /dɪ'bɑː(r)/ (-rr-)

de'bar sb from sth; de'bar sb from doing sth (*formal*) to prevent sb from doing sth, joining an organization, going somewhere, etc.: *Students who have not paid their fees will be debarred from taking examinations.* ◇ *He was debarred from holding public office.*

♦ v + n/pron + prep

decide /dɪ'saɪd/

de'cide on sb/sth (*also* **de'cide upon sb/sth** *more formal*) to choose sb/sth after careful thought: *We haven't decided on a date for the wedding yet.* ◇ *Have you decided on whether to take the job or not?* ◇ *Nothing has yet been decided on.*

SYN settle on/upon sth

♦ v + prep

deck /dek/

deck sb 'out; deck yourself 'out (**in/as/like sth**) to put on interesting and brightly coloured clothes or jewellery, usually for a special occasion: *He decked himself out in his best suit.* ◇ *A lot of supporters were decked out in the team's colours.*

SYN dress up (**as sth**), etc.

NOTE Deck **sb/yourself** (**in/with sth**) is also used on its own.
♦ v + adv + n ♦ v + n/pron + adv

ˌdeck sth ˈout (**with/in/like sth**) to decorate sth, especially a room or a building, for a special occasion: *The canteen was decked out with Christmas decorations.* ◇ *The room was decked out to look like the inside of a spaceship.*
OBJ room
NOTE Usually used in the passive.
♦ v + adv + n ♦ v + n/pron + adv

declare /dɪˈkleə(r); *AmE* dɪˈkler/

deˌclare aˈgainst sb/sth (*BrE, formal*) to say publicly that you do not support sb/sth: *The newspaper has declared against the government in the run-up to the election.*
♦ v + prep

deˈclare for sb/sth (*BrE, formal*) to say publicly that you support sb/sth: *Otto the Bald declared for the Emperor.*
♦ v + prep

deˈclare for sth (*AmE*) **1** (of a politician) to announce that you will take part in an election for a particular office: *Yesterday she declared for Governor in a press conference.* **2** (of a sports player) to announce that you will take part in the system by which teams choose players from a ranked group (the **draft**): *He's been thinking about declaring for the draft since last year.*
♦ v + prep

dedicate /ˈdedɪkeɪt/

ˈdedicate sth to sb to say at the beginning of a book, a piece of music or a performance that you are doing it for sb, as a way of thanking them or showing respect: *This book is dedicated to my parents.*
OBJ book, work, song
♦ v + n/pron + prep

ˈdedicate yourself/sth to sth; ˈdedicate yourself/sth to doing sth to give a lot of your time and effort to a particular activity or purpose because you think it is important: *She dedicates herself to her work.* ◇ *He dedicated his life to helping the poor.*
♦ v + n/pron + prep

defer /dɪˈfɜː(r)/ (-rr-)

deˈfer to sb/sth (*rather formal*) to accept sb's opinion or do what they suggest because you respect them: *I defer to your judgement in these matters.* ◇ *We are happy to defer to the committee's wishes.*
OBJ judgement, wishes
♦ v + prep

delight /dɪˈlaɪt/

deˈlight in sth; deˈlight in doing sth to get a lot of pleasure from sth or from doing sth, especially sth that annoys or upsets other people: *She seemed to delight in making her parents angry.* ◇ *From childhood, she delighted in reading.*
♦ v + prep

deliver /dɪˈlɪvə(r)/

deˈliver on sth if you **deliver on** a promise, a threat or an agreement, you do what you have said you would do, or what you are expected to do: *Can he be trusted to deliver on his promises?* ◇ *They failed to deliver on the agreement.*
OBJ promise, agreement
♦ v + prep

deˌliver sb/sth ˈover/ˈup (to sb), deˌliver yourself ˈover/ˈup (to sb) (*formal*) to give sb/sth/yourself to sb in authority, often because you have been ordered to do so: *The defendant has been ordered to deliver up the goods.* ◇ *She delivered the baby over to the care of her sister.* ◇ *He delivered himself up to the authorities.*
SYN hand sb/sth over (to sb), etc. (*less formal*)
♦ v + adv + n ♦ v + n/pron + adv

delve /delv/

ˌdelve ˈinto sth to try hard to find out more information about sth: *We should not delve too deeply into this painful matter.*
OBJ subject, reasons **SYN** probe (sth/into sth)
♦ v + prep

depart /dɪˈpɑːt; *AmE* dɪˈpɑːrt/

deˈpart from sth to behave in a way that is different from what is usual or expected: *The teachers are not encouraged to depart from the syllabus.* ◇ *They departed from tradition and got married in a hotel.*
OBJ principles, rules, tradition, decision
♦ v + prep

depend /dɪˈpend/

deˈpend on sb/sth (*also* deˈpend upon sb/sth *more formal*) **1** (for sth) (*not usually used in the progressive tenses*) to need help or support from sb/sth in order to live or to manage in a particular situation: *The organization depended heavily on voluntary help.* ◇ *She came to depend on her daughter for support.* ◇ *He depends on medication to stay alive.* **SYN** rely on/upon sb/sth (for sth) **2** (*not used in the progressive tenses*) to be affected by or decided by sb/sth: *I don't know if I'll come or not.* **It all depends on** *how tired I feel this evening.* ◇ *This may be a welcome change or not, depending on your point of view.* **3** to rely on sb/sth; to be able to trust sb: *I hope you'll be able to come—I'm depending on you to help me.* ◇ *We need someone who can be depended on.* **SYN** count on/upon sb/sth; rely on/upon sb/sth **4** (*not used in the progressive tenses*) to be sure that sth will happen: *You can depend on my sister to spoil things* (= she always

depend on/upon sb/sth

believe in sb ◆ **count on sb/sth** ◆ **depend on/upon sb/sth** ◆ **rely on/upon sb/sth** ◆ **trust sb/sth**

These verbs all mean to believe that sb/sth will do what you hope or expect of them or that what they tell you is correct or true.

believe in sb to feel that you can trust sb and/or that they will be successful: *They need a leader they can believe in.*

count on sb/sth (often used with *can, cannot, etc.*) to be sure that sb will do what you need them to do, or that sth will happen as you want it to happen: *I'm counting on you to help me.* ◇ *Can we count on your support in the next election?*

depend on/upon sb/sth (often used with *can, cannot, etc.*) to trust sb/sth to do what you expect or want, to do the right thing, or to be true or correct: *He knew he could depend on her to deal with the situation.*

rely on/upon sb/sth (used especially with *can, cannot, etc.*) to trust sb/sth to do what you expect or want, or to be honest, correct or good enough: *Can I rely on you to keep this secret?* ◇ *He can't be relied on to tell the truth.* ◇ *You can't rely on any figures you get from*

them. NOTE **Rely upon sb/sth** is more formal than **rely on sb/sth**.

trust sb/sth to believe that sb is good, honest, sincere, etc. and that they will do what you expect of them or do the right thing; to believe that sth is true or correct: *You can trust me not to tell anyone.* ◇ *I don't really trust his judgement.* ◇ *Don't trust what you read in the newspapers!*

WHICH WORD?

You can **trust** a person but **not** a thing or system. You can **trust** sb's *judgement* or *advice*, but **not** their support. You can **depend on** sb's *advice* or *support*, but **not** their judgement.

PATTERNS AND COLLOCATIONS

- to trust/depend on/rely on/count on sb/sth **to do** sth
- to trust/rely on/believe in **yourself**
- to trust/depend on/rely on **sb's advice**
- to trust/rely on **sb's judgement**
- to rely on/depend on/count on **sb's support**
- to **completely/fully** trust/depend on/rely on/count on/believe in sb/sth

does). SYN **count on/upon sb/sth**; **rely on/upon sb/sth**

◆ v + prep ◆ v + prep + n/pron + **to**+inf

deprive /dɪˈpraɪv/

de**ˈprive sb/sth/yourself of sth** to prevent sb/sth from having sth important; to take sth away from sb: *In prison they were starved and deprived of sleep.* ◇ *The baby's brain had been deprived of oxygen during the birth.* ◇ *There is no need to deprive yourself of food on this diet.* ◇ (*humorous*) *I couldn't deprive you of* (= take away from you) *your last few pence.*

◆ v + n/pron + prep

derive /dɪˈraɪv/

de**ˈrive from sth** to come or develop from sth: *The word history derives from the Latin word 'historia' meaning story.* ◇ *The criticism derives from a misunderstanding of our aims.*

◆ v + prep

de**ˈrive sth from sth 1** (*formal*) to get or obtain sth from sth: *She derived a great deal of satisfaction from this achievement.* OBJ **pleasure, satisfaction, information, benefits 2** to obtain a substance from sth: *These remedies are derived mainly from the natural world.* NOTE Of-

ten used in the passive. **3** to come or develop from sth: *Washington derives its name from the first US president.* ◇ *The name of the mountain appears to be derived from an old Norse word.* OBJ **name, word** NOTE Often used in the passive.

◆ v + n/pron + prep

descend /dɪˈsend/

be des**ˈcended from sb/sth** to be related to sb who lived a long time ago: *He claimed he was descended from the Vikings.* OBJ **ancestors, line, family**

◆ be + v + prep

des**ˈcend into sth** to get into a very bad condition or state: *The situation has descended into total chaos.* ◇ *There were fears that the country was descending into turmoil or even civil war.*

◆ v + prep

des**ˈcend on sb/sth** (*also* des**ˈcend upon sb/sth** *more formal*) **1** to arrive somewhere, especially suddenly and unexpectedly and in large numbers: *Dozens of police descended on the building.* ◇ (*humorous*) *My sister and her family are descending on us this weekend.* **2** to go towards sb/sth as if you are going to attack them/it: *The mosquitoes descended on us as soon as night fell.*

◇ *A large woman in a hat was descending on them.*
♦ v + prep

des'cend to sth to do or say sth that makes people lose their respect for you: *If you insult him back, you descend to his level.*
[SYN] **stoop to sth, stoop to doing sth**
♦ v + prep

despair /dɪˈspeə(r); *AmE* dɪˈsper/

de'spair of sb/sth; de'spair of doing sth (*formal* or *humorous*) to feel that there is no hope that sb/sth will improve, get better, etc. or that sth will happen: *I despair of you, Ian—act your age!* ◇ *I'd begun to despair of ever seeing him again.*
♦ v + prep

detract /dɪˈtrækt/

de'tract from sth (*not usually used in the progressive tenses*) to make sth seem less good than it really is: *These revelations should not detract from his achievements.* ◇ *Her tattered clothes in no way detracted from her beauty.*
[SYN] **diminish sth**
♦ v + prep

devolve /dɪˈvɒlv; *AmE* -ˈvɑːlv/

de'volve on/to/upon sb/sth (*formal*) (of work, duties, power or responsibility) to be given to a person or an organization by sb at a higher level of authority: *All the responsibility has devolved upon him.* ◇ *Additional powers will devolve to the regional governments.*
♦ v + prep

de'volve sth to sb/sth to give work, duties, power or responsibility to sb with less authority than you: *More powers are gradually being devolved to the regions.*
♦ v + n/pron + prep

devote /dɪˈvəʊt; *AmE* dɪˈvoʊt/

de'vote sth to sb/sth; de'vote sth to doing sth to give an amount of time, energy or attention to sb/sth: *He devoted his life to the struggle for justice.* ◇ *She gave up work to devote more time to her children.* ◇ *The museum is hosting an exhibition devoted to her work.* ◇ *Several courses are devoted to improving customer care.*
[OBJ] **time, attention, energy, life, chapter**
♦ v + n/pron + prep

de'vote yourself to sb/sth; de'vote yourself to doing sth to spend a large part of your time, energy and attention on a particular activity, especially sth good: *After her marriage, she couldn't devote herself totally to her music.* ◇ *They had devoted themselves entirely to building up their business.*
♦ v + pron + prep

dial /ˈdaɪəl/ (-ll-, *AmE* -l-)

,dial 'in; ,dial 'into sth (*also* ,dial 'up sth) (*computing*) to make a connection between one computer and another using a telephone line: *I dial in from my PC at home to get the files I need.* ◇ *Every time I try to dial into the Internet I can't get a connection.*
♦ v + adv ♦ v + prep

,dial sth 'in to push buttons to use a telephone or put information into a computer: *I dialled in the number and waited for someone to answer.*
♦ v + adv + n ♦ v + n/pron + adv

,dial 'out to make a call to sb outside the building you are in: *You can't dial out from that phone—it's for internal calls only.*
♦ v + adv

,dial 'up sb/sth 1 (*AmE*) to call sb/sth on the telephone: *Would you dial up the doctor's office for me?* [SYN] **call sb/sth up; call sb/sth** (*AmE*) **2** → DIAL INTO STH: *Customers can dial up the central computer from home and access the database.*
[NOTE] When the object of **dial up** is a noun, it comes after **up**, but when the object is a pronoun, it comes between **dial** and **up**: *Sit down and dial them up.*
♦ v + adv + n ♦ v + pron + adv
▶ **'dial-up** *adj* [only before noun] using a telephone line to connect your computer to the Internet

dictate /dɪkˈteɪt; *AmE* ˈdɪkteɪt/

dic'tate to sb to give orders to sb, especially in a rude or aggressive way: *You can't dictate to people how they should live.* ◇ *I'm not going to be dictated to by my little brother!*
♦ v + prep

diddle /ˈdɪdl/

,diddle a'round (*AmE, informal*) to spend your time doing things that are not important: *Stop diddling around and do some work!*
[SYN] **fiddle about/around** (*BrE*); **mess around**
♦ v + adv

die /daɪ/ (**dies, dying, died, died**)

,die a'way 1 (of a sound) to become so faint or weak that you can no longer hear it: *The sound of the car engine died away.* ◇ *Her laughter died away when she saw how angry he was.* [SYN] **fade away 2** (*also* ,die 'out) (of rain, wind or a storm) to gradually become weaker and stop: *The rain will largely die away overnight.* **3** (of a feeling or an emotion) to gradually become weaker and disappear: *The excitement over their affair soon died away.* [SYN] **fade away** ⊃ note at PETER OUT
♦ v + adv

,die 'back (*also* ,die 'down) if a plant **dies back**, its leaves die, although the roots are still alive: *The leaves die back in winter.*
♦ v + adv

die down

die down ◆ ebb away ◆ lessen ◆ wane

These verbs can all be used when the level or strength of sth goes down gradually or quickly. *See also* **dwindle away, peter out**.

die down (especially of noise, bad weather or fire) to become gradually less loud or strong: *When the applause had died down, she began her speech.* ◇ *As the flames died down, he felt cold air on his face.*

ebb away (*formal*) (especially of feelings) to become gradually weaker or less: *As night fell, our enthusiasm began to ebb away.* **NOTE** **Ebb** can be used on its own: *The pain was ebbing.*

lessen to become smaller, weaker or less important: *The dominance of Oxford and Cambridge had begun to lessen.* ▶ **lessening**

n: There has been a lessening of tension in the region.

wane (*used especially in newspapers*) to become gradually weaker or less important: *Her enthusiasm for the whole idea was waning rapidly.* ◇ *Their popularity waned during that period.* ▶ **wane** *n: Her popularity is on the wane.*

PATTERNS AND COLLOCATIONS

- **support/enthusiasm/confidence** wanes/ebbs (away)
- **anger/fear** ebbs (away)
- the **storm/wind/rain** dies down
- to **wane/die down quickly**
- to **wane/die down/lessen/ebb** (away) **gradually**

die 'down 1 (of a sound or flames) to gradually become less loud or strong: *He waited for the applause to die down.* ◇ *The fire had died down by the morning.* ⊃ note at GO OUT **2** (of wind, rain or a storm) to gradually become less strong or violent: *As it got dark, the wind died down.* **SYN** **subside 3** if sth such as excitement or confusion **dies down**, it gradually becomes less: *When all the fuss had died down, he just quietly went back home.* **SYN** **subside 4** → DIE BACK
◆ v + adv

be 'dying for sth (*informal*) (*only used in the progressive tenses*) if sb is **dying for** sth, they want it very much: *I'm dying for a glass of water.* **SYN** **be gagging for sth** (*BrE, slang*) **NOTE** You can also use **be dying to do sth**: *I'm dying to know what happened.*
◆ v + prep

die 'off if a group of people or animals **die off**, they die one by one over a short period of time until there are none left: *The survivors are dying off daily.*
◆ v + adv

die 'out 1 if a family, race, type of animal, etc. **dies out**, there are no longer any members left alive: *There are several theories about why dinosaurs died out so suddenly.* ◇ *Many plants and animals are in danger of dying out.* **SYN** **become extinct 2** (of a custom, tradition or skill) to no longer be used or practised: *Many May Day ceremonies have virtually died out now.* **3** → DIE AWAY 2: *The outbreaks of rain will die out later in the day.*
◆ v + adv

dig /dɪg/ (**digging, dug, dug** /dʌg/)

dig 'in; dig 'into sth 1 (*informal*) to begin to eat: *Dig in while it's hot!* ◇ *As soon as the food arrived he dug in hungrily.* ◇ *They dug into the pizza hungrily.* **SYN** **tuck in, etc.** (*especially BrE*) **NOTE** **Dig in** is used especially to tell sb to start eating. **2** (*AmE, informal*) to begin to do sth in a way that shows that you are determined to continue or finish it, even if it is difficult: *He looked at the stack of work and dug in straight away.* ◇ *She dug into the reports and finished them before the meeting.*
◆ v + adv ◆ v + prep

dig 'in; dig yourself 'in to make a safe place for yourself in the ground and prepare for the enemy to attack: *The troops dug in and organized their defences.* ◇ *The marines were dug in on the front line.* ◇ (*figurative*) *Hospital workers dug in, prepared for a long battle over pay increases.* **NOTE** Often used in the passive.
◆ v + adv ◆ v + pron + adv

dig sth 'in; dig sth 'into sth 1 to push sth into sth: *The bird dug its claws in and held onto its prey.* ◇ *She dug her nails into my arm.* **2** to mix a substance into soil by digging: *I've dug the fertilizer into the soil.*
◆ v + n/pron + adv ◆ v + adv + n ◆ v + n/pron + prep
IDM **dig your 'heels/'toes in** to refuse to do sth or to change your ideas or plans: *He dug his heels in and insisted she went with him.*

dig 'into sth to examine sth carefully to find out information: *It isn't a good idea to dig too deep into his past.*
◆ v + prep
IDM **dig (deep) into your 'pocket(s), 'savings, etc.** to spend some of the money you have or

have been saving: *I'll have to dig into my savings to buy a new car.*

,dig sb/sth 'out; ,dig sb/sth 'out of sth to get sb/sth out of a place by digging the ground around them/it: *It took them three hours to dig him out of the rubble.* ◇ *The car was buried in snow and had to be dug out.*

◆ v + n/pron + adv ◆ v + adv + n
◆ v + n/pron + adv + prep

▶ 'dugout *n* **1** a rough shelter made by digging a hole in the ground and covering it, used by soldiers **2** a shelter by the side of a sports field where a team's manager, etc. can sit and watch the game **3** a light narrow boat made by cutting out the inside of a tree

,dig sth 'out **1** (*informal*) to find sth that has been hidden or not used for a long time: *He dug out the shoes he'd bought 20 years before.* SYN **unearth** sth (*more formal*) **2** (*informal*) to find out facts or information by searching or asking questions: *I took the opportunity to dig out some interesting facts and figures about the island.*

SYN **hunt sth down/out; root sb/sth out**
◆ v + adv + n ◆ v + n/pron + adv

,dig sth 'over to prepare the ground thoroughly for plants by digging the soil: *The flower beds should be dug over in the spring.*

OBJ **ground, garden**
◆ v + n/pron + adv ◆ v + adv + n

,dig sth 'up **1** to break the ground into small pieces, especially before building sth, taking sth from underneath it, etc.: *Some Roman remains were found under a car park which was being dug up.* OBJ **road, garden 2** to remove sth from the ground by digging: *Archaeologists have dug up some human remains.* OBJ **weeds, roots** SYN **unearth sth** (*more formal*) **3** (*informal*) to discover information about sb/sth by searching or asking questions: *See what you can dig up on this man's past.* SYN **unearth sth** (*more formal*)

◆ v + n/pron + adv ◆ v + adv + n

dine /daɪn/

'dine on sth to eat a particular type of food: *We dined on freshly caught fish in a floating restaurant.* ◇ *They dined on a bland diet of soup and bread.*

◆ v + prep

,dine 'out (*formal*) to have dinner away from your home, for example at a restaurant or in sb else's home: *We dined out every night when we stayed in Paris.*

SYN **eat out** (*less formal*)
◆ v + adv

,dine 'out on sth (*BrE, humorous*) to tell people of sth that has happened to you in order to impress them: *She only actually said one sentence to Brad Pitt but she dined out on it for years.*

◆ v + adv + prep

ding /dɪŋ/

,ding 'down (*ScotE*) to snow or rain heavily: *It was dinging down.* ◇ *The snow was dinging down.* SUBJ **the snow, the rain, it**
◆ v + adv

,ding 'into sb/sth (*ScotE*) to hit sb/sth by accident: *In the dark I dinged into a chair.*
◆ v + prep

dink /dɪŋk/

,dink a'round (*AmE, informal*) to waste time doing unimportant things and not get very much done: *They came home from war to find all their friends dinking around and going nowhere.*
◆ v + adv

dip /dɪp/ (-pp-)

,dip sth 'in/'into sth; ,dip sth 'in to put sth very quickly into a liquid and take it out again: *She dipped her toes cautiously into the sea.* ◇ *She took off her shoes and cautiously dipped a toe in.* ◇ *The fruit had been dipped in chocolate.*
◆ v + n/pron + prep ◆ v + n/pron + adv ◆ v + adv + n

,dip 'into sth **1** to read or watch only small parts of a book, magazine, programme, etc.: *I've only had time to dip into the report.* ◇ *The continuous news services are intended for people to dip into.* OBJ **book, report** ➔ note at LOOK THROUGH STH **2** to put your hand into a container to take sth out of it: *She dipped into her purse and took out a coin.*
◆ v + prep

IDM **dip into your 'pocket, 'savings, etc.** to take an amount from money that you have been keeping or saving: *They have dipped into their savings to pay for the shares.*

disagree /ˌdɪsəˈɡriː/

disa'gree with sb (*not used in the progressive tenses*) **1** (**about/on/over sth**) to have a different opinion from sb: *He disagreed with his parents on most things.* **2** if sth such as food or the weather **disagrees with** you, it has a bad effect on you or makes you feel ill/sick: *I feel terrible—something I ate must have disagreed with me.* SYN **upset sb** NOTE **Not agree with sb** is used more often: *Mushrooms really don't agree with me.*
→ see also AGREE WITH SB
◆ v + prep

disa'gree with sth; disa'gree with doing sth to disapprove of sth and think it is bad or wrong: *We totally disagree with the ban on fox hunting.* ◇ *She disagrees with keeping animals locked up in cages.*
OBJ **decision, statement, principle** OPP **agree with sth, agree with doing sth**
◆ v + prep

disassociate /ˌdɪsəˈsəʊʃieɪt, -ˈsəʊs-; *AmE* -ˈsoʊ-/

ˌdisas'sociate yourself from sb/sth (*formal*)
→ DISSOCIATE YOURSELF FROM SB/STH

disbelieve /ˌdɪsbɪˈliːv/

disbe'lieve in sb/sth to not believe that sb/sth
exists: *to disbelieve in God/devils*
NOTE Not believe in sb/sth is used more
frequently.
→ see also BELIEVE IN SB/STH
♦ v + prep

discourse /dɪsˈkɔːs; *AmE* -ˈkɔːrs/

dis'course (with sb) on sth (*formal*) to talk for
a long time on a subject; to make a long speech
about sth: *He was able to discourse at great
length on the problems of education.*
♦ v + prep

dish /dɪʃ/

ˌdish sth 'out (to sb) **1** (*informal*) to give sth out
to large numbers of people or in large amounts:
He's always dishing out advice to people.
SYN hand sth out (to sb) (*more formal*)
NOTE In informal spoken language, **dish sb
out sth** is also used: *He dished me out a few
vitamin pills.* **2** to serve food to sb by putting it
on plates: *He's busy dishing out the dinner.*
SYN serve sth (to sb) (*more formal*)
♦ v + adv + n ♦ v + pron + adv ♦ v + n + adv (*rare*)
IDM ˌdish it 'out (*disapproving*) to criticize sb or
attack them: *He was good at dishing it out. It was
time he learned what it felt like.*

ˌdish 'up; ˌdish sth 'up (*BrE, informal*) to serve
food by putting it on plates: *You pour the wine
while I dish up.* ◇ *Come and wash your hands—
I'm just going to dish up the dinner.*
SYN serve sth out; serve, serve sth (*more
formal*)
♦ v + adv ♦ v + adv + n ♦ v + pron + adv
♦ v + n + adv (*less frequent*)

ˌdish 'up sth (*informal*) to present or offer sth to
sb, usually sth not very good: *She keeps on
dishing up the same old jokes in her shows.*
SYN serve sth up
NOTE When the object of **dish up** is a noun, it
comes after **up**, but when the object is a
pronoun, it comes between **dish** and **up**: *He
keeps dishing them up.*
♦ v + adv + n ♦ v + pron + adv

dispense /dɪˈspens/

di'spense with sb/sth (*formal*) to get rid of
sth; to stop using sb/sth because they are/it is
no longer necessary: *The programme dispensed
with its most popular presenter.* ◇ *The spread of
PCs has dispensed with the need for typists.* ◇ *His
services can now be dispensed with.*
OBJ services, need, requirement
♦ v + prep

dispose /dɪˈspəʊz; *AmE* dɪˈspoʊz/

di'spose of sb to defeat or kill sb: *The league
champions quickly disposed of the opposition.*
♦ v + prep

di'spose of sb/sth (*formal*) to get rid of sb/sth
that you do not want: *She tried to dispose of the
evidence.* ◇ *They decided to dispose of much of
their property.* ◇ *Ensure that all the waste is
properly and safely disposed of.*
OBJ waste, property, assets
♦ v + prep

di'spose of sth (*formal*) to successfully deal
with or finish with a problem, etc.: *There just
remains the matter of funding to dispose of.*
OBJ problem, matter, argument **SYN** deal
with sth (*less formal*)
♦ v + prep

dissociate /dɪˈsəʊʃieɪt, -ˈsəʊs-; *AmE* -ˈsoʊ-/

(*also* disassociate /ˌdɪsəˈsəʊʃieɪt, -ˈsəʊs-; *AmE*
-ˈsoʊ-/)

dis'sociate yourself from sb/sth (*formal*) to
say or do sth to show that you have no
connection with sb/sth and do not support or
agree with them/it: *The President dissociated
himself from the report.*
OPP associate yourself with sb/sth
♦ v + pron + prep

dissolve /dɪˈzɒlv; *AmE* -ˈzɑːlv/

dis'solve into sth **1** to suddenly start to laugh
or cry: *They dissolved into fits of laughter.*
◇ *I dissolved into giggles.* ◇ *When I mentioned
his name, she dissolved into tears.* **OBJ** laughter,
giggles, tears **2** to change gradually into a very
bad state: *His surprise slowly dissolved into fury.*
♦ v + prep

dive /daɪv/ (dived, dived, *AmE also* dove /dəʊv; *AmE* doʊv/, dived)

ˌdive 'in; ˌdive 'into sth **1** (*informal*) to start
doing sth with enthusiasm and without stopping to think: *She dived in with a question before
I had finished speaking.* ◇ *They had dived into the
new business without thinking it through.* **2** (*informal*) to start eating with enthusiasm: *As soon as
the food was served, she dived in.* **OBJ** food,
dinner **SYN** dig in; dig into sth
♦ v + adv ♦ v + prep

'dive into sth to move your hand quickly into
sth such as a pocket or bag to try to find sth: *She
dived into her handbag for the keys.*
OBJ bag, pocket
♦ v + prep

divest /daɪˈvest/

di'vest sb/yourself of sth (*formal*) to take
clothes off sb/yourself: *He swiftly divested himself of his clothes.*
♦ v + n/pron + prep

di'vest sb/sth of sth (*formal*) to take sth away from sb/sth: *The court order divests the company of all its assets.*
SYN **strip sb/sth of sth** (*less formal*)
◆ v + n/pron + prep

di'vest yourself of sth (*formal*) to get rid of sth you no longer want or that is no longer useful: *She managed to divest herself of the unwanted property.*
→ see also DIVEST SB/YOURSELF OF STH
◆ v + pron + prep

divide /dɪ'vaɪd/

di'vide by sth if a number **divides by** another number, the second number is contained in the first an exact number of times: *Does 612 divide by 13? ◇ 148 doesn't divide by 12.*
◆ v + prep

di'vide sth by sth if you **divide** a number by another number, you find out how many times the second number is contained in the first: *What's 48 divided by 3? ◇ 48 ÷ 3 = 16* (read: forty-eight divided by three equals sixteen)
◆ v + n/pron + prep

di'vide into sth if a number **divides into** another number, it is contained in the second number a particular number of times: *Does 300 divide into 1270?*
◆ v + prep

di'vide sth into sth if you **divide** a number **into** another number, you find out how many times the first number is contained in the second: *Can you divide 300 into 1270?*
◆ v + n/pron + prep

di,vide sth/sb 'off (**from sth/sb**) to separate two things or two people with a barrier such as a wall or fence; to form a barrier between two things or people: *A fence divided off one side of the garden. ◇ They put up a barrier to divide the women's section off from the men's.*
◆ v + adv + n ◆ v + n/pron + adv

di,vide 'up; **di,vide sb/sth 'up** (**into sth**) to separate, or to make sb/sth separate, into groups or parts: *Divide up into two teams. ◇ They divided the children up into groups. ◇ Divide up your time so that you don't spend too long on any of the questions.*
◆ v + adv ◆ v + n/pron + adv

di,vide sth 'up (**among/between sb**) to separate sth into parts and give one part to each of a number of people: *We divided the work up between us. ◇ The money was divided up among all three winners.*
OBJ **work**, **money**, **land**
◆ v + n/pron + adv ◆ v + adv + n

divorce /dɪ'vɔːs; *AmE* dɪ'vɔːrs/

di'vorce sb/sth from sth to separate a person, an idea, a subject, etc. from sth; to keep two things separate: *They believed that art*

should be divorced from politics. ◇ When he was depressed, he felt utterly divorced from reality.
SYN **separate sb/sth** (**from/and sth**)
◆ v + n/pron + prep

divvy /'dɪvi/ (**divvies**, **divvying**, **divvied**)

,divvy sth 'up (*informal, especially AmE*) to divide or share sth, especially money, between a number of people: *They divvied up the bill.*
OBJ **money** **SYN** **share sth out** (**among/between sb**) (*more formal*)
◆ v + n/pron + adv ◆ v + n + adv ◆ v + adv (*rare*)

do /du; strong form duː/ (**does** /dʌz/, **did** /dɪd/, **done** /dʌn/)

,do a'way with sb/yourself (*informal*) to kill sb/yourself: *She tried to do away with herself.*
◆ v + adv + prep

,do a'way with sth (*informal*) **1** to get rid of sth; to stop doing or having sth: *They've done away with the uniform at our school. ◇ A lot of the paperwork could easily be done away with.*
SYN **abolish sth** (*more formal*) **2** to make sth no longer necessary: *Computers have done away with a lot of the repetitive work.* **SYN** **eliminate sth**; **end sth** (*more formal*)
◆ v + adv + prep

,do sb 'down; **,do yourself 'down** (*BrE, informal*) to criticize sb or yourself in a way that makes them/you appear more stupid or less able than they/you really are: *Don't do him down, he's a good worker. ◇ She's always doing herself down.*
SYN **put sb down**, etc. (*more formal*)
◆ v + n/pron + adv ◆ v + adv + n (*less frequent*)

'do for sb/sth (*BrE, informal*) to damage or destroy sth; to injure or kill sb; to put sb/sth in a situation so bad that they/it have no chance of returning to normal: *The last bout of pneumonia nearly did for her.*
◆ v + prep

▶ **'done for** *adj* (*informal*) in serious trouble or danger; having no chance of succeeding at sth: *If anyone recognizes us, we're done for! ◇ After three days trapped in the cave they thought they were done for* (= they thought they would die).

,do sb 'in (*informal*) **1** if sth **does you in**, it makes you feel extremely tired: *That's done me in, lifting all those boxes.* **2** (*also* **,do yourself 'in**) (*informal, especially BrE*) to kill sb/yourself: *When we split up, I felt like doing myself in. ◇ Does he get done in at the end of the film?*
◆ v + n/pron + adv
◆ v + adv + n (*rare*) **2** also v + pron + adv
▶ **done 'in** *adj* (*informal*) very tired: *I felt absolutely done in by the end of the day! ◇ Come and sit down—you look done in.*

,do sth 'in (*BrE, informal*) to injure a part of your body: *He did his back in playing tennis.*
◆ v + n/pron + adv ◆ v + adv + n (*less frequent*)

IDM do sb's 'head in (*BrE, informal*) to make sb feel confused, upset and/or annoyed: *Shut up! You're doing my head in.*

,do yourself 'in → DO SB IN 2

,do sth 'out (*BrE, informal*) to clean or paint and decorate a room, a house, etc.: *He's done the whole house out in yellows and greens.* ◇ *They had the hall done out in striped wallpaper.*
 ♦ v + n/pron + adv ♦ v + adv + n

,do sb 'out of sth (*informal*) to prevent sb from getting or keeping sth they ought to have, in an unfair or dishonest way: *She tried to do me out of my inheritance.* ◇ *The residents of the home have been done out of a lot of money.*
 ♦ v + n/pron + adv + prep

,do sb 'over (*BrE, informal*) to attack sb and beat them severely: *They threatened to do her over if she didn't pay.*
 ♦ v + n/pron + adv ♦ v + adv + n

,do sth 'over 1 (*BrE, informal*) to enter a house, flat/apartment, etc. by force and steal things from it: *I got back to find the house had been done over.* **NOTE** Often used in the passive. 2 (*AmE*) to do sth again: *Your handwriting is too messy—you'd better do it over* (= write it out again).* ◇ *I'm glad the campaign was successful, but I wouldn't want to do it over.* **SYN** do sth again; redo sth (*more formal*) 3 (*AmE*) to clean or paint and decorate a room, house, etc.: *They've done over the whole store.*
 ♦ 1,3 v + n/pron + adv ♦ v + adv + n
 ♦ 2 v + n/pron + adv

,do 'up; ,do sth 'up (*especially BrE*) to be fastened with buttons, etc.; to fasten or close sth in this way: *This skirt does up at the back.* ◇ *Could you do up my dress?* ◇ *I can't do the zip up.*
 OBJ jacket, buttons, zip **SYN** fasten up, fasten sth up (*BrE*); fasten, fasten sth **OPP** undo, undo sth
 ♦ v + adv ♦ v + adv + n ♦ v + n/pron + adv

,do sth 'up 1 (*in sth*) to make sth into a package: *She was carrying some books done up in brown paper.* **SYN** wrap sth up (*in sth*) 2 (*especially BrE*) to repair or decorate a room, a house, etc. to make it look better and more modern: *They're looking for an old house so that they can do it up.* ◇ *We're having the kitchen done up.* **OBJ** house **SYN** fix sth up (*especially AmE*); decorate sth; renovate sth
 ♦ v + n/pron + adv ♦ v + adv + n

,do yourself 'up (*informal*) to make yourself more attractive by putting on make-up, attractive clothes, etc.: *She spent hours doing herself up for their first date.*
 SYN doll yourself up
 ♦ v + pron + adv

'do with sb/sth
 ♦ v + prep
 IDM be/have 'done with it to finish dealing with sth unpleasant, especially as quickly as possible: *Just tear up the contract and be done with it.* **I, you, etc. can't/couldn't be 'doing with sth/sth** (*BrE, informal*) used to say that you do not like sb/sth and find them/it very annoying: *I can't be doing with people like that.* ◇ *He couldn't be doing with her untidiness.* **I, you, etc. could 'do with sth/sb** used to say that you need or would like sth/sb: *I could do with a drink!*

'do sth with sth used with negatives and in questions to talk about where sb has put sth: *What have you done with my shoes?* ◇ *I haven't done anything with your keys* (= I haven't moved them).
 ♦ v + pron + prep

'do sth with yourself used in questions to talk about how sb spends their time: *She doesn't know what to do with herself while they're at school.*
 ♦ v + pron + prep + pron

,do with'out; ,do with'out sb/sth to manage without sb/sth: *If you can't afford a car, you'll just have to do without.* ◇ *I could do without* (= I wish I didn't have) *all this hassle.*
 SYN go without, go without sth
 ♦ v + adv ♦ v + prep

dob /dɒb; *AmE* dɑːb/ (**-bb-**)

,dob sb 'in (to sb) (*BrE, AustralE, informal*) to tell sb about sb bad that another person has done: *Kay wasn't sure who had dobbed her in to the teachers.*
 ♦ v + n/pron + adv

dole /dəʊl; *AmE* doʊl/

,dole sth 'out (to sb) (*informal*) to give money, food, etc. to a group of people: *She quickly doled out the food.* ◇ *The money was doled out to them on a weekly basis.*
 OBJ money, bread, etc.
 ♦ v + adv + n ♦ v + pron + adv
 ♦ v + n + adv (*less frequent*)

doll /dɒl; *AmE* dɑːl/

,doll yourself 'up (*in sth*) (*informal*) to make yourself look attractive by putting on fashionable clothes, doing your hair, etc.: *Every Friday she dolls herself up and goes out to a nightclub.*
 SYN do yourself up
 ♦ v + pron + adv

be/get ,dolled 'up (*in sth*) (*informal*) to be/get ready for a special occasion by putting on fashionable clothes, doing your hair, etc.: *She was all dolled up in a black dress and pearls.* ◇ *I got dolled up for the party.*
 ♦ be/get + v + adv

dope /dəʊp; *AmE* doʊp/

be/get ,doped 'up (*informal, especially AmE*) to be in a state where you cannot think clearly or act normally because you are under the influence of drugs: *Some of the patients were kept doped up most of the time.*

◆ be/get + v + adv

dose /dəʊs; AmE doʊs/

ˌdose sb/yourself ˈup (with sth) to give sb/ yourself a large amount of a medicine: *She dosed him up with aspirin and sent him to bed.*

NOTE **Dose sb/yourself** is used more often with the same meaning.

◆ v + n/pron + adv

doss /dɒs; AmE dɑːs/

ˌdoss aˈbout/aˈround (BrE, informal) to spend your time doing nothing or very little: *Everyone dosses about in geography classes. ◇ He just dossed around for a year before he got a job.*

◆ v + adv

ˌdoss ˈdown (BrE, informal) to sleep on the floor or somewhere uncomfortable because you have nowhere else to sleep: *We dossed down on Tony's floor after the party.*

SYN **bed down** (BrE, more formal)

NOTE **Doss** is sometimes used on its own with the same meaning.

◆ v + adv

dot /dɒt; AmE dɑːt/ (-tt-)

be ˌdotted aˈbout/aˈround; be ˌdotted aˈbout/aˈround sth (especially BrE) if things or people are **dotted about/around**, they are in several different places over an area: *A few farms were dotted about in the valley.*

◆ be + v + adv ◆ be + v + prep

ˈdot A on/over B; ˈdot B with A to spread very small amounts of sth in different places on a surface: *Dot the suncream on your face in tiny quantities and rub it in well. ◇ Dot the top of the cake with small sweets.*

◆ v + n/pron + prep

be ˈdotted with sth if an area is **dotted with** things or people, they are spread around in several places: *The hillside was dotted with houses.*

◆ be + v + prep

dote /dəʊt; AmE doʊt/

ˈdote on sb (also ˈdote upon sb more formal) to feel or show very great love for sb and ignore their faults: *They dote on their daughter. ◇ He was doted on (by his sisters).*

OBJ **daughter**, **child**, **mother**, etc.

◆ v + prep

double /ˈdʌbl/

ˈdouble as sth; ˌdouble ˈup as sth to have a second function in addition to the main use: *The garage doubles as his workshop. ◇ The school secretary doubled up as the nurse.*

◆ v + prep ◆ v + adv + prep

ˌdouble ˈback (on yourself, itself, etc.) to turn around and go back in the direction you have come from: *The road ahead was flooded so we had to double back to find another way around. ◇ The line of trees doubles back on itself at a bend in the river.*

◆ v + adv

ˌdouble ˈover, etc. → DOUBLE UP/OVER, ETC.

ˌdouble sth ˈover to bend or fold sth in the middle: *Use an A4 sheet doubled over.*

◆ v + n/pron + adv ◆ v + adv + n

ˌdouble ˈup 1 (with sb/on sth) to form pairs in order to share sth: *We've only got one room left; you'll have to double up with Peter. ◇ There were enough guitarists to double up on parts (= two played each part).* 2 (on sth) (rare) to do sth in addition to your main role: *The band are looking for a singer who can double up on guitar (= who can also play the guitar).*

◆ v + adv

ˌdouble ˈup as sth → DOUBLE AS STH, ETC.

ˌdouble ˈup/ˈover (in/with sth), ˌdouble sb ˈup/ˈover (in/with sth) to bend your body suddenly or quickly because you are in pain, for example; to make sb bend their body in this way: *He doubled up in/with pain. ◇ She doubled up with laughter. ◇ The punch hit him in the stomach, doubling him over.*

◆ v + adv ◆ v + n/pron + adv ◆ v + adv + n (rare)

doze /dəʊz; AmE doʊz/

ˌdoze ˈoff to go to sleep, especially during the day: *He dozed off during the film. ◇ I must have dozed off for a few minutes.*

SYN **nod off** (informal)

◆ v + adv

draft (also draught especially BrE) /drɑːft; AmE dræft/

ˌdraft sb ˈin; ˌdraft sb ˈinto sth to choose people and send them somewhere for a special task: *Extra police are being drafted in to control the crowds. ◇ Williams was drafted into the team to play France.*

◆ v + adv + n ◆ v + n/pron + adv
◆ v + n + adv (less frequent) ◆ v + n/pron + prep

drag /dræg/ (-gg-)

ˌdrag sb/sth/yourself aˈway (from sb/sth) to make sb or yourself stop doing sth when they/ you do not really want to: *She was enjoying herself at the party so much, I couldn't drag her away. ◇ I find it difficult to drag myself away from my computer. ◇ He couldn't **drag his eyes away** from her face.*

SYN **tear sb/sth/yourself away** (from sb/sth)

◆ v + n/pron + adv

ˌdrag sb/sth ˈdown 1 (to sth) to bring sb down to a lower standard of behaviour, or a lower social or economic level: *I'm worried the other children will be dragged down to his level*

(= because his behaviour is so bad). **2** to make sb feel depressed or weak: *Her parents' constant criticism began to drag her down.*

◆ v + n/pron + adv ◆ v + adv + n (*less frequent*)

ˌdrag sb/sth 'in; **ˌdrag sb/sth 'into sth 1** to make sb or sth become involved in a difficult or unpleasant situation when they do not want to be involved: *When violence breaks out in the streets, innocent people are always dragged in.* ◇ *Don't drag me into your argument!* **SYN involve sb** (**in sth**) (*more formal*) **2** to start talking about a person or a subject that has nothing to do with what is being talked about: *Do you have to drag politics into every conversation?*

◆ v + n/pron + adv ◆ v + adv + n ◆ v + n/pron + prep

ˌdrag sb 'off (**to sth**) to take sb somewhere by force: *I was dragged off to the head teacher's office.*

◆ v + n/pron + adv

ˌdrag 'on (*disapproving*) to progress very slowly and take too long: *The day dragged on interminably.* ◇ *Negotiations between the two sides dragged on through the summer.* **SUBJ months**, **time**, **meeting**, **negotiations**

◆ v + adv

ˌdrag sth 'out to make sth last longer than it should: *She dragged the meeting out for as long as possible.*

SYN prolong sth (*more formal*)

◆ v + n/pron + adv ◆ v + adv + n

ˌdrag sth 'out of sb to make sb give you information they do not want to give you: *They eventually dragged a confession out of her.*

OBJ confession, **truth**

◆ v + n/pron + adv + prep

ˌdrag 'up; **ˌdrag sb/yourself 'up** (*informal*) to dress in clothes which are usually worn by the opposite sex, often to entertain people; to dress sb in this way: *He did a karaoke number dragged up as Kylie Minogue.*

◆ v + adv ◆ v + n/pron + adv ◆ v + adv + n

ˌdrag sth 'up to mention in a conversation an unpleasant fact from the past that sb would prefer to forget: *It all happened years ago. There's no point dragging it up now.* ◇ *She's dragged up that story just to embarrass me.*

SYN bring sth up

◆ v + n/pron + adv ◆ v + adv + n

dragoon /drəˈɡuːn/

draˈgoon sb into sth; **draˈgoon sb into doing sth** (*formal* or *humorous*) to force sb to do sth that they do not want to do: *We were dragooned into the football team.*

NOTE Usually used in the passive.

◆ v + n/pron + prep

drain /dreɪn/

ˌdrain aˈway (of feelings or colours) to disappear gradually: *As she lay in the warm bath all the*

tension drained away. ◇ *The colour had drained away from her face.* **SUBJ anger SYN fade**

◆ v + adv

ˌdrain aˈway/ˈoff; **ˌdrain sth aˈway/ˈoff** (**from sth**) if a liquid **drains away/off**, or sb **drains it away/off**, it flows away: *The water drained away down the plughole.* ◇ *I drained the water away and hung up the blouse to dry.* ◇ (*figurative*) *Paying for private education for the children was draining away their resources.*

◆ v + adv ◆ v + adv + n ◆ v + n/pron + adv

draught /drɑːft; *AmE* dræft/

ˌdraught sb 'in, etc. (*especially BrE*) → DRAFT SB IN, ETC.

draw /drɔː/ (**drew** /druː/, **drawn** /drɔːn/)

ˌdraw 'back 1 to move away from sb/sth, especially sb/sth that makes you feel frightened: *She drew back from him in case anyone saw her.* **2** (**from sth/from doing sth**) to decide not to do sth, because you are afraid of what might happen: *The government has drawn back from making a commitment to reform the voting system.*

◆ v + adv

ˌdraw sth 'down (*especially AmE*) to reduce the amount of sth, especially money, by using it and spending it: *Higher production costs will draw down cash gains from rising farm prices.*

OBJ funds

◆ v + adv + n ◆ v + n/pron + adv

ˌdraw sth 'down (from sth); **ˌdraw 'down on sth** (*especially AmE, business*) to take money from a fund that a bank, etc. has made available: *If you draw down income from your investment too quickly, it may not last long.*

OBJ income

◆ v + adv + n ◆ v + n/pron + adv ◆ v + adv + prep

ˌdraw 'down on sb (*AmE, slang*) to pull a gun out and point it at sb: *What do you think you're doing, drawing down on a cop?*

◆ v + prep

ˈdraw sth from sth to get sth from a particular source: *Many artists and poets have drawn their inspiration from the landscape.* ◇ *At times of crisis, we drew strength from each other.*

OBJ inspiration, **comfort**, **support**

◆ v + n/pron + prep

ˌdraw 'in (*BrE*) (*usually used in the progressive tenses*) when evenings or nights are **drawing in**, it is gradually becoming darker earlier in the evening because winter is coming: *The nights are drawing in fast now.* ◇ *Evening was already drawing in.* ◇ *It was the end of September and the days had begun to draw in.*

SYN close in OPP draw out (*BrE*)

◆ v + adv

ˌdraw 'in; **ˌdraw 'into sth** (*especially BrE*) if a train **draws in**, or **draws into** a station, it slowly enters a station and stops at the platform: *The London train drew in late.* ◇ *I got to the platform just as the train was drawing into the station.*

SYN **pull in**, **pull into sth** **OPP** **draw out**, **draw out of sth**

♦ v + adv ♦ v + prep

,draw sb 'in; ,draw sb 'into sth; ,draw sb 'into doing sth to make sb become involved or take part in sth, although they do not want to: *I didn't like the book when I started it, but the strange story soon drew me in.* ◇ *I refuse to be drawn into this argument.*

OBJ **conversation**, **discussion**, **argument**, **situation** **SYN** **involve sb** (**in sth**)

NOTE Often used in the passive.

♦ v + n/pron + adv ♦ v + adv + n ♦ v + n/pron + prep

,draw sth 'in if you **draw in** a breath, you breathe deeply or quickly: *She drew in a deep breath at the magical sight of the city below.* ◇ *He drew in his breath sharply.*

OBJ only **a, your, etc. breath**

♦ v + adv + n ♦ v + n/pron + adv

,draw sth 'off to remove some liquid from a larger amount: *He drew off a glass of beer.*

♦ v + n/pron + adv ♦ v + adv + n

,draw 'on (of a time or a season) to slowly pass: *As night drew on, it became clear he wasn't coming.*

♦ v + adv

'draw on sth 1 (also 'draw upon sth *more formal*) to use sth that you have or that is available to help you do sth: *The assignment asked us to draw on our experiences while we were in England.* ◇ *I'll have to draw on my savings to pay for the car.* ◇ *Sections of the book should be drawn on as required.* **OBJ** **experience**, **work**, **resources**, **savings**, **tradition 2** if you **draw on** a cigarette or a pipe, etc., you breathe smoke into your mouth from it: *He drew on his cigar.* **OBJ** **cigar**, **cigarette**, **pipe**

♦ v + prep

,draw 'out (*BrE*) (*usually used in the progressive tenses*) when evenings or nights are **drawing out**, it is gradually becoming lighter for longer in the evening because spring is coming: *After March the evenings started drawing out.*

OPP **draw in** (*BrE*)

♦ v + adv

,draw 'out; ,draw 'out of sth (*especially BrE*) if a train **draws out** or **draws out of** a station, it begins to move and slowly leaves the station: *I arrived in time to see the train drawing out.* ◇ *The train drew slowly out of the station.*

SYN **pull out**, **pull out of sth** **OPP** **draw in**, **draw into sth**

♦ v + adv ♦ v + adv + prep

,draw sb 'out to encourage sb who is shy to talk freely: *I tried to draw him out on the subject of his life in Africa.*

♦ v + n/pron + adv

,draw sth 'out to make sth such as a meeting or an event last longer than usual or longer than it should: *They drew the interview out to over an hour.* ◇ *The process is likely to be drawn out over several months.*

♦ v + n/pron + adv ♦ v + adv + n

▸ ,drawn-'out (*also* ,long-drawn-'out, 'long-drawn *less frequent*) adj lasting longer than you expect or too long: *The negotiations were difficult and drawn-out.* ◇ *It was another long-drawn-out meeting.*

,draw sth 'out; ,draw sth 'out of sth to take money out of a bank account: *How much money did you draw out?* ◇ *Several thousand pounds had been drawn out of the account.*

SYN **take sth out**, **take sth out of sth**; **withdraw sth** (**from sth**) (*more formal*)

♦ v + n/pron + adv ♦ v + adv + n ♦ v + n/pron + adv + prep

,draw 'up; ,draw sth/sb 'up to come to a stop; to make sth/sb/yourself stop: *A taxi drew up outside.* ◇ *He drew the car up at the front door.* ◇ *He was walking towards the door when a loud knock drew him up sharply.*

SYN **pull up**; **pull sb up**; **pull yourself up**

♦ v + adv ♦ v + n/pron + adv

,draw sth 'up 1 to make or write sth that needs careful planning: *My solicitor is drawing up the contract.* ◇ *Clear guidelines need to be drawn up.* ◇ *We've drawn up a plan of action.* **OBJ** **contract**, **agreement**, **plan** **SYN** **formulate sth** (*more formal*) 2 to bring sth nearer to sb/sth: *She drew up another chair and sat with them.* ◇ *He drew his knees up to his chest.* **OBJ** **chair**, **knees** **SYN** **pull sth up**

♦ v + adv + n ♦ v + n/pron + adv

,draw yourself 'up to stand up very straight so that you are as tall as possible: *She **drew herself up to her full height** and glared at me.*

SYN **pull yourself up**

♦ v + pron + adv

'draw upon sth → DRAW ON STH 1

dream /driːm/ (**dreamt**, **dreamt** /dremt/ or **dreamed**, **dreamed**)

,dream sth a'way to spend time in a lazy way, thinking about things you would like to do but not actually doing anything: *She dreamt her life away, never really achieving anything.*

OBJ **life**

♦ v + n/pron + adv ♦ v + adv + n

'dream of sth to imagine and think about sth that you would like to happen: *She dreams of running her own business.* ◇ *It was the kind of trip most of us only dream about.*

♦ v + prep

IDM **wouldn't 'dream of sth/of doing sth** used to emphasize the fact that you would not even think about doing sth: *'Don't go without me, will you?' 'I wouldn't dream of it!'*

▶ un'dreamed-of (*BrE also* **un'dreamt-of**) *adj* much more or much better than you thought was possible: *undreamed-of happiness*

,**dream 'on** (*informal*) used to tell sb that you are certain that what they have just said will not happen: *You want a pay rise? Dream on!*
◆ v + adv

,**dream sth 'up** (*informal*) to have an idea or think of a plan, especially one that is not very practical: *The scheme was dreamed up by a local businessman.* ◇ *Trust you to dream up a crazy idea like this!*
OBJ **idea, scheme** ⊃ note at THINK STH UP
◆ v + adv + n ◆ v + pron + adv ◆ v + n + adv (*rare*)

dredge /dredʒ/

,**dredge sth 'up** (*usually disapproving*) **1** to mention sth that sb has forgotten or wants to forget because it is unpleasant or embarrassing: *She always dredges up that embarrassing story.*
OBJ **the past 2** to remember sth or to do sth with difficulty: *She was dredging up the little she knew about babies.* ◇ *He managed to dredge up a smile.*
◆ v + adv + n ◆ v + pron + adv
◆ v + n + adv (*less frequent*)

dress /dres/

,**dress 'down** (**in sth**) to wear clothes that are less formal than those you usually wear or those that are usually worn in a particular situation: *He deliberately dressed down for the party.* ◇ *More and more people are dressing down for the office these days.*
OPP **dress up** (**in sth**)
◆ v + adv
▶ '**dress-down** *adj* [only before noun] (*business*): *The company has a dress-down Friday* (= staff are allowed to wear clothes that are less formal than normal).

,**dress sb 'down** to criticize sb angrily for sth wrong that they have done: *The sergeant dressed down the new recruits.*
◆ v + adv + n ◆ v + n/pron + adv
▶ ,**dressing-'down** *n* [sing.] (*old-fashioned*, *informal*) an occasion when sb speaks angrily to a person because they have done sth wrong

,**dress 'up** (**as sb/sth**), ,**dress sb/yourself 'up** (**as sb/sth**) to put on special clothes in order to pretend to be sb else: *The kids love dressing up.* ◇ *They dressed themselves up as cartoon characters.* ◇ (*BrE*) *dressing-up clothes* ◇ (*AmE*) *dress-up clothes*
◆ v + adv ◆ v + n/pron + adv
◆ v + adv + n (*less frequent*)

,**dress 'up** (**in sth**), ,**dress yourself 'up** (**in sth**) to wear special or more formal clothes than you usually do or than those usually worn in a particular situation: *Don't bother to dress up— come as you are.* ◇ *She dressed herself up in a grey suit for the court appearance.*

OPP **dress down** (**in sth**) ⊃ note at PUT STH ON
◆ v + adv ◆ v + pron + adv

,**dress sth 'up** (**as sth**) to make sth seem different or better than it really is by the way that you present it: *You're sacking me. Don't try to dress it up as a career move.*
◆ v + n/pron + adv ◆ v + adv + n

drift /drɪft/

,**drift a'part** to become less close or less friendly with sb: *Over the years we just drifted apart.*
◆ v + adv

,**drift 'off** to fall asleep: *She soon drifted off.* ◇ *I drifted off to sleep on the sofa while I was watching the football.*
SYN **doze off**
◆ v + adv

drill /drɪl/

,**drill 'down** to go to deeper levels of an organized set of data on a computer or a website in order to find more detail: *Navigation is good and there's a display to show how far you've drilled down.*
◆ v + adv

,**drill sth 'into sb** to make sb learn or understand sth by repeating it frequently: *We had multiplication tables drilled into us at school.* ◇ *There's no need to drill things into them—they'll learn as they go along.*
SYN **drum sth into sb**
NOTE Often used in the passive.
◆ v + n/pron + prep

drink /drɪŋk/ (**drank** /dræŋk/, **drunk** /drʌŋk/)

,**drink sth 'down** to drink all of sth quickly: *He filled a cup with cold water and drank it down in one gulp.*
◆ v + n/pron + adv ◆ v + adv + n

,**drink 'in sth** to look at, listen to or experience sth with great pleasure and interest: *She wandered the streets, drinking in the atmosphere.* ◇ *His followers drink in every word he says.*
OBJ **sight, view, atmosphere, beauty**
NOTE When the object of **drink in** is a noun, it comes after **in**, but when the object is a pronoun, it comes between **drink** and **in**: *We sat gazing at the view, drinking it all in.* ◆ Not used in the passive.
◆ v + adv + n ◆ v + pron + adv

'**drink to sb/sth** to wish sb/sth good luck, success or happiness, by raising your glass and then drinking: *They all drank to the couple's health.* ◇ *'Things can only get better.' 'I'll drink to that!'*
SYN **toast sb/sth**
◆ v + prep

,**drink 'up**; ,**drink sth 'up** to finish all of a drink: *Drink up. It's time to go.* ◇ *Drink your milk up—it's good for you.* ◇ *drinking-up time*

(= the time allowed in pubs in Britain to finish your drink after the bar has closed)

NOTE Not used in the passive.

✦ v + adv ✦ v + n/pron + adv ✦ v + adv + n

drive /draɪv/ (**drove** /drəʊv/; *AmE* droʊv/, **driven** /'drɪvn/)

be 'driving at sth to try to express or say sth: *I'm not sure I understand **what you're driving at**.* ◇ *What's he driving at?*

SYN get at sth

NOTE Drive at sth is only used in the progressive tenses and in direct or indirect questions with '*what*'.

✦ v + prep

‚drive a'way/'off; **‚drive sb/sth a'way/'off** (of a car or a driver) to go away in a vehicle; to take sb away in a vehicle: *The cab drove slowly away.* ◇ *There's someone to drive your car away and park it.* ◇ *They were driven away in a police van.*

✦ v + adv ✦ v + n/pron + adv

‚drive sb/sth a'way (**from sth**) to make sb not want to go to a particular place or be with a particular person; to make sb/sth leave a place: *Rising prices are driving customers away.* ◇ *His violent behaviour has driven all his family away.*

OBJ business, customers

✦ v + n/pron + adv ✦ v + adv + n

‚drive sb/sth 'in (in baseball) to hit the ball in such a way that a runner can score: *Ramirez drove in three runs in the second inning.*

✦ v + n/pron + adv ✦ v + adv + n

‚drive 'off (in golf) to hit the ball to begin a game

✦ v + adv

‚drive 'off; **‚drive sb/sth 'off** → DRIVE AWAY/ OFF, DRIVE SB/STH AWAY/OFF: *The van drove off at high speed.* ◇ *The car was driven off at speed.* ◇ *Then he drove her off to the airport.*

‚drive sb/sth 'off; **‚drive sb/sth 'off sth** to force sb/sth to move away from a particular place: *The army was driven off by the fierce attacks of the rebels.* ◇ *We were driven off the island by the new owner.*

✦ v + n/pron + adv ✦ v + adv + n
✦ v + n/pron + prep

‚drive 'on to continue driving either without stopping or after stopping for a short time: *We drove on until we came to an open square full of cafes.* ◇ *Paula stopped to let Philip out of the car before driving on.*

✦ v + adv

‚drive sb/sth 'out; **‚drive sb/sth 'out of sth** to make sb/sth leave or disappear: *They're hoping that their competitive prices will drive out the rival company.* ◇ *They tried to drive her out of the village.*

✦ v + n/pron + adv ✦ v + adv + n
✦ v + n/pron + adv + prep

drone /drəʊn; *AmE* droʊn/

‚drone 'on (**about sth**) to talk about sth for a long time in a boring way: *I nearly fell asleep while he was droning on!* ◇ *She droned on for hours about the uses of the present tense.*

✦ v + adv

drool /druːl/

'drool over sb/sth to look at sb/sth in a way that shows you like and admire or want them/it, often in a silly or exaggerated way: *He was drooling all over you at the party!* ◇ *The boys drooled over the sports cars in the showroom.*

✦ v + prep

drop /drɒp; *AmE* drɑːp/ (-**pp**-)

‚drop a'round (*AmE*) → DROP BY

‚drop sth a'round (*AmE*) → DROP STH ROUND

‚drop a'way (*especially BrE*) **1** if the ground **drops away**, it slopes down steeply away from where you are: *The seabed suddenly dropped away and I was waist deep in the water.* **2** to become less strong or disappear: *He felt his dark mood dropping away.*

✦ v + adv

‚drop 'back if a person in a group **drops back**, they move to a position further back behind other people, often because they are not able to stay at the front: *The original leader in the race has now dropped back to third place.*

SYN fall back

✦ v + adv

‚drop be'hind; **‚drop be'hind sb/sth** if sb **drops behind** or **drops behind** sb/sth, they move to a position behind other people: *He dropped behind to walk with Sam.* ◇ *We cannot afford to drop behind our competitors.*

SYN fall behind, fall behind sb/sth

✦ v + adv ✦ v + prep

‚drop 'by (*also* **‚drop 'round** *BrE*, **‚drop a'round** *AmE*) (*informal*) to pay a short, informal visit to sb, often without arranging this in advance: *I just dropped by to check you were OK.* ◇ *I'm dropping round to Kate's later.*

SYN call by (*especially BrE*), **stop by** ⮑ note at VISIT WITH SB

→ see also DROP IN (ON SB/AT…), DROP INTO STH; DROP OVER

✦ v + adv

‚drop sth 'by (*AmE*) → DROP STH IN, ETC.

‚drop 'down to lower yourself from a high place: *We climbed the wall and dropped down on the other side.*

✦ v + adv

▶ **'drop-down** *adj* [only before noun] **1** used to describe sth that appears by moving down into view when it is needed: *a drop-down video screen* **2** used to describe a menu that appears on a computer screen when you choose it, and that stays there until you choose one of the functions on it: *a drop-down menu*

▶ **'drop-down** n a drop-down menu: *Select the item you want from the drop-down.*

,**drop 'in** (**on sb/at...**), ,**drop 'into sth** (*informal*) to pay a short, informal visit to sb, often without arranging this in advance: *Drop in any time you're passing.* ◊ *She drops in on her parents at least once a week.* ◊ *I dropped into the pub for a quick drink on my way home.*
SYN call in
→ see also DROP BY
◆ v + adv ◆ v + prep

▶ **'drop-in** adj [only before noun] used to describe a place where you can go without making an appointment: *a drop-in centre/surgery/clinic*

,**drop sb/yourself 'in it** (*BrE, informal*) to put sb in a difficult or embarrassing situation: *She got herself out of trouble by dropping Laura in it.*
◆ v + n/pron + prep + it

,**drop sth 'in** (**to sb/sth**), ,**drop sth 'into sth** (*especially BrE*) (*AmE usually* ,**drop sth 'by**) (*informal*) to deliver sth, especially when you are on the way to somewhere else: *She dropped the report in on her way out.* ◊ *I'll drop a note in to you when I know the arrangements.* ◊ *Could you drop my coat into the cleaner's on your way to work?* ◊ *I'll drop the brochures by later.*
◆ v + n/pron + adv ◆ v + adv + n ◆ v + n/pron + prep

,**drop 'into sth** → DROP IN (ON SB/AT...), ETC.
,**drop sth 'into sth** → DROP STH IN, ETC.

,**drop 'off 1** (*informal, especially BrE*) to fall into a light sleep: *He's always dropping off in front of the TV.* **SYN** doze off; nod off (*informal*) **2** if a number, an amount or a quality **drops off**, it decreases: *The numbers applying for membership have dropped off sharply.* **SYN** fall off
◆ v + adv

▶ **'drop-off** (**in sth**) n a decrease: *Managers are concerned by a recent drop-off in sales.*

☝,**drop sb/sth 'off** to stop and let sb get out of a car, etc.; to deliver sth to a place, often when you are on the way to somewhere else: *Could you drop me off at the station?* ◊ *I'm going past Jan's house—I could drop the cake off.* ◊ *She dropped off some clothes at the dry-cleaner's.*
◆ v + n/pron + adv ◆ v + adv + n

▶ **'drop-off** n a place where vehicles can stop for people to get out, or where sth can be left; the action of doing this: *It is easier to get a taxi at passenger **drop-off points** than at flight arrival stands.*

☝,**drop 'out**; ,**drop 'out of sth 1** to stop taking part in an activity, being a member of a group, etc.: *Several members of the team had to drop out at the last minute.* ◊ *She had to drop out of the race halfway through.* ◊ *The company had to drop out of the deal due to rising costs.* **SYN** pull out, pull out of sth; withdraw (from sth) (*more formal*) **2** to leave school, college, university, etc. without finishing your studies: *She dropped out of college after only a few weeks.* ◊ *Many*

students drop out or fail because they're not enjoying the course. **3** to reject the accepted ideas, morals and values of society: *There's a danger that when people lose their jobs they drop out (of society) altogether.*
◆ v + adv ◆ v + adv + prep

▶ **'dropout** n **1** a person who leaves school, college or university before they have finished their studies: *He might be a college dropout but he's made a fortune in business.* ◊ *There is a high **dropout rate** from some college courses.* **2** (*disapproving, especially BrE*) a person who rejects the accepted ideas, morals and values of society: *Many of the town's dropouts hang around the square.*

,**drop 'over** (*especially AmE*) to visit sb for a short time at their home, without arranging a time in advance: *I think I'll just drop over to Jim's for a while.* ◊ *Why don't you drop over this evening?*
SYN pop over/round
→ see also DROP BY
◆ v + adv

,**drop 'round** (*BrE*) → DROP BY
,**drop sth 'round** (*BrE*) (*AmE* ,**drop sth a'round**) (*informal*) to deliver sth to sb's home, etc.: *I'll drop those papers round later.*
→ see also DROP STH IN (TO SB/STH), DROP STH INTO STH
◆ v + n/pron + adv

drown /draʊn/

,**drown sb/sth 'out** if a sound **drowns out** sb/sth, it is so loud that they/it cannot be heard: *The music was playing at full volume, drowning out conversation.* ◊ *Her reply was drowned out by a passing motorbike.* **SUBJ** noise, sound, roar, music
NOTE Drown sb/sth can also be used with the same meaning: *Her voice was drowned by the crashing waves.*
◆ v + adv + n ◆ v + pron + adv
◆ v + n + adv (*less frequent*)

drum /drʌm/ (**-mm-**)

,**drum sth 'into sb** to make sb remember sth by repeating it often: *He drummed road safety into them before letting them out on their bicycles.* ◊ *Traditional values were drummed into him from an early age.* ◊ *I had it drummed into me that I shouldn't talk to strangers.*
SYN drill sth into sb
◆ v + n/pron + prep

,**drum sb 'out**; ,**drum sb 'out of sth** to force sb to leave a group or an organization, usually because they have done sth wrong: *He was drummed out of the club.*
SYN throw sb out, throw sb out of sth
◆ v + n/pron + adv ◆ v + n/pron + adv + prep

,**drum sth 'up** to work hard to get sth: *We're launching a campaign to drum up more business.*

◇ *We couldn't drum up enough cash to keep the club going.*
[OBJ] **business, support, customers**
♦ v + adv + n ♦ v + pron + adv ♦ v + n + adv (*rare*)

dry /draɪ/ (**dries, drying, dried**)

,dry 'off; ,dry sb/sth 'off; ,dry yourself 'off
to become dry; to make sb/sth/yourself dry: *We lay beside the pool to dry off in the sun.* ◇ *You can use this towel to dry yourself off.* ◇ *I dried the car off with a soft cloth.*
♦ v + adv ♦ v + n/pron + adv ♦ v + adv + n

,dry 'out; ,dry sb 'out (*informal*) to receive treatment to help you stop drinking alcohol or taking drugs; to cure sb of drinking too much alcohol or of taking drugs: *She went into a clinic to dry out.*
♦ v + adv ♦ v + n/pron + adv

,dry 'out; ,dry sth 'out to become very or too dry; to make sth become very or too dry: *Water the plant regularly and don't let the soil dry out.* ◇ *The wind and the sun had dried out my skin.*
♦ v + adv ♦ v + n/pron + adv ♦ v + adv + n

,dry 'up **1** if a supply of sth **dries up**, it is no longer available: *The plan was abandoned when the money dried up.* [SUBJ] **investment, supply, funds** [SYN] **run out 2** (*informal*) to stop talking suddenly because you cannot remember what to say next or are very nervous: *She dried up during the second act.* ◇ *I just dried up halfway through the interview.* **3** (*informal*) used to tell sb rudely to be quiet or stop talking
♦ v + adv

🔒,dry 'up; ,dry sth 'up **1** if a river or a lake, etc. **dries up**, or sth **dries it up**, it becomes completely dry: *The well dried up for the first time in a century.* ◇ *The sun dried up all the puddles.* **2** (*BrE, informal*) to dry dishes after they have been washed: *I'll dry up if you wash the dishes.* ◇ *He dried all the dishes up and put them away.* [NOTE] **Dry** and **dry sth** are also used on their own.
♦ v + adv ♦ v + adv + n ♦ v + pron + adv
♦ v + n + adv (*rare*)
▶ ,dried 'up *adj* **1** completely dry: *They camped in a dried-up river bed.* **2** [only before noun] (*disapproving*) (of a person) old, with many folds and lines on the skin, small and usually bitter or bad-tempered: *The librarian was a dried-up, bitter old man.*
▶ ,drying-'up *n* [U] (*BrE, informal*) the act of drying dishes after they have been washed: *to do the drying-up*

duck /dʌk/

,duck 'out; ,duck 'out of sth; ,duck 'out of doing sth (*informal*) to avoid a responsibility or duty, especially an unpleasant one: *She ducked out of visiting him in hospital.* ◇ *You have to go, so don't try ducking out.*

[NOTE] **Duck** can be used with an object with the same meaning: *Don't try to duck the issue.*
♦ v + adv ♦ v + adv + prep

dude /duːd/

,dude yourself 'up (*AmE, slang*) to make yourself more attractive and try to impress people by wearing expensive or special clothes: *He really duded himself up for the party.*
♦ v + pron + adv

duff /dʌf/

,duff sb 'up (*BrE, informal*) to hit or kick sb severely: *A couple of guys duffed him up.*
[SYN] **beat sb up**
♦ v + n/pron + adv

duke /djuːk; *AmE* duːk/

,duke it 'out (with sb) (*AmE, slang*) to fight with sb using your hands tightly closed: *You can't settle every argument by duking it out.* ◇ (*figurative*) *You'll have to duke it out over the last cookie.*
♦ v + it + adv

dumb /dʌm/

,dumb 'down; ,dumb sth 'down (*disapproving*) to make sth too simple and therefore less accurate and of poorer quality, by trying to make it easier for people to understand: *The programme producers claimed they had to dumb down.* ◇ *The new producer has really dumbed the show down.*
♦ v + adv ♦ v + n/pron + adv ♦ v + adv + n
▶ ,dumbing 'down *n* [U] the act or policy of making sth too simple and therefore less accurate and of poorer quality

dummy /dʌmi/ (**dummies, dummying, dummied**)

,dummy 'up (*AmE*) to say nothing: *If he dummies up, just try a little persuasion.*
[SYN] **clam up**
♦ v + adv

dump /dʌmp/

'dump on sb (*slang*) **1** to treat sb unfairly, especially by giving them too much to do or unpleasant tasks: *The boss dumps on Jane and she dumps on the junior staff.* **2** (*AmE*) to criticize sb and make them feel unimportant or stupid: *Quit dumping on me, I'm trying my best.* ◇ *Why do I always get dumped on?*
♦ v + prep

'dump on sb; 'dump sth on sb (*slang, especially AmE*) to tell sb all your problems: *He dumps on me every time she throws him out.* ◇ *She keeps phoning me and dumping all her problems on me.*
♦ v + prep ♦ v + n/pron + prep

dwindle away

dwindle away ◆ fall away ◆ fall off ◆ tail off
◆ taper off

These are all verbs that can be used when the amount or number of sth goes down gradually. *See also* **die down**, **peter out**.

dwindle away to become gradually less in number or amount: *Support for the party slowly dwindled away to nothing.*
NOTE **Dwindle** can be used on its own: *Membership of the club has dwindled from 70 to 20.*

fall away to become gradually fewer or smaller; to disappear: *The market for their products fell away to almost nothing.* ◇ *All our doubts fell away.*

fall off to become gradually lower or less in level or number: *Attendance at my lectures*

has fallen off considerably. ◇ *Public interest started to fall off after a while.*

tail off (*especially BrE*) (of a number, level or sb's voice) to become smaller or weaker: *The number of tourists tails off in October.* ◇ *'But why...?' Her voice tailed off in disappointment.*

taper off to become gradually less in number, amount, etc.: *The number of applicants for teaching posts has tapered off.*

PATTERNS AND COLLOCATIONS

- the **number/level of sth** dwindles (away)/falls away/falls off/tails off/tapers off
- **support** dwindles (away)/tails off
- sb's **voice** tails off
- to dwindle (away)/fall away/fall off/tail off/ taper off **gradually/slowly**

dust /dʌst/

,dust sb/sth 'off; ,dust yourself 'off (*BrE also* ,dust sb/sth 'down, ,dust yourself 'down) to remove the dust or dirt from sb/sth/yourself, for example with your hand or a brush: *She stood up and dusted herself down.*
→ see also DUST YOURSELF OFF
◆ v + n/pron + adv ◆ v + adv + n

,dust sth 'off (*BrE also* ,dust sth 'down) to bring sth out after it has not been used for a long time and start to use it again: *The government is dusting off its plans for offshore gas and oil exploration.* ◇ *Some of their early songs have been brought out and dusted down for re-release.*
◆ v + adv + n ◆ v + pron + adv
◆ v + n + adv (*less frequent*)

,dust yourself 'off (*BrE also* ,dust yourself 'down) to recover after a difficult or unpleasant experience and begin again: *After a disappointment I just dust myself down and start again.*
→ see also DUST SB/STH OFF, DUST YOURSELF OFF
◆ v + pron + adv

dwell /dwel/ (dwelt, dwelt or dwelled, dwelled)

'dwell on sth (*also* 'dwell upon sth *more formal*)
1 to think or talk about sth for too long, especially sth unpleasant: *It's time you stopped dwelling on the past.* **OBJ** the past, problems
2 (*literary*) to look at sth for a long time: *He smiled, his eyes dwelling on her face.*
◆ v + prep

dwindle /'dwɪndl/

,dwindle a'way (to sth) to become gradually less or smaller: *The audience for this kind of music has dwindled away to nothing.*
◆ v + adv

E e

ease /iːz/

,ease 'back **1** (*business*) if profits, prices, etc. **ease back**, they become a little lower, especially after they have been high: *The company's profits eased back from £15.1 million to £14.7 million.*
2 (**on sth**) if sb **eases back**, they go a little slower, do sth with a little less energy, are less strict, etc. than before: *The team played aggressively in the first half of the game, but were able to ease back in the second.* ◇ *The government should ease back on farming restrictions.*
◆ v + adv

,ease 'back into sth; ,ease sb/yourself 'back into sth to gradually become familiar again with sth you have not done for some time; to help sb become familiar again with sth they used to do: *Smith is gradually easing back into running after his injury.* ◇ *It's time to ease the kids back into the school routine.*
→ see also EASE INTO STH, ETC.
◆ v + adv + prep ◆ v + n/pron + adv + prep

,ease 'into sth; ,ease sb/yourself 'into sth to gradually become, or help sb become, familiar with sth new, especially a new job: *to ease into retirement* ◇ *a course for easing people into the world of computing*

→ see also EASE BACK INTO STH, ETC.
- v + prep ♦ v + n/pron + prep

ease 'off 1 to gradually become less strong or unpleasant: *Eventually the rain started to ease off.* ◇ *The pain eased off after a few hours.* **2** to go slower or make less effort: *He eased off in the last lap and still won.* SYN **slack off**
- v + adv

ease sb 'out; **ease sb 'out of sth** to make sb leave their job or position, especially by making it difficult or unpleasant for them over a period of time: *He was eased out of his job as presidential adviser.* NOTE Often used in the passive.
- v + n/pron + adv ♦ v + adv + n
- v + n/pron + adv + prep

ease 'up 1 (on sth) to go slower or make less effort; to do sth less: *The doctor told him to ease up.* ◇ *I'd ease up on the training a bit if I were you.* **2 (on sb)** to start being less severe with sb: *I think you should ease up on the kids a bit.*
- v + adv

eat /iːt/ (**ate** /et, eɪt; *especially AmE*)/, **eaten** /'iːtn/

eat sth a'way to gradually damage or destroy sth over a period of time: *Something was eating away the foliage.* ◇ *The stone had been eaten away by pollution.* ◇ *The sea is eating away the coastline.*
- v + adv + n ♦ v + n/pron + adv

eat a'way at sb to worry sb over a long period of time: *Jealousy is eating away at him.*
- v + adv + prep

eat a'way at sth to gradually damage or destroy sth over a period of time: *Pollution is eating away at the stone.* ◇ *Resentment ate away at their relationship.*
→ see also EAT STH AWAY
- v + adv + prep

eat 'in 1 to have a meal at home rather than at a restaurant: *Are you eating in tonight?* OPP **eat out 2** (*also* **eat sth 'in**) (*especially BrE*) to buy and eat food at a restaurant, rather than taking it away to eat: *Is this food to eat in or take away?* OPP **take sth away** (*especially BrE*)
- **1** v + adv
- **2** also v + n/pron + adv

eat 'into sth 1 to gradually damage or destroy sth: *Woodworm had eaten into most of the furniture.* **2** to use or take away a large part of sth valuable, especially money or time: *My work began to eat into the weekends.* OBJ **profits**, **time**
- v + prep

eat 'out to have a meal in a restaurant, etc. rather than at home: *We ate out almost every night.* SYN **dine out** (*formal*) OPP **eat in**
- v + adv

eat 'up used to tell sb to eat quickly or to eat everything they have been given: *Eat up! You'll be late for school.*
→ see also EAT STH UP 1
- v + adv

eat sb 'up if an emotion such as anger, etc. **eats sb up**, it worries them all the time and they cannot think of anything else: *The anger was eating her up inside.* ◇ *He's eaten up by jealousy.* SYN **consume sb** (*formal*)
NOTE Often used in the passive.
- v + n/pron + adv ♦ v + adv + n

eat sth 'up 1 to eat all the food you have been given: *Eat up your broccoli. It's good for you.*
→ see also EAT UP **2** (*informal, especially BrE*) to use large quantities of sth, for example fuel or electricity: *His extravagance is eating up our profits.* ◇ *The van really eats up petrol/gas.*
- v + adv + n ♦ v + pron + adv ♦ v + n + adv (*rare*)
IDM **eat it 'up** (*AmE, informal*) to be very happy about sth that has happened and want it to happen more: *He started telling jokes, and the audience just ate it up.*

ebb /eb/

ebb a'way to gradually become weaker and begin to disappear: *His confidence ebbed away.* SUBJ **strength**, **enthusiasm**, **anger** ⟳ note at DIE DOWN
- v + adv

edge /edʒ/

edge sb/sth 'out; **edge sb/sth 'out of sth** to gradually move sb out of their job or position, especially by taking their place yourself; to gradually defeat sb: *Be careful he doesn't edge you out of your job altogether.* ◇ *She was edged out of the semi-final by her younger rival.*
- v + n/pron + adv ♦ v + adv + n
- v + n/pron + adv + prep

edge 'up if prices, etc. **edge up**, they gradually increase: *Inflation is edging up.*
- v + adv

edit /'edɪt/

edit sth 'out; **edit sth 'out of sth** to remove words or phrases from a book, programme, etc. before it is published or shown: *The swear words were edited out (of the song).* ◇ *He must have edited a lot of the interview out.* ◇ *Read through your work and edit out anything irrelevant.*
- v + n/pron + adv ♦ v + adv + n
- v + n/pron + adv + prep

edit sth 'down (to sth) to reduce the length of film/movie, report, etc. by taking out parts of it: *We edited several hours of tape down to a short video.*
- v + n/pron + adv ♦ v + adv + n

eff /ef/

,eff 'off (*BrE*, △, *slang*) a rude way of telling sb to go away, used instead of **fuck off**
* v + adv

egg /eg/

,egg sb 'on (**to do sth**) to encourage sb to do sth, especially sth stupid or wrong: *Egged on by his classmates, he climbed a bit higher.* ◇ *The other lads were egging them on to fight.*
SYN urge sb/sth on (**to sth/to do sth**)
* v + n/pron + adv * v + adv + n

eke /iːk/

,eke sth 'out **1** to make a small supply of sth last longer by using only a little at a time or by adding sth else to it: *She eked out the stew to make another meal.* **OBJ** income, supplies
2 ,eke 'out sth (*literary*) to manage to live with very little money: *She eked out a living by selling what she could grow.* **OBJ** living, existence
NOTE Eke out is not used with a pronoun object in this meaning.
* **1** v + adv + n * v + pron + adv
* v + n + adv (*less frequent*)
* **2** v + adv + n

elaborate /ɪˈlæbəreɪt/

e'laborate on/upon sth to explain or describe sth in a more detailed way: *He said he was resigning but did not elaborate on his reasons.*
SYN enlarge on/upon sth
* v + prep

elbow /ˈelbəʊ; *AmE* -boʊ/

,elbow sb/sth a'side/'out; ,elbow sb/sth 'out of sth to force sb or sth out of a position or job: *The story was on the front page, elbowing aside the peace talks.* ◇ *He was elbowed out of power.* ◇ *Germany has elbowed America out of the top slot after just one year.*
* v + adv + n * v + n/pron + adv
* v + n/pron + adv + prep

embark /ɪmˈbɑːk; *AmE* ɪmˈbɑːrk/

em'bark on/upon sth (*formal*) to start to do sth new, important or difficult: *The government has embarked upon a programme of reforms.* ◇ *He travelled for a year, before embarking on graduate studies.*
OBJ programme, career, course, journey
⊃ note at START ON STH
* v + prep

empty /ˈempti/ (**empties, emptying, emptied**)

,empty 'out; ,empty 'out of sth if a place **empties out**, or people **empty out of** a place, it becomes empty of people: *At 11.30 the restaur-*

ant emptied out (= people left it). ◇ *People were emptying out of bars and clubs.*
NOTE Empty and **empty sth** are also used on their own.
* v + adv * v + adv + prep

,empty sth 'out; ,empty sth 'out of sth to remove all the things from inside a container: *He emptied the bag out onto the table.* ◇ *Don't empty the bath water out!* ◇ *I was asked to empty everything out of my pockets.*
NOTE Empty sth is used more frequently on its own than **empty sth out**.
* v + n/pron + adv * v + adv + n
* v + n/pron + adv + prep

encroach /ɪnˈkrəʊtʃ; *AmE* ɪnˈkroʊtʃ/

en'croach on sth (*also* **en'croach upon sth**) (*formal*) **1** to use up too much of sb's time, personal life, etc.; to begin to affect sb: *She tried to prevent her work from encroaching too far on her private life.* **SYN** cut into sth (*less formal*); trespass on sth **2** to gradually spread over more and more of an area: *New housing is starting to encroach upon the surrounding fields.* **OBJ** territory, land
* v + prep

end /end/

'end in sth to have sth as an ending or as a result: *Many adverbs in English end in -ly.* ◇ *His first attempt to run a marathon ended in disaster.* ◇ *The partnership between the two companies could all end in tears* (= have an unhappy result).
OBJ failure, disaster, divorce, a draw
* v + prep

,end 'up; ,end 'up doing sth to reach or come to a particular place or situation that you did not expect or intend to be in: *He ended up in prison.* ◇ *I don't want to end up worse off than when I started.* ◇ *I expect I'll end up paying, as usual.* ◇ *If you drive like that, you could end up dead!*
SYN finish up, finish up doing sth; wind up, wind up doing sth (*informal*)
NOTE Note that this phrasal verb does not mean the same as **end**: *Classes end at 4 p.m.*
* v + adv * v + adv + -ing

endear /ɪnˈdɪə(r); *AmE* -ˈdɪr/

en'dear sb/yourself to sb (*formal*) to make sb/yourself loved or liked by sb: *He managed to endear himself to my entire family.* ◇ *The government's record on employment did not endear them to the voters.*
* v + n/pron + adv + prep

endow /ɪnˈdaʊ/

en'dow sb/sth with sth (*formal*) **1** to give sb sth, such as a particular quality, responsibility, etc.: *They endowed their children with remark-*

able names. ◇ *The job endows its holder with great prestige.* **2** to imagine or believe that sb/sth has a particular quality: *They endowed certain plants with almost magical healing qualities.*

♦ v + n/pron + prep

be en'dowed with sth to naturally have a particular skill, quality, feature, etc.: *He is endowed with both intelligence and good looks.* ◇ *machines endowed with amazing powers* ◇ *The islands are well endowed with ponds, lakes and streams.*

♦ be + v + prep

engage /ɪnˈɡeɪdʒ/

en'gage in sth; **en'gage in doing sth**; **en'gage sb in sth**; **en'gage sb in doing sth** (*formal*) to take part in sth; to make sb take part in sth; to be busy doing sth: *Lecturers engage in teaching and research.* ◇ *She tried to engage him in conversation.* ◇ *He was engaged in running a small business.*

OBJ **activities**, **research**, **business**, **discussion**

♦ v + prep ♦ v + n/pron + prep

be en'gaged on/upon sth (*formal*) to do sth; to be involved in doing sth: *He is engaged on a biography of his father.*

♦ be + v + prep

enlarge /ɪnˈlɑːdʒ; AmE -ˈlɑːrdʒ/

en'large on/upon sth (*formal*) to say or write more about sth you have mentioned: *I'll enlarge on this point later.*

SYN **elaborate on/upon sth**

♦ v + prep

enquire (*also* inquire *especially AmE*) /ɪnˈkwaɪə(r)/

en'quire after sb (*formal*) to ask about sb's health or about what they are doing: *My mother enquired after you and the baby.*

SYN **ask after sb** (*less formal*)

♦ v + prep

en'quire into sth (*formal, especially BrE*) to try to find out the facts about sth: *The committee are enquiring into the employment of children.*

SYN **investigate sth**

♦ v + prep

en'quire sth of sb (*formal*) to ask sb sth: '*Are you able to come with us?*' *she enquired of Will.*

♦ v + n/pron + prep

enter /ˈentə(r)/

'**enter into sth** (*formal*) **1** (**with sb**) to begin to discuss or deal with sth: *The government agreed to enter into negotiations.* ◇ *The examiners cannot enter into any correspondence over the results.* OBJ **negotiations**, **correspondence**, **contract 2** (**with sb**) to begin or become involved in a formal agreement: *The government has entered into an agreement with the World*

Bank. ◇ *It is vital that the contract be freely entered into.* OBJ **agreement 3** to affect a situation or be an important part of it: *Luck didn't enter into it; I won because of my skill.* OBJ **it**

♦ v + prep

'**enter on/upon sth** (*formal*) to make a start on sth; to begin sth: *The economy entered on a period of sustained growth.* ◇ *In 1991, he entered upon a turbulent political career.*

♦ v + prep

entitle /ɪnˈtaɪtl/

en'title sb to sth to give sb a right to have or do sth: *This ticket entitles you to a free meal.* ◇ *All children are entitled to education.* ◇ *I think I'm entitled to an explanation.*

NOTE Often used in the passive.

♦ v + n/pron + prep

entrust /ɪnˈtrʌst/

en'trust A to B; **en'trust B with A** to make sb responsible for doing sth or for taking care of sb: *I couldn't entrust my children to strangers.* ◇ *Can you entrust an assistant with the task?*

♦ v + n/pron + prep

equate /iˈkweɪt/

e'quate to sth to be equal to sth: *Do my qualifications equate to any in your country?* ◇ *Production costs for the movie equated to around 30% of income.*

♦ v + prep

e'quate sth with sth to consider that sth is the same as sth else, or equal in value or importance: *He equates success with material wealth.*

♦ v + n/pron + prep

etch /etʃ/

be 'etched into/on sth; **be 'etched with sth** if a feeling is **etched into/on** sb's face or sb's face is **etched with** a particular feeling, that feeling can be seen very clearly: *Tiredness and despair were etched into his face.* ◇ *Anthea's face was etched with horror.*

♦ be + v + prep

IDM **be etched on your 'heart/'memory/'mind** if sth is **etched on your memory**, you remember it because it has made a very strong impression on you

even /ˈiːvn/

,**even 'out** if sth **evens out**, it becomes level or steady after a period when it has gone up and down or changed a lot: *The path evens out further on.* ◇ *House prices will eventually even out.*

♦ v + adv

fade

,**even sth 'out** to spread sth equally over a number of people or a period of time: *She tried to even out the work among the staff.*
◆ v + adv + n ◆ v + n/pron + adv

,**even sth 'up** to make a situation, a competition, etc. more equal: *If I give you another £5, that will even things up a bit.*
◆ v + n/pron + adv ◆ v + adv + n

expand /ɪkˈspænd/

ex'**pand on sth** (*also* ex'**pand upon sth** *more formal*) to give more information or details about sth you have said or written: *Could you expand on your earlier statement?*
OBJ **point**, **statement**
◆ v + prep

explain /ɪkˈspleɪn/

ex,**plain sth a'way** to give reasons why you should not be blamed for sth or why sth is not as important or as bad as people think: *How will you explain away the loss of two cars?*
◆ v + adv + n ◆ v + n/pron + adv

eye /aɪ/ (**eyeing** or **eying**, **eyed**, **eyed**)

,**eye sb 'up** (*informal, especially BrE*) to look at sb in a way that shows that you are interested in them, especially in a sexual way: *She's eyeing me up as a potential customer.* ◇ *He was eyeing up all the women at the party.*
◆ v + n/pron + adv ◆ v + adv + n

,**eye sth 'up** (*informal, especially BrE*) to look closely at sth, because you want it or are interested in it: *Are you eyeing up that strawberry tart?*
NOTE **Have your eye on sth** has a similar meaning
◆ v + adv + n ◆ v + n/pron + adv

Ff

face /feɪs/

,**face sb 'down** (*especially AmE*) to oppose or defeat sb by dealing with them directly and confidently: *The President is determined to face down his critics.*
◆ v + adv + n ◆ v + n/pron + adv

,**face 'off** (*AmE*) **1** (in ice hockey) to start the game: *The teams face off at 2.30.* **2** to get ready to argue, fight or compete with sb: *The candidates face off in a Democratic primary today.*
◆ v + adv
▶ '**face-off** *n* (*AmE*) **1** (in ice hockey) the beginning of the game **2** an argument or a fight

,**face 'onto sth** if a room or a building **faces onto** sth, the windows look in that direction: *The front bedroom faces onto a main road.*
◆ v + prep

,**face 'up to sth** to accept and deal with a difficult or unpleasant situation: *When is she going to face up to her responsibilities?* ◇ *He must face up to the fact that he is no longer young.* ◇ *This problem has got to be faced up to.*
OBJ **fact**, **reality**, **problem**, **responsibilities**
SYN **square up** (**to sb/sth**)
◆ v + adv + prep

factor /ˈfæktə(r)/

,**factor 'into sth** to have an influence on sth: *The report will factor into the committee's decision.*
◆ v + prep

,**factor sth 'in**; ,**factor sth 'into sth** (*especially AmE*) to include a particular fact or situation when you are calculating sth, or thinking about or planning sth: *When you estimated the cost of the repairs, you forgot to factor in the labour.*
OPP **factor sth out**, **factor sth out of sth**
◆ v + adv + n ◆ v + n/pron + adv ◆ v + n/pron + adv + prep

,**factor sth 'out**; ,**factor sth 'out of sth** (*especially AmE*) to not include a particular fact or situation when you are calculating sth, or thinking about or planning sth: *When inflation is factored out, the trade deficit fell 12.8%.*
OPP **factor sth in**, **factor sth into sth**
◆ v + n/pron + adv ◆ v + adv + n ◆ v + n/pron + adv + prep

fade /feɪd/

,**fade a'way 1** to gradually become less strong, clear or frequent and disappear: *His footsteps gradually faded away.* ◇ *Her enthusiasm will soon fade away.* SYN **die away** NOTE **Fade** can also be used on its own with this meaning, especially in more formal English. ➲ note at PETER OUT **2** (of a person) to become weaker and die: *She's fading away rapidly.*
◆ v + adv

,**fade 'in**; ,**fade sth 'in** if a sound or a picture in a film/movie, etc. **fades in**, or sb **fades it in**, it gradually becomes louder or clearer
OPP **fade out**, **fade sth out**
◆ v + adv ◆ v + n/pron + adv ◆ v + adv + n
▶ '**fade-in** *n* [U, C] an act of gradually making a picture appear at the beginning of a scene in a film/movie

,**fade 'out**; ,**fade 'out of sth** to become quieter, weaker, etc. and gradually disappear: *The protest eventually faded out.* ◇ *She looked a strong candidate, but then faded out of the picture.*
◆ v + adv ◆ v + adv + prep

,**fade 'out**; ,**fade sth 'out** if a sound or a picture in a film/movie, etc. **fades out** or sb **fades it out**, it gradually becomes quieter or less clear: *Near the end of the song he faded out the music.*
OPP **fade in**, **fade sth in**
◆ v + adv ◆ v + n/pron + adv ◆ v + adv + n

▶ **'fade-out** *n* [U, C] an act of gradually making a picture disappear at the end of a scene in a film/movie

faff /fæf/

,**faff a'bout/a'round** (*BrE, informal*) to waste time doing unimportant things and not get very much done: *Stop faffing about.*
◆ v + adv

fake /feɪk/

,**fake sb 'out** (*AmE, informal*) to trick sb; to make sb think you are going to do one thing and then do another: *He thought I was going to turn left, but I faked him out.*
◆ v + n/pron + adv ◆ v + adv + n

fall /fɔːl/ (**fell** /fel/, **fallen** /'fɔːlən/)

,**fall a'bout** (*BrE, informal*) to laugh a lot: *We all fell about at her idea.* ◇ *He's rude to the audience and yet they **fall about laughing**.*
◆ v + adv

⚡,**fall a'part 1** to be old or in bad condition and break or break into pieces: *If you buy cheap shoes, they'll fall apart after a few months.* ◇ *My dictionary is falling apart now.* **SYN come apart 2** to have so many problems that it is no longer possible to exist or operate: *The whole country's falling apart.* ◇ *After my marriage fell apart I moved away.* **3** (*informal*) to have so many problems or worries that you can no longer think or behave normally: *I fell apart when she left.*
◆ v + adv

IDM **be falling apart at the 'seams** to have a lot of problems and be starting to fail

,**fall a'way 1** (**from sth**) to break off or separate from a surface: *The plaster was falling away in* big chunks. **2** (of land, a road, etc.) to slope down: *The ground falls away abruptly to the right.* **3** to gradually disappear: *Gradually, all his cares and worries fell away.* ◇ *When things got difficult, his supporters all fell away.* ➔ note at DWINDLE AWAY **4** (*especially BrE*) to get less or smaller: *The number of applicants has fallen away sharply.* → see also FALL OFF
◆ v + adv

,**fall 'back 1** to fail to stay with people at the front in a race: *Betts had been leading, but fell back with ten laps to go.* **SYN drop back 2** to move or turn back away from sth or sb: *When the troops moved forward, the crowd fell back.* **SYN retreat** (*more formal*) **3** (*BrE, finance*) to decrease in value or amount: *Prices rose by more than 10% before falling back slightly.*
◆ v + adv

,**fall 'back on sb/sth** (*also* ,**fall 'back upon sb/sth** *more formal*) to use sb/sth when the situation is difficult or other people/things have failed: *It's very hard if you have no family to fall back on.* ◇ *He could always fall back on his old jokes.*
◆ v + adv + prep

▶ **'fallback** *n* a plan or course of action that you can use if sth else fails: *a fallback position*

,**fall be'hind**; ,**fall be'hind sb/sth** to fail to stay with other people or things, especially in a race or competition: *I fell further and further behind.* ◇ *The industry is falling behind the rest of Europe.* ◇ *He fell behind the rest of the class.* **SYN drop behind, drop behind sb/sth**
→ see also FALL BACK 1
◆ v + adv ◆ v + prep

,**fall be'hind with/in sth** to not do sth or pay sth at the right time: *She fell behind with the rent.* ◇ *He began falling behind in his schoolwork.*
OBJ payments, school work
◆ v + adv + prep

fall down

cave in ◆ **collapse** ◆ **fall down** ◆ **fall over** ◆ **topple over**

These verbs are all used to talk about buildings and other structures falling to the ground.

cave in (of a roof, wall, etc.) to fall down and towards the centre: *The ceiling suddenly caved in on top of them.*

collapse (of a building, etc.) to fall down or fall in suddenly, often after breaking apart: *The roof collapsed under the weight of snow.*

fall down to suddenly stop standing: *The house looked as if it was about to fall down.*

fall over to become unsteady and fall down: *I thought I was going to fall over.* ◇ *The chair had fallen over.*

topple over to become unsteady and fall down: *The pile of books toppled over.*

WHICH WORD?

Only **fall down** and **collapse** can be used to talk about whole buildings. **Cave in** is used with parts of buildings, and **fall over** and **topple over** are used to talk about other structures.

PATTERNS AND COLLOCATIONS

- a **building/house** falls down/collapses
- a **roof/wall/ceiling** collapses/caves in
- to **completely/suddenly** collapse
- to **be about to** fall down/fall over/collapse/ cave in/topple over

fall 'down 1 to suddenly stop standing: *I thought the whole house was falling down.* ◇ *Her legs were so weak that she fell down on her knees.* **2** to drop to the ground: *His trousers were falling down.* ◇ *A lump of the ceiling fell down.* **3 be falling down** (*only used in the progressive tenses*) (of a building) to be in extremely bad condition: *It's a beautiful house but it's falling down.* **4** (of an idea, an argument, a method, etc.) to be shown to be not true or not good enough: *That's where the theory falls down.*
♦ v + adv
▶ **'downfall** *n* the loss of sb's power, position, money, etc.; the thing that causes this

fall 'down on sth (*BrE, informal*) to fail to do sth correctly or successfully: *The suggestion was that he was falling down on the job.*
[OBJ] **job**

'fall for sb/sth (*informal*) to be attracted to sb/sth; to fall in love with sb/sth: *He fell for a young student.* ◇ *We fell for the farmhouse as soon as we saw it.*
♦ v + prep

'fall for sth (*informal*) to be tricked into believing sth is true when it is not: *You didn't fall for that old trick, did you?*
♦ v + prep

fall 'in 1 if a roof or a ceiling **falls in**, it drops to the ground: *The roof of the cave fell in.* **2** (of soldiers) to move into a line [OPP] **fall out**
♦ v + adv

fall 'in with sb (*informal*) to join sb; to become involved with sb: *She fell in with a bad crowd.*
♦ v + adv + prep

fall 'in with sth (*BrE*) to agree to or support a plan or an idea, especially when you do not really want to: *He always expects me to fall in with his plans.*
[OBJ] **plans** [SYN] **go along with sb/sth**
♦ v + adv + prep

fall 'into sth 1 to begin to be in a particular state: *He fell into a deep sleep.* ◇ *The tramway fell into disuse in the 1920s.* ◇ *We mustn't fall into this error* (= make this mistake). ◇ *He's fallen into arrears with the rent* (= he is late in paying it). [OBJ] **disuse, disrepair 2** to begin to do sth or become involved in sth: *I fell into the habit of having a nap after dinner.* ◇ *She fell into conversation with her neighbour.* [OBJ] **the habit of…, conversation 3** to be able to be divided into sth: *Computer viruses fall into three broad categories.* [OBJ] **two groups, three categories, etc. 4** to belong to a particular group or class: *Only 25% of people fall into this group.* [OBJ] **category, group, class, etc.**
♦ v + prep

fall 'off to decrease in quantity or quality: *Attendance has fallen off recently.* ◇ *The standard of cooking fell off when the old chef left.*
[SYN] **drop off**

→ see also FALL AWAY 4; ➔ note at DWINDLE AWAY
♦ v + adv
▶ **'fall-off** (*BrE also* **'falling-off** *less frequent*) (**in/of sth**) *n* [sing.] a decrease in the quality of sth: *a fall-off in attendance/interest/sales*

fall 'off; 'fall 'off sth if sth **falls off** or **falls off** sth, it becomes separated from the thing it is joined to: *The door handle has fallen off.* ◇ *Put the picture up properly—we don't want it to fall off the wall.*
♦ v + adv ♦ v + prep

'fall on sb/sth (*also* **'fall upon sb/sth** *more formal*) (*especially BrE*) **1** to be the responsibility or duty of a particular person or organization: *Most of the cost fell on us.* ◇ *When he died, the responsibility of the business fell on his son.* **2** if your eyes **fall on** sb/sth, you suddenly see or notice them/it: *My eye fell on a letter she had left on the table.* **3** to attack sb/sth with energy or enthusiasm: *The children fell on the food with cries of delight.* ◇ (*figurative*) *He fell on the drawings and examined them closely.* [OBJ] **food**
♦ v + prep

fall 'out 1 (of hair, teeth, etc.) to become loose and drop out: *The chemotherapy made her hair fall out.* **2** (**with sb**) (**over/about sth**) (*especially BrE*) to have an argument with sb and stop being friendly with them: *It's not worth falling out about this.* ◇ *Why have you fallen out with him?* ◇ *They fell out over their father's will.* **3** (of soldiers) to move out of lines [OPP] **fall in**
♦ v + adv
▶ **'falling-'out** *n* [sing.] (*especially BrE*) an argument or disagreement: *We've had a bit of a falling-out.*
▶ **'fallout** *n* [U] **1** dangerous (**radioactive**) dust that is in the air after a nuclear explosion or accident **2** the bad results of a situation: *the current crisis and its political fallout*

fall 'over 1 to be unable to stay standing and fall to the ground: (*especially BrE*) *He lost his balance and fell over.* ◇ *His bike fell over.* ➔ note at FALL DOWN **2** (of a computer or program) to stop working suddenly: *My spreadsheet keeps falling over.* [SYN] **crash**
♦ v + adv

fall 'over sb/sth to hit sb/sth with your foot when you are walking or running and fall or almost fall: *Mind you don't fall over the boxes.* [SYN] **trip over sb/sth**
♦ v + prep

[IDM] **,fall 'over yourself to do sth** (*informal*) to be very keen to do sth: *Recording companies were falling over themselves to sign the band.*

fall 'through to fail to be completed; to not happen: *Our travel plans have fallen through.* ◇ *The deal fell through.* [SUBJ] **deal**
♦ v + adv

'fall to sb (**to do sth**) to become the duty or responsibility of a particular person: *The task of*

telling them the news fell to me. ◇ *It falls to the police **to** ensure that demonstrations are well organized.*
  ♦ v + prep

'**fall to sth**; '**fall to doing sth** (*literary*) to start doing sth: *Little Red Riding Hood and the wolf fell to talking.* ◇ *They fell to it with gusto.*
  ♦ v + prep

'**fall under sth 1** to belong to or be included in a particular group of things: *What heading do these items fall under?* OBJ **heading 2** to begin to be controlled or influenced by sb/sth: *I realized I was **falling under her spell.*** ◇ *The education system fell under the control of the church.* OBJ **spell**
  ♦ v + prep

'**fall upon sb/sth** → FALL ON SB/STH

familiarize (*BrE also* familiarise) /fə-'mɪliəraɪz/

fa'**miliarize sb/yourself with sth** to teach sb about sth or to learn about sth until you know it well: *I familiarized myself with everyone's name before the meeting.*
  ♦ v + n/pron + prep

fan /fæn/ (-nn-)

,**fan 'out** to spread out over an area from a central point: *Searchers fanned out over the area where the missing child was last seen.* ◇ *Five main roads fan out from the village.*
  ♦ v + adv

,**fan sth 'out** if a bird **fans out** its feathers, it spreads them out: *The peacock fanned out its tail.*
  ♦ v + adv + n ♦ v + n/pron + adv

fancy /'fænsi/ (fancies, fancying, fancied)

,**fancy sth 'up** (*AmE, informal*) to make sth look more attractive by adding decoration to it: *I fancied up the dress with some pearls.* ◇ *You don't need to fancy up your web pages.*
  ♦ v + adv + n ♦ v + n/pron + adv

farm /fɑːm; *AmE* fɑːrm/

,**farm sb 'out** (**to sb**) (*informal, disapproving*) to arrange for sb you are responsible for, especially a child, to be cared for by other people: *When he was little, he was often farmed out to family friends.*
  ♦ v + n/pron + adv ♦ v + adv + n

,**farm sth 'out** (**to sb**) (*informal*) to send or give work to other people to do: *We farm a lot of the work out to other companies.*
  ♦ v + n/pron + adv ♦ v + adv + n

fart /fɑːt; *AmE* fɑːrt/

,**fart a'round** (*BrE also* ,fart a'bout) (△, *slang*) to waste time, especially by behaving in a silly way: *Stop farting around and behave yourself!*

NOTE A more polite, informal way to express this is **mess around** or, in British English, **mess about**.
  ♦ v + adv

fasten /'fɑːsn; *AmE* 'fæsn/

'**fasten on sb/sth**; '**fasten sth on sb/sth** if your eyes **fasten on** sb/sth, or you **fasten** your eyes **on** sb/sth, you look at them for a long time: *All eyes in the room fastened on me.* ◇ *She fastened her gaze on him.*
  ♦ v + prep ♦ v + n/pron + prep

'**fasten on/onto sth** (*also* '**fasten upon sth** *more formal*) **1** to hold sth firmly: *The cheetah's jaw fastened on the gazelle's throat.* **2** to choose sth and give it all your attention or interest: *When she fastens on an idea, there's no stopping her.* OBJ **idea, word, fact**
  ♦ v + prep

'**fasten sth on/onto sb/sth** to direct feelings such as blame, hope, etc. towards sb: *The blame hasn't been fastened on anybody yet.* OBJ **blame, hopes**
  ♦ v + n/pron + prep

,**fasten 'up**; ,**fasten sth 'up** (*BrE*) to close, or to make sth close, with buttons, etc.: *The dress fastens up at the front.* ◇ *Fasten your jacket up—it's getting cold.* OBJ **jacket, coat** SYN **do up, do sth up** (*especially BrE*)

NOTE **Fasten** and **fasten sth** can also be used on their own with the same meaning.
  ♦ v + n/pron + adv ♦ v + adv + n

'**fasten upon sth** → FASTEN ON/ONTO STH

fathom /'fæðəm/

,**fathom sb/sth 'out** (*BrE*) to understand how sb thinks and acts; to find an explanation for sth: *I can't fathom her out—she says one thing then does another.* ◇ *Have you fathomed out how to work the video yet?* SYN **work sb out; work sth out**

NOTE Not used in the passive.
  ♦ v + n/pron + adv

fatten /'fætn/

,**fatten 'up**; ,**fatten sb/sth 'up** to become fatter; to give an animal or a person a lot of food so that they become fatter: *The sheep fattened up quickly.* ◇ *We're fattening the livestock up for slaughter.*
  ♦ v + adv ♦ v + n/pron + adv ♦ v + adv + n

fax /fæks/

NOTE A **fax** is a message sent using a machine that sends and receives messages or documents along telephone wires and then prints them.

,**fax 'in**; ,**fax sth 'in** to send a fax to an organization, a company, a television or radio programme, etc.: *Viewers are invited to fax in*

with their comments. ◇ Orders can be either phoned or faxed in to us.
 ◆ v + adv ◆ v + n/pron + adv ◆ v + adv + n

,fax sth 'on (to sb/sth) to send a fax that you have received to sb else for them to see or deal with: Please email or fax this on to a friend.

,fax sth 'out to send a fax to a large number of people at the same time: Draft proposals will be faxed out for comment at the end of May.
 ◆ v + n/pron + adv ◆ v + adv + n

,fax sth 'through to send sb a fax with details of or information about sth
 ◆ v + n/pron + adv ◆ v + adv + n

fear /fɪə(r); AmE fɪr/

'fear for sb/sth (literary) to be anxious or worried about sb/sth: I fear for her safety. ◇ When he's away at sea, I really fear for him.
 OBJ life, safety, future
 ◆ v + prep

feed /fiːd/ (fed, fed /fed/)

,feed 'back (into/to sth) if sth **feeds back** to/into sth, it returns to the place, situation, idea, etc. that it started from and has an effect, usually a good one, on its development: Rising import prices tend to feed back into domestic prices. ◇ What the audience says feeds back into the development of the programme.
 ◆ v + adv

,feed sth 'back (to sb) to give information, advice or opinions about a product, sb's work, etc., especially so that it can be improved: We will feed this information back to the company. ◇ The results of the tests will be fed back to the schools.
 OBJ information
 ◆ v + n/pron + adv ◆ v + adv + n
 ▸ 'feedback n [U] **1** information, advice or opinions about how good a product, sb's work, etc. is: We got a lot of positive feedback about the programme. **2** an unpleasant noise produced by some electrical equipment when some of the power returns to the system

,feed sth 'in; ,feed A 'into B; 'feed B with A to put sth into a machine: You'll need to feed the paper in by hand. ◇ to feed information into a computer ◇ He fed coins into the meter. ◇ He fed the meter with coins.
 ◆ v + n/pron + adv ◆ v + adv + n ◆ v + n/pron + prep

,feed 'into sth to have an influence on the development of sth: The report's findings will feed into company policy.
 ◆ v + prep

'feed on/off sth **1** (of an animal, etc.) to use sth as food; to eat sth; to get strength from sth: This bat feeds on fruit. **2** (disapproving) to become stronger because of sth else: The media feed off each other's stories.
 ◆ v + prep

,feed 'through (to sb/sth/into sth) to reach sb/sth after going through a process or a system: Rises in prices feed through to higher wage claims. ◇ It will take time for the higher rates to feed through to investors.
 ◆ v + adv

,feed sb/sth 'up (BrE) to give extra food to a person or an animal to make them stronger and more healthy: You need feeding up a bit.
 ◆ v + n/pron + adv ◆ v + adv + n

feel /fiːl/ (felt, felt /felt/)

'feel for sb to have sympathy for sb: I really felt for her, bringing up her children alone. ◇ I do feel for you, honestly.
 ◆ v + prep

,feel sb 'out (AmE, informal) to try to discover sb's views, opinions, etc. on sth, especially in an indirect way: You have to feel them out and figure out whether they want to talk to you.
 SYN sound sb/sth out (formal)
 ◆ v + adv + n ◆ v + pron + adv ◆ v + n + adv

,feel sb 'up (informal) to touch sb in a sexual way when they do not want you to
 ◆ v + n/pron + adv

,feel 'up to sth; ,feel 'up to doing sth to feel capable of doing sth, physically or mentally: If you **feel up to it**, we could walk into town. ◇ I don't really feel up to seeing anyone.
 ◆ v + adv + prep

fence /fens/

,fence sb 'in to restrict sb's freedom: We've been fenced in by rules and regulations for too long.
 SYN hem sb/sth in
 NOTE Often used in the passive.
 ◆ v + n/pron + adv ◆ v + adv + n

,fence sth 'in to surround sth with a fence: The grounds are fenced in by barbed wire.
 NOTE Often used in the passive.
 ◆ v + n/pron + adv ◆ v + adv + n

,fence sth 'off to separate one area from another with a fence, often to stop people or animals from entering: We've fenced off the vegetable patch to stop the rabbits from getting in.
 ◆ v + adv + n ◆ v + n/pron + adv

fend /fend/

,fend for your'self to take care of yourself without needing any help from other people: We were brought up to fend for ourselves when we were still quite young.
 ◆ v + prep + pron

,fend sb/sth 'off to defend or protect yourself from sb/sth: The minister had to fend off some awkward questions. ◇ She managed to fend her attackers off for some time. ◇ She held up her arm to fend him off.
 OBJ attack, question, criticism
 ◆ v + adv + n ◆ v + pron + adv
 ◆ v + n + adv (less frequent)

ferret /ˈferɪt/

ˌferret ˈout sth (*informal*) to discover sth by searching thoroughly or asking a lot of questions: *She's determined to ferret out the truth.*
  □ **OBJ** **information**, **the truth**
  □ **NOTE** When the object of **ferret out** is a noun, it comes after **out**, but when the object is a pronoun, it comes between **ferret** and **out**: *It took us a while to ferret it out.*
  ◆ v + adv + n ◆ v + pron + adv

fess /fes/

ˌfess ˈup (**to sth**)/(**to sb**) (**about sth**) (*informal, especially AmE*) to admit that you have done sth wrong: *Come on, fess up. I know there's something you're not telling me.* ◇ *How many stolen cars did they fess up to?*
  □ **SYN** **own up** (**to sth/to doing sth**); **confess** (**to sth/to doing sth**) (*more formal*) ➔ note at ADMIT TO STH
  ◆ v + adv

fetch /fetʃ/

ˌfetch ˈup (*informal, especially BrE*) to arrive somewhere by chance: *The boat finally fetched up on a sandy beach.* ◇ *He travelled around Europe for a while and finally fetched up in Naples.*
  □ **SYN** **end up**
  ◆ v + adv

fiddle /ˈfɪdl/

ˌfiddle aˈbout/aˈround (*BrE, informal*) to spend your time doing nothing or doing sth that is not important: *He's fiddling around in the garage.*
  □ **SYN** **mess around**
  ◆ v + adv

fight /faɪt/ (**fought, fought** /fɔːt/)

ˌfight ˈback (**against sb/sth**) to defend yourself with actions or words when sb attacks you or causes problems: *The team fought back to win the game.* ◇ *Don't let them bully you. Fight back!*
  ◆ v + adv

ˌfight ˈback sth to try hard not to show your feelings or not to do sth: *She tried to fight back the tears.*
  □ **OBJ** **tears**, **urge**
  □ **NOTE** When the object of **fight back** is a noun, it comes after **back**, but when the object is a pronoun, it comes between **fight** and **back**: *The tears came, but she fought them back.*
  ◆ v + adv + n ◆ v + pron + adv

ˌfight ˈdown sth to try hard not to show an emotion that you are starting to feel: *He fought down a rush of panic.* ◇ *She fought down the anger that was rising in her.*
  □ **OBJ** **desire**, **impulse**, **panic**
  □ **NOTE** When the object of **fight down** is a noun, it comes after **down**, but when the object is a

pronoun, it comes between **fight** and **down**: *A feeling of rage rose in her, but she fought it down.*
  ◆ v + adv + n ◆ v + pron + adv

ˌfight sb/sth ˈoff to resist sb/sth or make them/it go away, by fighting against them/it: *She managed to fight her attackers off.* ◇ *The company fought off tough competition.*
  □ **OBJ** **attack**, **illness**
  ◆ v + n/pron + adv ◆ v + adv + n

ˌfight ˈout sth; **ˌfight it ˈout** to fight or argue about sth until it is settled: *We mustn't interfere. Let them fight it out between themselves.* ◇ *The teams fought out a 0-0 draw.*
  □ **OBJ** **battle**, **struggle**, **draw**
  □ **NOTE** When the object of **fight out** is a noun, it comes after **out**, but when the object is the pronoun **it**, it comes between **fight** and **out**.
  ◆ v + adv + n ◆ v + pron + adv

figure /ˈfɪɡə(r); AmE ˈfɪɡjər/

ˈfigure on sth; **ˈfigure on sb/sth doing sth** (*informal, especially AmE*) to include sth in your plans; to plan sth: *We hadn't figured on a long delay at the airport.* ◇ *I figure on being in New York in January.*
  ◆ v + prep

ˌfigure sb/sth ˈout to come to understand sb/ sth by thinking carefully: *I could never figure him out.* ◇ *Can you figure out what's going on?*
  □ **SYN** **work sb out**; **work sth out** ➔ note at WORK STH OUT
  □ **NOTE** **Figure out** is often followed by a question word such as *how, what, why*, etc: *I can't figure out why he quit his job.*
  ◆ v + n/pron + adv ◆ v + adv + n

ˌfigure sth ˈout to calculate the total amount of sth: *Have you figured out how much it will cost?*
  □ **SYN** **work sth out**
  □ **NOTE** **Figure out** is often followed by a question word such as *what, how much*, etc.
  ◆ v + adv + n ◆ v + n/pron + adv

file /faɪl/

ˌfile sth aˈway to put papers, documents, etc. away in a place where you can find them easily: *Everything is filed away in drawers.*
  ◆ v + n/pron + adv ◆ v + adv + n

fill /fɪl/

ˌfill ˈin (**for sb**) to take sb's place for a short time and do the work they normally do: *Who's filling in for you while you're away?*
  ◆ v + adv

ˌfill sb ˈin (**on sth**) to give sb all the details about sth that has happened: *Can you fill me in on what's been happening while I was away?*
  ◆ v + n/pron + adv ◆ v + adv + n

ˌfill sth ˈin 1 (*also* **ˌfill sth ˈout** *especially AmE*) to complete a form, etc. by writing information on it: *You could fill in an application form now.* ◇ *Fill in the blank spaces with one of these words.*

◇ *I've left gaps on the sheet for you to fill in the details.* [OBJ] **form**, **details 2** to fill sth, such as a hole, a crack, etc. completely with a substance: *We'll have to fill the holes in with cement.* [OBJ] **hole**, **crack 3** (*especially BrE*) to spend time while you are waiting for sb/sth: *How shall we fill in the time until he arrives?*
◆ v + adv + n ◆ v + n/pron + adv (*less frequent*)

ˌfill 'out to become larger, rounder or fatter: *The baby's filled out a lot recently.*
◆ v + adv

ˌfill sth 'out **1** to make sth larger or more complete: *We'll need to fill the story out to make a full page article.* **2** (*especially AmE*) → FILL STH IN 1
◆ v + n/pron + adv ◆ v + adv + n

ˌfill 'up; ˌfill sth 'up **1** (**with sb/sth**) if a container or a place **fills up** or sb **fills it up**, it becomes completely full: *The restaurant was beginning to fill up.* ◇ *She filled her glass up again.* ◇ *People began filling up the empty seats.* **2** (**with sth**) to fill your vehicle with petrol/gas, etc.: *I need to fill up with petrol before we go.* ◇ *Fill the tank up with diesel.*
◆ v + adv ◆ v + n/pron + adv ◆ v + adv + n
▶ 'fill-up *n* (*AmE*) the action of filling sth, particularly of filling a car with petrol/gas

ˌfill sb/yourself 'up to give sb a lot of food so that they feel full; to eat as much as you can: *The meals at school never fill me up.* ◇ *Eat lots of pasta to fill yourself up.*
◆ v + n/pron + adv

filter /ˈfɪltə(r)/

NOTE A **filter** is a device containing paper, sand, etc., or a substance used to remove unwanted substances.

ˌfilter sth 'out to remove sth using a filter: *Use a sun cream to filter out ultraviolet rays.*
◆ v + adv + n ◆ v + n/pron + adv

find /faɪnd/ (**found**, **found** /faʊnd/)

'find against sb (*law*) to decide in court that sb is guilty: *The court found against the defendant.*
◆ v + prep

'find for sb (*law*) to decide in court that sb is innocent: *The jury found for the defendant.*
◆ v + prep

ˌfind 'out; ˌfind sth 'out to learn a fact, a piece of information, or the truth about sth/sb: *She won't be happy when she finds out about this.* ◇ *'What did she say?' 'You'll find out soon enough.'* ◇ *When did you find out (that) she was ill?* ◇ *I never found out exactly what happened.* ◇ *How did you find that out?*
◆ v + adv ◆ v + adv + n ◆ v + pron + adv
◆ v + n + adv (*rare*)

ˌfind sb 'out (*informal*) to discover that sb has been dishonest or has done sth wrong: *If you're ever found out, you'll go to prison.*

find sth out

discover sth ◆ **find sth out** ◆ **hear about sb/sth** ◆ **learn of sth**

These verbs all mean to find information by being told by sb, reading, etc.

discover sth to find some information about sth: *We never discovered why she gave up her job.* ◇ *It was later discovered that the diaries were a fraud.*

find sth out to find some information about sth by asking, reading, etc.: *She didn't want her parents to find out about the relationship.* ◇ *We later found out that we'd been at the same school.*

hear about sb/sth to be told about sb/sth: *I was sorry to hear about your accident.* **NOTE** **Hear** can be used on its own with a clause: *I was surprised to hear (that) they'd got married.*

learn of sth to become aware of sth by hearing it from sb else: *I learnt of her arrival from a close friend.* **NOTE** **Learn** can be used on its own with a clause: *We were surprised to learn (that) that they're now divorced.*

WHICH WORD?

Find out is often used with question words such as *how, what, when,* etc.: *Did you ever find out who did it?* If you **find sth out**, you do so either by chance or by asking or studying. You can **discover** a piece of information that other people know but you didn't. **Hear about sth** and **learn of sth** are used to talk about news that is freely available.

PATTERNS AND COLLOCATIONS

- to **quickly/soon/eventually** find out/discover...
- to be **surprised/amazed/fascinated** to hear/discover/learn...
- to be **delighted/glad/pleased** to hear/discover/learn...
- to be **dismayed/horrified/shocked** to hear/discover/learn...
- to be **saddened/sorry** to hear/learn...
- to **aim/try/attempt** to find out/discover...

NOTE Often used in the passive.
◆ v + n/pron + adv

finish /ˈfɪnɪʃ/

ˌfinish ˈoff (with sth), ˌfinish sth ˈoff (with sth) (*informal*) to have sth as the last part of sth; to make sth end by doing one last thing: *After a delicious meal we finished off with coffee and mints.* ◇ *The concert finished off with the band's latest hit.* ◇ *The band finished off the show with their latest hit.* ◇ *I have to go now, can I leave you to finish off?* ◇ *Her outfit was finished off with navy shoes.*
NOTE **Finish** and **finish sth** are also used on their own with almost the same meaning.
◆ v + adv ◆ v + n/pron + adv ◆ v + adv + n

ˌfinish sb ˈoff (*informal*) to make sb so unhappy, tired, etc. that they cannot continue what they are doing: *Running in that heat nearly finished him off.*
NOTE **Finish sb** can also be used on its own with almost the same meaning.
◆ v + n/pron + adv ◆ v + adv + n (*rare*)

ˌfinish sb/sth ˈoff (*informal*) **1** to destroy or kill sb/sth, especially sb/sth that is already injured: *He thought the soldiers would come back and finish him off.* ◇ *We ought to finish the poor animal off.* ◇ (*figurative*) *The business had been finished off by financial difficulties.* **2** (*sport*) to defeat a person or team that you are competing against: *Murray finished him off in three sets.*
◆ v + n/pron + adv ◆ v + adv + n

ˌfinish sth ˈoff **1** to complete sth: *I'm going to try and finish off my work tonight.* **2** to use the last part of sth, especially food or drink: *He's finished off all the ice cream!*
NOTE **Finish sth** is used on its own with almost the same meaning.
◆ v + n/pron + adv ◆ v + adv + n

ˌfinish ˈup **1** [+ adj/prep] (*also* **finish up doing sth**) (*especially BrE*) to reach or come to a particular place, state or situation after a long series of events, often without planning it: *He lost control of the car and finished up in the river.* ◇ *She started out washing dishes and finished up as a chef.* ◇ *They all went home and I finished up doing most of the cleaning.* **SYN** **end up**; **wind up** (*informal*) **2** (*AmE*) to complete what you are doing; to do the last part of sth: *I'll finish up here and join you later.*
◆ **1** v + adv ◆ v + adv + -ing
◆ **2** v + adv

ˌfinish sth ˈup (*especially AmE*) to do the last part of sth; to use what is left of sth: *He stayed home to finish up his assignment.*
NOTE Not used in the passive.
◆ v + adv + n ◆ v + pron + adv
◆ v + n + adv (*less frequent*)

ˈfinish with sb (*informal*) **1** (*BrE*) to end a relationship with sb: *I've finished with Antonia.* **SYN** **break up** (**with sb**) **2** to stop punishing sb:

He'll never do that again once I've finished with him!
◆ v + prep

ˈfinish with sth **1** to no longer need to use sth: *Can you wash your cup when you've finished with it?* ◇ *Can I keep the book a little longer? I haven't finished with it yet.* **NOTE** Usually used in the perfect tenses. **2** (*BrE, informal*) to stop doing sth because you no longer want to do it or enjoy it: *He said he was finished with football.* **NOTE** Usually used in the perfect tenses or in the form **be finished with sth**.
◆ v + prep

fire /ˈfaɪə(r)/

ˌfire aˈway (*informal*) used to tell sb to begin asking questions or to begin to speak: *'Can I ask you some questions?' 'Fire away!'*
◆ v + adv

ˌfire sth ˈoff **1** to shoot a bullet from a gun: *He fired off a volley of shots.* **OBJ** **gun**, **shot 2** to ask a lot of questions, etc. quickly, one after the other: *He fired off a series of questions.* **OBJ** **questions 3** to write a letter, report, etc. quickly, often because you are angry: *She would fire off a letter of protest in the morning.* **OBJ** **letter 4** if you **fire off** an email, you send it: *I'm going to fire off an email to a newsgroup.* **OBJ** **email**
◆ v + adv + n ◆ v + pron + adv ◆ v + n + adv (*rare*)

ˌfire sb/sth ˈup to make sb/sth become excited or enthusiastic about sth: *The manager fired the team up at half-time.*
◆ v + n/pron + adv ◆ v + adv + n
▶ ˌfired ˈup adj: *She felt fired up by the challenge the new job presented.*

ˌfire sth ˈup **1** (*AmE*) to light a fire; to make sth hot: *I'll get the burgers—you fire up the grill.* **2** (*especially AmE*) to start a machine, piece of equipment, computer program, etc.: *We need to fire up one of the generators.* ◇ *Let me fire up another window* (= on the computer screen). **OBJ** **engine**
◆ v + adv + n ◆ v + n/pron + adv

firm /fɜːm; *AmE* fɜːrm/

ˌfirm sth ˈup (*also* ˌfirm ˈup *less frequent*) **1** if sb **firms up** an arrangement, an agreement, etc. it becomes more definite or less likely to change: *I'll phone on the 25th to firm up the details of the meeting.* ◇ *Prices will firm up later this year.* **OBJ** **plans**, **agreement 2** to make sth, especially part of the body harder, or more solid: *These exercises will firm up those difficult areas of your body.*
◆ v + adv + n ◆ v + pron + adv ◆ v + n + adv (*rare*)
◆ v + adv

fish /fɪʃ/

ˈfish for sth (*often used in the progressive tenses*) to try to make sb tell you sth, say sth nice to you, etc. by asking them a question: *Are you fishing for compliments?*

OBJ **information**, **compliment** SYN **angle for sth**

♦ v + prep

ˌfish sb/sth ˈout; ˌfish sb/sth ˈout of sth to take or pull sb/sth out of somewhere: *He fished some change out of his pocket.* ◇ *Several days later his car was fished out of the river.*

♦ v + n/pron + adv ♦ v + adv + n
♦ v + n/pron + adv + prep

fit /fɪt/ (**fitting**, **fitted**, **fitted**, *AmE usually* **fitting**, **fit**, **fit** except in the passive)

ˌfit ˈin (**with sth**) if sth **fits in**, it looks pleasant or suitable with other things or in a particular place: *The building doesn't fit in with the surrounding area.* ◇ *It's an old house, but our furniture fits in well.*

♦ v + adv

ˌfit ˈin; ˌfit ˈinto sth **1** to be the right size or shape to go in a particular place: *Will all your furniture fit in?* ◇ *The piano wouldn't fit into the room.* **2** to live or work easily and naturally with a group of people: *Tim never fitted in at college.* ◇ *Jane **fitted in** well **with** the rest of the staff.* ◇ *She's fitted into the team well.* **3** to have a particular role or part in a plan, a situation, etc.: *Where does he fit in?* ◇ *I like to know where I fit in and what I have to do.* ◇ *Where do I fit into all this?*

♦ v + adv ♦ v + prep

ˌfit sb/sth ˈin; ˌfit sb/sth ˈinto sth **1** to find a place for sb/sth, especially when there is not much space: *We can't fit a sofa in here.* ◇ *We will try to fit you in somewhere in the organization.* SYN **get sb in**, **get sb into sth**; **get sth in**, **get sth into sth 2** to manage to find time to see sb or to do sth: *The nurse will fit you in between other appointments.* ◇ *How do you manage to fit so much into your day?*

♦ v + n/pron + adv ♦ v + adv + n ♦ v + n/pron + prep

ˌfit ˈin with sth **1** if an activity or event **fits in with** sth else, they exist or happen together in an easy or convenient way: *My job fits in with looking after my family.* **2** to adapt to what sb else is planning or to sb else's way of doing things: *They've got to learn to fit in with our methods.* ◇ *I'll fit in with what you want to do.* **3** to agree with ideas or information that you already have about sb/sth: *That fits in with everything I've heard about her.*

♦ v + adv + prep

ˌfit sb/sth ˈout (*also* ˌfit sb/sth ˈup) (**with sth**) to supply sb/sth with the clothes, food, equipment, etc. they need: *The ship had to be fitted out before the voyage.* ◇ *the high cost of fitting out offices* ◇ *We fitted him out with a set of dry clothes.*

NOTE Often used in the passive.

♦ v + adv + n ♦ v + n/pron + adv

ˌfit sb ˈup (**for sth**) (*BrE*, *informal*) to make sb appear to be guilty of a crime that they have not committed: *They're trying to fit me up for the theft.*

SYN **frame sb** (*more formal*)

♦ v + n/pron + adv ♦ v + adv + n

ˌfit sb/sth ˈup, etc. → FIT SB/STH OUT, ETC.

fix /fɪks/

ˈfix on sth to decide to choose sth: *We haven't fixed on a date for the meeting yet.*

SYN **decide on/upon sth**; **settle on/upon sth**

♦ v + prep

ˈfix sth on sb/sth if you **fix** your eyes or your mind **on** sb/sth, you look at or think about them/it with great attention: *She fixed her eyes on his face.* ◇ *His attention was fixed on a dark car.*

OBJ **eyes**, **gaze**, **attention**

NOTE Often used in the passive.

♦ v + n/pron + prep

ˌfix sb ˈup; ˌfix yourself ˈup (*informal*) **1** (**with sth**) to arrange for sb to have sth; to provide sb with sth: *I can fix you up with somewhere to stay.* ◇ *I hope she soon gets herself fixed up with a job.*

NOTE In informal spoken language **fix sb up sth** is also used: *Can you fix me up an appointment for tomorrow?* **2** (**with sb**) to arrange for sb to meet sb who might become a boyfriend or girlfriend: *My brother says he wants me to fix him up with one of my friends.*

→ see also FIX YOURSELF UP; FIX STH UP 1; FIX UP TO DO STH, FIX UP FOR SB TO DO STH

♦ v + n/pron + adv ♦ v + adv + n (*less frequent*)

ˌfix sth ˈup **1** to arrange or organize sth; to arrange for sb to have sth: *Have you fixed your holiday up yet?* ◇ *Shall we fix up a meeting for next week?* OBJ **meeting** SYN **arrange sth** → see also FIX UP TO DO STH, FIX UP FOR SB TO DO STH **2** (*especially AmE*) to repair, decorate, etc. a room of a house: *They spent £30 000 fixing up their house.* ◇ *We fixed up the attic as a study.* OBJ **house**, **room** SYN **do sth up** (*BrE*) **3** (*especially BrE*) to build or make sth quickly; to make sth ready: *We fixed up a shelter for the night.*

♦ v + adv + n ♦ v + pron + adv
♦ v + n + adv (*less frequent*)

ˌfix yourself ˈup (*AmE*, *informal*) to make yourself neat and attractive: *Can you wait? I'll just go and fix myself up.*

→ see also FIX SB UP, FIX YOURSELF UP

♦ v + pron + adv

ˌfix ˈup to do sth; ˌfix ˈup for sb to do sth (*BrE*, *informal*) to make arrangements to do sth or for sb to do sth: *He's fixed up for her to see the doctor on Thursday.* ◇ *I've fixed up with the school to start in September.*

SYN **arrange (for sb) to do sth**

→ see also FIX STH UP 1; FIX SB UP, ETC.

♦ v + adv + **to**+inf ♦ v + adv + prep + n/pron + **to**+inf

,**fix sb with sth** (*formal*) if you **fix sb with** a look, etc., you look at them directly for a long time: *She fixed him with a cold stare.*
♦ v + n/pron + prep

fizzle /ˈfɪzl/

,**fizzle 'out** (*informal*) to fail or to end in a weak or disappointing way, often after having started strongly: *The romance fizzled out after a month.* ◇ *The coup attempt soon fizzled out.* ⌕ note at PETER OUT
♦ v + adv

flag /flæg/ (-gg-)

,**flag sb/sth 'down** to signal to the driver of a moving vehicle to stop, usually by waving your arm: *He managed to flag down a passing motorist.* ◇ *The police were flagging down all heavy goods vehicles.*
OBJ taxi/cab, motorist SYN **wave sb/sth down**
♦ v + adv + n ♦ v + n/pron + adv

,**flag sth 'up** to draw attention to sth: *The report flagged up the dangers of under-age drinking.*
♦ v + adv + n ♦ v + n/pron + adv

flake /fleɪk/

,**flake 'out** (*informal*) **1** to collapse or fall asleep because you are very tired: *I was so exhausted that I flaked out on the sofa.* **2** (*AmE*) to begin to behave in a strange way
♦ v + adv

flame /fleɪm/

,**flame 'out** (*AmE*) to fail, especially after succeeding for a while: *The team routinely wins 50 or 60 games in the season and then flames out in the play-offs.*
♦ v + adv
▶ **'flameout** *n* [C, U]: *Hollywood is experiencing box-office flameout. Fans love DVDs but not movie theaters.*

flare /fleə(r); AmE fler/

,**flare 'up 1** (of flames, a fire, etc.) to suddenly burn more strongly: *The fire flared up as I added more wood.* **2** if fighting, tension, anger, etc. **flares up**, it starts very suddenly and violently: *Violence flared up in several cities.* ◇ *The dispute could flare up into a major crisis.* **3** if a person **flares up**, they show sudden anger towards sb: *He flared up in a fury and shouted at her.* **4** if an illness or injury **flares up**, it suddenly starts again or becomes worse: *Her asthma has flared up again.*
♦ v + adv
▶ **'flare-up** *n* [usually sing.] **1** a sudden expression of anger, violent feeling, etc.: *the latest flare-up between the two countries* **2** an occasion when an illness or injury starts again or quickly becomes worse

flash /flæʃ/

,**flash sth a'round** (*also* ,**flash sth a'bout** *especially BrE*) (*disapproving*) to show sth valuable, especially money or jewellery to people, or let them see it, to impress them: *Stop flashing your money around.*
♦ v + n/pron + adv

,**flash 'back** (**to sth**) if your mind or your thoughts **flash back** to sth that happened in the past, you suddenly remember it: *My mind flashed back to my first day at college.*
♦ v + adv
▶ **'flashback** *n* **1** [C, U] a scene in a film/movie, book, etc. which shows sth that happened earlier **2** a sudden, very clear, strong memory of sth that happened to you in the past that is so real you feel that you are living through the experience again: *She still has nightmares and vivid flashbacks of the accident.*

,**flash 'by/'past**; ,**flash 'by/'past sb/sth** to go or pass very quickly; to go very quickly past sb/sth: *The days just flashed by.* ◇ *She watched the scenery flash past the train window.*
♦ v + adv ♦ v + prep

,**flash 'forward** (**to sth**) if a book, film/movie, etc. **flashes forward**, it describes or shows sth that will happen at a later time: *The movie then flashes forward to wartime London.* ◇ (*figurative*) *Flash forward to the present: we are still in the same mess as we were in back then.*
♦ v + adv
▶ ,**flash'forward** *n*

'**flash on sb** if sth **flashes on** you, you suddenly realize it: *It flashed on me that he was the man I'd seen in the hotel.*
SYN **hit sb**
♦ v + prep

'**flash on sth** (*AmE*, *informal*) to remember or realize sth: *I suddenly flashed on how horrible that day had been.*
♦ v + prep

flatten /ˈflætn/

,**flatten sth/yourself a'gainst/'on sb/sth** to press your body or part of your body on or against sb/sth: *She flattened her nose and lips against the window.* ◇ *I flattened myself against the wall to let them pass.*
♦ v + n/pron + prep

,**flatten 'out 1** if a road, an area of land, etc. **flattens out**, it gradually becomes flat: *After Oxford the countryside flattens out.* **2** to stop growing or going up: *Sales have flattened out in the last few years.*
♦ v + adv

,**flatten sth 'out** to make sth completely flat: *She flattened out the crumpled letter on the desk.*
♦ v + adv + n ♦ v + n/pron + adv

flesh /fleʃ/

,flesh sth 'out (**with sth**) to add more details or information to an argument, an idea, a drawing, etc.: *You need to* **flesh out the bones** *of your idea a bit more.* ◇ *They must be prepared to flesh out their strategy with some details.*
 ◆ v + adv + n ◆ v + n/pron + adv

flick /flɪk/

,flick sth 'off to switch sth off quickly: *He flicked the light off.*
 OBJ **light** SYN **switch sth off** OPP **flick sth on**
 ◆ v + n/pron + adv ◆ v + adv + n

,flick sth 'on to switch sth on quickly: *He flicked on the air conditioning.*
 OBJ **light** SYN **switch sth on** OPP **flick sth off**
 ◆ v + n/pron + adv ◆ v + adv + n

,flick 'through sth to turn the pages of a book, etc. quickly, or look through a pile of papers, etc. without reading everything: *He flicked through a magazine while he waited.*
 OBJ **pages, book, papers** SYN **flip through sth; leaf through sth; thumb through sth** ⊃ note at LOOK THROUGH STH
 ◆ v + prep

fling /flɪŋ/ (**flung** /flʌŋ/, **flung**)

'fling yourself at sb (*informal, disapproving*) to try too hard to show sb that you are interested in them in a sexual way and make them interested in you
 SYN **throw yourself at sb**
 ◆ v + pron + prep

'fling yourself into sth to start to do sth with a lot of energy, enthusiasm and effort: *When they split up she flung herself into her work to try to forget him.*
 SYN **throw yourself into sth**
 ◆ v + pron + prep

,fling sth 'off (*informal*) to take clothes off quickly and carelessly: *Flinging off her coat, she sank into an armchair.*
 SYN **throw sth off** OPP **fling sth on**
 ◆ v + n/pron + adv ◆ v + adv + n

,fling sth 'on (*informal*) to put clothes on quickly and carelessly: *Just fling a coat on over your pyjamas.*
 SYN **throw sth on** OPP **fling sth off**
 ◆ v + n/pron + adv ◆ v + adv + n

flip /flɪp/ (**-pp-**)

'flip for sb/sth (*AmE, slang*) to begin to like sb very much; to suddenly become very excited about sth attractive, pleasant, etc.: *She flipped for his red hair and freckles.*
 ◆ v + prep

'flip for sth, etc. (*AmE*) → TOSS FOR STH, ETC.

,flip sb 'off (*AmE, slang*) to raise your middle finger to sb in a very rude sign
 ◆ v + n/pron + adv ◆ v + adv + n

,flip sth 'off/on (*AmE, informal*) to turn off/on an electrical switch: *I flipped on the light to see what was making the noise.*
 ◆ v + n/pron + adv ◆ v + adv + n

,flip 'out (*informal, especially AmE*) to become very angry, excited or enthusiastic about sth: *She flipped out because I was late.* ◇ *People are flipping out over these new digital cameras.*
 NOTE **Flip** is often used on its own with this meaning, especially in British English.
 ◆ v + adv

,flip 'over; ,flip sth 'over to turn over, or to turn sth over, onto the other side or upside down: *The dolphin flipped over onto its back.* ◇ *A huge wave flipped the dinghy over.*
 ◆ v + adv ◆ v + n/pron + adv ◆ v + adv + n

'flip through sth to turn over the pages of a book, etc. quickly, or look through a pile of papers, etc. without reading everything: *He flipped through the photos quickly.*
 OBJ **pages, magazines** SYN **flick through sth; leaf through sth** ⊃ note at LOOK THROUGH STH
 ◆ v + prep

flirt /flɜːt; *AmE* flɜːrt/

'flirt with sth **1** to think about or be interested in sth for a short time, but not very seriously: *I flirted briefly with the idea of emigrating.*
 OBJ **idea, thought** SYN **toy with sth 2** to take risks or not worry about a dangerous situation: *to flirt with danger/death/disaster* OBJ **danger, disaster**
 ◆ v + prep

float /fləʊt; *AmE* floʊt/

,float a'round; ,float a'round sth (*BrE also* ,float a'bout/'round, ,float a'bout/'round sth) **1** (*usually used in the progressive tenses*) if an idea or a piece of news is **floating around/about**, it is being talked about by a lot of people: *There's a rumour floating about (the office) that she's leaving.* SUBJ **rumour, idea** SYN **go around, go around sth 2** if you say that an object is **floating around/about**, you mean that you have seen it somewhere but do not know exactly where it is: *Is there a pen floating about here somewhere?*
 ◆ v + adv ◆ v + prep

flog /flɒg; *AmE* flɑː/

,flog sth 'off to sell sth cheaply because you want to get rid of it or because you need the money: *We buy them cheaply and then flog them off at a profit.*
 ◆ v + adv + n ◆ v + n/pron + adv

flood /flʌd/

,flood 'back if a thought or a memory **floods back**, you remember sth suddenly and it affects you strongly: *Suddenly all my fears came flooding back.*

> **NOTE** **Flood back** is often used with the verb **come**: *His words came flooding back to me.*
> ◆ v + adv

,flood 'in; ,flood 'into sth **1** if water, etc. **floods in** or **floods into** a place, it moves to fill or cover it: *He opened the door and water came flooding in.* ◇ *Sunshine flooded into the room.* **2** to come to or arrive at a place in large numbers or great quantities: *Letters of support have been flooding in from all over the country.*

> **SYN** pour in, pour into sth
> ◆ v + adv ◆ v + prep

,flood sb 'out to force sb to leave their home because of a flood: *We were flooded out by a burst water main.*

> **NOTE** Often used in the passive.
> ◆ v + n/pron + adv ◆ v + adv + n

,flood 'over/'through sb if a feeling **floods over/through** you, it affects you very strongly: *A great sense of relief flooded through her.*

> **SUBJ** relief
> ◆ v + prep

flounder /'flaʊndə(r)/

,flounder a'round (*BrE also* ,flounder a'bout) to struggle to move or get somewhere because it is difficult, or because you do not know where you are going: *People were floundering about in the water, shouting and screaming.* ◇ (*figurative*) *I floundered around trying to decide what I ought to do.*

> ◆ v + adv

flow /fləʊ; *AmE* floʊ/

'flow from sth (*formal*) to come or result from sth: *What benefits might flow from joining the European Union?* **SUBJ** benefits/advantages, consequences

> ◆ v + prep

,flow 'through to sb/sth to reach sb/sth or have an effect on them/it: *It will take time for the drop in manufacturing costs to flow through to consumers.*

> ◆ v + adv + prep

fluff /flʌf/

,fluff sth 'out/'up to shake or brush feathers, fur, hair, etc. so that they look bigger or softer: *The bird fluffed out its feathers.* ◇ *Let me fluff up your pillows for you.*

> **OBJ** feathers
> ◆ v + adv + n ◆ v + n/pron + adv

flunk /flʌŋk/

,flunk 'out; ,flunk 'out of sth (*AmE, informal*) to have to leave school or college because your marks/grades are not good enough: *He flunked out (of college) last year.*

> ◆ v + adv ◆ v + adv + prep

flush /flʌʃ/

,flush sth a'way to get rid of sth with a sudden quick flow of water: *She flushed the unused tablets away.*

> ◆ v + n/pron + adv ◆ v + adv + n

,flush sb/sth 'out; ,flush sb/sth 'out of sth **1** to force a person or an animal to leave the place where they are hiding: *The dogs flushed out the deer that were left in the wood.* ◇ *The police flushed the gunmen out of the building.* **2** to force sb who is planning or doing sth secretly, especially sth dishonest, to say what they are planning or who they are: *Their offer is likely to flush out any rival bidders.*

> ◆ v + adv + n ◆ v + n/pron + adv
> ◆ v + n/pron + adv + prep

,flush sth 'out; ,flush sth 'out of sth to wash sth out; to get rid of sth with a rush of water: *Drink lots of water to flush the poisons out of your body.*

> ◆ v + n/pron + adv ◆ v + adv + n
> ◆ v + n/pron + adv + prep

flutter /'flʌtə(r)/

,flutter a'round; ,flutter a'round sth (*also* ,flutter a'bout, ,flutter a'bout sth *especially BrE*) **1** if a bird or an insect **flutters around**, it flies somewhere moving its wings very quickly: *Butterflies fluttered around (the garden).* **2** if a person **flutters around**, they move quickly in a nervous or excited way: *My mother fluttered about picking things up and putting things away.*

> ◆ v + adv ◆ v + prep

,flutter 'down to move gently through the air to the ground: *Wind shook the branches and several leaves fluttered down.*

> ◆ v + adv

fly /flaɪ/ (**flies, flying, flew** /fluː/, **flown** /fləʊn; *AmE* floʊn/)

,fly a'round; ,fly a'round sth (*also* ,fly a'bout, ,fly a'bout sth *especially BrE*) (*usually used in the progressive tenses*) if a story or a piece of news is **flying around**, it is being talked about by a lot of people and passed from one person to another: *Stories about his past are flying around among the students.* ◇ *Rumours have been flying around the office.*

> ◆ v + adv ◆ v + prep

'fly at sb (of a person or an animal) to attack sb suddenly and violently: *She flew at him, hitting and kicking.*

> ◆ v + prep

,fly 'by/'past **1** when time **flies by/past**, it seems to pass very quickly: *My three years at college flew by.* ◇ *When you have lots of things to do, time just flies past.* **SUBJ** time, days, hours,

etc. NOTE **Fly** can also be used on its own with this meaning, especially with the subject *time*: *There was so much to do, the time just flew.* **2** when miles, etc. **fly by/past**, a journey by car, bus, train or bicycle seems to pass very quickly: *As the miles flew past and we got closer and closer to the sea, the kids got more and more excited.*
SUBJ **miles, countryside**
♦ v + adv

fly 'in/out; **fly 'into sth**; **fly 'out of sth** to arrive/leave a place by plane: *She's flying out to join him in Nairobi next week.* ◇ *Several heads of state flew into London last night for talks with the Prime Minister.*
→ see also FLY SB/STH IN/OUT, ETC.
♦ v + adv ♦ v + prep ♦ v + adv + prep

fly sb/sth 'in/'out; **fly sb/sth 'into sth**; **fly sb/sth 'out of sth** to bring sb/sth by plane to a place or take them away: *They flew us in by helicopter.* ◇ *Food supplies are being flown out immediately.* ◇ *The travel company is flying 200 people out of the area tomorrow.*
→ see also FLY IN/OUT, FLY INTO, FLY OUT OF STH
♦ v + n/pron + adv ♦ v + adv + n ♦ v + n/pron + prep
♦ v + n/pron + adv + prep

fly 'into sth if sb **flies into a temper**, etc., they suddenly become extremely angry: *He flies into a rage when you mention her.*
OBJ **rage, temper, panic**
♦ v + prep

fly 'off; **fly 'off sth** to come off sth suddenly and with force: *The jolt caused her glasses to fly off.*
♦ v + adv ♦ v + prep
IDM **fly off the 'handle** (*informal*) to become suddenly very angry

fly 'out, etc. → FLY IN/OUT, ETC.

fly 'past → FLY BY/PAST

fob /fɒb; *AmE* fɑːb/ (**-bb-**)

fob sb 'off (**with sth**) (*BrE*) **1** to try to make sb stop asking questions or complaining by giving them answers or excuses that are not true: *Don't try to fob me off with excuses.* **2** to give sb sth that is different from or not as good as what they want: *We thought we'd been fobbed off with inferior goods.*
SYN **palm sb off** (**with sth**)
♦ v + n/pron + adv ♦ v + adv + n

fob sth 'off on/onto sb (*BrE, informal*) to trick sb into accepting sth that you do not want or sth that is not genuine: *She tried to fob all her junk off onto me.*
♦ v + n/pron + adv + prep

focus /'fəʊkəs; *AmE* 'foʊ-/ (**-s-** or **-ss-**)

'focus on sb/sth; **'focus sth on sb/sth** (*also* **'focus upon sb/sth, 'focus sth upon sb/sth** *more formal*) **1** to give all your attention, effort, etc. to a particular problem, subject or person: *Suspi-*

cion focused on her husband. ◇ *The programme was intended to focus attention on global warming.* **2** (of eyes, a camera, etc.) to be adjusted so that things can be seen clearly; to adjust sth so that you can see things clearly: *Rest your eyes by letting them focus on distant objects.* ◇ *The camera was focused on an old woman.*
♦ v + prep ♦ v + n/pron + prep

fog /fɒg; *AmE* fɔːg, fɑːg/ (**-gg-**)

fog 'up if a glass surface **fogs up**, it becomes covered with steam or drops of water so that it is difficult to see in or through it: *The windscreen started to fog up.*
SYN **mist up, mist sth up**; **steam up, steam sth up**
♦ v + adv

foist /fɔɪst/

'foist sth/sb/yourself on sb (*also* **'foist sth/sb/ yourself upon sb** *more formal*) to force sb to accept sth that they do not want, or take care of sb that they do not want to: *He tries to foist his beliefs on everyone.* ◇ *She resented having the child foisted on her while the parents were abroad.*
NOTE Often used in the passive.
♦ v + n/pron + prep

fold /fəʊld; *AmE* foʊld/

fold a'way/'down; **fold sth a'way/'down** to be able to be bent or arranged into a smaller or flatter shape that you can store or carry more easily; to bend or arrange sth in this way: *The bed can fold away.* ◇ *You can fold the table away to make more room.*
♦ v + adv ♦ v + n/pron + adv ♦ v + adv + n
▸ **'foldaway** (*also* **'fold-down, 'fold-up**) *adj* [only before noun] that can be folded so that you can carry it or store it more easily

fold sth a'way to fold sth and put it away: *She folded the newspaper away.*
♦ v + n/pron + adv ♦ v + adv + n

fold sth 'back, 'over, 'down, etc. to bend sth back, over, down, etc. so that one part of it lies flat on another: *He folded the corner of the page over to mark his place.*
♦ v + n/pron + adv ♦ v + adv + n

fold 'down, etc. → FOLD AWAY/DOWN, ETC.

fold sth 'into sth; **fold sth 'in** (in cooking) to mix one substance gently with another, usually with a spoon: *Gently fold the flour into the mixture.* ◇ *Fold in two egg whites.*
♦ v + n/pron + prep ♦ v + adv + n ♦ v + n/pron + adv

'fold A in B; **'fold B round/over A** to wrap sb/sth in sth: *She gently folded the baby in a blanket.* ◇ *She folded a blanket round the baby.* ◇ *He folded her in his arms* (= he put his arms around her).
♦ v + n/pron + prep

follow

ʖ̩fold ˈup; ̩fold sth ˈup to bend sth or fold it so that it is smaller: *The map folds up quite small.* ◇ *She folded the letter up and put it in her pocket.*
OPP unfold, unfold sth
♦ v + adv ♦ v + adv + n ♦ v + n/pron + adv
▶ **ˈfold-up** *adj* → FOLDAWAY at FOLD AWAY/DOWN

follow /ˈfɒləʊ; AmE ˈfɑːloʊ/

̩follow ˈon 1 (**from sth**) to continue or result from sth in a natural or logical way: *Listen carefully to the answer and make sure that your next question follows on.* ◇ *Following on from what Jill has said, I'd like to talk about the future of the company.* **2** to leave a place after sb else and meet them later: *You go now. I'll follow on later.*
♦ v + adv
▶ **ˈfollow-on** *n* (*especially BrE*) sth that continues or results from sth; the action of following on from sth: *'Jaws 2' was a follow-on to 'Jaws'.* ◇ *follow-on treatment/talks* ◇ *a follow-on call*

̩follow ˈthrough (in tennis, golf, etc.) to complete a stroke by continuing to move the club, etc. after you have hit the ball
♦ v + adv
▶ **̩follow-ˈthrough** (*also* **ˈfollow-through** *especially AmE*) *n* (in tennis, golf, etc.) the final part of a stroke after the ball has been hit

̩follow ˈthrough (**with sth**), **̩follow sth ˈthrough** to complete sth you have begun or already done: *The store did not follow through with the prosecution.* ◇ *He never follows things through.*
♦ v + adv ♦ v + adv + n ♦ v + n/pron + adv
▶ **̩follow-ˈthrough** *n* the actions that sb takes to complete or continue sth: *Your follow-through on the project was not very satisfactory.*

̩follow ˈup on sth; ̩follow sth ˈup 1 (**with sth**) to take further action about sth: *You should follow your letter up with a phone call* (= you should write first and then telephone). **2** to find out more about sth sb has told you or suggested to you: *The police are following up all the leads.* ◇ *It's worth following up his idea.* **OBJ lead, idea, complaint, matter SYN investigate sth** (*more formal*)
♦ v + adv ♦ v + n/pron + adv ♦ v + adv + n
▶ **ˈfollow-up** (**to sth**) *n* [usually sing.] sth that continues sth: *The survey is a follow-up to the questionnaire.* ◇ *follow-up treatment/studies*

fool /fuːl/

̩fool aˈround 1 (*BrE also* **̩fool aˈbout**) (**with sth**) to waste time or behave in a silly way: *Stop fooling about with that knife!* **2** (**with sb**) (*especially AmE*) to have a sexual relationship with another person's partner or with sb who is not your partner: *He's been fooling around with other women.* **3** (*AmE*) if two people **fool**

around, they kiss and touch each other in a sexual way: *We were fooling around on the couch when my dad walked in.*
♦ v + adv

ˈfool with sth (*AmE*) to touch or use sth in a careless and/or annoying way: *I caught him fooling with the buttons on the DVD.*
SYN mess with sth
♦ v + prep

force /fɔːs; AmE fɔːrs/

̩force ˈback sth to try very hard not to show an emotion: *Forcing back the tears, she nodded and smiled.*
OBJ tears
NOTE When the object of **force back** is a noun, it comes after **back**, but when the object is a pronoun, it comes between **force** and **back**: *Ruth was about to let out a scream, but she forced it back.* ♦ Not used in the passive.
♦ v + adv + n ♦ v + pron + adv

̩force sth ˈdown 1 to make yourself eat or drink sth when you do not want to: *She forced down her breakfast.* **2** to make a price, figure, etc. decrease
♦ v + adv + n ♦ v + n/pron + adv

ˈforce sth on sb (*also* **ˈforce sth upon sb** *more formal*) to make sb accept sth they do not want to: *I didn't want to take the money, but she forced it on me.* ◇ *Teachers feel that changes are being forced on them.*
OBJ change, cuts, decision
♦ v + n/pron + prep

ˈforce itself on sb (*also* **ˈforce itself upon sb** *more formal*) if sth **forces itself on** you, you cannot avoid becoming aware of it: *When he read the letter, the truth forced itself on him.*
♦ v + pron + prep

ˈforce yourself on sb (*also* **ˈforce yourself upon sb** *more formal*) to force sb to have sex with you when they do not want to, by using violence or by threatening them
♦ v + pron + prep

̩force sb ˈout; ̩force sb ˈout of sth to make sb leave a job or position against their wishes: *She was forced out of her job.*
♦ v + n/pron + adv ♦ v + adv + n
♦ v + n/pron + adv + prep

̩force sth ˈout of sb to make sb tell you sth, especially by threatening them: *I managed to force the truth out of him.*
OBJ truth
♦ v + n/pron + adv + prep

̩force sth ˈthrough to get a new law or plan officially accepted, even though some people do not want it: *The party wants to force through new environmental taxes.*
♦ v + adv + n ♦ v + n/pron + adv

̩force sth ˈup to make a price, figure, etc. increase
♦ v + adv + n ♦ v + n/pron + adv

forge /fɔːdʒ; AmE fɔːrdʒ/

ˌforge aˈhead **1** to move forward quickly: *He forged ahead, panting and breathless.* **2** (**with sth**) to make progress quickly: *The company is forging ahead with its plans.* ◇ *Jane's language skills enabled her to forge ahead on the career ladder.*
SYN press ahead/on (**with sth**)
◆ v + adv

fork /fɔːk; AmE fɔːrk/

ˌfork ˈout (**for sth**), ˌfork sth ˈout (**for/on sth**) (*informal*) to pay a lot of money for sth, especially when you do not want to: *I had to fork out for a cab home.* ◇ *I had to fork out $30 for a cab home.*
SYN shell out (**for sth**), shell sth out (**for sth**)
⟳ note at PAY OUT, PAY STH OUT
◆ v + adv ◆ v + adv + n ◆ v + pron + adv
◆ v + n + adv (*rare*)
ˌfork sth ˈover (*AmE, informal*) to pay for sth, especially when you do not want to: *I had to fork over the $10 I owed her.*
◆ v + adv + n ◆ v + pron + adv
◆ v + n + adv (*less frequent*)

form /fɔːm; AmE fɔːrm/

ˌform ˈup; ˌform sb ˈup if soldiers **form up**, or sb **forms them up**, they get into position in lines: *The general formed up his troops.* ◇ *The teams formed up into lines.*
◆ v + adv ◆ v + adv + n ◆ v + pron + adv
◆ v + n + adv (*rare*)

foul /faʊl/

NOTE A **foul** in sports is an action that is against the rules of the game.

ˌfoul ˈout (**of sth**) **1** (in basketball) if a player **fouls out**, or **fouls out of the game**, he/she makes more than the number of fouls allowed in a game and is no longer allowed to play in that game **2** (in baseball) if a player **fouls out**, he/she hits a ball into the foul area and it is caught by a player on the opposing team, so that the first player's turn to hit is over
◆ v + adv
ˌfoul ˈup; ˌfoul sth ˈup (*informal*) to do sth badly; to spoil sth, especially by making mistakes: *The team can't afford to foul up in this game.* ◇ *He admitted he'd completely **fouled things up**.*
SYN mess up, mess sth up
◆ v + adv ◆ v + adv + n ◆ v + n/pron + adv
▶ 'foul-up *n* (*informal*) a problem caused by bad organization or a stupid mistake: *an administrative foul-up* ◇ *There was a complete foul-up at the bank and the customers were sent the wrong statements.*

found /faʊnd/

ˈfound sth on sth (*also* ˈfound sth upon sth *more formal*) to base sth on sth: *Their conclusions were largely founded on guesswork.*
SYN base sth on/upon sth
NOTE Usually used in the passive.
◆ v + n/pron + prep

freak /friːk/

ˌfreak ˈout; ˌfreak sb ˈout (*informal*) if sb **freaks out** or if sth **freaks them out**, they react very strongly to sth that shocks, angers, excites or frightens them: *I don't know what happened in the exams. I just freaked out.* ◇ *I thought I'd seen a ghost—it really freaked me out.*
SYN bug out (*AmE*)
NOTE **Freak** and **freak sb** are used on their own less often with the same meaning.
◆ v + adv ◆ v + n/pron + adv
◆ v + adv + n (*less frequent*)

free /friː/

ˌfree sb/sth ˈup to do sth so that sb is able to do sth else; to make money, time, etc. available for a particular purpose: *Having a secretary frees me up to work on other things.* ◇ *I need to free up more disk space.*
NOTE **Free sb/sth** is also used on its own.
◆ v + adv + n ◆ v + pron + adv
◆ v + n + adv (*less frequent*)

freeze /friːz/ (**froze** /frəʊz; AmE froʊz/, **frozen** /ˈfrəʊzn; AmE ˈfroʊzn/)

ˌfreeze sb/sth ˈout; ˌfreeze sb/sth ˈout of sth (*informal*) to prevent sb from being part of a group or taking part in an activity, business, etc. by being very unfriendly or making things very difficult for them: *My colleagues were freezing me out.* ◇ *American rice farmers complained that their crops were being frozen out of the market.*
NOTE Often used in the passive.
◆ v + n/pron + adv ◆ v + adv + n
◆ v + n/pron + adv + prep
▶ 'freeze-out *n* (*informal, especially AmE*) an act of preventing sb from being part of a group or from taking part in an activity, a business, etc.
ˌfreeze ˈover to become covered by ice: *The river sometimes freezes over.*
SYN ice over/up
◆ v + adv
IDM till/until/when hell freezes over used to say that you think sth will never happen: *'They might give you a pay rise soon.' 'Yeah, right. When hell freezes over!'*
ˌfreeze ˈup **1** if sth **freezes up**, it becomes blocked with frozen liquid so that it cannot be used: *The pipes had frozen up.* **2** if sb **freezes up**, they are so nervous, frightened or excited that they are unable to move: *I was so nervous I froze up.*
◆ v + adv

freshen /ˈfreʃn/

,freshen 'up; ,freshen yourself 'up to wash and make yourself look clean and tidy after a journey, before a meeting, etc.: *I'll just freshen (myself) up before dinner.*
♦ v + adv ♦ v + pron + adv

,freshen sth 'up to make sth look cleaner and more attractive: *A coat of paint will freshen this room up.*
♦ v + n/pron + adv ♦ v + adv + n

frighten /ˈfraɪtn/

⌐,frighten sb/sth a'way/'off; ,frighten sb/sth a'way from sth **1** to make a person or an animal go away by making them feel afraid: *The noise frightened the birds away.* ◇ *I sometimes use a gun to frighten dogs away from the hens.* **2** to make a person or an organization so nervous that they are no longer interested in sth or no longer want to do sth: *Investment companies have been frightened off by fear of losing money.*
SYN **scare sb/sth away/off**
♦ v + n/pron + adv ♦ v + adv + n ♦ v + n/pron + prep

fritter /ˈfrɪtə(r)/

,fritter sth a'way (on sth) to waste time or money on things that are not useful or important: *He's frittered away the money his father left him.*
OBJ **money, time**
♦ v + adv + n ♦ v + n/pron + adv

front /frʌnt/

'front for sb/sth to represent a group or an organization in order to hide a secret or an illegal activity or protect the person who is controlling it: *The police could not discover who he was fronting for.*
♦ v + prep

,front 'onto sth if a building **fronts onto** sth, it faces it: *The apartment fronts onto the beach.*
♦ v + prep

frost /frɒst/; AmE frɔːst/

NOTE **Frost** is the thin white layer of ice that forms when the temperature drops below 0°C.

,frost 'over/'up to become covered with frost: *All the windows frosted up overnight.*
♦ v + adv

frown /fraʊn/

'frown on sb/sth (*also* 'frown upon sb/sth *more formal*) to disapprove of sb/sth: *Some restaurants frown on men not wearing jackets.* ◇ *Such behaviour is frowned upon.*
NOTE Often used in the passive.
→ see also SMILE ON/UPON SB/STH
♦ v + prep

fry /fraɪ/ (**fries, frying, fried**)

,fry sth 'up to cook food in oil especially in order to make a meal quickly: *He fried up some eggs and potatoes.*
♦ v + adv + n ♦ v + n/pron + adv
▶ 'fry-up *n* (*BrE, informal*) a meal of fried food

fuck /fʌk/

,fuck a'round (*BrE also* ,fuck a'bout) (**with sth**) (△, *slang*) to waste time by behaving in a silly way: *Stop fucking around and give me a hand.*
NOTE A more polite informal way of saying this is **mess around** or, in British English, **mess about**.
♦ v + adv

,fuck sb a'round (*BrE also* ,fuck sb a'bout) (△, *slang*) to treat sb in a way that wastes their time: *Don't fuck me around.*
NOTE A more polite informal way of saying this is **mess sb around** or, in British English, **mess sb about**.
♦ v + n/pron + adv

,fuck 'off (△, *slang*) used to tell sb very rudely to go away: *Fuck off and leave me alone!*
♦ v + adv

,fuck sb 'over (*AmE*, △, *slang*) to treat sb very badly or unfairly: *The company promised me a big pay-off but they really fucked me over.*
NOTE A more polite informal way to say this is **mess sb around**.
♦ v + n/pron + adv ♦ v + adv + n (*less frequent*)

,fuck 'up; ,fuck sth 'up (△, *slang*) to spoil sth or do sth badly; to make a stupid mistake: *It was my fault—I fucked up.* ◇ *He's fucked everything up.*
NOTE A more polite informal way to say this is **mess (sth) up** or **foul (sth) up**.
♦ v + adv ♦ v + n/pron + adv ♦ v + adv + n
▶ 'fuck-up *n* (△, *slang*) **1** a problem caused by bad organization or a stupid mistake NOTE A more polite informal way to say this is **foul-up**. **2** a person who is not in control of their life

,fuck sb 'up (△, *slang*) **1** to upset or confuse sb so much that they are not able to deal with problems in their life NOTE A more polite informal way to say this is **mess sb up**. **2** (*AmE*) to hit or kick sb hard many times NOTE A more polite informal way to say this is **beat sb up**.
♦ v + n/pron + adv ♦ v + adv + n
▶ ,fucked 'up *adj* (△, *slang*) extemely confused or disturbed
NOTE A more polite informal way to say this is **messed up**.
▶ 'fuck-up *n* (△, *slang*) **1** a person who is extemely confused or disturbed **2** a situation which is confused or full of problems

'fuck with sb (△, *slang*) to treat sb badly in a way that makes them annoyed

NOTE A more polite informal way to express this is **mess with sb**.

♦ v + prep

fuel /ˈfjuːəl/ (**-ll-**, AmE **-l-**)

,**fuel 'up**; ,**fuel sth 'up** to put fuel into a vehicle: *I need to fuel up before I begin the trip.* ◊ (*figurative*) *On a cold morning I like to fuel up with a hot breakfast.* ◊ *People in a hurry can fuel up their cars and themselves in one stop.*

♦ v + adv ♦ v + n/pron + adv ♦ v + adv + n

fumble /ˈfʌmbl/

,**fumble a'round** (*also* ,**fumble a'bout** *especially BrE*) to move awkwardly, especially using your hands to do sth or to find sth: *He fumbled around in the dark trying to find the lamp.*

♦ v + adv

furnish /ˈfɜːnɪʃ; AmE ˈfɜːrnɪʃ/

'**furnish sb/sth with sth** (*formal*) to supply or provide sb/sth with sth: *She furnished him with the facts surrounding the case.*

SYN supply sb/sth (with sth)

♦ v + n/pron + prep

fuss /fʌs/

'**fuss at sb** (*AmE*) to complain to sb about sb/sth very often in an annoying way: *She's always fussing at me about my smoking.*

♦ v + prep

'**fuss over sb/sth** to pay a lot of attention, or too much attention, to sb/sth: *She likes to have someone to fuss over.* ◊ *When she gets nervous she fusses over unimportant details.* ◊ *I hate being fussed over.*

♦ v + prep

futz /fʌts/

,**futz a'round** (*AmE, slang*) to spend time doing unimportant things: *I just futzed around all morning and got nothing done.*

SYN mess around (*BrE*)

♦ v + adv

G g

gabble /ˈɡæbl/

,**gabble a'way/'on** (**about sth**) to talk quickly and for a long time about sth so that people find it difficult to understand you or become bored: *Someone on the radio was gabbling away in a foreign language.* ◊ *Nicola gabbled on about her boyfriend for hours.*

♦ v + adv

gad /ɡæd/ (**-dd-**)

,**gad a'bout/a'round** (*old-fashioned*, *informal*, *humorous*, *especially BrE*) to go to different places looking for fun and excitement, especially when you should be doing sth else: *It's about time he stopped gadding about and settled down.*

♦ v + adv

gag /ɡæɡ/ (**-gg-**)

be '**gagging for sth** (*BrE, slang*) (*only used in the progressive tenses*) if sb is **gagging for** sth, they want it very much: *We were all gagging for a burger.* ◊ *Not all rock stars are gagging for it* (= wanting to have sex with sb).

SYN be dying for sth (*informal*)

NOTE You can also use **be gagging to do sth**: *footballers gagging to play for their country.*

♦ v + prep

gain /ɡeɪn/

'**gain in sth** to get more of a particular quality: *The students are slowly gaining in confidence.*

OBJ popularity, confidence, strength

♦ v + prep

'**gain on sb/sth** (*often used in the progressive tenses*) to come closer to sb/sth, especially sb/sth that you are chasing: *We were gaining on the car in front.*

♦ v + prep

gallop /ˈɡæləp/

,**gallop 'through sth** to do or say sth very quickly: *Don't gallop through your speech as if you can't wait to finish.*

♦ v + prep

gamble /ˈɡæmbl/

,**gamble sth a'way** to lose sth such as money, your possessions, etc. by risking it/them on a card game, horse race, etc.: *She gambled away all our money.*

OBJ money

♦ v + adv + n ♦ v + n/pron + adv

'**gamble on sth**; '**gamble on doing sth**; '**gamble on sb/sth doing sth** to take a risk with sth, hoping that you or it will be successful: *She's had two transplants and now her family are gambling on one last operation.* ◊ *We're gambling on the weather being fine on Saturday.*

♦ v + prep

gang /ɡæŋ/

,**gang 'up** (**against/on sb**) (*informal*) to join together, especially to oppose, threaten, hurt or frighten sb: *My brothers are always ganging up on me.*

♦ v + adv

gas /gæs/ (-ss-)

,gas 'up; ,gas sth 'up (AmE, informal) to put fuel in a vehicle: *I'll have to gas up before we leave.* ◇ *Have you gassed up the car?*
 SYN fuel up, fuel sth up
 ♦ v + adv ♦ v + adv + n ♦ v + n/pron + adv

gather /'gæðə(r)/

,gather a'round; ,gather a'round sb/sth (BrE also ,gather 'round, ,gather 'round sb/sth) to come together in one place, forming a group around sb/sth: *Everyone gathered around to hear the song.* ◇ *They all gathered round the table.*
 ♦ v + adv ♦ v + prep

,gather sth 'in to collect a quantity of things, especially crops, and put them all together in one place
 OBJ harvest, crop
 ♦ v + n/pron + adv ♦ v + adv + n

,gather 'round, etc. (BrE) → GATHER AROUND, ETC.

,gather sth to'gether/'up to bring together objects that have been spread around: *She gathered together her belongings and left.*
 OBJ papers, belongings, things
 NOTE Gather sth is used on its own with the same meaning.
 ♦ v + adv + n ♦ v + n/pron + adv

gaze /geɪz/

'gaze at sb/sth to look steadily at sb/sth for a long time, either because you are very interested or surprised, or because you are thinking of sth else: *She gazed lovingly at her baby.*
 ♦ v + prep

gear /gɪə(r); AmE gɪr/

'gear sth to/towards sb/sth; 'gear sth to/towards doing sth to make or change sth so that it is suitable for a particular need or an appropriate level or situation: *The programme is clearly geared to a teenage audience.* ◇ *We try to gear our services to customers' requirements.* ◇ *The policy is geared towards attracting nurses back to work.*
 NOTE Usually used in the passive.
 ♦ v + n/pron + prep

,gear 'up (for sth/to do sth), ,gear sb/sth/yourself 'up (for sth/to do sth) to be ready and able to do sth; to become or make sb/sth/yourself ready or able to do sth: *The players are gearing up for the big game.* ◇ *The hospital is gearing itself up to deal with new patients.*
 NOTE Usually used in the passive.
 ♦ v + adv ♦ v + n/pron + adv ♦ v + adv + n

gee /dʒiː/

,gee 'up (BrE) used to tell a horse to start moving or to go faster
 ♦ v + adv

,gee sb 'up (BrE) to encourage sb to work harder or faster or to perform better: *Their success last week will gee the team up.*
 ♦ v + n/pron + adv ♦ v + adv + n

gen /dʒen/ (-nn-)

,gen 'up; ,gen sb/yourself 'up (on sth) (old-fashioned, BrE, informal) to find out about sth; to get or give sb information on sth: *I must gen myself up for the interview.*
 ♦ v + adv ♦ v + n/pron + adv

get /get/ (getting, got, got /gɒt; AmE gɑːt/)

 NOTE In spoken American English, the past participle **gotten** is almost always used.

,get a'bout **1** (BrE also ,get a'round) if sb who is old or ill/sick gets about, they are able to move from place to place without difficulty: *She gets about with the help of a stick.* **2** (BrE) → GET AROUND
 ♦ v + adv

,get a'bout sth (BrE) → GET AROUND STH

,get a'bove yourself (especially BrE) (often used in the progressive tenses) to have too high an opinion of yourself; to behave as if you are better than other people: *She's been getting a bit above herself since winning that award.*
 ♦ v + prep + pron

,get a'cross (to sb) to be communicated to sb or understood by sb: *The message is finally getting across to the public.*
 ♦ v + adv

⚓,get a'cross; ,get a'cross sth to move from one side of a river, a bridge, a street, etc. to the other: *How can we get across to the island?* ◇ *The only way to get across the lake is by boat.* ◇ *Can we get across the city without having to use the subway?*
 ♦ v + adv ♦ v + prep

⚓,get sth a'cross (also ,get sth 'over less frequent) (to sb) to communicate sth to sb; to make sth clear to sb: *He's not very good at getting his ideas across to the class.* ◇ *You'll have to think of new ways of getting your message across effectively.*
 OBJ message, point, idea **SYN** put sth across
 NOTE Not used in the passive.
 ♦ v + n/pron + adv ♦ v + adv + n

,get sb/sth a'cross sth (also ,get sb/sth 'over sth) to move sb/sth, or to help sb/sth move, from one side of sth such as a road, river, bridge, wall, etc. to the other: *We've got to get supplies across the border somehow.* ◇ *We got all the injured soldiers across the river.* ◇ *Billy got the pony over the jumps with difficulty.*
 NOTE Not used in the passive.
 ♦ v + n/pron + prep

,get 'after sb (informal, AmE) **1** to keep asking or telling sb to do sth, often in an annoying way: *She's been getting after me to take a vacation.* ◇ *I had to get after Jack to clean his room.* **2** to

get sth across

communicate sth ◆ **convey sth** ◆ **get sth across** ◆ **pass sth on**

These verbs all mean to make sure sb receives and understands information, ideas or feelings about sth.

communicate sth to make information, ideas or feelings known to other people: *He was eager to communicate his ideas to the group.*

convey sth to make information, ideas or feelings known to sb: *He tried desperately to convey how urgent the situation was.* ◇ *Colours like red convey a sense of energy and strength.*

get sth across to succeed in communicating sth: *He's not very good at getting his ideas across.*

pass sth on to give information to sb else after receiving it yourself: *I passed your message on to my mother.*

WHICH WORD?

You can **convey**, **get across** or **pass on** information, etc. to one other person or to a group of people. You can **communicate** sth to a group of people or people in general, but not usually to one other person. **Pass on** is not used for communicating ideas or feelings. **Communicate** and **convey** are the most formal of these verbs.

PATTERNS AND COLLOCATIONS

- to convey/communicate/get across/pass on sth **to** sb
- to convey/communicate to sb **that…/what…**
- to convey/communicate/get across/pass on a **message**
- to convey/communicate/get across your **ideas**
- to convey/pass on **the news**
- to convey/communicate/get sth across **clearly/effectively**

---

try to catch sb, especially after they have committed a crime: *We need to get after drug users more.*
◆ v + prep

,get a'head; ,get a'head of sb to make more progress than other people, companies, etc.; to become successful in your life or career: *It isn't easy to get ahead in this business.* ◇ *By doing extra homework, he soon got ahead of his classmates.*
◆ v + adv ◆ v + adv + prep
IDM get a'head of yourself to tell sb before you have fully explained the background or the details that they need to know first

,get a'long (*informal*) **1** (*often used in the progressive tenses*) to leave a place: *It's late. We'd better be getting along.* ◇ *One more coffee and then I must get along.* → see also GET ON 5 **2** (**with sb/together**) → GET ON 1 **3** (**with sth**) → GET ON 4
◆ v + adv

,get a'round (*BrE also* ,get a'bout) **1** (*informal*) to move from place to place; to go to lots of different places: *You certainly get around! Paris one minute, Berlin the next.* ◇ *She can use my car to get around while she's here.* **2** (of news, a piece of information, etc.) to become known by a lot of people: *The news of her resignation soon got around.* ◇ *Word soon got around that they were having an affair.* **3** (*informal, disapproving*) to have sexual relationships with lots of different people **4** → GET ABOUT 1
◆ v + adv

,get a'round, etc. → GET ROUND, ETC.

,get a'round sth (*BrE also* ,get a'bout sth, ,get 'round sth) **1** to move around a city, a country, etc.: *It's easy to get around Amsterdam on a bicycle.* **2** (of news, a piece of information, etc.) to become known by a lot of people: *News soon gets round the office.* ◇ *It didn't take long for the rumour to get all around town.* **3** (*especially AmE*)
→ GET ROUND STH 3
◆ v + prep

,get a'round to sth, etc. → GET ROUND/AROUND TO STH, ETC.

'get at sb (*informal*) **1** (*usually used in the progressive tenses*) to keep criticizing sb: *Sam's parents are always getting at him.* ◇ *She feels she's being got at.* **2** to influence sb, especially illegally, for example by threatening them or offering money, in order to persuade them to say sth that is not true or act in an unfair way: *One of the witnesses had been got at.* ◇ *They even tried getting at the judge.*
◆ v + prep

'get at sb/sth to reach or obtain sb/sth; to find a way of entering a place, talking to sb, looking at sth, etc.: *The files are locked up and I can't get at them.* ◇ *I can't get at my inheritance until I'm 21.* ◇ *Put it in a place where it can be got at easily.*
◆ v + prep

'get at sth to learn, discover or find out sth: *We've got to get at the truth.*
OBJ truth **SYN** find sth out
◆ v + prep
IDM what are you, was he, etc. 'getting at? used to ask, often in an angry way, what sb is/was suggesting: *What exactly are you getting at?*

◇ *I see what you're getting at, but I'm afraid I can't help you with that.*

⸙ ,get a'way **1** (**from sth/…**) to succeed in leaving a place: *It was midday before we finally managed to get away.* ◇ *I won't be able to get away from the office before seven.* ⟳ note at GO AWAY **2** (**from sb/sth/…**) to escape from sb or a place: *The thieves got away in a blue van.* ◇ *You're not getting away from me so easily!* **3** to have a holiday/vacation: *We're hoping to get away for a few days at Easter.* ◇ *Will you manage to get away this year?* **4** ,get 'away (**with you**)! (*old-fashioned*, *BrE*) used to show that you find it difficult to believe what sb has just said: *Get away! You could never run that far!* ◇ *'I'm going to live in China.' 'Get away with you!'* **SYN** go on
♦ v + adv

▸ 'getaway *n* [usually sing.] **1** the act of leaving a place in a hurry, especially after committing a crime: *They made a quick getaway.* **2** a short holiday/vacation; a place for this: *the popular island getaway of Penang*

,get a'way from sth; ,get a'way from doing sth to start doing sth in a different way or talking about a different subject: *The club should get away from its old-fashioned image.* ◇ *I tried to get away from the subject of babies.*
♦ v + adv + prep

IDM get a'way from it all (*informal*) to have a short holiday/vacation in a quiet place where you can relax **there's no getting a'way from sth**; **you can't get a'way from sth** you have to admit that sth unpleasant is true: *There's no getting*

away from the fact that his mistake lost the game for his team.

,get sb/sth a'way from sth to remove sb/sth from somewhere: *Get that dog away from me!* ◇ *I tried to get Ana away from the window.* **NOTE** Not used in the passive.
♦ v + n/pron + adv + prep

⸙ ,get a'way with sth **1** to steal sth and escape with it: *Thieves raided the bank and got away with £50 000.* **2** (*also* ,get a'way with doing sth) (*informal*) to do sth wrong and not be punished or criticized for it: *I can't believe you cheated in the exam and got away with it!* ◇ *Nobody gets away with insulting me like that.* **3** to receive a relatively light punishment: *For such a serious offence he was lucky to get away with a fine.*
OBJ fine, warning
♦ v + adv + prep

⸙ ,get 'back **1** (**from/to sth/…**) to return, especially to your home: *What time did you get back last night?* ◇ *We only got back from our trip yesterday.* ◇ *It'll take us ten minutes to get there and five minutes to get back.* ⟳ note at COME BACK **2** (**from sb/sth**) (*used especially to give orders*) to move away from a place, a person or sth that is happening: *Get back or I'll shoot!*
SYN stand back; back off
♦ v + adv

,get sb 'back **1** to persuade sb to begin a romantic relationship with you again, after you have been apart for some time: *I've done everything I can to get her back.* **2** (**for sth/for doing sth**) (*informal*) → GET BACK AT SB

---

get sth back

get sth back ♦ recover sth ♦ regain sth ♦ retrieve sth ♦ reclaim sth

These verbs all mean to get back sth that you no longer have.

get sth back (*not formal*) to obtain sth again after having lost it or given it to sb: *She's got her old job back.* ◇ *I never lend books—you never get them back.*

recover sth to get back an amount of money that you have spent or that is owed to you; to get back or find sth that was lost, stolen or missing: *The police eventually recovered the stolen paintings.* ◇ *He is unlikely to ever recover his legal costs.*

regain sth to get back sth you no longer have, such as an ability, quality or position: *I struggled to regain some dignity.* ◇ *She paused on the edge, trying to regain her balance.*

retrieve sth (*formal*) to bring or get sth back, especially from a place where it should not

be: *She bent to retrieve her comb from the floor.* ◇ *The dog retrieved the ball from the water.* ◇ *The police have managed to retrieve some of the stolen money.*

reclaim sth to get sth back or to ask to have it back after it has been lost or taken away: *You'll have to go to the police station to reclaim your wallet.* ◇ *The team reclaimed the title from their rivals.*

PATTERNS AND COLLOCATIONS

- to recover sth/get sth back/retrieve sth **from** sb/sth
- to recover/regain/get back **control/the lead**
- to recover/get back/retrieve your **costs/ expenses/losses/money**
- to recover/get back **tax/your investment**
- to recover/get back/retrieve/reclaim **stolen property**

NOTE Not used in the passive.
♦ v + n/pron + adv

‚get sb/sth ‚back (**to sth/…**) to take sb/sth back to a place after they have been away from it: *We'll get her back home before midnight.*

NOTE Not used in the passive.
♦ v + n/pron + adv

‚get sth ‚back to obtain sth again after you have lost it, spent it, lent it to sb, etc.: *She's got her old job back.* ◊ *I never lend people books; you never get them back.* ◊ *If I don't like the dress, can I get my money back?* ◊ *There isn't much of a chance of getting the wallet back* (= it has been stolen).

NOTE Not used in the passive.
♦ v + n/pron + adv ♦ v + adv + n (*rare*)

IDM **get your ‚breath back** (*BrE*) to start breathing normally again after physical exercise: *It took me a while to get my breath back after running for the bus.* ◊ (*figurative*) *I haven't had a moment to get my breath back* (= I've been very busy) *since we came back from Prague.*

‚get ‚back at sb (*also* ‚get sb ‚back) (**for sth/for doing sth**) (*informal*) to punish or hurt sb because they have done sth unpleasant to you: *This is his way of getting back at me for arguing with him.* ◊ *I'll get her back for what she's done.*
SYN **pay sb back** (**for sth/for doing sth**)
♦ v + adv + prep ♦ v + n/pron + adv

‚get back ‚into sth to start being interested or involved in a particular activity again: *She'll try to get back into journalism when the kids start school.* ◊ *I should get back into serious training.*
♦ v + adv + prep

‚get ‚back to sb to reply to sb or contact them again by letter or by telephone: *Leave a message and I'll get back to you as soon as I can.* ◊ *They never got back to me about my order.*
♦ v + adv + prep

‚get ‚back to sth to start doing or talking about sth again; to return to sth: *To get back to what I was saying…* ◊ *Once I was awake I couldn't get back to sleep.* ◊ *Let's get back to the point.*
♦ v + adv + prep

‚get ‚back with sb; **‚get back to‚gether** to begin a romantic relationship with sb again, after you have been apart for some time: *Jack's getting back with his ex-girlfriend.* ◊ *Jack and his girlfriend are getting back together.*
→ see also GET TOGETHER 2
♦ v + adv + prep ♦ v + adv + adv

‚get be'hind (**with sth**) to not go as fast as is necessary or as other people; to not produce sth at the right time: *Once I get behind* (*with my work*) *it's very hard to catch up.* ◊ *We're getting behind with the rent.*
SYN **drop behind, drop behind sb/sth; fall behind, fall behind sb/sth** OPP **get ahead**
♦ v + adv

‚get be'hind sb/sth 1 to move into a position behind sb/sth: *If you get behind the tree, they won't see you.* ◊ *He seems to go mad when he gets*

behind the wheel of a car. **2** to reveal the truth about sth: *This is a programme that really gets behind the world of pop music.* **3** (*especially AmE*) to support sb/sth and help them to succeed: *The whole town got behind him/the campaign.*
♦ v + prep

‚get be'yond sth 1 (*also* ‚get 'past sth) to move or advance further than a particular place: *I haven't been able to get beyond chapter one.* ◊ *When we got beyond York, it started to snow.* **2** (*also* ‚get 'past sth) to make progress so that you no longer do or are interested in a particular thing: *Hasn't she got beyond/past the stage of sucking her thumb yet?* **3** to become more than sth: *What if our losses get beyond 10%?*
♦ v + prep

IDM **get beyond a 'joke** to become annoying and no longer acceptable: *This rain is getting beyond a joke. Let's go inside.*

‚get 'by to manage to live or do a particular thing using the money, knowledge, equipment, etc. that you have: *How does she get by on such a small salary?* ◊ *'Are you earning more money now?' 'I get by.'* ◊ *She's got a deadline to meet, so she's getting by on virtually no sleep.* ◊ *I don't know a lot of Italian, but I can get by.* ◊ *To begin with, you can get by with a few simple tools.* ◊ *Getting by isn't good enough for me. I want to be successful.*
♦ v + adv

‚get 'by; **‚get 'by sb/sth** → GET PAST, GET PAST SB/STH

‚get 'down 1 (**from sth**) to move from a higher position to a lower one: *The driver got down from his truck to help me.* OPP **get up 2** to bend downwards from a standing position and sit, lie, etc. on the ground: *The children got down on their hands and knees and pretended to be lions.* ◊ *He's going to shoot! Get down!* OPP **get up 3** (**to sth/…**) to visit or arrive at a place further south in the country than the place where you live: *How long did it take you to get down here?* OPP **get up 4** (**from sth**) (*BrE*) (of children) to leave the table after a meal: *Please may I get down* (*from the table*)? **5** (**to sth**) (*informal*) to go to a place: *I'll get down there straight away.* ◊ *I've got five minutes to get down to the store.* **6** (*AmE, informal*) to relax and enjoy yourself, especially in a very lively way: *Let's get down and party!*
♦ v + adv

‚get 'down; **‚get 'down sth** to move from a higher place to a lower one, for example using stairs, a rope, etc.: *What are you doing on the table? Get down now!* ◊ *Did you get down the hill without any difficulty?* ◊ *How does water get down the back of the sink?*
OPP **get up, get up sth**
♦ v + adv ♦ v + prep

,get sb 'down (*informal*) to make sb feel sad or depressed: *This weather is really getting me down.* ◇ *Don't let it get you down too much.*
SYN **depress sb**
NOTE Not used in the passive.
♦ v + n/pron + adv

,get sb/sth 'down 1 (to sth/...) to send or move sb/sth to a place, often a place further south in a country: *Get somebody down here straight away.* ◇ *We'll need to get the boat down to the south coast.* **OPP** **get sb/sth up 2** (**from sth**) to move sb/sth from a higher position to a lower one: *Can you get a jar down from the shelf for me?* ◇ *He got the baby down from the high chair and put her on the floor.* ◇ *Get your head down! He's going to shoot!* **NOTE** In informal spoken language **get sb down sth** and, less often, **get sb sth down**, are also used: *Can you get me down that book?* ◇ *Can you get me that book down?*
NOTE Not used in the passive.
♦ v + n/pron + adv

,get sth 'down 1 (*also* ,get sth 'down sb/you *informal*) to swallow sth, usually with difficulty: *The medicine was so horrible I could hardly get it down.* ◇ *Get this tea down you, then you'll feel better.* **SYN** **swallow sth 2** to make a note of or record sth: *Get it down in writing.* ◇ *I just managed to get down the car's registration number.* ◇ *Did you get his name and telephone number down?* **SYN** **note sth down**; **take sth down**; **write sth down 3** to reduce sth, especially the cost or price of sth: *If we bargain, we may be able to get the price down.* ◇ *How can I get my blood pressure down?* **SYN** **bring sth down**; **lower sth**
NOTE Not used in the passive.
♦ v + n/pron + adv
♦ v + adv + n (*less frequent*) **1** also v + n/pron + prep

,get sb/sth 'down sth to manage to move sb/sth from a higher place to a lower one, for example using stairs, a rope, etc.: *I can't get the bookcase down the stairs on my own.*
NOTE Not used in the passive.
♦ v + n/pron + prep

,get 'down on sb/sth (**for sth**) (*AmE, slang*) to think that sb/sth is wrong and to criticize them: *She's always getting down on me for coming in late.* ◇ *It's easy to get down on kids from day to day and forget their good points.*
♦ v + adv + prep

,get 'down to sth; ,get 'down to doing sth to begin to do sth; to give serious attention to sth: *Let's get down to business straight away.* ◇ *Isn't it about time you got down to work?* ◇ *Read the text all the way through before you get down to translating it.*
OBJ **business**, **work** ⊃ note at START ON STH
♦ v + adv + prep

,get 'in; ,get 'into sth 1 to arrive at a place: *When do you normally get in* (= arrive home) *from work?* ◇ *What time do you get into work in*

the morning? ◇ *The train got in late.* ◇ *What time does your flight get into Heathrow?* **2** (*also* ,get 'in sth *informal*) to succeed in entering a place, especially a building: *How did the burglars get in?* ◇ *They broke a window to get into the house.* ◇ *You can't get in without a ticket.* ◇ *Maybe we can get in the window?* **OPP** **get out**, **get out of sth 3** (*also* ,get 'in sth) to enter or go inside sth: *He ran to the car, got in and drove off.* ◇ *I saw Jan getting into a cab.* ◇ *Hurry up and get into bed.* ◇ *Get in the car!* ◇ *He needs help getting in the bath.* ◇ *Luckily the poison hasn't got into her bloodstream.* ◇ *The smell of smoke got into all my clothes.* **OPP** **get out**, **get out of sth** ⊃ note at GET ON, GET ON STH **4** to be elected to a political position: *They need 326 seats to get in.* ◇ *The Republican candidate got in with a small majority.* ◇ *When did she first get into Parliament?* **5** to gain a place at a school, college, university, etc.: *She's applied for Cambridge, but doesn't know if she'll get in.* ◇ *I tried to get into Harvard, but I wasn't accepted.* **6** (*also* ,get 'in sth *informal*) (*BrE, sport*) to be chosen as a member of a sports team: *He played well at the trials and got in.* ◇ *I'll never get into the senior side.* ◇ *Did you get in/into the team?*
→ see also GET INTO STH; GET INTO STH, GET SB/ YOURSELF INTO STH
♦ v + adv ♦ v + prep

,get 'in sth → GET IN, GET INTO STH 2,3,6

,get sb 'in 1 to call sb to your home, etc. to do a job for you: *We'll have to get a plumber in to mend the pipe.* **2** to attract a large audience: *A comedy usually gets the crowds in.* **SYN** **pull sb in 3** (*also* ,get sb 'into sth) to fit sb in a small place: *Can you get another person in?* (= in a car, for example) **SYN** **fit sb/sth in**, **fit sb/sth into sth 4** (*also* ,get sb 'into sth) to make it possible for sb to get into a place, attend an event, etc.: *If I come to the stage door, can you get me in?*
NOTE Not used in the passive.
♦ v + n/pron + adv ♦ v + adv + n (*rare*)

,get sth 'in 1 to collect or gather sth and bring it inside a place: *Did you get in the washing when it started raining?* ◇ *Can you get the bags in from the car?* ◇ *We worked hard all week to get the corn in.* **SYN** **bring sth in 2** to buy a supply of sth: *Have you got your coal in for the winter yet?* ◇ *Will you be getting any more of these dresses in?* ◇ (*informal*) *Who's going to get the beers in* (= buy beer for everybody)? **3** to manage to do, have, etc. sth, although there is not much time: *I can only get in an hour's piano practice a day.* ◇ *We ought to get in another meeting before the end of the month.* **SYN** **fit sth in 4** to manage to say sth, usually when there are lots of people talking: *She talks so much that it's impossible to get a word in.* ◇ *'Excuse me', I eventually got in, 'I think I can help you.'* **OBJ** **word 5** to manage to finish a piece of work and give it to sb, for example your teacher: *Did you manage to get* *your project in on time?* **6** (*also* ˌget sth 'into sth) to fit sth in a small place: *How are we going to get everything in?* SYN **fit sth in, fit sth into sth** NOTE Not used in the passive.

♦ v + n/pron + adv ♦ v + adv + n **3** v + adv + n
♦ v + n/pron + adv (*less frequent*)
♦ **4** also v + adv + speech

IDM **(not) get a word in 'edgeways** (*BrE*) (*AmE* **(not) get a word in 'edgewise**) to (not) be able to say anything because sb else is talking too much: *When those two get together, you can't get a word in edgeways.*

ˌget 'in on sth (*informal*) to become involved or take part in an activity: *How did she manage to get in on the deal?* ◊ *He's hoping to get in on any discussions about the new project.*

→ see also BE IN ON STH

♦ v + adv + prep

IDM **get ˌin on the 'act** (*informal*) to become involved in an activity that sb else has started, especially in to get sth for yourself: *Since the success of the first four-wheel drives, other companies are getting in on the act too.*

ˌget 'in with sb (*informal*) to try to become friendly with sb, especially in order to gain an advantage for yourself: *Have you noticed how he's trying to get in with the boss?* ◊ *She got in with a bad crowd at school.*

♦ v + adv + prep

ˌget 'into sb

♦ v + prep

IDM **what has got into sb?** used to say that sb has started to behave in a strange or different way: *What's got into you?* ◊ *I don't know what's got into Georgia recently—she's so bad-tempered.*

ˌget 'into sth **1** to put on a piece of clothing, especially with difficulty: *I can't get into those shoes.* ◊ *She wants to get into a size 40.* ◊ *Go upstairs and get into your pyjamas.* **2** to start a career in a particular profession: *Can you give me any advice on getting into advertising?* **3** (*also* 'get into doing sth) to become involved in an activity; to start sth: *We got into a conversation about pollution.* ◊ *He got into taking drugs at school.* ◊ *Sam's always getting into fights.* ◊ *Are you sure you know what you're getting into?* OBJ **conversation, fight, argument 4** to develop a habit, a routine, etc.: *I don't want to get into bad habits.* ◊ *We've got into a routine now.* ◊ *Get into the habit of checking your work carefully.* OBJ **habit, routine** OPP **get out of sth 5** (*informal*) to develop a taste for or an interest in sth: *I'm really getting into jazz these days.* **6** to become familiar with sth; to learn sth: *I haven't really got into my new job yet.* **7** to be found and used in a particular way or by particular people: *I hope the story doesn't get into the papers.* ◊ *I don't want this file **getting into the wrong hands** (= getting to people who should not see it).*

→ see also GET IN, GET INTO STH; GET INTO STH, GET SB/YOURSELF INTO STH

ˌget 'into sth; ˌget sb/yourself 'into sth to reach a particular state or condition, especially a bad or unpleasant one; to make sb do this: *Jerry was always getting into trouble as a boy.* ◊ *Her little brother was always getting her into trouble.* ◊ *My sense of humour often gets me into trouble!* ◊ *The company has got into difficulties* (= financial problems). ◊ *His passion for sailing has got him into debt.* ◊ *That's another fine mess I've got myself into!* ◊ *Do you realize what you're getting (yourself) into?*

OPP **get out of sth; get sb/yourself out of sth** NOTE Not used in the passive.

→ see also GET IN, GET INTO STH; GET INTO STH

♦ v + prep ♦ v + n/pron + prep

IDM **get sb into 'bed** to persuade sb to have a sexual relationship with you

ˌget sb/sth 'into sth → GET SB IN, GET SB IN STH

ˌget 'off **1** to leave a place or start a journey: *We ought to get off straight after breakfast.* ◊ *to get off to bed/work* **2** (**with sth**) to escape or nearly escape punishment: *He got off with a small fine.* ◊ *Companies who pollute the environment have been **getting off lightly**.* **3** (**with sth**) to escape or nearly escape injury in an accident: *She was lucky to get off with just a few bruises.* **4** (*BrE, informal*) to go to sleep: *I couldn't **get off to sleep** last night.* **5** (*AmE, informal, disapproving*) to be brave enough to say or do sth: *I don't know where you get off saying that musicians don't make much money.* **6** (△, *slang*) to achieve sexual satisfaction

♦ v + adv

IDM **get off to a flying 'start; get off to a 'flyer** to make a very good start: *The team have got off to a flying start this season.* **get off on the right/wrong 'foot** (*informal*) to start a relationship well/badly: *Mark and I managed to get off on the wrong foot.*

ˌget 'off; ˌget 'off sb (*informal*) used to tell sb to stop touching sb: *Get off (me)! You're hurting my arm!*

♦ v + adv ♦ v + prep

ˌget 'off; ˌget 'off sth **1** to leave a bus, train, plane, etc. that you are travelling in: *Ask the driver where to get off.* ◊ *Let's get off the bus and walk the rest of the way.* OPP **get on, get on sth** → see also GET OUT, GET OUT OF STH 2 ⟳ note on page 126 **2** to move your body from sth you are sitting, standing, lying, etc. on, down to the ground: *Get off the table at once!* ◊ *Your bike's got a flat tyre. You'd better get off and walk.* **3** to leave work with permission: *I normally get off at 5.30, but I'll try to get off earlier.* ◊ *What time do you get off work tomorrow?* **4** to stop touching sth: *Get off those cakes! They're for your grandparents.*

♦ v + adv ♦ v + prep

SYNONYMS

get off

alight ◆ disembark ◆ dismount (from sth) ◆ get off (sth) ◆ get out (of sth)

These verbs all mean to get out of a form of transport such as a car or bus, or get down from a form of transport such as a bicycle or horse.

alight (*formal*) to get out of a bus, train or other vehicle: *He would alight at Piccadilly Circus.*

disembark (*formal*) to leave a vehicle, especially a ship or plane, at the end of a journey: *We will be disembarking at midday.* ▶ disembarkation *n* [U]: *All crew should get ready for disembarkation.*

dismount (from sth) to get off a horse, bicycle or motorcycle: *She stopped her horse and dismounted.*

get off (sth) to leave a form of transport such as a bus, plane, train, etc.; to get down from a horse or bicycle: *Get off at the next stop.* ◇ *They were arrested when they got off the plane.*

get out (of sth) to get out of a vehicle such as a car: *She stopped the car and ordered him to get out.* ◇ *If you feel sleepy, get out of the car and walk around.*

PATTERNS AND COLLOCATIONS

■ to get out/get off/disembark/alight **at…**
■ to disembark/alight/dismount **from** sth
■ to get off/dismount from a **horse/motorcycle/ bicycle**
■ to get off a **bus/plane/train**
■ to get out of a **car**

,get 'off sth **1** to leave a place where you should not be: *Get off my land!* [OBJ] **land, property 2** to stop discussing a particular subject: *Doesn't she ever get off the subject of money?* [OBJ] **subject 3** to stop using the telephone: *Can you tell me when you get off the phone?* ◇ *Get off that phone! I'm waiting for a call.* [OBJ] **phone, line** [OPP] **get on sth 4** to stop using or doing sth that you have been using or doing as a habit: *I'm determined to get off the drugs.* [OBJ] **drugs, drink** → see also GET SB OFF STH 1 **5** (*AmE*) to say or write sth amusing
◆ v + prep

[IDM] ,get 'off it! (*AmE, informal*) used to tell sb to stop saying sth that you think is silly or annoying: *'I told you it wouldn't be easy!' 'Oh, get off it. I'm doing just fine.'* **get off my 'back/ 'case** (*informal*) used to ask sb to stop annoying you by criticizing you or telling you to do things **get (sth) off the 'ground** to start happening successfully; to make sth do this: *The project was slow to get off the ground.* ◇ *to get a new company off the ground*
,get sb 'off **1** (**to …**) to make or help sb leave a place or start a journey: *I'll come after I've got the children off to school.* **2** to make a baby, a child, etc. fall asleep: *She got the baby off to sleep by rocking her.* ◇ *When did you eventually get him off?* [OBJ] **baby 3** (*also* ,get sb 'off sth) to help sb to escape punishment: *She's relying on clever lawyers to get her off.* ◇ *They managed to get him off the charge.*
[NOTE] Not used in the passive.
◆ v + n/pron + adv **3** also v + n/pron + prep
,get sth 'off **1** to send sth by post/mail: *I must get these letters off tonight.* [SYN] **send sth off (to sb) 2** to remove sth from sth; to manage to

remove sth from sth: *Get your coat off and come and sit down.* ◇ *Her finger was so swollen that she couldn't get her ring off.* [OBJ] **clothes, coat** [SYN] **take sth off 3** to have permission from your employer not to go to work for a particular period of time: *Can you get some time off next week?* ◇ *I'll see if I can get the day off.* [OBJ] **time, day, week** [SYN] **take sth off** → see also GET STH OFF STH 2
[NOTE] Not used in the passive.
◆ v + n/pron + adv

[IDM] get it 'off (**with sb**) (*AmE,* △*, slang*) to have sexual relations with sb; to have strong feelings of sexual pleasure
,get sb 'off sth **1** to help sb to stop using or doing sth that they are in the habit of using or doing: *I need professional help to get me off the alcohol.* → see also GET OFF STH 4 **2** to stop sb from discussing a particular subject: *I couldn't get him off politics once he'd started* **3** → GET SB OFF 3
[OPP] get sb onto sth
[NOTE] Not used in the passive.
◆ v + n/pron + prep
,get sth 'off sb (*informal*) to succeed in getting sb to give you sth: *Did you get that money off him?* ◇ *Our team couldn't get the ball off them.*
[NOTE] Not used in the passive.
◆ v + n/pron + prep
,get sth 'off sth **1** to manage to remove sth from sth; to remove sth from somewhere: *Can you get the top off this bottle?* ◇ *She got a jar of coffee off the shelf.* ◇ *Get your feet off the chair!* **2** to get permission from your employer not to go to work during a particular period of time: *Do you think you can get the week off work?* [OBJ] **time, day, week** → see also GET STH OFF

SYN take sth off sth

NOTE Not used in the passive.

♦ **1** v + n/pron + prep

♦ **2** v + n/pron + prep + n

get 'off on sth; **get 'off on doing sth** (*informal*) to become very excited by sth, often in a sexual way or because of drugs: *She seems to get off on shouting at people.*

♦ v + prep

get 'off with sb; **get 'off together** (*informal, especially BrE*) to start a sexual or romantic relationship with sb: *Sam got off with Kate at the party.* ◇ *They got off together at the party.* ◇ *He was trying to get off with her.*

♦ v + adv + prep ♦ v + adv + adv

get 'on 1 (*BrE*) (*also* **get a'long**) (**with sb/together**) to have a friendly relationship with sb: *My mum and I never really got on (together).* ◇ *Do you get along all right with your boss?* ◇ *Do you and your boss get along all right?* ◇ *I'm glad you get on so well with her.* **2** (**with sth**) to start an activity or continue doing sth, especially after an interruption: *Be quiet and get on with your dinner!* ◇ *Let's get on with the meeting.* ◇ *She got on with the job quietly.* ◇ *If you're going to tell us, just get on with it!* ◇ *I'd love to talk but I must get on.* ◇ *All I want is to get on with my life.* **3** (**in sth**) to be successful in your career: *She's keen to get on in her career.* ◇ *Having contacts is the only way to get on in the art world.* **4** (*also* **get a'long**) (**with sth**) used to talk about how well sb is doing a task, managing a situation, etc.: *How's Jan getting on at college?* ◇ *Are you getting on alright with your project?* ◇ *I can get along without him easily.* ◇ *I'm not*

getting on very fast with this job. ◇ *How did you get on in your exams?* **5** (*often used in the progressive tenses*) to leave a place, because you have lots to do: *It's time we were getting on.*

→ see also GET ALONG 1

♦ v + adv

IDM **be getting 'on 1** (of a person) to be becoming old **2** (of time) to be becoming late: *The time's getting on—we ought to be going.* **be, getting 'on for...** to be near a particular time, age or number: *It must be getting on for midnight.* ◇ *I think he's getting on for 40.* **be, getting 'on towards/toward...** (*especially AmE*) to be near a particular time, especially a time that is late: *It must be getting on toward midnight by now.*

get 'on; **get 'on sth 1** (*also* **get 'onto sth**) to get into a bus, plane, train, etc.: *How did he manage to get on the wrong plane?* ◇ *Did Jack manage to get on?* ◇ *Did anyone see Sue getting onto the bus?* ◇ *He got on his bike and rode off.* **OBJ** **plane, bus, train, bicycle** **SYN** **board, board sth** (*more formal*) **OPP** **get off, get off sth** **NOTE** **Enter sth** cannot be used with this meaning. **2** (*also* **get 'onto sth**) to move your body so that you are standing, sitting or lying on sth: *How did the rabbit get onto the table?* **OPP** **get off, get off sth 3** to leave one road and join another: *You'll need to get on the motorway.*

♦ v + adv ♦ v + prep

get 'on sth 1 (**to sb**) to pick up the telephone and try to call sb: *Get on the phone (to them) and tell them you can't come.* **OBJ** **phone, telephone, line** **OPP** **get off sth 2** (*also* **get 'onto sth**) to be successful in being chosen to do sth such as be

get on (sth)

board (sth) ♦ **embark** ♦ **get in (sth)** ♦ **get on (sth)** ♦ **mount (sth)**

These verbs all mean to get inside or onto a form of transport.

board (sth) to get on a ship, plane, train, bus, etc.: *Passengers are waiting to board.* ◇ *She boarded a train for Philadelphia.* **NOTE** If a plane or ship is **boarding**, it is ready for passengers to get on.

embark to get onto a ship: *Will all foot passengers get ready to embark.* ◇ *The family embarked at Liverpool.* ► **embarkation** *n* [U]: *Embarkation will be at 14.20 hours.*

get in (sth) (*also* **get into sth**) to get inside a vehicle such as a car: *Rob got in beside me.* ◇ *She checked the tyres and got back into the van.*

get on (sth) (*also* **get onto sth**) to go onto or into a form of transport that carries several

people, such as a plane, bus or boat; to move your body onto a form of transport such as a bicycle or horse: *It was time to get on the plane.* ◇ *We can get on the bus at the end of the road.* ◇ *He was stopped from getting onto the ferry at the port.*

mount (sth) to get on a horse, bicycle, etc. in order to ride it: *He mounted his horse and rode away.* ◇ *Carla waved and mounted her bike again.* **NOTE** The use of **mount** without a direct object usually relates to getting on a horse: *Paul went up to the pony, mounted, and galloped off.*

PATTERNS AND COLLOCATIONS

■ to get in/get on/board/embark **at...**
■ to get on/mount a **horse/motorcycle/bicycle**
■ to get on/board a **bus/plane/train**
■ to get in a **car**

on a radio or television programme, etc.: *She'd do anything to get on the telly.* **3** (*also* ,get 'onto sth) to gain a place on a course, a committee, etc.: *I was very lucky to get onto the course.* **4** (*also* ,get 'onto sth) to be dropped, rubbed, etc. on sth; to fall on sth: *How did that mud get on the carpet? ◇ Be careful that the oil doesn't get onto your clothes.*
♦ v + prep

,get on 'sth; ,get sb on 'sth used especially in offices to mean to make telephone calls, or to contact sb by phone: *I'll get on the phone and find out exactly what he wants. ◇ I couldn't get him on the phone all day. ◇ Shall I get her on the line?*
NOTE Not used in the passive.
♦ v + prep ♦ v + n/pron + prep

,get sth 'on **1** to put on, or to manage to put on, an item of clothing, jewellery, etc.: *Get your coat on and we'll go for a walk. ◇ My finger's swollen and I can't get my ring on.* **OBJ** coat, shoes
OPP get sth off **2** to start preparing or cooking a meal, a drink, etc.: *It's nearly six o'clock. I must get the dinner on. ◇ Get the kettle on and make us a nice cup of tea.* **OBJ** dinner, kettle
SYN put sth on
NOTE Not used in the passive.
♦ **1** v + n/pron + adv ♦ v + adv + n (*less frequent*)
♦ **2** v + n/pron + adv
IDM ,get it 'on (with sb) (*slang, especially AmE*) to have sex with sb

,get sb/sth 'on sth (*also* ,get sb/sth 'onto sth *less frequent*) **1** to manage to put sb/sth onto a place: *It took four people to get the piano on the stage. ◇ Get him onto a chair and call an ambulance.* **2** to make sth reach a particular state or condition: *How did you get mud on your coat?*
NOTE Not used in the passive.
♦ v + n/pron + prep
IDM get your 'hands on sb/sth to find, obtain or catch sb/sth: *I'll need anything I can get my hands on. ◇ Just wait until I get my hands on him!*

,get 'on at sb to criticize sb a lot: *She's always getting on at me.*
♦ v + adv + prep

,get 'onto sb; ,get 'on to sb **1** (*informal*) to contact sb, especially by telephone or letter: *If you've got a complaint you'd better get onto the manager.* **2** to become aware of sb's activities, especially ones they want to keep secret: *I don't want the police getting onto me.* → see also BE ONTO SB
♦ v + prep ♦ v + adv + prep

,get 'onto sth **1** → GET ON STH 2,3,4 **2** (*also* ,get 'on to sth*) to begin to discuss a new subject: *We somehow got onto the subject of exams. ◇ It's time we got onto the question of cost.* **OBJ** subject, question **3** (*also* ,get 'on to sth) (*informal*) to start working on or thinking about sth: *I'll get*

onto it right away.* → see also BE ONTO STH
4 → GET ON, GET ON STH 1,2
♦ v + prep

,get sb 'onto sth; ,get sb 'on to sth **1** to introduce sb to sth, especially sth harmful: *Who got her onto drugs in the first place?* **2** to make sb start discussing a particular subject: *Don't get Ken onto politics or we'll be here all night!*
OPP get sb off sth
NOTE Not used in the passive.
♦ v + n/pron + prep ♦ v + n/pron + adv + prep

,get sb/sth 'onto sth → GET SB/STH ON STH

,get 'out **1** if news, etc. gets out, it becomes known, even though people are trying to keep it a secret: *If word gets out there'll be trouble. ◇ When it got out that we'd won the lottery, we couldn't escape press photographers.* **SYN** leak out **2** to have a social life outside your home: *You need to get out more.* **SYN** go out → see also GET AROUND 3 **3** Get out! (*AmE, informal*) used to show that you do not believe sth: *Get out! Ed actually said that?*
♦ v + adv

🔓,get 'out; ,get 'out of sth **1** to leave or go out of a place such as a car, a lift, a room or a house: *The car door opened and a tall man got out. ◇ I have a lot of trouble getting out of bed in the mornings. ◇ Close the door to stop the heat getting out. ◇ Get out and don't come back! ◇ Do you need help getting out of the bath?* **OPP** get in, get into sth ⊃ note at GET OFF, GET OFF STH **2** to leave a car, etc. that you are travelling in: *A car drew up and a stranger got out.* **OPP** get on, get on sth → see also GET OFF, GET OFF STH 1 **3** to manage to find a way out of a place: *It's very difficult getting out of the city in the rush hour. ◇ The thieves must have got out through the window.* **4** to leave a place, an organization, etc. in order to avoid difficulty or danger: *They were able to get out of the country before the war started. ◇ The company's in trouble—you should get out while you can.*
♦ v + adv ♦ v + adv + prep

,get sb 'out (in cricket) to end the time when sb is hitting the ball, for example by forcing them to make a mistake: *If England can get Richards out, they might win the match.*
♦ v + n/pron + adv ♦ v + adv + n (*less frequent*)

,get sb 'out; ,get sb 'out of sth to help or make sb leave a place: *Get everyone out* (= out of a building) *quickly! ◇ I couldn't get the kids out of bed this morning. ◇* (*figurative*) *I can't get her out of my mind.*
♦ v + n/pron + adv ♦ v + n/pron + adv + prep

,get sth 'out **1** to say sth with difficulty: *She was laughing so much she could hardly get the words out. ◇ I wanted to tell him how I felt, but I couldn't get it out.* **OBJ** words **2** to produce or publish sth: *Will we get the book out by the end of the year?*

NOTE Not used in the passive.
◆ v + n/pron + adv ◆ v + adv + n (*less frequent*)

get sth 'out; **get sth 'out of sth 1** to remove or take sth out of a place, a container, etc.: *Get your violin out and we'll start the lesson.* ◇ *He started to get his wallet out (of his pocket) but I insisted on paying.* ◇ *I'll need to get some money out* (= of the bank). ◇ *She got out her cigarettes and offered me one.* ◇ *I'll try and get that book out of the library.* ◇ (*figurative*) *I can't get the argument out of my mind.* **SYN** **take sth out**, **take sth out of sth 2** to remove a mark, etc. from sth: *Did you manage to get out that oil stain?* ◇ *I can't get the red wine out of the carpet.*
OBJ **stain**
◆ v + n/pron + adv ◆ v + adv + n (*less frequent*)
◆ v + n/pron + adv + prep

IDM **get sth out of your 'system** (*informal*) to do or say sth so that you no longer feel a very strong emotion or have a very strong desire: *I need to get the anger out of my system.* ◇ *You'll feel better once you've got it all out of your system.*

get 'out of sth 1 (*also* **get 'out of doing sth**) to avoid a responsibility or duty; to not do sth that you ought to do: *We promised we'd go—we can't get out of it now.* ◇ *I'll see if I can get out of going to the meeting.* **2** to stop having a particular habit: *I can't get out of the habit of waking up early.* ◇ *I don't want the children to get out of their routine.* ◇ *Try to get out of the habit of eating between meals.* **OBJ** **habit**, **routine** **OPP** **get into sth 3** to escape from a difficult situation: *Sometimes I feel I'll never get out of debt.* ◇ *How are we going to get out of this mess?* **OBJ** **debt**, **mess**, **trouble** **OPP** **get into sth 4** to remove an item of clothing: *Come in and get out of those wet clothes.* **OPP** **get into sth**
◆ v + adv + prep

▶ **'get-out** *n* [usually sing.] a way of avoiding sth; an excuse: *They're looking for a good get-out.* ◇ *The agreement contains a number of get-out clauses.*

get 'out of sth; **get sb/yourself 'out of sth** to escape from a particular state or condition, especially a bad or unpleasant one; to make or help sb do this: *Jack always uses his wits to get out of trouble.* ◇ *The situation is getting out of control.* ◇ *Who can get us out of this mess?* ◇ *This new job should help me get out of debt.* **OPP** **get into sth**; **get sb/yourself into sth** **NOTE** Not used in the passive.
◆ v + adv + prep ◆ v + n/pron + adv + prep

get sth 'out of sb to obtain sth from sb, usually by persuading or threatening them: *The police have got a confession out of her.* ◇ *It's not worth trying to get money out of him!* ◇ *I couldn't get a word out of her.*
OBJ **word**, **money**, **the best**
◆ v + n/pron + adv + prep

get sth 'out of sth; **get sth 'out of doing sth** to gain, obtain or achieve sth from a particular occasion, situation or activity: *She seems to get a lot out of life.* ◇ *He gets a lot of pleasure out of buying presents for the children.* ◇ *I didn't get much out of the conference.* ◇ *I don't feel she's getting the most out of her studies.* ◇ *John **gets a kick out of** (= gets a lot of pleasure and excitement from) driving fast cars.*
OBJ **pleasure**, **enjoyment**
◆ v + n/pron + adv + prep

get 'over (*also* **get yourself 'over** *informal*) [+adv/prep] to go to a place or to arrive somewhere: *How much will it cost you to get over to Ireland?* ◇ *I'd better get over there right now to see her.* ◇ *Get yourself over there now and tell him how you feel.*
◆ v + adv ◆ v + pron + adv

get 'over sb/sth to return to your usual state of health, happiness, etc. after the end of a relationship, an illness, a shock, etc.: *He never really got over Jennifer* (= when their relationship finished). ◇ *I'm still getting over my cold.* ◇ *My pride was hurt, but I'll get over it.*
◆ v + prep

get 'over sth 1 to deal with or gain control of sth: *Eddy's got to learn to get over his shyness.* ◇ *I think the problem can be got over without too much difficulty.* **OBJ** **shyness**, **problem** **SYN** **overcome sth 2** (*informal*) (*usually used in a negative sentence with **can't** or **couldn't**) to believe that sth surprising or unexpected really did happen or is true: *I can't get over* (= I'm very surprised by) *how much she's changed!* **3** to climb or cross sth high: *Can you get over the wall on your own?*
◆ v + prep

IDM **get 'over it** (*informal*) used to tell sb that they should stop worrying about sth which you think is not important or not their business: *These people don't like the way I dress. They should get over it!*

get 'over yourself (*informal*) to realize that you are not as good, important, etc. as you think you are: *She needs to get over herself!*
◆ v + prep

get sb 'over [+adv/prep] to arrange for sb to go or come to a place: *Get a reporter over here straight away!* ◇ *Shall we get my parents over for dinner tonight?*
NOTE Not used in the passive.
◆ v + n/pron + adv

get 'over 1 → GET STH ACROSS (TO SB) **2** (*informal*) to complete sth necessary and usually unpleasant: *Can we just get this test over?* ◇ *Let's tell her the news now and **get it over with**.* ◇ *I'll be glad to **get** the exam **over and done with**.*
NOTE Not used in the passive.
◆ **1** v + n/pron + adv ◆ v + adv + n
◆ **2** v + n/pron + adv

get

,get yourself 'over [+adv/prep] → GET OVER
,get sb/sth 'over sth → GET SB/STH ACROSS STH
,get 'past; ,get 'past sb/sth (also ,get 'by, ,get
'by sb/sth less frequent) **1** to manage to move
past sb/sth: *He tried to get past them and run for
the door.* ◇ *Once we get past this truck I can speed
up.* **2** to pass sb/sth without being noticed,
caught or stopped: *It'll be difficult to get past the
ticket collector without paying.* ◇ *The movie will
never get past the censors.* ◇ *Very few goals get
past the goalkeeper.*
 ◆ v + adv ◆ v + prep
,get 'past sth → GET BEYOND STH 1, 2
,get sb/sth 'past sb/sth **1** to manage to move
 sb/sth past sb/sth: *I couldn't get the baby's buggy
 past the car parked on the pavement.* **2** to make
 sb/sth go past sb/sth without being noticed,
 stopped or caught: *You won't get any goals past
 him!* ◇ *How did you get your article past the
 editor?*
 NOTE Not used in the passive.
 ◆ v + n/pron + prep
,get 'round; ,get 'round sth (BrE) (also ,get
 a'round, ,get a'round sth AmE, BrE) **1** (sport) to
 complete a course and return to the beginning:
 *How long did it take you to get round (the
 course)?* **2** to fit in a circle around a table, etc.:
 Can we all get round (the table)?
 ◆ v + adv ◆ v + prep
,get 'round sb (also ,get a'round sb especially
 AmE) to persuade sb to let you do or have sth, or
 to do what you want, often by being nice to
 them: *I'll try and get round my dad tonight and
 persuade him to give us a lift.*
 ◆ v + prep
,get 'round sth (BrE) **1** → GET AROUND STH 1
 2 → GET AROUND STH 2 **3** (also ,get a'round sth
 especially AmE) to deal with a problem successfully; to avoid sth: *There's no getting round it.
 We're just going to have to pay.* ◇ *A clever lawyer
 might be able to get round that clause.* ◇ *There
 must be a way these rules can be got round.*
 ◆ v + prep
ﬔget 'round/a'round to sth; ,get 'round/
 a'round to doing sth to find the time to do
 sth: *I haven't got round to asking him yet.* ◇ *One
 of these days I'll get around to buying a new car.*
 ◇ *I'm going to write to Uncle Joe, but I haven't got
 around to it yet.*
 ◆ v + adv + prep
ﬔget 'through **1** (to sb) to make contact with sb
 by telephone: *I tried ringing you but I couldn't
 get through.* ◇ *We had great trouble getting
 through to the right person on the phone.* **2** (to
 sb) to make sb understand or accept what you
 say to them, especially when you are trying to
 help them: *I don't feel I'm getting through (to
 her).* ◇ *Do you think the message is getting
 through?* ◇ *How can I **get it through to** him that
 he's wasting his life in that job?* **3** (to sb/sth) to
 succeed in reaching a place or a person:

*Thousands of refugees will die if these supplies
don't get through (to them).* **4** (to sth) to reach
the next stage of a competition: *Murray got
through to the final.* ◇ *I really wasn't expecting to
get through!*
 ◆ v + adv
ﬔget 'through; ,get 'through sth **1** to survive
 a difficult or unpleasant experience or period in
 your life: *He wouldn't have got through (it)
 without her.* ◇ *I don't know how I got through the
 day.* ◇ *These difficult times just have to be got
 through.* OBJ **day** SYN **survive, survive sth**
 → see also GET SB THROUGH, GET SB THROUGH
 STH 1 **2** to be successful in an examination,
 a test, etc.: *Tom failed but his sister got
 through.* ◇ *The whole class got through the exam.*
 OBJ **exam** SYN **pass, pass sth 3** to manage to
 pass through a hole, gap, etc. to reach the other
 side: *The gap's not very wide. Do you think you
 can get through?* ◇ *Sophie's probably small
 enough to get through the window.* ◇ *The sun
 was still trying to get through (the clouds).*
 OBJ **window** → see also GET STH THROUGH,
 GET STH THROUGH STH 2 **4** to be officially
 approved or accepted: *Do you think the bill will
 get through (Congress)?* OBJ **Parliament, Congress** → see also GET STH THROUGH, GET STH
 THROUGH STH 1
 ◆ v + adv ◆ v + prep
ﬔget 'through sth **1** (especially BrE) to use up the
 amount or quantity of sth mentioned: *She gets
 through forty cigarettes a day.* ◇ *Have we got
 through all that milk already?* **2** to manage to do
 or complete sth: *I've got a lot of work to get
 through today.* ◇ *We must get through the syllabus before the end of the year.* ◇ *There are a lot of
 jobs to be got through.* OBJ **work**
 ◆ v + prep
,get sb 'through; ,get sb 'through sth **1** to
 help sb survive a difficult or unpleasant experience or period in their life: *I'm depending on
 luck to get me through.* ◇ *A good breakfast will
 help you get through the morning.* SYN **bring sb
 through, bring sb through sth** (AmE) → see also
 GET THROUGH, GET THROUGH STH 1 **2** to help sb
 to be successful in an examination, a test, etc.:
 My mum got me through my driving test. ◇ *These
 grades should just get me through.* → see also
 GET THROUGH, GET THROUGH STH 2 **3** (to sth) to
 help a player or team to reach the next stage of
 a competition: *He was responsible for getting
 them through that round.* ◇ *A stroke of luck may
 get us through to the final.*
 NOTE Not used in the passive.
 ◆ v + n/pron + adv ◆ v + n/pron + prep
,get sth 'through (to sb/sth) to manage to send
 sth to a person or place: *I really need to get a
 message through to them.* ◇ *We must get food
 through to the hungry.*
 NOTE Not used in the passive.
 ◆ v + n/pron + adv

‚get sth 'through; ‚get sth 'through sth 1 to make sth be officially approved or accepted: *I'm still trying to get the proposal through.* ◇ *Will he manage to get the bill through parliament?* [OBJ] **bill 2** to cause sth to pass through sth: *Can you get your car through the gate?* ◇ *My hair was so tangled that I couldn't get a comb through it.* [NOTE] Not used in the passive.
→ see also GET THROUGH, GET THROUGH STH 3
♦ v + n/pron + adv ♦ v + n/pron + prep

'get to sb (*informal*) to begin to annoy, anger, upset or affect sb, even though they try not to let it: *His constant nagging is beginning to get to her.* ◇ *Don't let her get to you.* ◇ *Seeing him so sad really got to me.*
♦ v + prep

'get to sth to arrive at a place or reach a particular situation, age, time, etc.: *The train gets to London at six o'clock.* ◇ *I didn't get to bed until after midnight last night.* ◇ *It's got to the stage/point where I don't want to go home.* ◇ *When you get to my age you're a bit more relaxed about things.* ◇ *It got to four o'clock and she still hadn't arrived.* ◇ *I wonder **where** Anthony's **got to** (= where he is/what he is doing)?*
[OBJ] **bed, stage, point** ⊃ note at CATCH UP
♦ v + prep

'get to doing sth to reach the point where you do sth; to begin to do sth: *He got to thinking that perhaps she wouldn't come after all.*
♦ v + prep

‚get to'gether (with sb) 1 to meet with sb for social purposes or to discuss or organize sth: *We must get together for a drink some time.* ◇ *The management should get together with the union to discuss their differences.* ◇ *Local residents have got together and started a petition.* **2** to begin a relationship with sb: *Did you two get together (with each other) at university?* → see also GET BACK WITH SB, GET BACK TOGETHER
♦ v + adv

▶ **'get-together** *n* (*informal*) an informal social meeting; a small party: *a family get-together* ◇ *We're having a little get-together to celebrate Jane's exam results.*

‚get A and B to'gether to help two people begin a romantic relationship with each other: *I was the one who got them together.*
[SYN] **bring A and B together**
[NOTE] Not used in the passive.
♦ v + n/pron + adv

‚get sb/sth to'gether to bring people or things together in one place: *She's getting her things together ready to leave.* ◇ *Do you think you could get together a team for Saturday's match?* ◇ *We're getting a band together.* ◇ (*figurative*) *We'll need some time to **get our ideas together** and come up with a plan.* ◇ *Can you get the money together by Friday?* ◇ *Do you think you can get together a*

proposal by next week? ◇ *I haven't got anything together for the trip.*
♦ v + n/pron + adv ♦ v + adv + n

[IDM] **get your 'act together** (*informal*) to become organized in order to be able to deal with or achieve sth: *If he gets his act together he could be very successful.* ◇ *The government needs to get its act together on unemployment.* **get it to'gether (with sb)** (*informal*) **1** to start a romantic or sexual relationship with sb: *I didn't know Bill and Gina had got it together!* **2** to become organized in order to be able to deal with or achieve sth: *The team needs to get it together if they want to win the match.*

‚get yourself to'gether to manage to control your feelings in a difficult situation: *She paused outside the door to get herself together.*
[SYN] **pull yourself together**
♦ v + pron + adv

‚get 'up 1 to stand after sitting, lying, etc.: *Everyone got up when the President came in.* ◇ *He got up slowly from his chair.* ◇ *Get up off the floor!* ⊃ note at STAND UP **2** [+adv/prep] to visit or travel to a place (usually somewhere further north in the country): *When are you going to get up to Glasgow for a visit?* ◇ *He doesn't get up to see me very often.* ◇ *I won't be able to get up there until Wednesday.* [OPP] **get down 3** if the sea or the wind **gets up**, it increases in strength: *As the sun went down, a breeze got up.*
♦ v + adv

▶ **‚get-up-and-'go** *n* [U] (*informal*) the quality of being determined and full of energy: *She's got lots of get-up-and-go.*

‚get 'up; ‚get sb 'up to get out of bed; to make sb get out of bed: *What time do you usually get up?* ◇ *Could you get me up early tomorrow?* ◇ *Get up, you lazy thing!* ⊃ note at WAKE UP, WAKE SB UP
♦ v + adv ♦ v + n/pron + adv

‚get 'up; ‚get 'up sth to climb to the top of sth such as a hill, steps, etc.: *How did the cat get up there?* ◇ *He can't really get up the stairs on his own.* ◇ *We used ropes to get up the mountain.* ◇ *I had to get up on the desk and shout to get somebody's attention.*
[OBJ] **mountain, hill, stairs, steps** [OPP] **get down, get down sth**
♦ v + adv ♦ v + prep

‚get 'up sth 1 to make yourself feel excited, full of energy, etc.: *I'm trying to **get up the enthusiasm** to do some Christmas shopping.* [OBJ] **enthusiasm, energy 2** to organize sth such as a public event or action: *Parents are getting up a petition against the closure of the local school.* ◇ *We're getting up a party for her birthday.*
♦ **1** v + adv + n
♦ **2** v + adv + n ♦ v + pron + adv ♦ v + n + adv (*rare*)
[IDM] **get up 'speed** to start to go faster: *We'll be able to get up speed once we get onto the motorway.*

gin

,get sb/sth 'up 1 (to sth) to send or move sb/sth to another place, often a place further north in the country: *We need to get somebody up there straight away.* ◇ *How can we get all our equipment up to Leeds?* **OPP get sb/sth down 2** (*also* **,get sb/sth 'up sth**) to move sb/sth from a lower position to a higher one: *Can you get me up onto the chair?* ◇ *How did you get the bed up the stairs?* **OPP get sb/sth down; get sb/sth down sth**
NOTE Not used in the passive.
◆ v + n/pron + adv **2** *also* v + n/pron + prep

,get sth 'up 1 to build sth; to put sth into a standing position: *They got the building up in just a few months.* ◇ *Can you get the tent up while I go and find water?* **2** if sb **gets** their hopes **up**, they start to hope and believe that sth they want will happen: *I don't want to get your hopes up, but there will probably be a place on the course for you.* **OBJ** only **hopes**
NOTE Not used in the passive.
◆ v + n/pron + adv

IDM get sb's 'back up (*informal*) to annoy sb: *He really gets my back up when he behaves like that!*
get it 'up (*slang*) (of a man) to become sexually excited

,get sb/yourself 'up as/in sth to dress sb/ yourself in unusual or strange clothes: *She was got up as an Indian princess.*
◆ v + n/pron + adv + prep
▶ **'get-up** *n* (*old-fashioned, informal*) a set of clothes, usually an unusual or strange one: *He looked ridiculous in that get-up!*

,get 'up to sth 1 to reach a particular point: *We got up to page 72 last lesson.* ◇ *I've got to get up to intermediate level in French in a year.* **2** (*informal*) to be doing or be involved in sth, especially sth that is surprising or unpleasant: *What on earth will he get up to next?* ◇ *What have you kids been getting up to?* ◇ *The boys are lively and get up to mischief all day.* ◇ *She's been getting up to her old tricks again!*
◆ v + adv + prep

,get 'with sb to start a relationship with sb, usually a sexual relationship: *She knew her brother was trying to get with her.*

,get 'with sth (*informal*) to start to behave or think in a way that sb else wants you to behave or think; to accept sth as being true or right: *They never had a hit because they refused to get with the publicity machine.* ◇ *He shook his head. 'I just cannot get with that.'*
IDM get 'with it (*informal*) to become aware of what is in fashion and start to follow it: *You need to get with it!* **get with the 'programme** (*AmE* **get with the 'program**) (*informal*) used to tell sb to change their attitude and start doing what they are supposed to be doing: *You need to get with the programme!*

gin /dʒɪn/

,gin sth 'up (*AmE*) to invent sth or create sth that is artificial in order to achieve a goal: *Presidents will do anything in an election year to save the economy, including gin up inflation.*
◆ v + adv + n ◆ v + pron + adv ◆ v + n + adv (*rare*)

ginger /'dʒɪndʒə(r)/

,ginger sb/sth 'up (*BrE*) to make sb/sth more active, interesting or exciting: *Some dancing would ginger up the party.* ◇ *They need some excitement to ginger them up a bit.*
◆ v + adv + n ◆ v + n/pron + adv

give /gɪv/ (*gave* /geɪv/, *given* /'gɪvn/)

,give sb a'way 1 (in a marriage ceremony) to lead the woman who is getting married to the man she is going to marry and formally allow her to marry him: *Her father gave her away.* **2** (*BrE*) to give a baby or a child to another person to take care of as their own child: *She had never understood why her mother had given her away.* → see also GIVE SB UP 2
◆ v + n/pron + adv ◆ v + adv + n

,give sb/sth/yourself a'way to do or say sth that shows sth about sb/sth/yourself that was a secret: *It was her eyes that gave her away* (= showed how she really felt). ◇ *He never gives very much away about himself.* ◇ *She had given away state secrets to the enemy.* ◇ *I found I could tell lies confidently without giving myself away.*
OBJ nothing, anything, little SYN betray sb/ sth/yourself (*more formal*)
◆ v + adv + n ◆ v + n/pron + adv
IDM ,give the 'game away to tell a secret, especially by accident; to show sth that has been hidden: *I don't want to give the game away by telling you how the movie ends.*
▶ **'giveaway** *n* (*informal*) sth that makes you guess the real truth about sth: *He said he was French, but his accent was a dead giveaway!* (= showed clearly that he was not French)

,give sth a'way 1 to give sth to sb as a gift: *He decided to give most of his money away.* ◇ *We have 200 tickets to give away free to our viewers.* **2** (*AmE*) to do sth in an election or competition that allows the other side to win easily: *We could have won the play-offs if we'd tried, but we gave the final game away.*
◆ v + n/pron + adv ◆ v + adv + n
▶ **'giveaway** *n* (*informal*) sth that a company gives free, usually with a product for sale, to persuade people to buy it
▶ **'giveaway** *adj* [only before noun] (*informal*) (of prices) very low

,give sth 'back (to sb) 1 to return sth to its owner: *You can't have it. Give it back!* ◇ *Have you given back the money you borrowed from your father?* ◇ *Can you lend me $20? I'll give it back to you later.* ◇ *The new law gives some power back to the people.* ◇ (*figurative*) *The operation gave*

give sb/sth away

betray sb/sth ◆ **disclose sth** ◆ **divulge sth** ◆ **give sb/sth away** ◆ **reveal sth**

These verbs all mean to give information about sb/sth to sb, especially when that information is supposed to remain secret.

betray sb/sth to tell sb or make them aware of a piece of information or a feeling, usually without meaning to: *His voice betrayed the worry he was trying to hide.* ◇ *She was terrified of saying something that would make her betray herself* (= show her feelings or who she was).

disclose sth to make sth known to sb, especially sth that was previously secret: *The spokesman refused to disclose details to the press.*

divulge sth (*formal*) to give sb information that is supposed to be secret: *Police refused to divulge the identity of the suspect.*
NOTE **Divulge** is often used in the negative, or with a verb that has a negative meaning, like **refuse**.

give sb/sth away to make known sth that sb wants to keep secret: *She gave away state*

secrets to the enemy. ◇ *His voice gave him away* (= showed who he really was).

reveal sth to make sth known to sb, especially sth that was previously secret: *The doctors did not reveal the truth to him.* ◇ *It was revealed that important evidence had been suppressed.*

WHICH WORD?

A person who **gives sth away** should really be keeping the information secret; a person who **divulges** information is more likely to have the authority to do so. **Disclose** is always rather formal; **reveal** can be used in formal or less formal contexts, including popular newspapers.

PATTERNS AND COLLOCATIONS

- to reveal/disclose/betray/divulge/give away sth **to** sb
- to reveal/disclose/betray/divulge/give away **that/who/where...**
- to reveal/disclose/betray/divulge/give away a **secret**
- to reveal/disclose/give away **the truth**
- to reveal/disclose/divulge/give away **details** of sth

him back the use of his legs. SYN **hand sth back** (**to sb**); **return sth** (**to sb**) (*more formal*) NOTE In informal language **give sb back sth** and, less often, **give sb sth back** are also used: *Could you give me back my pen?* ◇ *Could you give me my pen back?* **2** to do sth which benefits a group of people because they have done sth for you: *I'd like to give something back to the community.*
◆ v + n/pron + adv ◆ v + adv + n

'**give sth for sth** to pay or give a particular amount to have or do sth: *How much did you give for the car?* ◇ *I'd give anything for a cold beer.*
NOTE Not used in the passive.
◆ v + n/pron + prep

,**give 'in** (**to sb/sth**) **1** to accept that you have been defeated or persuaded by sb: *I give in— you'll have to tell me the answer.* ◇ *Eventually I gave in to temptation and had an ice cream.* **2** to finally agree to do sth that you do not want to do: *We mustn't give in to terrorist demands.* ◇ *She gives in to the children all the time to avoid arguments.* OPP **hold out** (**against sb/sth**)
◆ v + adv

,**give sth 'in** (**to sb**) to hand sth to sb in authority, for example a teacher: *Please give your test in* (*to the teacher*) *when you've finished.* SYN **hand sth in** (**to sb**)
◆ v + n/pron + adv ◆ v + adv + n

'**give of sth**; '**give of yourself** (*formal*) to give your time or money willingly to help other people without expecting them to do anything for you: *She's always willing to give of her time to help the homeless.* ◇ *The teacher encourages all the children to give of their best.*
OBJ **time**, **best**
◆ v + prep ◆ v + prep + pron

,**give 'off sth 1** to produce sth such as heat, light, smoke, etc.: *Burning apple wood gives off a pleasing smell.* OBJ **smell**, **aroma**, **light**, **gas** → see also GIVE STH OUT **2 2** to give a particular impression by the way you look or behave: *She gave off an air of confidence.*
NOTE When the object of **give off** is a noun, it comes after **off**, but when the object is a pronoun, it comes between **give** and **off**: *They absorb radiation from the sun, then give it off at night.*
◆ v + adv + n ◆ v + pron + adv (*less frequent*)

'**give onto sth** (*BrE*) if a door, a window, etc. **gives onto** sth, it has a view of it or leads directly to it: *French windows give onto a balcony.*
◆ v + prep

,**give 'out 1** to come to an end; to be used up: *My patience finally gave out.* ◇ *We were fine until the batteries in the torch gave out.* SYN **run out 2** if an engine, a machine, etc. **gives out**, it stops working, especially because it is old or damaged: *One of the plane's engines gave out.* ◇ (*figurative*) *His heart gave out just before his eightieth birthday.* SYN **break down**

⟁**give sth 'out 1** to hand sth to a lot of people: *The teacher gave out the exam papers.* ◇ *I'll write up the report and give it out to the whole department.* OBJ **cards**, **leaflets** SYN **hand sth out** (**to sb**) NOTE In informal spoken language **give sb out sth** is also used: *I'll give you out the cards later.* **2** to produce sth, such as light or heat: *That lamp doesn't give out a lot of light.* OBJ **light**, **heat**, **noise** → see also GIVE OFF STH 1 **3** (*BrE*) to tell people sth or broadcast sth: *No details of the accident have been given out yet.* ◇ *The leader of the opposition has **given out that** she is resigning.* OBJ **information** NOTE Often used in the passive.
  ◆ v + adv + n ◆ v + n/pron + adv

,**give 'over** (*BrE, informal*) used to tell sb to stop doing sth: *Give over! I can't work with you shouting like that.*
  ◆ v + adv

,**give sb/sth 'over to sb** to let sb have sb/sth so that they can look after or have responsibility for them/it: *We gave the house over to my uncle when we went to live abroad.*
  ◆ v + n/pron + adv + prep ◆ v + adv + n + prep

,**give sth 'over to sth** to use sth only for a particular activity or purpose: *The newspapers*

gave six pages over to the tragedy. ◇ *Much of the countryside is given over to agriculture.*
NOTE Often used in the passive.
  ◆ v + n/pron + adv + prep ◆ v + adv + n + prep

,**give yourself 'over/'up to sth**; ,**give yourself 'over/'up to doing sth** to spend all your time and energy on sth; to allow sth to completely control your life: *After his wife's death, he seemed to give himself over to despair.* ◇ *I want to give myself over to writing full-time.*
  ◆ v + pron + adv + prep

⟁,**give 'up**; ,**give sth 'up**; ,**give 'up doing sth 1** to stop trying to do sth, usually because it is too difficult: *She doesn't give up easily.* ◇ *I tried to fix the car myself, but gave up the attempt after a couple of hours.* ◇ *I've given up trying to understand her.* → see also GIVE IN (TO SB/STH) **2** to stop doing or having sth that is not good for your health: *It's about time you gave up smoking.*
  ◆ v + adv ◆ v + adv + n ◆ v + pron + adv
  ◆ v + n + adv (*less frequent*) ◆ v + adv + -ing

,**give sb 'up 1** to stop having a friendship or a relationship with sb: *I'm not going to give up all my friends just because I'm getting married.* ◇ *He gave her up for a younger woman.* **2** to give a baby to sb else to bring up: *She gave the baby up for adoption.* → see also GIVE SB AWAY 2 **3** (*also* ,**give 'up on sb** *especially AmE*) to stop hoping

give sth up

give sth up ◆ **knock off** (**sth**) ◆ **leave off** (**sth**) ◆ **pack sth in** ◆ **quit** (**sth**) ◆ **stop** (**sth**)

These verbs all mean to no longer continue to do sth.

give sth up to stop doing or having sth: *She didn't give up work when she had the baby.* ◇ *We'd given up hope of ever having children.* ◇ *He gave up medicine for a career in show business.*

knock off (**sth**) (*informal*) to stop doing sth, especially work: *Do you want to knock off early today?*

leave off (**sth**) (*informal*) to stop doing sth, especially temporarily: *Start reading from where you left off last time.*

pack sth in (*informal*) to stop doing sth: *She decided to pack in her job.*

quit (**sth**) (*informal, especially AmE*) to stop doing sth: *I'm still trying to quit smoking.* ◇ *We only just started. We're not going to quit now.*

stop (**sth**) to no longer continue to do sth; to make sth no longer happen: *Please stop*

crying and tell me what's wrong. ◇ *He couldn't stop thinking about her.* ◇ *Stop it! You're hurting me.*

WHICH WORD?

Give up, **quit**, **leave off**, **knock off** and **pack sth in** are all informal ways of saying 'stop doing sth'. **Knock off** is usually used about work, when you stop work at the end of the day or for a short time. You can **give up**, **quit** or **pack in** your job if you leave to do something else. If you *give up/quit work* you leave your job and don't get another one. **Leave off** is also usually used when you stop sth temporarily and expect to start again later.

PATTERNS AND COLLOCATIONS

■ to stop/give up/quit/leave off **doing sth/ what…**
■ to give up sth **for/in favour of** sth else
■ to stop/give up/quit/leave off/knock off **work**
■ to give up/quit/pack in your **job**
■ to stop/give up/quit **smoking**

that sb will arrive or is still alive: *Where have you been? We'd given you up!*
- ◆ v + n/pron + adv ◆ v + adv + n **2** also v + adv + prep
- **IDM** give sb up for 'lost/'dead to no longer hope or expect that sb will arrive or is still alive

give sth 'up 1 to stop doing or having sth: *He's given up the idea of becoming a model.* ◇ *She'd given up all hope of seeing him again.* **2** (to sb) to let sb else have sth, sometimes because they need it more than you: *Children rarely give up their seats to older people on buses now.* **3** (to sb) to hand sth over to sb else: *Do I have to give up my old passport when I apply for a new one?* **4** to spend time doing sth when you would normally be doing sth else: *Thanks for giving up your time to come and help us.* **OBJ** time, the morning, etc. **5** (for sb/to do sth) to stop doing or having sth that you enjoy so that you can do or achieve sth that you consider more important: *I gave up everything for my family.* ◇ *She gave it all up to be with him.*
- **NOTE** Not often used in the passive.
- ◆ v + adv + n ◆ v + pron + adv
- ◆ v + n + adv (*less frequent*) **3** v + n/pron + adv
- ◆ v + adv + n
- **IDM** give it up for sb (*informal, especially AmE*) to clap to show you approve of sb or have enjoyed sth

give yourself 'up (to sb/sth) to allow yourself to be arrested or captured: *After a week on the run he gave himself up to the police.*
- **SYN** surrender (to sb/sth)
- ◆ v + pron + adv

give 'up on sb (*informal*) **1** to lose hope that sb will get better, change, etc.: *I've given up on her. She never replies to my letters.* ◇ *His teachers seem to have given up on him.* **2** (*especially AmE*) → GIVE SB UP 3
- ◆ v + adv + prep

give 'up on sth (*informal*) to stop hoping that sth will be successful or will happen: *I haven't given up on my marriage yet.* ◇ *Have you given up on the idea of emigrating?*
- ◆ v + adv + prep

give yourself 'up to sth → GIVE YOURSELF OVER/UP TO STH

glam /glæm/ (-mm-)

glam 'up; glam yourself/sb 'up to make yourself/sb look attractive by wearing clothes, make-up, etc. that look expensive: *We got all glammed up in preparation for our night out.*
- ◆ v + adv ◆ v + n/pron + adv ◆ v + adv + n

glance /glɑːns; AmE glæns/

glance 'off sth if a ball, etc. **glances off** sth, it touches it lightly and moves away from it in a different direction: *The ball glanced off the goalpost into the net.*
- ◆ v + prep

glance 'off/'on sth if light **glances off/on** sth, it flashes on a surface or is reflected from it: *the sun glancing on water*
- ◆ v + prep

glance 'over/'through sth to look at or read sth very quickly and not very thoroughly: *Could you glance over this document for me?* ◇ *I glanced through a magazine while I waited.*
- **OBJ** book, list
- ◆ v + prep

glare /gleə(r); AmE gler/

glare at sb/sth to look at sb/sth in an angry way: *He glared at me with open hostility.*
- ◆ v + prep

glaze /gleɪz/

glaze 'over if a person's eyes **glaze over**, the person begins to look very bored or tired: *Her eyes glazed over when they started talking about football.* ◇ *I started to glaze over at that point.*
- **NOTE** Glaze can also be used on its own: *Her eyes glazed with tears.*
- ◆ v + adv

glom /glɒm; AmE glɑːm/ (-mm-)

glom 'onto sth (*AmE, slang*) to become very interested in sth such as a new fashion or an idea: *The whole nation glommed onto the scandal.*
- ◆ v + prep

glory /'glɔːri/ (glories, glorying, gloried)

'glory in sth (*literary*) **1** to get great pleasure or enjoyment from sth: *He gloried in his son's success.* ◇ *I gloried in the beauty of the scenery.* **2** to take pleasure in sth: *She seemed to glory in his failure.*
- ◆ v + prep

gloss /glɒs; AmE glɔːs, glɑːs/

gloss 'over sth to treat sth such as a problem, mistake, etc. as if it was not important and avoid discussing it in detail: *The manager glossed over the team's recent defeat.* ◇ *The movie glosses over the real issues of the war.* ◇ *This question has been glossed over by politicians.*
- ◆ v + prep

gnaw /nɔː/

'gnaw at sb to make sb feel gradually more anxious or annoyed over a long period of time: *These doubts had been gnawing at him for some time.*
- ◆ v + prep

gnaw a'way at sth to gradually have a harmful effect on sth over a long period of time: *His attitude towards her gnawed away at her confidence.*
- ◆ v + adv + prep

go /gəʊ; *AmE* goʊ/ (**goes** /gəʊz; *AmE* goʊz/, **went** /went/, **gone** /gɒn; *AmE* gɔːn, gɑːn/)

NOTE Been is used as the past participle of **go** when sb has gone somewhere and come back.

ˌgo aˈbout, etc. (*BrE*) → GO AROUND, ETC.

ˈgo about sth to continue to do sth in your usual way, especially after sth unusual has happened; to keep busy with sth: *Everybody was going about their business as usual.*
OBJ your business, the business of…, work, task
♦ v + prep

ˌgo aˈbout sth; ˌgo aˈbout doing sth to start to work at sth; to approach or deal with sth: *I want to help, but I don't know how to go about it.* ◇ *How should I go about finding a job?* ◇ *You're not going about it the right way.* ◇ *It seems a strange way of **going about things**.*
OBJ things **SYN** set about sth, set about doing sth; tackle sth
♦ v + prep

ˌgo aˈcross; ˌgo aˈcross sth to cross a room, a road, a river, etc. in order to get to the other side: *We borrowed a boat and went across to the island.* ◇ *Can you go across the road to the store for me?*
♦ v + adv ♦ v + prep

ˌgo ˈafter sb/sth 1 to chase or follow a person or an animal to try to catch them: *He went after the burglars.* ◇ *Aren't you going to go after her to see if she's all right?* 2 to try to get or obtain sb/sth: *We're both going after the same job.*
♦ v + prep

ˌgo aˈgainst sb if a result, a judgement, etc. goes against sb, it is not in their favour or to their advantage: *The jury's verdict went against him.* ◇ *The war is going against us.*
♦ v + prep

ˌgo aˈgainst sb/sth to resist or oppose sb/sth; to act in a different way from what sth tells you or advises you to do: *Anyone who goes against me will be punished.* ◇ *He was going against his doctor's advice by continuing to work.* ◇ *Don't go against your parents' wishes.*
↻ note at STAND UP TO SB/STH
♦ v + prep

ˌgo aˈgainst sth to be opposed to sth; to not fit or agree with sth: *This goes against everything I believe in.* ◇ *Paying for my children's education goes against my principles.*
OBJ principles, beliefs
♦ v + prep

IDM go against the ˈgrain to be sth different from what is normal or natural for you and so sth you do not like doing: *It went against the grain to have to agree with my brother.*

ˌgo aˈhead 1 (*also* ˌgo aˈhead of sb) to go in front of other people who are going in the same direction and you arrive before them: *She went ahead of him into the house.* ◇ *You go ahead and we'll follow when we're ready.* 2 (of a

plan, a project, a deal, etc.) to be carried out or happen: *The building of the new bridge will go ahead as planned.* ◇ *Filming went ahead in spite of the bad weather.* **SYN** proceed (*formal*) 3 (**with sth**) if sb **goes ahead** with sth, they do it, although there may be a problem, or sb may have objected or expressed doubts: *In spite of her illness, Anna decided to go ahead with the wedding.* ◇ *'May I start now?' 'Yes, go ahead* (= I give you permission).*'* **SYN** proceed (**with sth**)
♦ v + adv 1 *also* v + adv + prep
▶ the ˈgo-ahead *n* [sing.] permission or approval for sth to start: *Has the boss **given** you **the go-ahead** for the project?*
▶ ˈgo-ahead *adj* [usually before noun] (*BrE*) trying hard to be successful, often by using new methods and ideas: *a go-ahead company*

ˌgo aˈlong 1 to progress; to develop or improve: *Things are going along nicely.* 2 (**to sth**) (**with sb**) to go somewhere or to an event with sb: *I went along to the club a couple of times.* ◇ *Sam said he'd go along to the party with us.* 3 (*especially AmE*) to do what sb else suggests or does: *Whatever Ed said, Max went right along.*
♦ v + adv
IDM as you go aˈlong while you are doing sth: *He made the story up as he went along.* ◇ *I was never taught how to use a computer. I just picked it up as I went along.*

ˌgo aˈlong; ˌgo aˈlong sth to move forward or from one end of sth towards the other: *The bus rattled as it went along.* ◇ *I went along a dark narrow passage, past several doors.*
♦ v + adv ♦ v + prep

ˌgo aˈlong with sb/sth 1 (*especially BrE*) to agree with sb/sth: *I can't go along with you on that point.* 2 to accept sth or do sth, especially when you do not really want to: *They didn't like the idea, but they went along with it.* ◇ *I didn't want to make him angry, so I just went along with him* (= I didn't argue with him). **SYN** fall in with sth (*BrE*) ↻ note at AGREE TO STH
♦ v + adv + prep

ˌgo aˈround (*AmE*) → GO ROUND

ˌgo aˈround; ˌgo aˈround sth (*BrE also* ˌgo ˈround, ˌgo ˈround sth) 1 to visit a group of people or places, one by one: *I'll go around and check all the doors are locked.* ◇ *We spent all afternoon going round the shops.* ◇ *She went round the table and said goodbye to everyone.* 2 (of a note, etc.) to be sent round a group of people so that everyone can read it: *A card's going around for people to sign.* ◇ *A memo went around the department.* 3 (*BrE also* ˌgo aˈbout, ˌgo aˈbout sth) if a piece of news, an illness, etc. goes around, it spreads from one person to another: *There's a rumour going around that Sam and Kate are having an affair.* ◇ *There's a nasty virus going round the school.* **SYN** float around, float around sth 4 to move or be placed in a circle: *The cyclist was going round the*

go around

circle (sth) ✦ go round/around (sth) ✦ revolve (round/around sth) ✦ rotate ✦ spin (round/around sth) ✦ turn

These verbs all mean to move around a central point.

circle (sth) to move in a circle, especially in the air: *Birds were circling overhead.* ◇ *The plane had to circle the airport for another 30 minutes before landing.*

go round/around (sth) to spin or move around in a circle: *The wheel was going round and round.* ◇ *The earth goes around the sun.*

revolve (round/around sth) to move in a circle around a central point: *People used to think that the sun revolved around the earth.* ◇ *The ceiling fan revolved slowly overhead.*

rotate to move in a circle around a fixed central point: *Make sure that the propeller can rotate freely.*

spin (round/around sth) to turn round and round quickly: *The dancers spun round and round.* ◇ *The Earth spins around a central axis.*

turn to move around a central point: *The wheels of the car began to turn.*

WHICH WORD?

When sth **rotates** or **spins**, it usually moves around its own centre; when sth **revolves**, it usually moves around a point outside itself. **Rotate**, **spin** and **turn** can be used with a direct object with the meaning of 'make sth go round': *Rotate the wheel through 180 degrees.* ◇ *Spin the coin.* ◇ *Turn the wheel slowly.*

PATTERNS AND COLLOCATIONS

▪ to spin/circle/rotate/revolve **about** sth
▪ to spin/turn/rotate **faster (and faster)/rapidly/quickly**
▪ to spin/turn/circle/rotate/revolve **slowly**

---

roundabout the wrong way. ◇ *The earth goes round the sun.* ◇ (*figurative*) *We're going round in circles in this argument.* **5** to be enough for everyone to have a share: *There aren't enough chairs to go round.* ◇ *Is there enough food to go around all the guests?* **6** to move around the outside of sth in order to get past sth or get to the other side: *We didn't go into the city. We went around it.* ◇ *Because of the flood, we had to go round by the minor roads to get to school.* **7** to travel in a country or place and visit lots of different things: *We travel around by bus.* ◇ *They're saving up to go around the world.* ◇ *We're planning to go round visiting all the temples.* **8** to visit every part of a room or building: *How long does it take to go around the museum?* ◇ *A guide will go round with you.*
◆ v + adv ◆ v + prep

IDM what ˌgoes around ˈcomes around whatever happens now will have an effect in the future

ˌgo aˈround; ˌgo aˈround sth; ˌgo aˈround doing sth (*BrE also* ˌgo ˈround/about, ˌgo ˈround/about sth, ˌgo ˈround/aˈbout doing sth) to dress or behave in a particular way; to do sth regularly: *She goes around barefoot most of the time.* ◇ *It's not safe to go about the streets alone.* ◇ *You can't go round spreading rumours like that.* ◇ *The kids went around in gangs, dressed completely in black.*
◆ v + adv ◆ v + prep

ˌgo aˈround sb/sth (*BrE also* ˌgo ˈround sb/sth) to surround or go in a circle around sb/sth: *I felt*

his arm going around my shoulder. ◇ *The belt won't go round my waist!*
◆ v + prep

ˌgo aˈround sth (*BrE also* ˌgo ˈround sth) to move or travel around a corner: *The car's tyres screeched as it went round the bend.* ◇ *Maggie watched until Jess had gone around the corner and was out of sight.*
OBJ only **corner, bend**
◆ v + prep

IDM go round the ˈbend/ˈtwist (*informal, especially BrE*) to go crazy: *If I have to stay in this place another day, I'll go round the bend!*

ˌgo aˈround with sb; ˌgo aˈround together (*BrE also* ˌgo aˈbout/ˈround with sb, ˌgo aˈbout/ˈround together) (*old-fashioned*) to spend a lot of time with sb or with a group of people: *Ann goes around with Sue.* ◇ *Ann and Sue go around together.* ◇ *These are the people I used to go around with.*
SYN hang around with sb, etc.
◆ v + adv + prep ◆ v + adv + adv

ˈgo at sb to attack sb: *He went at me like a wild animal.*
◆ v + prep

ˈgo at sth to make great efforts to do sth; to work hard and with enthusiasm at sth: *They went at the job as if their lives depended on it.* ◇ *He was going at the food as though he hadn't eaten for days.*
◆ v + prep

IDM go at it ˌhammer and ˈtongs if two people **go at it hammer and tongs**, they argue or fight with a lot of energy and noise

go away

clear off ◆ clear out ◆ depart ◆ get away ◆ go away ◆ leave (sth)

These verbs all mean to go away from a person or place.

clear off (*informal*) to leave a place quickly because you do not want to be found there or sb does not want you there: *They cleared off as soon as the police arrived.* ◇ *Clear off!*

clear out (*informal*) to leave a place quickly, especially taking all your things with you: *He cleared out with the money and left her with the kids.*

depart to leave a place, especially to start a trip: *She waited until the last of the guests had departed.*

get away to succeed in leaving a place: *I won't be able to get away from the office before seven.*

go away (used especially in orders) to leave a person or place: *Just go away and leave me alone!* ◇ *It's been over seven years since he went away.* NOTE **Go** can be used on its own: *I must be going now.*

leave (sth) to go away from a place: *If we leave now, we should make it in time.* ◇ *Are you ready to leave yet?* ◇ *John says he left the restaurant at around midnight.*

WHICH WORD?

In ordinary speech, **depart** is formal, but it is the usual official word used about planes, trains, etc. that are leaving: *This train will depart in three minutes.*

PATTERNS AND COLLOCATIONS

- to leave/depart **for...**
- to **plan to/be about to/be going to** leave/go/depart/go away
- to **decide to/intend to/refuse to** leave/go/go away
- to **be ready to/be forced to** leave/go/depart
- to **tell sb to** leave/go/go away/clear off
- to leave/go/depart/go away **at once/in a hurry/now/soon**

---

go a'way 1 to leave a place or a person: *Go away! You're annoying me!* ◇ *Go away and think about it a bit.* **2** to leave home for a period of time, especially for a holiday/vacation: *They went away for the weekend.* ◇ *Are you going away on holiday this year?* ◇ *She goes away on business a lot.* **3** to disappear gradually: *The smell still hasn't gone away.* ◇ *Has your headache gone away?* ◇ *The longing never went away.*
OPP **come back**
◆ v + adv

go a'way with sth to leave a place with a particular feeling or impression: *I don't want people to go away with the wrong idea.*
◆ v + adv + prep

go 'back 1 (**to sth/...**) to return to a place where you were before: *Can we go back inside?* ◇ *I made a cup of tea and went back to bed.* ◇ *When are you going back to Australia?* ⊃ note at COME BACK **2** (**to sth**) to return to school or work after a break: *The children have to go back to school next week.* **3** (**to sb/sth**) to be in a situation that you were in before: *We can never go back to how things were before* (= in a relationship, for example). ◇ *Once you have taken this decision,* **there's no going back.** ◇ *I don't think Emily will go back to her husband* (= live with him again). **4** (**to sth**) to return to work after being on strike: *The strikers won't go back* (*to work*) *until they get a pay rise.* **5** (**to sth**) (*informal*) (of sth that you have bought or

borrowed) to be returned to the place where you got it: *This toaster will have to go back to the shop—it doesn't work properly.* ◇ *When does this video have to go back?* **6** (of clocks and watches) to be set to an earlier time when the time changes at the end of summer: *The clocks go back tonight. We get an extra hour in bed.* OPP **go forward**
◆ v + adv

go 'back... 1 if two people **go back** a period of time, they have known each other and have been friends for that time: *Adam and I* **go back a long way. 2** (*also* **go 'back to sth**) to have existed since a particular time in the past: *Our friendship goes back fifteen years.* ◇ *This tradition goes back to medieval times.* SYN **date back...**, **date back to sth 3** (*also* **go 'back to sth**) to consider sth that happened in the past: *To trace the origins of the problem, we have to go back to the 18th century.* ◇ *I'm* **going back a few years** *now...* (= I'm talking about sth that happened some years ago)
◆ v + adv **2,3** also v + adv + prep

go 'back on sth to fail to keep a promise; to change your mind about sth: *She never* **goes back on her word** (= fails to do what she has said she will do). ◇ *He went back on his promise.* ◇ *I don't like to go back on what I said.*
OBJ **your promise, your word**
◆ v + adv + prep

,go **'back over sth** to think about sth again or often: *I went back over the day's events in my mind.*
   ♦ v + adv + prep

,go **'back to sth 1** to start talking about sth again: *To go back to what you were saying before...* SYN **return to sth 2** → GO BACK... 2 **3** → GO BACK... 3
   ♦ v + adv + prep

,go **'back to sth**; ,go **'back to doing sth 1** to start doing sth again that you had stopped doing: *Tom turned over and went back to sleep.* ◊ *I wouldn't go back to living in the city.* ◊ *She's decided to go back to teaching.* ◊ *John's going back to college to get some more qualifications.* **2** (of a situation) to return to what it was before sth else happened: *Things haven't gone back to normal yet.*
   SYN **return to sth**
   ♦ v + adv + prep

,go **be'fore** (*literary*) (*not used in the progressive tenses*) to exist or happen in an earlier time: *The present crisis is worse than any that have gone before.*
   NOTE **Go before** is usually used in the past or perfect tenses.
   ♦ v + adv

'go **before sb/sth** (of a legal case, a proposal or an issue) to be presented to sb/sth so that they can discuss it or make a decision or a judgement about it: *When does his case go before the judge?*
   ♦ v + prep

,go **be'yond sth** to be greater, better, etc. than sth: *The price we got for the painting went beyond*

all our expectations. ◊ *The matter has **gone beyond a joke*** (= has become very serious and is no longer amusing).
   SYN **exceed sth** (*formal*)
   ♦ v + prep

⚡,go **'by** (of time) to pass: *As time goes by, my memory seems to get worse.* ◊ *The weeks went slowly by.* ◊ *Hardly a day went by without Anthony's name being mentioned.*
   ♦ v + adv

⚡,go **by**; ,go **by sb/sth 1** to pass sb/sth without stopping: *Did you see a boy go by on a bicycle?* ◊ *We sat and **watched the world go by*** (= watched people passing). ◊ *They waved to us as we went by the window.* SYN **pass by, pass by sb/sth 2** (*AmE*) to stop somewhere or visit sb for a short time, often on your way to somewhere else: *I'll **go by and** see him on my way home.* ◊ *Would you go by the grocery store for me?* SYN **drop by**; **stop by**
   ♦ v + adv ♦ v + prep

'go **by sth 1** to be guided or directed by sth; to form an opinion or a judgement from sth: *That's a good rule to go by.* ◊ *If past experience **is anything to go by**, Tom will be late!* ◊ *I shall go entirely by what my solicitor says.* **2** to call yourself a particular name, which may not be your real name: *For her crime novels, she goes by the name of Monica Simon.* OBJ only **the name of...**
   ♦ v + prep

⚡,go **'down 1** (**to.../sth**) (**from.../sth**) to travel from one place to another, especially from the north of a country to the south: *We're going*

---

go by

elapse ♦ go by ♦ pass ♦ progress ♦ tick away ♦ wear on

These are all verbs that can be used to talk about time moving forward.

elapse (*not usually used in the progressive tenses*) (*formal*) (of time) to pass: *Many years elapsed before they met again.*

go by (of time) to pass: *Things will get easier as time goes by.* ◊ *The weeks went slowly by.*

pass if an hour, day, year, etc. passes, it moves forward in time: *Six months passed and we still had no news of them.*

progress (of time, an event or an activity) to pass: *The weather became colder as the day progressed.*

tick away (of time) to pass, especially when there is not much time to do sth: *I had to get to the airport by two, and the minutes were ticking away.*

wear on (of time) to pass, especially in a way that seems slow: *As the party wore on, she became more and more tired.*

WHICH WORD?

Wear on and **progress** are mainly used to say that a situation developed during a particular period of time: *The situation worsened as the year wore on.* ◊ *The visiting team's confidence increased as the game progressed.* You cannot usually use **progress** and **wear on** with *hours, days*, etc. as the subject.

PATTERNS AND COLLOCATIONS

- a day/a night/a year/time goes by/passes/ elapses/wears on/progresses/ticks away
- days/hours go by/pass/elapse/tick away
- time goes by/passes/wears on/ticks away slowly/uneventfully
- time goes by/passes **quickly**

go down

decline ♦ decrease ♦ drop ♦ fall ♦ go down ♦ slump

These verbs are all used to talk about a reduction in amount, level or number.

decline to become lower or less in level, number, size, strength or importance: *The number of tourists visiting the resort declined by 10% last year.*

decrease to fall in number or level: *The number of students decreased from 210 to 160 this year.* ◊ *Donations have decreased significantly in recent years.*

drop (*not used in the progressive tenses*) to become lower or less in level, number, or strength: *The temperature has dropped considerably.* ◊ *The team have dropped to fifth place.* ◊ *The wind dropped.*

fall to become lower or less in level, number, or strength: *Their profits have fallen by 30%.* ◊ *The temperature fell sharply in the night.* ◊ *Share prices fell 30p.*

go down to become less in level or value: *The temperature sometimes goes down to minus thirty.* ◊ *Coffee is going down in price.*
NOTE **Come down** is used when prices, etc.

return to their previous level: *The price of gas is coming down again.*

slump (*not used in the progressive tenses*) (*especially business*) to fall in price, value or number, suddenly and by a large amount: *Profits slumped by over 50%.*

WHICH WORD?

In many cases you can use any of these verbs: *Sales have fallen/declined/dropped by 20%.* They can all be used to talk about numbers, levels, rates, prices, profits and sales. To talk about a loss of economic strength, use **decline**: *The market has declined.*

PATTERNS AND COLLOCATIONS

■ **numbers/levels/rates** fall/decline/drop/ decrease

■ **prices/profits/sales** fall/decline/drop/slump/ decrease

■ **figures/temperature** fall/drop

■ to fall/decline/drop/decrease **sharply/significantly/considerably**

■ to fall/drop/decline/decrease **slightly/slowly/ gradually/steadily**

down to London next week. OPP **go up 2** to fall to the ground: *She tripped and went down with a bump.* **3** to become lower or smaller; to fall: *The price of petrol is going down/Petrol is going down (in price).* ◊ *The temperature went down by ten degrees overnight.* ◊ *Rental costs have gone down (£50) since last year.* ◊ *The floodwaters are going down.* ◊ *Membership numbers have gone down recently.* ◊ *The swelling has gone down a little.* SYN **drop**; **fall** OPP **go up 4** (*AmE also* ˌgo 'over) [+ adv] if a remark, a performance, an action, etc. **goes down** well or badly, etc., it gets a good or bad reaction from people: *Did your performance go down all right?* ◊ *The movie went down well in America.* ◊ *Jokes don't go down too well with my mother* (= she does not like them). ◊ *The band **went down a storm** (= people liked them very much).* **5** (of the sun and moon) to disappear below the point where the sky seems to meet the land or the sea (the **horizon**): *We watched the sun go down.* SYN **set** OPP **come up**; **rise 6** to get worse: *The quality of the product has gone down since the company was sold.* ◊ *He's certainly gone down in my estimation* (= I don't have the good opinion of him that I used to). ◊ *The food's gone down since the restaurant changed hands.* SYN **deteriorate** (*more formal*) OPP **go up 7** (*computing*) if a computer system **goes down**, it stops working

temporarily: *I lost all my work when the computer went down.* ➔ note at BREAK DOWN **8** (of food, a meal, etc.) to be partly or completely dealt with by your body: *Let your food go down before you go swimming.* **9** [+ adv] if food or drink will/will not **go down**, it is easy/difficult to swallow, or you enjoy it/do not enjoy it: *My drink **went down the wrong way** and I started coughing.* ◊ *A cup of tea would go down nicely* (= I would like one). **10** when the curtain in a theatre **goes down**, it is the end of the performance: *The audience were cheering as the curtain went down.* ◊ (*figurative*) *After 25 years, the curtain has finally gone down on his sparkling career.* OPP **go up 11** when lights **go down** in a theatre, the performance is about to start: *She quickly found a seat before the lights went down.* OPP **go up 12** [+ adv/prep] to reach down to a particular point: *Pepita's coat is so big it goes right down to her ankles.* **13** (of a tyre) to lose air: *My tyre's gone down again.* **14** (*BrE, informal*) to be sent to prison: *He's gone down for twenty years.* **15** (of a carpet) to be put on the floor: *It'll feel a lot warmer when the carpet goes down.* **16** (of a plane) to fall from the sky; to be brought to the ground: *'The plane's going down!'* he cried. **17** (of a ship) to sink: *Hundreds died when the ferry went down.* **18** to fail; to behave badly and lose people's respect: *If the business* goes down, we go down with it. **19** (**to sb**) to be defeated by sb, especially in a sports game or competition: *Liverpool went down 2-0 to Everton.* **20** (**to sth**) (*especially BrE*) to be made to move to a lower position, rank, class, status, etc.: *We need to win the next two games to avoid going down.* **OPP** **go up** **21** (**in sth**) (**as sth**) to be written down; to be recorded or remembered in a particular way: *Everything I said went down in his little book.* ◇ *1998 will go down as the company's best year.* ◇ *He will go down in history as a great statesman.* **22** (*slang, especially AmE*) to be happening: *She always knows what's going down.* ◇ *What's going down?* **23** (**from…**) (*BrE, formal*) to leave a university (especially Oxford or Cambridge) at the end of a term or after finishing your studies: *She went down (from Cambridge) in 2004.* **OPP** **go up**

◆ v + adv

go 'down; **go 'down sth** to move from a higher position to a lower one; to go along sth from one end towards the other: *One end of the see-saw goes up while the other end goes down.* ◇ *The pain goes down my arm.* ◇ *I've just got to go down to Jim's office with these papers.* ◇ *Will we go down any steep hills?* ◇ *You'll see the museum if you go down the road a bit.* ◇ *It was hard enough to get up here* (= a mountain, for example), *and now we've got to go down!* ◇ *Their company has decided to **go down the same path*** (= do the same things) *as ours.* ◇ *I **went down on my hands and knees** to look for the pen.* ◇ *I'm not going to go down on my knees and beg him to forgive me.*

OBJ road, stairs, hill **OPP** go up, go up sth

◆ v + adv ◆ v + prep

IDM **go down the 'drain** (*BrE also* **go down the 'plughole**) to be wasted; to get much worse **go down 'that road** to follow a particular course of action, especially a difficult or harmful one: *He said he'd never used drugs because he'd seen too many talented kids go down that road.*

go 'down on sb (*slang*) to perform a sex act on sb with your mouth

◆ v + adv + prep

go 'down to sth to go to a place near where you are, or a place you often go to: *Shall we go down to the beach for a swim?* ◇ *I'm going down to the corner shop for some milk.*

◆ v + adv + prep

go 'down with sth (*especially BrE*) to become ill/sick with sth: *I think I'm going down with a cold.*

SYN come down with sth; sicken for sth; catch sth; get sth

◆ v + adv + prep

go for sb/sth 1 to attack sb/sth: *She went for him with a knife.* ◇ (*figurative*) *The newspapers really went for him over his defence of terrorism.* **2** to apply to sb/sth; to be true of sb/sth: *What I said about Tim helping goes for you too, Alex.*

◇ *We may have high unemployment, but the same goes for many other countries.* ◇ *Terry needs to relax more, and **the same goes for you**.* **3** to go to get sb/sth: *Shall I go for a doctor?* ◇ *She's gone for some milk.* **4** to be attracted by sb/sth; to like or prefer sb/sth: *He's not the type I usually go for.* ◇ *Children usually go for colourful packaging.*

◆ v + prep

IDM (**have**) **a lot, nothing, etc. 'going for it/you** (to have) many/not many advantages: *She has a good job, she's attractive and intelligent—she has a lot going for her.* ◇ *The town doesn't really have much going for it.*

'go for sth 1 to choose sth: *I think I'll go for the steak.* ◇ *Which computer system are they going for?* **2** to try to get or achieve sth: *Did you go for that job?* ◇ *He's going for the world record.* ◇ *Go for it! You've got nothing to lose.* ◇ *That's a great idea! Go for it!* **3** to be sold for the price mentioned: *These computers usually go for under £1 000.*

◆ v + prep

go 'forth (*literary*) to leave a place and go somewhere, especially in order to do sth good or brave

◆ v + adv

go 'forward 1 to make progress; to begin to happen or be successful: *The project is going forward nicely.* ◇ *Now that we have his agreement, the deal can go forward.* **2** (of clocks and watches) to be set one hour ahead at the beginning of summer: *The clocks go forward tonight. We have an hour less in bed.* **OPP** **go back 3** to be suggested as a candidate for a job or an elected position, etc.: *Her name has gone forward for the job.* **4** (**to sth**) to win one stage of a competition, etc. and be able to take part in the next stage: *Which teams will go forward to the second round?*

◆ v + adv

go 'in 1 (of the sun or moon) to disappear behind a cloud: *The sun went in and it grew colder.* **OPP** **come out 2** (*informal*) (of facts, information, etc.) to be absorbed, understood and remembered: *I keep studying, but these dates just won't go in.* **SYN** sink in **3** (of a piece of equipment, furniture, etc.) to be built or fitted in a place: *The kitchen will be finished once the fridge has gone in.*

◆ v + adv

go 'in; **go 'in sth**; **go 'into sth 1** to enter a room, a house, etc.: *It's getting cold; let's go in.* ◇ *Let's go in the kitchen—it's warmer.* ◇ *Why did you go into my office?* ◇ *Are you going into town today?* **2** to fit into a container, etc.: *The suitcase is full already—those shoes definitely won't go in.* ◇ *I'm amazed that all the luggage went in the car.* ◇ *All the photos will go into this box.* **3** (*informal*) to join an organization, especially one of the armed forces or the police: *He was 17 when he went 'in the army.* ◇ *Ed wants to go into the*

go in

come in ♦ **enter (sth)** ♦ **go in** ♦ **set foot in/on sth**

All these words mean to come or go into sth.

come in (also **come into sth**) to enter a place, especially a building, room, etc.: *It's getting cold. Why don't you come in now?* ◇ *Come in!* (= used to give sb permission to enter a room)

enter (sth) (*formal*) to come or go into a place: *Please knock before you enter.* ◇ *Where did the bullet enter the body?*

go in (also **go into sth**) to enter a place, especially a building, room, etc.: *It's getting cold. Let's go in.* ◇ *They went into the dining room.*

set foot in/on sth to enter or visit a place: *He was the first person to set foot on the moon.*

◇ *I vowed never to set foot in the place again.*
◇ *It was the first time I'd set foot on African soil.*

WHICH WORD?

Come in implies movement in the direction of the speaker; **go in** implies movement in the opposite direction: *Come in and help me tidy up.* ◇ *The door was open but we were too scared to go in.* **Enter** can imply movement in either direction.

PATTERNS AND COLLOCATIONS

■ to enter/come into/go into/set foot in a **room/ building/country/town**
■ to enter/come in/go in **by/through** sth
■ to **allow sb/permit sb/give permission for sb** to enter/come in/go in

---

Marines. **4** (of the ball in sports played with a ball, etc.) to enter the goal, net, hole, etc. and score points: *Did you see if the ball went in?* ◇ *He kicked the ball hard enough to go into the back of the goal.*
♦ v + adv ♦ v + prep

‚go 'in; ‚go 'into sth 1 to go to an office or another place of work in order to work, do a particular task, have some work done for you, etc.: *I've got to work tomorrow, but I can always go in late.* ◇ *The car needs to go in* (= into the garage) *for a service.* ◇ *Are you going into work tomorrow?* **2** to go to a hospital to receive treatment, tests, etc.: *I'm going in on Friday for an X-ray.* ◇ *When is Cara going into hospital?* **3** (of soldiers, an army, etc.) to go to a place where there is fighting or a war and become involved in it: *Troops are going in tonight.*
♦ v + adv ♦ v + prep

⚑‚go 'in for sth (*especially BrE*) **1** to take part in a competition; to take an exam: *She goes in for all the competitions in the magazines and never wins anything.* ◇ *Which events are you going in for at the school sports?* ◇ *She's going in for the Cambridge First Certificate.* **2** → GO INTO STH 3: *He decided to go in for politics.*
SYN enter sth
♦ v + adv + prep

‚go 'in for sth; ‚go 'in for doing sth to like sth and regularly use it, do it, etc.; to have sth as an interest or a hobby: *She goes in for very bright colours.* ◇ *He doesn't really go in for making long speeches.* ◇ *We don't go in for that sort of thing.* ◇ *She never went in for dancing.*
♦ v + adv + prep

‚go 'in with sb (**on sth**) to join sb in a particular project, activity, business, etc.: *Jack went in with some friends to start a car hire business.* ◇ *I'll go in with you on it* (= I'll give you some money for) *Mary's present.* ◇ *My brothers are opening a garage and they want me to go in with them.*
♦ v + adv + prep

⚑‚go 'into sth 1 (of a vehicle) to hit sth violently; to crash into sth: *The car skidded and went into a tree.* **2** (of a vehicle or driver) to start a particular movement: *The truck went into a spin on a patch of ice.* ◇ *The plane went into a nosedive.* **3** (*also* ‚go 'in for sth) to decide to do a particular kind of work as your job or career: *When did you decide to go into politics?* ◇ *She's going into publishing.* ◇ *Sanjay's gone into business with his father.* OBJ **politics SYN take sth up 4** to begin to be in a particular state or situation: *She went into a coma after the accident.* ◇ *The country is going into a decline.* ◇ *The company has gone into liquidation.* ◇ *The family has gone into hiding.* OBJ **liquidation, production, decline, hiding, exile, a coma 5** to begin to act or behave in a particular way: *He went into a long explanation of the affair.* ◇ *Divers were there, ready to go into action if the stunt went wrong.* **6** to examine or discuss sth carefully: *I won't go into details now.* ◇ *We need to go into the question of costs.* ◇ *She's not coming, for reasons which I won't go into now.* **7** (*also* ‚go 'into doing sth) (of money, time, effort, etc.) to be spent on sth; to be used to do sth: *More money needs to go into rebuilding the inner cities.* ◇ *I can see that a lot of time and effort has gone into your project.* ◇ *A huge amount of work went into making the occasion*

a success. ◇ *A lot of skill, love and work had gone into the garden.* **8** to start taking part in an exam, a competition, an election, etc.: *I can't go into the exam unprepared.* **9** if one number **goes into** a larger number, it is contained in that number the number of times mentioned: *5 goes into 25 five times.* ◇ *Does 13 go into 39?*
♦ v + prep

go 'off 1 (**to sth**) to leave a place, especially in order to do sth: *You go off and have fun.* ◇ *When are you going off on your trip?* ◇ *Have the children gone off to school yet?* ◇ *Everyone went off happy.* ◇ *I can't believe Ed went off without saying goodbye!* ◇ *My parents have just gone off to bed.* **2** (of a weapon, etc.) to be fired; to explode: *The gun went off by accident.* ◇ *The bomb went off in a crowded street.* SUBJ **gun, bomb 3** (of an alarm) to make a sudden loud noise or flash: *She got up as soon as the alarm clock went off.* ◇ *The thieves ran away when the burglar alarm went off.* SUBJ **alarm, alarm clock, fire alarm 4** if a light, the electricity, etc. **goes off**, it stops working: *Suddenly all the lights went off.* ◇ *The heating goes off at nine.* SUBJ **lights** OPP **come on; go on 5** [+ adv] if a performance, etc. **goes off** well/badly, it is successful/not successful: *The show went off very well.* ◇ *How did the concert go off?* ◇ *The performance went off without a hitch* (= without any problems at all). **6** (*BrE*) if food or drink **goes off**, it becomes bad and not fit to eat or drink: *This milk has gone off.* SUBJ **milk, meat 7** (*especially BrE*) to become worse in quality: *Her books have gone off in recent years.* **8** (*informal, especially BrE*) to fall asleep: *Hasn't the baby gone off (to sleep) yet?* SYN **drop off**
♦ v + adv

go 'off; go 'off sth 1 to move away from sth large or important and go in a different direction: *The road you want goes off on the right.* ◇ (*figurative*) *She's always going off the point* (= not talking about the main topic). **2** to leave the stage, the sports field, etc. during a play or a game: *Hamlet goes off in the middle of the scene.* ◇ *Johnson went off at half-time.*
♦ v + adv ♦ v + prep

go 'off (**on sb**) to suddenly become angry with sb: *He just went off on her and started yelling.* ◇ (*BrE*) *I spilt coffee on the sofa and my mum went off on one.*
♦ v + adv

go 'off sb/sth (*informal, especially BrE*) to lose interest in sb/sth; to stop liking sb/sth: *I think she's going off me.* ◇ *He's gone off his food.* ◇ *I've gone off the idea of a holiday in Scotland.*
♦ v + prep

go 'off with sb to leave your husband, wife, etc. in order to have a relationship with sb else: *Eddie's gone off with his wife's best friend.*
SYN **run away/off with sb**
♦ v + adv + prep

go 'off with sth to leave a place with sth that does not belong to you: *Who's gone off with my new pen?*
SYN **make off (with sth)**
♦ v + adv + prep

go 'on 1 (of a situation or a state of affairs) to continue to happen or exist without changing: *We can't let this dispute go on.* ◇ *Things can't go on as they are.* ◇ *In spite of everything, life must go on.* ◇ *We can't go on like this!* SYN **carry on; continue 2** to last for a particular time: *The meeting went on for hours.* ◇ *How much longer will this hot weather go on (for)?* SYN **carry on; last 3** (**with sth**) to continue an activity, especially after a pause or a break: *I'm sorry I interrupted. Go on with your story.* ◇ *The children quietly went on with their work.* ◇ *Let's take a break. We'll go on when you're ready.* SYN **carry on (with sth) 4** (**with sth**) (*also* **go 'on doing sth**) to continue an activity without stopping: *When I came into the room, the boss just went on with what she was doing and didn't look up.* ◇ *I could have gone on listening to Ted's stories all night.* ◇ *I'd prefer to go on doing things my own way.* SYN **carry on (with sth), carry on doing sth 5** to continue speaking after a short pause: *'You know', he went on, 'I never liked her.'* ◇ *Go on then! Tell me what happened!* ◇ *She hesitated for a moment, and then went on.* SYN **carry on 6** (of a light, the electricity, etc.) to start to work; to be switched on: *Suddenly all the lights went on.* OPP **go off 7** (of time) to pass: *Things will improve as time goes on.* ◇ *She became more miserable as the evening went on.* SYN **go by 8** (*usually used in the progressive tenses*) to take place; to happen: *What's going on here?* ◇ *Who knows what goes on when I'm away.* ◇ *There must be a party going on next door.* ◇ *She ignores a lot of what goes on.* **9** (**to sth/to do sth**) to do sth after you have finished sth else: *Do all the students go on to work in catering?* ◇ *Let's go on to the next item on the agenda.* ◇ *The boys went on to a club, but I decided to go home.* **10** **go 'on!** (*informal*) used to encourage or dare sb to do sth: *Go on! Have another cake.* ◇ *Go on! Try it!* ◇ *Go on! Ask her out! I dare you!* **11** (**about sb/sth**) to continue talking to sb for a long time about the same person or thing, usually in an annoying way: *They keep going on about their trip.* ◇ *What is she going on about?* ◇ *My parents went on and on about how successful my sister is.* SYN **bang on about sb/sth** (*BrE, informal*) **12** (**at sb**) (**about sth**) (*especially BrE*) to complain to sb about their behaviour, work, etc.: *My dad went on at me about not having a job.* ◇ *Stop going on at me!* ◇ *She keeps going on at me to dress better.* SYN **carry on (at sb) (about sth); criticize sb 13** to continue to travel in the direction you are going: *I'm too tired to go on.* ◇ *They had an accident and couldn't go on.* SYN **carry on**

14 (**ahead/to sth**) to travel in front of sb else: *Jack's going on ahead to get the house ready.* ◇ *Shall we wait for Ray or shall we go on into town without him?* **15** (of a road, a piece of land, etc.) to cover a particular distance in a particular direction: *The desert seemed to go on forever.* **16** (of an actor or a performer) to walk onto the stage to begin their performance: *She doesn't go on till Act 2.* **17** (*sport*) (of a player) to join a team instead of another player during a game: *Allen went on (in place of Brown) just before half-time.* **18** go on (*informal, especially BrE*) used to agree to do or allow sth that you do not really want to do or allow, after sb has persuaded you: '*Are you sure you won't come?*' '*Oh go on then, but I won't be able to stay long.*' **19** go on! (*old-fashioned, BrE, informal*) used to show that you do not believe what sb is saying: *Go on! You didn't eat it all yourself!* **SYN** **get away** (**with you**)
♦ v + adv **4** also v + adv + -ing
♦ **5** also v + adv + speech

IDM **be ˌgoing ˈon** (**for**) **sth** (*BrE*) to be nearly a particular age, time or number: *It was going on (for) midnight.* ◇ *She's 20, going on 21.* **enough, plenty, etc. to be going ˈon with** enough, plenty, etc. for our present needs: *That should be enough food to be going on with.*
▶ **ˌgoings-ˈon** *n* [pl.] (*informal*) activities or events that are strange or amusing: *There have been some strange goings-on at their house.*
▶ **ˈongoing** *adj* [usually before noun] continuing to exist or develop: *an ongoing process* ◇ *the ongoing debate* ◇ *an ongoing situation* ◇ *The problem is ongoing.*

ˌgo ˈon; **ˌgo ˈon sth** to fit or be put on top of another object: *The lid won't go on.* ◇ *This shoe won't go on my foot at all.*
♦ v + adv ♦ v + prep

ˈgo on sth 1 (*used in negative sentences and questions*) to base an opinion or a judgement on sth: *The police don't have much evidence to go on.* ◇ *I'm only going on what she told me.* **2** to begin doing, following, enjoying or using sth: *to go on a course/trip* ◇ *I'm going on a diet on Monday.* ◇ *When are you going on holiday?* ◇ *to go on the dole* (= to start to receive government unemployment benefit) ◇ *When do the band go on tour?*
♦ v + prep

ˈgo on sth; **ˈgo on doing sth** (of money, time, energy, etc.) to be spent or used for sth: *All his money goes on drink.* ◇ *Most of the electricity we use goes on running the computers.*
→ see also GO ON 4
♦ v + prep

ˌgo ˈout 1 (**for/to sth**) to leave your house to go to social events, etc.: *Shall we go out for a meal tonight?* ◇ *Ellie goes out a lot.* ◇ *She goes out dancing most weekends.* ◇ *Jenny usually goes out*

SYNONYMS

go out

burn (itself) out ♦ **die down** ♦ **go out**
These verbs all mean to stop burning. *See also* **put sth out**.

burn (itself) out to stop burning because there is nothing more to burn: *The fire had burnt (itself) out before the fire engines arrived.*

die down to burn less strongly: *As the flames died down he felt cold air on his face.*

go out to stop burning: *The candles had all gone out and I was left in darkness.*

PATTERNS AND COLLOCATIONS

- a **fire/blaze** goes out/burns (itself) out/dies down
- **flames** go out/die down
- a **candle/cigarette** goes out
- to **gradually** burn (itself) out/die down
- to **suddenly** go out

with her friends on Friday evenings. **OPP** **stay in 2** (**with sb/together**) (*informal*) (especially of young people) to spend time with sb and have a romantic or sexual relationship with them: *Sam has been going out with Kate for six months.* ◇ *How long have Sam and Kate been going out together?* ◇ *When did they start going out?* **SYN** **date**, **date sb 3** (of a letter, a message, etc.) to be sent, announced, etc.: *Have the invitations gone out yet?* ◇ *A memo went out about the director's resignation.* **4** (of news, information, etc.) to be made public; to be published: *Word went out that the Prime Minister had resigned.* ◇ *The magazine goes out six times a year.* **5** (*especially BrE*) (of a radio or television programme) to be broadcast: *The first episode goes out next Friday at 8.00 p.m.* ◇ *The show will go out live from the studio.* **6** (of a fire or a light) to stop burning or shining: *The fire has gone out.* ◇ *There was a power cut and all the lights went out.* **SUBJ** **lights, fire** **SYN** **be extinguished** (*formal*) **7** if money **goes out**, it is spent on bills and expenses: *We need to have more money coming in than going out.* **OPP** **come in 8** (**to …**) to leave your country and travel to another one, especially one far away: *We went out to see him when he was living in Australia.* ◇ *Have you been out to India recently?* **9** if the **tide goes out**, the sea moves away from the land: *When does the tide go out?* **SUBJ** only **the tide** **SYN** **ebb** (*more formal*) **OPP** **come in 10** to fail in a competition, contest, etc.: *She went out in the first round of the tournament.*
♦ v + adv

IDM go out like a 'light to fall asleep very quickly: *I went out like a light as soon as my head hit the pillow.*

▶ 'outgoing *adj* **1** very friendly and liking to meet and talk to other people: *Annie's sister is much more outgoing than she is.* **2** [only before noun] about to leave a position of responsibility: *the outgoing government* **3** [only before noun] going away from a particular place: *outgoing calls/flights/passengers* ◇ *the outgoing tide*

▶ 'outgoings *n* [pl.] (*BrE*) the money which a person or a company spends regularly on bills and other necessary expenses: *They haven't got enough money to cover their outgoings.*

,go 'out; ,go 'out of sth **1** to leave a room, building, etc.: *It's too cold to go out.* ◇ *The talking started as soon as the teacher went out of the room.* ◇ *It isn't a good idea to go out alone at night.* ◇ *I'm going out for a walk.* ◇ *He's just gone out to get a newspaper.* ◇ *My grandmother never* **went out to work** (= away from the home). ◇ *She went straight out and spent £200 on a new coat.* **OPP** go in, go in sth, go into sth **2** to become no longer fashionable or used: *That hairstyle* **went out of fashion** *years ago.* ◇ *Styles like that have completely gone out now.* ◇ *The word 'leathern' has gone out of use in modern English.* **OPP** come in, come in sth, come into sth

♦ v + adv ♦ v + adv + prep

,go 'out for sth (*AmE*) to try to gain a place in a sports team, a band or a group that does some other activity: *I had to talk Greg into going out for the basketball team.* ◇ *'Did she make the band?' 'She didn't go out for it.'*

SYN try for sth (*especially BrE*); **try out (for sth)** (*especially AmE*)

♦ v + adv + prep

,go 'out of sb/sth (of a quality or feeling) to no longer be present in sb/sth; to disappear from sb/sth: *He relaxed and the tension went out of him.* ◇ *The heat had gone out of the day.*

♦ v + adv + prep

,go 'out to sb if you say that your heart, thoughts, prayers, etc. **go out to** sb, you are expressing sympathy for them: *Our hearts go out to all the victims of the disaster.*

♦ v + adv + prep

,go 'over **1** (to sb/sth) to move towards sb/sth, especially crossing a room, etc.: *He went over to the window for a closer look at the parade.* ◇ *I went over and sat beside Jane.* **2** (to sth) to visit sb for a short time, usually at their house: *I'm going over to my daughter's for lunch.* → see also GO ROUND 1 **3** (to …) to travel to a place in another country, especially by sea: *My family live in Belgium and I'm going over to see them next week.* **4** [+ adv] (*AmE*) → GO DOWN 4: *My suggestion didn't go over well with my boss.* ◇ *The*

news *of her promotion went over well with her colleagues.*

♦ v + adv

,go 'over; ,go 'over sth to pass above or over the top of sb/sth: *Planes were going over all night.* ◇ *We were shaken as the car went over the bumps in the road.*

♦ v + adv ♦ v + prep

,go 'over sth **1** to do more, spend more, etc. than a particular amount or than you are allowed to do: *Don't go over the speed limit.* ◇ *Did you go over budget on your project?* **SYN** exceed sth (*more formal*) **2** to examine the details of sth; to check sth: *I'll go over the figures again to make sure they're right.* ◇ *Go over your work carefully before you hand it in.* ⊃ note at CHECK SB/STH OVER **3** to study sth carefully; to repeat sth: *I've gone over and over what happened in my mind.* ◇ *She went over her lines* (= in a play) *until she knew them perfectly.* **4** to look at or check sth carefully: *Police went* (back) *over all the evidence again.* ◇ *My dad went over the car thoroughly and advised us not to buy it.* **5** to draw, paint, etc. over the top of sth that has already been drawn or painted: *I've gone over the original drawing in pen.* **6** to clean sth by passing sth across the surface: *He went over the surfaces with a duster.*

♦ v + prep

▶ ,going-'over *n* [sing.] (*informal*) **1** an act of examining, cleaning or repairing sth thoroughly: *I've given the flat a good going-over* (= a thorough clean). ◇ *The garage gave the car a thorough going-over* (= a careful check). **2** a serious attack on sb, physically or in words: *The gang gave him a real going-over.*

,go 'over to sb/sth **1** to leave a group of people in order to join a competing group; to change from one side, opinion, habit, system, etc. to another; to start using sth different: *Two MPs went over to the opposition.* ◇ *We've recently gone over to semi-skimmed milk.* **2** (in broadcasting) to transfer to a different person, place, etc. for the next part of a programme: *Let's go over to the news desk for an important announcement.*

♦ v + adv + prep

,go 'past (of time) to pass: *Half an hour went past while we were sitting there.*

♦ v + adv

,go 'past; ,go 'past sb/sth to pass in front of sb/sth: *I stood back to let Jack go past.* ◇ *The shop is empty whenever I go past it.*

♦ v + adv ♦ v + prep

,go 'round (*BrE*) (*AmE* ,go a'round) **1** (to sth) to visit sb for a short time, usually at their house: *Why don't you go round and see Annie?* ◇ *I've got to go around to my sister's* (= to her house) *in the morning.* → see also GO OVER 2 **2** to spin or turn: *When I found the bicycle, the wheels were still going round.* ◇ (figurative) *I've got so many ideas going around in my head at the moment.*

→ see also GO AROUND, ETC.
♦ v + adv

,go 'through 1 (to sth) (*informal*) used especially to ask sb to enter a room, etc.: *Shall we go through to my office?* ◊ *Go through and make yourself comfortable.* **2** if a law, a contract, etc. **goes through**, it is officially approved, accepted or completed: *The bill went through without any objections.* ◊ *The adoption* (= of a child) *has finally gone through.* **3** if a business deal, etc. **goes through**, it is completed successfully: *We are almost certain the deal will go through.* ◊ *If the merger goes through, we may lose our jobs.* **4** (to sth) to pass to the next stage of a competition, etc., having won the first part(s): *Four teams will go through to the semi-final.*
♦ v + adv

,go 'through; ,go 'through sth to enter and cross a room, an area of land, a town, a country, etc.; to pass through sth: *The gates opened and we went through.* ◊ *Lots of huge trucks go through the town.* ◊ *You have to go through the lounge to reach the kitchen.* ◊ *The defence was weak, and the ball went through into the goal.* ◊ *The bullet went straight through the window.* ◊ *This is the hole where the bullet went through.*
♦ v + adv ♦ v + prep

,go 'through sb **1** if a feeling **goes through** you, it passes through your body: *A shudder went through her.* **2** if a particular type of food **goes through** you, your body cannot deal with it easily and it is emptied from your body quickly or in liquid form: *I can't eat sushi—it goes right through me.*
♦ v + prep

'go through sb/sth to ask a person or an organization to deal with sth for you or give you permission to do sth: *If you want to book the cruise, you'll have to go through a travel agent.*
♦ v + prep

,go 'through sth **1** to pass through sth from one end to the other: *We went through the woods to get to the lake.* ◊ (*figurative*) *What went through your mind when you saw her?* **2** if you **go through** an event, a period of time, etc., you pass through it from the beginning to the end: *He went through the day in a state of shock.* ◊ *She can't go through life always depending on her parents.* **3** to experience or suffer sth: *You don't realize what I've been going through.* ◊ *She's been through a bad patch recently.* ◊ *We've been through a lot together.* ◊ *It's a phase/stage all teenagers go through.* OBJ **phase**, **experience**, **a bad, difficult, etc. patch** SYN **undergo sth** (*more formal*) **4** to look at, check or examine sth closely and carefully, especially in order to find sth: *I've gone through all my pockets but I can't find my keys.* ◊ *After his death, his daughter had to go through his papers.* OBJ **pockets**, **papers 5** to discuss or study sth in detail, especially repeating it: *Let's go through*

the arguments again. ◊ *Could we go through Act 2 once more?* SYN **run through sth 6** to perform a series of actions; to follow a method: *This is the process you have to go through to become a club member.* ◊ *I made a mistake when I was logging out and had to go through the whole process again.* ◊ *Have you seen him go through his exercise routine in the mornings?* OBJ **process**, **routine**, **procedure 7** to use up sth: *I seem to be going through a lot of money at the moment.* ◊ *Have we gone through all that milk already?* SYN **get through sth 8** to wear or make a hole in sth: *I've gone through the elbows of my jumper.*
♦ v + prep

IDM **go through the 'motions** (of sth/of doing sth) **1** to pretend to do sth: *He just went through the motions of being a poet.* **2** to do or say sth without being serious or sincere about it: *Her heart wasn't in the game—she was just going through the motions.* **go through the 'roof 1** (of prices, etc.) to rise very quickly: *House prices have gone through the roof.* **2** to become very angry: *My mum will go through the roof if she finds out!*

,go 'through with sth to do what is necessary to complete sth or achieve sth, even though it may be difficult or unpleasant: *She decided not to go through with the operation* (= she decided not to have it). ◊ *He says he'll take us to court, but he'll never go through with it.*
♦ v + adv + prep

,go 'to it (*AmE, informal*) used to tell sb to start doing sth: *You need to get it finished by six. Go to it!* ◊ *We better go to it before it gets dark.*
♦ v + prep + it

'go to sb/sth **1** to be given to sb/sth; to pass to sb else when sb dies: *Proceeds from the concert will go to charity.* ◊ *Some of the credit for the book should go to the illustrator.* ◊ *The first prize went to Peter.* ◊ *The contract has gone to a private firm.* ◊ *The property went to his eldest daughter* (= when he died). **2** to approach sb/sth for help or information; to ask sb for sympathy or advice: *Sue goes to her friends for support rather than her family.* ◊ *He's the only person I can go to for advice.* ◊ *I always go to my dictionary when I come across a word I don't know.* SYN **turn to sb/sth**
♦ v + prep

▶ 'go-to *adj* [only before noun] (*AmE, informal*) a **go-to** guy, etc. is one that you can approach for help, information, etc.: *Jimmy's the go-to guy if you're looking for advice about your car.*

'go to sth **1** to start to do sth; to begin to be in a particular state or condition: *The two countries are set to go to war over the dispute.* ◊ *I hate to see food going to waste.* ◊ *My brain went to work on* (= started to think about) *what I should do next.* OBJ only **war**, **waste**, **work 2** to make a lot of effort, spend a lot of money, etc. in order

to do or achieve sth: *Don't **go to any trouble** on my behalf.* ◇ *Why **go to the expense** of buying a car?* ◇ *He **went to great pains** to persuade us.* ◇ *It's amazing the lengths people will go to to get a job.* ⌊OBJ⌋ only **trouble**, **expense**, **pains**, **lengths**
♦ v + prep + n

⌊IDM⌋ **go to the 'dogs** (*informal*) to get into a very bad state: *Some people think this country is going to the dogs.* **go to sb's 'head 1** (of alcohol) to make sb feel drunk **2** (of success, praise, etc.) to make sb feel very proud of themselves, especially in a way that other people find annoying **go to 'pieces** (*informal*) if sb **goes to pieces**, they become so upset or frightened that they cannot live or work normally: *It seems he goes to pieces in a crisis.* **go to 'pot** (*informal*) to be spoiled because people are not working hard or taking care of things: *His plan to make money had gone to pot.* **go to 'sleep 1** to fall asleep **2** if part of your body **goes to sleep**, you lose the sense of feeling in it **go to 'town (on sth)** to do sth with a lot of energy and enthusiasm, especially spending a lot of money: *They hadn't got a garden, so they really went to town on indoor plants.* **go to the 'wall** if a company or a business **goes to the wall**, it fails because of a lack of money

,go to'gether **1** (of two or more things) to exist at the same time; to be often found together: *Money and happiness don't always go together.* → see also GO WITH STH 2 **2** to look, taste, sound, etc. good together; to combine well with sth: *These colours go together well.* ◇ *Curry and pasta don't go together.* ⌊NOTE⌋ **Go** is also used: *Curry and pasta don't really go.* ◇ *These colours don't really go.* → see also GO WITH STH 1 **3** (*old-fashioned, especially AmE*) (*usually used in the progressive tenses*) (of two people) to spend time with each other and have a romantic or sexual relationship: *They haven't been going together long.* → see also GO OUT 2
♦ v + adv

'go towards sth; 'go towards doing sth to be used as part of the payment for sth; to be used as part of sth: *The money will go towards buying a computer.* ◇ *All these marks go towards my final diploma.*
♦ v + prep

,go 'under **1** to sink below the surface of the water: *They had to swim to shore when the boat went under.* ◇ *Someone rushed to help him when he went under.* **2** (*informal*) to fail, lose power, etc.; to be unable to pay what you owe: *A large number of small companies have gone under.*
♦ v + adv

'go under sth to be known by a particular name or title: *Does he go under any other names?* ⌊OBJ⌋ **the name of…**, **a different, etc. name**, **the title of…**
→ see also GO BY STH 2
♦ v + prep

,go 'up **1** to become higher in price, level, etc.; to rise: *The price of cigarettes is going up.* ◇ *Cigarettes are going up (in price).* ◇ *My pension has gone up (by) £5 a week.* ⌊SUBJ⌋ **price**, **temperature** ⌊SYN⌋ **rise** ⌊OPP⌋ **come down**; **go down 2 (to sb/ sth)** to go towards sb/sth: *He went up to the*

go up

climb ♦ go up ♦ grow ♦ increase ♦ rise

These are all verbs that can be used when an amount, level or number of sth gets bigger or higher. *See also* **put sth up**, **shoot up**.

climb to become greater in level or value: *The dollar/temperature/price of oil has been climbing all week.*

go up to become greater in level or value: *The price of cigarettes is going up.* ◇ *Do you think interest rates will go up again?*

grow to become greater in size, number or strength: *The company profits are expected to grow by 5% next year.* ◇ *She is growing in confidence all the time.*

increase to become greater in amount, level, number, degree, value, size or strength: *The population has increased from 1.2 million to 1.8 million.* ◇ *The rate of inflation increased by 2%.*

rise to become greater in number, level or amount: *rising fuel bills/crime rates* ◇ *Unem-*

ployment has risen by 3%. ◇ *Gas rose sharply in price.*

WHICH WORD?

Rise is most often used to talk about the number or level of sth; **grow** and **increase** can also be used about size and strength: *Profits/ Numbers have risen/grown/increased.* ◇ *Her confidence/fear grew/increased.* **Climb** is usually used about a number rather than an amount.

PATTERNS AND COLLOCATIONS

■ the **price/number** rises/increases/climbs/goes up
■ the **level/cost/temperature** rises/increases/ goes up
■ the **size/amount** grows/increases
■ to rise/grow/increase/climb/go up **slightly/ steadily/slowly/rapidly/dramatically/sharply**
■ to rise/grow/increase/go up **significantly/substantially/considerably**

house and knocked on the door. **3** (**to…**) to travel from one place to another, especially from the south of a country to the north: *She's gone up to Scotland to see her son.* ◇ *Are you going up to London tomorrow?* **4** to be built; to be put up: *New office blocks are going up everywhere.* **5** to be destroyed by fire or an explosion: *If one of the gas tanks goes up, there will be massive damage.* ◇ *The whole building* **went up in flames**. **6** to be fixed in a public place: *Notices have gone up all over the university.* **7** if the curtain across the stage in a theatre **goes up**, it is raised or opened: *The stage was empty when the curtain went up.* ⟦SUBJ⟧ **curtain** ⟦OPP⟧ **come down 8** if a loud sound such as a shout **goes up**, it is made by lots of people: *A huge cheer went up from the crowd.* ⟦SUBJ⟧ **cheer**, **cry 9** (**to/into sth**) (of a sports team or a student) to move to a higher rank, position or class: *Oxford went up in the second division.* ◇ *Is she going up into the sixth form this year?* ⟦OPP⟧ **go down 10** (**to…**) (*BrE*) to begin your studies at a university, especially Oxford or Cambridge; to begin a term at university: *She went up (to Oxford) in 1996.* ⟦OPP⟧ **go down**
  ◆ v + adv

⚓ **go** '**up**; ˌ**go** '**up sth** to move from a lower position to a higher one or upstairs in a building: *The lift goes up and down all day.* ◇ *Go up the ladder.* ◇ *She went up the stairs very slowly.* ◇ *Julie's gone up to her room to change.* ⟦OBJ⟧ **stairs**, **hill**, **road** ⟦SYN⟧ **ascend**, **ascend sth** (*formal*) ⟦OPP⟧ **go down, go down sth**; **descend**, **descend sth** (*formal*)
  ◆ v + adv ◆ v + prep

ˌ**go** '**up against sb/sth** (*AmE*, *informal*) to face sb/sth difficult, for example in a competition: *He went up against the champion in the second round.* ◇ *In a consumer taste test, Coke went up against Pepsi.*
  ◆ v + adv + prep

ˌ**go** '**up to sth** to come close to a particular point or time, or go in a particular direction: *This diary only goes up to November.* ◇ *The road goes up to the school.*
  ◆ v + adv + prep

'**go with sb** (*old-fashioned*, *informal*) to have a sexual or romantic relationship with sb; to have sex with sb: *She's been going with him for quite a while.*
  → see also GO OUT 2
  ◆ v + prep

'**go with sb/sth** (*informal*, *especially AmE*) to support a plan, an idea, etc. or the person suggesting it: *I'm prepared to go with her decision.* ◇ *I like Ted's idea. Let's go with it.* ◇ *Which candidate shall we go with?*
  ◆ v + prep

⚓'**go with sth 1** to look, taste, sound, etc. good with sth; to combine well with sth: *This sauce*

goes well with lamb. ◇ *Does this skirt go with my jumper?* → see also GO TOGETHER 2 **2** (of two or more things) to exist at the same time or in the same place as sth; to be often found together: *Disease often goes with poverty.* ◇ *She loves all the attention that goes with being famous.* → see also GO TOGETHER 1 **3** to be included with or as a part of sth: *A new car goes with the job.*
  ◆ v + prep

⚓ˌ**go with'out**; ˌ**go with'out sth**; **go with'out doing sth** to manage without sth which you usually have: *I never want the children to have to go without.* ◇ *She went without sleep for three days.*
  ⟦SYN⟧ **do without, do without sth**
  ◆ v + adv ◆ v + prep

goad /ɡəʊd; *AmE* ɡoʊd/

ˌ**goad sb** '**on** to drive and encourage sb to do sth: *They goaded him on to break the window.* ◇ *The boxers were goaded on by the shrieking crowd.*
  ◆ v + n/pron + adv

gobble /ˈɡɒbl; *AmE* ˈɡɑːbl/

ˌ**gobble sth** '**down/'up** (*informal*) to eat food very quickly: *I gobbled down my breakfast and ran out of the house.*
  ⟦SYN⟧ **wolf sth down**
  ◆ v + adv + n ◆ v + n/pron + adv

ˌ**gobble sth** '**up** (*informal*) **1** to use all of sth, especially money, very quickly: *The rent gobbles up half his earnings.* **2** if a business, company, etc. **gobbles up** a smaller one, it takes control of it: *Small family businesses are being gobbled up by larger firms.*
  ⟦SYN⟧ **swallow sth up**
  ◆ v + adv + n ◆ v + n/pron + adv

goof /ɡuːf/

ˌ**goof a'round** (*informal*, *especially AmE*) to waste your time doing silly or stupid things: *Come on, quit goofing around—this is serious.*
  ⟦SYN⟧ **mess around**
  ◆ v + adv

ˌ**goof** '**off** (*AmE*, *informal*) to waste time when you are supposed to be working
  ◆ v + adv
  ▶ '**goof-off** *n* (*AmE*, *informal*, *disapproving*) a lazy person who does not work hard

ˌ**goof** '**up** (**on sth**), ˌ**goof sth** '**up** (*AmE*, *informal*) to make a mistake; to spoil sth by making a mistake or doing it badly: *He always goofs up (on exams).* ◇ *He really goofed up his exam.*
  ⟦SYN⟧ **mess up, mess sth up**
  ◆ v + adv ◆ v + n/pron + adv ◆ v + adv + n

gouge /ɡaʊdʒ/

ˌ**gouge sth** '**out**; ˌ**gouge sth** '**out of sth** to remove sth, or form sth, by digging into a surface with a sharp tool, your fingers, etc.:

I wanted to gouge her eyes out. ◇ *Glaciers gouged out valleys from the hills.*

OBJ eyes
♦ v + adv + n ♦ v + n/pron + adv
♦ v + n/pron + adv + prep

grab /græb/

'**grab at sb/sth** to try to take hold of sb/sth: *She grabbed at the branch, missed and fell.*
SYN clutch at sb/sth
♦ v + prep

'**grab at sth** to take advantage of an opportunity to do or have sth: *He'll grab at any excuse to avoid doing the dishes.*
OBJ chance, opportunity, excuse **SYN** seize on sth
♦ v + prep

grapple /'græpl/

'**grapple with sth** to try to deal with a difficult situation or solve a difficult problem: *I've spent all afternoon grappling with these accounts.* ◇ *This is an issue that is being grappled with by the council.*
OBJ problem, issue **SYN** wrestle with sth
♦ v + prep

grasp /grɑːsp; AmE græsp/

'**grasp at sth/sb** to try to take hold of sth/sb in your hands: *She grasped at his coat.*
SYN catch at sth/sb; clutch at sth/sb
♦ v + prep

'**grasp at sth** to try to take advantage of an opportunity, especially because you are unhappy with the present situation: *He grasped at any hope of escape.*
SYN clutch at sth
♦ v + prep

IDM grasp at '**straws** to try very hard to find a solution to a problem or some hope in a difficult situation, even though this seems very unlikely

grass /grɑːs; AmE græs/

,**grass sth** '**over** to cover an area of ground with grass: *The garden had been grassed over.*
NOTE Often used in the passive.
♦ v + adv + n ♦ v + n/pron + adv

,**grass sb** '**up** (*BrE, informal*) to inform the police or sb in authority about a crime or sth bad that sb has done: *My girlfriend grassed me up.*
NOTE It is also possible to say: *My girlfriend grassed (on me).*
♦ v + n/pron + adv ♦ v + adv + n

gravitate /'grævɪteɪt/

'**gravitate to/toward(s) sb/sth** to move towards sb/sth that you are attracted to: *Most visitors to New York gravitate to Times Square.*
♦ v + prep

grey (BrE) (AmE gray) /greɪ/

,**grey sth** '**out** (*computing*) to show writing, etc. in a faint colour on a computer screen to show that a particular option cannot be chosen: *That option is greyed out.*
NOTE Usually used in the passive.
♦ v + adv + n ♦ v + pron + adv ♦ v + n + adv (*rare*)

grind /graɪnd/ (**ground, ground** /graʊnd/)

,**grind sb** '**down** to treat sb in an unkind way or annoy them for a long time until they can no longer defend themselves or fight back: *Don't let your colleagues grind you down!* ◇ *The villagers had been ground down by years of poverty.*
SYN wear sb down
♦ v + n/pron + adv ♦ v + adv + n

,**grind sth** '**down** to rub sth against a hard surface in order to make it smooth and shiny
SYN wear sth down
♦ v + n/pron + adv ♦ v + adv + n

,**grind** '**on** to continue for a long time in a boring or unpleasant way: *The negotiations ground on for months.*
♦ v + adv

,**grind sth** '**out 1** to produce sth in large quantities over a long period of time, especially sth that is not interesting or of good quality: *He grinds out a novel a month.* **SYN** churn sth out **2** to press a burning cigarette down firmly with your hand or your foot in order to stop it burning: *He ground out the cigarette with his heel.* **SYN** stub sth out
♦ v + adv + n ♦ v + n/pron + adv

,**grind sth** '**up** to break or crush sth into very small pieces: *I ground up the nuts to put in the cake.*
♦ v + n/pron + adv ♦ v + adv + n

grope /grəʊp; AmE groʊp/

'**grope for sth** to try hard to find sth: *I stepped in the door and groped for the light switch.* ◇ (*figurative*) '*Yes, but...*' *He was groping for words.*
OBJ light, word, answer
♦ v + prep

'**grope towards sth** (*rare*) to try to find an agreement, an answer to a problem, etc.: *The two parties are groping towards a compromise.*
♦ v + prep

gross /grəʊs; AmE groʊs/

,**gross sb** '**out** (*informal, especially AmE*) to make sb feel disgusted: *His greasy hair really grosses me out!*
♦ v + n/pron + adv ♦ v + adv + n (*less frequent*)
▶ '**gross-out adj** [only before noun] (*informal, especially AmE*): *Hollywood's latest gross-out comedy*

ground /graʊnd/

be 'grounded in/on sth to be based on sth: *Is the story grounded in fact?*
* be + v + prep

,ground 'out (*AmE*) (in baseball) to hit a ball along the ground, which is then caught by an opposing player and thrown to first base before you can run there, so that you are out: *Miller singled and grounded out.*
* v + adv

grow /graʊ; *AmE* groʊ/ (**grew** /gruː/, **grown** /graʊn; *AmE* groʊn/)

,grow a'part to become less close to sb in a relationship: *We used to be good friends, but we've grown apart.*
* v + adv

,grow a'way from sb to come to have a less close relationship with sb; to depend on sb less: *She has grown away from her parents.*
* v + adv + prep

,grow 'back if hair, fur, etc. **grows back**, it starts to grow again after it has been cut or damaged: *His hair grew back thicker after it fell out.*
SUBJ **hair**
* v + adv

,grow 'into sth 1 to gradually become sth over a period of time: *She had grown into a beautiful young woman.* **2** if a child **grows into** clothes, he/she becomes big enough to fit into them: *This coat's too big for him now, but he'll grow into it.* OBJ **coat, trousers**, etc. OPP **grow out of sth 3** to become familiar with and confident in a new job, activity, etc.: *He needs time to grow into the job.* OBJ **job, role**
* v + prep

'grow on sb if sb/sth **grows on** you, you gradually like them/it more and more: *That painting's really grown on me.*
* v + prep

,grow 'out if the colour or style of your hair **grows out**, it disappears as your hair grows: *I had my hair coloured six weeks ago, but it's growing out now.*
* v + adv

,grow sth 'out to let your hair grow so that the colour or style changes or disappears: *I've decide to grow the layers out.*
* v + n/pron + adv ◆ v + adv + n

,grow 'out of sth 1 if a child **grows out of** clothes, he/she becomes too big to wear them: *She grows out of her clothes so fast!* OBJ **coat, trousers**, etc. SYN **outgrow sth** OPP **grow into sth 2** to stop doing sth or suffering from sth as you become older: *He grew out of his eczema as he got older.* ◇ *He was a very rebellious teenager, but he grew out of it.* SYN **outgrow sth 3** to develop from sth: *These laws grew out of a need to protect children.*
* v + adv + prep

SYNONYMS

grow up

develop ◆ **grow up** ◆ **mature** ◆ **shoot up**
These verbs are all used to talk about children becoming bigger or more adult.

develop to gradually become bigger, stronger and more like an adult: *The child is developing normally.*

grow up to develop into an adult: *My children have grown up and left home.* ◇ *Children grow up fast.*

mature to develop emotionally and start to behave like a sensible adult: *He has matured a lot over the past year.*

shoot up to become bigger very quickly: *The kids have shot up since I last saw them.*

WHICH WORD?

Grow up never means 'to become larger in size'. Use **grow** instead.

PATTERNS AND COLLOCATIONS

* to grow up **fast/quickly/rapidly**
* to develop/mature **quickly/rapidly**
* to develop/mature **emotionally/physically**
* to grow up/develop/mature **into** an adult, etc.

,grow 'up 1 when a person **grows up**, they become an adult: *Kate's growing up fast.* ◇ *Oh, grow up* (= behave in a more sensible way) *and stop making such a fuss!* ◇ *He was a difficult teenager, but grew up to be a responsible adult.* **2** [+adv/prep] to spend the time you are a child in a particular place or in a particular way: *He grew up in Portugal.* ◇ *Mel and I grew up together.* ◇ *This generation has grown up on MTV.* **3** to develop gradually: *The town had grown up around the abbey.* ◇ *A cult had grown up around him.* SYN **develop**
* v + adv

▸ **,grown-'up** *adj* (*informal*) **1** mentally and physically an adult: *He has two grown-up children.* **2** like an adult in behaviour: *Susie is very grown-up for her age.*

▸ **'grown-up** *n* (*informal*) (*used especially by adults when talking to children, or by children*) an adult person: *The grown-ups will sit at one table and the children at another.*

grub /grʌb/ (**-bb-**)

,grub sth 'out/'up (*rare*) to dig sth out of the ground: *Thousands of miles of hedgerows have been grubbed up.*
SYN **dig sth out**; **dig sth up**
* v + adv + n ◆ v + n/pron + adv

guard /gɑːd; AmE gɑːrd/

'guard against sth; **'guard against doing sth** to do sth to prevent sth happening or to protect yourself from sth: *Clean the wound to guard against the danger of infection.* ◇ *We should guard against the possibility of this happening again.* ◇ *Regular exercise can help to guard against heart disease.* ◇ *This danger must be guarded against.*

[OBJ] **danger, risks, possibility**

♦ v + prep

guess /ges/

'guess at sth to try to imagine sth or make a judgement without knowing all the facts: *We can only guess at the reason for his actions.* ◇ *Her feelings can only be guessed at.*

♦ v + prep

gulp /gʌlp/

ˌgulp sth 'back (*rare*) to stop yourself showing that you are upset by swallowing hard: *She gulped back her tears.*

[OBJ] **tears**

♦ v + adv + n ♦ v + n/pron + adv

ˌgulp sth 'down to swallow sth quickly and noisily: *He gulped down a glass of water.*

[OBJ] **water, coffee, etc.**

[NOTE] **Gulp** can also be used on its own with a similar meaning.

♦ v + adv + n ♦ v + n/pron + adv

gum /gʌm/ (-mm-)

ˌgum sth 'up (*BrE, informal, rare*) to fill sth with a sticky substance so that it cannot move or work: *My eyes were all gummed up.* ◇ *The substance gummed the machine up.*

[NOTE] Often used in the passive.

♦ v + n/pron + adv ♦ v + adv + n

gun /gʌn/ (-nn-)

ˌgun sb 'down (*informal*) to shoot sb, especially so as to kill or seriously injure them: *He was gunned down outside his home.* ◇ *Terrorists gunned down six people in the town last month.*

[SYN] **shoot sb**; **shoot sb down** ⤴ note at SHOOT SB/STH DOWN

[NOTE] Often used in the passive.

♦ v + adv + n ♦ v + pron + adv ♦ v + n + adv (*rare*)

be 'gunning for sb (*informal*) (*only used in the progressive tenses*) to try to blame sb or cause trouble for them: *She's been gunning for me since I came to work here.*

♦ v + prep

be 'gunning for sth (*informal*) (*only used in the progressive tenses*) to try hard to get sth; to aim for sth: *They are both gunning for places in the championship.*

♦ v + prep

gussy /'gʌsi/ (gussies, gussying, gussied)

ˌgussy sb/sth 'up; **ˌgussy yourself 'up** (*AmE, informal*) to dress sb/yourself in special, attractive clothes; to decorate sth to make it look attractive: *She gussied herself up for the big party.* ◇ *Jim's got all gussied up!* ◇ *My dress was plain, but I gussied it up with some jewellery.* ◇ *The city was gussied up for the President's visit.*

[SYN] **doll yourself up**; **be/get dolled up**

[NOTE] Usually used in the passive.

♦ v + adv + n ♦ v + pron + adv

gut /gʌt/ (-tt-)

ˌgut it 'out (*AmE, informal*) to work in a very determined way to achieve sth, often despite great problems or physical pain: *Those kids went into the game and gutted it out. And they won!*

[SYN] **tough it out**

♦ v + it + adv

H h

hack /hæk/

ˌhack sth a'bout (*BrE, informal, disapproving*) to cut or change sth in a rough and careless way: *The hairdressers have hacked her hair about a bit.* ◇ (*figurative*) *The script was hacked about by several people before the movie was finished.*

♦ v + n/pron + adv

'hack at sth; **ˌhack a'way (at sth)** to try to cut sth using strong rough blows with a knife, scissors, etc.: *She's really hacked at my hair. It's a complete mess.* ◇ *He was hacking away at the trees with an axe.* ◇ *Don't hack at it! Cut it carefully!*

♦ v + prep ♦ v + adv

ˌhack sth 'down to cut a tree, etc. roughly so that it falls to the ground: *They are hacking down the forests to sell the timber.*

[OBJ] **tree** [SYN] **chop sth down**

♦ v + n/pron + adv ♦ v + adv + n

ˌhack 'into sth (*computing*) to find a way of looking at or changing the information on sb else's computer without their knowledge or permission: *A teenage girl managed to hack into the bank's computer.*

♦ v + prep

ˌhack sb 'off (*BrE, informal*) to make sb feel extremely annoyed or irritated: *He was hacked off with the whole situation.* ◇ *She always wants me to be there. That really hacks me off.*

[NOTE] Usually used in the passive.

♦ v + n/pron + adv ♦ v + adv + n

ˌhack sth 'off; **ˌhack sth 'off sth** to cut sth off sth with rough heavy blows: *They hacked off the dead branches.* ◇ *He hacked the padlock off the*

door. ◇ *She was always threatening to hack her lovely long hair off with the kitchen scissors.* **SYN** **chop sth off**, **chop sth off sth**
◆ v + adv + n ◆ v + n/pron + adv ◆ v + n/pron + prep

,hack sth 'up to cut sth very roughly into large pieces: *He hacked up the meat with a large knife.* **SYN** **chop sth up**
◆ v + adv + n ◆ v + n/pron + adv

hail /heɪl/

'hail from ... (*formal*) (*not used in the progressive tenses*) to come from or to live in a particular place: *Which part of Ireland does he hail from?*
◆ v + prep

ham /hæm/ (-mm-)

,ham it 'up (*informal*) to act in a deliberately artificial or exaggerated way: *The actors were really hamming it up.*
◆ v + it + adv

hammer /'hæmə(r)/

,hammer a'way at sth to work hard in order to finish or achieve sth; to repeat sth again and again: *He kept hammering away at the same point all through the meeting.*
◆ v + adv + prep

,hammer sth 'in; ,hammer sth 'into sb to force sb to learn sth by repeating it many times: *I'll manage to hammer the point in somehow.* ◇ *They have had English grammar hammered into them.*
◆ v + n/pron + adv ◆ v + adv + n ◆ v + n/pron + prep

,hammer sth 'out 1 to discuss a plan, a deal, etc. for a long time and with great effort, until sth is decided or agreed on: *It took weeks to hammer out an agreement.* **OBJ** **deal**, **agreement**, **policy 2** to play music loudly, especially on a piano: *She hammered out 'Happy Birthday' on the piano.*
◆ v + adv + n ◆ v + n/pron + adv

hand /hænd/

,hand sth a'round (*especially AmE*) → HAND STH ROUND

,hand sth 'back (**to sb**) **1** to give sth back to the person, country, etc. who used to have it or who owns it legally: *The territory was handed back to Egypt.* ◇ *We will not press charges if the money is handed back.* **OBJ** **money**, **control 2** to give sth back to the person who gave it to you: *She looked quickly at my passport and then handed it back.* **OBJ** **passport**, **letter**, **glass** **NOTE** In informal spoken language **hand sb back sth** and, less often, **hand sb sth back** are also used: *I handed her back her pen.* ◇ *I handed her her pen back.*
SYN **give sth back** (**to sb**); **return sth** (**to sb**)
◆ v + n/pron + adv ◆ v + adv + n

,hand sth 'down 1 (*also* ,hand sth 'on) (**to sb**) to give or leave sth to a younger person: *All my*

clothes were handed down to me by my brother. ◇ *These skills have been handed down from generation to generation.* ◇ *He's got no one to hand the family house on to.* **OBJ** **tradition**, **custom**, **skills** **SYN** **pass sth down** (**to sb**) **NOTE** Usually used in the passive. **2** (*especially AmE*) (of a court, etc.) to announce an official decision: *The judge handed down a sentence of six years.* **OBJ** **decision**, **sentence**, **verdict**
◆ v + n/pron + adv ◆ v + adv + n

▶ 'hand-me-down n [usually pl.] (*especially AmE*) clothing that is no longer wanted and is given to sb else, especially a younger brother or sister: *I had to wear my brother's hand-me-downs.*

,hand sth 'in (**to sb**) **1** to give a piece of work to sb, such as a teacher, so that they can correct, read or deal with it; to give sth to sb in authority because it belongs to them or is lost: *Make sure you hand in your homework on time.* ◇ *Hand your room keys in by 10 a.m.* **OBJ** **essay**, **homework** **SYN** **give sth in** (**to sb**) **2** to tell sb officially that you intend to leave your job: *I've just handed in my notice.* **OBJ** only **your notice**, **your resignation** **SYN** **give sth in** (**to sb**); **resign**
◆ v + adv + n ◆ v + n/pron + adv

,hand sb 'off (*BrE*, *sport*) to push away a player who is trying to stop you, with your arm straight
◆ v + adv + n ◆ v + n/pron + adv

,hand sth 'on (**to sb**) **1** to send or give sth to another person after you have finished with it: *Hand on the magazine to your friends.* ◇ *The task has been handed on to me.* **2** → HAND STH DOWN 1 **SYN** **pass sth on** (**to sb**)
◆ v + adv + n ◆ v + n/pron + adv

,hand sth 'out (**to sb**) **1** to give sth to each person in a group: *She handed textbooks out to the new students.* **OBJ** **leaflets**, **money** **SYN** **give sth out**; **pass sth out** (**to sb**) **2** to give advice, criticism, a punishment, etc. to sb: *The courts are handing out tough sentences to frequent offenders.* **OBJ** **information**, **punishment**, **sentence** **SYN** **dish sth out** (**to sb**) (*informal*)
◆ v + n/pron + adv ◆ v + adv + n

▶ 'handout n **1** sth that is given free to people, especially food, money or clothes **2** a document giving information about sth, especially one that is given to a group or a class by a teacher, speaker, etc.

,hand 'over to sb; ,hand sb 'over to sb (*especially BrE*) to give sb else a turn to speak when you have finished talking: *I'd like to hand over now to our guest speaker.* ◇ *I'll hand you over to Dad for a chat.*
◆ v + adv + prep ◆ v + n/pron + adv + prep

,hand 'over to sb; ,hand sth 'over to sb to give sb else your position of power or authority; to give sb else the responsibility for dealing with a particular situation: *I am resigning and hand-*

ing over to my deputy. ◇ *My father has handed over the business to me.*
- ◆ v + adv + prep ◆ v + adv + n + prep
- ◆ v + n/pron + adv + prep
- ▶ **'handover** *n* [C, U] the act of moving power or responsibility from one person or group to another; the period during which this happens

hand sb/sth 'over (**to sb**), **hand yourself 'over** (**to sb**) to give sb/sth officially to sb else, especially sb in authority: *They handed him over to the police.* ◇ *He forced me to hand over the keys.*
- SYN **deliver sb/sth over/up** (**to sb**), **deliver yourself over/up** (**to sb**) (*more formal*)
- ◆ v + n/pron + adv ◆ v + adv + n
- ▶ **'handover** *n* [C, U] the act of giving a person or a thing to sb in authority

hand sth 'round (*especially BrE*) (*AmE usually* **hand sth a'round**) to offer or pass sth (especially food and drink) to each person in a group of people or in a room: *Could you hand round the sandwiches, please?*
- ◆ v + adv + n ◆ v + n/pron + adv

hang /hæŋ/ (**hung, hung** /hʌŋ/)

hang a'bout, etc. (*BrE*) **1** (*informal*) → HANG ON 3 **2** → HANG AROUND, ETC.

hang a'bout with sb; **hang a'bout together** (*BrE*) → HANG AROUND WITH SB, HANG AROUND TOGETHER

hang a'round (*BrE also* **hang a'bout/'round**) (*informal*) **1** to wait: *Sorry to keep you hanging around for so long.* ◇ *I won't hang about for you if you're late.* SYN **wait around** (**for sb/sth**) **2** to delay doing sth; to be slow to do sth: *Have you finished already? You don't hang about do you?*
- ◆ v + adv

hang a'round; **hang a'round sth** (*BrE also* **hang a'bout/'round**, **hang a'bout/'round sth**) (*informal*) to spend time somewhere, without doing very much: *We spent most of the day hanging about doing nothing.* ◇ *Children hang around the streets because there's nowhere for them to play.* ◇ *Why are they always hanging round our house?*
- ◆ v + adv ◆ v + prep

hang a'round with sb; **hang a'round together** (*BrE also* **hang a'bout/'round with sb**, **hang a'bout/'round together**) (*informal*) to spend a lot of time with sb or with a group of people: *Bob hangs around with Tim.* ◇ *Bob and Tim hang around together.* ◇ *I don't like the kind of people she hangs about with.*
- SYN **go around with sb**, **go around together**
- ◆ v + adv + prep ◆ v + adv + adv

hang 'back 1 to not move forwards because you are nervous or afraid: *She hung back, afraid to go near the dog.* **2** to stay behind in a place such as a school or an office after most of the other people have left: *My friends rushed out, but I hung back to talk to the teacher.* **3** to be

unwilling to do sth; to hesitate: *This is a great opportunity. We can't afford to hang back.*
- ◆ v + adv

hang 'on 1 (**to sb/sth**) to hold sb/sth firmly: *Hang on tight and you won't fall off.* ◇ *The horse suddenly galloped off and I tried to hang on as best as I could.* ◇ *Hang on to my hand while we cross the road.* → see also HANG ONTO STH/SB; ⟳ note at HOLD ON **2** (*BrE, informal*) used to ask sb to wait for a short time: *Hang on a minute—I'm nearly ready.* ◇ *The line's engaged. Would you like to hang on?* **3** (*BrE also* **hang a'bout**) (*informal*) used to tell sb to stop what they are doing or saying, because you have just realized sth, or because you do not understand sth: *Hang on! I've had an idea.* ◇ *Hang on! How much did you say it was?* ◇ *Hang on! That's not what I said!* **4** to continue doing sth even when the situation is difficult: *How much longer can their troops hang on in that position?* **5** to wait for sth to happen: *I need an answer soon—don't keep me hanging on.*
- SYN **hold on**
- ◆ v + adv
- IDM **hang** (**on**) 'in there (*informal*) to continue trying to do sth, even though it is very difficult: *Hang on in there! The exams will soon be over.*

hang on sth to depend on sth: *My whole future hung on his decision.*
- OBJ **decision** SYN **depend on sth**
- ◆ v + prep
- IDM **hang on sb's words/sb's every word** to listen with great attention to sb you admire

hang sth on sb (*informal, especially AmE*) to blame sb for sth, often unfairly: *You can't hang the damage to your computer on me—I wasn't even there!* ◇ *They tried to hang the blame on me.*
- ◆ v + n/pron + prep

hang 'on to sb/sth (*informal*) to keep sb/sth; to not sell, give away or lose sth: *Hang on to the receipt in case you want to change the dress.* ◇ *You can hang on to the book for a bit longer if you want.* ◇ *I hope she manages to hang on to her job.* ◇ *The company seems to be incapable of hanging on to its staff.* ◇ *He's a great guy—you should hang on to him!*
- SYN **hold onto sb/sth**, **hold on to sb/sth**
- ◆ v + prep ◆ v + adv + prep
- ▶ **hanger-'on** *n* a person who tries to be friendly with a famous person or who goes to important events, in order to get some advantage: *It's not the monarchy I object to, it's all the hangers-on that go with it.*

hang 'out (*informal*) **1** [+adv/prep] to spend a lot of time in a place or with a person or a group of people: *Where does he hang out these days?* ◇ *She used to hang out with the Beatles in the sixties.* **2** to spend time relaxing, doing very little: *We've just been hanging out and listening to music.*
- ◆ v + adv

▶ ˈhang-out *n* (*informal*) a place where you live or enjoy spending time with friends: *a popular hang-out for teenagers*

ˌhang sth ˈout to attach things that you have washed to a piece of string or rope outside so that they can dry; to attach sth such as a flag outside a window or in a street: *Have you hung the washing out?* ◊ *Many houses hung out a banner supporting the march.*
〈OBJ〉 **washing**, **clothes**, **flags**, **banner**
→ see also HANG UP, HANG STH UP 1
♦ v + n/pron + adv ♦ v + adv + n

ˌhang ˈover sb/sth if a problem, a threat or sth sad **hangs over** you, you think about it or worry about it a lot: *A question mark hangs over the future of the club* (= no one knows what is going to happen). ◊ *The threat of dismissal hung over our heads.* 〈SUBJ〉 **question mark**, **threat**
〈OBJ〉 **head**, **future**
♦ v + prep

ˌhang ˈround, etc. (*BrE*, *informal*) → HANG AROUND, ETC.

ˌhang toˈgether 1 to be well organized and fit together well; to have parts that all agree with each other: *The book doesn't really hang together.* ◊ *This account of what happened doesn't hang together.* 2 (*especially AmE*) when people **hang together**, they support or help one another: *We need to all hang together against those who want to remove our freedoms.* 〈SYN〉 **cooperate**; **pull together**; **stick together** (*informal*)
♦ v + adv

ˌhang ˈup, ˌhang sth ˈup 1 to attach sth from the top to a hook, a piece of string, etc. so that the lower part is free or loose; to be attached in this way: *My dress is hanging up in the wardrobe.* ◊ *Shall I hang your coat up?* ◊ *He took off his suit and hung it up carefully.* 〈OBJ〉 **coat**, **clothes**
→ see also HANG STH OUT 2 (**on sb**) to end a telephone conversation, often very suddenly, by putting down the part of the telephone that you speak into (the **receiver**) or switching the telephone off: *She hung up on me.* ◊ *Don't hang up. I'd like to talk to Dad too.* ◊ *I was so upset I hung up the phone.* 〈OBJ〉 **phone**, **receiver** 3 to finish using sth for the last time; to give up a particular activity, profession, etc.: *After twenty years playing football, he's finally hanging up his boots.* 〈OBJ〉 **boots**
♦ v + adv ♦ v + adv + n ♦ v + n/pron + adv

be/get ˌhung ˈup 1 (**on/about sth/sb**) (*informal*, *disapproving*) to be very worried about sth/sb; to think about sth/sb too much: *You're not still hung up on that girl?* ◊ *Don't get too hung up about fitness.* 2 (*AmE*) to be delayed: *I got hung up in traffic.* ◊ *Sorry I'm late—I got hung up at the office.*
♦ get + v + adv

▶ ˈhang-up *n* 1 an emotional problem about sth that makes you embarrassed or worried: *He's got a real hang-up about his height.* 2 (*AmE*)

a problem that delays sth being agreed or achieved

ˈhang with sb (*AmE*, *slang*) to spend a lot of time with sb: *Are you still hanging with those loser guys?*
♦ v + prep

hanker /ˈhæŋkə(r)/

ˈhanker after/for sth to want sth very much: *He hankered after city life.*
〈SYN〉 **long for sth**
♦ v + prep

happen /ˈhæpən/

ˌhappen aˈlong/ˈby (*informal*) to arrive or appear unexpectedly: *A police car happened along just at that moment.*
♦ v + adv

ˈhappen on/upon sb/sth (*old-fashioned*) to find or meet sb/sth by chance: *I happened upon the book I wanted in a second-hand bookshop.*
〈SYN〉 **come across sb/sth**
♦ v + prep

hark /hɑːk; *AmE* hɑːrk/

ˈhark at sb (*humorous*) used only in the form **hark at** sb, to show that you think what sb has just said is stupid, or shows too much pride: *'I need to lose some weight.' 'Hark at her! She's so thin I can hardly see her!'*
♦ v + prep

ˌhark ˈback to sth 1 to talk about or remember sth that happened in the past or was mentioned before: *You can't keep harking back to the past.* 〈OBJ〉 **the past**, **youth** 〈NOTE〉 Often used in the progressive tenses. 2 (*BrE*) to be like sth in the past: *The melody harks back to one of his earlier symphonies.* 〈NOTE〉 Not used in the progressive tenses.
♦ v + adv + prep

harp /hɑːp; *AmE* hɑːrp/

ˌharp ˈon (**about sth**), ˈharp on sth (*informal*) to keep talking about sth in a way that other people find annoying: *He's still harping on about his accident.* ◊ *He's always harping on the same theme.*
〈SYN〉 **go on** (**about sth**)
♦ v + adv ♦ v + prep

harsh /hɑːʃ; *AmE* hɑːrʃ/

ˈharsh on sb (*AmE*, *slang*) to criticize sb: *In his blog he harshed on actresses who jump on the anti-war bandwagon.*
♦ v + prep

hash /hæʃ/

ˌhash sth ˈout (*AmE*, *informal*) to discuss sth in detail for a long time in order to reach an agreement: *They are still hashing out the details of the contract.*

SYN thrash sth out
◆ v + adv + n ◆ v + n/pron + adv

,hash sth 'over (*AmE, informal*) to discuss sth for a long time in a lot of detail: *We hashed over the events of the previous evening, but couldn't come up with any answers.*
◆ v + adv + n ◆ v + n/pron + adv

hatch /hætʃ/

,hatch 'out (*BrE*) when a bird, an insect, etc. **hatches out**, it comes out of the egg; when an egg **hatches out**, it breaks open and a bird, an insect, etc. comes out: *The chicks hatch out after fifteen days.* ◊ *Have the eggs hatched out yet?* ◊ *When will the caterpillars hatch out?*
NOTE **Hatch** is used on its own instead of **hatch out** in American English. It can also be used in British English.
◆ v + adv

haul /hɔːl/

,haul sb be'fore sb/sth (*also* ,haul sb 'up before sb/sth) (*informal*) to make sb appear in court to be judged: *They were hauled before the courts.* ◊ *They hauled her up in front of senior officers.*
SYN bring sb before sb/sth (*more formal*)
NOTE In front of sb/sth can be used instead of **before**: *They hauled her up in front of senior officers.* ◆ Often used in the passive.
→ see also HAUL SB UP
◆ v + n/pron + prep

,haul sth 'in (*AmE, informal*) to win or earn sth: *The thirty-year-old hauled in five gold medals.*
◆ v + n/pron + adv ◆ v + adv + n

,haul sb 'off (to sth/…) (*informal*) to take sb somewhere by force: *They hauled him off to jail.*
SYN drag sb off (to sth)
◆ v + n/pron + adv ◆ v + adv + n (*rare*)

,haul sb 'up (*informal*) to make sb appear in court to be judged: *He was hauled up on a charge of dangerous driving.*
NOTE Often used in the passive.
→ see also HAUL SB BEFORE SB/STH
◆ v + n/pron + adv ◆ v + adv + n (*rare*)

have /həv, əv, hæv/ (**has, having, had, had**)

NOTE Phrasal verbs with **have** are not normally used in the passive.

,have sth a'gainst sb/sth (*also* have ,got sth a'gainst sb/sth) (*not used in the progressive tenses*) to dislike sb/sth for a particular reason: *I've got nothing against her family personally!* ◊ *I don't know what she had against me.*
OBJ nothing, anything, something
◆ v + pron + prep

,have sb a'round (*especially AmE*) → HAVE SB OVER

,have it a'way (with sb) (*BrE, slang*) → HAVE IT OFF (WITH SB)

,have sb 'back (*especially BrE*) **1** to allow a husband, wife or partner that you are separated from to return: *He had his wife back time and time again.* **SYN** take sb back **2** to invite sb to your house after you have been somewhere with them: *After the cinema we had everybody back for coffee.* **SYN** ask sb back; invite sb back (*more formal*)
◆ v + n/pron + adv

,have sth 'back to receive sth that has been borrowed or taken from you: *Can I have the book back by Thursday?*
◆ v + n/pron + adv ◆ v + adv + n (*rare*)

,have sb 'down as sth (*especially BrE*) to think that sb is a particular type of person, especially when in fact they are not: *I didn't have you down as the jealous type.*
◆ v + n/pron + adv + prep

,have sb 'in (*also* have ,got sb 'in) to have sb doing some work in your home or office: *They've got the builders in all week.* ◊ *We had the inspectors in on Tuesday.*
◆ v + n/pron + adv

,have sth 'in (*also* have ,got sth 'in) (*not used in the progressive tenses*) to have a supply of sth in your home, etc.: *Do we have enough food in for the holiday?* ◊ *I wanted to get a new swimsuit, but the store didn't have any in yet.*
◆ v + n/pron + adv

have it 'off (*also* ,have it a'way (with sb)) (*BrE, slang*) to have sex with sb
◆ v + it + adv

,have sb 'on (*informal*) (*usually used in the progressive tenses*) to joke with sb by pretending sth is true when it is not: *'We've won a new car!' 'You're having me on!'*
◆ v + n/pron + adv

,have sth 'on (*also* have ,got sth 'on) **1** (*not used in the progressive tenses*) to be wearing sth: *She's got her best dress on.* ◊ *He had nothing (= no clothes) on!* ◊ *He had on a blue and white checked shirt and jeans.* **OBJ** clothes, coat, hat, etc. **SYN** be wearing sth **2** to have a piece of electrical equipment switched on: *I didn't hear you come in because I had the radio on.* **OBJ** television, radio **3** to have sth planned or arranged: *I've had a lot on recently.* ◊ *What do you have on (for) tomorrow?* **OBJ** nothing, something, a lot
◆ v + n/pron + adv **1** also v + adv + n (*less frequent*)

,have sth 'on sb/sth (*also* have ,got sth 'on sb/sth) (*informal*) (*not used in the progressive tenses*) to know sth bad about sb/sth that can be used against them/it: *The police had nothing on him (= no evidence that he had committed a crime).*
OBJ something, nothing
◆ v + n/pron + prep

,have sth 'out **1** to have a tooth or an organ of your body removed: *I had to have a tooth out.* **OBJ** tooth, appendix, tonsils **2** (with sb) to talk

have sth on

dress up ◆ get dressed ◆ have sth on ◆ put sth on ◆ wear sth

These verbs mean to put or have clothes on your body.

dress up to wear clothes that are more formal than those you usually wear; to put on special clothes or a costume: *I like to dress up on a Saturday night.* ◇ *We decided to dress up as fairies.*

get dressed to put clothes on yourself: *I got up and got dressed.* **NOTE** Dress can be used on its own with this meaning, but is more formal. It is also used to talk about the kind of clothes a person wears: *She always dresses well.*

have sth on (*not used in the progressive tenses*) to be wearing sth: *She had a red jacket on.* ◇ *He had nothing on.*

put sth on to dress yourself in sth: *Put your coat and scarf on!*

wear sth to have clothes on your body: *He was wearing a tie.* ◇ *I don't know what to wear.*

PATTERNS AND COLLOCATIONS

- to wear/put on/have on a **dress/hat/jacket**
- to **tend to/refuse to/be entitled to** wear sth
- to get dressed/put sth on **hurriedly/quickly/carefully**
- to dress **casually/elegantly/fashionably/neatly/nicely/smartly/well**

---

to sb openly to try to settle a disagreement: *She finally decided to **have it out with** him.*
◆ v + n/pron + adv

,have sb 'over (*also* ,have sb a'round *especially AmE*) (*BrE also* ,have sb 'round) to invite sb to come to your house: *They had some friends over last night.* ◇ *We're having people round for dinner tonight.*
◆ v + n/pron + adv

,have sb 'up (**for sth**) (*BrE, informal*) to accuse sb of sth and bring them to court to be examined by a judge: *He was had up for dangerous driving.*
◆ v + n/pron + adv

hawk /hɔːk/

,hawk sth a'bout/a'round/'round; ,hawk sth a'bout/a'round/'round sth (*BrE*) to try to sell things by going from place to place asking people to buy them: *Pirate copies of their CD were being hawked around.* ◇ *They hawked their newsletter around student bars.*
◆ v + n/pron + adv ◆ v + adv + n (*less frequent*)
◆ v + n/pron + prep

head /hed/

⌐'head for/towards sth (*also* be 'headed for/ towards sth *especially AmE*) (*often used in the progressive tenses*) **1** to be going in a particular direction or to a particular place: *It's time I was heading for home.* ◇ *Jane headed for the door.*
SYN make for sb/sth **2** to be likely to experience sth, especially sth bad: *They're heading for trouble.* ◇ *The country is headed for an economic disaster.*
OBJ trouble, defeat, disaster, victory, a fall
◆ v + prep ◆ be + v + prep

,head 'off to leave a place to go somewhere else or do sth else: *It's time we headed off to get the train.*
◆ v + adv

,head sb 'off to get in front of sb in order to make them turn back or go in a different direction: *Police tried to head off the demonstrators before they got to the city hall.*
SYN intercept sb (*more formal*)
◆ v + adv + n ◆ v + n/pron + adv

,head sb/sth 'off to prevent sth; to stop sb from doing sth: *Their attempts to head off criticism have failed.*
◆ v + adv + n ◆ v + n/pron + adv

'head towards sth, etc. → HEAD FOR/ TOWARDS STH, ETC.

,head 'up sth to be in charge of sth such as a department, a company, an organization, etc.: *She heads up our finance division.* ◇ *The new company will be headed up by Graham Hart.*
OBJ operation, company
NOTE When the object of **head up** is a noun, it comes after **up**, but when the object is a pronoun, it comes between **head** and **up**: *This new company—who will head it up?*
NOTE Head sth is also used on its own: *She heads our finance division.*
◆ v + adv + n ◆ v + pron + adv

heal /hiːl/

,heal 'up/'over if a cut, a wound, etc. **heals up/ over**, it closes and becomes healthy again: *Her leg took a long time to heal up.* ◇ *The cut has healed over now.*
NOTE Heal is often used on its own with the same meaning.
➔ note at PULL THROUGH
◆ v + adv

heap /hiːp/

ˈheap A on B; ˈheap B with A (*also* ˈheap A upon B *more formal*) **1** to put a lot of sth in a pile on sth: *She heaped food on my plate.* ◇ *The food was heaped on the plate.* ◇ *The chairs were heaped with cushions.* **2** to offer or give sb a lot of sth, especially praise or criticism: *They heaped scorn upon his proposal.* ◇ *Praise was heaped on the police for their handling of the case.*

OBJ praise, scorn

NOTE Often used in the passive.

◆ v + n/pron + prep

ˌheap sth ˈup to put sth into a pile: *A huge pile of washing was heaped up in a corner.*

SYN pile sth up

◆ v + n/pron + adv ◆ v + adv + n

hear /hɪə(r)/; *AmE* hɪr/ (**heard, heard** /hɜːd; *AmE* hɜːrd/)

ˈhear about sb/sth to be told news or information about sb/sth: *I'm so sorry to hear about your mother* (= for example, that she is ill). ◇ *Have you heard about your job yet* (= if you have got it)? ➔ note at FIND OUT, FIND SB OUT

◆ v + prep

ˈhear from sb; ˈhear sth from sb **1** to receive news or information from sb, usually by letter or telephone: *Do you ever hear from any of your school friends?* ◇ *I look forward to hearing from you.* ◇ *I haven't heard anything from Kate for ages.* **2** to formally get sb's opinion about sth or their description of sth that has happened, such as an accident, etc.: *Can we hear from some of the women in the audience?* ◇ *The police would like to hear from anyone who witnessed the accident.* ◇ *I'd like to hear something from somebody who's had experience of studying abroad.*

◆ v + prep ◆ v + n/pron + prep

ˈhear of sb/sth to know about sb/sth because you have been told about them/it: *I've heard of the Alexander technique, but I don't know anything about it.* ◇ *I've never heard of him.*

NOTE Hear of sb is often used in the present perfect tense with *have*.

◆ v + prep

ˈhear of sb/sth; ˈhear sth of sb/sth to have news of sb/sth: *I was sorry to hear of your accident.* ◇ *He was last heard of in Liverpool.* ◇ *You're going abroad? This is the first I've heard of it!* ◇ *From what I've heard of Andy, he's become very successful.* ◇ *I expect we'll hear more of this band in the future.*

NOTE Often used in the passive.

→ see also NOT HEAR OF STH, ETC.

◆ v + prep ◆ v + n/pron + prep

▶ unˈheard-of *adj* that has never been known or done; surprising: *It's almost unheard-of for it to rain there in July.*

not ˈhear of sth; not ˈhear of sb doing sth to not allow sth or not allow sb to do sth:

I offered to go but she wouldn't hear of it. ◇ *They wouldn't hear of us postponing the trip.*

◆ v + prep

ˌhear sb ˈout to listen until sb has finished saying what they want to say: *I know you don't believe me, but please hear me out!*

◆ v + n/pron + adv

heat /hiːt/

ˌheat ˈup (*AmE*) → HOT UP

ˌheat ˈup; ˌheat sth ˈup to become warm or hot; to make sth warm or hot: *The pipes will expand as they heat up.* ◇ *We can heat up the soup in the microwave.*

SYN warm up, warm sth up

◆ v + adv ◆ v + adv + n ◆ v + n/pron + adv

hedge /hedʒ/

ˌhedge sth aˈbout/aˈround/ˈround with sth (*BrE, formal*) to surround and limit sth with conditions or restrictions: *Employment is hedged around with legislation nowadays.*

NOTE Usually used in the passive.

◆ v + n/pron + adv + prep

ˌhedge sb/sth ˈin to surround sb/sth with sth; to restrict the freedom of sb to do sth: *The cathedral is hedged in by other buildings.* ◇ *He felt hedged in by all the rules and regulations.*

SYN fence sb in; hem sb/sth in

NOTE Often used in the passive.

◆ v + n/pron + adv ◆ v + adv + n

help /help/

ˌhelp sth aˈlong to try to make sth happen more quickly or easily: *My mother always says that a cup of tea **helps things along**.* ◇ *His father's name helped along his career in the early days.*

◆ v + n/pron + adv ◆ v + adv + n (*less frequent*)

ˌhelp sb ˈoff/ˈon with sth to help sb to take off or put on a piece of clothing, such as a coat: *Can I help you off with your coat?* ◇ *She helped him on with his dressing gown.*

◆ v + n/pron + adv + prep

ˌhelp ˈout (with sth), ˌhelp sb ˈout (with sth) to help sb in order to make things easier for them, for example by doing some of their work or by giving them money: *Thank you for helping out.* ◇ *My dad said he'd help me out with money.*

NOTE Help (with sth) and help sb (with sth) can be used with the same meaning.

◆ v + adv ◆ v + n/pron + adv ◆ v + adv + n (*rare*)

ˈhelp sb to sth; ˈhelp yourself to sth to give sb/yourself some food or drink: *Can I help anyone to more chicken?* ◇ *Please help yourselves to salad.*

◆ v + n/pron + prep

hem /hem/ (**-mm-**)

ˌhem sb/sth ˈin to surround sb/sth with sth so that they cannot move freely: *The thick trees*

hemmed *them* in *on all sides.* ◇ *The ship was hemmed in by the ice.* ◇ (*figurative*) *We felt hemmed in by restrictions.*
SYN **fence sb in**
NOTE Often used in the passive.
◆ v + n/pron + adv ◆ v + adv + n

herd /hɜːd; *AmE* hɜːrd/

,herd to'gether; ,herd sb/sth to'gether to move or make sb/sth move in a particular direction: *They were herded together into trucks and driven away.*
NOTE Often used in the passive.
◆ v + adv ◆ v + n/pron + adv ◆ v + adv + n

hew /hjuː/ (**hewed**, **hewed** or **hewn** /hjuːn/)

'hew to sth (*AmE*) to agree with or match sth closely: *His comments hewed to the line of other senior government officials.*
◆ v + prep

hide /haɪd/ (**hid** /hɪd/, **hidden** /'hɪdn/)

,hide a'way; ,hide yourself a'way to go to a place secretly because you do not want anyone to find you: *She used to hide away in her room when she got depressed.* ◇ *She hid herself away until she felt better.*
◆ v + adv ◆ v + pron + adv
▶ 'hideaway *n* a place where sb goes to be alone

,hide sb/sth a'way to put sb/sth in a secret place so that no one else can find them/it: *You won't find your present—I've hidden it away!*
◆ v + n/pron + adv ◆ v + adv + n (*less frequent*)

,hide 'out to go to a secret place to escape from sb who is trying to find you: *He hid out in the woods.*
◆ v + adv
▶ 'hideout *n* a place where sb goes when they do not want to be found

hike /haɪk/

,hike sth 'up **1** (*informal*) to lift or pull up a piece of clothing that you are wearing: *He hiked up his trousers and waded into the water.* **SYN** **hitch sth up 2** to increase a price or rate suddenly and by a large amount: *They hiked up the price by 40%.* **SYN** **jack sth up** (*informal*); **put sth up** **NOTE** Hike sth is used on its own less often with this meaning.
◆ v + adv + n ◆ v + pron + adv ◆ v + n + adv (*rare*)

hinge /hɪndʒ/

'hinge on sth (*also* 'hinge upon sth *more formal*) if an action, a result, etc. **hinges on/upon** sth, it depends on it completely or is strongly influenced by it: *My whole career could hinge on the results of these exams.* ◇ *The success of the project hinges on how well everyone works together.*
◆ v + prep

hint /hɪnt/

'hint at sth to suggest in an indirect way that sth is true or likely: *In his speech the Prime Minister hinted at an early election.* ◇ *The problem was only hinted at.*
◆ v + prep

hire /'haɪə(r)/

,hire sb 'out; ,hire yourself 'out (**to sb**) (**as sth**) to arrange for sb to work for sb else; to arrange to work for sb: *The agency hires out cleaning staff.* ◇ *He hires himself out to farmers at harvest time.* ◇ *He had been hired out to them as an expert.*
◆ v + adv + n ◆ v + n/pron + adv

,hire 'on; ,hire sb 'on (*AmE*) to take a particular job or position; to give sb a job: *I'm just trying to do what I hired on to do.* ◇ *She* **hired on as** *a claims adjuster with an insurance company.* ◇ *We've hired on thirty new staff members this month alone.*
◆ v + adv ◆ v + adv + n ◆ v + n/pron + adv

,hire sth 'out (**to sb**) to allow sb to use sth for a short period of time in return for payment: *The club will hire out tennis rackets to guests.*
OBJ **equipment**, **boat** **SYN** **let sth out** (**to sb**); **rent sth out** (**to sb**)
◆ v + adv + n ◆ v + n/pron + adv

hit /hɪt/ (**hitting**, **hit**, **hit**)

,hit 'back (**at sb/sth**) to criticize or attack sb who has criticized or attacked you: *In an interview she hit back at her critics.*
SYN **bite back** (**at sb/sth**); **strike back** (**at/ against sb/sth**)
◆ v + adv

'hit sb for sth (*also* ,hit sb 'up for sth) (*slang, especially AmE*) to ask sb for sth, especially money: *They hit us for a commission as well.* ◇ *She's always hitting me up for the cab fare home.* ◇ *Does he always hit you for cash when he wants new clothes?*
◆ v + n/pron + prep ◆ v + n/pron + adv + prep

,hit it 'off (**with sb**) (*informal*) if two people **hit it off** with each other, they like each other and become friendly immediately: *We hit it off from the start.* ◇ *She didn't really hit it off with the office manager.*
◆ v + it + adv

'hit on sb (*AmE, slang*) to talk to sb in a way that shows you are sexually attracted to them: *He was hitting on my girlfriend!*
◆ v + prep

'hit on sth (*also* 'hit upon sth *more formal*) (*not used in the progressive tenses*) to think of a plan, a solution, etc. suddenly or by chance: *She hit on an idea for raising money.* ◇ *I realized I'd hit upon a solution to one of our main problems.*
OBJ **idea**, **method**, **formula**, **solution** **SYN** **light on/upon sb/sth** ⟳ note at THINK STH UP
◆ v + prep

hit out (at sb/sth)

attack sb/sth ✦ **condemn sb/sth** ✦ **criticize sb/ sth** ✦ **denounce sb/sth** ✦ **hit out (at sb/sth)**

These verbs all mean to say that you disapprove of sb/sth, especially because you think they have done sth bad.

attack sb/sth (*used especially in newspapers*) to criticize sb/sth strongly, especially in order to make people stop respecting them: *Newspapers attacked the minister for her stance.*

condemn sb/sth (*used especially in newspapers*) to express very strong disapproval of sb/sth, usually for moral reasons: *The government issued a statement condemning the killings.*

criticize sb/sth (*BrE also* **criticise**) to say that you disapprove of sb/sth; to say what you do not like or think is wrong about sb/sth: *The decision was criticized by the unions.* ◇ *Who are they to criticize my dress sense?*

denounce sb/sth (*formal*) to criticize sb/sth strongly, usually in public: *She denounced the government's handling of the crisis.*

hit out (at sb/sth) (*used especially in newspapers*) to criticize sb/sth strongly, especially because you think their views or actions are bad or because they have criticized you unfairly: *The Duchess has hit out at journalists who criticize her dress sense.*

WHICH WORD?

You **denounce** things because you think they are wrong, not just because you do not like them.

PATTERNS AND COLLOCATIONS

- to criticize/condemn/attack/denounce sb/sth **for** sth
- to criticize/condemn/attack/denounce **the government/the President/a decision**
- to criticize/condemn/attack/denounce sb/sth **strongly/publicly**
- to be **severely/roundly** criticized
- to be **widely** blamed/criticized/condemned/ attacked/denounced

ˌhit ˈout (at sb/sth) **1** to attack sb violently, especially sb who is trying to hit or capture you: *She hit out at the policeman as he tried to arrest her.* ◇ *I just hit out blindly in all directions.* **SYN strike out (at sb/sth) 2** to criticize sb or sth strongly: *He hit out at the government's decision.* **SYN lash out (at sb/sth)**
◆ v + adv

ˌhit sb ˈup for sth (*AmE*) → HIT SB FOR STH

ˈhit upon sth → HIT ON STH

hitch /hɪtʃ/

ˌhitch sth ˈup to pull up a piece of your clothing: *We hitched up our skirts and climbed over the wall.* **SYN hike sth up** (*informal*)
◆ v + adv + n ◆ v + n/pron + adv

hive /haɪv/

ˌhive sth ˈoff (**into/to sth**) (*business*) to separate sth from a larger group; to sell part of a company: *Some of the firm's operations have been hived off into a separate company.* **NOTE** Often used in the passive.
◆ v + adv + n ◆ v + pron + adv ◆ v + n + adv (*rare*)

hoe /həʊ; *AmE* hoʊ/

ˌhoe ˈin (*AustralE, informal*) to eat with enthusiasm
◆ v + adv

hoist /hɔɪst/

ˌhoist sb/sth ˈup; ˌhoist yourself ˈup to raise sb/sth/yourself to a higher position or level, often with difficulty or using ropes or special equipment: *She hoisted the box up onto the shelf.*
↻ note at LIFT SB/STH UP
◆ v + n/pron + adv ◆ v + adv + n

hold /həʊld; *AmE* hoʊld/ (**held**, **held** /held/)

ˌhold sth aˈgainst sb to allow sth bad that sb has done to make you like or respect them less: *I was stupid—I hope you won't hold it against me.* ◇ *Do you hold any grudges against him?* ◇ *I don't hold it against him that he lied to me.* **OBJ it, grudge NOTE** Hold sth against sb is often used with a negative such as *don't* or *won't*.
◆ v + n/pron + prep

ˌhold ˈback (**from doing sth**), ˌhold sb ˈback (**from doing sth**) to hesitate, or to make sb hesitate: *Don't hold back! This opportunity is too good to miss!* ◇ *Phil walked forward confidently but something held Ben back.* ◇ *I nearly told him what I thought of him, but I held back.*
◆ v + adv ◆ v + n/pron + adv

ˌhold sb/sth ˈback **1** to prevent sb/sth from moving forward or from entering or leaving a place: *The police were unable to hold back the fans.* **2** to prevent the progress or development of sb/sth: *Now that he's got this job, there'll be **no holding him back**.* ◇ *Teaching all the children* together can hold the brighter children back. ◇ Low rates of investment will hold back technical progress. ◇ Parents claim the tests are being used to hold children back (= not let them progress to the next class).

◆ v + n/pron + adv ◆ v + adv + n

ͺhold sth ˈback 1 to stop yourself from expressing or showing how you feel: They couldn't hold back their laughter. ◇ He struggled to hold back his tears. OBJ **your tears**, **your laughter** SYN **keep sth back**; **contain sth** (more formal) **2** to not tell sb sth that you wish to keep secret: I think he's holding something back; he knows more than he's admitting. OBJ **something**, **anything**, **information** SYN **withhold sth** (more formal) **3** to keep sth such as money to use later: £1 000 of the grant will be held back until the project is completed. NOTE Often used in the passive.

◆ v + adv + n ◆ v + n/pron + adv

ͺhold ˈback on sth to try to spend only a little time, money, etc. on sth; to show control in what you do: She never held back on the tea and cakes when we visited. ◇ She held back on her questioning (= she did not ask too many questions).

◆ v + adv + prep

ͺhold sb ˈdown to prevent sb from having their freedom or rights

SYN **oppress sb**

◆ v + adv + n ◆ v + n/pron + adv

ͺhold sb/sth ˈdown to use force to hold sb/sth in a particular position and stop them/it from moving: He was held down and kicked by the two

men. ◇ Hold the mouse button down as you move the cursor.

◆ v + n/pron + adv ◆ v + adv + n

ͺhold sth ˈdown 1 to manage to keep a job, position, etc. even though it may be difficult for you to do so: He doesn't seem able to hold down a full-time job. OBJ **a job 2** (especially BrE) to keep sth at a low level: The company is trying to hold down costs. ◇ The rate of inflation must be held down. OBJ **prices**, **wages**, **inflation**, **costs** SYN **keep sth down 3** (AmE, informal) to limit sth, especially a noise: Hold it down, will you? I'm trying to sleep! **4** (usually used in negative sentences) to be able to eat food without bringing it back out of your mouth: She hasn't been able to hold any food down since the operation. OBJ **food** SYN **keep sth down 5** to not allow yourself to show or express a strong emotion: I had to hold down the urge to hit him.

◆ v + adv + n ◆ v + n/pron + adv

ͺhold ˈforth (**on/about sth**) (formal or humorous) to speak for a long time and often in a boring or annoying way: He was holding forth about how successful his business is.

◆ v + adv

ͺhold sth ˈin 1 to keep sth inside a place so that it cannot fall out or escape: The straps hold the baby in securely. ◇ I had to hold my stomach in (= pull the muscles flat) to zip up my jeans. OBJ **your stomach**, **your tummy 2** to not show or express how you feel: I couldn't hold in my anger any longer. OPP **let sth out**

◆ v + n/pron + adv ◆ v + adv + n

ͺhold ˈoff 1 if rain or a storm, etc. **holds off**, it does not start: I hope the rain holds off for the

hold on (to sth/sb)

clasp sth ◆ cling to sth ◆ clutch sth ◆ grip sth ◆ hang on (to sth) ◆ hold on (to sb/sth)

These verbs all mean to have sb/sth in your hands, arms, etc.

clasp sth to hold sb/sth tightly in your hand or in your arms: He leaned forward, his hands clasped tightly together. ◇ She clasped the children in her arms.

cling to sth to hold sb/sth tightly, especially with your whole body: Survivors clung to pieces of floating debris.

clutch sth to hold sb/sth tightly, especially in your hand; to take hold of sth suddenly: She clutched her bag tightly in one hand.

grip sth to hold sth very tightly with your hand: Grip the rope as tightly as you can.
▶ **grip** n [C, usually sing.]: Keep a tight **grip** on the rope. ◇ The climber slipped and lost his grip.

hang on (to sth) to hold sth very tightly, especially in order to support yourself or stop yourself from falling: I hung on to him for support. ◇ She was standing at the top of the stairs, hanging on to the banister.

hold on (to sth/sb) (also **hold onto sb/sth**) to continue to hold sb/sth; to put your hand on sb/sth and keep it there: Hold on and don't let go. ◇ It's very windy—you'd better hold on to your hat. ◇ He held on to the back of the chair to stop himself from falling.

PATTERNS AND COLLOCATIONS

■ to clutch/grip/clasp sth in your **hand/hands/arms**

■ to hold on to/cling to/clutch/grip/clasp/hang on to sb/sth **tight/tightly/firmly**

■ to hold on to/cling on to/clutch/grip/clasp/hang on to sb's **hand**

wedding. **SYN** **keep off 2** (*also* ˌhold ˈoff sth, ˌhold ˈoff (**from**) **doing sth**) to delay doing sth: *I need to make a decision soon, but I'll hold off until next week.* ◇ *The committee will hold off their decision until they receive the report.* ◇ *I'm holding off buying a dress until the sales start.* **NOTE** **Hold off** is not used with a pronoun object.

♦ **1** v + adv

♦ **2** v + adv ♦ v + adv + n ♦ v + adv + -ing

ˌhold sb/sth ˈoff to resist an attack by an enemy or an opponent: *How long do you think you can hold off the attack?* ◇ *He held off a late challenge from Davies to win the race.*

♦ v + adv + n ♦ v + n/pron + adv

ˌhold ˈon 1 (*informal*) used to ask sb to wait or stop for a short time: *Hold on a minute—I'm not ready.* ◇ *Hold on! That doesn't sound right.* **2** to survive in a difficult or dangerous situation; to continue doing sth although it is difficult: *They managed to hold on until help arrived.*

SYN **hang on**

♦ v + adv

ˌhold ˈon (**to sth/sb**) to hold sth/sb tightly; to not let go of sth/sb: ***Hold on tight**—I'm going to speed up!* ◇ *Hold on to your hat or it'll blow away.*

SYN **hang on**

NOTE **Hold on to sth** can also be spelt **hold onto sth**: *I had to hold onto the chair for support.*

♦ v + adv ♦ v + prep ♦ v + adv + prep

ˌhold sth ˈon to keep sth in position so that it cannot fall off: *It is these nuts and bolts that hold the wheels on.*

♦ v + n/pron + adv ♦ v + adv + n

ˌhold ˈonto sb/sth; ˌhold ˈon to sb/sth to keep sth/sb; to not lose sth/sb: *Hold on to the magazines for as long as you like.* ◇ *The party will hold on to its majority at the next election.* ◇ *She's a good worker. You should hold on to her.* ◇ *You must pass the ball and not hold onto it.*

SYN **hang onto sb/sth, hang on to sb/sth** (*informal*)

→ see also HOLD ON

♦ v + prep ♦ v + adv + prep

ˌhold ˈout 1 if money or supplies, etc. **hold out**, they last or remain: *I'm staying here for as long as my money holds out.* ◇ *Do you think the fine weather will hold out?* **SYN** **last out 2** (**against sb/sth**) to resist an attack: *The town continues to hold out against enemy bombing.* **3** (**against sth**) to refuse to accept sth that you do not agree with: *We can't hold out against industrialization any longer.* **OPP** **give in** (**to sb/sth**)

♦ v + adv

▶ ˈholdout *n* a person or group of people that resists an attack, an enemy or an opponent, or refuses to accept sth

ˌhold ˈout sth to offer a chance, hope or possibility of sth: *He may come, but I don't **hold out much hope**.* ◇ *This method seems to hold out the greatest promise of success.*

OBJ the promise/prospect/possibility of…, hope

NOTE **Hold out** is never used with a pronoun object.

♦ v + adv + n

ˌhold sth ˈout to hold sth such as your hand or sth in your hand, in front of you towards sb else: *She held her cup out for more coffee.* ◇ 'You must be Kate,' he said, holding out his hand.*

OBJ hand

♦ v + n/pron + adv ♦ v + adv + n

ˌhold ˈout for sth to deliberately delay reaching an agreement in the hope that you will gain sth; to refuse to accept anything less than what you are asking for: *Union leaders are holding out for a better deal.*

♦ v + adv + prep

ˌhold ˈout on sb (*informal*) to refuse to tell or give sb sth: *You promised to give me the money. Stop holding out on me.*

♦ v + adv + prep

ˌhold sth ˈover 1 to leave sth to be dealt with later: *We decided to hold the matter over until the next meeting.* **SYN** **postpone sth 2** (*AmE*) to show a film/movie or play for longer than planned because it is so successful: *The show is being held over for another month.*

NOTE Often used in the passive.

♦ v + n/pron + adv ♦ v + adv + n

▶ ˈholdover *n* (*AmE*) a person who keeps a position of power, for example sb who had a particular position in one government and who still has it in the next

ˌhold sth ˈover sb to use sth that you know about sb in order to threaten them and to make them do what you want: *I don't want to give him anything to hold over me.*

♦ v + n/pron + prep

ˈhold to sth if you **hold to** an opinion, a belief, etc., you do not change it: *She always holds to her principles.*

SYN **keep to sth; stick to sth**

♦ v + prep

ˈhold sb to sth 1 to make sb keep a promise: '*I promise I'll take you out to dinner if we win.*' '*I'll hold you to that!*' **2** (*sport*) to stop your opponent in a sports competition winning more points than you: *Spain held France to a 1-1 draw.*

♦ v + n/pron + prep

ˈhold sth to sth to place sth close to sth else: *He held a knife to her throat.*

♦ v + n/pron + prep

ˌhold toˈgether; ˌhold sth toˈgether 1 to remain, or to keep sb/sth, united: *The coalition has held together for longer than expected.* ◇ *Strong bonds of loyalty hold the family together.* **2** if ideas, arguments, etc. **hold together**, or sth **holds them together**, they are logical and the parts agree with each other: *His ideas don't really hold together.* ◇ *Words like 'however', 'therefore', 'although', etc. can hold* *your text together.* **3** to remain in one piece; to stay in good condition: *It's a miracle that his car is still holding together.* ◊ *His trousers were held together by safety pins.*

♦ v + adv ♦ v + n/pron + adv ♦ v + adv + n

,hold 'up **1** to remain healthy, in good condition or working effectively, especially when there are difficulties: *Sales have held up well, in spite of economic difficulties.* ◊ *How did your tent hold up in the storm?* **2** if an idea, an argument, etc. **holds up**, it remains strong when you analyse it carefully: *I don't think his argument really holds up.* SYN **stand up**

♦ v + adv

,hold sb/sth 'up **1** to raise sb/sth in the air: *She held up her hand to stop him.* ◊ *He held up his trophy as the crowd applauded.* **2** to support sb/ sth and prevent it/them from falling: *Her trousers were held up with string.* ◊ *The two pillars were holding up the ceiling up.* SYN **keep sth up 3** to block or delay the progress of sb/sth: *Roadworks on the motorway are holding up traffic.* ◊ *She phoned to say she'd been held up at the office.* ◊ *I don't want to hold you up.* **4** to rob a person, a bank, a shop/store, etc. using a gun: *Have they caught the people who held up the bank?*

NOTE Often used in the passive.

♦ v + adv + n ♦ v + n/pron + adv **4** v + adv + n
♦ v + pron + adv ♦ v + n + adv (*rare*)

▶ 'hold-up *n* **1** a delay or sth which causes a delay: *What's the hold-up?* **2** an act of robbing a person, a bank, a shop/store, etc. using a gun

,hold sb/sth 'up as sth to present sb/sth as an example of sth: *My mother held up my cousin as an example of a good student.*

♦ v + n/pron + adv + prep
♦ v + adv + n + prep

'hold with sth to agree with or approve of sth: *I don't hold with these new theories on education.* NOTE **Hold with sth** is only used in negative sentences and questions.

♦ v + prep

hole /həʊl; *AmE* hoʊl/

,hole 'up; be ,holed 'up (*informal*) to hide somewhere: *The thieves holed up in an empty warehouse.* ◊ *The police couldn't find out where the gang were holed up.*

♦ v + adv ♦ be + v + adv

hollow /ˈhɒləʊ; *AmE* ˈhɑːloʊ/

,hollow sth 'out **1** to make a space inside sth by removing part of it: *We hollowed out the pumpkin and put a candle in it.* ◊ *a hollowed-out tree trunk* **2** to form sth by making a hole in sth else: *The waves have hollowed out caves along the cliff.*

♦ v + adv + n ♦ v + pron + adv
♦ v + n + adv (*rare*)

home /həʊm; *AmE* hoʊm/

,home 'in on sb/sth **1** to move or be aimed straight towards sb/sth: *She homed in on me as soon as she saw me.* **2** to turn all your attention to sth: *The lawyer homed in on the inconsistencies in her story.*

♦ v + adv + prep

hook /hʊk/

,hook sb 'into sth; ,hook sb 'into doing sth (*AmE, informal*) to persuade sb to do sth when they do not want to: *I didn't want to be involved but I got hooked into helping.* ◊ *He tried to hook me into going with them.*

NOTE Nearly always used in the passive.

♦ v + n/pron + prep

,hook 'up (with sb) **1** (*informal*) to agree to work with sb: *We've hooked up with a firm in Ireland.* **2** (*informal, especially AmE*) to meet sb and spend time with them: *On vacation we hooked up with some Texans.* ◊ *Let's hook up when you get back from your trip.* **3** (*informal, especially AmE*) to start a relationship with sb, especially a sexual relationship: *They hooked up at Kyle's party.* ◊ *Judith hoped to hook up with a cowboy at the rodeo.*

▶ 'hook-up *n* (*AmE, informal*) a new relationship with sb, especially a sexual relationship: *The magazine has all the latest gossip about celebrity hook-ups.*

♦ v + adv

,hook 'up; ,hook sb/sth 'up (to sth) to connect sb/sth to a piece of electronic equipment or to a power supply: *All the speakers hook up to a single amplifier.* ◊ *The boat was hooked up to the shore power supply.* ◊ *They've hooked him up to a life-support machine.*

♦ v + adv ♦ v + adv + n ♦ v + n/pron + adv

▶ 'hook-up *n* a connection between two or more pieces of equipment: *an international phone hook-up*

,hook sb 'up with sth (*AmE, informal*) to give sb a valuable gift because of their job or position: *My clients from the music industry often hook me up with free tickets.*

♦ v + n/pron + adv + prep

hoover /ˈhuːvə(r)/

NOTE A **Hoover**™ (*BrE*) is an electric machine that cleans floors, carpets, etc. by sucking up dirt and dust.

,hoover sth 'up (*BrE*) **1** to remove dust, dirt, etc. from a carpet or floor with a Hoover: *to hoover up all the dust* **2** get or collect sth in large quantities: *The US and Canada usually hoover up all the gold and silver medals.*

♦ v + adv + n ♦ v + n/pron + adv

hop /hɒp; *AmE* hɑːp/ (-**pp**-)

be/get ,hopped 'up (on sth) (*AmE, informal*) **1** to be behaving in a very excited or enthusi-

astic way: *I remember the first time they came to my office, hopped up on their new ideas for the Internet.* **2** to be behaving in an excited or unusual way because of the effects of alcohol or drugs: *Some psycho hopped up on heroin pulled a gun.*
◆ get + v + adv
▸ ‚hopped-'up *adj* [only before noun] (*AmE, informal*): *a hopped-up crowd at Dodger Stadium*
◇ *hopped-up street thugs*

horn /hɔːn; *AmE* hɔːrn/

‚horn 'in (*AmE*) **1** (on sb/sth) to rudely interrupt sb when they are speaking: *She kept trying to horn in on our conversations.* **2** (on sb/sth) to interfere in a situation that does not concern you: *Stop horning in on my private life!*
◆ v + adv

horse /hɔːs; *AmE* hɔːrs/

‚horse a'round (*BrE also* ‚horse a'bout) (*informal*) to play in a noisy and careless way that is likely to damage sth or hurt sb: *If you two don't stop horsing around you'll hurt yourselves.*
SYN mess around (*BrE*)
◆ v + adv

hose /həʊz; *AmE* hoʊz/

NOTE A hose is a long rubber or plastic tube.

‚hose sth 'down (*AmE also* ‚hose sth 'off) to wash or clean sth using water from a hose: *I hosed the car down to get rid of the mud.* ◇ *She stood in the driveway hosing off her newly washed car.*
◆ v + n/pron + adv ◆ v + adv + n

hot /hɒt; *AmE* hɑːt/ (-tt-)

‚hot 'up (*BrE*) (*also* ‚heat 'up *informal*) to become more lively or exciting: *Things are hotting up as the election approaches.* ◇ *As the pace hotted up, he dropped back into third place.*
◆ v + adv

hound /haʊnd/

‚hound sb 'out; ‚hound sb 'out of sth; 'hound sb from sth to force sb to leave a place or their job: *They were hounded out of the town.* ◇ *She was hounded from politics by her rivals.*
NOTE Usually used in the passive.
◆ v + n/pron + adv ◆ v + adv + n (*rare*)
◆ v + n/pron + adv + prep ◆ v + n/pron + prep

huddle /'hʌdl/

‚huddle to'gether to move, stand or sit close to one another for warmth or protection: *We huddled together for warmth.*
◆ v + adv

‚huddle 'up (against/to sb/sth) to press yourself into a small space for warmth or protection: *She huddled up against him to keep warm.*
◆ v + adv

hunger /'hʌŋgə(r)/

'hunger after/for sth (*literary*) to have a strong desire for sth and try to get it: *She hungers after wealth and prestige.*
◆ v + prep

hunker /'hʌŋkə(r)/

‚hunker 'down (*especially AmE*) **1** to sit on your heels with your knees bent up in front of you: *We hunkered down around the fire.* **SYN** squat **2** to refuse to change an opinion, a way of behaving, etc.: *The Democrats have hunkered down and won't be moved.* **3** to start to work at sth or study very hard: *It's time you hunkered down and started studying.*
◆ v + adv

hunt /hʌnt/

‚hunt sb 'down to search for sb until you find or catch them: *He vowed to hunt down the killer.*
◆ v + adv + n ◆ v + n/pron + adv

‚hunt sth 'down/'out to find sth after a long and difficult search: *I managed to hunt out those files you wanted.* ◇ *Can you hunt down his phone number for me?*
SYN dig sth out; root sb/sth out
◆ v + adv + n ◆ v + pron + adv ◆ v + n + adv (*rare*)

'hunt for sb to look for sb in order to catch them or harm them: *Detectives are hunting for thieves who broke into a warehouse yesterday.*
◆ v + prep

'hunt for sb/sth to look for sth that is difficult to find: *She is still hunting for a new job.*
⊃ note at SEARCH FOR SB/STH
◆ v + prep

‚hunt sb/sth 'up to search for sb/sth, especially sb/sth that is hidden or difficult to find: *We hunted up anyone who might have known him.*
◆ v + adv + n ◆ v + pron + adv ◆ v + n + adv (*rare*)

hurry /'hʌri; *AmE* 'hɜːri/ (hurries, hurrying, hurried)

‚hurry sb/sth a'long to do or say sth to make sb move or work faster; to do sth to make sth happen faster: *Hurry the kids along or we'll miss the train.* ◇ *Try to **hurry things along** a bit.*
◆ v + n/pron + adv

‚hurry 'on (to sth) to continue speaking, without allowing anyone to interrupt or speak: *She hurried on to the next topic before I could object.* ◇ *'Just leave that to me,' she hurried on.*
◆ v + adv ◆ v + adv + speech

‚hurry 'up used to tell sb to move or do sth more quickly: *Hurry up, we have to leave in five minutes!* ◇ *I wish the bus would hurry up and*

come. ◊ *I wish the waiter would hurry up with our soup.*
* v + adv

,**hurry sb/sth 'up** to encourage sb to move or work faster; to do sth to make sth happen faster: *Hurry your brother up or we'll be late.* ◊ ***Hurry it up**—we haven't got all day!* ◊ *Is there a way of **hurrying things up**?*
* v + n/pron + adv * v + adv + n (*rare*)

hush /hʌʃ/

,**hush sth 'up** to hide information about a situation, especially sth bad or shocking, because you do not want people to know about it: *The government tried to hush the affair up.* ◊ *The scandal was hushed up.*
NOTE Often used in the passive.
* v + n/pron + adv * v + adv + n

hype /haɪp/

,**hype sb/sth 'up** (*informal*) to advertise or talk about sb/sth in an exaggerated way in order to get a lot of public attention for them/it: *His latest movie is being hyped up by the media.*
NOTE Often used in the passive. * **Hype sb/sth** is also used on its own.
* v + n/pron + adv * v + adv + n

▶ ,**hyped 'up** *adj* (*informal*) **1** (of a person) very excited or worried about sth: *She gets very hyped up before a race.* **2** (of a film/movie, a book, an event, etc.) advertised or talked about in an exaggerated way to get public attention: *a hyped-up movie*

ice /aɪs/

,**ice sth 'down** (*AmE*) to put ice on, around, or in sth to keep it cold: *Have you iced down the champagne?*
* v + adv + n * v + n/pron + adv

,**ice 'over/'up**; be ,**iced 'over/'up** to become covered by a layer of ice: *The road had iced over during the night.* ◊ *The windscreen had iced up.* ◊ *The lake was iced up.*
SYN **freeze over, freeze up**
* v + adv * be + v + adv

identify /aɪ'dentɪfaɪ/ (**identifies, identifying, identified**)

i**'dentify with sb/sth** to feel that you can understand and share the feelings of sb else: *He's a character that readers feel they can identify with.*
* v + prep

i**'dentify sb with sb/sth** to consider sb to be sth or to be closely connected with sb/sth: *The*

last thing she wanted was to be identified with her parents. ◊ *Many of these artists were closely identified with Cubist painting.*
NOTE Often used in the passive.
* v + n/pron + prep

i**'dentify sth with sth** to consider sth to be the same as sth else: *Beauty is often identified with youth.*
* v + n/pron + prep

i**'dentify yourself with sb/sth; be i'dentified with sb/sth** to support sb/sth; to be closely connected with sb/sth: *He refused to identify himself with the new political party.*
→ see also IDENTIFY SB WITH SB/STH

idle /'aɪdl/

,**idle sth a'way** to spend time doing nothing very useful: *They idled away their time watching television.*
OBJ **day, time**
* v + adv + n * v + n/pron + adv

imbue /ɪm'bjuː/

im**'bue sb/sth with sth** to fill sb/sth with a strong feeling, quality, etc.: *He managed to imbue his employees with team spirit.* ◊ *The painting is imbued with energy and life.*
SYN **infuse B with A**
NOTE Often used in the passive.
* v + n/pron + prep

immerse /ɪ'mɜːs; AmE ɪ'mɜːrs/

im**'merse sb/yourself in sth** to become, or to make sb become, completely involved in sth: *He immersed himself in his studies.* ◊ *I was completely immersed in the story.*
NOTE Often used in the passive.
* v + n/pron + prep

impact /ɪm'pækt/

im**'pact on sb/sth** (*also* im**'pact upon sb/sth** *more formal*) to have an effect on sb/sth: *Government cuts will impact directly on education.* ◊ *This decision may impact on the unemployed.*
SYN **affect sb/sth**
* v + prep

impinge /ɪm'pɪndʒ/

im**'pinge on sb/sth** (*also* im**'pinge upon sb/sth** *more formal*) to have a strong effect on sb/sth, especially a bad one: *She didn't allow her personal problems to impinge on her work.*
SYN **affect sb/sth**
* v + prep

impose /ɪm'pəʊz; AmE ɪm'poʊz/

im**'pose on sb** to expect sb to do sth for you or spend time with you when they do not have much time, or when it may not be convenient for them: *Tim never says 'No', so people are always imposing on him.*

♦ v + prep

impress /ɪmˈpres/

imˈpress sth on sb (*also* **imˈpress sth upon sb** *more formal*) to emphasize to sb how important or serious sth is: *I wanted to impress on him that it was a very serious offence.* ◇ *She impressed on her staff the importance of keeping accurate records.*

NOTE The object of **impress** usually comes after **on sb.**

♦ v + n/pron + prep

imˈpress sth/itself on sth (*also* **imˈpress sth/ itself upon sth** *more formal*) if sb **impresses sth on** or sth **impresses itself on** your mind, memory, etc., it has a great effect on you so that you do not forget it: *Her beauty impressed itself on everyone who met her.* ◇ *His words impressed themselves on my memory.*

♦ v + n/pron + prep

imprint /ɪmˈprɪnt/

imˈprint A in/on B; imˈprint B with A 1 to have a great effect on sth so that it cannot be forgotten, changed, etc.: *The scene was imprinted on my mind.* ◇ *The picture is imprinted with his own style.* **2** to print or press a mark or design on sth: *T-shirts imprinted with the logos of sports teams*

NOTE Often used in the passive.

♦ v + n/pron + prep

improve /ɪmˈpruːv/

imˈprove on sth (*also* **imˈprove upon sth** *more formal*) to achieve or produce sth of a better standard or quality than sth else: *There are a few points in your work that you could improve on.* ◇ *The Kenyan girl improved on her previous best performance* (= in a race). ◇ *These results cannot be improved upon.*

♦ v + prep

impute /ɪmˈpjuːt/

imˈpute sth to sb/sth (*formal*) to say, often unfairly, that sb/sth is responsible for sth, or has a particular quality: *Why do you impute selfish motives to her?*

♦ v + n/pron + prep

incline /ɪnˈklaɪn/

inˈcline to/towards sth; inˈcline sb to/ towards sth (*formal*) to tend to think or behave in a particular way; to make sb do this: *I incline to the view that we should take no action.* ◇ *Her love of languages inclined her towards a career as a translator.*

♦ v + prep ♦ v + n/pron + prep

indulge /ɪnˈdʌldʒ/

inˈdulge in sth 1 to allow yourself to have or do sth that you like, often sth that is bad for you: *She indulged in the luxury of a long bath.* ◇ *He now has time to indulge in his favourite hobby: photography.* ◇ *It's a luxury that can only be indulged in from time to time.* ◇ *I'm going to indulge in a chocolate cake!* **2** to take part in an activity, especially sth bad or illegal: *We shouldn't indulge in speculation as to what really happened.*

♦ v + prep

inform /ɪnˈfɔːm; AmE ɪnˈfɔːrm/

inˈform on sb to give evidence about sb or accuse sb of sth, to the police or sb in authority: *One of the gang informed on the rest.*

♦ v + prep

infringe /ɪnˈfrɪndʒ/

inˈfringe on sth (*also* **inˈfringe upon sth** *more formal*) to limit sb's freedom, rights, etc.: *The media is accused of infringing on people's privacy.*

OBJ **liberty, rights**

♦ v + prep

infuse /ɪnˈfjuːz/

inˈfuse A into B; inˈfuse B with A (*formal*) to fill sb/sth with a particular quality: *His arrival infused new life and energy into the team.* ◇ *Her work is infused with anger.*

SYN **imbue sth with sth**

♦ v + n/pron + prep

ink /ɪŋk/

ˌink sth ˈin (*BrE*) to write or draw in ink over sth that has been written or drawn in pencil: *I did the answers in pencil first and then inked them in.* ◇ (*figurative*) *The company has inked in June 1st* (= made it definite) *for the launch.*

♦ v + n/pron + adv ♦ v + adv + n

inquire /ɪnˈkwaɪə(r)/

inˈquire into sth, etc. (*especially AmE*) → ENQUIRE

insinuate /ɪnˈsɪnjueɪt/

inˌsinuate yourself ˈinto sth (*formal, disapproving*) to get yourself into a position of advantage, especially by clever talk or by gaining the favour or respect of sb important: *She cleverly insinuated herself into his family.*

♦ v + pron + prep

insist /ɪnˈsɪst/

inˈsist on sth; inˈsist on doing sth (*also* **inˈsist upon sth, inˈsist upon doing sth** *more formal*) to demand sth and refuse to be persuaded to accept anything else: *They are insisting on a meeting tomorrow.* ◇ *I always insist on*

skimmed milk. ◇ He insisted on walking home with her. ◇ This format must be insisted on.
- v + prep

in'sist on doing sth (also **in'sist upon doing sth** more formal) to continue doing sth even though other people find it annoying: She will insist on shouting at the top of her voice.
- v + prep

insure /ɪnˈʃʊə(r), -ˈʃɔː(r); AmE -ˈʃʊr/

in'sure against sth 1 to buy an insurance policy which will pay you money if the event mentioned happens: Everyone needs to insure against fire. **2** to take action to prevent sth unpleasant happening: This is to insure against a repetition of previous disasters.
- v + prep

interest /ˈɪntrəst, -trest/

'interest sb in sth to persuade sb to buy, do or eat sth: Could I interest you in this model (= of car), Sir?
- v + n/pron + prep

interfere /ˌɪntəˈfɪə(r); AmE ˌɪntərˈfɪr/

inter'fere with sb (BrE) to touch a child in a sexual way
- v + prep

⚡ **inter'fere with sth 1** to get in the way of sth; to prevent sth from being done or making progress: Don't let anything interfere with your training. ◇ We don't want to interfere with your plans. **2** to touch, adjust or change sth without permission, and damage it: Who's been interfering with the clock? ◇ The evidence has been interfered with. **SYN** **tamper with sth 3** if sth **interferes with** radio or sound waves, etc., it

stops them being heard easily or clearly: The computer is interfering with the radio.
- v + prep

inure /ɪˈnjʊə(r); AmE ɪˈnjʊr/

i'nure sb/yourself to sth to make sb/sth get used to sth unpleasant so that they are no longer strongly affected by it: The prisoners quickly became inured to the harsh conditions.
- v + n/pron + prep

invalid /ˈɪnvəlɪd, ˈɪnvəliːd/

ˌinvalid sb 'out; **ˌinvalid sb 'out of sth** (BrE) to make sb leave a job, especially in the armed forces, because they are ill/sick or injured: He was invalided out of the army because of his injuries.
NOTE Usually used in the passive.
- v + n/pron + adv ◆ v + adv + n
- v + n/pron + adv + prep

inveigh /ɪnˈveɪ/

in'veigh against sb/sth (formal) to criticize sb/sth strongly: The article went on to inveigh against political correctness and all the perceived evils of the modern world.
- v + prep

invest /ɪnˈvest/

in'vest in sth (informal, often humorous) to buy sth or spend money on sth useful, especially sth expensive: It's time we invested in a new sofa—this one is falling to bits.
- v + prep

in'vest sb/sth with sth (formal) to make sb/sth seem to have a particular quality: Being the boss invests her with a certain glamour.
NOTE Often used in the passive.
- v + n/pron + prep

SYNONYMS

interfere with sth

disrupt sth ◆ interfere with sth ◆ interrupt sth ◆ upset sth

These verbs all mean to make it difficult for sth to continue in the normal or planned way.

disrupt sth to make it difficult for sth to continue in the normal way or in the way that was planned: Demonstrators succeeded in disrupting the meeting.

interfere with sth to prevent sth from succeeding or from continuing as normal or as planned: She doesn't allow her personal feelings to interfere with her work. ▶ interference n [U]: We will not allow any interference with the normal democratic processes.

interrupt sth to stop the continuous progress of sth for a short time: The game was

interrupted several times by rain. ◇ We interrupt this programme to bring you an important news bulletin. ▶ interruption n [C,U]: The service was maintained without interruption throughout the war.

upset sth to make a plan, event or situation go wrong: He arrived an hour late and upset all our arrangements. ◇ The disagreement further upset relations between the two countries.

PATTERNS AND COLLOCATIONS

- to disrupt/interfere with/interrupt **work**
- to disrupt/interrupt **services/a meeting**
- to disrupt/interfere with/upset **plans**
- to interfere with/upset **arrangements**
- to disrupt/interfere with **sb's life**

invite /ɪnˈvaɪt/

in‚vite sb aˈlong to ask sb if they would like to go with you to an event or activity: *Shall I invite Dave along (to the concert)?*
> **SYN** ask sb along (*less formal*)
> ◆ v + n/pron + adv ◆ v + adv + n (*rare*)

in‚vite sb aˈround (*AmE*) → INVITE SB OVER/ROUND

in‚vite sb ˈback (to sth) (*especially BrE*) to ask sb to go back to your home after you have been out somewhere together: *She invited me back to her place for coffee after the movie.*
> **SYN** ask sb back (to sth); have sb back (*less formal*)
> ◆ v + n/pron + adv ◆ v + adv + n (*less frequent*)

in‚vite sb ˈin/ˈup to politely ask sb to enter a room, your house, etc.: *Aren't you going to invite me in for a coffee?*
> **SYN** ask sb in/up (*less formal*)
> ◆ v + n/pron + adv ◆ v + adv + n (*less frequent*)

in‚vite sb ˈout to ask sb to go out with you, especially as a way of beginning a romantic relationship: *We've been invited out for dinner this evening.* ◇ *He eventually found the courage to invite Julia out.*
> **SYN** ask sb out (*less formal*)
> ◆ v + n/pron + adv ◆ v + adv + n (*less frequent*)

in‚vite sb ˈover/ˈround (*BrE*) (*AmE* ‚invite sb aˈround*) to ask sb to come and visit you in your home: *I've invited a few friends round to watch the game with us on TV.* ◇ *We ought to invite the new neighbours over for coffee.*
> **SYN** ask sb over/round (*less formal*)
> ◆ v + n/pron + adv

in‚vite sb ˈup → INVITE SB IN/UP

involve /ɪnˈvɒlv; *AmE* ɪnˈvɑːlv/

inˈvolve sb in sth to make sb experience or do sth, especially sth unpleasant: *The new exams have involved teachers in a lot of extra work.*
> ◆ v + n/pron + prep

iron /ˈaɪən; *AmE* ˈaɪərn/

‚iron sth ˈout **1** to remove the folds that you do not want from clothes, etc. by using an iron: *Iron out all the creases.* **OBJ** creases **2** to get rid of any problems or difficulties that are affecting sth: *We must iron out the problems before next week.* **OBJ** difficulties, problems **SYN** resolve sth (*more formal*)
> ◆ v + adv + n ◆ v + pron + adv ◆ v + n + adv (*rare*)

issue /ˈɪʃuː; *BrE also* ˈɪsjuː/

ˈissue from sth (*formal*) to come, go or flow out of sth or somewhere: *I could see smoke issuing from the window.*
> ◆ v + prep

itch /ɪtʃ/

ˈitch for sth (*usually used in the progressive tenses*) to want sth very much: *They were just itching for a fight.*
> **OBJ** a fight, a chance
> **NOTE** Itch to do sth can also be used with the same meaning: *He was itching to find out more.*
> ◆ v + prep

Jj

jab /dʒæb/ (**-bb-**)

ˈjab at sb/sth (with sth) to push a sharp or pointed object quickly or roughly into sb/sth or in the direction of sb/sth: *He kept jabbing at the paper cup with his pencil.* ◇ *She jabbed at the papers with her finger.*
> ◆ v + prep

jabber /ˈdʒæbə(r)/

‚jabber aˈway (*informal*) to speak or talk quickly in an excited way: *She jabbered away, trying to distract his attention.* ◇ *He was jabbering away in Russian.*
> ◆ v + adv

jack /dʒæk/

‚jack sb aˈround (*AmE, informal*) to treat sb in a way that is deliberately not helpful to them or wastes their time: *Let's go. We're being jacked around here.*
> **SYN** mess sb around (*informal*)
> ◆ v + n/pron + adv

‚jack ˈin; ‚jack ˈinto sth (*informal*) to connect to a computer system: *I'm jacking into the Internet now.*
> ◆ v + adv ◆ v + prep

‚jack sth ˈin (*BrE, informal*) to stop doing sth, especially your job: *She decided to jack in her job.* ◇ *After such a bad day I feel like jacking it all in.*
> **OBJ** job **SYN** chuck sth in/up; pack sth in
> **NOTE** Not used in the passive.
> ◆ v + adv + n ◆ v + n/pron + adv

‚jack ˈoff (*AmE, △, slang*) if a man jacks off, he gives himself sexual pleasure by rubbing his sexual organs
> ◆ v + adv

‚jack ˈup (*slang*) to take an illegal drug by putting it into your body using a needle
> ◆ v + adv

‚jack sth ˈup **1** to lift sth such as a vehicle off the ground using a special device (a **jack**) **OBJ** car **2** (*informal*) to increase the cost or the price of sth: *The wholesalers have jacked up their*

prices. [OBJ] cost, price [SYN] put sth up; increase sth (*more formal*) ⊃ note at PUT STH UP
♦ v + adv + n ♦ v + n/pron + adv

,be/get ,jacked 'up (*AmE, slang*) **1** to be ruined or spoiled: *My PC is all jacked up right now.* **2** to be nervous or excited: *The whole school is jacked up about the game tonight.* **3** to be drunk: *Don't drive if you're too jacked up.*
♦ get + v + adv

jam /dʒæm/ (-mm-)

,jam sth 'on if you **jam on the brakes** of a vehicle, you operate them suddenly and with force: *A child ran into the road and I jammed on the brakes.*
[OBJ] only **the brakes, the handbrake** [SYN] **slam sth on**
♦ v + adv + n ♦ v + n/pron + adv

,jam 'up; ,jam sth 'up (**with sth**) (*especially BrE*) if a machine, a road, etc. **jams up**, or sth **jams it up**, it becomes blocked, stops working, etc.: *Let's get moving before the traffic jams up.* ◊ *People were jamming up the aisles in their rush to get out of the theatre.* ◊ *That photocopier is always getting jammed up.*
♦ v + adv ♦ v + adv + n ♦ v + pron + adv
♦ v + n + adv (*less frequent*)

jazz /dʒæz/

,jazz sth 'up (**with sth**) (*informal*) **1** to make sth more lively or interesting: *Jazz up that plain dress with some jewellery.* [SYN] **liven sth up**; **spice sth up** (*more formal*) **2** to make a piece of music sound more modern, or more like jazz or popular music: *jazzed-up Bach*
♦ v + adv + n ♦ v + n/pron + adv

jerk /dʒɜːk; AmE dʒɜːrk/

,jerk sb a'round (*informal, especially AmE*) to treat sb badly and cause them problems, especially by not telling the truth: *He won't give us an answer—he keeps jerking us around.*
[SYN] **mess sb about/around** (*BrE*)
♦ v + n/pron + adv ♦ v + adv + n

,jerk 'off (⚠, *slang*) if a man **jerks off**, he gives himself sexual pleasure by rubbing his sexual organs
♦ v + adv

jet /dʒet/ (-tt-)

,jet 'off (**to ...**) to fly somewhere, especially somewhere far away: *They're jetting off to Florida tomorrow.*
♦ v + adv

jibe /dʒaɪb/

'jibe with sth (*AmE*) to agree with sth; to be the same as sth or match sth: *Her story didn't jibe with the witnesses' account.*
♦ v + prep

jockey /'dʒɒki; AmE 'dʒɑːki/

'jockey for sth to try very hard to gain an advantage, a favour, etc. for yourself and stop other people getting it: *Several employees are jockeying for the manager's position.*
[OBJ] **position, power**
♦ v + prep

jog /dʒɒg; AmE dʒɑːg/ (-gg-)

,jog a'long (*BrE, informal*) to continue in a steady way, with little or no excitement or progress: *For years the business just kept jogging along.*
♦ v + adv

join /dʒɔɪn/

⚲,join 'in (**with sb/sth**), ,join 'in sth to become involved in sth; to take part in an activity with other people: *Can I join in (the game)?* ◊ *We all joined in with the singing.*
[SYN] **participate** (**in sth**) (*more formal*)
♦ v + adv ♦ v + prep

,join 'up **1** (**with sb/sth**) to meet or combine with sb/sth to do sth together: *They joined up with the rest of the party later.* **2** to become a member of the armed forces: *We both joined up in 1939.*
[SYN] **enlist** (*more formal*)
♦ v + adv

⚲,join 'up; ,join sth 'up (*especially BrE*) to be connected to sth; to connect sth to sth: *The dots join up to form a solid line.* ◊ *Join up the dots to see the picture.*
[SYN] **connect** (**sth**) (*more formal*)
♦ v + adv ♦ v + adv + n ♦ v + n/pron + adv
▶ ,joined 'up *adj* [usually before noun] (*especially BrE*) things that are **joined up** are connected or linked together: *joined-up writing* ◊ (*figurative*) *joined-up thinking* ◊ (*figurative*) *the government's joined-up policy on health care*

'join with sb (**in sth/in doing sth**) (*formal*) to do or say sth with sb else or with a group of people: *I'm sure you'll join with me in congratulating Jo and Mark.* ◊ *Parents joined with teachers to protest against the closure of the school.*
♦ v + prep

joke /dʒəʊk; AmE dʒoʊk/

,joke a'round (*AmE*) to make jokes or do things to make people laugh: *I'm always joking around, trying to lighten the mood.*
♦ v + adv

jolly /'dʒɒli; AmE 'dʒɑːli/ (**jollies, jollying, jollied**)

,jolly sb a'long (*BrE, informal*) to keep encouraging sb in a friendly way: *She tried to jolly him along but he couldn't forget his problems.*
♦ v + n/pron + adv

,jolly sb/sth 'up (*BrE*) to make sb/sth brighter or more cheerful: *Do you think you can jolly Anthony up a bit?*

SYN cheer sb/sth up; liven sb/sth up
♦ v + n/pron + adv ♦ v + adv + n

jostle /'dʒɒsl; AmE 'dʒɑːsl/

'jostle for sth to compete strongly with other people for sth: *People in the crowd were jostling for the best positions.*
♦ v + prep

jot /dʒɒt; AmE dʒɑːt/ (-tt-)

,jot sth 'down to write sth down quickly: *I'll jot down their address before I forget it.*
SYN note sth down
♦ v + adv + n ♦ v + n/pron + adv

juice /dʒuːs/

,juice sth 'up (*informal, especially AmE*) **1** to make sth more lively, exciting or interesting: *Juice up your talk with pictures.* **SYN** jazz sth up **2** to make sth more powerful: *I can juice up the engine for you.* **SYN** soup sth up **3** to put petrol in a vehicle: *We need to juice up the car before we leave.* [OBJ] car **SYN** fill sth up
♦ v + adv + n ♦ v + n/pron + adv

jumble /'dʒʌmbl/

,jumble sth 'up/to'gether to mix things up in a confused way: *Make sure you don't jumble everything up.* ◇ *The details of the accident were all jumbled together in his mind.*
SYN mix sth up ➭ note at MIX STH UP
NOTE Often used in the passive: *All her papers had been jumbled up.*
♦ v + n/pron + adv ♦ v + adv + n

jump /dʒʌmp/

'jump at sb (*AmE*) → JUMP ON SB
'jump at sth to accept an opportunity, a chance, etc. with enthusiasm: *I jumped at the chance of a trip to Italy.*
[OBJ] chance, idea **SYN** leap at sth
♦ v + prep
,jump 'in 1 (**with sth**) to interrupt a conversation: *I jumped in while there was a brief pause in the conversation.* **2** to become involved in a situation suddenly or quickly: *She had jumped in to help while he was ill.*
♦ v + adv
'jump on sb (*AmE also* **'jump at sb**) (*informal*) to criticize sb sharply: *She jumped on me before I had a chance to explain.*
♦ v + prep
,jump 'out at sb to be very easy to see; to be noticeable: *The headline jumped out at me.* ◇ *The mistakes are so obvious they jump out at you.*
SYN leap out at sb
♦ v + adv + prep
,jump 'up to stand quickly and suddenly when you have been sitting: *He jumped up off the floor.*

SYN leap up
♦ v + adv
▶ **'jumped-up** *adj* [only before noun] (*BrE, informal, disapproving*) thinking that you are more important than you really are, particularly when you have risen in social status but do not deserve to: *I won't take orders from a jumped-up office girl!*

jut /dʒʌt/ (-tt-)

,jut 'out (**from sth**), **,jut 'out of sth** to stand out from sth; to stick out further than the surrounding surface: *The tops of the flooded houses jutted out of the water.*
SYN stick out, stick out of sth
♦ v + adv ♦ v + adv + prep

K k

keel /kiːl/

,keel 'over 1 (*informal*) to fall over: *I'm so tired, all I want to do is keel over and sleep for a week.*
SYN collapse **2** (of a boat) to turn on its side: *The boat keeled over in the strong winds.*
SYN capsize
♦ v + adv

keep /kiːp/ (**kept, kept** /kept/)

,keep 'after sb (**about sth/to do sth**) (*AmE*) to ask or tell sb repeatedly to do sth: *She keeps after me to fix the TV.*
→ see also KEEP ON 2
♦ v + prep
,keep a'head; **,keep a'head of sb/sth** to continue to be more advanced or successful than other people, groups, etc.: *We need to keep ahead of our competitors.* ◇ *If you want to keep ahead in this industry, you have to be ruthless.*
SYN stay ahead, stay ahead of sb/sth
♦ v + adv ♦ v + adv + prep
,keep 'at sth; **,keep sb 'at sth** to continue to work hard at sth, or to make sb work hard at sth, particularly sth which is difficult or takes a long time: *Keep at it, you've nearly finished!* ◇ *He kept them at the job until it was finished.*
♦ v + prep ♦ v + n/pron + prep
,keep a'way (**from sb/sth**) to not go near sb/sth: *Keep away from me!* ◇ *The police told us to keep well away from the area.*
SYN stay away (**from sb/sth**)
♦ v + adv
,keep sb/sth a'way (**from sb/sth**) to prevent sb/ sth from going near sb/sth: *Keep him away from the kitchen while we make his birthday cake.* ◇ *We turned off the lights to keep the mosquitoes away.* ◇ *Her parents are keeping her away from*

keep

school for a few days. ◇ (*figurative*) *A healthy diet can help to keep colds and flu away.*
♦ v + n/pron + adv ♦ v + adv + n (*less frequent*)

▶ '**keep-away** *n* [U] a game, usually played by children, in which two or more people throw a ball and try to stop another person from catching it

,keep '**back** (**from sb/sth**) to remain at a distance from sb/sth: *Keep back or I'll shoot!* ◇ *I kept well back from the road.*
SYN **stay back**
♦ v + adv

,keep sb '**back 1** (*BrE*) → KEEP SB IN 1: *I was kept back after school for being cheeky.* **2** (*AmE*) → KEEP SB DOWN 1

,keep sb/sth '**back** (**from sb/sth**) to make sb/sth remain at a distance from sb/sth; to prevent sb from moving forwards: *Keep the children back from the fire.* ◇ *The police were trying to keep back the crowds.*
♦ v + n/pron + adv ♦ v + adv + n

,keep sth '**back 1** (*especially BrE*) to keep a part of sth to use later: *Have you kept some money back to pay the bills?* ◇ *Keep a piece of cake back for Alex.* **2** (**from sb/sth**) to refuse to tell sb sth; to hold sth back: *I'm sure she's keeping something back* (*from us*). **OBJ** **something, anything, nothing** **SYN** **withhold sth** (*more formal*) **3** to try not to let other people see or know how you feel: *He could hardly keep back the tears.*
OBJ **tears** **SYN** **hold sth back**
♦ **1,2** v + n/pron + adv ♦ v + adv + n
♦ **3** v + adv + n ♦ v + n/pron + adv

,keep sb be'**hind** (*AmE*) → KEEP SB IN 1

,keep '**down** to hide yourself by not standing up straight: *Keep down! Don't let anybody see you.*
SYN **stay down**
♦ v + adv

,keep sb '**down 1** (*BrE*) (*AmE* ,keep sb '**back**) to make a student repeat a year at school, college, etc. because of poor marks/grades: *I was kept down because I failed the exam.* **2** to control a people, a nation, etc. so that they have no power or freedom: *The people have been kept down for years by a brutal regime.* **SYN** **repress sb**
♦ **1** v + n/pron + adv
♦ **2** v + n/pron + adv ♦ v + adv + n

⚥,keep sth '**down 1** to make sth remain at a low level; to avoid increasing sth: *We're trying to keep costs down.* ◇ *He exercises a lot to keep his weight down.* ◇ *Keep your voice down!* ◇ *Keep it down* (= Make less noise)! *I'm trying to concentrate.* **OBJ** **costs, prices, voice, noise** **SYN** **hold sth down 2** to manage to keep food or drink in your stomach and avoid bringing it back through your mouth: *He can't keep anything down.* **OBJ** **food** **SYN** **hold sth down 3** to not raise a part of your body: *Keep your head down!* ◇ *She kept her eyes down while he was talking.* **OBJ** **eyes, head, face**

NOTE Not used in the passive in meanings 2 and 3.
♦ **1,2** v + n/pron + adv ♦ v + adv + n
♦ **3** v + n/pron + adv

IDM **keep/get your** '**head down** to avoid attracting attention

'keep **from doing sth**; '**keep yourself from doing sth** to prevent yourself from doing sth: *She bit her lip to keep from laughing.*
♦ v + prep ♦ v + pron + prep

'keep **sb from sth**; '**keep sb from doing sth** to prevent sb from doing sth: *Don't let me keep you from your work.* ◇ *I've been trying to keep him from finding out the truth.* ◇ *Her pride kept her from crying in front of them.*
♦ v + n/pron + prep

'keep **sth from sb** to avoid telling sb sth: *I think he's keeping secrets from me.* ◇ *Are you keeping something from us?*
OBJ **secrets, something**
♦ v + n/pron + prep

,keep '**in** (*BrE*) to stay near the edge of the road or path while you are driving, walking, etc.: *If you keep in, the van can overtake.*
♦ v + adv

,keep sb '**in** (*especially BrE*) **1** (*BrE also* ,keep sb '**back**) (*AmE also* ,keep sb be'**hind**) to make a child stay after normal school hours as a punishment: *The teacher kept them all in after school.* **2** to not allow a child to go outdoors: *I'm keeping the children in because it's raining outside.* **3** to keep sb in hospital: *She's much better, but they're keeping her in overnight.*
♦ v + n/pron + adv

,keep sth '**in 1** to stop yourself expressing an emotion: *He could hardly keep in his anger.* **SYN** **restrain sth 2** to not allow sth to escape, be lost or taken out: *Close the door to keep in the warmth.* ◇ *She wanted to cut the sex scene* (= in a play or film/movie), *but we kept it in.* **OBJ** **warmth, heat 3** to not allow an animal to go outdoors
♦ v + n/pron + adv ♦ v + adv + n

IDM **keep your** '**hand in** to do an activity occasionally so that you do not lose your skill at it: *I play squash from time to time, just to keep my hand in.*

'keep **sb/yourself in sth** (*informal*) to give or allow sb/yourself a regular supply of sth: *This part-time job keeps me in cigarettes.*
♦ v + n/pron + prep

,keep '**in with sb** (*BrE*) to continue to be friendly with sb, especially in order to gain some advantage for yourself: *He keeps in with anyone who might be useful to him.*
♦ v + adv + prep

,keep '**off** (*especially BrE*) if rain, snow, etc. **keeps off**, it does not fall, even though it looks as if it might: *The party will go ahead provided the rain keeps off.*

SYN hold off
- v + adv

,**keep 'off**; ,**keep 'off sth** to not go onto a particular area: *Keep off (the grass)!* ◇ *We kept off the main roads to avoid the traffic.*
OBJ grass
- v + adv ◆ v + prep

,**keep 'off sth**; ,**keep sb 'off sth 1** to not eat, drink or smoke sth; to not let sb eat, drink or smoke sth: *The doctor's told me to keep off red meat.* **2** to not mention a particular topic; to stop sb talking about a particular topic: *It's best to keep off the subject of politics with my father.* ◇ *Keep her off the subject of teenage girls!*
OBJ subject, topic
SYN stay off sth
- v + prep ◆ v + n/pron + prep

,**keep sb/sth 'off**; ,**keep sb/sth 'off sb/sth** to stop sb/sth from coming near or going into (a place); to stop sb/sth from touching or harming sb/sth: *He covered the sandwiches to keep the flies off.* ◇ *Keep your animals off my land!* ◇ *Working helps* **keep my mind off** *my problems.* ◇ *I kept the children off (school) until they felt better.*
OBJ flies, hands, mind, eyes
- v + n/pron + adv ◆ v + n/pron + prep

,**keep 'on 1** (*also* ,**keep 'on doing sth**) to continue without stopping: *He'll get into trouble if he keeps on like this!* ◇ *Keep on trying—don't give up!* ◇ *The rain kept on all night.* **SYN** carry on (with sth), carry on doing sth **2** (at sb) (about sb/sth) (*BrE*) to continue to talk about sb/sth in a boring or annoying way: *Don't keep on (about it)!* ◇ *My mum keeps on at me to cut my hair.* **SYN** go on (about sb/sth) → see also KEEP AFTER SB (ABOUT STH/TO DO STH)
- v + adv **1** also v + adv + -ing

,**keep 'on**; ,**keep 'on sth** to continue to follow a particular route: *Keep on until you come to the road.* ◇ *Keep on the path until you see a gate.*
- v + adv ◆ v + prep

,**keep sb 'on** to continue to employ sb, even though circumstances have changed: *We can only afford to keep a few workers on.*
- v + n/pron + adv ◆ v + adv + n (*less frequent*)

,**keep sth 'on 1** to continue to wear sth; to not take sth off: *It was so cold that we kept our socks on in bed.* ◇ *Keep the lid on while the tea is brewing.* **OPP** take sth off **2** to not switch sth off: *Do you keep the heating on all day?* **SYN** leave sth on **OPP** switch sth off **3** to stop sth coming or falling off: *How do you keep that bandage on?* **4** to continue to rent or be the owner of a house, flat/apartment, etc.: *Can you afford to keep this place on while you're abroad?*
- v + n/pron + adv ◆ v + adv + n (*less frequent*)
IDM keep your 'hair on (*BrE, informal*) used to tell sb not to become angry

'**keep sth on sb/sth** if you **keep** your mind, eyes, etc. **on** sb/sth, you fix your attention on them/it: *I can't keep my mind on my work.* ◇ *She kept one eye on the traffic and the other on the map.*
OBJ mind, attention, eye
- v + n/pron + prep
IDM keep an eye on sb/sth (*informal*) to watch or check sb/sth to make sure that they are safe, etc.; to look after sb/sth: *Will you keep an eye on the baby for five minutes?*

,**keep 'out**; ,**keep 'out of sth** to not enter a place; to remain outside: *There was a sign saying 'Keep out!'.* ◇ *Please keep out of the office while I'm working.*
- v + adv ◆ v + adv + prep

,**keep 'out of sth**; ,**keep sb 'out of sth 1** to avoid sth; to prevent sb/yourself from being affected by sth: *The doctor has advised me to keep out of the sun.* ◇ *They always kept their daughter out of the spotlight* (= away from the public). ◇ *I try to keep out of his way.* **OBJ** the sun, sight, sb's/the way **2** to avoid becoming involved in sth; to stop sb from becoming involved in sth: *Keep out of this! It's got nothing to do with you!* ◇ *Try to keep the kids out of mischief while I'm out.* **SYN** stay out of sth
- v + adv + prep ◆ v + n/pron + adv + prep

,**keep sth 'out** to not put sth away that you have taken out of a cupboard, etc.; to keep sth ready to use: *Keep the butter out for your dad's breakfast.*
OPP put sth away
- v + n/pron + adv ◆ v + adv + n (*less frequent*)

,**keep sb/sth 'out**; ,**keep sb/sth 'out of sth** to prevent sb/sth from entering a place: *We hung a curtain at the door to keep out the cold.* ◇ (*figurative*) *She tried to keep the anger out of her voice.*
- v + n/pron + adv ◆ v + adv + n
- v + n/pron + adv + prep

'**keep to sth 1** to not leave a path, a road, etc.: *Keep to the footpath.* ◇ *Keep to the left* (= on a road, etc.). **OBJ** path **2** to talk or write only about a particular subject: *Keep to the point!* ◇ *Will you please keep to the subject under discussion?* **OBJ** subject, point **3** to follow a plan, an agreement, a rule, etc. exactly as you are supposed to do: *She hasn't kept to the agreement, so neither will I.* ◇ *We must keep to the schedule.* ◇ *He never keeps to the speed limit.* ◇ *Was the agenda kept to at the meeting?* **OBJ** rules, agreement, schedule **SYN** adhere to sth (*formal*)
SYN stick to sth
- v + prep

,**keep to your'self**; ,**keep your'self to your'self** to avoid meeting people socially or becoming involved in other people's affairs: *He keeps (himself) to himself and nobody knows very much about him.*
- v + prep + pron ◆ v + pron + prep + pron

'**keep to sth**; '**keep sth to sth** to use only one thing or a limited number or amount of sth; to

make sure that the number or amount of sth does not become any bigger than a particular size: *We've decided to keep to pale colours for the bedroom.* ◇ *I'm trying to keep the number of guests to a minimum.*
◆ v + prep ◆ v + n/pron + prep

,keep sth to your'self to not tell anyone about sth or what you think about sth: *I know who's won, but I'm keeping it to myself.* ◇ *Keep your opinions to yourself in future!* ◇ (*figurative*) *Keep your hands to yourself!* (= do not touch me)
[OBJ] **opinions**
◆ v + n/pron + prep + pron

,keep to'gether; ,keep sb/sth to'gether to remain together in a group; to make sb/sth do this: *Keep together, kids, when we cross the road.* ◇ *Use a paper clip to keep your papers together.*
◆ v + adv ◆ v + n/pron + adv
◆ v + adv + n (*less frequent*)

,keep sb 'under (*BrE*) to control sb: *The local people are kept under by the army.*
[SYN] **oppress sb** (*more formal*)
◆ v + n/pron + adv

,keep 'up **1** if rain, snow, etc. **keeps up**, it continues without stopping: *The rain kept up all afternoon.* **2** (**with sb/sth**) to move at the same rate or speed as sb/sth: *I had to run to keep up with him.* [OPP] **fall behind, fall behind sb/sth 3** to work at the necessary speed so that you progress at the same speed as other people: *She's having trouble keeping up with the rest of the class.* ◇ *Do keep up! I can't keep repeating everything.* **4** (**with sth**) to rise at the same rate as sth else: *Salaries are not keeping up with inflation.* **5** (**with sth**) to do all the work necessary in order to finish on time or deal successfully with a situation that changes rapidly: *We're finding it hard to keep up with demand.* ◇ *Things were happening too fast to keep up with.*
◆ v + adv

,keep sb 'up to prevent sb from going to bed or from sleeping: *I hope we're not keeping you up.* ◇ *The baby kept us up half the night.*
◆ v + n/pron + adv

,keep sth 'up **1** to continue sth at the same, usually high, level; to continue to practise or observe sth: *Keep up the good work!* ◇ *You're doing a great job! Keep it up!* ◇ *We kept up a fast pace all the way.* ◇ *We're having difficulty keeping up our mortgage payments.* ◇ *The press is keeping up the pressure on the government.* ◇ *Do you still keep up your Portuguese?* [OBJ] **it, pace, pressure, tradition 2** to prevent sth from falling down: *You'll have to wear a belt to keep your trousers up.* [OBJ] **trousers/pants** [SYN] **hold sth up 3** to make sth stay at a high level: *High transport costs are keeping food prices up.* ◇ *They sang songs to keep their spirits up.* [OBJ] **price, spirits, strength, morale 4** to keep a house, garden/yard, etc. in good condition by spending money on it or

working hard on it: *The house is becoming too expensive for them to keep up.* [SYN] **maintain sth**
◆ v + n/pron + adv ◆ v + adv + n

[IDM] **keep up ap'pearances** to hide the true situation and pretend that things are better than they are: *There's no point keeping up appearances when everyone knows we've lost.* **keep your 'chin up!** (*informal*) used to tell sb to remain cheerful in difficult circumstances

▶ 'upkeep *n* [U] **1** the cost or process of keeping a building, piece of land, etc. in good condition: *Who is responsible for the day-to-day upkeep of the house?* **2** the cost or process of giving a child or an animal the things that they need

,keep 'up with sb to continue to be in contact with sb by writing, phoning or seeing them regularly: *How many of your old school friends do you manage to keep up with?*
◆ v + adv + prep

,keep 'up with sth **1** to learn about the news, events, etc. that are happening: *I try to keep up with current affairs.* ◇ *Susie likes to keep up with the latest fashions.* **2** to continue to pay or do sth regularly: *He couldn't keep up with the repayments on the loan.* ◇ *Are you keeping up with your homework?*
◆ v + adv + prep

key /kiː/

,key sth 'in; ,key sth 'into sth to put information into a computer, using a keyboard: *Key in your personal number.* ◇ *All the information has been keyed into the computer.*
[OBJ] **data, information** [SYN] **enter sth (into sth)**
◆ v + adv + n ◆ v + n/pron + adv ◆ v + n/pron + prep

,key 'in on sth → KEY ON STH

,key 'into sth **1** to use a computer or information stored on a computer: *A hacker keyed into a vital database at the newspaper's office.* [SYN] **access sth** (*more formal*) **2** if sth **keys into** sth else, it goes well with it and agrees with it, producing a good result: *remedies that key into the body's basic metabolism*
◆ v + prep

'key on sth (*also* **key 'in on sth**) (*AmE*) to focus on sth or begin to pay attention to it: *Keying on the public's interest in the first airplane flight, the Pilots Association launched a new ad campaign today.* ◇ *Police dogs keyed in on a briefcase left in the baggage area.*
◆ v + prep ◆ v + adv + prep

'key sth to sth/sb to make sth suitable for sth/ sb; to link sth with sth else: *The farm was keyed to the needs of the local people.* ◇ *The timing of the concerts was keyed to the World Cup soccer games.*
[NOTE] Usually used in the passive.
◆ v + n/pron + prep

kick /kɪk/

'**kick against sth** to protest about sth or resist sth: *It's no use kicking against the system.*
- ◆ v + prep

,**kick a'round**; ,**kick a'round sth** (*BrE also* ,**kick a'bout**, ,**kick a'bout sth**) (*informal*) **1** (*usually used in the progressive tenses*) to be present or lying somewhere not being used: *His letter is kicking about somewhere.* ◇ *The idea has been kicking around for years.* **2** (of a person) to be somewhere, or to go from one place to another, with no particular purpose: *I decided to kick around the States for a couple of months.*
- **SYN** knock around, knock around sth
- ◆ v + adv ◆ v + prep

,**kick sb a'round** (*BrE also* ,**kick sb a'bout**) (*informal*) to treat sb in an unkind or unfair way: *Don't let the boss kick you around.*
- **SYN** push sb around
- ◆ v + n/pron + adv

,**kick sth a'round** (*BrE also* ,**kick sth a'bout**) **1** to play with a ball by kicking it with your foot: *They were kicking a ball around in the street.*
- **OBJ** ball **2** (*informal*) to discuss plans, ideas, etc. in an informal way: *They're kicking around the idea of a merger.* **OBJ** idea **SYN** discuss sth (*more formal*); knock sth around
- ◆ v + n/pron + adv ◆ v + adv + n

,**kick 'back** (*AmE, informal*) to relax: *I spent the evening kicking back in the hotel's piano bar.*
- ◆ v + adv

,**kick sth 'back** (**to sb**) (*AmE, informal*) to pay money illegally in order to get some advantage for yourself: *Contractors winning construction jobs had to kick back two per cent of the contract price to the mafia.*
- ◆ v + adv + n ◆ v + n/pron + adv
- ▶ '**kickback** *n* (*informal, especially AmE*) money that is paid to sb in order to get an advantage for yourself

,**kick sth 'down** to break sth and make it fall by kicking it: *If you don't open up, we'll kick the door down.*
- **OBJ** door
- ◆ v + n/pron + adv ◆ v + adv + n

,**kick 'in** (*informal*) to start to work or have an effect: *After a couple of minutes the emergency electricity supply kicked in.* ◇ *You'll feel better when the antibiotics kick in.*
- ◆ v + adv

,**kick sth 'in** to break sth and make it fall by kicking it: *They had kicked the front door in.*
- **OBJ** door
- ◆ v + n/pron + adv ◆ v + adv + n (*less frequent*)
- **IDM** ,**kick sb's 'head/'teeth in** (*informal*) to kick sb very violently

,**kick 'off 1** (in football/soccer) when a game or team **kicks off**, the game starts: *The game kicks off at 7.30.* **2** (**with sth**) (*informal*) to start: *The tour kicks off with a concert in Nottingham.* ➲ note at START OFF **3** (*BrE, informal*) to start

fighting: *Jamie is always kicking off and causing trouble.*
- ◆ v + adv
- ▶ '**kick-off** *n* **1** [C, U] (in football/soccer) the start of a game: *It's an afternoon kick-off.* **2** [C] (*BrE*) a fight: *There were kick-offs in the town centre every Friday night.*

,**kick sb 'off**; ,**kick sb 'off sth 1** (*informal, computing*) to break the connection between sb's computer and the Internet, so that they can no longer use the Internet: *I keep getting kicked off the Internet.* **OBJ** the Internet, server, website **SYN** disconnect sb (**from sth**) **2** (*especially AmE*) to force sb to stop being a member of a team or organization, usually because they have done sth wrong: *He was kicked off his college team for using steroids.* **OBJ** team
- **NOTE** Usually used in the passive.
- ◆ v + n/pron + adv ◆ v + n/pron + prep

,**kick sth 'off 1** to remove sth by kicking: *She kicked off her shoes and lay down on the bed.* **2** (**with sth**) to begin a meeting, an event, etc.: *Who's going to kick off the discussion?*
- ◆ v + adv + n ◆ v + pron + adv ◆ v + n + adv (*rare*)

,**kick 'on** (*BrE, sport*) to continue playing: *We need to kick on and take advantage of our lead.* ◇ (*figurative*) *Kick on, I thought. Don't get left behind.*
- ◆ v + adv

,**kick 'out** (**at sb/sth**) **1** to kick your foot into the air to try to hit sb, especially because you are angry or upset: *She kicked out wildly at him as he tried to grab her.* **2** to react violently to sb/sth that makes you angry or upset: *She kicked out against traditional ideas about painting portraits.*
- ◆ v + adv

,**kick sb 'out**; ,**kick sb 'out of sth** (*informal*) to make sb leave; to send sb away by force: *His parents kicked him out* (= made him leave home) *when he was seventeen.* ◇ *They were kicked out of the nightclub for fighting.*
- **SYN** boot sb out, etc. (*informal*); throw sb out, etc.
- **NOTE** Often used in the passive.
- ◆ v + n/pron + adv ◆ v + adv + n
- ◆ v + n/pron + adv ◆ v + n/pron + prep

,**kick sth 'over** to make sth fall on its side by kicking it: *She almost kicked the bucket over.*
- **SYN** knock sth over
- ◆ v + n/pron + adv ◆ v + adv + n

,**kick 'up** if a wind, a storm, etc. **kicks up**, it becomes stronger
- **SUBJ** only wind, storm
- ◆ v + adv

,**kick sth 'up** to make dust, sand, etc. rise into the air: *The horse kicked up a cloud of dust.*
- **OBJ** dirt, dust, sand
- ◆ v + adv + n ◆ v + n/pron + adv ◆ v + n + adv (*rare*)
- **IDM** ,**kick up a 'fuss/'stink etc.** (**about sth**) to complain loudly about sth

kid /kɪd/ (-dd-)

,kid a'round (*informal, especially AmE*) to behave in a silly way; to joke: *A lot of what I said was just kidding around, but people took me seriously.*
SYN mess around
♦ v + adv

kill /kɪl/

,kill sb/sth 'off **1** to make a lot of plants, animals, etc. die: *Antibiotics should kill off the bacteria.* ◇ *The plant life was killed off by air pollution.* **2** to get rid of sb/sth; to stop sth: *The hero is killed off in the last chapter.* ◇ *It is difficult to kill off old traditions or myths.*
NOTE Often used in the passive.
♦ v + adv + n ♦ v + pron + adv ♦ v + n + adv (*rare*)

kip /kɪp/ (-pp-)

,kip 'down (*BrE, informal*) to sleep in a place that is not your own bed: *Is there anywhere to kip down for the night?*
♦ v + adv

kiss /kɪs/

,kiss sth a'way to stop sb feeling sad or angry by kissing them: *Let mummy kiss away your tears.*
OBJ tears, worries
♦ v + adv + n ♦ v + pron + adv ♦ v + n + adv (*rare*)

,kiss 'off (*AmE, informal*) used to tell sb rudely to leave or stop bothering you: *If he asks me for any more money I'll tell him to kiss off.*
♦ v + adv
▸ 'kiss-off *n* [sing.] (*informal*): *He had just bought her a ring, and she gave him the kiss-off* (= told him she did not want to have a relationship).

,kiss sb/sth 'off (**as sth**) to consider that sb/sth is a failure or not important: *The record companies kissed us off as a second-rate punk band.*
♦ v + adv + n ♦ v + pron + adv ♦ v + n + adv

,kiss 'up to sb (*AmE, informal*) if you **kiss up to** sb in authority, you try to please them in order to gain an advantage for yourself
SYN suck up to sb
♦ v + adv + prep

kit /kɪt/ (-tt-)

,kit sb/sth 'out (*also* ,kit sb/sth 'up *less frequent*) (**in/with sth**) (*BrE*) to supply sb/sth with the clothes or equipment that they need for a particular purpose: *The kids are all kitted out for the new school year.* ◇ *The studio is kitted out with modern sound equipment.*
NOTE Usually used in the passive.
♦ v + n/pron + adv ♦ v + adv + n

kneel /niːl/ (**knelt, knelt** /nelt/, *AmE also* **kneeled, kneeled**)

,kneel 'down to get into a position where one or both knees are resting on the ground: *He knelt down beside the chair.* ◇ *She was kneeling down, looking for something on the floor.*
♦ v + adv

knit /nɪt/ (-tt-)

,knit to'gether (***Knit*** *is usually used for the past tense and past participle*) when broken bones **knit together**, they grow together again: *The ribs are broken, but they'll knit together.*
NOTE **Knit** is also used on its own.
♦ v + adv

knock /nɒk; *AmE* nɑːk/

,knock a'round; ,knock a'round sth (*BrE also* ,knock a'bout, ,knock a'bout sth) (*informal*) **1** (*especially BrE*) (*often used in the progressive tenses*) used to say that sb/sth is in a particular place, but is not doing anything or being used: *These chocolates have been knocking around since New Year.* ◇ *His book was knocking around the lounge for ages.* ◇ *There were a few kids knocking about in the street outside.* **2** to travel and live in various places: *He spent a few years knocking about Europe.* ◇ *Jeff will know what to do—he's knocked about a bit* (= has had a lot of experience of different situations).
SYN kick around, kick around sth
♦ v + adv ♦ v + prep

,knock sb a'round (*BrE also* ,knock sb a'bout) (*informal*) to hit sb again and again: *Her husband knocks her about.*
♦ v + n/pron + adv

,knock sth a'round (*BrE also* ,knock sth a'bout) **1** to treat sth roughly; to hammer or hit sth: *The builders have started knocking our kitchen about.* **2** (*BrE*) to kick sth around: *We spent a few hours knocking a ball about.* **OBJ** a ball **SYN** kick sth around **3** (*informal*) to discuss an idea or a suggestion with several people: *We knocked a few ideas about at the meeting.* **OBJ** idea
SYN kick sth around
♦ v + n/pron + adv ♦ v + adv + n
▸ 'knockabout *n* (*BrE*) a period of time spent kicking a ball around with other people: *We had a knockabout in the park.*
▸ 'knockabout *adj* [usually before noun] (*BrE*) **knockabout** entertainment involves people acting in a deliberately silly way, for example falling over or hitting other people, in order to make the audience laugh

,knock a'round/a'bout with sb; ,knock a'round/a'bout together (*BrE, informal*) to spend a lot of time with sb: *She knocks around with Sahan.* ◇ *She and Sahan knock around together.* ◇ *He knocks about with some strange people!*
SYN hang around with sb, etc.
♦ v + adv + prep ♦ v + adv + adv

,knock sb 'back **1** to prevent sb from achieving sth or making progress, especially by rejecting them or sth that they suggest or ask: *He had*

been knocked back twice by the selection committee. **2** to surprise or shock sb: *The news really knocked me back.*
♦ v + n/pron + adv ♦ v + adv + n (*rare*)

▶ ˈknock-back n (*BrE*) an occasion when sb rejects you or sth that you suggest or ask; a refusal: *I don't think I could stand another knock-back.*

ˌknock sb ˈback sth (*BrE*, *informal*) to cost sb a particular amount of money: *Those books knocked me back £50.* ◇ *That car must have knocked you back a bit!*
SYN set sb back sth
NOTE Not used in the passive.
♦ v + n/pron + adv + n

ˌknock sth ˈback (*informal*) to drink sth quickly: *He knocked back two pints of beer.*
OBJ beer, coffee, etc. **SYN** swig sth
♦ v + adv + n ♦ v + n/pron + adv

ˌknock sb ˈdown **1** if a car or another vehicle knocks sb down, it hits them, often killing or injuring them: *She was knocked down by a bus.*
SYN run sb over **NOTE** Often used in the passive. **2** to hit or push sb so that they fall to the ground or the floor: *The wind was strong enough to knock you down.* ◇ *He knocked down his opponent in the first round* (= in boxing).
→ see also KNOCK SB OVER
♦ v + n/pron + adv ♦ v + adv + n

IDM you could have knocked me down with a ˈfeather used to express great surprise

▶ ˈknock-down n (in boxing, etc.) an occasion when one person taking part hits the other so hard that they fall to the ground

▶ ˈknock-down adj [only before noun] **1** using a lot of force: *a knock-down punch* **2** very convincing: *a knock-down argument*

▶ ˌknock-down-ˈdrag-out adj [only before noun] (*AmE*, *informal*) (of a fight or an argument) very aggressive and unpleasant

ˌknock sb/sth ˈdown to persuade sb to accept a lower price for sth; to make the price of sth lower: *He knocked Simon down to $5.* ◇ *We knocked the price down to £10.* ◇ *How did you manage to knock them down from $5 000 to $4 000?* ◇ *He managed to knock the price down from £350 to £320.*
SYN beat sb/sth down
NOTE Knock sb down (by) sth and knock sth down (by) sth can also be used: *We should be able to knock them down (by) a few pounds.* ◇ *He knocked the price down (by) five dollars.*
♦ v + n/pron + adv ♦ v + adv + n (*less frequent*)

▶ ˌknock-down n sth that has been reduced in price: *I can never resist a knock-down.*

ˌknock sth ˈdown **1** to destroy sth and make it fall down: *If you don't open up, I'm going to knock the door down.* ◇ *These old houses are going to be knocked down.* **OBJ** house, door
SYN demolish sth (*more formal*) **2** (**to sb**) to sell sth to the person who offers most money at a public sale (an **auction**): *The painting was knocked down to me for £5 000.* **3** (*AmE*) to take

knock sth down

demolish sth ♦ knock sth down ♦ pull sth down ♦ tear sth down

These are all verbs that can be used to talk about destroying buildings or trees.

demolish sth to destroy a building or part of a building by breaking its walls, usually deliberately: *The old slums are being demolished to make way for a new housing project.*
▶ **demolition** n [U,C]: *The whole row of houses is scheduled for demolition.*

knock sth down to deliberately destroy a building, wall or fence: *These old houses are going to be knocked down.* ◇ *You could knock this wall down and make one large room.*

pull sth down to deliberately destroy a building or part of a building by breaking its walls: *This tower is being pulled down in a few weeks' time.*

tear sth down to deliberately destroy a building, wall or barrier: *They're tearing down these old houses to build a new office*

block. ◇ (*figurative*): *We need to tear down the barriers that divide the two communities.*

WHICH WORD?

Buildings are usually **demolished** deliberately, because they are not safe or are no longer needed, or the land is needed for sth else. In informal usage, especially in American English, buildings, vehicles and other objects can be **demolished** by accident: *The hurricane demolished trailers and blew roofs off houses.* **Tear sth down** can suggest that unnecessary violence was used, or that the speaker has negative feelings about what was done. **Demolish**, **knock sth down** and **pull sth down** are neutral in meaning.

PATTERNS AND COLLOCATIONS

■ to demolish/tear down/knock down/pull down a **building/house/factory/wall**
■ to be **due to be** demolished

sth apart, especially furniture, so that it can be sent or carried somewhere more easily

◆ v + n/pron + adv ◆ v + adv + n

▶ ˈknock-down price *n* a much lower price than usual: *I got these books at a knock-down price.*

ˌknock sth ˈin; ˌknock sth ˈin/ˈinto sth **1** to make sth enter sth by hitting it, for example with a hammer: *She knocked some nails into the wall.* ⟨OBJ⟩ **nail 2** to make sth go into sth by hitting or kicking it: *Barnes knocked in two goals.* ◇ *She knocked the ball into the net.* ⟨OBJ⟩ **goal, ball**

◆ v + n/pron + adv ◆ v + adv + n ◆ v + n/pron + prep

ˌknock sth ˈin sth to make sth such as a hole in sth by hitting: *They knocked a hole in the wall for the window.*

⟨OBJ⟩ **hole**

◆ v + n/pron + prep

ˌknock ˈoff; ˌknock ˈoff sth (*informal*) to stop doing sth, especially work: *What time do you knock off (work) today?*

⟨OBJ⟩ **work** ⟳ note at GIVE UP, GIVE STH UP

◆ v + adv ◆ v + prep

ˌknock it ˈoff (*informal*) used to tell sb to stop doing sth annoying: *Knock it off! I'm trying to concentrate!*

◆ v + it + adv

ˌknock sb ˈoff (*slang*) **1** to murder sb: *He was knocked off by another gang.* ⟨SYN⟩ **bump sb off** (*informal*) **2** (*BrE*, ⚠, *slang*) to have sex with sb **3** (*AmE, informal*) to defeat sb in a competition or election: *She easily knocked off her Republican opponent in the last election.*

◆ v + n/pron + adv ◆ v + adv + n

ˌknock sb ˈoff; ˌknock sb ˈoff sth to make sb fall off sth by hitting them: *I was knocked off my bike this morning* (= by a car).

◆ v + n/pron + adv ◆ v + n/pron + prep

ˌknock sth ˈoff **1** (*also* ˌknock sth ˈout) (*informal*) to complete sth quickly and without much effort: *They expect me to knock off* (= write) *a thousand words a day.* **2** (*BrE, slang*) to steal sth: *He's knocking off TVs and video recorders.* ◇ *These bikes have been knocked off.* **3** (*AmE, informal*) to make a copy of a popular product to sell at a cheaper price, often illegally

◆ v + adv + n ◆ v + n/pron + adv

▶ ˈknock-off *n* (*AmE, informal*) a copy, often illegal, of a popular product sold at a cheaper price

ˌknock sth ˈoff; ˌknock sth ˈoff sth **1** to reduce the price, value, etc. of sth: *We've knocked £20 off the price.* ◇ *The short cut knocks about half an hour off the journey.* ◇ *That hairstyle knocks years off your age.* **2** to remove sth, and usually make it fall to the ground, by hitting it: *Who knocked that glass off the table?* ◇ *She knocked my glasses off.*

◆ v + n/pron + adv ◆ v + adv + n ◆ v + n/pron + prep

⟨IDM⟩ **I'll knock your ˈblock/ˈhead off** (*BrE, informal*) used to show that you are very angry with sb, by threatening to hit them **knock/blow sb's ˈsocks off** to impress or surprise sb very much

ˌknock sb ˈout **1** (*also* ˌknock yourself ˈout) to make sb/yourself fall asleep or become unconscious: *The bump on the head knocked me out cold.* ◇ *He ran straight into a lamp post, knocking himself out.* ◇ *That sleeping pill knocked me out.* **2** (in boxing) to hit an opponent so hard that they fall to the ground and cannot get up within a limited time, so losing the fight: *He was knocked out in the seventh round.* **3** (*also* ˌknock yourself ˈout*) to make sb/yourself very tired, ill/sick, etc.: *The course completely knocked me out.* ◇ *She's knocking herself out with all that work.* **4** (*informal*) to surprise sb very much; to have a strong emotional effect on sb: *The movie was fantastic. It knocked me out.* ⟨SYN⟩ **blow sb away** (*informal*); **bowl sb over**

◆ **1,2,3** v + n/pron + adv

◆ v + adv + n (*less frequent*)

◆ **4** v + n/pron + adv

▶ ˈknockout (*also* ˈknock-out) *n* **1** a person, a piece of clothing, a performance, etc. that is extremely attractive or impressive: *Her daughter's an absolute knockout.* **2** (in boxing) a blow that is so hard that your opponent falls to the ground and cannot get up within a limited time, so losing the fight

ˌknock sb/sth ˈout; ˌknock sb/sth ˈout of sth (*sport*) to defeat a person or a team so that they cannot continue in the competition: *France knocked Belgium out of the European Cup.*

◆ v + n/pron + adv ◆ v + adv + n

◆ v + n/pron + adv + prep

▶ ˈknockout (*also* ˈknock-out) *n* (*especially BrE, sport*) a competition in which the winning player or team at each stage goes on to the next stage, but the losing one no longer takes part in the competition: *the European cup knockout* ◇ *a knockout competition*

ˌknock sth ˈout **1** (*informal*) → KNOCK STH OFF 1: *Can you knock out a quick report for me?* **2** to remove sth with a hard blow: *She knocked out her front teeth in the fall.* ⟨OBJ⟩ **teeth 3** to stop a machine, system, etc. from working: *The hurricane knocked out power to over a million customers.* ◇ *Scientists are now able to knock out this gene.*

◆ v + adv + n ◆ v + n/pron + adv

ˌknock yourself ˈout **1** → KNOCK SB OUT 1 **2** → KNOCK SB OUT 3 **3** (*informal, humorous, especially AmE*) used to encourage sb to do sth they have said they would like to do, even though you do not understand why they want to do it: *You want to help? Great, knock yourself out!* ◇ *Sure you can take over the cooking—knock yourself out!*

◆ v + pron + adv

knock sth 'out of sb to make sb lose their breath, because of a fall, a blow, etc.: *The force of the impact knocked the breath out of her.*
⬛ **breath**, **wind**
◆ v + n/pron + adv + prep

IDM **knock the 'stuffing out of sb** (*informal*) to make sb lose their energy, enthusiasm or confidence

knock sb 'over if a car or another vehicle **knocks sb over**, it hits them and often kills or injures them: *He got knocked over by a bus.*
SYN **run sb/sth over**
NOTE Often used in the passive. ◆ **Knock sb over** is not used as often as **knock sb down** or **run sb over**.
→ see also KNOCK SB DOWN
◆ v + n/pron + adv ◆ v + adv + n

knock sth 'over 1 to push or hit sth, making it fall or turn on its side: *You've knocked my drink over!* ◇ *I'll put the candle here so that it doesn't get knocked over.* **2** (*AmE*, *informal*) to rob a bank or other business: *The two men were wanted for knocking over a bank.* ⬛ **bank**
◆ v + n/pron + adv ◆ v + adv + n

knock 'through (*BrE*) to knock down the wall between two rooms: *I intend to knock through on the ground floor.*
◆ v + adv

knock to'gether (*especially BrE*) if two things **knock together**, they touch each other with some force and make a sound: *His knees were knocking together with fright.*
◆ v + adv

knock sth to'gether 1 (*also* **knock sth 'up**) to make or complete sth quickly and often not very well: *I'll quickly knock some lunch together.* **2** (*BrE*) to join two or more rooms or houses to make a single one: *They've knocked the two rooms together to make one big living room.*
◆ v + n/pron + adv ◆ v + adv + n

knock 'up (*BrE*, *sport*) (in tennis, etc.) to practise for a short time before the beginning of a game: *We knocked up for a few minutes before the match.*
◆ v + adv
▶ **'knock-up** *n* (*BrE*) (in tennis, etc.) a short practice before a game

knock sb 'up (*informal*) **1** (*BrE*) to wake sb by knocking on their door: *Would you like me to knock you up in the morning?* **2** (*especially AmE*) to make a woman pregnant
◆ **1** v + n/pron + adv
◆ **2** v + n/pron + adv ◆ v + adv + n

knock sth 'up → KNOCK STH TOGETHER 1

know /nəʊ; *AmE* noʊ/ (**knew** /njuː; *AmE* nuː/, **known** /nəʊn; *AmE* noʊn/)

'know sb/sth as sth to call sb/sth by a particular name; to think that sb/sth has a particular characteristic or is a particular type of person or thing: *She is known to her friends as*
Beth. ◇ *It became known as the worst local company to work for.*
NOTE Usually used in the passive.
◆ v + n/pron + prep

be 'known for sth to be well known because of a particular characteristic, achievement or feature: *The town is best known for its ancient university.* ◇ *He is not known for his tact!* (= he is often rude)
◆ be + v + prep

'know A from B to be able to recognize the difference between two things: *She doesn't know a Rolls Royce from a Renault.*
NOTE Not used in the passive.
◆ v + n/pron + prep

IDM **not know your ,arse from your 'elbow** (*BrE*, ⚠, *slang*) to be very stupid or completely lacking in skill: *He doesn't know his arse from his elbow.*

'know of sb/sth to have heard of sb/sth, but not have very much information about or experience of them/it: *'Has he ever been in trouble with the police?'* *'Not that I know of.'* ◇ *I know of one student who failed the exam twice.* ◇ *I know of her, but we've never actually met.*
◆ v + prep

knuckle /'nʌkl/

knuckle 'down (**to sth**) (*informal*) to begin to work seriously at sth, usually after a period when you have not worked hard: *It's time to knuckle down* (*to some hard work*).
SYN **buckle down** (**to sth**)
◆ v + adv

knuckle 'under (**to sb/sth**) (*informal*) to accept or admit defeat and do what you are told or what you have to do: *Those who refused to knuckle under were imprisoned.*
◆ v + adv

kowtow /ˌkaʊ'taʊ/

kow'tow to sb/sth (*informal*) to show sb/sth too much respect and be too willing to obey them: *I refuse to kowtow to anyone.*
◆ v + prep

L l

labour (*BrE*) (*AmE* **labor**) /'leɪbə(r)/

'labour under sth (*BrE*, *formal*) **1** (*often used in the progressive tenses*) to believe sth that is not true: *to be labouring under a delusion* ◇ *She was labouring under the impression that he loved her.* ⬛ **misapprehension**, **delusion**, **impression** **2** to find a situation very difficult because of sth: *The new government is labouring under a huge debt.*
◆ v + prep

lace /leɪs/

NOTE Laces (or **shoelaces**) are strings that go through the holes on a shoe to fasten it.

ˌlace **'up**; ˌlace sth **'up** to be fastened with laces; to fasten sth with laces: *She laced her shoes up.*
OBJ shoes, boots **SYN** do up, do sth up
NOTE Lace sth is also used on its own.
♦ v + n/pron + adv ♦ v + adv + n
▸ **'lace-up** n [usually pl.] (*BrE*) shoes fastened with laces: *As a child, she always wore lace-ups.*
◇ *lace-up shoes*

ˈlace sth **with sth 1** to put a small amount of sth, such as alcohol, a drug, poison, etc. into a drink: *Someone had laced the cat's milk with alcohol.* **2** (*especially BrE*) to put a lot of a particular quality into sth such as a speech, a piece of writing, etc.: *The show is laced with black humour.* ◇ *She laces her stories with irony.*
NOTE Usually used in the passive.
♦ v + n/pron + prep

ladle /'leɪdl/

NOTE A **ladle** is a large deep spoon with a long handle.

ˌladle sth **'out 1** to serve food with a ladle, etc., or in large quantities: *He ladled out the soup.*
2 (*sometimes disapproving*) to give sb a lot of sth, especially money or advice
♦ v + adv + n ♦ v + n/pron + adv

lag /læg/ (**-gg-**)

ˌlag be'hind; ˌlag be'hind sb/sth **1** to be behind sb/sth because you are walking more slowly: *Everyone ran down to the beach, but Amy lagged behind.* ◇ *Susie lagged behind the other children.* **2** (**in sth/in doing sth**) to progress or develop more slowly than others: *We are lagging far behind our European competitors in using new technology.*
♦ v + adv ♦ v + prep

lager /'lɑːɡə(r)/

be/get ˌlagered **'up** (**on sth**) (*BrE, informal*) to be behaving in an excited or violent way because of the effects of alcohol: *They just sit in front of the TV, getting lagered up and shouting at the referee.*
♦ be/get + v + adv
▸ ˌlagered-ˈup *adj* [only before noun] (*BrE, informal*): *The town centre is full of lagered-up lads looking for a fight.*

land /lænd/

ˈland **in sth**; ˈland sb/yourself **in sth** (*informal*) to get sb/yourself into trouble or a difficult situation: *She landed in court for stealing a car.* ◇ *Being too outspoken landed her in trouble.* ◇ *How did I land myself in such a mess?* ◇ *He really* **landed** *us* **in it!** (= got us into trouble)
♦ v + prep ♦ v + n/pron + prep

ˈland **on sb** (*AmE, informal*) to criticize sb angrily: *My professor really landed on me for turning my paper in late.*
♦ v + prep

ˌland **'up** (*BrE, informal*) **1** [**+adv/prep**] to reach a final position or situation: *She landed up in hospital with a broken leg.* ◇ *The train was diverted and we landed up in York.* ◇ *The dish slipped out of my hands and landed up on the floor.* ◇ *I landed up with more work than I could manage.* **2** ˈland up **doing sth** to end by doing sth or having to do sth that you had not planned to do: *They landed up paying for the damage.* ◇ *We landed up spending the night at the airport.*
SYN end up; finish up
♦ **1** v + adv
♦ **2** v + adv + -ing

ˈland **sb/yourself with sb/sth**; ˈland **sb/yourself with doing sth** (*informal, especially BrE*) to give sb/yourself an unpleasant or difficult task to deal with: *We've landed ourselves with the most boring job of the lot.* ◇ *I got landed with clearing up the mess.* ◇ *They landed the organization with a huge bill.*
SYN saddle sb/yourself with sb/sth, etc.
NOTE Often used in the passive, usually with **get**: *Guess who got landed with washing the dishes?*
♦ v + n/pron + prep

lap /læp/ (**-pp-**)

ˌlap sth **'up 1** to receive sth such as praise or a kind remark with pleasure without thinking about whether it is true or not: *The baby was lapping up the attention he was getting.* ◇ *She lapped up his flattery.* **2** to drink all of sth with great enjoyment: *The cat lapped up the cream.*
♦ v + adv + n ♦ v + pron + adv
♦ v + n + adv (*less frequent*)

lapse /læps/

ˈlapse **into sth 1** to pass gradually into a worse or less active state or condition: *They lapsed into silence.* ◇ *The country lapsed into chaos.* ◇ *to lapse into unconsciousness/a coma* **OBJ** silence, unconsciousness **2** to start speaking or behaving in a different way, often one that is less acceptable: *She lapses into English when she can't think of a word in French.*
♦ v + prep

lard /lɑːd; *AmE* lɑːrd/

ˈlard **sth with sth** (*often disapproving*) to include particular words or expressions in a speech or in a piece of writing: *His conversation was larded with Russian proverbs.*
NOTE Nearly always used in the passive.
♦ v + n/pron + prep

lark /lɑːk; AmE lɑːrk/

,lark a'bout/a'round (*old-fashioned, informal, especially BrE*) to enjoy yourself by behaving in a silly way: *Some kids were larking about in the shopping centre.*
SYN mess around
♦ v + adv

lash /læʃ/

,lash 'down if rain **lashes down**, it falls heavily: *The rain lashed down.*
♦ v + adv

,lash 'out (at sb/sth) **1** to make a sudden violent attack on sb: *He lashed out at us.* ◇ *Jim lashed out with both fists.* **2** to criticize sb/sth in an angry way: *She lashed out at the company for treating her so badly.*
SYN hit out (at sb/sth)
♦ v + adv

,lash 'out on sth (*BrE, informal*) to spend a lot of money on sth
SYN splash out (on sth)
♦ v + adv + prep

last /lɑːst; AmE læst/

,last 'out; ,last sth 'out **1** to survive for a period of time: *How long can we last out without water?* ◇ *The doctors thought he might not last out the night.* **2** to continue in the same situation or manage to do sth for a particular length of time: *He made it to the summit, but at one point I thought he wasn't going to last out.* ◇ *She lasted out for a week without smoking.* ◇ *Can you last out the day without using your phone?* **3** to be enough for a particular length of time: *Our supplies should last out until the end of the month.* ◇ *Will the food last out the week?*
SYN hold out
NOTE Not used in the passive. ♦ **Last** and **last sth** are used frequently on their own with the same meanings.
♦ v + adv ♦ v + adv + n ♦ v + pron + adv
♦ v + n + adv (*less frequent*)

,last sb 'out (*often humorous*) to live or continue longer than sb else: *My grandmother is so fit and healthy she'll probably last us all out!*
♦ v + n/pron + adv

latch /lætʃ/

,latch 'on; ,latch 'onto sb (*also* ,latch 'on to sb) (*informal*) to follow sb around, often when they do not want you with them: *He latched onto us and we couldn't get rid of him.*
♦ v + adv ♦ v + prep ♦ v + adv + prep

,latch 'on; ,latch 'onto sth (*also* ,latch 'on to sth) **1** to become attached to sth: *The virus latches onto the red blood cells.* **2** to be interested in an idea, a fashion, etc. and use it for your own purposes: *The government have latched onto environmental issues to win votes.* ◇ *They have a reputation for latching onto all the latest crazes.*

◇ *Young children latch onto phrases and repeat them over and over.* **3** (*BrE, informal*) to understand an idea, what sb is saying, etc.: *It took him a while to latch onto their style of humour.* ◇ *She soon latched onto the idea.* ◇ *It was a difficult concept to grasp, but Sam latched on very quickly.*
♦ v + adv ♦ v + prep ♦ v + adv + prep

laugh /lɑːf; AmE læf/

🔒'laugh at sb/yourself to make sb/yourself seem stupid by making jokes about them/yourself; to not be too serious about sb/yourself: *They were laughing at him behind his back.* ◇ *We all laughed at Jane when she said she believed in ghosts.* ◇ *I laughed at myself for believing such an unlikely story.* ◇ *Nobody likes to be laughed at.*
♦ v + prep

🔒'laugh at sth **1** to show that you find sth funny or amusing: *You never laugh at my jokes.* ◇ *The whole class was laughing at him clowning around.* **2** to make sth seem stupid by making jokes about it: *He was laughing at my accent.* ◇ *He doesn't like his ideas being laughed at.*
SYN ridicule sth (*more formal*)
♦ v + prep

,laugh sth 'off (*informal*) to try to make people think that you do not care about sth, or that it is not serious or important, by making a joke about it: *He laughed off suggestions that he had been approached to be manager of the England team.* ◇ *It was an embarrassing situation, but she managed to laugh it off.*
♦ v + adv + n ♦ v + pron + adv
♦ v + n + adv (*less frequent*)

launch /lɔːntʃ/

'launch into sth; 'launch yourself into sth to start doing sth in a very enthusiastic or emotional way: *She launched into an explanation of how the machine worked.* ◇ *We don't want to launch ourselves into the wrong enterprise.* ◇ *The band launched into one of their best known songs.* ◇ *He launched into a tirade of abuse against the police officer.*
OBJ speech, explanation, challenge
♦ v + prep ♦ v + pron + prep

,launch 'out (into sth) to begin to do sth new or different in a confident way: *She's decided she has enough experience to launch out on her own.*
♦ v + adv

lavish /ˈlævɪʃ/

'lavish sth on sb/sth (*also* 'lavish sth upon sb/sth *more formal*) to give a lot of sth, often too much, to sb/sth: *They lavished such care on that house!* ◇ *He was jealous of the attention lavished on his sister.* ◇ *Millions of pounds were lavished on restoring the building.*
OBJ attention, praise, care
NOTE Often used in the passive.
♦ v + n/pron + prep

lay /leɪ/ (**laid**, **laid** /leɪd/)

,lay a'bout sb (**with sth**) (*especially BrE*) to attack sb violently physically or with words: *He started to lay about me with his walking stick.*
  ♦ v + prep

,lay sth a'side (*formal*) **1** to put sth to one side and not use it or think about it: *I laid my book aside and picked up the letter.* ◇ (*figurative*) *They laid aside their differences until the crisis was over.* **2** (*also* ,lay sth ' by *less frequent*) to keep sth to use in the future; to save sth: *Have you laid anything aside for your old age?*
  SYN put sth aside; set sth aside
  ♦ v + n/pron + adv ♦ v + adv + n

,lay sth be'fore sb/sth to present a proposal, some information, etc. to sb for them to think about and decide on: *The bill was laid before Parliament.*
  ♦ v + n/pron + prep

,lay sth 'by → LAY STH ASIDE

,lay sth 'down **1** to put sth down or stop using it: *He stopped writing and laid down his pen.* ◇ *They refused to* **lay down their arms**. **SYN** put sb/sth down **2** if you **lay down** a rule, or a principle, you state officially that people must obey it or use it: *The government has laid down procedures for negotiating teachers' pay.* ◇ *Clear guidelines have been laid down for religious teaching in schools.* **OBJ** guidelines, rules, conditions **3** to establish sth that will develop or be useful in the future: *Good eating habits can be laid down in childhood.* **4** to produce sth that is stored and gradually increases: *If you eat too much, the surplus is laid down as fat.* **OBJ** fat **NOTE** Usually used in the passive. **5** (*BrE*) to store sth, especially wine, to use in the future: *She has laid down hundreds of bottles of port.* **OBJ** bottles, wine **6** to record music for a CD, etc.: *We laid down a couple of tracks in the studio this morning.* **OBJ** track
  ♦ **1,4** v + adv + n ♦ v + n/pron + adv
  ♦ **2,3,5,6** v + adv + n ♦ v + pron + adv
  ♦ v + n + adv (*rare*)
  IDM lay down the 'law to tell sb firmly what they can or cannot do **lay down your 'life** (**for sb/sth**) to die willingly in order to save sb or because of sth that you believe in

,lay sth 'in (*formal*) to get a supply of sth and store it to use in the future: *I've laid in enough logs for the winter.*
  SYN get sth in
  ♦ v + adv + n ♦ v + n/pron + adv

,lay 'into sb/sth (**with sth**) (**for sth/for doing sth**) (*informal*) to attack sb/sth violently, with words or blows: *She laid into him with her fists.* ◇ *He laid into the government for spending millions of pounds on buildings nobody wanted.*
  SYN rip into sb/sth, etc.
  ♦ v + prep

,lay 'off; ,lay 'off sb/sth; ,lay 'off doing sth (*informal*) used to tell sb to stop doing sth that irritates or annoys you: *Lay off! You're messing up my homework!* ◇ *Lay off him, he's still learning.* ◇ *Lay off bullying your brother!*
  ♦ v + adv ♦ v + prep

SYNONYMS

lay sb off

dismiss sb ♦ fire sb ♦ lay sb off ♦ make sb redundant ♦ sack sb

These verbs all mean to officially remove sb from their job.

dismiss sb (*usually passive*) (*formal*) to officially remove sb from their job: *She claims she was unfairly dismissed from her post.*

fire sb (*often passive*) to officially remove sb from their job: *We had to fire him for dishonesty.* ◇ *She got fired from her first job.*

lay sb off (*often passive*) to stop employing sb, often for a temporary period, because there is not enough work for them to do: *200 workers at the factory have been laid off.*

make sb redundant (*usually passive*) to remove sb from their job because there is no more work available for them: *She was made redundant from her job.*

sack sb (*often passive*) (*informal, especially BrE*) to dismiss sb from a job, usually because they have done sth wrong: *She was sacked for* refusing to work on Sundays. **NOTE** It is also possible to say **give sb the sack** or **get the sack** in British English.

WHICH WORD?

Dismiss is the preferred term in legal contexts, especially in the phrase *unfairly/wrongfully dismissed*. **Sack** can sound more sudden or dramatic than **give sb the sack**, and is used more in newspapers. **Give sb the sack** is more frequent in everyday spoken English: *She got the sack/was given the sack for refusing to work on Sundays.*

PATTERNS AND COLLOCATIONS

- to fire sb/dismiss sb/lay sb off/sack sb/make sb redundant/get the sack **from** a job
- to fire sb/dismiss sb/sack sb/give sb the sack **for** sth
- **staff/workers** are fired/dismissed/laid off/sacked/made redundant
- to be **unfairly/summarily** fired/dismissed/sacked

lead

lay 'off sth; **lay 'off doing sth** (*informal*) to stop doing or using sth harmful: *You should lay off alcohol/drinking for a while.*
 ◆ v + prep

lay sb 'off to dismiss workers, usually for a short time, because there is not enough work: *We've had to lay off hundreds of workers.*
 ◆ v + n/pron + adv ◆ v + adv + n
 ▶ **'lay-off** *n* **1** [C] an act of dismissing workers because there is not enough work: *The crisis has caused thousands of lay-offs.* **2** [usually sing.] a period of time when sb is not able to take part in an activity or a sport that they usually do

lay sth 'on (*BrE, informal*) to provide or arrange sth for sb, for example food, transport or entertainment: *Extra buses were laid on during the train strike.* ◇ *She had laid on tea for the players.*
 ◆ v + adv + n ◆ v + n/pron + adv
 IDM **lay it/sth on with a 'trowel**; **lay it on 'thick** (*informal*) to talk about sb/sth in a way that makes them seem much better or worse than they really are; to exaggerate sth: *He was laying on the flattery with a trowel.* ◇ *Calling him a genius is laying it on a bit thick!*

lay sth 'on sb (*informal*) **1** to force sb to deal with sth unpleasant or difficult: *I'm sorry to lay all this work on you.* **2** (*AmE*) to break bad or surprising news to sb: *Sorry to **lay this on you**, but he's never coming back.*
 ◆ v + n/pron + prep

lay 'out (*AmE*) to stop taking part in a group activity for a short time, especially in order to let others take part: *He's always happy to lay out for a while and let other people be heard.*
 ◆ v + adv

lay sb 'out 1 (*informal*) to knock sb unconscious: *He laid his opponent out with a single blow.* **2** to prepare a dead body to be buried
 ◆ v + n/pron + adv ◆ v + adv + n

lay sth 'out 1 to spread sth out ready to use or so that it can be seen easily: *Lay out all the clothes you want to take.* ◇ *Lay all the cards out on the table.* **2** to plan how sth should look and arrange it in this way: *They laid the streets out on a grid pattern.* ◇ *a well-laid-out CV/résumé* **3** to present or explain sth clearly and carefully: *At the meeting, he laid out his plans for the company.* **4** (**on sth**) (*informal*) to spend money: *He laid out thousands renovating the house.*
 ◆ v + n/pron + adv ◆ v + adv + n
 ▶ **'layout** *n* [usually sing.] the way in which sth is arranged: *He still recalled the layout of the house perfectly.* ◇ *The magazine has a very attractive layout.*
 ▶ **'outlay** *n* [C, U] the money that you spend on sth, especially when you start a new project: *an outlay of $400 000* ◇ *What was your initial outlay on equipment?*

lay 'over (**in/at …**) (*AmE*) to stop somewhere for a short time when you are on a journey by plane: *Several passengers were laying over in Chicago for a few hours.*
 ◆ v + adv
 ▶ **'layover** *n* a short stay somewhere during a plane journey: *a four-hour layover*

lay 'up to hide somewhere or do nothing for a while: *They lay up in a cave until it got dark.*
 ◆ v + adv

lay sb 'up (*informal*) if sb is **laid up**, they are unable to work or take part in an activity because they are ill/sick or injured: *I was laid up for a month with a broken leg.* ◇ *He has been laid up with flu for a week.*
 NOTE Nearly always used in the passive.
 ◆ v + n/pron + adv ◆ v + adv + n

lay sth 'up 1 (**for yourself**) (*BrE*) if you **lay up** trouble or problems for yourself, you do sth that will result in difficulties later: *You're laying up problems for yourself by not tackling this now.*
 OBJ **trouble**, **problems** **2** to stop using a vehicle, ship, etc. because you do not need it, or it has to be repaired: *Our boat is laid up during the winter months.* **NOTE** Often used in the passive.
 ◆ v + adv + n ◆ v + n/pron + adv

laze /leɪz/

laze a'round; **laze a'round sth** (*BrE also* **laze a'bout**, **laze a'bout sth**) to spend your time relaxing and doing very little: *He lazed about all day.* ◇ *They lazed around the pool in the afternoon.*
 SYN **lie around**, **etc.**; **lounge about/around**, **etc.**
 ◆ v + adv ◆ v + prep

laze sth a'way to spend a period of time relaxing and doing very little: *We lazed away the summer on the beach.*
 ◆ v + n/pron + adv ◆ v + adv + n

lead /liːd/ (**led**, **led** /led/)

lead 'into sth 1 if a subject or a discussion **leads into** sth, it moves naturally into a second subject or discussion: *This led into a discussion on gender differences.* ◇ *Pair and group work often leads into a whole-class discussion.* **2** if a room, a door, a street, etc. **leads into** a place, it opens into it or connects with it: *The door led into a tiny kitchen.* **SUBJ** **door**, **room**, **road**
 ◆ v + prep
 ▶ **'lead-in** (**to sth**) *n* an introduction to a subject, a story, etc.: *We want a striking lead-in to the new programme.*

lead 'off (**with sth**) (*especially AmE*) to start a discussion, meeting, etc.: *Everyone will have a chance to speak. Would you like to lead off?*
 ◆ v + adv

lead 'off sth; **lead 'off from sth 1** if a street **leads off** (from) a place, it starts there and goes away from it: *He pointed to a street leading off (from) the corner of the square.* **2** if a room, a

leaf

door, etc. **leads off** (from) a place, it connects directly with it: *All the rooms lead off the main hall.*

◆ v + prep ◆ v + adv + prep

,**lead sb 'on** (*informal*) to make sb believe sth that is not true, especially that you love them or find them attractive: *You shouldn't have led him on like that.*

◆ v + n/pron + adv

◆ v + adv + n (*less frequent*)

⚡'**lead to sth**; '**lead sb to sth** (*also* ,**lead 'on to sth**, ,**lead sb 'on to sth**) to result in a particular action or event; to force or persuade sb to take a particular action: *Living in damp conditions can lead to serious health problems.* ◇ *What led you to this conclusion?* ◇ *The increase in the number of motor vehicles has led to an increase in vehicle crime.* ◇ *The police have offered a reward for information leading to the conviction of the child's killers.* ◇ *She described how her early life had led her to her profession as an artist.* ◇ ***One thing led to another*** *and before long Sue and I were engaged.*

NOTE **Lead sb to do sth** can also be used with this meaning: *She described how her early life led her to become an artist.*

◆ v + prep ◆ v + n/pron + prep ◆ v + adv + prep
◆ v + n/pron + adv + prep

,**lead 'up to sth** **1** to be the introduction to or the cause of sth: *The book describes the period leading up to the start of the war.* ◇ *Police are investigating the chain of events that led up to her death.* **2** to prepare to talk about sth or ask a difficult question by gradually introducing the subject you want to talk about: *What exactly are you leading up to?* ◇ *He seemed to be leading up to asking a difficult question.*

◆ v + adv + prep

▶ ,**lead-'up** (**to sth**) *n* [sing.] (*BrE*) a period of time or an event or series of events before another event or activity: *in the lead-up to the election*

leaf /liːf/

,**leaf 'through sth** to turn over the pages of a book, a magazine, etc. quickly without reading them carefully or in detail: *She picked up a brochure and leafed through it.*

OBJ **pages** **SYN** **flick through sth** ⟳ note at
LOOK THROUGH STH

◆ v + prep

leak /liːk/

,**leak 'out** if secret information **leaks out**, it becomes known to the public when it should remain secret: *He was worried about what might happen if the news leaked out.*

SYN **get out**

◆ v + adv

lean /liːn/ (**leaned**, **leaned**, *BrE also* **leant**, **leant** /lent/)

⚡'**lean a'gainst/on sth/sb**; ,**lean 'up against sth** to rest against or on sth/sb for support: *Laura leaned weakly against the door.* ◇ *We left our bikes leaning up against the wall.* ◇ *You can lean on my arm.*

→ see also LEAN ON SB/STH

◆ v + prep ◆ v + adv + prep

⚡'**lean sth against/on sth**; ,**lean sth 'up against sth** to make sth rest against or on sth in a sloping position: *He leaned his head on his hand and closed his eyes.* ◇ *Maggie leant the broom up against the wall.*

◆ v + n/pron + prep ◆ v + n/pron + adv + prep

'**lean on sb** (*informal*) to try to make sb do sth by threatening them: *They are leaning on him to make him withdraw his complaints.* ◇ *I was being leaned on.*

◆ v + prep

'**lean on sb/sth** (*also* '**lean upon sb/sth** *more formal*) to depend on sb/sth: *It's good to have someone to lean on.* ◇ *She was unsure of herself and leaned heavily on her friends for support.*

→ see also LEAN AGAINST/ON SB/STH

◆ v + prep

,**lean to'wards sth** (*also* ,**lean to'ward sth**) to support or tend to prefer a particular idea or political party: *I'm not sure how I'm going to vote but I'm leaning towards the Democrats.*

◆ v + prep

,**lean up a'gainst sth** → LEAN AGAINST/ON STH/SB

,**lean sth up a'gainst sth** → LEAN STH AGAINST/ON STH

'**lean upon sb/sth** → LEAN ON SB/STH

leap /liːp/ (**leapt**, **leapt** /lept/ or **leaped**, **leaped**)

'**leap at sth** to accept sth with enthusiasm, without hesitating: *She leapt at the chance of working in Paris.*

OBJ **chance**, **opportunity** **SYN** **jump at sth**

◆ v + prep

'**leap on sth** (*also* '**leap upon sth** *more formal*) (*especially BrE*) to suddenly become very interested in an idea or a suggestion, especially because you think it will give you an advantage: *The press leapt on the story.*

◆ v + prep

,**leap 'out at sb** if sth, especially sth written, **leaps out at** you, you see it immediately: *His name leapt out at me from the page.*

SYN **jump out at sb**

◆ v + adv + prep

,**leap 'up** to stand quickly and suddenly when you have been sitting: *He leapt up and ran to answer the door.*

SYN **jump up**

◆ v + adv

'**leap upon sth** (*especially BrE*) → LEAP ON STH

learn /lɜːn; *AmE* lɜːrn/

,**learn of sth** to become aware of sth by hearing about it from sb else: *I learnt of her arrival from a close friend.* ➣ note at FIND OUT, FIND SB OUT
♦ v + prep

leave /liːv/ (**left, left** /left/)

,**leave sth a'side** to not discuss or consider a particular idea or issue: *Leaving aside car parking space, the housing development is well planned.* ◇ *Let us **leave aside the question of** costs for the moment.* ◇ *Leaving that aside…*
[OBJ] **question, that/this problem**
♦ v + adv + n ♦ v + pron + adv
♦ v + n + adv (*less frequent*)

,**leave sb/sth be'hind** to make progress much faster than sb else: *The new car is going to leave the competition far behind.*
♦ v + n/pron + adv

,**leave sb/sth be'hind**; ,**leave sb/sth be'hind sb 1** to go away from a place without taking sb/sth because you have forgotten them/it: *Somebody has left their umbrella behind.* ◇ *Wait—don't leave me behind!* **2** to go away from a place while the result of sth you have done stays there: *They wore gloves so as not to leave any fingerprints behind (them).* **3** to leave a person or place permanently, especially in order to begin a new life: *He was anxious to leave the past behind (him).* ◇ *She disappeared a year ago, leaving behind a boyfriend and a small baby.* **4** to have sb/sth remaining after your death: *He died at the age of 33, leaving behind a wife and three young children.*
[NOTE] **Leave sb/sth** is sometimes used on its own with these meanings: *They wore gloves so as not to leave any fingerprints.*
♦ v + n/pron + adv ♦ v + adv + n ♦ v + n/pron + prep

,**leave sth 'in** to not remove sth, for example from a book, a piece of writing, etc.: *Make sure you leave that paragraph in.*
[OPP] **leave sth out**
♦ v + n/pron + adv ♦ v + adv + n

,**leave 'off**; ,**leave 'off sth**; ,**leave 'off doing sth** (*BrE, informal*) to stop doing sth: *Lee shouted at him, but he wouldn't leave off.* ◇ *Would you leave off what you are doing for a moment?* ◇ *We're going to try and begin where they left off.* ◇ *'Will you leave off nagging?' he shouted.* ➣ note at GIVE UP, GIVE STH UP
♦ v + adv ♦ v + adv + n ♦ v + adv + -ing

,**leave sb/sth 'off**; ,**leave sb/sth 'off sth** to not include or mention sb/sth, especially on a list: *Have I left anyone off the list?*
♦ v + n/pron + adv ♦ v + adv + n ♦ v + n/pron + prep

,**leave sth 'on 1** if you **leave** clothes **on**, you continue wearing them: *Leave your shoes on.*
[SYN] **keep sth on 2** to not switch sth off: *I found* the television had been left on all night. ◇ *Do you mind if I leave the tape recorder on while you talk?* [OPP] **leave sth off; switch sth off**
♦ v + n/pron + adv ♦ v + adv + n

,**leave it 'out** (*BrE, informal*) **1** used to tell sb to stop doing sth silly or annoying **2** used to tell sb that you think what they have said is stupid, or that you do not believe it: *Two million dollars? Leave it out!*
♦ v + it + adv

,**leave sb 'out**; ,**leave sb 'out of sth** to not include sb deliberately: *It seemed unkind to leave Daisy out, so we invited her too.* ◇ *There was an outcry when he was left out of the team.*
[SYN] **exclude sb** (*more formal*)
♦ v + n/pron + adv ♦ v + adv + n
♦ v + n/pron + adv + prep
▸ **left 'out** *adj* unhappy because you have not been included in sth: *I felt a bit left out.*

,**leave sb/sth 'out**; ,**leave sb/sth 'out of sth 1** to not involve sb/sth in sth: *Leave my brother out of this—he had nothing to do with it.* **2** to not include sth either accidentally or deliberately: *Have I left anyone out?* ◇ *You can leave out the gory details.* ◇ *This is spelt wrongly. You've left out the 'e'.* ◇ *You've left the second 'm' out of 'committee'.* ◇ *You've left out an 'm' in 'committee'.* [SYN] **omit sth** (*more formal*); **miss sth out** (*BrE*)
♦ **1** v + n/pron + adv ♦ v + n/pron + adv + prep
♦ **2** v + adv + n ♦ v + n/pron + adv
♦ v + n/pron + adv + prep

▸ **be ,left 'over** (**from sth**) (of food or money) if food, money, etc. is **left over**, it remains when the rest has been eaten or used up: *After I've paid my rent and bought food there isn't much left over to spend on books.* ◇ *There was plenty of food left over after the party.* ◇ *There's some rice left over from lunch.*
♦ be + v + adv
▸ **'leftover** *n* (*BrE*) **1** [usually pl.] food that has not been eaten and remains after a meal **2** a custom, tradition, etc. that belongs to an earlier time but still exists: *These narrow roads are a leftover from the days of horse-drawn carriages.*
▸ **'leftover** *adj* [only before noun] remaining because it has not been eaten or used: *leftover vegetables/fabric*

'leave sb to sth to go away from sb so that they can continue what they were doing before you came, or do sth without your help: (*informal*) *If you don't need me any more, I'll **leave you to it**.* ◇ *I'll leave you to your lunch.*
♦ v + n/pron + prep

[IDM] **leave sb to their own de'vices** to leave sb alone to do as they wish: *Once I've explained things to him I tend to leave him to his own devices.*

lend /lend/ (**lent**, **lent** /lent/)

,lend sth 'out (**to sb**) to allow sb to borrow sth for a period of time: *The reference books cannot be lent out.*
‹ v + n/pron + adv ‹ v + adv + n

'lend itself/themselves to sth (*formal*) to be suitable for sth: *Science in elementary schools lends itself well to learning through play.* ◇ *Not all materials lend themselves to scientific dating.*
‹ pron + prep

let /let/ (**letting**, **let**, **let**)

,let sb 'down 1 to fail to help or support sb in the way that they hoped or expected: *She said she would help, but let them down at the last minute.* ◇ *It's important our decision doesn't let down our customers.* ◇ *The car has never let me down.* ◇ *I felt I'd been badly let down by the company.* 2 to tell sb some bad news in a kind way so that they will not be too disappointed or upset: *The kids will be really upset that the trip's been cancelled—try to let them down gently.*
‹ v + n/pron + adv 1 also v + adv + n
IDM let the 'side down (*BrE*) to disappoint your family, friends, team, etc. by not being as successful as they expect, or not helping or supporting them: *John would never let the side down.* ◇ *I knew I was letting the side down* (= disappointing my family, etc.) *by not going to college.*
▶ 'let-down *n* [C, usually sing., U] sth that is not as good as you thought or hoped it would be: *The book was great but the ending was a bit of a let-down.*

,let sb/sth 'down; ,let yourself 'down to make sb/sth/yourself less successful or impressive than they/it/you should be: *Her pronunciation lets her down.* ◇ *His clothes let him down.* ◇ *If you don't work hard for these exams, you'll only be letting yourself down.*
‹ v + n/pron + adv ‹ v + adv + n

,let sth 'down 1 to make sth go lower: *We let the bucket down on a rope.* **SYN** lower sth (*more formal*) 2 to make sth longer, especially an item of clothing: *I'm going to let the hem down a couple of centimetres.* **OPP** take sth up 3 (*BrE*) to allow the air to come out of sth, such as a tyre: *The tyres on his car had been let down during the night.* **OBJ** tyre **SYN** deflate sth (*formal*)
‹ v + n/pron + adv ‹ v + adv + n
IDM let your 'hair down (*informal*) to relax and enjoy yourself, often in a lively way: *I saw my parents letting their hair down on the dance floor.*

,let sb/sth 'in; ,let yourself 'in; ,let sb/sth/ yourself 'into sth to allow sb/sth/yourself to enter a room or a building: *Let me in! It's cold out here.* ◇ *The guard refuses to let anyone in without a security pass.* ◇ *She let herself into the flat.*
‹ v + n/pron + adv ‹ v + adv + n ‹ v + n/pron + prep

,let sth 'in to allow sth such as water or light to enter a place through a hole: *There was a hole in the roof that let the rain in.* ◇ *I drew the curtains back to let in some light.*
OBJ light, rain, water
NOTE Not used in the passive.
‹ v + n/pron + adv ‹ v + adv + n
▶ 'inlet *n* 1 a narrow strip of water which goes from the sea or a lake into the land: *a narrow/ sheltered inlet* 2 the part of a machine through which air, gas or fuel enters: *a fuel/power inlet*

,let sb/yourself 'in for sth (*informal*) to allow yourself to become involved in sth difficult or unpleasant: *If I'd known what I was letting myself in for, I'd never have agreed to help.* ◇ *What have you let me in for?*
NOTE Not used in the passive. ‹ Often used in questions with *what*.
‹ v + n/pron + adv + prep

,let sb 'in on sth (*BrE also* ,let sb 'into sth) (*informal*) to allow sb to share a secret: *Are you going to let them in on your plans?* ◇ *I wanted to let Chris in on the secret.* ◇ *I'll let you into a little secret.*
OBJ secret, plans
‹ v + n/pron + adv + prep ‹ v + n/pron + prep

be ,let 'into sth (*BrE*) to be put into the surface of sth: *A large window was let into the wall.*
‹ be + v + prep

,let 'off (*BrE, informal*) to let air from the body come out through your bottom
SYN break wind (*more formal*); fart (*slang*)
‹ v + adv

,let sb 'off (**with sth**) to punish sb lightly for sth wrong they have done; to not punish sb at all: *She was let off with a fine.* ◇ *I'll let you off this time, but don't do it again.*
‹ v + n/pron + adv

,let sb 'off; ,let sb 'off sth 1 to allow sb not to do sth or not to go somewhere: *You really ought to help with the shopping, but I suppose I could let you off.* ◇ *Mum let me off the household chores during exams.* 2 to allow sb to get out of a vehicle, especially a bus: *Can you let me off here?*
‹ v + n/pron + adv ‹ v + n/pron + prep
IDM let sb off the 'hook to free sb from a difficult or unpleasant task or situation: *He wasn't going to let the senator off the hook easily; he kept asking difficult questions.*

,let sth 'off to fire a gun; to make sth explode: *The boys were letting off fireworks.* ◇ *He let off a warning shot.*
OBJ firework, shot
‹ v + adv + n ‹ v + n/pron + adv
IDM ,let off 'steam (*AmE also* ,blow off 'steam) to get rid of your energy, emotions, etc. by shouting or doing sth active: *He let off steam by hitting a pillow.* ◇ (*AmE*) *I decided to go for a jog to blow off some steam.*

,let 'on (**to sb**) (*informal*) to tell sb sth that is supposed to be a secret: *She doesn't know I've*

bought her a watch, so don't **let on**, will you? ◇ The children knew he was coming, but they didn't **let on** to anyone. ◇ There were holes in Jack's shoes, but Kate didn't **let on** (that) she'd noticed.
 ◆ v + adv

,**let 'out** (*AmE*) when schools, classes, offices, etc. **let out**, they come to an end and students, workers, etc. go home at the end of a day or a term: *Classes* **let out** *in June.* ◇ *More than 30 000 people are expected in the square after work* **lets out.**
 ◆ v + adv

,**let sb 'out**; ,**let sb 'out of sth 1** to allow sb not to do sth they have promised or are expected to do; to free sb from a difficult situation: *I've got school tomorrow, so that* **lets** *me* **out** (*of helping*). **2** to allow sb to leave a hospital, prison, etc., especially for a short time or earlier than expected: *The doctors might* **let** *me* **out** *tomorrow.* ◇ *I was amazed they* **let** *her* **out** *of hospital so soon.* ◇ *He was* **let out** *on parole last week.*
 ◆ v + n/pron + adv ◆ v + adv + n
 ◆ v + n/pron + adv + prep
 ▶ '**let-out** *n* [sing.] (*especially BrE*) something that allows you to avoid an unpleasant or difficult situation: *a* **let-out** *clause* (= in a contract) ◇ *'I think it's too hot to go jogging today,' I said, looking for a* **let-out.**

,**let sb/sth 'out**; ,**let sb/sth 'out of sth**; ,**let yourself 'out**; ,**let yourself 'out of sth** to allow sb/sth/yourself to go out of a room or a building: *Shall I* **let** *the dog* **out**? ◇ *Can you* **let** *yourself* **out**?
 ◆ v + n/pron + adv ◆ v + adv + n
 ◆ v + n/pron + adv + prep
 IDM **let the 'cat out of the bag** to tell a secret carelessly or by mistake: *I was trying to keep my promotion quiet, but Steve went and* **let the cat out of the bag.**

,**let sth 'out 1** to give a cry; to make a sound: *She* **let out** *a scream of terror.* ◇ *He* **let out** *a sigh of relief.* **OBJ** **cry, sigh, scream** **OPP** **hold sth in**
 2 to allow secret information to become known: *He's the only person who could have* **let** *the secret* **out.** ◇ *The company* **let out** *that they were putting in a bid for KFC.* **OBJ** **secret** **SYN** **reveal sth** (*more formal*) **3** (**to sb**) (*BrE*) to make a house, etc. available for rent: *The apartment's been* **let out** *to a couple.* **OBJ** **flat/apartment, house** **SYN** **hire sth out** (**to sb**); **rent sth out** (**to sb**) **4** to make an item of clothing looser or larger: *I've eaten so much I'll have to* **let** *my belt* **out**! **OBJ** **skirt, trousers** **OPP** **take sth in 5** (*also* ,**let sth 'out of sth**) to allow air, liquid, etc. to escape: *We need to* **let** *the air* **out** *of the radiator.*
 ◆ v + adv + n
 ◆ v + n/pron + adv **5** also v + n/pron + adv + prep
 ▶ '**outlet** *n* **1** (**for sth**) a way of expressing or using energy, strong feelings, ideas, etc.: *Chil-*

dren need an **outlet** *for all their energy.* **2** a shop/store or an organization that sells goods made by a particular company or of a particular type: *a retail/fast food* **outlet 3** (*especially AmE*) a shop/store that sells goods of a particular make/makes at reduced prices: *designer* **outlets 4** a pipe or hole through which water, steam, etc. can flow out **5** (*AmE*) a device in a wall that you use to connect a piece of electrical equipment to a power supply: *an electrical* **outlet 6** the end of a river where it flows into a lake or the sea

,**let sb/sth 'past** to allow sb/sth to go past you: *Can you* **let** *me* **past**, please?
 ◆ v + n/pron + adv

,**let sb/sth 'through 1** to allow sb/sth to pass or go through sth that is blocking the way: *The crowd moved aside to* **let** *the ambulance* **through.** ◇ *Let me* **through**—*I'm a doctor.* ◇ *These blinds don't* **let** *much light* **through.** **2** (*especially BrE*) to say that sb/sth is good enough for sth or is correct: *We were worried the council wouldn't* **let** *the plans for the new building* **through.**
 ◆ v + n/pron + adv ◆ v + adv + n (*rare*)

,**let 'up** (*informal*) **1** to become less strong: *The rain showed no sign of* **letting up. 2** to do sth with less effort or energy than before, or stop doing it: *We mustn't* **let up**, *even though we're winning.* ◇ *Doesn't she ever* **let up**? *She's been complaining all day.*
 ◆ v + adv
 ▶ '**let-up** (**in sth**) *n* [U, sing.] a reduction in the strength of something; a period of time when sth unpleasant stops: *There can be no* **let-up** *in the war against drugs.* ◇ *The rain continued all afternoon with no* **let-up.**

level /'levl/ (**-ll-**, *AmE* **-l-**)

,**level sth at sb/sth 1** (*also* ,**level sth a'gainst sb/sth**) to say publicly that sb is to blame for sth, especially a mistake or a crime: *The charges* **levelled** *against him are unjust.* ◇ *Environmental groups have* **levelled** *a number of criticisms at the proposal.* ◇ *Accusations of incompetence have been* **levelled** *at the principal.* **OBJ** **criticism, accusation, charge** **NOTE** Usually used in the passive. **2** to point sth, especially a gun, at sb: *She* **levelled** *the pistol at his head.*
 ◆ v + n/pron + prep

,**level sth 'down/'up** to make standards, amounts, etc. be the same low/high or lower/higher: *The government is accused of* **levelling down** *standards in schools rather than* **levelling them up.**
 ◆ v + adv + n ◆ v + n/pron + adv

,**level 'off/'out 1** to become level or steady after a period of sharp rises and falls: *House prices showed no sign of* **levelling off. 2** to become level or horizontal after rising or falling: *The road began to* **level off** *as we approached the coast.* ◇ *The plane* **levelled off** *at 20 000 feet.*
 ◆ v + adv

_¡**level sth 'off/'out** to make sth smooth or flat: *Level the ground out before sowing the seed.*
  ♦ v + n/pron + adv ♦ v + adv + n
_¡**level sth 'up** → LEVEL STH DOWN/UP
'level with sb (*informal*) to speak or deal with sb in an honest and direct way: *I'm going to level with you now—your work hasn't been up to standard for some time.* ◊ *I've got the feeling that he's not levelling with me.*
  ♦ v + prep

lick /lɪk/

_¡**lick sth 'off/'up**; _¡**lick sth 'off sth** to eat or drink sth by moving your tongue over the surface of it: *She licked the jam off* (*the spoon*). ◊ *The cat licked up the milk from the dish.*
  ♦ v + n/pron + adv ♦ v + adv + n ♦ v + n/pron + prep

lie /laɪ/ (**lies**, **lying**, **lay** /leɪ/, **lain** /leɪn/)

_¡**lie a'bout, etc.** (*BrE*) → LIE AROUND, ETC.
_¡**lie a'head**; _¡**lie a'head of sb** to be in the future; to be in front of sb: *Great opportunities lie ahead.* ◊ *Who knows what problems might lie ahead of us?*
  ♦ v + adv ♦ v + adv + prep
_¡**lie a'round**; _¡**lie a'round sth** (*BrE also* _¡**lie a'bout**, _¡**lie a'bout sth**) **1** (of a person) to spend time being lazy and not doing anything in particular: *She's been lying around the house all day doing nothing.* **SYN** **laze around**, **laze around sth**; **lounge about/around**, **lounge about/around sth 2** (of a number of things) to be left somewhere in a careless or untidy way: *His clothes lay around all over the floor.* ◊ *'Have you seen my purse?' 'It was lying about in the kitchen when I last saw it.'* ◊ *You shouldn't* **leave** valuables **lying around** *the changing rooms.*
  ♦ v + adv ♦ v + prep
  ▶ **'layabout** *n* (*old-fashioned*, *BrE*, *informal*) a lazy person who does very little work
_¡**lie 'back** (**in/on sth**) to rest, relax and do very little: *Just lie back and enjoy the peace and quiet.* ◊ *She lay back on the pillows and closed her eyes.*
  ♦ v + adv
_¡**lie be'fore sb** (*literary*) **1** to be in front of sb: *A terrible sight lay before them.* **2** to be in the future: *Your whole life lies before you.*
  ♦ v + prep
_¡**lie be'hind sth** to be the real explanation or reason for sth: *She understood the feelings that lay behind his angry words.* ◊ *We will probably never know what lay behind his decision to resign.*
  ♦ v + prep
_¡**lie 'down** to be or move into a horizontal position on a bed, etc. in order to sleep or rest: *Go and lie down for a while.* ◊ *He lay down on the sofa and went to sleep.* ◊ *The coughing is worse when he's lying down.* ◊ *She was lying down on the bed.*

NOTE Do not confuse this sense of **lie down** with **lay sth down**, which must always have an object: *I'm going to lie down for a while* (not *I'm going to lay down for a while*). ◊ *They were told to lay their guns down* (not *They were told to lie their guns down*).
  ♦ v + adv
IDM **lie down on the 'job** to not do sth that you are responsible for doing or expected to do: *Someone at City Hall is obviously lying down on the job, or this would be done by now.* **take sth lying 'down** to accept an insult, a criticism, a violent attack, etc. without protesting or reacting to it: *He has been accused of bribery, but he won't take this lying down.*
  ▶ _¡**lie-'down** *n* [sing.] (*BrE*, *informal*) a short rest, especially in bed: *to have a lie-down*
_¡**lie 'in** (*BrE*, *informal*) to stay in bed after the time you usually get up: *It's Saturday tomorrow, so you can lie in.*
  SYN **sleep in**
  ♦ v + adv
  ▶ _¡**lie-'in** *n* [sing.] (*BrE*, *informal*) an act of staying in bed longer than usual in the morning: *to have a lie-in*
_¡**lie 'up** (*BrE*) to hide somewhere: *The fugitives lay up in the caves until it got dark.*
  ♦ v + adv
'lie with sb/sth (**to do sth**) (*formal*) to be the duty or responsibility of sb/sth: *It lies with you to accept or reject the proposal.* ◊ *The decision on whether to proceed lies with the minister.*
  SYN **rest with sb**
  ♦ v + prep

lift /lɪft/

_¡**lift 'off** (of a rocket, etc.) to rise from the ground into the air: *The rocket lifts off next Monday.*
  ♦ v + adv
  ▶ **'lift-off** *n* [C, U] the moment when sth lifts off: *We have lift-off!*
_¡**lift sb/sth 'up**; _¡**lift yourself 'up** to raise sb/sth/yourself to a higher position or level: *I can't lift you up—you're too heavy!* ◊ *She lifted herself up on one elbow.* ◊ *She lifted up the box and put it on the table.*
  NOTE **Lift sb/sth/yourself** can also be used on its own with this meaning.
  ↻ note on page 187
  ♦ v + n/pron + adv ♦ v + adv + n

light /laɪt/ (**lit**, **lit** /lɪt/)

'light on/upon sb/sth (*literary*) **1** to suddenly see sb/sth: *Her gaze lighted on her daughter.* **SYN** **alight on/upon sb/sth 2** to suddenly find sb/sth or think of sth: *The research team has lit upon important new material.* **SYN** **hit on sth**
  NOTE **Lighted** is also used for the past tense and past participle.
  ♦ v + prep

lift sb/sth up

hoist sb/sth up ♦ **lift sb/sth up** ♦ **pick sb/sth up** ♦ **scoop sb/sth up**

These verbs all mean to take hold of sb/sth and raise, move or pull it/them.

hoist sb/sth up to raise or pull sth up to a higher position, often with difficulty or using ropes or special equipment: *He hoisted himself upon to a high stool.* NOTE **Hoist** can be used on its own: *The cargo was hoisted aboard by crane.*

lift sb/sth up to take hold of sb/sth and move them/it to a different position: *Can you lift up the computer so I can clean underneath?* NOTE **Lift** can be used on its own: *I lifted the lid of the box and looked in.*

pick sb/sth up to take hold of sb/sth and lift them/it up: *She went over to the crying child and picked her up.* ◊ *He picked up the phone and dialled the number.*

scoop sb/sth up to move or lift sth with a spoon or similar object; to pick sb up in your arms: *He scooped the child up in his arms.*

NOTE **Scoop** can be used on its own: *She scooped ice cream into the bowls.*

WHICH WORD?

Pick up is usually used to talk about things and people that are not very heavy; when you use **lift up** or **hoist up** you are suggesting that the person or thing is quite heavy. **Lift** is also used to talk about moving heavy people or things in different directions: *to lift sth up/down/into sth/from sth.* **Pick up**, on the other hand, can only be used to talk about raising a person or thing to a higher position.

PATTERNS AND COLLOCATIONS

■ to pick up/lift (up)/hoist (up)/scoop (up) sb/sth **sharply/smoothly/carefully/gently**
■ to **try to/manage to/be able to** pick up/lift (up)/hoist (up)/scoop (up) sb/sth
■ to pick up/lift (up)/hoist (up)/scoop (up) a **bag/suitcase/child/body**
■ to pick up/lift the **phone/telephone/receiver**

ˌlight 'out for sth (*AmE*) to go somewhere quickly because you are keen to get there: *At 22 he lit out for Hollywood and was in his first movie the next year.*
♦ v + adv + prep

ˌlight 'up; ˌlight sth 'up **1** to become or to make sth bright with light or colour: *Flashes of lightning lit up the sky.* ◊ *The waterfall was lit up at night with pink and green floodlights.* **2** (of a computer system, etc.) to start working; to make sth start working: *She switched the monitor on and the screen lit up.* ◊ *I lit up the spreadsheet application on my PC.* ◊ *They expect to start lighting up the network by early 2011.* **3** if a person's eyes or face **light up**, or sth **lights them up**, they become bright with excitement or happiness: *Her eyes lit up when she saw them.* ◊ *A smile of delight lit up his face.* ◊ *His face lit up with pleasure.* **4** (*informal*) to begin to smoke a cigarette, etc.: *She took out a cigarette and lit up.* ◊ *He lit up one cigarette after another.*
♦ v + adv ♦ v + adv + n ♦ v + pron + adv
♦ v + n + adv (*less frequent*)

ˌlight sb 'up (*AmE*) **1** to hit or kick sb repeatedly: *If he doesn't watch what he says, someone's going to light him up.* **2** to defeat your opponent easily in a game or competition: *The White Sox lit up the Cubs last night at Wrigley Field.*
♦ v + adv + n ♦ v + n/pron + adv

'light upon sb/sth → LIGHT ON/UPON SB/STH

lighten /ˈlaɪtn/

ˌlighten 'up used to tell sb to be less serious or to complain or worry less about sth: *Come on, lighten up! It was only a joke.*
♦ v + adv

ˌlighten sth 'up (*informal*) to make sth more cheerful and less serious or depressing: *He did his best to lighten things up.* ◊ *She tried to lighten up her speech with a few jokes.*
♦ v + n/pron + adv ♦ v + adv + n

liken /ˈlaɪkən/

'liken sb/sth to sb/sth (*formal*) to compare sb/sth to sb/sth else and say that they are similar: *He has been likened to a young George Best.* ◊ *She likened the building to a ship.*
NOTE Often used in the passive.
♦ v + n/pron + prep

limber /ˈlɪmbə(r)/

ˌlimber 'up (for sth) to do exercise to prepare to take part in a sport, a race, etc.; to warm up: *The players were limbering up for the game.* ◊ (*figurative*) *The candidates are already limbering up for the election campaign.*
SYN warm up
♦ v + adv

limit /ˈlɪmɪt/

'limit sth to sb/sth to make sth exist or happen only in a particular place or within a particular group: *Violent crime is not limited to big cities.*

◊ *The teaching of history should not be limited to dates and figures.*

SYN **confine sth to sb/sth**

NOTE Usually used in the passive.

♦ v + n/pron + prep

line /laɪn/

,line 'out (*BrE, sport*) to go onto the sports field at the beginning of a game, etc.: *Nobody will line out tomorrow unless they're fully fit.*

♦ v + adv

,line 'up **1** (**for sth/to do sth**) if people **line up**, they form a line, standing one behind the other or beside each other: *A group of people were lining up for tickets.* ◊ *They lined up to shake the President's hand.* ◊ *The runners lined up at the starting line.* → see also QUEUE UP (FOR STH/TO DO STH) **2** (**against sth**) (**behind sb/sth**) to join with sb in order to do sth: *Several newspapers lined up to demand his resignation.* ◊ *Local groups are lining up against the new development* (= joining together to oppose it). ◊ *All the residents have lined up behind the caretaker* (= they support him).

♦ v + adv

▶ 'line-up *n* [usually sing.] a row of people that is formed so that sb who saw a crime can try to recognize the person who did it: *She picked him out of a line-up* (= she recognized him as the person who committed the crime).

,line 'up; ,line sth 'up to be, or to put sth, in the correct position in relation to sth else: *The three holes should all line up* (*with each other*).

♦ v + adv ♦ v + n/pron + adv ♦ v + adv + n

,line sb/sth 'up **1** to arrange people or things in a line or a row: *She lined the children up for the*

photograph. ◊ *His CDs were lined up on the shelf.* **2** (**for sb/sth**) to organize an event or an activity; to arrange for sb to do sth at an event, a competition, etc.: *He's lined up a band for the party.* ◊ *We've lined up a few things for the weekend.* ◊ *They already had a buyer for their car lined up.*

♦ v + adv + n ♦ v + pron + adv

♦ v + n + adv (*less frequent*)

▶ 'line-up *n* [usually sing.] **1** a group of people who have been chosen or invited to take part in an event: *an impressive line-up of performers* ◊ *The line-up for tonight's game is still not known.* **2** a set of events, people or things: *Several new dramas are included in the line-up of programmes for next year.*

linger /ˈlɪŋɡə(r)/

,linger 'on **1** to remain for a long time: *The memory of that day lingers on in the minds of local people.* ◊ *The smell lingered on for days after.* **2** to remain alive, but becoming gradually weaker: *We should be thankful that she didn't linger on.* **NOTE** **Linger** is used more frequently on its own with the same meanings.

♦ v + adv

link /lɪŋk/

,link 'up **1** (**with sb**) to join with sb in order to do sth together: *We are trying to link up with other charities working in the area.* **2** (**with sth**) to make a connection with sth: *The two spacecraft will link up in orbit.*

♦ v + adv

,link sb/sth 'up (**to sth**) to connect sb/sth with sb/sth else: *The alarm is linked up to the police*

SYNONYMS

listen in (on sth)

bug sth ♦ **eavesdrop (on sb/sth)** ♦ **listen in (on sth)** ♦ **overhear sb/sth** ♦ **tap sth**

These verbs all mean to listen to a conversation in which you are not involved.

bug sth to put a special electronic listening device (= a bug) somewhere in order to listen secretly to sb's private conversations: *They bugged her hotel room.*

eavesdrop (on sb/sth) to listen secretly to what other people are saying; to listen secretly to electronic communications in order to collect information: *We caught him eavesdropping outside the window.* ◊ *Hackers eavesdropped on phone networks to steal data.*

listen in (on sth) to listen to a conversation that you are not supposed to hear, especially by means of electronics: *You shouldn't listen*

in on other people's conversations. ◊ *They did not know that the police were secretly listening in.*

overhear sb/sth to hear, especially by accident, a conversation in which you are not involved: *We talked quietly so as not to be overheard.* ◊ *I overheard a conversation between two boys on the bus.*

tap sth to fit a device to a telephone or telephone line so that sb's calls can be listened to secretly: *He was convinced his phone was being tapped.*

PATTERNS AND COLLOCATIONS

- to overhear/eavesdrop on/bug/listen in on a **conversation**
- to eavesdrop on **communications**
- to tap/bug sb's **telephone**

listen to sb/sth

catch sth ◆ **hear sb/sth** ◆ **listen to sb/sth** ◆ **pay attention (to sb/sth)**

These verbs all mean to be aware of the sound made by sb/sth, or to understand the meaning of sb's words.

catch sth to manage to hear or understand sth: *Sorry, I didn't quite catch what you said.* ◇ *Did you catch that programme on the radio?*

hear sb/sth (*not used in the progressive tenses*) to be aware of sounds with your ears: *Can you hear me?* ◇ *She heard footsteps behind her.*

listen to sb/sth to give your attention to the sound produced by sb/sth; to take notice of what sb says to you so that you follow their advice or believe them: *He enjoys listening to music.* ◇ *None of this would have happened if you'd listened to me.*

pay attention (to sb/sth) to listen to sb/sth carefully: *Can you all pay attention please?* ◇ *Don't pay any attention to what they say.*

WHICH WORD?

Hear usually describes what happens when a sound comes to your ears, whether you are giving the sound your attention or not. **Listen** means that you are deliberately trying to hear a sound. **Catch** is used especially in negative sentences to say that sb did not hear or understand sth.

PATTERNS AND COLLOCATIONS

■ to hear/listen to/catch a **radio programme**
■ to hear/listen to **music**
■ to hear/listen to/pay attention to **a conversation/advice/a warning**
■ to hear/listen to/pay attention to **sb's words/what sb says**

---

station. ◇ *The new network links us up to organizations around the country.*
◆ v + n/pron + adv ◆ v + adv + n
▶ **'link-up** *n* a connection between two systems, organizations or machines: *They did a live satellite link-up with the show.*

liquor /ˈlɪkə(r)/

be/get ˌliquored 'up (*AmE, informal*) to be/get drunk: *We got liquored up on Saturday night.*
◆ be/get + v + adv

listen /ˈlɪsn/

'listen for sb/sth; **ˌlisten 'out for sb/sth** to listen carefully to see if you can hear sb/sth: *She lay awake, listening out for the sound of the key in the lock.* ◇ *Will you listen for the phone while I'm in the bath?* ◇ *Farmers should listen out for flood warnings this weekend.*
OBJ **sound, knock, doorbell**
◆ v + prep ◆ v + adv + prep

ˌlisten 'in 1 (**on/to sth**) to listen to sth or sb secretly: *Have you been listening in on my phone calls?* ◇ *They were sure that the police were listening in to their conversations.* **2** (**to sth**) to listen to a radio programme, etc.: *Listen in on Friday for our interview with Britney.*
◆ v + adv

ˌlisten 'out, etc. → LISTEN FOR SB/STH, ETC.

'listen to sb/sth 1 to pay attention to sb/sth that you can hear: *I enjoy listening to music.* ◇ *Listen carefully to what I have to say.* **2** to take notice of what sb says to you so that you follow

their advice or believe them: *If you had listened to me, none of this would have happened.*
◆ v + prep

ˌlisten 'up (*especially AmE*) used to tell sb to pay attention to what you are going to say: *Listen up, everyone—this is important!*
◆ v + adv

live /lɪv/

'live by sth to follow a particular belief or set of principles: *Some people live by the rule 'anything for the sake of peace'.* ◇ *Women working in a man's world have to live by men's rules.*
OBJ **principles, standards, rules**
◆ v + prep

IDM **live by your 'wits** to earn money or survive by clever and sometimes dishonest means: *He had no job and was living by his wits.*

'live by sth; **'live by doing sth** to earn the money that you need by using or doing a particular thing: *people who live by the land* (= for example, farmers) ◇ *She lived by giving private lessons.*
◆ v + prep

ˌlive sth 'down to make people forget sth very embarrassing or bad that you have done in the past: *I can't believe I fell in the river—I'll never be able to* **live it down**.
NOTE Not used in the passive.
◆ v + n/pron + adv ◆ v + adv + n

'live for sb/sth to consider sb/sth as the main purpose of or the most important person or thing in your life: *She lives for her work.* ◇ *What have I got to live for now?*
◆ v + prep

liven

live 'in to live at the place where you work or study: *They have a nanny living in.* ◇ *(BrE) Most students live in during their first year.*
OPP live out
♦ v + adv
▶ '**live-in** *adj* [only before noun] **1** (of an employee) living in the house where they work: *a live-in housekeeper/position* **2** (of a boyfriend, girlfriend, etc.) living in the same house as their sexual partner: *a live-in lover/boyfriend*

'**live off sb/sth** (*disapproving*) to get the money or the things you need from sb/sth: *You can't live off your parents forever!* ◇ *He had to live off his savings.*
♦ v + prep

'**live off sth** to eat one type of food very frequently or all the time: *When I was a student I lived off bread and cheese.*
→ see also LIVE ON STH 2
♦ v + prep

IDM **live off the 'land** to eat food that you can grow, kill or find yourself: *The army was forced to live off the land.* ◇ *It's a farming area and most of the people still live off the land.* **live off the fat of the 'land** (*disapproving*) to have enough money to be able to buy expensive food, drink, clothes, etc.: *It was a time when landlords and merchants lived off the fat of the land.*

'**live 'on** to continue to live or exist: *He may be dead but his music lives on.*
♦ v + adv

'**live on sth** **1** to have a particular amount of money with which to buy everything you need: *How did you manage to live on a student grant?* ◇ *They don't earn enough to live on.* **2** to eat a particular type of food very frequently or all the time: *She was living on fruit and raw vegetables.* ◇ *birds that live on insects* → see also LIVE OFF STH
♦ v + prep

'**live 'out** (*BrE*) to live away from the place where you work or study: *I lived out during my final year at college.*
OPP live in
♦ v + adv

'**live 'out sth** **1** to do in reality sth that you think about, believe in, dream of, etc.: *On holiday in Texas I lived out my childhood fantasy of being a cowboy.* **OBJ** fantasy, dream **2** to spend your life or the rest of your life in a particular way: *She lived out the rest of her life in poverty.* ◇ *Maybe I'll live out my days in the peace of the mountains.* **OBJ** life, days
NOTE When the object of **live out** is a noun, it comes after **out**, but when the object is a pronoun, it comes between **live** and **out**: *I always dreamt of crossing the desert, and now I've lived it out.*
♦ v + adv + n ♦ v + pron + adv

'**live 'through sth** to experience sth difficult or unpleasant and survive: *He lived through both*

world wars. ◇ *It's something I never want to live through again.*
♦ v + prep

'**live together** (*also* '**live with sb**) **1** to live in the same house, flat/apartment, etc.: *There are six students living together in the house.* ◇ *I'm living in a flat with Meg.* **2** to share a home and have a sexual relationship, but without being married
♦ v + adv ♦ v + prep

'**live it 'up** (*informal*) to have a very exciting and enjoyable time, usually spending a lot of money: *I've heard that Tom's living it up in L.A.*
♦ v + it + adv

'**live 'up to sth** to behave as well as or be as good or successful as people expect: *The hotel failed to live up to expectations.* ◇ *Mr Mean lived up to his name.* ◇ *I've got a lot to live up to.*
OBJ expectations, name, reputation
↻ note at MEASURE UP
♦ v + adv + prep

'**live with sb** → LIVE TOGETHER

'**live with sth;** '**live with yourself** to accept an unpleasant situation and continue with your life and work: *You might not like the situation, but you'll have to learn to live with it.* ◇ *She wouldn't be able to live with herself if she hurt him.*
♦ v + prep

liven /'laɪvn/

'**liven 'up;** '**liven sb/sth 'up** to become or to make sb/sth more lively, interesting or exciting: *She livened up when Alan asked her to dance.* ◇ *Put some music on to liven things up.* ◇ *A few pictures would liven up the room.*
SYN brighten up; brighten sth up
♦ v + adv ♦ v + n/pron + adv ♦ v + adv + n

load /ləʊd; AmE loʊd/

'**load sb/sth 'down** (**with sth**) **1** to give sb/sth too many things to carry: *She was loaded down with books.* **2** to give sb/sth too much work or too many responsibilities: *We've been loaded down with work recently.*
NOTE Usually used in the passive.
♦ v + n/pron + adv ♦ v + adv + n

'**load 'up** (**with sth**), '**load sth 'up** (**with sth**) to put a lot of things in/on sth, especially a vehicle: *Bring the car to the door and we'll help you load up.* ◇ *I loaded up the van with all my possessions.* ◇ *We've loaded up all the furniture and are just about ready to go.*
NOTE Load and load sth are used more frequently on their own with this meaning.
♦ v + adv ♦ v + adv + n ♦ v + n/pron + adv

loaf /ləʊf; AmE loʊf/

'**loaf a'round;** '**loaf a'round sth** (*BrE also* '**loaf a'bout,** '**loaf a'bout sth**) (*informal*) to spend your time in a lazy way, doing very little: *kids*

Study pages

Recording phrasal verbs

Phrasal verbs usually have a meaning which is different from the normal meaning of the verb plus the normal meaning of the particle. For that reason it is advisable to learn phrasal verbs as units. You should record the verb, its meaning and a short example sentence to help you remember the context. You could also record a translation in your own language, but make sure that the context is the same.

Look at these examples of how to record phrasal verbs and complete them using the dictionary.

verb:	drop off
meaning:	to fall asleep, often when you don't intend to
example:	He usually drops off in front of the television.
translation:	

verb:	mess around
meaning:	
example:	
translation:	

The position of objects

If the verb has an object, it is useful to record the possible positions of the object. In this dictionary you will find this after the definitions and examples in every phrasal verb entry. (Look at page xi for more information.) You can record the information as it is given in the dictionary, or by putting examples in your notebook.

Look at these examples and complete them using the dictionary.

verb:	try sth out
grammar code:	v+n/pron+adv, v+adv+n
examples:	She tried out the new recipes/She tried the new recipes out/She tried them out.

verb:	head up sth
grammar code:	
examples:	

Collocations

Many phrasal verbs are frequently used with particular nouns as subjects or objects. It is a good idea to record these too. In the dictionary you will find them marked with SUBJ and OBJ.

Use your dictionary to add typical objects from the box.

> changes   a conversation   a form   information
> negotiations   a problem   a solution   a story

to find out	**information**	to phase in	
to play down		to break off	
to work out		to make up	
to fill in		to butt in on	

Organizing phrasal verbs

When you record the verbs there are ways of organizing them that may make them easier to remember.

Organizing by particles

The particles used in phrasal verbs often have particular meanings which can help you to understand the meaning of the whole verb. (These meanings are listed in the *Guide to the particles* on page 380.) You can record verbs under these meanings.

In this example, match the meanings with the phrasal verbs.

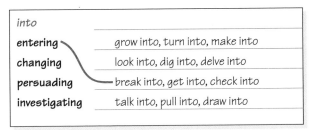

into	
entering	grow into, turn into, make into
changing	look into, dig into, delve into
persuading	break into, get into, check into
investigating	talk into, pull into, draw into

Organizing by topics

Sometimes it can help you to remember verbs if you record them in groups according to the topics they relate to. This is because these verbs often appear together in the same context.

In this example, match the topics with the phrasal verbs.

computers	*get carried away; fall out; get on with*
feelings	*take off; check in; touch down*
travel	*get away with; break into; track down*
crime	*log on; boot up; mouse over*

Organizing by opposites

You may find it easier to learn a word together with its opposite.
In this example, match each phrasal verb with its opposite.

pass out	*turn down*
go away	*switch off*
switch on	*come round*
bring forward	*get together*
turn up	*come back*
break up	*put back*

Organizing according to the verb

Sometimes phrasal verbs formed from the same verb will have meanings in common, which should make them easier to remember. For example, all of these phrasal verbs share the meaning of 'asking someone to go somewhere':

invite sb back
invite sb in
invite sb over/round
invite sb out
invite sb up

Key phrasal verbs

Some of the most frequently used vocabulary items in English are phrasal verbs. In this dictionary, these very frequent items are marked with a key symbol: ⚷. Often it is not possible to replace these with a single-word equivalent (for example, **find out** is not the same as **discover**). It is therefore essential to learn the most frequently used phrasal verbs if you want to understand and speak English well. These exercises will help you to use the most common ones more confidently.

Particles

These exercises are organized according to the meaning of the particle. See the *Guide to the particles* on page 380.

1 Up

Match the sentence beginnings on the left with the endings on the right.

increasing or improving

1 Many people   a grow up so fast and soon leave home.
2 Students   b bring up their children to be well-mannered.
3 Peter,   c cheer up when their university exams are over.
4 Children   d hurry up or we'll miss the train.

completing or finishing

1 Add up   a the phone – you've been talking for ages.
2 Hang up   b early if you want to get to work on time.
3 Give up   c your expenses and give them to my secretary.
4 Wake up   d chocolate if you want to get fit.

2 On

Match the sentence beginnings on the left with the endings on the right.

Continuing

1 The professor   a went on for months until we solved it.
2 The customer   b keeps on talking to me and interrupting my work.
3 My boss   c carried on talking even though the seminar had finished.
4 The problem   d held on for several minutes then put the phone down.

3   Down

Put the correct verb from the box into the gaps below. You may have
to change the form of the verb.

> turn   close   break   let

failing

1   When your car ___breaks___ down, it no longer works.

2   If somebody _____ you down, you feel disappointed with them.

3   If you are _____ down for a job, you are not accepted.

4   The company was forced to _____ down.

> bend   keep   lie   put   sit

movement

1   Every day, at eight, we all _____ down to have dinner together.

2   If you don't want him to see you, you'd better _____ your head down.

3   That bag looks heavy! You can _____ it down over there.

4   The coach made us _____ down and touch our toes. It was quite
difficult.

5   I'm so tired – I'm going to _____ down on the bed. Wake me up if
I fall asleep.

4   In

Put the correct phrasal verb from the box into the gaps below. You may
have to change the form of the verb.

> break in   check in   come in   let in

Entering or arriving

1   When you _____ somewhere you enter a place, often somewhere
familiar such as your home, or when a friend invites you to their house.

2   When you _____ , you register at a hotel or an airport desk.

3   When you _____ somebody _____ , you open the door and
allow them to come in.

4   If someone _____ , they enter a building illegally.

5 Off

Match the sentence beginnings on the left with the endings on the right.

Departing

1 Get off
2 Go off
3 Run off
4 Set off

a early so you miss the traffic on the motorway.
b the bus at the next stop if you want the city centre.
c on holiday by yourself if you really want to relax.
d and play in the garden – you need some fresh air.

6 Out

Put the correct verb from the box into the gaps below. You may have to change the form of the verb.

Leaving

> break   come   fall   get

1 Some medical treatments can make your hair _____ out.

2 As I was _____ out of the car, I fell over.

3 Several prisoners have _____ out of jail.

4 As we _____ out of the hotel we saw the beach right in front of us.

7 Verbs with an adverb and a preposition

Put the correct verb from the box into the gaps below. You may have to change the form of the verb.

> look forward to   get on with   hang on to   run out of   put up with

1 You should _____ your baggage at the airport in case it gets stolen.

2 I've been really _____ meeting your family.

3 Oh no, we've _____ milk again – will you go to the shop and get some?

4 I don't know how you _____ his temper – you must be very patient.

5 I _____ my father very well – we always have a laugh together.

Phrasal verb or single word?

Phrasal verbs are very common in everyday language. A single word which means the same is often more formal. Look at this description of an excursion from a printed brochure:

DAY 4: Temple Tour

The coach will <u>depart</u> at 09.00. Leaving the city, it will <u>ascend</u> the mountain passes to <u>reach</u> the temple at 10.30. A local guide will conduct the tour and will answer any questions that <u>arise</u>. Visitors will not be <u>admitted</u> unless they are wearing suitable clothing, and will be expected to <u>remove</u> their shoes before <u>entering</u> the temple. The group will return via the 'Lost Valley', where lunch will be <u>provided</u> for those who have <u>requested</u> it.

Now look at this letter, which Penny wrote to her friend when she got back from her holiday. In this letter the words that are underlined in the brochure text would be too formal. Use a form of one of each of the phrasal verbs in the box to fill the gaps in her letter.

ask for	come back	come up	get to		go in	go up
lay on	let in		set off	show round	take off

For me, the highlight of the whole holiday was the trip to the temple. We ¹ _set off_ at nine in the morning and were soon ² _____ _____ some hair-raisingly steep roads. We ³ _____ _____ the temple about half ten. We had to wear long-sleeved tops and long trousers or they wouldn't have ⁴ _____ us _____ . Of course, we had to ⁵ _____ our shoes _____ before we ⁶ _____ _____ the temple, too. A local guide ⁷ _____ us _____ , which was good, because lots of questions ⁸ _____ _____ about the history of the place. The temple itself was absolutely breathtaking, but that wasn't the best thing, because we ⁹ _____ _____ through what they call the 'Lost Valley'. Lunch was ¹⁰ _____ _____ for the people who'd ¹¹ _____ _____ it, but we'd taken a packed lunch with us, and we agreed that it was the most spectacular picnic spot we'd ever seen!

Opposites

The following verbs are organized into pairs with their opposites.
Match the phrase on the right with the phrase on the left.

1 If we set off early,   a and put a T-shirt on.
2 I decided to carry on with tennis   b Get up and do something.
3 I put my bag down here.   c we'll get back before dark.
4 You've been lying down all day.   d Did you pick it up by mistake?
5 Take your jumper off   e and give up volleyball.

Multi-meaning verbs

The following verbs have more than one meaning. Complete the
pairs of sentences with one of the verbs listed below.

catch up	give up	meet up	pick up	take off	come out	fall out

1 If you want to _catch up_ you will have to run.

   You will have to work hard to _catch up_ with the other students.

2 That shampoo made my hair _____ in handfuls.

   I hate to have arguments and _____ with my friends.

3 My little daughter always _____ her clothes by herself.

   When the plane _____ we will be able to see the fields below.

4 I'm going to _____ smoking in the New Year.

   I don't think the rebels will _____ their fight easily.

5 If she waits by the station, I'll _____ her _____ in my car.

   The cat was so light , I could _____ it _____ with one hand.

6 The mark on my skirt wouldn't _____ even when I washed it.

   We know that the stars _____ at night but we can't always see them.

7 Do you want to _____ for dinner after work?

   I'm so surprised to _____ with you here – I haven't seen you for ages.

Formal and informal in the dictionary

Phrasal verbs are especially common in informal language, but it is important to know whether a phrasal verb is informal or not to be able to use it appropriately.

Look at the dictionary entry below and notice how information on the formality of the phrasal verb is given:

> **bust** /bʌst/ (**bust, bust** or **busted, busted**)
> **NOTE** Bust is an informal way of saying **break**.
> ˌbust ˈout; ˌbust ˈout of sth; ˌbust sb ˈout;
> ˌbust sb ˈout of sth (*informal*) to escape from
> somewhere, usually prison; to help sb do this:
> *His last movie was about a guy busting out of
> Alcatraz.* ◇ *His friends busted him out of jail.*
> **SYN** break out, break out of sth (*more formal*)

Look up the following phrasal verbs in your dictionary and complete the table.

formal	*informal*	*neutral*
	boot sb out	

a   boot sb out
b   provide for sth
c   turn up
d   barge into sb
e   throw sth aside
f   put sb up
g   bounce around
h   attend to sb/sth
i   dispense with sb/sth
j   hash sth over
k   safeguard against sth
l   fade away

Phrasal verbs in informal language

Replace all the words *in italics* with one phrasal verb from the box, remembering to change the verb into the correct form.

freak out	cotton on	chicken out	level with	throw together
check out	rustle up	crack up	whip through	clam up

1 OK, I'll *level with you*
~~tell you the situation in an honest way~~. I'm afraid we're not able to accept your proposals at this time.

2 Greg was all ready to do the bungee jump, but at the last moment he *decided not to do it because he was afraid*.

3 We're going to visit the new bar in town to *see if it's any good*. Would you like to come?

4 Dinner? I haven't had time to go the shops, but I guess I'll be able to *provide something quickly and without planning*.

5 Our class was really behind the others, so we *did* the last three chapters *very quickly*.

6 I don't like watching horror movies – they *make me feel really shocked and scared*.

7 He's usually pretty quick, but it took him ages to *understand what I meant without being told directly*.

8 As soon as I asked her about her family, she just *refused to speak because she didn't want to talk about it*.

9 I think Dave's great – he really *makes me laugh a lot*.

10 I don't think much of this book. It looks like they've just *made it quickly or carelessly*.

Phrasal verbs in emails

Emails are often written in informal language. Read the following email from Helen to her friend Katy. Underline all the phrasal verbs that you can find.

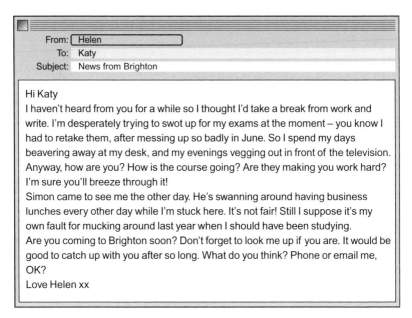

From: Helen
To: Katy
Subject: News from Brighton

Hi Katy
I haven't heard from you for a while so I thought I'd take a break from work and write. I'm desperately trying to swot up for my exams at the moment – you know I had to retake them, after messing up so badly in June. So I spend my days beavering away at my desk, and my evenings vegging out in front of the television. Anyway, how are you? How is the course going? Are they making you work hard? I'm sure you'll breeze through it!
Simon came to see me the other day. He's swanning around having business lunches every other day while I'm stuck here. It's not fair! Still I suppose it's my own fault for mucking around last year when I should have been studying.
Are you coming to Brighton soon? Don't forget to look me up if you are. It would be good to catch up with you after so long. What do you think? Phone or email me, OK?
Love Helen xx

Now write one of the phrasal verbs from the email next to its definitions below.

1 work very hard (at sth) _____

2 study very hard, especially when you are preparing for an exam _swot up_

3 go from one place to another feeling pleased with yourself _____

4 do sth very badly _____

5 visit or contact sb when you are in the place where they live _____

6 find out about things that have happened to somebody _____

7 behave in a silly way, especially when you should be doing sth else _____

8 succeed in sth very easily _____

9 relax in a lazy way and do very little _____

Phrasal verbs in formal language

Not all of the phrasal verbs in this section are marked 'formal' in the Dictionary, but they can all be used in formal language, such as essays and reports.

Phrasal verbs in essays

These phrasal verbs are often used in essays. Match the beginnings of the sentences with their endings.

1	These figures refer to	the main points we have examined.
2	The rise can be attributed to	changes in living standards.
3	It should be pointed out	the conclusion reached by others.
4	I shall now sum up	why this happened?
5	I shall deal with	each point individually.
6	How can we account for	the years 1960 to 1989.
7	The statistics do not bear out	that no action was ever taken.

Phrasal verbs in business

In the sentences below, choose the best verb to fill the gap.

1 This document _____ the brochures you were sent earlier this week.
   a consists of   **b** refers to   **c** accounts for

2 It is important to _____ that our prices have been reduced.
   a set out   **b** sum up   **c** point out

3 The director would like you to _____ the list carefully and check the figures.
   a go through   **b** draw up   **c** deal with

4 The secretary reported that the papers had been _____ in the wrong order.
   a filed away   **b** accounted for   **c** put forward

5 It is useful to _____ all the important points in a presentation.
   a draw up   **b** write down   **c** edit out

6 It is essential to _____ the main points discussed in your report.
   a put forward   **b** file away   **c** sum up

7 This afternoon the MD will _____ on our success in the new markets.
   a sum up   **b** write down   **c** report back

8 The presentation will _____ the issue of customer complaints.
   a deal with   **b** account for   **c** point out

Phrasal verbs in reports

Read the following extract from a report and replace the underlined words with the phrasal verbs listed below.

> consists of   gone through   summed up   deals with
> puts forward   drawn up   refers to   sets out
> enlarges upon   reported back   accounts for

This report *concerns* [1]_____ the delivery services we wish to expand for our clients. Our market research company has already *given the information* [2]_____ to the marketing department on their recent research. The main points of this information will be *given* [3]_____ in a series of short reports for the committee to examine in their own time.

The marketing department has now *made* [4]_____ a plan of action for increasing our delivery service. The Managing Director has *examined* [5]_____ this carefully and given it his approval. Essentially it *presents* [6]_____ three suggestions for discussion and *explains* [7]_____ the reasons why we should consider a slow rather than a rapid expansion.

This report summarizes those reasons and *is in* [8]_____ three parts:

(a) it *gives more details about* [9]_____ the difficulties we have had with recruiting staff,

(b) it *explains* [10]_____ why our delivery service had problems last month,

(c) it *briefly discusses* [11]_____ the problems caused by rising inflation.

Computers

Have you noticed how many phrasal verbs are used in computing? Try this crossword to see how many you know. Use the dictionary to help you if you need to. Use a verb from the top box and a particle from the lower box to complete each sentence. The answer can be a verb, an adjective or a noun. The solid lines in the crossword show the divisions between words.

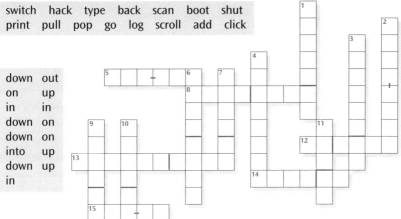

switch hack type back scan boot shut
print pull pop go log scroll add click

down out
on up
in in
down on
down on
into up
down up
in

Down

1 _____ the link below to visit our website.

2 Select 'options' from the _____ menu.

3 The printer didn't work because I'd forgotten to_____ it_____ !

4 I stuck a_____ of the email on the wall.

6 Close all programs before you _____ your computer.

7 You can_____ your photos and email them to friends.

9 _____ vital documents on floppy disk to avoid losing them.

10 The computer sometimes takes ages to_____ when I turn it on.

11 You'll need a password to_____

Across

5 You can download various _____ that allow your existing software to do even more things.

8 A teenager managed to _____ the bank's main database.

12 I hope the computer doesn't _____ again or I'll never finish this work.

13 _____ the page until you find the item you want.

14 _____ your password and press 'enter'.

15 If you click on the right mouse button a_____ menu will appear.

The environment

Use your environmental knowledge and your dictionary to help you do this exercise. Match the beginnings and endings of the sentences, then write the sentences in a logical order under the appropriate heading.

The algae use up	heat that should escape into space.
Humans burn or cut down	the nitrates and multiply uncontrollably.
This pushes up	too many trees.
Some species die out	when fossil fuels are burned.
Algae feed on	desert.
Greenhouse gases are given off	the soil and end up in rivers and lakes.
Nitrates from fertilizers soak into	the oxygen in the water, and fish die.
Some areas turn into	because they have lost their habitat.
These greenhouse gases soak up	temperatures on earth.

The greenhouse effect

1   Greenhouse gases are given off when fossil fuels are burned.

2

3

Algae

1

2

3

Deforestation

1

2

3

Business

The story of a company

Here is the history of Hall Motors. Use the dictionary to help you fill in the missing particles and follow the rise and fall of this company.

1888 Frank Hall designs and builds the 'Hall safety cycle' in his back yard. The design really catches ___*on*___ and Hall soon has to take _____ five workers to help him produce bicycles.

1902 Hall, who now has a workforce of 50, teams _____ with his cousin Jack, a motor mechanic, and they build their first car. They set _____ 'Hall Motors' and sell _____ the bicycle side of the business.

1906 Hall Motors is the country's second biggest car manufacturer, turning _____ 20 cars a week.

1945 Frank Hall dies and his son Bill takes _____ the company.

1960 Hall Motors revolutionizes the design of the small car with the 'Townie'. Sales take _____ immediately, bringing _____ record profits.

1969 The company buys _____ its main rivals, Wallace Cars and Ryder-Pratt.

1974 Workers at the Leeds plant walk _____ in protest at the latest pay offer, sparking _____ several years of management-union unrest.

1989 Hall Motors' market share has been gradually worn _____ by cheaper foreign imports. With sales falling _____ as quickly as debts mount _____ , the company seems set to go _____ , but is bailed _____ by a last-minute government loan.

1999 As sales continue to decline, Europe Motors takes _____ the company, announcing that its aim is to break even within two years. After investing heavily in new models, Europe Motors is caught _____ as the value of the pound shoots _____ , causing exports to plunge. The decision is taken to wind _____ Hall Motors.

2000 6000 workers are laid _____ as the last remaining Hall Motors plant closes _____ .

Sport

Here are three extracts from a sports news programme on the radio. Complete the extracts with phrasal verbs, using either a verb from the box on the left or a particle from the box on the right in each gap. You will need to change the form of the verb in some cases. Use your dictionary to help you if you need to.

bring	Football, and tonight's match in the European Cup ended in	away
end	controversy after Italy *came* _____ from 2–0 down to beat	back
play	Spain. At 2–2, the Italian goalkeeper Alberti appeared to	for
rule	_____ *down* Rojas, the Spanish centre forward. As the	off
send	Spanish players *appealed* _____ a penalty, the Italians	up
	_____ *on* and *broke* _____ to score. The Spanish	
	captain Martín was then _____ _____ for arguing with	
	the referee. Italy _____ *up* fortunate winners, but their	
	goalkeeper *picked* _____ a hand injury and has been	
	_____ *out* of the next two games.	

catch	The Tokyo marathon has been won by Takeshi Saito of Japan.	ahead
drop	_____ *on* by the home crowd, Saito *forged* _____ after	back
hold	just 5 kilometres and built up a 2-minute lead. The chasing	off
urge	runners did not *give* _____ , and gradually reduced the lead.	up
	The hot weather and the fast pace caused several leading	
	athletes to _____ *out*. Saito's recent training in the Sahara	
	desert *paid* _____ as he _____ *off* the strong challenge	
	of the Kenyan Daniel Nyanga, who _____ *up* with 5	
	kilometres to go, then *fell* _____ in the final kilometre.	

go	Tennis, and the unseeded Sofia Adamou of Greece has beaten	against
hold	Russia's Irena Markova in three sets to _____ _____ to	through
knock	the final of the French Open. Adamou said afterwards, "I've	up
pick	never _____ *up* _____ such a tough opponent. Before I	
settle	came here I thought I'd get _____ *out* in the first round, but	
take	now I've got a chance of winning." Adamou, who only _____	
come	_____ the sport four years ago, will _____ *up* a cheque	
	for $100 000. The loser will have to _____ *for* just $50 000!	

Where do new phrasal verbs come from?

New phrasal verbs turn up all the time, but where do they come from? One answer is that new verbs are invented to talk about new types of activity. But in fact they are not usually completely new verbs, but new combinations of existing verbs and particles, or old ones which have found new uses.

1 New verbs from nouns or adjectives.

New phrasal verbs don't have to come from verbs. Nouns and adjectives, too, can be used. So, from the noun **luck** comes the phrasal verb **luck out**, meaning 'to be very lucky'. Sometimes a short form of the noun or adjective is used to form the phrasal verb, for example **max out**, from **maximum**.

Complete these sentences with phrasal verbs derived from the nouns and adjectives in the box.

| flag | glamorous | ice | mouse | tear |

1 The problem of the river drying up has only recently been _____ *up*.

2 Don't forget to _____ *down* the champagne for the party.

3 Lola has had to _____ herself *up* for her television appearance.

4 Bradley began to _____ *up* as he thought of his children.

5 When you _____ *over* this button, it plays a sound.

2 Modern life

New phrasal verbs (or new meanings of existing phrasal verbs) are often brought in to talk about new inventions, new concepts, etc. that have developed or become current in the modern world. In many cases these phrasal verbs have nouns or adjectives derived from them, such as **drop-down** (as in *a drop-down menu*) from **drop down**.

Put these phrasal verbs or derivatives into columns according to the area of modern life they are connected with.

| armoured-up | click through | dial-up | roll sth out | stand sb/sth down |
| charge sth up | crossover | lay sth down | spin-out | top-up |

Internet	telecoms	business	music	military
_____	_____	_____	_____	_____
_____	_____	_____	_____	_____

3   Figurative meanings

Plough back originally meant 'to return a crop that you have grown to the soil, in order to produce more'. It is easy to see how this can change to being used about reinvesting profits in a business.

In this exercise, replace the words in italics with a phrasal verb from the box. You may have to change the form of the phrasal verb.

| button up | chew up | give away | haul in | land on | lock in |

1   The fashion industry has *destroyed the careers of* so many young models. _____

2   Norway *won* a clutch of medals at the Winter Olympics. _____

3   When I asked him about his past, he just *refused to say anything*. _____

4   Her boss *criticized* her for her poor performance over the past year. _____

5   Germany was in good form and Mexico *lost* the game with sloppy play. _____

6   How can we *make permanent* all the improvements we've made to our procedures? _____

4   New particles

New phrasal verbs can be created by taking an existing phrasal verb and using it with a different particle to express a meaning which is the opposite of or different from the original meaning. For example, **dress down** (wear more casual clothes) can be easily understood to be the opposite of **dress up** (wear more formal clothes). New particles can also be added to verbs which are not normally used with particles, sometimes keeping the same meaning and sometimes acquiring a different meaning.

Say whether these pairs of verbs are similar or opposite in meaning.

1   beat sb down, beat sb up *similar*

2   print sth off, print sth up _____

3   flash forward, flash back _____

4   head sth, head sth up _____

5   ratchet sth up, ratchet sth down _____

6   slow up, slow down _____

7   hire sb, hire sb on _____

8   ramp up, ramp down _____

9   gobble sth up, gobble sth down _____

10   bomb, bomb out _____

Synonyms

Look up the verb in column **A** and match it with the verb in column **B** that is closest to it in meaning. You will find synonyms given in the dictionary after the symbol **SYN**.

A	**B**
invite sb out	mull sth over
fork out	cut sth back
egg sb on	shell out
think sth over	ask sb out
cheer sth up	urge sb on
pare sth down	liven sth up
knock sb down	run sb over

Opposites

Look up the verb in column **A** and match it with the verb in column **B** that is opposite in meaning. You will find opposites given in the dictionary after the symbol **OPP**.

A	**B**
breathe in	disconnect sth
connect sth	hold sth in
do sth up	let sth down
go out	put sth together
let sth out	stay in
take sth apart	undo sth
blow sth up (tyre)	breathe out

Rewrite these sentences so that the meaning is the opposite of the original.

1 I plugged the DVD player in. _I unplugged the DVD player._

2 The price of coffee has come down again. _____

3 The scandal blew up after the report came out. _____

4 I checked into the clinic yesterday. _____

5 I need to let out this skirt a little. _____

6 She buttoned up her jacket. _____

Synonym notes

Synonym notes in this dictionary compare phrasal verbs and single-word verbs which have a similar meaning, helping you to choose the right word. You can find them printed on a blue background throughout the dictionary.

Pull through

Look at the note at *pull through* and choose the best word or phrase to complete these sentences.

1 That cut has _____ very quickly.

2 _____ soon!

3 It took a long time to _____ from his illness.

4 Despite being gravely ill, she _____ and made a good recovery.

5 Tamara is gradually _____ .

Look up to sb

Look at the note at *look up to sb* and choose the best word or phrase to complete these sentences.

1 I completely disagree with you, but I _____ your opinion.

2 She is widely _____ in the field of child psychology.

3 When I was young I _____ my elder brother.

4 Fiona's teachers _____ her.

Choosing the best word

In these sentences the words *in italics* are not used correctly. Look at the synonym note for the phrasal verb in italics and choose a more appropriate one. In some cases more than one alternative is possible.

1 My olive tree has *grown up* a lot since last year. ____*grown*____

2 I *got off* the car and started to walk. _____

3 I'll *call* you *up* as soon as I arrive in Inverness. _____

4 Support for these proposals has *died down*. _____

5 What time do you *give up* work? _____

6 I'm sorry, I didn't *listen to* your name. _____

7 I *looked at* a film, then went to bed. _____

8 I *mixed up* the cards then dealt seven to each player. _____

loafing about with nothing to do ◇ *She just loafs around the streets all day.*
SYN **lie around, lie around sth**
♦ v + adv ♦ v + prep

loan /ləʊn; *AmE* loʊn/

,**loan sth/sb 'out** (**to sb**) to lend sth/sb to sb, sometimes in return for money: *Several players have been loaned out to other teams.* ◇ *Sometimes we loan out these buses.*
♦ v + adv + n ♦ v + n/pron + adv

lock /lɒk; *AmE* lɑːk/

,**lock sb a'way** → LOCK SB UP/AWAY

,**lock sth a'way** → LOCK STH UP 1

,**lock yourself a'way** to shut yourself in a place away from other people so that you are not disturbed: *He locked himself away (in his room) until he'd finished his work.*
SYN **shut yourself away** (**from sb/sth**)
→ see also LOCK SB UP/AWAY
♦ v + pron + adv

,**lock sth 'down** (*AmE*) (of the police, etc.) to strictly control who goes in and out of a particular building, area, city, etc. during an emergency: *It would take more officers than we have to lock down the whole city.*
♦ v + n/pron + adv ♦ v + adv + n
▶ '**lockdown** *n* [C, U] (*AmE*): *The school was under lockdown for two hours after the shooting incident.*

,**lock sb/sth 'in**; ,**lock yourself 'in** to put sb/sth/yourself in a room or building and lock the door: *The prisoners are locked in every night.* ◇ *He rushed to his bedroom and locked himself in.*
♦ v + n/pron + adv ♦ v + adv + n
▶ '**lock-in** *n* (*BrE*) an occasion when customers are locked into a bar or pub after it has closed so that they can continue drinking privately

,**lock sth 'in** to carry out measures to ensure that improvements in a system are permanent: *Formal treaties help lock in the benefits of arms control.*
♦ v + adv + n ♦ v + n/pron + adv

be '**locked in sth** to be involved in a difficult or unpleasant situation, especially an argument or a legal battle, that seems unlikely to end soon: *The parents are locked in a bitter legal battle over the future of the twins.*
♦ be + v + prep

,**lock 'in on sth** → LOCK ONTO STH

be ,**locked 'into sth** (*also* **become/get** ,**locked 'into sth**) to be in a particular situation, or behave in a particular way, that you cannot change: *The government is locked into a policy of reducing taxes.* ◇ *Older horses can get locked into bad habits.*
♦ be + v + prep

,**lock 'onto sth** (*also* ,**lock 'in on sth**) if a weapon that is sent through the air **locks onto** sth or **is locked onto** sth that it is aimed at, it finds it and follows it: *The missile can lock onto a target from a kilometre away.* ◇ *The missile was locked onto the target.* **SUBJ** **missile** **OBJ** **target**
♦ v + prep ♦ v + adv + prep

,**lock sb/sth 'out 1** (*also* ,**lock sb/sth 'out of sth**) to prevent sb/sth from entering a place by locking a door: *I arrived home to find the landlady had locked me out.* **2** to prevent workers from entering their place of work until they agree to the conditions given by the employer: *The management will lock out anyone who refuses to sign the new contract.*
♦ v + n/pron + adv
♦ v + adv + n **1** also v + n/pron + adv + prep
▶ '**lockout** *n* a situation when an employer refuses to let workers enter their place of work until they agree to particular conditions: *The strikers faced a lockout.*

,**lock yourself 'out**; ,**lock yourself 'out of sth** to accidentally leave your keys inside a car, building, etc. when you go out, so that you are unable to get inside again: *I've managed to lock myself out of my room three times!*
♦ v + pron + adv ♦ v + pron + adv + prep

,**lock 'up** to stop working correctly: *My brakes had locked up.* ◇ *The computer locks up when I try to load the program.*
♦ v + adv
▶ '**lock-up** *n*: *This computer game has a history of technical problems, including lock-ups.*

,**lock 'up**; ,**lock sth 'up** to make a building safe by locking the doors and windows: *Make sure you lock up before you leave.* ◇ *She locked the shop up and went home.*
♦ v + adv ♦ v + n/pron + adv ♦ v + adv + n
▶ '**lock-up** *n* (*BrE*) a small shop/store that the owner does not live in; a place that the owner does not need and rents to sb else, for example to keep a car in: *a lock-up garage/shop*

,**lock sb 'up/a'way** (*informal*) to put sb in prison or in a guarded hospital: *People like that should be locked up!* ◇ *They should lock her up and throw away the key.* ◇ *He was locked away for the rest of his life.*
♦ v + n/pron + adv ♦ v + adv + n
▶ '**lock-up** *n* a small prison where prisoners are kept for a short time

,**lock sth 'up 1** (*also* ,**lock sth a'way**) to put sth valuable in a safe place and lock it: *Lock your valuables up in the safe.* ◇ *She locked the money away in a cupboard.* **2** (**in sth**) to invest money in sth and not be able to turn it into cash to spend: *Huge sums of money are locked up in pension funds.* **OBJ** **capital, money** **SYN** **tie sth up** **NOTE** Usually used in the passive. **3** (*also* **have sth ,locked 'up**) (*especially AmE*) to be sure that you will win sth or achieve a goal you have been

log

aiming for: *The Senator knew he had the nomination locked up.*
- v + n/pron + adv ◆ v + adv + n

▶ **'lock-up** *n* (*finance*) an agreement not to sell or exchange shares for a particular period of time: *The shares will be subject to a lock-up for 180 days.*

▶ **'lock-up** *adj* [only before noun] (*finance*): *A lock-up agreement prevented the shares from being sold for six months.*

log /lɒɡ; *AmE* lɔːɡ, lɑːɡ/ (-gg-)

log 'in/'on; **log 'into/'onto sth** (*computing*) to perform the actions that allow you to begin using a computer system: *I got an error message when I tried to log in/on.* ◇ *The password allows the user to log onto the system.*
[OBJ] **system, network, computer** [OPP] **log off/out; log off/out of sth**
[NOTE] **Log into/onto sth** can be used in the pattern **be logged into/onto sth**: *I was logged onto the Internet.*
- v + adv ◆ v + prep

log sb 'in/'on to allow sb to begin using a computer system: *The system is unable to log you on.*
[OPP] **log sb off/out**
- v + n/pron + adv ◆ v + adv + n

log 'off/'out; **log 'off/'out of sth** (*computing*) to perform the actions that allow you to finish using a computer system: *Try logging off and logging on again.*
[OBJ] **system, computer** [OPP] **log in/on; log into/onto sth**
[NOTE] **Log off/out of sth** can be used in the pattern **be logged off/out of sth**: *Wait until all the users are logged off.*
- v + adv ◆ v + prep

log sb 'off/'out to cause sb to finish using a computer system: *The system will automatically log you off after 30 minutes.*
[OPP] **log sb in/on**
- v + n/pron + adv ◆ v + adv + n

loll /lɒl/

loll a'round; **loll a'round sth** (*BrE also* **loll a'bout, loll a'bout sth**) to sit, lie or stand in a relaxed way, doing very little: *There were several kids lolling around outside the club.* ◇ *Jim should get a job instead of lolling around the house all day.*
[SYN] **lie around, lie around sth**; **loaf around, loaf around sth**
- v + adv ◆ v + prep

long /lɒŋ; *AmE* lɔːŋ/

'long for sb/sth; **'long for sb to do sth** to want sb/sth very much: *to long for a baby* ◇ *I was longing for a chat and a good laugh.*

◇ *She found herself longing for her visitors to leave.*
- v + prep ◆ v + prep + n/pron + **to**+inf

▶ **'longed-for** *adj* [only before noun] that sb has been wanting or hoping for very much: *a longed-for child*

look /lʊk/

look a'bout, etc. (*BrE*) → LOOK AROUND, ETC.

look a'cross/'over (**at/to sb/sth**) to look quickly across a room: *I looked across to where they were sitting.* ◇ *She knew I was there, but they didn't look over at me.*
- v + adv

look 'after sb/sth/yourself (*especially BrE*)
1 to make sure that sb/sth is safe; take care of sb/sth: *His parents are looking after the children for the weekend.* ◇ *She doesn't look after her clothes.* ◇ *Sophie will look after the visitors.* ◇ *They're old enough to look after themselves now* (= they don't need any help). ◇ *Would you mind looking after my bag for a minute?* ◇ *He needs to be properly looked after.* ◇ *See you soon—look after yourself* (= when saying goodbye to sb). [NOTE] **Take care of sb** is used in both British and American English with the same meaning: *My mother is going to look after/take care of the kids while we're away.* → see also BRING SB UP 1; ➔ note at CARE FOR SB **2** to make sure that things happen to sb's advantage: *He's good at looking after his own interests.*

look 'after sth (*BrE*) to deal with sth; to be responsible for sth: *Their accountant looks after the financial side of things.* ◇ *Everything's being looked after.*
[SYN] **attend to sth** (*more formal*)
[NOTE] **Take care of sth** is used in both British and American English with the same meaning.
- v + prep

look a'head (**to sth**) to think about what is going to happen in the future: *The team is looking ahead to next season.* ◇ *Looking ahead to the weekend, the weather will stay fine.*
- v + adv

look a'round (*BrE also* **look 'round**) **1** (**at sb/sth**) to turn your head in order to see sb/sth behind you: *The people in front kept looking round at us.* ◇ *He looked round to see if I was still there.* **2** (**for sb/sth**) to examine various choices or possibilities: *We're looking around for a new car.* ➔ note at LOOK FOR SB/STH
- v + adv

look a'round; **look a'round sth** (*BrE also* **look 'round, look 'round sth**) to visit a place or a building as a tourist or because you are interested in buying it, etc.: *Take your time looking around.* ◇ *They've gone to look round the* cathedral. ◇ I spent the day looking around the town.

♦ v + adv ♦ v + prep

ˌlook aˈround; ˌlook aˈround sth; ˌlook aˈround you (BrE also ˌlook aˈbout/ˈround, ˌlook aˈbout/ˈround sth, ˌlook aˈbout/ˈround you) to turn your head in different directions so that you can see sth or see what is there: She came into the room, looked around, then went out again. ◇ He looked round the classroom angrily. ◇ I looked about me at the other passengers on the plane.

♦ v + adv ♦ v + prep

ˈlook at sb/sth 1 to turn your eyes towards sb/ sth so that you can see them/it: Don't look at me like that! ◇ What are you looking at? 2 to examine sth/sb closely: I'd like the doctor to look at him. ◇ Can you look at this watch for me? I think it might be broken. ◇ I took the car to the garage to get it looked at. 3 (usually used in negative sentences or questions) to consider or be prepared to accept sb/sth: They wouldn't even look at someone wanting part-time work. 4 used to draw sb's attention to sb/sth, often as an example that you want them to follow or not follow: I wouldn't take advice from her—just look at the mess she's made of her own life! ◇ He left school without any qualifications, but look at him now! (= he is very successful now) ◇ Money doesn't always bring happiness—just look at Frank (= he is rich but not happy).

♦ v + prep

ˈlook at sth 1 to read sth, usually quickly, without reading all the details: She sat in the waiting room, looking at a magazine. ◇ Don't hand the form in until it's been looked at by a teacher. 2 to think about or study sth: Have you looked at the possibility of adopting a child? ◇ The film looks at the events leading up to the war. ◇ Four possible routes were looked at for the new road. 3 to consider sth in a particular way: If you look at it like that, it's a good thing we didn't go. 4 be ˈlooking at sth (informal) (always used in the progressive tenses) to have to consider or deal with sth; to be faced with sth: You're looking at £600 to get the car fixed. ◇ If he's found guilty he's looking at a six-year prison sentence.

♦ v + prep

ˌlook aˈway (from sb/sth) to look in the opposite direction; to turn your eyes away from sb/sth: She looked at him then looked away. ◇ He mumbled a reply and looked away from me.

♦ v + adv

ˌlook ˈback (at/on/to sth) to think about sth that has happened in your past: Looking back, I'm not surprised she left. ◇ He looked back on his time in England with a sense of nostalgia.

♦ v + adv

IDM never/not look ˈback (informal) to become more and more successful: He started work on a market stall in 1970 and he's never looked back.

ˌlook ˈdown (at sb/sth) to turn your eyes downwards to the floor, especially because

look at sb/sth

check sb/sth out ♦ look at sb/sth ♦ observe sb/sth ♦ view sth ♦ watch sb/sth

These verbs all mean to turn your eyes in a particular direction in order to see sth.

check sb/sth out (informal) to look at or examine sb/sth that seems interesting or attractive: Check out the prices at our new store!

look at sb/sth to turn your eyes in a particular direction towards sb/sth: She looked at me and smiled.

observe sb/sth (not used in the progressive tenses) (formal) to watch sb/sth carefully, especially to learn more about them: I felt he was observing everything I did. ◇ The patients were observed over a period of several months.

view sth (formal) to look at sth, especially when you look carefully; to watch television, a film/movie, etc.: The eclipse should only be viewed through a special lens. ◇ It's an opportunity to view the movie before it comes out.

watch sb/sth to look at sb/sth for a time, paying attention to what happens: I only let my kids watch television at the weekends. ◇ A capacity crowd watched the semi-final match.

WHICH WORD?

All of these verbs imply a deliberate action, unlike see. However, you can talk about seeing a film/movie/programme (or going to see a film/ movie). See is never used with television. Watch is used especially when you are interested in something which is happening or moving, unlike look at: Watch me while I show you how. ◇ Look at my new shoes!

PATTERNS AND COLLOCATIONS

■ to watch/see/view a film/movie/programme
■ to watch/see a match/game/fight
■ to look at/watch/observe sb/sth carefully/ closely/intently
■ to look at/watch sb/sth thoughtfully/suspi- ciously/expectantly
■ to watch/observe what/who/how…

look

SYNONYMS

look for sb/sth

be after sb/sth ◆ **have a look (for sb/sth)**
◆ **look around (for sb/sth)** ◆ **look for sb/sth**
◆ **seek sb/sth**

These verbs all mean to try to find sb/sth that is lost or that you need or want. *See also* **search for sth.**

be after sb/sth (*informal*) to try to find or catch sb/sth: *The police are after him.* ◇ *He's after a job at our place.* ◇ *What are you after now?*

have a look (for sb/sth) to try to find sth, especially quickly or only in one place: *I'll just have a quick look for my glasses.* ◇ *'Have you seen my keys?' 'Have a look in the kitchen.'*

look around (for sb/sth) to try to find sth in a number of different places; to try to get sth by considering different possibilities: *She looked around for a towel to dry his hands.* ◇ *I'm looking around for a new secretary.*

look for sb/sth to try to find sb/sth: *We've been looking for you.* ◇ *Are you still looking for a job?*

seek sb/sth (*formal*) to try to find sb/sth; to try to obtain or achieve sth: *Drivers are advised to seek alternative routes.* ◇ *to seek funding for a project* ◇ *to seek medical advice*

WHICH WORD?

Seek is the most formal of these verbs. It is used especially in business or work contexts, and in newspapers. It is not normally used to talk about trying to find things that are lost. The most neutral of these verbs is **look for sth.**

PATTERNS AND COLLOCATIONS

- to look for/look around for/seek/be after **work/a job**
- to look for/look around for/seek/have a look for your **keys/glasses/wallet**
- to **carefully** look for sth

---

you are embarrassed, shy, etc.: *The little boy blushed and looked down.* ◇ *She looked down at her hands.*
◆ v + adv

look 'down on sb/sth to consider sb/sth as less good or important than yourself: *She tends to look down on people who haven't been to college.* ◇ *They looked down on our little house.* ◇ *He was looked down on at school.*
◆ v + adv + prep

look for sb/sth to search for sb/sth, either because you have lost them/it, or because you need them/it: *Sue's been looking for you.* ◇ *'Can I help you?' 'Yes, I'm looking for this shirt in blue.'* ◇ *They were looking for an easy solution to the problem.*
◆ v + prep

look for sth to hope for sth or expect sth: *The examiners will be looking for good grammar and spelling.* ◇ *This could be just the opportunity he's been looking for.*
◆ v + prep

IDM **look for 'trouble** to behave in a way that is likely to cause an argument, a fight, etc.: *Are you looking for trouble?*
▸ **un'looked-for** *adj* (*formal*) not expected: *unlooked-for success*

look 'forward to sth; look 'forward to doing sth to feel excited about sth that is going to happen because you expect to enjoy it: *Are you looking forward to your trip?* ◇ *I'm not looking forward to going to the dentist.* ◇ *We're looking forward to the concert!* ◇ *I look forward to hearing from you* (= at the end of a letter).

◇ *The President's visit is eagerly looked forward to.*
NOTE Remember that **to** is a preposition in this phrasal verb and must be followed by a noun or the *-ing* form of a verb.
◆ v + adv + prep

look 'in (on sb) to make a short visit to a place, especially sb's house when they are ill/sick or need help: *I asked Sarah to look in on her grandmother on her way home.* ◇ *The doctor will look in again this evening.*
⊃ note at VISIT WITH SB
◆ v + adv

look 'into sth to examine sth or consider it carefully: *The committee is looking into the matter.* ◇ *The manager is looking into your complaint.* ◇ *We're looking into the possibility of moving to France.* ◇ *This situation should be looked into.*
◆ v + prep

look 'on 1 to watch an event or an incident without taking part in it yourself: *People looked on in alarm as the car began to roll down the hill.* ◇ *Passers-by just looked on as he was attacked.* **2** (**with sb**) (*AmE*) to share a book, etc. with another person in a group: *There aren't enough books so you'll have to look on with your neighbor.*
◆ v + adv
▸ **'onlooker** *n* a person who watches sth without becoming involved in it: *A crowd of onlookers formed around the fight.*

'look on sb/sth (*also* **'look upon sb/sth** *more formal*) [+ **adv/prep**] to consider sb/sth in a

look out

beware ◆ look out ◆ watch out

These verbs are all used to warn sb about sb/sth that is dangerous.

beware (used only in infinitives and orders) used to warn sb that sb/sth is dangerous and that they should be careful: *Motorists have been warned to beware of icy roads.*

look out used to warn sb to be careful, especially when there is danger: *Look out! There's a snake! ◇ If they don't look out they're going to get in trouble.*

watch out used to warn sb about sth dangerous: *Watch out! There's a car coming.*

WHICH WORD?

There is very little difference in the meaning or use of these verbs. **Watch out** is a little more frequent in spoken English than **look out**.

PATTERNS AND COLLOCATIONS

- to look out/watch out **for** sth
- sb/sth **had better** beware/watch out/look out

particular way: *I look on you as my friend. ◇ She looked upon the assignment as a challenge. ◇ I looked on life in a different way after that. ◇ She was always looked on with distrust. ◇ The job was looked upon as glamorous.*

◆ v + prep

,look 'out used to tell sb to be careful, especially when there is some danger: *Look out! There's a car coming. ◇ You're going to burn that food if you don't look out.*

SYN watch out

◆ v + adv

,look sth 'out **(for sb/sth)** *(BrE)* to search for sth from among your possessions: *I'll look out that book for you.*

NOTE Not used in the passive.

◆ v + adv + n ◆ v + n/pron + adv

,look 'out for sb/yourself to take care of sb/ yourself and think about their/your own interests: *Once he was in London he had to look out for himself. ◇ Emily's brothers always looked out for her.*

◆ v + adv + prep

,look 'out for sb/sth **1** to try to find sb/sth or meet sb: *I was looking out for Pete but I didn't see him. ◇ Look out for this movie at your local multiplex.* **2** to try to avoid sth bad happening or doing sth bad: *Look out for pickpockets.*

SYN watch out for sb/sth

◆ v + adv + prep

▸ 'lookout *n* **1** a place where sb watches from to see if there is any danger: *a lookout post/ tower* **2** a person who watches for danger: *The burglars posted a lookout outside the house.*

,look 'out on/over sth (of a room, etc.) to have a view of sth: *Our room looked out over the square.*

◆ v + adv + prep

,look 'over **(at/to sb/sth)** → LOOK ACROSS/OVER (AT/TO SB/STH)

,look 'over sth **1** to make a tour of a place: *We were invited to look over the new classrooms.* **2** to read sth quickly: *I need to look over my notes before the test. ◇ Your tutor will look over your work with you.*

◆ v + prep

,look sb/sth 'over to check or examine sb/sth to see how good, big, etc. they are/it is: *He looked the painting over carefully. ◇ I'd like the doctor to look him over. ◇ We'll get a mechanic to look the car over before we buy it.*

SYN check sb/sth over; examine sb/sth ⊃ note at CHECK SB/STH OVER

NOTE When **look sb/sth over** is used with the pronouns *it* and *them* referring to things, these pronouns can also come after **over**: *We'd like a mechanic to look it over for us.*

◆ v + n/pron + adv ◆ v + adv + n

,look 'round, etc. *(BrE)* → LOOK AROUND, ETC.

,look 'through sb to look at sb and not show that you have seen or recognized them: *I smiled at him, but he just looked straight through me.*

◆ v + prep

,look 'through sth **1** to read sth quickly: *She looked through her notes before the exam. ◇ I looked through the paper while I was waiting.* **2** to examine a collection of things or what is inside sth: *What are you doing looking through my bag?*

⊃ note on page 196

◆ v + prep

'look to sb/sth **(for sth/to do sth)** to rely on sb/ sth or expect sb to provide sth or do sth: *They looked to us for help. ◇ We must look to other means to generate the funds we need. ◇ Many students can't look to their parents for financial support.*

SYN turn to sb

◆ v + prep

'look to sth *(especially BrE)* **1** to think about sth that will happen in the future: *We are looking to the future with confidence.* **OBJ** the future **2** *(formal)* to make sure that sth is safe or in good condition; to think about how to improve sth: *You should look to your own behaviour before criticizing others.*

◆ v + prep

,look 'up **1** **(from sth)** to raise your eyes: *She looked up from her book and smiled.* **2** *(informal)* *(usually used in the progressive tenses)* (of a business, a situation etc.) to become better; to

look through sth

dip into sth ◆ **flick/flip through sth** ◆ **leaf through sth** ◆ **look through sth** ◆ **scan through sth**

These verbs all mean to look at and understand the meaning of printed or written words without reading everything.

dip into sth to read only parts of sth: *It's a good book to dip into now and again.*

flick/flip through sth to quickly turn the pages of a book, magazine, etc. and look at them without reading everything: *She was flicking through a magazine.* ◇ *While he was out I flipped through his address book.*

leaf through sth to quickly turn the pages of a book, without reading them or looking at them closely, especially in order to find sth in particular: *She leafed through the guidebook until she found the page she wanted.*

look through sth to turn the pages of a book, magazine, etc., and look at them without

reading everything: *I caught him looking through my confidential files.*

scan through sth to read sth quickly but not very carefully and not reading every word: *I scanned through the list quickly, looking for my name.* **NOTE** **Scan** can be used on its own: *I scanned the list quickly, looking for my name.*

WHICH WORD?

If you **flick/flip through sth**, you do it more quickly than if you **look through sth**, which is usually more deliberate.

PATTERNS AND COLLOCATIONS

- to flick through/look through/leaf through/flip through a **book/magazine/newspaper**
- to flick through/look through/leaf through/scan/flip through **the pages of** sth
- to scan (through) **a list/a menu**

---

improve: *Things started to look up for me after I got a job.* ◇ *Business is looking up at last.*
◆ v + adv

,**look sb** '**up** (*informal*) to visit or contact sb when you are in the place where they live, especially when you have not seen them for a long time: *Look me up next time you're in London.* **NOTE** Not used in the passive.
◆ v + n/pron + adv ◆ v + adv + n (*less frequent*)
IDM **look sb** ,**up and** '**down** to look at sb in a suspicious, careful or critical way

,**look sth** '**up** to search for a word or some information in a dictionary or another book: *I looked the word up in the dictionary.* ◇ *Hang on, I'll just look up her telephone number.*
◆ v + n/pron + adv ◆ v + adv + n

,**look** '**up to sb** to admire or respect sb: *She always looked up to her older sister.* ◇ *She was looked up to by the rest of her family.*
↪ note on page 197
◆ v + adv + prep

'**look upon sb/sth** → LOOK ON SB/STH

loom /luːm/

,**loom a**'**head** if sth dangerous, difficult or unpleasant **looms ahead**, it is likely to happen soon: *Further problems are looming ahead.*
◆ v + adv

,**loom** '**up** to appear as a large shape that is not clear, often in a way that seems frightening or threatening: *A shape loomed up out of the fog.* **NOTE** **Loom up** is usually followed by an adverb or a phrase beginning with a preposition: *A man*

loomed up out of the darkness. ◆ **Loom** is also used on its own.
◆ v + adv

loosen /'luːsn/

,**loosen** '**up**; ,**loosen sb** '**up** (*informal*) to become more relaxed and comfortable; to make sb feel like this: *He began to loosen up and enjoy the evening.*
◆ v + adv ◆ v + n/pron + adv ◆ v + adv + n

,**loosen** '**up**; ,**loosen sb/sth** '**up** to relax your muscles or parts of the body, or make them relax, before taking exercise, etc.: *I swam a short distance to loosen up.* ◇ *A massage will help loosen you up.* ◇ *These exercises will loosen up your shoulders.*
◆ v + adv ◆ v + n/pron + adv ◆ v + adv + n

lop /lɒp; AmE lɑːp/ (-pp-)

,**lop sth** '**off**; ,**lop sth** '**off sth 1** to remove sth from sth, especially branches from a tree, by cutting it: *Several branches had been lopped off (the tree).* ◇ *They lopped 20p off the price of each unit.* **SYN** **chop sth off**, **chop sth off sth**, **cut sth off**, **cut sth off sth 2** to make sth smaller or less: *The new rail link has lopped an hour off the journey.* **SYN** **knock sth off**, **knock sth off sth**
◆ v + n/pron + adv ◆ v + adv + n ◆ v + n/pron + prep

lord /lɔːd; AmE lɔːrd/

'**lord it over sb** to behave in a superior way to sb: *She likes to lord it over the junior staff.*
◆ v + it + prep

lose /luːz/ (**lost, lost** /lɒst; AmE lɔːst/)

'**lose yourself in sth** to become so interested in sth that you are not aware of anything else: *I soon lost myself in the excitement of the play.*
♦ v + pron + prep

,**lose 'out (on sth)** (*informal*) to be unsuccessful in getting sth that you want or think you should have: *Some youngsters are taking day jobs and losing out on schooling.* ◇ *If things go wrong, I'm the one who'll lose out.* ◇ *While the stores make big profits, it's the customer who loses out.*
♦ v + adv

,**lose 'out to sb/sth** (*informal*) to not get the business you expected or hoped to get, because sb else has got it: *Small stores are losing out to the big supermarkets.*
♦ v + adv + prep

lounge /laʊndʒ/

,**lounge a'round; ,lounge a'round sth** (BrE also ,**lounge a'bout, ,lounge a'bout sth**) to spend your time in a relaxed way doing very little: *She was always lounging about while the rest of us were working!* ◇ *They were lounging around the hotel pool.*
SYN **laze around, laze around sth; lie about/around, lie about/around sth**
♦ v + adv ♦ v + prep

louse /laʊs/

,**louse sth 'up** (*slang*) to spoil or ruin sth: *He loused up my promotion chances.*
SYN **mess sth up** (BrE)
♦ v + adv + n ♦ v + n/pron + adv

love /lʌv/

be/get ,loved 'up (BrE, *informal*) to be/start to be full of happy, loving or romantic feelings, because you are in love or because of the effects of drugs, music, etc.
♦ be/get + v + adv

▸ ,**loved-'up** *adj* [only before noun] (BrE, *informal*): *a bunch of loved-up clubbers*

luck /lʌk/

,**luck 'into sth** (AmE, *informal*) to get sth you want by chance: *I lucked into some free tickets for the show.*
♦ v + prep

,**luck 'out** (AmE, *informal*) to be very lucky: *We lucked out in a big way.* ◇ *We really lucked out with the weather.*
♦ v + adv

lug /lʌg/ (**-gg-**)

,**lug sth a'round** (BrE also ,**lug sth a'bout, ,lug sth 'round**) (**with you**) (*informal*) to carry or pull sth large, awkward or heavy from one place to another, or everywhere you go: *Can I leave my bag somewhere? It's very heavy to lug around.*
SYN **carry sth around (with you)** (*more formal*); **cart sth around (with you)**
♦ v + n/pron + adv ♦ v + adv + n

lull /lʌl/

,**lull sb 'into sth; ,lull sb 'into doing sth** to make sb feel confident and relaxed, especially so that they do not expect it when sth bad happens: *Don't let success in the test lull you into thinking you do not need to work hard.* ◇ *His calm manner **lulled me into a false sense of security** (= made me feel safe with him when I was not).*
♦ v + n/pron + prep

lumber /'lʌmbə(r)/

be/get 'lumbered with sb/sth (BrE, *informal*) to give sb a responsibility or a problem that they do not want and cannot get rid of: *I'm sorry you've been lumbered with driving me home.* ◇ *The movie was about somebody who sees a*

SYNONYMS

look up to sb

admire sb ♦ **look up to sb** ♦ **respect sb** ♦ **think highly of sb**

These verbs all mean to have a good opinion of sb.

admire sb to respect sb for what they have done: *I don't agree with her, but I admire her for sticking to her principles.*

look up to sb to admire or respect sb, especially sb who is older: *Children need somebody to look up to.* ◇ *Everyone looks up to her because of who she is.*

respect sb to have a very good opinion of sb; to admire sb: *She had always been honest*

with me, and I respect her for that. ◇ *a much loved and highly respected teacher*

think highly of sb to have a very good opinion of sb: *His teachers think very highly of him.*

WHICH WORD?

If you **respect** sb, you do not necessarily like them or agree with them.

PATTERNS AND COLLOCATIONS

■ to **deeply/greatly** admire/respect sb
■ a **highly** respected doctor, teacher, etc.
■ to be **generally/widely** admired

murder and then gets lumbered with the dead man's child.
* be/get + v + prep

lump /lʌmp/

ˌlump A and B toˈgether; ˈlump A with B; ˈlump A in with B (*informal*) to put or consider two or more people or things together in the same group: *A large number of plants are lumped together under the name of 'herbs'.* ◇ *You can't lump the elderly and the disabled together.* ◇ *You can't lump the elderly with the disabled.*
NOTE Often used in the passive.
* v + n/pron + adv * v + adv + n * v + n/pron + prep
* v + n/pron + adv + prep

lust /lʌst/

ˈlust after sb (*often disapproving*) to feel a strong sexual desire for sb
* v + prep

ˈlust after/for sth to have a strong desire to possess or have sth: *She was lusting after/for revenge.*
* v + prep

luxuriate /lʌɡˈʒʊərieɪt; *AmE* -ˈʒʊr-/

luˈxuriate in sth (*formal*) to take great pleasure in sth that is very pleasant and relaxing: *Alison likes to luxuriate in a long, hot bath.*
* v + prep

M m

magic /ˈmædʒɪk/ (-ck-)

ˌmagic sb/sth aˈway/ˈup (*BrE*) to use magic to make sb/sth disappear or appear; to make sb/sth disappear or appear so quickly or suddenly that it seems as if you have used magic: *I wish my problems could be just magicked away.* ◇ *Sarah magicked up a meal in a very short time.*
* v + adv + n * v + n/pron + adv

mail /meɪl/

ˌmail sth ˈin to send sth by post/mail to a place where it will be dealt with: *Don't forget to mail in your entry form for the contest!*
SYN send sth in
* v + n/pron + adv * v + adv + n

ˌmail sth ˈoff (to sb) to send sth to sb by post/mail: *I mailed off an application the next day.*
OBJ letter, package **SYN** post sth off (*BrE*); send sth off (to sb)
NOTE You can also use **mail a letter**, etc., but this often refers to the action of putting the letter in the mailbox: *I'm sorry—I forgot to mail your letter.*
* v + n/pron + adv * v + adv + n

ˌmail sth ˈout to send sth to a lot of different people or places at the same time: *Catalogues will be mailed out next week.*
SYN send sth out
NOTE **Mail sth** can also be used with this meaning.
* v + n/pron + adv * v + adv + n

major /ˈmeɪdʒə(r)/

ˈmajor in sth (*AmE*) to study sth as your main subject at a university or college; to get a degree in that subject: *He majored in chemistry.*
* v + prep

make /meɪk/ (made, made /meɪd/)

ˌmake aˈway with sth to steal sth and take it away with you: *Thieves made away with a computer and two televisions.*
→ see also MAKE OFF (WITH STH)
* v + adv + prep

ˈmake for sb/sth to move in the direction of sb/sth: *He jumped up and made for the door.* ◇ *She made straight for me.*
SYN head for/towards sth
* v + prep

ˈmake for sth (*not used in the progressive tenses*) to help to make sth possible; to produce a particular result: *The two-hour journey to work makes for a long day.* ◇ *The large print makes for easier reading.*
* v + prep

ˈmake sb/sth into sth to change sb/sth into sth: *They made the extra bedroom into a bathroom.* ◇ *You're trying to make her into something she isn't.* ◇ *Their story is being made into a movie.*
SYN turn sb/sth into sth
* v + n/pron + prep

ˈmake sth of sb/sth to have an impression or an understanding of sb/sth: *What did you make of the play?* ◇ *I never knew quite what to make of Nick.* ◇ *The information we have is so confused, it's hard to make anything of it.*
* v + n/pron + prep

ˌmake ˈoff (with sth) to hurry or rush away, especially when sb is trying to escape or has stolen sth: *The youths made off in a stolen car.* ◇ *Two boys made off with our bags.*
→ see also MAKE AWAY WITH STH; ↻ note at RUN AWAY
* v + adv

ˌmake ˈout (*informal*) **1** used to ask sb how they have managed or survived in a particular situation: *How are you making out in your new home?* ◇ *'Did you make out all right in the interview?' 'Yes, fine.'* **2** (with sb) (*AmE*) to kiss and touch sb in a sexual way; to have sex with sb: *I saw her making out with Billy.*
* v + adv

ˌmake ˈout (that …), ˌmake sb/sth/yourself ˈout to be … to claim that sth is true that may

make sb/sth out

discern sth ◆ **distinguish sb/sth** ◆ **identify sb/sth** ◆ **make sb/sth out** ◆ **pick sb/sth out**

These verbs all mean to be able to see or hear sb/sth and especially to be able to say who or what they are.

discern sth (*not used in the progressive tenses*) (*formal*) to recognize or know sth, especially sth that is not obvious: *He discerned a certain coldness in their welcome.*

distinguish sb/sth (*not used in the progressive tenses*) to manage to see or hear sb/sth that is not very clear: *I could not distinguish her words, but she sounded agitated.* ◇ *She could not distinguish the make of the car.*
NOTE **Distinguish** is often used in the negative, or with a verb that has a negative meaning.

identify sb/sth to be able to say who or what sb/sth is: *The bodies were identified as those of two suspected drug dealers.* ◇ *First of all we must identify the problem areas.*

make sb/sth out (*not used in the progressive tenses*) to manage to see or hear sb/sth that is

not very clear: *I could just make out a figure in the darkness.*

pick sb/sth out to recognize sb/sth from among other people or things: *See if you can pick me out in this photo.*

WHICH WORD?

Distinguish is more formal than **make sb/sth out** and is more likely to have a noun phrase as object: *I was able to distinguish the bird's yellow beak.* **Make sb/sth out** is more likely to have a clause with *what* or *who* as object: *I couldn't make out what she was saying.*

PATTERNS AND COLLOCATIONS

- to identify/distinguish sb/sth **by** sth
- to identify/make out/discern/distinguish **who/what/how...**
- to **clearly/easily/barely/hardly** identify/make out/discern/pick out/distinguish sb/sth
- to **accurately/correctly** identify/discern/pick out/distinguish sb/sth
- to **attempt/try/enable sb/help (sb)** to identify/make out/discern/pick out/distinguish sb/sth

not be; to try to make people believe sth: *She made out (that) she was earning a fortune.* ◇ *Things aren't as bad as he makes out.* ◇ *The brochure made the place out to be a quiet resort.* ◇ *He makes himself out to be a big shot in the city.* ◇ *The hotel wasn't quite what it was made out to be* (= it was not as good as the advertisement said it was).
◆ v + adv ◆ v + n/pron + adv + **to**+inf

,make sb/sth 'out 1 to manage to see sb/sth or read sth: *I could just make out the shape of a house in the darkness.* ◇ *She could just make out the sound of distant voices.* ◇ *I couldn't make out what he was saying.* ◇ *Can you make out his handwriting?* **2** (*used especially in negative sentences and questions*) to understand sb/sth; to see the reasons why sth happens or why sb behaves in the way that they do: *She couldn't make out the expression on his face as he spoke.* ◇ *I can't make her out at all.* ◇ *He couldn't make out what was going on.* ◇ *You need to apply for a permit, as far as I can make out.* ◇ *How do you make that out* (= how did you reach that conclusion)?
NOTE Not used in the passive.
◆ **1** v + adv + n ◆ v + pron + adv
◆ v + n + adv (*less frequent*)
◆ **2** v + adv + n ◆ v + n/pron + adv

,make sth 'out to write out or complete a form or document: *He made out a cheque for £100.* ◇ *Who shall I make the cheque out to* (= whose name shall I write on it)? ◇ *Shall I make the*

invoice out to the company? ◇ *Would you make out a list for me of everyone who's coming?*
OBJ **cheque**, **list**
NOTE In informal spoken language **make sb out sth** can also be used: *I'll make you out a list.*
◆ v + adv + n ◆ v + n/pron + adv

,make sb/sth 'over (*informal, especially AmE*) to change sb/sth to give them/it a new appearance; to change sth to give it a new use: *They decided to make over the whole house when they moved in.*
◆ v + adv + n ◆ v + n/pron + adv

▶ **'makeover** *n* the process of improving the appearance of a person or a place: *She won a complete makeover* (= new clothes, hairstyle, etc.) *in a competition.*

,make sth 'over to sb to legally give sth you own to sb else: *He made his estate over to his eldest son.* ◇ *The government has made a lot of its power over to the regions.* ◇ *The house was made over to the charity three years ago.*
OBJ **estate**, **money**
◆ v + n/pron + adv + prep ◆ v + adv + n + prep

'make towards sb/sth to go in the direction of sb/sth: *I saw them making towards the exit.*
◆ v + prep

,make 'up; **,make sb/sth 'up**; **,make yourself 'up** (*BrE*) to put make-up on to make sb/yourself attractive or to prepare for an appearance in the theatre, on television, etc.: *It takes her an hour to make up before going on stage.*

◇ *She spends ages making herself up.* ◇ *The children had been made up to look like clowns.*
♦ v + adv ♦ v + n/pron + adv ♦ v + adv + n
▶ ˌmade-'up *adj* wearing make-up: *a heavily made-up face* ◇ *She's always carefully made-up.*
▶ 'make-up *n* [U] substances that people put on their eyes, lips and face to make themselves more attractive, or that actors, etc. use: *to put on your make-up* ◇ *a make-up bag*

ˌmake 'up; ˌmake it 'up (with sb) (*BrE*) to end an argument or a disagreement with sb: *Let's kiss and make up.* ◇ *He's made it up with his parents.*
♦ v + adv ♦ v + it + adv

🔑ˌmake up 'up **1** to invent sth, often in order to trick sb: *He was making up stories for the children.* ◇ *She made up an excuse for being late.* ◇ *Did you think I was making it all up?*
OBJ story, excuse **2** ˌmake 'up sth to form a particular part of sth: *Rice makes up a large part of their diet.* ◇ *Women make up 55% of the student population.* **SYN** account for sth; constitute sth (*formal*) ⊃ note at CONSIST OF STH/SB **3** ˌmake 'up sth to put sth together from several different things: *the cultures and races that make up the nation* ◇ *The course is made up of five modules.* **SYN** constitute sth; be composed of sth (*formal*) → see also CONSIST OF STH/SB, CONSIST OF DOING STH **NOTE** When the object of **make up** is a noun, it comes after **up**, but when the object is a pronoun, it comes between **make** and **up**: *the United Kingdom and the regions that make it up.* **4** to complete sth, especially a number or an amount: *We need one more player to make up a team.* **5** to replace sth that has been lost or missed: *We need to make up lost time.* ◇ *He was late for work but he made the*

time up the following day. **6** to prepare sth; to make sth ready to use: *The pharmacist made up the prescription* (= the medicine). ◇ *She made up a basket of food for the picnic.* ◇ *The bed's already made up.* ◇ *She bought a length of material for making up into a skirt.* **NOTE** In informal spoken language **make sb up sth** is also used: *Can you make us up a packed lunch?*
♦ v + adv + n ♦ v + n/pron + adv **2** v + adv + n
♦ **3** v + adv + n ♦ v + pron + adv
IDM make up your 'mind to decide sth: *I like both—I can't make up my mind.* ◇ *Have you made up your minds where to go for your honeymoon?* ◇ *You'll never persuade him to stay—his mind's made up* (= he has definitely decided to go). ◇ *Come on—it's make your mind up time!*
▶ ˌmade-'up *adj* invented; not true or real: *It was a true story, not a made-up one.*
▶ 'make-up *n* **1** the different things, people, qualities, etc. that combine to form sth: *Aggression is part of our genetic make-up.* ◇ *The country has a complicated ethnic make-up.* **2** (*AmE*) a school test that you were not present for and that you take later: *The make-up will be on Friday.* ◇ *a make-up test*
▶ 'make-up *adj* [only before noun] intended to replace sth that has been lost or missed: *There will be a make-up party in January for those who can't come to the one in December.*

🔑ˌmake 'up for sth; ˌmake 'up for doing sth to do or provide sth good to balance or reduce the effects of sth bad: *I bought myself a new dress to make up for not getting the job.* ◇ *After two years in prison he's now making up for lost time* (= doing the things he was not able to do before).

---

make sth up

concoct sth ♦ fabricate sth ♦ invent sth ♦ make sth up

These verbs all mean to say or describe sth that is not true.

concoct sth to invent a story or plan, especially in order to trick people: *She concocted some elaborate story to explain her absence.*

fabricate sth (*often passive*) to invent false information in order to trick people: *The prisoners claimed their confessions had been fabricated by police.*

invent sth to say or describe sth that is not true, especially in order to trick people; to think of and use a new word, phrase or name: *I did not have to invent any tales about my past.* ▶ invention *n* [C,U]: *The story is apparently a complete invention.*

make sth up to invent a story, name, etc., especially in order to trick or entertain sb: *He made up some excuse about his daughter being sick.* ▶ made-up *adj*: *a made-up story/word/ name*

WHICH WORD?

Make sth up is slightly less formal than **invent**. It is often used where the object of the verb is not specific: *You're making it up.* ◇ *It turned out she had made the whole thing up.*

PATTERNS AND COLLOCATIONS

■ to invent/make up/fabricate/concoct **a story**
■ to invent/make up **an excuse/a name/a word**
■ to make up/fabricate **evidence**

make up for sth

cancel sth out ◆ **compensate (for sth)** ◆ **make up for sth** ◆ **offset sth**

These verbs all mean to reduce or remove the effect of sth else.

cancel sth out to have an equal but opposite effect to sth, so that the situation does not change: *Recent losses have cancelled out any profits made at the start of the year.* ◇ *The advantages and disadvantages would appear to cancel each other out.*

compensate (for sth) to provide or do sth good to balance or reduce the bad effects of sth: *Nothing can compensate for the death of a loved one.*

make up for sth to provide or do sth good that makes a bad situation better: *Nothing can make up for the loss of a child.* ◇ *The warm welcome we received more than made up for our horrendous journey there.*

offset sth to use one cost, payment, or situation to reduce or remove the effect of

another: *The company's losses in the US were more than offset by gains everywhere else.*

WHICH WORD?

Compensate is more formal than **make up for sth** but can be used in a wider range of structures, with or without *for*: *You should be able to eat more on this diet without having to compensate by going hungry.* **Offset** is often used in technical contexts.

PATTERNS AND COLLOCATIONS

- to be compensated/offset/cancelled out/made up for **by** sth
- to compensate for/offset/cancel out the **effect** of sth
- to compensate for/offset a **problem**
- to **help (to)** compensate for/offset/make up for sth
- to **partly/partially/more than** compensate for/offset/make up for sth

---

SYN compensate **(for sth)** (*more formal*)
◆ v + adv + prep

make ˈup for sth; **make it ˈup to sb** (*informal*) to do sth good for sb because you have treated them badly or because they have done sth good for you: *An apology won't make up for the way you've behaved.* ◇ *He said he was sorry and promised to make it up to her.* ◇ *You've done me a real favour—I don't know how to make it up to you.*
◆ v + adv + prep ◆ v + it + adv + prep

make ˈup to sb (*BrE, informal, disapproving*) to be pleasant to sb in order to get an advantage for yourself: *He's always making up to the boss.*
SYN kiss up to sb (*AmE*); suck up to sb
◆ v + adv + prep

make with sth (*informal*) to do sth or use sth: *Just make with the apology and buzz off.* ◇ *Stop talking and make with the duster* (= start cleaning).
◆ v + prep

map /mæp/ (-pp-)

map sth ˈon/onto sth to link a group of qualities, items, etc. with their source, cause, position on a scale, etc.: *Grammar information enables students to map the structure of a foreign language onto their own.*
◆ v + n/pron + prep

map sth ˈout to plan or arrange sth in detail: *I've mapped out a route for you.* ◇ *She felt as though her future had been mapped out for her.*

OBJ future, route, strategy, plan
◆ v + adv + n ◆ v + pron + adv ◆ v + n + adv (*rare*)

march /mɑːtʃ; AmE mɑːrtʃ/

march ˈon 1 to continue marching; to continue walking quickly: *I tried to speak to her but she just marched on.* **2** to move on or pass quickly: *Time marched on and we still hadn't finished.*
SUBJ time
◆ v + adv

march on sth to march to a place in order to attack it or make a protest: *Demonstrators marched on the American embassy.*
◆ v + prep

march ˈpast; **march ˈpast sb/sth** (of soldiers) to march past an important person or building: *At eleven o'clock the army began to march past.*
◆ v + adv ◆ v + prep
▶ **ˈmarch past** n a ceremony in which soldiers formally march past an important person, etc.

mark /mɑːk; AmE mɑːrk/

mark sb/sth ˈdown to reduce the marks given to sb in an examination, etc.: *She was marked down for poor spelling.*
◆ v + n/pron + adv ◆ v + adv + n

mark sth ˈdown 1 to reduce the price of sth: *All goods have been marked down by 15%.*
SYN reduce sth **2** to write sth down; to make a note of sth for future action: *The teacher had marked me down as absent.* ◇ *The council had*

the old square *marked down for new develop-ment.*
  ◆ v + n/pron + adv ◆ v + adv + n
  ▸ '**markdown** *n* a reduction in price: *a mark-down of 12%*
,**mark sb** '**down as sth** (*BrE*) to consider sb to be a particular type of person: *I had him marked down as a promising player from the start.*
  ◆ v + n/pron + adv + prep
,**mark sb/sth** '**off** (*BrE*) → MARK SB/STH OUT
,**mark sth** '**off 1** to separate sth by marking a line between it and sth else: *We've marked the playing area off with a white line.* **2** to write or draw a mark beside a name or an item on a list, for example, for a particular reason: *The students I want to see are marked off on the list.*
  ◆ v + n/pron + adv ◆ v + adv + n
,**mark sb/sth** '**out** (*BrE also* ,**mark sb/sth** '**off** *less frequent*) to make sb or sth different from other people or things: *There was something about her which marked her out from the other students.*
  ◆ v + n/pron + adv ◆ v + adv + n
,**mark sth** '**out** to draw lines to show the edges of sth: *She marked out a circle on the ground.*
  ◆ v + adv + n ◆ v + n/pron + adv + prep
,**mark sth** '**up 1** to increase the price of sth: *Shares were marked up by 8%.* **2** to mark or correct a text: *The text had already been marked up with corrections* (= for printing).
  NOTE Often used in the passive.
  ◆ v + n/pron + adv ◆ v + adv + n
  ▸ '**markup** *n* [usually sing.] **1** the difference between the cost of producing sth and the price it is sold at **2** the symbols used in computer documents which give information about the structure of the document, etc.: *a markup language*

marry /'mæri/ (**marries**, **marrying**, **married**)

,**marry be**'**neath you/yourself** to marry sb who belongs to a lower social class than your own: *She thought her son was marrying beneath him.*
  ◆ v + prep + pron
,**marry** '**into sth** to become a part of a family or a group because you have married sb who belongs to it: *She married into a wealthy family.*
  OBJ **family, aristocracy**
  ◆ v + prep
,**marry sb** '**off** (**to sb**) (*disapproving*) to get rid of a daughter or a son by finding a husband or wife for them: *He had married his daughter off to a man twice her age.*
  ◆ v + n/pron + adv ◆ v + adv + n
,**marry** '**up**; ,**marry sth** '**up** (**with sth**) (*BrE*) **1** to join up or connect successfully; to make two things or two parts do this: *The two halves of the structure didn't marry up.* ◊ *He couldn't marry up the two parts of the lock.* **2** to match; to make two things match: *The two versions of*

the story *don't quite marry up.* ◊ *The lawyers couldn't marry up her story with the facts.*
  ◆ v + adv ◆ v + adv + n ◆ v + n/pron + adv

marvel /'mɑːvl; *AmE* 'mɑːrvl/ (**-ll-**, *AmE* **-l-**)

'**marvel at sth** to be very surprised or impressed by sb/sth: *Everyone marvelled at his courage.* ◊ *Massimo marvelled at how quickly he had got used to life in Britain.*
  SYN **wonder at sth**
  ◆ v + prep

masquerade /ˌmæskə'reɪd; *BrE also* ˌmɑːsk-/

masque'**rade as sb/sth** to pretend to be sth that you are not: *commercial advertisers masquerading as private individuals* ◊ *The local paper is full of gossip masquerading as news.*
  ◆ v + prep

match /mætʃ/

'**match sb/sth against/with sb/sth** to make sb/sth compete with another person or thing: *Jobson will be matched against a far more experienced player.* ◊ *Match your skill against the experts in our weekly quiz.*
  NOTE Often used in the passive.
  ◆ v + n/pron + prep
'**match sth against sth** to compare sth to sth else to see how the two things are similar or different: *We are able to match the details he gave us against the information held on the computer.*
  ◆ v + n/pron + prep
,**match** '**up 1** (**with sth**) to be the same or similar: *Do their names match up with any in our database?* ◊ *The two statements don't match up.* SYN **tally** (**with sth**) **2** (**to sb/sth**) (*especially BrE*) (*usually used in negative sentences*) to be as good as or equal to sb/sth: *The movie didn't match up to my expectations.* ◊ *He knows what he wants and I just don't match up.* SYN **measure up** (**to sb/sth**) ⟳ note at MEASURE UP
  ◆ v + adv
,**match sb/sth** '**up** (**with sb/sth**) to find things or people that are suitable for each other or fit well with each other: *The agency matched me up with a suitable job.* ◊ *They were unable to match up his tissue type with any of the possible donors.* NOTE Match **sb/sth** (**with sb/sth**) can be used with the same meaning.
  ◆ v + n/pron + adv ◆ v + adv + n
'**match sb/sth with sb/sth** → MATCH SB/STH AGAINST/WITH SB/STH

max /mæks/

,**max** '**out**; ,**max sth** '**out** (*informal, especially AmE*) to reach the limit at which nothing more is possible: *The car maxed out at 180 mph.* ◊ *I just maxed out my credit card.*
  ◆ v + adv ◆ v + adv + n ◆ v + n/pron + adv

mellow

measure up (to sb/sth)

come up to sth ♦ **live up to sth** ♦ **match up (to sb/sth)** ♦ **measure up (to sb/sth)**

These verbs all mean to be good enough for a particular purpose or as good as sb expects.

come up to sth to reach an acceptable level or standard: *His performance didn't really come up to his usual high standard.* ◇ *Their trip to France didn't come up to expectations.*

live up to sth to do sth as well or be as good as sb expects: *The island definitely lives up to its reputation as an ideal holiday destination.*

match up (to sb/sth) to be as good or successful as expected or needed: *I tried to compete, but found I couldn't match up.*

measure up (to sb/sth) to be as good or successful as expected or needed: *The job failed to measure up to her expectations.*

WHICH WORD?

There is little difference in meaning or use between these verbs, but **measure up** is the most common. **Come up to**, **match up to** and **measure up** are usually used in the negative, or with a verb that has a negative meaning; **live up to** can be used in the negative, but is also used with positive meanings.

PATTERNS AND COLLOCATIONS

- to measure up **as** sb/sth
- to measure up/match up **against** sb/sth
- to measure up to/live up to/come up to **expectations**
- to **fail to** live up to sth/measure up/come up to sth/match up

measure /'meʒə(r)/

'measure sb/sth/yourself against sb/sth to compare sb/sth/yourself with sb/sth else: *The quality of the water is measured against EU standards.* ◇ *We have nothing to measure our performance against.* ◇ *She always measured herself against her sisters.* ◇ *I had no one to measure myself against.*
♦ v + n/pron + prep

ˌmeasure 'off to mark out a particular length on sth such as a piece of cloth: *She measured off two metres of cloth.*
♦ v + adv + n ♦ v + pron + adv
♦ v + n + adv (*less frequent*)

ˌmeasure sth 'out to measure the quantity of sth that you need from a larger amount: *He measured out the ingredients for the cake.*
♦ v + adv + n ♦ v + pron + adv
♦ v + n + adv (*less frequent*)

ˌmeasure 'up (to sb/sth) (*informal*) to be of a good enough standard or as good as sb/sth else: *The new assistant didn't measure up* (= he was not good enough to do the job)*, so we had to replace him.* ◇ *The procedures don't measure up to today's standards.*
SYN match up (to sb/sth)
NOTE Measure up is often used in negative sentences and questions.
♦ v + adv

ˌmeasure 'up (for sth), **ˌmeasure sb/sth 'up (for sth)** (*especially BrE*) to find the exact size of sth by measuring: *We need to measure up and decide where the furniture can go.* ◇ *They've come to measure up* (the room) *for the new carpet.* ◇ *He was being measured up for a suit.*
♦ v + adv ♦ v + n/pron + adv ♦ v + adv + n

meet /miːt/ (**met**, **met** /met/)

ˌmeet 'up 1 (**with sb**) to meet sb by arrangement: *We're meeting up with Gary after work, if you want to come.* ◇ *Where shall we meet up?* **2** (**with sb**) to meet sb by chance: *It was lucky we met up with them.* ◇ *I expect we'll meet up again some time.* **3** (**with sth**) (of two or more roads, rivers, etc.) to join up: *The two paths meet up just below the summit.* ◇ *This road eventually meets up with the A40.* **SYN join up**
♦ v + adv

'meet with sb to have a meeting with sb: *The Prime Minister met with other European leaders this morning.*
♦ v + prep

'meet with sth (*formal*) **1** to experience sth unpleasant: *The chief witness met with an accident on his way to the court.* ◇ *Our attempts to save her met with failure.* **OBJ an accident, fate, failure 2** to be received or treated by sb in a particular way: *The proposal met with considerable opposition.* ◇ *My explanation met with a blank stare.* **OBJ opposition, approval, hostility, resistance**
♦ v + prep

'meet sth with sth to react to sth in a particular way, especially a bad or negative way: *The proposal was met with anger and dismay.*
NOTE Usually used in the passive.
♦ v + n/pron + prep

mellow /'meləʊ; AmE -loʊ/

ˌmellow 'out (*informal, especially AmE*) to relax and do very little: *We could just put on some music and mellow out.*

SYN chill out
- v + adv

‚mellow sb 'out (*informal, especially AmE*) to make sb more relaxed: *A week on the beach should mellow him out.*
- v + n/pron + adv ◆ v + adv + n

melt /melt/

‚melt a'way; ‚melt sth a'way to disappear gradually; to make sth disappear gradually: *His anger melted away.* ◊ *The crowd dispersed, melting away into the side streets.* ◊ *His smile melted away all the tension.*
- v + adv ◆ v + adv + n ◆ v + n/pron + adv

‚melt sth 'down to heat sth until it is in a liquid state, usually so that it can be made into sth else: *Aluminium cans can be melted down and recycled.*
OBJ gold, silver, etc.
- v + n/pron + adv ◆ v + adv + n

▶ 'meltdown *n* [U, C] **1** a serious accident in which the central part of a structure that produces nuclear energy melts: *A meltdown at the reactor had only just been avoided.* **2** a disaster or serious collapse: *The meltdown on Wall Street caused chaos in markets worldwide.*

'melt into sth to gradually become part of sth and difficult to see: *I tried hard to melt into the background.*
- v + prep

merge /mɜːdʒ; AmE mɜːrdʒ/

‚merge 'in (with sth), ‚merge 'into sth if sth merges in (with sth), or merges into sth, it is so similar to the second thing that you cannot really see the differences between them or where one ends and the other begins: *The new college building does not merge in with the old buildings.* ◊ *Autumn is merging into winter.* ◊ *Saturday and Sunday seemed to merge into each other.*
→ see also BLEND IN; BLEND INTO STH
- v + adv ◆ v + prep

IDM merge into the 'background (of a person) to behave quietly when you are with a group of people so that they do not notice you

mess /mes/

‚mess a'bout, etc. (*BrE*) → MESS AROUND, ETC.
‚mess a'bout/a'round (*BrE, informal*) to treat sb badly, making them waste time, changing your mind a lot, etc.: *They messed us around so much, I wrote to complain.* ◊ *I don't like being messed about.*
SYN muck sb about/around (*BrE*)
- v + n/pron + adv

⚷‚mess a'round (*BrE also* ‚mess a'bout) (*informal*) **1** (with sb/sth) to spend time and enjoy yourself doing sth with no particular purpose: *We just messed around at home all day.* ◊ *Children love to mess about in water.* **2** (with sb/sth) to behave

in a silly way, especially when you should be working or doing sth else: *He was messing around in class.* ◊ *She messed about all year and failed her exams.* ◊ *Stop messing around with Tony and get on with your work.* ◊ *'They fixed that quickly!' 'Yeah, they don't mess around.'* (= they do things quickly) **3** to joke, to say silly things: *I'm not messing about, it's true!* **SYN** kid around (*informal*)
SYN muck about/around (*BrE*)
→ see also MESS AROUND WITH STH
- v + adv

‚mess sb a'round (*BrE*) → MESS SB ABOUT/AROUND

‚mess a'round with sb (*BrE also* ‚mess a'bout with sb) (*informal*) to have a sexual relationship with sb
- v + adv + prep

⚷‚mess a'round with sth (*BrE also* ‚mess a'bout with sth) (*informal*) **1** to keep touching or moving sth in an annoying way: *Stop messing around with the video!* ◊ *Don't mess around with your food like that!* ◊ *This package has been messed around with.* **2** to get involved in sth that you do not know much about or understand: *Who knows what might happen if we mess around with nature?* **3** to get involved with sth dangerous: *He started messing around with drugs when he was just a kid.*
SYN muck about/around with sth (*BrE*)
→ see also MESS AROUND
- v + adv + prep

⚷‚mess 'up; ‚mess sth 'up (*informal*) to spoil sth; to do sth very badly: *I was so nervous I totally messed up at the interview.* ◊ *She messed up all our arrangements by arriving late.* ◊ *You've really messed things up for me.*
SYN foul up, etc.; screw up, etc. (*slang*)
- v + adv ◆ v + adv + n ◆ v + n/pron + adv

‚mess sb 'up (*informal*) **1** to spoil sb's life; to make sb suffer emotionally or mentally: *His parents really messed him up.* ◊ *He came back into her life and messed her up again.* **2** (*AmE*) to physically hurt sb, especially by hitting them
SYN screw sb up (*slang*)
- v + n/pron + adv ◆ v + adv + n

▶ ‚messed 'up *adj* (*informal*) confused and upset, especially because of sth bad that has happened to you in the past: *He's just a messed-up kid.*

⚷‚mess sth 'up to make sth untidy or dirty: *She comes in, messes the place up and then goes out again.* ◊ *The wind is going to mess up my hair.*
SYN muck sth up (*informal*)
- v + n/pron + adv ◆ v + adv + n

'mess with sb (*informal*) (*usually used in negative sentences*) **1** to get involved with sb who may react in a dangerous or violent way: *I wouldn't mess with Frank if I were you.* **2** to have or try to have a sexual relationship with sb

mess sth up

clutter sth up ◆ **litter sth** ◆ **mess sth up**
These verbs all mean to make a place untidy.

clutter sth up (*often passive*) (*disapproving*) to fill a place with too many things, so that it looks untidy: *I don't want all these boxes cluttering up the place.* NOTE **Clutter** can be used on its own: *Don't clutter the page with too many diagrams.*

litter sth (*often passive*) to be spread around a place, making it look untidy: *Piles of books and newspapers littered the floor.* ◇ *The*

tables were littered with old newspapers and ashtrays.

mess sth up (*informal*) to make a place untidy, especially by leaving things in the wrong place or spreading them around: *I don't want you messing up my nice clean kitchen.*

PATTERNS AND COLLOCATIONS

■ to **be** littered/cluttered (**up**) **with** sth
■ to litter/clutter (up)/mess up **the place**
■ to litter/clutter (up) the **room/table/floor**

→ see also MESS AROUND WITH SB
◆ v + prep

'mess with sth (*informal, especially AmE*) **1** to use or treat sth carelessly, causing damage: *Who's been messing with the answering machine?* ◇ *Read the label carefully before you start messing with dangerous products.* **2** to get involved with sth dangerous: *How long has he been messing with drugs?* OBJ **drugs**
→ see also MESS AROUND WITH STH
◆ v + prep

mete /miːt/

ˌmete sth 'out (**to sb**) (*formal*) to give sb a punishment, etc.: *Severe penalties were meted out by the court.* ◇ *The commission was appalled at the treatment meted out to prisoners.*
OBJ **punishment**, **treatment**, **justice**, **penalty**
NOTE Usually used in the passive.
◆ v + adv + n ◆ v + pron + adv ◆ v + n + adv (*rare*)

militate /ˈmɪlɪteɪt/

ˌmilitate a'gainst sth (*formal*) to prevent sth; to make it difficult for sth to happen: *Lack of funds militated against the success of the campaign.*
◆ v + prep

mill /mɪl/

ˌmill a'round; **ˌmill a'round sb/sth** (*BrE also* **ˌmill a'bout**, **ˌmill a'bout sb/sth**) if a large number of people **mill around**, or **mill around** a place, they move around without going anywhere in particular, often while waiting for sth to happen: *Photographers milled around outside the hotel, waiting for the prince to appear.* ◇ *People milled about the room, shaking hands and chatting.*
◆ v + adv ◆ v + prep

mind /maɪnd/

ˌmind 'out (*BrE*) **1** used to warn sb to be careful: *Mind out! You nearly knocked me off my bike!*

◇ *I've got you fish and chips. Mind out for the bones!* SYN **watch out 2** (*informal*) used to tell sb to move so that you or sb else can pass: *Mind out, Joe—you're in the way!*
◆ v + adv

minister /ˈmɪnɪstə(r)/

'minister to sb/sth (*old-fashioned, formal*) to care for sb; to make sure that sb/sth has everything necessary: *She felt it was her vocation to minister to the sick.* ◇ *Servants ministered to his needs.* ◇ *He would not be ministered to by strangers.*
OBJ **needs, the sick**
◆ v + prep

minor /ˈmaɪnə(r)/

'minor in sth (*AmE*) to study another subject as well as your main subject at a university or college: *He minored in Art History.*
◆ v + prep

miss /mɪs/

ˌmiss 'out (**on sth**) to lose an opportunity to benefit from sth or enjoy yourself, by not doing sth or taking part in an activity: *I felt I missed out because I didn't go to college.* ◇ *She missed out on the school trip.* ◇ *He just missed out on a gold medal in the last Olympics* (= he was just beaten). ◇ *There are lots of things happening during Carnival, so don't miss out on the fun!*
◆ v + adv

ˌmiss sb/sth 'out (*BrE*) to not include sb/sth either deliberately or by accident: *Have I missed anybody out?* ◇ *You've missed out the most important piece of information!* (= you haven't mentioned it) ◇ *She missed out a few chapters in the middle.*
SYN **leave sb/sth out**
◆ v + n/pron + adv ◆ v + adv + n

mist /mɪst/

,mist 'over **1** if glass **mists over**, it becomes covered with very small drops of water so that you cannot see through it: *As soon as I stepped inside, my glasses misted over.* **2** if your eyes **mist over**, they fill with tears: *His eyes misted over.*
NOTE Mist is often used on its own.
◆ v + adv

,mist 'up; ,mist sth 'up to cover glass, a mirror, etc. with small drops of water so that you cannot see clearly: *The inside of the car was beginning to mist up.* ◇ *The windows were misted up.*
SYN fog up; steam up, steam sth up
NOTE Mist and mist sth are also used on their own.
◆ v + adv ◆ v + n/pron + adv ◆ v + adv + n

mistake /mɪˈsteɪk/ (mistook /mɪˈstʊk/, mistaken /mɪˈsteɪkən/)

⚑ mi'stake sb/sth for sb/sth to think wrongly that sb/sth is sb/sth else: *I mistook him for his brother.* ◇ *The toy could easily be mistaken for a real gun.*
◆ v + n/pron + prep

SYNONYMS

mistake sb/sth for sb/sth

confuse sb/sth (with sb/sth) ◆ mistake sb/sth for sb/sth ◆ mix sb/sth up (with sb/sth) ◆ take sb/sth for sb/sth
These verbs all mean to think that sb/sth is sb/sth else.

confuse sb/sth (with sb/sth) to think wrongly that sb/sth is sb/sth else: *People often confuse me and my twin sister.* ◇ *Be careful not to confuse quantity with quality.*

mistake sb/sth for sb/sth to think wrongly that sb/sth is sb/sth else: *She was quite annoyed when I mistook her for a waitress.* ◇ *These tablets can be easily mistaken for sweets.*

mix sb/sth up (with sb/sth) (*not formal*) to think wrongly that sb/sth is sb/sth else: *I think you must be mixing me up with someone else.* ◇ *She always gets her left and right mixed up.*

take sb/sth for sb/sth (*not used in the progressive tenses*) to consider sb/sth to be sb/sth, especially when you are wrong: *I mistakenly took her for the Senator's wife.* ◇ *He's not the fool you take him for.*

PATTERNS AND COLLOCATIONS
■ to easily confuse/mistake sth
■ you can't mistake sth

---

mix /mɪks/

,mix sth 'in (**with sth**), ,mix sth 'into sth to combine one substance with others, especially in cooking: *Mix the eggs in slowly.* ◇ *Mix a little cream into the sauce.*
SYN blend sth in; stir sth in, stir sth into sth
◆ v + n/pron + adv ◆ v + adv + n ◆ v + n/pron + prep

⚑ mix sb 'up; be/get ,mixed 'up to make sb unable to think clearly or understand what is happening; to be in or get into this state: *Now you've mixed me up completely! I'm really confused.* ◇ *He got mixed up and caught the wrong train.*
SYN muddle sb up (*informal, especially BrE*); confuse sb (*more formal*)
NOTE Often used in the passive with *be* or *get*: *I think you're getting mixed up.*
◆ v + n/pron + adv ◆ v + adv + n ◆ be/get + v + adv
▶ ,mixed 'up adj (*informal*) confused because of social or emotional problems: *She's a very mixed-up kid.*

⚑ mix sb/sth 'up (**with sb/sth**) to think wrongly that sb/sth is sb/sth else; to be unable to distinguish between two or more people or things: *You're mixing me up with my brother.* ◇ *The hospital mixed up the babies' name tags.*
SYN muddle sb/sth up, etc. (*especially BrE*)
⟳ note at MISTAKE SB/STH FOR SB/STH
◆ v + n/pron + adv ◆ v + adv + n
IDM get A and B mixed up; get A mixed up with B to think wrongly that sb/sth is sb/sth else; to be unable to distinguish between two or more people or things: *My bag got mixed up with somebody else's at the airport.* ◇ *People who are colour-blind usually get red and green mixed up.*

⚑ mix sth 'up (**with sth**) to change the order or arrangement of things in a confused or untidy way: *I'd sorted those papers out and now you've mixed them all up again.* ◇ *My letters have all been mixed up with yours.*
SYN muddle sth up (**with sth**) (*especially BrE*)
⟳ note at MISTAKE SB/STH FOR SB/STH
NOTE Often used in the passive with *be* or *get*: *The clean clothes got all mixed up with the dirty ones.*
◆ v + n/pron + adv ◆ v + adv + n
▶ 'mix-up n a mistake that causes confusion; a situation that is full of confusion: *There was a mix-up over the tickets.*
▶ ,mixed 'up adj untidy; in a state of confusion: *My papers were all mixed up.* ◇ *mixed-up papers*

be/get ,mixed 'up in sth to be/become involved in sth dangerous or illegal: *He would never have got mixed up in anything criminal.* ◇ *How did you get mixed up in all this?*
◆ be/get + v + adv + prep

be/get ,mixed 'up with sb to be/become friendly with or involved with sb dangerous or dishonest: *I'll never understand how she got*

mix sth up

jumble sth up ◆ **mix sth up** ◆ **muddle sth up** ◆ **shuffle sth**

These verbs all mean to put things together in the wrong order or a different order.

jumble sth up (*usually passive*) to mix things together without any order and in an untidy way: *The letters in these words have been jumbled up.* NOTE **Jumble** can be used on its own: *Books, shoes and clothes were jumbled together on the floor.*

mix sth up to change the order or arrangement of a group of things, often by mistake or in a way that you do not want: *Someone has mixed up all the application forms.*

muddle sth up (*often passive*) (*especially BrE*) to accidentally change the order or arrangement of a group of things, usually in a way that you do not want: *All the cups and saucers have been muddled up.* NOTE **Muddle** can be used on its own: *Don't do that—you're muddling my papers.*

shuffle sth to move paper or things into different positions or a different order; to completely change the order of playing cards before playing a game: *He nervously shuffled the papers on his desk.* ◇ *Shuffle the cards and deal out seven to each player.*

WHICH WORD?

You can **mix** or **jumble** things **up** by mistake or deliberately; things are always **muddled** by mistake. You can **mix up** or **muddle** papers or forms by getting them in the wrong order; things that are **jumbled** are usually objects that are not in any order at all.

PATTERNS AND COLLOCATIONS

■ to **be** jumbled/mixed/muddled up
■ to be jumbled/muddled up **together**
■ to jumble/mix up **letters/words**
■ to mix up/muddle sb's **papers**

---

mixed up with Phil. ◇ *He was mixed up with the wrong crowd for a while.*
◆ be/get + v + adv + prep

mix it 'up with sb (*AmE, informal*) **1** to fight with sb: *Some guys came into the bar obviously in the mood to mix it up with someone.* **2** to start an argument with sb: *Do they really mean what they say, or are they just trying to mix it up with the other side?*
◆ v + it + adv + prep

'mix it with sb (*BrE, informal*) **1** to compete with sb; to argue or fight with sb: *He'll be mixing it with the world's best players.* ◇ *He can mix it with the best of them.* **2** to meet and spend time with people in a friendly way: *She loves mixing it with the rich and famous.*
◆ v + it + prep

mock /mɒk/

mock sth 'up to produce a copy of sth that is going to be made, so that it can be tested or people can see what it will be like: *We mocked up the front page to see how it would look.*
◆ v + adv + n ◆ v + n/pron + adv

▶ **'mock-up** *n* a copy of sth that is produced to show people what it will be like, or to test it: *a mock-up of the next day's front page*

model /'mɒdl/; *AmE* 'mɑːdl/ (-**ll**-, *AmE* -**l**-)

'model sb/sth/yourself on sb/sth (*also* **'model sb/sth/yourself upon sb/sth** *more formal*) (*AmE also* **'model sb/sth after sb/sth**) to make or create sth that looks or behaves like sth

else; to take sb, especially sb you like, as an example and copy them: *The house was modelled on a French chateau.* ◇ *He modelled the main character on his friend.* ◇ *He still models himself on Elvis.*
NOTE Often used in the passive: *The ship was modelled on/after a Greek pirate ship.*
◆ v + n/pron + prep

monkey /'mʌŋki/

monkey a'bout/a'round (**with sth**) (*BrE, informal*) to behave in a silly way; to touch or change sth in a careless way: *They were monkeying around in class.* ◇ *He's monkeyed about with the original words of the song.*
SYN **mess around; mess around with sth**
◆ v + adv

mooch /muːtʃ/

mooch a'bout/a'round; mooch a'bout/ a'round sth (*informal, especially BrE*) to spend time doing nothing in particular: *We went into town and mooched about for a while.* ◇ *They spent an hour mooching around the shops.*
◆ v + adv ◆ v + prep

moon /muːn/

moon a'bout/a'round; moon a'bout/ a'round sth (*BrE, informal*) to spend time doing nothing in particular, often because you are feeling unhappy: *He mooned around the streets, hoping to see Anna.*

SYN mope around; mope around sth
♦ v + adv ♦ v + prep

'**moon over sb** (*informal*) to spend your time in a dream thinking about sb that you love: *He spends most of his time mooning over Helen.*
♦ v + prep

mop /mɒp; *AmE* mɑːp/ (**-pp-**)

,**mop 'up**; ,**mop sth 'up 1** to clean up liquid or remove liquid from somewhere, using sth that absorbs it: *I always have to mop up after he's had a shower.* ◇ *Can you mop up the water on the bathroom floor?* ◇ *She mopped up the sauce with a piece of bread.* ◇ *Mopping-up operations have begun after the floods.* **2** to use up all of sth: *The new factory should mop up the pool of surplus labour.* **3** to take control of sth: *The company started mopping up smaller firms.*
♦ v + adv ♦ v + adv + n ♦ v + pron + adv
♦ v + n + adv (*less frequent*)

,**mop sb/sth 'up** to get rid of the last few people who continue to oppose you; to finish tasks that remain: *The army mopped up some isolated pockets of resistance.* ◇ *There are a few things to mop up before we go.*
♦ v + adv + n ♦ v + pron + adv
♦ v + n + adv (*less frequent*)

mope /məʊp; *AmE* moʊp/

,**mope a'round**; ,**mope a'round sth** (*BrE also* ,**mope a'bout**, ,**mope a'bout sth**) to walk about a place in an unhappy way, with no particular purpose: *He's been moping about all day.* ◇ *You spend too much time moping around the house.*
SYN moon about/around; moon about/around sth (*BrE*)
♦ v + adv ♦ v + prep

mount /maʊnt/

,**mount 'up** (**to sth**) to increase gradually in size or quantity: *The paperwork soon mounts up if you don't deal with it immediately.* ◇ *My debts have mounted up to over a thousand dollars.*
♦ v + adv

mouse /maʊs/

,**mouse 'over sth** (*computing*) to move a computer mouse so that you point to a particular area on the screen: *When you mouse over these hot spots, they change colour.*
SYN roll over sth
♦ v + prep
▸ '**mouseover** *n* [C, U]: *Most browsers support mouseovers.* ◇ *mouseover buttons*

mouth /maʊð/

,**mouth 'off** (**at/about sb/sth**) (*informal*) (*often used in the progressive tenses*) to give your opinion about sb/sth loudly; to complain loudly about sb/sth: *I could hear him mouthing off about how*

they should have won. ◇ *She was mouthing off at all the other drivers on the road.*
♦ v + adv

move /muːv/

,**move a'bout, etc.** (*especially BrE*) → MOVE AROUND, ETC.

,**move a'cross**; ,**move a'cross sth** to move from one side of sth to the other: *He moved across to the window and looked out.*
OBJ room
♦ v + adv ♦ v + prep

,**move a'head** to advance or develop, often after there has been a delay: *The project is moving ahead again now.*
SYN proceed (*more formal*)
♦ v + adv

,**move a'head of sb/sth** to move faster than sb/sth; to develop more quickly than sb/sth else: *'Speed up!' he said, moving ahead of her.* ◇ *Our foreign competitors are moving ahead of us.*
SYN overtake sb/sth
♦ v + adv + prep

,**move a'long**; ,**move a'long sth** to go forward: *The convoy of cars was moving slowly along the road.*
OBJ road
♦ v + adv ♦ v + prep

,**move a'long/'on**; ,**move sb a'long/'on** to leave a particular place or go to a new position; to make sb do this: *Move along now. You're blocking the entrance.* ◇ *The police arrived to move the demonstrators along.*
♦ v + adv ♦ v + n/pron + adv

,**move a'long**; ,**move sth a'long** if a project, etc. **moves along**, or if sb **moves it along**, it continues to make good progress: *Can you move the story along a bit faster? What happened in the end?*
♦ v + adv ♦ v + n/pron + adv

,**move a'part** if two or more things or people **move apart**, they become separated by a distance: *They quickly moved apart when I walked in.* ◇ (*figurative*) *The two sides in the dispute are moving further and further apart.*
♦ v + adv

,**move a'round**; ,**move a'round sth** (*also* ,**move a'bout/'round**, ,**move a'bout/'round sth** *especially BrE*) to keep moving from one place to another: *Use the mouse to move around the screen.* ◇ *I have to move around a lot with my job.* ◇ *She sang as she moved about the room.*
♦ v + adv ♦ v + prep

,**move sb/sth a'round** (*also* ,**move sb/sth a'bout/round** *especially BrE*) to move sb/sth from one place to another: *It's not fair to keep moving the children around from school to school.* ◇ *The chair is light and easy to move about.*
♦ v + n/pron + adv

,**move a'round sth** (*also* ,**move 'round sth** *especially BrE*) to move in a circle around sth that

is blocking your path: *She moved round the table to open the window.*
SYN go around sb/sth
♦ v + prep

,**move a**'**side** to move to one side, usually to allow sb or sth to pass: *I moved aside to let her go past.*
♦ v + adv

,**move sb/sth a**'**side** to put sb/sth to one side away from the centre of a place, usually to make room for sb/sth else: *We moved the tables aside so that we could dance.*
♦ v + n/pron + adv

,**move a**'**way** to leave the place where you live to go and live in another place: *All her friends have moved away from the area.*

,**move a**'**way** (**from sb/sth**), ,**move sth a**'**way** (**from sb/sth**) to leave the place or position you are in and go to another; to take sth from one place or position and put it in another: *Move away from the window in case anyone sees you.* ◊ *Can you move the scissors away from the baby?*
♦ v + adv ♦ v + n/pron + adv ♦ v + adv + n

,**move a**'**way from sth** to stop doing, following or believing sth: *The party seems to be moving away from its original aims.*
♦ v + adv + prep

,**move** '**back**; ,**move sth** '**back 1** to go, or to move sth, to a new position at a distance away from the front or behind sb/sth: *He moved back a few steps.* ◊ *She moved her chair back from the fire.* **OPP move forward, move sth forward 2** to go, or to move sth, to the place or position it was in before: *His eyes moved back to her face.* ◊ *It took a long time to move the furniture back after the party.* **SYN return** (**sth**) (**to sth**) **3** if an event **moves back**, or sb **moves it back**, it takes place at a later date or time than was first planned: *They've moved back the date of the wedding.* **OPP bring sth forward; move forward; move sth forward**
→ see also PUT STH BACK
♦ v + adv ♦ v + n/pron + adv
♦ v + adv + n (*less frequent*)

,**move** '**down** (of a level or an amount) to decrease: *Prices move up and down according to demand.*
SYN go down OPP move up
♦ v + adv

,**move** '**down**; ,**move** '**down sth 1** to move from a higher position to a lower one: *I watched her move nervously down the slope.* **OBJ hill, ladder OPP go up, go up sth 2** to move to a new position to make more space for sb else: *Can you move down (the bus) so more people can get on?* **SYN move up, move up sth**
♦ v + adv ♦ v + prep

,**move** '**down**; ,**move sb** '**down** (at school) to move, or to move sb, to a lower class, grade or

level: *I was worried that if I failed the test I would have to move down.* ◊ *If you don't work harder, you'll be moved down (to the class below).*
OPP move up, move sb up
♦ v + adv ♦ v + n/pron + adv

,**move sb/sth** '**down**; ,**move sb/sth** '**down sth** to move sb/sth from a higher position to a lower one: *Move the boxes down from the top of the wardrobe.*
♦ v + n/pron + adv ♦ v + n/pron + prep

,**move** '**forward**; ,**move sth** '**forward 1** to go, or to make sth go, to a place or position that is in front: *The car began to move forward slowly.* **OPP move back, move sth back 2** to develop, or to make sth develop, towards a good result: *It's time to move this project forward.* **3** to move, or to make sth move, towards the future: *The company must keep moving forward.* ◊ *The story then moves forward to 1999.* **4** if an event **moves forward**, or sb **moves it forward**, it takes place at an earlier date or time than was planned: *My operation has been moved forward two weeks.*
OPP move back, move sth back
♦ v + adv ♦ v + n/pron + adv

,**move** '**in 1** (**on sb/sth**) to move towards sb/sth, especially in a threatening way, or to make a dangerous situation calm: *I moved in close and stuck the gun in his back.* ◊ *The police moved in to control the crowd.* **SYN close in** (**on sb/sth**) **2** to arrive and begin work, especially when people do not really want you there: *The developers moved in and built a housing estate in the grounds of the old house.* **3** (**on sth**) to begin to try to have control of or responsibility for a company, a project, etc.: *They are moving in on another drugs company.*
♦ v + adv

,**move** '**in**; ,**move** '**into sth** to go to a new house and begin to live there: *How soon can you move in?* ◊ *When are you moving into your new flat?*
OPP move out, move out of sth
♦ v + adv ♦ v + prep

,**move** '**in together**; ,**move** '**in with sb** to start living with sb, especially a partner: *They've decided to move in together.*
♦ v + adv + adv ♦ v + adv + prep

,**move** '**into sth 1** → MOVE IN, MOVE INTO STH **2** to start to be involved in a new area of activity or business: *The company is looking to move into new markets.* ◊ *After teaching for ten years he moved into publishing.* **3** to develop or advance into a new position, stage, etc.: *The project is now moving into its second year.* ◊ *The team has moved into fourth place after their victory.*
♦ v + prep

,**move sb/sth** '**into sth** to take sb/sth and put them/it in a new place: *We've moved the phone into the hall.* ◊ *The doctors at the hospital have*

moved my father into a room on his own. ◇ I've moved my savings into a different bank account.
◆ v + n/pron + prep

,move 'off (*especially BrE*) (especially of a vehicle) to start a journey; to begin to move: *Check your mirrors before you move off.*
◆ v + adv

,move 'off sth; ,move sb/sth 'off sth to leave the place where you are; to remove sb/sth from a particular place: *Farmers are rapidly moving off the land.* ◇ *Can you move your car off the pavement please?*
◆ v + prep ◆ v + n/pron + prep

,move 'on **1** to continue your journey after stopping for a short while; to leave the place where you are and go to a new place: *After a few minutes, the bus moved on again.* ◇ *The police told them to move on and go home!* ◇ *When I looked round, I realized everyone else had moved on.* **2** if ideas, beliefs, etc. **move on**, they change and develop: *Things have moved on a lot since my parents were young.* ◇ *The debate does not seem to have moved on much.* ◇ *Fashions are moving on all the time.* **3** (**to sth**) to start doing or discussing sth new: *I want to move on to my next point now.* ◇ *When her contract here runs out in April, Tessa will move on.* ◇ *She moved on to become senior editor of a magazine.* **SYN pass on** (**to sth**)
◆ v + adv

,move 'on; ,move sb 'on → MOVE ALONG/ON, MOVE SB ALONG/ON: *Every time they stopped they got moved on by the police.*

,move 'out; ,move 'out of sth to leave your home and go to live somewhere else: *The lodger moved out yesterday.* ◇ *He wants to move out of London.* ◇ *They've recently moved out of the city and gone to live in the country.*
OPP move in, move into sth
◆ v + adv ◆ v + adv + prep

,move sb 'out; ,move sb 'out of sth **1** to make sb leave a place, especially their home: *The landlord is moving the tenants out.* ◇ *The emergency services are moving people out of their homes.* **2** to remove sb, especially soldiers, from a place: *Many countries are moving their troops out of the area.* **SYN withdraw sb (from sth)**
◆ v + n/pron + adv ◆ v + adv + n (*less frequent*)
◆ v + n/pron + adv + prep

,move sth 'out; ,move sth 'out of sth to remove sth from a place, especially in order to make more space: *We'll need to move some chairs out to make more room.* ◇ *When can you move your belongings out of my apartment?* ◇ *That table will have to be moved out of the way.*
◆ v + n/pron + adv ◆ v + adv + n (*less frequent*)
◆ v + n/pron + adv + prep

,move 'out of sth **1** to leave a particular place, area or situation: *We watched the boat moving out of the harbour.* ◇ *The country is moving out of recession.* **2** to stop being involved in a

particular activity or area of business: *Many people have been forced to move out of farming.*
◆ v + adv + prep

,move 'over **1** (**to sb/sth**) to go towards sb/sth: *He moved over to her.* **2** (**to sth**) (*especially BrE*) to begin to do sth in a different way or with different people; to change the system you are using: *I'm an interpreter, but I'd like to move over to translation work.* ◇ *We've just moved over to a new computing system.* **3** to move to one side, usually to make room for sb/sth else: *I wish the car in front would move over and let me overtake.* ◇ *Move over! I want to sit down too.* ◇ (*figurative*) *Older managers should move over to make room for younger people.* → see also MOVE UP 2
◆ v + adv

,move 'over sth; ,move sb/sth 'over sth **1** to go forward slowly across a surface; to make sth do this: *The tank adapts to the ground it is moving over.* ◇ *Just move the brush lightly over the paper.* **2** if sb's hands, eyes, etc. **move over** sth, or sb **moves them over** sth, they slowly move across sth: *His eyes moved over her face.* ◇ *She moved her hands gently over his injured ankle.*
◆ v + prep ◆ v + n/pron + prep

,move 'past sb/sth to pass in front of sb/sth: *He moved past her into the lounge.*
SYN go past sb/sth
◆ v + prep

,move 'round, etc. (*especially BrE*) → MOVE AROUND, ETC.

,move to'wards sb/sth to approach sb/sth: *She began to run as the car moved towards her.*
◆ v + prep

,move to'wards sth; ,move to'wards doing sth (*especially BrE*) (*AmE usually* ,move to'ward sth, ,move to'ward doing sth) (*often used in the progressive tenses*) to prepare to do or achieve sth; to approach or move nearer to sth: *We are moving towards a better understanding of the situation.* ◇ *Is the group moving towards finding a solution?*
OBJ understanding, settlement
◆ v + prep

,move 'up (of a rate, a level or an amount) to increase: *What will we do if interest rates move up?*
SYN go up OPP go down
◆ v + adv

,move 'up; ,move sb 'up to move, or to make sb move, to a higher level, grade or class: *She's been moved up into the Advanced class.* ◇ *I see Tim has **moved up in the world** (= has got a better job, more money, a higher social position, etc.)*
OPP move down, move sb down
◆ v + adv + adv ◆ v + n/pron + adv

,move 'up; ,move 'up sth; ,move sb/sth 'up; ,move sb/sth 'up sth **1** to move from a lower to a higher position; to make sb/sth do

this: *Hold the ladder tightly and move up a rung at a time.* ◇ *We watched the group moving up the hill.* ◇ (*figurative*) *This is your chance to move up the career ladder and get a better job.* ◇ *Move your hand up and down.* ◇ *We had to move the piano up three flights of stairs.* **SYN** **go up**, etc. **OPP** **move down**, etc. **2** to change your position to make room for sb else; to make sb/sth do this: *Come on, move up a bit and let your mother sit down!* → see also MOVE DOWN, MOVE DOWN STH 2; MOVE OVER 3
♦ v + adv ♦ v + prep ♦ v + n/pron + adv
♦ v + n/pron + prep

mow /məʊ; *AmE* moʊ/ (**mowed**, **mown** /məʊn; *AmE* moʊn/ or **mowed**)
,mow sb 'down **1** to kill sb, often large numbers of people, with a gun: *The demonstrators were mown down by the soldiers.* ➜ note at SHOOT SB/STH DOWN **2** (of a vehicle or a driver) to kill/hit sb, because the driver has been driving in a careless or dangerous way: *A mother and her two children were mown down by joyriders.* **SYN** **run sb down**
NOTE Often used in the passive.
♦ v + adv + n ♦ v + n/pron + adv

muck /mʌk/
,muck a'bout/a'round (*BrE*, *informal*) **1** (**with sb/sth**) to spend time and enjoy yourself doing sth with no particular purpose: *They were mucking about outside, kicking a ball around.* **2** (**with sb/sth**) to behave in a silly way, especially when you should be working or doing sth else: *Stop mucking around and go to bed.* ◇ *She mucked around all year and failed her exams.* **3** to joke; to say silly things: *I thought he was mucking about until I saw it was real blood on his face.*
SYN **mess around**
♦ v + adv
,muck sb a'bout/a'round (*BrE*, *informal*) to treat sb badly, making them waste time, changing your mind a lot, etc.: *I'm sick of being mucked about by employers.*
SYN **mess sb about/around**
♦ v + n/pron + adv
,muck a'bout/a'round with sth (*BrE*, *informal*) to keep touching, moving or changing sth in an annoying way: *Who's been mucking about with my computer?* ◇ *Don't muck around with the words of the song—I think they're fine.*
SYN **mess around with sth**, etc.
♦ v + adv + prep
,muck a'round, etc. (*BrE*) → MUCK ABOUT/ AROUND, ETC.
,muck 'in (*BrE*, *informal*) **1** to join in with other people in order to complete a task: *If we all muck in, we'll soon get the job finished.* **2** to share food, accommodation, costs, etc. with other

people: *Money was short, but we all mucked in together.*
♦ v + adv
,muck 'out; ,muck sth 'out to clean the place where an animal lives, especially a horse: *It's your turn to muck out today.*
♦ v + adv ♦ v + adv + n ♦ v + n/pron + adv
,muck sth 'up (*informal*, *especially BrE*) **1** to do sth very badly; to spoil sth: *This is your last chance, so don't muck it up.* ◇ *Her surprise visit totally mucked up my plans.* **2** to make sth dirty: *Take your shoes off! You're mucking up my floor!* **3** to make sth untidy: *Stop that, you're mucking up my hair.*
SYN **mess sth up**
♦ v + adv + n ♦ v + n/pron + adv

muddle /'mʌdl/
,muddle a'long (*also* ,muddle 'on *less frequent*) (*especially BrE*) to continue living or doing sth with no clear purpose or plan: *We muddle along from day to day.*
♦ v + adv
,muddle 'through to achieve your aims although you are not efficient, do not know what you are doing, do not have the right equipment, etc.: *I'll muddle through somehow.*
♦ v + adv
,muddle sb 'up (*especially BrE*) to make sb confused: *I won't explain now—it might muddle you up.* ◇ *You're muddling me up!* ◇ *I got muddled up and took the wrong turning.*
SYN **mix sb up**; **confuse sb** (*more formal*) ➜ note at MIX STH UP
NOTE Often used in the passive with *get*. ♦ **Muddle sb** is used more frequently on its own with the same meaning.
♦ v + n/pron + adv ♦ v + adv + n (*less frequent*)
,muddle sb/sth 'up (**with sb/sth**), ,muddle A 'up with B (*especially BrE*) to confuse one person or thing with another; to think that sb/ sth is sb/sth else: *He muddled up our passports and gave me back the wrong one.* ◇ *I keep muddling her up with her sister.*
SYN **mix sb/sth up** (**with sb/sth**)
NOTE Muddle sb/sth is also used on its own.
♦ v + n/pron + adv ♦ v + adv + n
IDM **get A and B muddled 'up**; **get A muddled 'up with B** to confuse one person or thing with another: *I always get the twins muddled up.*
,muddle sth 'up (**with sth**) (*especially BrE*) to carelessly put things in the wrong order; to mix things together in an untidy way: *The money was muddled up with everything else in his pocket.* ◇ *The kids have muddled up all the photos.*
SYN **mix sth up** (**with sth**) ➜ note at MIX STH UP
NOTE Muddle sth is also used on its own.
♦ v + adv + n ♦ v + n/pron + adv
IDM **get sth muddled 'up** (**with sth**) to put things in the wrong order; to mix things

together in an untidy way: *The words seemed to have got muddled up.*

mug /mʌg/ (-gg-)

,mug 'up (on sth), ,mug sth 'up (*BrE*, *informal*) to quickly learn sth, especially sth that you should already know, before an exam, etc.: *He spent the whole night mugging up for the exam.* ◇ *I'd better mug up on the subject before I meet her.* ◇ *I'm going to mug up as much as I can about Delhi before I go there.*
SYN swot up (on sth) (*BrE*); review sth (*especially AmE*); revise sth (*BrE*)
◆ v + adv ◆ v + adv + n ◆ v + n/pron + adv

mull /mʌl/

,mull sth 'over to think about or consider sth for a long time before you decide to do it: *I've been mulling over what you said last night.*
⊃ note at THINK STH OVER
◆ v + n/pron + adv ◆ v + adv + n

muscle /'mʌsl/

,muscle 'in (on sb/sth) (*informal*) to get involved in a situation that you have no right to be involved in, especially sth that will give you an advantage or a profit: *I don't want Matt muscling in on our deal.*
◆ v + adv

,muscle 'up to develop your muscles so that you become stronger and fitter: *Once you muscle up, you'll find that your body burns more calories.*
◆ v + adv

,muscle 'up; ,muscle sth 'up to become stronger, better or more powerful; to make sth stronger, better or more powerful: *The unions need to muscle up if they want to become a force in this country again.* ◇ *The BBC is trying to muscle up its winter schedules.*
◆ v + adv ◆ v + adv + n ◆ v + pron + adv
◆ v + n + adv (*rare*)

muss /mʌs/

,muss sth 'up (*AmE*) to make sth look untidy: *My skirt got mussed up when I sat down.*
SYN mess sth up
NOTE Often used in the passive. ◆ **Muss sth** is often used on its own.
◆ v + n/pron + adv ◆ v + adv + n

muster /'mʌstə(r)/

,muster sth 'up to find the courage, strength, etc. that you need in order to do sth difficult or unpleasant: *She could barely muster up the strength to get out of bed.*
OBJ strength, energy **SYN** summon sth up
NOTE Muster sth is often used on its own.
◆ v + adv + n ◆ v + n/pron + adv

N n

naff /næf/

,naff 'off (*old-fashioned*, *BrE*, *slang*) used by some people to tell sb rudely to go away and stop annoying them: *Just naff off and leave me alone!*
SYN clear off (*especially BrE*)
◆ v + adv

nag /næg/ (-gg-)

,nag at sb 1 to keep complaining to sb about their behaviour; to keep asking sb to do sth: *He keeps nagging at me to get more exercise.* 2 to worry or irritate sb continuously: *The suspicion that she was lying continued to nag at me.*
◆ v + prep

nail /neɪl/

,nail sb 'down (to sth) to force sb to state exactly what they think, what they intend to do, etc.: *He says he'll come, but I can't nail him down to a date.*
SYN pin sb down (to sth)
◆ v + n/pron + adv ◆ v + adv + n

,nail sth 'down 1 to fasten sth down with nails: *She got him to nail the loose floorboard down.* 2 to know or understand exactly what sth is: *Something seems strange here, but I can't nail it down.* 3 to reach an agreement or a decision, usually after a lot of discussion: *They managed to nail down an agreement with the management.*
OBJ agreement
◆ 1 v + n/pron + advv + adv + n ◆ v + n/pron + adv
◆ 3 v + adv + n ◆ v + n/pron + adv

,nail sth 'up 1 to attach sth to a wall, a post, etc. with nails: *I nailed up a notice saying: Keep out!* 2 to fasten a door, a window, etc. with nails so that it cannot easily be opened: *He nailed up the door to keep intruders out.*
◆ v + adv + n ◆ v + n/pron + adv

name /neɪm/

'name sb/sth 'after sb/sth (*AmE also* 'name sb/sth 'for sb/sth) to give sb/sth the name of sb/sth else that you like or admire, for example a family member or a famous person or place: *We named her after her grandmother.* ◇ *The Miller fire was named for the canyon in which it began.*
◆ v + n/pron + prep

narrow /'nærəʊ; *AmE* -roʊ/

,narrow sth 'down (to sth) to gradually reduce the number of possibilities: *I've narrowed the list of candidates down to three.*
◆ v + n/pron + adv ◆ v + adv + n

nestle /'nesl/

,nestle 'up (to sb/sth) to make yourself warm and comfortable by moving close to sb: *Jamie nestled up to his mother on the sofa.*
 ◆ v + adv

nibble /'nɪbl/

'nibble at sth **1** to eat sth by taking very small bites: *The mouse nibbled at the peanuts.* ◇ *You've only nibbled at your lunch.* **2** to show a slight interest in sth: *Several companies have nibbled at our offer.*
 ◆ v + prep

,nibble a'way at sth (*especially BrE*) to gradually reduce or use up the total amount of sth: *Inflation began to nibble away at their savings.*
 ◆ v + adv + prep

nip /nɪp/ (-pp-)

,nip sth 'off to remove a part of sth by squeezing it with your fingers, cutting it quickly with scissors, etc.: *She nipped off the dead leaves.*
 SYN cut sth off
 ◆ v + adv + n ◆ v + n/pron + adv

nod /nɒd; AmE nɑːd/ (-dd-)

,nod 'off (*informal*) to fall asleep: *She nodded off in front of the television.*
 SYN doze off (*more formal*)
 ◆ v + adv

nose /nəʊz; AmE noʊz/

,nose a'round (*BrE also* ,nose a'bout) (for sth) (*informal*) to go around trying to find out sth about sb/sth, particularly when you should not do this: *I'm just nosing about for clues.*
 ◆ v + adv

,nose sb 'out (*informal*) to defeat sb by a small amount, for example in a race or an election: *She was nosed out of first place by her old rival.*
 ◆ v + n/pron + adv ◆ v + adv + n

,nose sth 'out (*informal*) to discover some information by searching for it: *That man can nose a news story out anywhere.*
 SYN sniff sth out
 ◆ v + n/pron + adv ◆ v + adv + n

notch /nɒtʃ; AmE nɑːtʃ/

,notch sth 'up (*informal*) to achieve a win or a high score: *He notched up ten points in the first five minutes of the game.*
 OBJ victory, points, score **SYN** clock sth up
 ◆ v + adv + n ◆ v + n/pron + adv

note /nəʊt; AmE noʊt/

,note sth 'down to write sth down so that you will remember it: *The class noted down every word she said.*
 SYN take sth down; write sth down ⊃ note at WRITE STH DOWN
 ◆ v + adv + n ◆ v + n/pron + adv

number /'nʌmbə(r)/

'number sb/sth among sth (*formal*) to include sb/sth in a particular group: *I number her among my closest friends.* ◇ *He is numbered among the world's top experts.*
 SYN count sb/sth among sth
 ◆ v + n/pron + prep

nut /nʌt/

,nut sth 'out (*AustralE, informal*) to calculate sth or find the answer to sth: *I'm going to have to nut it out on a piece of paper.*
 SYN work sth out
 ◆ v + adv + n ◆ v + n/pron + adv

nuzzle /'nʌzl/

,nuzzle 'up against/to sb/sth to press your head, face, etc. against sb/sth to show affection or keep warm, etc.: *He nuzzled up to his mother with a happy sigh.*
 ◆ v + adv + prep

O o

object /əb'dʒekt/

ob'ject to sb/sth; ob'ject to doing sth; ob'ject to sb doing sth to say that you disagree with, disapprove of or oppose sth: *Many local people object to the new airport.* ◇ *I really object to being charged for parking.*
 ◆ v + prep

occur /ə'kɜː(r)/

oc'cur to sb if an idea or a thought **occurs to** you, it suddenly comes into your mind: *Hasn't it ever occurred to you that he might be lying to you?* ◇ *A strange thought suddenly occurred to me.* **SUBJ** thought, possibility
 ◆ v + prep

offend /ə'fend/

of'fend against sth (*formal*) to go against what people believe is morally right: *The book offends against good taste.*
 ◆ v + prep

offer /'ɒfə(r); AmE 'ɔːf-, 'ɑːf-/

,offer sth 'up (for sth) to give sth to God: *She offered up a prayer for her husband's safe return.*
 OBJ prayer, sacrifice
 ◆ v + adv + n ◆ v + n/pron + adv (*less frequent*)

ooze /uːz/

,ooze 'out; ,ooze 'out of/'from/'through sth if a thick liquid **oozes out** or **oozes from** somewhere, it flows out slowly: *Cream was*

oozing out of the cake. ◇ *cakes with cream oozing out at the sides* ◇ *Blood was oozing from the cut.*
◆ v + adv ◆ v + adv + prep ◆ v + prep

open /ˈəʊpən; *AmE* ˈoʊ-/

,open 'into/'onto sth if a door or a room **opens into/onto** sth, it leads directly to it: *The door opened onto a small yard.* ◇ *The kitchen opens into a large sitting room.*
◆ v + prep

,open 'off sth if a door or a room **opens off** sth, it connects directly with it: *Several doors opened off the hall.* ◇ *The offices opened off the reception area.*
◆ v + prep

,open 'out **1** (**into/onto sth**) to become wider or bigger; to become more open and not surrounded by anything: *The valley opened out in front of us.* ◇ *The narrow lane opened out into a field.* **2** (**to sb**) (*BrE*) → OPEN UP 1: *He only opened out to her very slowly.* **3** to spread out; to become open and larger or flatter: *The table opens out so that more people can sit at it.* ◇ *The buds on the trees have all opened out.*
◆ v + adv

,open sth 'out to spread sth out; to make sth open and flat: *He opened the map out.*
◆ v + n/pron + adv ◆ v + adv + n

,open 'up **1** (*BrE also* ,open 'out) (**to sb**) (*informal*) to talk freely and openly about what you feel or think: *Will you open up to me and tell me what's worrying you?* **2** to start firing: *The anti-aircraft guns opened up.* **3** (*often used in orders, etc.*) to open a door: *Open up or we'll break the door down!*
◆ v + adv

,open sb 'up to cut sb open in order to do a medical operation: *They opened her up but didn't find anything wrong.*
◆ v + n/pron + adv ◆ v + adv + n

Ŗ,open 'up; ,open sth 'up **1** to become or to make sth possible, available or able to be reached: *If you have good qualifications, a whole range of possibilities open up for you.* ◇ *The whole region has been opened up for trade by the new rail link.* ◇ *They opened up the sports hall to house the flood victims.* ◇ *Writing to penfriends can open up a whole new world.* **2** to start a new business: *The company are opening up a new factory in Wales.* ⊙₽₽ **close down, close sth down 3** to begin business for the day: *If you're feeling tired this morning, I'll open up* (*the store*). ⊙₽₽ **close up, close sth up 4** (*usually in sport*) to develop or start to happen; to produce sth or make sth start to happen: *An increasing gap is opening up between girls and boys in exams.* ◇ *United have opened up a three-point lead after five games.* **5** to become wider; to make sth wider, especially sth that has been closed: *Coughing might open up your wound.* ◇ *She wished the floor would open up and swallow her*

(= *because she felt very embarrassed*). ◇ *Cutting down the trees opened up the view from the house.*
◆ v + adv ◆ v + n/pron + adv ◆ v + adv + n

Ŗ,open sth 'up to make sth that is shut, locked, etc. open: *Can you open up that box of books for me?*
◆ v + n/pron + adv ◆ v + adv + n

opt /ɒpt; *AmE* ɑːpt/

'opt for sth to choose sth; to make a decision about sth: *More students are now opting for computer courses.* ◇ *You can stay in the hotel or opt for one of the bungalows near the beach.*
◆ v + prep

,opt 'in; ,opt 'into sth to choose to take part in sth: *We offer a pension plan, and all staff have the chance to opt in.* ◇ *The government decided to opt into the new European treaty.*
⊙₽₽ **opt out, opt out of sth**
◆ v + adv ◆ v + prep

,opt 'out; ,opt 'out of sth **1** to choose not to take part in sth: *You can opt out of the company's pension plan.* **2** (of a school or a hospital in Britain) to choose not to be under the control of the local authority: *A majority of parents were in favour of opting out.*
⊙₽₽ **opt in, opt into sth**
◆ v + adv ◆ v + adv + prep

▶ 'opt-out *n* (*often used as an adjective*) **1** the act of choosing not to take part in sth **2** (in Britain) the action of a school or a hospital that decides to manage its own money and is therefore no longer controlled by a local authority: *Nurses and health workers voted against the opt-out.*

order /ˈɔːdə(r); *AmE* ˈɔːrd-/

,order sb a'round (*BrE also* ,order sb a'bout) to keep on telling sb to do things in an unpleasant way: *Stop ordering me around!* ◇ *Even as a child, he ordered his friends about.*
◆ v + n/pron + adv

,order 'in; ,order 'in sth (*AmE*) to telephone and buy a meal from a restaurant that cooks the food and brings it to you: *I'm too tired to cook—let's order in.* ◇ *Let's order in Chinese tonight.*
◆ v + adv ◆ v + adv + n

,order sb 'off; ,order sb 'off sth **1** to tell sb to leave sth such as a bus, a train, etc.: *The driver ordered the boys off for messing around on the bus.* **2** (**for sth**) (*especially BrE*) (in a sports game) to make sb leave the field because they have broken the rules of the game: *He was ordered off for arguing with the referee.* ⊙ᴮᴶ **player** ꜱʏɴ **send sb off** (**for sth**) (*BrE*) ɴᴏᴛᴇ Often used in the passive.
◆ v + n/pron + adv ◆ v + adv + n ◆ v + n/pron + prep

,order 'out (**for sth**) (*AmE*) to telephone and buy a meal from a restaurant that cooks the food and brings it to you: *We could order out for a Chinese.*

⬩ v + adv

own /əʊn; *AmE* oʊn/

‚own ˈup (**to sth/to doing sth**) to admit that you are the person responsible for sth that has happened: *Nobody owned up to breaking the window.*

SYN confess (**to sth/to doing sth**) (*more formal*)

⊃ note at ADMIT TO STH

⬩ v + adv

P p

pace /peɪs/

‚pace ˈout sth (*also* ‚pace ˈoff sth *less frequent*) to measure sth by taking regular steps across it: *She paced out the length of the room.*

NOTE When the object of **pace out** is a noun, it comes after **out**, but when the object is a pronoun, it comes between **pace** and **out**: *To measure your plot, either use a tape measure or just pace it out.*

⬩ v + adv + n ⬩ v + pron + adv

pack /pæk/

‚pack aˈway if sth **packs away**, it can be folded up small when you are no longer using it: *The jacket packs away neatly into its own pocket.*

⬩ v + adv

‚pack sth aˈway **1** to put sth into a box, cupboard, etc. when you are no longer using it: *We packed away the picnic things and put them in the car.* **2** (*informal*) to eat a lot of sth: *She can certainly pack it away!*

SYN put sth away

⬩ v + n/pron + adv ⬩ v + adv + n

‚pack sb ˈin to attract large numbers of people to a show, a play, etc.: *The film is still packing in the crowds.*

OBJ the crowds

NOTE Not used in the passive.

⬩ v + adv + n ⬩ v + n/pron + adv ⬩ v + n + adv (*rare*)

‚pack sb/sth ˈin; ‚pack sb/sth ˈin/ˈinto sth **1** to do a lot of things, see a lot of people, etc. in a limited period of time: *She managed to pack a lot of sightseeing into three days.* ◇ *We packed in a lot yesterday afternoon.* **2** to put a lot of things or people into a limited space: *Somehow we managed to pack everyone in.*

SYN cram sb/sth in, cram sb/sth in/into sth

⬩ v + n/pron + adv ⬩ v + adv + n ⬩ v + n/pron + prep

‚pack sth ˈin (*BrE, informal*) **1** to give sth up, especially a job: *She's packed in her job as a teacher.* ◇ *Smoking's bad for you. You ought to pack it in.* ◇ *I was so depressed I felt like packing it all in.* **OBJ** job **SYN** chuck sth in/up (*BrE*);

jack sth in (*BrE*); give sth up → see also PACK UP, PACK STH UP 2; ⊃ note at GIVE UP, GIVE STH UP **2** ‚pack it ˈin used to tell sb to stop behaving badly or doing sth that is annoying you: *Just pack it in, will you?*

⬩ **1** v + adv + n ⬩ v + n/pron + adv

⬩ **2** v + it + adv

‚pack ˈinto sth if people **pack into** a place, they go there in large numbers and fill it completely: *All six of us packed into the tiny car.* ◇ *More than 70 000 people packed into Trafalgar Square on New Year's Eve.*

SYN cram into sth

⬩ v + prep

‚pack sb/sth ˈinto sth → PACK SB/STH IN, ETC,

‚pack sb ˈoff (**to …**) (*informal*) to send sb away, especially because you do not want them with you: *She was packed off to boarding school at the age of eight.* ◇ *He packed the children off to bed.*

NOTE Often used in the passive.

⬩ v + n/pron + adv ⬩ v + adv + n

‚pack sth ˈout (*BrE*) if a show, a performer, etc. **packs out** a place, large numbers of people go to see it/them: *The band packs out venues all over the country.* ◇ *The movie has been packing out cinemas for weeks.*

⬩ v + adv + n ⬩ v + n/pron + adv

▶ ‚packed ˈout *adj* (*BrE*) very full: *The town is packed out with tourists in the summer.* ◇ *a packed-out stadium*

‚pack ˈup (*BrE, informal*) if a machine, an engine, etc. **packs up**, it stops working: *My car's packed up again.*

SYN break down; give out

⬩ v + adv

‚pack ˈup; ‚pack sth ˈup **1** to put your possessions, equipment, etc. into bags or boxes before you leave a place: *It's time to pack up and go home.* ◇ *All our things were packed up, waiting to be moved.* **OBJ** things, belongings **2** (*BrE, informal*) to stop doing sth, especially a job: *He used to smoke but he packed up last year.* ◇ *You'd feel better if you packed up smoking.* ◇ *When did you pack up your job at the shop?* **OBJ** smoking, work, job **SYN** give sth up → see also PACK STH IN 1

⬩ v + adv ⬩ v + adv + n ⬩ v + pron + adv

⬩ v + n + adv (*rare*)

package /ˈpækɪdʒ/

‚package sth ˈup (*especially AmE*) to wrap sth and make it into a package so that you can send it somewhere: *She packaged up his books and mailed them to him.*

SYN parcel sth up (*BrE*)

⬩ v + adv + n ⬩ v + n/pron + adv

pad /pæd/ (**-dd-**)

‚pad sth ˈout (**with sth**) **1** to put soft material into a piece of clothing in order to change its shape: *She padded the costume out with foam.*

2 to make sth, such as a book, an article, a speech, etc., longer by adding unnecessary material: *I padded out the article with lots of quotations.*
♦ v + adv + n ♦ v + pron + adv ♦ v + n + adv

page /peɪdʒ/

,page 'down/'up (*computing*) to move forward/ backwards in a computer document, web page, etc.: *You can page up or down using the scroll bar at the side of the screen.*
♦ v + adv

,page 'through sth (*AmE*) to turn the pages of a book, a magazine, etc. and look at them without reading them in detail: *She paged through the report looking for her name.*
SYN leaf through sth
♦ v + prep

,page 'up → PAGE DOWN/UP

paint /peɪnt/

,paint sth 'out (*especially BrE*) to cover sth, such as a mark, part of a picture, etc. by putting paint on top of it so that no one can see it: *The markings on the plane had been hurriedly painted out.*
♦ v + adv + n ♦ v + pron + adv ♦ v + n + adv (*rare*)

,paint 'over sth to cover sth with a layer of paint: *We'll have to paint over the dirty marks on the wall. ◇ I don't like the way the painting has turned out so I'll just paint over it. ◇ The name had been painted over.*
♦ v + prep

,paint sth 'up to paint sth, decorating it in a bright, attractive way: *Their house had been painted up in amazing colours. ◇ The bus was painted up with advertisements.*
♦ v + n/pron + adv ♦ v + adv + n

pair /peə(r); *AmE* per/

,pair 'off; ,pair sb 'off (with sb) to form a pair or pairs, especially in order to have a romantic relationship; to bring two people together in this way: *By the end of the course, everyone had paired off. ◇ (especially BrE) They tried to pair their daughter off with the neighbour's son.*
♦ v + adv ♦ v + n/pron + adv ♦ v + adv + n

,pair 'up; ,pair sb 'up (with sb/sth) to form a pair or pairs (with sb/sth) in order to work, play a game, etc. together; to bring two people together for this purpose: *The job is a lot easier if you pair up with someone else. ◇ Writers have been paired up with artists to write articles on paintings.*
♦ v + adv ♦ v + n/pron + adv ♦ v + adv + n

pal /pæl/ (-ll-)

,pal a'round (with sb) (*AmE*) to become friends with sb and spend time with them: *I used to pal around with Brad.*
♦ v + adv

,pal 'up (with sb) (*BrE*) to become friends with sb: *They palled up at college.*
♦ v + adv

palm /pɑːm/

,palm sb 'off (with sth) (*informal*) **1** to persuade sb to believe an explanation for sth that is not true, in order to stop them asking questions or complaining: *Don't let him palm you off with an excuse.* **2** to persuade sb to accept sth that has little value or is not what they really want: *Make sure he doesn't palm you off with faulty goods.*
SYN fob sb off (with sth)
♦ v + n/pron + adv ♦ v + adv + n

,palm sth 'off as sth (*informal*) to persuade sb that sth is better than it really is, or is sth different, especially in order to sell it: *She was trying to palm copies off as original paintings.*
♦ v + n/pron + adv + prep

,palm sb/sth 'off on/onto sb (*informal*) to get rid of sb/sth that you do not want by persuading sb else to accept them/it: *He tried to palm his uncle off on me for the whole afternoon. ◇ I think she palmed off the stolen necklace on some unsuspecting old lady.*
♦ v + n/pron + adv + prep ♦ v + adv + n + prep

pan /pæn/ (-nn-)

,pan 'out (*informal*) (of events or a situation) to develop in a particular way: *I don't know why things panned out the way they did. ◇ How do you see your career panning out?*
SYN turn out
♦ v + adv

pander /ˈpændə(r)/

'pander to sb/sth (*disapproving*) to try to please sb by doing or providing what they want although you know it is probably wrong to do so: *He panders to her every whim. ◇ His movies never pandered to public taste. ◇ I don't think children should be pandered to.*
♦ v + prep

panic /ˈpænɪk/ (-ck-)

'panic sb into sth; 'panic sb into doing sth to make sb do sth too quickly because they are afraid: *Don't let them panic you into a decision. ◇ She refused to be panicked into making rash promises.*
NOTE Often used in the passive.
♦ v + n/pron + prep

paper /ˈpeɪpə(r)/

,paper 'over sth **1** to cover sth such as a wall with thick paper in order to hide sth: *We papered over the stains on the wall.* **2** to hide sth such as a problem, a disagreement, etc., especially quickly or not very well: *The divisions in*

the party had been papered over during the election campaign.
* v + prep

IDM **paper over the 'cracks (in sth)** to try to hide a problem or fault, especially in a way that is unlikely to be successful

parachute /ˈpærəʃuːt/

,parachute sb 'in; ,parachute sb 'into sth
to put sb from outside an organization into a senior position in the organization: *She was parachuted in last year to resolve the pensions crisis.*
NOTE Often used in the passive.
* v + n/pron + adv ◆ v + adv + n ◆ v + n/pron + prep

parcel /ˈpɑːsl/ ; *AmE* /ˈpɑːrsl/ (-ll-, *AmE* -l-)

NOTE A **parcel** is something that is wrapped in paper so that it can be sent by mail, carried easily, or given as a present.

,parcel sth 'off to sell or transfer a set of things that are part of a larger set: *They'll parcel off some of the stores to the other companies.*
* v + n/pron + adv ◆ v + adv + n

,parcel sth 'out to divide sth into parts: *They parcelled out the land into small plots. ◇ The work was parcelled out among the staff.*
* v + adv + n ◆ v + pron + adv ◆ v + n + adv (*rare*)

,parcel sth 'up (*BrE*) to wrap sth and make it into a parcel: *She parcelled up the books ready to send.*
SYN **package sth up** (*especially AmE*); **wrap sth up**
NOTE Parcel sth on its own is used less often with the same meaning.
* v + adv + n ◆ v + n/pron + adv

pare /peə(r)/ ; *AmE* /per/

,pare sth a'way/'off to remove the thin outer layer from sth in thin strips: *Pare off the rind from the orange using a sharp knife. ◇ (figurative) Their rights had been pared away under the last three kings.*
NOTE Pare sth can also be used on its own with this meaning: *Pare the rind from the lemons. ◇ thinly pared rind.*
* v + adv + n ◆ v + n/pron + adv

,pare sth 'down (*also* ,pare sth 'back *less frequent*) (to sth) to gradually reduce sth considerably in size or amount: *We've pared our expenses down to a minimum.*
SYN **cut sth back**; **cut sth down (to sth)**
NOTE Pare sth can also be used on its own with this meaning: *We pared costs by doing much of the work ourselves.*
* v + n/pron + adv ◆ v + adv + n

parlay /ˈpɑːleɪ/ ; *AmE* /ˈpɑːrleɪ/

,parlay sth 'into sth (*AmE, informal*) to use an advantage that you have, such as money or a skill, in order to get sth or make it worth more: *He parlayed his relationship with his boss into an important job.*
* v + n/pron + prep

part /pɑːt/ ; *AmE* /pɑːrt/

'part with sth to give sth away that you would prefer to keep: *It was my grandmother's necklace and I'll never part with it. ◇ (humorous) We won't be sorry to part with that old sofa. ◇ He hates parting with* (= spending) *his money.*
OBJ **money**
* v + prep

partake /pɑːˈteɪk/ ; *AmE* /pɑːrˈt-/ (partook /-ˈtʊk/, partaken /-ˈteɪkən/)

par'take of sth (*old-fashioned* or *humorous*) to eat or drink sth: *Would you care to partake of some refreshment?*
* v + prep

partition /pɑːˈtɪʃn/ ; *AmE* /pɑːrˈt-/

par,tition sth 'off to separate one area, one part of a room, etc. from another with a wall or screen: *The dining area is partitioned off with screens.*
NOTE Often used in the passive.
* v + adv + n ◆ v + n/pron + adv

partner /ˈpɑːtnə(r)/ ; *AmE* /ˈpɑːrtnər/

,partner 'up (with sb) to join one other person in order to play a game, dance, etc.: *Our dancing coach got us to partner up. ◇ Who have you partnered up with?*
* v + adv

pass /pɑːs/ ; *AmE* /pæs/

⚡,pass sth a'round; ,pass sth a'round sth (*BrE also* ,pass sth 'round, ,pass sth 'round sth) to offer sth to each person in a group: *Would you mind passing the sandwiches round? ◇ A picture was passed around the class.*
SYN **hand sth round, hand sth around**
* v + n/pron + adv ◆ v + adv + n ◆ v + n/pron + prep

'pass as sb → PASS FOR/AS SB

⚡,pass a'way **1** (*also* ,pass 'on) people say **pass away** to avoid saying 'die': *She passed away peacefully in her sleep.* **2** to disappear: *Many of these customs have passed away.*
↪ note on page 218
* v + adv

,pass be'tween sb if sth such as a look, a word, etc. **passes between** two people, they look quickly at each other, speak to each other, etc.: *A look of understanding passed between Ann and Carla. ◇ I never knew what passed between them* (= what they said to each other) *on that day.*
* v + prep

,pass 'by if time **passes by**, it goes past: *The weeks passed by and she didn't call.*
SYN **go by**

pass away

die ✦ pass away ✦ perish ✦ bite the dust
These verbs all mean to stop living.

die to stop living: *Her father died of cancer.*
◇ *Her husband died suddenly last week.*

pass away to die: *His mother passed away last year.*

perish (*formal* or *literary*) to die, especially in a sudden violent way: *A family of four perished in the fire.* ◇ *Thousands perished at the hands of the invading forces.*

bite the dust (*informal*, *humorous*) to die: *At the end of the film the baddies all bite the dust.*

WHICH WORD?

People say **pass away** to avoid saying 'die'. **Perish** is usually used in texts describing the results of war and accidents. **Bite the dust** is used humorously, and so should usually be avoided when talking about real people. It can be used to talk about businesses, plans, etc.

PATTERNS AND COLLOCATIONS

- to die/perish **of/from** sth
- to die/perish **in** an accident, a fire, etc.
- to die/pass away **peacefully**

NOTE **Pass** on its own is used more frequently: *The weeks passed.*
✦ v + adv

pass 'by; ,pass 'by sb/sth to go past sb/sth without stopping: *He saw the procession pass by.*
◇ *The boat passed close by the island.*
SYN go by, go by sb/sth
NOTE **Pass** and **pass sb/sth** are also used on their own: *We watched the procession pass.*
✦ v + adv ✦ v + prep
▶ 'bypass *n* **1** a road that goes around a town, etc. and which is intended to keep traffic out of the town centre **2** a medical operation on the heart in which blood is directed along a different route so that it does not flow through a part that is damaged or blocked; the new route that the blood takes: *a bypass operation*
▶ ,passer-'by *n* a person who is walking past sb/sth, especially when sth unexpected happens: *Several passers-by stopped to help.*

,pass sb/sth 'by to happen without affecting sb/sth: *She feels that life is passing her by* (= that she is not enjoying the opportunities and pleasures of life). ◇ *The whole business passed him by* (= he was hardly aware that it was happening).
✦ v + n/pron + adv

pass sth 'down (to sb) to give sth or teach sth to your children or people who are younger than you, who will then give or teach it to their children, etc.: *These stories were passed down from one generation to the next.* ◇ *Some of the furniture has been passed down through the family.*
SYN hand sth down (to sb)
NOTE Often used in the passive.
✦ v + n/pron + adv ✦ v + adv + n

pass for sth (*disapproving*) used to say that although sth is said to be a particular thing, you do not think it is good enough to be called that:

I got used to drinking what passes for tea in that part of the world.
✦ v + prep

pass for/as sb to be so much like another person, or another type of person, that people could easily think you were that person or type: *He speaks French well enough to pass for a Frenchman.* ◇ *She's in her forties but she could pass for ten years younger.* ◇ *They could pass as twins.*
✦ v + prep

pass into sth (*formal*) to become a part of sth: *Many foreign words have passed into English.*
✦ v + prep

,pass 'off (*BrE*) **1** [+ adv/prep] if an event **passes off** in a particular way, it takes place and is finished in the way mentioned: *The election has passed off without incident.* ◇ *The celebrations passed off peacefully.* **2** if pain, the effects of a drug, etc. **pass off**, they gradually disappear: *The symptoms should pass off within 24 hours.*
✦ v + adv

,pass sth 'off to act as if a difficult or awkward remark or situation is less important than you really think it is: *He had really upset her, but she smiled and tried to pass it off.* ◇ *He managed to pass the question off lightly.*
✦ v + n/pron + adv ✦ v + adv + n

,pass sb/sth 'off as sb/sth; ,pass yourself 'off as sb/sth to pretend that sb or sth is sth that they are not: *She tried to pass the picture off as an original.* ◇ *He succeeded in passing himself off as a doctor.*
✦ v + n/pron + adv + prep
✦ v + adv + n + prep (*less frequent*)

pass 'on **1** (to sth) (*BrE*) to begin a new activity, discussion, etc.: *Let's pass on to the next item on the agenda.* ◇ *If you can't answer one question, pass on to the next.* SYN move on (to sth)
2 → PASS AWAY 1
✦ v + adv

,pass sth 'on (to sb) **1** to give sth to sb else, especially after receiving or using it yourself: *I'll pass this book on to you when I've finished with it.* ◊ *I'll pass on your news to the rest of the family.* ☜ **hand sth on (to sb) 2** to give sth that you have, such as a disease, a quality, etc. to sb else: *HIV can be passed on from parent to child.* ◊ *Parents pass these attitudes on to their children.* **3** if a company, a shop/store, etc. **passes on** higher or lower costs to its customers, it makes them pay more or less for sth: *The supermarket did not pass on its profit to customers by cutting prices.*
   ◆ v + n/pron + adv ◆ v + adv + n

,pass sb 'on to sb to arrange for sb else to help or deal with a particular person: *I'm afraid I can't answer your question, but I'll pass you on to my colleague.*
   ◆ v + n/pron + adv + prep

,pass 'out **1** to become unconscious: *He almost passed out with the pain.* ☜ **black out**; **faint** → see also COME ROUND/COME TO **2** (*also* ,pass 'out of sth) (*BrE*) to leave a military college after completing a course of training
   ◆ v + adv **2** also v + adv + prep

,pass sth 'out (to sb) to give something to each person in a group: *The teacher asked me to pass the books out.*
   ☜ **give sth out**; **hand sth out (to sb)**
   ◆ v + n/pron + adv ◆ v + adv + n

,pass 'over sb (for sth) to not consider sb for a better job, especially when they deserve it or think they deserve it: *I was passed over for promotion again.* ◊ *He was passed over in favour of a younger man.*
   NOTE When the object of **pass over** is a noun, it comes after **over**, but when the object is a pronoun, it comes between **pass** and **over**: *Her distinguished career made it impossible to pass her over.* ◆ Often used in the passive.
   ◆ v + adv + n ◆ v + pron + adv

,pass 'over sb/sth **1** to move over the top of sb/ sth: *The planes pass directly over the hospital.* ◊ *The eye of the storm was passing over us.* **2** to ignore or avoid sth: *They chose to pass over her rude remarks.* ◊ *For years this painting was passed over by experts.* ☜ **ignore sb/sth**
   ◆ v + prep
   ▶ 'overpass *n* (*especially AmE*) a bridge that carries one road or railway above another; a bridge over a road for people who want to cross: *Don't try to cross the highway—use the overpass.*

,pass sb/sth 'over (to sb) **1** to give sth to sb, especially when they ask for it or you do not want it any more; to give sb, or the responsibility for sb, to sb else: *Jeff passed the phone over so that I could speak to Clare.* ◊ *The doctor passed the baby over to the nurse.* ◊ *Control of the budgets has been passed over to individual schools.* ☜ **hand sb/sth over (to sb) 2** to let

sb listen or speak to sb else when you have finished talking: *If there are no more questions, I'll pass you over to Ted.* ☜ **hand over to sb**, **hand sb over to sb**
   ◆ v + n/pron + adv ◆ v + adv + n

,pass sth 'round, etc. (*BrE*) → PASS STH AROUND, ETC.

,pass 'through; ,pass 'through sth to go or travel through a place, only stopping for a short time: *We're not staying here, we're just passing through.* ◊ *We passed through Paraty on our way to Rio.*
   ◆ v + adv ◆ v + prep

,pass 'through sth (*especially BrE*) to experience a particular kind of situation or period of time, especially a difficult or unpleasant one, and develop during it: *She passed through a difficult period after her divorce.* ◊ *The industry is passing through a period of change.*
   OBJ **period**, **stage** ☜ **go through sth**
   ◆ v + prep

'pass to sb/sth to begin to be owned by sb new: *When she died, the house passed to her niece.*
   ◆ v + prep

,pass sth 'up (*informal*) to decide not to take advantage of an opportunity, an offer, etc.: *She passed up the chance of a trip to Rome.* ◊ *Imagine passing up an offer like that!*
   OBJ **opportunity**, **chance**, **offer**
   ◆ v + adv + n ◆ v + pron + adv
   ◆ v + n + adv (*less frequent*)

pat /pæt/ (-tt-)

,pat sb 'down (*AmE*) (of a police officer, etc.) to feel sb's body, legs, arms, etc. with your hands in order to check whether the person has a gun: *The policeman had stopped two teenagers and was patting them down.*
   ☜ **frisk sb**; **search sb**
   ◆ v + adv + n ◆ v + n/pron + adv
   ▶ 'pat-down *n* (*AmE*): *Five or six passengers were given pat-downs as they entered the station.*

patch /pætʃ/

,patch sb/sth 'through to connect telephone or electronic equipment temporarily: *The radio was patched through to army headquarters.*
   ◆ v + n/pron + adv

,patch sth to'gether to arrange sth quickly, especially by putting several different parts together, without taking any care over it: *An interim government was quickly patched together.*
   ◆ v + adv + n ◆ v + n/pron + adv

,patch sb/sth 'up to give quick or temporary medical treatment to sb who is injured: *They patched him up and sent him back onto the field* (= for example in a game of football). ◊ *The doctor did his best to patch up their wounds.*
   ◆ v + n/pron + adv ◆ v + adv + n

,patch sth 'up **1** to repair sth, especially quickly or temporarily: *The car was patched up and*

paw

resold. ◇ *We patched up the hole in the roof and got it repaired the next day.* **2** to end an argument or disagreement with sb and be friends again: *They patched up their differences.* ◇ *Can't you two try to patch things up?* OBJ **differences, quarrel, things 3** to agree on sth, especially after long discussions and even though the result is not as good as hoped: *They managed to patch up a peace.*
♦ **1** v + n/pron + adv ♦ v + adv + n
♦ **2,3** v + adv + n ♦ v + n/pron + adv

paw /pɔː/

NOTE An animal's **paw** is its foot.

'**paw at sb/sth** (*informal*) if an animal **paws at** sb/sth, it touches sb/sth repeatedly with its paw: *a horse pawing at the ground* ◇ (*figurative*) *One of the children was pawing at my sleeve.*
♦ v + prep

pawn /pɔːn/

,**pawn sth 'off as sth** to pretend that sth is better, more valuable, etc. than it really is: *There is so much misinformation pawned off as fact these days.*
♦ v + n/pron + adv + prep ♦ v + adv + n + prep

,**pawn sth 'off on sb** (*AmE*) to get rid of sb/sth that you do not want by persuading sb else to accept them/it: *New economies are trying to pawn off old processes on poorer countries.*
♦ v + n/pron + adv + prep ♦ v + adv + n + prep

pay /peɪ/ (**paid, paid** /peɪd/)

,**pay sb 'back** (**for sth/for doing sth**) to punish sb because they have made you or sb else suffer: *I'll pay him back for getting me into trouble!*
SYN **get back at sb** (**for sth/for doing sth**)
♦ v + n/pron + adv ♦ v + adv + n (*less frequent*)
▶ '**payback** n [C, U] a reward or a punishment that sb receives for sth they have done

,**pay sb 'back; ,pay sth 'back** (**to sb**) to return money that you have borrowed from sb: *I'll pay you back next week.* ◇ *She's trying to pay the loan back over five years.* ◇ *He'll never be able to pay back the money.*
SYN **repay sb** (**sth**), **repay sth** (**to sb**) (*more formal*)
NOTE In informal language **pay sb back sth** and, less often, **pay sb sth back** are also used on their own: *When are you going to pay me back that $100 you owe me?* ◇ *Can you pay me that money back soon?*
♦ v + n/pron + adv ♦ v + adv + n
▶ '**payback** n [C, U] the money that you receive back on money that you have invested; the time that it takes to get your money back: *I'm waiting to get the maximum payback on my investment.* ◇ *a ten-year payback*

,**pay sth 'down** to give an amount of money as the first payment for sth: *You can pay $200 down and the rest in 12 monthly instalments.*
♦ v + adv + n ♦ v + n/pron + adv

'**pay for sth 1** (*also* '**pay sb for sth**) to give sb money for work, goods, services, etc.: *I'll pay for the tickets.* ◇ *You need to pay Paul for all that work he did for you.* **2** to suffer or be punished for sth wrong that you have done or said, or for sth you believe: *Someone's going to pay for this!* ◇ *They are paying dearly for their mistake.*
OBJ **mistake, crime**
♦ v + prep

,**pay sth 'in; ,pay sth 'into sth** to put money into a bank account: *I had to go to the bank to pay a cheque in.* ◇ *Her wages are paid directly into her account.*
OBJ **cheque, money** SYN **deposit sth** (**in sth**) (*more formal*)
♦ v + n/pron + adv ♦ v + adv + n ♦ v + n/pron + prep

,**pay 'off** if sth that involves risk **pays off**, it is successful and brings the results that you want: *The gamble paid off.* ◇ *Their hard work is beginning to pay off.* ◇ *All the training you've been doing seems to have paid off handsomely* (= has had very good results).
♦ v + adv
▶ '**pay-off** n (*informal*) a reward or a benefit that you receive as a result of sth you do: *What are the pay-offs of working at home?*

,**pay sb 'off 1** to give sb money to persuade them not to do sth or not to tell sb about sth illegal or dishonest you have done: *She refused to be paid off.* SYN **buy sb off 2** to pay sb the money they have earned and dismiss them from their job: *The store has paid off many of the full-time staff and offered them part-time work.*
♦ v + n/pron + adv ♦ v + adv + n
▶ '**pay-off** n (*informal*) **1** a payment you make to sb to persuade them not to do sth or not to tell sb about sth illegal or dishonest you have done: *Police have been accused of receiving pay-offs from local gangs.* **2** a payment made to sb to persuade them to leave their job: *She has received a £10 000 pay-off.*

,**pay sth/sb 'off 1** to finish paying money that you owe for sth: *I used the money to pay off my overdraft.* ◇ *They're still paying off their mortgage.* ◇ *to pay off creditors/a bank manager* OBJ **mortgage, loan, debts** SYN **repay sth/sb** (*more formal*) **2** (*especially BrE*) to pay for a taxi journey: *She paid the taxi off and walked the rest of the way.* OBJ **taxi/cab**
♦ **1** v + adv + n ♦ v + pron + adv
♦ v + n + adv (*less frequent*)
♦ **2** v + n/pron + adv ♦ v + adv + n

,**pay 'out; ,pay sth 'out** (**for sth**) (*especially BrE*) to pay a large amount for sth: *The insurance company refused to pay out.* ◇ *The government*

pay (sth) out

cough (sth) up ◆ **fork out (sth)** ◆ **pay (sth) out** ◆ **pay up** ◆ **shell (sth) out**

These verbs all mean to give money to pay for goods or services.

cough (sth) up (*informal*) to pay or give money unwillingly: *His family shouldn't have to cough up for his gambling debts.* ◇ *She finally coughed up the money she owed us.*

fork out (sth) (*informal*) to spend a lot of money on sth, especially unwillingly: *Furious rail passengers had to fork out for taxis.* ◇ *We've forked out a small fortune on home improvements.*

pay (sth) out to pay a lot of money for sth or to sb: *I had to pay out £500 to get my car repaired.* **NOTE** *Pay* can be used on its own: *I had to pay £500 to get my car repaired.*

pay up (*not formal*) to pay all the money that you owe to sb, especially when you do not

want to or when the payment is late: *I had a hard time getting him to pay up.*

shell (sth) out (*informal*) to spend a lot of money on sth: *The band shelled out $100 000 for a mobile recording studio.*

WHICH WORD?

You **fork out** for sth more unwillingly than you **shell out** for sth. You can **cough up** money that you or sb else owes. You cannot **pay up** for sb else's debts, only your own. **Pay up** does not take an object.

PATTERNS AND COLLOCATIONS

- to pay out/fork out/shell out **on** sth
- to pay out/pay up/cough up/fork out/shell out **for** sth
- to pay out/cough up/fork out/shell out **money/£1 000/a lot**

pays out millions of pounds in benefits. ◇ *I can't afford to pay out for private treatment.*
- v + adv ◆ v + adv + n ◆ v + pron + adv
- v + n + adv (*rare*)

▶ **'payout** *n* a large amount of money that is given to sb: *People injured in the crash won record payouts from the rail company.*

,**pay sth 'out** (*BrE*) to pass a rope, etc. through your hands: *He started paying out the rope.*
- v + adv + n ◆ v + pron + adv ◆ v + n + adv (*rare*)

,**pay 'up** (*informal*) to give sb the money that you owe them, especially if you do not want to: *In the end we threatened to take them to court and they paid up.*
SYN **cough up** (*especially BrE*)
- v + adv

▶ **'paid-up** *adj* [only before noun] **1** having paid all the money necessary to be a member of a club or an organization **2** (*informal*) strongly supporting sth: *a fully paid-up football fan*

peck /pek/

'**peck at sth** to eat only very small amounts of sth, because you are not hungry: *He was so nervous he only pecked at his lunch.*
- v + prep

peel /piːl/

,**peel a'way/'back (from sth)**, ,**peel a'way/ 'back (from sth)** to come off the surface of sth; to remove a thin layer from the surface of sth: *The wallpaper had started to peel away.* ◇ *The paint was peeling away from the wood.* ◇ *She peeled back the blankets and jumped into bed.* ◇ *He peeled away the plastic wrapping.*

→ see also PEEL STH OFF, PEEL STH OFF STH
- v + adv ◆ v + n/pron + adv
- v + adv + n

,**peel 'off 1** to come away from the surface of sth: *The wallpaper was peeling off.* **SUBJ** **paper, skin, paint 2** (of cars, aircraft, etc.) to leave a group and turn to one side: *The planes peeled off, one by one.*
- v + adv

,**peel sth 'off 1** to remove some or all of your clothing, especially sth that fits tightly: *He peeled off his wet clothes.* **OBJ** **clothes, gloves, T-shirt, etc. 2** to remove some notes from a thick pile of folded or rolled paper money: *He peeled off two hundred dollars and handed them to her.*
- v + adv + n ◆ v + pron + adv
- v + n + adv (*rare*)

,**peel sth 'off**; ,**peel sth 'off sth** to remove a thin layer from the surface of sth: *He peeled off the sweet wrapper.* ◇ *She peeled all the wallpaper off the bathroom ceiling.*
OBJ **wallpaper, paint, wrapper**
- v + n/pron + adv ◆ v + adv + n ◆ v + n/pron + prep

,**peel 'out** (*AmE, informal*) to leave quickly and in a noisy way, especially in a car, on a motorcycle, etc.: *She peeled out of the driveway and sped down the street.*
- v + adv

peer /pɪə(r); *AmE* pɪr/

'**peer at sth** to look closely or carefully at sth, especially when you cannot see it clearly: *She peered closely at the dusty old letters.*
- v + prep

peg /peg/ (**-gg-**)

,peg a'way (**at sth**) (*informal*) to continue to work hard at or try to achieve sth difficult: *He keeps pegging away at his novel.*
  ◆ v + adv

,peg sb/sth 'back (*sport*) to stop sb/sth from winning or from increasing the amount by which they are ahead: *Italy were winning 2-0, but were pegged back to a draw by Spain's late goal.*
  NOTE Often used in the passive. ◆ It is common in newspapers.
  ◆ v + n/pron + adv ◆ v + adv + n (*less frequent*)

,peg 'out (*BrE, informal*) to die: *I thought she was going to peg out right in front of me!*
  ◆ v + adv

pelt /pelt/

'pelt down (*informal*) to rain very heavily: *It's pelting down (with rain) outside.*
  SYN pour down
  ◆ v + adv

pen /pen/ (**-nn-**)

,pen sb/sth 'in; ,pen sb/sth 'in sth to shut sb/sth in a small space with walls or fences, etc. all around: *We penned the sheep in the yard.* ◇ *The troublemakers were penned in by the police.* ◇ (*figurative*) *She felt penned in living in the heart of the city.*
  NOTE Often used in the passive.
  ◆ v + n/pron + adv ◆ v + adv + n ◆ v + n/pron + prep

,pen sb/sth 'up (*especially BrE*) to shut sb/sth in a place with walls, fences, etc. all around, and not let them leave: *It was good to go outside after being penned up in the house all day.* ◇ *They penned us up in a little room and wouldn't let anyone leave.*
  NOTE Usually used in the passive.
  ◆ v + n/pron + adv ◆ v + adv + n

pencil /'pensl/ (**-ll-**, *AmE* **-l-**)

,pencil sb/sth 'in (**for sth**) to write down sb's name for an appointment, or the details of an arrangement, although you know that this might have to be changed later: *Let's pencil in the third of May for the meeting.*
  ⮌ note at WRITE STH DOWN
  ◆ v + n/pron + adv ◆ v + adv + n

pension /'penʃn/

,pension sb 'off to allow or force sb to retire, especially because they are old or ill/sick, and pay them a pension: *She was pensioned off at the age of 56.* ◇ (*figurative*) *We've pensioned our old TV off and bought a new one.*
  NOTE Usually used in the passive.
  ◆ v + n/pron + adv ◆ v + adv + n

pep /pep/ (**-pp-**)

,pep sb/sth 'up (*informal*) to make sb/sth more interesting; to make sb feel more lively or full of energy: *The company needs to pep up its image.*
  ◆ v + adv + n ◆ v + n/pron + adv

pepper /'pepə(r)/

'pepper sb/sth with sth to hit sb/sth with lots of small things such as bullets: *They said they were peppered with shotgun pellets as they walked in the forest.* ◇ (*figurative*) *The interviewer peppered her with questions.*
  NOTE Usually used in the passive.
  ◆ v + n/pron + prep

'pepper sth with sth to include a large number of sth in sth: *She peppers her conversation with references to famous people.* ◇ *Her hair is peppered with grey.*
  NOTE Usually used in the passive.
  ◆ v + n/pron + prep

perk /pɜːk; *AmE* pɜːrk/

,perk 'up; ,perk sb 'up (*informal*) to become, or make sb, more lively or more cheerful, especially after they have been ill/sick: *You've perked up since this morning.* ◇ *A shower would soon perk you up.*
  SYN liven up, liven sb up ⮌ note at CHEER UP
  ◆ v + adv ◆ v + n/pron + adv ◆ v + adv + n

,perk 'up; ,perk sth 'up (*informal*) to improve or increase in value, to make sth increase in value, etc.: *The weather seems to be perking up.* ◇ *The recent demand for houses has perked up the prices.* ◇ *House prices are expected to perk up.*
  SYN improve, improve sth
  ◆ v + adv ◆ v + n/pron + adv ◆ v + adv + n

,perk sth 'up (*informal*) to make sth more interesting or more attractive: *Perk up a dark kitchen with a coat of paint.* ◇ *A vegetable stew can be perked up with a dash of chilli sauce.* ◇ *ideas for perking up bland food*
  SYN liven sth up
  ◆ v + adv + n ◆ v + pron + adv
  ◆ v + n + adv (*less frequent*)

permit /pə'mɪt; *AmE* pər'm-/ (**-tt-**)

per'mit of sth (*formal*) to make sth possible; to allow sth to happen: *The situation does not permit of any delay.*
  NOTE Permit of sth is usually used in negative sentences.
  ◆ v + prep

pertain /pə'teɪn; *AmE* pər't-/

per'tain to sth (*formal*) to be connected with a particular subject, person, event or situation: *The committee was reviewing all the laws pertaining to adoption.*
  ◆ v + prep

peter out

die away ◆ **fade away** ◆ **fizzle out** ◆ **peter out**

These verbs can all be used when sth gradually becomes less or weaker, and eventually disappears or stops happening. *See also* **die down, dwindle away**.

die away (especially of noise) to become gradually weaker or fainter and finally disappear: *The sound of their laughter died away.*

fade away to disappear gradually: *Hopes of reaching an agreement seem to be fading away.* ◇ *The laughter faded away.* NOTE **Fade** can be used on its own: *Her smile faded.*

fizzle out (*informal*) to gradually become less successful and end in a disappointing way: *The threatened revolt just fizzled out.* ◇ *Her parents are hoping that the relationship will fizzle out.*

peter out to gradually become smaller, quieter or weaker and then end: *The campaign petered out for lack of support.* ◇ *The conversation eventually petered out.*

PATTERNS AND COLLOCATIONS

- the **storm/wind/rain** peters out/dies away
- sb's **voice** peters out/dies away/fades away
- sb's **words** peter out/die away/fade away
- a **revolt/relationship** peters out/fizzles out

peter /ˈpiːtə(r)/

ˌpeter 'out (into sth) to decrease or fade gradually before coming to an end: *The road petered out into a dirt track.* ◇ *By midday their enthusiasm had petered out.* ◇ *The conversation gradually petered out.*
◆ v + adv

phase /feɪz/

ˌphase sth 'down to reduce sth gradually in stages over a period of time: *We are phasing down production of less profitable items.*
◆ v + adv + n ◆ v + n/pron + adv

ˌphase sth 'in to introduce sth gradually or in stages: *The government will phase in the new tax.* ◇ *The scheme will be phased in over 15 years.*
OPP **phase sth out**
NOTE Often used in the passive.
◆ v + adv + n ◆ v + n/pron + adv

ˌphase sth 'out to stop using sth gradually or in stages: *They agreed to phase out chemical weapons.* ◇ *The old system is being phased out.*
OPP **phase sth in**
NOTE Often used in the passive.
◆ v + adv + n ◆ v + n/pron + adv

phone /fəʊn; *AmE* foʊn/

NOTE **To phone** is the most common way to say 'to telephone' in British English. **To ring** and **to call** are also used. The most common verb in American English for this is **to call**.

ˌphone a'round/'round; ˌphone a'round/ 'round sb/sth (*especially BrE*) to make phone calls to several different people or places, usually to try to find out some information: *I spent the morning phoning round hotels.* ◇ *He phoned around to tell everyone about the meeting.*
◆ v + adv ◆ v + prep

ˌphone 'back; ˌphone sb 'back (*especially BrE*) to telephone sb again or to telephone sb who telephoned you earlier: *I left a message but they never phoned back.* ◇ *Tom called while you were out. He asked if you could phone him back.* ◇ *The travel agent phoned back to confirm your booking.* ◇ *It's engaged—I'll phone back later.*
◆ v + adv ◆ v + n/pron + adv ◆ v + adv + n (*rare*)

ˌphone 'in (*especially BrE*) **1** to telephone your place of work: *I'll phone in to say I won't be in until lunchtime.* ◇ *He phoned in sick* (= to say he was ill/sick and could not go to work) *this morning.* **2** to phone a television or radio programme: *Hundreds of listeners phoned in to complain.*
◆ v + adv

▶ 'phone-in *n* (*especially BrE*) a radio or TV programme in which people can phone and ask questions, give their opinions, etc. as the programme is being broadcast: *He hosts a radio phone-in.* ◇ *a phone-in programme*

ˌphone sth 'in **1** (*especially BrE*) to make a telephone call to the place where you work in order to give sb some information: *Our reporter phoned the story in this afternoon.* **2** (*informal*) to do sth such as play a role in a film/movie, play in a sports competition, etc. without making much effort: *Cruise is just phoning it in in this new release.* ◇ *Pavarotti's performance was phoned in.*
◆ v + n/pron + adv ◆ v + adv + n

ˌphone 'round, etc. (*especially BrE*) → PHONE AROUND/ROUND, ETC.

ˌphone sth 'through (*especially BrE*) to phone sb with details of or information about sth: *Phone your order through to the store.*
◆ v + n/pron + adv ◆ v + adv + n

ˌphone 'up; ˌphone sb/sth 'up (*especially BrE*) to make a telephone call to sb/sth: *I'll phone up and cancel my appointment.* ◇ *Phone Mike up and ask him if he wants to come.* ◇ *I phoned up the bank this morning.*
NOTE **Phone** and **phone sb** are also frequently used on their own. **Phone up** and **phone sb up** are very common in spoken English.
⊃ note at CALL UP, CALL SB/STH UP
◆ v + adv ◆ v + n/pron + adv ◆ v + adv + n

pick /pɪk/

,**pick at sth 1** to eat very small amounts of food because you are not hungry: *She picked at her food for a while, then left the table.* ⟦OBJ⟧ **food, meal 2** to pull sth with your fingers several times: *She picked nervously at her skirt until she made a hole.*
 ◆ v + prep

,**pick sb/sth 'off 1** to shoot a person, an animal, a bird, an aircraft, etc. especially one of a group, after aiming carefully: *One of our men was picked off by a sniper.* ⟳ note at SHOOT SB/STH DOWN **2** to choose the best people or things for your own use: *The company continues to pick off the brightest young graduates.*
 ◆ v + adv + n ◆ v + n/pron + adv

,**pick sth 'off**; ,**pick sth 'off sth** to remove sth from sth with your nails or a tool: *She watered the plants and picked off the dead leaves.*
 ◆ v + n/pron + adv ◆ v + adv + n ◆ v + n/pron + prep

'**pick on sb 1** to treat sb badly or unfairly, especially repeatedly: *You're always picking on me!* ◇ *The manager was accused of picking on a member of the department.* ◇ *It's difficult being the younger sister—you always get picked on.* **2** (*especially BrE*) to choose sb for a task, especially an unpleasant one: *The teacher always picked on Tom to answer the difficult questions.*
 ◆ v + prep

,**pick sb/sth 'out 1** to choose sb/sth from a number of people or things: *He picks out people from the audience to come up on stage.* ◇ *The brightest students were picked out for special training.* ◇ *He picked out the most expensive suit in the shop.* ⟦SYN⟧ **select sb/sth** (*more formal*) **2** to recognize sb/sth from among people or things: *Can you pick me out in this old school photo?* ◇ *The suspect was picked out at an identity parade.* **3** to manage to see sb/sth: *We could just pick out a car in the distance.* ⟦SYN⟧ **make sb/sth out** (*more formal*) ⟳ note at MAKE SB/STH OUT **4** if a light, etc. **picks sb/sth out**, it shines on sb/sth so that they/it are easier to see: *The car's headlights picked out a road sign.*
 ◆ v + adv + n ◆ v + n/pron + adv

,**pick sth 'out 1** to discover or recognize sth after careful study: *It was difficult to pick out the important points from the mass of facts.* ◇ *They were asked to pick out exactly what made his style so distinctive.* **2** if you **pick out** a tune on a musical instrument, you play it slowly, note by note, without using written music: *Buddie was picking out a simple tune on his guitar.* ⟦OBJ⟧ **melody, tune 3** usually be ,**picked 'out** (*BrE*) to paint, draw or write sth in such a way that it is very easy to see, especially by using a colour that is different from the background: *The details of the flowers were picked out in blue and gold.*
 ◆ v + adv + n ◆ v + n/pron + adv

,**pick sth 'over 1** (*also* ,**pick 'through sth** *less frequent*) to look carefully at a group of things, choosing what you want and rejecting anything you do not want: *He picked over the apples, checking for bad ones.* ◇ *Bargain hunters picked over a pile of sale items.* **2** (*especially BrE*) to examine or analyse sth carefully: *We spent the meeting picking over last month's results.*
 ◆ v + adv + n ◆ v + pron + adv

,**pick 'up 1** to become better; to improve: *The market always picks up in the spring.* ◇ *The game started very slowly but picked up in the second half.* ◇ *We're waiting until the weather picks up a bit.* **2** if the wind **picks up**, it starts to blow more strongly: *The wind seems to be picking up.* **3** to start again; to continue: *The new series picks up where the old one left off.* → see also PICK STH UP 9 **4** if your speed **picks up**, you start to go faster: *After the first mile (= in a race) I started to feel stronger and my speed picked up.* → see also PICK UP SPEED/MOMENTUM at PICK STH UP **5** if a bus, etc. **picks up** somewhere, it stops there to allow passengers to get on: *The bus picks up outside the Post Office* → see also PICK STH UP 1 **6** (**after sb**) (*informal, especially AmE*) to collect things that have been dropped or left on the ground and put them away: *I shouldn't have to pick up after you!* → see also PICK STH UP 12; ⟳ note at TIDY UP
 ◆ v + adv

▶ '**pickup** n **1** an improvement: *There are no signs of a pickup in consumer spending.* **2** (*AmE*) the ability of a vehicle to increase its speed

,**pick 'up**; ,**pick sth 'up** to answer the telephone: *Pick up if you're there, Tom!* ◇ *At last someone picked up the phone.*
 ◆ v + adv ◆ v + pron + adv ◆ v + adv + n

,**pick sb 'up 1** ,**pick 'up sb** if a bus, etc. **picks up** sb, it stops and allows them to get on: *The bus stopped to pick up some passengers.* ⟦NOTE⟧ When the object of **pick up** is a noun, it comes after **up**, but when the object is a pronoun, it comes between **pick** and **up**: *The bus stopped to pick us up.* → see also PICK UP 5 **2** to rescue sb, for example from the sea: *Lifeboats picked up all the survivors.* **3** to arrest sb; to take sb somewhere in order to question them: *She was picked up by the police as she was leaving her hotel.* **4** (*informal*) to start talking to sb you do not know, because you want to have a sexual relationship with them: *He picked her up at a club.* **5** if sth **picks you up**, it makes you feel better: *A cup of tea will soon pick you up.* → see also PICK YOURSELF UP
 ◆ v + n/pron + adv ◆ v + adv + n **2** v + adv + n
 ◆ v + pron + adv

▶ '**pick-me-up** n (*informal*) sth that makes you feel better or happier, etc.: *The country air was the perfect pick-me-up.*

▶ '**pickup** n **1** an occasion when sb gets in a car, on a bus, etc. to be taken to another place:

pick sb/sth up

collect sb/sth ♦ fetch sb/sth ♦ get sb/sth ♦ pick sb/sth up

These verbs all mean to go to a place where sb/sth is and bring them/it back.

collect sb/sth to go to a place where sb is waiting or sth is ready or has been left for you, and bring them/it back or take them/it somewhere: *Your package is ready to be collected.* ◇ *(BrE) What time do you have to collect the kids from school?* ▸ **collection** n [U]: *Your car will be ready for collection on Monday.*

fetch sb/sth *(especially BrE)* to go to a place where sb/sth is and bring them/it back: *She's gone to fetch the kids from school.* ◇ *He fetched a couple of towels from the bathroom.* ◇ *Can you fetch me a towel?*

get sb/sth *(not formal)* to go to a place where sb/sth is and bring them/it back: *Quick—go and get a cloth!* ◇ *Get a drink for John.* ◇ *Get John a drink.*

pick sb/sth up to go to a place where sb is waiting or sth is ready or has been left for you, and bring them/it back or take them/it somewhere: *He's gone to pick up Jan from the airport.* ◇ *I'll pick up your dry-cleaning for you if you like.*

WHICH WORD?

Get has a wider range of meaning than **fetch**: you usually **fetch** people or things that are in a place and just need to be collected; you can **get** things that need to be prepared or obtained. When you are talking about people, **collect** can be used in British English; in American English it is more usual to say **pick sb up**. You might be on foot or in a car when you **pick sth up** but you always **pick sb up** in a car.

PATTERNS AND COLLOCATIONS
- to get/fetch/pick up/collect sb/sth **from** sth/somewhere
- to get/fetch/collect sth **for** sb
- to **go/come to** get/fetch/pick up/collect sb/sth
- to **go/come and** get/fetch sth
- to get/fetch **help/a doctor**

The coach driver made several pickups before heading for the airport. ◇ *a pickup point* **2** *(informal)* a situation in which sb is trying to start a sexual relationship with a person they do not know; the person they are trying to start a sexual relationship with: *Nothing ever came of his pickups.* ◇ *a pickup joint* ▸ **'pickup** adj [only before noun] *(AmE)* not planned in advance or open for anyone to join in: *a pickup game of basketball* ◇ *The children ate pickup meals next to the stove.* ◇ *a pickup dance troupe*

ˌpick sb/sth ˈup 1 to take hold of and lift sb/sth: *I always pick the baby up when she cries.* ◇ *I picked up your bag by mistake.* ◇ *Pick your coat up off the floor!* ⟳ note at LIFT SB/STH UP **2** to go to sb's home or a place you have arranged and take them somewhere in your car; to collect sth from a place you have arranged: *I'll pick you up at seven o'clock.* ◇ *He picked up a hitchhiker.* ◇ *I went to pick her up from the airport.* ◇ *We can pick up the tickets an hour before the show starts.* **NOTE** **Pick sb/sth up** is used much more often than **collect sb/sth** in spoken English.

♦ v + n/pron + adv ♦ v + adv + n

ˌpick sth ˈup 1 to obtain or buy sth **2** to learn a language, a skill, etc., or to get information, without making an effort: *She picks up languages really easily.* ◇ *I showed her the software and she picked it up quickly.* ◇ *I picked up lots of tips on home entertainment from the magazine.* ◇ *She picked up the idea for the novel from a news story.* [OBJ] **languages, French, tips, etc. 3** to get or obtain sth: *He picked up a virus at school.* ◇ *The children have picked up the local accent.* [OBJ] **cold, habits 4** to identify or recognize sth: *The early signs of the disease were not picked up.* [OBJ] **signs** [SYN] **detect sth 5** if a machine **picks sth up**, it receives a sound, a signal or a picture: *The microphone picks up every sound.* ◇ *Signals from the satellite are picked up at ground stations.* ◇ *We were able to pick up the BBC World Service.* **6** to buy sth, especially cheaply or by good luck: *He picked up some bargains in the sales.* ◇ *You can pick up a second-hand bike for about £60.* [OBJ] **bargain 7** to win a prize or an award: *The movie picked up several Oscars.* [OBJ] **award, cheque 8** to find and follow a route, etc.: *A police dog picked up his scent.* ◇ *The French police picked up the trail and traced her to Lille.* [OBJ] **trail, scent 9** to discuss sth further; to return to a topic or theme and continue it: *Can I pick up the point you made earlier?* ◇ *We pick the story up again in London, five years later.* [OBJ] **point, story** → see also PICK UP 3 **10** to manage to see or hear sth that is not very clear: *I just picked up the sound of a car in the distance.* **11** *(especially AmE)* to collect things that have been dropped or left on the ground and put them away: *Will you pick up your toys now?* **12** *(AmE)* to tidy a room, etc. and put

things away: *Pick up your room before you go out.* [OBJ] **room** [SYN] **tidy sth up** (*BrE*); **tidy sth** (*BrE*) ⊃ note at TIDY UP → see also PICK UP 6 **13** (*informal*) if you **pick up** a bill for sth, you pay it for sb else: *We ended up picking up the bill.* [OBJ] **bill, tab**
◆ v + adv + n ◆ v + n/pron + adv **13** v + adv + n
◆ v + pron + adv ◆ v + n + adv (*rare*)
[IDM] **pick up the 'pieces** to return, or to help sb return, to a normal situation, particularly after a shock or a disaster: *He walked out on his family, leaving his wife to pick up the pieces.* **pick up 'speed/mo'mentum** to go faster: *The bus picked up speed as it went down the hill.*
▶ '**pickup 1** (*also* '**pickup truck**) a light motor vehicle with low sides and no roof at the back, used, for example, by farmers **2** the part of a record player or musical instrument that changes electrical signals into sound, or sound into electrical signals **3** (*AmE, sport*) a player who is bought by a particular team: *The young left-handed slugger was a great pickup for the Braves.*

,**pick yourself 'up** to get to your feet, especially after a fall: *She picked herself up and stumbled on.* ◇ (*figurative*) *We have to pick ourselves up after yesterday's defeat and start again.*
→ see also PICK SB UP
◆ v + pron + adv

,**pick 'up on sth 1** to notice sth: *He picked up on her feelings of unease.* ◇ *Children soon pick up on tensions between their parents.* **2** to return to a point in order to talk about it in more detail: *I'd like to pick up on Mr Finlay's point.* [OBJ] **point**
◆ v + adv + prep

,**pick sb 'up on sth** (*BrE*) to correct sth that sb has said or done: *If you make a mistake, he always picks you up on it.*
◆ v + n/pron + adv + prep

piece /piːs/

,**piece sth to'gether 1** to discover a story, etc. by putting together separate facts or pieces of evidence: *Detectives are piecing together the events of the last hours of his life.* ◇ *Investigators are still trying to piece together the evidence to find out what caused the crash.* [OBJ] **evidence, story, events 2** to make sth by putting a lot of separate parts together: *Archaeologists have worked for years to piece together the huge mosaic.*
◆ v + adv + n ◆ v + pron + adv
◆ v + n + adv (*less frequent*)

pig /pɪɡ/ (-gg-)

,**pig 'out** (**on sth**) (*informal*) to eat too much or a lot of food: *We pigged out at lunch for four bucks each.* ◇ *It isn't a good idea to pig out on sugar.*
◆ v + adv

▶ '**pig-out** *n* an occasion on which you eat too much or a lot of food: *We had a real pig-out last night.* ◇ *a pig-out party*

piggyback /'pɪɡibæk/

'**piggyback on/onto sth** to use sth that already exists as a support for your own work; to use a larger organization, etc. for your own advantage: *We can piggyback on the other departments for our stationery supplies.*
◆ v + prep

pile /paɪl/

,**pile 'in/'out**; ,**pile 'into/'out of sth** to go in or out of somewhere without order or control: *The taxi arrived and we all piled in.* ◇ *Crowds of children piled out of the building.* [OBJ] **car, taxi, room**
◆ v + adv ◆ v + prep

,**pile 'into sb/sth** to crash into sb/sth: *She stopped dead in the middle of the pavement and we all piled into her.* ◇ *As many as 30 cars and trucks piled into each other in the fog this morning.*
→ see also PILE UP, PILE STH UP
◆ v + prep

,**pile 'on** if sb's weight **piles on**, it increases rapidly: *The pounds have just piled on since I got married!*
◆ v + adv

,**pile sth 'on 1** to express a feeling in a much stronger way than is necessary: *I admit I'm piling on the drama a bit, but I'm trying to make a serious point.* **2** to give sb a lot or too much of sth: *United piled on the pressure in the second half* (= of the football game). [OBJ] **pressure, guilt 3** to make sth increase rapidly: *As soon as she stops dieting she piles on the pounds.* ◇ *The team were piling on the points.* [OBJ] **pounds, weight**
◆ v + adv + n ◆ v + n/pron + adv

,**pile 'out, etc.** → PILE IN/OUT, ETC.

,**pile 'up**; ,**pile sth 'up 1** to form a pile; to make a lot of things into a pile: *Snow was piling up against the windows.* ◇ *They piled the stones up in a corner of the yard.* **2** to increase or to make sth increase in quantity or amount: *Rubbish was piling up in the streets.* ◇ *The bills were piling up and we had no money to pay them.* ◇ *Liverpool should have gone on to pile up a big score* (= in a game of football).
◆ v + adv ◆ v + n/pron + adv ◆ v + adv + n **2** v + adv
◆ v + adv + n ◆ v + pron + adv ◆ v + n + adv (*rare*)
▶ '**pile-up** *n* a road accident in which several vehicles crash into each other: *Eleven cars were involved in a pile-up on the motorway.* ◇ *Three people were killed in a multiple pile-up.*

pin /pɪn/ (-nn-)

,**pin sb 'down 1** to make sb unable to move, especially by holding them firmly: *The older boy* had pinned Jimmy down on the floor. ◇ *The rebels were pinned down* (= they could not move from their position) *just south of the border.* **2** (**to sth/to doing sth**) to make sb say clearly exactly what they are going to do: *You'll find it difficult to pin him down to a price.* ◇ *They pinned the builders down to finishing by June.* **SYN** **nail sb down** (**to sth**) **3** to find sb and make them answer a question or tell you what you need to know: *She tried to pin him down for an interview, but he was always busy.*

◆ v + n/pron + adv ◆ v + adv + n

pin sth 'down to identify or understand sth exactly: *There's something wrong with this photograph but I can't quite pin it down.* ◇ *Doctors have been unable to pin down the cause of her symptoms.*

◆ v + n/pron + adv ◆ v + adv + n

pin sth on sb to make sb seem responsible or take the blame for sth they have not done: *They tried to pin the blame on me!*

OBJ **blame**

◆ v + n/pron + prep

IDM ,**pin (all) your 'hopes on sb/sth**; ,**pin your 'faith on sb/sth** to rely on sb/sth completely for success or help: *Police are pinning their hopes on finding the murder weapon.*

,**pin sth 'up 1** to fasten sth to a wall, etc. with pins: *He pinned up a notice on the board.* ◇ *Can I pin this poster up?* **2** to fix your hair in place with pins: *She was pinning her hair up in front of the mirror.* **OBJ** **hair**

◆ v + n/pron + adv ◆ v + adv + n

▶ '**pin-up** *n* **1** a picture of an attractive person, designed to be put up on the wall for people to look at: *The walls of his room were covered in pin-ups.* ◇ *He was football's first pin-up boy.* **2** a person who appears in a pin-up

pine /paɪn/

,**pine a'way** to become very sad, and sometimes ill/sick or weak because sb has died or gone away: *After his wife died, he just pined away.* ◇ *He seemed to be pining away from love.*

◆ v + adv

'**pine for sb/sth** to want or miss sb/sth very much: *She wasn't really pining for Brazil at all.* ◇ *a dog pining for its master*

◆ v + prep

pipe /paɪp/

,**pipe 'down** (*informal*) used to tell sb to be less noisy or to stop talking: *OK, everybody pipe down!*

◆ v + adv

,**pipe 'up** (**with sth**) (*informal*) to begin to speak: *Debbie suddenly piped up with 'I've seen this film before!'*

◆ v + adv ◆ v + adv + speech

piss /pɪs/

,**piss a'bout/a'round** (*BrE*, △, *slang*) to waste time by acting in a silly way: *We haven't got time to piss about.*

NOTE A more polite, informal way of saying this is **mess around** or, in British English, **mess about**.

◆ v + adv

,**piss sb a'bout/a'round** (*BrE*, △, *slang*) to treat sb in a way that wastes their time: *Don't piss me about, just tell me the truth!*

NOTE A more polite, informal way of saying this is **mess sb around**, or, in British English, **mess sb about**.

◆ v + n/pron + adv

'**piss down**; '**piss it down** (*BrE*, △, *slang*) to rain very heavily: *It's still pissing (it) down out there.* ◇ *The rain was pissing down.*

SYN **pour down** (*BrE*, *more formal*)

NOTE A more polite, informal way of saying this is **chuck it down**.

◆ v + adv ◆ v + it + adv

,**piss 'off** (△, *slang*, *especially BrE*) used to tell sb rudely to go away: *I told him to piss off.* ◇ *Piss off and leave me alone!*

◆ v + adv

,**piss sb 'off** (△, *slang*) to make sb annoyed or bored: *Everybody's pissed off with what's going on.* ◇ *It really pisses me off when I see people behaving like that.*

NOTE **Pissed off** (*BrE*) and **pissed** (*AmE*) are often used as adjectives: *I was really pissed off with him.* A more polite way of saying **piss sb off** is **get on sb's nerves**: *It really gets on my nerves when I see people behaving like that.*

◆ v + n/pron + adv ◆ v + adv + n (*rare*)

pit /pɪt/ (-**tt**-)

,**pit sb/sth/yourself a'gainst sb/sth** to test sb/sth/yourself in a struggle or competition with sb/sth: *It's a chance to pit yourself against the champion.* ◇ *I'd like to* **pit my wits against** *the best minds in the country* (= to test my intelligence). ◇ *I like sailing as I enjoy* **pitting my strength** *against the wind and the waves.*

◆ v + n/pron + prep

,**pit 'out**; ,**pit sth 'out** (*AmE*, *slang*) to spoil a shirt, etc. by sweating a lot: *I was so nervous, and my T-shirt was totally pitted out.* ◇ *I tried to defend myself, turned red, and totally pitted out.*

◆ v + adv ◆ v + n/pron + adv ◆ v + adv + n

pitch /pɪtʃ/

,**pitch 'in** (**with sb/sth**) (*informal*) to join in willingly with sb to help with an activity: *We all pitched in and soon finished the job.* ◇ *Lots of people pitched in with advice.* ◇ *Ruth pitches in with the adults before she goes to school.*

◆ v + adv

,pitch 'into sb (*informal, especially BrE*) to attack or criticize sb: *They really pitched into me when I refused to cooperate.*
♦ v + prep

,pitch 'into sth (*informal, especially BrE*) to start doing sth with energy and enthusiasm: *I rolled up my sleeves and pitched into the cleaning.* ◇ *All of them pitched into the fight.*
SYN launch into sth
♦ v + prep

,pitch 'up (*BrE, informal*) to arrive somewhere, especially late or without planning: *You can't just pitch up and expect to get in without a ticket.*
SYN turn up
♦ v + adv

pivot /'pɪvət/

'pivot on/around sth to depend on a central point; to develop from a central idea or point: *The success of the project pivots on investment from abroad.* ◇ *The novel pivots around a long conversation between two characters.*
SYN hinge on sth
♦ v + prep

plan /plæn/ (-nn-)

,plan a'head (for sth) to make arrangements in advance: *It's impossible to plan ahead when things keep changing!* ◇ *We need to plan ahead for our retirement.*
♦ v + adv

'plan on sth; 'plan on doing sth; 'plan on sb doing sth 1 to intend to do sth: *We'd planned on having a quiet evening at home tonight.* ◇ *I'm not planning on going to bed yet.* 2 (*often used in negative sentences*) to expect sth to happen: *We hadn't planned on a storm!* ◇ *They hadn't planned on so many people visiting the exhibition.*
♦ v + prep

,plan sth 'out to plan carefully and in detail sth that you are going to do in the future: *to plan out your time/route* ◇ *I knew exactly where I was going—I'd got it all planned out.*
♦ v + adv + n ♦ v + n/pron + adv

plant /plɑːnt; AmE plænt/

,plant sth 'out to put plants in the ground so that they have enough room to grow
♦ v + adv + n ♦ v + n/pron + adv
♦ v + n + adv (*less frequent*)

plaster /'plɑːstə(r); AmE 'plæs-/

NOTE Plaster is a substance that is put on walls and ceilings to give them a smooth hard surface.

,plaster 'over sth to cover sth such as a crack or a wall with plaster: *The old brick had been plastered over.*
NOTE Often used in the passive.
♦ v + prep

plate /pleɪt/

,plate 'up; ,plate sth 'up (in a restaurant, etc.) to arrange food on a plate so that it is ready to be served: *The food was plated up and ready to go.* ◇ *Just before you plate up, add the cheese and cream to the rice.*
OBJ food
♦ v + adv ♦ v + n/pron + adv ♦ v + adv + n

play /pleɪ/

,play a'bout, etc. (*BrE*) → PLAY AROUND, ETC.

,play a'long (with sb/sth) to pretend to agree with sb/sth, to believe sb/sth, etc., to gain an advantage, amuse yourself, avoid trouble, etc.: *He realized they'd mistaken him for the gardener, but decided to play along.* ◇ *I knew he was lying, but I decided to play along with him.*
♦ v + adv

,play a'round (*BrE also* ,play a'bout) 1 (with sb/sth) to behave in a careless way, without thinking about the results: *Stop playing about and get on with your work!* ◇ *Don't play around with matches!* **SYN** mess around (with sb/sth); mess around with sth (*BrE*) → see also PLAY AROUND WITH STH 2 (with sb) (*informal*) to have a sexual relationship with sb who is not your usual partner ⊃ note at CHEAT ON SB
♦ v + adv

,play a'round with sth (*BrE also* ,play a'bout with sth) to test or try new ideas, methods, etc. to see how good or effective they are before you make a final decision: *Play around with the spreadsheet until you find the best way to display the data.* ◇ *We're still playing around with ideas for a new programme.*
♦ v + adv + prep

'play at doing sth (*especially BrE*) to do sth without any effort or real interest: *He's just playing at being in love.*
♦ v + prep
IDM 'two can play at 'that game used to tell sb who has played a trick on you that you can do the same to them **what is sb playing at?** (*informal*) used to ask in an angry way what sb is doing: *What do you think you're playing at?*

,play a'way; ,play away from 'home (*BrE*) 1 (of a sports team) to play a match at the opponent's ground or stadium 2 (of a person who is married or who has a regular sexual partner) to have a secret sexual relationship with sb else
♦ v + adv

,play sth 'back (to sb) to play music, sound, images, etc. that have been recorded on a tape, video, etc.: *Can you play back what we've just recorded?*
OBJ tape
♦ v + n/pron + adv ♦ v + adv + n
▶ 'playback n [U, C] the act of playing music, showing a film/movie or listening to a telephone message that has been recorded before;

a recording that you listen to or watch again: *A TV playback showed exactly what had happened.*

play sth 'down to try to make sth appear less important than it is: *The government is trying to play down its involvement in the affair.*

OPP play up sth, play it/them up

NOTE Downplay sth is also used with the same meaning: *The report downplayed the effects of large class sizes in schools.*

♦ v + adv + n ♦ v + pron + adv ♦ v + n + adv (*rare*)

play 'off (*especially BrE*) if two teams, players, etc. that have the same number of points in a competition **play off**, they play a final game to decide who has won: *The two Germans played off for a place in the final.*

♦ v + adv

▶ **'play-off** *n* a game or games between two players or teams with equal points in a competition to decide who the winner is: *We're unlikely to reach the play-offs.* ◇ *The title was decided by a sudden-death play-off.* ◇ *a play-off final*

play A 'off against B (*BrE*) (*AmE*) **'play A off B**) to make two people or groups oppose each other, especially in order to gain an advantage for yourself: (*BrE*) *He tries to play one parent off against the other.* ◇ (*AmE*) *The children played their parents off each other.* ◇ *She played her two rivals off against each other and got the job herself.*

♦ v + n/pron + adv + prep ♦ v + n/pron + prep

play 'on 1 (*sport*) to continue to play; to start playing again: *They claimed a penalty but the referee told them to play on.* **2** to continue to play music: *Despite the uproar, the musicians played on.*

♦ v + adv

'play on sth (*also* **'play upon sth** *more formal*) to deliberately use sb's fears, etc. for your own advantage: *He played on my feelings of guilt to make me stay.* ◇ *The government played on people's fears of rising crime to get support for their policies.*

OBJ fears **SYN** exploit sth (*formal*)

♦ v + prep

play 'out (*informal*) if a band, etc. **plays out**, it performs in front of an audience: *Serious bands should be playing out regularly.* ◇ *Playing out is the best way for a DJ to build a following.*

♦ v + adv

play 'out; play itself/themselves 'out (*formal*) to develop and come to an end or be no longer useful or important: *The crisis has yet to play out.* ◇ *The revolution soon played itself out.*

♦ v + adv ♦ v + pron + adv

▶ **played 'out** *adj* completely finished; too tired or weak to continue: *She was played out—too exhausted even to cry.*

play sth 'out 1 when an action **is played out**, or sb **plays it out**, it happens: *The negotiations*

are being played out behind closed doors.* ◇ *She continued to play out her role of dutiful daughter.*

NOTE Often used in the passive. **2** (*especially AmE*) to continue to play sth until it finishes: *We'll play out this game and then go to bed.* **3** to let a length of rope pass through your hands bit by bit

♦ v + adv + n ♦ v + n/pron + adv

play 'up; play sb 'up (*informal, especially BrE*) **1** if sth **plays up** or **plays you up**, it causes you problems: *The car started playing up about six months ago.* ◇ *The computer's been playing me up recently.* ◇ *My leg's playing up again* (= it is painful). ◇ *My back plays me up from time to time.* **2** if children **play up** or **play sb up**, they behave very badly: *The kids have been playing up all day.* ◇ *All kids play new teachers up.*

NOTE Play up, play sb up are often used in the progressive tenses.

♦ v + n/pron + adv ♦ v + adv + n

play 'up sth to try to make sth appear more important than it really is: *She played up her achievements in an attempt to impress us.*

OPP play sth down

NOTE When the object of **play up** is a noun, it comes after **up**, but when the object is a pronoun, it comes between **play** and **up**: *He has some financial problems, but the newspapers have really played them up.*

♦ v + adv + n ♦ v + pron + adv

play 'up to sb (*BrE*) to behave towards sb in a way that you think they will like and will bring you an advantage: *She always played up to her father.*

♦ v + adv + prep

play 'up to sth (*especially BrE*) to behave in the way that people expect you to: *People think she's only twenty, and she plays up to this all the time.*

♦ v + adv + prep

'play upon sth → PLAY ON STH

'play with sb/sth (*disapproving*) to behave towards sb in a way that is not serious, especially by pretending to feel sth you do not feel: *She was just playing with my emotions.*

♦ v + prep

'play with sth 1 to keep touching or moving sth: *She was playing with her hair.* ◇ *Stop playing with your food!* **2** to use things in different ways to produce an interesting or humorous effect, or to see what effect they have: *In this poem Fitch plays with words which sound alike.* ◇ *The composer plays with the exotic sounds of Japanese instruments.* **3** (*usually used in the progressive tenses*) if you **play with** an idea, you think about it, but do not really intend to do anything about it: *She's playing with the idea of starting her own business.*

OBJ idea **SYN** toy with sth

♦ v + prep

'**play with yourself** (*informal*) to touch your sexual organs in order to give yourself pleasure
♦ v + prep

plod /plɒd; *AmE* plɑːd/ (**-dd-**)

,**plod a'long/'on** to continue doing sth, especially difficult or boring work, at a very slow rate: *Keep plodding on—you'll soon be finished!* ◇ *They're still plodding along with their investigation.*
♦ v + adv

,**plod a'way** (**at sth**) to work steadily but slowly at a difficult or boring task: *He plodded away all night at his project to get it finished.*
♦ v + adv

plonk (*especially BrE*) /plɒŋk; *AmE* plɑːŋk, plɔːŋk/ (*AmE usually* **plunk**)

,**plonk 'down**; ,**plonk yourself 'down** (*informal*) to sit down heavily and quickly: *She plonked herself down in front of the telly.*
SYN **plump down, plump yourself down**
♦ v + adv ♦ v + pron + adv

,**plonk sb/sth 'down** (*informal*) to drop sth or put sth down heavily without taking great care: *She plonked the food down in front of them.* ◇ *Don't just plonk the baby down on the floor.*
♦ v + n/pron + adv ♦ v + adv + n (*less frequent*)

plough (*BrE*) (*AmE* **plow**) /plaʊ/

NOTE A **plough** is a large piece of farming equipment with one or several curved blades, used for digging and turning over soil.

,**plough sth 'back** (**into sth**); ,**plough sth back 'in** to put profits back into the business that produced them: *All the profits are ploughed back into the company.* ◇ *The director confirmed that every penny had been ploughed back in.*
OBJ **profits, money**
NOTE Usually used in the passive.
♦ v + n/pron + adv ♦ v + adv + n

,**plough 'into sb/sth** (of a vehicle or a driver) to crash violently into sb/sth: *The car hit a lamp post before ploughing into a wall.*
➔ note at CRASH INTO SB/STH
♦ v + prep

,**plough sth 'into sth**; ,**plough sth 'into doing sth** to invest a large amount of money in a project, a business, etc.: *$50 million will be ploughed into the area over the next five years.*
SYN **sink sth into sth**
♦ v + n/pron + prep

,**plough 'on** (**with sth**) to continue to say or do sth even though it becomes difficult: *No one was listening to him but he **ploughed on regardless**.* ◇ *The path was steep, but we ploughed on until we got to the top.*
♦ v + adv

,**plough 'through sth**; ,**plough your way 'through sth 1** to force a way through sth: *The car ploughed its way through the snow and*
ice. ◇ *The journey involved ploughing through 50 miles of swampland.* **2** (of a vehicle or an aircraft) to crash violently through sth: *The car ploughed through the hedge.* **3** to slowly do, read or eat all of sth even though it is difficult or boring: *It took me hours to plough through all my emails.* ◇ *I had to plough my way through a mountain of pasta because I didn't want to appear rude.*
♦ v + prep ♦ v + n + prep

,**plough sth 'up 1** to break the surface of an area of land that has not been used for growing crops before, and turn it over using a plough: *He ploughed up the field ready for sowing.* ◇ *action to prevent farmers ploughing up footpaths* **2** to break up the surface of the ground by walking or driving across it: *He got so angry he ploughed up his neighbour's lawn with his motorbike.*
♦ v + adv + n ♦ v + n/pron + adv

plow (*AmE*) /plaʊ/

,**plow** (*AmE*) → PLOUGH

pluck /plʌk/

'**pluck at sth** to take hold of sth with your fingers and pull it towards you in a quick, sharp movement: *He plucked at my sleeve.*
♦ v + prep

plug /plʌg/ (**-gg-**)

,**plug a'way** (**at sth**) (*informal*) to work hard and steadily at sth for a long time, especially sth difficult or boring: *Scientists have been plugging away at the problem for years.*
♦ v + adv

'**plug for sth** to support sth or keep asking for sth because you think it is important: *For years I've been plugging for a new assistant for the office.*
♦ v + prep

,**plug 'in**; ,**plug 'into sth 1** to be able to be connected to a source of electricity or another piece of electrical equipment: *Where does the TV plug in?* ◇ *The guitar plugs into this amplifier.* **2** to become involved with a particular activity or group of people: *The company hopes to plug into new markets in Asia.* **3** (*computing*) to have access to a computer network: *We plug into the Institute's research network.*
♦ v + adv ♦ v + prep

,**plug sth 'in**; ,**plug sth 'into sth** to connect a piece of electrical equipment to the electricity supply or to another piece of electrical equipment: *Don't forget to plug the printer in.* ◇ *Where can I plug in my hairdryer?*
OPP **unplug sth** (**from sth**)
♦ v + n/pron + adv ♦ v + adv + n
♦ v + n/pron + prep

▶ '**plug-in** *adj* [only before noun] that can be connected to an electricity supply with a plug: *a plug-in kettle*

▶ **'plug-in** *n* **1** (*computing*) a piece of software that can be added to a computer system to give extra features: *plug-ins for a palmtop computer* ◇ *a plug-in graphics card* **2** (*Canadian English*) an electric socket in a garage or car park where a car can be plugged in when it is parked, used to heat the engine and prevent it from freezing: *Medicine Hat Hotel offers free parking with plug-ins.* ◇ *plug-in facilities*

be/get ,plugged 'in (to sth), **be/get ,plugged 'into** sth (*informal, especially AmE*) to be aware of or understand sth: *The good thing about this job is that I'm plugged into what's going on in the industry.* ◇ *Colin is always plugged in to what is fashionable with the kids.*
♦ be/get + v + adv ♦ be + v + prep

▶ **,plugged-'in** *adj* [only before noun] (*informal, especially AmE*) aware of what is happening, what is new, etc.: *a group of plugged-in editors and designers*

,plug sth 'up to fill or block a hole with a substance or a piece of material that fits tightly into it: *We plugged up all the holes around the window to stop the wind coming in.*
OBJ **hole** SYN **block sth up**
NOTE **Plug sth** is often used on its own with the same meaning.
♦ v + adv + n ♦ v + n/pron + adv

plumb /plʌm/

,plumb sth' in (*BrE*) to connect a washing machine, a bath, etc. to a water system: *He's plumbed in the new washing machine for me.*
♦ v + adv + n ♦ v + n/pron + adv

plump /plʌmp/

,plump 'down; ,plump yourself 'down (*informal*) to sit down quickly and heavily: *She plumped herself down in the armchair.*
SYN **plonk down, plonk yourself down**
♦ v + adv ♦ v + pron + adv

,plump sth 'down (*informal*) to put sth down suddenly and carelessly: *He plumped his books down on the table.*
♦ v + n/pron + adv ♦ v + adv + n

'plump for sb/sth (*BrE, informal*) to choose or vote for sb/sth after thinking about it carefully: *I think I'll plump for the steak.*
♦ v + prep

,plump 'up to become rounder or fatter: *Soak the raisins until they plump up.*
♦ v + adv

,plump sth 'up to make sth which is stuffed with feathers, etc. rounder and softer by shaking it: *Let me plump up your pillows for you.*
OBJ **cushion, pillow**
♦ v + adv + n ♦ v + n/pron + adv

plunge /plʌndʒ/

,plunge 'in; ,plunge 'into sth 1 to jump or fall into sth, usually with some force: *He plunged*

into the pool. ◇ *The car plunged into a gorge.* ◇ *We ran down to the sea and plunged in.* **2** to begin doing sth or talking about sth without preparing for it or thinking carefully: *He plunged into the task of clearing the office.* ◇ *I plunged in and started telling him all about it.*
♦ v + adv ♦ v + prep

,plunge sth 'in; ,plunge sth 'in/'into sth to put sth quickly and with force into sth else: *She plunged the knife into his leg.* ◇ *He opened the sack and plunged his arm in.*
OBJ **knife, hand**
♦ v + n/pron + adv ♦ v + adv + n ♦ v + n/pron + prep

,plunge 'into sth → PLUNGE IN, PLUNGE INTO STH

,plunge 'into sth; ,plunge sb/sth 'into sth to be or to make sb/sth suddenly be in a bad state: *The country plunged into recession.* ◇ *The city was plunged into chaos as a result of the strike.* ◇ *The room was suddenly plunged into darkness.*
OBJ **recession, despair**
NOTE Often used in the passive.
♦ v + prep ♦ v + n/pron + prep

,plunge sth 'into sth → PLUNGE STH IN, ETC.

plunk /plʌŋk/

,plunk 'down; ,plunk yourself 'down (*AmE, informal*) → PLONK DOWN, PLONK YOURSELF DOWN
♦ v + adv

,plunk sb/sth 'down (*AmE, informal*) → PLONK SB/STH DOWN: (*figurative*) *Movie goers **plunked down** $1.7 billion for tickets* (= spent that amount on tickets) *this summer.*
♦ v + n/pron + adv ♦ v + adv + n

ply /plaɪ/ (**plies, plying, plied**)

'ply sb with sth 1 to keep giving sb large amounts of sth, especially food and drink: *They plied us with tea and cakes.* **2** to keep asking sb questions: *They plied me with questions about my visit to England.*
♦ v + n/pron + prep

point /pɔɪnt/

'point at/to sb/sth to stretch out your finger or sth held in your hand towards sb/sth in order to show sb where a person or thing is: *He pointed to the spot where the house used to stand.* ◇ *He pointed at the computer screen with his pen.*
♦ v + prep

'point sth at sb/sth to aim sth at sb/sth: *He pointed the gun at her head.*
OBJ **gun** SYN **aim sth at sb/sth**
♦ v + n/pron + prep

,point sb/sth 'out (to sb) to show sb which person or thing you are referring to, for example by moving your head, by describing them/it, etc.: *Will you point his wife out to me if you see her?* ◇ *He drove them around Beverley*

Hills, pointing out where the stars lived. ◇ *The guide pointed out various historic monuments.*
◆ v + n/pron + adv ◆ v + adv + n

🔑 **point sth 'out** (**to sb**) to mention sth in order to give sb information about it or make them notice it: *He thanked me for pointing out the mistakes in his report.* ◇ *I must point out that my part in the rescue was very small.* ◇ ***It must be pointed out that*** *this new drug is not a miracle cure.* ◇ *He doesn't like having his faults pointed out to him.* ◇ *'He's not my father, he's my stepfather,' he pointed out angrily.*
NOTE **Point sth out** is often used in the pattern **point out that...**
◆ v + adv + n ◆ v + n/pron + adv ◆ v + adv + speech

point to sb/sth → POINT AT/TO SB/STH

point to sth 1 to mention sth that you think is important and/or the reason why a particular situation exists: *She pointed to unemployment as a reason for rising crime.* **2** if a fact, event or situation **points to** sth, it suggests that this is true or likely to happen: *All the signs pointed to a successful year ahead.* ◇ *The facts seem to point to him having been murdered.* ◇ *She had symptoms which pointed to a diagnosis of kidney failure.*
◆ v + prep

point 'up sth (*BrE, formal*) to give special emphasis to one particular aspect of a problem, fact or opinion; to show sth very clearly: *This incident points up the hostility between the two sides.*
NOTE When the object of **point up** is a noun, it comes after **up**, but when the object is a pronoun, it comes between **point** and **up**: *There are divisions in the party, and the conference has pointed them up.*
◆ v + adv + n ◆ v + pron + adv

poke /pəʊk; *AmE* poʊk/

poke a'bout/a'round; **poke a'bout/a'round sth** (*informal*) **1** (*also* **poke 'through sth** *especially AmE*) to look for sth, especially sth that is hidden among other things that you have to move: *They were poking around in the bushes, looking for their ball.* ◇ *What were you doing poking about in my room?* ◇ *He spent his weekends poking around dusty old bookshops.* ◇ *Customs officials poked through the containers looking for weapons.* **2** to try to find out information, especially secret or hidden information; to get involved in sth that does not concern you: *A reporter had been poking around, trying to discover something in my past.*
◆ v + adv ◆ v + prep

poke a'long (*AmE, informal*) to move somewhere very slowly: *The bus poked along at about 30 mph, stopping in every tiny town.*
◆ v + adv

poke a'round; **poke a'round sth** (*AmE, informal*) to move or do things slowly, without

hurrying: *I was just poking around in town all morning.*
◆ v + adv ◆ v + prep

poke at sth to push your finger, a stick, etc. into sth, often several times: *She poked at her salad with her fork.*
SYN **prod at sth**
◆ v + prep

poke 'out; **poke 'out of sth** (*also* **poke 'through**, **poke 'through sth**) if sth **pokes out** or **pokes out of** sth, you can see it because a small part is coming through a hole or is no longer covered: *His toes were poking through the holes in his socks.* ◇ *Two feet poked out from under the bed.* ◇ *There were flowers poking out of holes in the wall.*
SYN **stick out**, **stick out of sth**; **stick through**, **stick through sth**
◆ v + adv ◆ v + adv + prep ◆ v + prep

poke sth 'out; **poke sth 'out of sth** to move sth suddenly forwards or out of sth: *The door opened and Max poked his head out.* ◇ *The pony poked its nose out of the door as I went past.*
OBJ **head**, **tongue** **SYN** **stick sth out**, **stick sth out of sth**
◆ v + n/pron + adv ◆ v + adv + n (*less frequent*)
◆ v + n/pron + adv + prep

poke 'through; **poke 'through sth** → POKE OUT, POKE OUT OF STH

poke 'through sth (*especially AmE*) → POKE ABOUT/AROUND, POKE ABOUT/AROUND STH 1

poke 'up to become visible because a small part is coming through a hole, etc.: *The grass had begun to poke up through the snow.*
SYN **stick up**
◆ v + adv

polish /'pɒlɪʃ; *AmE* 'pɑːl-/

polish sb 'off (*informal, especially AmE*) to kill sb: *She hired an assassin to polish him off.*
◆ v + n/pron + adv ◆ v + adv + n

polish sth 'off (*informal*) to finish sth quickly, especially food or drink: *They polished off the pudding in no time.* ◇ *I'll polish off this last bit of work, then we can go out.*
◆ v + adv + n ◆ v + n/pron + adv

polish sth 'up 1 to make changes to sth in order to improve it: *The college needs to polish up its image.* **OBJ** **act**, **image 2** to improve your skills in sth that you have learned but have not used for a long time: *She went on a course to polish up her German.* **OBJ** **French**, **Italian**, etc.
SYN **brush sth up**
◆ v + adv + n ◆ v + pron + adv ◆ v + n + adv (*rare*)

ponce /pɒns; *AmE* pɑːns/

ponce a'bout/a'round (*BrE, informal*) to do silly things in a way that looks ridiculous, especially to attract attention; to waste time: *He ponces around on the show, interviewing mem-*

bers of the audience. ◇ *I could have finished that job while you've been poncing around!*
♦ v + adv

ponder /ˈpɒndə(r); AmE ˈpɑːn-/

ˈponder about/on/over sth to think about sth carefully for a period of time: *She pondered over what he had said.* ◇ *They were left to ponder on the implications of the announcement.*
➲ note at THINK STH OVER
♦ v + prep

pony /ˈpəʊni; AmE ˈpoʊni/ (**ponies, ponying, ponied**)

ˌpony ˈup; ˌpony ˈup sth (*AmE, informal*) to pay money for sth: *If you really want it, you have to pony up.* ◇ *Each guest had to pony up $40 for the meal.*
♦ v + adv + n ♦ v + pron + adv

poop /puːp/

ˌpoop ˈout (*AmE, slang*) **1** (**on sb/sth**) (*also* ˌpoop ˈout of sth) to fail to do sth that you have arranged to do; to stop doing sth because you are very tired or afraid: *I was supposed to go out last night but I pooped out.* ◇ *I'm sorry to poop out on you, but I have the worst headache.* **2** (**on sb**) if a machine **poops out**, it stops working: *The horn on my old Toyota pooped out on me.*
♦ v + adv **1** also v + adv + prep

ˌpoop sb ˈout (*AmE, informal*) to make sb very tired: *A long day at the office poops me out.*
➲ note at TIRE SB OUT
♦ v + n/pron + adv
▸ ˌpooped ˈout *adj* [not before noun] (*informal, especially AmE*) very tired: *I was pooped out after a long day at the office.*

pop /pɒp; AmE pɑːp/ (**-pp-**)

ˌpop ˈin (*informal, especially BrE*) to visit sb/sth for a short time: *She often pops in for coffee.* ◇ *I'll pop in to see you at the weekend.*
SYN drop in (on sb/at …) ➲ note at VISIT WITH SB
♦ v + adv

ˌpop sth ˈin/ˈround (*BrE*) to deliver sth to sb on your way to another place: *I'll pop the library books in on my way home.* ◇ *Could you pop those photos round later?*
SYN drop sth by; drop sth in (to sb/sth); drop sth off
♦ v + n/pron + adv

ˌpop ˈoff (*informal, especially BrE*) **1** to go or leave somewhere, especially for a short time: *I'm going to pop off early tonight* (= leave work early). ◇ *They just pop off to France whenever they feel like it.* **2** to die: *When I pop off, all my money goes to you.* **3** (**to sb**) (*AmE*) to talk angrily about sb/sth or to criticize sb/sth in public: *The*

assistant coach popped off to the press about the team's poor performances.
♦ v + adv

ˌpop sth ˈon (*BrE, informal*) **1** to put on a piece of clothing quickly: *He popped on his jacket and went out.* **2** to turn on a piece of electrical equipment: *I'll pop the kettle on for some tea.*
♦ v + n/pron + adv ♦ v + adv + n

ˌpop ˈout 1 (*also* ˌpop ˈout of sth) to come out from a place suddenly: *He just popped out from behind a tree.* ◇ (*figurative*) *I didn't mean to tell them—it just popped out* (= I spoke) *before I realized.* ◇ (*figurative*) *His eyes nearly popped out of his head* (= he was very surprised) *when he saw what she was wearing.* **2** (*especially BrE*) to leave somewhere for a very short time: *John's just popped out to get a newspaper.*
♦ v + adv **1** also v + adv + prep

ˌpop ˈover/ˈround (*BrE*) to visit sb's home for a short time: *Pop over if you feel lonely.*
SYN drop by; drop over (*especially AmE*)
♦ v + adv

ˌpop ˈup (*informal*) to appear or happen when you do not expect it: *He seems to pop up in the most unlikely places.* ◇ *When you click with the mouse, a menu pops up.*
♦ v + adv
▸ ˈpop-up *adj* [only before noun] **1** (*computing*) a **pop-up** function is one that appears quickly on the screen when you choose it while you are working on another document: *a pop-up menu/window* **2** (of a book, etc.) having pictures that stand up when you open the pages: *a pop-up book* **3** (*AmE*) a **pop-up** store is a shop/store that opens for a short time in a place where many people will see it, in order to advertise the company that owns it: *a pop-up store on Fifth Avenue*

ˌpop ˈup; ˌpop sth ˈup (*AmE*) (in baseball) to hit a ball very high, so that it can be easily caught by the opposing team: *He popped it up into left field and Haines caught it.* ◇ *Miller popped up and the inning was over.*
♦ v + adv ♦ v + n/pron + adv ♦ v + adv + n
▸ ˈpop-up *n* (*AmE*) (in baseball) a ball which is popped up: *He hit a pop-up into center field.*

pore /pɔː(r)/

ˈpore over sth to study sth by looking at it or thinking about it very carefully: *She was poring over an old map.*
♦ v + prep

post /pəʊst; AmE poʊst/

ˌpost sth ˈoff (**to sb**) (*BrE*) to send sth to sb by post/mail: *I posted a letter off to you this morning.*
OBJ letter, parcel **SYN** mail sth off; send sth off (to sb)

NOTE You can also use **post a letter, etc.**, but this refers to the action of putting the letter in the mailbox: *Did you remember to post my letter?*
  ◆ v + n/pron + adv ◆ v + adv + n

,post sth 'up to put a notice, etc. up on a wall so that people can see it: *The exam results will be posted up in the hall.*
  ◆ v + n/pron + adv ◆ v + adv + n

potter (*BrE*) /ˈpɒtə(r)/; *AmE* ˈpɑːt-/ (*AmE* **putter**)

,potter a'bout/a'round; **,potter a'bout/a'round sth** to do things or move without hurrying, especially when you are doing sth that you enjoy and that is not important: *They spent the day pottering about by the river.* ◇ *She was happy just pottering around the house.*
  OBJ the house, the garden
  ◆ v + adv ◆ v + prep

pounce /paʊns/

'pounce on sb/sth (*also* **'pounce upon sb/sth** *more formal*) to quickly notice sth that sb has said or done, and criticize it or use it for your own advantage: *As soon as I opened my mouth, the teacher pounced on me.* ◇ *He said something silly and the other boys pounced on it at once.* ◇ *His mistake was pounced on by the press.*
  SYN seize on sth (*more formal*)
  ◆ v + prep

'pounce on sth (*also* **'pounce upon sth** *more formal*) to accept an opportunity, etc. with enthusiasm: *She pounced on the opportunity to work with them.*
  SYN seize sth (*more formal*)
  ◆ v + prep

pound /paʊnd/

,pound sth 'out to play a tune on a musical instrument very loudly: *Cole was pounding out a tune on the piano.* ◇ (*figurative*) *She pounded out her poems on an old typewriter.*
  ◆ v + adv + n ◆ v + pron + adv
  ◆ v + n + adv (*less frequent*)

pour /pɔː(r)/

,pour sth a'way to get rid of a liquid by emptying it out of its container: *He poured the water away after he finished washing the car.*
  ◆ v + n/pron + adv ◆ v + adv + n

'pour down to rain heavily: *It's pouring down.* ◇ *The rain poured down all weekend.*
  SYN pelt down
  NOTE **Pour** is also used on its own, but only with the subject *it*: *It's pouring (with rain).*
  ◆ v + adv
  ▶ **'downpour** *n* a heavy shower of rain

,pour 'forth; **,pour 'forth sth** (*formal*) to appear or to produce sth from somewhere in large numbers or amounts: *The doors opened* *and a crowd of people poured forth.* ◇ *He poured forth a stream of bitter accusations.*
  ◆ v + adv ◆ v + adv + n

,pour 'in; **,pour 'into sth** to arrive somewhere in large numbers or amounts: *Complaints poured in after last night's programme.* ◇ *Sunlight poured in through the windows.* ◇ *Fans were still pouring into the stadium.*
  SYN flood in, flood into sth
  ◆ v + adv ◆ v + prep

,pour sth 'into sth to provide a large amount of money for sth: *The council has been pouring money into the area.*
  ◆ v + n/pron + prep

,pour sth 'off to remove some of the liquid from a container, cooking pot, etc. by pouring: *When the fish is cooked, pour off the water.*
  ◆ v + adv + n ◆ v + n/pron + adv

,pour it 'on (*AmE*) (*informal*) **1** (of a team or sports player) to play very well against your opponent, so that you are difficult to defeat: *The Rangers came onto the ice and poured it on from the very beginning.* **2** to talk or behave in an exaggerated way in order to impress sb: *She was really pouring it on, making sure he knew she was available.*
  ◆ v + it + adv

,pour 'out; **,pour sth 'out 1** (*also* **,pour 'out of sth**, **,pour sth 'out of sth**) to come out or to produce sth from somewhere in large amounts or numbers: *Black smoke poured out of the engine.* ◇ *People poured out through the gates.* ◇ *Factory chimneys poured out smoke.* **2** when feelings or words **pour out**, or sb **pours them out**, they are expressed, usually after they have been kept hidden for some time: *All her feelings of resentment just came pouring out.* ◇ *The whole story then came out.* ◇ *He poured out his troubles to me.*
  ◆ v + adv ◆ v + adv + n ◆ v + pron + adv
  ◆ v + n + adv (*less frequent*)
  1 also v + adv + prep ◆ v + n/pron + adv + prep
  ▶ **'outpouring** *n* **1** [usually pl.] a strong and sudden expression of feeling: *She hated having to listen to his passionate outpourings.* **2** a large amount of sth produced in a short time: *a remarkable outpouring of scholarship*

power /ˈpaʊə(r)/

,power 'up; **,power sth 'up** if a machine **powers up**, or sb/sth **powers it up**, it is switched on and becomes ready to use: *Switch on the computer then wait for it to power up.* ◇ *This switch will power up the monitor.*
  ◆ v + adv ◆ v + adv + n ◆ v + n/pron + adv

precede /prɪˈsiːd/

'precede sth with sth (*formal*) to do or say sth before the main thing that you want to do or say: *They often precede their performances with a short talk or display.*

♦ v + n/pron + prep

predispose /ˌpriːdɪˈspəʊz; AmE -ˈspoʊz/

predi'spose sb to sth (also predi'spose sb towards sth *less frequent*) (*formal*) to make sb more likely to do sth or to suffer from a particular illness: *Cigarette advertising predisposes children to smoking.* ◇ *His lifestyle predisposed him to high blood pressure.* ◇ *Certain people may be predisposed to mental illness.* NOTE Often used in the passive: *He believes that some people are predisposed to criminal behaviour.*

♦ v + n/pron + prep

preface /ˈprefəs/

'preface sth by/with sth; 'preface sth by doing sth (*formal*) to say sth before you start making a speech, answering a question, etc.: *It is helpful if an interviewer prefaces each group of questions with a brief explanation.*

♦ v + n/pron + prep

prefix /ˈpriːfɪks/

'prefix A to B; 'prefix A with B to add letters, numbers or words to the beginning of a number or word: *Prefix 020 to the number you want to call.* ◇ *Prefix the number you want to call with 020.*

♦ v + n/pron + prep

preside /prɪˈzaɪd/

pre'side over sth (*formal*) to lead or be in charge of a meeting, ceremony, etc.: *She presided over the meeting.* ◇ *The court is presided over by a single judge.* ◇ (*figurative*) *His government presided over* (= were responsible for) *a massive increase in unemployment.*

♦ v + prep

press /pres/

ˌpress aˈhead/ˈon (*also* ˌpress ˈforward *less frequent*) (with sth) to continue moving forward quickly; to continue to do a task in a determined way: *He pressed on, even though it was now dark.* ◇ *They decided to press ahead with their plans.* SYN forge ahead (with sth)

♦ v + adv

'press for sth; 'press sb for sth to make repeated and urgent requests for sth: *The unions are pressing for a pay rise.* ◇ *I must press you for a reply.* SYN push for sth, push sb for sth

♦ v + prep

ˌpress ˈforward → PRESS AHEAD/ON

ˌpress ˈin (on/upon sb) to move nearer to sb in a way that seems likely to cause harm: *He felt as if the walls were pressing in on him.*

SYN close in (on sb/sth)

♦ v + adv

ˌpress ˈon → PRESS AHEAD/ON

'press sth on sb to try to make sb accept sth, even though they may not want it: *She pressed cake and tea on us.*

♦ v + n/pron + prep

presume /prɪˈzjuːm; AmE -ˈzuːm/

pre'sume on/upon sth (*formal*) to use sb's friendship or kindness for your own advantage in an unfair way: *I felt it would be presuming on our friendship to keep asking her for help.* OBJ friendship, hospitality

♦ v + prep

pretend /prɪˈtend/

pre'tend to sth (*formal*) (*usually used in negative sentences and questions*) to claim to be or have sth, especially when it is not true: *I don't pretend to any great knowledge of the situation.*

♦ v + prep

pretty /ˈprɪti/ (pretties, prettying, prettied)

ˌpretty sth ˈup (*especially AmE*) to make sth look or seem better than before: *She had prettied up the front porch with a few plants.*

♦ v + n/pron + adv

prevail /prɪˈveɪl/

pre'vail on/upon sb (to do sth) (*formal*) to persuade sb to do sth: *Can I prevail on you to play the piano for us?* ◇ *She was prevailed upon to give one final performance.*

♦ v + prep

prey /preɪ/

'prey on sb (*also* 'prey upon sb *more formal*) to treat sb who is weaker than you in an unfair or dishonest way in order to get sth or gain an advantage for yourself: *The thieves have been preying on elderly people living alone.* SYN exploit sb

♦ v + prep

IDM prey on sb's 'mind if a problem or a thought preys on your mind, you think and worry about it all the time

'prey on sth (*also* 'prey upon sth *more formal*) if a bird or an animal preys on/upon another bird or animal, it hunts and kills it for food: *They prey on small mammals.* ◇ *These small fish are preyed upon by sharks and other fish.*

♦ v + prep

pride /praɪd/

'pride yourself on sth; 'pride yourself on doing sth to be proud of sth such as a personal quality or a skill: *She had always prided herself on her appearance.*

♦ v + pron + prep

print /prɪnt/

,**print sth 'off/'out** to produce a document or information from a computer in printed form: *I'll print off enough copies for everyone to have one.* ◇ *I'm waiting for the results to be printed out.*

[OBJ] **copy**

◆ v + adv + n ◆ v + n/pron + adv

▶ '**printout** *n* a printed copy of information in a computer file: *She asked for a printout of the previous year's accounts.*

,**print sth 'up** to produce sth in printed form, especially quickly or in large quantities: *He printed up 200 000 catalogues for the new season.*

◆ v + adv + n ◆ v + n/pron + adv

prise (*BrE*) (*AmE* **prize**) /praɪz/ (*also* **pry** /praɪ/ (*especially AmE*)

,**prise sth 'out of sb**; '**prise sth from sb** to obtain some information, etc. from sb with great difficulty: *I finally managed to prise his new address out of her.* ◇ *She had a way of prising secrets from people.* ◇ *You'll be lucky to prise any money out of him!*

◆ v + n/pron + adv + prep ◆ v + n/pron + prep

proceed /prə'siːd; *AmE* proʊ-/

pro'**ceed against sb** (*formal*, *law*) to start a court case against sb: *I shall instruct my solicitor to proceed against you for trespass.*

◆ v + prep

pro'**ceed from sth** (*formal*) to be caused by or be the result of sth: *The dispute proceeded from a wrong interpretation of the law.*

◆ v + prep

prod /prɒd; *AmE* prɑːd/ (-**dd**-)

'**prod at sth** to press sth with your finger or with a pointed object, especially to see what it is, or what it is made of, etc.: *He prodded at the plate of fish with his fork.*

[SYN] **poke at sth**

◆ v + prep

pronounce /prə'naʊns/

pro'**nounce for/against sb/sth** to give a judgement in court for or against sb/sth

◆ v + prep

pro'**nounce on/upon sth** (*formal*) to express an opinion or give a judgement on sth: *The minister will pronounce on the situation today.*

◆ v + prep

prop /prɒp; *AmE* prɑːp/ (-**pp**-)

,**prop sb 'up** to support sb by putting sth under or behind them: *We propped her up with a pillow.* ◇ *He tried to prop himself up on his elbow.*

◆ v + n/pron + adv ◆ v + adv + n

,**prop sth 'up 1** to keep sth standing or stop sth from falling by putting sth under or behind it: *A*

family photo was propped up against some books on her desk. ◇ *The tree had to be propped up with thick posts.* **2** to support sth that is having financial, political, etc. difficulties: *The regime is being propped up by foreign aid.* ◇ *The government will no longer prop up inefficient industries.*

◆ v + n/pron + adv ◆ v + adv + n

provide /prə'vaɪd/

pro'**vide against sth** (*formal*) to make plans in order to deal with or prevent a bad or unpleasant situation: *Does your insurance provide against loss of income?*

◆ v + prep

pro'**vide for sb** to give sb the things that they need to live, such as food, money and clothing: *How will she provide for six children?* ◇ *My family will be well provided for if I die.*

[OBJ] **children**, **family**

◆ v + prep

pro'**vide for sth** (*formal*) **1** to make plans or arrangements to deal with sth that may happen in the future: *The budget provides for rising inflation.* [SYN] **allow for sth 2** (of a law, etc.) to make it possible for sth to be done: *European legislation provides for expansion of the EU.*

◆ v + prep

prowl /praʊl/

,**prowl a'round**; ,**prowl a'round sth** (*also* ,**prowl a'bout/'round**, ,**prowl a'bout/'round sth** *especially BrE*) **1** to move quietly and carefully around an area, often with the intention of committing a crime: *There was someone prowling around outside.* ◇ *Why were you prowling about the building so late?* **2** to walk around a room, a building, etc., because you are worried, bored or unable to relax: *Her husband prowled about restlessly.* ◇ *She got up and prowled around the room.*

◆ v + adv ◆ v + prep

pry (*AmE*) /praɪ/ (**pries**, **prying**, **pried**)

,**pry sth 'out, etc.** → PRISE STH OUT, ETC.

psych /saɪk/

,**psych sb 'out** (*informal*) to make an opponent feel less confident by saying or doing things that make you seem better, stronger, etc. than them: *The other team tried to psych us out before the game started.*

◆ v + n/pron + adv ◆ v + adv + n

,**psych sb 'up**; ,**psych yourself 'up** (**for sth**) (*informal*) to prepare sb/yourself mentally for sth difficult, such as a game, an exam, an interview, etc.: *Boxers need to psych themselves up for the fight.* ◇ *I'd got psyched up for the interview but then it was cancelled at the last minute!*

◆ v + n/pron + adv ◆ v + adv + n

puff /pʌf/

,puff a'way (at/on sth) (*informal*) (*usually used in the progressive tenses*) to smoke a pipe, cigarette, etc., often when you are thinking deeply: *He stood looking out of the window, puffing away at his pipe.*
 ◆ v + adv

,puff sth 'out to make sth larger and rounder by filling it with air: *She puffed out her cheeks in anger.* ◊ *Her hair was puffed out round her face.*
 OBJ cheeks, chest
 ◆ v + n/pron + adv ◆ v + adv + n

,puff 'up; ,puff sth 'up to swell or to make sth swell and increase in size: *He could feel his face puffing up where Mark had hit him.* ◊ *He puffed up his chest like an exotic bird.* ◊ *The medicine makes my ankles puff up.*
 ◆ v + adv ◆ v + adv + n ◆ v + n/pron + adv
 IDM be puffed up with 'pride, etc. to be too full of pride, etc.: *She was so puffed up with conceit she didn't notice people were avoiding her.*

pull /pʊl/

,pull a'head; ,pull a'head of sb/sth to move in front of sb/sth, especially suddenly or unexpectedly: *I pulled ahead of the other runners on the last straight.*
 ◆ v + adv ◆ v + adv + prep

,pull sb/sth a'part 1 to separate sb/sth, often people or animals that are fighting: *It took several of us to pull them apart.* **SYN** separate sb/sth (*more formal*) 2 to severely criticize sb/sth: *She pulled my work apart and made me do it again.*
 ◆ v + n/pron + adv ◆ v + adv + n (*less frequent*)

,pull sth a'part to destroy sth or separate sth into pieces by pulling parts of it in different directions: *I pulled the machine apart, but couldn't find what was wrong with it.* ◊ *The fox was pulled apart by the dogs.*
 ➮ note at TEAR STH UP
 ◆ v + n/pron + adv ◆ v + adv + n (*less frequent*)

,pull sb a'side to take sb to a quiet corner or place to talk to them privately: *I pulled him aside to warn him not to say anything.*
 SYN take sb a'side
 ◆ v + n/pron + adv

,pull sth a'side to move sth such as a curtain so that you can see sth: *She pulled the curtain aside to reveal a small door.*
 OBJ curtain
 ◆ v + n/pron + adv ◆ v + adv + n

'pull at sth 1 to pull sth lightly several times especially to gain attention: *The little boy pulled anxiously at her sleeve.* 2 → PULL ON/AT STH
 SYN tug at sth
 ◆ v + prep

,pull a'way (from sth) 1 when a vehicle **pulls away**, it begins to move: *The train was pulling away as we reached the station.* ◊ *I started the engine and pulled away from the kerb.* 2 to

gradually move further in front of sb/sth; to start to win a game or competition by getting more points than your opponent: *The British boat began to pull away from the Italians* (= in a race). ◊ *The German pair pulled away to finish three games ahead* (= in tennis). 3 (from sb/sth) to move quickly away from sb/sth: *She pulled away from him in horror.*
 ◆ v + adv

,pull sb/sth a'way (from sb/sth) to make sb/sth move away from sb/sth: *I pulled her away from the edge.*
 ◆ v + n/pron + adv ◆ v + adv + n

,pull 'back 1 (from sb/sth) to move backwards away from sb/sth: *He pulled back and stared at her in disbelief.* ◊ *The camera then pulled back to a wider view.* 2 to decide not to do sth you were intending to do, usually because of possible problems: *Their sponsors pulled back from financing the movie.* **SYN** withdraw
 ◆ v + adv

,pull 'back; ,pull sb/sth 'back 1 to move back from a place; to make an army move back from a place 2 (*BrE*, *sport*) to improve a team's position in a game: *Rangers pulled back to 4–3.* ◊ *They pulled back a goal in the last few minutes of the game.*
 ◆ v + adv ◆ v + adv + n ◆ v + n/pron + adv

,pull sb/sth 'back to hold sb/sth and move them/it backwards, sideways or away from sth: *I pulled the child back from the edge.* ◊ *He pulled back the curtain.* ◊ *She pulled the sheet back to show us the wound.*
 ◆ v + n/pron + adv ◆ v + adv + n

,pull sb 'down (*informal*, *especially AmE*) to have a bad effect on sb's health or happiness: *The strain is really pulling me down.*
 SYN get sb down
 ◆ v + n/pron + adv ◆ v + adv + n

,pull sth 'down 1 to move sth from a higher to a lower position: *She pulled down the blinds and locked the door.* ◊ *He dried his hands and pulled down his sleeves.* **OBJ** blinds, trousers 2 (*especially BrE*) to destroy a building completely: *My old school has been pulled down.* **OBJ** house, building **SYN** demolish sth (*more formal*) ➮ note at KNOCK STH DOWN 3 (*computing*) to make a list of possible choices appear on a computer screen by pressing one of the buttons on the mouse 4 (*informal*) → PULL STH IN
 ◆ v + n/pron + adv ◆ v + adv + n
 ▶ 'pull-down adj [only before noun] used to describe a list of possible choices that appears on a computer screen below a title: *a pull-down menu*

'pull for sb/sth (*AmE*) to support and encourage sb/sth and hope they will be successful: *Hang in there, we're all pulling for you to win!*
 SYN root for sb/sth
 ◆ v + prep

ᴪ,pull 'in; ,pull 'into sth 1 if a train or a bus **pulls in**, it arrives somewhere and stops: *The express pulled in on time.* ◇ *The coach pulled into bay 27.* **2** (*BrE*) if a vehicle or a driver **pulls in**, they move to the side of the road and stop: *Pull in in front of the bus.* ◇ *He pulled into the parking lot and turned off the engine.*
ꜱʏɴ draw in, draw into sth **ᴏᴘᴘ** pull out, pull out of sth
◆ v + adv ◆ v + prep

,pull sb 'in 1 (*informal*) to bring sb to a police station in order to ask them questions: *The police have pulled him in for questioning.* **ꜱʏɴ** bring sb in **2** if an event or a show **pulls** people **in**, it attracts people in large numbers: *The show is still pulling in the crowds.*
ᴏʙᴊ crowds, customers **ꜱʏɴ** get sb in
◆ **1** v + n/pron + adv ◆ v + adv + n
◆ **2** v + adv + n ◆ v + n/pron + adv

,pull sth 'in (*also* ,pull sth 'down) (*informal*) to earn a particular amount of money: *He must be pulling in a hundred thousand.*
◆ v + adv + n ◆ v + n/pron + adv (*rare*)

ᴪpull 'off; ,pull 'off sth (of a vehicle or its driver) to leave the road in order to stop for a short time: *He pulled off onto the verge.* ◇ *I pulled off the main road and stopped.*
◆ v + adv ◆ v + prep + n

,pull sb/sth 'off; ,pull sb/sth 'off sb/sth to strongly pull away sb/sth that is attacking sb/sth else: *They tried to pull off the dogs with their hands.* ◇ *He had to be pulled off the older man by two policemen.*
◆ v + adv + n ◆ v + n/pron + adv ◆ v + n/pron + prep

,pull sth 'off 1 to remove an item of clothing quickly or with difficulty: *She pulled off her hat and gloves.* **ꜱʏɴ** take sth off **ᴏᴘᴘ** pull sth on **2** (*informal*) to succeed in doing or achieving sth difficult: *The goalie pulled off a terrific save.* ◇ *If anyone can pull it off, I'm sure you can.* **ꜱʏɴ** bring sth off
◆ **1** v + n/pron + adv ◆ v + adv + n
◆ **2** v + adv + n ◆ v + pron + adv ◆ v + n + adv (*rare*)

,pull sth 'on to put an item of clothing on quickly or with difficulty: *I pulled my shorts on and ran outside.*
ꜱʏɴ put sth on **ᴏᴘᴘ** pull sth off
◆ v + n/pron + adv ◆ v + adv + n

'pull on/at sth to take long deep breaths from a cigarette, etc.: *She pulled on her cigar.*
ᴏʙᴊ cigarette, cigar
◆ v + prep

ᴪ,pull 'out 1 (*also* ,pull 'out of sth) if a train or bus **pulls out**, it leaves a place: *The train pulled out (of the station) on time.* **ꜱʏɴ** draw out, draw out of sth **ᴏᴘᴘ** pull in, pull into sth **2** [+ adv/prep] (of a vehicle or its driver) to move away from the side of a road, from behind sth, etc.: *I pulled out onto the main road.* ◇ *A white van suddenly pulled out in front of me.*
◆ v + adv **1** also v + adv + prep

ᴪpull 'out; ,pull 'out of sth; ,pull sb/sth 'out; ,pull sb/sth 'out of sth 1 to move or to make sb/sth move away from sth or stop being involved in it: *They are pulling their troops out of the war zone.* **2** (*also* ,pull 'out of doing sth, ,pull sb/sth 'out of doing sth) to stop being involved in sth or decide not to do sth you had promised to do; to make sb do this: *The other firm wanted to pull out of the deal.* ◇ *The manager has pulled the team out of the competition.* ◇ *The company is pulling out of sponsoring the team.*
ꜱʏɴ back out, back out of sth, back out of doing sth; withdraw (from sth), withdraw sb/sth (from sth) (*more formal*)
◆ v + adv ◆ v + prep ◆ v + n/pron + adv ◆ v + adv + n
◆ v + n/pron + adv + prep
▶ **'pull-out** *n* an act of taking an army away from an area; an act of taking an organization out of a system, a deal, etc.: *their unexpected pull-out from the competition*

ᴪpull sth 'out; ,pull sth 'out of sth 1 to take sth out of somewhere by pulling: *He pulled an envelope out of his pocket.* ◇ *The woman suddenly pulled out a knife.* **2** to remove sth from sth else; to separate sth from sth else: *I pulled out the middle page of the magazine to show him.*
◆ v + n/pron + adv ◆ v + n/pron + adv + prep
▶ **'pull-out** *n* a part of a magazine, newspaper, etc. that can be taken out easily and kept separately: *an eight-page pull-out* ◇ *a pull-out guide to health*

ᴪpull 'over; ,pull sb/sth 'over to move or to make sb/sth move, to the side of the road and stop: *He pulled over and jumped out of the car.* ◇ *I pulled over to let the ambulance pass.* ◇ *A police car pulled me over.*
◆ v + adv ◆ v + n/pron + adv ◆ v + adv + n

ᴪpull 'through; ,pull 'through sth; ,pull sb 'through; ,pull sb 'through sth 1 to get better after an illness; to help sb get better after an illness: *Few people expected him to pull through after the accident.* ◇ *She has pulled through the operation remarkably well.* ◇ *He suffered terrible injuries, but his courage pulled him through.* **2** to succeed in doing sth very difficult or in dealing with difficult problems; to help sb do this: *He's got his problems at school, but with help he'll pull through.* ◇ *It's going to be tough but we'll pull through it together.* ◇ *She relied on her business experience to pull her through.*
◆ v + adv ◆ v + prep ◆ v + n/pron + adv

,pull sth 'to if you **pull** a door **to**, you close it or almost close it by pulling it towards you: *Pull the door to on your way out.*
ᴏʙᴊ door **ꜱʏɴ** shut sth **ᴏᴘᴘ** push sth to
◆ v + n/pron + adv

pull through

get better ◆ get well ◆ heal up ◆ pull through ◆ recover

These verbs all mean to stop suffering from an illness or injury.

get better (of a person or a part of the body) to become healthy again after being ill or hurt: *I hope you get better soon.* ◇ *My wrist is getting better.*

get well (of a person) to recover from an illness: *Get well soon!* ◇ *They sent me a get-well card.*

heal up (of a wound or injury) to become healthy again; to make a wound or injury healthy again: *The cut healed up without leaving a scar.* NOTE Heal can be used on its own: *It took a long time for the wounds to heal.*

pull through (*not formal*) to get better after a serious illness or operation: *The doctors think she will pull through.*

recover (of a person) to become healthy again after being ill or hurt: *He's still recovering from his operation.* ◇ *Mother and baby are recovering well.* ▶ **recovery** *n*: *He made a full recovery.*

WHICH WORD?

Get well is used especially to talk about the wish or need for sb to recover; it is not used much in the past tense.

PATTERNS AND COLLOCATIONS
- to recover **from** sth
- to **gradually** recover/get better/heal (up)
- to **completely/partially** recover/heal (up)

,pull to'gether if a group of people **pull together**, they act or work together in order to achieve sth: *If we all pull together, we'll finish by Friday.* SYN cooperate; **hang together** (*especially AmE*); **stick together** (*informal*)
◆ v + adv

,pull sth to'gether **1** to make all the different parts of an organization, an activity, etc. work together in a successful way: *His inspired leadership pulled the party together.* **2** to organize a variety of ideas, etc. in a logical and careful way: *This lecture pulls together several recent theories.*
◆ v + n/pron + adv ◆ v + adv + n

,pull yourself to'gether to gain control of your feelings and start to act in a calm and sensible way: *She made a great effort to pull herself together.* ◇ *Stop crying and pull yourself together!*
◆ v + pron + adv

,pull sb/sth 'under to make sb/sth become completely covered in water: *He felt the waves pulling him under.*
◆ v + n/pron + adv

,pull 'up (of a vehicle, or its driver) to stop, especially for a short time: *He pulled up alongside me at the traffic lights.* ◇ *A taxi pulled up outside.* SYN draw up
◆ v + adv

,pull sb 'up **1** (on/for sth) (*BrE, informal*) to criticize sb for sth they have done badly or wrong: *She pulled him up on his untidy handwriting.* ◇ *I was pulled up for not using the*

correct procedure. **2** to make sb stop doing or saying sth very suddenly: *The shock of his words pulled me up short.* ◇ *The expansion of industry was pulled up sharply by an economic crisis.* SYN draw sb up
◆ v + n/pron + adv ◆ v + adv + n

,pull sth 'up **1** to move sth from a lower to a higher position: *She pulled her shorts up and put a T-shirt on.* **2** to remove sth from the ground with force: *Kids had pulled all the shrubs up.* **3** (to sth) to bring sth such as a chair closer to sb/sth: *Pull up a chair and sit down.* SYN draw sth up
◆ v + n/pron + adv ◆ v + adv + n

IDM pull your 'socks up (*BrE*) to try to develop a more serious, responsible attitude to your work; to improve your behaviour: *He'll have to pull his socks up if he wants to pass that exam.*

▶ 'pull-up *n* an exercise in which you hold onto a high bar above your head and pull yourself up towards it: *She does 50 pull-ups and 100 sit-ups every morning.*

,pull yourself 'up **1** to move your body into a standing position, especially by holding sth firmly and using force: *Julia pulled herself up from the sofa.* ◇ *I pulled myself up to my full height and glared angrily at Dan.* **2** to stop doing or saying sth very suddenly: *I started to ask about her family, but pulled myself up sharply when I saw she was getting upset.* SYN draw yourself up
◆ v + pron + adv

IDM pull yourself 'up by your (own) 'bootstraps (*informal*) to improve your situation yourself, without help from other people

pump

pump /pʌmp/

NOTE A **pump** is a machine that is used to force liquid, gas or air into or out of sth.

pump sth 'in; **pump sth 'into sth** to give large amounts of money or resources to sth: *Millions have been pumped into this industry.*
OBJ **money** SYN **inject sth (into sth)**
◆ v + n/pron + adv ◆ v + adv + n ◆ v + n/pron + prep

pump 'out; **pump 'out of sth**; **pump sth 'out**; **pump sth 'out of sth 1** (of a liquid) to come out of somewhere or to be produced from somewhere with force and in large amounts: *Blood was pumping out of the wound.* ◇ *Cars are pumping out tons of pollutants every year.* **2** if music, sound, etc. **pumps out** or sb **pumps it out**, it is produced from somewhere very loudly and for a long time: *Heavy metal was pumping out of huge speakers.*
◆ v + adv ◆ v + adv + prep ◆ v + adv + n
◆ v + n/pron + adv ◆ v + n/pron + adv + prep

pump sth 'out; **pump sth 'out of sth** to remove a gas, liquid, etc. from inside sth with a pump: *The fire brigade pumped out the basement.* ◇ *The fire brigade pumped the water out of the basement.*
◆ v + n/pron + adv ◆ v + adv + n
◆ v + n/pron + adv + prep

pump sb 'up; **pump yourself 'up** (*informal, especially AmE*) to make sb feel more excited or determined about sth: *I was really pumped up for the race.*
NOTE Often used in the passive.
◆ v + adv + n ◆ v + n/pron + adv

pump sth 'up 1 to fill a tyre, etc. with air using a pump: *Pump your tyres up before you set off.* **2** (*informal, especially BrE*) to increase the amount, value or volume of sth: *They always pump their prices up before Christmas.*
◆ v + n/pron + adv ◆ v + adv + n

punch /pʌntʃ/

punch 'in/'out; **punch sb 'in/'out** (*AmE*) to record the time that you arrive at or leave work, by putting a card into a machine; to do this for sb else: *He punched in ten minutes late.* ◇ *I was in such a hurry to leave that I forgot to punch out.* ◇ *Would you punch me in? I'm going to be late.*
SYN **clock in/on**, **clock sb in/on** (*BrE*); **clock off/out** (*BrE*)
◆ v + adv ◆ v + n/pron + adv

punch sth 'in; **punch sth 'into sth** to put information into a computer, etc. by pressing keys: *She punched in the security code and the door opened.*
◆ v + adv + n ◆ v + n/pron + adv ◆ v + n/pron + prep

punch 'out, etc. (*AmE*) → PUNCH IN/OUT, ETC.

punch sb 'out (*AmE, informal*) to hit sb repeatedly: *Touch my car and I'll punch you out.*
SYN **beat sb up**
→ see also PUNCH IN/OUT, PUNCH SB IN/OUT
◆ v + n/pron + adv

punch sth 'out 1 to press a combination of buttons or keys on a computer, telephone, etc.: *He picked up the phone and punched out Donna's number.* **2** to hit sth very hard and make a hole in it or make sth fall out: *The burglar had punched out a pane of glass to open the window.*
◆ v + adv + n ◆ v + n/pron + adv

push /pʊʃ/

push sb a'bout (*especially BrE*) → PUSH SB AROUND

push a'head/'forward/'on (with sth) to continue with a plan in a determined way: *They pushed ahead with the modernization programme.*
→ see also PUSH ON
◆ v + adv

push sb a'round (*also* **push sb a'bout** *especially BrE*) (*informal*) to order sb to do things in a threatening or unpleasant way: *Don't let him push you around.*
SYN **kick sb around**
◆ v + n/pron + adv

push sb/sth a'side 1 to move sb/sth to a position where you are not prevented from going somewhere or doing sth: *He pushed her aside and went into the room.* ◇ *I pushed the curtain aside to get a better view.* **2** to treat sb/sth as if they are/it is not important; to avoid thinking about sb/sth: *When his sister brought home a school friend, he felt pushed aside and abandoned.* ◇ *Emma immediately pushed the unpleasant thought aside.*
◆ v + n/pron + adv ◆ v + adv + n

push sb/sth a'way to remove sb/sth from in front of you with your hands or arms, to show that you do not want them/it: *He offered to help, but she pushed him away.* ◇ *She pushed her plate away. 'I'm not hungry.'* ◇ (*figurative*) *Had he lied to me? I pushed the thought away.*
◆ v + n/pron + adv ◆ v + adv + n

push 'back (at sb) (*AmE*) to respond to sth that you think is wrong by telling the person responsible that you do not like it: *Minority groups are pushing back at the city's police department, after years of being mistreated.*
◆ v + adv
▶ **'pushback** *n* [U] (*AmE*): *The pushback from left-wing groups on the subject of tax cuts has been strong and loud.*

push sb 'back 1 to use force to make sb move backwards, especially by using your hands or arms: *The police pushed the protesters back.* **2** if sb **pushes** soldiers, an army, etc. **back**, they force them to move away from a place: *Magnus's army was gradually pushed back into a defensive circle.*
◆ v + n/pron + adv ◆ v + adv + n

push sth 'back 1 to make sth move backwards by using your hands, arms, legs, etc.: *He pushed his chair back and stood up.* **2** to make the time

or date of a meeting, etc. later than originally planned: *The release of their new album has been pushed back until early next year.*
 ♦ v + n/pron + adv ♦ v + adv + n

,push 'by/'past; ,push 'by/'past sb to use force to go past other people, rudely making them move to one side: *She pushed by without saying a word.* ◊ *He followed me to the door and pushed past me into the house.*
 ♦ v + adv ♦ v + prep

'push for sth; 'push sb for sth to keep asking for sth, or asking sb to do sth, because you think it is very important: *We are pushing hard for electoral reform.* ◊ *They're pushing me for a decision on the matter.*
 SYN press for sth, press sb for sth
 ♦ v + prep ♦ v + n/pron + prep

,push 'forward **1** to move forward through a group of people until you are near the front: *She pushed forward through the crowd.* **2** → PUSH AHEAD/FORWARD/ON **3** if soldiers, an army, etc. **push forward**, they move forward against the enemy, especially with some difficulty
 ♦ v + adv

,push sb/yourself 'forward to try to make sb notice sb/yourself, especially in order to obtain sth such as a job or a move to a more important job: *He's not the sort of person who pushes himself forward.*
 ♦ v + n/pron + adv

,push 'in (*BrE, informal*) to move in front of other people who are waiting in a line: *They thought I was trying to push in at the head of the queue.*
 SYN cut in (*AmE*)
 ♦ v + adv

,push 'off **1** (*informal, especially BrE*) used to tell sb rudely to go away: *Push off and leave me in peace!* **2** to leave sb/a place, especially in order to go home: *It's time I pushed off and did some work.* **3** (**from sth**) to move away from land in a boat, or from the side of a swimming pool: *He pushed off from the bank and rowed downstream.*
 ♦ v + adv

,push 'on **1** (**to…**) to continue travelling somewhere: *We decided to push on to Stonehaven.* **2** → PUSH AHEAD/FORWARD/ON
 ♦ v + adv

'push sth on/onto sb to try to make sb accept or buy sth they do not really want: *He keeps pushing his attentions on her.*
 ♦ v + n/pron + prep

,push sb 'out; ,push sb 'out of sth to make sb leave a place or an organization: *He refused to resign, so his colleagues pushed him out.* ◊ *Patients are being pushed out of hospital before they are really ready.*
 ♦ v + n/pron + adv ♦ v + adv + n
 ♦ v + n/pron + adv + prep

,push sb/sth 'out to make sb/sth less important than before; to replace sb/sth with sb/sth else:

My parents didn't want me to feel pushed out by my younger brother. ◊ *'Harry Potter' is pushing out more traditional children's stories.*
 ♦ v + n/pron + adv ♦ v + n/pron + adv + n

,push sb/sth 'over to make sb/sth fall to the ground; to make sth fall onto its side or turn over: *I was pushed over in the playground.*
 ♦ v + n/pron + adv

▶ 'pushover n (*informal*) **1** a task that is easy to do; a contest that you win easily: *The game against Sheffield will be a pushover.* **2** a person who is easy to influence or persuade

,push 'past, etc. → PUSH BY/PAST, ETC.

,push 'through; ,push 'through sth to use force to cross a barrier, especially one formed by a crowd of people: *He pushed his way through to the front of the crowd.*
 ♦ v + adv ♦ v + prep

,push sth 'through; ,push sth 'through sth to get a new law, plan or proposal officially accepted: *We're trying to push through the reforms as quickly as possible.* ◊ *The Prime Minister promised to push the bill through Parliament quickly.*
 OBJ bill, reforms, legislation
 ♦ v + n/pron + adv ♦ v + adv + n ♦ v + n/pron + prep

,push sth 'to if you **push** a door **to**, you close it or almost close it by moving it away from you: *I pushed the door to.*
 OBJ only door **SYN** shut sth **OPP** pull sth to
 ♦ v + n/pron + adv

,push to'wards sth to make progress towards achieving an aim: *We are pushing towards full membership of the EU.*
 ♦ v + prep

,push sb to'wards sth; ,push sb to'wards doing sth to make sb try to do or achieve sth: *The need for aid finally pushed them towards cooperation with the USA.*
 ♦ v + n/pron + prep

,push sth 'up to make sth rise or increase: *A shortage of land pushed property prices up.*
 OBJ prices, rates, costs
 ♦ v + n/pron + adv ♦ v + adv + n

pussyfoot /'pʊsifʊt/

pussyfoot a'bout/a'round to be careful or anxious about expressing your opinion in case you upset sb: *Alison should stop pussyfooting around and tell him what she really thinks.*
 ♦ v + adv

put /pʊt/ (putting, put, put)

,put a'bout (*technical*) if a ship **puts about**, it changes direction: *The ship put about and headed back to port.*
 ♦ v + adv

,put it a'bout (*also* ,put yourself a'bout) (*BrE, slang*) to have sexual relationships with a lot of

different people: *He had a reputation for putting it about when he was at college.*
◆ v + it + adv

,**put sth a'bout** (*informal*, *especially BrE*) to spread information, stories, etc. among a group of people: *Someone has been **putting it about that** you're leaving.* ◇ *This was an idea put about by the government.* ◇ *Rumours were put about that the shop was closing.*
[OBJ] **rumour**, **idea**, **it**
[NOTE] Often used in the passive.
◆ v + n/pron + adv ◆ v + adv + n

,**put yourself a'bout** (*BrE*) **1** (*informal*) to be sociable and friendly in public, especially in order to become well-known: *Politicians like that are always putting themselves about at parties.* **2** (*informal*, *sport*) to be very involved in a game and play with enthusiasm: *Christian is a no-nonsense defender who puts himself about and is popular with the fans.* **3** → PUT IT ABOUT
◆ v + it + adv

'**put sb/sth above sb/sth** → PUT SB/STH BEFORE SB/STH

⚑,**put sth a'cross** (*also* ,**put sth 'over**) (**to sb**) to communicate your ideas, feelings, etc. to sb clearly and successfully: *The campaign failed to put the message across.* ◇ *She's very good at putting across her ideas.*
[OBJ] **message**, **idea**, **point** [SYN] **get sth across**
◆ v + n/pron + adv ◆ v + adv + n
[IDM] **put one a'cross sb** (*informal*) to trick sb

,**put yourself a'cross** (*also* ,**put yourself 'over**) (**to sb**) (*BrE*) to make sb understand your ideas, your personality, etc.: *She puts herself across well at interviews.*
◆ v + pron + adv

,**put sth a'side 1** to place sth to one side: *She put the newspaper aside and stood up.* [SYN] **lay sth aside 2** to keep an item for a customer to collect later: *I asked them to put the dress aside for me.* **3** (*also* ,**put sth 'by** *especially BrE*, ,**put sth a'way**) to save some money to use later: *He had been putting some money aside every month.*
[OBJ] **money 4** to decide to keep a period of time for a particular task or activity: *We need to put aside some time to deal with this.* [OBJ] **time 5** to ignore or forget sth: *Doctors have to put their personal feelings aside.* ◇ *They decided to put aside their differences.* [SYN] **set sth aside**; **disregard sth** (*more formal*)
◆ v + adv + n ◆ v + n/pron + adv

'**put sth/sb at sth** to calculate or estimate sth to be a particular size, amount, etc.: *I'd put his age at about sixty.* ◇ *I'd put him at about sixty.* ◇ *The cost of the project is put at two million pounds.*
[OBJ] **figure**, **cost**
◆ v + n/pron + prep + n

,**put sb a'way** (*informal*) **1** to send sb to prison, to a hospital for people who are mentally ill, etc.: *He was put away for 15 years.* ◇ *If you're found guilty, they'll put you away for a long time.*

[NOTE] Often used in the passive. **2** (*AmE*, *slang*) to kill sb: *He was ordered to put the hostage away.*
◆ v + n/pron + adv ◆ v + adv + n

⚑,**put sth a'way 1** to put sth in a box, drawer, etc. because you have finished using it: *He washed the dishes and put them away.* ◇ *I'm just going to put the car away* (= in the garage). ◇ *Kids, will you put away your toys now?* **2** → PUT STH ASIDE 3: *She's putting some money away for college.* ◇ *I'm **putting** something **away for a rainy day*** (= for difficult times). **3** (*informal*) to eat or drink large quantities of sth: *They put away five bottles of wine between them!* ◇ *I don't know how he manages to put it all away!* **4** (*BrE*, *informal*, *sport*) to score a goal: *He had a couple of chances which he failed to put away.* **5** (*AmE*) → PUT STH DOWN 4
◆ v + n/pron + adv ◆ v + adv + n

⚑,**put sth 'back 1** to return sth to its usual place; to return sth to the place it was before: *He uses my things and never puts them back.* ◇ *Put the book back on the shelf, will you?* ◇ *She carefully put the letters back where she'd found them.* [SYN] **replace sth** (*more formal*) **2** (**to…**) to move sth to a later time or date: *The meeting has been put back to next week.* ◇ *The game has been put back 24 hours.* [SYN] **postpone sth** (*more formal*) [OPP] **bring sth forward 3** to cause sth to be delayed: *The strike has put back our deliveries by over a month.* [SYN] **set sth back 4** to move the hands of a clock back to give the correct earlier time, especially at the end of summer: *We forgot to put the clocks back last night.* [OBJ] **the clocks**, **your watch** [OPP] **put sth forward 5** (*informal*) to drink a large quantity of alcohol: *I had just put back my sixth beer of the evening.* [SYN] **knock sth back 6** (**into sth**) to give sth to or do sth for an organization, a society, etc. that has given you sth: *The school has been so good to me. I really want to put something back into it.* [OBJ] **something** [SYN] **give sth back 7** to spend more money on sth in order to make it better or more successful: *The government isn't putting enough money back into the economy.*
[OBJ] **money**
◆ **1,2,4** v + n/pron + adv ◆ v + adv + n
◆ **3,5** v + adv + n ◆ v + n/pron + adv
[IDM] **put the 'clock back** to return to a situation that existed in the past: *I wish I could put the clock back and give our marriage another chance.*

'**put sb/sth before sb/sth** (*also* '**put sb/sth above sb/sth**) to give sb/sth more importance than sb/sth else: *He puts his children before anyone else.* ◇ *They have always put business before pleasure.* ◇ *Some young men put their own career above their partner's.*
◆ v + n/pron + prep

,**put sth be'fore sb/sth** to present sth to sb/sth: *She will put her arguments before the* committee. ◇ *The new evidence was put before the court.*

[OBJ] **proposal, evidence, plan**

♦ v + n/pron + prep

,put sth be'hind you to try to forget about sth unpleasant that has happened and not allow it to affect your future: *She wanted to put the past behind her.*

[OBJ] **your/the past, your problems**

♦ v + n/pron + prep + pron

,put sth 'by: (*especially BrE*) → PUT STH ASIDE 3: *He puts a few pounds by every week.* ◇ *She's got some money put by.*

,put 'down (*especially BrE*) if a plane or its pilot **puts down**, the plane comes down to the ground: *The plane put down at Manchester airport.* ◇ *He had to put down in a field.*

[SYN] **set down, set sth down; land, land sth**

♦ v + adv

,put sb 'down 1 (*also* ,put yourself 'down) to criticize sb and make them feel stupid, especially in front of other people; to say sth that suggests that you have a low opinion of yourself: *She's always putting people down.* ◇ *Don't put yourself down!* [SYN] **do sb down, do yourself down** (*BrE, informal*) 2 (*BrE*) (of a bus, etc.) to allow sb to get off: *The bus stopped to put down some passengers.* ◇ *Ask the driver to put you down outside the City Hall.* [SYN] **set sb down** (*especially BrE*) [OPP] **pick sb up** 3 to put a baby to bed: *She's just put the baby down.* [OBJ] **baby**

♦ **1,3** v + n/pron + adv ♦ v + adv + n (*rare*)

♦ **2** v + n/pron + adv ♦ v + adv + n

▶ 'put-down n (*informal*) a remark or an action that is intended to make sb look stupid: *She produces some wonderful put-downs.*

,put yourself 'down 1 → PUT SB DOWN 1

2 → PUT SB/STH DOWN, PUT YOURSELF DOWN

,put sb/sth 'down to place sb/sth that you are holding onto the floor or another surface: *She put her bag down by the door.* ◇ *Put me down!* ◇ (*figurative*) *It's a great book. I couldn't put it down!* (= stop reading it)

[OPP] **pick sb/sth up**

♦ v + n/pron + adv ♦ v + adv + n

,put sb/sth 'down; ,put yourself 'down (for/as sth) (to do sth) to add sb's name or your own name to a list; to write sth down: *She put herself down for an aerobics class.* ◇ *I've put Jack's name down for the local school.* ◇ *We've been put down to go to a class at 4 p.m.* ◇ *I'll put the meeting down in my diary.* ◇ *He put himself down on the form as 'unfit'.* ◇ *I've put some ideas down on paper.* ◇ *Could you put down in writing what you feel?* ◇ *I've put you* (= your name) *down where it says 'next of kin'* (= on a form).

⊃ note at WRITE STH DOWN

♦ v + n/pron + adv ♦ v + adv + n

,put sth 'down 1 to replace the part of the telephone that you speak into (the **receiver**) of a telephone and end your conversation: (*BrE*) *She put the phone down on me!* [OBJ] only **the phone, the receiver** 2 to pay part of the cost of sth: *I've put down a deposit on our trip.* [OBJ] **deposit** 3 to move sth from a higher to a lower position: *The sun's in my eyes—can I put the blind down?* ◇ *Put your feet down, please!* (= off the table/chair) ◇ *The rain stopped so she put her umbrella down.* 4 (*AmE also* ,put sth a'way) to kill an animal because it is old or sick: *The horse was injured and had to be put down.* ◇ *We had to* **have** *our cat put down.* [NOTE] Often used in the passive. 5 to stop sth by force: *The revolt was swiftly put down.* [OBJ] **rebellion, uprising, revolt** [SYN] **suppress sth; crush sth** 6 to spread sth on the floor or ground: *We decorated the room and put a new carpet down.* ◇ *I'm going to put some poison down for the rats.* 7 (in a game of cards) to play a card: *She put down the ace of spades.* ◇ *Each player puts down a card in turn.* [OBJ] **card, ace, etc.** 8 to present sth formally for discussion by a parliament or a committee: *to put down a motion/an amendment* [SYN] **table sth** (*formal*)

♦ v + n/pron + adv ♦ v + adv + n

[IDM] **put your 'foot down 1** (*BrE*) to drive faster; to drive very fast **2** to be very firm in opposing sth: *You'll just have to put your foot down and say no.* **put your 'head down** to go to sleep: *Why don't you put your head down for a while?*

,put sb 'down as sth to think that sb is a particular type of person, especially when you do not know them very well: *I put the boy down as a troublemaker as soon as I saw him.* ◇ *I would never have put you down as an athlete!*

♦ v + n/pron + adv + prep + n

,put sb 'down for sth to write down that sb is willing or wishes to buy sth, give an amount of money, etc.: *Put me down for three tickets for the Saturday show.*

♦ v + n/pron + adv + prep

,put sth 'down to sth to consider that sth is caused by sth: *They put everything down to fate.* [SYN] **attribute sth to sth** (*formal*); **chalk sth up to sth** (*informal*)

♦ v + n/pron + adv + prep

,put sth 'forth (*formal or literary*) 1 (*especially AmE*) → PUT STH FORWARD 3 2 (*AmE*) to make a strong physical or mental effort to do sth: *He isn't putting forth the necessary effort.* [OBJ] **effort**

♦ v + adv + n ♦ v + n/pron + adv (*rare*)

,put sb/sth 'forward; ,put yourself 'forward (for/as sth) to suggest sb/yourself as a candidate for a job, a position, etc.: *Can I put your name forward for the job?* ◇ *Only one woman has put herself forward as a candidate.* ◇ *We would like to put you forward as head of department.* ◇ *My name was put forward for the scholarship by the principal.*

[OBJ] **name**

♦ v + n/pron + adv ♦ v + adv + n

ˌput sth ˈforward 1 to move sth to an earlier time or date: *We've put the meeting forward a couple of days.* **SYN** bring sth forward 2 to move the hands of a clock forward to give the correct time, especially at the beginning of summer: *We forgot to put the clocks forward last night.* ◇ *France is an hour ahead, so you'll have to put your watch forward when you get there.* **OBJ** the clocks, your watch **OPP** put sth back 3 (*also* ˌput sth ˈforth *formal, especially AmE*) to suggest an idea or a plan so that it can be discussed: *She put forward several ideas for new projects.* ◇ *This theory was originally put forward by Darwin.* **OBJ** argument, proposal, idea **SYN** bring sth forward

♦ **1** v + n/pron + adv ♦ v + adv + n
♦ **2** v + n/pron + adv ♦ v + adv + n (*rare*)
♦ **3** v + adv + n ♦ v + n/pron + adv

ˌput ˈin (at …), ˌput ˈinto … (*BrE*) (of a ship or its sailors) to stop in port for a short time: *The ship put in at Lisbon.* ◇ *The captain was instructed to put into Calais for repairs.* **OPP** put out (to/from…)

♦ v + adv ♦ v + prep

ˌput ˈin; ˌput ˈin sth to interrupt another speaker in order to say sth: *'But what about us?' he put in quickly.* ◇ *Could I put in a word?* **SYN** interject sth (*more formal*)

♦ v + adv + speech ♦ v + adv + n ♦ v + n/pron + adv

ˌput sb ˈin (*especially BrE*) to elect a political party as the government; to choose sb officially to do a particular job: *The voters put the Conservatives in with a large majority.*

♦ v + n/pron + adv ♦ v + adv + n

ˌput sb ˈin/ˈinto sth 1 to make sb go to a particular institution, such as a school, hospital, etc.: *He was put in prison for five years.* ◇ *An accident put him in hospital for three weeks.* ◇ *We had to put granny in/into a nursing home.* **NOTE** When this meaning of the phrasal verb is used with *hospital* and *prison*, in is usually used rather than into. 2 to give sb a particular job to do: *We put her in/into sales and she did really well.*

♦ v + n/pron + prep

IDM put sb in the ˈpicture (*informal*) to give sb the information they need in order to understand a situation: *You should put Mike in the picture as soon as possible.* put sb in their ˈplace to make sb feel stupid or embarrassed when they have shown too much confidence put yourself in sb's shoes to imagine that you are in another person's situation, especially when it is an unpleasant or difficult one: *Don't be angry with your brother. Try to put yourself in his shoes.*

ˌput sth ˈin 1 to fit a piece of equipment, furniture, etc. into a particular place: *Steve put the shower in by himself.* ◇ *They had central heating put in when they moved into the flat.* **SYN** install sth (*more formal*) 2 to officially make a claim, a request, etc.: *I've put in a request for*

some extra funding. ◇ *They've put in an offer on the house* (= to buy it). **OBJ** offer, claim 3 to give sth, such as time or money, in order to help sb/sth: *We all put in five pounds for Lucy's present.* 4 to plant sth in the ground: *Have you put any bulbs in this autumn?* **OBJ** bulbs, seeds

♦ v + n/pron + adv ♦ v + adv + n

IDM put in an apˈpearance to go somewhere for a short time: *I can't stay long at the party, but I'd better put in an appearance.*

ˌput sth ˈin; ˌput sth ˈin/ˈinto sth 1 to include sth in a story, a letter, etc.: *He didn't put anything in his letter about coming to stay.* ◇ *When you write the report, make sure you put in the latest figures.* 2 to pay money into a bank account: *He put £500 into his account.* **OBJ** money **SYN** pay sth in, pay sth into sth; deposit sth 3 (*also* put sth into doing sth) to give a lot of time or effort to sth or to doing sth: *She's put a lot of effort into improving her French.* ◇ *Thank you for all the hard work you've put in.* **OBJ** effort 4 (*also* put sth into doing sth) to provide money for sth: *The school has put a lot of money into* (buying) *new equipment.* **OBJ** money, resources **SYN** invest sth

♦ v + n/pron + adv ♦ v + adv + n ♦ v + n/pron + prep

▶ ˈinput n [C, U] time, knowledge, ideas or work that you put into a project, etc. in order to make it succeed: *Nurses should have more input into the way patients are treated.* ◇ *Thank you for your input to the discussion.* **NOTE** There is also a verb **input sth** meaning *to put information into a computer* and a related noun **input**.

ˌput ˈin for sth (*especially BrE*) to apply formally for sth: *Are you going to put in for that job?* ◇ *She's going to put in for a transfer.* **OBJ** transfer, job

♦ v + adv + prep

ˌput sb/sth/yourself ˈin for sth to enter sth/yourself for a competition: *She's put herself in for the 100 metres.* ◇ *You should put that photo in for the competition.*

♦ v + n/pron + adv + prep

ˌput ˈinto… (*BrE*) → PUT IN (at …), PUT INTO…
ˌput sb ˈinto sth → PUT SB IN/INTO STH
ˌput sth ˈinto sth 1 to add a quality to sth: *Do you need to put some excitement into your life?* 2 → PUT STH IN, PUT STH IN/INTO STH

♦ v + n/pron + prep

ˌput sth into doing sth → PUT STH IN, PUT STH IN/INTO STH 3,4
ˌput ˈoff doing sth → PUT STH OFF 1
ˌput sb ˈoff 1 to cancel a meeting or sth you had arranged with sb: *He was supposed to come yesterday, but I put him off.* ◇ *Tell her you want to talk to her and don't be put off.* 2 (*BrE*) (of a vehicle, a driver, a ship, etc.) to stop in order to allow sb to get off: *I asked the bus driver to put me off near the town centre.*

♦ v + n/pron + adv ♦ v + adv + n (*less frequent*)

ˌput sb ˈoff; ˌput sb ˈoff sb/sth; ˌput sb ˈoff doing sth to make sb stop liking sb/sth; to make sb lose interest in sb/sth: *His manner tends to put people off.* ◇ *Your story is putting me off my food!* ◇ *The accident put her off driving for life.* ◇ *The way he treated his wife really put me off him.* ◇ *Don't be put off by her appearance—she's really very sweet.*
◆ v + n/pron + adv ◆ v + adv + n (*rare*)
◆ v + n/pron + prep
▶ **ˈoff-putting** *adj* (*informal, especially BrE*) unpleasant; making sb dislike or not be interested in sth/sb: *The computer made a buzzing noise that she found off-putting.* ◇ *I find it very off-putting to have someone watching me all the time.* ◇ *His manner is very off-putting.*

ˌput sb ˈoff; ˌput sb ˈoff sth to disturb sb who is trying to give all their attention to sth: *Don't put me off when I'm trying to concentrate.* ◇ *The sudden noise put her off her game.*
SYN **distract sb (from sth)**
◆ v + n/pron + adv ◆ v + adv + n (*rare*)
◆ v + n/pron + prep

ˌput sth ˈoff 1 (*also* **ˌput ˈoff doing sth**) to change sth to a later date or time: *We'll have to put the meeting off until next week.* ◇ *He keeps putting off going to the dentist.* SYN **delay sth** **2** (*especially BrE*) to switch sth off: *Could you put the lights off before you leave?* OBJ **lights, the television, etc.** SYN **switch sth off; turn sth off**
◆ v + n/pron + adv ◆ v + adv + n **1** also v + adv + -ing

ˌput sb ˈon (*AmE, informal*) (*usually used in the progressive tenses*) to laugh at sb, especially by pretending that sth is true that is not: *I thought you were putting me on!*
SYN **have sb on** (*BrE*)
NOTE Not used in the passive.
◆ v + n/pron + adv
▶ **ˈput-on** *n* [C, usually sing.] (*AmE, informal*) an act of laughing at sb by telling them that sth is true that is not; a joke or trick: *Don't take it so seriously—it was just a put-on.*

ˌput sb ˈon; ˌput sb ˈon sth to give sb the telephone so that they can speak to the person calling: *She put Tim on the phone.* ◇ *Put Jane on for a minute, will you?*
◆ v + n/pron + adv ◆ v + n/pron + prep

ˌput sb ˈon sth 1 to make sure that sb gets on a plane, train, etc.: *We put Ruth on the bus to Carlisle.* **2** to make sb follow a particular diet, take a particular medicine, etc.: *The doctor put him on antibiotics.* ◇ *Tim's been put on a low-fat diet.* **3** to decide that sb should do a particular job: *They're going to put someone else on that project.*
◆ v + n/pron + prep

ˌput sth ˈon 1 to put an item of clothing, etc. on your body: *Aren't you going to put your coat on?* ◇ *Hang on, I need to put my glasses on.* ◇ *I can't find anything clean to put on!* ◇ *Have you put your seat belt on?* (= in a car) ◇ *Could you put his shoes on for him?* OBJ **coat, shoes, glasses, etc.** OPP **take sth off** ➲ note at HAVE STH ON **2** to

SYNONYMS

put sth on

affect sth ◆ **assume sth** ◆ **fake sth** ◆ **feign sth** ◆ **put sth on**

These verbs all mean to behave in a particular way, in order to make other people believe sth that is not true.

affect sth (*formal, often disapproving*) to pretend to be thinking or feeling sth or to have a particular way of speaking, often in order to impress other people: *She affected a calmness she did not feel.*

assume sth (*formal*) to pretend to be thinking or feeling sth; to pretend to have a particular way of speaking: *She assumed an air of concern.*

fake sth (*not formal*) to pretend that you are ill, injured or have a particular physical feeling: *She's not really sick—she's just **faking** it.*

feign sth (*formal*) to pretend that you have a particular emotion or that you are ill, injured, asleep or dead: *'Who cares?' said Alex, feigning indifference.*

put sth on (*not formal*) to pretend to be thinking or feeling sth; to pretend to have a particular way of speaking: *I don't think she was hurt. She was just **putting it on**.*

WHICH WORD?

Put on is often used with a phrase describing sb's face or voice: *to put on a look of concern/an artificial accent.* **Put on** is rather informal; **assume** and **affect** are both formal. **Affect** is often more disapproving than **assume**, suggesting that you think the person's behaviour is silly.

PATTERNS AND COLLOCATIONS

- to feign/assume/affect **indifference**
- to feign/assume **interest**
- to feign/affect **surprise**
- to feign/fake **illness/injury**
- to put on/assume/affect an **accent**
- to put on/assume an **air of** concern, indifference, etc.

apply sth to your skin: *She's putting her make-up on.* ◇ *Make sure you put some sun cream on before you go out.* ⏹OBJ **lipstick, make-up, perfume** SYN **apply sth** OPP **take sth off 3** (*especially BrE*) to switch sth on: *Shall I put the light on?* ◇ *Let's put the kettle on and have a cup of tea.* ⏹OBJ **the light, the heating, the radio, the kettle** SYN **switch sth on; turn sth on** OPP **put sth off; switch sth off; turn sth off 4** to begin to cook food: *I need to get home and put the dinner on.* SYN **get sth on 5** to make a CD, etc. begin to play: *Do you mind if I put some music on?* ◇ *She put on a Bob Marley CD.* ⏹OBJ **some music, CD, video 6** to operate the brakes on a vehicle (= a device for slowing or stopping the vehicle): *Don't forget to put the handbrake on.* ◇ *She put on the brakes suddenly.* ⏹OBJ **the brakes, the handbrake** SYN **apply sth** (*more formal*) **7** to grow heavier by the amount mentioned: *He's* **put on** *a lot of* **weight** *since I last saw him.* ◇ *I've put on two kilos in two weeks.* ⏹OBJ **weight** SYN **gain sth** (*more formal*) OPP **lose sth** NOTE Not used in the passive. **8** to provide sth specially: *They put on extra trains during the holiday period.* ◇ *A splendid lunch was put on for the visitors.* ⏹OBJ **bus, train** SYN **lay sth on** OPP **take sth off 9** to produce or present a play, an exhibition, etc.: *The local drama group are putting on 'Macbeth'.* ◇ *The museum put on a special exhibition about dinosaurs.* ⏹OBJ **play, exhibition, show** SYN **stage sth** (*more formal*) OPP **take sth off 10** to pretend to have a particular feeling or quality: *He put on a hurt expression.* ◇ *Can you put on an American accent?* ◇ *She isn't really upset—she's just* ***putting it on.*** ◇ *He seemed furious, but I think it was all put on.* ⏹OBJ **accent, expression** SYN **assume sth** (*formal*) ⏹ note on page 245
◆ v + n/pron + adv ◆ v + adv + n
▶ **'put-on** *n* [C, usually sing.] (*AmE, informal*) sth that is done to trick people: *Kate's shabby appearance is just a put-on. Her parents are both lawyers.*

,**put sth 'on sth 1** to add an amount of money to the price or cost of sth: *The new tax put 20p on the price of a packet of cigarettes.* OPP **knock sth off sth 2** to bet money on sth: *I've put £10 on Sultan's Promise* (= a horse) *in the next race.* ⏹OBJ **bet (on sth), money**
◆ v + n/pron + prep

,**put sb 'onto sb/sth** (*also* ,**put sb 'on to sb/sth**) **1** to tell sb about a person, an organization, etc. that could help them, or sth that they might like or find useful: *Could you put me onto a good accountant?* **2** to connect sb by telephone to sb else: *Could you put me onto the manager, please?* **3** to inform the police, etc. about a crime or a criminal: *Do you know who put the police onto the hackers?*
◆ v + n/pron + prep ◆ v + n/pron + adv + prep

,**put 'out 1** (**to/from…**) (*BrE*) (of a boat or a crew) to move out to sea from a port: *The ship put out to sea by night.* ◇ *We put out from Liverpool.* OPP **put in (at …) 2** (*AmE, slang*) (of a woman) to agree to have sex with sb: *She won't put out on a first date.* NOTE Sometimes considered offensive.
◆ v + adv

⏳,**put sb 'out 1** to make trouble, problems, extra work, etc. for sb: *I hope our arriving late didn't put you out at all.* **2** be ,**put 'out** to be upset or offended: *Jeff wasn't at all put out by what I said.* ◇ *I was a bit put out that I hadn't been invited.* **3** (*informal*) to make sb go to sleep or become unconscious: *These pills should put him out for a few hours.* → see also PUT YOURSELF OUT
◆ v + n/pron + adv ◆ v + adv + n (*less frequent*)

⏳,**put sth 'out 1** to make sth stop burning: *Firefighters soon put the fire out.* ◇ *He put his cigarette out.* ⏹OBJ **fire, cigarette, candle** SYN **extinguish sth** (*more formal*) **2** (*especially BrE*) to switch sth off: *Put the light out before you come to bed.* ⏹OBJ **the light** SYN **put sth off; switch sth off; turn sth off 3** to take sth out of your house and leave it, often for sb to collect: (*BrE*) *Remember to put the dustbins/rubbish out.* ◇ (*AmE*) *Remember to put the garbage/trash out.* ◇ *She put the washing out to dry.* OPP **bring sth in 4** to place sth where it will be noticed and used: *Have you put out clean towels for the guests?* **5** to stretch part of your body away from yourself towards sb else: *He put his hand out to shake mine.* ⏹OBJ **hand, tongue 6** (*also* ,**put sth 'out of sth**) to put a part of your body through a door or window to the outside: *She opened the window and put her head out.* ◇ *Sam put the cat out of the door roughly.* **7** (*BrE*) to broadcast sth; to publish or issue sth: *The programme will be put out on Channel 4.* ◇ *The CD was put out for the American market.* ◇ *The police put out an urgent appeal for witnesses.* ⏹OBJ **appeal, statement** SYN **broadcast sth 8** (*informal*) to produce sth: *The factory puts out 500 new cars a week.* ◇ *They put out a new software package last month.* SYN **produce sth 9** (*also* ,**put sth 'forth** *more formal*) (of a plant) to develop or produce new leaves, etc.: *The roses are putting out new shoots already.* ⏹OBJ **flowers, shoots, leaves 10** to make a figure, a result, etc. wrong: *A price increase put our estimates out by £650.* **11** (**to sb**) to give a job, a task, etc. to a worker who is not your employee or to another company so that the work will be done in another place: *A lot of editing is put out to freelancers.* ◇ *The cleaning contract was* ***put out to tender*** (= companies were asked to make offers to supply these services). ⏹OBJ **work 12** (*informal*) to push a bone out of its normal position: *She fell off her horse and put her shoulder out.* ◇ *I put my back out lifting those*

put sth out

blow sth out ◆ **extinguish sth** ◆ **put sth out**
◆ **smother sth** ◆ **stub sth out**

These verbs all mean to stop a fire, etc. from burning.

blow sth out to put out a flame, etc. by blowing: *Maisie blew out the candles on her birthday cake.*

extinguish sth to make a fire stop burning: *Firefighters tried to extinguish the flames.*

put sth out to stop sth from burning: *Firefighters soon put the fire out.*

smother sth to make a fire stop burning by covering it with sth: *He tried to smother the flames with a blanket.*

stub sth out to stop a cigarette, etc. from burning by pressing the end against sth hard: *He stubbed out his cigarette in the ashtray.*

WHICH WORD?

Extinguish has a similar meaning to **put out**, but is more formal.

PATTERNS AND COLLOCATIONS

- to extinguish/put out/smother **a fire/the flames/a blaze**
- to blow out/extinguish/put out a **candle**
- to extinguish/put out/stub out a **cigarette**

---

boxes. OBJ **your back, shoulder** SYN **dislocate sth** (*formal*)
◆ v + n/pron + adv ◆ v + adv + n
▶ **'output** *n* [U, sing.] **1** the amount of sth that a person, machine, company, etc. produces: *The company aims to increase output in the coming year.* ◇ *His musical output has diminished in recent years.* **2** (*computing*) the information produced by a computer: *data output* NOTE There is also a verb **output sth**, related to this meaning. **3** the power, energy, etc. produced by a piece of equipment: *an output of 100 watts*
put yourself 'out to make a special effort to do sth for sb: *Please don't put yourself out on our account.* ◇ *She really put herself out for the visitors.*
→ see also PUT SB OUT 1
◆ v + pron + adv
be ,put 'out → PUT SB OUT 2
,put yourself 'over (**to sb**) → PUT YOURSELF ACROSS (TO SB)
,put sth 'over → PUT STH ACROSS
IDM **put one 'over on sb** (*informal*) **1** to persuade sb to accept sth that is not true; to trick sb: *No one is going to put one over on him.* **2** to show that you are better, stronger, etc. than sb else by defeating them: *We'd love to put one over on the Welsh team.*
,put sth 'past sb (**to do sth**) (*informal*) (*always used in negative sentences with* **wouldn't**) to be surprised that sb has done sth wrong, illegal, etc.: *I wouldn't put it past him to use force to get what he wants.* ◇ *'She won't tell the teacher, will she?' 'I wouldn't put it past her!'* ◇ *Personally I wouldn't put anything past him!*
OBJ only **it, anything, that**
NOTE Not used in the passive.
◆ v + n/pron + prep

,put sb/yourself 'through sth 1 to make sb/yourself experience sth unpleasant or difficult: *He put his parents through hell.* ◇ *Why put yourself through it?* ◇ *She never forgot the terrible ordeal he had put her through.* **2** to pay for sb to attend a school, college, etc.: *She worked part-time to put herself through university.*
◆ v + n/pron + prep
,put sb/sth 'through (**to sb/sth**) to connect sb to sb else by telephone: *Could you put me through to the manager, please?* ◇ *The call was put through to the wrong extension.* ◇ *Hold the line, I'm putting you through.*
◆ v + n/pron + adv
,put sb/sth 'through sth to test sb/sth to see what they are able to do: *We put the machines through a series of tests.* ◇ *The team are put through a fitness programme.*
◆ v + n/pron + prep
IDM **put sb/sth through their/its 'paces** to give sb/sth tasks to perform in order to find out what they are/it is able to do: *He put the car through its paces.* ◇ *She watched the team being put through their paces.*
,put sth 'through; **,put sth 'through sth** to complete a plan, programme, etc. successfully: *This was the last deal James put through.* ◇ *Has the legislation been put through parliament?*
◆ v + n/pron + adv ◆ v + adv + n ◆ v + n/pron + prep
,put sth 'through sth to change sth by using a machine, a process, etc.: *She put some oranges through the juicer.* ◇ *The fish is then put through the smoking process* (= to produce smoked fish).
◆ v + n/pron + prep
▶ **'throughput** *n* [U, C, usually sing.] (*technical*) the number of people that are dealt with, or the amount of work that is done, in a particular period: *Hospitals have increased the throughput of patients.*

put

248

put sth together

assemble sth ♦ erect sth ♦ put sth together ♦ put sth up ♦ set sth up

These verbs all mean to make sth, especially by putting different parts together.

assemble sth to fit together all the separate parts of sth such as a piece of furniture or a machine: *The shelves are extremely easy to assemble.*

erect sth (*formal*) to build sth; to put sth in position and make it stand upright: *Police had to erect barriers to keep the massive crowds back.*

put sth together to make or prepare sth by fitting or collecting parts together: *to put together a model plane/an essay/a meal*

put sth up to build sth or place sth somewhere: *I'm putting up shelves in the garage this weekend.*

set sth up to build sth or place sth somewhere: *The police set up roadblocks on routes out of the city.*

WHICH WORD?

Assemble, **put together** and **set up** are not used for permanent buildings, whereas the others can be: *to set up/put up a fence/barrier/shelter* ◊ *They're putting up new hotels in the area.* You *set up camp* but *put up a tent*.

PATTERNS AND COLLOCATIONS

- to assemble/put together a **machine**
- to erect/set up/put up a **barrier**
- to erect/put up a **house/shelter/wall/fence/tent/statue/monument**
- to erect/put up some **shelves**
- to assemble/put together the **parts/sections** of sth

ˈput sb to sth to make trouble, problems or extra work for sb: *I hope we're not putting you to too much trouble.*
♦ v + n/pron + prep + n

ˈput sth to sb **1** to suggest sth to sb for them to consider: *Your proposal will be put to the board of directors.* ◊ *The question of strike action must be put to union members.* ◊ *When are you going to put the idea to your parents?* ◊ *I'll put it to you straight* (= tell or ask you sth in an honest and direct way). OBJ **proposal**, **idea**, **view 2** to ask sb a question: *The audience were invited to put questions to the panel.* OBJ **question**
♦ v + n/pron + prep

ˌput sth toˈgether **1** to make or repair sth by fitting parts together: *He took the clock apart and couldn't put it together again.* ◊ *Can you put a team together in time for the game on Saturday?* SYN **assemble sth** (*more formal*) OPP **take sth apart 2** to create sth: *He's putting together a travel guide for the British Isles.* ◊ *The band are putting their first album together.* **3** to combine things: *What reaction will we get if we put these two chemicals together?* ◊ *This painting is worth more than all the rest put together.*
♦ **1,3** v + n/pron + adv ♦ v + adv + n (*less frequent*)
♦ **2** v + adv + n ♦ v + n/pron + adv

IDM put our/your/their ˈheads together to discuss sth as a group in order to reach a plan of action, a solution to a problem, etc.: *We put our heads together and decided what had to be done.*

ˈput sth towards sth to use or give an amount of money to pay part of the cost of sth: *We will put the money towards a new computer.* ◊ *The*

city council will put £5 000 towards equipment for the nursery.
OBJ **money**
♦ v + n/pron + prep

ˌput sb ˈunder (*informal*) to make sb unconscious before a medical operation: *I'm afraid we'll need to put you under for the operation.*
♦ v + n/pron + adv

ˌput ˈup [+ adv/prep] (*old-fashioned, especially BrE*) to stay somewhere for the night: *We put up at a hotel.*
♦ v + adv

ˌput ˈup sth **1** to resist strongly or fight hard in a game, a contest, an argument, etc.: *The other team didn't put up much of a fight.* ◊ *She's not likely to put up much resistance to the idea.* OBJ **fight**, **resistance 2** to show a good level of skill in a game or a competition: *The team put up a great performance* (= played very well). OBJ **performance**, **show 3** to suggest an idea for other people to discuss: *to put up a proposal for a new book* OBJ **argument**, **proposal**
♦ v + adv + n

ˌput sb ˈup **1** to let sb stay at your home; to arrange for sb to stay somewhere: *We can put you both up for the night.* ◊ *They put us up at a hotel in town.* **2** (**for sth**) to present sb as a candidate in an election; to propose sb for an official position: *We hope to put up more women candidates in the next election.* ◊ *We want to put you up for club secretary.* OBJ **candidates**
♦ **1** v + n/pron + adv ♦ v + adv + n (*less frequent*)
♦ **2** v + n/pron + adv ♦ v + adv + n

ˌput sth ˈup **1** to raise sth from a lower to a higher position: *Put your hand up if you want to ask a question.* ◊ *It started raining so I put my*

umbrella up. ◇ I've decided to put my hair up for the party. ◇ to put up a flag [OBJ] **your hand, your hair 2** to fix or fasten sth in a place where it will be seen; to display sth: Several warning signs have been put up. ◇ The exam results haven't been put up on the noticeboard yet. ◇ Annie's put posters up all over her bedroom. ◇ They've put their Christmas decorations up already. [OBJ] **sign, poster, curtains, notice** [OPP] **take sth down 3** to build sth; to put sth into a standing position: These apartments were put up in the sixties. ◇ We had trouble putting the tent up in the dark. ◇ We need to put some shelves up for our books. [OBJ] **tent, shelf, fence** [OPP] **take sth down; pull sth down** ⟹ note at PUT STH TOGETHER **4** to increase the price, cost or level of sth: The theatre has put up ticket prices. ◇ The banks have put up their interest rates again. ◇ The landlord wants to put up the rent by £20 a month. [OBJ] **prices** [SYN] **raise sth** [OPP] **bring sth down 5** (informal) to provide or lend money: James put up half the money for the car. ◇ A local businessman has put up the £500 000 needed to save the football club. [OBJ] **money 6** put sth 'up **for sth** to offer sth to sb else for them to buy, etc.: The house has been **put up for sale.** ◇ Why did Jess **put** her baby **up for adoption**? [OBJ] **house, baby, child**
♦ **1,2,3,4** v + n/pron + adv ♦ v + adv + n
♦ **5** v + adv + n ♦ v + pron + adv
♦ v + n + adv (less frequent)
♦ **6** v + n/pron + adv ♦ v + adv + n (rare)

[IDM] **put your 'feet up** to sit down and relax: I can't wait to get home and put my feet up for a while. a **,put-up 'job** (BrE, informal) a plan or an event that has been arranged secretly in order to trick sb: The kidnapping was a put-up job.
,put sb 'up to sth; ,put sb 'up to doing sth (informal) to encourage or persuade sb to do sth wrong or stupid: Some of the older boys must have put him up to it. ◇ Her sister put her up to climbing into the house through an open window.
♦ v + n/pron + adv + prep
,put 'up with sb/sth to accept sb/sth that is annoying or unpleasant without complaining: I don't know how your parents put up with you! ◇ We put up with that car for years. ◇ I don't see why I should put up with being spoken to like that. ◇ I can put up with the rain—it's the cold I don't like. ◇ She has a lot to put up with.
[SYN] **tolerate sth** (more formal); **endure sth** (more formal)
♦ v + adv + prep
'put upon sb (BrE) to use sb's kindness for your own advantage by asking them to do things for you that you should not expect them to do: I felt that my mother had been put upon.
[NOTE] Often used in the passive.
♦ v + prep
▶ **'put-upon** adj badly treated by sb who uses your kindness for their own advantage: She is the most put-upon member of the family.

SYNONYMS

put sth up

boost sth ♦ **increase sth** ♦ **jack sth up** ♦ **put sth up** ♦ **raise sth**

These verbs all mean to make the amount, number or level of sth bigger or greater.

boost sth (often approving, used especially in newspapers) to make sth increase: A last-minute rush by Christmas shoppers boosted sales.

increase sth to make sth greater in amount, number, level, degree or value: We need to increase productivity. ◇ They've increased the price by 50%. ◇ increased demand/pressure/ spending

jack sth up (informal, disapproving) to increase sth, especially prices, by a large amount: Florists always jack up the price of roses just before Valentine's Day.

put sth up to raise or increase sth: They've put up the rent by £20 a month.

raise sth to increase the amount or level of sth: The government has promised not to raise

taxes. ◇ How can we raise standards of teaching in our schools?

WHICH WORD?

Increase is slightly more common than **raise** when talking about numbers, prices and figures; **raise** is more useful for abstract nouns such as feelings and qualities: to raise interest/ awareness. **Boost** is always used about a positive increase: to boost productivity/sales/spending ◇ to boost sb's morale/career/confidence. **Jack sth up** is nearly always used about an unwanted increase.

PATTERNS AND COLLOCATIONS

■ to increase/raise/boost sth **by.../from.../to...**
■ to increase/raise/boost/jack up **prices**
■ to increase/raise/boost your **income/profits**
■ to increase/raise **salaries/taxes**
■ to increase/raise/boost **awareness/interest/ support/confidence**

putter /ˈpʌtə(r)/

,putter a'round, etc. (AmE) → POTTER ABOUT, ETC.

putz /pʌts/

,putz a'round (AmE, informal) to waste time not doing anything useful or important: *You need to stop putzing around and do some real work.*
 ♦ v + adv

puzzle /ˈpʌzl/

,puzzle a'bout sth → PUZZLE OVER/ABOUT STH
,puzzle sth 'out to find the solution to a difficult problem by thinking carefully about it: *She couldn't puzzle out where her keys could have gone.* ◇ *I spent hours trying to puzzle out an explanation for his behaviour.* ◇ *I can't puzzle out how the box opens.*
 SYN work sth out
 NOTE Puzzle sth out is often used with the question words *how, what, why*, etc. ♦ It cannot be used in the passive.
 ♦ v + adv + n ♦ v + pron + adv
 ♦ v + n + adv (*less frequent*)
,puzzle 'over/about sth to think hard about sth because you want to understand it: *Police are still puzzling over the incident.* ◇ *She puzzled over the postmark on the letter.*
 ♦ v + prep

Q q

quarrel /ˈkwɒrəl; AmE ˈkwɔːr-, ˈkwɑːr-/ (-ll-, AmE -l-)

'quarrel with sth/sb (*especially BrE*) (*usually used in negative sentences*) to disagree with sth/ sb: *Few would quarrel with the principle of free education for all.*
 ♦ v + prep

queue /kjuː/ (queuing or queueing)

,queue 'up (for sth/to do sth) (BrE) to wait or stand in a line with other people in order to get sth or do sth: *They spent four hours queueing up for tickets.* ◇ *We had to queue up to get our visas.*
 NOTE Queue is often used with the same meaning: *We spent four hours queueing for tickets.*
 → see also LINE UP 1
 ♦ v + adv
be ,queuing 'up for sth/to do sth if you say that people **are queuing up** for sth, you mean that a lot of people want to have sth or do sth: *Actors are queuing up to work with this company.*
 ♦ be + v + adv + prep ♦ be + v + adv + **to**+inf

quieten (BrE) /ˈkwaɪətn/ (AmE quiet /ˈkwaɪət/)

,quieten 'down; ,quieten sb/sth 'down (AmE ,quiet 'down, ,quiet sb/sth 'down) to become, or to make sb/sth, calmer, less noisy or less active: *We've been really busy at work during the summer but **things** should **quieten down** now.* ◇ *It took a long time for the baby to quieten down.* ◇ *Can you quieten the kids down?*
 NOTE Quieten/quiet and quieten/quiet sb/sth are also used on their own, especially in more formal language: *The class quietened.* ⊃ note at SHUT SB UP
 ♦ v + adv ♦ v + n/pron + adv
 ♦ v + adv + n (*less frequent*)

quit /kwɪt/ (quitting, quit, quit, BrE also quitting, quitted, quitted)

'quit on sb (AmE, informal) **1** to stop helping, working with or supporting sb when they need you most: *I can't believe he quit on the team after only two games!* ◇ *You can't quit on me now, we're almost there!* **2** if a machine, a vehicle, etc. **quits on** you, it stops working at a time when you really need it: *The air conditioning quit on us in mid-July.*
 ♦ v + prep

R r

rabbit /ˈræbɪt/

,rabbit 'on (about sb/sth) (BrE, informal, disapproving) to talk about sth for a long time in a boring way: *What's he rabbiting on about?*
 SYN go on (about sb/sth)
 ♦ v + adv

rack (also wrack less frequent) /ræk/

,rack 'up sth (informal, especially AmE) to get or collect a large amount or quantity of sth, such as profits or losses in a business or points in a competition: *The company racked up $20 billion in sales.* ◇ *Bush has racked up victories in another five states.*
 NOTE When the object of **rack up** is a noun, it comes after **up**, but when the object is a pronoun, it comes between **rack** and **up**: *Even more impressive than the goals he scored was the effortless way he racked them up.*
 ♦ v + adv + n ♦ v + pron + adv (*less frequent*)

raffle /ˈræfl/

 NOTE A **raffle** is a competition where people buy tickets with a number on and some of the numbers are later chosen to win prizes.

raffle sth 'off to offer sth as a prize in a raffle: *The cake will be raffled off to raise money for the school.*
NOTE **Raffle sth** is used more frequently on its own with this meaning.
◆ v + adv + n ◆ v + n/pron + adv

rag /ræg/ (-gg-)

rag on sb (*AmE, informal*) to complain to sb about their behaviour, work, etc.: *My boss is always ragging on me.*
◆ v + prep

rail /reɪl/

rail against/at sb/sth (*formal*) to protest about sb/sth in an angry or bitter way: *to rail against the government/authorities* ◇ *There's no point in railing against the decision.*
◆ v + prep

rain /reɪn/

rain 'down (on/upon sb/sth), **rain sth 'down (on/upon sb/sth)** to fall or to make sth fall on sb/sth in large quantities: *Huge boulders rained down on us.* ◇ *He rained blow after blow down on my skull.*
◆ v + adv ◆ v + n/pron + adv ◆ v + adv + n

be ,rained 'off (*BrE*) (*AmE* **be ,rained 'out**) (*informal*) if an event such as a sports game is **rained off**, it stops or it does not take place because of rain: *The game was rained off.* ◇ *It looks as if the concert is going to be rained off.*
◆ be + v + adv

rake /reɪk/

NOTE A **rake** is a tool with a long handle and a row of metal points at the end.

rake sth 'in (*informal*) to earn large amounts of money without difficulty: *The company rakes in about £190 million.* ◇ *Since she moved to London she's been **raking it in**.*
◆ v + adv + n ◆ v + pron + adv
◆ v + n + adv (*less frequent*)

rake sth 'off to take part of the profits of sth, especially secretly or dishonestly: *Landlords have been raking off commission from inflated insurance premiums.*
◆ v + adv + n ◆ v + pron + adv
◆ v + n + adv (*less frequent*)

rake 'over sth (*BrE, informal, disapproving*) to examine sth that happened in the past in great detail and keep talking about it, when it should be forgotten: *There's no point in raking over the events of the past.*
OBJ the past
◆ v + prep

IDM **rake over old 'coals/'ashes** to discuss sth that happened in the past in detail, when it should be forgotten **rake sb over the 'coals** (*AmE*) (*BrE* **haul sb over the 'coals**) to criticize sb severely because they have done sth wrong

rake 'through sth to examine a collection of things or what is inside sth: *I raked through my bag but couldn't find my ticket.*
SYN **search through sth** ⟳ note at SEARCH FOR SB/STH
◆ v + prep

rake sth 'up 1 to talk about sth unpleasant that has happened in the past, which people would like to forget: *I didn't come here to rake up old arguments.* **2** to collect sth into a pile using a rake: *I raked up all the leaves.*
◆ v + adv + n ◆ v + n/pron + adv

rally /'ræli/ (rallies, rallying, rallied)

rally a'round/'round; ,rally a'round/ 'round sb if people **rally around** or **rally around sb**, they work together to help and support sb who is in a difficult situation: *When she was ill, the neighbours all rallied round to help her.* ◇ *His friends rallied around him when they heard the news.*
◆ v + adv ◆ v + prep

ram /ræm/ (-mm-)

ram 'into sb/sth; ,ram sth 'into sth to hit sth violently; to make sth hit sth violently: *He was going too fast and rammed into the car in front.* ◇ *The thieves rammed their truck into the jeweller's window.*
◆ v + prep ◆ v + n/pron + prep

ramble /'ræmbl/

ramble 'on (about sb/sth) (*BrE*) to talk or write a lot about sb/sth in a confused and boring way: *What is she rambling on about?* ◇ *There's me rambling on, and you haven't told me your news yet.*
◆ v + adv

ramp /ræmp/

ramp 'down; ,ramp sth 'down to decrease in stages; to make sth decrease in stages: *As the fighting ramps down, the soldiers are looking forward to going home to their families.* ◇ *We are ramping down our activities in the region.*
◆ v + adv ◆ v + adv + n ◆ v + pron + adv
◆ v + n + adv (*rare*)

ramp 'up; ,ramp sth 'up to increase in stages; to make sth increase in stages: *The manufacturer has ramped up production of this popular new model.* ◇ *Internet sales have been ramping up over the past year.*
◆ v + adv ◆ v + adv + n ◆ v + pron + adv
◆ v + n + adv (*rare*)

range /reɪndʒ/

be ,ranged a'gainst/'with sb/sth; ,range yourself a'gainst/'with sb/sth (*formal*) to join with other people to oppose sb/sth: *He felt as though the whole family was ranged against*

him. ◇ *She ranged herself more with her parents than with her brother.*
 ◆ be + v + prep ◆ v + pron + prep

rap /ræp/ (**-pp-**)

,rap sth '**out** to say sth quickly and sharply: *The officer rapped out orders.*
 OBJ **command, order** SYN **bark sth out**
 ◆ v + adv + n ◆ v + pron + adv ◆ v + n + adv (*rare*)
 ◆ v + adv + speech

rat /ræt/ (**-tt-**)

'rat on sb (*informal*) to give information to people in authority, causing trouble for sb: *Say what you like about Ali but he has never ratted on his friends.*
 ◆ v + prep

'rat on sth (*BrE, informal*) to fail to keep a promise you have made: *They accused the government of ratting on promises to the disabled.*
 OBJ **promise, pledge**
 ◆ v + prep

ratchet /ˈrætʃɪt/

,ratchet sth '**up** to make prices, etc. increase a little at a time: *The interest rates have been ratcheted up sharply.* ◇ *The hormone rushes around the brain, ratcheting the heart rate up from 60–80 to about a hundred.* ◇ (*figurative*) *The government have ratcheted up the pressure on the protest organizers.*
 ◆ v + adv + n ◆ v + n/pron + adv

,ratchet sth '**down** to make prices, etc. decrease a little at a time: *Management were determined to ratchet down costs.*
 ◆ v + adv + n ◆ v + n/pron + adv

ration /ˈræʃn/

,ration sth '**out** to divide sth that there is not very much of between a group of people in such a way that everyone gets a small share: *They rationed the water out among the survivors.*
 OBJ **food, water**
 ◆ v + n/pron + adv ◆ v + adv + n

rattle /ˈrætl/

,rattle a'**round**; ,rattle a'**round sth** (*informal*) to live, work, etc. somewhere that is much too big for your needs: *There are only two of us, rattling around in this massive office.* ◇ *They're rattling around that house now that the children have left.*
 ◆ v + adv ◆ v + prep

,rattle sth '**off** to say or repeat sth from memory, quickly and without any effort: *She rattled off the names of the movies Hitchcock had directed.*
 SYN **reel sth off**
 ◆ v + adv + n ◆ v + pron + adv ◆ v + n + adv (*rare*)

,rattle '**on** (**about sth**) (*informal*) to talk quickly and for a long time about sth that is not important or interesting: *He rattled on about his job for over an hour.*
 SYN **waffle on (about sth)**
 ◆ v + adv

,rattle '**through sth** (*BrE, informal*) to do sth very quickly: *He rattled through his homework then went out.*
 ◆ v + prep

reach /riːtʃ/

,reach sth '**down** (**for sb**) to get sth down from a high place: *Could you reach that vase down for me?* ◇ *She reached down a box from the top shelf.*
 NOTE In informal spoken language **reach sb down sth** is also used: *Could you reach me down that vase?*
 ◆ v + n/pron + adv ◆ v + adv + n

,reach '**out**; ,reach sth '**out** to stretch your arm or your hand in order to touch or get sth: *He reached out to switch on the light.* ◇ *I reached out a hand to touch her face.* ◇ *The child reached out for her hand.*
 ◆ v + adv ◆ v + adv + n ◆ v + pron + adv
 ◆ v + n + adv (*rare*)

,reach '**out to sb** to show sb that you are interested in them and/or want to help them; to try to get people's interest or attention: *The organization is trying to reach out to people of all ages and from all levels of society.* ◇ *The party has failed to reach out to young people.* ◇ *The makers of this movie have tried to reach out to an older audience.*
 ◆ v + adv + prep
 ▶ '**outreach** *n* the activity of an organization that provides a service or advice to people in the community, especially those who cannot come to an office, a hospital, etc. for help: *a rural outreach programme* ◇ *outreach work*

read /riːd/ (**read, read** /red/)

,read sth '**back** to read a message, a letter, etc. aloud in order to check that it is correct: *I got her to read the message back to me to make sure it was right.*
 ◆ v + n/pron + adv ◆ v + adv + n

,read sth '**into sth** to think that sth has a meaning or an importance that it probably does not have: *It's a mistake to read too much into the results of one opinion poll.* ◇ *You can read anything you want into horoscopes.* ◇ *Her voice was cold and I wasn't sure what to read into it.*
 OBJ **too much, something, anything**
 ◆ v + n/pron + prep

,read sth '**off** to look at the measurement shown on a machine or measuring device: *The speed can be read off from the graph.* ◇ *I looked at the thermometer and read off the temperature.*
 ◆ v + adv + n ◆ v + n/pron + adv

read 'on to continue reading: *The book was so exciting he read on until dawn.* ◇ *The idea is to make the reader want to read on.* ◇ *If you want to find out more, read on!*
◆ v + adv

read sth 'out (**to sb**) **1** to read sth aloud, especially to other people: *She read out the names of the winners.* ◇ *The teacher read my poem out to the class.* ◇ *There's a letter from Tom. Shall I read it out to you?* **2** (*especially AmE, computing*) to get back information that is stored on a computer; to produce a display of the information on a screen
◆ v + adv + n ◆ v + n/pron + adv ◆ v + adv + speech
▶ **'read-out** *n* (*computing*) a record or display of information on a computer screen: *The computer will work out the best route for you and give you a read-out on the screen.*

read sth 'through (*also* ,**read sth 'over** *less frequent*) to read sth from the beginning to the end, usually in order to find any mistakes: *I read through my translation, checking for mistakes.* ◇ *When she read her letter through the next day, she decided not to send it.* ◇ *When she'd finished, Emily read over what she'd written.*
◆ v + adv + n ◆ v + n/pron + adv

read 'up on sb/sth; ,**read sb/sth 'up** (*also* ,**read 'up about sb/sth** *less frequent*) to read a lot about a particular subject in order to learn about it: *Have you been reading up on the history of the island?* ◇ *I've been reading this place up in the library.*
◆ v + adv + prep ◆ v + adv + n ◆ v + n/pron + adv

rear /rɪə(r); *AmE* rɪr/

rear sb/sth on sth to give a person or an animal a particular type of food, entertainment, etc. when they are young: *I was reared on jazz, but later discovered rock.*
NOTE Usually used in the passive.
◆ v + n/pron + prep

,**rear 'up 1** if a horse, etc. **rears up**, it stands on its back legs with its front legs in the air: *The horse reared up and she fell off.* **2** if a building, mountain, etc. **rears up**, it seems to lean over you in a threatening way: *The cliff reared up before them.*
NOTE Rear is also used on its own with these meanings, especially meaning 1: *The horse reared and she fell off.*
◆ v + adv

reason /'ri:zn/

,**reason sth 'out** to think carefully about sth in a logical way in order to understand it: *Let's try to reason out why he behaved as he did.* ◇ *Reason it out for yourself—why do you think she didn't say where she was going?*
SYN figure sb/sth out; work sth out
◆ v + n/pron + adv ◆ v + adv + n

'**reason with sb** to talk to sb in order to persuade them to be more sensible: *It's impossible to reason with her when she's in this mood.* ◇ *He can't be reasoned with.*
◆ v + prep

rebound /rɪ'baʊnd/

re'bound on sb (*also* **re'bound upon sb** *more formal, less frequent*) if sth that you do, especially sth that is intended to be unpleasant for sb else, **rebounds on** you, it has an unpleasant effect for you instead: *His trick seems to have rebounded on him.* ◇ *These measures could rebound on the poorest families* (= affect them instead of the people they were intended to affect).
◆ v + prep

reckon /'rekən/

'**reckon on sb/sth**; '**reckon on doing sth**; '**reckon on sb/sth doing sth** to rely on sb/sth or on sth happening; to expect sb to do sth or sth to happen: *We were reckoning on a profit of about half a million.* ◇ *You can reckon on my support.* ◇ *We hadn't reckoned on them arriving so early.* ◇ *You can't always reckon on having good weather in June.* ◇ *The company thought they would easily get permission to build a hotel, but they hadn't reckoned on the local people.*
SYN count on sb/sth, count on doing sth, count on sb/sth doing sth
◆ v + prep

,**reckon sth 'up** (*especially BrE*) to add figures or numbers together: *That'll be £20.50, if I've reckoned it up correctly.*
SYN add sth up; calculate sth (*more formal*)
◆ v + n/pron + adv ◆ v + adv + n

'**reckon with sb/sth 1** (*usually used in negative sentences*) to consider sb/sth as a possible problem that you should be prepared for: *Unfortunately, we hadn't reckoned with Emily.* ◇ *We must reckon with the possibility of failure.* **2** to consider or deal with sb/sth as a serious opponent or problem: *He had to reckon with a great deal of opposition.* ◇ *The team are still* **a force to be reckoned with** (= they will be difficult to defeat).
◆ v + prep

'**reckon without sb/sth** (*especially BrE*) to not consider sb/sth as a possible problem and therefore not be prepared for it: *We allowed an hour to get there, but we'd reckoned without the traffic.*
◆ v + prep

reconcile /'rekənsaɪl/

'**reconcile sb/yourself to sth**; '**reconcile sb/yourself to doing sth** to make sb/yourself accept an unpleasant situation because nothing can be done to change it: *They were reconciled to the fact that he wouldn't be coming*

back. ◇ *I've reconciled myself to having no money while I'm a student.*
♦ v + n/pron + prep

reduce /rɪ'djuːs; AmE -'duːs/

re'duce sb/sth to sth to bring sb/sth to a particular state, especially a worse one: *She was reduced to tears by their criticism.* ◇ *The building was reduced to a heap of rubble.* ◇ *Her questioning reduced him to a state of confusion.*
♦ v + n/pron + prep

re'duce sb to doing sth to make sb do sth they do not approve of or are ashamed of because there is no other choice for them: *I was reduced to borrowing money from friends.*
NOTE Nearly always used in the passive.
♦ v + n/pron + prep

re'duce sth to sth to change sth into a simpler or more general form: *His arguments can be reduced to four points.*
♦ v + n/pron + prep

reek /riːk/

'reek of sth (*disapproving*) **1** to smell very strongly of sth unpleasant: *His breath reeked of tobacco.* **2** if sth **reeks of** sth, it suggests very strongly that there is sth unpleasant or suspicious about it: *His statement reeks of hypocrisy.* ◇ *The whole place reeked of neglect.*
♦ v + prep

reel /riːl/

NOTE A **reel** is a round object around which you wind such things as thread or wire.

,reel sth 'in/'out to wind sth on/off a reel: *He slowly reeled the fish in.* ◇ *The firefighters reeled out the hose.* ◇ *The line caught on something in the water as he reeled it in.*
♦ v + n/pron + adv ♦ v + adv + n

,reel sth 'off **1** to say a long list of things quickly and without having to think about it: *He reeled off the names of the people he'd invited.* **OBJ** list, names, figures **SYN** rattle sth off **2** (*informal, especially BrE*) (in a sports competition) to win a series of games or a number of points: *The Bulls reeled off nine consecutive points.* ◇ *Sharapova reeled off three straight games.* **OBJ** points, games **SYN** chalk up sth
♦ v + adv + n + prep ♦ v + n/pron + adv
♦ v + n + adv (*less frequent*)

,reel sth 'out → REEL STH IN/OUT

refer /rɪ'fɜː(r)/ (-rr-)

⚡ re'fer to sb/sth **1** (as sth) to mention or talk about sb/sth: *She never referred to the incident again.* ◇ *Passengers are now referred to as 'customers'.* **2** to describe or be connected to sb/sth: *This paragraph refers to the events of last year.* ◇ *This phenomenon is referred to in detail in chapter nine.* ◇ *The term 'visually handi-*

refer to sb/sth

allude to sb/sth ♦ cite sth ♦ mention sth/sb
♦ refer to sb/sth

These verbs all mean to write or speak about sb/sth, especially in order to give an example or prove sth.

allude to sb/sth (*formal*) to mention sth in an indirect way: *The problem had been alluded to briefly in earlier discussions.*

cite sth (*formal*) to mention sth as a reason or an example, or in order to support what you are saying: *He cited his heavy workload as the reason for his breakdown.*

mention sth/sb to write or speak about sth/sb, especially without giving much information: *Nobody mentioned anything to me about it.*

refer to sb/sth to mention or speak about sb/sth: *I promised not to refer to the matter again.*

PATTERNS AND COLLOCATIONS

- sth is **commonly/frequently/often** mentioned/referred to/cited/alluded to
- to mention/refer to/allude to sb/sth **briefly/casually/in passing**
- to mention/refer to sb/sth **directly/explicitly**
- the example mentioned/referred to/cited/alluded to **above/earlier/previously**
- to mention/refer to/cite **an example/an instance/a case** of sth

capped' refers to students who have serious difficulties in seeing.
♦ v + prep

re'fer to sth to look at sth for information: *You don't need to refer to a dictionary for this exercise.* ◇ *It is important to provide a record that can be referred to.*
OBJ book, dictionary, manual, instructions **SYN** consult sth (*more formal*)
♦ v + prep

re'fer sb/sth to sb/sth to send sb/sth to a different place or person in order to get help, advice or a decision: *The case was referred to the Court of Appeal.* ◇ *My tutor referred me to a counsellor.* ◇ (*formal*) *I refer you to my letter of 2 June.*
♦ v + n/pron + prep

reflect /rɪ'flekt/

re'flect on sb/sth (*also* re'flect upon sb/sth *more formal*) to make sb have a particular opinion of sb/sth: *When the department performs badly, it reflects on me as manager* (= it makes people think I am a bad manager). ◇ *This*

incident **reflects badly** *on everyone involved.*
◇ *When our students are successful it* **reflects well** *on the whole school.*

NOTE **Reflect on sb/sth** is often used with adverbs, especially *badly* or *well*.

‣ v + prep

IDM **reflect great credit on sb/sth** to show that sb/sth is very good or has done sth very well: *The fine condition of the cars reflects great credit on their owners.* ◇ *The young orchestra's performance reflected great credit on their training.*

regale /rɪˈɡeɪl/

reˈgale sb with sth to entertain sb with stories, jokes, etc.: *She was regaling us with tales of her youth.*

‣ v + n/pron + prep

rein /reɪn/

ˌrein ˈin; ˌrein sth ˈin (*also* ˌrein ˈback, ˌrein sth ˈback *less frequent*) to pull on the reins of a horse (= the leather bands that go around its neck) to make it go more slowly or stop: *Felipe reined back and rode beside her.* ◇ *She reined in her horse and waited for John to catch up.*

‣ v + adv ‣ v + adv + n ‣ v + n/pron + adv

ˌrein sb/sth ˈin (*also* ˌrein sb/sth ˈback *less frequent*) to control sb or sth more strictly: *We need to rein in public spending.* ◇ *The new President is faced with the task of reining in the military.* ◇ *He was unable to rein back his impatience.*

‣ v + adv + n ‣ v + pron + adv ‣ v + n + adv

relate /rɪˈleɪt/

reˈlate to sb/sth **1** to feel that you can understand a person, a situation, sth that sb does or feels, etc. and have sympathy with them/it: *She was unable to relate to her youngest child.* ◇ *I find him very difficult to relate to.* ◇ *I just couldn't relate to that movie at all.* ◇ *She could relate to his feelings of guilt about his children.* **2** to be connected to sb/sth; to refer to sb/sth: *All the documents relating to the matter were destroyed.* ◇ *The new law relates only to children born after 1996.*

‣ v + prep

relieve /rɪˈliːv/

reˈlieve sb of sth **1** (*formal*) to carry out a difficult or unpleasant task for sb else, or instead of them: *Robots can relieve people of dull and repetitive work.* ◇ *Can I relieve you of some of your bags* (= carry them for you)? **2** (*formal*) to dismiss sb from a job or responsibility: *He was relieved of his post as manager.* **NOTE** Often used in the passive. **3** (*informal, ironic*) to rob sb of sth: *The thief relieved him of his wallet.*

‣ v + n/pron + prep

rely /rɪˈlaɪ/ (**relies, relying, relied**)

‣ **reˈly on sb/sth** (*also* **reˈly upon sb/sth** *more formal*) **1** (**for sth**) to need or depend on sb/sth: *She still has to rely on her parents for money.* ◇ *He hasn't got a car, and relies on public transport to get around.* ◇ *We relied on Anna to translate for us.* ◇ *Before they got a piped water supply, local people had to rely on getting their water from wells and tanks.* **SYN** **depend on/upon sb/sth** (**for sth**) ⊃ note at DEPEND ON SB/STH **2** to trust or have confidence in sb/sth: *You can safely rely on her judgement.* ◇ *You can rely on Jon to turn up late!* (= he always does) ◇ *For the first time in years she had someone she could rely on.* ◇ *We relied on the advice of our solicitor.* ◇ *She cannot be relied on to tell the truth.* **SYN** **count on/upon sb/sth; depend on/upon sb/sth**

‣ v + prep

remember /rɪˈmembə(r)/

reˈmember sb to sb (*BrE*) (*not used in the progressive tenses*) used to ask sb to say hello and give your good wishes to sb else: *Remember me to your mother.*

‣ v + n/pron + prep

remind /rɪˈmaɪnd/

‣ **reˈmind sb of sb/sth** (*not used in the progressive tenses*) if sb/sth **reminds you of** sb/sth, they make you think of sb/sth because they are similar: *The smell of bread baking reminds me of home.* ◇ *When Clare smiled, she reminded me of her mother.* ◇ *Listening to her, he was reminded of Helen.* ◇ *Watching his serious face, with its big round glasses, she was reminded of an owl.*

⊃ note on page 256

‣ v + n/pron + prep

renege /rɪˈniːɡ, rɪˈneɪɡ/

reˈnege on sth to break a promise, an agreement, etc.: *Clarke claimed that she had reneged on her promise to marry him.*

OBJ **deal, debt, contract**

‣ v + prep

rent /rent/

ˌrent sth ˈout (**to sb**) to allow sth that you own to be used by another person in return for payment: *They rented the house out to students.* ◇ *Most of these houses are rented out.*

OBJ **room, house, etc.** **SYN** **hire sth out** (**to sb**); **let sth out** (**to sb**) (*BrE*)

NOTE **Rent sth** can also be used on its own with the same meaning: *You could rent a room to a student.*

‣ v + n/pron + adv ‣ v + adv + n

remind sb of sb/sth

bring sb/sth to mind ◆ **conjure sth up** ◆ **evoke sth** ◆ **remind sb of sb/sth** ◆ **take sb back**

These verbs both mean to bring a feeling, a memory or an image into your mind.

bring sb/sth to mind (*formal*) to remind you of sb/sth: *The painting brings to mind some of Picasso's early works.*

conjure sth up to make sth appear as a picture in your mind: *That smell always conjures up memories of holidays in France.*

evoke sth (*formal*) to bring a memory, feeling or image into your mind: *The music evoked memories of her youth.* ◇ *His case is unlikely to evoke public sympathy.*

remind sb of sb/sth (*not used in the progressive tenses*) (of a person, place, thing or event) to make sb think of another person, place, etc. because they are similar in some way: *You remind me of your father when you say that.* ◇ *That smell reminds me of Italy.*

take sb back to make sb remember a time in the past: *The smell of the sea took him back to his childhood.* ◇ *That song takes me back 30 years.*

WHICH WORD?

Conjure sth up can be more visual than **evoke** and usually means to remember sth in pictures or images. **Evoke** is used more for talking about memories and feelings. **Remind** and **take back** refer specifically to memories.

PATTERNS AND COLLOCATIONS

- to remind sb of/evoke/conjure up/take sb back to **the past/past times**
- to evoke/conjure up **a memory/a picture/an image/a feeling**
- to **vividly** remind sb of sth/evoke sth/conjure sth up

repair /rɪˈpeə(r)/; *AmE* -ˈper/

re·**pair to...** (*formal* or *humorous*) to go to a place: *After dinner, they repaired to the lounge for coffee.*
◆ v + prep

report /rɪˈpɔːt; *AmE* rɪˈpɔːrt/

re·**port ˈback 1** (**to sb**) (**on sb/sth**) to give a spoken or written account of some information that you were asked to find out about: *I have to report back to the manager on our progress.* **2** (**to...**) to return to a place, especially in order to start work again: *When do you have to report back for duty?*
◆ v + adv

re·**port ˈin** (**to sb/sth**) to contact sb to let them know where you are or what you are doing: *The officer briefly reported in (to the police station).*

re·**port to sb** (*business*) (*not used in the progressive tenses*) if you **report to** sb in a company or an organization, they are responsible for your work and tell you what to do: *She reports directly to the chief executive.* ◇ *A new team will be put together for the project, reporting to me.*
◆ v + prep

reside /rɪˈzaɪd/

re·**side in sb/sth** (*formal*) to be in sb/sth; to be caused by sth: *The attraction of the book resides in its illustrations.* ◇ *The interests of the child reside in getting the best possible education.*
◆ v + prep

re·**side in/with sb/sth** (*formal*) to be present in or belong to sb/sth: *Supreme authority resides with the President.* ◇ *Political power seems to reside increasingly in Brussels.*
◆ v + prep

resign /rɪˈzaɪn/

re·**sign yourself to sth; re·sign yourself to doing sth** to be ready to accept sth unpleasant because you cannot avoid it: *She resigned herself to her fate.* ◇ *They resigned themselves to being defeated.* ◇ *I've resigned myself to staying in again tonight.*
◆ v + pron + prep

resolve /rɪˈzɒlv; *AmE* rɪˈzɑːlv/

re·**solve into sth; re·solve sth into sth** to separate or to be separated into its parts: *The design resolved into a number of different patterns.* ◇ *a lawyer's ability to resolve facts into their legal categories*
◆ v + prep ◆ v + pron + prep

re·**solve into sth; re·solve itself into sth 1** if sth you see or hear at a distance **resolves into** sth or **resolves itself into** sth, you gradually see it or hear it clearly as a particular thing: *The grey shape resolved into a group of walkers.* ◇ *The white light resolved itself into the headlights of a car.* **2** to gradually become or be understood as sth: *The discussion eventually resolved itself into two main issues.* ◇ *The question resolves itself into whether individuals should be allowed to choose such a course of action.*
◆ v + prep ◆ v + pron + prep

resonate /ˈrezəneɪt/

'**resonate with sth** (*formal*) (*not usually used in the progressive tenses*) to be full of a particular quality or feeling: *She makes a simple story resonate with complex themes and emotions.*
♦ v + prep

resort /rɪˈzɔːt; AmE rɪˈzɔːrt/

re'**sort to sth**; re'**sort to doing sth** to make use of sth, especially sth bad or unpleasant, as a way of achieving sth, often because no other course of action is possible: *They should be able to settle their differences without resorting to violence.* ◊ *They resorted to bribery to get what they wanted.* ◊ *Various measures were resorted to.*
OBJ **violence, bribery**
♦ v + prep

rest /rest/

'**rest on sb/sth** (*also* '**rest upon sb/sth** *more formal*) **1** to depend on sb/sth: *Britain's hopes of a medal now rest on Henderson.* **2** if your eyes **rest on** sb/sth, you look at them/it: *Her eyes rested on a photograph on the desk.* SUBJ **eyes, gaze**
♦ v + prep

'**rest on sth** (*also* '**rest upon sth** *more formal*) to be based on sth: *The whole case rests on one man's evidence.* ◊ *His argument seemed to rest on a false assumption.*
♦ v + prep

,**rest 'up** (*informal*) **1** (*old-fashioned, especially BrE*) to rest after an illness or injury: *He was advised to rest up for a week after his fall.* NOTE **Rest** on its own is more usual. **2** (*especially AmE*) to rest in order to gain energy and strength, for example after an illness or before a sports competition: *You should rest up if you're going to be fit for the game.* ◊ *The climbers decided to rest up for a couple of days before continuing up to the summit.* NOTE **Rest** can also be used on its own with this meaning.
♦ v + adv

'**rest with sb** (**to do sth**) (*formal*) (*not used in the progressive tenses*) to be sb's responsibility: *The decision rests entirely with you.* ◊ *The responsibility for bringing up children rests with the parents.* ◊ ***It rests with** the bus company **to** prove they were not responsible for the accident.*
SYN **lie with sb** (**to do sth**)
♦ v + prep

result /rɪˈzʌlt/

re'**sult in sth** to have a particular effect; to make sth happen: *The accident resulted in 67 deaths.* ◊ *The agreement will result in employers working more closely with students and teachers.*
OBJ **death, increase, loss**
♦ v + prep

retail /ˈriːteɪl/

'**retail at/for sth** (*business*) to be sold at a particular price: *The DVDs retail at £15 each.*
♦ v + prep

return /rɪˈtɜːn; AmE rɪˈtɜːrn/

re'**turn to sth 1** to go back to a previous state: *Train services have **returned to normal** after the strike.* SYN **go back to sth 2** to start discussing a subject you were discussing earlier: *He returns to this topic later in the report.* SYN **come back to sth**
♦ v + prep

rev /rev/ (**-vv-**)

,**rev 'up**; ,**rev sth 'up** if the engine of a vehicle **revs up**, or sb **revs it up**, it runs quickly although the vehicle does not move: *The car revved up and roared away.*
NOTE **Rev** and **rev sth** are also used on their own.
♦ v + adv ♦ v + n/pron + adv ♦ v + adv + n

,**rev 'up** (**for sth**), ,**rev sb/sth 'up** (**for sth**) (*especially AmE*) to become, or to make sb/sth, more active or excited: *The team are revving up for next week's game.* ◊ *It's his job to rev up the audience before the show starts.*
♦ v + adv ♦ v + n/pron + adv ♦ v + adv + n

revel /ˈrevl/ (**-ll-, -l-**)

'**revel in sth**; '**revel in doing sth** to enjoy a situation or an experience very much: *I think he's secretly revelling in all the attention.* ◊ *She seems to revel in annoying her parents.*
♦ v + prep

revert /rɪˈvɜːt; AmE rɪˈvɜːrt/

re'**vert to sb** (*law*) (of property and land) to return legally to the owner: *After his death the house reverted to its original owner.*
♦ v + prep

re'**vert to sth**; re'**vert to doing sth** (*formal*) **1** to go back to a previous condition or activity, especially a worse one: *When the pressure is on, players revert to bad habits.* ◊ *After a good year the team **reverted to type** in their last game* (= they played badly again). ◊ *After 80 years as a school, the building has reverted back to being a house again.* **2** to start talking or thinking again about a subject you were considering earlier: *To revert to your earlier question…*
♦ v + prep

revise /rɪˈvaɪz/

re,**vise sth 'down** to decrease an estimate in order to correct or improve it: *The company was forced to revise down its earnings forecast.*
♦ v + n/pron + adv ♦ v + adv + n

re,vise sth 'up to increase an estimate in order to correct or improve it: *US growth forecasts have been revised up.*
◆ v + n/pron + adv ◆ v + adv + n

revolve /rɪˈvɒlv; *AmE* rɪˈvɑːlv/

re'volve around sb/sth; re'volve around doing sth (*also* revolve round sb/sth, revolve round doing sth *especially BrE*) to have sb/sth as the main subject or interest: *His whole life revolved round cars.* ◊ *You think the whole world revolves around you.* ◊ *Much of a dolphin's life revolves around finding and eating food.*
◆ v + prep

re'volve around sth (*also* re'volve round sth *especially BrE*) to move around sth in a circle: *The earth revolves around the sun.*
◆ v + prep

rid /rɪd/ (ridding, rid, rid)

'rid sb/sth/yourself of sb/sth (*formal*) to remove sth/sb unpleasant from a person, a place or an organization: *The government pledged to rid the country of nuclear weapons.* ◊ *How could she rid herself of Charles?*
NOTE Get rid of sb/sth is a more common way of saying rid yourself of sb/sth: *How could she get rid of Charles?*
◆ v + n/pron + prep

riddle /ˈrɪdl/

'riddle sb/sth with sth to fill sb/sth with bullets or with holes: *His body was riddled with bullets.* ◊ *wooden beams riddled with holes* ◊ *a bullet-riddled car*
NOTE Often used in the passive.
◆ v + n/pron + prep

be 'riddled with sth to be full of sth, especially sth unpleasant or bad: *The whole organization is riddled with corruption.*
◆ be + v + prep

ride /raɪd/ (rode /rəʊd/; *AmE* roʊd/, ridden /ˈrɪdn/)

'ride on sth (*usually used in the progressive tenses*) to depend on sth: *My whole future is riding on this interview.* ◊ *There's a lot of money riding on this deal.* ◊ *She has **a lot riding on** this film after the failure of the last two.*
◆ v + prep

,ride sth 'out to manage to survive a difficult period or situation without suffering serious harm: *Do you think the president will be able to ride out this latest crisis?* ◊ *Of course your parents were angry, but you should have stayed to **ride out the storm**.*
OBJ storm, recession
◆ v + adv + n ◆ v + n/pron + adv

,ride 'up if an item of clothing rides up, it gradually moves upwards, out of position: *His*

waistcoat was riding up over his stomach. ◊ *My skirt tends to ride up.*
◆ v + adv

rifle /ˈraɪfl/

,rifle 'through sth to search quickly through sth such as drawers, cupboards or papers, in order to find or steal sth: *Sally rifled through her wardrobe looking for something to wear.* ◊ *The room looked as if a burglar had rifled through it.* ◊ *The drawers had been rifled through.*
◆ v + prep

rig /rɪɡ/ (-gg-)

'rig sb/sth 'out (in/with sth) (*old-fashioned*, *BrE*) to provide sb/sth with clothes or equipment: *We rigged them out from top to bottom* (= bought them new clothes, shoes, etc.). ◊ *The ship had been rigged out with state-of-the-art equipment.*
SYN kit sb/sth out (in/with sth) (*BrE*)
NOTE Often used in the passive.
◆ v + adv + n ◆ v + n/pron + adv
▶ 'rig-out *n* (*BrE*, *informal*, *disapproving*) a set of clothes worn together: *Where are you going in that rig-out?*

,rig sth 'up **1** to fix a piece of equipment into place: *We've rigged up lights in the garden for the party.* ◊ *He was rigged up to a machine so that the nurses could check his heartbeat.* **2** to make or build sth quickly, using whatever materials are available: *He had rigged up a sort of tent, using his jacket and shirt.*
◆ v + adv + n ◆ v + n/pron + adv

ring /rɪŋ/ (rang /ræŋ/, rung /rʌŋ/)

NOTE To ring is not used in American English to mean 'to telephone'. To call is the most common verb for this in American English. It is also used in British English, as well as to phone.

,ring a'round/'round; ,ring a'round/ 'round sb/sth (*BrE*) to phone several people or places to find out information or discuss sth: *I've spent the morning ringing round travel agents.*
◆ v + adv ◆ v + prep

,ring 'back; ,ring sb 'back (*BrE*) to telephone sb again or to telephone sb who telephoned you earlier: *I'll ring you back later with more details.* ◊ *Your mother called. She wants you to ring back.* ◊ *I've only got a few coins for this call* (= from a public telephone). *Can you ring me back?*
◆ v + adv ◆ v + n/pron + adv
▶ 'ringback *n* [U, C] a telephone service that you can use if you call sb and their telephone is being used, so that your telephone will ring when the line is free

,ring 'in (*BrE*) **1** to telephone the place where you work: *She felt so exhausted she rang in sick* (= to say she could not come to work). ◊ *The boss rings in several times a day, even when he's on* *holiday.* **2** to telephone a radio programme, etc.: *Listeners were asked to ring in with their opinions.*

,ring **'off** (*BrE*) to end a telephone conversation, and put the telephone down: *He rang off before I could explain.*

SYN hang up
◆ v + adv

,ring **'out** to be heard loudly and clearly: *His clear voice rang out across the hall.* ◇ *Suddenly shots rang out nearby.*
◆ v + adv

,ring **'round, etc.** (*BrE*) → RING AROUND/ROUND, ETC.

,ring **'through** (to **sb/sth**) (*BrE*) to make a telephone call to sb, especially within the same building: *Reception rang through to say my visitor had arrived.*
◆ v + adv

,ring **'up**; ,ring **sb/sth 'up** (*BrE*) to telephone sb/sth: *He rang up to apologize.* ◇ *We must ring Jenny up tonight.* ◇ *Can you ring up the station to check the train times?* ◇ *My dad was once rung up by someone claiming to be John Lennon.*
NOTE Ring and ring sb are also frequently used on their own. **Ring up** and **ring sb up** are very common in spoken English.
➔ note at CALL UP, CALL SB/STH UP
◆ v + adv ◆ v + n/pron + adv ◆ v + adv + n

,ring **sth 'up** to record the cost of goods being bought in a shop/store on a machine (a **cash register**); to make sales of the value mentioned: *She rang up the drinks on the till.* ◇ *The company rang up profits of $160 million last year.*
◆ v + adv + n ◆ v + n/pron + adv

rinse /rɪns/

,rinse **sth 'out 1** to make sth clean by washing it in water: *Ruth finished her coffee and rinsed out her cup under the tap.* ◇ *Rinse your mouth out to get rid of the taste.* **NOTE** Rinse sth is also used on its own: *She quickly rinsed her cup and plate.* **2** (*also* ,rinse **sth 'out of sth**) to remove sth such as soap from sth else with water: *Leave the conditioner on your hair for three minutes and then rinse it out.*
SYN wash sth out
◆ v + n/pron + adv
◆ v + adv + n **2** also v + n/pron + adv + prep

rip /rɪp/ (-pp-)

,rip **sb/sth a'part 1** to criticize sb/sth very severely: *After she'd gone, we ripped her apart.* ◇ *My tutor ripped my essay apart.* **SYN** rip into sb/sth; tear sb/sth apart **2** to defeat sb/sth easily: *We ripped the other team apart in the second half.* **SYN** tear sb/sth apart
◆ v + n/pron + adv ◆ v + adv + n (*rare*)

,rip **sth a'part** to destroy sth completely: *The hooligans had **ripped the place apart**.*

SYN tear sth apart; tear sth up
◆ v + n/pron + adv ◆ v + adv + n (*rare*)

'rip **at sth** to attack sth violently and tear it or cut it: *The bird ripped at its rival's throat.* ◇ (*figurative*) *The hurricane tore at their skin and ripped at their clothes.*
◆ v + prep

,rip **'into sb/sth** (with **sth**) (for **sth/for doing sth**) (*informal*) to criticize sb in an angry way for sth they have done or said: *He ripped into me for being late.*
SYN lay into sb/sth (with sth) (for sth/for doing sth)
◆ v + prep

,rip **'into/'through sb/sth** to go very quickly or violently into or through sb/sth: *An explosion ripped through a four-storey apartment building.*
◆ v + prep

,rip **sb 'off** (*informal*) to cheat sb, for example by charging them too much for sth, selling them sth of poor quality, etc.: *The bank was accused of ripping off its customers.* ◇ *The tickets were very expensive. We felt we'd been ripped off.* ◇ *The law protects tenants from being ripped off by landlords.*
◆ v + adv + n ◆ v + n/pron + adv
▶ 'rip-off n [usually sing.] (*informal*) a situation where you pay too much for sth; sth that is not worth what you pay for it: *They charged you £25 for a T-shirt? What a rip-off!* ◇ *The meal was a total rip-off.* ◇ *rip-off prices*

,rip **sb/sth 'off** (*informal*) to copy sb/sth, by stealing ideas, designs, etc. especially in order to make money for yourself: *Another band has ripped off our song.* ◇ *She was accused of ripping off other people's ideas.*
◆ v + adv + n ◆ v + n/pron + adv
▶ 'rip-off (of sth) n (*informal*) a copy of sth, especially one that is not as good as the original: *He has a stall that sells designer rip-offs* (= clothes).

'rip **'off** (*slang*) to steal sth: *Thieves broke in and ripped off five computers.*
SYN nick sth (*BrE, slang*)
◆ v + n/pron + adv ◆ v + adv + n
▶ 'rip-off n (*informal*) an act of stealing sth: *It was a scandalous rip-off of public funds.*

,rip **sth 'off**; ,rip **sth 'off sb/sth** to remove sth, especially clothing, very quickly by pulling sharply: *The fans were trying to rip his clothes off.* ◇ *She ripped the poster off the wall.*
SYN tear sth off, tear sth off sb/sth
◆ v + n/pron + adv ◆ v + adv + n

'rip **on sb** (*AmE*) to laugh at sb or make jokes about them: *My buddies were ripping on me about a poem I had written.*
◆ v + prep

,rip **'through sb/sth** → RIP INTO/THROUGH SB/STH

,rip **sth 'up 1** to tear sth to pieces: *I ripped the letter up without reading it.* ➔ note at TEAR STH

UP **2** to pull sth quickly or violently from the floor or ground: *A gang of teenagers ripped up fences and plants.* ◇ *We've ripped up the old carpets and painted the walls.*
SYN tear sth up
♦ v + n/pron + adv ♦ v + adv + n
IDM rip/tear up the 'rule book to start doing things in a way that is different from the way things are usually done, usually resulting in an improvement: *What we were able to do was rip up the rule book and design a car that doesn't damage the environment.*

rise /raɪz/ (**rose** /rəʊz/; *AmE* roʊz/, **risen** /ˈrɪzn/)
,rise a'bove sth **1** to not be affected or limited by problems, insults, etc.; to be able to deal with problems: *She was able to rise above her disability.* **2** to be too wise or good to do sth wrong or to think or behave in the way other people do: *He had an unusual ability to rise above the prejudices of his generation.* ◇ *There will always be gossip. You have to try and rise above it.* **3** to be better than other similar things: *Her articles never rise above the level of a gossip column.*
♦ v + prep
'rise to sth **1** to deal successfully with a situation or problem that you do not expect or do not usually have to face: *The job wasn't easy but Sam was ready to rise to the challenge.* ◇ *The play was a challenge for the actors but they rose to the occasion.* **2** to react when sb is deliberately trying to make you angry or get you interested in sth: *I refuse to rise to that sort of comment.* ◇ *I decided to flatter him and he rose to the bait* (= he reacted in the way that I wanted).
♦ v + prep
,rise 'up **1** (**against sb/sth**) (*formal*) to start to fight against or refuse to obey people in authority, for example a government or king: *The people rose up against the invaders.*
SYN rebel (**against sb/sth**) **2** (*literary*) to appear as a tall shape above the surroundings: *A magnificent palace rose up before her.*
♦ v + adv
▶ 'uprising *n* a situation in which a group of people join together to fight against or to refuse to obey people in authority: *The uprising was ruthlessly suppressed.*

roar /rɔː(r)/
roar back (*AmE*) (of a sports team) to start beating your opponent easily after losing: *The Sixers won the first two games, but the Trail Blazers roared back with four straight wins.*
♦ v + adv

rock /rɒk; *AmE* rɑːk/
,rock 'up (*BrE, AustralE, informal*) to arrive, especially in a relaxed way or without giving

advance warning: *You can't just rock up to that kind of restaurant without booking—they're very selective.*
SYN roll up (*informal*)
♦ v + adv

roll /rəʊl; *AmE* roʊl/
,roll a'round (*BrE also* ,roll 'round) (*informal*) **1** (*BrE also* ,roll a'bout) to be laughing so much that you can hardly control yourself: *Her speech had everyone rolling around with laughter.* **2** (of a regular event) to arrive; to happen at the usual time: *We have to be ready when election time rolls around again.* **SYN** come round, come around
♦ v + adv
,roll sth 'back **1** to reduce the amount of influence, power or importance that sth has; to change sth so that it is the opposite of what it was: *They were determined to roll back union power.* **2** to reduce prices, wages, etc.: *We must roll back inflation.* **OBJ** prices **3** to make sth go back or further away: *to roll back the frontiers of space/science* ◇ *The former star rolled back the years with a brilliant performance last night* (= he played as he did when he was younger).
OBJ frontiers
♦ v + adv + n ♦ v + pron + adv ♦ v + n + adv (*rare*)
▶ 'rollback (**of sth**) *n* **1** (*especially AmE*) a reduction or decrease in sth: *a 2% rollback in taxes* **2** (*computing*) a return to the condition that existed before there was an error in a computer system
,roll sth 'down **1** to open out a piece of clothing, etc. that has been folded over and over: *She rolled down her sleeves and buttoned the cuffs.* **OBJ** sleeves **2** to lower sth; to open a window in a car, especially by turning a handle: *He rolled down the car window and waved to us.*
OBJ car window **OPP** roll sth up
♦ v + adv + n ♦ v + pron + adv + n/pron + adv
,roll 'in (*informal*) **1** to arrive in great numbers or quantities: *Offers of help continue to roll in.* **2** to arrive somewhere, usually late and without being worried or sorry: *Rob finally rolled in at lunchtime.*
♦ v + adv
roll off sth to be produced, usually in large numbers, in a factory: *By next year, 60 000 cars will be rolling off its assembly lines.*
♦ v + prep
,roll 'on **1** (of time) to pass steadily: *As the years rolled on the painful memories began to fade.* **2** to continue without changing very much: *For the next few weeks the debate rolled on.* **3** roll on... (*BrE, informal*) used to say that you wish sth would come soon: *Roll on summer!*
♦ v + adv
,roll sb/sth 'out (*informal, especially AmE*) to use sb/sth to help you achieve sth: *He rolled out all*

his old friends to help him win the election. ◇ *The circus rolled out bears to announce its arrival.*

◆ v + adv + n ◆ v + pron + adv ◆ v + n + adv

‚roll sth 'out 1 to make a substance flat and thin by rolling sth over it: *Roll out the pastry with a clean rolling pin.* [OBJ] **pastry, dough 2** to open sth that is in a roll and put it flat on the ground: *I rolled out my sleeping bag and crawled in.* [OPP] **roll sth up 3** to officially make a new product available or start to use a new system: *The Air Force will roll out its new planes in November.* [SYN] **launch sth**

◆ v + adv + n ◆ v + n/pron + adv

[IDM] **roll out the red 'carpet (for sb)** to treat sb like a very important visitor

▶ **'roll-out** *n* an occasion when a company introduces or starts to use a new product or system: *a roll-out ceremony* ◇ *the global roll-out of the new corporate identity*

‚roll 'over (*informal*) to be easily defeated without even trying: *We can't expect them to just roll over for us.* ◇ *They thought the unions would roll over.*

◆ v + adv

‚roll 'over; ‚roll sb/sth 'over 1 (of a person) to turn from lying on one side of your body to the other side; to move sb in this way: *She rolled over onto her back.* ◇ *I rolled the baby over and sat up.* **2** (of a vehicle, a boat, etc.) to turn onto its side or upside down; to move sth in this way: *The car rolled over into a ditch.*

[SYN] **turn over, turn sb/sth over**

◆ v + adv ◆ v + n/pron + adv

‚roll 'over sth (*computing*) to move a computer mouse so that you point to a particular area on the screen: *When you roll over these hot spots, they change colour.* [SYN] **mouse over sth**

◆ v + prep

▶ **'rollover** *n* [C, U]: *Most browsers support rollovers.* ◇ *rollover buttons*

‚roll sb 'over (*BrE, informal*) to defeat sb easily: *They rolled us over in the replay.*

◆ v + adv + n ◆ v + n/pron + adv

‚roll sth 'over 1 (*finance*) to allow money that sb owes to be paid at a later date: *The government agreed to roll over the debt.* [OBJ] **debt, loan 2** to save points, credits, etc. that are supposed to be used in one time period and use them at a later time: *My mobile phone network allows me to roll over any unused minutes from one month to the next.* **3** (*BrE*) to add the prize money in a competition in a particular week to the prize money the next week, if no one has won it: *This week's lottery jackpot will be rolled over until next week.*

◆ v + adv + n ◆ v + n/pron + adv

▶ **'rollover** *n* **1** [C] (*BrE*) a prize of money in a competition that is formed by adding the prize from one week when no one has won it to the prize for the next week: *This week there is a*

rollover of £14 million. ◇ *a rollover jackpot/week* **2** [U] (*finance*) the act of allowing money that is owed to be paid at a later date

‚roll 'round (*BrE*) → ROLL AROUND

‚roll 'up (*informal*) to arrive, especially in a relaxed way or without giving advance warning: *He finally rolled up an hour late.* ◇ *Roll up! Roll up for the greatest show on earth!* (= used to invite people who are passing to come and form an audience)

[SYN] **rock up** (*BrE, AustralE, informal*)

◆ v + adv

‚roll sth 'up 1 to turn the end of a piece of clothing over and over to make it shorter: *He rolled up his sleeves and started washing the dishes.* [OBJ] **sleeves, trousers** [OPP] **roll sth down 2** to fold sth to make the shape of a tube or a ball: *She rolled up the sleeping bag.* [OPP] **roll sth out 3** to close the window in a car, especially by turning a handle; to raise sth: *She rolled up the window and drove off.* [OBJ] **car window** [OPP] **roll sth down**

◆ v + adv + n ◆ v + n/pron + adv

▶ **'roll-up** *n* (*BrE, informal*) a cigarette that you make yourself: *Simon lit a roll-up.*

‚roll sb/sth 'up to defeat or gain an advantage against a group of enemy soldiers, etc.: *Counter-intelligence services rolled up many of Moscow's spy networks.* ◇ *Numerous terrorist cells have been rolled up.*

◆ v + adv + n ◆ v + n/pron + adv

romp /rɒmp; *AmE* rɑːmp/

‚romp a'head/a'way (*BrE*) to make progress, increase or win quickly and easily: *The home team romped away to win by three goals.*

[NOTE] This verb is mostly used in newspapers.

◆ v + adv

‚romp 'through sth (*BrE, informal*) to do sth easily and quickly: *She romped through the exam questions.*

[NOTE] This verb is mostly used in newspapers.

◆ v + prep

root /ruːt/

‚root a'round; ‚root a'round/'through sth (*BrE also* **‚root a'bout, ‚root a'bout sth**) (**for sth**) to move things around to try to find sth: *He was rooting around in the drawer for his keys.* ◇ *Someone had been rooting through the rubbish.*

◆ v + adv ◆ v + prep

'root for sb/sth (*informal*) (*usually used in the progressive tenses*) to support or encourage sb in a sports competition or when they are in a difficult situation: *Good luck—I'll be rooting for you!*

↻ note at CHEER SB ON

◆ v + prep

‚root sb/sth 'out 1 to find the person or thing that is causing a problem and remove or get rid of them/it: *The government has promised to root*

out police corruption. ◇ *The troublemakers seem to have been rooted out.* OBJ **corruption 2** (*informal*) to find sb/sth when it is not easy or it takes a long time: *They eventually rooted out two witnesses.* ◇ *I've got some instructions for the camera somewhere—I'll see if I can root them out.* ◇ *I'll root out the photo for you.* SYN **dig sth out**; **hunt sth down/out**
  ◆ v + adv + n ◆ v + pron + adv
  ◆ v + n + adv (*less frequent*)

,root 'through sth → ROOT AROUND, ETC.

'root sb to sth if fear, shock, etc. **roots you to** a place, it makes you unable to move: *She stood **rooted to the spot** in horror.*
  ◆ v + n/pron + prep

,root sth 'up to dig or pull up a plant, tree, etc. with its roots: *Kids have been rooting up plants.*
  ◆ v + adv + n ◆ v + n/pron + adv

rope /rəʊp; *AmE* roʊp/

,rope sb 'in; ,rope sb 'into sth; ,rope sb 'into doing sth (*informal*) to persuade sb to take part in an activity or to help you, even when they do not want to: *We'll rope Colin in to help us.* ◇ *I got roped into washing all the dirty dishes.*
  NOTE Often used in the passive.
  ◆ v + n/pron + adv ◆ v + adv + n ◆ v + n/pron + prep

,rope sth 'off to separate one area from another with ropes, in order to stop people from entering it: *The scene of the crime had been roped off.*
  OBJ **area**
  NOTE Often used in the passive.
  ◆ v + n/pron + adv ◆ v + adv + n

rot /rɒt; *AmE* rɑːt/ (-tt-)

,rot a'way to gradually decay: *The window frame had rotted away.*
  ◆ v + adv

rough /rʌf/

,rough sth 'out to draw or write the main parts of sth without including all the details: *She roughed out the design on the back of an envelope.* ◇ *I've roughed out a few ideas for the book.*
  ◆ v + adv + n ◆ v + pron + adv
  ◆ v + n + adv (*less frequent*)

,rough sb 'up (*informal*) to hurt sb by hitting or kicking them, especially in order to frighten or warn them: *They didn't want to kill him, just rough him up a little.* ◇ *Demonstrators claimed they had been roughed up by the police.*
  SYN **beat sb up** (*more formal*)
  ◆ v + n/pron + adv ◆ v + adv + n

round /raʊnd/

,round sth 'down → ROUND STH UP/DOWN

,round sth 'off 1 (*AmE also* ,round sth 'out) (**with sth**) to end or complete sth in an accept-

able way: *We rounded off the meal with coffee.* ◇ *The team rounded off a successful season with another brilliant victory.* ◇ *The evening was rounded off with a disco.* OBJ **the day**, **the evening 2** to give a smooth curved shape to the edge of sth: *I rounded off the corners with sandpaper.*
  ◆ v + adv + n ◆ v + n/pron + adv

'round on sb to suddenly speak angrily to sb and criticize or attack them: *He rounded on her angrily and told her to keep her mouth shut.*
  ◆ v + prep

,round sth 'out (*AmE*) → ROUND STH OFF 1

,round sb/sth 'up to bring together a number of people, animals or objects in one place: *to round up cattle/sheep* ◇ *The gang were rounded up and put in jail.* ◇ (*humorous*) *We've rounded up some good speakers for the conference.*
  ◆ v + adv + n ◆ v + n/pron + adv
  ▶ 'round-up n [usually sing.] **1** a brief summary of the most important points of news or sport, for example on a television or radio news programme: *a news round-up* ◇ *a round-up of the day's events* **2** an act of bringing people or animals together in one place: *a round-up of wild ponies* ◇ *a round-up of suspects*

,round sth 'up/'down (**to sth**) to increase/ decrease a number to the next highest or lowest whole number: *He rounded the price down to $900.* ◇ *Totals should be rounded up to the nearest whole number.*
  ◆ v + n/pron + adv ◆ v + adv + n

rub /rʌb/ (-bb-)

,rub a'gainst sb/sth; ,rub 'up against sb/ sth if an animal **rubs** (**up**) **against** sb/sth, it moves backwards and forwards and presses itself against them/it: *The cat rubbed (up) against her.*
  ◆ v + prep ◆ v + adv + prep

,rub a'long (**with sb/together**) (*BrE*, *informal*) to live or work together with sb in an acceptable way: *We rub along all right with the neighbours.*
  SYN **get on/along** (**with sb/together**)
  ◆ v + adv

,rub sb/sth 'down; ,rub yourself 'down to rub the skin of a person, an animal, etc. with sth such as a towel, to make it clean and dry: *She rubbed herself down with a towel.* ◇ *After exercise each horse must be rubbed down.*
  ◆ v + n/pron + adv ◆ v + adv + n
  ▶ 'rub-down n [usually sing.] an act of rubbing sb/sth/yourself with a towel, for example

,rub sth 'down 1 (*especially BrE*) to make sth clean by rubbing it with a cloth, etc.: *Rub the walls down well before painting them.* **2** to make the surface of sth smooth by rubbing it with special paper, etc.: *He rubbed the woodwork down with sandpaper.*
  ◆ v + n/pron + adv ◆ v + adv + n

▶ **'rub-down** *n* [usually sing.] (*especially BrE*) **1** an act of cleaning the surface of sth with a cloth, etc. **2** an act of rubbing the surface of sth to make it smooth

,**rub sth 'in** to say sth to sb which reminds them of sth that they feel embarrassed or guilty about and would like to forget: *I already know it was my fault—there's no need to **rub it in**.* ◇ *Was he trying to rub in the fact that he didn't like me?*

OBJ it

NOTE Not used in the passive.

◆ v + n/pron + adv ◆ v + adv + n

IDM **rub sb's 'nose in it** to remind sb of sth they feel embarrassed or guilty about and would like to forget

,**rub sth 'in**; ,**rub sth 'into sth** to spread a substance over a surface while pressing firmly with your fingers, a cloth, etc.: *Rub the lotion into your skin with your fingers.* ◇ *Spray on the polish and rub it in well.*

OBJ cream, lotion

◆ v + n/pron + adv ◆ v + adv + n ◆ v + n/pron + prep

,**rub 'off (on/onto sb)** if sth, such as a good quality that sb has, **rubs off** onto you, you gain some of that quality by spending time with the person: *Let's hope some of his good luck rubs off on me!* ◇ *None of her love for nature has rubbed off onto her children.*

◆ v + adv

,**rub 'off**; ,**rub sth 'off**; ,**rub sth 'off sth** to be removed from sth by rubbing; to remove sth from sth by rubbing: *Somebody's used the wrong kind of pen on the whiteboard and it won't rub off.* ◇ *He quickly rubbed the mud off his face.*

◆ v + adv ◆ v + n/pron + adv ◆ v + adv + n

◆ v + n/pron + prep

,**rub sb 'out** (*AmE, slang*) to murder sb: *He was rubbed out before he could talk.*

SYN **bump sb off** (*informal*); **do away with sb** (*informal*); **murder sb**

NOTE Often used in the passive.

◆ v + n/pron + adv ◆ v + adv + n

,**rub sth 'out** (*BrE*) to remove the marks made by a pen, pencil, etc. from a piece of paper, a board, etc.: *Draw the outline with a soft pencil, so that you can rub it out later.*

SYN **erase sth** (*more formal*)

◆ v + n/pron + adv ◆ v + adv + n

,**rub 'up against sb/sth** → RUB AGAINST SB/STH

ruck /rʌk/

,**ruck 'up**; ,**ruck sth 'up** (*BrE*) to form untidy folds; to make sth do this: *Your blouse has rucked up at the back.* ◇ *Her skirt was rucked up.*

◆ v + adv ◆ v + adv + n ◆ v + n/pron + adv

rule /ruːl/

,**rule sth 'in**; ,**rule sth 'into sth** (*formal*) if sb **rules sth in**, they decide that it is possible, or that it can or should happen: *He asked for all possible results to be ruled into the discussions.*

OPP **rule sth out, rule sth out of sth**

◆ v + n/pron + adv ◆ v + adv + n ◆ v + n/pron + prep

⚡,**rule sb 'out (as sth)**, ,**rule sb 'out of sth 1** if sb **rules** sb else **out**, they decide that it is not possible for them to have done sth or to do sth, or that they are not suitable for sth: *The police soon ruled out her husband as a suspect.* ◇ *The producer ruled out an older actress for the role.* ◇ *Ramsay has been ruled out as too old for the job.* **2** if sth **rules sb out**, it makes it impossible for sb to have done sth or to do sth, or makes them not suitable for sth: *Several people saw her at the restaurant at 9.00 p.m. so that seems to rule her out as the murderer.* ◇ *Beckham has been ruled out of tonight's game with a knee injury.*

→ see also RULE YOURSELF OUT, ETC.

◆ v + n/pron + adv ◆ v + adv + n

◆ v + n/pron + adv + prep

⚡,**rule sth 'out (as sth)**, ,**rule sth 'out of sth 1** if sth **rules sth out**, they decide that it is not possible, or that it cannot or should not happen: *The police have ruled out suicide.* ◇ *I wouldn't rule anything out.* ◇ *Detectives have not ruled out the possibility that she was abducted.* ◇ *Paris has been ruled out as the site for the next Olympics.* ◇ *Sabotage was ruled out of the investigation.*

OPP **rule sth in, rule sth into sth 2** if sth **rules** sth out, it makes it impossible for sth to happen, or makes sth not suitable for a particular purpose: *The latest developments **rule out the possibility** of peace.* ◇ *The change in the weather ruled out any climbing the next day.* ◇ *The size of the house ruled it out as a family home.*

◆ v + adv + n ◆ v + n/pron + adv

◆ v + n/pron + adv + prep

,**rule yourself 'out**; ,**rule yourself 'out of sth** to decide you do not want to or are not able to do sth; to decide that you are not suitable for sth: *Smith has not ruled himself out of Saturday's game.*

◆ v + pron + adv ◆ v + pron + adv + prep

rumble /ˈrʌmbl/

,**rumble 'on** (*especially BrE*) if an argument, a disagreement, etc. **rumbles on**, it continues slowly and steadily for much longer than it should: *The dispute rumbled on through the summer.* ◇ *The row has been rumbling on for two years.*

◆ v + adv

run /rʌn/ (**running, ran** /ræn/, **run**)

,**run a'bout, etc.** (*BrE*) → RUN AROUND, ETC.

▶ **'runabout** *n* (*informal*) **1** a small car, boat or aircraft, used mainly for short journeys **2** (*AmE*) a person who moves from place to place

,**run a'cross sb/sth** to meet sb or find sth by chance: *I ran across Mary in town yesterday.*

SYN **come across sb/sth**

◆ v + prep

run 'after sb (*informal*) to try to persuade sb to have a romantic or sexual relationship with you: *He's always running after younger women.*
◆ v + prep

run 'after sb/sth to run to try to catch sb/sth; to chase sb/sth: *They ran after the thief but he got away.*
◆ v + prep

run a'long (*old-fashioned*, *informal*) used to tell sb, especially a child, to go away and not disturb you: *Run along now, children, I'm busy.*
◆ v + adv

run a'round; **run a'round sth** (*BrE also* **run a'bout/'round**, **run a'bout/'round sth**) **1** to run in different directions, especially in an excited way: *It's a lovely park to run around in.* ◇ *The children were running round the house with no clothes on.* ◇ *They stopped the car to let the dogs run about.* **2** to move very quickly from place to place, being very busy: *I ran around like a mad thing all day.* ◇ *He's been running about the place organizing the party.* ◇ *I've been running round everywhere looking for you!* ◇ *He's had the police* **running around in circles** (= being very busy but not achieving anything). **SYN** **rush around**, **rush around sth**; **tear around**, **tear around sth**
◆ v + adv ◆ v + prep
▶ **'runaround** *n* if you give sb the **runaround**, you treat them badly by delaying them, not telling them the truth, etc.: *You know where she is, but you're just* **giving me the runaround**.

run a'round after sb (*BrE also* **run 'round after sb**) to be very busy doing a lot of things for sb, when they should be able to do them for themselves: *His mother shouldn't have to run around after him.* ◇ *She spends all her time running round after the children.*
◆ v + adv + prep

run a'round with sb (*disapproving*) to spend a lot of time with sb: *Their son is running around with a bad crowd.*
◆ v + adv + prep

'run at sb to run towards sb to attack them or as if you were going to attack them: *He ran at me with a knife.*
◆ v + prep

'run at sth (*often used in the progressive tenses*) to be at or near a particular level or rate: *Inflation is running at 26%.* ◇ *Interest rates were running at record levels.* **SUBJ** **inflation**, **unemployment**
◆ v + prep

run a'way 1 (**from sb/sth**) to move quickly away from sb/a place; to escape from sb/a place: *A man was seen running away from the shop.* ◇ *'Bye then,' she said, and ran away without looking back.* ◇ *His first instinct was to run away.* → see also RUN OFF 1 **2** (**from sth**) to leave the place where you are living or staying suddenly and secretly because you are unhappy: *She ran away from home.* ◇ *He ran away and joined a*

SYNONYMS

run away

flee ◆ **make off** ◆ **run away** ◆ **run off** ◆ **take off**

flee to leave a place very quickly, especially because you are in danger: *Refugees fled from the city.* ◇ *The robbers fled empty-handed from the shop.*

make off to hurry away, especially in order to escape from sb/sth: *The robbers made off before the police arrived.*

run away to leave a person or place suddenly; to escape from sb/sth: *He turned and ran away.* ◇ *I tried to* **run away from home** *several times when I was a kid.*

run off to escape from sb/sth by running: *She ran off when I tried to talk to her.*

take off (*informal*) to leave a place, especially in a hurry: *When he saw me coming he took off in the opposite direction.*

PATTERNS AND COLLOCATIONS

▪ to flee/run away/run off/take off/make off **in terror/in panic/empty-handed**
▪ to flee/run away/take off/make off **from** sb/sth
▪ to flee/run away/run off/take off/make off **to safety**
▪ to **be forced to/have to** flee/run away
▪ to **try to/attempt to/manage to** flee/run away/run off/take off/make off

circus. → see also RUN OFF 2 **3** to leave a person or a place to try to avoid doing sth: *Don't run away—I want your advice.* **4** used to tell a child to go away and not disturb you: *Run away and play.*
◆ v + adv
▶ **'runaway** *adj* [only before noun] **1** (of a situation or an event) happening quickly and easily and not able to be controlled: *The movie has been a runaway success.* ◇ *The game was a runaway victory for Liverpool.* ◇ *runaway inflation* **2** (of an animal or a vehicle) moving, but no longer under the control of the rider or driver: *a runaway horse* **3** (of a person) having secretly left their home or the place where they are staying: *runaway children/teenagers*
▶ **'runaway** *n* a person who has left their home or the place where they are staying suddenly and secretly because they are unhappy there: *a 16-year-old runaway*

run a'way/'off; **run a'way/'off with sb**; **run a'way/'off together** to leave your home, husband, wife, etc. secretly with sb else in order to marry them or have a sexual relationship with them: *They ran away to Scotland.* ◊ *We think John and Susie have run off together.*

♦ v + adv ♦ v + adv + prep ♦ v + adv + adv

,**run a'way from sth** to try to avoid dealing with or thinking about sth because it is difficult or unpleasant: *He is running away from his responsibilities.* ◊ *You can't just run away from difficult situations—you must face up to them.* ◻OBJ responsibilities

♦ v + adv + prep

,**run a'way with sb, etc.** → RUN AWAY/OFF, ETC.

,**run a'way with sb** if a feeling, an emotion, etc. **runs away with you**, you are not able to control it: *Her imagination tends to run away with her.* ◊ *My tongue ran away with me and I said things I regretted.* ◻SUBJ imagination, tongue

♦ v + adv + prep

,**run a'way with sth 1** to win sth clearly or easily: *Their team are running away with the championship.* ◊ *She ran away with the show* (= she was easily the best performer). **2** (*especially AmE*) (*also* ,**run 'off with sth**) to escape with sth that you have stolen or taken without asking: *The treasurer ran away with all the funds.* **3** (*informal*) to believe sth that is not true: *Don't run away with the idea that everything was perfect in our marriage.* ◻OBJ idea, impression

♦ **1,2** v + adv + prep
♦ **3** v + adv + prep + noun

,**run sth 'by/'past sb** (*informal*) to show sb sth or tell them about an idea, a proposal, etc. in order to get their reaction to it: *I've got a few ideas I'd like to run by you.* ◊ *Run that past me again.*

♦ v + n/pron + prep

,**run 'down**; ,**run sth 'down 1** to lose power or stop working; to make sth do this: *I think the batteries are running down.* ◊ *If you leave your headlights on, you'll run the battery down.* ◻SUBJ battery **2** to stop functioning gradually or become smaller in size or number; to make sth do this: *Oil supplies in the region will start to run down in the next decade.* ◊ *The company are running down their operations in the UK.* ◊ *Businesses in the town have been allowed to run down during the last few years.*

♦ v + adv ♦ v + n/pron + adv ♦ v + adv + n

▶ '**rundown** (**in/of sth**) *n* [usually sing.] (*BrE*) a reduction in the size, number, amount or importance of sth: *The public are complaining about the rundown of health services.*

▶ ,**run-'down** *adj* **1** (of a building or place) in very bad condition; that has not been taken care of: *run-down inner-city areas* **2** (of a business, etc.) not as busy or as active as it used to be: *run-down transport services* **3** [not before noun] (of a person) tired or slightly ill/

sick, especially from working hard: *I'm feeling rather run-down.*

,**run 'down sth**; ,**run sth 'down sth 1** to look quickly at a list; to quickly read and mention the items on it: *Her eyes ran down the figures on the page.* ◊ *She ran her eyes down the page.* **2** to pass, or to make sth pass, downwards over a surface: *She ran her finger down the page.*

▶ '**rundown** (**on/of sth**) *n* [usually sing.] an explanation or a description of sth: *I can give you a brief rundown on each of the job applicants.* ◊ *We would like a full rundown on the progress of the project so far.* ◊ *a rundown of the history of each team*

♦ v + prep ♦ v + n/pron + prep

,**run sb/sth 'down 1** (of a vehicle or its driver) to hit a person or an animal and knock them/it to the ground: *The cyclist was run down by a lorry.* ◊ *You nearly ran down that pedestrian.* ◻SYN knock sb down; knock sb over ◻NOTE Often used in the passive. It can also suggest that the driver of the vehicle intended to hit the person or animal: *The officer challenged the thief and tried to make the car stop, but the driver ran him down.* → see also RUN SB/STH OVER **2** to criticize sb/sth in an unkind way: *She's always running her husband down in front of their friends.* ◻SYN disparage sb/sth (*formal*) ◻NOTE Not used in the passive. → see also RUN YOURSELF DOWN **3** to find sb/sth after looking for a long time: *I finally ran the book down in the college library.* ◻SYN track sb/sth down; trace sb/sth ◻NOTE Not used in the passive.

♦ v + n/pron + adv ♦ v + adv + n

,**run yourself 'down** to criticize yourself, often unfairly: *You're always running yourself down!* → see also RUN SB/STH DOWN 2

♦ v + pron + adv

,**run 'in**; ,**run 'into sth** (*AmE, informal*) to visit sb for a short time in an informal way; to go somewhere quickly on your way to somewhere else: *I'll run in on my way home.* ◊ *Can you run into the dry-cleaner's on your way to work?*

♦ v + adv ♦ v + prep

,**run sb 'in** (*old-fashioned, informal*) to arrest sb and take them to a police station: *She was run in for shoplifting.*

♦ v + n/pron + adv ♦ v + adv + n (*rare*)

▶ '**run-in** *n* **1** (**with sb**) (*informal*) an argument or a disagreement: *I had a run-in with my mum this evening.* **2** (*also* '**run-up**) (**to sth**) (*BrE*) a period of preparation just before an event takes place: *the final run-in to the World Cup* **3** the action of approaching sth or the distance you cover: *the final run-in to the target*

,**run sb 'in**; ,**run sb 'into sth/...** to take sb by car to the centre of town, etc.: *I need to go into town. Can you run me in?*

♦ v + n/pron + adv ♦ v + n/pron + prep

,run sth 'in (*BrE*) (in the past) to drive a vehicle slowly and carefully when it is new so that you do not damage the engine: *I'm not going on motorways until I've run the car in.*
◆ v + n/pron + adv ◆ v + adv + n

,run 'into sb to meet sb by chance: *Guess who I ran into today?* ◇ *You rarely run into people you know in London.*
SYN **bump into sb** (*informal*)
◆ v + prep

⚡'run into sb/sth; 'run sth into sb/sth to accidentally crash into sb/sth; to make a vehicle do this: *The car went out of control and ran into a tree.* ◇ *The lorry behind ran into the back of me* (= my car). ◇ *He ran his car into a tree.*
◆ v + prep ◆ v + n/pron + prep

⚡'run into sth 1 to meet or enter an area of bad weather while travelling: *We ran into a patch of thick fog just outside the city.* OBJ **bad weather** 2 to experience difficulties or problems: *We ran into problems right from the beginning of the project.* OBJ **trouble**, **difficulties**, **problems**, **opposition** 3 to reach a particular level or amount: *The bill will run into hundreds of pounds.* 4 if things **run into** each other, or sth **runs into** sth else, they join so that they can only be separated with difficulty: *I tried to explain, but my words all ran into each other.*
◆ v + prep

,run sb 'into sth → RUN SB IN, RUN SB INTO STH
'run sth into sb/sth → RUN INTO SB/STH, ETC.

,run 'off 1 to move quickly away from sb/a place; to escape from sb/a place: *The thief ran off down a side street.* ◇ *They ran off laughing.* → see also RUN AWAY 1 2 to leave a place secretly: *She ran off in the middle of the night.* → see also RUN AWAY 2; RUN AWAY/OFF, RUN AWAY/OFF WITH SB, RUN AWAY/OFF TOGETHER
◆ v + adv

,run 'off; ,run 'off sth if a road, path, etc. **runs off** or **runs off** a place, it leads away from it: *Can you see that road running off to the right?* ◇ *Several doors ran off the corridor.*
◆ v + adv ◆ v + prep

,run 'off; ,run 'off with sb, etc. → RUN AWAY/OFF, ETC.

,run 'off sb/sth to flow away from sb/sth: *Water runs off the fields into the valley.* ◇ *Sweat was running off him.* SUBJ **water**, **sweat**
◆ v + prep

▶ 'run-off *n* [U, C] (*technical*) rain, water or other liquid that runs off land and into rivers, etc.

,run 'off sth; ,run sth 'off sth (of a machine, etc.) to use a particular type of power in order to operate a machine: *The outboard motor runs off an ordinary car battery.*
→ see also RUN ON STH, RUN STH ON STH
◆ v + prep ◆ v + n/pron + prep

,run sth 'off 1 to produce copies of a piece of writing, etc. on a machine: *They ran off hundreds of copies of the leaflet.* ◇ *Can you run these letters off for me?* NOTE In informal spoken language, **run sb off sth** and **run sb sth off** are also used: *I'll just run you off a copy.* ◇ *I'll run you a copy off now.* 2 to produce sth that is usually difficult to write, such as a poem, speech, etc. quickly and easily: *She ran off a fantastic speech in no time at all.*
◆ v + adv + n ◆ v + n/pron + adv

,run 'off with sb; ,run 'off together → RUN AWAY/OFF WITH SB, RUN AWAY/OFF TOGETHER

,run 'off with sth → RUN AWAY WITH STH 2

,run 'on 1 to continue to run in the same direction: *I'll stop here, you run on ahead.* 2 to continue longer than is necessary or expected: *I don't want the meeting to run on.* 3 (**about sth**) (*especially AmE*) to continue talking for a long time about unimportant things: *She does tend to run on!* ◇ *She ran on with great enthusiasm about her latest project.* 4 [+ **adv/prep**] (of a road or a track) to continue in the same direction: *The road runs on into the desert.* 5 (of a line of text) to continue into the next line: *This line runs on into the next verse of the poem.*
SYN **go on**
◆ v + adv

'run on sth if your thoughts, etc. **run on** a particular subject, you think or talk about it a lot: *Her thoughts kept running on their last meeting.*
◆ v + prep

⚡'run on sth; 'run sth on sth to use a particular type of power or fuel to make a machine or a vehicle work: *You can run the car on any type of unleaded petrol.*
→ see also RUN OFF STH, RUN STH OFF STH
◆ v + prep ◆ v + n/pron + prep

⚡,run 'out 1 if a supply of sth **runs out**, it is finished or used up: *I'm going to keep travelling until my money runs out.* ◇ *We have to eat quickly as time is running out.* ◇ *One day his luck will run out.* ◇ *My patience with her suddenly ran out.* SUBJ **money**, **petrol**, **time**, **luck**, **patience** 2 (*also* ,run 'out of sth) if a person or a machine **runs out** of a supply of sth, they finish it or use it all up: *We're running out of money.* ◇ *Could you get some more milk? We've run out.* ◇ *I've run out of patience with her.* ◇ *You've run out of space on the disk.* ◇ *The band seems to have run out of ideas.* OBJ **money**, **ideas**, **petrol**, **patience**, **time** 3 if a contract or other legal document **runs out**, it is no longer valid: *His contract with the club runs out at the end of the season.* SYN **expire** (*more formal*)
◆ v + adv 2 also v + adv + prep

IDM ,run out of 'steam (*informal*) to have less energy and enthusiasm and stop doing sth or do it less well: *I ran out of steam halfway up the hill.* ◊ *The campaign seems to have run out of steam.*

,run sb 'out; ,run sb 'out of sth/... (*especially AmE*) to force sb to leave a place: *He vowed to run them out of town.*

♦ v + n/pron + adv ♦ v + n/pron + adv + prep

,run sb 'out; ,run yourself 'out (in cricket, etc.) to make a player end their turn at hitting the ball by throwing the ball so that it hits the set of sticks, (the **wicket**), while they are still running: *He was run out for 73.*

NOTE Often used in the passive.

♦ v + n/pron + adv ♦ v + adv + n

,run 'out on sb to leave sb that you live or work with, especially when they need your help: *She ran out on them as soon as things got difficult.*

♦ v + adv + prep

,run 'over **1** if a container or the liquid in it **runs over**, the liquid flows out of it over the edge: *Don't let the bath run over!* ◊ *The tea ran over into the saucer.* SYN **overflow 2** to continue longer than expected or planned: *We've already run over so let's try to end the meeting soon.*

♦ v + adv

,run 'over sb/sth; ,run sth 'over sb/sth to move over a surface; to make sth do this: *I let the cold water run over me.* ◊ *She ran her eye over the figures on the page.*

♦ v + prep

,run 'over sth to read through or think about sth quickly; to practise sth: *Let's run over the plans again.* ◊ *I ran over the possibilities in my mind.*

SYN **go over sth**

♦ v + prep

,run sb/sth 'over (of a vehicle or its driver) to knock a person or an animal down and often pass over their body or part of it: *Two children were run over by a truck and killed.* ◊ *I ran over a cat last night.* ◊ *You nearly ran me over!*

SYN **knock sb over**

→ see also RUN SB/STH DOWN 1

♦ v + n/pron + adv ♦ v + adv + n

,run sth 'past sb (*informal*) → RUN STH BY/ PAST SB

,run 'round, etc. (*BrE*) → RUN AROUND, ETC.

,run 'through sb/sth if a feeling **runs through** sb/sth, it passes quickly through them/it: *A thrill of excitement ran through her.* ◊ *She felt a tremor run through his body.* ◊ *An angry murmur ran through the crowd.* SUBJ **tremor, shiver, shudder, fear, relief**

♦ v + prep

,run 'through sth **1** to be present in every part of sth: *There is a common theme running through all of her novels.* ◊ *The English title picks up a thread running through the film.* **2** to discuss, examine or read sth quickly: *He ran through his list one more time.* ◊ *Can you run through some of these figures with me?* ◊ *She mentally ran through the list of who to invite.* ◊ *Let's run*

through what I'm meant to do again. SYN **go through sth 3** to perform, act or practise sth: *Could we run through Act 3 again, please?* SYN **go through sth 4** (*informal*) to use up or spend money carelessly: *She ran through a lot of money in her first year at college.* SYN **go through sth**

♦ v + prep

▶ 'run-through *n* a practice for an event or a performance: *We're having the main technical run-through of the play tonight.*

'run to sb to go to sb for help, advice, protection, etc.: *If you get hurt, don't come running to me.*

♦ v + prep

'run to sth **1** to reach the amount, or size mentioned, especially a large one: *The total cost runs to hundreds of pounds.* ◊ *The report already runs to 800 pages.* **2** (*BrE*) (*often used in negative sentences and with **can***) if a person or their money can **run to sth**, they have enough money to pay for it: *We couldn't quite run to private education for the children.* **3** if your taste or your mind, etc. **runs to** sth, you enjoy it or can do it: *His taste in music runs to pop and jazz, but that's about it.*

♦ **1** v + prep + n
♦ **2,3** v + prep

,run 'up **1** to move quickly towards sb/sth: *She ran up to me, smiling.* **2** (in cricket and other sports) to run in order to gain speed before you throw a ball, jump, etc.: *Gough is now running up to bowl.* **3** to increase: *Product prices have run up faster than expected.*

♦ v + adv

▶ 'run-up *n* (*BrE*) **1** (*sport*) the act of running or the distance you run in order to gain speed before you throw a ball, jump, etc.: *She took a run-up and kicked the ball.* **2** (also 'run-in *less frequent*) (**to sth**) the period of preparation before an important event: *She's been training hard in the run-up to the big competition.* ◊ *the run-up to the election*

,run sth 'up **1** to allow a bill, debt, etc. to reach a large total: *I ran up a few debts while I was abroad.* ◊ *He's run up a huge bill on his credit card.* OBJ **bill, debts, overdraft 2** (**for sb**) to make sth very quickly, especially an item of clothing: *I'll run up some new dresses for the girls.* NOTE In informal spoken language, **run sb up sth** and, less often, **run sb sth up** can also be used: *Could you run me up some curtains/run me some curtains up?* **3** to raise sth, especially a flag: *They ran up a white flag and surrendered.* OBJ **flag 4** to achieve sth: *The team have run up their best victory yet.* OBJ **victory, results**

♦ v + adv + n ♦ v + pron + adv
♦ v + n + adv (*less frequent*)

,run 'up against sb/sth to experience a difficulty or a problem: *The project keeps running up against the problem of lack of funds.* ◊ *In this round, he will run up against the previous year's champion.*

OBJ **problems** SYN **come up against sb/sth**
 ◆ v + adv + prep

'**run with sb** → RUN AWAY/OFF, RUN AWAY/OFF WITH SB, RUN AWAY/OFF TOGETHER

'**run with sth** to accept or start to use a particular idea or method: *OK, let's run with Jan's suggestion.*
 ◆ v + prep

rush /rʌʃ/

,**rush a'round**; ,**rush a'round sth** (*BrE also* ,**rush a'bout/'round**, ,**rush a'bout/'round sth**) to move very quickly from place to place, being very busy: *I've been rushing around all day.* ◇ *He rushed about the room tidying.*
 SYN **run around**, **run around sth**; **tear around**, **tear around sth**
 ◆ v + adv

,**rush 'in** to do or decide sth very quickly, often without thinking about it for long enough: *He's very wary of rushing in and making changes.*
 ◆ v + adv ◆ v + prep

IDM **fools rush in** (**where angels fear to tread**) used to say that people with little experience will try to do the difficult or dangerous things that people with more experience would not do

,**rush 'into sth**; ,**rush 'into doing sth**; ,**rush sb 'into doing sth** to do or decide sth quickly without thinking about it carefully; to make sb do this: *Don't go rushing into anything.* ◇ *You shouldn't rush into getting married.* ◇ *She won't be rushed into a decision.* ◇ *Don't let anyone rush you into accepting the job.*
 ◆ v + prep ◆ v + n/pron + prep

,**rush 'off** to leave quickly: *Don't rush off, I haven't finished.*
 ◆ v + adv

,**rush sth 'out** to produce sth very quickly: *They rushed out the posters in time for the festival.* ◇ *The book was rushed out by the publishers.*
 ◆ v + adv + n ◆ v + n/pron + adv

,**rush 'round, etc.** (*BrE*) → RUSH AROUND, ETC.

,**rush 'through**; ,**rush sth 'through sth** to make sth become official policy, etc. much quicker than normal: *The legislation has been rushed through.* ◇ *They rushed the bill through Parliament.*
 OBJ **bill, legislation**
 ◆ v + n/pron + adv ◆ v + adv + n (*rare*)
 ◆ v + n/pron + prep

rustle /'rʌsl/

,**rustle sb/sth 'up** (*informal*) to prepare or provide sth for sb very quickly without planning; to find sb sth very quickly: *I'll rustle some lunch up for you.* ◇ *I rustled up a few helpers to hand out leaflets.*
 ◆ v + adv + n ◆ v + n/pron + adv

Ss

sack /sæk/

,**sack 'out** (*AmE, informal*) to lie down to rest or relax: *We sacked out on the couch and watched a video.*
 ◆ v + adv

saddle /'sædl/

NOTE A **saddle** is a leather seat for a rider on a horse.

,**saddle 'up**; ,**saddle sth 'up** to prepare to ride a horse by placing a saddle on it: *Have you saddled up the horses yet?* ◇ *Saddle up, we're leaving right away.*
 OBJ **horse**
 ◆ v + adv ◆ v + adv + n ◆ v + n/pron + adv

'**saddle sb/yourself with sb/sth**; '**saddle sb/yourself with doing sth** to give sb/yourself a difficult or unpleasant task or responsibility to deal with: *I've been saddled with my brother's kids for the weekend* (= I have to take care of them). ◇ *He had saddled himself with huge debts.* ◇ *I've been saddled with organizing the conference.*
 SYN **land sb/yourself with sb/sth**, **land sb/yourself with doing sth**
 NOTE Often used in the passive.
 ◆ v + n/pron + prep

safeguard /'seɪfɡɑːd; *AmE* -ɡɑːrd/

,**safeguard a'gainst sth**; ,**safeguard sb/sth/yourself a'gainst sth** (*formal*) to prevent sth bad from happening; to keep sth safe from harm or damage: *Safeguard against theft by installing a burglar alarm.* ◇ *The leaflet shows you how to safeguard your home against accidents.*
 ◆ v + prep ◆ v + n/pron + prep

sail /seɪl/

,**sail 'through**; ,**sail 'through sth** to succeed in an examination, a test, etc. very easily: *She sailed through her final exams.*
 OBJ **exam**
 ◆ v + adv ◆ v + prep

sally /'sæli/ (**sallies**, **sallying**, **sallied**)

,**sally 'forth** (*also* ,**sally 'out** *less frequent*) (*old-fashioned* or *literary*) to leave a place in a determined or enthusiastic way: *After lunch she sallied forth for a short walk.*
 ◆ v + adv

salt /sɔːlt; *BrE also* sɒlt/

,**salt sth a'way** to save money, etc. for the future, often secretly or dishonestly: *He claimed*

she had salted money away in accounts in Brazil.
◊ *$10 billion had been salted away in banks.*
`OBJ` **money**
♦ v + n/pron + adv ♦ v + adv + n

sand /sænd/

,sand sth 'down to make sth smooth by rubbing it with strong, rough paper: *Sand the doors down before you paint them.*
`NOTE` **Sand sth** can be used on its own: *Sand the doors before you paint them.*
♦ v + n/pron + adv ♦ v + adv + n

sandwich /'sænwɪtʃ, -wɪdʒ/

'sandwich sb/sth between sb/sth to fit sth/sb into a very small space between two other things or people: *I was sandwiched between two large men on the back seat.* ◊ *The shop is sandwiched between a bank and a cafe.*
`NOTE` Nearly always used in the passive.
♦ v + n/pron + prep

,sandwich A and B to'gether (with sth) to put sth between two things to join them: *Sandwich the cakes together with cream.*
♦ v + n/pron + adv ♦ v + adv + n

save /seɪv/

'save on sth; 'save sth on sth to use less of sth or not more than necessary: *He saved on electricity by using candles.* ◊ *Get your tickets early and save $5 on the cost of an adult ticket.*
♦ v + prep ♦ v + n/pron + prep

,save 'up; ,save sth 'up (for sth) to keep your money instead of spending it, especially because you want to buy a particular thing: *She's saving up for a new computer.* ◊ *I saved up all my wages to buy my parents a present.*
`NOTE` **Save** and **save sth** are used more frequently on their own with this meaning, especially in more formal English.
♦ v + adv ♦ v + adv + n ♦ v + n/pron + adv

,save sth 'up to keep sth to use or enjoy in the future: *I save up the week's newspapers to read at weekends.*
`NOTE` **Save sth** is used more frequently on its own with this meaning, especially in more formal English.
♦ v + adv + n ♦ v + n/pron + adv

saw /sɔː/ (sawed, sawn /sɔːn/, *AmE also* sawed, sawed)

`NOTE` A **saw** is a tool with a long blade and sharp points along the edge.

,saw sth 'down to cut sth down and bring it to the ground, using a saw: *We had to saw down two trees.*
`OBJ` **tree**
♦ v + adv + n ♦ v + n/pron + adv

,saw sth 'off; ,saw sth 'off sth to remove sth from sth by cutting it with a saw: *I sawed the lower branches off the apple tree.*

`OBJ` **branch**
♦ v + n/pron + adv ♦ v + adv + n ♦ v + n/pron + prep
▸ 'sawn-off (*BrE*) (*AmE* 'sawed-off) [only before noun] (of a gun) having had the long tube through which the bullets are fired, (the **barrel**), cut short: *a sawn-off shotgun*

,saw sth 'up (into) to cut sth into pieces using a saw: *All the trees were sawn up into logs.*
♦ v + adv + n ♦ v + n/pron + adv

scale /skeɪl/

,scale sth 'down (*AmE also* ,scale sth 'back) to reduce sth in size or importance: *The company has scaled down its training programmes this year.* ◊ *Police are scaling down the search for the attacker.* ◊ *Colin's tools were a scaled-down version of his father's.*
`OBJ` **programme, project** `OPP` **scale sth up** (*less frequent*)
↻ note at CUT STH BACK
♦ v + adv + n ♦ v + n/pron + adv

,scale sth 'up to increase the size or importance of sth: *We're deciding how to scale up our operation.*
`OPP` **scale sth down**
♦ v + adv + n ♦ v + n/pron + adv

scan /skæn/ (-nn-)

,scan sth 'in; ,scan sth 'into sth to pass light over a picture or document using a special machine (a **scanner**) in order to copy it and put it in the memory of a computer: *Text and pictures can be scanned into the computer.*
♦ v + adv + n ♦ v + n/pron + adv ♦ v + n/pron + prep

,scan 'through sth to look quickly but not very carefully at a document, etc.: *She scanned through the newspaper over breakfast.*
♦ v + prep

scare /skeə(r); *AmE* sker/

,scare sb/sth a'way/'off to make sb/sth leave or stay away by frightening them: *She used a whistle to scare away her attacker.* ◊ *The noise scared the birds off.*
`SYN` **frighten sb/sth away/off** (*especially BrE*)
♦ v + adv + n ♦ v + n/pron + adv

'scare sb into sth; ,scare sb 'into doing sth to make sb do sth by frightening them: *He was scared into signing a confession.* ◊ *Her threats finally scared him into action.*
♦ v + n/pron + prep

,scare sb 'off to accidentally make sb afraid of or nervous about sth they are planning to do: *Many investors were scared off by the rumours.* ◊ *Don't act too interested or you'll scare him off.*
`SYN` **frighten sb off** (*especially BrE*)
♦ v + n/pron + adv ♦ v + adv + n

,scare sb/sth 'off → SCARE SB/STH AWAY/OFF

,scare 'up sth (*AmE, informal*) to find sb/sth or to make sth by using whatever is available: *I'll see*

if I can scare up enough chairs for us all. ◇ *I'll to scare up some friends to come and help us.*
NOTE When the object of **scare up** is a noun, it comes after **up**, but when the object is a pronoun, it comes between **scare** and **up**: *I'll try to scare some up for you.*
◆ v + adv + n ◆ v + pron + adv (*less frequent*)

scarf /skɑːf; *AmE* skɑːrf/

,scarf sth 'down (*AmE, informal*) to eat sth very quickly: *He came home and scarfed down a piece of blueberry pie.*
SYN scoff sth (*BrE, informal*); wolf sth down (*informal*)
◆ v + n/pron + adv ◆ v + adv + n

,scarf sth 'up (*AmE, informal*) to eat sth very quickly: *The kids sat down and started scarfing up everything in sight.*
SYN scoff sth (*BrE, informal*); wolf sth down (*informal*)
◆ v + n/pron + adv ◆ v + adv + n

scoop /skuːp/

,scoop sth 'out **1** (*also* ,scoop sth 'out of sth) to remove sth from the inside of sth else using a curved tool, such as a spoon, or your hand: *Scoop all the seeds out of the fruit.* **OBJ** seeds, flesh **2** to make sth hollow by removing the inside with a spoon, etc.: *First scoop out the melon using a spoon.* **SYN** hollow sth out
◆ **1** v + n/pron + adv ◆ v + adv + n
◆ v + n/pron + adv + prep
◆ **2** v + adv + n ◆ v + n/pron + adv

,scoop sb/sth 'up to move or lift sb/sth using a quick continuous movement: *I scooped up a handful of sweets.* ◇ *She scooped the baby up into her arms.*
➔ note at LIFT SB/STH UP
◆ v + adv + n ◆ v + n/pron + adv

,scoop sth 'up to win or get sth easily, especially a large sum of money or a prize: *The Liberals scooped up four fifths of the seats.*
OBJ seats, prizes
NOTE Scoop sth can also be used on its own: *The movie scooped nine Oscars.*
◆ v + adv + n ◆ v + n/pron + adv

scoot /skuːt/

,scoot 'over (*AmE, informal*) to move along on a seat to make room for another person: *Scoot over and make room for your sister.* ◇ (*figurative*) *Scoot over, men! Women golfers are on the increase.*
SYN move over
◆ v + adv

scope /skəʊp; *AmE* skoʊp/

,scope sb/sth 'out (*AmE, informal*) to look for sb/sth interesting or attractive; to search out sb/sth: *We scoped out a place to spend the weekend.*
◆ v + adv + n ◆ v + n/pron + adv

score /skɔː(r)/

'score off sb (*especially BrE*) to show that you are better than sb, especially by making clever remarks, for example in an argument: *He's always trying to score off his colleagues.*
◆ v + prep

,score sth 'out/'through (*BrE*) to draw a line or lines through sth in a text to show that you do not want it: *The last paragraph had been scored out.* ◇ *He neatly scored through the word 'impossible'.*
SYN cross sth out/through; delete sth
◆ v + adv + n ◆ v + n + adv (*rare*)

scout /skaʊt/

,scout a'round; ,scout a'round sth (*BrE also* ,scout 'round, ,scout 'round sth) (for sb/sth) to search an area or different places to try to find sb/sth: *I'll go and scout around for some water.*
◆ v + adv ◆ v + prep

,scout sth 'out to find out what sth is like or where sth is, by searching: *A team travelled to Moscow to scout out possible places for a meeting.* ◇ *The company is scouting out business opportunities in Vietnam.*
◆ v + adv + n ◆ v + n/pron + adv

scrabble /'skræbl/

,scrabble a'round (*BrE also* ,scrabble a'bout, ,scrabble 'round) (for sth) to use your fingers to search for sth quickly or with difficulty: *She scrabbled around in her bag for her glasses.*
◆ v + adv

,scrabble at sth to scratch at sth with small, hurried movements: *She was scrabbling at the earth with her fingers.*
◆ v + prep

scrape /skreɪp/

,scrape 'by (on sth) to manage to live on the money you have, although you do not have much: *I can just scrape by on what my parents give me.*
◆ v + adv

,scrape 'in; ,scrape 'into sth (*BrE*) to manage to get a job, a position, a place at college, etc., but with difficulty: *I just managed to scrape into university.* ◇ *He scraped in with 180 votes.*
◆ v + adv ◆ v + prep

,scrape sth 'off; ,scrape sth 'off sth to remove sth from a surface by moving sth sharp and hard like a knife across it: *He spent all day scraping paint off the walls.*
◆ v + n/pron + adv ◆ v + adv + n ◆ v + n/pron + prep

,scrape sth 'out **1** (*also* ,scrape sth 'out of sth) to remove sth from the inside of sth else using sth sharp and hard like a knife: *I scraped all the seeds out of the melon.* ◇ *He scraped out the bowl* (= removed everything from it) *with a teaspoon.* **2** (*AmE*) to just manage to make enough money to live: *He **scraped out a living** by drawing* cartoons for local newspapers. [OBJ] **living, existence**

♦ v + adv + n
♦ v + n/pron + adv + prep **1** v + n/pron + adv + prep

,scrape **'through**; ,scrape **'through sth** to succeed with difficulty in doing sth, especially in passing an exam: *I might scrape through* (*the exam*) *if I'm lucky.* ◇ *She just scraped through law school.*

[OBJ] **exam**

♦ v + adv ♦ v + prep

,scrape sth to'**gether** (*also* ,scrape sth **'up** *less frequent*) to obtain or collect sth such as an amount of money with difficulty: *They managed to scrape together $1 200.* ◇ *We* **scraped up enough money** *to buy a small car.*

♦ v + adv + n ♦ v + n/pron + adv

scratch /skrætʃ/

,scratch a'**round** (*BrE also* ,scratch a'**bout**) (**for sth**) to search for sth in a way that is not very organized, by looking at different things, looking on the ground, etc.: *He was scratching around on the ground for clues.*

♦ v + adv

,scratch sth **'off**; ,scratch sth **'off sth** to remove sth from a surface by rubbing with your nails, etc.: *She scratched the paint off to see what was underneath.*

♦ v + n/pron + adv ♦ v + adv + n ♦ v + n/pron + prep

,scratch sth **'out** to remove a word, especially a name, from sth written, usually by putting a line through it: *Their names had been scratched out.*

♦ v + n/pron + adv ♦ v + adv + n

scream /skriːm/

,scream **'out 1** to give a loud, high cry, because you are hurt, frightened, etc.: *She screamed out in pain.* ⊃ note at CRY OUT **2** (**for sth**) to be very obvious or noticeable; to demand attention: *The mistakes just scream out at you.* ◇ *The cake was screaming out to be eaten.* ◇ *The market has been screaming out for a product like this.*

♦ v + adv

screen /skriːn/

,screen sth **'off** to separate or hide an area of a room, etc. from another area by putting a tall piece of furniture or equipment in front of it or around it: *Part of the room had been screened off with a curtain.*

[NOTE] Often used in the passive.

♦ v + adv + n ♦ v + n/pron + adv

,screen sb/sth **'out** to not include sb/sth, or not allow sb to join an organization, enter a country, etc. because you think they may not be suitable or may cause trouble: *Unsuitable candidates were screened out.* ◇ *His job is to screen out inquiries unlikely to result in a sale.*

◇ *Insurance companies often screen out people who are high risk.*

♦ v + adv + n ♦ v + n + adv (*less frequent*)
♦ v + pron + adv

,screen sth **'out** to prevent sth harmful from entering or going through sth: *It is essential to screen out ultraviolet rays.* ◇ *A window blind will screen out too much light.*

♦ v + adv + n ♦ v + n + adv (*less frequent*)
♦ v + pron + adv

screw /skruː/

,screw a'**round** (⚠, *slang*) **1** to have sex with a lot of different people [NOTE] A more polite, informal way to say this is **sleep around**. **2** (*AmE*) to waste time doing silly or useless activities: *Stop screwing around and do some work!* [NOTE] A more polite, informal way to say this is **mess around**, or, in British English, **mess about**.

♦ v + adv

,screw sb a'**round** (*BrE*, ⚠, *slang*) to treat sb in a way that is deliberately not helpful to them or wastes their time: *Stop screwing me around and tell me the truth!*

[NOTE] A more polite, informal way of saying this is **mess sb about/around** (*BrE*).

♦ v + n/pron + adv

,screw sth **'down** to attach sth firmly to sth else using screws: *Screw the lid of the box down securely.*

♦ v + n/pron + adv ♦ v + adv + n

,screw sth **'on**; ,screw sth **'onto sth** to fasten the top on a container by twisting it around: *Is the top screwed on tightly?*

[OBJ] **lid, top**

♦ v + n/pron + adv ♦ v + adv + n ♦ v + n/pron + prep

[IDM] **have your head screwed on** (**right/the right way**) (*informal*) to be a sensible person

,screw sb **'out of sth** (*slang*) to cheat sb and prevent them from having sth that they should have: *She tried to screw him out of his winnings.* [NOTE] A more polite way to say this is **cheat sb out of sth**.

♦ v + n/pron + adv + prep

,screw sth **'out of sb** (*slang*) to force sb to give you sth; to get sth from sb with great difficulty: *They screwed the money out of her by threatening to hit her.*

♦ v + n/pron + adv + prep

,screw sb **'over** (*AmE*, ⚠, *slang*) to trick sb in order to obtain sth valuable from them; to treat sb badly, especially by telling lies: *He screwed her over and took all her money.*

♦ v + n/pron + adv ♦ v + adv + n

,screw **'up**; ,screw sth **'up** (*slang, especially AmE*) to do sth badly or spoil sth: *I was trying to be helpful, but I screwed up again.* ◇ *She screwed up all the arrangements.*

[SYN] **mess up, mess sth up**

♦ v + adv ♦ v + adv + n ♦ v + n/pron + adv

▶ **'screw-up** *n* (*slang, especially AmE*) a situation that has been dealt with very badly; a bad mistake: *There was a screw-up over the bookings.*

,**screw sb 'up** (*slang*) to make sb so upset or confused that they are unable to deal with problems in life: *Her parents have really screwed her up.*
SYN mess sb up
◆ v + n/pron + adv ◆ v + adv + n

▶ ,**screwed-'up** *adj* (*informal*) upset and anxious, especially because of sth bad that has happened to you in the past: *a screwed-up kid*

,**screw sth 'up 1** (*BrE*) to squeeze sth into a tight ball: *She screwed up the note and threw it away.* **OBJ** paper, letter **SYN** scrunch sth up **2** if you **screw up** your eyes or your face, your muscles become tight because you are in pain, the light is too bright, etc.: *He screwed up his face in disgust.* **OBJ** face, eyes
◆ v + adv + n ◆ v + n/pron + adv

IDM screw up your 'courage (*especially BrE*) to force yourself to be brave enough to do sth: *I finally screwed up my courage and went to the dentist.*

▶ ,**screwed-'up** *adj* (*BrE*) squeezed and twisted into a ball: *a screwed-up sheet of paper*

scribble /'skrɪbl/

,**scribble sth 'down** to write sth quickly and carelessly: *She scribbled down the directions on her pad.*
◆ v + adv + n ◆ v + n/pron + adv

scrimp /skrɪmp/

'**scrimp on sth** to spend too little money on sth or buy sth that is of poor quality: *If you're going to do a good job of renovating an old house, don't scrimp on materials.*
◆ v + prep

scroll /skrəʊl; AmE skroʊl/

,**scroll 'down/'up** (*computing*) to move down/up or backwards/forwards in the text on a computer screen so that you can read different parts of it: *She scrolled down to the end of the document.*
◆ v + adv

,**scroll 'through sth** to move through a text on a computer screen quickly, without reading everything: *You can scroll through the document using the wheel on your mouse.*
◆ v + prep

scrounge /skraʊndʒ/

,**scrounge a'round** (**for sth**) (*AmE, informal*) to search around in different places for sth, especially if it is difficult to find or there is not much available: *He scrounged around in his desk drawer for a paper clip.*
◆ v + adv

,**scrounge sth 'up** (*AmE, informal*) to discover information about sb/sth by searching or asking questions: *It would be great if you could scrounge up some information on this.*
◆ v + n/pron + adv

scrub /skrʌb/ (-bb-)

,**scrub 'in** (*AmE*) → SCRUB UP

,**scrub sth 'off**; ,**scrub sth 'off sth** to remove sth from the surface of sth by rubbing it hard with a brush, etc.: *Scrub all that mud off the walls.*
◆ v + n/pron + adv ◆ v + adv + n ◆ v + n/pron + prep

,**scrub sth 'out** to clean the inside of sth by rubbing it hard with a brush and usually with soap and water: *He scrubbed out the pans.* ◇ *The cupboards are scrubbed out every week.*
◆ v + adv + n ◆ v + n/pron + adv

,**scrub 'up** (*especially BrE*) (*AmE usually* ,**scrub 'in**) (of a doctor, nurse, etc.) to wash your hands and arms very thoroughly before performing a medical operation: *The surgeon scrubbed up and put on his gloves.* ◇ *He asked to scrub in for surgery.*
◆ v + adv

IDM scrub 'up well if sb **scrubs up well**, they look very attractive when they are clean and tidy

scrunch /skrʌntʃ/

,**scrunch sth 'up** (*informal*) **1** to squeeze sth into a small round shape in your hands: *He scrunched up the piece of paper and threw it at me.* **OBJ** paper, letter **SYN** ball sth up (*AmE*); **crumple sth up**; **wad sth up** (*especially AmE*) **2** to twist your face or part of it into a different shape: *He scrunched up his face, trying to concentrate.* **OBJ** face, eyes
◆ v + adv + n ◆ v + n/pron + adv

seal /siːl/

,**seal sth 'in** to keep sth inside a container so that none of it can escape: *The foil packet seals in the flavour.*
◆ v + adv + n ◆ v + n/pron + adv

,**seal sth 'off** if the police, the army, etc. **seal** a place or an area **off**, they put barriers there to prevent anyone from entering it: *The police have sealed off the town centre.* ◇ *Seal off all the exits!*
OBJ area, road, building
◆ v + adv + n ◆ v + n + adv (*less frequent*)
◆ v + pron + adv

,**seal sth 'up 1** to close an envelope, etc. by sticking the edges of the opening together: *He sealed up the envelope and wrote the address on it.* **2** to close sth completely so that nothing can get in or out: *I sealed up the windows to keep out the fumes.* **NOTE** Seal sth is used more frequently on its own with these meanings.
◆ v + adv + n ◆ v + n/pron + adv

see

search for sth

hunt for sb/sth ♦ **rake through sth** ♦ **search for sth** ♦ **search through sth** ♦ **trawl through sth**

These verbs all mean to try very carefully to find sb/sth that is lost or that you need or want, especially sb/sth that is difficult to find. *See also* **look for sb/sth**.

hunt for sb/sth to try to find sb/sth that is difficult to find: *I'm still hunting for a job.* ◇ *Police are hunting for a serial killer.*

rake through sth to look in sth carefully to find sth that is missing: *I raked through my bag for the keys.*

search for sb/sth to try to find sb/sth by looking carefully: *I've been searching for those files.*

search through sth to look in sth carefully to try to find sth that is missing or hidden: *The*

customs officers searched through our bags. ◇ *I searched through my files for the information.*
NOTE Search can be used on its own: *The customs officers searched our bags.*

trawl through sth to search through a large amount of information or a large number of people, places, etc. looking for a particular thing or person: *The police are trawling through their files for similar cases.*

■ to search through/rake through/trawl through sth **for** sb/sth
■ to **carefully** search for sth
■ to search **thoroughly/diligently/painstakingly** (for sb/sth)
■ to search **eagerly/desperately/frantically/in vain** (for sb/sth)
■ to search **far and wide/high and low**

search /sɜːtʃ; *AmE* sɜːrtʃ/

⟐**'search for sb/sth** to look carefully for sb/sth: *I searched everywhere for my passport.*
♦ v + prep

⟐**search sb/sth 'out** to look for sb/sth until you find them: *He's searching out some old pictures to show us.* ◇ *She wanted to search out her real parents.* ◇ *John searched me out and gave me a note.*
SYN seek sb/sth out
♦ v + adv + n ♦ v + n + adv (*less frequent*)
♦ v + pron + adv

⟐**search 'through sth** to examine a collection of things or what is inside sth: *I searched through my bag but couldn't find my ticket.*
SYN rake through sth ⟿ note at SEARCH FOR SB/STH
♦ v + prep

see /siː/ (**saw** /sɔː/, **seen** /siːn/)

⟐**'see about sth**; **'see about doing sth** to deal with sth; to make arrangements for sth to be done: *I'll go and see about lunch.* ◇ *I must see about getting someone to help you with the kids.* ◇ *He says he won't help, does he? Well, we'll soon see about that* (= I will demand that he does help).
♦ v + prep

see sb 'in; **see sb 'into sth** to go with sb into a room, building, etc. to make sure that they get there safely: *After seeing her in* (= into her home), *he rode away without a word.*
→ see also SEE SB/YOURSELF OUT, SEE SB/YOURSELF OUT OF STH
♦ v + n/pron + adv ♦ v + n/pron + prep

see sth 'in if you **see in** an occasion such as New Year, you are there when it happens: *They saw in the New Year with friends.* ◇ *He lived long enough to see in the new millennium.*
OBJ New Year
♦ v + adv + n ♦ v + n/pron + adv

'see sth in sb/sth to believe that sb/sth has a particular quality or characteristic, especially a good one: *I don't know what she sees in him* (= I can't understand why she likes him or finds him attractive). ◇ *He sees good in everyone.* ◇ *I can see value in each argument.*
♦ v + n/pron + prep

see sb 'off 1 to go to a station, an airport, etc. to say goodbye to sb who is going on a journey: *We all went to the airport to see her off.* **2** (*BrE*) to force sb to leave a place, for example by chasing them: *The dogs soon saw off the burglars.* **3** to defeat sb: *She saw off her opponent and now goes into the final.*
♦ v + n/pron + adv ♦ v + adv + n

see sth 'off (*BrE*) to be strong enough to resist sth: *The company saw off the threat of a takeover.*
♦ v + adv + n ♦ v + n/pron + adv

see sb 'out (*BrE*) (*not used in the progressive tenses*) to last longer than the rest of sb's life: *I've had this coat for years, and I'm sure it will see me out.*
♦ v + adv + n ♦ v + n/pron + adv

see sb/yourself 'out; **see sb/yourself 'out of sth** to go with sb out of a building, etc. to make sure that they find the way: *Jay saw the last guests out and locked the door.* ◇ *Don't get up. I'll see myself out.*

→ see also SEE SB IN, SEE SB INTO STH
* v + n/pron + adv * v + adv + n
* v + n/pron + adv + prep

,see sth 'out (*not used in the progressive tenses*)
1 to stay in the same place, do the same things, or survive, until the end of sth: *She promised to see out the rest of her contract.* **2** to last until the end of sth: *We have enough fuel to see the winter out.*

NOTE Not used in the passive.
* v + adv + n * v + n/pron + adv

,see 'over/'round sth (*BrE*) to visit and look at a place carefully: *We'd like to see over the flat again before we rent it.*
SYN **look over sth; look around sth**
* v + prep

,see 'through sb/sth (*not used in the progressive tenses*) to realize the truth about sb/sth: *We saw through him straight away.* ◇ *I can see through your little game* (= trick).
* v + prep

,see sb 'through; ,see sb 'through sth to give sb support to enable them to survive a difficult experience or a particular period of time: *His courage and good humour saw him through.* ◇ *She saw him through the months after his accident.* ◇ *I only have $20 to see me through the week.*
* v + n/pron + adv * v + n/pron + prep

,see sth 'through (*not usually used in the progressive tenses*) to not give up a task, project, etc. until it is completed: *She's determined to see the job through.*
OBJ **project, job**
* v + n/pron + adv

⚡'see to sb/sth to deal with sb/sth that needs attention: *I'll see to the kids.* ◇ *Lin was great and saw to everything.* ◇ *Don't worry, I'll* **see to it!** ◇ *We must get that door seen to.*
SYN **attend to sb/sth** (*formal*)
* v + prep

▶ 'seeing-to *n* [sing.] (*BrE*) **1** an act of hitting sb hard in a fight: *If he wasn't so big I'd give him a right seeing-to!* ◇ (*figurative*) *The England squad got a thorough seeing-to in the final.* **2** an act of sex

'see to it that… to make sure that sth happens: *Can you see to it that everyone knows the date of the meeting?*
* v + prep

seek /siːk/ (**sought, sought** /sɔːt/)

,seek sb/sth 'out to look for and find sb/sth, especially when this means using a lot of effort: *He sought her out to ask her advice.* ◇ *She's always seeking out new business opportunities.*
OBJ **opportunities, information** SYN **track sb/sth down** (*less formal*)
➔ note at LOOK FOR SB/STH
* v + adv + n * v + n/pron + adv

seep /siːp/

,seep a'way to flow away slowly and in small quantities: *Water had been slowly seeping away from the pond.* ◇ (*figurative*) *My anger began to seep away.*
* v + adv

segue /'segweɪ/

,segue 'into sth to move smoothly from one song, subject, place, etc. to another: *a spiritual that segued into a singalong chorus* ◇ *He then segued into a discussion of children's rights.*
* v + prep

seize /siːz/

'seize on sth (*also* 'seize upon sth *more formal*) to suddenly show a lot of interest in sth, especially because you can use it to your advantage: *The scandal was immediately seized upon by the press.* ◇ *Peter seized eagerly on all opportunities for conversation.*
SYN **pounce on sth**
* v + prep

,seize 'up **1** if a machine or a part of a machine **seizes up**, it stops moving or working correctly: *The engine seized up after only three weeks.* ◇ (*figurative*) *The whole city seized up* (= no traffic, etc. was able to move) *during the blizzard.* **2** if a part of your body **seizes up**, it becomes stiff and you are unable to move it easily: *My legs were beginning to seize up and I needed a rest.*
* v + adv

sell /sel/ (**sold, sold** /səʊld; *AmE* soʊld/)

⚡,sell sth 'off **1** to sell all or part of an industry, a company or a piece of land: *Unwanted land next to the farm was sold off.* ◇ *The government decided to sell off state companies.* OBJ **assets, land, business, company 2** to sell things cheaply because you no longer want them or because you need the money: *The store is selling off the old stock.* ◇ *The family silver was sold off to pay the debts.*
* v + adv + n * v + n/pron + adv

▶ 'sell-off *n* (*BrE*) **1** the sale by the government of an industry or a service to individual people or private companies: *the proposed sell-off of the rail company* ◇ *sell-off plans* **2** (*AmE, business*) the sale of a large number of shares in a company, after which their value usually falls

,sell sth 'on (to sb) to sell sth to sb else that you have bought not long before, usually in order to make a profit: *She managed the business for a year and then sold it on.*
* v + n/pron + adv * v + adv + n

be 'sold on sth (*informal*) to be convinced that sth is very good: *I could see she was sold on the idea.* ◇ *I'm not really sold on American music.*
OBJ **idea**
* be + v + prep

sell sth off

auction sth off ◆ sell sth off ◆ sell (sth) up

These verbs all mean to give sth to sb in exchange for money.

auction sth off to sell sth at an auction (= an event where things are sold to the person who offers the most money), especially sth that is no longer needed or wanted: *The Army is auctioning off a lot of surplus equipment.* NOTE **Auction** can be used on its own: *The costumes from the movie are to be auctioned for charity.*

sell sth off to sell things cheaply because you want to get rid of them or because you need the money; to sell all or part of an industry, a company or land: *In the nineties most state-owned industries were sold off.* NOTE **Sell** can be used on its own: *They sold the business at a profit/loss.*

sell (sth) up (*especially BrE*) to sell your home, possessions, business, etc., usually because you are leaving the country or retiring: *They sold up and moved to France.* ◊ *I sold up everything I had and bought a farm.*

PATTERNS AND COLLOCATIONS

- to sell sth (off)/auction sth (off) **to sb/for** £100, £47 000, etc.
- to sell (off)/auction (off) **assets/a collection/ land/property**
- to sell (off) **shares/a company**
- to sell/auction **a house**
- to be **forced to/obliged to** sell sth (off)/sell sth up
- to sell sth (off) **cheaply/at a loss**

---

sell 'out; be ,sold 'out 1 if tickets for a concert, a game, etc. **sell out** or are **sold out**, they are all sold and there are none left: *The tickets for the game will sell out quickly.* ◊ *To-night's performance is completely sold out.* ◊ *The first 5 000 copies of the book have sold out.* **2** (*also* **,sell 'out of sth, be ,sold 'out of sth**) if sb **sells out** of sth or is **sold out** of sth, they have sold all of it and have nothing left: *I'm sorry, we've sold out of milk.* ◊ *We are already sold out for tonight's concert.*

◆ v + adv ◆ be + v + adv **2** *also* v + adv + prep
◆ be + v + adv + prep

▸ **'sell-out** n [usually sing.] a play, concert, etc. for which all the tickets have been sold: *The gig is a sell-out.* ◊ *a sell-out tour/crowd*

,sell 'out (to sb/sth) (*disapproving*) **1** to ignore or change your principles or beliefs, especially to gain an advantage for yourself: *The rest of the gang accused him of selling out to the law.* ◊ *a talented British movie director who's sold out to Hollywood* **2** to sell your business or a part of your business: *The company sold out to its rival.*

◆ v + adv

▸ **'sell-out** n [usually sing.] a situation in which sb is not loyal to sb who trusted them, by not doing sth that they promised to do, or by doing sth that they promised not to do: *a dreadful sell-out of their cause* ◊ *The deal was seen as a union sell-out to management.*

,sell sb/sth 'out (to sb/sth) to not be loyal to sb: *They discovered who had sold them out to the enemy.*

◆ v + n/pron + adv ◆ v + adv + n

,sell 'out of sth → SELL OUT, ETC.

,sell 'up; ,sell sth 'up to sell your home, possessions, business, etc., usually because you need the money, are moving to another place or are stopping work: *They sold up and moved to France.* ◊ *We decided to sell up everything and buy a farm.* ⊃ note at SELL STH OFF

◆ v + adv ◆ v + adv + n ◆ v + pron + adv

send /send/ (**sent, sent** /sent/)

,send sb/sth a'head to arrange for sb/sth to go or be taken to the place you are going to, before you arrive there: *The rest of the equipment was sent ahead by air.*

◆ v + n/pron + adv

,send a'way (for sth) → SEND OFF (FOR STH)

,send sb a'way 1 to tell sb to leave: *The reporters were sent away empty-handed* (= without any news). **2** (**to…**) to arrange for sb to go somewhere away from home: *He was sent away to boarding school at the age of seven.*

◆ v + n/pron + adv ◆ v + adv + n (*less frequent*)

,send sb/sth 'back (to sb/sth) to return sb/sth to where they/it came from: *The refugees were sent back to their own country.* ◊ *You can send the goods back if you're not satisfied.*

SYN **return sb/sth (to sb/sth)** (*more formal*)

◆ v + n/pron + adv ◆ v + adv + n

,send sb 'down (*BrE*) **1** (*informal*) to send sb to prison: *He was sent down for ten years.* SYN **put sb away 2** (*old-fashioned*) to make a student leave a university, especially Oxford or Cam-bridge, because of bad behaviour: *She was sent down from Oxford.* SYN **expel sb**

NOTE Often used in the passive.

◆ v + n/pron + adv ◆ v + adv + n

,send for sb to send a message to sb to ask them to come and see you, especially in order to help you: *Send for a doctor.* ◊ *Has the doctor been sent for?*

OBJ **doctor, police** SYN **call sb in**
 ◆ v + prep

'**send for sth** to ask sb to bring or deliver sth to you: *Send for an ambulance.* ◇ *Have you sent for a catalogue* (= *by post/mail*)? ◇ *More equipment has been sent for.*
 ◆ v + prep

,**send sb 'in 1** to order sb to go to a place to deal with a difficult situation: *Troops were sent in to restore order.* OBJ **troops, police, army 2** to tell sb to go into a room, where sb else is waiting to see them: *Send the next candidate in, please.*
 ◆ v + n/pron + adv ◆ v + adv + n

,**send sth 'in** to send sth by post/mail to a place where it will be dealt with: *500 schools sent in entries for the competition.* ◇ *Viewers are invited to send in their suggestions for next week's programme.*
 ◆ v + n/pron + adv ◆ v + adv + n

,**send 'off** (*also* ,**send a'way** *especially AmE*) (**for sth**) to write to sb and ask them to send you sth by post/mail: *If you save enough packets, you can send off and get a free toy.* ◇ *You can send off for a free booklet.*
 SYN **write away/off** (**to sb**) (**for sth**)
 ◆ v + adv

,**send sb 'off 1** (**for sth**) (*BrE*) (in a sports game) to make sb leave the field because they have broken the rules of the game: *He was sent off for a foul.* ◇ *Three players got sent off in the first half.* OBJ **player** NOTE Often used in the passive. **2** (**to …**) to ask or tell sb to go somewhere: *The bank sent him off for four months' study at Harvard.* ◇ *I always send the kids off to school looking clean and tidy.* ◇ *The men were sent off to find water.*
 ◆ **1** v + n/pron + adv ◆ v + adv + n
 ◆ **2** v + n/pron + adv
 ▶ ,**sending-'off** *n* (*BrE*) (in a sports game) a situation when a player is told to leave the field because they have broken the rules: *It's his third sending-off this year.* ◇ *The match saw three penalties and two sendings-off.*
 ▶ '**send-off** *n* (*informal*) an occasion when people come together to say goodbye to sb who is leaving: *She was given a good send-off by all her colleagues.*

,**send sth 'off** (**to sb**) to send sth by post/mail: *Have you sent that letter off yet?*
 OBJ **letter, parcel** SYN **mail sth off** (**to sb**) (*AmE*); **post sth off** (**to sb**) (*BrE*)
 ◆ v + n/pron + adv ◆ v + adv + n

,**send sth 'on 1** (**to…**) to send a letter, etc. that has arrived at sb's old address to their new one: *I've asked a neighbour to send on any important letters.* OBJ **letter** SYN **forward sth** (**to sb/sth**) (*more formal*) **2** (**to sb/sth**) to send sth you have received to sb else for them to see or deal with: *I'll send the photos on to you.* **3** to send sth to a place so that it arrives before you get there: *We*

sent our furniture on by ship. ◇ *We've arranged for your belongings to be sent on.*
 ◆ v + n/pron + adv ◆ v + adv + n

,**send sb 'out** to send sb somewhere for a particular purpose: *I'll ask them to send someone out straightaway to fix the car.* ◇ *If I'm not back by midnight, send out a search party!*
 ◆ v + n/pron + adv ◆ v + adv + n

,**send sth 'out 1** to send sth to a lot of different people or places: *I sent out fifty invitations.* ◇ *Have we sent letters out to all the applicants?* OBJ **letter, information** SYN **mail sth out 2** to produce sth, such as light, a signal, sound, etc.: *a fire sending out waves of warmth* ◇ *His brain was sending out warning signals telling him to be careful.* OBJ **signal** SYN **emit sth** (*more formal*)
 ◆ v + n/pron + adv ◆ v + adv + n

,**send 'out for sth** to ask a restaurant or shop/store to deliver food to you at home or at work: *We could send out for a takeaway.*
 ◆ v + adv + prep

,**send sb 'up** (*AmE, informal*) to send sb to prison NOTE Often used in the passive.
 ◆ v + n/pron + adv ◆ v + adv + n

,**send sb/sth 'up** (*BrE, informal*) to make people laugh, especially by copying sb/sth in an amusing way: *a TV programme that sends up politicians* ◇ *Everyone was sending her up.* ◇ *The teacher heard me sending up her accent.*
 ◆ v + adv + n ◆ v + pron + adv ◆ v + n + adv (*rare*)
 ▶ '**send-up** *n* (*BrE, informal*) an act of making sb/sth look silly by copying them/it in an amusing way: *The movie is a hilarious send-up of the Hollywood western.*

separate /'sepəreɪt/

,**separate sth 'off** (**from sth**) to remove sth from a larger thing or group; to keep sth apart: *The property agency has been separated off from the main business.*
 ◆ v + adv + n ◆ v + pron + adv ◆ v + n + adv (*rare*)

,**separate 'out**; ,**separate sb/sth 'out** (**from sth**) to divide into different parts; to divide sb/sth into different parts or groups: *The mixture separates out into layers.* ◇ *Plastics must be separated out into different types for recycling.* ◇ *We need to separate out fact from speculation.* ◇ *The process separates out the different gases.* NOTE **Separate** and **separate sb/sth** can also be used on their own with this meaning.
 ◆ v + adv + n ◆ v + pron + adv ◆ v + n + adv (*rare*)

serve /sɜːv; *AmE* sɜːrv/

'**serve as/for sth** to be used instead of sth else when there is nothing better available: *An old box served as a table.* ◇ *Small temporary buildings had to serve for offices.*
 SYN **act as sth**
 ◆ v + prep

'**serve sth on sb** (*also* '**serve sth upon sb** *more formal*) '**serve sb with sth** (*law*) to give or send sb an official document, especially one that orders them to appear in court: *The police have served a summons on Mr Jackson.* ◇ *The police have served him with a summons.*

OBJ summons, notice, writ

◆ v + n/pron + prep

serve sth 'out 1 to continue doing sth until the end of a fixed period of time: *She served out the rest of her sentence in an open prison.* **OBJ** notice, sentence, term **NOTE** Not used in the passive. **2** (*especially BrE*) → SERVE STH UP

◆ v + adv + n ◆ v + pron + adv ◆ v + n + adv (*rare*)

serve sth 'up 1 (*also* **serve sth 'out** *especially BrE*) to put food onto plates and give it to people: *He served up a delicious meal.* **SYN** dish sth out; dish up, dish sth up **2** (*disapproving*) to give or offer sth: *All the TV channels served up the usual old movies during the holidays.*

◆ v + n/pron + adv ◆ v + adv + n

serve sth u'pon sb; **'serve sb with sth** → SERVE STH ON SB

set /set/ (setting, set, set)

'set about sb (**with sth**) (*old-fashioned*, *BrE*) to attack sb: *He set about me with a stick.*

◆ v + prep

'set about sth; **'set about doing sth 1** to begin a task or an activity, especially with energy or enthusiasm: *We set about the task of cleaning the apartment.* **2** to approach a problem or task in a particular way: *You've set about this problem the wrong way.* ◇ *How should I set about finding a job?* **SYN** go about sth, go about doing sth

◆ v + prep

'set sb a'gainst sb to make sb oppose a friend, relative, etc.: *The civil war set brother against brother.*

◆ v + n/pron + prep

set sth a'gainst sth 1 to consider sth by comparing good points with bad ones: *Set against the benefits of the new technology is the possibility that jobs will be lost.* **SYN** balance A against B **2** (*also* **set sth 'off against sth**) (*finance*) to record sth as a business cost as a way of reducing the amount of tax you must pay: *The cost of looking for oil can be set against tax as business expenditure.* **3** be set against sth if sth is **set against** sth else, it is placed near it or next to it so that the difference between the two is very noticeable: *views of rocky islands set against fiery sunsets* ◇ *Set against her white dress, her hair seemed even darker.* **4** be set against sth if a story, a film/movie, etc. is **set against** a particular time, event or place, the action happens at that time or place: *It is a love story set against a backdrop of rural Irish life.* **NOTE** In meanings 3 and 4 **set sth against sth** is only used in the passive.

◆ **1,2** v + n/pron + prep
◆ **3,4** be + v + prep

set sth a'head (*AmE*) to change a clock or watch to show the correct later time: *Don't forget to set your clocks ahead tonight* (= because the time has officially changed).

OBJ clock, watch **SYN** put sth forward (*BrE*)
OPP set sth back (*AmE*); put sth back (*BrE*)

◆ v + n/pron + adv

set sb/sth a'part (**from sb/sth**) to make sb/sth different from or better than others: *His confidence sets him apart from his classmates.* ◇ *It's the service at the restaurant that sets it apart.*

◆ v + n/pron + adv ◆ v + adv + n (*less frequent*)

set sth a'part (*BrE*) (*also* **set sth a'side** *AmE, BrE*) to keep sth such as money or time for a special use or purpose: *A room was set apart for quiet reading.*

◆ v + adv + n ◆ v + pron + adv
◆ v + n + adv (*less frequent*)

set sth a'side 1 to place sth to one side: *I set her letter aside, meaning to read it later.* **SYN** put sth aside **2** to save or keep sth for a particular purpose: *She sets aside £50 every month for her daughter's college fees.* ◇ *We need to set aside some time to deal with this.* **OBJ** money, time **SYN** put sth aside **3** to ignore sth such as your feelings or opinions, because other things are important: *We decided to set our differences aside.* ◇ *Let's set aside my personal feelings for now.* **SYN** put sth aside **4** → SET STH APART: *Restaurants must set aside an area for non-smokers.* **OBJ** area, room **SYN** put sth aside **5** (*law*) to reject a previous decision made by a court: *The verdict was set aside by the Appeal Court.* **OBJ** decision, conviction **SYN** overturn sth (*more formal*)

◆ v + adv + n ◆ v + n/pron + adv

▶ **'set-aside** *n* [U] a system in which the government pays farmers not to use some of their land for growing crops; the land that the farmers are paid not to use: *750 acres of set-aside*

set sb 'back sth (*informal*) to cost sb a large amount of money: *That new car must have set her back a bit.* ◇ *This watch set me back £200.*
SYN knock sb back sth (*BrE, informal*)
NOTE Not used in the passive.

◆ v + n/pron + adv + n

set sb/sth 'back to delay the progress of sb/sth: *The rain set the building programme back by several weeks.* ◇ *He was starting to play very well, but his injury has really set him back.*

◆ v + n/pron + adv ◆ v + adv + n

▶ **'setback** *n* a problem or difficulty that delays the progress of sb/sth: *Parry's broken ankle was a major setback for the team.*

set sth 'back (*AmE*) to change a clock or watch to show the correct earlier time: *I forgot to set my watch back last night* (= when the time officially changed).

◻OBJ◻ **clock**, **watch** ◼SYN◼ **put sth back** (*BrE*) ◼OPP◼ **put sth forward** (*BrE*); **set sth ahead** (*AmE*)
♦ v + n/pron + adv

be ˌset ˈback (**from sth**) if a building is **set back**, it is a long way from sth, especially a road: *Their house is the only one that's set back (from the road).*
♦ be + v + adv

ˌset ˈdown; ˌset sth ˈdown (of a plane, a pilot, passengers, etc.) to land: *We set down on the beach.* ◇ *The pilot set the plane down in a field.*
◼SYN◼ **put down** (*especially BrE*), **land**, **land sth**
♦ v + adv ♦ v + n/pron + adv ♦ v + adv + n

ˌset sb ˈdown (*BrE*) (of a vehicle or its driver) to stop and allow sb to get off/out: *The taxi set me down at the end of the road.*
◼SYN◼ **drop sb/sth off** ◼OPP◼ **pick sb up**
♦ v + n/pron + adv ♦ v + adv + n

ˌset sth ˈdown **1** (**on sth**) (*literary*) to place an object down on a surface: *He set his glass down before he spoke.* ◇ *She set the tray down on the table.* ◼SYN◼ **put sth down 2** to write sth down on paper in order to record it: *I wanted to set my thoughts down on paper.* ◇ *It's a good idea to set down your complaint in writing.* ◼SYN◼ **put sth down 3** to give sth as a rule, etc.: *to set down guidelines/rules* ◇ *qualifying standards set down by the Athletics Association*
♦ **1,2** v + n/pron + adv ♦ v + adv + n
♦ **3** v + adv + n ♦ v + pron + adv ♦ v + n + adv (*rare*)

ˌset ˈforth (*literary*) to start a journey: *They set forth for Crete.*
◼SYN◼ **set out** (*less formal*)
♦ v + adv

ˌset ˈforth sth (*formal*) to state sth clearly; to make sth known: *The President set forth his views in a long television broadcast.* ◇ *Her beliefs have been clearly set forth.*
◼NOTE◼ When the object of **set forth** is a noun, it comes after **forth**, but when the object is a pronoun, it comes between **set** and **forth**: *I have my opinions on the matter, but I would never set them forth in public.*
♦ v + adv + n ♦ v + pron + adv

ˌset ˈin if bad weather, an unpleasant feeling, an illness, etc. **sets in**, it begins and seems likely to continue: *I need to mend the roof before winter sets in.* ◇ *Panic set in when she realized how much work there was to do.* ◇ *He eventually agreed to stay in bed, but it was too late—pneumonia had set in.* ◼SUBJ◼ **panic**, **winter**
♦ v + adv

◼IDM◼ **the ˈrot set in** used to describe the fact that a situation has become very bad and will continue like that: *She had problems at her first school, but when she changed schools the rot really set in.*

ˌset sth ˈin/ˈinto sth to fix sth in a space so that it does not stick out beyond the surface: *A small safe had been set into the wall.*

SYNONYMS

set off

leave ♦ **set off** ♦ **set out** ♦ **start**
These verbs all mean to begin a journey.

leave to go away from a person or place: *It was raining when we left.*

set off to begin a journey: *We set off at dawn.* ◇ *Check all the doors and windows are locked before setting off.* ◇ *The group set off for Rome the next day.*

set out to leave a place and begin a journey: *They set out on the last stage of their journey.*

start out to begin a journey: *They started out at five o'clock in the morning.* ◼NOTE◼ **Start** can be used on its own: *I should get there by the afternoon if I start early.*

PATTERNS AND COLLOCATIONS

▪ to set off/start (out)/set out **late/early/at midday/at 9 o'clock**
▪ to set off/start (out)/set out **for/from...**
▪ to set off/start/set out **back (to ...)**
▪ to set off/start (out)/set out **on a journey/voyage/trip**
▪ **before** setting off/starting (out)/setting out

◼NOTE◼ Usually used in the passive. ♦ The verb **inset sth** has a similar meaning.
♦ v + n/pron + prep
▸ ˈinset *n* **1** a small picture, map, etc. inside a larger one: *The committee members' names appeared in an inset.* **2** a piece of material, a small stone, etc. that is added on to sth else or put inside sth else: *a silver brooch with ruby insets*

ˌset ˈoff to begin a journey: *I set off for work at seven.* ◇ *Check your oil before setting off on a long journey.* ◇ *When are you planning to set off?*
♦ v + adv

ˌset sb ˈoff; ˌset sb ˈoff doing sth (*informal, especially BrE*) to make sb start doing sth such as laughing, crying or talking: *Those photos always set her off (crying).* ◇ *Just seeing him laughing sets me off!* (= makes me start laughing)
◼SYN◼ **start sb off**, **start sb off doing sth**
♦ v + n/pron + adv

ˌset sth ˈoff **1** to make a bomb, etc. explode: *to set off fireworks* ◇ *They set the bomb off as soon as they were a safe distance away.* ◻OBJ◻ **bomb**, **firework 2** to make an alarm start: *The burglars set the alarm off.* ◇ *If you burn the toast you'll set the smoke alarm off.* ◻OBJ◻ **alarm 3** to start a process or series of events: *The news set off a wave of panic on world markets.* ◇ *The girl's death set off a terrible chain of events.* ◻OBJ◻ **panic**, **chain/series of events** → see also SET STH UP 4 **4** to make sth appear more attractive by being placed near it: *That scarf sets off the blue of her eyes.*

♦ **1,2** v + n/pron + adv ♦ v + adv + n
♦ **3,4** v + adv + n ♦ v + n/pron + adv

,set sth 'off against sth → SET STH AGAINST STH 2

NOTE The verb **offset sth** (**against sth**) has a similar meaning: *There are certain expenses that you can offset against tax.*

'set on/upon sb (*formal*) to attack sb: *I was set upon by a gang of youths.*

NOTE Often used in the passive.

♦ v + prep

'set sb/sth on sb to make a person or an animal attack sb: *The farmer threatened to set his dogs on us if we didn't leave at once.*

♦ v + n/pron + prep

,set 'out **1** to leave a place and begin a journey, especially a long journey: *They set out on the last stage of their journey.* ◇ *We set out at dawn.* **2** ,set 'out to do sth to begin to do sth with a particular aim or purpose: *She set out to break the world record.* ◇ *They succeeded in what they had set out to do.*

♦ v + adv **2** also v + adv + **to**+inf

▶ 'outset *n* the beginning of sth: *We knew the danger at/from the outset.*

,set sth 'out **1** to arrange or display sth: *She began setting out plates and glasses.* ◇ *Set out your answers neatly.* **2** to present ideas, facts, etc. in a clear, organized way, in speech or writing: *This document sets out our objections to the proposal.* **OBJ** **terms**, **reasons**, **policies**, **conditions**

♦ **1** v + adv + n ♦ v + n/pron + adv

♦ **2** v + adv + n ♦ v + pron + adv ♦ v + n + adv (*rare*)

,set 'to (*old-fashioned, formal, especially BrE*) **1** to begin doing sth in a busy or determined way: *She set to with a scrubbing brush* (= she started cleaning). **2** to begin fighting: *They took off their jackets and set to.*

♦ v + adv

▶ ,set-'to *n* [sing.] (*informal, especially BrE*) a fight or an argument: *He had a set-to with one of his workmates.*

,set 'up; ,set sth 'up to make a machine, some equipment, etc. ready to use: *He helped me to carry my equipment in and set up.* ◇ *It took hours to set up all the equipment.*

♦ v + adv ♦ v + adv + n ♦ v + n/pron + adv

,set 'up; ,set yourself 'up to start running your own business: *He left the firm and set up in business on his own.* ◇ *She set herself up as a hairdresser.*

♦ v + adv ♦ v + pron + adv

,set sb 'up **1** to provide sb with the money they need, for example to start a business, buy a home, etc.: *A bank loan helped to set her up in business.* ◇ *He set his daughter up in her own apartment.* ◇ *If you win tonight's fight, you'll* ***be set up for life*** (= have all the money you will

ever need). **2** (*informal*) to trick sb, especially by making them appear to be guilty of sth that they have not done: *He claimed he had been set up by the police.* **3** (*informal*) to make sb feel healthier, stronger, more active, etc.: *A good breakfast will set you up for the day.* **4** (**with sb**) (*informal*) to arrange for sb to meet sb so that they can have a romantic or sexual relationship: *He set me up with his sister.*

♦ v + n/pron + adv ♦ v + adv + n

♦ v + n + adv (*less frequent*)

▶ 'set-up *n* [usually sing.] (*informal*) **1** a situation in which sb tricks you or makes it seem as if you are guilty of sth that you have not done: *I didn't do it, this is a set-up!* **2** a situation when sb arranges for you to meet sb in order to begin a romantic or sexual relationship: *a set-up date*

,set sth 'up **1** to create sth or start a business, an organization, etc.: *She gave a talk on setting up a business.* ◇ *A committee was set up to investigate the problem.* ◇ *young people* ***setting up home*** *for the first time* **OBJ** **business**, **committee**, **system**, **company** **2** to build sth or put sth somewhere: *The police set up roadblocks on all main roads.* ⊃ note at PUT STH TOGETHER **3** to organize or arrange sth; to make the arrangements for sth to happen: *to set up a meeting* ◇ *We'll set up the transport arrangements.* **OBJ** **meeting** **4** to start a process or a series of events: *The crisis set up a chain reaction in other European markets.* **OBJ** **chain reaction**, **chain of events** → see also SET STH OFF 3

♦ v + adv + n ♦ v + n/pron + adv

▶ 'set-up *n* [usually sing.] (*informal*) the way sth is organized or arranged; a system: *I've only been here a week so I don't really know the set-up.*

,set yourself 'up → SET UP, SET YOURSELF UP

,set yourself 'up as sth to claim to be very important, know a lot about sth, etc.: *He set himself up as an authority on modern art.*

♦ v + pron + adv + prep

'set upon sb (*formal*) → SET ON/UPON SB

settle /'setl/

,settle 'down **1** (*also* ,settle yourself 'down) to get yourself into a comfortable position when you are sitting or lying: *She settled down in an armchair to read.* ◇ *Tom settled himself down at the table.* **2** to start to have a calmer or quieter way of life, without many changes, especially living in one place: *He got married and settled down.* **3** to become relaxed and confident in a new situation; to get used to a new way of life, job, etc.: *She's settling down well at her new school.* ◇ *He just couldn't settle down in the city.* **4** to become calmer and less active: *I've been really busy at work, but things should settle down again soon.* ◇ *Their speed settled down to a steady fifty miles an hour.*

♦ v + adv **1** also v + pron + adv

,settle 'down; ,settle sb 'down to become or to make sb become calmer, less excited, etc.: *The children finally settled down and started work.* ◇ *The teacher had trouble settling the class down.*
 ◆ v + n/pron + adv
,settle yourself 'down → SETTLE DOWN
,settle 'down to sth (*also* 'settle to sth *BrE*) to begin to think about sth or give your attention to doing sth: *They had just settled down to dinner when the phone rang.* ◇ *I'm so worried that I can't settle to anything.*
 ◆ v + adv + prep ◆ v + prep
'settle for sth; 'settle for doing sth to accept sth that is not quite what you wanted but is the best that you can get: *Both teams were happy to settle for a draw.* ◇ *He'd hoped to get £8 000 for the car but had to settle for a lot less.* ◇ *I refuse to settle for (being) second best!*
 OBJ less
 ◆ v + prep
,settle 'in; ,settle 'into sth to become used to sth new, such as a new home, school or job: *She soon settled in at school.* ◇ *It took her a while to settle into her new job.*
 OBJ routine, school, job
 ◆ v + adv ◆ v + prep
'settle on sth (*also* 'settle upon sth *more formal*) to choose sth; to make a decision about sth: *We couldn't decide where to go but we eventually settled on Italy.* ◇ *A date was finally settled on.*
 SYN decide on/upon sth
 ◆ v + prep
'settle sth on/upon sb (*formal, law*) to arrange to give property or money to sb, for example after your death: *He settled his entire estate on his son.*
 OBJ money, estate
 ◆ v + n/pron + prep
'settle to sth (*BrE*) → SETTLE DOWN TO STH
,settle 'up (with sb) to pay sb the money you owe them: *We need to settle up with them for the hire of the room.* ◇ *I'll pay now—we can settle up later.*
 ◆ v + adv
'settle upon sth, etc. → SETTLE ON STH, ETC.

sew /səʊ/; *AmE* soʊ/ (**sewed, sewn** /səʊn/; *AmE* soʊn/ *or* **sewed**)
,sew sth 'up **1** to join or repair sth using a needle and thread: *Sew up the tear before it gets any worse.* ◇ *They cleaned the wound and sewed it up.* OBJ seam, tear, wound **2** (*informal*) to arrange sth in an acceptable way; to bring sth to an acceptable conclusion: *They'd sewn the deal up by midday.* OBJ deal **3** (*informal*) to have control of sth; to be likely to win sth: *Her company* **have got** *the market* **sewn up**. ◇ *By half-time they* **had** *the game* **sewn up**. OBJ market, game, election

NOTE Often used in the passive in meanings 2 and 3, and in the phrase **have (got)** sth sewn up.
 ◆ v + adv + n ◆ v + n/pron + adv

sex /seks/
,sex sb 'up (*informal*) to make sb feel sexually excited
 ◆ v + adv + n ◆ v + pron + adv ◆ v + n + adv
,sex sth 'up (*informal*) to make sth seem more exciting and interesting: *The profession is trying to sex up its image.*
 ◆ v + adv + n ◆ v + pron + adv ◆ v + n + adv

shack /ʃæk/
,shack 'up with sb; be ,shacked 'up with sb (*also* ,shack 'up together) (*slang, disapproving*) to live with sb you are having a sexual relationship with but are not married to: *He's shacked up with some girl he met in Berlin.*
 ◆ v + adv + prep ◆ be + v + adv + prep ◆ v + adv + adv

shade /ʃeɪd/
,shade sth 'in to make part of a picture darker, either with colours or using black: *He shaded in part of the graph.*
 ◆ v + adv + n ◆ v + n/pron + adv
,shade 'into sth to gradually change into sth else so that you cannot tell where one thing ends and the other begins: *The blue gradually shades into purple.* ◇ *Sometimes nervousness can shade into fear.*
 ◆ v + prep

shake /ʃeɪk/ (**shook** /ʃʊk/, **shaken** /'ʃeɪkən/)
,shake 'down (*informal*) to become comfortable and confident in a new situation: *Once the team shakes down, results should improve.*
 ◆ v + adv
 ▶ 'shakedown n (*AmE, informal*) the test of a vehicle or an aircraft before it is generally used, to see if there are any problems: *a shakedown flight*
,shake sb 'down (*AmE, slang*) to threaten sb in order to get money from them: *They've found the guy who shook George down.* ◇ *police who shake down motorists for bribes*
 ◆ v + n/pron + adv ◆ v + adv + n
 ▶ 'shakedown n (*AmE, slang*) an act of trying to get money from sb with violence or threats: *He was stabbed during a shakedown.*
,shake sb/sth 'down (*AmE, informal*) to search a person or place in a very thorough way: *Police shook down the club, looking for drugs.*
 ◆ v + adv + n ◆ v + n/pron + adv
 ▶ 'shakedown n (*AmE, informal*) a thorough search of sb/sth: *a police shakedown of the area*
,shake sb 'off **1** to escape from sb; to get rid of sb who is following you: *He twisted and turned in a desperate attempt to shake off his pursuer.* ◇ *I think we've shaken them off.* **2** to escape from

sb who is holding you and will not let go: *She clung to him, but he shook her off.*
♦ v + adv + n ♦ v + n/pron + adv

,shake sth 'off to get rid of sth, such as an illness, that is causing you problems: *I can't shake off this cold.* ◇ *She struggled to shake off her image as a beauty with no brains.*
[OBJ] (a) **cold**
♦ v + adv + n ♦ v + n/pron + adv

'shake on sth to shake hands with sb in order to show that you agree to sth: *Let's shake on it.*
[OBJ] **deal, agreement, it**
♦ v + prep

,shake sth 'out **1** to open or spread sth by shaking it: *He shook the blanket out and spread it on the grass.* **2** to open sth by shaking it in order to get rid of bits of dirt, dust, etc.: *She went outside to shake out the tablecloth.*
♦ v + n/pron + adv ♦ v + adv + n

,shake sb 'up **1** to shock or upset sb: *She has been badly shaken up by the experience.*
[NOTE] Often used in the passive. ♦ **Shake sb** is also used frequently on its own with this meaning: *She was badly shaken by the experience.* **2** to surprise sb in order to make them think or behave in a different way, become more active, etc.: *He was asked to shake the staff up a bit.*
♦ v + n/pron + adv ♦ v + adv + n

,shake sth 'up to make important changes in an organization, a profession, etc. in order to make it more efficient: *The company needs shaking up a bit.*
♦ v + n/pron + adv ♦ v + adv + n
▶ 'shake-up (*also* 'shake-out) *n* a major change to a company or an organization in order to improve it: *The police force is facing the biggest shake-up in its history.*

shame /ʃeɪm/

'shame sb into sth; 'shame sb into doing sth to persuade sb to do sth by making them feel ashamed not to do it: *They shamed him into apologizing.*
♦ v + n/pron + prep

shape /ʃeɪp/

,shape 'up (*informal*) **1** [+ adv/prep] to develop in a particular way, often in the way that you had hoped for: *Our plans are shaping up nicely.* ◇ *How's the new team shaping up?* **2** to improve your work or your behaviour: *If you don't shape up, you'll lose your job.* **3** (*especially BrE*) to become thin and physically fit: *It's time to slim down and shape up for the summer.*
♦ v + adv
[IDM] **shape up or ship 'out** (*AmE, informal*) used to tell sb that if they do not improve their work or their behaviour they will have to leave their job, etc.

share /ʃeə(r); AmE ʃer/

,share sth 'out (**among/between sb**) to divide sth such as money, food or work and give an amount to each person: *The work was shared out equally.* ◇ *How can we share out the pizza between the five of us?*
♦ v + adv + n ♦ v + n/pron + adv

sharpen /'ʃɑːpən; AmE 'ʃɑːrpən/

,sharpen 'up; ,sharpen sb/sth 'up to become, or to make sb/sth, better, more skilful, more effective, etc. than before: *She needs to sharpen up before next month's competition.* ◇ *This exercise will help students sharpen up their reading skills.* ◇ *Discipline has sharpened them up.*
♦ v + adv ♦ v + adv + n ♦ v + n/pron + adv

shave /ʃeɪv/

,shave sth 'off to remove hair from your face, head, etc.: *Dad's shaved his beard off.* ◇ *She shocked everyone by shaving all her hair off.*
[OBJ] **beard, moustache, hair**
♦ v + n/pron + adv ♦ v + adv + n

,shave sth 'off; ,shave sth 'off sth **1** to cut very thin pieces from the surface of a piece of wood, etc.: *I had to shave a bit off the door to make it shut.* ◇ *Use a sharp knife to shave off thin rolls of chocolate.* **2** to make sth smaller or lower by a very small amount: *We managed to shave 5% off the cost.* ◇ *He shaved half a second off the world record.*
♦ v + n/pron + adv ♦ v + adv + n ♦ v + n/pron + prep

shear /ʃɪə(r); AmE ʃɪr/ (sheared, shorn /ʃɔːn; AmE ʃɔːrn/ or sheared)

be 'shorn of sth (*literary*) to have sth important taken away from you: *a political party shorn of power*
♦ be + v + prep

,shear 'off; ,shear sth 'off (*technical*) (especially of sth metal) to break under pressure; to cut through sth and make it break: *The bolts holding the wheel in place sheared off.*
♦ v + adv ♦ v + n/pron + adv ♦ v + n + adv

sheer /ʃɪə(r); AmE ʃɪr/

,sheer a'way/'off to suddenly move away in a different direction, especially to avoid hitting sth: *The car sheered wildly away, just missing the truck.* ◇ *Her mind sheered away from images she did not wish to dwell on.*
[SYN] **veer off, veer away (from sth)**
♦ v + adv

shell /ʃel/

,shell 'out (**for sth**), ,shell sth 'out (**for sth**) (*informal*) to pay for sth, especially when it is a lot of money or you do not really want to: *I'm not shelling out for another computer.* ◇ *I had to shell out $500 for the air fare.*

SYN **fork out** (**for sth**), **fork sth out** (**for sth**)
➔ note at PAY OUT, PAY STH OUT
◆ v + adv ◆ v + adv + n ◆ v + pron + adv
◆ v + n + adv (*less frequent*)

shin (*BrE*) /ʃɪn/ (*AmE* **shinny**) (**-nn-**)
‚shin 'down/'up; ‚shin 'down/'up sth (*BrE*)
(*informal*) to climb down or up sth, using your
hands and legs to hold it tightly: *He shinned
down the drainpipe.* ◇ *You might be able to see if
you shin up that tree.*
[OBJ] **drainpipe**, **rope**
◆ v + adv ◆ v + prep

shine /ʃaɪn/ (**shone**, **shone** /ʃɒn; *AmE* ʃoʊn/)
‚shine 'out **1** to shine brightly: *A light shone out
across the field.* **2** if a person or a thing **shines
out**, you notice them because they are very
much better than the others: *She seemed to shine
out from the rest.*
◆ v + adv
‚shine 'through; ‚shine 'through sth to be
seen clearly and easily: *In the last game her
talent really shone through.* ◇ *His love of life
shines through the pages of his book.*
◆ v + adv ◆ v + prep

shinny (*AmE*) /'ʃɪni/ (**shinnies**, **shinnying**,
shinnied)
‚shinny 'down/'up; ‚shinny 'down/'up sth
(*AmE*) ➔ SHIN DOWN/UP, SHIN DOWN/UP STH:
*Burglars broke into the art gallery through the
roof, shinnied down the rope and stole five
valuable paintings.*

ship /ʃɪp/ (**-pp-**)
‚ship sb 'off (**to…**) (*informal*) to send sb away
somewhere, especially when they do not want
to go: *They shipped the children off to camp.*
◇ *I was shipped off to Canada.*
NOTE Often used in the passive.
◆ v + n/pron + adv ◆ v + adv + n
‚ship sb/sth 'off (**to…**) to send goods or people
somewhere by ship: *They shipped all their
possessions off to Australia.* ◇ *The goods were
shipped off last week.*
NOTE Often used in the passive.
◆ v + n/pron + adv ◆ v + adv + n
‚ship sb/sth 'out (**to…**) to send goods or people
somewhere, especially by ship: *They shipped the
sculpture out to the States.* ◇ *Fresh supplies were
shipped out.*
NOTE Often used in the passive.
◆ v + n/pron + adv ◆ v + adv + n
[IDM] **shape up or ship 'out** ➔ SHAPE

shoo /ʃuː/ (**shoos**, **shooing**, **shooed**)
‚shoo sb/sth a'way to get rid of sb/sth by
waving your arms, making a noise, etc.: *We tried
to shoo the flies away.*
◆ v + n/pron + adv ◆ v + adv + n
‚shoo sb/sth 'in; ‚shoo sb/sth 'into sth
(*informal, especially AmE*) **1** to send sb/sth into a
room, building, etc.: *Our friends unloaded our
bags and shooed us into the house.* ◇ *After a
minute, she opened the door and shooed me in.*
NOTE Often used in the passive. **2** to ensure
that sb wins a competition or an election or gets
a job without going through the proper procedures: *They're trying to shoo in their first choice
without even giving her an interview.* ◇ *I'm not

SYNONYMS

shoot sb down

blow sb away ◆ **gun sb down** ◆ **mow sb down**
◆ **pick sb off** ◆ **shoot sb/sth down**
These verbs all mean to kill or wound a person
or animal with a gun.

blow sb away (*especially AmE, informal*) to kill
sb by shooting them: *He thought that he
would be the next to be blown away.*

gun sb down (*usually passive*) (*used especially
in newspapers*) to shoot sb and kill or
seriously injure them: *The policeman was
gunned down while on duty.*

mow sb down to kill sb using a gun or a
vehicle, especially when several people are
all killed at the same time: *The gunmen
opened fire, mowing down at least seven
people.*

pick sb off (*informal*) to aim carefully at a
person, animal or aircraft, especially one of a

group, and then shoot them: *Snipers were
picking off innocent civilians.*

shoot sb/sth down (*usually passive*) to make a
person or plane fall to the ground by shooting
them/it: *Several planes were shot down by
enemy fire.*

WHICH WORD?

Planes, people in planes, or people on the
ground can be **shot down**; only people on the
ground can be **gunned down**.

PATTERNS AND COLLOCATIONS

■ to **threaten/be going** to shoot sb down/blow
sb away
■ to be shot down/gunned down **in cold blood**
■ to be picked off **one by one/at random**

shop

shoot up

jump ◆ **leap** ◆ **rocket** ◆ **shoot up** ◆ **soar**
◆ **spiral** ◆ **surge**

These are all verbs that can be used when an amount, level or number increases quickly. See also **go up**.

jump (*used especially in newspapers*) to increase suddenly and by a large amount: *Prices jumped by 60% last year.* ◇ *Sales jumped from $2.7 billion to $3.5 billion.*

leap (*usually approving*) to increase suddenly and by a large amount: *Shares leapt in value from 476p to close at 536p.*

rocket (of an amount or rate) to increase very quickly and suddenly: *The total has rocketed from 376 to 532.*

shoot up (*often disapproving*) to increase suddenly and by a large amount: *Ticket prices shot up last year.* ◇ *Burglaries in the city have shot up by nearly seventy per cent.*

soar to increase very quickly in value, amount or level: *Soaring costs/prices/temperatures have made progress difficult.* ◇ *Unemployment has soared to 18%.*

spiral (*disapproving*) to increase quickly in level or amount: *You must be aware of the spiralling cost of health care in this country.* ◇ *Prices are spiralling out of control.*

surge (*especially business*) (of prices, profits or the rate of sth) to suddenly increase in value or level: *Profits from cigarettes surged to $225m last year.*

Leap is usually used when the increase is seen as a positive thing: *profits, shares* and *prices* can **leap** or **jump**, but *costs* **jump**. **Leap** usually suggests a more dramatic, surprising or significant increase: *Raw material costs jumped 1 per cent last month.* **Shoot up** is used in more informal contexts, and especially when the increase is seen as a negative thing: *Prices/ charges/interest rates have shot up.* **Spiral** is nearly always used with a negative meaning: *spiralling debt/prices.*

- to soar/jump/shoot up **in price/in number**
- to soar/jump/rocket/leap/shoot up **from…/ to…/by…**
- the **price/cost of sth** soars/jumps/surges/spirals/rockets/shoots up
- **profits** soar/jump/surge/leap
- **numbers/levels of sth** soar/jump/shoot up
- to soar/jump/surge/leap/shoot up **suddenly/ dramatically**

---

going to sit back and watch my rival get shooed in. ◇ *She was surprised when she got shooed into the top job.* NOTE Usually used in the passive.
◆ v + n/pron + adv ◆ v + adv + n ◆ v + n/pron + prep
▶ **'shoo-in** (**for sth/to do sth**) *n* (*informal, especially AmE*) a person or team that will win easily: *Tiger Woods is a shoo-in for the championship.*

shoot /ʃuːt/ (**shot, shot** /ʃɒt; *AmE* ʃɑːt/)

shoot sb/sth 'down 1 to shoot at sb/sth and make them/it fall to the ground: *They were shot down in cold blood.* ◇ *They shot down a civilian aircraft by mistake.* **2** (*informal*) to strongly criticize sb or their ideas, etc.: *When I made a suggestion, they shot me down in flames.* ◇ *My ideas were shot down one by one.*
◆ v + adv + n ◆ v + n/pron + adv

'shoot for sth (*AmE, informal*) (*usually used in the progressive tenses*) to try to get or achieve sth difficult: *They're shooting for another victory this season.*
◆ v + prep

shoot 'off (*informal*) to leave somewhere very quickly: *She had to shoot off to meet someone.* ◇ *I'm sorry, I've got to shoot off.*
◆ v + adv

shoot sth 'off to remove sth by shooting: *They shot the lock off.*
◆ v + n/pron + adv ◆ v + adv + n

shoot 'through (*informal, AustralE*) to leave, especially in order to avoid sb/sth: *I was only five when my dad shot through.*
◆ v + adv

shoot 'up 1 (**to sth**) to rise or increase very quickly: *The inflation rate has shot up to 20%.* **2** to grow taller in a short time: *She's shot up in the last few months.* ➲ note at GROW UP
◆ v + adv

shoot 'up; shoot 'up sth (*slang*) to make an illegal drug enter your body using a needle
OBJ **heroin, drugs**
◆ v + adv ◆ v + adv + n

shoot sb/sth 'up to injure sb or damage sth severely by shooting: *An armed gang shot up the nightclub.*
OBJ **house, bar, club**
◆ v + adv + n ◆ v + n/pron + adv

shop /ʃɒp; *AmE* ʃɑːp/ (**-pp-**)

shop a'round (**for sth**), **shop a'round sth** (**for sth**) to look at different shops/stores to compare the prices of goods or services so that you can buy the ones that are the best value: *If* *you're buying a new MP3 player, shop around for the best price.* ◇ *It's worth shopping around the travel agents to find the best deal.* ◇ *When you open a bank account, it's a good idea to shop around first.*

◆ v + adv ◆ v + prep

shore /ʃɔː(r)/

shore sth 'up 1 to support part of a building or other large structure by placing large pieces of wood or metal against or under it so that it does not fall down: *Engineers shored up the tunnel with wooden beams.* ◇ *The building was shored up to make it safe.* **2** to support sth that is weak or failing: *to shore up the economy/dollar/pound*

◆ v + adv + n ◆ v + pron + adv
◆ v + n + adv (*less frequent*)

shout /ʃaʊt/

shout sb 'down to shout to prevent sb who is speaking from being heard, because you do not like what they are saying or you disagree with them: *I tried to explain but they just shouted me down.* ◇ *The speaker was shouted down by angry protesters.*

◆ v + n/pron + adv ◆ v + adv + n

shout 'out (**to sb**), **shout sth 'out** (**to sb**) to suddenly say sth in a loud voice: *I shouted out to them but they didn't hear me.* ◇ *She shouted out a warning.* ◇ *He shouted out, 'Over here!'*

SYN call out (**to sb**), call sth out (**to sb**)

◆ v + adv ◆ v + adv + n ◆ v + n/pron + adv
◆ v + adv + speech

▶ '**shout-out** *n* an act of mentioning sb's name by a performer at a concert or by a disc jockey (= a person who plays music on the radio or at a club), in order to give a message, say hello, etc.: *A big shout-out to my boyfriend Flavio on his birthday!*

shove /ʃʌv/

shove 'off (*BrE*) used to tell sb rather rudely to go away: *Just shove off and leave me alone!*

SYN push off

◆ v + adv

shove 'up (*BrE*) used to ask sb to move to make a space for sb else to sit down: *We can get one more in if you shove up.* ◇ *Shove up a bit!*

SYN budge up (*BrE*); move up

◆ v + adv

show /ʃəʊ; *AmE* ʃoʊ/ (**showed**, **shown** /ʃəʊn; *AmE* ʃoʊn/ or, rarely, **showed**)

show sb a'round; **show sb a'round sth** (*BrE also* **show sb 'round**, **show sb 'round sth**) to go with sb when they visit a place for the first time, showing them what is interesting: *There are guides in the palace who will show visitors around.* ◇ *I'll arrange for someone to show you around the school.*

SYN take sb around, take sb around sth

→ see also SHOW SB OVER STH

◆ v + n/pron + adv ◆ v + n/pron + prep

show sb 'in; **show sb 'into sth** to lead a visitor to a place where they can wait, or to the room where sb is waiting to see them: *Sarah showed the visitors in.* ◇ *I was shown into a waiting room.*

OPP show sb out, show sb out of sth

◆ v + n/pron + adv ◆ v + adv + n ◆ v + n/pron + prep

show 'off (*informal*, *disapproving*) to try to impress other people with your abilities, wealth, intelligence, etc.: *Stop showing off!* ◇ *Bonnie was showing off to her friends, doing handstands on the grass.*

◆ v + adv

▶ '**show-off** *n* (*informal*, *disapproving*) a person who likes to impress other people with their abilities, wealth, etc.: *You're such a show-off!*

show sb/sth 'off 1 to try to make people pay attention to sb/sth because you are proud of them/it: *He was showing his CD collection off to his friends.* ◇ *She brought her new boyfriend along to show him off.* **2** to make sb/sth look attractive or seem interesting or exciting by showing their best features: *The black sweater showed off her figure to full advantage.* ◇ *The music shows the band off in their best light.*

◆ v + n/pron + adv ◆ v + adv + n

show sb 'out; **show sb 'out of sth** to lead a visitor to the door out of a room, a building, etc.: *I'll show you out.*

OPP show sb in, show sb into sth

◆ v + n/pron + adv ◆ v + adv + n ◆ v + n/pron + prep

show sb 'over sth (*BrE*) to take sb around a place they are visiting and show them what is interesting: *They showed me over the house.*

→ see also SHOW SB AROUND, SHOW SB AROUND STH

◆ v + n/pron + prep

show sb 'round, etc. (*BrE*) → SHOW SB AROUND, ETC.

show 'through; **show 'through sth** to be visible through sth or behind sth: *This paper is so thin the ink shows through.* ◇ *His skull showed through his thin hair.* ◇ *When he spoke, his bitterness showed through.*

◆ v + adv ◆ v + prep

show 'up (*informal*) to arrive or appear at the place you have arranged: *She finally showed up at lunchtime.* ◇ *I arranged to meet him but he didn't show up.*

SYN turn up ⟳ note at TURN UP

◆ v + adv

show 'up; **show sth 'up** to become or to make sth easy to see: *His striped tie showed up well against his dark red shirt.* ◇ *Something odd has shown up on the X-ray.* ◇ *Her lack of experience was shown up by the test.*

◆ v + adv ◆ v + adv + n ◆ v + n/pron + adv

show sb/sth off

flaunt sth ◆ **parade sb/sth** ◆ **show sb/sth off**

These verbs all mean to show people sb/sth that you are proud of.

flaunt sth (*disapproving*) to show sth you are proud of to other people, in order to impress them: *He did not believe in flaunting his wealth.*

parade sb/sth to show sb/sth in public so that people can see them/it: *The trophy was paraded around the stadium.* ◇ *The prisoners were paraded in front of the crowd.*

show sb/sth off to show people sb/sth that you are proud of: *She wanted to show off her new husband at the party.* ◇ *He likes to show off how well he speaks French.* ▶ **show-off** *n* a person who tries to show off: *You're such a show off!*

WHICH WORD?

Show sb/sth off can be either approving or disapproving, but **flaunt sth** is nearly always disapproving. **Flaunt** is most commonly used with words relating to money, such as *wealth, prosperity* and *possessions*, but it is also often used with words for parts of the body and relationships: *He wore a tight T-shirt which really showed off his muscles.* People **parade** things either because they are proud of them and want to impress other people, or because they want to make other people feel ashamed.

PATTERNS AND COLLOCATIONS

- to show off/flaunt/parade sth **in front of** sb
- to show off/flaunt your **wealth/possessions**
- to show off/flaunt your **body/breasts**
- to show off/parade your **knowledge/skills/talents/medals**

,**show sb 'up** (*informal*) to make sb else feel embarrassed by behaving badly or by doing sth better than them: *He said I'd shown him up in front of his friends.* ◇ *You really showed me up by snoring during the concert!* ◇ *Don't worry about being shown up by the kids.*
◆ v + n/pron + adv ◆ v + adv + n

,**show sb/sth 'up as/for sth** to show what sb/sth is really like, when this is worse than people thought: *The book shows her up for what she really is: a fraud.* ◇ *We were shown up as the second-rate team that we were.*
◆ v + n/pron + adv + prep

shower /'ʃaʊə(r)/

,**shower 'down**; ,**shower 'down on sb/sth**; '**shower on sb/sth**; ,**shower sth 'down on sb/sth**; ,**shower sth on sb/sth** to fall onto sb/sth, especially in a lot of small pieces: *Volcanic ash showered down on the town after the eruption.* ◇ *The bottle broke and showered glass fragments on us.*
◆ v + adv ◆ v + adv + prep ◆ v + prep
◆ v + n/pron + adv + prep ◆ v + n/pron + prep

'**shower sb with sth** to drop a lot of small things onto sb: *The bride and groom were showered with rice as they left the church.* ◇ *The roof collapsed, showering us with dust and debris.* ◇ (*figurative*) *He showered her with gifts.*
◆ v + n/pron + prep

shrink /ʃrɪŋk/ (shrank /ʃræŋk/, shrunk /ʃrʌŋk/ or shrunk, shrunk)

,**shrink a'way/'back** (**from sb/sth**) to move backwards or away from sb/sth, especially

because you are frightened or disgusted: *She shrank away from him in horror.*
◆ v + adv

'**shrink from sth**; '**shrink from doing sth** (*often used in negative sentences*) to be unwilling to do or accept sth that you find frightening, unpleasant or immoral: *She recognized her responsibility and did not shrink from it.* ◇ *He shrank from confronting his son face to face.* ◇ *She never shrank from difficult tasks.*
[OBJ] **task**, **duty** [SYN] **back away from sth**
◆ v + prep

shrivel /'ʃrɪvl/ (-ll-, *AmE* -l-)

,**shrivel 'up** to become dry and develop deep lines because of heat, lack of water, etc.: *The apples left on the tree had shrivelled up.*
[NOTE] **Shrivel** is used on its own with a similar meaning.
◆ v + adv
▶ ,**shrivelled 'up** *adj*: *shrivelled-up apples*

shroud /ʃraʊd/

be '**shrouded in sth 1** to be covered or hidden by sth: *The city was shrouded in mist.* ◇ *furniture shrouded in dust sheets* **2** if information, etc. is shrouded in mystery, it is hidden or kept secret: *His family background is shrouded in mystery.* ◇ *Their work is shrouded in secrecy.*
◆ be + v + prep

shrug /ʃrʌɡ/ (-gg-)

,**shrug sth 'off 1** (*also* ,**shrug sth a'way** *less frequent*) to push sth back or away with your shoulders: *She shrugged off her jacket.* ◇ *She put her hand on his shoulder but he shrugged it away.*

OBJ **jacket**, **hand 2** (*also* ˌshrug sth a'side *less frequent*) to treat sth as if it is not important: *He shrugged off all the objections I raised.* ◇ *Barnes is trying to shrug of an ankle injury.* **OBJ** **injury**, **criticism**

♦ v + adv + n ♦ v + n/pron + adv

shuck /ʃʌk/

ˌshuck sth 'off (*AmE*) to take off a piece of clothing in a careless way: *He shucked off his bathrobe and got into the shower.*

♦ v + adv + n ♦ v + n/pron + adv

shut /ʃʌt/ (**shutting**, **shut**, **shut**)

ˌshut sb/sth a'way to put sb/sth in a place where other people cannot see or find them/it: *He shut the files away in the safe.* ◇ *prisoners shut away in jail for a long time*

SYN **lock sb up/away; lock sth up/away**

♦ v + n/pron + adv ♦ v + adv + n

ˌshut yourself a'way (*from sb/sth*) to stay in your room or go somewhere where you will be completely alone: *He shut himself away in his study to finish the book.* ◇ *You can't just shut yourself away from the world.*

SYN **lock yourself away**

♦ v + pron + adv

ˌshut 'down; ˌshut sth 'down **1** to stop opening for business; to stop sth from opening: *The mine shut down last month.* ◇ *The club was shut down by the police.* **SYN** **close down**, **close sth down 2** if a machine **shuts down**, or sb **shuts it down**, it stops working: *The machine shuts down if there's an overload.* ◇ *The computer system will be shut down over the weekend.*

♦ v + adv ♦ v + adv + n ♦ v + n/pron + adv

▶ 'shutdown *n* **1** the act of closing a factory or business, either temporarily or permanently: *The shutdown has put hundreds out of work.* **2** the act of stopping a large machine from working, either temporarily or permanently: *There was a fault in the nuclear reactor's emergency shutdown procedures.*

ˌshut sb/sth 'in; ˌshut sb/sth 'in sth; ˌshut yourself 'in; ˌshut yourself 'in sth to put sb/sth in a room, a vehicle, etc. and keep them there; to go into a room, a building, a vehicle, etc. and stay there: *They shut the animals in at night.* ◇ *Liz rushed out and shut herself in her room.*

♦ v + n/pron + adv ♦ v + adv + n ♦ v + n/pron + prep

▶ 'shut-in *n* (*old-fashioned*, *AmE*) a person who cannot leave their home because they are ill/sick or cannot move easily

'shut sth in sth to trap or injure sth by closing sth tightly around it: *I shut my finger in the car door.*

OBJ **finger**

♦ v + n/pron + prep

ˌshut 'off; ˌshut sth 'off **1** if a machine **shuts off**, or sb **shuts it off**, it stops working: *The*

heating will shut off automatically at 9.30. ◇ *I stopped the car and shut off the engine.* **SYN** **switch off**, **switch sth off**; **turn off**, **turn sth off** **OPP** **switch on**, **switch sth on**; **turn on**, **turn sth on 2** if a supply of gas, electricity, etc. **shuts off** or sb/sth **shuts it off**, it stops flowing: *The water shuts off automatically when the tank is full.* ◇ *A valve shuts off the gas when the lid is closed.*

♦ v + adv ♦ v + n/pron + adv ♦ v + adv + n

▶ 'shut-off *n* **1** a device that stops sth working or stops power, gas, etc. from flowing: *a shut-off valve* **2** a period when power, gas, etc. is prevented from flowing: *a shut-off of the water supply*

ˌshut sb/sth 'off (*from sth*) to keep sb/sth separate from other people or things: *A range of mountains shuts Bosnia off from the Adriatic.* ◇ *The kitchen area is shut off from the rest of the room.*

♦ v + n/pron + adv ♦ v + adv + n

ˌshut yourself 'off (*from sb/sth*) to deliberately separate yourself physically or socially from other people: *After her son died, she just wanted to shut herself off from the world.*

SYN **cut yourself off (from sb/sth)**

♦ v + pron + adv

ˌshut sb 'out **1** (*also* ˌshut sb 'out of sth) to refuse to allow a person to share your thoughts, feelings or activities: *Don't shut me out—I want to help you.* ◇ *I was shut out of the decision-making process.* ◇ *When he saw her with the baby he felt shut out.* **SYN** **exclude sb** (*more formal*) **2** (*AmE*, *informal*) to stop an opponent from scoring in a game or contest: *They shut out the Mets in their last game.*

♦ v + n/pron + adv

♦ v + adv + n **1** also v + n/pron + adv + prep

▶ 'shutout *n* (*AmE*, *informal*) a game in which one team does not score

ˌshut sb/sth 'out; ˌshut sb/sth 'out of sth to stop sb/sth from entering a place: *He closed the door firmly, shutting us out of the room.* ◇ *I drew the curtains to shut out the light.*

OBJ **light**, **noise**

♦ v + adv + n ♦ v + n/pron + adv

♦ v + n/pron + adv + prep

ˌshut sth 'out; ˌshut sth 'out of sth to stop yourself from having particular feelings or from thinking about particular things: *She tried to shut out all the painful memories.*

OBJ **pain**, **memories** **SYN** **block sth out**, **block sth out of sth**

♦ v + adv + n ♦ v + n/pron + adv

♦ v + n/pron + adv + prep

ˌshut yourself 'out; ˌshut yourself 'out of sth to be unable to enter your home because you have closed the door and left your keys inside: *I've shut myself out of the house again!*

SYN **lock yourself out**, **lock yourself out of sth**

♦ v + pron + adv ♦ v + pron + adv + prep

shut up

be quiet ◆ **fall silent** ◆ **quieten (sb/sth) down** ◆ **shut (sb) up** ◆ **silence sb/sth**

These verbs all mean to stop talking or making a noise, or to make people stop talking.

be quiet a way of telling sb to stop talking or making a noise: *'Be quiet!' said the teacher.* ◇ *Will you please be quiet? I'm trying to read.*

fall silent (*formal*) to stop talking or crying: *As the curtain rose, the audience fell silent.*

quieten (sb/sth) down to become or make sb/sth calmer or less noisy: *Things seem to have quietened down now.* ◇ *A night in the cells will quieten him down.* **NOTE** Quieten can be used on its own: *The chatter of voices gradually quietened.*

shut (sb) up (*informal*) to stop talking or make sb stop talking; a rude way of telling sb to stop talking: *Just shut up and listen!* ◇ *Will*

you tell Mike to shut up? ◇ *Somebody should shut him up.*

silence sb/sth to make sb/sth stop speaking or making a noise; to stop sb expressing their opinions: *She silenced him with a glare.* ◇ *All protest has been silenced.*

WHICH WORD?

Be quiet and **shut up** are used to tell people to stop making a noise. **Be quiet** and **shut up** are not polite. **Fall silent** is used to describe what people do, not to tell them what to do.

PATTERNS AND COLLOCATIONS

- to **tell/ask** sb to shut up/be quiet
- the audience/class/room **falls silent/quietens down**
- to silence **rumours/your critics**

,shut 'up (*informal*) used to tell sb rudely to stop talking or making a noise: *Shut up and go away!* ◇ *If you'd shut up, I could hear what the speaker is saying.*
SYN belt up (*BrE*)
◆ v + adv

,shut sb 'up (*informal*) to make sb stop talking or making a noise: *I couldn't shut the kids up!*
◆ v + n/pron + adv

,shut sb/sth 'up (in sth), ,shut yourself 'up (in sth) to keep sb/sth in a place and prevent them/it from going anywhere; to stay in a room and not go out: *He had been shut up in a cell for ten years.* ◇ *Shut the dog up in the shed.* ◇ *My father used to shut himself up with his books for days.*
◆ v + n/pron + adv ◆ v + adv + n

,shut sth 'up (*especially BrE*) to close a room, house, etc. and not use it for a period of time: *We shut the summer house up again for another year.*
SYN close sth up
◆ v + n/pron + adv ◆ v + adv + n

IDM shut up 'shop (*BrE, informal*) to close a business permanently; to stop working for the day: *It's time to shut up shop and go home for the day.*

shy /ʃaɪ/ (shies, shying, shied /ʃaɪd/)

,shy a'way (from sth/from doing sth) to avoid doing sth because you are nervous or frightened: *She shies away from close friendships.* ◇ *Don't shy away from saying what you think.*
◆ v + adv

sic (*also* sick) /sɪk/ (-cc-)

'sic sth on sb (*AmE, informal*) to tell a dog to attack sb: *Back off or I'll sic the dog on you.*
OBJ dog **SYN** set sth on sb (*BrE*)
◆ v + n/pron + prep

sick /sɪk/

,sick sth 'up (*BrE, informal*) to bring food up from the stomach: *The baby sicked up her milk.*
SYN throw sth up; vomit sth (*more formal*)
◆ v + adv + n ◆ v + n/pron + adv

'sick sth on sb (*AmE, informal*) → SIC STH ON SB

sicken /'sɪkən/

'sicken for sth (*BrE*) (*usually used in the progressive tenses*) to show signs that you may be becoming ill/sick: *I feel as if I'm sickening for something.* ◇ *You must be sickening for flu.*
SYN go down with sth; get sth
◆ v + prep

side /saɪd/

'side with sb (against sb) to support sb in an argument, a disagreement, etc.: *The children always sided with their mother (against their father).*
◆ v + prep

sidle /'saɪdl/

,sidle 'over/'up (to sb) to approach sb in a shy, uncertain or secret way: *She sidled up to him and whispered in his ear.*
◆ v + adv

sift /sɪft/

'sift sth from sth; ˌ**sift sth 'out from sth** to separate sth, usually sth you want, from a group of things: *to sift (out) the good from the bad*
- v + n/pron + prep ◆ v + adv + n + prep
- v + n/pron + adv + prep

ˌ**sift sth 'out** to separate sth, usually sth you do not want, from a group of things: *We need to sift out unsuitable applications.* ◇ *He helped me sift out the bad songs I'd written.*
- v + adv + n ◆ v + n/pron + adv

ˌ**sift 'through sth** (**for sth**) to carefully examine a large amount of sth in order to find sth important or decide what is useful: *I sifted through his papers for clues.* ◇ *The judges sifted through 8 000 entries and finally picked the winner.* ◇ *This pile of reports needs to be sifted through by the end of this week.*
- v + prep

sign /saɪn/

ˌ**sign sth a'way** to give up your rights, property, etc. by signing a document: *The artist lost millions by signing away his rights to the cartoon character he created.*
[OBJ] **rights**
- v + adv + n ◆ v + n/pron + adv

'sign for sth 1 to sign a form, etc. as proof that you have received sth: *The postman asked me to sign for the packet.* ◇ *This letter hasn't been signed for.* **2** (*sport*) if a player **signs for** a club, he/she formally agrees to play for that team: *When did Rooney sign for United?*
- v + prep

ˌ**sign 'in**; ˌ**sign sb 'in** to write your name or the name of a guest when you arrive at an office, a club, etc.: *All visitors must sign in on arrival.* ◇ *You have to be signed in by a member.*
[OPP] **sign out**, **sign sb out**
- v + adv ◆ v + n/pron + adv ◆ v + adv + n

ˌ**sign 'off 1** (*BrE*) to end a letter, email, etc.: *I'll sign off now and post this.* **2** to end a broadcast by saying goodbye or playing a piece of music: *I'll sign off with a reminder to tune in again tomorrow.*
- v + adv
  ▸ **'sign-off** *n* a way of ending a letter, email, etc.: *His letter ended with an indecipherable sign-off which could have been 'lots of love'.*

ˌ**sign sb 'off** (*BrE*) to say officially that sb is too ill/sick to work for a particular period: *The doctor signed him off for a week.* [SUBJ] **doctor**
- v + n/pron + adv ◆ v + adv + n

ˌ**sign sth 'off** (*BrE*) to give your formal approval to sth, by signing your name: *She signed off all the invoices.*
- v + adv + n ◆ v + n/pron + adv

ˌ**sign 'off on sth** (*AmE*, *informal*) to express your approval of sth formally and definitely: *The President hasn't yet signed off on this report.*
- v + adv + prep

ˌ**sign 'on 1** (*BrE*, *informal*) to sign a form stating that you are unemployed so that you can receive payment from the government: *He had to sign on when the factory closed.* **2** (*old-fashioned*, *AmE*) to announce the start of broadcasting for the day: *This is Jack Grainger signing on.*
- v + adv

ˌ**sign 'on**; ˌ**sign sb 'on** → SIGN UP, SIGN SB UP: *Eric has been signed on for the team as goalkeeper.* ◇ *Shall I sign you on for the painting class?* ◇ *I tried to sign on as a medical assistant.*
- v + adv ◆ v + n/pron + adv

ˌ**sign 'out**; ˌ**sign sb 'out** to write your name or the name of a guest when you leave an office, a club, etc.: *Don't forget to sign out when you go.* ◇ *You must sign your guests out when they leave the club.*
[OPP] **sign in**, **sign sb in**
- v + adv ◆ v + n/pron + adv

ˌ**sign sth 'out** to sign a document to say officially that sth can be removed from a place or that you have taken it: *There is no record of the file being signed out again.*
- v + n/pron + adv ◆ v + adv + n

ˌ**sign sth 'over** (**to sb**) to give your rights or property to sb else by signing a document: *He signed the house over to his daughter.*
- v + n/pron + adv ◆ v + adv + n

ˌ**sign 'up**; ˌ**sign sb 'up** (*also* ˌ**sign 'on**, ˌ**sign sb 'on** *less frequent*) **1** (**with/for sb**) to sign a document saying that you agree to work for sb, play for their team, etc.; to persuade sb to do this: *She's signed up with an employment agency.* ◇ *We've signed up three new players.* ◇ *Who has been signed up to star in the new movie?* **2** (**for sth**) to arrange to do a course of study by adding your name or sb else's name to the list of people doing it: *I've signed up for a pottery course.* ◇ *Shall I sign you up for the workshop too?* **3** to agree to become a member of the armed forces; to persuade sb to do this: *He tried to sign up when he was only fifteen.*
- v + adv ◆ v + adv + n ◆ v + n/pron + adv

silt /sɪlt/

[NOTE] **Silt** is sand, mud, etc. that has been brought in by flowing water.

ˌ**silt 'up**; ˌ**silt sth 'up** to become blocked with silt; to block sth in this way: *The old harbour has silted up.* ◇ *Mud is silting up the stream.*
- v + adv ◆ v + adv + n ◆ v + n/pron + adv

simmer /ˈsɪmə(r)/

ˌ**simmer 'down** (*informal*) to become calm after a period of anger, excitement, violence, etc.: *Just simmer down and we'll discuss this calmly.*
[SYN] **cool down**, **calm down**
- v + adv

sing /sɪŋ/ (**sang** /sæŋ/, **sung** /sʌŋ/)

ˌsing aˈlong (**with sb/sth**), ˌsing aˈlong (**to sth**)
to sing together with sb who is already singing
or while a record, radio, or musical instrument
is playing: *He sang along with the CD.* ◇ *We sang
along to all the songs.*
♦ v + adv

▸ 'singalong *n* an informal occasion at which
people sing songs together: *We had a great
singalong in the pub last night.*

ˌsing ˈout; ˌsing sth ˈout to sing or say sth
clearly and loudly: *Sing out so that everyone can
hear.* ◇ *If you need anything, just sing out.*
♦ v + adv ♦ v + adv + speech ♦ v + adv + n
♦ v + n/pron + adv

ˌsing ˈup (*BrE*)   to sing more loudly: *Sing up, I
can't hear you.*
♦ v + adv

single /'sɪŋgl/

ˌsingle sb/sth ˈout (**for sth/as sb/sth**) to choose
sb/sth from among a group for special comment
or treatment: *They singled her out for particular
praise.* ◇ *He was singled out as the best student.*
NOTE Often used in the passive: *Why had Aidan
been singled out for special treatment?*
♦ v + adv + n ♦ v + n/pron + adv

sink /sɪŋk/ (**sank** /sæŋk/, **sunk** /sʌŋk/ or (*less
frequent*) **sunk**, **sunk**)

ˌsink ˈback (**into sth**) to move or fall backwards,
or lie down, especially when you are feeling
tired: *She sank back into her chair.* ◇ *He sank
back against the pillows, exhausted.*
♦ v + adv

ˌsink ˈin; ˌsink ˈinto sth **1** (of liquids) to go
down into another substance: *Apply the mois-
turizer and let it sink in.* ◇ *The rain sank into the
dry ground.* **SYN** **be absorbed** (**into sth**) **2** (of
words, etc.) to be fully understood or realized: *It
took a while for the news to sink in.* ◇ *He paused
to let his words sink into her brain.* **SUBJ** **words,
news, meaning**
♦ v + adv

IDM **be ˈsunk in sth** to be in a state of
unhappiness or deep thought: *She just sat there,
sunk in thought.*

'sink into sth to go gradually into a less active,
happy or pleasant state: *She sank into a deep
sleep.* ◇ *He sank deeper into depression.*
OBJ **depression** **SYN** **descend into sth** (*more
formal*)
♦ v + prep

ˌsink ˈinto sth; ˌsink sth ˈinto sth to go deep
into sth solid, to make sth sharp do this: *Sharp
teeth sank into his arm.* ◇ *The dog sank its teeth
into my leg.*
♦ v + prep ♦ v + n/pron + prep

ˌsink sth ˈinto sth to spend a lot of money on a
business or an activity, for example in order to

make money from it in the future: *We sank all
our savings into the new company.*
OBJ **a fortune** **SYN** **plough sth into sth**
♦ v + n/pron + prep

sip /sɪp/ (-**pp**-)

'sip at sth to drink sth slowly, taking a very
small amount each time: *She sipped at her coffee.*
OBJ **drink**
♦ v + prep

siphon (*also* **syphon**) /'saɪfn/

ˌsiphon sth ˈoff (**from sth**) (*informal*) to move
money or resources from one place to another,
usually illegally: *She siphoned off profits into her
own bank account.*
OBJ **money, funds** **SYN** **divert sth** (*more formal*)
♦ v + adv + n ♦ v + n/pron + adv

sit /sɪt/ (**sitting**, **sat**, **sat** /sæt/)

ˌsit aˈround; ˌsit aˈround sth (*BrE also* ˌsit
aˈbout/'round, ˌsit aˈbout/'round sth) to spend
time sitting down doing very little: *I'm far too
busy to sit around here all day.* ◇ *We sat about
talking for most of the morning.* ◇ *All we could
do was sit around and wait.* ◇ *They were sitting
around the house chatting.*
♦ v + adv + n ♦ v + prep

ˌsit ˈback **1** to sit or lean comfortably in a chair:
He sat back in his chair and closed his eyes.
2 (**and do sth**) to relax, especially by not getting
too involved in or anxious about sth: *Now all the
work's done we can **sit back and** enjoy things!*
◇ *Are you going to sit back and let me do
everything?*
♦ v + adv

'sit ˈby to do nothing to stop sth bad or
unpleasant happening: *I'm not going to sit by
and let an innocent man go to jail.*
SYN **stand by**
♦ v + adv

ˌsit ˈdown **1** to lower your body until you are
sitting on a chair, etc.: *Please sit down!* ◇ *We sat
down on the sofa.* ◇ *When everyone was sitting
down, he began.* → see also SIT YOURSELF DOWN;
↺ note on page 290 **2** (**and do sth**) to give time
and attention to sth in order to try to solve a
problem or achieve sth: *We've never actually **sat
down and** talked the problem through.* **3** (**with
sb**) to meet with sb to discuss sth: *If you're
feeling undervalued, it might be a good idea to sit
down with your boss and talk about it.*
♦ v + adv

▸ 'sit-down *n* **1** [C] a strike, protest, etc.
involving people sitting down and refusing to
leave a place: *to stage a sit-down* ◇ *a sit-down
protest* **2** [sing.] (*BrE, informal*) a short rest while
sitting: *I need a sit-down.* **3** [C] (*AmE*) a meeting
to discuss sth: *Oprah will host a sit-down with
some of Hollywood's hottest stars.*

sit down

be seated ◆ **sit (yourself) down** ◆ **take a seat**

These verbs all mean to rest your weight on your bottom with your back upright, for example on a chair.

be seated (*formal*) to be sitting: *She was seated at the head of the table.* ◇ *Wait until all the guests are seated.* **NOTE Be seated** is often used as a formal way of inviting sb to sit down: *Please be seated.*

sit (yourself) down to move from a standing position to a sitting position: *Please sit down.* ◇ *He sat down on the bed.* ◇ *Come in and sit yourselves down.* **NOTE Sit** can be used on its own: *May I sit here?*

take a seat to sit down **NOTE Take a seat** is used especially as a polite way of inviting sb

to sit down: *Please take a seat. I'll be with you shortly.*

WHICH WORD?

All of these are used to ask people to sit. **(Please) be seated** is the most formal, and **sit yourself down** is the least formal. **Sit**, **be sitting** and **be seated** can also refer to the position sb is in: *He sat and stared at the letter in front of him.* ◇ *Where were you sitting?* ◇ *We were seated in the front row.*

PATTERNS AND COLLOCATIONS

- to sit/sit down/be seated/take a seat **on/in** sth
- to sit/sit down/be seated **astride** sth
- to sit/sit down/be seated/take a seat **beside/opposite/next to** sb/sth

---

▶ **'sit-down** *adj* [only before noun] a **sit-down meal**, etc. is one where people sit on chairs instead of standing up

sit 'sb down to help or persuade sb to sit down either for a rest or to discuss sth: *She sat him down in front of the fire.* ◇ *We need to sit him down and explain the situation.* **NOTE** Not used in the passive.
◆ v + n/pron + adv

sit yourself 'down (*informal*) to lower your body until you are sitting on a chair, etc.: *Come in and sit yourself down.*
→ see also SIT DOWN 1
◆ v + pron + adv

sit for sb/sth to be a model for an artist or a photographer: *She sat for some of the most famous artists of her day.*
◆ v + prep

sit 'in (on sth) to attend a meeting, a class, etc. to watch it, not to take part: *I was allowed to sit in on the meeting.* ◇ *I sat in on some English classes.*
◆ v + adv

▶ **'sit-in** *n* a form of protest in which people refuse to leave a factory, a building, etc.: *Workers decided to stage a sit-in.*

sit 'in for sb to do sb's job or perform sb's duties while they are away: *The chief reporter often sat in for George as editor.*
SYN stand in for sb
◆ v + adv + prep

sit on sth 1 to be a member of a group of people such as a committee: *How many people sit on the committee?* ◇ *My mother sat on the jury during a famous murder trial.* **OBJ committee**, **council**
2 (*informal*) to do nothing about a letter, report, etc. that sb has sent you: *They've been sitting on my application for a month now.*
◆ v + prep

IDM sit on the 'fence to avoid becoming involved in deciding or influencing sth: *You can't go on sitting on the fence trying not to upset anybody.* **(be) sitting on a 'fortune/'gold mine** (*informal*) to own sth very valuable, often when you do not realize it: *His paintings are in great demand. If you have one, you could be sitting on a gold mine.*

sit 'out to sit outside somewhere rather than inside: *It's too cold now to sit out.* ◇ *Let's sit out on the balcony.*
◆ v + adv

sit sth 'out 1 to not take part in a dance, game or other activity: *I think I'm going to sit this one out.* **OBJ dance 2** to stay in a place and wait for sth unpleasant or boring to finish: *to sit out a recession/slump/war* ◇ *We'll just have to sit it out here until things improve.*
NOTE Not used in the passive.
◆ v + adv + n ◆ v + pron + adv ◆ v + n + adv (*rare*)

sit over sth to have a meal or a drink in a slow relaxed way: *We sat over breakfast and planned the day ahead.*
OBJ breakfast, **dinner**, etc.
◆ v + prep

sit 'round; **sit 'round sth** (*BrE*) → SIT AROUND, SIT AROUND STH

sit through sth to stay until the end of a performance, speech, meeting, etc. that you think is boring or too long: *We had to sit through a whole dinner without a cigarette.* ◇ *I can't sit through four hours of Shakespeare!*
◆ v + prep

sit 'up 1 to be or to move yourself into a sitting position, for example, from lying down: *He sat up, turned the light on, and looked at his watch.* ◇ *Do you feel well enough to sit up yet?* **2** to not go to bed until later than usual: *We sat up late*

watching a movie. **SYN** **stay up 3 (and do sth)** to suddenly give your attention to sth: *We need an advert that will make people **sit up and take notice**.* ◇ *This will make them sit up and listen.*
♦ v + adv

▶ **'sit-up** *n* an exercise in which you move from lying down to a sitting position: *I do about sixty sit-ups a day.*

,**sit sb 'up** to move sb from lying to a sitting position: *She sat the baby up in the pram.*
♦ v + n/pron + adv

size /saɪz/

,**size sb/sth 'up** (*informal*) to form a judgement or an opinion of sb/sth: *The two opponents were sizing each other up.* ◇ *I sized up the situation very quickly.*
OBJ situation **SYN** sum sb/sth up (as sb/sth)
♦ v + n/pron + adv ♦ v + adv + n

skate /skeɪt/

,**skate 'over/a'round sth** (*BrE also* ,**skate 'round sth**) to talk about sth difficult or embarrassing quickly, without giving attention to details: *She skated over the next part of her story.*
♦ v + prep

sketch /sketʃ/

,**sketch sth 'in 1** to give more information or details about sth: *He sketched in the background to the case.* ◇ *I'll sketch in the details later for you.* ◇ *You need to sketch in his character a little more.* **OBJ** background, history **2** to add sth to a drawing quickly or roughly: *She sketched in a few more trees.* ◇ *I sketched in the outline of the house.*
♦ v + adv + n ♦ v + n/pron + adv

,**sketch sth 'out 1** to draw all the main features of sth without showing exact details: *He sketched out some preliminary designs.* **2** to give a brief general description of a plan or an idea: *She sketched out the plots of her novels in an exercise book.* **SYN** outline sth (*more formal*)
♦ v + adv + n ♦ v + n/pron + adv

skim /skɪm/ (-mm-)

,**skim sth 'off 1** to remove a substance such as fat from the surface of a liquid: *Skim off the fat and reheat the stew.* **2** to take the best part of sth for yourself, often in an unfair or dishonest way: *She's been skimming off a percentage of the profits for years.*
♦ v + adv + n ♦ v + n/pron + adv

,**skim 'through sth** to read sth very quickly in order to get a general impression or to find a particular point: *I only had time to skim through the report.* ◇ *He skimmed through the article trying to find his name.*
OBJ book, letter
♦ v + prep

skimp /skɪmp/

'**skimp on sth** to spend less money or time on sth than is normal or necessary: *Older people shouldn't skimp on food or heating.*
SYN hold back on sth
♦ v + prep

skin /skɪn/

,**skin 'up** (*informal*) to make a cigarette containing an illegal drug (**marijuana**)
♦ v + adv

skip /skɪp/ (-pp-)

,**skip 'off** (*BrE*) (*also* ,**skip 'out** *AmE, BrE*) (*informal*) to leave a place secretly or suddenly, especially for a dishonest reason, for example to avoid paying for sth: *They skipped off without paying.*
♦ v + adv

,**skip 'out on sb/sth** (*AmE, informal*) to leave sb, especially when they need you; to try to avoid a difficult situation by leaving a place: *He just skipped out on his wife leaving her with four kids to take care of.* ◇ *He was found 22 years after he skipped out on drugs charges.*
SYN run out on sb (*especially BrE*)
♦ v + adv + prep

skirt /skɜːt; AmE skɜːrt/

,**skirt a'round sth** (*BrE also* ,**skirt 'round sth**) **1** to be or move around the edge: *We skirted around the pond and crossed the bridge.* **2** to avoid discussing or dealing with a difficult or embarrassing subject: *She tactfully skirted around the subject of money.* ◇ *The issue was skirted around for years.* **OBJ** subject, question
NOTE Skirt sth is also used on its own with both these meanings: *the road that skirted the lake* ◇ *to skirt laws/duties.*
♦ v + prep

skive /skaɪv/

,**skive 'off**; ,**skive 'off sth** (*BrE, informal*) to avoid work or school by staying away or leaving early: *I can skive off for a few hours.* ◇ *I decided to skive off school.*
OBJ school, work **SYN** bunk off, bunk off sth (*BrE*)
NOTE Skive can also be used on its own, but not skive sth: *Where's Tom? I expect he's skiving again!*
♦ v + adv ♦ v + prep

slack /slæk/

,**slack 'off** to do sth more slowly or work less hard than before: *We can't slack off until everything is finished.*
SYN ease off
♦ v + adv

slacken

slacken /ˈslækən/

,**slacken 'off** to become less busy or active: *We've been really busy, but things are starting to slacken off now.*
  ◆ v + adv

slag /slæɡ/ (**-gg-**)

,**slag sb/sth 'off** (*BrE, slang*) to criticize sb/sth in a cruel, unkind way: *He's always slagging his brother off.*
  SYN **run sb/sth down** (*BrE*); **cut sb/sth down** (*AmE, more formal*)
  ◆ v + n/pron + adv ◆ v + adv + n

slam /slæm/ (**-mm-**)

,**slam a'gainst sb/sth, etc.** → SLAM INTO/ AGAINST SB/STH, ETC.

,**slam sth 'down** (**on/onto sth**) to put sth down with a lot of force, especially when you are angry: *She slammed the book down on the table.* ◇ *I slammed down the phone* (= put the receiver down and ended the phone conversation) *in a rage.*
  OBJ **phone, receiver**
  ◆ v + n/pron + adv ◆ v + adv + n

,**slam 'into/a'gainst sb/sth**; ,**slam sb/sth 'into/a'gainst sb/sth** to crash, or to make sth crash, into sth with a lot of force: *The jeep slammed into the wall.* ◇ *In the crash she was slammed against the back of the seat.*
  ⊃ note at CRASH INTO SB/STH
  ◆ v + prep ◆ v + n/pron + prep

,**slam sth 'on** if you **slam on the brakes** of a vehicle, you operate them suddenly and with force: *A child suddenly ran out into the road and I had to slam on the brakes.*
  OBJ only **brakes** **SYN** **jam sth on**
  ◆ v + adv + n ◆ v + n/pron + adv

slap /slæp/ (**-pp-**)

,**slap sb a'bout/a'round** (*informal, especially BrE*) to hit sb regularly or often, used especially of a man hitting a woman: *He used to come back drunk and slap his wife around.*
  SYN **knock sb around**
  ◆ v + n/pron + adv

,**slap sb 'down** (*informal*) to criticize sb or their ideas or suggestions in an unfair way, often in public: *He tried to object, but was immediately slapped down.* ◇ *If you ask a question, she just slaps you down.*
  SYN **cut sb down** (*AmE*)
  ◆ v + n/pron + adv ◆ v + adv + n

,**slap sth 'down** (**on/onto sth**) to put sth onto a surface in a quick and often noisy way, especially because you are angry: *He slapped down a copy of the book on the table.*
  ◆ v + n/pron + adv ◆ v + adv + n

,**slap sth 'on**; ,**slap sth on sb/sth** (*informal*) to announce suddenly that sb must have a punishment, obey a new rule, etc., often when this

is unfair: *Judges have been slapping on longer prison sentences.* ◇ *The government slapped a new tax on high earners.*
  ◆ v + n/pron + prep

,**slap sth 'on**; ,**slap sth 'on/'onto sth** (*informal*) to spread a substance on a surface quickly and carelessly: *I'd better slap some make-up on before I go out.*
  OBJ **paint, make-up**
  ◆ v + n/pron + adv ◆ v + adv + n ◆ v + n/pron + prep

,**slap sth on sth** (*informal*) to increase the price of sth suddenly: *They've slapped 50p on the price of cigarettes.*
  ◆ v + n/pron + prep

,**slap sth 'onto sth** → SLAP STH ON, SLAP STH ON/ONTO STH

,**slap sb 'up** (*slang*) to hit sb hard with your hand, many times
  ◆ v + n/pron + adv ◆ v + adv + n (*rare*)

slash /slæʃ/

'**slash at sb/sth** (**with sth**) to attack sb violently with a knife, etc. and try to cut them/it: *He slashed at his opponent's face with a knife.*
  ◆ v + prep

slave /sleɪv/

,**slave a'way** (**at sth**) (*usually used in the progressive tenses*) used to emphasize how hard you are working, especially when you think people do not recognize this or feel grateful: *I've been slaving away all day trying to get this work finished.*
  ◆ v + adv

sleep /sliːp/ (**slept, slept** /slept/)

,**sleep a'round** (*informal, disapproving*) to have sex with many different partners
  ◆ v + adv

,**sleep 'in 1** to remain in bed longer than usual in the morning: *She usually sleeps in on Sundays.* **SYN** **lie in** (*BrE, informal*) **2** (*ScotE*) to sleep longer than you intended: *I slept in and missed the bus.* **SYN** **oversleep**
  ◆ v + adv

,**sleep sth 'off** to get better after sth, especially drinking too much alcohol, by sleeping: *He's still sleeping off yesterday's hangover.* ◇ *Go home and sleep it off.*
  ◆ v + adv + n ◆ v + n/pron + adv

'**sleep on sth** to delay making a decision about sth until the next day so that you can think about it: *Sleep on it and let me know tomorrow.*
  ◆ v + prep

,**sleep 'out** to sleep outdoors: *We slept out most nights when we were in Greece.*
  ◆ v + adv

,**sleep 'over** to stay the night at sb else's home: *The kids are sleeping over with friends.* ◇ *It's very late now—why don't you sleep over?*
  ◆ v + adv

▶ **'sleepover** *n* a party for children or young people when a group of them spend the night at one house

,sleep 'through sth to not be woken up by sth such as a loud noise or a lot of activity: *She slept right through the thunderstorm.* ◇ *I'm afraid I slept through the alarm.* ◇ *Did he sleep through the whole incident?*
♦ v + prep

'sleep together; **'sleep with sb** (*informal*) to have sex with sb, especially sb you are not married to: *They have been sleeping together for months now.*
♦ v + adv ♦ v + prep

slice /slaɪs/

,slice sth 'off; **,slice sth 'off sth 1** to remove a thin piece of sth from sth larger by cutting: *The top of his finger was sliced off in an accident.* ◇ *She sliced a piece of meat off the joint.* **2** to reduce sth by a particular amount: *He sliced two seconds off the world record.*
♦ v + adv + n ♦ v + n/pron + adv ♦ v + n/pron + prep

,slice 'through sth (*especially BrE*) to pass through sth very easily: *The axe sliced through the wood like butter.* ◇ (*figurative*) *He sliced through all my objections.*
♦ v + prep

,slice sth 'up to cut sth into flat thin pieces: *Would you slice the cucumber up?*
♦ v + n/pron + adv ♦ v + adv + n

slick /slɪk/

,slick sth 'back/'down if you **slick** your hair **back/down**, you make it lie flat by putting oil, water, etc. on it: *His hair was slicked back.* ◇ *He still slicks down his hair with oil.*
OBJ **hair**
NOTE Often used in the passive.
♦ v + n/pron + adv ♦ v + adv + n

slim /slɪm/ (-mm-)

,slim 'down to become thinner, for example as a result of eating less: *She slimmed down to 60 kilos before her wedding.*
SYN **trim down**
♦ v + adv

,slim 'down; **,slim sth 'down** to make sth, such as an organization or a company, smaller by employing fewer people, reducing the amount of work done, etc.: *The coal industry has had to slim down.* ◇ *The firm had to slim down its workforce.* ◇ *a slimmed-down curriculum*
SYN **trim down, trim sth down**
♦ v + adv ♦ v + adv + n ♦ v + n/pron + adv

sling /slɪŋ/

,sling 'off at sb (*AustralE, informal*) to laugh at sb in an unkind way
♦ v + adv + prep

slip /slɪp/ (-pp-)

,slip a'way 1 (*also* **,slip 'off**) to leave quietly without attracting attention: *I slipped away to my room to write some letters.* ◇ *He managed to slip off alone for an hour.* **2** (*also* **,slip 'by**) if a period of time **slips away**, it passes more quickly than you realize: *She could see her childhood slipping away.* ◇ *The afternoon slipped by.* **3** (**from sb**) to disappear; to die or to stop existing: *He slipped away peacefully during the night.* ◇ *I felt the game was slipping away from me* (= I was losing).
♦ v + adv

,slip 'by 1 → SLIP AWAY 2: *Time just seemed to slip by.* **2** if an opportunity, etc. **slips by**, it passes and you do not use it: *I try never to let a chance to travel slip by.*
♦ v + adv

,slip sth 'in; **,slip sth 'into sth** to add sth to a speech, conversation or written text quickly or secretly: *He usually slips a couple of jokes into his lectures.* ◇ *She slipped in a few comments about her boyfriend.*
♦ v + adv + n ♦ v + n/pron + adv ♦ v + n/pron + prep

,slip 'into sth 1 to put clothes on quickly and easily: *I'll just slip into something more comfortable.* OBJ **dress, shoes, etc.** OPP **slip out of sth**
→ see also SLIP STH OFF; SLIP STH ON **2** to pass into a particular state or situation, especially a difficult or unpleasant one: *The patient slipped into a coma.* ◇ *The economy has slipped into recession.* OBJ **coma, sleep, recession, debt**
♦ v + prep

,slip 'off → SLIP AWAY 1
,slip sth 'off to take clothes or shoes off quickly and easily: *She slipped her shoes off by the door.* ◇ *Slip off your coat and I'll make some tea.*
OBJ **coat, shoes, etc.** OPP **slip sth on**
→ see also SLIP INTO STH; SLIP OUT OF STH
♦ v + n/pron + adv ♦ v + adv + n

,slip sth 'on to put clothes or shoes on quickly and easily: *Hold on, I'll just slip my coat on, then I'll be ready.*
OBJ **shoes, jacket, etc.** OPP **slip sth off**
→ see also SLIP INTO STH; SLIP OUT OF STH
♦ v + n/pron + adv ♦ v + adv + n

▶ **'slip-on** *n* [usually pl.] a shoe that you can put on and take off quickly and easily without having to tie or fasten anything: *a pair of cheap slip-ons* ◇ *slip-on shoes*

,slip 'out (*informal*) if sth **slips out**, you say it when you do not intend to: *I didn't mean to tell him—it just slipped out.*
♦ v + adv

,slip 'out of sth to take off clothes quickly and easily: *She slipped out of her clothes and got into the shower.*
OBJ **clothes, dress, etc.** OPP **slip into sth**
→ see also SLIP STH OFF; SLIP STH ON
♦ v + prep ♦ v + adv + prep

,**slip** '**over** to slide a short distance and fall: *He slipped over on the ice and broke his leg.*
♦ v + adv

,**slip** '**through**; ,**slip** '**through sth** if sth or sth **slips through** or **slips through** a system, etc., a person or a system fails to find and deal with it/them: *Mistakes occasionally slip through.* ◊ *Somehow he slipped through the company's screening process.*
♦ v + adv ♦ v + prep

IDM (**let sth**) **slip through your** '**fingers** if sb/sth **slips through your fingers**, you fail to keep or use it/them: *The thief had slipped through their fingers yet again.* ◊ *You've let your chances slip through your fingers.* **slip through the** '**net** when sb/sth slips through the net, an organization or a system fails to find them and deal with them: *We tried to contact all the former students, but some slipped through the net.*

,**slip** '**up** (**over sth**) (*informal*) to make a careless mistake: *I slipped up over the date of the meeting.* ◊ *He slipped up in his calculations.* ◊ *We slipped up there, didn't we?*
♦ v + adv
▶ '**slip-up** *n* (*informal*) a careless mistake: *One small slip-up could cost us the election.*

slob /slɒb; *AmE* slɑːb/ (**-bb-**)

,**slob** a'**round**/'**out**; ,**slob** a'**round sth** (*BrE, slang*) to spend time being lazy and doing nothing: *We just slobbed out in front of the telly last night.* ◊ *Are you going to slob around in your pyjamas all morning?* ◊ *I decided to slob around the campsite instead of going swimming.*
♦ v + adv ♦ v + prep

slobber /'slɒbə(r); *AmE* 'slɑːb-/

'**slobber over sb/sth** (*informal*) to show, without any pride or control, how much you like or want sb/sth: *I know he's in love with you but does he have to slobber over you in public?*
♦ v + prep

slog /slɒg; *AmE* slɑːg/ (**-gg-**)

,**slog** a'**way** (**at sth**) (*informal*) to work hard and steadily at sth, especially a boring or difficult task, for a long time: *He slogged away at that report for weeks.*
♦ v + adv

,**slog it** '**out** (*BrE, informal*) → SLUG IT OUT

,**slog** '**through sth** (*informal*) to work hard and steadily at sth, especially a boring or difficult task, for a long time: *I seem to have been slogging through this book for weeks.*
♦ v + prep

slop /slɒp; *AmE* slɑːp/ (**-pp-**)

,**slop** a'**bout**/a'**round 1** (**in sth**) (of a liquid) to move around in a container, often so that some liquid comes over the edge: *Water was slopping about in the bottom of the boat.* **SYN slosh**

around/**about 2** (**in sth**) to move around in water, mud, etc.: *She slopped around in the cooling water.* **SYN slosh around**/**about 3** (*BrE, informal, disapproving*) to spend time relaxing or being lazy: *She used to slop around all day in old jeans and sweatshirts.* **SYN slouch about**/**around** (*BrE*); **hang around**

,**slop** '**out** (*BrE*) when prisoners **slop out**, they empty the containers that they use as toilets
♦ v + adv

,**slop** '**over**; ,**slop** '**over sth** (of a liquid) to move around in a container so much that some liquid comes out over the edge: *Some tea had slopped over into the saucer.* ◊ *Water slopped over the edge of the bath.*
♦ v + adv ♦ v + prep

slope /sləʊp; *AmE* sloʊp/

,**slope** '**off** (*BrE, informal*) to go away, especially without being noticed, in order to avoid doing work, talking to sb, etc.: *He always slopes off if there's any work to be done.* ◊ *Where are you trying to slope off to?*
♦ v + adv

slosh /slɒʃ; *AmE* slɑːʃ/

,**slosh** a'**round** (*also* ,**slosh** a'**bout** *especially BrE*) (**in sth**) (*informal*) **1** (of a liquid) to move around noisily in a container: *The water was sloshing about in the bucket.* **SYN slop about**/**around 2** to move around noisily in sth liquid: *The children were sloshing around in the puddles.* **SYN slop about**/**around 3** (*BrE*) (especially of money) to be present in large quantities: *There seems to be lots of money sloshing around in professional tennis.*
♦ v + adv

slot /slɒt; *AmE* slɑːt/ (**-tt-**)

,**slot** '**in**; ,**slot** '**into sth** if sth **slots in** or **slots into sth**, it fits easily and exactly into a space, especially the space made or designed for it: *This bit slots in neatly just here.* ◊ *This piece is meant to slot into this groove.* ◊ (*figurative*) *I didn't understand everything at the time, but later it all slotted into place.*
→ see also SLOT STH IN, SLOT STH INTO STH
♦ v + adv ♦ v + prep

,**slot sb/sth** '**in** to manage to find a time to see sb or to do sth: *I can slot you in tomorrow at four.*
SYN fit sb/sth in
♦ v + n/pron + adv ♦ v + adv + n

,**slot sth** '**in**; ,**slot sth** '**into sth** to put sth into a space that is available or designed for it: *He slotted a coin into the machine.* ◊ (*figurative*) *The final pieces of the puzzle had been slotted into place.*
→ see also SLOT IN, SLOT INTO STH
♦ v + n/pron + adv ♦ v + adv + n ♦ v + n/pron + prep

,slot to'gether; ,slot A and B to'gether if two things **slot together**, or sb **slots them together**, they fit together easily and exactly: *The base comes in sections that simply slot together.* ◇ *The parts are ready to be slotted together.*
◆ v + adv ◆ v + n/pron + adv ◆ v + adv + n

slouch /slaʊtʃ/

,slouch a'bout/a'round; ,slouch a'bout/ a'round sth (*BrE, disapproving*) to spend time relaxing or being lazy: *He slouches around all day reading comics.* ◇ *She wasted the day slouching about the house.*
SYN slop about/around (*BrE*); **hang around**
◆ v + adv ◆ v + prep

slough /slʌf/

,slough sth 'off **1** to remove or get rid of a layer of dead skin, etc.: *Slough off dry skin once a week.* **SYN** shed sth **2** (*formal*) to get rid of sth that you no longer want: *He was not able to slough off the memories of the past.* ◇ *Responsibilities are not sloughed off so easily.*
◆ v + adv + n ◆ v + pron + adv ◆ v + n + adv (*rare*)

slow /sləʊ; AmE sloʊ/

,slow 'down; ,slow sb/sth 'down (*also* ,slow 'up, ,slow sb/sth 'up *less frequent*) **1** to go, or to make sb/sth go, at a slower speed: *Slow down, I can't keep up with you.* ◇ *The bus slowed up as it approached the junction.* ◇ *The heat slowed us down.* ◇ *The roadworks are slowing the traffic up in the mornings.* **2** to be less active or develop more slowly; to make sb/sth do this: *He looks ill, he should slow down.* ◇ *The economy has slowed down.* ◇ *They claim they can slow up the ageing process.*
◆ v + adv ◆ v + n/pron + adv ◆ v + adv + n
▶ '**slowdown** *n* **1** a decrease in the rate of activity or production: *a slowdown in the economy* **2** (*AmE*) a protest that workers make by doing their work more slowly than usual: *The union threatened a slowdown if their demands were not met.*

slug /slʌg/ (-gg-)

,slug it 'out (*BrE also* ,slog it 'out) (*informal*) to fight; to compete until sb has won: *The two companies slugged it out for their share of the market.* ◇ *The Democrats and the Republicans will be slugging it out in November.*
◆ v + it + adv

sluice /sluːs/

,sluice sth 'down/'out (*especially BrE*) to wash or clean the surface of sth with large amounts of water: *They sluice the streets down every morning.* ◇ *An attendant was sluicing out the changing rooms.*
◆ v + adv + n ◆ v + n/pron + adv

smack /smæk/

'smack of sth to seem to contain an unpleasant attitude or quality: *His comments smack of racism.*
◆ v + prep

,smack sb 'up (*slang*) to hit sb hard with your hand, many times
◆ v + n/pron + adv ◆ v + adv + n (*rare*)

smart /smɑːt; AmE smɑːrt/

,smart 'off (**to sb**) (*AmE, informal*) to say sth that does not show respect to sb in authority: *You are more likely to get a ticket from a cop if you smart off to him or her.*
◆ v + adv

smarten /'smɑːtn; AmE 'smɑːrtn/

,smarten 'up **1** (*also* ,smarten yourself 'up) to make yourself neater, tidier, or more attractive: *You need to smarten (yourself) up before you go out.* **SYN** spruce yourself up **2** (*especially AmE*) to become more clever and aware of things: *You'll have to smarten up if you want to pass those exams.*
◆ v + adv **1** also v + pron + adv

'smarten sb/sth 'up (*especially BrE*) to make a person or a place neater, tidier or more attractive: *The hotel has been smartened up by the new owners.* ◇ *She did her best to smarten her husband up.*
SYN spruce sb/sth up
◆ v + adv + n ◆ v + n/pron + adv

smash /smæʃ/

,smash sth 'down to make sth fall by hitting it very hard and breaking it: *The police decided to smash the door down.*
OBJ door
◆ v + n/pron + adv ◆ v + adv + n

,smash sth 'in to make a hole in sth or destroy it by hitting it very hard: *The doll's face had been smashed in.* ◇ (*informal*) *He threatened to smash my head in* (= hit my head very hard).
OBJ door, face, head **SYN** bash sth in (*informal, especially BrE*)
◆ v + n/pron + adv ◆ v + adv + n

,smash 'into sb/sth (of a vehicle or a driver) to hit sb/sth very hard, causing damage: *The car smashed into a tree.* ◇ *I smashed into the car in front.*
➷ note at CRASH INTO SB/STH
◆ v + prep

,smash sth 'up to damage or destroy sth by hitting it very hard: *A bunch of thugs broke in and smashed the place up.* ◇ *He smashed his car up last week* (= he had a crash).
OBJ car, things, place
➷ note at BREAK STH UP
◆ v + n/pron + adv ◆ v + adv + n

smell /smel/ (**smelled**, **smelled**, *BrE also* **smelt**, **smelt** /smelt/)

⚡'smell of sth to have the smell of sth: *The baby smelled of soap and milk.* ◇ *Can you put your cigarette out? I don't want my room smelling of smoke.*
♦ v + prep

IDM **come up/out of sth smelling of 'roses** (*informal*) to still have a good reputation, even though you have been involved in sth that might have given people a bad opinion of you

,smell sb/sth 'out 1 to be aware of fear, danger, trouble, etc. in a situation: *He could smell out weakness in others.* **2** (of dogs) to find sb/sth, by smelling: *The dogs are trained to smell out drugs.*
SYN **sniff sb/sth out**
♦ v + adv + n ♦ v + n/pron + adv

,smell sth 'out (*BrE*) (*AmE* **smell sth 'up**) to fill a place with an unpleasant smell: *That fish smelt the whole house out.* ◇ *I burned some milk and smelled up the whole house.*
SYN **stink sth out** (*BrE*); **stink sth up** (*AmE*)
♦ v + n/pron + adv ♦ v + adv + n

smile /smaɪl/

'smile on/upon sb/sth (*formal* or *literary*) if **fortune, fate, etc. smiles on you**, you are very lucky and successful: *Fortune smiled on us that night and the plane landed safely.*
→ see also **FROWN ON SB/STH**
♦ v + prep

smoke /sməʊk; *AmE* smoʊk/

,smoke sb/sth 'out 1 to make sb/sth come out of a place by filling it with smoke: *The fire is used to smoke the bees out.* **2** to find sb/sth that is causing a problem; to make sth that is secret publicly known: *The police are determined to smoke out the leaders of the gang.*
♦ v + adv + n ♦ v + n/pron + adv

smooth /smuːð/

,smooth sth a'way/'out to reduce or remove problems and difficulties: *The group was set up to smooth away local difficulties.* ◇ *His anxieties were quickly smoothed away.*
♦ v + adv + n ♦ v + n/pron + adv

,smooth sth 'down to make your hair or your clothes smooth and flat with your hands: *He smoothed down his hair.*
OBJ **hair, skirt**
♦ v + adv + n ♦ v + n/pron + adv

,smooth sth 'out 1 to make sth such as a piece of paper or cloth smooth and flat with your hands: *She tried to smooth out the crumpled letter.* **OBJ** **wrinkles, paper 2** → SMOOTH STH AWAY/OUT: *We are here to smooth out any practical problems for you.* **OBJ** **differences, problems**
♦ v + adv + n ♦ v + n/pron + adv

,smooth sth 'over to make a problem or difficulty seem less serious or easier to deal with, especially by talking to the people involved: *She tried to calm her parents down and smooth things over.* ◇ *The leaders managed to smooth over their differences.*
OBJ **differences, things**
♦ v + adv + n ♦ v + n/pron + adv

snack /snæk/

'snack on sth to eat small amounts of food between or instead of meals: *It's healthier to snack on fruit rather than chocolate.*
♦ v + prep

snap /snæp/ (**-pp-**)

,snap 'back (**into sth**) (*AmE*) → BOUNCE BACK (FROM STH): *After the initial shock, he soon snapped back.* ◇ *She snapped back into her daily routine soon after the operation.*
SYN **recover** (**from sth**)
♦ v + adv

,snap sth 'off; **,snap sth 'off sth**; **,snap 'off** to break sth suddenly with a sharp noise; to be broken in this way: *He snapped a twig off a bush.* ◇ *The branch she was standing on must have snapped off.*
➲ note at BREAK OFF, BREAK STH OFF
♦ v + adv + n ♦ v + n/pron + adv
♦ v + n/pron + prep

,snap sth 'out to say sth in a sharp or unpleasant way: *The sergeant snapped out an order.*
NOTE **Snap sth** can be used on its own with this meaning: *She snapped instructions to the team.*
♦ v + adv + n ♦ v + pron + adv
♦ v + n + adv (*less frequent*) ♦ v + adv + speech

,snap 'out of sth; **,snap sb 'out of sth** (*informal*) to make yourself, or help sb else, stop feeling upset, in a bad mood, etc.: *Come on, Joe. Snap out of it.* ◇ *She was snapped out of her reverie by the sound of the door opening.*
♦ v + adv + prep ♦ v + n/pron + adv + prep

,snap 'to it (*informal*) used to tell sb to start working harder or more quickly: *This place has to be clean by this evening so snap to it!*
♦ v + prep + it

,snap sb/sth 'up to buy or take sth quickly and with enthusiasm: *Fans quickly snapped up the tickets.* ◇ (*figurative*) *He was snapped up by United.*
♦ v + adv + n ♦ v + n/pron + adv

snarl /snɑːl; *AmE* snɑːrl/

,snarl 'up; **,snarl sth 'up** if sth **snarls up**, or sth **snarls** it **up**, it becomes so confused, twisted, etc. that no part of it can move: *The dog's lead got snarled up in a bush.* ◇ *The traffic snarls up at that junction every evening.* ◇ *The accident snarled up the traffic for the whole day.*

NOTE Often used in the passive with *get*: *The city centre gets snarled up with tourists in the summer.*

◆ v + adv ◆ v + adv + n ◆ v + n/pron + adv

▸ **'snarl-up** *n* (*BrE, informal*) a situation in which traffic is unable to move

snatch /snætʃ/

'snatch at sth 1 to try to take hold of sth: *She snatched at the letter in his hand.* **2** (*BrE*) to take an opportunity to do sth quickly and with enthusiasm: *They snatched at the chance to be happy.*

◆ v + prep

sneak /sniːk/

NOTE The usual past form is **sneaked**, but **snuck** is now common in informal speech, especially in American English. However, many people consider it incorrect.

,sneak 'up (on sb) to approach sb very quietly, so that they do not see or hear you until you reach them: *He loves sneaking up on me to scare me.*
◇ *She snuck up behind them and suddenly shouted.*

◆ v + adv

sniff /snɪf/

,sniff a'round; **,sniff a'round sth/sb** (*BrE also* **,sniff 'round**, **,sniff 'round sth/sb**) (*informal*) to go somewhere to try to find secret information about sth/sb or to look for a particular person or thing: *The studio was sniffing around for new talent.* ◇ *It won't be long before the press come sniffing around the club.*

◆ v + adv ◆ v + prep

'sniff at sth (*informal*) to show a lack of interest in or respect for sth: *At first he sniffed at her foreign ways.*

◆ v + prep

IDM **not to be 'sniffed at** (*informal*) good enough to be accepted or considered seriously: *Her achievement is not to be sniffed at.*

,sniff sb/sth 'out 1 (especially of dogs) to find sb/sth by smelling: *These dogs can sniff out explosives.* **SYN** **smell sb/sth out 2** (*informal*) to find information about sth/sb: *journalists trained to sniff out a scandal* ◇ *They're quick to sniff out a deception.* **SYN** **nose sth out**

◆ v + adv + n ◆ v + n/pron + adv

,sniff 'round, etc. (*BrE*) → SNIFF AROUND, ETC.

snow /snəʊ; AmE snoʊ/

be/get ,snowed 'in/'up to be unable to go anywhere or leave a place because of heavy snow: *We got snowed in for three days.*

◆ be/get + v + adv

be/get ,snowed 'under (**with sth**) to have so much work that you have problems dealing

with it: *We're snowed under with work at the moment.*

◆ be/get + v + adv

be/get ,snowed 'up (*BrE*) **1** → BE/GET SNOWED IN/UP **2** (of a road, etc.) to be/become blocked with snow: *The driveway was still snowed up.*

◆ be/get + v + adv

snuff /snʌf/

,snuff sb 'out (especially *AmE*) to kill sb: *He was snuffed out by the Mafia.*

◆ v + n/pron + adv ◆ v + adv + n

,snuff sth 'out 1 to stop a flame from burning: *She snuffed out the candles.* **OBJ** **candle**, **flame** **NOTE** Snuff sth can also be used on its own with this meaning. **2** to suddenly end or destroy sth: *A moment of mindless violence snuffed out his life.* ◇ *The revolution was quickly snuffed out.* **OBJ** **life**, **hope**

◆ v + adv + n ◆ v + n/pron + adv
◆ v + n + adv (*less frequent*)

snuggle /'snʌgl/

,snuggle 'down to make yourself warm and comfortable in your bed: *He snuggled down and went to sleep.*

◆ v + adv

,snuggle 'up (to/against sb/sth), **,snuggle 'up (in sth)** to get into a warm and comfortable position close to sb/sth or in sth: *She snuggled up to him.* ◇ *I'd love to snuggle up in bed right now!* **SYN** **cuddle up (to/against sb)**

◆ v + adv

soak /səʊk; AmE soʊk/

,soak 'in; **,soak 'into sth** (of a liquid) to pass into sth: *Apply the oil to the wood and leave it to soak in.* ◇ *The wine had soaked into the carpet.*

◆ v + adv ◆ v + prep

,soak 'through; **,soak 'through sth** (of a liquid) to pass into or through sth: *Blood had soaked through the bandage.*

◆ v + adv ◆ v + prep

,soak sth 'up 1 to take in or absorb sth, especially a liquid: *Use a paper towel to soak up the excess oil.* ◇ (*figurative*) *The farmers soak up* (= use up) *£1 billion of government aid a year.* **OBJ** **water**, **debts 2** to absorb sth into your senses, your body or your mind: *We walked around the town, soaking up the atmosphere.* **OBJ** **the sun, the atmosphere** **SYN** **absorb sth** (*more formal*)

◆ v + adv + n ◆ v + n/pron + adv (*less frequent*)

sober /'səʊbə(r); AmE 'soʊ-/

,sober 'up; **,sober sb 'up** to become, or to make sb, no longer drunk: *I decided to walk home to sober up.* ◇ *I need a black coffee to sober me up.* ◇ (*figurative, especially BrE*) *We all laughed at what Liam said, but soon sobered up*

(= became serious) *when we saw his wife's expression.*
* v + adv * v + n/pron + adv * v + adv + n

sock /sɒk; *AmE* sɑːk/

,**sock** sth a'**way** (*AmE, informal*) to save money by putting it in a bank or by buying shares in a company, etc.: *She already has $500 socked away for college.* ◊ *He socks away half his salary every month for the house.*
[OBJ] **money**
* v + adv + n * v + n/pron + adv

'**sock it to sb** (*informal* or *humorous*) used to encourage sb to do or say sth that will have a strong effect, for example before an interview, a sports game, etc.: *You'll be fine. Just get in there and sock it to them.*
* v + it + prep

sod /sɒd; *AmE* sɑːd/ (-**dd**-)

,**sod** '**off** (*BrE*, ⚠, *slang*) used to tell sb to go away: *Just sod off and leave me in peace!*
* v + adv

soften /'sɒfn; *AmE* 'sɔːfn/

,**soften sb** '**up** (*informal*) to try to make sb more willing to do sth for you by being very nice to them first: *I know you, you're just trying to soften me up!* ◊ *They softened the voters up with promises they had no intention of keeping.*
[SYN] **butter sb up**
* v + adv + n * v + n/pron + adv

,**soften sb/sth** '**up** to make an enemy weaker and easier to attack: *It'll take more than a few bruises to soften him up.* ◊ *The artillery was used to soften up the advancing enemy.*
* v + n/pron + adv * v + adv + n

soldier /'səʊldʒə(r); *AmE* 'soʊl-/

,**soldier** '**on** (**with sth**) to continue with sth you are doing although it is difficult or unpleasant: *She soldiered on with the course in spite of her personal problems.* ◊ *I'm having to soldier on alone since Bill left.*
* v + adv

sort /sɔːt; *AmE* sɔːrt/

,**sort sb** '**out** (*informal, especially BrE*) to deal with sb who has been causing trouble: *They sent the lads round to sort him out.*
[SYN] **deal with sb**
* v + n/pron + adv * v + adv + n

,**sort sb/yourself** '**out** (*BrE, informal*) **1** to find a solution to sb's/your own problems, etc.: *It took her months to sort herself out after the divorce.* ◊ *He was so upset it took us an hour to calm him down and sort him out.* [SYN] **straighten sb/yourself out 2** to organize sb or yourself: *You load the car and I'll sort the kids out.* ◊ *She's in her room sorting herself out for the trip.*
* v + n/pron + adv

,**sort sb** '**out with sth** (*informal, especially BrE*) to provide sb with sth they need: *I'm sure we can sort you out with some dry clothes.*
* v + n/pron + adv + prep

🔑,**sort sth** '**out 1** to put sth in order; to tidy and organize sth: *I spent the afternoon sorting out my study.* [OBJ] **room, stuff** ⊃ note at TIDY UP **2** (*especially BrE*) to organize or arrange sth: *First you have to sort out a work permit.* **3** (*especially BrE*) to decide on sth: *I need to sort out what clothes to take with me on the trip.* [OBJ] **details, priorities** [NOTE] Usually used with question words such as *what, where*, etc. **4** to solve a problem: *We've sorted the problem out.* [OBJ] **problem, mess 5** (**from sth**) to separate sth from a larger group: *Sort out the ripe pears from the rest.* ◊ *She sorted out the clothes that she didn't wear any more.*
* v + n/pron + adv * v + adv + n
▶ '**sort-out** *n* (*BrE, informal*) an act of arranging or organizing things in a neat and tidy way and getting rid of things you do not want

,**sort itself** '**out** (*especially BrE*) if a problem **sorts itself out**, it stops being a problem without anyone having to do anything: *He woke up feeling ill, but thought the problem would soon sort itself out.*
[SYN] **work itself out**
* v + pron + adv

,**sort** '**through sth** to look through a number of things either in order to find a particular thing or to put them in groups: *She sorted through her wardrobe for something to wear.* ◊ *They sorted through thousands of old photos.*
* v + prep

sound /saʊnd/

,**sound** '**off** (**about sth**) (*informal, disapproving*) to express your opinions loudly or in an aggressive way: *He should check his facts before sounding off like that.*
* v + adv

,**sound sb/sth** '**out** (**about/on sth**) to try to discover sb's views, opinions, etc. on sth, especially in an indirect way: *I want to sound him out about a possible job.* ◊ *We should sound out opinions on these changes.*
* v + adv + n * v + pron + adv
* v + n + adv (*less frequent*)

soup /suːp/

,**soup sth** '**up** (*informal*) if you **soup up** a car, a computer, etc., you make changes to it so that it is more powerful or exciting: *He makes a living buying old cars and souping them up.*
* v + adv + n * v + pron + adv
* v + n + adv (*less frequent*)
▶ '**souped-up** *adj* [only before noun] (*informal*) a **souped-up** car, etc. has been changed to make it more powerful or exciting: *a souped-up Mini*

space /speɪs/

,space 'out; ,space sb 'out (slang, especially
AmE) to be confused, unable to think clearly, or
not aware of what is happening around you, for
example as a result of taking drugs; to put sb in
a state like this: *I was supposed to meet her for
lunch but I spaced out and forgot.* ◇ *The drugs I
was taking for my illness spaced me out so I
couldn't think clearly.*
♦ v + adv ♦ v + n/pron + adv
▸ ,spaced 'out *adj* (slang) confused, unable to
think clearly and not completely conscious of
what is happening around you, for example
because of taking drugs: *He sat in the corner
looking completely spaced out.*
,space sth 'out to arrange things with a regular
distance or time between them, especially a
fairly large amount: *Try spacing the words out
more on the page.* ◇ *Should I space out the baby's
feeds over 24 hours?*
♦ v + n/pron + adv ♦ v + adv + n

spark /spɑːk; AmE spɑːrk/

,spark sth 'off (informal) to cause sth to
suddenly happen or develop: *The incident
sparked off riots across the country.* ◇ *His resignation sparked off a political crisis.*
OBJ **riots, debate, incident, protest, crisis**
NOTE **Spark sth** is also used on its own: *The TV
programme sparked a storm of protest.*
♦ v + adv + n ♦ v + pron + adv ♦ v + n + adv (rare)
,spark 'up if a fire **sparks up**, it starts to burn
brightly again after a period when it was almost
out: *The fire is still smoking and could spark up at
any moment.* ◇ (figurative) *They sparked up
(= became more lively and interested) when
they heard the music.*
♦ v + adv
,spark sth 'up (informal) **1** if you **spark up** a
conversation, a debate, a friendship, etc., you
start one, often suddenly: *I sat down beside
Helen and tried to spark up a conversation with
her.* **2** to add interest or excitement to sth: *Spark
up pasta dishes with fresh herbs.* ◇ *Send a card
and spark up someone's day.* SYN **spice sth up**
3 spark up sth to light a fire, etc.: (slang) *Time to
spark up a cigarette.* ◇ (figurative) *There is
nothing in the book to spark up the reader's
interest.* NOTE When the object of **spark up** is a
noun, it comes after **up**, but when the object is a
pronoun, it comes between **spark** and **up**: *If
your dress looks boring, spark it up with some
sequins.*
♦ v + adv + n ♦ v + pron + adv ♦ v + n + adv (rare)

speak /spiːk/ (past spoke /spəʊk; AmE spoʊk/,
spoken /'spəʊkən; AmE 'spoʊ-/)

'speak for sb **1** to state the wishes or views of
sb; to act as a representative for sb: *I can't speak
for the others, but I'd love to come.* ◇ *She speaks
for a whole generation of disillusioned youngsters.*
SYN **answer for sb 2** to give evidence to
support sb in court: *Many people spoke for her
at the trial.*
♦ v + prep
IDM **speak for it'self/them'selves** if sth **speaks
for itself**, it is so clear and easy to understand
that it does not need to be explained: *The facts
speak for themselves.*
,speak for your'self to express your own
opinion, although you know that others might
not agree with you: *Speaking for myself, I'd
prefer to go by train.* ◇ *He speaks for himself
when he says we need a smoking area.*
♦ v + prep
IDM **speak for my'self/her'self/him'self/them-
'selves** to express your opinion yourself, rather
than sb else doing it for you: *I can speak for
myself, thank you!* **speak for your'self** (informal)
used to tell sb that sth they have said is not true
of you: *'We're all tired.' 'Speak for yourself—I'm
fine!'*
be 'spoken for **1** to be married or to have a
partner already: *You can forget about him, he's
already spoken for!* **2** to be set aside for a
particular purpose: *Half the money is already
spoken for.*
♦ be + v + adv
'speak of sth (formal, literary) to be evidence of
sth; to suggest sth: *The pictures in the room
spoke of dreams of faraway places.*
♦ v + prep
,speak 'out (against/in favour of/on sth) to say
what you think clearly and publicly, often
criticizing or opposing sb/sth, in a way that
needs courage: *People are no longer afraid to
speak out.* ◇ *She spoke out forcefully against the
regime.*
♦ v + adv
▸ out'spoken *adj* saying openly exactly what
you think, even if you know other people will
disagree or be offended: *Her outspoken views
often get her into trouble.*
▸ 'speakout *n* (AmE) an organized public
meeting at which people talk about their
experiences of a particular subject: *Speakouts
are good because they encourage people to talk
about things in a positive way.*
,speak 'up **1** used to ask sb to speak louder:
Please speak up—we can't hear you at the back.
2 (for sb/sth/yourself) to say what you think
clearly and freely, especially to support or
defend sb/sth: *Several players spoke up for their
manager.* ◇ *She's learned to speak up for herself.*
◇ *It's time to speak up about what is happening
in our schools.*
♦ v + adv

speed /spiːd/ (**speeded, speeded, or sped**, **sped** /sped/)

,speed a'way/'off to leave very quickly, usually in a vehicle of some kind: *The car sped away from the house.* ◇ *She sped off on her bike.*
NOTE Sped is usually used as the past tense and past participle of this verb.
♦ v + adv

,speed 'up; ,speed sth 'up to start to move or happen faster; to make sth do this: *The train started to speed up.* ◇ *Parking restrictions were introduced to try to speed up the traffic.* ◇ *They worked slowly at first, speeding up as they got used to it.* ◇ *The new tool **speeds things up**.*
NOTE Speeded is used as the past tense and past participle of this verb.
♦ v + adv ♦ v + adv + n ♦ v + n/pron + adv

spell /spel/ (**spelt, spelt** /spelt/ or **spelled, spelled**)

,spell sth 'out **1** to make sth clear and easy to understand; to explain sth in detail: *His reasons for leaving are spelt out in detail in his letter.* ◇ *Surely I don't have to spell it out?* (= it should be obvious) **2** to say or write the letters of a word in the correct order: *Could you spell that word out for me again?*
NOTE Spell sth on its own is more usual.
♦ **1** v + adv + n ♦ v + pron + adv
♦ v + n + adv (*less frequent*)
♦ **2** v + adv + n ♦ v + n/pron + adv ♦ v + adv + speech

spew /spjuː/

,spew 'out; ,spew sth 'out to flow out quickly in large amounts; to make sth do this: *lava spewing out from a volcano* ◇ *fumes spewed out by cars and trucks*
NOTE Spew and spew sth are also used on their own: *a volcano spewing clouds of ash.*
♦ v + adv ♦ v + adv + n ♦ v + n/pron + adv

,spew 'up; ,spew sth 'up (*BrE, slang*) to bring food from the stomach back out through the mouth: *He spewed up all over my jacket.*
SYN throw up, throw sth up; vomit, vomit sth (*more formal*)
♦ v + adv ♦ v + n/pron + adv ♦ v + adv + n

spice /spaɪs/

,spice sth 'up to add spice to food in order to give it more flavour and make it more interesting: *Casseroles can be spiced up with a dash of tabasco sauce.* ◇ (*figurative*) *He exaggerated the details to spice up the story.*
SYN jazz sth up (*informal*); liven sth up
♦ v + adv + n ♦ v + n/pron + adv

spiff /spɪf/

,spiff sb/sth 'up; ,spiff yourself 'up (*AmE, informal*) to make sb/sth/yourself look more attractive: *We went home to **get spiffed up** for the party.* ◇ *Here are some easy ways to spiff up spreadsheets.*
♦ v + adv + n ♦ v + n/pron + adv
♦ v + n + adv (*less frequent*)

spill /spɪl/ (**spilled, spilled**, *BrE also* **spilt, spilt** /spɪlt/)

,spill 'out; ,spill 'out of sth **1** to accidentally flow out of a container: *The contents of her bag spilled out everywhere.* ◇ *Water had spilled out onto the floor.* **2** to come out in large numbers or amounts: *The theatre crowds spilled out onto the pavement.* ◇ *The children spilled out into the yard.* **SYN** pour out, pour out of sth
♦ v + adv

,spill 'out; ,spill sth 'out to tell sb a secret, your fears, worries, etc. without intending to: *When she started to speak, the words just **came spilling out**.* ◇ *She spilled out her troubles to her parents.*
♦ v + adv ♦ v + adv + n ♦ v + n/pron + adv

,spill 'over (into/to sth) to start in one situation or area and then have an effect on another situation or in another area: *Unrest has spilt over into areas outside the city.* ◇ *Anger spilled over into violence at yesterday's demonstration.* ◇ *Her excitement spilled over to the rest of the group.*
♦ v + adv

▶ 'overspill *n* [U, sing.] (*BrE*) people who move from a town or city because it is too crowded and go and live somewhere else: *These towns were built to house overspill populations from the big cities.*

▶ 'spillover [C, U] **1** sth that is too large or too much for the place where it starts and spreads to other places: *a spillover of riots* ◇ *a spillover room* (= a room where extra people can go) **2** the results and effects of sth that have spread to other situations or areas: *Other resorts could benefit from the spillover* (*of tourists*). ◇ *spillover effects/benefits*

,spill 'over; ,spill 'over sth to flow over the edge of a container that is too full: *The water spilled over the rim of the glass.* ◇ *Her tears suddenly spilled over* (= she started to cry). ◇ *The goods were spilling over from the shops onto the pavements.* ◇ (*figurative*) *His emotions suddenly spilled over.*
♦ v + adv ♦ v + prep

spin /spɪn/ (**spinning, spun, spun** /spʌn/)

,spin a'round; ,spin sb/sth a'round (*BrE also* ,spin 'round, ,spin sb/sth 'round) **1** to turn very quickly to face in the opposite direction; to turn sb/sth in this way: *She heard her name and spun around to see the speaker.* ◇ *He spun her round to face him.* **2** to turn round and round quickly; to make sth do this: *The propeller started to spin around.* ◇ *The room seemed to be spinning* *round.* ◊ *The wheels were spinning round in the mud.*

♦ v + adv ♦ v + n/pron + adv

,spin 'off (from sth), ,spin sth 'off (from sth) (*especially BrE, business*) to produce a new product, material, service, etc. that is connected with sth successful that already exists; to be produced in this way: *Calendars and diaries spinning off from familiar books and TV shows are always popular.* ◊ *'A Different World' was spun off from 'The Cosby Show'.* ◊ *Their research has spun off many useful applications.*

♦ v + adv ♦ v + n/pron + adv ♦ v + n + adv
♦ v + n + adv (*rare*)

▶ 'spin-off *n* **1** an unexpected but useful result of an activity that is designed to produce sth else: *commercial spin-offs from medical research* ◊ *spin-off effects* **2** a product or a book, film/movie, etc. that is based on a very successful book, film/movie or television series: *'The Cosby Show' and its spin-off* ◊ *a spin-off movie*

,spin sth 'off (*business*) to separate part of a company or an organization from the main part in order to form a new one: *The fast food chain could be spun off as a separate company.*

♦ v + adv + n ♦ v + pron + adv ♦ v + n + adv (*rare*)

▶ 'spin-off *n* [C, U] the act of forming a new, independent company from part of an existing one; a company formed in this way

,spin 'out (of/from sth), ,spin sth 'out (of/from sth) (*especially AmE, business*) to form a new and independent company from part of an existing one by selling shares in it: *a newly spun-out company*

NOTE Usually used in the passive.

♦ v + adv ♦ v + adv + n ♦ v + pron + adv ♦ v + n + adv

▶ 'spin-out *n* **1** a company that is formed to develop and use the results of research done at a university, etc.: *Cambridge has produced 120 spin-outs over the last ten years.* **2** → SPIN-OFF

,spin sth 'out to make sth last as long as possible: *I managed to spin my talk out to an hour.* ◊ *She had to spin out her money until payday.*

♦ v + adv + n ♦ v + n/pron + adv

,spin 'round, etc. (*BrE*) → SPIN AROUND, ETC.

spirit /'spɪrɪt/

,spirit sb/sth a'way/'off (to sth) to remove sb/sth quickly, secretly or as if by magic: *He was spirited away by his friends before the police arrived.* ◊ *An enormous amount of money had been spirited away in only two months.*

♦ v + n/pron + adv ♦ v + adv + n

spit /spɪt/ (spitting, spat, spat /spæt/ or spitting, spit, spit, especially AmE)

,spit it 'out used to tell sb to reveal a piece of information or to say sth when they are feeling nervous or unwilling to speak: *Come on, spit it out! Who did it?*

♦ v + it + adv

,spit sth 'out **1** to force sth out of your mouth: *It tasted so horrible he had to spit it out.* **2** to say sth very angrily: *'Men!' She spat the word out.*

OBJ word

♦ v + n/pron + adv
♦ v + adv + n **2** also v + adv + speech

,spit 'up; ,spit sth 'up (*AmE*) if a baby **spits up** or **spits sth up**, it brings milk back from its stomach out through its mouth: *Put this cloth on your shoulder in case she spits up.* ◊ *Lots of babies spit up some milk after feeding.*

♦ v + adv ♦ v + n/pron + adv ♦ v + adv + n

SYN vomit, vomit sth; be sick (*BrE*)

▶ 'spit-up *n* [U] the milk that a baby brings back out of its mouth

splash /splæʃ/

,splash a'bout (*BrE*) → SPLASH AROUND

,splash sth a'bout/a'round (*informal, especially BrE*) to spend money freely or carelessly: *He splashes his wages about just to impress her.*

♦ v + n/pron + adv ♦ v + adv + n

,splash sth a'cross/o'ver sth to publish a photograph, a news story, etc. in a place where a lot of people will see it, especially in a newspaper: *The next day her name was splashed across all the front pages.* ◊ *I don't want my private life splashed all over the tabloids.*

NOTE Often used in the passive.

♦ v + n/pron + prep

,splash a'round (*BrE also* ,splash a'bout) (in sth) to move about in water making it fly everywhere: *The children splashed about in the river all afternoon.*

♦ v + adv

,splash sth a'round → SPLASH STH ABOUT/AROUND

,splash 'down when a spacecraft **splashes down**, it returns to earth and lands in the sea/ocean: *The capsule splashed down in the Pacific.*

♦ v + adv

▶ 'splashdown *n* [C, U] the return of a spacecraft to earth when it lands in the sea/ocean: *Splashdown is expected 300 kilometres west of Valparaíso.*

,splash 'out (on sth), ,splash sth 'out (on/for sth) (*informal*) to spend a lot of money on sth: *She splashed out on a new pair of shoes.* ◊ *Why don't we splash out and go out for a meal?* ◊ *The band splashed out thousands on new equipment.* ◊ *Don't splash it all out at once!*

♦ v + adv ♦ v + adv + n ♦ v + pron + adv
♦ v + n + adv (*rare*)

,splash sth 'over sth → SPLASH STH ACROSS/OVER STH

split /splɪt/ (**splitting**, **split**, **split**)

ˌsplit aˈway/ˈoff (**from sth**), **ˌsplit sth aˈway/ ˈoff** (**from sth**) to separate from, or be separated from, a large object or a group: *The branch had split away from the trunk.* ◇ *The wind split the door away from its frame.* ◇ *Some of the members split away to form a new party.* ◇ *Should the ownership of the rail track be split off from the running of the train services?*
◆ v + adv ◆ v + adv + n ◆ v + n/pron + adv

ˈsplit on sb (**to sb**) (*BrE*, *informal*) to tell sb in authority about sth bad or wrong that sb has done: *Promise you won't split on me.*
SYN tell on sb
◆ v + prep

ˌsplit ˈup (**with/from sb**), **ˌsplit sb ˈup** (*informal*) to end a relationship or a marriage; to make two people stop having a relationship with each other: *He told me he had split up with his girlfriend.* ◇ *The band split up at the height of their fame.* ◇ *My friend is doing her best to split Maria and me up.*
SYN break up (with sb), break sb up
◆ v + adv ◆ v + n/pron + adv ◆ v + adv + n

ˌsplit ˈup (**into sth**), **ˌsplit sb/sth ˈup** (**into sth**) if a group of people or a family **splits up**, or sb **splits it up**, the members separate and do not stay together: *We split up into groups to discuss the question.* ◇ *The class was split up into groups.* ◇ *We got split up in the crowd.*
SYN break up, break sb/sth up
◆ v + adv ◆ v + n/pron + adv ◆ v + adv + n

ˌsplit sth ˈup (**into sth**) to divide sth into smaller parts: *The day was split up into six one-hour classes.* ◇ *We split the profits up between us.*
◆ v + n/pron + adv ◆ v + adv + n

spoil /spɔɪl/ (**spoiled**, **spoiled** /spɔɪld/, *BrE also* **spoilt**, **spoilt** /spɔɪlt/)

be ˈspoiling for sth (*informal*) (*only used in the progressive tenses*) to be wanting to fight sb: *He was spoiling for a fight.*
OBJ a fight
◆ v + prep

sponge /spʌndʒ/

ˌsponge sb/sth ˈdown to wash sb/sth with a wet cloth or a soft material: *I sponged the coat down to remove the mud.* ◇ *She tried sponging the baby down to lower his temperature.*
◆ v + n/pron + adv ◆ v + adv + n

ˈsponge off sb (*also* **ˈsponge on sb** *less frequent*) (*informal*, *disapproving*) to get money, food, etc. from other people, without doing anything for them or offering to pay: *He's constantly sponging off his friends.*
◆ v + prep

ˌsponge sth ˈoff; **ˌsponge sth ˈoff sth** (*especially BrE*) to remove a mark, some dirt, etc. with a wet cloth or a piece of a soft material: *It was*

impossible to sponge the mark off. ◇ *I couldn't sponge the stain off my dress.*
◆ v + n/pron + adv ◆ v + adv + n ◆ v + n/pron + prep

ˈsponge on sb → SPONGE OFF SB

spout /spaʊt/

ˌspout ˈoff/ˈon (**about sth**) (*informal*, *disapproving*) to talk about sth in a boring or annoying way: *He's always spouting off about the behaviour of young people today.* ◇ *What are you spouting on about now?*
◆ v + adv

sprawl /sprɔːl/

ˌsprawl ˈout to sit or lie down with your arms and legs spread out in a relaxed or awkward way: *He came home and just sprawled out on the sofa.*
NOTE Sprawl is used more frequently on its own: *Tom sprawled in the armchair.*
◆ v + adv

spread /spred/ (**spread**, **spread**)

ˌspread ˈout 1 to gradually cover a wider area: *The city has spread out into what used to be countryside.* ◇ *The ripples spread out across the water.* ◇ (*figurative*) *A bright future spread out before him.* **NOTE** Spread is also frequently used on its own with this meaning: *The fields spread for miles along the river.* **2** (*also* **ˌspread yourˈselves ˈout**) to move away from others in a group so as to cover a wider area: *The search party spread out over the moor.* ◇ *Don't all sit together. Spread yourselves out.* **3** (*also* **ˌspread yourself ˈout**) to stretch your body or arrange your things over a large area: *There's more room to spread out in business class.* ◇ *Do you have to spread yourself out all over the sofa?*
◆ **1** v + adv
◆ **2,3** also v + pron + adv

ˌspread ˈout; be ˌspread ˈout to cover a wide area: *The valley spread out beneath us.* ◇ *We looked down at the city spread out below us.*
NOTE This verb is often used in descriptions of cities, views, etc. ◆ Spread and be spread are also frequently used with this meaning: *The valley lay spread before us.*
◆ v + adv ◆ be + v + adv

ˌspread sth ˈout 1 to arrange a group of objects on a surface so that you can see them all clearly: *Spread out all the pieces before you begin the jigsaw.* ◇ *All the brochures were spread out on the floor.* **2** to open sth that is folded and put it down on a flat surface: *They spread the blanket out on the grass.* ◇ *The map had been spread out on the table.* **OBJ** map, newspaper, blanket **3** to stretch your fingers, arms, etc. so that they are apart: *The boy spread out his arms, pretending to be an aeroplane.* **OBJ** arms, hands **NOTE** Spread sth is also frequently used on its own with this meaning. **4** (**over sth**) to separate sth into parts

and arrange them over a period of time or divide them between different people: *The cost can be spread out over two years.* ◇ *I'll try to spread out the work evenly.* **OBJ** **cost**, **work** **SYN** **divide sth** (*more formal*) **NOTE** Spread sth (**over sth**) is also frequently used on its own with this meaning: *Payments can be spread (over five years).*
◆ v + n/pron + adv ◆ v + adv + n

spring /sprɪŋ/ (**sprang** /spræŋ/, **sprung** /sprʌŋ/, *AmE also* **sprung**, **sprung**)

'**spring for sth** (*AmE*, *slang*) to pay for sth for other people: *I'll spring for lunch.*
◆ v + prep

'**spring from sth 1** to be caused by sth; to start from sth: *The idea for the novel sprang from a trip to India.* ◇ *Aggression often springs from fear.* **2** (*informal*) (*usually used in questions*) to appear suddenly or unexpectedly from somewhere: *Where on earth did you spring from?*
◆ v + prep

'**spring sth on sb** to suddenly do or say sth that people do not expect: *I hate to spring this on you at such short notice.* ◇ *They were planning to spring a surprise on us.* ◇ *I didn't know about Rob's new job until he sprang it on me this morning.*
◆ v + n/pron + prep

,**spring 'up** to appear, develop, grow, etc. quickly or suddenly: *Weeds were springing up everywhere.* ◇ *Several new cafes sprang up in the area.* ◇ *A cool breeze had sprung up.* ◇ *New industries were springing up all over the country.*
◆ v + adv

spruce /spruːs/

,**spruce sb/sth 'up**; ,**spruce yourself 'up** to make sb/sth/yourself tidy and clean: *We spruced up the room with a coat of paint.* ◇ *He spruced himself up for the interview.*
SYN **smarten up**, **smarten yourself up**; **smarten sb/sth up**
◆ v + adv + n ◆ v + pron + adv
◆ v + n + adv (*less frequent*)

spur /spɜː(r)/ (**-rr-**)

,**spur sb 'on** (**to sth/to do sth**) to encourage sb to act in a particular way, especially to work harder or to try to achieve sth: *Her difficult childhood spurred her on to succeed.* ◇ *His parents' encouragement spurred him on to greater efforts.* ◇ *Spurred on by this victory, we went on to win the championship.* ◇ *Their shouts of encouragement spurred us on.*
SYN **encourage sb**
NOTE Often used in the passive. ◆ **Spur sb** followed by an infinitive or a phrase beginning with a preposition is also used: *His criticism spurred me to try harder.*
◆ v + n/pron + adv ◆ v + adv + n

spurt /spɜːt; *AmE* spɜːrt/

,**spurt 'out**; ,**spurt 'out of sth**; ,**spurt sth 'out**; ,**spurt sth 'out of sth** to come out of sth in a sudden or fast stream; to pour out a sudden fast stream of liquid or flames: *Water spurted out of the hole.* ◇ *The volcano was spurting out rivers of molten lava.*
◆ v + adv ◆ v + adv + prep ◆ v + adv + n
◆ v + n/pron + adv ◆ v + n/pron + adv + prep

spy /spaɪ/ (**spies**, **spying**, **spied**)

'**spy on sb/sth** (*also* '**spy upon sb/sth** *more formal*) to watch sb/sth secretly: *He hired a detective to spy on his wife.* ◇ *He knew he was being spied on.*
◆ v + prep

,**spy sth 'out** (*BrE*) to go somewhere secretly to try to find out information: *I arrived early to spy out the land* (= collect information before deciding what do do). ◇ *He studied the map and spied out the quickest route.*
◆ v + adv + n ◆ v + pron + adv ◆ v + n + adv (*rare*)

square /skweə(r); *AmE* skwer/

,**square sth a'way** (*AmE*) to finish dealing with sth; to put sth in order: *We need to get everything squared away before you leave.*
NOTE Often used in the passive.
◆ v + n/pron + adv ◆ v + adv + n

,**square 'off** (**against sb**) (*AmE*) to fight or to prepare to fight sb: *The two candidates will square off in a TV debate tomorrow.* ◇ *Protesting students squared off against police.*
◆ v + adv

,**square 'up 1** (**to sb**) (*BrE*) to stand facing sb as if you are prepared to fight or argue with them: *Kath put her hands on her hips and squared up to him.* **2** (**to sb/sth**) to face a difficult situation and deal with it in a determined way: *He must square up to the reality of being out of work.* **SYN** **face up to sth 3** (**with sb**) to pay sb the money you owe them: *Can I leave you to square up with the waiter?* **SYN** **settle up** (**with sb**)
◆ v + adv

'**square with sth**; '**square sth with sth** to agree with another fact, idea or situation; to make two facts, etc. agree with each other: *This doesn't square with what you told me earlier.* ◇ *How do you square your profession with your religious beliefs?* ◇ *The interests of farmers need to be squared with those of consumers.*
◆ v + prep ◆ v + n/pron + prep

'**square sth with sb** to get sb's approval before you do sth: *You'd better square it with the boss if you want to leave early.*
◆ v + n/pron + prep

squash /skwɒʃ; *AmE* skwɑːʃ, skwɔːʃ/

,**squash 'in, etc.** → SQUEEZE IN, ETC.: *Can I squash in?* ◇ *We all squashed into the back of the van.*

,**squash sb/sth to'gether** to press people or things tightly together in a small space: *people living squashed together in terrible conditions* NOTE Usually used in the passive.
  ◆ v + n/pron + adv ◆ v + adv + n (*rare*)

,**squash 'up, etc.** (*BrE*) → SQUEEZE UP, ETC.: *If we squash up there'll be room for one more.* ◊ *I was squashed up against Samantha in the back of the van.*

squeak /skwiːk/

,**squeak 'by** (*AmE*, *informal*) to achieve a successful result with great difficulty: *We just squeaked by in the semi-final.*
  ◆ v + adv

,**squeak 'through**; ,**squeak 'through sth** (*informal*) to manage to achieve sth or get a successful result with great difficulty: *Andrew squeaked through the qualifying rounds of the championship.*
  SYN **scrape through**, **scrape through sth**
  ◆ v + adv ◆ v + prep

squeeze /skwiːz/

,**squeeze 'in**; ,**squeeze 'into sth** to just manage to fit into a small space: *The bus was so full not one more passenger could have squeezed in.*
  ◆ v + adv ◆ v + prep

,**squeeze sb/sth 'in**; ,**squeeze sb/sth 'into sth 1** (*also* ,**squash sb/sth 'in**, ,**squash sb/sth 'into sth**) to just manage to put sb/sth into a small space: *Can you squeeze anything else into that case?* **2** to just manage to fit sb/sth into a short period of time: *The doctor can squeeze you in on Tuesday morning.* ◊ *All my classes are squeezed into four days a week.*
  ◆ v + n/pron + adv ◆ v + adv + n ◆ v + n/pron + prep

,**squeeze sb/sth 'out**; ,**squeeze sb/sth 'out of sth** to prevent sb/sth from doing sth or from doing business: *Small firms are being squeezed out by larger companies.* ◊ *One candidate has already been squeezed out of the leadership race.*
  SYN **crowd sb/sth out**, **crowd sb/sth out of sth**; **exclude sb/sth** (**from sth**)
  ◆ v + n/pron + adv ◆ v + adv + n
  ◆ v + n/pron + adv + prep

,**squeeze sth 'out 1** (*also* ,**squeeze sth 'out of sth**) to remove liquid from sth by pressing it hard: *She squeezed the cloth out.* ◊ *Squeeze the juice out of four oranges.* **2** (*also* ,**squeeze sth 'out of sb/sth**) to get sth such as information or money from sb by putting pressure on them, threatening them, etc.: *The government will try to squeeze more money out of the taxpayer.* ◊ *The police squeezed the truth out of him.* ◊ *They finally squeezed some concessions out of the employers.*
  ◆ v + n/pron + adv ◆ v + adv + n
  ◆ v + n/pron + adv + prep

,**squeeze 'up** (**against sth**), ,**squeeze sb/sth 'up** (**against sth**) (*also* ,**squash 'up**, ,**squash sb/sth 'up**) to move closer towards sb so that you are pressed tightly together: *There'll be enough room if we all squeeze up a bit.* ◊ *I'll walk—it's better than being squeezed up in the back of the car.*
  ◆ v + adv ◆ v + n/pron + adv ◆ v + adv + n

squirrel /'skwɪrəl; *AmE* 'skwɜːrəl/ (-**ll**-, *AmE* -**l**-)

,**squirrel sth a'way** to put sth, especially money, in a safe place so that you can use it later: *She had money squirrelled away in various accounts.*
  ◆ v + n/pron + adv ◆ v + adv + n

stack /stæk/

,**stack 'up 1** to increase gradually until there is a large pile, a long line, etc.: *Over the months he just let the paperwork stack up.* ◊ *The traffic quickly stacked up behind the bus.* SYN **pile up 2** (**against sb/sth**) (*informal*) to compare with sb/sth: *How does this washing powder stack up against your usual brand?* ◊ *Let's try him in the team and see how he stacks up.* SYN **compare** (**with sb/sth**)
  ◆ v + adv

,**stack 'up**; ,**stack sth 'up** if planes **stack up** or are **stacked up** over an airport, there are a lot of them flying around waiting to land: *Planes stacked up at Heathrow after an accident on the runway.* NOTE **Stack** and **stack sth** are sometimes used on their own: *a queue of planes stacked in the air over the closed airport*
  ◆ v + adv ◆ v + adv + n ◆ v + n/pron + adv

,**stack sth 'up 1** to arrange things in a tall pile: *He stacked up the dishes on the draining board.* SYN **pile sth up** NOTE **Stack sth** is often used on its own. **2** (*AmE*, *informal*) to gradually get more of sth: *She's stacking up the college credits with all of her night classes.*
  ◆ v + n/pron + adv ◆ v + adv + n

stake /steɪk/

'**stake sth on sth**; '**stake sth on doing sth** to risk money or sth very important on the result of sth or on sth happening: *He staked twenty pounds on the favourite* (= in horse racing, for example). ◊ *Several journalists staked their reputation on Bush winning the election.* ◊ *He'll never let you down—I'd **stake my life on it**.*
  ◆ v + n/pron + prep

,**stake sth 'out 1** to mark the position and the limits of a piece of land or an area to show that you own it: *The male stakes out his territory and defends it from other birds.* **2** to state your position or opinion on sth clearly: *The President staked out his position on the issue.* **3** if police **stake out** a building, they watch it secretly and continuously because they think sth illegal is happening there: *Armed police have been staking out the house for two weeks.* ◇ *The cops had the building staked out.*

◆ v + adv + n ◆ v + pron + adv ◆ v + n + adv (*rare*)

▶ '**stake-out** *n* a situation when police watch a building continuously and secretly because they think sth illegal is happening there: *The stake-out at the house produced nothing.*

stamp /stæmp/

'**stamp on sth** **1** to bring your foot down on sth with force: *The child stamped on the spider.* ◇ *She stamped on his foot as hard as she could.* ◇ *The victim had been kicked and stamped on.* ◇ *A child ran out into the road and I had to stamp on the brakes.* **2** (*especially BrE*) to control sth or stop sth from happening by force: *This kind of disobedience must be stamped on at once.*

◆ v + prep

'**stamp sth on sth** to make sth have an important effect or influence on sth: *She stamped her own interpretation on the role.* ◇ *The new director has worked hard to stamp his authority on the board.* ◇ *The date is forever stamped on her memory.*

OBJ your authority, your mark

◆ v + n/pron + prep

,**stamp sth 'out 1** to destroy or get rid of sth bad or unpleasant by force or with a lot of effort: *They aim to stamp out drug dealing in schools.* ◇ *The party chairman is determined to stamp out corruption.* OBJ **a problem**, **drug abuse** SYN **eradicate sth** (*more formal*) **2** to put out a fire by pressing down on it hard with your foot: *He stamped out the flames before they spread any further.*

◆ **1** v + n/pron + adv ◆ v + adv + n
◆ **2** v + adv + n ◆ v + pron + adv ◆ v + n + adv (*rare*)

stand /stænd/ (**stood**, **stood** /stʊd/)

,**stand a'round**; ,**stand a'round sb/sth** (*BrE also* ,**stand a'bout/'round**, ,**stand 'round sb/sth**) to stand in a place doing nothing, either waiting for sb/sth or with no particular purpose: *Don't just stand around watching me, give me a hand.* ◇ *There were a few people standing around the square.* ◇ *A group of people stood around watching.* ◇ *Young men stood about in groups, chatting.*

◆ v + adv ◆ v + prep

,**stand a'side 1** to move to one side to let sb/sth pass: *Stand aside please and let her through.* **2** to take no part in events; to do nothing: *I can't stand aside and let you waste an opportunity like that.* **3** to stop doing a job so that sb else can do it: *It's time he stood aside and let somebody younger take his place.*

◆ v + adv

,**stand 'back** (**from sth**) **1** to move a short distance away from sb/sth: *Stand well back*

from the flames. **2** to be located at a distance from sth: *The house stands back from the road.* **3** to think about a situation as if you are not involved in it: *She found it hard to stand back from the situation.* ◇ *This is an opportunity to stand back and think about what you have achieved.*

SYN **step back** (**from sth**)

◆ v + adv

,**stand be'tween A and B** to prevent sb from doing or having sth, or being in a particular situation: *Only three people stood between him and the crown* (= becoming king). ◇ *Your lack of confidence is all that stands between you and a much better job.*

◆ v + prep

,**stand 'by 1** to be present when sth bad or unpleasant is happening, but not become involved: *I can't stand idly by and let him take the blame for what happened.* ◇ *I can't stand by and see you ruin your life.* **2** (**for sth**) to be ready to take appropriate action: *The pilot was instructed to stand by for take-off.* ◇ *Fire crews are standing by in case of an explosion.*

◆ v + adv

▶ '**bystander** *n* a person who is present but is not involved in sth: *Two innocent bystanders were hit by stray bullets.*

▶ '**standby** *n* **1** [C] a person or a thing that can be used if sb/sth else is not available: *Keep some candles as a standby in case the power fails.* ◇ *Mia made a delicious meal from standbys in the store cupboard.* **2** [U] a state of being ready to act if necessary: *All local hospitals have been put on standby.* **3** [U] if an electrical device such as a television is **on standby**, the power supply is switched on but it is not actually functioning: *Do you leave the TV on standby?*

▶ '**standby** *adj* [only before noun] **1** that can be used if other things are not available: *standby supplies* ◇ *Two divers work together while a standby diver remains on the surface.* **2** a **standby** ticket for a flight, a theatre, etc. is one that cannot be bought in advance and is only available a very short time before the plane leaves or the performance starts: *standby passengers* ◇ *to fly standby* (= with a standby ticket)

,**stand 'by sb** to support or help sb in a difficult situation: *I'll stand by you whatever happens.*

SYN **stick by sb** (*informal*)

◆ v + prep

'**stand by sth** to continue to believe sth you said earlier even though the situation may now be different: *I'll stand by what I said earlier.* ◇ *The committee stood by their decision.*

◆ v + prep

,**stand 'down 1** (**as/from sth**) to leave a job or position; to stop taking part in a race or a competition, etc.: *She stood down after only three months as chairman.* ◇ *He stood down from the committee for personal reasons.* SYN **step**

down (**as/from sth**) **2** (in court) to leave the place where you stand to give evidence: *The witness was allowed to stand down.*
◆ v + adv

,**stand sb/sth** '**down** to give an official order that a group of people, equipment, etc. should no longer be in operation: *The regiment will be stood down from next month.*
◆ v + n/pron + adv ◆ v + adv + n

⚡'**stand for sth 1** (*not used in the progressive tenses*) to be a shorter form of sth: *What does DVD stand for?* **2** to support sth; to be in favour of sth: *Our party stands for racial harmony.* ◇ *I hated him and all he stood for.* **3** (*used in negative sentences and questions*) to allow sth to happen or sb to do sth: *I won't stand for this behaviour.* **SYN** **put up with sth**; **tolerate sth**
◆ v + prep

,**stand** '**in** (**for sb**) to take sb's place: *We'll need someone to stand in for you while you're away.* **SYN** **deputize** (**for sb**) (*formal*)
◆ v + adv

▸ '**stand-in** n **1** a person who does sb's job for a short time while they are away or not available: *Tom acted as my stand-in while I was abroad.* ◇ *a stand-in goalkeeper* **2** a person who replaces an actor in some scenes in a film/movie, especially dangerous ones: *rehearsing with stand-ins*

stand out

excel ◆ shine ◆ stand out

These verbs all mean to be much better than other people or things, especially at doing sth.

excel to be very good at doing sth: *She has always excelled in foreign languages.* ◇ *Music was something at which he excelled.*

shine to be very good at sth: *He failed to shine academically, but was extremely popular with the other students.*

stand out to be much better or more important than other people or things: *Of all the members of the cast, two in particular stood out.* ◇ *There will be lots of applications for the job, so yours really needs to stand out.*

WHICH WORD?

Shine is used especially in the phrase *shining example* and when talking about people doing well at school or college. **Excel** is used especially to talk about people being good at particular subjects or skills.

PATTERNS AND COLLOCATIONS

▪ to excel **at** sth
▪ to excel/stand out **as** sth
▪ to shine/excel **academically**

⚡,**stand** '**out 1** (**against/from sth**) to be clearly visible: *His yellow jacket stood out clearly against the grey hillside.* ◇ *The tower stands out against the sky.* ◇ *A small figure in red stood out from the rest of the group.* **SYN** **stick out 2** (**as/from sb/sth**) to be much better or more important than other people or things: *This building stands out from the rest because of its design.* ◇ *She's the sort of person who always **stands out in a crowd**.* **3** (**against/for sb/sth**) to oppose or refuse to accept sth that you believe is wrong: *Parents often stand out against troublesome behaviour for some time, then give in.* **SYN** **stick out for sth**; **hold out against/for sth**
◆ v + adv

IDM **stand out like a sore thumb** to be very noticeable in an unpleasant way: *Dressed like that, you'll stand out like a sore thumb.*

▸ **out**'**standing** adj **1** excellent: *an outstanding young actress* **2** [usually before noun] very obvious or important: *Lake Baikal is one of earth's outstanding features.* **3** (of payment, work, problems, etc.) not yet paid, done, solved, etc.: *to repay outstanding debts* ◇ *I don't have any urgent work outstanding.*

▸ **out**'**standingly** adv **1** used to emphasize the good quality of sth: *outstandingly beautiful/successful* **2** extremely well: *Owen has played outstandingly this season.*

▸ '**standout** n (*informal, especially AmE*) a person or thing that is better, more impressive, etc. than others of a similar type: *This is my list of standouts in this week's CD chart.*

▸ '**standout** adj [only before noun] (*informal, especially AmE*) better, more impressive, etc. than others of a similar type: *There are a few real standout moments which put this movie ahead of others in its class.*

,**stand** '**over sb** to remain close to sb and watch them, usually to make sure that they behave or do sth correctly: *She won't do her homework unless I stand over her.* ◇ *I can't concentrate with you standing over me.*
◆ v + prep

,**stand** '**round**; ,**stand** '**round sb/sth** (*BrE*)
→ STAND AROUND, STAND AROUND SB/STH

⚡,**stand** '**up 1** to rise to your feet from a sitting or lying position; to be on your feet: *Darcy stood up when Emma came into the room.* ◇ *There was silence when the President stood up to speak.* ◇ *Stand up straight* instead of *slouching.* ◇ *Horses can sleep standing up.* **2** (**to sth**) to remain true or correct even when tested, examined closely, etc.: *Your theory doesn't stand up to close examination.* ◇ *His story won't stand up under cross-examination.* **SYN** **hold up 3** (**to sth**) to be strong enough not to be harmed by sth: *The children **stood up well** under questioning from the police.* ◇ *The players are standing up to the tour well.*
◆ v + adv

stand up

be on your feet ✦ **get to your feet** ✦ **get up** ✦ **rise** ✦ **stand up**

These verbs all mean to be in an upright position with your weight on your feet, or to put yourself in this position.

be on your feet to be in a standing position: *I've been on my feet all day.*

get to your feet to stand after sitting, kneeling or lying: *I helped her to get to her feet.* ◊ *'I'd better be going,' he said, getting to his feet.*

get up to get into a standing position from a sitting, kneeling or lying position: *Please don't get up! I can let myself out.* ◊ *She got up and left the room.*

rise (*formal*) to get into a standing position from a sitting, kneeling or lying position: *They rose from the table.* ◊ *She rose to her feet.*

stand up to be in a standing position; to stand after sitting: *Stand up straight!* ◊ *I've been standing up for hours.* ◊ *He stood up and put*

on his coat. **NOTE** **Stand** can be used on its own: *Everyone stood when the President entered the room.*

WHICH WORD?

Stand usually means 'to be in a standing position': *to stand talking*; but it can also mean 'to get into a standing position'. **Stand up** can be used with either of these meanings, but its use is more restricted: it is used especially when sb tells sb or a group of people to stand, or when sb has to stand up (for example, because there is nowhere to sit). **Get up** is the most frequent way of saying 'get into a standing position', and this can be from a sitting, kneeling or lying position; if you **stand up**, this is nearly always after sitting, especially on a chair.

PATTERNS AND COLLOCATIONS

- to get up/rise/stand up **from** sth
- to stand/get up/rise/stand up **quickly/slowly**
- to stand/stand up **straight**

▶ '**stand-up** *adj* [only before noun] **1** a **stand-up comedian** is an entertainer who tells jokes to an audience: *stand-up comedy* ◊ *a stand-up act* **2** (*especially BrE*) a **stand-up** argument, fight, etc. is one in which people shout loudly at each other or are violent towards each other: *He had a stand-up row with the team captain.* **3** (*AmE, informal*) honest and easy to trust or depend on: *He was known in business circles as a stand-up guy.*

,**stand** sb '**up** (*informal*) to deliberately fail to meet sb you have arranged to meet, especially sb you are having a romantic relationship with: *We agreed to meet at the cinema but she stood me up.* ◊ *I've been stood up!*
✦ v + n/pron + adv ✦ v + adv + n (*less frequent*)

,**stand** sb/sth '**up** (*especially AmE*) to prepare a group of people, equipment, etc. to do a particular job: *The authorities have stood up a special team to deal with the disaster.*
✦ v + n/pron + adv ✦ v + adv + n

,**stand** '**up for** sb/sth/yourself to support or defend sb/sth/yourself, especially when sb is criticizing them/it/you: *She's always stood up for her friends.* ◊ *You should stand up for what you believe in.* ◊ *He's always telling her what to do. It's time she stood up for herself!* ◊ *James doesn't need you to stand up for him.*
OBJ your rights, your interests
✦ v + adv + prep

,**stand** '**up to** sb/sth to resist sb/sth; to defend your position against a more powerful person or

organization that is treating you badly or unfairly: *If you don't stand up to him he'll treat you like dirt.* ◊ *It was difficult for Paul to stand up to his father's rage.*
➲ note on page 308
✦ v + adv + prep

,**stand** '**up to** sth (of a product, material, etc.) to be able to stay in good condition even though it is treated roughly: *Will your china and glass stand up to family wear and tear?*
SYN withstand sth (*formal*)
✦ v + adv + prep

stare /steə(r); *AmE* ster/

'**stare at** sb/sth to look at sb/sth for a long time: *I stared blankly at the paper in front of me.*
✦ v + prep

,**stare** sb '**out** (*BrE*) (*also* ,**stare** sb '**down** *AmE*, *BrE*) to look sb directly in the eyes for a long time until they feel forced to lower their eyes or look away: *He was looking at her intently but she stared him out.* ◊ (*figurative*) *The two nations are trying to stare each other down.*
✦ v + n/pron + adv ✦ v + adv + n (*less frequent*)

start /stɑːt; *AmE* stɑːrt/

,**start** '**back** to begin to return somewhere: *It's time we started back.*
✦ v + adv

'**start for** ... to leave one place to go to another: *We started for home.*
SYN head for ...
✦ v + prep

stand up to sb

defy sb/sth ♦ go against sb/sth ♦ oppose sth
♦ resist sth ♦ stand up to sb/sth

These verbs all mean to speak or act against
things that you disagree with.

defy sb/sth to refuse to obey or show respect
for sb/sth in authority, a law, rule or
decision: *I wouldn't have dared to defy my
teachers.* ◇ *Hundreds of people today defied
the ban on political gatherings.*

go against sb/sth to disagree with a rule or
sb's wishes and do the opposite of what they
say: *He would not go against his parents'
wishes.*

oppose sb/sth to disagree strongly with a
person, plan or policy, and to speak or act
against them: *This party would bitterly
oppose the re-introduction of the death penalty.* ◇ *He found himself opposed by his own
deputy.*

resist sth to refuse to accept a change or what
sb wants to do, and try to stop it from
happening: *They are determined to resist pressure to change the law.*

stand up to sb/sth to refuse to accept bad
treatment from a more powerful person or
organization without complaining: *It was
brave of her to stand up to those bullies.*

PATTERNS AND COLLOCATIONS

■ to oppose/resist **change/a plan/a proposal/an
idea**
■ to oppose a **decision**
■ to oppose/defy **a ban/the law/sb's wishes**
■ to oppose/defy/stand up to **the government**
■ to defy **your parents/authority/a rule/an
order**
■ to **effectively/fiercely/bitterly/strongly**
oppose/resist sth

,**start** '**in** (**on sth**) (*informal, especially AmE*) to
begin to do sth: *Let's start in now and get the job
done quickly.* ◇ *It's time you started in on your
homework.*
 ♦ v + adv

,**start** '**in on sb/sth** (*especially AmE*) **1** → START
ON SB/STH **2** → START ON AT SB

⁊,**start** '**off 1** (*also* ,**start** '**off doing sth**, ,**start sth**
'**off**) [+ **adv/prep/adj**] to begin happening in a
particular way; to begin doing sth in a particular way: *The game started off well, but gradually
got worse.* ◇ *We started off with some gentle
exercises.* ◇ *She started off by welcoming everyone.* ◇ *He started off as a plumber.* ◇ *I started off
working quite hard, but it didn't last.* ◇ *The
discussion started off calmly enough.* ◇ *The
leaves start off green but turn red later.* ◇ *We always
started off the lessons with a quiz.* ◇ *The teacher
started things off by asking us what we had done
at the weekend.* **2** [**+adv/prep**] to begin to move
or travel: *The bus started off with a jolt.* ◇ *We
started off for home.*
 ♦ **1** v + adv ♦ v + adv + -ing ♦ v + adv + n
 ♦ v + pron + adv ♦ v + n + adv (*rare*)
 ♦ **2** v + adv

,**start sb** '**off 1** (**on sth**) (*also* ,**start sb** '**off doing
sth**)) to help sb begin an activity, an exercise, a
job, etc.: *I'll start you off on the first exercise.*
◇ *His father started him off farming.* **2** (*also*
,**start sb** '**off doing sth**) to make sb react in
a particular way or begin doing sth: *Just
mentioning 'The Simpsons' started her off
again* (= made her start laughing). ◇ *Don't
shout—you'll start the baby off* (*crying*) *again.*
SYN **set sb off**, **set sb off doing sth**

NOTE Not used in the passive.
 ♦ v + n/pron + adv

,**start sth** '**off** → START OFF 1

'**start on sb/sth** (*also* ,**start** '**in on sb/sth**
especially AmE) (*informal*) to attack sb physically
or with words: *He hit me first and then he started
(in) on my friend.* ◇ *Don't start on me, I'm tired.*
◇ *My mum started on me about doing my
homework as soon as I got home.*
 ♦ v + prep ♦ v + adv + prep

⁊'**start on sth** to begin to deal with sth; to begin
to do sth: *When she'd finished cleaning the
kitchen, she started on the bathroom.*
 ⮑ note on page 310
NOTE **Start sth** has a similar meaning.
 ♦ v + prep

,**start** '**on at sb** (*BrE*) (*also* ,**start** '**on about sth**,
,**start** '**in on sb/sth** *AmE, BrE*) (*informal*) to begin
to criticize sb or complain to sb about sth:
He started on at me again about my hair. ◇ *Don't
start on about that dog barking.*
 ♦ v + adv + prep

⁊,**start** '**out 1** to begin a journey: *Check the oil
before you start out.* ◇ *What time did they start
out?* **SYN** **set off 2** (**as sth**) to begin in a
particular way, especially in business or work:
We started out originally as a taxi firm. ◇ *When
the band started out, they had hardly any
equipment.* ◇ *Did you know the tower started
out leaning the other way?* **3** (*also* ,**start** '**out to
do sth**, ,**start** '**out doing sth**) to have a particular
idea or intention when you begin to do sth:
*I had no idea what I was going to write when I
started out.* ◇ *She had started out to write a short
story but it ended up as a novel.* ◇ *He started out*

start off

begin ◆ commence ◆ kick off ◆ open ◆ start off

These verbs are all used to talk about things happening from the beginning.

begin to start to happen or exist; to start in a particular way or from a particular point: *When does the concert begin?* ◇ *It was beginning to snow.*

commence (*formal*) to start happening: *The meeting is scheduled to commence at noon.*

kick off (*informal*) (of an event, activity, film or book) to start, especially in a particular way: *The festival kicks off on Monday September 13.*

open (of an event, film or book) to start, especially in a particular way: *The story opens with a murder.*

start off (of an event or thing) to start in a particular way or from a particular point: *The discussion started off mildly enough.* ◇ *Let's start off with some gentle exercises.*
NOTE Start can be used on its own: *Have you any idea where the rumour started?*

WHICH WORD?

Start (off) is more frequent in spoken English and in business contexts than **begin**, which is more frequent in written English and is often used when you are describing a series of events: *The story begins on the island of Corfu.* **Open** is a less informal way of saying **kick off**; however, it is **not** usually used for shorter or more informal activities: *What time do we kick off?* You can use it for longer or more formal events: *The conference opens on 15 March.*

PATTERNS AND COLLOCATIONS

- to start/begin/start off/kick off/commence/ open **by doing/with** sth
- to start/begin/start off/commence **as** sth
- a **campaign/season/tour** starts/begins/starts off/kicks off/commences/opens
- a **film/book/chapter** starts/begins/starts off/ opens
- an **enquiry/investigation** starts/begins/commences/opens
- **work/production** starts/begins/starts off/kicks off/commences

with no political opinions, but soon got involved in student politics. ◇ *She'd started out meaning to apologize but couldn't.* **SYN** set out to do sth
◆ v + adv **3** also v + adv + **to**+inf ◆ v + adv + -ing

start 'over; **start sth 'over** (*especially AmE*) to begin doing sth again, especially because you were not successful the first time: *I messed up and had to start over.* ◇ *She spelled my name wrong and had to start over.* ◇ *His wife has walked out and he must start life over.*
◆ v + adv ◆ v + n/pron + adv

start 'up to begin happening: *After a moment's silence, the music started up again.*
◆ v + adv

start 'up; **start sth 'up 1** to start operating; to make sth start operating: *The engine started up with a roar.* ◇ *It took me a while to start up the generator.* ◇ *I heard the car starting up.* **2** (**in sth**) to start operating or trading; to establish a business: *When I started up in business, I needed a lot of help.* ◇ *There are a lot of small businesses starting up in the area.* ◇ *My father helped me start up my own company.* **OBJ** business, company
◆ v + adv ◆ v + adv + n ◆ v + n/pron + adv

▶ **'start-up** *adj* connected with beginning a new business: *the new company's start-up costs*

▶ **'start-up** *n* a company that is just beginning to operate, especially an Internet company: *This is just one of the problems facing start-ups in this highly competitive area.*

starve /stɑːv; *AmE* stɑːrv/

'starve for sth; **'starve sb/sth for sth** (*AmE*) to feel you do not have sth that you really need; to prevent sb/sth from having sth necessary or very important: *Sam was starving for a kind word from Clare.* ◇ *The children were starved for affection.*
NOTE Starve for sth is usually used in the progressive tenses. Usually used in the passive.
→ see also STARVE SB/STH OF STH
◆ v + prep ◆ v + n/pron + prep

'starve sb into sth; **'starve sb into doing sth** to force sb to do sth or accept sth by preventing them from getting food or money: *The aim was to* **starve** *the enemy* **into submission**.
◆ v + n/pron + prep

'starve sb/sth of sth to prevent sb/sth from having sth that they want or need: *The project is being starved of funds.* ◇ *The baby had been starved of oxygen at birth.* ◇ *Teachers described the students as starved of attention and affection.*
SYN deprive sb/sth/yourself of sth
NOTE Usually used in the passive.
→ see also STARVE FOR STH, ETC.
◆ v + n/pron + prep

starve sb 'out to force sb to leave a place by not allowing them to get food: *It took a month to*

start on sth

begin sth ◆ embark on/upon sth ◆ get down to sth ◆ start on sth ◆ take sth up
These verbs all mean to do the first part of sth, or to do sth or make sth happen or exist for the first time.

begin sth to do the first part of sth; to do sth that you were not doing just before; to make sth happen or exist for the first time: *He always begins his lessons with a warm-up exercise.* ◇ *She began to cry.* ◇ *Everyone began talking at once.*

embark on/upon sth to begin doing sth new or difficult: *She is about to embark on a new career.*

get down to sth to begin giving serious attention to sth: *Let's get down to business.* ◇ *It's time I got down to thinking about that essay.*

start on sth to begin doing sth; to make sth begin to happen: *It's time you started on your homework.* **NOTE** Start sth can be used on its own: *It's time you started your homework.*

take sth up to begin sth such as a job or hobby: *He takes up his duties next week.* ◇ *They've taken up golf.*

WHICH WORD?

Start sth (up) is more frequent in spoken English and in business contexts than **begin**, which is more frequent in written English. **Start**, but *not* **begin**, can also mean 'to make sth start happening or working': *Who started the fire?* ◇ *I can't start the car.*

PATTERNS AND COLLOCATIONS

- to begin/start/get down to **doing sth**
- to begin/start **to do sth**
- to begin/start sth **by doing/with** sth
- to begin/start **a discussion/a conversation/negotiations/an argument/a fight/a riot**
- to begin/start/get down to **work**
- to begin/start/take up **a job/employment/your duties/a hobby**
- to begin/start/embark on a **journey/hunt/search/relationship/career**

---

starve them out. ◇ *A few rebels remain in the area. The rest have been starved out.*
◆ v + n/pron + adv ◆ v + adv + n

stash /stæʃ/

ˌstash sth aˈway (*informal*) to store sth in a secret or safe place: *She has a fortune stashed away in various bank accounts.*
SYN hide sth away
◆ v + n/pron + adv ◆ v + adv + n

stave /steɪv/

ˌstave sth ˈin to break sth by hitting it with force and making part of it fall: *The side of the boat was staved in when it hit the rocks.*
◆ v + n/pron + adv ◆ v + adv + n

ˌstave sth ˈoff to prevent sth unpleasant from happening for a period of time; to delay sth unpleasant: *to stave off hunger/illness* ◇ *desperate attempts to stave off civil war* ◇ *I staved off jet lag with a bath and an early night.*
SYN avert sth
◆ v + adv + n ◆ v + pron + adv ◆ v + n + adv (*rare*)

stay /steɪ/

ˌstay aˈhead; ˌstay aˈhead of sb/sth to succeed in remaining further forward in space, time, development, success, etc.: *We need to keep an eye on our competitors if we want to stay ahead.* ◇ *He stayed ahead of me throughout the race.* ◇ *More investment is needed if we are to*

stay ahead of the game (= be more successful than our competitors). **SUBJ** competitors
SYN keep ahead, keep ahead of sb/sth
◆ v + adv ◆ v + adv + prep

ˌstay aˈround to not leave somewhere: *I'll stay around in case you need me.* ◇ *I don't know if he'll be angry with us or not, but I'm not staying around to find out!*
◆ v + adv

ˌstay aˈway (**from sb/sth**) to not go near sb/sth dangerous or unpleasant; to have nothing to do with sb/sth: *Stay away from the edge!* ◇ *He advised us to stay away from drugs.* ◇ *The police have asked the public to stay away.*
SYN keep away (**from sb/sth**)
◆ v + adv

ˌstay ˈback to remain in a place and not move forward: *The police shouted to the crowd to stay back.*
SYN keep back (**from sb/sth**)
◆ v + adv

ˌstay beˈhind (**after sth**) to remain in a place at the end of an event after other people have left: *I had to stay behind after class.* ◇ *She stayed behind after the meeting for a chat.*
◆ v + adv

ˌstay ˈdown **1** to remain in a low position: *The blind won't stay down.* ◇ *Get down and stay down or he'll see you!* **SYN** keep down **2** (of food) to remain in the stomach: *Nothing she ate would stay down.*
◆ v + adv

,stay 'in **1** to remain in a position inside sth: *This nail won't stay in.* **2** to remain at home or inside a building: *I was ill and had to stay in all week.* ◇ *Let's stay in this evening.*
♦ v + adv

,stay 'off to keep away; to not return: *If the rain stays off, we'll got out for a walk.* ◇ *She's always dieting, but she can never get the weight to stay off.*
♦ v + adv

,stay 'off; ,stay 'off sth (*BrE*) to not go to work, school, etc., especially because you are ill/sick: *He injured his back and stayed off for a week.* ◇ *Can I stay off school today?*
[OBJ] **work, school**
♦ v + adv ♦ v + prep

,stay 'off sth to stop yourself from eating or drinking sth, especially sth that could be harmful: *The doctor told him to stay off alcohol.*
[SYN] **keep off sth**
♦ v + prep

,stay 'on **1** to remain in position on top of sth: *The lid won't stay on.* **2** to not leave a job, school, place, etc. when you are expected to, or when other people do: *We hope he will stay on as manager at the end of his contract.* ◇ *We couldn't persuade Jane to stay on at school for an extra year.* **3** to continue operating: *The light stays on until dawn.*
♦ v + adv

,stay 'out **1** to remain out of the house or outdoors, especially at night: *Sam was allowed to stay out until 11.30 on a Saturday.* ◇ *I don't like you staying out so late.* **2** to remain on strike: *The miners stayed out for fifteen months.*
♦ v + adv

,stay 'out; ,stay 'out of sth to remain outside a place: *Stay out, the floor's wet.* ◇ *Stay out of the kitchen, I'm busy.*
♦ v + adv ♦ v + adv + prep

,stay 'out of sth **1** to not become involved in sth that does not concern you: *I try to stay out of their little quarrels.* ◇ *Stay out of this, it's none of your business.* **2** to avoid sth: *Try to stay out of trouble!*
[SYN] **keep out of sth, keep sb out of sth**
♦ v + adv + prep

,stay 'over to sleep at sb's house for a night: *It got late, so we stayed over.* ◇ *Can I stay over at Gareth's (house) tonight?*
[SYN] **sleep over**
♦ v + adv

,stay 'up **1** if sth **stays up**, it remains in a standing or higher position where it has been put, built, etc.: *These trousers won't stay up without a belt.* ◇ *I'm not very good at putting up shelves—I'm amazed they've stayed up!* **2** to not go to bed: *Don't **stay up** too **late**.* ◇ *We let him stay up to watch the movie.*
♦ v + adv

'stay with sth/sb (*informal*) to continue to do sth, especially when it is difficult or you do not really want to: *Several students weren't enjoying the course, but they stayed with it.* ◇ *Stay with me, I've nearly finished.*
[SYN] **stick with sth**
♦ v + prep

steal /stiːl/ (**stole** /stəʊl; *AmE* stoʊl/, **stolen** /'stəʊlən; *AmE* 'stoʊ-/)

,steal a'way to go away from a place quietly and secretly: *He stole away under cover of darkness.*
♦ v + adv

,steal 'over sb (*formal*) if a feeling **steals over** you, you gradually feel it: *A chill stole over her body.* ◇ *Exhaustion stole over me as I sat there.*
♦ v + prep

,steal 'up (on sb) to approach sb quietly so that they do not see or hear you coming: *She stole up on him in the dark.*
♦ v + adv

steam /stiːm/

,steam sth 'off; ,steam sth 'off sth to remove a piece of paper from another piece using steam to melt the glue that is holding them together: *He steamed the stamp off the envelope.*
♦ v + n/pron + adv ♦ v + adv + n ♦ v + n/pron + prep

,steam 'up; ,steam sth 'up to become, or to make sth become, covered with steam: *The windows had steamed up.* ◇ *The warmth in the room steamed all the windows up.*
[SYN] **fog up; mist up, mist sth up**
♦ v + adv ♦ v + n/pron + adv ♦ v + adv + n

[IDM] **be/get (all) steamed 'up (about/over sth)** (*BrE, informal*) to be/become very angry or excited about sth: *I realized I had got all steamed up over nothing.*

steep /stiːp/

'steep sth in sth to put food in a liquid and leave it for some time so that it becomes soft and flavoured by the liquid: *Raspberries are delicious steeped in brandy.*
♦ v + n/pron + prep

'steep yourself in sth; be 'steeped in sth (*formal*) to spend a lot of time doing sth or thinking about sth and learn a lot about it: *teenagers steeping themselves in pop culture* ◇ *He was steeped in the family business from an early age.*
♦ v + pron + prep ♦ be + v + prep

be 'steeped in sth to have a lot of a particular quality: *a city steeped in history*
[OBJ] **history, tradition**
♦ be + v + prep

steer /stɪə(r); *AmE* stɪr/

,steer a'way from sth to avoid discussing sth or becoming involved with sb/sth, because it may cause problems: *I tried to steer away from*

the subject of divorce. ◊ *Jane tends to steer away from sugary foods.*
◆ v + adv + prep

stem /stem/ (**-mm-**)
'**stem from sth** (*not used in the progressive tenses*) to be caused by sth; to be the result of sth: *Many of her problems stem from the fact that her parents are famous.* ◊ *Their opposition stems from fear and ignorance.* [SUBJ] **problem**, **difficulty** [OBJ] **the fact that...**
◆ v + prep

step /step/ (**-pp-**)
,**step a'side/'down** (**as/from sth**) to leave an important job or position in order to let sb else take your place: *After ten years as party leader, it's time for him to step aside.* ◊ *He decided to step aside as director to make way for his son.* ◊ *I intended to step down as Chairman.* ◊ *She's stepping down from her post next year.*
◆ v + adv
,**step 'back 1** (**from sth**) to try to think calmly about a situation in which you have been closely involved, as if you are not involved in it: *You should try to step back from the problem and look for a new way to deal with it.* [SYN] **stand back** (**from sth**) **2** to feel as if you have moved backwards to an earlier period of history: *When*

you enter the cathedral you **step back in time** to the 15th century.
◆ v + adv
,**step 'down** (**as/from sth**) → STEP ASIDE/DOWN [SYN] **stand down** (**as/from sth**)
,**step 'forward** to offer to help sb, give information, money, etc.: *A soft drinks company has stepped forward to sponsor the team.*
◆ v + adv
,**step 'in** to help in an argument or a difficult situation: *When my mum was ill, my aunt stepped in to help.* ◊ *The Youth Club was going to close, but a local bank stepped in with a generous donation.*
◆ v + adv
'**step on it** (*informal*) used especially to tell sb to drive faster: *Step on it! We're late!* ◊ *We'll have to step on it to be there by noon.* ◊ (*figurative*) *Step on it! I need those figures soon.*
◆ v + prep + it
,**step 'out** (*especially AmE*) to leave a place for a short period: *He's just stepped out for ten minutes.*
◆ v + adv
,**step 'up** (**to sb/sth**) to come forward: *He stepped up to receive his award.* ◊ *The runners stepped up to the line.*
◆ v + adv
,**step sth 'up** to increase the rate, level, amount, etc. of sth: *Security has been stepped up at the*

SYNONYMS

step sth up

boost sth ◆ **heighten sth** ◆ **intensify sth** ◆ **step sth up**
These verbs all mean to make the amount or level of sth bigger or greater.

boost sth (*often approving, used especially in newspapers*) to make sth become stronger, better or more successful: *to boost productivity/sales/spending* ◊ *to boost sb's morale/career/confidence* [NOTE] **Boost** is always used about a positive increase.

heighten sth to increase an effect or feeling or make it stronger: *The campaign is intended to heighten public awareness of the disease.* ◊ *Fears of further conflict were heightened by news of the riots.*

intensify sth to increase an activity or feeling in degree or strength: *The leader has intensified his attacks on the government.* ◊ *The reforms served only to intensify the misery of the poor.* ▶ **intensification** *n* [U, sing.]

step sth up to increase the level of an activity: *He has stepped up his training to prepare for*

the race. ◊ *Security has been stepped up in response to the recent threat.*

WHICH WORD?

Heighten and **intensify** can also be used without an object, though **heighten** is more commonly used with an object. **Heighten** is used especially about feelings and attitudes; **intensify** can apply to actions too: *a heightened sense of loneliness/well-being* ◊ *to intensify the campaign/battle.*

PATTERNS AND COLLOCATIONS

■ to boost/step up sth **by.../from.../to...**
■ to boost/heighten **awareness/interest**
■ to boost **support/confidence/your income/prices/profits/numbers**
■ to intensify/step up **the pressure/a campaign/your efforts**
■ to heighten **the tension**
■ to intensify/heighten/step up **security**
■ to boost sth **considerably/significantly/dramatically**

airport since the bomb scare. ◊ Police have stepped up their search for the missing schoolgirl. OBJ **campaign**, **pressure**, **security**, **production**, **efforts**
♦ v + adv + n ♦ v + n/pron + adv

stick /stɪk/ (stuck, stuck /stʌk/)

NOTE **Stick** is often used as an informal way of saying **put**.

,stick a'round (*informal*) to stay in or near a place, waiting for sth to happen, sb to arrive, etc.: *Stick around—we need all the help we can get.* ◊ *I'll stick around here in case Maya arrives.*
♦ v + adv

'stick at sth to work continuously at sth in a determined way: *If we **stick at it**, we should finish the job today.* ◊ *She never sticks at anything for very long.*
SYN **keep at sth**; **persevere with sth** (*more formal*)
♦ v + prep

,stick sth 'back (*informal*) to return sth to its usual place; to return sth to the place it was before: *Stick the cake back in the oven for ten minutes.* ◊ *When you've finished with the dictionary, just stick it back on the shelf.*
SYN **put sth back**
♦ v + n/pron + adv

'stick by sb (*informal*) to be loyal to sb and continue to support them in difficult times: *She stuck by him through thick and thin.*
SYN **stand by sb**
♦ v + prep

'stick by sth to do what you said, planned or promised you would do, even though the situation might have changed: *In spite of what's happened, we must stick by our decision.* ◊ *The developer wants to stick by his original plan.*
SYN **stand by sth**
♦ v + prep

'stick sth 'down **1** to fix a piece of paper, etc. to sth else using glue: *I can't stick the letter in my wallpaper down.* ◊ *The envelope hadn't been stuck down properly.* **2** (*informal*) to place sth that you are holding onto the floor or another surface: *Stick your coat on the chair and come and sit down here.* SYN **put sth down 3** (**in/on sth**) (*informal*) to write or note sth down quickly: *Stick it all down on paper before you forget.*
SYN **put sth down**; **note sth down**; **jot sth down**
♦ v + n/pron + adv ♦ v + adv + n

,stick sth 'in/'into sth; ,stick sth 'in **1** (*informal*) to put sth into sth: *I stuck the letter in my pocket to read later.* ◊ *He saw the hole and stuck his finger in.* ◊ *I stuck my feet into my slippers.* ◊ *Timmy stuck his thumb in his mouth.* SYN **put sth in, put sth in/into sth 2** to put sth sharp into sth, making a small hole: *Ouch! I've stuck the needle in my finger!* OBJ **knife**, **needle 3** (*informal*) to include sth in a story, a letter, etc.:

Should I stick this paragraph in or leave it out? ◊ *I'll stick in something about football to make the article more interesting.* SYN **put sth in, put sth in/into sth 4** to attach sth firmly to sth, using tape or glue: *I'm going to stick the photos in my album.*
♦ v + n/pron + adv ♦ v + adv + n ♦ v + n/pron + prep

IDM **stick/poke your 'oar/'nose into sth** (*informal*) to try to become involved in sth that does not concern you

,get stuck 'in; ,get stuck 'into sth (*BrE*, *informal*) to start doing sth in an enthusiastic way; to become very interested and involved in sth: *You must be hungry. Get stuck in!* (= start eating) ◊ *I was too tired to get really stuck into the debate.*
♦ get + v + adv ♦ get + v + prep

,stick sth 'on (*informal*) **1** to switch on a piece of electrical equipment: *I'll stick the kettle on for a cup of tea.* **2** to put on clothes: *I'll just stick a jacket on, and I'm ready.* **3** to begin to cook food: *I'll stick the potatoes on.* **4** to make a CD, etc. begin to play: *Stick on some music, if you like.*
SYN **put sth on**
♦ v + n/pron + adv ♦ v + adv + n

,stick sth 'on; ,stick sth 'on/'onto sth to attach sth firmly to a surface, using glue, tape, etc.: *I stuck the label on with adhesive tape.* ◊ *He sealed the envelope, and stuck a stamp on it.*
♦ v + n/pron + adv ♦ v + adv + n ♦ v + n/pron + prep
▸ 'stick-on *adj* [only before noun] a **stick-on** object has glue on one side so that it can be attached to sth: *stick-on badges/labels*

,stick sth 'on sth (*informal*) **1** to put sth somewhere in a careless or rough way: *Stick your report on my desk when you've finished it.* **2** to add an amount of money to the price or cost of sth: *They can't just stick an extra 20p on the price of cigarettes!*
SYN **put sth on sth**
♦ v + n/pron + prep

,stick 'out to be very noticeable or easy to see: *They wrote the notice in red so that it would stick out.* ◊ (*figurative*) *One of the boys in the class sticks out in my mind.*
SYN **stand out** (*more formal*)
♦ v + adv

IDM **stick out a 'mile** to be very noticeable or easy to see: *Dressed like that, you stick out a mile.* ◊ *It stuck out a mile that she was lying.*
stick out like a sore 'thumb to be very different from others, especially in an unpleasant way: *The red house stuck out like a sore thumb among the old stone cottages.*

,stick 'out; ,stick 'out of sth to be further out than sth else; to be partly outside sth such as a container: *His ears stick out.* ◊ *There was a newspaper sticking out of her coat pocket.*
♦ v + adv ♦ v + adv + prep

,stick sth 'out; ,stick sth 'out of sth to make sth, especially part of your body, come through

sting

a hole: *If you want to turn right, stick out your hand.* ◇ *I stuck my head out of the window to see what was happening.*

OBJ **head, tongue** **SYN** **poke sth out**, etc.
- v + adv + n • v + n/pron + adv
- v + n/pron + adv + prep

IDM **stick your 'neck out** (*informal*) to do or say sth when there is a risk you may be wrong: *I'm going to stick my neck out and say that we'll have a dry summer.*

,**stick it/sth 'out** to continue doing sth difficult or boring until it is finished: *I don't like being on my own, but I'll stick it out until my parents come back.* ◇ *I'm amazed that she's stuck the course out this long.*
- v + n/pron + adv

,**stick 'out for sth** (*BrE, informal*) to refuse to give up until you get what you want: *They're sticking out for a higher pay rise.*

SYN **hold out for sth**
- v + adv + prep

,**stick 'through**; ,**stick 'through sth** if sth **sticks through** or **sticks through** sth, it goes from one side to the other and it is partly outside: *His head was sticking through the railings.*
- v + adv • v + n/pron + adv

⸙ '**stick to sth 1** to continue doing sth even if it is difficult or you have problems: *He found it difficult to stick to a diet.* → see also STICK WITH STH 1 **2** to continue doing or using sth and not want to change it: *I'm sticking to my previous statement.* ◇ *That's her story and she's sticking to it.* → see also STICK WITH STH 2 **3** to keep inside the limits of a particular subject, etc.: *I'm not interested in your opinions—just stick to the facts.*
- v + prep

IDM **stick to your 'guns** to refuse to change your mind about sth even when other people are trying to persuade you that you are wrong

⸙ **stick to**'**gether** (*informal*) **1** to remain friendly and loyal to one another; to support each other: *The family should stick together at a time like this.* ◇ *The children from the village tended to stick together.* **2** (*informal*) to stay physically close to each other: *Let's all stick together until we find the way out.*
→ see also STICK WITH SB 1
- v + adv

,**stick sth to**'**gether** to attach things or parts of things to each other: *Cut out the shapes and stick them together to make a bird.*
- v + n/pron + adv • v + adv + n

⸙,**stick 'up** to point upwards: *The branch was sticking up out of the water.* ◇ *Is my hair sticking up?*
- v + adv

,**stick sb/sth 'up** (*AmE, informal*) → HOLD SB/STH UP: *He stuck up a liquor store in Oregon.*

▶ '**stick-up** *n* (*AmE, informal*) an act of robbing sb/sth using a gun: *This is a stick-up, nobody move!*

,**stick sth 'up** to attach sth to a wall, a board, a window, etc. so that people can see it: *They had stuck up posters everywhere advertising the show.* ◇ *If you want to sell your bike, just stick a notice up in the shop window.*

SYN **put sth up**
- v + adv + n • v + n/pron + adv

,**stick sth 'up**; ,**stick sth 'up sth** (*informal*) to place sth in a high position; to move sth upwards, especially inside sth: *Stick your hand up if you know the answer.* ◇ *Jeff stuck his hand up the pipe to see what was blocking it.*

OBJ **hand, finger**
- v + n/pron + adv • v + adv + n

,**stick 'up for sb/yourself/sth** (*informal*) to support or defend sb, yourself or sth, when they are being criticized: *She always sticks up for her little sister.* ◇ *You must stick up for what you believe in.* ◇ *Don't be so weak—you should stick up for yourself.*
- v + adv + prep

'**stick with sb 1** (*informal*) to stay physically close to sb: *Stick with me until we get out of the forest.* → see also STICK TOGETHER 2 **2** (*informal*) to remain in sb's memory: *His words will stick with me for ever.*
- v + prep

'**stick with sth** (*informal*) **1** to continue to do sth in spite of difficulties: *If we stick with it we should finish soon.* ◇ *I stuck with the job for as long as I could.* **2** to continue doing or using sth and not want to change: *I've decided to stick with my usual method.* → see also STICK TO STH 2
- v + prep

be/get 'stuck with sb/sth (*informal*) to be forced to do sth, take care of sb/sth, etc. that you do not want to: *How did I get stuck with all the cleaning?* ◇ *If we're stuck with each other for the next two weeks, we might as well be polite.* ◇ *I got stuck with defending my brother's wild behaviour* (= but I really thought he was wrong).
- be/get + v + prep

sting /stɪŋ/ (**stung, stung** /stʌŋ/)

'**sting sb for sth** (*informal*) **1** to trick or cheat sb into paying more money than they should or than they expected to: *Motorists are being stung for another £25 road tax.* **2** (*BrE*) to borrow money from sb, especially when they are unwilling to give it to you: *Can I sting you for a fiver?*
- v + n/pron + prep

stink /stɪŋk/ (**stank** /stæŋk/, **stunk** /stʌŋk/ or **stunk, stunk**)

,**stink sth 'out** (*BrE*) (*AmE* ,**stink sth 'up**) (*informal*) to fill a room, a building, etc. with a very

unpleasant smell: *He stank the whole place out with his cigarettes.*
OBJ **the place** SYN **smell sth out** (*BrE*); **smell sth up** (*AmE*)
♦ v + n/pron + adv ♦ v + adv + n

stir /stɜ:(r)/ (-rr-)

‚stir sth 'in; ‚stir sth 'into sth to mix one substance into another by moving a spoon, etc.: *Stir in the cream.* ◇ *Stir the pasta into the sauce.*
SYN **mix sth in** (**with sth**), **mix sth into sth**
♦ v + adv + n ♦ v + n/pron + adv ♦ v + n/pron + prep

‚stir sb 'up to encourage sb to do sth; to make sb feel they must do sth: *He was accused of stirring up the slaves against their masters.*
♦ v + adv + n ♦ v + n/pron + adv

‚stir sb/sth 'up 1 to cause trouble, especially by making people feel strong emotions: *I don't want to stir up any more trouble.* ◇ *The government has been accused of stirring up racial hatred.* OBJ **hatred**, **trouble**, **things**, **controversy** SYN **rouse sb/sth 2** to make sb have a particular feeling or attitude: *Her story stirred up a lot of old memories for me.* ◇ *I can't seem to stir up any interest in the campaign.* OBJ **memories**, **interest**, **emotions 3** to make sth such as sand or dust move around in water or air: *The helicopter stirred up a cloud of dust.* OBJ **dust**
♦ v + adv + n ♦ v + n/pron + adv

IDM **stir up a 'hornets' nest** to cause a difficult situation in which a lot of people get very angry: *His criticisms of the president stirred up a hornets' nest.*

stitch /stɪtʃ/

‚stitch sb 'up (*BrE, informal*) to make sb appear to be guilty of sth they have not done, for example by giving false information; to cheat sb: *I didn't do it! I've been stitched up!*
SYN **frame sb**
♦ v + n/pron + adv ♦ v + adv + n

▶ 'stitch-up *n* (*BrE, informal*) a situation in which sb deliberately cheats you or causes you to be wrongly blamed for sth: *It was a stitch-up!*

‚stitch sth 'up 1 to join things together using a needle and thread: *This wound has to be stitched up urgently.* OBJ **wound 2** (*BrE, informal*) to arrange sth; to complete a business deal: *He has managed to stitch up major deals all over the world.* ◇ *The company has the US market stitched up.* OBJ **deal**
SYN **sew sth up**
♦ v + adv + n ♦ v + n/pron + adv

stock /stɒk; *AmE* stɑːk/

‚stock 'up (**on/with sth**) to buy or get a lot of sth so that you can use it later: *The shops are very busy with people stocking up for the holidays.* ◇ *I need to stock up on food before all the family arrive.*
♦ v + adv

‚stock sth 'up (**on/with sth**) to fill sth with goods, food, etc.: *Mum stocked up the freezer for us before she went to the conference.*
♦ v + adv + n ♦ v + n/pron + adv

stoke /stəʊk; *AmE* stoʊk/

‚stoke 'up (**on/with sth**) (*informal*) to eat a lot of sth so that you will not feel hungry later: *We'd better stoke up now—we've got a long journey in front of us.*
♦ v + adv

‚stoke sth 'up 1 to keep a fire, etc. burning by adding more fuel: *He stoked up the fire before going to bed.* OBJ **fire 2** to make people feel sth more strongly: *He continued to stoke up hatred in his speeches.*
NOTE **Stoke sth** can also be used on its own with the same meanings.
♦ v + adv + n ♦ v + n/pron + adv

stoop /stu:p/

‚stoop to sth; ‚stoop to doing sth to do sth bad or unpleasant in order to gain an advantage for yourself: *I can't believe he would stoop to blackmail.* ◇ *He's the kind of person who would stoop to making personal attacks on a rival.*
SYN **descend to sth** (*more formal*)
♦ v + prep

stop /stɒp; *AmE* stɑːp/ (-pp-)

‚stop a'round; ‚stop a'round sth (*AmE*) to make a short visit to sb, usually at their home: *I'll stop around this evening when I finish work.* ◇ *Let's stop around the Smiths' house for a drink.*
SYN **drop round; pop over/round** (*BrE*)
♦ v + adv ♦ v + prep

‚stop a'way to deliberately decide not to go somewhere: *Many of the people invited to the dinner had stopped away in protest.*
SYN **stay away**
NOTE **Stay away** is more frequent.
♦ v + adv

‚stop 'back (*AmE*) to return to somewhere that you visited earlier: *I'll stop back on my way home.*
♦ v + adv

‚stop be'hind (**after sth**) (*informal*) to remain somewhere at the end of an event after other people have left: *She stopped behind after the meeting to talk to him.*
NOTE **Stay behind** is more frequent.
♦ v + adv

‚stop 'by; ‚stop 'by sth to make a short visit to sb/sth, especially when you are on the way to somewhere else: *Stop by for a chat on your way home.* ◇ *Could you stop by the store for some milk?*
SYN **come by, come by sth; drop by** ⟳ note at VISIT WITH SB
♦ v + adv ♦ v + prep

store

,stop 'in (*BrE, informal*) to stay at home rather than go out: *We've decided to stop in tonight because it's raining.*
NOTE Stay in is more frequent.
◆ v + adv

,stop 'off (at/in...) to stop somewhere for a short time when you are on the way to somewhere else: *We stopped off for lunch just north of Paris.* ◇ *I stopped off at the supermarket on the way home.*
◆ v + adv
▶ 'stop-off *n* **1** a short stay somewhere during a trip: *a stop-off in Sydney* **2** a place where you stop for a short time during a trip

,stop 'on [+ adv/prep] (*BrE, informal*) to stay somewhere longer than you planned or after other people have left: *I'll stop on an hour after work.*
NOTE Stay on is more frequent.
◆ v + adv

,stop 'out (*BrE, informal*) to stay out late at night or all night instead of going home: *He often stops out till three in the morning.*
NOTE Stay out is more frequent.
◆ v + adv

,stop 'over (in/at ...) to stop somewhere for a short time when you are on a long journey, especially a journey by plane: *I stopped over in Mérida on the way to Havana.*
◆ v + adv
▶ 'stopover *n* **1** a short stay somewhere during a long journey: *We had a three-day stopover in Hawaii.* **2** a place where you stay for a short time during a long journey

,stop 'up (*BrE, informal*) to not go to bed until later than usual: *She stopped up to see the football match.*
NOTE Stay up is more frequent.
◆ v + adv

,stop sth 'up to cover or fill a hole, a crack, etc. so that nothing can get through: *I stopped up all the holes to keep out the draught.*
SYN block sth up
◆ v + adv + n ◆ v + n/pron + adv

store /stɔː(r)/

,store sth a'way to put sth in a safe place and keep it there so that you can use it later: *We stored away the baby clothes.* ◇ *It's amazing how much knowledge he's got stored away in his memory.* ◇ *I stored away the information for future use.*
◆ v + adv + n ◆ v + n/pron + adv

,store 'up sth to make trouble for yourself in future: *Smokers may be storing up health problems for their unborn children.* ◇ *Children who store up their bad feelings often develop headaches or stomach pains.*
OBJ problems, trouble

NOTE A pronoun always comes between the verb and **up**.
◆ v + adv + n ◆ v + pron + adv

,store sth 'up **1** to keep sth so that it can be used later: *animals storing up food for the winter* ◇ *The batteries store up enough energy for a week.* **NOTE** Store sth is also used on its own. **2** to keep information or facts in your memory to use later: *He stored up all the amusing and interesting things that happened during the day to tell his family in the evening.*
◆ v + adv + n ◆ v + n/pron + adv

storm /stɔːm; *AmE* stɔːrm/

,storm 'off to leave a place or a person suddenly because you are very angry: *We had a big argument and he stormed off.*
◆ v + adv

stow /stəʊ; *AmE* stoʊ/

,stow a'way (on sth) to hide on a vehicle, especially a ship or a plane, in order to travel without paying or without being seen: *He stowed away on a ship bound for Vigo.*
◆ v + adv
▶ 'stowaway *n* a person who hides on a ship or a plane in order to travel without paying or without being seen

,stow sth a'way to put sth in a place where it will be safe or will not be found: *He stowed his passport away safely in a drawer.*
◆ v + n/pron + adv ◆ v + adv + n

straighten /'streɪtn/

,straighten 'out; ,straighten sth 'out to become or to make sth straight: *After the bridge, the road straightens out.* ◇ *attempts to straighten out the river*
◆ v + adv ◆ v + adv + n ◆ v + n/pron + adv

,straighten sb 'out; ,straighten yourself 'out to help sb deal with problems or understand a difficult situation; to help yourself in this way: *A few sessions talking to a counsellor should straighten him out.*
SYN sort sb/yourself out
◆ v + n/pron + adv ◆ v + adv + n

,straighten sth 'out to deal with problems or a difficult situation; to organize things that are confused: *I was left to straighten out the mess.* ◇ *He's trying to straighten out his finances.*
SYN sort sth out
◆ v + adv + n ◆ v + n/pron + adv

,straighten 'up to stand up straight from a bent position: *She slowly straightened up and rubbed her back.*
◆ v + adv

,straighten sth 'up to make a room, etc. neat and tidy: *We'd better straighten up the house before they get back.*
SYN tidy sth up
◆ v + adv + n ◆ v + n/pron + adv

strain /streɪn/

strain at sth to pull very hard on sth: *The dog was straining at its lead.*

   ◆ v + prep

IDM **strain at the 'leash** (*informal*) to want to do sth very much, especially when sb/sth is trying to stop you: *He's straining at the leash to get on with his research.*

strain sth 'off to separate a liquid from sth solid by pouring it through sth that has very small holes in it: *Strain off any excess liquid.*

   ◆ v + adv + n ◆ v + n/pron + adv

strap /stræp/ (-pp-)

NOTE A **strap** is a strip of leather, cloth, etc. that is used to fasten sth or keep sth in place.

strap sb 'in; ˌstrap yourself 'in; ˌstrap sb/ yourself 'into sth to fasten sb/yourself in a seat, etc. using straps: *All passengers in the plane must be securely strapped in.* ◇ *Make sure you strap the baby firmly into the high chair.* ◇ *Have you strapped yourselves in?*

   ◆ v + n/pron + adv ◆ v + n/pron + prep

strap sth 'on; ˌstrap sth 'onto sth to attach sth to sth else with straps: *He strapped on his helmet and rode away.* ◇ *She strapped the suit-cases onto the roof of the car.*

   ◆ v + adv + n ◆ v + n/pron + adv ◆ v + n/pron + prep

strap sth 'up to tie bandages around sth, especially an injured part of the body, to support it or prevent it from moving: *Your wrist needs to be strapped up.*

   ◆ v + n/pron + adv ◆ v + adv + n

stress /stres/

stress sb 'out (*informal*) to make sb very anxious and tired so that they are unable to relax: *My job really stresses me out.* ◇ *My dad stressed me out by criticizing me all the time.*

   ◆ v + n/pron + adv

  ▶ ˌstressed 'out *adj* too anxious and tired to be able to relax: *When I'm stressed out, I try to go for a long walk.* ◇ *stressed-out executives*

stretch /stretʃ/

ˌstretch a'way/'out [+ **adv/prep**] to spread over a large area of land, especially away from where you are: *The mountains stretched away into the distance.* ◇ *Banana plantations stretched away as far as the eye could see.*

   SYN **extend**

   ◆ v + adv

ˌstretch 'out; ˌstretch yourself 'out to lie down, with your arms or legs out straight, especially in order to relax or sleep: *He stretched out on the floor and fell asleep.*

   ◆ v + adv ◆ v + pron + adv

ˌstretch sth 'out 1 to put your arm or leg out straight, especially in order to reach sth: *She stretched out a hand to touch his face.* ◇ *He leant back and stretched his legs out in front of him.*

OBJ **arm**, **hand**, **leg 2** to make sth last as long as possible by not using very much at a time: *It's hard to stretch my money out to the end of the month.* **SYN** **spin sth out**

   ◆ v + n/pron + adv ◆ v + adv + n

strew /struː/ (**strewed**, **strewed** or **strewn** /struːn/)

be 'strewn with sth to be covered with a lot of things: *The floor was strewn with clothes.* ◇ (*figurative*) *The way ahead is strewn with difficulties.*

   ◆ be + v + prep

strike /straɪk/ (**struck**, **struck** /strʌk/, *AmE* *also* **struck**, **stricken** /'strɪkən/)

'strike at sb/sth 1 to try to hit sb/sth, especially with a weapon: *She screamed and struck at the wolf with a stick.* **2** to cause damage or have a serious effect on sb/sth: *The proposals **struck at the roots of** community life.* ◇ *This legislation strikes at the most vulnerable people in society.*

   ◆ v + prep

ˌstrike 'back (**at/against sb/sth**) to criticize or attack sb who has criticized or attacked you: *Sarah used the article to strike back at her critics.* **SYN** **hit back** (**at sb/sth**)

   ◆ v + adv

ˌstrike sb 'down (*formal*) **1** if a disease **strikes sb down**, it kills them or makes them very ill/ sick: *She was struck down by polio at the age of four.* ◇ *I was struck down by flu and had to cancel the trip.* **2** to hit sb very hard so that they fall to the ground; to kill sb: *Fights broke out near the shop and one girl was struck down by a handbag.* ◇ *the spot where Kennedy was struck down*

   NOTE Often used in the passive.

   ◆ v + n/pron + adv ◆ v + adv + n

ˌstrike sth 'down (*especially AmE*) to reject sth; to make sth no longer valid: *Only the Supreme Court has the power to strike down this legisla-tion.* ◇ *Parents tried to have the ban struck down.*

   ◆ v + n/pron + adv ◆ v + adv + n

ˌstrike 'off → STRIKE OUT 3

ˌstrike sb/sth 'off; ˌstrike sb/sth 'off sth (*BrE*) to remove sb's name from the list of members of a profession so that they can no longer work in that profession: *She was struck off for professional misconduct.* ◇ *These doctors should be struck off the medical register.* ◇ *I'm going to strike Ashok off my guest list for the party.*

   ◆ v + n/pron + adv ◆ v + adv + n ◆ v + n/pron + prep

ˌstrike sth 'off (*formal*) to remove sth with a sharp blow; to cut sth off: *They struck off his head with a sword.* **SYN** **chop sth off** (*less formal*)

   ◆ v + adv + n ◆ v + n/pron + adv

ˌstrike 'out 1 (**at sb/sth**) to aim a violent blow at sb: *He struck out at me with his fist.* **SYN** **hit out** (**at sb/sth**) **2** to start being independent and do

sth new: *Sanjay left the firm and struck out on his own.* **3** (*also* ˌstrike ˈoff *less frequent*) [+ **adv/prep**] to start to go somewhere in a determined way: *He struck out across the fields towards the farmhouse.* **4** (**with sb**) (*AmE, informal*) to fail; to be unsuccessful: *I tried to get a job but struck out completely.* ◇ *He must have struck out with her because he came home early.* **5** (**at sb/sth**) to criticize sb/sth, especially publicly: *striking out at your critics* **SYN** **hit out** (**at sb/sth**)
◆ v + adv

ˌstrike ˈout; ˌstrike sb ˈout (*AmE*) (in baseball) to fail to hit the ball successfully three times and so finish your turn; to make sb do this: *He struck out in the third inning.* ◇ *The pitcher struck out three batters.*
◆ v + adv ◆ v + adv + n ◆ v + n/pron + adv
▶ ˈstrikeout *n* (in baseball) an occasion when sb is struck out

ˌstrike sth ˈout/ˈthrough (*especially BrE*) to remove sth from a text or a list by drawing a line through it: *I struck out some words to make the message shorter.* ◇ *He insisted that I strike out all references to his family.*
SYN **cross sth out/through**
◆ v + adv + n ◆ v + n/pron + adv
▶ ˈstrikethrough (*also* ˈstrikeout) *n* [U] a style of print in which words have a line through them, usually to show that they are wrong: *strikethrough text*

ˌstrike ˈup (**with sth**), ˌstrike ˈup sth if musicians **strike up**, they begin to play: *Everyone was waiting for the band to strike up.* ◇ *The orchestra struck up a lively tune.*
OBJ **tune**
◆ v + adv ◆ v + adv + n

ˌstrike ˈup sth (**with sb**) to begin a friendship, a relationship, a conversation, etc. with sb: *My mother will strike up a conversation with anyone she meets.* ◇ *Children of the same age don't always strike up friendships (with each other).*
OBJ **conversation, friendship, relationship**
◆ v + adv + n

string /strɪŋ/ (**strung, strung** /strʌŋ/)

ˌstring aˈlong (**with sb**) (*informal*) to go somewhere or do sth with sb else, especially because you have nothing else to do: *Can I string along with you when you go to the shops?*
SYN **tag along** (**behind/with sb**)
◆ v + adv

ˌstring sb aˈlong (*informal*) to allow sb to believe sth that is not true for a long time, especially when you encourage them to have false hopes: *They never intended to give her a job. They were just stringing her along.* ◇ *He strung her along for years and then married Kate.*
◆ v + n/pron + adv

ˌstring ˈout (**across/along sth**) to spread out in a line: *As we climbed, we tended to string out, with the fittest people taking the lead.*
◆ v + adv

ˌstring sth ˈout to make sth last longer than expected or necessary: *I didn't want to string out the argument.*
◆ v + adv + n ◆ v + n/pron + adv

ˌstring sth toˈgether **1** to combine words, phrases, sentences, etc. to form sth that has some meaning: *I can barely string together two words of German.* ◇ *The report should be written by somebody who can string two sentences together.* **OBJ** **words, a sentence 2** to join a series of things together: *pearls strung together on a necklace* ◇ *The student of kung fu learns various movements that are then strung together.*
◆ v + n/pron + adv ◆ v + adv + n

ˌstring sb ˈup (*informal*) to kill sb by hanging them, especially illegally: *They'll string him up if they catch him.*
◆ v + n/pron + adv ◆ v + adv + n

ˌstring sth ˈup to hang or tie sth in place: *She strung up a banner saying 'Happy 40th Birthday'.*
◆ v + n/pron + adv ◆ v + adv + n

strip /strɪp/ (**-pp-**)

ˌstrip sth aˈway **1** (**from sth**) to completely remove a layer of sth that is covering sth else: *Strip away the paint to reveal the wood underneath.* ◇ *The bark has been stripped away from the tree.* **2** to remove anything that is not true and necessary to reveal what sb/sth is really like: *When you strip away the jargon, he really has nothing sensible to say.* ◇ *The programme stripped away the mystery surrounding the royal family.* **3** to remove or get rid of sth that has existed for a long time: *Our basic rights are being stripped away by these laws.*
◆ v + adv + n ◆ v + n/pron + adv

ˌstrip sth ˈdown to separate a machine or an engine into parts, especially in order to clean or repair it: *We had to strip down the engine and replace the worn parts.* ◇ *The car was stripped down and sold for parts.*
SYN **dismantle sth** (*more formal*)
◆ v + adv + n ◆ v + n/pron + adv

ˌstrip ˈdown to sth to take off your clothes until you are only wearing the items mentioned: *I stripped down to my underwear for the massage.*
◆ v + adv + prep + noun

ˌstrip sth ˈfrom sth → STRIP STH OFF, ETC.

ˈstrip sb/sth of sth to take away a right, property, etc. that sb has, as a punishment: *He was stripped of his title for refusing to fight in Britain* (= for example, in boxing). ◇ *They stripped me of my citizenship and deported me.*
SYN **divest sb/sth of sth** (*formal*)
NOTE Often used in the passive.
◆ v + n/pron + prep

,strip 'off; ,strip sth 'off (*BrE*, *informal*) if you **strip off**, or **strip sth off**, you take off all or nearly all your clothes: *She stripped off and dived into the water.* ◇ *Strip off your wet clothes and put on these dry ones.*
➔ note at TAKE STH OFF
◆ v + adv ◆ v + adv + n ◆ v + n/pron + adv

,strip sth 'off; ,strip sth 'off/'from sth to remove a layer of sth: *It was hard work stripping the old wallpaper off.* ◇ *All the leaves had been stripped off the branches.*
◆ v + n/pron + adv ◆ v + adv + n ◆ v + n/pron + prep

,strip sth 'out to completely remove things you do not want; to remove everything from a place and leave it empty: *They had stripped out all the original features of the house.*
◆ v + adv + n ◆ v + n/pron + adv

struggle /'strʌgl/

,struggle a'long/'on to manage to continue in spite of great difficulties: *The country's economy is still struggling along.* ◇ *The government struggled on with a tiny majority.*
◆ v + adv

stub /stʌb/ (-bb-)

,stub sth 'out to stop a cigarette, etc. burning: *He stubbed the cigarette out with his foot.*
OBJ **cigarette**, **cigar** **SYN** **grind sth out**; **put sth out**; **extinguish sth** (*more formal*) ➔ note at PUT STH OUT
◆ v + n/pron + adv ◆ v + adv + n

stuff /stʌf/

,stuff 'up; ,stuff sth 'up (*BrE*, *slang*) to do sth very badly; to fail at sth: *I'm afraid I stuffed up again.* ◇ *I'm not having them stuff up my plans.*
SYN **mess up**; **mess sth up**
◆ v + adv ◆ v + adv + n ◆ v + n/pron + adv

stumble /'stʌmbl/

,stumble a'cross/'on/u'pon sb/sth to find sb/sth unexpectedly or by chance: *We stumbled on the solution by accident.* ◇ *I stumbled across an old school friend today.*
◆ v + prep

'stumble into sth to become involved in sth by chance: *She stumbled into engineering because of her love of maths.*
◆ v + prep

stump /stʌmp/

,stump 'up (for sth), ,stump 'up sth (for sth) (*BrE*, *informal*) to pay the amount of money for sth that sb asks, often when you do not want to: *He had no money so I had to stump up for his ticket.* ◇ *We had to stump up an extra five hundred pounds for insurance.*
OBJ **the cash** **SYN** **cough up**, **cough sth up**
◆ v + adv ◆ v + adv + n

subject /səb'dʒekt/

sub'ject sb/sth/yourself to sth (*formal*) to make sb/sth/yourself experience, suffer or be affected by sth, usually sth unpleasant: *to subject sth to scrutiny/analysis* ◇ *All our products are subjected to thorough tests.* ◇ *to be subjected to criticism/harassment/abuse/torture* ◇ *Why did I subject myself to another evening of arguments?* ◇ *The city was subjected to repeated bombings.*
NOTE Often used in the passive.
◆ v + n/pron + prep

subscribe /səb'skraɪb/

sub'scribe to sth (*formal*) to agree with an opinion, a theory, etc.: *It's not an opinion I tend to subscribe to.* ◇ *The company subscribe to the view that if you can encourage children to use your products, they will continue to use them when they are adults.* ◇ *It's not a theory that is commonly subscribed to.*
OBJ **view**, **theory**, **opinion**
◆ v + prep

substitute /'sʌbstɪtjuːt; *AmE* -tuːt/

'substitute for sb/sth to take the place of sb/sth else: *Can you substitute for me at the meeting?* ◇ *Nothing can substitute for the advice your doctor is able to give you.*
◆ v + prep

succeed /sək'siːd/

suc'ceed in doing sth to achieve sth that you have been trying to do or get; to have the result or effect that was intended: *He succeeded in getting top marks in chemistry.* ◇ *The Labour Party succeeded in capturing the female vote* (= they persuaded women to vote for them). ◇ (*ironic*) *I tried to mend my watch, but only succeeded in breaking it* (= that was not what I intended).
◆ v + prep

suck /sʌk/

,suck sb 'in; ,suck sb 'into sth to gradually involve sb in an activity, a situation, etc., especially one that they do not at first want to be involved in: *There is a danger we could be sucked into a war.* ◇ *Don't let yourself get sucked in.* ◇ *In his youth he had been sucked into a hippy cult.*
NOTE Nearly always used in the passive.
◆ v + n/pron + adv ◆ v + adv + n ◆ v + n/pron + prep

,suck it 'up (*AmE*, *informal*) to accept an unpleasant or difficult situation, and continue living, working, etc. in the usual way: *I know he has a cold, but he'll just have to suck it up like everyone else does.*
◆ v + it + adv

,suck 'up to sb (*informal*, *disapproving*) to try to please sb by helping them, saying nice things to them, etc. in order to gain an advantage for

yourself: *He's always sucking up to the teacher.*
◇ *We don't suck up to anyone!*
♦ v + adv + prep

sucker /'sʌkə(r)/
,**sucker sb 'into sth**; ,**sucker sb 'into doing
sth** (*AmE*, *informal*) to persuade sb to do sth they
do not really want to do, especially by using
their lack of knowledge or experience: *He got
suckered into the scheme.* ◇ *I was suckered into
helping.*
NOTE Usually used in the passive.
♦ v + n/pron + prep

sue /su:; *BrE also* sju:/
'**sue for sth** (*formal*) to formally ask for sth,
especially in court: *to sue for divorce* ◇ *The rebels
were forced to sue for peace.*
OBJ **divorce**, **peace**
♦ v + prep

suffer /'sʌfə(r)/
🔑'**suffer from sth 1** to have a particular illness or medical condition: *She suffers from hay
fever.* ◇ *Some of the victims are suffering from
shock.* **2** to have a particular problem: *Many
companies are suffering from a shortage of skilled
staff.*
♦ v + prep

suit /su:t; *BrE also* sju:t/
'**suit sth to sb/sth** to make sth appropriate for
sb/sth: *He can suit his conversation to whoever
he's with.*
♦ v + n/pron + prep

,**suit 'up** (*AmE*) to put on the clothing that you
wear to do a particular job, play a sport, etc.:
*OK, everyone. Time to suit up. The game starts in
a half hour.*
♦ v + adv

sum /sʌm/ (**-mm-**)
🔑,**sum 'up**; ,**sum sth 'up 1** to give the main
points of sth in a few words: *Before we conclude
the meeting, let me sum up.* ◇ *To sum up*, there
are three main ways of tackling the problem...
◇ *In her conclusion, she summed up what had
been agreed.* **SYN** **summarize**, **summarize sth**
(*more formal*) **2** (of a judge) to give the main
points of the evidence or arguments in a legal
case, near the end of the trial: *When he summed
up, the judge reminded the jury of the seriousness
of the case.*
♦ v + adv ♦ v + adv + n ♦ v + pron + adv
♦ v + n + adv (*less frequent*)
▸ ,**summing-'up** *n* **1** a speech made by the
judge to the court near the end of the trial,
giving the main points of the evidence and the
arguments in the case: *The judge will begin her
summing-up on Monday.* **2** an occasion when sb
states the main points of an argument, etc.:
There was a final summing-up by each of the

suffer from sth

**catch sth ♦ come down with sth ♦ contract
sth ♦ get sth ♦ have sth ♦ suffer from sth**

These verbs all mean to be or become ill with
a disease or illness.

catch sth to get an infectious illness: *I think I
must have caught this cold from you.* ◇ *It is
unusual to catch measles more than once.*

come down with sth to get an illness that is
not very serious: *I think I'm coming down
with something.*

contract sth to get a disease, especially a
serious one: *He contracted malaria while
abroad.*

get sth to begin to have an illness, to suffer
from a pain: *I think I'm getting a cold.* ◇ *She
gets really bad headaches.*

have sth (also **have got**) (*not used in the
progressive tenses*) to suffer from an illness or
pain: *I had a cold yesterday and I couldn't
come to work.* ◇ *I've got a headache.*

suffer from sth to be badly affected by a
disease, an illness or pain: *He suffers from*

asthma. ◇ *The driver was taken to hospital
suffering from shock.*

WHICH WORD?

Have sth and **suffer from sth** are used to talk
about sb having an illness. The other verbs are
used to talk about sb *starting* to have an illness.
Contract is often used in technical contexts.

PATTERNS AND COLLOCATIONS

- to suffer from/have/get/catch/contract **a dis-
  ease/an illness**
- to suffer from/have/get/catch/contract/come
  down with a **a bug/flu**
- to suffer from/have/get/contract **cancer/AIDS**
- to suffer from/have/get/catch/contract **a virus/
  HIV/malaria**
- to suffer from/have/get/catch/come down
  with a **a cold**
- to suffer from/have/get **a headache/a condi-
  tion/arthritis/diarrhoea**

speakers. ◇ *The speakers gave brief summings-up of their talks.*

ˌsum sb/sth ˈup 1 to describe or show the most typical characteristics of sb/sth, especially in a few words: *His speech summed up the mood of the whole country.* ◇ *Totally lazy—that just about sums him up.* **2** (**as sb/sth**) to decide or express what you think about sb/sth: *The two of them stood there, summing each other up.* ◇ *He had already summed her up as someone who hated to admit defeat.* ◇ *I summed up the situation immediately* (= realized what was happening and what needed to be done). **SYN** **size sb/sth up**

- v + adv + n ◆ v + pron + adv
- v + n + adv (*less frequent*)

summon /ˈsʌmən/

ˌsummon sth ˈup 1 to manage to produce a particular feeling in yourself, although this is difficult: *She eventually summoned up the courage to knock at the door.* ◇ *He managed to summon up a smile.* ◇ *I can't summon up much enthusiasm for grammar!* ◇ *I don't think I can summon up the energy to go for a run.* **OBJ** **courage**, **smile**, **energy**, **strength** **SYN** **muster sth up** **NOTE** Not used in the passive. ◆ **Summon sth** is sometimes used on its own with this meaning. **2** to make an idea, a feeling, a memory, etc. come into your mind: *It's a smell that summons up memories of my childhood.* **OBJ** **memories**, **vision**, **image** **SYN** **evoke sth** (*more formal*)

- v + adv + n ◆ v + pron + adv ◆ v + n + adv (*rare*)

surge /sɜːdʒ; AmE sɜːrdʒ/

ˌsurge ˈthrough sb if a feeling **surges through** you, you suddenly feel it very strongly: *A thrill of excitement surged through Isobel.* **SUBJ** **relief**, **excitement**, **anger**
→ see also SURGE UP
- v + prep

ˌsurge ˈup (*literary*) if an emotion **surges up** in you, you suddenly feel it very strongly: *Panic surged up inside her.*
→ see also SURGE THROUGH SB
- v + adv

▶ **ˈupsurge** (**in/of sth**) *n* [*usually* sing.] a sudden great increase in sth: *There has been a recent upsurge of violence in the area.* ◇ *an upsurge of interest in science and technology*

surrender /səˈrendə(r)/

surˈrender to sb/sth; surˈrender yourself to sb/sth (*formal*) to stop trying to resist a feeling, a particular person, etc. and let them control what you do do: *He surrendered to his natural instinct to run away.* ◇ *She surrendered to Leo's charm.* ◇ *He surrendered himself to sleep.*

- v + prep ◆ v + pron + prep

suss /sʌs/

ˌsuss sb/sth ˈout (*BrE, informal*) to find out what sb/sth is really like; to understand the important things about sb/sth: *My classmates were sussing me out, seeing how tough I was.* ◇ *We'll need to suss out our opponents before the game.* ◇ *I've got him sussed out now.* ◇ *Jen had sussed out right away that there was something strange going on.* ◇ *Simon always did what his family wanted. I soon sussed that out.*
NOTE **Suss sb/sth** can be used on its own with a similar meaning: *I've got him sussed.*
- v + n/pron + adv ◆ v + adv + n

swallow /ˈswɒləʊ; AmE ˈswɑːloʊ/

ˌswallow sb/sth ˈup to completely cover sb/sth or absorb them, so that they can no longer be seen or do not exist separately: *He watched them walk away until the darkness swallowed them up.* ◇ *She was so embarrassed she wished that the ground would open and swallow her up.* ◇ *The countryside is rapidly being swallowed up by building developments.* ◇ *Many small businesses have been swallowed up by larger companies.*
NOTE **Swallow sb/sth** is sometimes used on its own with this meaning: *She wished that the ground would open up and swallow her.*
- v + n/pron + adv ◆ v + adv + n

ˌswallow sth ˈup to use sth such as money or resources completely: *Practising the piano swallows up all her free time.* ◇ *Pay rises were quickly swallowed up by price increases.* ◇ *Nuclear weapons swallowed up a third of the country's defence spending.* ◇ *The extra money was swallowed up by debts.*
OBJ **time**, **money** **SYN** **use sth up**
NOTE Often used in the passive.
- v + adv + n ◆ v + pron + adv ◆ v + n + adv (*rare*)

swan /swɒn; AmE swɑːn/ (**-nn-**)

ˌswan aˈbout/aˈround; ˌswan aˈbout/aˈround sth (*BrE, informal, disapproving*) to move around or go from one place to another enjoying yourself, but with no real purpose: *Stop swanning about pretending to be clever.* ◇ *She's swanning around Europe for the summer.*
- v + adv ◆ v + prep

ˌswan ˈoff (**to…**) (*BrE, informal, disapproving*) to go off to enjoy yourself with no real purpose: *He's always swanning off to Spain on holiday!*
- v + adv

swap (*also* swop) /swɒp; AmE swɑːp/ (**-pp-**)

ˌswap aˈround/ˈover/ˈround (*informal, especially BrE*) if two people **swap around/over/round**, they move to where the other person was before or start doing each other's jobs: *I'll drive there and you can read the map. We'll swap over on the way back.*
SYN **change over/round** (*BrE*)
- v + adv

swarm

,swap sb/sth a'round/'over/'round (*informal*, *especially BrE*) to replace sb/sth with sb/sth else: *At half-time the manager swapped some of the players around.*
SYN change sb/sth round/around
♦ v + n/pron + adv ♦ v + adv + n (*rare*)

,swap 'over (to sth), ,swap sb/sth 'over (to sth) to change from one situation, position, etc. to another; to make sb do this: *We swapped over from an electric cooker to gas.* ◇ *Have you been swapped over to the new computer system yet?*
SYN switch over, etc.
♦ v + adv ♦ v + n/pron + adv
♦ v + adv + n (*less frequent*)

swarm /swɔːm/; *AmE* swɔːrm/

'swarm with sb/sth (*usually used in the progressive tenses*) if a place is **swarming with** sb/sth, it is very full of people or things moving around: *The museum was swarming with tourists.* ◇ *The room was hot and swarming with flies.*
♦ v + prep

swear /sweə(r)/; *AmE* swer/ (swore /swɔː(r)/, sworn /swɔːn/; *AmE* swɔːrn/)

'swear by sb (*not used in the progressive tenses*) used to show that you are making a serious promise: *I swear by Almighty God that I will tell the truth* (= for example, said in a British court).
♦ v + prep

'swear by sth/sb (*not used in the progressive tenses*) to believe strongly that sth/sb is very useful and helpful: *My brother swears by lemon and honey drinks as a cold remedy.* ◇ *Why don't you go and see Dr Nash? My mother swears by him.*
♦ v + prep

,swear sb 'in; ,swear sb 'into sth to introduce sb publicly to a new position, responsibility, etc. by getting them to promise that they will do the job correctly, be loyal to the organization, their country, etc.: *He was sworn in as President in January.* ◇ *The new President was hurriedly sworn into office.*
NOTE Often used in the passive.
♦ v + adv + n ♦ v + n/pron + adv ♦ v + n/pron + prep
▶ ,swearing-'in n [U, sing.] the act of swearing sb in: *The swearing-in of the new president will take place tomorrow.* ◇ *a swearing-in ceremony*

,swear 'off sth (*informal*, *especially AmE*) to make a serious promise that you will give sth up, especially sth that is bad or harmful: *He's intending to swear off alcohol.* ◇ *Ever since her boyfriend left she has sworn off men.*
♦ v + prep

'swear to sth (*informal*) to say that sth is definitely true: *I think I've met him somewhere before, but I* **couldn't swear to it** (= I'm not completely certain).
♦ v + prep

'swear sb to sth to make sb promise sth, especially that they will not tell other people sth: *The actors know how the series will end but they are* **sworn to secrecy**. ◇ *Jeff told me about his promotion and* **swore** me **to silence**.
♦ v + n/pron + prep

sweat /swet/

,sweat sth 'off to lose weight by doing a lot of hard exercise: *I sweated off the extra weight by playing squash every day.*
♦ v + adv + n ♦ v + pron + adv ♦ v + n + adv (*rare*)

,sweat sth 'out **1** to get rid of a cold, fever, etc. by staying warm so that you produce sweat: *Whenever I get a bad fever I go to bed and sweat it out.* **OBJ** cold, fever **2** ,sweat it 'out to wait for sth that you feel nervous or anxious about to happen or to end: *They made us sweat it out for two hours until the result was announced.*
NOTE Not used in the passive.
♦ v + pron + adv ♦ v + n + adv
♦ v + adv + n (*less frequent*)

'sweat over sth (*informal*) to work very hard on sth; to spend a lot of time doing sth or worrying about sth: *I've been sweating over my letter of resignation for several days.*
♦ v + prep

sweep /swiːp/ (swept, swept /swept/)

,sweep sb a'long/a'way to make sb feel very enthusiastic about sth or involved in sth; to affect sb so much they forget everything else: *Ana was swept along by her father's enthusiasm.*
SYN carry sb along; be/get carried away
NOTE Usually used in the passive.
♦ v + n/pron + adv

,sweep sb a'side to defeat sb easily: *United swept Liverpool aside with ease.*
♦ v + n/pron + adv ♦ v + adv + n

,sweep sth a'side to ignore sth; to treat sth as though it is not important: *All their objections were swept aside.* ◇ *She sweeps aside every suggestion I make.*
OBJ objections, protests, restrictions, opposition, criticism
NOTE Often used in the passive.
♦ v + n/pron + adv ♦ v + adv + n

,sweep sb a'way → SWEEP SB ALONG/AWAY

,sweep sth a'way to destroy or get rid of sth completely: *The President's speech swept away all our doubts.* ◇ *Poverty will be swept away!* ◇ *The old way of life has been swept away by the electronic revolution.*
♦ v + adv + n ♦ v + n/pron + adv

,sweep sth 'back/'up if you **sweep** your hair **back** or **up**, you brush or push it away from your face: *She swept her hair back from her face with both hands.* ◇ *Long hair can be swept up on top of your head.*
OBJ hair
♦ v + n/pron + adv ♦ v + adv + n

,sweep sth 'off; ,sweep sth 'off sth to remove sth from somewhere, especially by brushing with your hands, a brush, etc.: *He swept the crumbs off the table.* ◇ (*figurative*) *The wind swept her hat off.*
♦ v + n/pron + adv ♦ v + adv + n ♦ v + n/pron + prep

IDM ,sweep sb off their 'feet to make sb fall suddenly and deeply in love with you: *Maria was swept off her feet by Mark's charm.*

,sweep sth 'out to clean a room, a cupboard, etc. with a large brush with a long handle (a **broom**): *Brad was busy sweeping out the yard.*
♦ v + adv + n ♦ v + n/pron + adv

,sweep sb 'up **1** to lift sb with a sudden smooth movement: *He ran forward and swept her up in his arms.* **2** to make sb become very involved in sth so that they are unable to think clearly: *The whole country was swept up in the excitement.* **SYN** be/get caught up (in sth) **NOTE** Often used in the passive.
♦ v + n/pron + adv ♦ v + adv + n (*rare*)

,sweep 'up; ,sweep sth 'up to remove dust, dirt, etc. from a floor with a brush: *We had to sweep up before we left.* ◇ *We'd better sweep up all the bits of broken glass quickly.*
♦ v + adv ♦ v + adv + n ♦ v + n/pron + adv

,sweep sth 'up → SWEEP STH BACK/UP

sweeten /ˈswiːtn/

,sweeten sb 'up (*informal*) to try to persuade sb to help you, agree to sth, etc. by giving them gifts, being very nice to them, etc.: *If you sweeten him up he'll do the work for you.* ◇ *They sweeten up customers with special offers.*
♦ v + n/pron + adv ♦ v + adv + n

swell /swel/ (**swelled** /sweld/, **swollen** /ˈswəʊlən; *AmE* ˈswoʊ-/ or **swelled, swelled**)

,swell 'up if part of the body **swells up**, it becomes much larger and rounder than usual as a result of illness, injury, etc.: *My foot swelled up to twice its normal size.* ◇ (*figurative*) *A feeling of admiration swelled up in her.*
♦ v + adv

swill /swɪl/

,swill sth 'down (*informal*) to drink a large amount of sth quickly: *He just swilled down his beer and walked out.*
♦ v + adv + n ♦ v + n/pron + adv

swing /swɪŋ/ (**swung, swung** /swʌŋ/)

,swing a'round; ,swing sb/sth a'round (*BrE also* ,swing 'round, ,swing sb/sth 'round) **1** to turn around fast to face the other way; to make sb/sth do this: *Luke suddenly swung round and glared at me.* ◇ *I swung the car round and drove back down the road.* **2** to change from one idea, opinion, etc. to another, especially the opposite one: *The Labour Party has now swung round to*

supporting Europe. ◇ *You should be able to swing people round to your point of view.*
♦ v + adv ♦ v + n/pron + adv

'swing at sb; 'swing sth at sb to try to hit sb: *She swung at me with the iron bar.*
♦ v + prep ♦ v + n/pron + prep

,swing 'by; ,swing 'by sth (*AmE, informal*) to visit a person or place for a short time, especially when you are going somewhere else: *She swung by* (= came here) *on her way home.* ◇ *Let's swing by Dave's house after the movie.*
SYN drop by
♦ v + adv ♦ v + prep

,swing 'round, etc. (*BrE*) → SWING AROUND, ETC.

switch /swɪtʃ/

,switch 'off (*informal*) to stop giving your attention to sb or sth: *I just switch off when Jo starts talking.* ◇ *Do you find it hard to switch off* (= stop thinking about work) *when you get home?*
SYN turn off
♦ v + adv

,switch 'off; ,switch sth 'off; ,switch itself 'off to stop an electrical device, a machine or an engine working by pressing a switch, a button, etc.: *The heating switches off at 10.00 p.m.* ◇ *Shall I switch the lights off?* ◇ *The electricity has been switched off.* ◇ *Her smile switched off suddenly when she saw him come in.* ◇ *Please switch off your mobile phones.*
SYN turn off, turn itself off; turn sth off
OPP switch on, switch sth on, switch itself on
♦ v + adv ♦ v + n/pron + adv ♦ v + adv + n

,switch 'on; ,switch sth 'on; ,switch itself 'on to start an electrical device, a machine or an engine by pressing a switch, a button, etc.: *She walked in and switched on the light.* ◇ *The machine switches* (*itself*) *on automatically.* ◇ *How do you switch this thing on?* ◇ (*figurative*) *He can switch on the charm whenever he likes.*
SYN turn on, turn itself on; turn sth on
OPP switch off, switch sth off, switch itself off
♦ v + adv

,switch 'over (to sth), ,switch sth 'over (to sth) **1** (*BrE*) to change from one television station to another: *I switched over to watch the news.* **SYN** change over (to sth); turn over (to sth), turn sth over (to sth) **2** (*also* ,switch sb 'over) to change from one position, situation, job, etc. to another: *We've finally switched over to a computerized system.* ◇ *The country gradually switched over from imperial to metric.* ◇ *35 000 customers have been switched over to the new system.* **SYN** change over (from sth) (to sth)
♦ v + adv ♦ v + n/pron + adv ♦ v + adv + n

swivel /ˈswɪvl/ (-ll-, *AmE* -l-)

,swivel a'round; ,swivel sb/sth a'round (*also* ,swivel 'round, ,swivel sb/sth 'round *espe-*

cially BrE) **1** to turn or move your body, eyes or head around quickly to face another direction: *He swivelled around to look at her.* **2** to turn or make sth turn around a fixed central point: *She swivelled the chair around to face them.*
◆ v + adv ◆ v + n/pron + adv

swop /swɒp; *AmE* swɑːp/ (-pp-)
,swop a'round, etc. → SWAP AROUND, ETC.

swot /swɒt; *AmE* swɑːt/
,swot 'up (on sth) (*BrE, informal*) to study a subject very hard, especially when you are preparing for an exam: *I have to swot up on phrasal verbs for a test tomorrow.* ◇ *It's time to start swotting up for the exam.*
SYN brush sth up, brush up on sth (*especially BrE*); mug up (on sth), mug sth up (*BrE*); review sth (*especially AmE*); revise sth (*BrE*)

syphon /'saɪfn/
,syphon sth 'off → SIPHON STH OFF

Tt

tack /tæk/
,tack sth 'on; ,tack sth 'on to sth (*informal*) to add sth as an extra item, especially in a careless way: *The last paragraph seems to have been tacked on at the last minute.* ◇ *An extra day has been tacked onto the New Year holiday.* ◇ *a porch tacked on to the front of the house*
SYN add sth on, add sth on to sth
NOTE Often used in the passive.
→ see also TAG STH ON, TAG STH ON TO STH
◆ v + n/pron + adv ◆ v + adv + n
◆ v + n/pron + adv + prep

tag /tæg/ (-gg-)
,tag a'long (behind/with sb) (*informal*) to go somewhere with sb, especially when you have not been invited: *The children tagged along behind their mother.* ◇ *Can I tag along (with you) when you go to the shops?*
SYN string along (with sb)
→ see also TAG ON, TAG ON TO SB
◆ v + adv
,tag 'on; ,tag 'on to sb/sth (*especially BrE*) to follow sb closely and go somewhere with them, although you have not been invited: *Kate's friend tagged on and spoiled the day.* ◇ *We tagged on to the end of the procession.*
→ see also TAG ALONG (BEHIND/WITH SB)
◆ v + adv ◆ v + adv + prep
,tag sth 'on; ,tag sth 'on to sth (*informal*) to add sth as an extra item to the end of sth, especially in a careless way: *An apology was tagged on to the end of the letter.* ◇ *Online*

security is being built into the system, not tagged on.
SYN add sth on, add sth on to sth
NOTE Often used in the passive.
→ see also TACK STH ON, TACK STH ON TO STH
◆ v + n/pron + adv ◆ v + adv + n
◆ v + n/pron + adv + prep

tail /teɪl/
,tail a'way → TAIL OFF
,tail 'back (*BrE*) if traffic **tails back**, it forms a long line that moves very slowly or not at all: *After the accident, traffic tailed back ten miles.*
◆ v + adv
▶ 'tailback *n* (*BrE*) a long line of traffic that tails back: *The crash caused a six-mile tailback.*
,tail 'off (*also* ,tail a'way *less frequent*) to become smaller, fewer, weaker, etc.: *Sales tailed off in the summer.* ◇ *The number of tourists starts to tail off in September.* ◇ *Her voice tailed away.* ◇ *'Did you want to see...' she tailed off.*
↻ note at DWINDLE AWAY
◆ v + adv

tailor /'teɪlə(r)/
'tailor sth to/for sb/sth to make or adapt sth for a particular purpose, a particular person, etc.: *Special programmes of study are tailored to the needs of specific students.*
◆ v + n/pron + prep

take /teɪk/ (took /tʊk/, taken /'teɪkən/)
,take sb a'back to shock or surprise sb: *I was taken aback by his rudeness.*
NOTE Usually used in the passive.
◆ v + n/pron + adv
,take 'after sb **1** (*not used in the progressive tenses*) to look like or behave like an older member of your family: *I'm told I take after my grandmother.* ◇ *Your daughter doesn't take after you at all.* ◇ *He's always been shy—he takes after his father.* **2** (*old-fashioned, AmE*) to begin to follow sb quickly in order to catch them: *A man rushed out of the bank and two men took after him.* ◇ *She ran out into the night and he took after her.*
◆ v + prep
,take a'gainst sb/sth (*old-fashioned, BrE*) to begin to dislike sb/sth: *Why have you suddenly taken against Laura?*
OPP take to sb/sth
◆ v + prep
,take sb/sth a'long (to sth) to take sb or sth with you when you go somewhere: *Tom took his sister along to the party.* ◇ *When you travel with young children, take along some favourite toys or a book.*
◆ v + n/pron + adv ◆ v + adv + n
,take sb/sth a'part (*informal*) **1** (*sport*) to defeat sb easily: *He took the American apart in the third set* (= in a game of tennis). ◇ *We took the other*

team *apart.* **2** to attack or criticize sb/sth severely: *Touch her again and I'll take you apart!* ◊ *Her second novel was taken apart by the critics.*
◆ v + n/pron + adv ◆ v + adv + n (*less frequent*)

ˌtake sth aˈpart to separate a machine, a piece of equipment, etc. into its parts: *She took the clock apart and couldn't put it back together.* ◊ *You can take the mixer apart to clean it.* ◊ *The police took the room apart* (= examined everything very carefully)*, looking for evidence.*
SYN **dismantle sth** (*more formal*) **OPP** **put sth together**
◆ v + n/pron + adv ◆ v + adv + n (*less frequent*)

ˌtake sb aˈround; ˌtake sb aˈround sth (*BrE also* ˌtake sb ˈround, ˌtake sb ˈround sth) to visit a place with sb; to show sb the interesting or important parts of a place: *If you'd like to see the town, I could take you around.* ◊ *We got a guide to take us round the temples.*
SYN **show sb around, show sb around sth; take sb over sth**
◆ v + n/pron + adv ◆ v + n/pron + prep

ˌtake sb/sth aˈround (*especially AmE*) → TAKE SB/STH ROUND

ˌtake sb aˈside to separate sb from the rest of a group in order to talk to them privately: *She took me aside and explained the situation.*
◆ v + n/pron + adv

ˌtake sb aˈway (**from sb/sth**) **1** to remove sb from somewhere; to lead or move sb to another place: *The injured were taken away by ambulance.* ◊ *I can take you away from all this* (= all this trouble)*.* **2** to remove sb, especially a child, from sb's care: *The children were taken away from them and put into a children's home.* ◊ *My father took me away from school and taught me himself.* **3** to take sb with you on a trip or holiday/vacation: *He takes the whole family away for two weeks in the summer.* **4** to make it necessary for sb to leave a place, especially temporarily: *Sam's work takes him away from his family for months at a time.*
◆ v + n/pron + adv ◆ v + adv + n (*less frequent*)

ˌtake sth aˈway **1** to remove sth and place it somewhere else: *They had to take the computer away to fix it.* ◊ *You can take the book away with you.* **2** (**from sb/sth**) to remove sth from a person, a place or an organization so that they no longer have it: *These books must not be taken away from the library.* ◊ *They can't take our rights away from us.* **3** to make a feeling, pain, etc. disappear: *These tablets should help take the pain away.* ◊ *I need a drink of water to take the bad taste away.* **OBJ** **pain**, **taste**, **appetite** **4** (**from sth**) (*mathematics*) to take one number from another: *If you take four away from ten, that leaves six.* ◊ *Ten take four away four leaves six.* **5** (*BrE*) (*AmE* ˌtake sth ˈout) (*usually used in the infinitive with 'to'*) to buy a cooked dish at a restaurant and carry it away to eat at home, in the street, etc.: *A cheeseburger and a coffee* **to**

take away, please. ◊ *Is that to eat here or take away?* **6** (**from sth**) to form an opinion or impression of sb/sth that is still there when you go away: *We didn't take away a very favourable impression of the hotel.* ◊ *What do we want students to take away* (= to learn) *from this course?*
◆ v + n/pron + adv ◆ v + adv + n

IDM **take sb's ˈbreath away** to surprise or please sb very much: *The first sight of the waterfall takes your breath away.*
▶ ˈtakeaway (*BrE*) *n* **1** a restaurant that cooks and sells food that you eat somewhere else: *a Chinese/Indian takeaway* ◊ *a takeaway restaurant* **2** (*AmE* **takeout, 'carry-out**) a meal that you buy from this type of restaurant: *We could get a takeaway tonight.* ◊ *a takeaway pizza* **3** (*AmE*) an idea that you learn about in a meeting or discussion that you remember and use later: *The key takeaway is that there should be more growth next quarter.*

ˌtake aˈway from sth to make the effect or value of sth seem less: *I don't wish to take away from his achievements, but he couldn't have done it without our help.*
SYN **detract from sth** (*more formal*)
◆ v + adv + prep

ˌtake sb aˈway from sth to take sb's attention away from sth: *These minor problems are taking us away from the real issue.*
SYN **distract sb** (**from sth**)
◆ v + n/pron + adv + prep

ˌtake sb ˈback **1** (**to sth**) to go with sb to the place where they were or to your/their home: *Can you take me back to the hotel?* ◊ *I'll take the kids back now—they're getting tired.* **2** to allow sb such as your husband, wife or partner to come home after they have left because of a problem; to allow sb to return to their job: *I agreed to take her back if she promised to be faithful in future.* ◊ *An employer cannot be forced to take you back.* **SYN** **have sb back 3** (**to sth**) to make sb's thoughts return to a past time: *The smell of the sea took me back to his childhood.* ◊ *That song takes me back a bit!* **SYN** **carry sb back** (**to sth**) ⮕ note at REMIND SB OF SB/STH
◆ v + n/pron + adv

ˌtake sth ˈback **1** (**to sb/sth**) if you **take sth back** to a shop/store, or a shop/store **takes sth back**, you return sth that you have bought because it is the wrong size or does not work, for example: *The sweater had a hole in it so I took it back.* **SYN** **return sth** (*more formal*) **2** to return sth you have borrowed, hired, etc.: *I forgot to take my books back to the library.* ◊ *It's your turn to take the videos back.* **SYN** **return sth** (*more formal*) **NOTE** In informal spoken language **take sb back sth**, or, less often, **take sb sth back** can also be used: *I took him back his CD.* ◊ *I took him his CD back.* **3** to take sth you have bought, etc. home with you after you have been away:

We were looking for presents to take back for the kids. NOTE In informal spoken language **take sb back sth** is also used: *We took the kids back some presents.* **4** to receive or take sth that you own from sb who has borrowed it: *When I'd read the letter he took it back and put it in his pocket.* ◇ *No attempt was ever made to take back the land* (= to take control of it again). **5** to admit that sth you said was wrong or that you should not have said it: *I take back what I said about you being lazy.* SYN **retract sth**; **withdraw sth** (*more formal*)

◆ v + n/pron + adv ◆ v + adv + n **5** v + adv + n
◆ v + pron + adv ◆ v + n + adv (*less frequent*)

,take sb '**down** (*AmE*) **1** to make sb fall to the ground, especially in a sport: *He ran for 40 yards before being taken down.* **2** to arrest sb

◆ v + n/pron + adv ◆ v + adv + n

▸ '**takedown** n (*AmE*) **1** a situation in which sb is made to fall to the ground: *his ninth takedown of the game* **2** a situation in which sb is arrested: *When it comes to the takedown, we only take the best officers along.*

,take sb/sth '**down**; ,take sb/sth '**down sth** to go with sb/sth to a lower level, to a more southern part of a country, etc., or to a different part of a building, town, etc.: *The nurse will take you down in the lift.* ◇ *The injured climbers were taken down the mountain on a sledge.* ◇ *You promised to take me down to London next time you went!* ◇ *Tony's just taking the car down to the garage—he'll be back soon.*

OPP **take sb/sth up, take sb/sth up sth**
◆ v + n/pron + adv ◆ v + adv + n (*less frequent*)
◆ v + n/pron + prep

,take sth '**down 1** to remove sth from a high level: *She took a book down from the top shelf.* **2** to remove sth that is hanging on a wall, etc.: *Will you help me take the curtains down?* OBJ **curtains**, **pictures** OPP **put sth up 3** to remove a structure by separating it into pieces: *They were taking their tent down as we left.* OBJ **a tent**, **scaffolding** OPP **put sth up 4** to pull down a piece of clothing worn below the waist, without actually removing it: *She took her trousers down to show the doctor her leg wound.* OBJ **trousers**, **pants 5** to write sth down: *She took down my name, address and phone number.* OBJ **details**, (**telephone**) **number** SYN **note sth down** ↻ note at WRITE STH DOWN **6** (*computing*) to remove a website or material on a website from the Internet: *All offensive advertisements will be taken down immediately.* OBJ **website**

◆ v + n/pron + adv ◆ v + adv + n

,'**take sb/sth for sb/sth** (*not used in the progressive tenses*) to consider sb/sth to be sb/sth, especially when you are wrong: *The experts took the painting for a genuine Matisse.* ◇ *What do you take me for?* (= what kind of person do you think I am?)

↻ note at MISTAKE SB/STH FOR SB/STH

◆ v + n/pron + prep

,take sb '**in 1** to allow sb to stay in your home: *She takes in paying guests.* ◇ *When my parents died, my uncle took me in.* OBJ **guests**, **lodgers 2** if the police **take sb in**, they take them to a police station to question them about a crime: *Two young men have been taken in for questioning.* **3** (of an organization, an institution, etc.) to accept sb as a member, a student, a patient, etc.: *The college took in more students than ever before last year.* **4** to make sb believe sth that is not true: *How could I have been taken in by his charm?* ◇ *She took me in completely with her story.* SYN **deceive sb** (*more formal*) NOTE Usually used in the passive.

◆ v + n/pron + adv ◆ v + adv + n

▸ '**intake** n **1** [C, U] the number of people who join a college or other organization at a particular time: *a new intake of students* **2** (*AmE*) a first test, meeting, etc. that you have when you go to a hospital or have an interview for a job or school, etc.

,take sb/sth '**in** (**to sth**), ,take sb/sth '**into sth** to go with sb or to take sth into a building or another place: *I'm going into town, so I'll take you in if you like.* ◇ *I took Jack into the kitchen for a quiet chat.* ◇ *I'll take you in to meet the manager now.* ◇ *If you take your camera in (to the shop), they'll have a look at it for you.* ◇ *My dad has been taken into hospital.*

NOTE In informal spoken language **take sth in** (**for sb**) can also be used in the patterns **take sb in sth** and, less often, **take sb sth in**: *I took him in a cup of tea.* ◇ *I took him a cup of tea in.*

→ see also TAKE STH IN, TAKE STH INTO STH
◆ v + n/pron + adv ◆ v + adv + n ◆ v + n/pron + prep

,take sth '**in 1** to notice sth with your eyes: *He took in every detail of her appearance.* ◇ *She started to relax and take in her surroundings.* **2** to understand or absorb sth that you hear or read; to accept sth as true: *I read the whole page without taking anything in.* ◇ *He just couldn't take in what had happened.* **3** to include or cover sth: *The trip takes in six European capitals.* ◇ *The study takes in women from 15 different countries.* NOTE Not used in the passive. **4** (*informal*) to go to see or visit sth such as a film/movie, especially when you are in a place for a different reason: *She always tries to take in a show when she's in New York.* OBJ **a show**, **the sights** NOTE Not used in the passive. **5** to make a piece of clothing narrower or tighter: *This dress needs to be taken in at the waist.* OBJ **a dress**, **a skirt**, etc. OPP **let sth out 6** if a boat **takes in** water, water comes in to it, usually through the bottom or sides OBJ only **water 7** (*old-fashioned*) to do particular kinds of work for other people in your home, in order to earn money: *My grandmother used to take in washing.* OBJ **washing**, **ironing**, **sewing 8** (*AmE*) to

SYNONYMS

take sth in

detect sth ◆ notice sth ◆ observe sth
◆ perceive sth ◆ take sth in

These verbs all mean to see or be aware of sth, especially when you pay careful attention to it.

detect sth to discover or notice sth, especially sth that is not easy to see, hear, etc.: *The tests are designed to detect the disease early.* ◇ *Do I detect a note of criticism in your voice?*

notice sth (*not usually used in the progressive tenses*) to see, hear or become aware of sb/sth; to pay attention to sb/sth: *The first thing I noticed about the room was the smell.* ◇ *I couldn't help noticing that she was wearing a wig.*

observe sth (*not used in the progressive tenses*) (*formal*) to see or notice sb/sth: *Have you observed any changes lately?*

perceive sth (*formal*) to notice or become aware of sth, especially sth that is not obvious: *I perceived a change in his behaviour over those months.*

take sth in to notice sth with your eyes: *He took in every detail of her appearance.* ◇ *She took in the scene at a glance.*

WHICH WORD?

All of these verbs can mean to become aware of sth with your eyes. **Detect, notice** and **perceive** can also be used in connection with other senses, such as hearing or smell.

PATTERNS AND COLLOCATIONS

- to notice/detect/observe/perceive **that/how/ what/where/who…**
- to notice/observe **sth happen/sb do sth**
- to **barely/hardly/scarcely** notice/detect/ observe/take in sth
- to be **worth** noticing/observing
- sb **can't/couldn't help** noticing/observing/ taking in sth
- to **fail to/not appear to/not seem to** notice/ detect/observe/perceive/take in sth

---

receive or earn an amount of money: *How much did the show take in?*
- ◆ v + adv + n ◆ v + pron + adv
- ◆ v + n + adv (*less frequent*)

,take sth 'in; ,take sth 'into sth to absorb sth into the body by breathing or swallowing it: *Fish take in oxygen through their gills.* ◇ *She took in deep breaths of sea air.* ◇ *When we breathe we take oxygen into the body.*
- ◆ v + adv + n ◆ v + n/pron + adv ◆ v + n/pron + prep
- ▶ 'intake n **1** [U, C] the amount of food, drink, etc. that you take into your body: *a high intake of vitamin C* ◇ *to reduce your calorie intake* **2** [C, usually sing.] an act of taking sth in, especially a breath: *a sharp intake of breath*

,take sb 'into sth to accept sb into an institution, an organization, etc.: *They had to* **take** *the children* **into** *care* (= to be looked after by the local authority). ◇ *Five men were* **taken into custody** (= to prison). ◇ *They took him into the firm as a partner last year.*
NOTE Often used in the passive.
- ◆ v + n/pron + prep

,take sb/sth 'into sth to bring sb/sth into a particular situation, activity, period of time, etc.: *Improved graphics took computer games into a new era.* ◇ *Owen's goal took England into the lead* (= they were winning). ◇ *the government that took Britain into Europe*
- ◆ v + n/pron + prep

, take 'off **1** (of an aircraft, etc.) to leave the ground and begin to fly: *The flight was due to take off from Heathrow at 13.15.* ◇ *The high*

jumper *took off at a bad angle.* **OPP land 2** (*informal*) if an idea, a product, etc. **takes off**, it suddenly becomes successful or popular: *The new dictionary has really taken off.* ◇ *Her career is just starting to take off.* ◇ *Sales of mobile phones have really taken off in the last few years.*
- ◆ v + adv
- ▶ 'take-off n [U, C] **1** the moment when an aircraft, etc. leaves the ground: *The plane is ready for take-off.* ◇ *take-off point/speed/run* ◇ (*figurative*) *The economy is poised for take-off.* **2** the moment when your feet leave the ground when you jump

,take 'off; ,take yourself 'off to leave somewhere suddenly or in a hurry: *Whenever things get tough, she takes off.* ◇ *He stayed for a year, then took off for a job in New York.* ◇ *I'm going to take myself off to bed.*
- ⊃ note at RUN AWAY
- ◆ v + adv ◆ v + pron + adv

,take sb 'off (*especially BrE*) **1** to copy sb in an annoying way: *She was taking off the woman next door.* **2** (in sports, entertainment, etc.) to remove a player from the field, an actor from the stage, etc. and not allow them to continue playing or acting.: *Their best striker was taken off after 30 minutes.*
- ◆ **1** v + adv + n ◆ v + pron + adv ◆ v + n + adv
- ◆ **2** v + n/pron + adv ◆ v + adv + n (*less frequent*)
- ▶ 'take-off n an act of copying sb in an amusing way

take

,take sb 'off; ,take sb 'off sth to rescue sb from a ship, a mountain, etc.: *The injured men were taken off the boat by helicopter.* NOTE Often used in the passive.
* v + n/pron + adv ◆ v + adv + n (*less frequent*)
* v + n/pron + prep

'take sb/sth 'off (to sth) to make sb go with you to another place; to take sth to another place: *They took him off to the police station.* ◇ *She collected our passports and took them off somewhere.*
* v + n/pron + adv ◆ v + adv + n (*rare*)

,take sb 'off sth 1 to stop sb from continuing a particular medicine, treatment, etc.: *His doctor took him off tranquillizers.* OPP put sb on sth 2 to remove sb from a job, position, etc. and not allow them to continue: *One of the lawyers has been taken off the case.*
* v + n/pron + prep

‖,take sth 'off 1 to remove an item of clothing from your/sb's body: *She took her coat off and hung it up.* ◇ *It's the custom to take off your shoes when you go into the house.* ◇ *Can you take off Tommy's jacket for me?* OBJ clothes, shoes, coat, jacket, etc. OPP put sth on 2 to remove a bus, train, etc. from service; to stop a television or radio programme, performances of a show, etc.: *The 17.13 bus to Bristol will be taken off next month.* ◇ *The play was taken off after a week.* OPP put sth on 3 to cut off hair or a part of the body: *The hairdresser asked me how much she should take off.* ◇ *His leg had to be taken off above the knee.* 4 (*AmE*) to lose weight by exercising or following a diet: *Several people reported that they had taken off more than 15 pounds.*
* v + n/pron + adv ◆ v + adv + n

‖,take sth 'off; ,take sth 'off sth 1 to remove sth from somewhere: *Sam took off the lid and looked inside.* ◇ *Sam took the lid off the box.* ◇ *Can you take your feet off the sofa?* ◇ *I've got an assistant now, which will take the pressure off a bit.* ◇ *Always take your make-up off before you go to bed.* SYN remove sth (*more formal*) OPP put sth on 2 to remove an amount of money, a number of points, etc. from sth in order to reduce the total: *Can you take any money off this shirt* (= sell it at a cheaper price)? ◇ *Marks will be taken off for bad spelling.* 3 to have a period of time as a break from work or school: *I'm going to take next week off.* ◇ *She took a day off work.* 4 to remove a name, an item, etc. from a list: *The soup has been taken off* (*the menu*). ◇ *I took my name off the list.*
* v + n/pron + adv ◆ v + adv + n ◆ v + n/pron + prep
IDM take your 'eyes off sb/sth to stop looking at sb/sth: *He couldn't take his eyes off the cake.* ◇ *I only took my eyes off her for a second and she disappeared.* take sb's 'mind off sb/sth to make sb stop thinking about sb or about sth unpleasant: *We thought going out for the evening might take her mind off things.*

,take sth 'off sb (*informal, especially BrE*) to use force or your authority to get sth from sb: *Another child took his teddy off him.* ◇ *The teacher took the cigarettes off me.*
* v + n/pron + prep
IDM take 'years off sb to make sb feel or look younger than they are: *That hairstyle takes ten years off you!*

---

take sth off

peel sth off ◆ remove sth ◆ strip off ◆ take sth off ◆ undress

These verbs mean to take clothes off your body.

peel sth off to take off all or most of your clothes, especially when they are tight or wet: *He peeled off his shirt.*

remove sth to take off clothes, etc. from the body: *Please remove your shoes before entering the temple.* ◇ *He removed his glasses.*

strip off to take off all or most of your clothes: *We stripped off and ran down to the sea.* NOTE Strip can be used on its own: *I stripped and washed myself all over.*

take sth off to remove a piece of clothing from your/sb's body: *Sit down and take off*

your shoes. ◇ *She took off her glasses, rubbed her eyes, then put them back on again.*

undress to take off your clothes: *I undressed and got into bed.* NOTE It is also possible to say **get undressed**: *You can get undressed behind the screen.*

WHICH WORD?

Remove sth is more formal than **take sth off** or **peel sth off**.

PATTERNS AND COLLOCATIONS

- to take off/remove a **dress/hat/jacket**
- to take off/remove your **glasses/shoes**
- to strip **down to** your underwear, etc.

take sb on

employ sb ◆ **engage sb** ◆ **hire sb** ◆ **recruit sb** ◆ **sign sb up** ◆ **take sb on**

These verbs all mean to give sb a job to do for payment.

employ sb to have sb working for you for payment; to give sb a job: *How many people does the company employ?* ◊ *For the past three years he has been employed as a firefighter.*

engage sb (*formal*) to employ sb to do a particular job: *We will have to engage the services of a translator.*

hire sb (*especially AmE*) to give sb a job; to find new people to work for a company or organization: *She was hired three years ago.* **NOTE** In both British and American English **hire** also means 'to employ sb for a short time to do a particular job': *They hired a firm of consultants to design the new system.*

recruit sb to find new people to join a company, an organization or the armed forces: *The police are trying to recruit more officers from ethnic minorities.*

sign sb up (*not formal*) to arrange for sb to sign a form or contract agreeing to do a job: *The company has signed up three top models for the fashion show.* **NOTE** **Sign** can be used on its own to talk about arranging for a professional sports player to join a team, or a musician to work with a recording company: *United have just signed a new goalie.*

take sb on to give sb a job: *We're not taking on any new staff at present.*

PATTERNS AND COLLOCATIONS

- to employ/hire/recruit/sign/engage/take on/ sign up sb **as sth/to do sth**
- to employ/hire/recruit/take on **workers/staff/ a manager**
- to employ/hire/engage a **lawyer**
- to sign/sign up a **player**
- to employ/take on sb **temporarily/permanently**

,take sth 'off sth (*informal*) to make sth shorter by the amount mentioned: *Smoking takes six years off the average life.*
◆ v + n/pron + prep

,take yourself 'off → TAKE OFF, TAKE YOURSELF OFF

,take 'on sth to begin to have a particular quality, appearance, etc.: *Lisa's voice took on a more serious tone.* ◊ *His words suddenly took on a different meaning.* ◊ *The car suddenly seemed to take on a life of its own* (= move by itself without anyone controlling it).
OBJ meaning, shape, expression, appearance
SYN assume sth (*more formal*)
◆ v + adv + n

,take sb 'on 1 to employ sb: *She was taken on as a graduate trainee.* ◊ *They take on extra staff for summer.* **SYN** employ sb 2 to accept sb as a patient, a customer, etc.: *The dentist has stopped taking on new patients.* **OBJ** patients, clients 3 to play against sb in a game or contest; to fight against sb: *She took her father on at chess and beat him.* ◊ *The rebels took on the entire Roman army.*
◆ v + n/pron + adv ◆ v + adv + n

,take sb/sth 'on (of a bus, plane, ship, etc.) to allow sb/sth to enter or come on board: *The bus stopped to take on more passengers.* ◊ *The plane was taking on fuel from a tanker.*
◆ v + adv + n ◆ v + n/pron + adv

,take sth 'on to decide to do sth; to agree to be responsible for sth: *She took on more responsi-*

bilities when she was promoted. ◊ *If we're short of money, I'll just have to take on extra work.*
OBJ responsibility, job, task, work
◆ v + adv + n ◆ v + n/pron + adv

'take sth on/upon yourself to decide to do sth without asking permission or talking to anyone else: *She took the responsibility for what had happened upon herself.* ◊ *Reg took it upon himself to tell the newspapers the truth.*
◆ v + n/pron + prep + pron

,take sb 'out (for/to sth) to invite sb to go with you to the theatre, a restaurant, etc.: *He took Susie out for a meal.*
◆ v + n/pron + adv

,take sb 'out; ,take sb 'out of sth to remove sb from a place; to take sb outside a building: *The prisoners were taken out and shot.*
◆ v + n/pron + adv ◆ v + n/pron + adv + prep

,take sb/sth 'out (*informal*) to kill sb or destroy sth; to injure or damage sb/sth so that they cannot work or be used: *Enemy missiles took out two of our planes.* ◊ *Police think he was taken out by a rival gang.*
◆ v + adv + n ◆ v + n/pron + adv

,take sth 'out 1 to remove a part of the body from inside sb: *She had to have her appendix taken out.* ◊ *I'm afraid we'll have to take the tooth out.* **OBJ** tonsils, teeth, appendix **SYN** remove sth (*more formal*) 2 to obtain an official document or a service: *She took out a loan to buy a new car.* ◊ *Did you remember to take out travel insurance?* **OBJ** insurance, loan, mortgage 3 (**against sb**) to start a legal process

take

against sb by means of an official document: *They took out an injunction against the newspaper.* OBJ **summons**, **injunction 4** (**for sth**) to leave your house with sth in order to do a particular activity: *Shall we take the car out for a drive this afternoon?* **5** (*AmE*) → TAKE STH AWAY **5**

♦ v + adv + n ♦ v + n/pron + adv

take sth 'out; ˌtake sth 'out of sth **1** to remove sth from somewhere: *Jack felt in his pocket and took out his keys.* ◇ *How many books did you take out of* (= borrow from) *the library?* ◇ *You're not allowed to take so much money out of the country.* ◇ *He took out his wallet and pulled out a £50 note.* **2** to carry sth with you outside: *I'll take the cases out to the car.* **3** to remove money from your bank account: *I took some more money out (of my account) yesterday.* OBJ **money** SYN **draw sth out**, **draw sth out of sth**; **withdraw sth** (**from sth**) (*more formal*) **4** to remove an amount of money from a larger amount to pay for sth: *£20 will be taken out of your wages to pay for the damage.* ◇ *Contributions to your pension will be taken out of your salary.* **5** to stop your career, studies, etc. for a period of time in order to do sth else: *She took a year out of college to work abroad.* ◇ *He took a year out between school and college.* ◇ *We need to take time out to think things through.* OBJ **a year**, **time** NOTE Not used in the passive. **6** to make sth disappear from somewhere: *Soaking should help to take the stain out.* OBJ **stain**

♦ v + adv + n ♦ v + n/pron + adv
♦ v + n/pron + adv + prep **5** v + n + adv
♦ v + adv + n (*rare*)

IDM **take a leaf out of sb's 'book** to follow sb's example: *I'm going to take a leaf out of your book and get to work early.* **take sth out of sb's 'hands** to remove sth from sb's control and deal with it yourself: *The decision has been taken out of my hands.* **take the 'mickey out of sb/sth** (*also* **take the 'piss out of sb** ⚠, *slang*) both (*BrE, informal*) to make sb look or feel silly by copying sth that they do, or making them believe sth that is not true: *They used to take the mickey out of Ade because of the way he spoke.*

▶ 'takeout (*AmE*) → TAKEAWAY at TAKE STH AWAY

ˈtake it/sth 'out of sb to make sb feel very tired: *That flu really took it out of me.* ◇ *Looking after three young children really takes a lot out of you.*

OBJ **a lot, so much** SYN **wear sb out**

♦ v + it + adv + prep ♦ v + pron + adv + prep

ˌtake sb 'out of themselves (*especially BrE*) to make sb forget their worries, thoughts, concerns, etc.: *Seeing his old friends again took him out of himself.*

♦ v + n/pron + adv + prep

ˌtake sth 'out on sb/sth to behave in an unpleasant way towards sb/sth because you feel angry, disappointed, etc.: *When he's had a bad day, he always takes it out on me.* ◇ *You shouldn't take your frustrations out on the kids.*

♦ v + it + adv + prep ♦ v + n/pron + adv + prep

ˌtake 'over **1** (**from sth**) (**as sth**) to become more important than sth else and replace it: *Computers are rapidly taking over from books as children's learning resources.* ◇ *Patras took over from Cork as European Capital of Culture.* **2** to become stronger, more powerful or more noticeable: *It's hard not to let negative feelings take over.* ◇ *When she saw the accident, her training as a doctor immediately took over.*

♦ v + adv

ˌtake 'over; ˌtake sth 'over **1** (**from sb**) (**as sth**) to take responsibility for sth after sb else has finished; to do sth instead of sb else: *Who's going to take over from Bill as manager when he retires?* ◇ *If you're tired of driving, I'll take over for a while.* ◇ *I'll take over the driving if you want.* ◇ *Anita took the business over from her father.* ◇ *More and more jobs are being taken over by machines.* **2** to gain control of a political party, a country, etc.: *Things will change when the Socialist Party takes over.* ◇ *In the film, aliens take over the world.*

♦ v + adv ♦ v + adv + n ♦ v + pron + adv
♦ v + n + adv (*rare*)

ˌtake sb 'over sth **1** to go with sb around a building and show them what is interesting or important: *A guide took us over the house.* SYN **take sb around/round sth 2** to look at or discuss sth with sb and explain important points: *Would you mind taking us over the procedure again?* → see also TAKE SB THROUGH STH

♦ v + n/pron + prep

ˌtake sb/sth 'over **1** to affect sb so strongly that they are unable to think of anything else or do anything else: *His ambition had taken him over.* ◇ *My job is starting to take over my life.* **2** [+**adv/prep**] to take sb/sth from one place to another: *I took Mia over to Cambridge to meet my parents.*

♦ **1** v + n/pron + adv ♦ v + adv + n
♦ **2** v + n/pron + adv

ˌtake sth 'over **1** to gain control of a business, a company, etc. by buying it or by buying most of its shares: *The company was taken over last September.* ◇ *They have already taken over several smaller airlines.* OBJ **company** SYN **buy sth out 2** if you **take over** a place, you fill it or use the whole of it so that other people cannot use it: *We're taking over the whole hotel for the conference.* **3** to start living in a place or using it: *The flat was a mess when we took it over.* ◇ *This building used to be a school until the hotel took it over.*

♦ v + adv + n ♦ v + n/pron + adv

▶ 'takeover *n* [C, U] **1** an act of gaining control of a company by buying most of its shares: *The company have abandoned their takeover bid.*

2 an act of gaining control of a country, region or city, especially by force: *a military takeover*

,take sb 'round, etc. (*BrE*) → TAKE SB AROUND, ETC.

,take sb/sth 'round (*BrE*) (*also* ,take sb/sth a'round *AmE, BrE*) to take sb/sth with you to another place, sb else's home, etc.: *I'm taking the photos straight round to Phil's to show him.* ◊ *Joe took us round to see his mother.*
◆ v + n/pron + adv ◆ v + adv + n

,take sb/sth 'through; ,take sb/sth 'through sth to lead or carry a person or a thing through one place to another: *Let's take our tea through to the lounge.* ◊ *The journey takes you through some beautiful scenery.* ◊ (*figurative*) *We have plenty of work to take us through to the end of the year.*
◆ v + n/pron + adv ◆ v + n/pron + prep

'take sb 'through sth to discuss sth with sb or explain it to them so that they know what to do: *Your solicitor will take you through the contract.* ◊ *The director took us through the play scene by scene.*
→ see also TAKE SB OVER STH 2
◆ v + n/pron + prep

'take to sb/sth to start liking sb/sth: *I didn't take to Elena's husband at all.* ◊ *He hasn't taken to his new school.*
OPP take against sb/sth
◆ v + prep

IDM not take 'kindly to sb/sth to not like sb/sth: *I don't take kindly to being told how to run my life.*

'take to sth to go away to a particular place, especially to escape from sth difficult or dangerous: *She felt so ill that she took to her bed.* ◊ *The rebels took to the hills.* ◊ *Thousands of people took to the streets* (= went out in to the streets) *in protest.*
◆ v + prep

IDM take to your 'heels to start running: *They took to their heels and fled.*

'take to sth **1** (*also* 'take to doing sth) to begin to do sth, especially as a habit: *For some reason he took to walking the New York streets at night.* ◊ *She gave up painting and took to sculpture.* **2** to develop an ability for sth: *He took to tennis as if he'd been playing all his life.* ◊ *Jeremy took to teaching like a duck to water* (= very naturally).
◆ v + prep

'take sth to sth (*informal*) to use a tool or piece of equipment in order to do sth, especially sth violent: *He took a hammer to the radio* (= he destroyed it).
◆ v + n/pron + prep

,take 'up to continue with sth, especially after sb/sth else has finished: *The band's new album takes up where the last one left off.*
◆ v + adv

,take sb/sth 'up; ,take sb/sth 'up sth to go with sb or take sth to a higher place or to another part of a building, country, etc.: *Someone will take you up to your room.* ◊ *Why don't we take our picnic up the hill?* ◊ *She took a hot drink up to bed with her.*
OPP take sb/sth down, take sb/sth down sth
NOTE In informal spoken language **take sb up sth** and, less often, **take sb sth up** are also used: *He took her up a cup of tea.* ◊ *He took her a cup of tea up.*
◆ v + n/pron + adv ◆ v + adv + n (*less frequent*)
◆ v + n/pron + prep

,take sth 'up **1** to remove sth that is fixed on a floor or on the ground: *They took the road up to repair the water pipes.* **OBJ** road, pavement, carpet, floorboards **SYN** pull sth up **2** to start to do a new activity, especially for pleasure: *She took up yoga a few years ago.* ◊ *I've decided to take up Japanese.* ◊ *Alex only took up the piano when he was 14.* ⊅ note at START ON STH **3** to start or begin sth, especially a job: *She took up a post at Kyoto University.* **OBJ** post **4** to make an item of clothing, a curtain, etc. shorter: *This skirt will need taking up.* **OPP** let sth down **5** to absorb sth such as a liquid, a gas, etc.: *Plants take up carbon dioxide from the atmosphere.* **SYN** absorb sth **6** to continue sth after sb else has stopped; to continue to discuss sth that was mentioned earlier: *I'd like to take up the point you raised earlier.* ◊ *Paula took up the story.* **OBJ** story **SYN** pick sth up **7** to accept a suggestion, a policy, an invitation, etc.: *The union have taken up her case.* ◊ *The idea was never taken up.* ◊ *I'd like to take up their invitation to visit them in Rio.* **OBJ** case, idea, challenge, offer **8** to join in saying or singing sth: *The cry was taken up by the rest of the crowd.* **OBJ** the cry, the refrain **9** to move into a particular position: *We took up our positions by the door.* ◊ (*formal*) *She has taken up residence* (= begun to live) *in London.* **OBJ** position **10** (*old-fashioned, formal*) to take sth in your hand: *She took up a book and began to read.* **SYN** pick sth up
◆ v + adv + n ◆ v + n/pron + adv

▶ 'take-up *n* [U, sing.] the rate at which people accept sth that is offered to them or made available to them: *a low take-up of government benefits*

▶ 'uptake *n* [U, sing.] **1** the process by which sth is taken into a body or system; the rate at which this happens: *The experiment measured the uptake of oxygen by the muscles.* **2** an act of making or starting sth; the number of people who do this: *There has been an increase in the uptake of these courses.*

,take 'up sth to fill a particular amount of space or time: *This table takes up too much room.* ◊ *Virtually all the memory is taken up with this one program.* ◊ *I mustn't take up any more of*

talk

your time. ◇ *Her whole day was taken up with making phone calls.*

NOTE Take up is not used with a pronoun object in this meaning.

◆ v + adv + n

OBJ room, space, time SYN occupy sth

,take sb 'up on sth (*informal*) **1** to question sb or argue with sb about sth because you do not agree: *I thought he was wrong but I didn't take him up on it.* ◇ *I'd like to take you up on what you said about unemployment.* **SYN pick sb up on sth 2** to accept an offer, an invitation that sb has made: *I think I'll take you up on your offer to help.* ◇ *'You can borrow the car if you like.' 'I might take you up on that.'*

◆ v + n/pron + adv + prep

,take 'up with sb (*informal*) to become friendly with sb; to start a relationship with sb, especially sb who might have a bad influence on you: *I heard Tom has taken up with a supermodel!* ◇ *She's taken up with a bunch of losers.*

◆ v + adv + prep

,take sth 'up with sb to speak or write to sb about sth they may be able to help you with: *You'll have to take your complaint up with the manager.*

◆ v + n/pron + adv + prep

be ,taken 'up with sb/sth; be ,taken 'up with doing sth to be very busy with sb or with doing sth: *She is very taken up with the children.* ◇ *I've been completely taken up with preparing for exams.*

◆ be + v + adv + prep

,take sth u'pon yourself → TAKE STH ON/UPON YOURSELF

be 'taken with sb/sth to find sb/sth attractive or interesting: *We were all very taken with Zoe.*

◆ be + v + prep

talk /tɔːk/

,talk a'round sth (*BrE also* ,talk 'round sth) to talk in a general way about a subject or a problem without discussing the difficult or important parts of it: *We talked around the subject for some time before coming to the real issue.*

OBJ subject

◆ v + prep

'talk at sb to speak to sb without listening to what they say in reply: *My father always listened to our point of view—he never just talked at us.* ◇ *I was being talked at rather than talked to.*

◆ v + prep

,talk a'way (**to sb**) to talk without stopping for a period of time: *They were soon talking away to each other as if they'd known each other for years.* ◇ *Marie was **talking away nineteen to the dozen** (= talking a lot without stopping).*

◆ v + adv

,talk 'back (**to sb**) to reply rudely to sb in authority: *She was sent out for talking back to the teacher.*

SYN answer back, answer sb back (*especially BrE*)

◆ v + adv

▶ 'back talk *n* [U] (*AmE, informal*) a rude reply or comment: *I said no, and don't give me any more back talk.*

,talk sb 'down **1** to talk to sb who is threatening to kill themselves by jumping from a tall building, etc. and persuade them not to: *The police were trying to talk down a youth threatening to jump from the bridge.* **2** to prevent sb from speaking by talking loudly or without stopping: *I tried to argue but they talked me down.*

◆ v + n/pron + adv ◆ v + adv + n

,talk sb/sth 'down **1** to help a pilot bring a plane to the ground by giving detailed instructions from the ground: *The pilots were talked down by the Ground Controllers.* ◇ *to talk a plane down* **2** to persuade sb to lower their prices: *He's asked for $1000. Can we talk him down any further?* **3** to talk about sth in a way that makes it seem less important or successful than it really is: *The opposition was attacked for talking the country down.* ◇ *He tends to talk his achievements down.* **OPP talk sb/sth up**

◆ v + n/pron + adv ◆ v + adv + n

,talk 'down to sb to speak to sb as if they are younger or less intelligent than you or than they really are: *He makes the mistake of talking down to his students.* ◇ *I hate being talked down to.*

SYN patronize sb

◆ v + adv + prep

,talk sb/yourself 'into/'out of sth; ,talk sb/yourself 'into/'out of doing sth to persuade sb/yourself to do/not to do sth: *Why did you let James talk you into this crazy scheme?* ◇ *I talked myself into believing I was happy.* ◇ *I'm leaving this minute and don't try to talk me out of it.*

◆ v + n/pron + prep ◆ v + n/pron + adv + prep

IDM talk your way out of sth/of doing sth to make excuses and give reasons for not doing sth; to manage to get yourself out of a difficult situation: *I managed to talk my way out of having to give a speech.* ◇ *I'd like to see him talk his way out of this!*

,talk sth 'out to discuss sth thoroughly until you find a solution, an agreement, etc. or make a decision: *to talk out your thoughts/feelings/problems with sb* ◇ *It might help to talk things out.*

OBJ things, problem

◆ v + n/pron + adv ◆ v + adv + n

,talk yourself 'out to talk until you have nothing left to say: *They spent all the evening discussing the problem until they talked themselves out.*

♦ v + pron + adv

,talk sb/yourself 'out of sth → TALK SB/
YOURSELF INTO/OUT OF STH, ETC.

⚑,talk sth 'over (with sb) to discuss sth with sb in order to find a solution, make a decision, etc.: *I need to talk it over with my parents.* ◇ *You'll find it helpful to talk things over with a friend.* ◇ *You both need to talk over what happened.*

OBJ **things**, **feelings**, **problems**

♦ v + n/pron + adv ♦ v + adv + n

,talk 'round sth (*BrE*) → TALK AROUND STH

,talk sb 'round (to sth) (*BrE*) to persuade sb to accept sth or to agree to sth: *My parents didn't want me to go to study in Britain, but I managed to talk them round (to the idea).*

♦ v + n/pron + adv

,talk sb 'through sth to explain sth to sb in detail so that they understand it: *The technical support staff will talk you through any difficulties you have with the software.* ◇ *I can talk you through the application form.*

SYN **walk sb through sth** (*AmE*)

♦ v + n/pron + prep

,talk sth 'through to discuss sth thoroughly so that you can understand it, come to an agreement, or make a decision about it: *Throughout their marriage they have always talked things through.* ◇ *It's helpful to talk the problem through with a counsellor.* ◇ *We talked through what had happened.*

OBJ **things**, **problems**

♦ v + n/pron + adv ♦ v + adv + n

⚑'talk to sb 1 (*also* 'talk with sb *especially AmE*) to have a conversation with sb 2 to speak to sb seriously, especially about sth wrong that they have done, or sth that they have not done: *I'd like to talk to you in my office now.*

♦ v + prep

▸ 'talking-to *n* [sing.] (*informal*) a serious talk with sb who has done sth wrong: *to give sb a good talking-to*

,talk sb/sth 'up to praise sb/sth in order to make other people interested in them/it; to describe sb/sth in a way that makes them sound better or more successful than they really are: *They talked up the tourist attractions to encourage more visitors.* ◇ *He was being talked up as a future presidential candidate.* ◇ *It's too early to tell if the new President will talk the dollar up or down.*

OPP **talk sb/sth down**

♦ v + n/pron + adv ♦ v + adv + n

'talk with sb (*especially AmE*) → TALK TO SB 1

tamper /'tæmpə(r)/

'tamper with sth to do sth to sth to change it without permission: *Two policemen were accused of tampering with the evidence.* ◇ *The lock has been tampered with.*

OBJ **evidence**, **controls**, **brakes** SYN **interfere with sth**

♦ v + prep

tangle /'tæŋgl/

,tangle sth 'up; be/get ,tangled 'up (in/with sth) to twist sth into an untidy mass; to become twisted in this way: *My long skirt got tangled up in the wheel of my bike.* ◇ (*figurative*) *Kurt didn't want to get tangled up with a girl while he was trying to study.*

NOTE Usually used in the passive.

♦ v + n/pron + adv ♦ v + adv + n ♦ be/get + v + adv

'tangle with sb (*informal*) to become involved in an argument or a fight with sb: *You've chosen the wrong man to tangle with.*

♦ v + prep

tank /tæŋk/

,tank 'up; ,tank sth 'up (*AmE, informal*) to fill a vehicle with fuel: *We'd better tank up before we get on the thruway.*

♦ v + adv ♦ v + n/pron + adv ♦ v + adv + n

,tank 'up (on sth) (*slang*) to drink a lot of alcohol: *The lads had spent all evening tanking up on scotch.*

♦ v + adv

▸ ,tanked 'up *adj* very drunk: *She got totally tanked up and couldn't drive home.*

tap /tæp/ (-pp-)

'tap sb for sth 1 (*BrE, informal*) to persuade sb to give you sth, especially money: *Can't you tap your father for a loan?* ◇ *to tap sb for information* 2 (*AmE, informal*) to choose sb for a particular role or job: *A British actress has been tapped for a part in the movie.* NOTE Usually used in the passive.

♦ v + n/pron + prep

,tap sth 'in/'out to put information, numbers, letters, etc. into a machine by pressing buttons: *Tap in your password.* ◇ *I picked up the phone and tapped out Joe's number.*

♦ v + adv + n ♦ v + n/pron + adv

,tap 'into sth 1 to use a computer to obtain information from another computer: *He had managed to tap into the company's database.* 2 to use sth from a supply of energy, knowledge, etc. for your own advantage: *Schools should tap into the knowledge and experience of people in the local community.* ◇ *His talk about bullying tapped into parents' anxieties.*

♦ v + prep

,tap 'out; ,tap sb/sth 'out (*AmE*) to have nothing left of a supply of money, resources, ideas, etc., or to make sb have nothing left: *I've given to so many charities lately and its tapping me out.* ◇ *If the US were to tap out, the global system would lose its best customer.* ◇ *The city has tapped out the groundwater supply.*

♦ v + adv ♦ v + n/pron + adv ♦ v + adv + n

▶ ,tapped 'out *adj* (*AmE*): *He is a creative guy and far from tapped out.* ◇ *a tapped-out TV series*

,tap sth 'out **1** to hit a surface lightly, making a rhythm: *He tapped out the rhythm with his foot.* **2** → TAP STH IN/OUT
♦ v + n/pron + adv ♦ v + adv + n

tape /teɪp/

,tape sth 'up **1** to fasten tape around sth firmly: *Put it in a box and tape it up securely.* **2** (*AmE*) to tie a bandage firmly around a wound: *That's a nasty cut—come on, we'll get it all taped up.*
NOTE **Tape sth** can also be used on its own: *Put it in a box and tape it securely.*
♦ v + n/pron + adv ♦ v + adv + n

taper /'teɪpə(r)/

,taper 'off to gradually become smaller in size, volume, amount, etc.: *Our profits have begun to taper off.*
↪ note at DWINDLE AWAY
♦ v + adv

tart /tɑːt; *AmE* tɑːrt/

,tart sth 'up (*BrE*, *informal*) to decorate or improve the appearance of sth, often in a way that other people do not think is attractive: *They've tarted up the restaurant but the food hasn't improved.*
♦ v + adv + n ♦ v + n/pron + adv

,tart yourself 'up (*BrE*, *informal*, *disapproving*) (especially of a woman) to make yourself more attractive by putting on special clothes, jewellery and make-up: *She spends ages tarting herself up for a night out.*
SYN **doll yourself up** (**in sth**)
♦ v + pron + adv

task /tɑːsk; *AmE* tæsk/

'task sb with sth to give sb a task to do: *forces tasked with keeping the peace*
NOTE Usually used in the passive. ♦ You can also use the pattern **task sb to do sth**: *soldiers tasked to provide medical support.*
♦ v + n/pron + prep

tax /tæks/

'tax sb with sth (*formal*) to accuse sb of doing sth wrong: *Critics taxed the government with not acting quickly enough.*
♦ v + n/pron + prep

team /tiːm/

,team 'up (**with sb**) to work together with another person or group in order to do sth: *The two companies have teamed up to produce new software.* ◇ *We've teamed up with XL Records to give away 25 tickets for the live concert.* ◇ *How did the two of you come to team up?*
♦ v + adv

tear¹ /teə(r); *AmE* ter/ (**tore** /tɔː(r)/, **torn** /tɔːn; *AmE* tɔːrn/)

,tear a'bout; ,tear a'bout sth (*BrE*) → TEAR AROUND, TEAR AROUND STH

,tear sb/yourself a'part to make sb/yourself suffer very much or feel very unhappy: *Being separated from the children was tearing her apart.* ◇ *Don't tear yourself apart thinking about the past.*
♦ v + n/pron + adv

,tear sb/sth a'part **1** (*also* ,tear itself, themselves, etc. a'part) to separate people in a family, an organization, a country, etc. and make them argue with or fight against each other: *The civil war is tearing the country apart.* ◇ *The family was torn apart by conflicting loyalties.* ◇ *The region was tearing itself apart.* ◇ *Jealousy tore them apart.* **2** to destroy or defeat sb/sth: *We tore the other team apart in the second half.* **3** to criticize sb/sth severely: *You can't write that—you'll be torn apart.*
♦ v + n/pron + adv ♦ v + adv + n

,tear sth a'part **1** to destroy sth by pulling it violently so that it breaks into pieces: *The dogs tore the fox apart.* **OBJ** **prey** **SYN** **rip sth apart**
↪ note at TEAR STH UP **2** to destroy a building, etc.: *Hundreds of homes were torn apart by the hurricane.* ◇ *The police tore the room apart looking for drugs.*
♦ v + n/pron + adv ♦ v + adv + n (*rare*)

,tear itself, themselves, etc. a'part → TEAR SB/STH APART 1

,tear a'round; ,tear a'round sth (*BrE also* ,tear a'bout/'round, ,tear a'bout/'round sth) to move very quickly from place to place, being very busy: *The children were tearing around shouting.* ◇ *No wonder you're tired, tearing about like that all the time.*
SYN **run around, run around sth**; **rush around, rush around sth**
♦ v + adv ♦ v + prep

'tear at sth (**with sth**) to attack sth violently, especially by pulling pieces off it: *The brambles tore at her legs.* ◇ *He tore at the meat with his bare hands.*
♦ v + prep

,tear sb/yourself/sth a'way (**from sb/sth**) to make sb/yourself stop doing sth they/you enjoy in order to do sth else: *I can't tear myself away from this book.* ◇ *Come and visit us, if you can tear Bill away from his computer!* ◇ *He couldn't* **tear his eyes away** *from* (= stop looking at) *Mina.*
SYN **drag sb/sth/yourself away** (**from sb/sth**)
♦ v + n/pron + adv

▶ 'tearaway *n* (*informal*) a young person who behaves in a wild way: *Her son's a bit of a tearaway.* ◇ *The ten-year-old tearaway had burgled several houses.*

,**tear sth a'way** to pull sth violently from the thing it is attached to: *The floods had torn away the base of the bridge.*
  ◆ v + n/pron + adv ◆ v + adv + n

be '**torn between A and B** to have to make a very difficult choice between two things, people, etc.: *I was torn between my parents and my friend.* ◇ *Thomas was torn between going to college or working for his father.*
  ◆ be + v + prep

,**tear sth 'down** to pull or knock down a building, a wall, etc.: *They're tearing down some old houses to build a new office block.*
  OBJ building, house, trees **SYN** pull sth down; demolish sth (*more formal*) ⊃ note at KNOCK STH DOWN
  ◆ v + adv + n ◆ v + n/pron + adv

,**tear 'into sb/sth** to attack sb/sth physically or with words: *He tore into Jed with his fists.* ◇ *She tore into the students if they were late.* ◇ *They tore into their food* (= started eating) *as if they were starving.*
  ◆ v + prep

,**tear sth 'off**; ,**tear sth 'off sb/sth** to remove sth quickly by pulling violently: *Alice tore off her ring and threw it on the ground.* ◇ *The door was nearly torn off its hinges.* ◇ *If you need a piece of paper I'll tear some off my pad.*
  ◆ v + n/pron + adv ◆ v + adv + n
  ◆ v + n/pron + prep
  IDM **tear sb 'off a strip**; **tear a 'strip off sb** (*BrE, informal*) to speak angrily to sb you think has done sth wrong: *The boss tore him off a strip.*

,**tear sth 'out**; ,**tear sth 'out of sth** to separate sth from sth it is attached to, especially with your hands: *Several pages had been torn out of the book.*
  ◆ v + n/pron + adv ◆ v + adv + n
  ◆ v + n/pron + adv + prep
  IDM **tear your 'hair out** (*informal*) to show that you are very angry or very worried about sth: *I was tearing my hair out trying to work out what to do.*

,**tear 'round**; ,**tear 'round sth** (*BrE*) → TEAR AROUND, TEAR AROUND STH

,**tear sth 'up 1** to destroy a piece of paper, a letter, etc. by pulling it into pieces: *She tore up all the letters he had sent her.* ◇ (*figurative*) *The union accused the management of tearing up* (= ignoring) *the agreement.* **OBJ** letter, agreement, treaty **SYN** rip sth up **2** to destroy or damage sth, especially by removing it violently from the ground: *Trees and bushes were torn up by the storm.* **OBJ** trees **SYN** pull sth up; rip sth up **3** (*AmE, informal*) to perform or do an activity with a lot of energy or emotion: *Two of the couples were tearing up the dance floor.* ◇ *Ray Charles was **tearing it up** at the piano, and the crowd was going wild.*
  ◆ v + n/pron + adv ◆ v + adv + n
  IDM **rip/tear up the 'rule book** to start doing things in a way that is different from the way things are usually done, usually resulting in an improvement: *What we were able to do was tear up the rule book and design a car that doesn't damage the environment.*

---

tear sth up

pull sth apart ◆ **rip sth up** ◆ **shred sth** ◆ **tear sth apart** ◆ **tear sth up**

These verbs all mean to pull sth apart by force.

pull sth apart to separate sth into pieces by pulling different parts of it in different directions, sometimes violently: *The wolves will pull the carcass apart.*

rip sth up to destroy sth by tearing it into small pieces, often suddenly or violently: *He ripped up the letter.* **NOTE** Rip can be used on its own: *She ripped the letter to shreds.* ▶ rip n: *The jacket had a rip in the sleeve.*

shred sth to cut or tear sth into lots of small pieces: *Serve the fish on a bed of shredded lettuce.* ◇ *He was accused of shredding documents relating to the case.*

tear sth apart to destroy sth violently, especially by pulling it to pieces: *The dogs tore the fox apart.* ◇ *They tore the room apart, looking for money.*

tear sth up to destroy a document, etc. by pulling it in different directions: *She tore up the letter.* **NOTE** Tear can be used on its own: *She tore the letter into tiny pieces.* ▶ tear n: *There's a tear in your coat.*

WHICH WORD?

Ripping is usually more violent than **tearing**. Both verbs, but especially **rip**, are often used with a preposition or adverb to show violent movement as the thing is ripped/torn. **Shredding** paper is usually done in a machine called a **shredder** or **shredding machine**; if you do it with your hands you **tear** it **up** or **rip** it **up**.

PATTERNS AND COLLOCATIONS

■ to rip (up)/shred **paper/a letter**
■ to rip **fabric/flesh**
■ to shred **vegetables**
■ to shred sth **finely**

tear² /tɪə(r); AmE tɪr/

,tear 'up (AmE) to start crying: *I saw Mom tear up as they said 'I do'.*
◆ v + adv

tease /tiːz/

,tease sth 'out; ,tease sth 'out of sth **1** to try to find some information or the meaning of sth when this is hidden or not clear: *teasing out meanings from texts* ◇ *These issues will be teased out in the course of the book.* ◇ *to tease information/the truth out of somebody* OBJ **information, answers, truth 2** to remove sth such as knots from hair, wool, etc. by gently pulling or brushing it: *Lisa dried her hair carefully, teasing it out between her fingers.* **3** to separate sth carefully from sth else: *birds teasing out ripe seeds (from plants)* ◇ *He took a screwdriver and teased out the remaining screws.*
◆ v + n/pron + adv ◆ v + adv + n
◆ v + n/pron + adv + prep

tee /tiː/ (**teed**, **teed**)

NOTE In golf, a **tee** is a flat area from which players hit the ball.

,tee 'off (in golf) to start a game by hitting the ball for the first time: *The players eventually teed off two hours late.* ◇ *(figurative) What time does the party tee off tonight?*
◆ v + adv

,tee sb 'off (AmE, informal) to make sb angry or annoyed
◆ v + n/pron + adv ◆ v + adv + n
▶ ,teed 'off adj (AmE, informal) annoyed or angry: *Her friend was teed off about what she said.*

,tee 'up; ,tee sth 'up (in golf) to prepare to hit a ball by placing it on a tee: *The crowd fell silent as he teed up.* ◇ *She teed up the ball and took a few practice swings.*
◆ v + adv ◆ v + n/pron + adv

teem /tiːm/

,teem 'down to rain hard: *It was absolutely teeming down.* ◇ *The rain teemed down.*
SUBJ only **the rain, it** SYN **pour down**
NOTE You can also say: *It was* **teeming with** *rain.*
◆ v + adv

'teem with sb/sth (usually approving) (usually used in the progressive tenses) to have large numbers of people or things moving around: *cities teeming with life/people* ◇ *The lake was teeming with fish.*
◆ v + prep

---

tell sb off

rebuke sb ◆ **reprimand sb** ◆ **scold sb** ◆ **tell sb off** ◆ **tick sb off**

These verbs all mean to tell sb that you disapprove of sth they have done.

rebuke sb (often passive) (formal) to tell sb, publicly or privately, that you blame them for doing sth wrong: *The company was publicly rebuked for having neglected safety procedures.* ▶ **rebuke** n [C, usually sing., U]: *He was silenced by her stinging rebuke.*

reprimand sb (formal) to tell sb officially that you disapprove of their actions, especially if they have broken a rule or law: *The officers were severely reprimanded for their unprofessional behaviour.* ▶ **reprimand** n: *He received a severe reprimand for his behaviour.*

scold sb to tell sb, especially a child, that you disapprove of sth they have done: *Rose scolded the child gently for her behaviour.* ▶ **scolding** n [C, usually sing.]: *She got a scolding from her mother.*

tell sb off (informal) to speak angrily to sb for doing sth wrong: *I told the boys off for making so much noise.* ◇ *Did you get told off?* ▶ **telling-off** n [C, usually sing.] (BrE, infor-

mal): *The nurse gave him a telling-off for smoking.*

tick sb off (BrE, informal) to speak angrily to sb, especially a child, because they have done sth wrong: *He was ticked off by the headmaster.* ▶ **ticking off** n [sing.] (BrE, informal): *She got a ticking off for being late.*

WHICH WORD?

There is no verb for telling sb that you disapprove of their actions that is neither formal nor informal. **Scold** is the most frequent of these verbs in written English, particularly in stories, but it is not used much in spoken English. **Tell sb off** is the most frequent in spoken English but it is not used much in written English.

PATTERNS AND COLLOCATIONS

■ to scold sb/tell sb off/rebuke sb/reprimand sb **for** sth
■ to scold/rebuke/reproach **yourself**
■ to scold sb/tell sb off/rebuke sb/reprimand sb **severely**
■ to scold/rebuke/reprimand sb **gently**
■ to **publicly** rebuke/reprimand sb

tell /tel/ (**told**, **told** /təʊld; *AmE* toʊld/)

,tell a'gainst sb (*formal*, *especially BrE*) to be a serious disadvantage to sb: *Her lack of experience told against her.*
SYN **count against sb** (*less formal*)
◆ v + prep

,tell sb/sth a'part to be able to distinguish sb/sth from other similar people or things: *I can never tell the twins apart.*
◆ v + n/pron + adv

'tell sb/sth from sb/sth to distinguish sb/sth from another person or thing: *It needs skill to tell a real diamond from a fake.* ◇ *Can you tell Tom from his twin brother?*
NOTE Not used in the passive.
◆ v + n/pron + prep

'tell of sth (*formal*, *literary*) to make sth known; to give an account of sth: *The report told of a series of design errors.* ◇ *The story tells of the love between a prince and a young girl.*
◆ v + prep

,tell sb 'off (**for sth/for doing sth**) (*informal*) to speak angrily to sb, especially a child, because they have done sth wrong: *I told the boys off for making so much noise.* ◇ *You'll get told off if you're caught doing that.*
SYN **tick sb off**; **reprimand sb**; **scold sb** (*formal*)
◆ v + n/pron + adv ◆ v + adv + n (*less frequent*)
▶ ,telling-'off (**for sth/for doing sth**) *n* [usually sing.] (*informal*, *especially BrE*) an act of speaking angrily to sb, especially a child, because they have done sth wrong: *You've already been given one telling-off today!* ◇ *How many tellings-off have you had this week?*

'tell on sb **1** (*informal*) (*used mainly by children*) to tell a teacher or sb in authority that sb has done sth wrong: *Don't tell on me, will you?* **2** (*formal*) to have a bad effect on sb/sth: *The long wait was telling on his nerves.*
◆ v + prep

tend /tend/

'tend to sb/sth to care for sb/sth, especially when there is a problem: *I'll look after the child—you tend to the mother.* ◇ *The injured were already being tended to.*
SYN **attend to sb/sth**; **see to sb/sth** ⊃ note at CARE FOR SB
NOTE **Tend sb/sth** can also be used: *farmers tending their cattle.*
◆ v + prep

'tend towards sth; 'tend towards doing sth (*less frequent*) to take a particular direction or have a particular opinion; to have a lot of a particular quality: *We're tending towards the view that all students should study two languages.* ◇ *His views tend towards the extreme.*
SYN **incline to/towards sth**
◆ v + prep

tense /tens/

,tense 'up; ,tense sth 'up if you **tense up** or **tense sth up**, you make your muscles stiff and tight because you are not relaxed: *If you feel that you're tensing up, take a few moments to relax.* ◇ *Tense up your arm and leg muscles and then let them go.*
NOTE **Tense** and **tense sth** are used on their own with the same meaning.
◆ v + adv ◆ v + adv + n ◆ v + pron + adv ◆ v + n + adv

test /test/

'test for sth; 'test sb/sth for sth to examine sb/sth to see if a particular substance, etc. is present: *They are testing for oil in the area.* ◇ *She was tested for hepatitis.* ◇ *The software has been tested for viruses.*
◆ v + prep ◆ v + n/pron + prep

,test sb 'out to try to find out what qualities sb has, how they will react in a particular situation, etc.: *My new boss gave me the most difficult clients to deal with. I felt he was really testing me out to see if I would cope.*
◆ v + n/pron + adv ◆ v + adv + n (*less frequent*)

,test sth 'out (**on sb/sth**) to try an idea, a machine, a product, etc. to see if it works well or if people like it: *Let me test this idea out on you.* ◇ *When you buy a bed, test it out in the shop.*
OBJ **idea**, **theory**, **equipment** **SYN** **try sb/sth out** (**on sb/sth**)
NOTE **Test sth** can also be used on its own with the same meaning.
◆ v + n/pron + adv ◆ v + adv + n

testify /'testɪfaɪ/ (**testifies**, **testifying**, **testified**)

'testify to sth to show or be evidence that sth is true: *James's school reports testified to his ability.*
◆ v + prep

thaw /θɔː/

,thaw 'out if ice or snow **thaws out**, it melts: *Britain is thawing out after the freeze.*
◆ v + adv

,thaw 'out; ,thaw sth 'out **1** to become, or to let frozen food become, soft and ready to cook: *He took the meat out of the freezer and left it to thaw out.* ◇ *to thaw out meat/fish* **SYN** **defrost**, **defrost sth 2** (*informal*) to become, or to let sth become, warmer after being very cold: *Come in and thaw out by the fire!* ◇ *My feet are frozen! I need to thaw them out.* ◇ (*figurative*) *She was very shy at first, but she soon thawed out.* **NOTE** **Thaw** and **thaw sth** can also be used on their own with these meanings.
◆ v + adv ◆ v + n/pron + adv ◆ v + adv + n

thin /θɪn/ (**-nn-**)

,thin sth 'down (**with sth**) to make a liquid less thick or strong, for example by adding water to

think

it: *The paint needs to be thinned down with water before you use it.*

NOTE **Thin sth** is used on its own more frequently.

♦ v + adv + n ♦ v + n/pron + adv

,thin 'out to become fewer in number, or less thick: *The crowd had thinned out and only a few people were left.* ◇ *Once they were clear of the city, the traffic started to thin out.* ◇ *The trees began to thin out as we climbed higher.*

SUBJ **crowd**, **trees**, **traffic**

♦ v + adv

,thin sth 'out to reduce the number of sth so that there is more space between them: *Thin out the seedlings to about 10 cm apart.*

OBJ **plants**

♦ v + adv + n ♦ v + n/pron + adv

think /θɪŋk/ (**thought**, **thought** /θɔːt/)

'think about sb/sth **1** to have ideas or images in your mind; to remember sb/sth: *I can't stop thinking about her.* ◇ *All he ever thinks about is money.* ◇ *It doesn't bear thinking about.* ◇ *When I was alone, I just sat and thought about things.* **2** (*also* 'think of sb/sth) to consider sb/sth: *It's time you stopped being so selfish and started thinking about other people!* **SYN** **take sb/sth into account**

♦ v + prep

IDM if/when you 'think about it used to draw attention to a fact that is not obvious or has not been mentioned before: *It must have been terrible when you think about it.*

'think about sth; 'think about doing sth to use your mind to consider sth, such as your future plans, to try to solve problems, etc.: *I'll think about it and let you know tomorrow.* ◇ *She's thinking about changing her job.* ◇ *Have you thought about what you'll do if you don't get a place at college?* ◇ *'What did I do wrong?' 'Just think about it!'*

♦ v + prep

IDM think 'twice about sth/about doing sth to think carefully before you decide to do sth: *I'd think twice about calling him if I were you.*

,think a'head (**to sth**) to think carefully about what might happen in the future; to plan for the future: *Even when their children are very young, parents are thinking ahead to exams and jobs.* ◇ *Pilots are trained to think ahead.*

♦ v + adv

,think 'back (**to sth**) to remember or think about sth that happened in the past: *She thought back to the day they first met.* ◇ *Thinking back, I'm sure I noticed there was something strange.*

♦ v + adv

,think for your'self to make your own decisions, form your own opinions, etc. without depending on other people: *You need to learn to think for yourself.* ◇ *Our parents always encouraged us to think for ourselves.*

♦ v + prep + pron

'think of sb/sth **1** to have an image or idea of a particular person or thing in your mind: *When I said that, I wasn't thinking of anyone in particular.* ◇ *He thought of how happy his parents would*

SYNONYMS

think sth over

chew sth over ♦ **consider sth** ♦ **mull sth over** ♦ **ponder about/on/over sth** ♦ **think sth over**

These verbs all mean to use your mind in order to try to understand sth, make a decision, solve a problem, etc.

chew sth over (*not formal*) to think about or discuss sth slowly and carefully, especially when sb cannot decide or a group of people cannot agree about sth: *I was chewing things over in my head.*

consider sth to think carefully about sth, especially in order to make a decision: *She considered her options.* ◇ *Let us consider the facts.* ◇ *He was considering an appeal.* ◇ *He was considering what to do next.*

mull sth over to spend time thinking carefully about sth such as a plan or proposal: *I need some time to mull it over before making a decision.*

ponder about/on/over sth to think carefully about sth, especially in order to understand

it: *She pondered over his words.* **NOTE** **Ponder** can be used on its own: *We intend to ponder all the alternatives before acting.*

think sth over to consider sth carefully, especially before reaching a decision: *He'd like more time to think it over.* **NOTE** It is also possible to use **think about sth** with this meaning: *I can't tell you now—I'll have to think about it.*

PATTERNS AND COLLOCATIONS

- to consider/think about/ponder (over) **how/ what/whether...**
- to **leave sb/pause** to consider sth/think about sth/think sth over/ponder (over) sth
- to consider sth/think about sth/think sth over/ ponder (over) sth **carefully/briefly**
- to consider sth/think sth over/think about sth **seriously/rationally**
- to think about sth/ponder sth **long and hard**

think

think sth up

come up with sth ♦ conceive of sth ♦ devise sth ♦ dream sth up ♦ hit on/upon sth ♦ think sth up

These verbs all mean to think of an idea, plan, solution, etc.

come up with sth (*not formal*) to think of or produce an idea, a plan, a solution, etc.: *He's come up with a really good design for a solar-powered car.*

conceive of sth (*formal*) to form an idea, a plan, etc. in your mind: *They conceived of a theory and stuck to it.* NOTE **Conceive** can be used on its own: *He conceived the idea of transforming the old power station into an arts centre.*

devise sth to invent sth new or a new way of doing sth: *Scientists have devised a method of recycling the contaminated oil.*

dream sth up (*not formal*) to think of an idea, especially a very unusual or silly one: *Trust you to dream up a crazy idea like this! ◇ It was a scheme dreamt up by some advertising guru.*

hit on/upon sth (*not formal*) to think of a good idea suddenly or by chance: *She hit on the perfect title for her new novel.*

think sth up (*not formal*) to think of an idea, plan or excuse: *Can't you think up a better excuse than that?*

PATTERNS AND COLLOCATIONS

- to come up with/devise/conceive (of)/hit on/think up/dream up a **plan/scheme**
- to come up with/conceive (of)/hit on/think up/dream up **an idea/the idea of doing sth**
- to come up with/devise/hit on/think up a **way of doing sth/method/formula**
- to come up with/devise a **solution**
- to come up with an **answer**
- to come up with/think up/dream up an **excuse**

---

be to see him. **2** → THINK ABOUT SB/STH 2: *Just think of the consequences if you give up your job.* **3** to create an idea in your imagination: *Who first thought of the idea? ◇ Can you think of anyone who could help? ◇ Hasn't this idea ever been thought of before?* **4** (*used especially with* **can**) to remember sb/sth: *I can't think of his name at the moment. ◇ I was just thinking of the wonderful trip we had.* **5** (**as sb/sth**) to consider sb/sth from a particular point of view: *I still think of Oxford as my home. ◇ Franco thought of his landlady as his 'English mother'. ◇ She is not thought of as a businesswoman. ◇ Elisa hates being thought of as a little girl.*
♦ v + prep

IDM **come to 'think of it** used when you suddenly remember sth or realize that it might be important: *Come to think of it, he did mention you.* **not think much of sb/sth** to not have a very high opinion of sb/sth: *I didn't think much of her new boyfriend.* **think 'better of it/of doing sth** to decide not to do sth you had planned to do after you have thought about it: *I was about to tell him the truth, but I thought better of it.* **think the 'world of sb** to have a very high opinion of sb; to love sb very much: *He thinks the world of his daughter.*

'think of doing sth **1** to consider that you might do sth: *They're thinking of moving to America. ◇ I did think of resigning, but I decided against it.* SYN **contemplate sth** (*more formal*) **2** to imagine an actual or a possible situation: *I'd never have thought of doing that! ◇ I couldn't think of letting you take the blame* (= I wouldn't allow you to do this). NOTE Often used in negative sentences.
♦ v + prep

IDM **think 'nothing of doing sth** to consider that doing sth is normal and not very difficult: *She thinks nothing of walking home in the rain.*

think sth 'out to consider all the details of sth carefully, especially in order to find an answer or a solution to a problem: *She needed to be alone to think things out. ◇ I thought out what I was going to say before I phoned. ◇ a well-thought-out training programme*
♦ v + n/pron + adv ♦ v + adv + n

think sth 'over to consider sth carefully, especially before making a decision: *Please think over what I've said. ◇ I'd like more time to think things over.*
SYN **mull sth over**
♦ v + adv + n ♦ v + n/pron + adv

think sth 'through to consider a problem fully: *Careers advisers can help you think through your choices. ◇ Take my advice and think things through before you do anything.*
♦ v + adv + n ♦ v + n/pron + adv

think sth 'up (*informal*) to create an idea, a plan, a story, etc. in your mind: *We need to think up a new name for the group. ◇ Can't you think up a better excuse than that?*
SYN **devise sth** (*more formal*); **invent sth** (*more formal*)
♦ v + adv + n ♦ v + pron + adv ♦ v + n + adv (*rare*)

thirst /θɜːst; *AmE* θɜːrst/

ˈthirst for sth (*literary*) to want sth very much:
Our opponents were thirsting for revenge.
 ◆ v + prep

thrash /θræʃ/

ˌthrash aˈround (*also* ˌthrash aˈbout *especially BrE*) to move about in a violent, uncontrolled way: *He thrashed around in the water, gasping for breath.*
 ◆ v + adv

ˌthrash sth ˈout to discuss sth thoroughly and in an open and honest way to try to find a solution: *He called a meeting to thrash out the problem.* ◇ *Eventually they thrashed out an agreement.*
 OBJ **problem, details, agreement, deal**
 SYN **hash sth out** (*AmE, informal*)
 ◆ v + adv + n ◆ v + pron + adv
 ◆ v + n + adv (*less frequent*)

thrill /θrɪl/

ˈthrill to sth (*formal*) to feel very excited at sth:
Audiences thrilled to his performance in Macbeth.
 ◆ v + prep

thrive /θraɪv/ (**thrived, thrived**, *AmE also* **throve** /θrəʊv; *AmE* θroʊv/, **thriven** /ˈθrɪvn/)

ˈthrive on sth to enjoy or be successful in a situation or condition that other people would not like: *He thrives on hard work.* ◇ *Sue and Jack seem to thrive on arguments.*
 ◆ v + prep

throttle /ˈθrɒtl; *AmE* ˈθrɑːtl/

ˌthrottle ˈback (*also* ˌthrottle ˈdown *less frequent*) to control the supply of fuel or power to an engine in order to reduce the speed of a vehicle: *The pilot got very low before he throttled back.*
 ◆ v + adv

ˌthrottle ˈup (*rare*) to control the supply of fuel or power to an engine to increase the speed of a vehicle
 ◆ v + adv

throw /θrəʊ; *AmE* θroʊ/ (**threw** /θruː/, **thrown** /θrəʊn; *AmE* θroʊn/)

ˌthrow sb/yourself aˈround; ˌthrow sb/yourself aˈround sth (*BrE also* ˌthrow sb/yourself aˈbout, ˌthrow sb/yourself aˈbout sth) to make sb/yourself move about suddenly and violently, often causing injury: *The passengers were thrown around in the crash.* ◇ *The child was screaming and throwing himself around.* ◇ *The band threw themselves around the stage like madmen.*
 ◆ v + n/pron + adv ◆ v + n/pron + prep

ˌthrow sth aˈround (*BrE also* ˌthrow sth aˈbout)
 1 to say sth, discuss sth, etc. in a general way:
You can't just throw accusations around like that!
◇ *Let's have an initial meeting to **throw some ideas about**.* OBJ **accusations, ideas** SYN **toss sth around 2** to spend time throwing sth such as a ball from one person to another, in a not very serious way: *They were in the yard throwing a ball around.* OBJ **ball 3** to move part of your body around violently: *She was speaking excitedly, throwing her arms around.* OBJ **arms, head**
 ◆ v + n/pron + adv

 IDM **throw your ˈmoney around** to spend a lot of money in a very careless way, often in order to impress people: *John hates people throwing their money about.* **throw your ˈweight around** (*informal*) to use your authority in an aggressive way to achieve what you want: *She enjoys throwing her weight about and getting her way.*

ˌthrow sth aˈround; ˌthrow sth aˈround sth (*also* ˌthrow sth aˈbout/ˈround, ˌthrow sth aˈbout/ˈround sth *especially BrE*) to send sth from your hand in different directions, often because you are angry: *How do you stop babies throwing their food around?* ◇ *Jeff got so angry that he started throwing furniture about.* ◇ *People were throwing glasses round the room.*
 ◆ v + n/pron + adv ◆ v + n/pron + prep

ˌthrow sth aˈround sb/sth (*BrE also* ˌthrow sth aˈbout/ˈround sb/sth) **1** if you **throw** your arms **around** sb, you hold them tightly to show that you love them or wish to thank them for sth: *Diana threw her arms around him/his neck and kissed him.* **2** to put sth quickly around sb/sth: *We threw blankets around ourselves to keep warm.* ◇ *a silk scarf thrown casually around the shoulders* **3** to put a barrier around a place so that people cannot enter or leave: *A security cordon had been thrown around the area.*
 ◆ v + n/pron + prep

ˌthrow sth aˈside **1** to put sth quickly to one side, often because you are angry or in a hurry: *She read the letter and immediately threw it aside.* SYN **cast sth aside** (*formal*); **toss sth aside** (*formal*) **2** to reject sth such as an attitude, an idea, a way of life, etc.: *All loyalties were thrown aside once the competition started.* ◇ *to throw aside sentimentality/nervousness* ◇ *to throw aside a system* SYN **cast sth aside** (*formal*)
 ◆ v + n/pron + adv ◆ v + adv + n

ˈthrow sth at sb **1** to direct sth such as a remark, a question, etc. at sb, often in an aggressive way: *She threw a look of contempt at me.* ◇ *to throw insults/accusations at somebody* ◇ *He has an answer for any question you can throw at him.* OBJ **question, look, accusation** NOTE You can also say: *She threw me a look of contempt.* **2** to do sth or give sb sth that tests their abilities and skills: *You never know what life's going to throw at you.* ◇ *We can cope with anything our opponents throw at us.* OBJ **everything, anything, whatever**
 ◆ v + n/pron + prep

'throw sth at sb/sth to throw an object in the direction of sb/sth, trying to make it hit them: *He threw stones at the window to try to catch their attention.*
♦ v + n/pron + prep
IDM throw the 'book at sb (*informal*) to punish sb who has committed an offence very severely
throw 'money at sth (*disapproving*) to try to solve a difficult situation or problem by spending lots of money on it rather than considering other ways of dealing with it: *You can't solve the problem by throwing money at it.*

'throw yourself at sb (*informal, disapproving*) to be too anxious to try to attract sb, because you want to have a romantic relationship with them: *He was flattered that such an attractive woman as Nell was throwing herself at him.*
SYN fling yourself at sb
♦ v + pron + prep

'throw yourself at sb/sth to rush or jump violently towards or onto sb/sth: *The dogs threw themselves at the gate.*
♦ v + pron + prep

throw sth a'way 1 (*also* ˌthrow sth 'out) to get rid of sth that has no use or that you no longer need: *She never throws anything away.* ◊ *The average household throws away three kilos of waste every week.* **SYN** discard sth (*more formal*) **2** to fail to make good use of sth; to waste sth: *She's throwing away a great opportunity.* ◊ *The team threw away a 2-0 lead* (= they were winning, but then lost the game). **OBJ** chance, lead, money, opportunity
♦ v + n/pron + adv ♦ v + adv + n
▶ **'throwaway** *adj* [only before noun] **1** a **throwaway** product is intended to be used only once, or for a short time and then to be got rid of: *a throwaway lighter/razor* ◊ *our throwaway culture/society* (= we expect to use things once and then throw them away) **2** a **throwaway** remark, line or comment is sth you say without careful thought, often in order to be funny: *Some people overreacted to a throwaway remark.*

ˌthrow yourself a'way (**on sb**) to have a relationship with sb, or work for sb, who is not good enough for you or does not deserve you: *Don't throw yourself away on somebody like him.*
♦ v + pron + adv

ˌthrow sth 'back 1 to return sth with a sharp movement of your arm or wrist: *Can you throw the ball back to me?* **2** to put sth quickly and carelessly in the place where it was before: *Just throw those papers back in the drawer when you've finished with them.* **3** if you **throw back** your head or your shoulders, you move them backwards suddenly: *She threw back her head and laughed.* **OBJ** head, shoulders **4** to pull or fold back a covering, especially on a bed: *He*

threw back the bedclothes and jumped out of bed.
OBJ covers, bedclothes
♦ v + n/pron + adv ♦ v + adv + n
▶ **'throwback** (**to sth**) *n* [C, usually sing.] sb/sth that is similar to sb/sth that existed long ago: *This music is a real throwback to the seventies.*

ˌthrow sth 'back at sb **1** to remind sb of sth they have said or done in the past, especially to upset or annoy them: *His unwise remark was frequently thrown back at him by his colleagues.* **OBJ** words, remark **2** to reply angrily to sb: *'It was your fault!' he threw back at her.*
♦ **1** v + n/pron + adv + prep
♦ **2** v + speech + adv + prep

be ˌthrown 'back on sth to be forced to rely on sth which you have not needed for a while because nothing else is available: *The television broke down so we were thrown back on our own resources* (= we had to entertain ourselves).
♦ be + v + adv + prep

ˌthrow 'down (*AmE, slang*) **1** to do sth with as much energy and pleasure as possible: *We were throwing down at the party last night.* **2** to fight or argue with sb, or to say sth that starts a fight or argument: *She was mad as hell and ready to throw down.*
♦ v + adv
▶ **'throwdown** *n* (*AmE, slang*) a fight or argument: *You could tell he was ready for a throwdown.*

ˌthrow sb/sth 'down; ˌthrow sb/sth 'down sth to send sb/sth from your hand suddenly and violently downwards: *Ellie threw the book down on the table.* ◊ *Jed threw her down on the sofa.* ◊ *Throw the rest of the medicine down the sink.* ◊ *Her husband threw her down the stairs.*
♦ v + n/pron + adv ♦ v + adv + n ♦ v + n/pron + prep

ˌthrow sth 'down **1** to drop or put your weapons down to show that you do not wish to fight any longer: *The rebels have thrown down their arms.* **OBJ** weapons, arms **2** to eat or swallow food or drink very quickly: *He threw his dinner down in two minutes.* **3** to suggest that sb should do sth you think they will not be willing or able to do: *She threw down a direct challenge for him to tell them the truth.* **OBJ** only challenge
♦ **1,2** v + adv + n ♦ v + pron + adv ♦ v + n + adv (*rare*)
♦ **3** v + adv + n ♦ v + n + adv (*rare*)
IDM throw down the 'gauntlet to invite sb to fight or compete with you

ˌthrow yourself 'down to move suddenly and violently so that you fall down to the ground: *She threw herself down on the grass.*
→ see also THROW SB/STH DOWN
♦ v + pron + adv

ˌthrow sb 'in/into sth to force or order sb to enter a prison and stay there: *I'll have you thrown in jail for that!* ◊ *He was thrown into a police cell overnight.*

NOTE Usually used in the passive.
◆ v + n/pron + prep

,throw sb/sth/yourself 'in; ,throw sb/sth/ yourself 'in/'into sth to push or move sb/sth/ yourself roughly or violently into sth, such as water or a building: *Sam opened the door of the shed and threw his bike in.* ◇ *Did Eva throw herself in the river or was she pushed?*
◆ v + n/pron + adv ◆ v + adv + n (*less frequent*)
◆ v + n/pron + prep

IDM **throw sb in at the 'deep end** (*informal*) (*usually used in the passive*) to introduce sb to the most difficult part of an activity or job, especially an activity they have not been prepared for

▶ **'throw-in** *n* (in football (soccer) and rugby) the act of throwing the ball back onto the playing field after it has gone outside the area

,throw sth 'in 1 to include sth with what you are selling or offering, without increasing the price: *The job pays £25 000, with a company car thrown in.* **2** to add a remark, comment, etc. without careful thought: *Jack threw in the odd encouraging comment.* ◇ *'I wouldn't mind coming,' she threw in casually.*
◆ v + adv + n
◆ v + n/pron + adv **2** also v + adv + speech

IDM **throw in your 'lot with sb/sth** (*informal*) to decide to join sb/sth and share all their successes and problems **throw in the 'towel; throw in your 'hand** (*informal*) to admit that you are defeated and stop trying to do sth: *Decorating my apartment isn't easy, but I'm not ready to throw in the towel yet.*

,throw sb 'into sth → THROW SB IN/INTO STH

,throw sb/sth 'into sth to put sb/sth suddenly in a particular state, especially a bad one: *His announcement **threw** everyone **into confusion**.* ◇ *Her arrival **threw** him **into a panic**.* ◇ *Traffic was **thrown into chaos** by the accident.*
◆ v + n/pron + prep

IDM **throw sth into 'doubt/'question** to make people wonder whether sth is true, correct, appropriate, etc. or whether it will be able to continue: *The future of the company has been thrown into question by recent events.* **throw sth into (sharp) relief 1** to make an object more noticeable than others around it: *The sunlight threw the objects in the room into sharp relief.* **2** to make a particular situation, problem, etc. more noticeable than before: *Their differences have been thrown into sharp relief by the present crisis.*

,throw sb/sth/yourself 'into sth → THROW SB/STH/YOURSELF IN, ETC.

,throw sth 'into sth 1 to use a lot of energy or resources to try to make sth successful: *He's thrown all his energy into this project.* **2** → THROW SB/STH/YOURSELF IN, ETC.
◆ v + n/pron + prep

,throw yourself 'into sth 1 (*also ,throw yourself 'into doing sth*) to begin to do sth with energy and often enthusiasm: *Laura threw herself into her work to try and forget him.* ◇ *He threw himself into writing his report.* SYN **fling yourself into sth 2** → THROW SB/STH/YOURSELF IN, ETC.
◆ v + pron + prep

,throw sb 'off; ,throw sb 'off sth to order sb to leave a place: *Farmers are being thrown off their land.* ◇ *If he finds you on his property, he'll throw you off.*
◆ v + n/pron + adv ◆ v + adv + n (*less frequent*)
◆ v + n/pron + prep

,throw sb/sth 'off; ,throw sb/sth 'off sth 1 to get rid of sb/sth that is making you suffer, annoying you, following you, etc.; to free yourself from sb/sth: *to throw off repression* ◇ *to throw off anger/family worries/troublesome thoughts* ◇ *They waded through a stream to throw the dogs off.* ◇ *I tried every way I could think of to throw him off.* ◇ *She wants to throw off her old image.* ◇ *I can't seem to throw off this cold.* **2** to disturb sb/sth who is trying to do sth, making them fail or not behave as usual: *The director came in while I was speaking and that threw me off a bit.* SYN **put sb off, put sb off sth**
◆ v + n/pron + adv ◆ v + adv + n ◆ v + n/pron + prep

IDM **throw sb off 'balance 1** to make sb unsteady and likely to fall: *I was thrown off balance by the sudden gust of wind.* **2** to make sb surprised and no longer calm: *The senator was thrown off balance by the unexpected question.* **throw sb off 'course 1** if sb/sth is **thrown off course**, they are forced away from the direction they should be travelling in: *The plane was thrown off course.* **2** to force sb to change the direction in which their ideas or actions are moving: *The government was thrown off course by economic problems.* **throw sb off the 'scent** to do sth to stop sb finding you or discovering a secret: *She changed taxis to throw her pursuers off the scent.* ◇ *Lisa told her parents she was going to a friend's house to throw them off the scent* (= she was really going somewhere else).

,throw sth 'off to remove your clothes or sth covering your body quickly and carelessly: *She threw off her clothes and leapt into the river.*
SYN **fling sth off** OPP **throw sth on**
◆ v + adv + n ◆ v + n/pron + adv

,throw sb/sth/yourself 'off; ,throw sb/sth/ yourself 'off sth to send or push sb/sth violently from a high place; to jump from a high place: *Ed was threatening to throw himself off the roof.* ◇ *The sledge hit a bump and threw me off into the snow.*
◆ v + n/pron + adv ◆ v + n/pron + prep

,throw sth 'on to put on a piece of clothing quickly and carelessly: *He threw on his clothes and ran downstairs.* ◇ *I'll just throw a coat on and then I'll be ready.*

SYN **fling sth on** **OPP** **throw sth off**
 ◆ v + adv + n   ◆ v + n/pron + adv

,**throw sb/sth 'on**; ,**throw sb/sth 'on/'onto
sth**; ,**throw yourself 'on/'onto sth** to send
or push sb/sth violently onto sth: *Jamie angrily
threw the book onto the table.* ◇ *The fire wasn't
burning well, so we threw on more wood.*
 ◆ v + adv + n   ◆ v + n/pron + adv   ◆ v + n/pron + prep

'**throw sth on sb/sth** (*also* ,**throw sth u'pon sb/
sth** *more formal*) **1** if sb/sth **throws** doubt or
suspicion **on** sb/sth, people start to wonder if
sth is true, will continue, etc.: *New evidence
threw doubt on Tom's innocence.* ◇ *This controversy throws doubt on her political future.* ◇ *The
murder was carefully planned to throw suspicion
on the woman's husband* (= to make him appear
guilty). ◇ *They tried to throw suspicion on us.*
 OBJ **doubt**, **suspicion 2** (*formal*) to cover sb/sth
in light or shadows: *The lamp threw strange
shadows on his face.* **OBJ** **light**, **shadows**
 ◆ v + n + prep

IDM **throw 'light on sth** to make a problem, etc.
easier to understand: *I might be able to throw
some light on the matter.* ◇ *Recent research has
thrown new light on the cause of the disease.*

'**throw yourself on sb/sth** (*also* '**throw yourself onto sb/sth** *less frequent*) to run towards sb/
sth and fall onto them: *She threw herself on him
and burst into tears.*
 → see also THROW SB/STH ON, ETC.
 ◆ v + pron + prep

IDM **throw yourself on sb's 'mercy** (*formal*) to
put yourself in a position where you must rely
on sb to be kind to you and not harm or punish
you: *He threw himself on the mercy of his captors.*
throw sb/sth/yourself 'onto sth → THROW
SB/STH ON, ETC.

,**throw sb 'out**; ,**throw sb 'out of sth** to force
sb to leave a place, their home, a job, etc.: *Tim's
parents threw him out when he was 18.* ◇ *When
the mine closed down, 50 people were thrown out
of their jobs.* ◇ *When she failed her exams, she
was thrown out of college.* ◇ *Many families have
been **thrown out into the street** (= out of their
homes).*
 SYN **boot sb out**, **boot sb out of sth**; **kick sb
out**, **kick sb out of sth** (*informal*)
 NOTE Often used in the passive.
 ◆ v + n/pron + adv   ◆ v + adv + n
 ◆ v + n/pron + adv + prep

,**throw sb/sth 'out** to confuse sb/sth; to make
sb make a mistake; to make sth wrong: *One of
the figures was wrong and it threw me out
completely.* ◇ *Some unexpected costs threw our
calculations out by £4 000.*
 OBJ **calculations**
 ◆ v + n/pron + adv   ◆ v + adv + n

,**throw sb/sth 'out**; ,**throw yourself 'out** (**of
sth**) to push or send sb/sth/yourself forward and

out of a place: *Frank quickly opened the window
and threw his cigarette out.* ◇ *He threw himself
out of the window and was killed.*
 ◆ v + n/pron + adv   ◆ v + adv + n
 ◆ v + n/pron + adv + prep

,**throw sth 'out 1** → THROW STH AWAY 1: *It's
time we threw that old chair out.* **2** to reject sth
such as a proposal, an idea, etc.: *The committee
have thrown out the proposal for a new supermarket.* ◇ *The case was **thrown out of court**.*
 OBJ **bill**, **case**, **proposals** **NOTE** Often used in
the passive. **3** to mention sth, usually without
thinking carefully, for people to think about: *She
threw out a few ideas for us to consider.* ◇ *We are
throwing out a challenge to residents to help
clean up our neighbourhood.* **OBJ** **idea**, **challenge** ⊃ note at TURN SB/STH DOWN **4** to
produce sth such as heat, light, smoke, etc.:
The fire throws out a lot of heat. ◇ *The lamp
threw out just enough light to read by.* **OBJ** **heat**,
light **SYN** **emit sth 5** to move a hand or arm
suddenly away from your body: *She threw her
arm out to protect herself as she fell.* **OBJ** **hand**,
arm
 ◆ v + adv + n   ◆ v + n/pron + adv

IDM **throw the baby out with the 'bathwater**
(*informal*) to lose sth that you want at the same
time as you are trying to get rid of sth that you
do not want

,**throw sb 'over** (*old-fashioned*) to end a relationship with sb: *His girlfriend threw him over
for somebody else.*
 SYN **chuck sb** (*BrE, slang*); **dump sb** (*informal*)
 ◆ v + n/pron + adv   ◆ v + adv + n

,**throw sb/sth/yourself 'over**; ,**throw sb/
sth/yourself 'over sth** to move or push sb/
sth so that they move over the top of sth and
land on the other side of it; to move yourself
violently in this way: *Throw a rope over and I'll
catch it.* ◇ *The neighbours have been throwing
rubbish over our wall.* ◇ *I threw myself over the
wall to escape from the dog.* ◇ *Jay took off his
coat and threw it over a chair* (= so it rested on
the back of a chair).
 ◆ v + n/pron + adv   ◆ v + adv + n (*less frequent*)
 ◆ v + n/pron + prep

,**throw sth 'over** (**to sb**) (*informal*) to pass sth to
sb in a careless or rough way: *He threw the paper
over to me.* ◇ *Will you throw over those keys?*
 NOTE You can also use **throw sb over sth** and
throw sb sth over: *Will you throw me over the
paper?* ◇ *Will you throw me the paper over?*
 ◆ v + n/pron + adv   ◆ v + adv + n

,**throw sth 'over sb/sth** to quickly place sth so
that it covers sb/sth: *I threw a blanket over the
baby to keep him warm.* ◇ *He threw a coat over
his pyjamas and ran out into the street.*
 ◆ v + n/pron + prep

ˌthrow sth ˈround, etc. → THROW STH AROUND, ETC.

ˌthrow sb toˈgether to bring people into contact with each other, often unexpectedly: *Fate had thrown them together.* ◇ *We were strangers, thrown together by circumstance.* **NOTE** Often used in the passive.
✦ v + n/pron + adv ✦ v + adv + n

ˌthrow sth toˈgether to make or produce sth roughly or quickly, often with things that you can find easily: *I'll just throw together a quick supper.* ◇ *Can you throw a report together by tomorrow morning?*
✦ v + adv + n ✦ v + n/pron + adv

ˌthrow ˈup; ˌthrow sth ˈup (*informal*) to bring food you have eaten back out of your mouth: *The smell made me want to throw up.* ◇ *He ate the meal and immediately threw it all up.*
SYN bring sth up; vomit, vomit sth (up)
✦ v + adv ✦ v + adv + n ✦ v + n/pron + adv

ˌthrow sb/sth ˈup to lift sb/sth and make them move upwards into the air by moving your hand quickly: *The baby loved being **thrown up into the air**.*
✦ v + n/pron + adv

ˌthrow sth ˈup 1 to produce sth; to show or make people notice sth: *Her research has thrown up some interesting facts.* ◇ *The competition threw up some promising players.* **OBJ** problems, questions, ideas, facts 2 (*BrE, informal*) to leave your job suddenly and often unexpectedly: *He threw up a highly paid job to travel round the world.* **OBJ** job **SYN** chuck sth in/up (*BrE, informal*); give sth up (*informal*) 3 to build sth suddenly or quickly, and often carelessly: *These buildings were thrown up hurriedly after the war.* **OBJ** buildings 4 if you **throw up** your arms or hands, you raise them quickly in the air: *He threw up his hands to protect his face as he fell.* ◇ *She threw her arms up in horror.* **OBJ** hand, arm 5 to make sth such as dust or water rise up into the air: *The wheels threw up a shower of mud and water.* **OBJ** dust, mud
✦ v + adv + n ✦ v + n/pron + adv

ˌthrow sth uˈpon sb/sth → THROW STH ON SB/STH

thrust /θrʌst/ (thrust, thrust)

ˌthrust sth aˈside to refuse to listen to sb's complaints, comments, etc.: *All our objections were thrust aside.*
✦ v + n/pron + adv ✦ v + adv + n

ˈthrust sb/sth on sb (*also* ˈthrust sb/sth upon sb *more formal*) to force sb to accept sb/sth or do sth that they do not want to: *Responsibility for the family was thrust upon him at an early age.* ◇ *She was annoyed at having three extra guests suddenly thrust upon her.*
OBJ role, responsibility, change
NOTE Often used in the passive.
✦ v + n/pron + prep

thumb /θʌm/

ˌthumb ˈthrough sth to turn the pages of a book, a magazine, etc. looking at them quickly: *She thumbed through her diary.*
OBJ book, pages **SYN** flick through sth
✦ v + prep

tick /tɪk/

ˌtick aˈway; ˌtick sth aˈway if a clock **ticks away** or **ticks** the minutes or seconds **away**, it makes continuous short light regular sounds to mark time passing: *The clock ticked away in the silence.* ◇ *We waited as the clock ticked away the last few seconds of the old millennium.*
✦ v + adv ✦ v + adv + n ✦ v + n/pron + adv

ˌtick aˈway/ˈby/ˈpast (of time) to pass, especially when you feel it is passing too quickly or too slowly: *The seconds ticked by as I tried to think of something to say.* ◇ *Two long minutes ticked past.* **SUBJ** minutes, seconds, time ⟳ note at GO BY
✦ v + adv

ˌtick sb ˈoff 1 (for sth/for doing sth) (*BrE, informal*) to speak angrily to sb, especially a child, because they have done sth wrong: *I was ticked off for forgetting my books.* **SYN** tell sb off; scold sb (*more formal*) ⟳ note at TELL SB OFF 2 (*informal, especially AmE*) to annoy sb: *This type of thing really ticks me off.* **SYN** hack sb off (*BrE*)
✦ v + n/pron + adv ✦ v + adv + n
▸ ˌticked ˈoff adj (*informal, especially AmE*) annoyed: *I was really ticked off about it.*
▸ ˌticking ˈoff (for sth/for doing sth) n [sing.] (*old-fashioned, BrE, informal*) the act of speaking to sb angrily because they have done sth wrong: *He gave me a ticking off for being late.*

ˌtick sb/sth ˈoff (*BrE*) (*AmE* ˌcheck sb/sth ˈoff) to put a mark next to sth on a list to show that it has been dealt with: *Alex ticked off the names of the people who had replied.* ◇ *Everything on the list had been ticked off.* ◇ *She ticked the points off on her fingers.*
OBJ points, items
✦ v + adv + n ✦ v + n/pron + adv

ˌtick ˈover (*especially BrE*) (*usually used in the progressive tenses*) 1 if an engine is **ticking over**, it is running slowly but the vehicle is not moving: *Don't leave the engine ticking over while you are in the shop.* ◇ (*figurative*) *Learning Japanese keeps my brain ticking over!* **SUBJ** engine **SYN** idle 2 to continue slowly without producing or achieving much: *Try and keep things ticking over while I'm away.* **SUBJ** things
✦ v + adv

ˌtick ˈpast → TICK AWAY/BY/PAST

tide /taɪd/

ˌtide sb ˈover; ˌtide sb ˈover sth to help sb through a difficult period by providing what they need: *We've got enough money to tide us over until next month.* ◇ *Our savings should tide us over the next couple of months.* [SUBJ] **money, loan**

[NOTE] **Tide sb over** is usually used in the infinitive form. It cannot be used in the passive.

◆ v + n/pron + adv ◆ v + n/pron + prep

---

tidy /ˈtaɪdi/ (**tidies, tidying, tidied**)

,**tidy sth aˈway** (*BrE*) to put things in a particular place where they cannot be seen so that a room, etc. appears tidy: *Harry was busy tidying away his papers in the office.*

[SYN] **clear away, clear sth away**

◆ v + adv + n ◆ v + n/pron + adv

,**tidy sth ˈout** (*BrE*) to make a room, a cupboard, etc. tidy by removing things you do not want and arranging the rest neatly: *It's time to tidy out the kitchen cupboards.*

[OBJ] **cupboard, drawer, room** [SYN] **clear sth out**

◆ v + adv + n ◆ v + n/pron + adv

,**tidy ˈup**; ,**tidy sth ˈup** (*especially BrE*) to make a room, a group of things, etc. tidy by arranging things neatly in the correct places: *Don't forget to tidy up when you've finished.* ◇ *The whole place needs tidying up.* ◇ *I've just got a bit of tidying up to do.* ◇ *I'd better tidy my desk up.*

[OBJ] **room, mess, house** [SYN] **clear up, clear sth up**

◆ v + adv ◆ v + n/pron + adv ◆ v + adv + n

,**tidy sb ˈup**; ,**tidy yourself ˈup** (*especially BrE*) to make sb/yourself look cleaner and neater: *How about tidying yourself up before we go out?*

◆ v + n/pron + adv ◆ v + adv + n

,**tidy sth ˈup** (*BrE*) **1** to finish sth such as a piece of written work by dealing with the last details well or correctly: *My lecture still needs tidying*

up. **2** to make sure that things are dealt with correctly: *He had to go to Boston to tidy up his brother's affairs* (= after his brother died).

◆ v + n/pron + adv ◆ v + adv + n

---

tie /taɪ/ (**ties, tying, tied, tied**)

,**tie sb ˈdown 1** (*also* ,**tie yourself ˈdown**) (**to sth/ to doing sth**) to restrict sb's activities or freedom, for example by making them accept particular conditions or by keeping them busy: *We managed to tie him down to a date for the meeting.* ◇ *She didn't want to be tied down by a full-time job.* ◇ *I don't want to be tied down to coming back at a particular time.* ◇ *Do you really want to tie yourself down at 18 with a husband, a home and a baby?* **2** to do sth so that an enemy force is kept busy and has to stay in a particular area: *Guerrilla activity kept the army tied down in the mountains.* [OBJ] **troops, police**

◆ **1** v + n/pron + adv

◆ **2** v + adv + n ◆ v + n/pron + adv

,**tie ˈin** (**with sth**) to fit or be in agreement with sth: *This new evidence ties in with the witness's statement.* ◇ *That doesn't tie in with what you said yesterday.*

◆ v + adv

,**tie ˈin** (**with sth**), ,**tie sth ˈin** (**with sth**) to link sb or be linked to sth; to happen or to arrange for sth to happen at the same time as sth else: *The book was intended to tie in with the TV series.* ◇ *Jack couldn't be tied in with the murder.* ◇ *The release of their new album will be tied in with the tour.*

◆ v + adv ◆ v + n/pron + adv ◆ v + adv + n

▶ **ˈtie-in** *n* **1** (*BrE*) a product such as a book or a toy that is sold in close connection with a film/ movie, television programme, etc.: *television/*

SYNONYMS

tidy (sth) up

clear (sth) up ◆ **pick (sth) up** ◆ **sort sth out** ◆ **tidy (sth) up**

These verbs all mean to make sth look neat by putting things away in the place where they belong.

clear (sth) up to make sth clean and neat, especially by putting things in the place where they belong: *It's time to clear up.* ◇ *Just give me a few moments to clear up my things.*

pick (sth) up (*AmE*) to put things away and make a room neat: *to pick up a room* ◇ *Will you pick up your toys now?*

sort sth out to organize the contents of sth; to tidy sth: *I've got to sort out all my cupboards.* ◇ *She spent the afternoon sorting out her office.*

tidy (sth) up (*especially BrE*) to make sth look neat by putting things in the place where they belong: *I spent all morning tidying up my room.* ◇ *She was always tidying up.* [NOTE] **Tidy** can be used on its own: ◇ *He spent a few minutes tidying his desk.*

WHICH WORD?

Tidy up, pick up and **clear up** can be used without an object: *I spend all my time tidying up.*

PATTERNS AND COLLOCATIONS

■ to tidy (up)/clear up/sort out/pick up your **room/apartment/bedroom**

■ to tidy (up)/sort out a **cupboard/closet/desk/ drawer**

■ to tidy (up)/clear up/sort out the **mess**

■ to tidy (up)/clear up/pick up **after** sb

tie (sth) up

anchor (sth) ◆ beach (sth) ◆ dock (sth) ◆ moor (sth) ◆ tie (sth) up

These verbs all mean to attach a boat, ship, etc. to a fixed object or to the land to stop it from floating away.

anchor (sth) to lower an anchor from a boat or ship to prevent it from floating away: *We anchored off the coast of Spain.* ◇ *Larger boats were anchored further up the quay.*

beach (sth) to bring a boat out of the water and onto the shore: *He beached the boat and lifted the boy onto the shore.*

dock (sth) to bring a ship into a harbour and stay there: *The ferry is expected to dock at about six.* ◇ *They docked at Liverpool on the way back from India.*

moor (sth) (*often passive*) to attach a boat, ship, etc. to a fixed object or to the land with a rope, chain, or anchor: *We moored off the north coast of the island.* ◇ *I walked down to where the boat was moored.*

tie (sth) **up** to attach a boat to a fixed object with a rope to stop it from floating away: *We tied up alongside the quay.* ◇ *They tried to find a sheltered spot where they could tie the boat up.*

PATTERNS AND COLLOCATIONS

- to moor/dock/tie up/beach/anchor **safely/securely**
- to moor/dock/tie up/anchor **off/in/at...**
- to moor/dock/tie up/beach/anchor **on/alongside/beside** sth

film tie-ins ◇ tie-in books/toys/sales **2** (*especially AmE*) a link or a relationship with sth: *a tie-in to the main subject*

,tie sb 'into sb/sth to restrict sb to a particular situation, person, organization, etc.: *They were tied into an agreement to buy from particular suppliers.*
◆ v + n/pron + prep

,tie sth 'off to put a knot in the end of sth; to close sth with string, thread, etc.: *to tie off a rope/an artery*
◆ v + adv + n ◆ v + n/pron + adv

⚡,tie 'up; ,tie sth 'up **1** to attach a boat to a fixed point with a rope: *The barge tied up at the quay.* ◇ *Ben tied the boat up and jumped ashore.* **2** to close or fasten sth with a knot; to be closed or fastened in this way: *I'm so fat my bathrobe won't tie up!* ◇ *to tie up a garbage bag*
◆ v + adv ◆ v + n/pron + adv ◆ v + adv + n

⚡,tie sb 'up **1** to tie sb's arms and legs tightly so that they cannot move or escape: *The gang tied up the security guard and put a gag in his mouth.* **2** to keep sb so busy that they have no time for other things: *I'm tied up in a meeting until three.* ◇ *Sorry I'm late—I was tied up at the office.* **NOTE** Usually used in the passive.
◆ v + n/pron + adv ◆ v + adv + n

⚡,tie sth 'up **1** to make sth secure by putting string, rope, etc. around it, or attaching it to sth else: *He tied the parcel up with a ribbon.* ◇ *He tied the dog up outside.* **2** (with sth) to connect or link sth to sth else: *Her behaviour is tied up with her feelings of guilt.* ◇ *Do you think these two incidents are tied up?* **NOTE** Usually used in the passive. **3** (in sth) to invest money so that it is not easily available for use: *Most of our capital is tied up in property.* **OBJ** **money, capital, resources, assets** **SYN** **lock sth up** **NOTE** Often

used in the passive. **4** to deal with all the remaining details of sth: *to tie up a deal* ◇ *We're hoping to* **tie up all the loose ends** *as quickly as possible.* **OBJ** **deal, loose ends 5** to bring sth to a stop; to prevent sb from doing sth or using sth: *The strike tied up production for a week.* ◇ *You've been tying up the phone for hours!*
◆ v + n/pron + adv ◆ v + adv + n

▶ 'tie-up *n* **1** (**with sb/sth**) (*BrE*) an agreement between two companies to join together: *They're negotiating a tie-up with Ford.* **2** (**between A and B**) (*BrE*) a connection between two or more things: *a tie-up between politics and economics* **3** (*especially AmE*) a situation in which sth, especially traffic, stops moving: *A tie-up on the highway caused major delays.*

tighten /'taɪtn/

,tighten 'up; ,tighten sth 'up **1** to become or to make sth tight or tighter: *His face muscles tightened up in anger.* ◇ *to tighten up a screw/wheel/muscle* **NOTE** **Tighten** and **tighten sth** can also be used on their own with this meaning. **2** to become more careful or strict about sth; to make sth more strict: *Laws on gambling have tightened up recently.* ◇ *The police are* **tightening up on** *drink-driving.* ◇ *to tighten up laws/rules/legislation/security*
◆ v + adv ◆ v + adv + n ◆ v + pron + adv
◆ v + n + adv (*less frequent*)

time /taɪm/

,time 'out if sth **times out**, it goes beyond a particular time limit and stops working, is no longer valid, etc.: *Your Internet session will time out after a few minutes if there is no activity.* ◇ *The demo will time out after three weeks.*
◆ v + adv

toddle

tinker /'tɪŋkə(r)/

tinker a'round (*also* **tinker a'bout** *especially BrE*) (**with sth**) to make small changes to sth in order to repair or improve it, especially in a way that may not be helpful: *He's outside tinkering around with his bike.* ◊ *They haven't made any real changes to the system—they've just been tinkering around a bit.*
◆ v + adv

tinker with sth to make small changes to sth in order to repair or improve it, especially in a way that may not be helpful: *The government should stop tinkering with the education system.*
◆ v + prep

tip /tɪp/ (-pp-)

tip down (*BrE, informal*) (*usually used in the progressive tenses*) to rain very heavily: *It was absolutely tipping down outside.*
SYN **pour down** (*BrE, more formal*)
◆ v + adv

tip sb 'off (**about sth**) (*informal*) to give sb a warning about sth which they should know about, especially sth illegal: *The police were tipped off about the bank robbery.*
OBJ **police**
◆ v + adv + n ◆ v + pron + adv
◆ v + n + adv (*less frequent*)
▶ **'tip-off** *n* (*informal*) a piece of useful or secret information that sb gives, for example to the police, to warn them about an illegal or unexpected activity: *The police received an anonymous tip-off about the attack.*

tip 'over; **tip sth 'over** to become no longer stable and fall over; to make sth do this: *The bottle tipped over and all the water spilled out.* ◊ *Watch you don't tip the jug over.*

SYN **overturn, overturn sth** (*more formal*)
◆ v + adv ◆ v + n/pron + adv ◆ v + adv + n

tip 'up; **tip sth 'up** to become unsteady and fall forwards, backwards or sideways; to make sth do this: *One after another the canoes tipped up.* ◊ *The pile of books on the end of the table nearly tipped it up.*
◆ v + adv ◆ v + n/pron + adv ◆ v + adv + n

tip sth 'up to change the angle of sth so that it leans to one side: *She tipped her glass up and drained it.* ◊ *He tipped his face up towards the light.*
◆ v + n/pron + adv ◆ v + adv + n

tire /'taɪə(r)/

'tire of sb/sth; **'tire of doing sth** to become bored with sb/sth or begin to enjoy them/it less: *They soon tired of the beach and went for a walk.*
◆ v + prep

IDM **never tire of doing sth** to do sth a lot, especially in a way that annoys people: *Jack travelled all over the world when he was a student, as he never tires of telling us.*

tire sb 'out; **tire yourself 'out** to make sb/yourself feel very tired: *I took the children to the beach to tire them out.* ◊ *Try not to tire yourself out too soon in the race.*
SYN **wear sb/yourself out** (**with sth**)
◆ v + n/pron + adv ◆ v + adv + n (*less frequent*)
▶ **tired 'out** *adj* very tired: *We finally reached home tired out.*

toddle /'tɒdl; AmE 'tɑːdl/

toddle 'off (*BrE, informal, humorous*) to leave: *It's late—it's time you toddled off to bed.*
◆ v + adv

SYNONYMS

tire sb/yourself out

exhaust sb/yourself ◆ poop sb out ◆ tire sb/yourself out ◆ wear sb/yourself out

These verbs all mean to make sb/yourself feel tired and want to sleep or rest.

exhaust sb/yourself to make sb/yourself feel very tired: *Even a short walk exhausted her.* ◊ *There's no need to exhaust yourself cleaning up—we'll do it.*

poop sb out (*AmE, informal*) to make sb feel very tired: *That walk really pooped me out!*

tire sb/yourself out to make sb/yourself feel very tired: *Working twelve hour shifts would really tire me out.* **NOTE** Tire can be used on its own, but is more formal: *Long conversations tired her.*

wear sb/yourself out to make yourself/sb feel very tired: *The kids have totally worn me*

out. ◊ *You'll wear yourself out if you carry on working so hard.*

WHICH WORD?

There is very little difference in meaning between these verbs. **Exhaust** is the most frequent, and the most suitable for use in formal writing, but it can be used in less formal contexts too. **Tire sb/yourself out** is less formal, and is used mostly in spoken English.

PATTERNS AND COLLOCATIONS

- to tire/exhaust **yourself**; to wear/tire **yourself** out
- to **quickly** tire sb/yourself (out)
- to **completely/totally** exhaust sb/wear sb out

tog /tɒg; AmE tɑːg, tɔːg/ (-gg-)

be/get ,togged 'out/'up (in sth) (*BrE*, *informal*) to be wearing clothes for a particular activity or occasion: *He got togged up in a suit and tie for the interview.* ◇ *We were all togged out in our best clothes.*
♦ be/get + v + adv

toil /tɔɪl/

,toil a'way (at sth) to work extremely hard at sth difficult or boring: *He toiled away at his homework all the evening.*
♦ v + adv

tone /təʊn; AmE toʊn/

,tone sth 'down 1 to make sth such as a speech, an opinion, etc. less offensive, critical or unkind than it was originally: *He had to tone down his article before it was published.* **2** to make sth, especially your clothes, less bright and noticeable: *She toned down her style of dress when she started her new job.* **3** to make a colour less bright: *We toned down the yellow paint with a little white.* ◇ *Petra used powder to tone down her rosy cheeks.*
♦ v + adv + n ♦ v + pron + adv
♦ v + n + adv (*less frequent*)

,tone 'in (with sth) (*BrE*) to match or fit with the colour or style of sth else: *The cushions tone in well with the carpet.* ◇ *The new bridge doesn't tone in with the buildings around it.*
♦ v + adv

,tone 'up; ,tone sth 'up to make your muscles or a part of your body firmer, stronger, and healthier: *It's time I toned up and slimmed down.* ◇ *This exercise will tone up your stomach muscles.*
◻ᴮᴶ **body, muscles**
♦ v + adv ♦ v + adv + n ♦ v + pron + adv
♦ v + n + adv (*less frequent*)

tool /tuːl/

,tool a'round; ,tool a'round sth (*AmE*) to drive a car around an area: *We tooled around Canada in his VW van.*
♦ v + adv ♦ v + prep

,tool 'up; ,tool sth 'up (for sth/to do sth) (*BrE*, *technical*) to get or provide sb/sth with the equipment, machines, etc. necessary to do or produce sth: *It took several months to tool up to produce the new model.* ◇ *A new plant in Scotland is being tooled up to produce these screws.*
♦ v + adv ♦ v + adv + n ♦ v + pron + adv
♦ v + n + adv (*rare*)

▶ **,tooled 'up** *adj* **1** having the equipment necessary for a particular job: ◇ *The factory is not tooled up to do this particular job.* **2** (*BrE*, *slang*) carrying a gun

top /tɒp; AmE tɑːp/ (-pp-)

,top sth 'off (with sth) to complete sth in a successful or pleasant way, especially by adding one final thing: *Jane was wearing a very colourful outfit, topped off with a dramatic hat.*
ɴᴏᴛᴇ Often used in the passive.
♦ v + n/pron + adv ♦ v + adv + n

,top 'out (at sth) to stop increasing after reaching a high level: *Your annual salary will top out at seventy thousand dollars.*
♦ v + adv

,top sb 'up (*BrE*) to fill sb's glass or cup by adding some more liquid: *Can I top you up?*
♦ v + n/pron + adv ♦ v + adv + n

▶ **'top-up** *n* (*BrE*) an amount of liquid that you add to some already in a glass, cup or other container: *Can I give you a top-up?*

,top sth 'up (*especially BrE*) **1 (with sth)** to add some more liquid to some already in a glass, cup or other container in order to fill it: *Can I top your glass up?* ◇ *We should top the car up with oil before we set off.* ◻ᴮᴶ **glass, cup 2** to increase the amount of sth to the level you want or need: *She relies on tips to top up her wages.* ◇ *I need to top up my mobile* (= pay money in advance to be able to make mobile phone/cellphone calls).
◻ᴮᴶ **income, pension**
♦ v + adv + n ♦ v + n/pron + adv

▶ **'top-up** *n* (*BrE*) a sum of money, etc. that is added to what you already have in order to increase it to the amount that you need: *a salary top-up* ◇ *a top-up loan* ◇ *university top-up fees* (= fees that are above the basic level) ◇ *a top-up card* (= a card that you buy for a mobile phone/cellphone which enables you to make calls to the value of the card)

topple /'tɒpl; AmE 'tɑːpl/

,topple 'over to become unsteady and fall over: *The vase wobbled and then toppled over.*
➔ note at FALL DOWN
♦ v + adv

toss /tɒs; AmE tɔːs/

,toss sth a'round (*also* ,toss sth a'bout *especially BrE*) to discuss ideas in a casual or general way: *We sat and tossed around a few suggestions.* ◇ *This is a problem that has been tossed around for more than a century.*
ꜱʏɴ **throw sth around**
♦ v + n/pron + adv ♦ v + adv + n

,toss sth a'side 1 to put sth quickly to one side because you are angry or in a hurry: *He tossed aside the newspaper angrily and stood up.* ◇ (*figurative*) *When he's bored with people he just tosses them aside.* ꜱʏɴ **cast sth aside** (*formal*); **throw sth aside 2** to reject sth such as an attitude, an idea, a way of life, etc.: *The idea of buying a new car was quickly tossed aside.* ꜱʏɴ **cast sth aside** (*formal*); **throw sth aside**
♦ v + n/pron + adv ♦ v + adv + n

toss sth a'way to throw sth away carelessly: *She finished her drink and tossed the can away.* ◇ (*figurative*) *He's tossed away so many opportunities.*
♦ v + adv + n ♦ v + n/pron + adv

toss sth 'back 1 (*also* ,**toss sth 'down** *less frequent*) to drink sth very quickly, especially alcohol: *She tossed back glass after glass of champagne.* ◇ *He tossed back the rest of his drink and walked out.* [OBJ] **drink, whisky, wine, etc.**
2 to move sth, especially your head, quickly backwards, especially when you are angry or impatient: *Sam tossed back his head in defiance.* ◇ *She tossed back her hair and smiled.* [OBJ] **hair, head**
♦ v + adv + n ♦ v + n/pron + adv

toss for sth; **'toss sb for sth** (*especially BrE*) (*BrE also* ,**toss 'up (for sth)**) (*AmE also* **'flip for sth, 'flip sb for sth**) to make a decision about sth by spinning a coin in the air and seeing which side is on top when it lands: *We can't both go, so why don't we toss for it?* ◇ *There's only one ticket left—I'll toss you for it.*
♦ v + prep ♦ v + n/pron + prep

toss 'off; ,**toss sb 'off**; ,**toss yourself 'off** (*BrE,* △, *slang*) to give yourself sexual pleasure by rubbing your sex organs; to give sb else sexual pleasure in this way
♦ v + adv ♦ v + n/pron + adv ♦ v + adv + n

toss sth 'off (*especially BrE*) to do sth quickly, easily and often with little care or effort: *He tossed this novel off in two months.*
♦ v + n/pron + adv ♦ v + adv + n

toss 'up (for sth) (*BrE*) → TOSS FOR STH, TOSS SB FOR STH: *They tossed up for the best seat.*
♦ v + adv

▸ **'toss-up** *n* [sing.] (*informal*) a situation where it is difficult to decide between two things, or where there are two possible results: *It was a toss-up between spending the night in the van and walking ten miles for help.*

tot /tɒt; *AmE* tɑːt/ (**-tt-**)

,**tot sth 'up** (*informal, especially BrE*) to add together several numbers or amounts in order to get a total: *Can you tot up how much I owe you?*
[OBJ] **figures, the number of sth** [SYN] **add sth up**
♦ v + adv + n ♦ v + pron + adv
♦ v + n + adv (*less frequent*)

total /'təʊtl; *AmE* 'toʊtl/ (**-ll-**, *AmE also* **-l-**)

,**total 'up (to sth)** to reach a particular total: *The costs total up to over a million.*
♦ v + adv

,**total sth 'up** to add amounts together to get a total: *Let's total up what we've spent.*
♦ v + adv + n ♦ v + n/pron + adv

touch /tʌtʃ/

,**touch 'down 1** (of a plane, a spacecraft, etc.) to land: *The plane touched down safely.* ◇ (*figurative*) *A tornado touched down in Colorado.* [SUBJ] **plane, aircraft, helicopter** [SYN] **land** [OPP] **take off** ⊃ note at COME DOWN **2** (in rugby) to score points by putting the ball on the ground behind the other team's goal line: *Williams touched down in the first few minutes of the game.*
♦ v + adv

▸ **'touchdown** *n* **1** the moment when a plane or a spacecraft lands **2** (in rugby) an act of scoring points by touching down **3** (in American football) an act of scoring points by crossing the other team's goal line while carrying the ball, or receiving the ball when you have crossed it

,**touch sb for sth** (*BrE, informal*) to persuade sb to give or lend you money: *He tried to touch me for twenty pounds.*
♦ v + n/pron + prep

,**touch sth 'off** to make sth begin, especially an explosion or a violent or difficult situation: *The explosion was touched off by a single spark.* ◇ *His arrest touched off a riot.*
♦ v + adv + n ♦ v + pron + adv ♦ v + n + adv (*rare*)

'touch on/upon sth to mention or deal briefly with a topic, a problem, etc.: *He touched on the need for increased funding.* ◇ *Some of these issues were touched on in Chapter 7.*
[OBJ] **subject, point, issue**
♦ v + prep

,**touch sb 'up** (*BrE, informal*) to touch sb in an unpleasant sexual way
♦ v + adv + n ♦ v + n/pron + adv

,**touch sth 'up** to improve sth by making small changes or additions: *He had to touch up the paintwork to cover the scratches.* ◇ *The photo had been touched up.*
♦ v + adv + n ♦ v + pron + adv
♦ v + n + adv (*less frequent*)

'touch upon sth → TOUCH ON/UPON STH

tough /tʌf/

,**tough 'out** to stay firm and determined in a difficult situation: *He decided not to resign, but to stay and* **tough it out**. [SYN] **gut it out** (*AmE, informal*)
♦ v + n + adv ♦ v + pron + adv
♦ v + adv + n (*less frequent*)

toughen /'tʌfn/

,**toughen 'up**; ,**toughen sb 'up** to become stronger and better able to deal with difficult situations; to make sb stronger in this way: *He had toughened up during military service.* ◇ *His parents sent him away to boarding school to toughen him up.*
♦ v + adv ♦ v + n/pron + adv ♦ v + adv + n

tout

,toughen sth 'up to make sth such as a law or a rule more strict: *The legislation on this trade needs to be toughened up.*
♦ v + adv + n ♦ v + n/pron + adv

tout /taʊt/

,tout sth a'round; ,tout sth a'round sth (*BrE also* ,tout sth 'round, ,tout sth 'round sth) to take sth to many different places or companies in the hope of selling it: *He's been touting his novel around publishers for years.*
♦ v + n/pron + adv ♦ v + adv + n ♦ v + n/pron + prep

'tout for sth (*especially BrE*) to try to get business, work, etc. by asking people directly: *cab drivers touting for business at the airport*
OBJ **business, trade, custom**
♦ v + prep

tow /təʊ; *AmE* toʊ/

,tow sth a'way (**from sth**) to remove sth, especially a vehicle, from a place, by pulling it behind another one: *They'll tow your car away if you park it here.*
♦ v + n/pron + adv ♦ v + adv + n

towel /'taʊəl/ (-ll-, *AmE* -l-)

,towel 'off (*AmE*) to dry your body with a towel after a shower, swim, etc.: *OK, kids, time to get out of the pool and towel off.*
♦ v + adv

tower /'taʊə(r)/

,tower a'bove/'over sb/sth **1** to be much higher or taller than other things or people that are near: *The new offices tower above the rest of the town.* ◇ *Amy towers over her mother.* **2** to be much better, more famous, etc. than other people or things: *He towers above all other poets of his generation.*
♦ v + prep

toy /tɔɪ/

'toy with sth **1** to consider sth but not very seriously or for very long: *He had toyed with the idea of living in Germany.* OBJ **the idea of 2** to play with sth; to move sth around carelessly without really thinking about it: *Stop toying with your food!* ◇ (*figurative*) *He accused the young man of toying with his daughter's affections.* ◇ *The possibility had been toyed with but rejected.*
SYN **dally with sth/sb**
♦ v + prep

trace /treɪs/

,trace sth 'back (**to sth**) to find the origin or cause of sth by following evidence backwards from the present time: *Many different childhood illnesses can be traced back to certain foods.* ◇ *Boston has a large population that traces its*

roots back to Ireland. ◇ *She can trace her family back as far as the 13th century.*
OBJ **roots, origins, history**
♦ v + n/pron + adv ♦ v + adv + n

,trace sth 'out to draw a shape or a mark clearly: *I traced out our route on the map.* ◇ (*figurative*) *She traced out how working patterns had changed in the last 50 years.*
♦ v + n/pron + adv ♦ v + adv + n

track /træk/

,track sb/sth 'down (**to sth**) to find sb/sth after a long and difficult search: *We finally tracked Sam down to his parents' house.* ◇ *It has taken ten years to track down the wreckage of the plane.*
♦ v + n/pron + adv ♦ v + adv + n

trade /treɪd/

,trade 'down (**to sth**) **1** to spend less money on things than you used to: *People are trading down and buying cheaper food.* **2** to sell sth large or expensive and buy sth smaller or less expensive: *They traded down to a house with fewer bedrooms.* OPP **trade up (to sth)**
♦ v + adv

,trade sth 'in (**for sth**) to give sth that you have used to sb you are buying sth new from as part of your payment: *He traded his motorbike in for a new van.*
♦ v + n/pron + adv ♦ v + adv + n

▶ 'trade-in *n* a method of buying sth by giving a used item as part of the payment for a new one; the used item that you give: *the trade-in value of a car* ◇ *Do you have a trade-in?*

,trade sth 'off (**against sth**) to balance two things or situations that are opposed to each other: *The government were attempting to trade off inflation against unemployment.* ◇ *They were willing to trade off information to keep the hostages alive.*
♦ v + adv + n ♦ v + pron + adv
♦ v + n + adv (*less frequent*)

▶ 'trade-off (**between sth and sth**) *n* the act of balancing two things that you need or want but which are opposed to each other: *a trade-off between inflation and unemployment* ◇ *There is a trade-off between the benefits of the drug and the risk of side effects.*

'trade on sth (*also* 'trade upon sth *more formal*, *less frequent*) (*disapproving*) to unfairly make use of sth for your own advantage: *He traded on his father's name to get himself a job.*
SYN **exploit sth**
♦ v + prep

,trade 'up (**to sth**) to sell sth small or not expensive in order to buy sth larger or more expensive: *He traded up to a larger car.*
OPP **trade down (to sth)**
♦ v + adv

'trade upon sth → TRADE ON STH

traffic /'træfɪk/ (-ck-)

'traffic in sth to buy and sell sth, especially
drugs or weapons, illegally: *He was accused of
trafficking in stolen works of art.*
OBJ **drugs, weapons**
♦ v + prep

trail /treɪl/

,trail a'way/'off if sb's speech **trails away/off**, it
gradually becomes quieter and then stops:
Mark's voice trailed away to a whisper. ◇ *'I only
hope…' She trailed off.* SUBJ **voice**
♦ v + adv

train /treɪn/

'train sth on/upon sb/sth (*formal*) to point sth
such as a gun, a camera, a light, etc. at sb/sth:
*The police marksmen trained their weapons on
the building.* ◇ *She trained the camera on the
bride.* ◇ *He kept his eyes trained on the road
ahead.*
OBJ **gun, camera, eyes**
♦ v + n/pron + prep

,train sb 'up to make sb ready to do a job or an
activity by teaching them the skills they need:
We need to train up extra staff for Christmas.
♦ v + adv + n ♦ v + n/pron + adv

traipse /treɪps/

,traipse a'round; ,traipse a'round sth (*BrE
also* ,traipse 'round, ,traipse 'round sth) (*informal*) to walk from place to place slowly because
you are tired and unwilling: *I've been traipsing
around all day with Jenny trying to buy a coat for
her.* ◇ *We spent the afternoon traipsing around
the town.*
♦ v + adv ♦ v + prep

trample /'træmpl/

'trample on/over sb/sth to ignore sb's feelings or rights and treat them as if they are not
important: *The government is trampling on the
views of ordinary people.* ◇ *Don't let Jack **trample
all over** you!*
♦ v + prep

trawl /trɔːl/

,trawl 'through sth (**for sth/sb**) to search
through a large amount of information or a
large number of people, places, etc., looking for
a particular thing or person: *The police are
trawling through their files for similar cases.*
⊃ note at SEARCH FOR SB/STH
♦ v + prep

treat /triːt/

'treat sb to sth to entertain sb with sth special:
Visitors will be treated to a spectacular show.
◇ *We were treated to* (= we had to suffer) *a two-
hour lecture.*

NOTE Often used in the passive.
♦ v + n/pron + prep

trespass /'trespəs/

'trespass on sth (*formal*) to make unfair use of
sb's time, help, etc.: *I mustn't trespass on your
time any longer.*
SYN **encroach on sth**
♦ v + prep

trick /trɪk/

,trick sb 'into sth; ,trick sb 'into doing sth
to manage to get sb to do sth by tricking them:
She felt she'd been tricked into marriage. ◇ *He
tricked me into lending him £100.*
NOTE Often used in the passive.
♦ v + n/pron + prep

,trick sb 'out of sth to take sth away from sb by
tricking them: *An 80-year old woman was tricked
out of her life savings.*
♦ v + n/pron + adv + prep

trickle /'trɪkl/

,trickle 'down (especially of money) to spread
from rich to poor people through the economic
system of a country: *If the wealthy pay less tax,
the benefits should trickle down to poorer people.*
♦ v + adv

▶ 'trickle-down n [U] the theory that if the
richest people in society become richer this will
have a good effect on poorer people as well, for
example by creating more jobs: *the trickle-down
effect*

trifle /'traɪfl/

'trifle with sb/sth (*used especially in negative
sentences*) to treat sb/sth without respect as if
they are not very important: *He is not a man to
be trifled with.* ◇ *He was a man who trifled with
women's affections.*
♦ v + prep

trigger /'trɪgə(r)/

,trigger sth 'off to make sth happen suddenly:
Nuts can trigger off a violent allergic reaction.
♦ v + adv + n ♦ v + pron + adv
♦ v + n + adv (*rare*)

trim /trɪm/ (-mm-)

,trim sth a'way/'off to cut off a small part of
sth because it is not needed: *My hair is too long
now. Can you trim off about two centimetres?*
♦ v + adv + n ♦ v + n/pron + adv

,trim 'down; ,trim sth 'down to become, or to
make sth, smaller in size: *He's trimmed down
from 90 kilos to 70.* ◇ *The movie was trimmed
down to two and a half hours.*
SYN **slim down; slim down, slim sth down**
♦ v + adv ♦ v + adv + n ♦ v + n/pron + adv

trip /trɪp/ (-pp-)

,trip 'out **1** (of an electrical device, system, etc.) to stop working because the electricity stops flowing: *The device can operate at low temperatures without tripping out.* **2** (*informal*) to be under the influence of a drug that makes you see, hear, etc. things that are not real **3** (*informal*) to feel amazed or excited by sth, especially sth you have not seen or done before: *The first time I saw the ocean I totally tripped out.* **4** (*AmE, informal*) to get very angry: *I'm sorry I tripped out that night. I shouldn't have gotten mad at you.*
  ♦ v + adv

,trip sb 'out (*AmE, informal*) **1** to make sb laugh: *That movie really tripped me out.* **2** to make sb feel surprised, shocked, or nervous: *Girl, you're tripping me out! Are you OK?* ◇ *I think it **tripped him out that** our family was so close.*
  ♦ v + adv + n ♦ v + n/pron + adv

,trip 'over; ,trip 'over sb/sth to fall or almost fall because you have accidentally hit your foot against sth while you are walking or running: *I tripped over the rug and fell heavily.* ◇ *He kept tripping over.* ◇ (*figurative*) *He tripped over his words in his excitement.*
  ♦ v + adv ♦ v + prep

,trip 'up; ,trip sb 'up **1** (*especially BrE*) to fall or almost fall because you have accidentally hit your foot against sth while walking or running; to make sb fall or almost fall by catching their foot while they are walking or running: *I tripped up as I ran across the room.* ◇ *She tripped him up with her stick.* **2** to make a mistake; to deliberately make sb do this: *I knew I had to think carefully in the interview or I might trip up.* ◇ *She was trying to trip me up with her questions.*
  ♦ v + adv ♦ v + n/pron + adv ♦ v + adv + n

trot /trɒt; AmE trɑːt/ (-tt-)

,trot 'off to go somewhere, walking quite quickly: *She trotted off to school happily with her new lunch box.*
  ♦ v + adv

,trot sth 'out (*informal, disapproving*) to say or repeat sth such as an excuse, an explanation, etc. without thinking about it or being sincere about it: *The airline trotted out the same old excuses to explain the delays.* ◇ *He's just trotting out the party line again* (= in politics).
  ♦ v + adv + n ♦ v + pron + adv (*less frequent*)

trump /trʌmp/

,trump sth 'up to make up a false story about sb/sth, especially accusing them of doing sth wrong: *Several of his colleagues trumped up a complaint to get him removed from the job.* ◇ *She was arrested on **trumped-up charges.***
  [OBJ] charge(s)
  ♦ v + adv + n ♦ v + pron + adv ♦ v + n + adv (*rare*)

trundle /'trʌndl/

,trundle sth 'out (*disapproving, especially BrE*) to mention sb/sth or do sth that you have often mentioned or done before: *The government trundled out the same old clichés to justify their actions.*
  ♦ v + adv + n ♦ v + n/pron + adv

truss /trʌs/

,truss sb/sth 'up (*old-fashioned*) to tie a person or an animal up very tightly so that they cannot move or escape: *The victims had been trussed up with rope and beaten.*
  [NOTE] Often used in the passive.
  ♦ v + n/pron + adv ♦ v + adv + n

trust /trʌst/

'trust in sb/sth (*formal*) to have confidence in sb/sth; to rely on sb completely: *I was scared before the operation, but I trusted in the skill of the doctors.* ◇ *He urged them to trust in God.*
  [OBJ] God
  ♦ v + prep

'trust to sb/sth to leave the result or progress of events to be decided by luck, chance, etc., because there is nothing or no one else to help you: *I stumbled along in the dark, **trusting to luck** to find the right door.*
  [OBJ] luck
  ♦ v + prep

'trust sb with sb/sth to give sb/sth to a person to take care of because you believe they will be careful with them/it: *Would you trust her with the children?* ◇ *I'd trust him with my life.*
  ♦ v + n/pron + prep

try /traɪ/ (tries, trying, tried)

,try 'back; ,try sb 'back (*AmE*) to telephone sb again when you have already telephoned them but have not managed to speak to them: *Can you try back later?* ◇ *She's not there. I'll have to try her back after lunch.*
  [SYN] phone back, phone sb back (*especially BrE*), call back, call sb back
  ♦ v + adv ♦ v + n/pron + adv ♦ v + adv + n

'try for sth (*especially BrE*) to make an attempt to get or win sth: *Are you going to try for that job?* ◇ *They've been trying for a baby* (= the woman has been trying to become pregnant).
  [OBJ] a baby
  ♦ v + prep

,try it 'on (with sb) (*informal, disapproving, especially BrE*) to behave badly towards sb or try to get sth from them just to see what you can do before they become angry or stop you: *The kids sometimes try it on with a new babysitter.*
  ♦ v + it + adv

▶ 'try-on n (*BrE*) an act of trying to behave badly and hoping that no one will stop you

,try sth 'on to put on a piece of clothing to see if it fits and how it looks: *Can I try on the blue one?* ◇ *If you like it, why don't you try it on?*

◆ v + adv + n ◆ v + n/pron + adv

,try 'out (for sth) (*especially AmE*) to compete for a place in a sports team, a part in a play, etc.: *He tried out for the school band.* ◇ *It's a pretty good team. I think I'll try out.*

◆ v + adv

▶ **'tryout** *n* (*AmE*) a test, etc. to choose players for a team, actors for a play, etc.: *The team is holding tryouts this Thursday.* ◇ *Did you have a tryout for the school play?*

,try sb/sth 'out (on sb) to test sb/sth to see how good and useful they are or how suitable for a particular task or purpose before you decide to use them/it: *We've been trying out some new musicians for our band.* ◇ *He couldn't wait to try out his new invention.* ◇ *I've got an idea I'd like to try out on you.* ◇ *The drug has not been tried out on humans yet.*

SYN test sth out (on sb/sth)

◆ v + n/pron + adv ◆ v + adv + n

▶ **'tryout** *n* an act of testing how good or suitable sb/sth is before you decide to use them/it: *The play had an out-of-town tryout in Oxford.*

tuck /tʌk/

,tuck sth a'way 1 be ,tucked a'way to be in a quiet or hidden place where not many people go: *The house is tucked away right at the end of a rough track.* **SYN** hide sth away **NOTE** Be tucked away is usually followed by a phrase with a preposition: *The cafe was tucked away in the basement.* **2** (in sth) to put sth in a safe place, especially sth valuable: *She tucked the photos away in her wallet.* ◇ *We've got some money tucked away for emergencies.* **SYN** stash sth away **3** (*BrE, informal*) to eat a lot of food: *He can certainly tuck it away!* **SYN** put sth away

◆ **1** be + v + adv
◆ **2,3** v + n/pron + adv ◆ v + adv + n

,tuck 'in; ,tuck 'into sth (*informal, especially BrE*) to eat food, especially quickly or with enthusiasm: *We tucked in hungrily.* ◇ *He was tucking into a huge plateful of pasta.* ◇ *Tuck in, everybody!*

SYN dig in; dig into sth

◆ v + adv ◆ v + prep

,tuck sb 'in/'up to cover sb, especially a child, comfortably in bed by pulling the covers around them: *Will you come and tuck me in, Mummy?* ◇ *The children were all tucked up in bed by eight o'clock.*

◆ v + n/pron + adv ◆ v + adv + n

,tuck sth 'in; ,tuck sth 'into sth 1 to push or fold the loose end of a piece of clothing, a sheet, rope, hair, etc., in sth, to make it tidy or hold it in position: *Tom, tuck your shirt in!* ◇ *Why don't you tuck your trousers into your socks?* ◇ *Tuck the flap of the envelope in.* **OBJ** shirt **2** to pull a

part of your body towards the centre: *Keep your chin tucked in.*

◆ v + n/pron + adv ◆ v + adv + n ◆ v + n/pron + prep

,tuck sb 'up → TUCK SB IN/UP

,tuck sth 'up to move or put sth in a small space, especially to hide it or keep it safe or comfortable: *She kicked off her shoes and tucked her feet up under her.* ◇ *She sat with her legs tucked up under her.*

OBJ legs, feet

NOTE Often used in the passive.

◆ v + n/pron + adv ◆ v + adv + n

tug /tʌg/ (-gg-)

'tug at sth to give sth a quick, strong pull: *Daniel tugged at my sleeve.*

OBJ sb's arm, sb's hair, sb's sleeve **SYN** pull at sth

◆ v + prep

tumble /'tʌmbl/

,tumble 'down to fall suddenly to the ground in a dramatic way: *One push and the wall came tumbling down.* ◇ *Her long dark hair tumbled down around her face.* ◇ (*figurative*) *She felt herself tumbling down into the hole.*

◆ v + adv

▶ **'tumbledown** *adj* [usually before noun] a **tumbledown** building is old and in a very bad condition, with parts falling down: *He lived in a small, tumbledown hut.*

,tumble 'over to fall to the ground: *She knocked the statue and it tumbled over.*

◆ v + adv

'tumble to sb/sth (*BrE, informal*) to suddenly realize, understand, or become aware of what sb/sth is really like: *I've tumbled to Isabel now.* ◇ *I've tumbled to what he is trying to do.*

◆ v + prep

tune /tjuːn; AmE tuːn/

,tune 'in (to sth), ,tune 'into sth 1 to turn on the radio or television in order to listen or watch a programme or channel: *We tuned in to watch the football.* ◇ *Tune into next week's exciting episode!* **2** to be aware of, or understand other people's thoughts feelings or needs: *You must tune into the needs of the people you love.*

◆ v + adv ◆ v + adv + prep

,tune sth 'in 1 to adjust the controls on a radio or television so that you can hear or see a programme or channel clearly: *The radio isn't properly tuned in.* ◇ *I keep the radio tuned in to the BBC.* **2** (*AmE*) to turn on the radio or television in order to listen to or watch a programme: *Tune in our TV special tonight at nine.*

◆ v + adv + n ◆ v + n/pron + adv

be ,tuned 'in (to sth), be ,tuned 'into sth to be aware of or understand sth, especially other people's feelings: *Parents should be tuned in to*

the needs of their child. ◇ I'm tuned in to what I have to do.
◆ be + v + adv ◆ be + v + prep

‚tune 'out; ‚tune sb/sth 'out to stop listening to sb/sth; to ignore sb/sth: *When Lee started talking about her job, Tim just tuned out.*
◆ v + adv ◆ v + n/pron + adv ◆ v + adv + n

'tune sth to sth to adjust the controls of a radio or television so that you can listen to or watch a particular programme: *All the TVs in the store were tuned to the same channel.*
◆ v + n/pron + prep

‚tune 'up; ‚tune sth 'up when musicians **tune up** or **tune up** their instruments, they adjust them so that they can play together: *We could hear the orchestra tuning up. ◇ The quartet tuned up and began to play.*
◆ v + adv ◆ v + n/pron + adv ◆ v + adv + n

turf /tɜːf; *AmE* tɜːrf/

‚turf sb/sth 'out; ‚turf sb/sth 'out of sth (*also* **‚turf sb 'off, ‚turf sb 'off sth**) (*BrE, informal*) to force sb/sth to leave a particular place or an organization: *We need to turf the governing party out. ◇ Several families have been turfed out of their homes. ◇ The boys should have been turfed off the bus.*
SYN **kick sb out, kick sb out of sth; throw sb/sth out, throw sb/sth out of sth**
◆ v + n/pron + adv ◆ v + adv + n (*less frequent*)
◆ v + n/pron + adv + prep ◆ v + n/pron + prep

‚turf sth 'out (*BrE, informal*) to get rid of sth you do not want: *The shop is full of beautiful clothes that people have turfed out.*
◆ v + adv + n ◆ v + n/pron + adv

turn /tɜːn; *AmE* tɜːrn/

‚turn a'bout (*especially BrE*) to turn around quickly so as to face in the opposite direction: *She turned about and went into the kitchen.*
→ see also TURN AROUND, ETC.
◆ v + adv

▶ **a‚bout-'turn** *n* (*BrE*) **1** an act of turning around quickly so as to face in the opposite direction: *He did a rapid about-turn when he saw me and went back inside.* **2** a complete change of opinion, plan or behaviour: *Hours later the management did an about-turn and agreed to our demands. ◇ a dramatic about-turn in government policy*

▶ **'turnabout** *n* [sing.] **1** an act of turning around quickly so as to face in the opposite direction **2** a sudden and complete change in attitude or opinion

‚turn a'gainst sb/sth; ‚turn sb a'gainst sb/sth to stop, or to make sb stop, being friendly towards sb; to stop, or to make sb stop, supporting sb/sth: *Her old friends were turning against her. ◇ He's trying to turn his family*

against me. ◇ *What has made them turn against the government?*
◆ v + prep ◆ v + n/pron + prep

‚turn a'round (*BrE also* **‚turn 'round**) if sb **turns around** and does sth, they do sth unexpectedly and often unfairly: *What will we do if he **turns around and** says it was all our fault?*
◆ v + adv

‚turn a'round; ‚turn sb/sth a'round (*BrE also* **‚turn 'round, ‚turn sb/sth 'round**) to move your head and shoulders or your whole body so that you face in the opposite direction; to make sb/sth change position in this way: *She turned around to stare at the man behind her. ◇ He walked away without turning round. ◇ I turned the bottle round to look at the label. ◇ The nurse turned him around to face the window.*
→ see also TURN ABOUT
◆ v + adv ◆ v + n/pron + adv
◆ v + adv + n (*less frequent*)

▶ **'turnaround** (*BrE also* **'turnround**) *n* [usually sing.] **1** the amount of time it takes to unload a plane or ship at the end of a journey and load it ready for the next one **2** the amount of time that it takes to do a piece of work that you have been given and return it **3** a complete change in sb's opinion, plans, behaviour, etc.

‚turn a'round; ‚turn sth a'round (*BrE also* **‚turn 'round, ‚turn sth 'round**) if a business or an economy **turns around**, or sb **turns it around**, it becomes successful after it has been unsuccessful: *The economy is slowly turning around. ◇ His job is to turn the company around.*
◆ v + n/pron + adv ◆ v + adv + n

▶ **'turnaround** (*BrE also* **'turnround**) *n* [C, usually sing.] a sudden improvement in a business, an economy, etc.: *The predicted economic turnaround failed to happen.*

‚turn sth a'round (*BrE also* **‚turn sth 'round**) to deliberately understand sth that sb says in the wrong way, especially for your own advantage: *You turn everything I say around to make me look stupid.*
◆ v + n/pron + adv ◆ v + adv + n

‚turn a'side to change direction and go to one side, especially in order to avoid sb/sth: *He turned aside in embarrassment.*
◆ v + adv

‚turn sb/sth a'side to make sb/sth move to one side, especially in order to avoid sth difficult or dangerous: *As he bent to kiss her, she turned her head aside. ◇ (figurative) He cleverly turned all her questions aside* (= he did not answer them).
◆ v + n/pron + adv ◆ v + adv + n (*less frequent*)

‚turn a'way; ‚turn sth a'way (**from sb/sth**) to move or to move your head in a different direction, often to avoid sth difficult or dangerous: *Will turned away and walked out of the door. ◇ He turned away from her with a sigh.*

◇ *Tina turned her head away and looked out of the window.*

♦ v + adv ♦ v + n/pron + adv ♦ v + adv + n

turn sb a'way 1 (from sth) to refuse to allow sb to enter a place: *We had to turn hundreds of fans away from the game* (= because the place was full). **2** to refuse to help sb: *They had nowhere to stay so I couldn't just turn them away.*

♦ v + n/pron + adv ♦ v + adv + n

turn a'way from sth; turn sb a'way from sth to stop, or to make sb stop, supporting sb/sth or being interested in sth: *Younger voters are turning away from the party.* ◇ *The recent scandals have turned many people away from politics.*

♦ v + adv + prep ♦ v + n/pron + adv + prep

turn 'back; turn sb/sth 'back to return in the direction that you have come from; to make sb/sth do this: *The weather got so bad that we turned back.* ◇ *We were turned back at the border.* ◇ (*figurative*) **There'll be no turning back** (= you can't change your mind) *once you sign the agreement.*

➲ note at COME BACK

♦ v + adv ♦ v + n/pron + adv ♦ v + adv + n

IDM **turn the 'clock back** to return to a situation that existed in the past; to return to old-fashioned methods or ideas: *This new law is an attempt to turn the clock back.*

turn sth 'back to fold sth back on itself: *She straightened the bedclothes and turned back the top sheet.*

♦ v + n/pron + adv ♦ v + adv + n

turn 'down (*rare*) if your mouth **turns down**, it forms a line with the ends curved downwards, because you are sad or annoyed: *'Don't be cross with me,' she said, her mouth turning down at the corners.*

OPP **turn up**

♦ v + adv

turn sb/sth 'down to reject or refuse sb/sth: *Why did Clare turn down your invitation?* ◇ *He asked her to marry him, but she turned him down.* ◇ *They turned down my offer of help.* ◇ *She turned the job down because it paid too little.* ◇ *My book was turned down by eight publishers.*

OBJ **offer, application, invitation, request, job, proposal** **SYN** **reject sb/sth**

♦ v + adv + n ♦ v + n/pron + adv

turn sth 'down 1 to adjust the controls on a piece of equipment in order to reduce the amount of heat, noise, light, etc. produced: *Turn that radio down, I can't sleep.* ◇ *It's warmer today. I'll turn down the heating.* ◇ *She turned the lights down low.* **OBJ** **volume, heating, sound, television** **OPP** **turn sth up 2** to fold sth so that one part is covering another: *The corner of the page had been turned down.* ◇ *He turned down the blankets and the children climbed into bed.*

♦ v + n/pron + adv ♦ v + adv + n

▸ **'downturn** *n* [C, usually sing.] a fall in economic activity or profits: *a downturn in sales*

turn 'in (*old-fashioned, informal*) to go to bed: *It's time for me to turn in.*

SYN **retire** (*formal*)

♦ v + adv

turn 'in; turn sth 'in to place or fold sth so that it bends or faces towards the centre; to be

---

turn sb/sth down

refuse sb/sth ♦ reject sb/sth ♦ throw sth out ♦ turn sth down

These verbs all mean to say that you do not want sth that has been offered to you or that you will not give sb sth that they want.

refuse sb/sth to say that you do not want sth that has been offered to you; to say that you will not give sb sth that they want or need: *I politely refused their invitation.* ◇ *They refused him a visa.*

reject sb/sth to refuse to accept or consider sth; to refuse to accept sb for a job, position, etc.: *The proposal they put forward was firmly rejected.* ◇ *I've been rejected by all the universities I applied to.*

throw sth out to decide not to accept a proposal, an idea, etc.: *All my suggestions for improvements were thrown out.*

turn sb/sth down to reject or refuse to consider an offer, a proposal, etc. or the person who makes it: *Why did she turn down your invitation?* ◇ *He has been turned down for ten jobs so far.* ◇ *He asked her to marry him but she turned him down.*

WHICH WORD?

Refuse sth and **turn sb/sth down** imply a more polite or sympathetic attitude than **reject sb/sth** and **throw sth out**.

PATTERNS AND COLLOCATIONS

■ to refuse/reject/throw out/turn down an **application/a request**
■ to refuse/reject/turn down an **invitation/offer**
■ to reject/throw out/turn down an **proposal/suggestion**
■ to **politely** refuse sth/turn sth down

placed or folded in this way: *Her feet turn in as she walks.*
◆ v + adv ◆ v + n/pron + adv ◆ v + adv + n

ˌturn ˈin sth to achieve a good result, perform-ance, profit, etc.: *The champion turned in a brilliant performance.* ◇ *The company turned in $150 000 last month.*
[OBJ] **performance, profit**
◆ v + adv + n

ˌturn sb ˈin (to sb), ˌturn yourself ˈin (to sb) (*informal*) to give sb or yourself to sb in authority because they/you have done sth wrong: *He turned his own brother in to the police.* ◇ *Things will be better for you if you turn yourself in.*
◆ v + n/pron + adv ◆ v + adv + n

ˌturn sth ˈin 1 to give back sth that you no longer need or should have: *Turn in your pass before you leave.* **2** (*especially AmE*) to give sth such as a piece of written work to the person who asked you to do it: *Have you turned in your assignment yet?* [SYN] **hand sth in (to sb) 3** to give sth to the police or sb in authority: *Only a few guns have been turned in so far.* [SYN] **hand sth in (to sb); give sth in**
◆ v + adv + n ◆ v + n/pron + adv

ˌturn ˈin on yourself to become very con-cerned with your own problems and stop communicating with others: *He completely turned in on himself after his wife left him.*
◆ v + adv + prep

ˌturn inside ˈout; ˌturn sth inside ˈout to make the inside of sth face out: *It was so windy my umbrella turned inside out.* ◇ *She pulled off her jumper, turning the sleeves inside out.*
◆ v + adv + adv ◆ v + n/pron + adv

ˌturn sb/sth inside ˈout to make great changes in sb's life: *The shock turned her world inside out.*
[SYN] **turn sb/sth upside down**
◆ v + n/pron + adv

ˌturn ˈinto sth; ˌturn sb/sth ˈinto sth to change, or to make sth change, into sth differ-ent: *We need to stop this problem from turning into a crisis.* ◇ *The house had been turned into three apartments.* ◇ *As the fruit ripens, the starch turns into sugar.* ◇ *The director turned her into a star.* ◇ *In one year she turned from a problem child into a model student.*
[SYN] **change into sth, change sb/sth into sth**
◆ v + prep ◆ v + n/pron + prep

ˌturn ˈoff (*informal*) to stop listening to or thinking about sb/sth: *I couldn't understand the lecture so I just turned off.*
[SYN] **switch off**
◆ v + adv

ˌturn ˈoff; ˌturn ˈoff sth to leave one road in order to travel on another: *She turned off onto a side street.* ◇ *The car turned off the main road.*
◆ v + adv ◆ v + prep

▸ **ˈturn-off** *n* a place where one road leads off a larger or more important road: *the turn-off for the airport*

ⱳturn ˈoff; ˌturn itself ˈoff if a machine or a piece of equipment **turns off,** or **turns itself off,** it stops operating: *The heating turns off automatically at 9.30.* ◇ *The computer will turn itself off if you leave it.*
[SYN] **switch off, switch itself off** [OPP] **turn on, turn itself on**
◆ v + adv ◆ v + pron + adv

ˌturn sb ˈoff; ˌturn sb ˈoff sb/sth 1 (*informal*) to make sb lose interest or become bored: *People had been turned off by both candidates in the election.* ◇ *His political views turned her off him.* **2** (*informal*) to stop sb feeling attracted to sb/sth; to make sb feel disgusted: *If I tell her I'm only 17 it might turn her off.* ◇ *The sight of all that raw meat turned me off.* ◇ *The smell turned me off my food.*
[OPP] **turn sb on; turn sb on to sb/sth**
◆ v + n/pron + adv ◆ v + adv + n ◆ v + n/pron + prep

▸ **ˈturn-off** *n* [C, usually sing.] (*informal*) a person or thing that people do not find inter-esting or attractive: *Unlike many other women she found his beard a real turn-off.*

ⱳturn sth ˈoff to stop the flow of electricity, gas, water, etc. by moving a switch or a button: *to turn the radio/television off* ◇ *I forgot to turn the tap off.* ◇ *Turn all the lights off when you leave.* ◇ *You'll need to turn off the water to mend the pipe.*
[OBJ] **light, television, tap, water, gas**
[SYN] **switch sth off** [OPP] **turn sth on**
→ see also TURN STH OUT
◆ v + n/pron + adv ◆ v + adv + n

ˈturn on sb to attack sb suddenly and unex-pectedly: *The dog turned on him and bit his finger.* ◇ *She suddenly turned on me and started shouting.*
◆ v + prep

ˈturn on sth (*also* **ˈturn upon sth** *more formal*) **1** (*BrE*) to depend on sth in order to have a successful result: *Her future career turns on this interview.* ◇ *The case turns on whether the police can prove that the driver knew he had hit something.* ◇ *Much turns on the outcome of the peace talks.* [SYN] **hinge on sth 2** if a conversa-tion, an argument, etc. **turns on** sth, it has that as its main subject: *Their talk turned on the likelihood of his return* (= if he was likely to return or not).
◆ v + prep

ⱳturn ˈon; ˌturn itself ˈon if a machine or a piece of equipment **turns on,** or **turns itself on,** it starts operating: *I've set the oven to turn on at 5 p.m.* ◇ *I don't know why the radio suddenly turned itself on.*
[SYN] **switch on, switch itself on** [OPP] **turn off, turn itself off**
◆ v + adv ◆ v + pron + adv

,**turn sb 'on** (*informal*) **1** to make sb enthusiastic about sth: *What really turns him on is motorbikes.* ◇ *If live theatre turns you on, there is plenty to choose from.* **2** to make sb feel sexually excited: *That's not the kind of thing that turns me on.* ◇ *I get turned on by men in uniform.*
OPP turn sb off
◆ v + n/pron + adv ◆ v + adv + n
▶ **'turn-on** *n* [C, usually sing.] (*informal*) a person, a thing, a situation, etc. that sb finds sexually exciting: *Being the centre of attention for four or five guys was a real turn-on.*

,**turn sth 'on** to start the flow of electricity, gas, water, etc. by moving a switch or a button: *Did you turn the central heating on?* ◇ *Turn the tap on slowly.* ◇ *I checked the fuses and turned the electricity back on.* ◇ *I didn't know you were in the room until I turned the light on.* ◇ *Leo turns the television on as soon as he comes home from school.*
OBJ light, tap, television, water, gas, etc.
SYN switch sth on **OPP** turn sth off
◆ v + n/pron + adv ◆ v + adv + n
IDM turn on the 'charm to be very pleasant and polite to sb in order to gain sth for yourself: *She's turning on the charm to get what she wants.*

'**turn sth on sb/sth** (*also* '**turn sth upon sb/sth** *more formal*) to point sth such as gun, a camera, a light, etc. at sb/sth: *Officers turned hoses on the demonstrators.*
SYN train sth on sb/sth
◆ v + n/pron + prep

,**turn sb 'on to sb/sth** (*informal*) to make sb interested in sb/sth or use sth for the first time: *What was it that first turned you on to jazz?*
OPP turn sb off sb/sth
◆ v + n/pron + adv + prep

,**turn 'out 1** to be present at an event; to attend sth or go somewhere: *The whole village turned out to welcome us.* ◇ *Only half the team turned out for the practice.* ◇ *I'm not going to turn out to meet you in this weather.* **2** (*used with an adverb, an adjective or in questions with* **how**) to take place or happen in the way mentioned; to develop or end in a particular way: *The article she wrote had turned out well.* ◇ *The day turned out fine again.* ◇ *You never know how things will turn out.* ◇ *I couldn't have gone anyway, as it turned out.* ◇ *The children have turned out well.* **3** to be discovered to be; to prove to be: *It turned out that she was a friend of my sister.* ◇ *My decision turned out to have been a mistake.* ◇ *Ruth's illness turned out not to be serious after all.*
◆ v + adv
▶ '**turnout** *n* [C, usually sing., U] **1** the number of people who come to take part in or watch an activity: *There was a good turnout for the concert.* **2** the number of people who vote in a particular election: *a high/low/poor turnout*

,**turn 'out**; ,**turn sth 'out** to point, or to make sth point, towards the outside: *His feet turn out as he walks.* ◇ *She turns her toes out when she walks.*
◆ v + adv ◆ v + n/pron + adv ◆ v + adv + n

,**turn sb 'out** (**from sth**), ,**turn sb 'out of sth** to force sb to leave or go out of a place: *The landlord turned them out of their house just before the New Year.* ◇ *You can't turn us out in this storm!*
SYN chuck sb out, chuck sb out of sth; kick sb out, kick sb out of sth; turf sb out, turf sb out of sth (*BrE, informal*)
◆ v + n/pron + adv ◆ v + n/pron + adv + prep

,**turn sth/sb 'out** to produce sth/sb: *The factory turns out 900 cars a week.* ◇ *This school has turned out several well-known engineers.*
◆ v + adv + n ◆ v + n/pron + adv (*less frequent*)

,**turn sth 'out 1** to switch off sth such as a light or a source of heat: *Remember to turn out the lights.* **OBJ** only light, gas **SYN** switch sth off **OPP** turn sth on → see also TURN STH OFF **2** (*BrE*) to clean a room, a cupboard, etc. thoroughly by removing the contents and organizing them again: *She turned the kitchen cupboards out at the beginning of the year.* ◇ *I'm going to turn out my bedroom during the holidays.* **SYN** clear sth out **3** to remove the contents of sth; to empty sth completely: *I turned out all the drawers looking for my keys.* ◇ *Turn out your pockets.* ◇ *She turned the rice out of the packet into a bowl.* **SYN** empty sth
◆ v + adv + n ◆ v + n/pron + adv

be ,**turned 'out** [**+ adv/prep**] to dress sb/ yourself with special care or effort: *The children were always* **beautifully turned out***.* ◇ *She was fashionably* **turned out** *in a red sweater.*
NOTE Always used in the passive.
◆ be + v + adv

,**turn 'over**; ,**turn sb/sth 'over** to change your position, or the position of sb/sth, so that the other side is facing out or up: *He turned over onto his back.* ◇ *The van skidded and turned over.* ◇ *Jack was driving too fast and turned the car over on the bend.* ◇ *The nurse turned Adam over onto his back.* ◇ *Turn the pancake over when one side is cooked.* ◇ (*figurative*) *The smell made my stomach turn over.*
◆ v + adv ◆ v + n/pron + adv
◆ v + adv + n (*less frequent*)

,**turn 'over**; ,**turn sth 'over 1** (of an engine) to run steadily at a low speed; to start: *I turned the key and the engine turned over quietly.* ◇ *The engine was turning over too fast.* **SYN** tick over **2** (**to sth**) (*BrE*) to change to a different channel when watching television: *Can I turn over to Channel 4? This is boring. Let's turn it over.* **SYN** change over (**to sth**); switch over (**to sth**), switch sth over (**to sth**) **3** to move a page or a piece of paper so that you can see the other side: *Turn over (the page) for more details.*

NOTE Turn and **turn sth** are used more frequently on their own: *I turned the page quickly.* ◇ *Turn to page 23.* **4** to sell goods and replace them; to be sold and replaced: *Large supermarkets turn over their stock very rapidly.* ◇ *This brand turns over twice as fast as the others.*
◆ v + adv ◆ v + n/pron + adv ◆ v + adv + n
IDM **turn over a new 'leaf** to change your way of life to become a better, more responsible person

▶ **'turnover** *n* [sing.] **1** the rate at which employees leave a company and are replaced by others: *a high turnover of staff* **2** the rate at which goods are sold in a shop/store and are replaced by others: *a fast turnover of stock*

turn sb/sth 'over (**to sb/sth**) to deliver sb/sth to the control and care of sb in authority, especially the police: *He was turned over to the Belgian police at the border.*
◆ v + n/pron + adv ◆ v + adv + n

turn sth 'over 1 (**to sb**) to give the responsibility for sth important to sb else: *He had to turn over some of his duties to his assistant.* ◇ *She's planning to turn the business over to her daughter.* **SYN** **hand over to sb**, **hand sth over to sb** **2** if a business **turns over** a particular amount of money, it deals with that amount in a particular period of time: *The company turned over a million pounds in its first year.* **3** to think about sth carefully: *Diana turned over what James had said in her mind.* ◇ *He lay in the dark, turning over the day's extraordinary events.* **SYN** **chew sth over**; **mull sth over 4** (*BrE*, *slang*) to enter a place illegally and steal valuable things from it: *The burglars had turned the house over.* **NOTE** Often used in the passive. **5** (*BrE*) to search a place very thoroughly, making it very untidy: *His room had been turned over by the police.* **NOTE** Often used in the passive. **6** (*AmE*) (in American football and basketball) if you **turn the ball over**, you make a mistake or break a rule resulting in lost possession of the ball
◆ **1,3,4,5,6** v + adv + n ◆ v + n/pron + adv
◆ **2** v + adv + n ◆ v + pron + adv

▶ **'turnover** *n* **1** [C, usually sing., U] the total amount of goods and services sold by a company during a particular period of time: *an annual turnover of twenty million* **2** [C] (*AmE*) (in American football and basketball) the loss of possession of the ball by a team, because players have made a mistake or broken a rule: *After the third turnover, the coach started yelling.*

turn 'over to sth; **turn sth 'over to sth** if an area, a factory, etc. **turns over** or sb **turns it over** to sth, it starts to be used for sth different: *The whole area has turned over to rice production.* ◇ *The factory was turned over to the production of aircraft parts.*
◆ v + adv + prep ◆ v + n/pron + adv + prep

turn 'round, etc. (*BrE*) → TURN AROUND, ETC.

'turn to sb to move your head or body so as to face sb: *He turned to me and smiled.*
◆ v + prep

'turn to sb/sth to go to sb/sth for help or information; to ask sb for sympathy or advice: *Sue turns to her friends for support rather than her family.* ◇ *You're the only person I can turn to for advice.* ◇ *I always turn to my dictionary when I come across a word I don't know.*
SYN **go to sb/sth**
◆ v + prep

'turn to sth to start to become involved in sth or start to do sth, especially sth illegal or harmful, often because you are in a difficult situation: *He was forced to turn to crime to pay off his debts.* ◇ *I cope with stress by turning to food for comfort.*
◆ v + prep

'turn to sth; **'turn sth to sth** to turn your attention, your thoughts, etc. to a new subject: *Our conversation soon turned to the kind of music that we liked.* ◇ *Let's turn our attention to next week's conference.*
OBJ **attention**
◆ v + prep ◆ v + n/pron + prep

turn 'up 1 (of a person) to arrive: *He finally turned up at three o'clock.* ◇ *The taxi didn't turn up so we walked.* **SYN** **show up** (*informal*) **2** to be found, especially by chance, after being lost: *The missing letter turned up in the waste basket.* **3** (of an opportunity) to happen, especially unexpectedly: *I haven't got a job at the moment, but I'm sure that something will turn up.* ◇ *References to Irina turn up in many of his poems.*
◆ v + adv

IDM **turn up/come up 'trumps** to do more than people expect and so make a situation very successful: *The team's new player turned up trumps and scored three goals.* ◇ *That was a wonderful meal! You've turned up trumps again.*

▶ **'turn-up** *n* [sing.] (*BrE*, *informal*, *humorous*) sth surprising or unexpected that happens: *Nick's handed his work in on time? That's a turn-up for the books!*

▶ **'upturn** *n* an improvement or an increase in sth: *an upturn in the economy*

turn 'up; **turn sth 'up** to point, or to make sth point, upwards: *Her nose turns up at the end.* ◇ *She turned her face up towards the sun.*
OPP **turn down**; **turn sth down**
◆ v + adv ◆ v + n/pron + adv ◆ v + adv + n

▶ **'turned up** *adj* pointing upwards: *a turned-up nose*

▶ **'upturned** *adj* [only before noun] pointing or facing upwards: *an upturned nose* ◇ *upturned faces*

turn sth 'up 1 to adjust the controls of a piece of electrical equipment in order to increase the heat, noise, etc.: *Turn the TV up, I can't hear what she's saying.* ◇ *Let's turn the heating up, I'm*

turn up

appear ◆ arrive ◆ get here/there ◆ show up ◆ turn up

These verbs all mean to get to a place.

appear to arrive at a place: *By ten o'clock Lee still hadn't appeared.* ◇ *One day a note appeared on my desk.*

arrive to get to a place, especially at the end of a journey: *They all arrived home safely.* ◇ *I arrived late.* ◇ *The train is due to arrive any time now.* ◇ *A pile of letters arrived on my desk.*

get here/there to arrive somewhere: *Why did it take you so long to get here?* ◇ *Make sure you get there early.*

show up (*informal*) to arrive somewhere: *He showed up at my door late one night.* ◇ *An ambulance showed up about an hour later.* ◇ *Jeff usually showed up drunk.* NOTE **Show** can be used on its own: *I waited till ten o'clock but she didn't show.*

turn up to arrive somewhere: *She turned up late, as usual.* ◇ *What time should we turn up?* ◇ *If you don't turn up to work, you won't get paid.*

WHICH WORD?

All of these can be used with people or things as the subject. Things like letters or emails **arrive** or **get here/there**. **Show up** and **turn up** can also be used with things like buses, cars, etc.

PATTERNS AND COLLOCATIONS

- to arrive/get here/get there/turn up/show up/ appear/show **late/early/on time**
- to arrive/get here/get there **safely**
- to **finally/eventually** arrive/get here/get there/turn up/show up/appear/show
- to be **due to/scheduled to/about to** arrive/get here/get there/appear
- to arrive/turn up/show up/appear **at/in/on…**
- to arrive/get **home**

freezing. ◇ *The music was turned up loud.* OBJ **heating, music, radio/television** OPP **turn sth down 2** to make a piece of clothing, or part of a piece of clothing, shorter by folding it back and sewing it: *The sleeves were too long and had to be turned up.* ◇ *Will you turn the hem up for me?* OBJ **hem** OPP **let sth down 3** to discover sth, such as information or sth hidden: *Their enquiries turned up a number of interesting facts.* ◇ *Our efforts to trace him turned up nothing.*
◆ **1,2** v + n/pron + adv ◆ v + adv + n
◆ **3** v + adv + n ◆ v + n/pron + adv
▶ **'turn-up** *n* (*BrE*) the bottom of the leg of a pair of trousers/pants that has been folded over on the outside: *Turn-ups seem to be coming back into fashion.*

'**turn upon sth, etc.** → TURN ON STH, ETC.

,**turn upside 'down**; ,**turn sth upside 'down** to move sth so that the bottom is facing upwards: *The car hit a wall, turned upside down, and ended up in a field.* ◇ *I turned the box upside down and everything fell out.*
◆ v + adv ◆ v + n/pron + adv

,**turn sth upside 'down 1** to make a place very untidy while you are searching for sth: *The burglars turned the flat upside down.* **2** to make large changes and confusion in sb's life: *The divorce turned his whole world upside down.*
SYN **turn sb/sth inside out**
◆ v + n/pron + adv
▶ '**upturned** *adj* [only before noun] turned upside down: *upturned chairs* ◇ *We sat on an upturned box.*

twist /twɪst/

,**twist sth 'off**; ,**twist sth 'off sth** to remove sth or break sth off by turning and pulling it with your hand: *He twisted off the lid and looked inside.* ◇ *She twisted the cap off the bottle and took a mouthful of water.*
◆ v + n/pron + adv ◆ v + adv + n ◆ v + n/pron + prep

type /taɪp/

,**type sth 'in**; ,**type sth 'into sth** to put data into a document using a computer, etc.: *Type in the file name then press return.* ◇ *Type the relevant details into the boxes provided.*
SYN **key sth in, key sth into sth**
◆ v + adv + n ◆ v + n/pron + adv ◆ v + n/pron + prep

,**type sth 'out/'up** to produce a copy of sth on a computer, etc.: *I'm typing up the report this morning.* ◇ *It took me ages to type my notes out.*
◆ v + adv + n ◆ v + n/pron + adv

U u

urge /ɜːdʒ; *AmE* ɜːrdʒ/

,**urge sb/sth 'on** (**to sth/to do sth**) to encourage sb; to support sb so that they can do sth better: *The supporters were urging the team on.* ◇ *Urged on by the Prime Minister, the police tried to end the strike.* ◇ *The driver urged the horses on.*
SYN **encourage sb/sth** ⊃ note at CHEER SB ON
◆ v + n/pron + adv ◆ v + adv + n

use /juːz/ (**used, used** /juːzd/)

,**use sth 'up** to use all of sth until no more is left: *I've used up all the milk.* ◇ *These eggs need to be used up quickly.* ◇ *This program will use up a lot of memory on the hard disk.*
◆ v + n/pron + adv ◆ v + adv + n

usher /ˈʌʃə(r)/

,**usher sth 'in** (*formal*) to mark or be the start of sth new: *The elections ushered in a new period of change in the country.* ◇ *Firework displays ushered in the New Year.*
OBJ **period, era** **SYN** **herald sth** (*formal*)
◆ v + adv + n ◆ v + pron + adv

V v

veer /vɪə(r)/; *AmE* vɪr/

,**veer 'off**; ,**veer 'off sth** (*also* ,**veer a'way** (**from sth**)) **1** to suddenly change direction: *The car suddenly veered off to the left.* ◇ *The truck veered off the road and crashed into a tree.* ◇ *The plane was going straight towards the mountain, but veered away at the last minute.* **2** (of a conversation or a way of behaving or thinking) to change: *The conversation veered off into more personal matters.* ◇ *Throughout his career, he's veered away from jazz into other areas.*
◆ v + adv ◆ v + prep

veg /vedʒ/ (**vegges, vegging, vegged, vegged**)

NOTE Although these forms are spelt with -*gg*-, they are all pronounced /vedʒ-/.

,**veg 'out** (*informal*) to relax and do very little: *All she does is veg out in front of the telly.*
SYN **laze about/around; lounge about/around**
◆ v + adv

venture /ˈventʃə(r)/

'**venture into/on sth** (*also* '**venture upon sth** *more formal*) to dare to do sth that could involve risk: *As soon as he arrived, he ventured on a trip up the Amazon.* ◇ *This is the first time the company has ventured into movie production.*
◆ v + prep

verge /vɜːdʒ; *AmE* vɜːrdʒ/

'**verge on sth** (*also* '**verge upon sth** *more formal*) to be very close or similar to an extreme state or condition: *I was treated with suspicion that verged on hostility.* ◇ *Her hair was dark brown, verging on black.*
SYN **border on sth**
◆ v + prep

vest /vest/

'**vest in sb/sth** (*law*) (of power, property, etc.) to belong to sb/sth legally: *In the case of bankruptcy, the property shall vest in the trustee.*
◆ v + prep

'**vest sth in sb/sth**; '**vest sb with sth** (*formal*) **1** to officially or legally give sb the power or authority to do sth: *It is unwise to vest absolute power in a single institution.* ◇ *The court is vested with certain rights.* **2** to make sb the legal owner of land or property **NOTE** Often used in the passive.
◆ v + n/pron + prep

vie /vaɪ/ (**vies, vying** /ˈvaɪɪŋ/, **vied, vied**)

'**vie with sb/sth** (**for sth/to do sth**), '**vie for sth** (*formal*) (*often used in the progressive tenses*) to compete strongly with sb/sth: *There'll be a lot of people vying for those posts.* ◇ *The children were vying for the teacher's attention.* ◇ *The boys were vying with each other to impress her.* ◇ *There were several restaurants vying with each other for customers.*
SYN **compete** (**with sb/sth**) (**for sth**)
NOTE You can also use **vie to do sth**: *The boys were vying to impress her.*
◆ v + prep

visit /ˈvɪzɪt/

be '**visited on sb/sth** (*also* be '**visited upon sb/ sth**) (*old-fashioned, formal*) to be punished with sth: *He listed the horrors visited upon the region during the conflict.* ◇ *Each new indignity visited on her was worse than the previous one.*
◆ be + v + prep

'**visit with sb** (*AmE, informal*) to spend time with sb talking in an informal and casual way: *I visited with my neighbour yesterday.*
◆ v + prep

vomit /ˈvɒmɪt; *AmE* ˈvɑːmɪt/

,**vomit sth 'up** to bring food you have eaten back out of your mouth: *He vomited up his breakfast.*
SYN **bring sth up; throw sth up** (*informal*)
◆ v + adv + n ◆ v + n/pron + adv

visit with sb

call by, round, etc. ◆ **drop by, in, etc.** ◆ **look in** ◆ **pop in, over, etc.** ◆ **stop by** ◆ **visit with sb**
These verbs all mean to go to see a person for a short period of time.

call by, round, etc. (*BrE*) to visit sb: ***Call by*** *any time!* ◇ *Last time she **called round** she only stayed for a few minutes.* ◇ *She **called on** Keith while she was in town.*

drop by, in, etc. to pay an informal visit to a person or place: ***Drop by*** *whenever you feel like it.* ◇ *We **dropped in** to see Ellie on the way.* ◇ *Don't forget to **drop in on** Harry.* ◇ *You should **drop over** some time.*

look in (*BrE*) to make a short visit to a place, especially the place where sb lives: *I'll try to look in on my way home.* ◇ *Could you **look in on** Dad some time?*

pop in, over, etc. (*BrE, informal*) to visit sb: *I **popped in** to see Jill on the way home.* ◇ *She often **pops over** in the afternoons.* ◇ ***Pop by*** *next time you're around.* ◇ *I'll **pop round** later if I get time.*

stop by to visit a place for a short time: *I'll stop by later.* ◇ *Perhaps you'd like to stop by for a chat?* ◇ *I'll **stop by at** your place.*

visit with sb (*AmE*) to go to see a person or place for a short period of time: *Come and visit with me some time.* **NOTE** **Visit** is used more often on its own: *He visits his children regularly.*

- to **regularly/often/occasionally** visit/call by, etc./pop in, etc./stop by/look in/drop in
- to call/pop in/look in/drop in **on sb**
- to **promise to/decide to/plan to/invite sb to** visit/call by, etc./pop in, etc./stop by/look in/drop in

---

vote /vəʊt; *AmE* voʊt/

ˌvote sb/sth ˈdown to reject or defeat a candidate or a proposal by voting: *The Senate has voted down efforts to raise taxes.* ◇ *If he demands too much, the unions will vote him down.*
◆ v + n/pron + adv ◆ v + adv + n

ˌvote sb ˈin; ˌvote sb ˈinto/ˈonto sth to choose sb for a particular position by voting: *I was voted in as treasurer.* ◇ *When was this government voted into office?* ◇ *Who voted her onto the Board of Governors?*
SYN **elect sb (to sth)** (*more formal*)
NOTE Often used in the passive.
◆ v + adv + n ◆ v + pron + adv ◆ v + n + adv (*rare*)
◆ v + n/pron + prep

ˌvote sb ˈoff sth → VOTE SB OUT, ETC.

ˈvote on sth to make a decision about sth by voting: *The committee is voting on the proposal tonight.* ◇ *Workers have begun voting on whether to hold a series of one-day strikes.* ◇ *The proposal was voted on and agreed.*
OBJ **proposal, resolution, issue**
◆ v + prep

ˌvote sb ˈonto sth → VOTE SB IN, VOTE SB INTO/ONTO STH

ˌvote sb ˈout; ˌvote sb ˈout of/ˈoff sth to decide as a group to remove sb from a particular position by voting: *The government may be voted out of office at the next election.* ◇ *What will he do if he gets voted out?* ◇ *Parsons was voted off the Board.*
OBJ **government, party**

NOTE Often used in the passive.
◆ v + n/pron + adv ◆ v + adv + n
◆ v + n/pron + adv + prep ◆ v + n/pron + prep

ˌvote sth ˈthrough to approve sth or bring a proposal, etc. into force by voting for it: *Congress voted the bill through without a debate.*
OBJ **bill, proposal**
NOTE Often used in the passive.
◆ v + n/pron + adv ◆ v + adv + n

---

vouch /vaʊtʃ/

ˈvouch for sb/sth 1 to say that you know sb, that you believe they have a good character and that you are prepared to be responsible for their actions: *They asked whether I was prepared to vouch for him.* ◇ *You should give the names of two people who can vouch for your honesty and reliability.* ◇ *I can vouch for the fact that he is a good worker.* **SYN** **answer for sth 2** to say that you know sth is true because you have seen it yourself: *I was in bed with flu. My wife can vouch for that/me.* ◇ *I can't vouch for this hotel* (= I have no personal experience of it) *but it looked wonderful from the brochure.*
◆ v + prep

Ww

wad /wɒd; *AmE* wɑːd/ (**-dd-**)

,wad sth 'up (*especially AmE*) to fold or press sth into a tight mass: *She wadded up the first draft and threw it away.*
SYN ball sth up (*AmE*); **crumple sth up**; **scrunch sth up**
♦ v + adv + n ♦ v + n/pron + adv

wade /weɪd/

,wade 'in; ,wade 'into sth (*informal*) to get involved in a discussion, an argument, a difficult situation, etc. in a determined and not very sensitive way: *She waded in with an attack on company policy.* ◇ *The Senator waded into a new argument over defence spending.*
♦ v + adv ♦ v + prep

,wade 'into sb (*informal*) to attack sb physically or with words: *Marty was terrific—he just waded into the skinheads without a thought.* ◇ *She waded straight into her critics.*
SYN launch into sb; attack sb (*more formal*)
♦ v + prep

,wade 'through sth to spend a lot of time and effort reading sth or dealing with sth: *I had to wade through pages and pages of statistics.*
OBJ pages **SYN** plough through sth
♦ v + prep

waffle /ˈwɒfl; *AmE* ˈwɑːfl/

,waffle 'on (**about sth**) (*informal, especially BrE*) to talk or write a lot about sth without giving any useful information: *He waffled on for ages about his garden.*
SYN go on (**about sth**); rattle on (**about sth**)
♦ v + adv

wait /weɪt/

,wait a'round (*BrE also* ,wait a'bout) (**for sb/sth**) to stay in a place without doing anything, waiting for sth to happen or for sb to arrive: *I wouldn't bother waiting around for him.* ◇ *She didn't wait about to hear his reply.*
SYN hang around
♦ v + adv

,wait be'hind (*especially BrE*) to stay after other people have gone, especially in order to speak to sb privately: *He asked her to wait behind after the meeting.*
♦ v + adv

ℹ'wait for sb/sth **1** to stay where you are or delay doing sth until sb/sth comes or sth happens: *Wait for me!* ◇ *We're waiting for the rain to stop before we go out.* **2** to hope or watch for sth to happen, especially for a long time: *Leeds United had waited for success for eighteen*

wait for sb/sth

await sb/sth ♦ **expect sb/sth** ♦ **wait for sb/sth**
These verbs all mean to stay where you are or not act until sth happens.

await sb/sth (*formal*) to wait for sb/sth; to be going to happen to sb: *He is in custody awaiting trial.* ◇ *Her latest novel is eagerly awaited.* ◇ *A warm welcome awaits all our guests.*

expect sb/sth to be waiting for sb/sth to arrive, as this has been arranged; to think or believe that sth will happen or that sb will do sth: *to expect a visit/call/letter from sb* ◇ *Are you expecting visitors?* ◇ *We are expecting a rise in food prices this month.*

wait for sb/sth to stay where you are or delay doing sth until sb/sth comes or sth happens: *Are you waiting for a bus?*

WHICH WORD?

Await sb/sth is more formal than **wait for sb/sth**, and is generally used for events, news, etc. rather than an actual person or thing.

PATTERNS AND COLLOCATIONS

- to wait for a **bus/taxi**
- to wait for/await sth **anxiously/patiently**
- to wait for/await the **outcome/result** of sth
- to **confidently/fully** expect sth

years. ◇ *This is just the opportunity I've been waiting for.*
♦ v + prep

,wait 'in (**for sb/sth**) (*BrE*) to stay at home because you are expecting sb to arrive or telephone: *I've got to wait in for the TV repair man.* ◇ *She waited in all day in case he called.*
♦ v + adv

'wait on sb **1** (*also* 'wait on sth *especially AmE*) to bring food and drink to people at a table, usually in a restaurant: *My daughter will wait on us this evening!* ◇ *When I started, I didn't know anything about **waiting on tables**.* ◇ *We were waited on by a very polite young man.* **2** (*also* 'wait upon sb *more formal*) to bring sb everything they want or need: *She spoiled the children, always **waiting on them hand and foot*** (= doing everything for them, like a servant). **3** (*AmE*) to serve customers in a shop/store: *Is anybody waiting on you?* ◇ *There is no one in the furniture department to wait on me.*
♦ v + prep

'wait on sb/sth (*informal, especially AmE, ScotE*) to wait until sb arrives or until sth is available:

Judd was late and she was sick of waiting on him.
◊ *I'm still waiting on the result of the blood test.*
◊ *She was waiting on my decision.*

NOTE In British English, **wait for sb/sth** is usually used.

♦ v + prep

'**wait on sth** (*especially AmE, ScotE*) → WAIT ON
SB 1

,**wait sth 'out** to stay in a place until sth difficult or unpleasant has passed or finished: *We sheltered in a doorway to wait out the storm.* ◊ *It was difficult to wait out the hours until I could phone her to hear the news.* ◊ *Their strategy has always been to wait the recession out.*

♦ v + adv + n ♦ v + n/pron + adv

,**wait 'up 1** (**for sb**) to not go to bed until sb comes home or arrives: *Don't wait up (for me), I may be late.* **SYN** **stay up 2** (*AmE, informal*) used to tell sb to wait for you: *Wait up! I'll be right there.* ◊ *Hey you guys, wait up!* **SYN** **hang on**; **hold on**

♦ v + adv

'**wait upon sb** → WAIT ON SB 2

---

wake up

awake ♦ **get up** ♦ **wake up**

These verbs all mean to stop sleeping.

awake (*formal*) to wake up: *She awoke to the sound of birds singing.* **NOTE** **Awaken** can also be used, but it is more formal and is found mainly in literature.

get up to get out of bed after sleeping: *What time do you get up in the morning?* ◊ *She always gets up early.* ◊ *We'll have to get up at six o'clock tomorrow.*

wake up to stop sleeping: *What time did you wake up this morning?* ◊ *I woke up in the middle of the night.* ◊ *Wake up! It's ten o'clock!* **NOTE** **Wake** can be used on its own, but is more formal: *When he woke, the sun was already shining.* ◊ *She woke from a deep sleep.*

WHICH WORD?

Awake, **awaken** and **wake** are mostly used in written English, especially literary English. In everyday spoken English, use **wake up**.

PATTERNS AND COLLOCATIONS

■ to wake up/wake/awake/awaken **from** sth
■ to wake up/get up/wake/awake/awaken **late/early/in the morning/at seven o'clock**
■ to wake up/wake/awake/awaken **suddenly**

---

wake /weɪk/ (**woke** /wəʊk/, **woken** /'wəʊkən/ or **waked**, **waked**)

,**wake 'up** to become conscious again: *When she woke up after the operation, her sister was sitting beside her bed.*
⊃ note at COME ROUND
♦ v + adv

,**wake 'up**; ,**wake sb 'up**; ,**wake yourself 'up 1** to stop sleeping; to make sb stop sleeping: *How many times does the baby wake up in the night?* ◊ *I usually wake up early in the summer.* ◊ *You look as if you've only just woken up!* ◊ *Can you wake me up at eight?* ◊ *He was woken up by the sound of breaking glass.* **2** to become, or to make sb, more lively and interested: *You need to wake up and start paying attention.* ◊ *Wake up! I don't want to have to repeat all this.* ◊ *The class needs waking up.*

♦ v + adv ♦ v + n/pron + adv ♦ v + adv + n

IDM **wake ,up and smell the 'coffee** (*informal*) used to tell sb to become aware of what is really happening in a situation, especially when this is sth unpleasant

▶ '**wake-up** *adj* [only before noun] that is intended to wake you up: *What time would you like your wake-up call* (= for example, in a hotel)?

,**wake 'up to sth** to become aware of sth; to realize sth: *People are finally waking up to the fact that the natural world must be conserved.* ◊ *The hospitals have woken up to the value of experienced nurses.* ◊ *He hasn't yet woken up to the seriousness of the situation.*

♦ v + adv + prep

walk /wɔːk/

,**walk a'way** (**from sb/sth**) **1** to leave a difficult or unpleasant situation in order to avoid it, instead of staying to deal with it: *to walk away from a situation/deal* ◊ *You can't just walk away from the problem.* ◊ *He just walked away from everything—his job, his home and his family.* **2** if you **walk away** from an accident, etc., you are not seriously injured: *Both drivers walked away with minor cuts and bruises.* ◊ *He walked away unhurt.*

♦ v + adv

,**walk a'way/'off with sth 1** to win sth very easily: *The team walked away with the championship.* **2** to steal sth; to take sth without the owner's permission: *The thief walked away with jewellery worth £24 000.*

♦ v + adv + prep

,**walk 'in on sb/sth** to go into a room and see what sb is doing when they did not expect you and did not want anyone to see them: *Sorry, I didn't mean to walk in on you.* ◊ *I'd obviously walked in on a very serious conversation.*

♦ v + adv + prep

,**walk 'into sb/sth** to crash into sb/sth while you are walking: *Look where you're going! You*

walked straight into me. ◇ *He keeps bumping into things and walking into walls.*
♦ v + prep

,walk 'into sth (*informal*) **1** to become caught in sth that you are not expecting, especially because you are not careful: *He realized he'd walked into a trap.* **2** to succeed in getting a job without having to make an effort: *She walked straight into a job in publishing.*
♦ v + prep

,walk 'off; ,walk 'off sth to leave a place or a person suddenly because you are angry or upset: *She turned and walked off without a word.* ◇ *The rest of the team walked off the field in protest.*
♦ v + adv ♦ v + prep

,walk sth 'off to go for a walk in order to get rid of the feeling that you have eaten too much or an emotion such as anger: *I need to walk off that lunch.* ◇ *It'll do her good to walk some of her temper off.*
NOTE Not used in the passive.
♦ v + adv + n ♦ v + n/pron + adv

,walk 'off with sth (*informal*) **1** → WALK AWAY/ OFF WITH STH 1: *They've walked off with most of the film awards.* **2** (*humorous*) → WALK AWAY/ OFF WITH STH 2: *Who's walked off with my pen?* ◇ *That dog's just walked off with our ball!*

⚡,walk 'out **1** (*also* ,walk 'out of sth) to leave a meeting, a performance, etc. suddenly before the end, because you do not like it or are angry: *Several students walked out of the debate before the vote.* ◇ *Some of the audience walked out in disgust.* **2** (of workers) to stop working and go on strike: *The cameramen have walked out over working conditions.* **3** (on sb/sth) (*informal*) to leave sb you have a close relationship with and a responsibility for: *He walked out on his wife/ marriage after 35 years.*
♦ v + adv **1** also v + adv + prep
▶ 'walkout *n* **1** a sudden strike by workers: *The staff* **staged a** *one-day* **walkout**. **2** a protest in which you leave a meeting, a performance, etc. to show your anger or disapproval

,walk 'over sb (*informal*) **1** to treat sb badly and not consider their wishes or feelings: *We're not prepared to let the management* **walk all over** *us.* **2** to defeat sb easily in a competition: *They'll* **walk all over** *you on Saturday.* ◇ *Don't let yourselves be walked over.*
♦ v + prep
▶ 'walkover *n* (*informal*) an easy victory in a game or competition; a situation in which you are considered to have won a game although you did not in fact play: *The race was no walkover* (= it was not easy to win). ◇ *The other team didn't turn up so we had a walkover into the final.*

,walk 'through sth **1** to practise or perform a play in a simple way, just using basic moves and

positions **2** to practise a television programme without the cameras
♦ v + prep
▶ 'walk-through *n* [usually sing.] **1** a practice of a play without the clothes, objects, etc. that are used for a real performance **2** a practice of a television programme without the cameras

,walk sb 'through sth to show or tell sb how to do sth by carefully explaining or showing each part separately: *She walked me through the complicated document.* ◇ *He'll walk you through the procedure.*
SYN talk sb through sth
♦ v + n/pron + prep
▶ 'walk-through *n* [usually sing.] a careful explanation of the details of a process

,walk 'up (to sb/sth) to approach sb/sth in a confident way: *She walked straight up to the desk and asked to see the manager.*
♦ v + adv

wall /wɔːl/

,wall sth 'in to put a wall or a barrier around sth: *Apartment blocks walled in the playground completely.*
♦ v + adv + n ♦ v + n/pron + adv

,wall sth 'off to build a wall or a barrier around an area to separate it from another area: *Part of the yard had been walled off.*
NOTE Often used in the passive.
♦ v + adv + n ♦ v + n/pron + adv

,wall sb 'up to keep sb as a prisoner in a place surrounded by walls: *a story of a woman who was walled up in a small room and left to die*
NOTE Often used in the passive.
♦ v + adv + n ♦ v + n/pron + adv

,wall sth 'up to block a space with bricks or a wall so that it can no longer be used: *The entrance had been walled up in the 17th century.*
NOTE Often used in the passive.
♦ v + adv + n ♦ v + n/pron + adv

wallow /'wɒləʊ; AmE 'wɑːloʊ/

'wallow in sth (*often disapproving*) to enjoy sth that gives you pleasure, especially when it is sth unpleasant and you do it in a way that makes other people think you enjoy being unhappy or want sympathy from them: *Stop wallowing in self-pity.* ◇ *She wallows in nostalgia for the past.*
OBJ self-pity, nostalgia
♦ v + prep

waltz /wɔːls; AmE wɔːlts/

,waltz 'off (with sth) (*informal*) to leave a person or place in an annoying way, often taking sth without the owner's permission: *The tenants waltzed off with half our possessions.* ◇ *He just waltzed off and left me!*
SYN walk away/off (with sth)
♦ v + adv

wander /ˈwɒndə(r); AmE ˈwɑːn-/

,wander 'off/a'way; ,wander 'from/'off sth
to leave the place where you ought to be, or the
person or group of people you are with without
thinking about it: *Don't wander off and get lost.*
◇ *The child had wandered away from her mother.*
◇ *We had wandered off the path.*
♦ v + adv ♦ v + prep

want /wɒnt; AmE wɑːnt, wɔːnt/

'want for sth (*formal*) (*usually used with a
negative word*) to suffer because you do not
have sth: *I work hard so that my children want
for nothing.*
[OBJ] little, nothing
♦ v + prep

,want 'in (on sth) 1 (*also* ,want 'into sth)
(*informal, especially AmE*) to want to be involved
in sth, especially a business deal: *Do you want in
(on this project)?* ◇ *Does Jack want into the club?*
2 (*AmE, ScotE, informal*) to want to come inside a
place: *The cat wants in. Can you open the door?*
[OPP] want out, want out of sth
♦ v + adv 1 also v + prep

,want 'out; ,want 'out of sth 1 (*informal*) to
no longer want to be involved in sth, especially
a business deal: *I want out before we get into
difficulties.* ◇ *I want out of this mess.* [OPP] want
in (on sth), want into sth 2 (*AmE, ScotE,
informal*) to want to go out of a place: *I want
out of here.* [OPP] want in
♦ v + adv ♦ v + adv + prep

ward /wɔːd; AmE wɔːrd/

,ward sb/sth 'off to prevent sb/sth dangerous
or unpleasant from affecting or harming you:
She put up a hand to ward off the blows. ◇ *I'm
taking vitamin C to ward off a cold.* ◇ *He keeps
dogs to ward off unwanted visitors.*
[OBJ] evil, blows, criticism, danger
♦ v + adv + n ♦ v + n/pron + adv

warm /wɔːm; AmE wɔːrm/

,warm 'down to do gentle exercises to help your
body relax after doing a particular sport or
activity
▶ 'warm-down n [usually sing.]: *Remember to
do your warm-down when you've finished your
work-out.*

'warm to sb to start to like a person: *I warmed
to the teacher immediately.*
♦ v + prep

'warm to sth to become more interested in or
enthusiastic about sth: *The speaker was warming
to his theme now.*
[OBJ] theme, task, idea
♦ v + prep

,warm 'up 1 (of the weather, the earth, etc.) to
become warmer: *Research shows that the sea is
warming up.* ◇ *When spring comes, the earth
begins to warm up.* 2 to do gentle exercise or

practice to prepare for exercise, a performance,
etc.: *I'm always careful to warm up before I go
jogging.* ◇ *Peter was warming up with a few
scales.* [SYN] limber up (for sth) 3 (of a machine,
an engine, etc.) to run for a short time in order
to reach the temperature at which it will
operate well: *This computer takes a long time
to warm up.*
♦ v + adv
▶ 'warm-up n [usually sing.] a series of gentle
exercises or a short practice to prepare for
exercise, a performance, etc.: *What do you do as
a warm-up?* ◇ *warm-up exercises*

,warm 'up; ,warm sb/sth 'up 1 to become, or
to make sb or a part of sb's body, feel warmer:
Come and warm up by the fire. ◇ *They stamped
their feet to warm them up.* 2 to become, or to
make sb/sth, more lively or enthusiastic: *By
midnight the party was only just warming up.*
◇ *His role is to warm up the audience before the
main event.*
♦ v + adv ♦ v + n/pron + adv ♦ v + adv + n

,warm sth 'up 1 to make sth become warmer:
The fire had begun to warm the room up. 2 to
heat cooked food again before you eat it: *The
soup just needs warming up.*
[SYN] heat sth up
♦ v + n/pron + adv ♦ v + adv + n

warn /wɔːn; AmE wɔːrn/

,warn sb/sth a'way to tell a person, a ship, an
aircraft, etc. not to come near a place because it
is dangerous: *The male birds sing to warn other
males away.* ◇ *An electric fence warned away
anyone who came too close.*
♦ v + n/pron + adv ♦ v + adv + n

,warn sb 'off; ,warn sb 'off sb/sth; ,warn
sb 'off doing sth 1 to tell sb to leave or not to
come near a place, often in a threatening way:
*The farmer warned us off his land when we tried
to camp there.* 2 to advise sb not to do sth or to
stop doing sth: *He was warned off smoking after
his first heart attack.* ◇ *She warned him off a
career in acting.* ◇ *We were warned off renting
the apartment.*
♦ v + n/pron + adv ♦ v + n/pron + prep

wash /wɒʃ; AmE wɑːʃ, wɔːʃ/

,wash sb/sth a'way if water, a wave, etc.
washes sb/sth away, it removes or carries
them/it away to another place: *A freak wave
washed the two children away.* ◇ *The bridge was
washed away by the floods.*
♦ v + n/pron + adv ♦ v + adv + n

,wash sth a'way to use water to remove a mark,
dirt, etc. from sth: *She tried to wash away some
of the dirt and blood from the boy's face.* ◇ (*figurative*) *A hot bath soon washed my tiredness
away.*
♦ v + adv + n ♦ v + n/pron + adv

,wash sth 'down **1** (**with sth**) to clean sth by using a large quantity of water: *I washed the car down with a hose.* **2** (**with sth**) to drink sth after, or at the same time as, eating food: *We washed our lunch down with iced tea.* ◇ *He had a huge plate of pasta washed down with several bottles of beer.* **3** (of a river, a flood, etc.) to carry sth downwards away from its original position: *Tons of earth had been washed down by the storm.*
◆ v + n/pron + adv ◆ v + adv + n

ᶭ,wash 'off; ,wash sth 'off; ,wash sth 'off sth to be removed from clothes, etc. by washing; to remove sth in this way: *However hard you rub, an ink stain won't wash off.* ◇ *Wash off the dirt with soap and water.* ◇ *Wash the mud off your boots before you go in.*
◆ v + adv ◆ v + n/pron + adv ◆ v + adv + n
◆ v + n/pron + prep

ᶭ,wash 'out; ,wash sth 'out; ,wash sth 'out of sth to be removed from a fabric, hair, etc. by washing; to remove sth in this way: *The hair colour will wash out in a few weeks.* ◇ *Take care to wash all the shampoo out of your hair.*
◆ v + adv ◆ v + n/pron + adv ◆ v + adv + n
◆ v + n/pron + prep

▶ ,washed 'out *adj* (of fabric, clothes or colours) no longer brightly coloured, often as a result of frequent washing: *Washed-out jeans were very fashionable at that time.*

,wash sb 'out to make sb very tired: *That long walk has washed me out.*
◆ v + n/pron + adv ◆ v + adv + n

▶ ,washed 'out *adj* (of a person) tired and pale: *You look washed out—go and rest.*

,wash sth 'out **1** (**with sth**) to wash the inside of a container in order to remove dirt, etc.: *He carefully washed the bottles out with disinfectant.* **2** if rain **washes out** a sports game, an event, etc., it makes it end early or prevents it from starting: *The game was washed out.* **3** (*AmE*) (of a flood or heavy rains) to destroy a road: *The storm surge washed out a huge chunk of the highway.* **4** (*AmE*, *formal*) to end sth: *Baltimore washed out the Indians' six-game win streak with an 8-3 win.*
◆ v + n/pron + adv ◆ v + adv + n

▶ ,washed 'out *adj* [only before noun] flooded; damaged by floods: *Washed-out towns are appealing for help.*

▶ 'washout *n* (*informal*) **1** an event that stops early or does not happen, because of rain: *The game was a washout.* **2** an event that is a complete failure: *The party was a total washout.* **3** (*AmE*) a part of a road that has been destroyed by a flood or heavy rains: *a hundred-foot washout*

,wash 'over sb **1** (*also* ,wash 'through sb) to suddenly affect sb very strongly: *A wave of guilt washed over her.* **2** (*informal*) to happen all

around sb without affecting them: *All their criticism seems to wash over him.*
◆ v + prep

ᶭ,wash 'up (*AmE*) to wash your hands and face: *I went to the men's room to wash up.*
◆ v + adv

ᶭ,wash 'up; ,wash sth 'up **1** (*BrE*) to wash dirty plates, glasses, etc. after a meal: *It's your turn to wash up.* ◇ *Don't forget to wash up the glasses as well.* **2** to be carried along in the water and then left on land; to carry sth along and leave it in this way: *A number of dead dolphins have washed up on the shore.* ◇ *His body was washed up on the beach two days later.*
◆ v + adv ◆ v + n/pron + adv ◆ v + adv + n

▶ ,washed 'up *adj* (*informal*, *especially AmE*) to be no longer successful and unlikely to succeed again in the future: *a washed-up cabaret singer*

▶ ,washing-'up *n* [U] (*BrE*) **1** the act of washing dirty dishes, glasses, etc. after a meal: *Don't forget to do the washing-up before you go out.* ◇ *washing-up liquid* **2** the dirty dishes, glasses, etc. that have to be washed after a meal: *a sink full of washing-up*

waste /weɪst/

,waste a'way (of a person, part of the body, etc.) to grow thin or weak because you are not in good health: *He was clearly wasting away.* ◇ *The muscles in her arm had wasted away.*
◆ v + adv

watch /wɒtʃ; *AmE* wɑːtʃ, wɔːtʃ/

'watch for sb/sth **1** to look and wait for sth to happen or for sb to come: *My parents were watching for me coming off the plane.* ◇ *Watch for the sign.* **2** → WATCH OUT FOR SB/STH 1: *There are several points to watch for.*
◆ v + prep

,watch 'out used to warn sb about sth dangerous: *Watch out, there's a car coming!* ◇ *He'll get in a terrible mess if he doesn't watch out.*
SYN look out ⊃ note at LOOK OUT
◆ v + adv

,watch 'out for sb/sth **1** (*also* 'watch for sb/ sth**) to be quick to notice or be aware of sb/sth, especially sb/sth that might cause you trouble: *The staff were asked to watch out for forged banknotes.* ◇ *Watch out for their striker; he could cause us all sorts of problems.* ⊃ note at LOOK OUT **2** to be ready to see sb/sth new or interesting: *Watch out for a new feature in next month's magazine.*
SYN look out for sb/sth
◆ v + adv + prep

,watch 'over sb/sth (*formal*) **1** to take care of sb/sth, by being near them; to protect or guard sb/sth: *The child needed to be watched over 24 hours a day.* ◇ *He believed his mother was still watching over him, even though she had died when he was very young.* **SYN** protect sb/sth

(more formal) **2** to watch sb/sth carefully to make sure that everything is done or happens correctly: *There is a committee to watch over government policy.* **SYN** **supervise sb/sth** *(more formal)*
♦ v + prep

water /'wɔːtə(r); AmE also 'wɑːt-/

‚water sth 'down **1** to make a liquid weaker by adding water: *The beer had been watered down.* **OBJ** **beer** **SYN** **dilute sth** *(more formal)* **2** to change sth such as a speech, a piece of writing, etc. to make it less strong and less likely to offend people: *The criticisms had been watered down to avoid giving offence.* ◊ *The government has watered down its policy to make it more acceptable.* **OBJ** **proposal** **SYN** **dilute sth** *(more formal)*
NOTE Often used in the passive.
♦ v + adv + n ♦ v + pron + adv
♦ v + n + adv *(rare)*
▶ ‚watered 'down *adj* **1** made weaker because water has been added: *watered-down beer* **2** made less strong or critical in order not to offend people: *watered-down language* ◊ *It's a watered-down version of the original proposal.*

wave /weɪv/

‚wave sth a'round *(BrE also* ‚wave sth a'bout*)* if you **wave** your arms, hands, etc. **around**, you move them violently, often to attract attention: *She ran out into the yard, waving her arms about.* ◊ *Stop waving that knife around!*
♦ v + n/pron + adv
‚wave sth a'side/a'way to not accept sth because you think it is not important or necessary: *Their protests were waved aside.* ◊ *He waved away my question without trying to answer it.*
OBJ **objection, protest** **SYN** **brush sth aside; dismiss sth** *(more formal)*
♦ v + n/pron + adv ♦ v + adv + n
‚wave sb/sth 'down to signal to sb/sth to stop, by waving your hand: *We waited while Richard waved down a taxi.* ◊ *The police had set up a roadblock and waved several drivers down.*
OBJ **driver, taxi, vehicle** **SYN** **flag sb/sth down**
♦ v + n/pron + adv ♦ v + adv + n
‚wave sb 'off to wave goodbye to sb as they leave: *I waved the children off to school and went back inside.*
♦ v + n/pron + adv ♦ v + adv + n
‚wave sb/sth 'on to signal to sb/sth to go forwards, by waving your hand or arm: *The police waved the traffic on.* ◊ *We stopped, but the cab driver waved us on.*
♦ v + n/pron + adv ♦ v + adv + n
‚wave sb/sth 'through; ‚wave sb/sth 'through sth to signal to sb to continue forwards through a gate or a barrier, by waving

your hand or arm: *The soldier gave us back our passports and waved us through.*
♦ v + n/pron + adv ♦ v + adv + n ♦ v + n/pron + prep

wean /wiːn/

'wean sb/yourself off/from sth to make sb/yourself gradually stop doing sth or using sth that is bad or harmful: *The hospital managed to wean her off the drug.* ◊ *The patch enables smokers to wean themselves off cigarettes gradually.* ◊ *It can be extremely difficult to wean children off junk food.*
♦ v + n/pron + prep
be 'weaned on sth to have learned about or experienced sth from an early age: *I was weaned on a regular diet of Hollywood fantasy.*
♦ be + v + prep

wear /weə(r); AmE wer/ (past wore /wɔː(r)/, worn /wɔːn; AmE wɔːrn/)

‚wear a'way if time **wears away**, it passes very slowly: *The afternoon was wearing away.*
SYN **pass by**
♦ v + adv
‚wear a'way; ‚wear sth a'way to become, or to make sth become, thinner, smoother, etc. by using or rubbing it over a long period of time: *The picture on the coin had worn away.* ◊ *The steps had been worn away by the feet of thousands of visitors.*
♦ v + adv ♦ v + adv + n ♦ v + pron + adv
♦ v + n + adv *(rare)*
‚wear a'way at sb/sth to slowly and gradually make sth thinner or smoother: *a drop of water wearing away at a stone* ◊ *(figurative)* *Stress can wear away at your ability to think straight.*
OBJ **stone** **SYN** **erode sth** *(more formal)*
♦ v + adv + prep
‚wear 'down; ‚wear sth 'down to become or to make sth become, gradually smaller, thinner, etc. by continuously using or rubbing it: *The tyres had worn right down.* ◊ *The path has been worn down in places to bare rock.*
♦ v + adv ♦ v + adv + n ♦ v + n/pron + adv
‚wear sb/sth 'down to make sb/sth weaker or less determined, especially by continuously attacking or putting pressure on them/it over a period of time: *Constantly being criticized was wearing her down.* ◊ *to wear down sb's patience/ resistance*
SYN **grind sb down**
♦ v + adv + n ♦ v + pron + adv ♦ v + n + adv *(rare)*
‚wear sth 'in *(BrE)* to wear boots or shoes for a short period of time until they become comfortable: *These boots were so comfortable they didn't need to be worn in at all.*
OBJ **boots, shoes** **SYN** **break sth in**
♦ v + n/pron + adv ♦ v + adv + n
‚wear 'off if a feeling or an effect **wears off**, it gradually disappears: *The effects of the medicine*

slowly wore off. ◇ *Children love new toys, but the novelty soon wears off.*
♦ v + adv

ˌwear ˈon when time **wears on**, it passes in a way that seems slow: *As the evening wore on, she became more and more nervous.*
⭢ note at GO BY
♦ v + adv

⚡ˌwear ˈout; ˌwear sth ˈout to become, or to make sth become, thin or no longer able to be used, usually because it has been used too much: *Our carpets always seem to wear out quickly.* ◇ *I wore out two pairs of boots on the walking trip.* ◇ (*figurative*) *Her patience finally wore out.*
♦ v + adv ♦ v + adv + n ♦ v + n/pron + adv
▸ ˌworn ˈout *adj* badly damaged and no longer useful because it has been used a lot: *worn-out clothes/equipment*

⚡ˌwear sb/yourself ˈout (**with sth**) to make sb/yourself extremely tired: *It's no good wearing yourself out by working so late.* ◇ *The kids have worn me out today.*
SYN tire sb out; exhaust sb (*more formal*)
⭢ note at TIRE SB OUT
♦ v + n/pron + adv
▸ ˌworn ˈout *adj* [not usually before noun] extremely tired: *I went to bed feeling worn out after the busy week.* ◇ *You look worn out!* ◇ *He died a worn-out man overcome by the injustices of life.*

weary /ˈwɪəri; *AmE* ˈwɪri/ (**wearies, wearying, wearied**)

ˈweary of sb/sth; ˈweary of doing sth (*literary*) to lose your interest in or enthusiasm for sth/sb: *As the day went on, we wearied of the long journey.*
SYN tire of sb/sth, etc. (*less formal*)
♦ v + prep

weasel /ˈwiːzl/ (-**ll**-, *AmE* -**l**-)

ˌweasel ˈout; ˌweasel ˈout of sth (*informal, disapproving, especially AmE*) to avoid keeping a promise, doing your duty, etc.: *I should be punished. I'm not going to try and weasel out.* ◇ *He's trying to weasel out of the deal.*
♦ v + adv ♦ v + adv + prep

weed /wiːd/

ˌweed sb/sth ˈout to remove or get rid of sb/sth that you do not want from a group of people or things: *a plan intended to weed out poor teachers* ◇ *Weak or sick animals were weeded out.*
♦ v + adv + n ♦ v + n/pron + adv

weigh /weɪ/

ˌweigh aˈgainst sb/sth (*formal*) to make sb less likely to achieve sth or to be successful: *The fact that he's had five jobs in two years will weigh against his application.*

SYN count against sb
♦ v + prep

ˌweigh sth aˈgainst sth to consider the importance or the advantages of sth compared to sth else: *Potential benefits need to be weighed against the obvious risks.*
SYN set sth against sth
♦ v + n/pron + prep

ˌweigh sb ˈdown (**with sth**) to make sb feel anxious or depressed: *The responsibilities of the job are weighing her down.* ◇ *He was weighed down with grief.*
NOTE Often used in the passive.
♦ v + adv + n ♦ v + pron + adv ♦ v + n + adv (*rare*)

ˌweigh sb/sth ˈdown (**with sth**) to put a heavy weight on sb/sth so that it is difficult for them to move easily: *We were weighed down with bags of shopping.* ◇ *The snow was weighing down the branches of the fir trees.*
SYN burden sb (**with sth**)
NOTE Often used in the passive.
♦ v + adv + n ♦ v + pron + adv ♦ v + n + adv (*rare*)

ˌweigh ˈin **1** (**at sth**) to have your weight measured, especially before a race, a competition, etc.: *Both boxers weighed in at several pounds below their limit.* ◇ *Baby Sam weighed in at four kilos.* **2** (**with sth**) (*informal*) to join in a discussion, an argument, etc. by saying sth important or doing sth to help: *We all weighed in with helpful suggestions.*
♦ **1** v + adv
♦ **2** v + adv ♦ v + adv + speech
▸ ˌweigh-in *n* the occasion when the weight of a person who is taking part in a sports event is measured just before the start: *The champion arrived five minutes late for the weigh-in*

ˈweigh on sb/sth (*also* ˈweigh upon sb/sth *more formal*) to make sb feel worried or depressed; to be a difficult duty or task for sb/sth: *The responsibilities are clearly **weighing heavily on** his **shoulders**.* ◇ *The debt burden weighs heavily on the government.*
SYN burden sb/sth
♦ v + prep

ˌweigh sth ˈout to measure a quantity of sth by weight: *Weigh out all the ingredients before you start making the cake.*
♦ v + adv + n ♦ v + pron + adv ♦ v + n + adv (*rare*)

ˌweigh sb ˈup to form an opinion of sb by watching them or talking to them: *She stared at him, weighing him up.* ◇ *The two women weighed each other up for a few moments.* ◇ *He's certainly got Jeff weighed up.*
♦ v + adv + n ♦ v + pron + adv ♦ v + n + adv (*rare*)

ˌweigh sth ˈup (**against sth**) to think carefully about a situation before you decide what to do: *I weighed up the pros and cons of giving up my job.* ◇ *We have to weigh up whether we can afford a trip to Italy this year.* ◇ *It's important to weigh up all possible courses of action.*
♦ v + adv + n ♦ v + pron + adv ♦ v + n + adv (*rare*)

'**weigh upon sb/sth** → WEIGH ON SB/STH

weight /weɪt/

,**weight sth 'down** (**with sth**) to add a weight to sth so that it feels very heavy, bends down, sinks, etc.: *The canvas sheet was weighted down to stop it blowing away.* ◇ *My pockets were weighted down with lots of small coins.*
NOTE Often used in the passive.
♦ v + adv + n ♦ v + pron + adv ♦ v + n + adv (*rare*)

welch /weltʃ, welʃ/

'**welch on sb/sth** → WELSH ON SB/STH

weld /weld/

,**weld sb/sth 'into sth**; ,**weld sb/sth to'gether** to unite sb/sth into an effective whole: *The manager has welded the players into a strong team.* ◇ *The crisis helped to weld the community together.*
♦ v + n/pron + prep ♦ v + n/pron + adv

well /wel/

,**well 'up 1** if a liquid **wells up**, it rises to the surface and starts to flow: *Tears welled up in his eyes.* ◇ *Spots of blood began to well up on her skin.* **2** (**in/inside sb**) if an emotion **wells up**, you start to feel it very strongly: *She felt anger welling up inside her.*
♦ v + adv

welsh /welʃ/ (*also* **welch**)

'**welsh on sb/sth** (*informal, disapproving*) to not do sth that you have promised to do, for example to not pay money that you owe a person: *'I'm not in the habit of welshing on deals,'* said Don.
♦ v + prep

whack /wæk/

,**whack 'off** (△, *slang*) if a man **whacks off**, he gives himself sexual pleasure by rubbing his sexual organs
♦ v + adv

,**whack sb 'out** (*informal, especially AmE*) to murder sb: *They never found out who whacked out that old tramp.*
♦ v + n/pron + adv ♦ v + adv + n

▶ ,**whacked 'out** *adj* **1** (*informal*) under the influence of drugs, so that you are not aware of what is happening around you: *Those guys must be whacked out on something.* **2** (*BrE, informal*) very tired: *I was whacked out by the time I reached home.*

whale /weɪl/

'**whale at/into/on sb** (*AmE, informal*) to attack sb by hitting them repeatedly with force: *We came in the room and found him whaling on his*

brother. ◇ *I was so angry, I simply whaled into him.*
♦ v + prep

wheel /wiːl/

,**wheel a'round**; ,**wheel sb/sth a'round** (*BrE also* ,**wheel 'round**, ,**wheel sb/sth 'round**) (*literary*) to turn around very quickly to face the opposite direction; to make sb/sth do this: *I wheeled around to scream at Miles.* ◇ *He wheeled his horse around* and started for home.
SYN spin around, spin sb/sth around
♦ v + adv ♦ v + n/pron + adv

,**wheel sb/sth 'out** (*BrE, informal*) to produce sb/sth to help you do sth, even though they have often been used before: *He wheels out the same old arguments every time he makes a speech.* ◇ *The company wheeled out some big guns* (= very important people) *to launch the new car.*
♦ v + n/pron + adv ♦ v + adv + n

while /waɪl/

,**while sth a'way** if you **while away** a period of time, you spend it in a pleasant, lazy way: *There were plenty of cafes in which to while away a pleasant evening.* ◇ *We whiled away the time at the airport reading magazines.*
♦ v + adv + n ♦ v + pron + adv ♦ v + n + adv (*rare*)

whip /wɪp/ (**-pp-**)

,**whip sth 'out**; ,**whip sth 'out of sth** to take sth out quickly and suddenly: *He whipped out his camera and started taking photos.*
♦ v + n/pron + adv ♦ v + adv + n
♦ v + n/pron + adv + prep

,**whip 'through sth** (*informal*) to do sth very quickly: *She whipped through the paperwork.*
♦ v + prep

,**whip sb/sth 'up** to deliberately make sb feel strong emotions or get excited about or interested in sth: *The studio audience was whipped up into a frenzy.* ◇ *They're trying to whip up support for their candidate.*
OBJ crowd, support, resistance **SYN** stir sb/sth up; rouse sb/sth (*more formal*)
♦ v + n/pron + adv ♦ v + adv + n

,**whip sth 'up 1** to prepare a meal or some food very quickly: *I can easily whip up an omelette.*
SYN put sth together; throw sth together (*informal*) **2** if the wind **whips up** dust, waves, etc., it makes it/them rise quickly: *The wind whipped up the sand in gusts.* **SUBJ** wind
♦ v + adv + n ♦ v + pron + adv
♦ v + n + adv (*less frequent*)

whisk /wɪsk/

,**whisk sb/sth a'way/'off** to remove sb/sth from a place very quickly: *The president was* *whisked away by his bodyguards.* ◇ *The food was whisked away before we had finished.*

◆ v + n/pron + adv ◆ v + adv + n

white /waɪt/

ˌwhite sth 'out (*especially AmE*) **1** to cover a mistake that you make when you are writing or typing, by covering it with a white liquid (**correction fluid**): *I noticed that my name had been whited out.* **2** (of weather conditions) to make it difficult to enter, leave or move round a place, or to stop an event from taking place, because there is so much snow that it is impossible to see anything: *Blizzards had whited out the whole county.* ◇ *Snowstorms almost whited out the final day of the tournament.*

◆ v + adv + n ◆ v + pron + adv ◆ v + n + adv (*rare*)

▶ 'white-out *n* weather conditions in which there is so much snow or cloud that it is impossible to see anything

whittle /'wɪtl/

ˌwhittle sth a'way (*also* ˌwhittle a'way at sth) to gradually reduce the size, importance or value of sth: *Inflation has been whittling away their savings.* ◇ *Our lead* (= in a sports competition, for example) *was being gradually whittled away.*

◆ v + adv + n ◆ v + n/pron + adv

ˌwhittle sb/sth 'down to reduce the size or number of sb/sth gradually: *The government's majority has been whittled down to eight.*

SYN reduce sb/sth

◆ v + adv + n ◆ v + n/pron + adv

whizz (*especially BrE*) (*AmE usually* whiz) /wɪz/

ˌwhizz 'through sth to do, read sth, etc. very quickly: *She whizzed through the work and was finished before lunch.*

◆ v + prep

whoop /wuːp; *AmE* wʊp/

ˌwhoop it 'up (*informal*) **1** to enjoy yourself in a noisy and excited way: *I've been working hard while you've been whooping it up in Berlin.* **2** (*AmE*) to try to make people excited or enthusiastic about sb/sth

SYN live it up

NOTE Not used in the passive.

◆ v + it + adv

wig /wɪg/

ˌwig 'out; ˌwlg sb 'out (*AmE, slang*) to become, or to make sb, very excited or very anxious about sth; to go, or to make sb, crazy, often as a result of the effect of drugs

◆ v + adv ◆ v + n/pron + adv

wimp /wɪmp/

ˌwimp 'out (on sb/sth) (*informal, disapproving*) to decide not to do sth you had intended to do because you are too frightened: *Did you wimp*

out on any of the tests? ◇ *Dave wimped out and refused to dive off the top board.*

SYN bottle out, etc.; chicken out, etc.

◆ v + adv

win /wɪn/ (winning, won, won /wʌn/)

ˌwin sb/sth 'back to get again by your own efforts sb/sth that you had before: *I'm hoping to win back my place in the team soon.* ◇ *Jack had tried everything to win Martha back.* ◇ *You do have a chance to win your money back.*

◆ v + n/pron + adv ◆ v + adv + n

ˌwin 'out (over sb/sth) (*informal*) if sb/sth wins out, they are/it is stronger or more successful than other things: *It is not clear if the archae-ologists will win out over the builders and save the temple.*

SYN prevail (*more formal*)

◆ v + adv

ˌwin sb 'over (*BrE also* ˌwin sb 'round) (to sth) to gain sb's support or approval, especially by persuading them that you are right: *My dad's against the idea, but I'm sure I can win him over.* ◇ *My parents were won over by Anthony's charm.*

SYN bring sb round/around (to sth)

◆ v + n/pron + adv ◆ v + adv + n

ˌwin 'through to finally succeed after trying very hard: *We are faced with a lot of problems but we'll win through in the end.* ◇ *United won through to the final in an exciting game.*

◆ v + adv

wind /waɪnd/ (wound, wound /waʊnd/)

ˌwind 'down **1** to relax, after a period of stress or excitement: *It takes a while for me to wind down after work.* **SYN** unwind **2** if a machine winds down, it goes slowly and then stops: *The old clock had wound right down.* **3** if a business winds down, it gradually reduces the amount of work it does until it closes completely: *Next week the mill winds down for a summer break.*

◆ v + adv

ˌwind sth 'down **1** to bring a business or an activity gradually to an end over a period of time: *The government is winding down its nuclear programme.* **OBJ** business, programme **SYN** reduce sth **OPP** expand sth **2** to make a car window open and go downwards by moving a handle, pushing a button, etc.: *She wound down the driver's window and called to him.* **OBJ** car window **SYN** open sth **OPP** wind sth up

◆ v + n/pron + adv ◆ v + adv + n

ˌwind 'up; ˌwind 'up doing sth (*informal*) to find yourself after a long time in a particular place or situation: *I always said she would wind up in jail.* ◇ *Bill wound up marrying the girl next door!* ◇ *If he isn't careful, he'll wind up dead.*

SYN end up, etc.; finish up, etc.

◆ v + adv

wind 'up; wind sth 'up 1 to make a machine, etc. work by turning a handle several times: *Does the clock have a battery or does it wind up?* ◇ *This is a great little toy. You just wind it up and off it goes!* **2** to bring sth such as a speech, a meeting or a discussion to an end: *Before I wind up, I'd like to make one final point.* ◇ *If we all agree, let's wind up the discussion.*
◆ v + adv ◆ v + adv + n ◆ v + n/pron + adv
▸ **'wind-up** *adj* [only before noun] a **wind-up** device is one that you operate by turning a handle several times: *a wind-up clock/toy*

wind sb 'up (*BrE, informal*) **1** to deliberately make sb very angry or annoyed: *Are you deliberately winding me up?* ◇ *Ignore them. They're just trying to wind you up.* **SYN annoy sb** (*more formal*) **2** to tell sb sth that is not true in order to make a joke: *Come off it, you're winding me up!* **SYN tease sb**
◆ v + n/pron + adv ◆ v + adv + n
▸ **'wind-up** *n* (*BrE, informal*) sth that sb says or does in order to annoy sb or to make a joke: *It sounded so crazy I thought it was a wind-up.*

wind sth 'up 1 to close a business, a company, etc.: *The company was wound up last year.* **OBJ business, company 2** to close a car window by turning a handle, pressing a button, etc.: *I wound up the window and locked the door.* **OBJ car window OPP wind sth down**
◆ v + adv + n ◆ v + n/pron + adv
▸ **winding-'up** *n* the act of officially closing a business, a company, etc.: *a voluntary winding-up of the company* ◇ *a winding-up order/petition*

wink /wɪŋk/

'wink at sth to pretend that you have not noticed sth, especially sth bad or illegal: *The authorities have chosen to wink at the illegal trade.*
◆ v + prep

winkle /'wɪŋkl/

winkle sb/sth 'out; winkle sb/sth 'out of sth (*BrE*) to get sb/sth out of somewhere slowly and with difficulty: *The bird uses its beak to winkle insects out of tree trunks.* ◇ *The terrorists have been winkled out of their hiding place.* ◇ *Leila was working in the library, so we sent Tim to winkle her out.*
◆ v + n/pron + adv ◆ v + adv + n
◆ v + n/pron + adv + prep

winkle sth 'out; winkle sth 'out of sb (*BrE*) to get sth such as information, money, etc. from sb with difficulty: *She's very good at winkling out secrets.* ◇ *He wouldn't tell you? Don't worry, I'll winkle it out of him.*
◆ v + n/pron + adv ◆ v + adv + n
◆ v + n/pron + adv + prep

wipe /waɪp/

wipe sth a'way to remove sth, such as dirt or tears, with a cloth or your hand: *Wipe away mud splashes with a wet cloth.* ◇ *He wiped away a tear.*
OBJ stain, tear
◆ v + adv + n ◆ v + n/pron + adv

wipe sth 'down to clean a surface with a cloth: *I'll just wipe the table down before you put your books there.*
◆ v + n/pron + adv ◆ v + adv + n

wipe sth 'off; wipe sth 'off sth 1 to remove sth from a surface with a cloth: *Wipe off any surplus glue with a rag before it dries.* ◇ *Tom had carefully wiped his fingerprints off the glass.*
OBJ stain, fingerprints 2 to remove sth that has been recorded on a tape or a video tape: *He wiped the conversation off the tape.* **3** to reduce the value of sth, especially shares: *Over £5 billion was wiped off share values worldwide today.* **4** to get rid of sth: *Wipe that smile off your face!* ◇ *Our secret plan will wipe the smile off her face* (= will stop her from being so confident).
OBJ smile
◆ v + n/pron + adv ◆ v + adv + n ◆ v + n/pron + prep

wipe 'out (**on sth**) (in surfing and other sports) to fall or crash in a sport, especially to fall from a board (a **surfboard**): *I caught a huge wave but then wiped out on the next.*
◆ v + adv
▸ **'wipeout** *n* (in surfing and other sports) a fall or a crash, especially a fall from a board (a **surfboard**): *I had so many bad wipeouts while I was learning to surf.*

wipe sb 'out 1 (*informal*) to defeat sb easily in a sports competition: *The Welsh side was wiped out 24–3.* **2** (*informal*) to make sb very tired: *All that travelling wiped her out.* **3** (*slang*) to murder sb
◆ v + n/pron + adv ◆ v + adv + n
▸ **wiped 'out** *adj* [not before noun] (*informal*) very tired
▸ **'wipeout** *n* (*especially AmE*) a situation where one team easily defeats another team in a sports competition: *Dallas's wipeout of the Giants*

wipe sb/sth 'out to kill large numbers of people or animals: *The whole village was wiped out by the flood.* ◇ *Pollution has wiped out half the species of fish in the river.*
↪ note on page 372
NOTE Often used in the passive.
◆ v + adv + n ◆ v + n/pron + adv

wipe sth 'out 1 to destroy sth completely: *The disease has been virtually wiped out.* ◇ *The government is trying to wipe out drug trafficking.* **OBJ disease 2** to remove information from a computer, writing from a board, etc.: *The virus could wipe out your hard disk.* ◇ (*figurative*) *I'll never be able to wipe out the memory of that day.* **OBJ memory 3** to remove or deal with a debt completely: *He secured a loan to wipe out the club's debts.* ◇ *Their lead was wiped out by four*

wipe sb/sth out

annihilate sb ◆ destroy sb/sth ◆ devastate sth ◆ exterminate sb/sth ◆ wipe sb/sth out

These verbs all mean to damage, remove or kill sb/sth so that they no longer exist.

annihilate sb to destroy or defeat sb completely: *The human race has enough weapons to annihilate itself.* ▸ **annihilation** *n* [U]: *the annihilation of the whole human race*

destroy sb/sth to kill sb; to damage sth so badly that it no longer exists or works: *The building was completely destroyed by fire.* ◇ *They've destroyed all the evidence.* ◇ (*figurative*): *Failure was slowly destroying him* (= making him less confident and happy). ▸ **destruction** *n* [U]: *the destruction of the rainforests*

devastate sth to completely destroy a place, area or building: *The bomb devastated much of the old part of the city.* ▸ **devastation** *n* [U]: *The bomb caused widespread devastation.*

exterminate sb/sth to deliberately kill all the members of a group of people or animals: *They used poison to exterminate the rats.*

wipe sb/sth out to destroy or remove sb/sth completely: *Whole villages were wiped out by the earthquake.* ◇ *a campaign to wipe out malaria*

WHICH WORD?

Devastate is stronger than **destroy**, but is only used about places or buildings. When used about people, it has a different meaning: *I was devastated* (= very upset) *to hear I'd failed my exams.* If people **exterminate** animals or people, they deliberately kill all of them. With the other expressions the cause can be natural, although **annihilate** is usually used to talk about the effects of war.

PATTERNS AND COLLOCATIONS

■ to destroy/wipe out/devastate a **village/town/ city**
■ a **bomb/blast** destroys/devastates **buildings**
■ to destroy/wipe out/annihilate/exterminate **the enemy**
■ **an earthquake/a flood/a fire** destroys/devastates sth

---

goals in ten minutes. ◇ *This year's losses have wiped out last year's profits.* OBJ **profits, debts**
◆ v + adv + n ◆ v + n/pron + adv

,wipe 'up; ,wipe sth 'up (*BrE, informal*) to dry dishes with a cloth: *You wash and I'll wipe up.* SYN **dry sth, dry sth up; dry, dry sth**
◆ v + adv ◆ v + n/pron + adv ◆ v + adv + n

▓,wipe sth 'up to clean a substance, especially a liquid, from a surface with a cloth: *Keep a cloth handy to wipe up any mess.*
◆ v + adv + n ◆ v + n/pron + adv

wire /ˈwaɪə(r)/

,wire sb/sth 'up (to sth) to connect sb/sth to a piece of electrical equipment by using electrical wires: *You will be wired up to a machine which will record your heartbeat.* ◇ *The police suggested I should be wired up* (= to record the conversation) *before I met the dealer.* ◇ *The band's instruments were all wired up for sound.* ◇ *The microphone hadn't been wired up properly.*
NOTE Often used in the passive.
◆ v + adv + n ◆ v + n/pron + adv

wise /waɪz/

,wise 'up (to sth) (*informal, especially AmE*) to become aware of the unpleasant truth about a situation: *Employees should wise up about how the industry works.* ◇ *You need to wise up to the*

fact that he's never coming back. ◇ *Wise up! Try and see her for what she really is.* ◇ *You need to wise up to how serious this situation is.*
◆ v + adv

wish /wɪʃ/

,wish sb/sth a'way to try to get rid of sth by wishing it did not exist; to wish that sb was somewhere else: *These complications can't just be wished away, you know.* ◇ *Don't wish your life away* (= said to sb who spends a lot of time looking forward to the future).
◆ v + n/pron + adv ◆ v + adv + n

'wish sb/sth on sb (*also* 'wish sb/sth upon sb *more formal*) (*used in negative sentences, especially with* **wouldn't**) to hope very much that sth unpleasant will happen to sb or that they will have to deal with sb unpleasant: *I wouldn't wish this pain on my worst enemy.* ◇ *I wouldn't wish my daughter on anyone at the moment—she's very difficult!*
◆ v + n/pron + prep

wither /ˈwɪðə(r)/

,wither a'way to become less or weaker, especially before disappearing completely: *All our hopes just withered away.* ◇ *They predicted that the bad schools would wither away.*
◆ v + adv

wolf /wʊlf/

,wolf sth 'down (*informal*) to eat sth very quickly, especially in large quantities: *He wolfed down his breakfast and rushed out of the house.*
SYN gobble sth down/up; scarf sth down (*AmE*, *informal*); scarf sth up (*AmE*, *informal*); scoff sth (*BrE*); wolf sth down (*informal*)
NOTE Wolf sth is also sometimes used on its own with this meaning: *wolfing tea and cakes.*
◆ v + adv + n ◆ v + n/pron + adv

wonder /'wʌndə(r)/

'wonder at sth to be very surprised by sth: *He wondered at her beauty.* ◇ *She wondered at her own stupidity.* ◇ ***It's hardly to be wondered at*** *that he behaves as he does, considering his family background.*
SYN marvel at sth
◆ v + prep

work /wɜːk; *AmE* wɜːrk/

,work a'gainst sb/sth if sth **works against** sb/sth, it has the effect of making it harder for sb to do or achieve sth: *The engineering career structure works against women.* ◇ *The new policy has worked against the interests of farmers.*
◆ v + prep

,work a'round sth (*BrE also* ,work 'round sth) to find a way of doing what you want to do in spite of situations, rules, etc. that could prevent you doing it: *If we can't get rid of the problem, we'll just have to work round it.* ◇ *He urged the two sides to work around their disputes and reach an agreement.* ◇ *My uncle couldn't read, but he'd found ways to work around it because he was too embarrassed to tell anyone.*
◆ v + prep
▶ 'work-around *n* a way of dealing with a problem which allows you achieve the result you want, without actually getting rid of the problem: *a work-around solution*

,work a'round to sth (*BrE also* ,work 'round to sth) to gradually turn a conversation towards a particular topic: *I wondered when he would work around to the subject of money.*
◆ v + adv + prep

'work at sth; 'work at doing sth to make great efforts to achieve sth or do sth well: *She worked hard at her French and passed the exam.* ◇ *You've got to work at losing weight.* ◇ *You've got to work at it.* ◇ *Marriage has to be worked at.*
◆ v + prep

,work a'way (at sth) (*often used in the progressive tenses*) to continue to work hard for a period of time: *I've been working away in a gym, trying to get fit.* ◇ *Ruth spends hours in the library, working away at Japanese.*
◆ v + adv

,work sth 'in; ,work sth 'into sth 1 to add one substance to another and mix them together: *Work the butter in with your fingers.* ◇ *Use plenty of polish and work it well into the wood.* 2 to try to include sth in a piece of writing, a speech, etc.: *Try and work in something about your own experience.* ◇ *He usually manages to work something topical into his act.*
◆ 1 v + n/pron + adv ◆ v + adv + n ◆ v + n/pron + prep
◆ 2 v + adv + n ◆ v + n/pron + adv ◆ v + n/pron + prep

,work yourself 'into sth to become very angry, excited, etc.: *She's working herself into a state about the exams.* ◇ *He was working himself into a rage.*
→ see also WORK SB UP, WORK YOURSELF UP
◆ v + pron + prep

'work off sth (of a machine, a piece of electrical equipment, etc.) to use a supply of power or another machine in order to operate: *The lighter works off the car battery.*
◆ v + prep

,work sth 'off 1 to get rid of sth by physical effort: *He went for a run to work off some calories.* ◇ *By the time she had finished cleaning, she had worked off her anger.* 2 to earn money to pay off a debt: *They worked off their huge bank loan over five years.* 3 if you work off a punishment, etc., you do what you have been told to do because you have done sth wrong or committed a crime: *Keane has started to work off his eight-match suspension.*
◆ v + adv + n ◆ v + n/pron + adv

'work on sb to try to persuade sb to agree to sth or to do sth: *My father hasn't said he will lend me the car yet, but I'm working on him.*
◆ v + prep

'work on sth 1 to be busy with a particular activity, project, piece of research, etc.: *What are you working on at the moment?* ◇ *The committee worked on ways to raise money.* ◇ *Tara is currently working on a solo album.* 2 to practise or work hard in order to improve sth: *Your designs are great, but you need to work on them a bit more.* ◇ *You need to work on your technique* (= for example, in a sport). ◇ *Jack's been working on building up his confidence.* ◇ *'Have you sorted things out with your parents yet?' 'No, but **I'm working on it*** (= I'm trying hard to do this).' 3 to consider that sth is true when you are saying or doing sth, planning sth, etc.: *We are **working on the assumption** that everyone invited will come.* ◇ *The police are working on the theory that she was attacked by somebody she knew.*
◆ v + prep

,work 'out 1 to happen or develop in a particular way, especially in a successful way: *I'm glad my plan worked out* (= was successful). ◇ *Their marriage didn't work out* (= was not successful). ◇ *It is all working out very well.* ◇ *Don't worry now, everything will work out all right in the end.* 2 (at sth) if sth **works out** at sth, you calculate that it will be a particular amount: *The rent works out at £50 a week each.* ◇ *It'll **work out cheaper** to go by bus.*

work

NOTE Work out is often used with *cheaper, more expensive*, etc. **3** to train the body by physical exercise: *I try and work out three times a week.* **4** if a sum, a maths problem, etc. **works out**, it gives a result: *The equation won't work out if x is negative.*

◆ v + adv

▸ **'workout** *n* a period of physical exercise: *I did a two-hour workout in the gym.*

,**work sb 'out** (*especially BrE*) to understand sb's character: *I've never been able to work my mother out.*

SYN figure sb out
NOTE Not used in the passive.

◆ v + n/pron + adv ◆ v + adv + n (*rare*)

work sth 'out 1 to calculate sth: *You'll have to work out the costs involved.* ◊ *Can you work out the answer to number 2?* ◊ *I worked out that we owe him £30.* ◊ *Let me pay for now and we'll work it out later.* **OBJ** cost, answer **SYN** figure sth out **2** to find the answer to a question or sth that is difficult to understand or explain: *I couldn't work out how Jack had got there so quickly.* ◊ *We worked out that we were second cousins.* ◊ *Can you work out what's going on?* ◊ *The game was fairly simple once we'd worked out the rules.* **SYN** figure sth out **NOTE** Work sth out is often used with *how, where, why*, etc. **3** to

plan sth; to think of sth: *I've worked out a better way of doing it.* ◊ *The details still have to be worked out.* **OBJ** details, plan, way **4** to organize sth or deal with problems in an acceptable way: *Ed and Jane seem to have **worked things out** between them.* **SYN** sort sth out **5** to continue to work at your job until the end of the period of time mentioned: *They didn't make me work out my notice* (= the period of time that is officially fixed before you can leave your job). ◊ *He didn't want to work out the rest of his years in an office.* **6** to remove all the coal or metal from a mine: *Most of the mines had been worked out.* **SYN** exhaust sth **NOTE** Often used in the passive.

◆ v + n/pron + adv ◆ v + adv + n

,**work itself 'out** if a problem **works itself out**, it gradually stops being a problem without anyone having to do anything: *Did you think everything would just work itself out?* **SYN** sort itself out

◆ v + pron + adv

,**work sb 'over** to attack sb physically and injure them, either as a punishment or to get information from them: *They sent the boys round to work him over.*

◆ v + n/pron + adv ◆ v + adv + n

,**work 'round sth, etc.** (*BrE*) → WORK AROUND STH, ETC.

work sth out

clear sth up ◆ **crack sth** ◆ **figure sb/sth out** ◆ **solve sth** ◆ **unravel sth** ◆ **work sth out**

These verbs all mean to find the correct answer or explanation for sth.

clear sth up (*not formal*) to solve or explain sth that is mysterious or confusing: *Police are desperate to have this murder cleared up.*

crack sth (*not formal*) to find the solution to sth such as a crime or problem: *We need some more solid evidence if we're going to crack the case.* ◊ *I think we've **cracked it**.*

figure sb/sth out (*not formal*) to think about sth until you understand it, especially how to do sth, what has happened, etc.: *I can't figure out how to do this.* ◊ *I've never been able to figure her out.*

solve sth to find the solution to a problem or explanation for sth that is difficult to understand or explain: *We were given clues to help us solve the puzzle.* ◊ *The mystery has not yet been completely solved.*

unravel sth to explain sth that is mysterious or difficult to understand: *The discovery will help us unravel the secrets of the Ice Age.*

work sth out (*not formal*) to think about sth until you understand it, especially how to do sth, what has happened, etc.: *I'm trying to work how I could possibly have spent $150 last night.*

WHICH WORD?

Work sth out is used more in British English and **figure sb/sth out** is used more in American English. However, if you are talking about understanding sb's character and behaviour **figure sb out** is used in both British and American English.

PATTERNS AND COLLOCATIONS

- to work out/figure out **how/what/where/who/why…**
- to solve/work out **a puzzle/an equation**
- to solve/clear up/crack/unravel a **case/mystery**
- to solve/clear up a **crime/murder/question/problem**
- to work out/figure out **the answer/solution**

,work 'through to work without stopping for a particular period of time: *At harvest time we work through until it gets dark.*
♦ v + adv

,work 'through; ,work 'through sth **1** to start to have an effect somewhere: *These pressures have worked through to the staff.* ◇ *The full effects of the change will take time to work through the system.* **2** to move or pass through sth gradually until you reach a particular point: *I started at page one and slowly* **worked my way through** *to the end.* ◇ *You shouldn't try to work through the course too fast.* ◇ *Allow time for the drug to work through your body.*
♦ v + adv ♦ v + prep

,work 'through sth **1** to experience a problem, a difficult situation, etc., and deal with it until you eventually find a solution: *to work through grief/emotions* ◇ *Counselling is helping him work through this trauma.* ◇ *The situation was difficult for the family, but they were able to work through it and come out the other side.* **2** (*also* **work sth 'through** *less frequent*) to think or talk about sth carefully until you can find a solution: *If you are having problems in your relationship, take time to work through it with your partner.* ◇ *Work the problem through together.*
♦ **1** v + prep
♦ **2** v + prep ♦ v + n/pron + adv (*less frequent*)

'work to sth to follow a plan, etc.: *We're working to a very tight schedule.* ◇ *They have to work to a budget.*
♦ v + prep

,work to'wards sth (*also* ,work to'ward sth *especially AmE*) to try to reach or achieve a goal: *She's working towards her PhD.* ◇ *The two groups are working towards the same end.* ◇ *Jo's working towards obtaining a Master's degree.*
♦ v + prep

,work sb 'up; ,work yourself 'up (into sth) to gradually make sb/yourself become very upset, angry or excited about sth: *She had worked herself up into a rage.* ◇ *He worked the crowd up into a frenzy.* ◇ *You've worked yourself up into a state again. Try and relax.*
♦ v + n/pron + adv ♦ v + adv + n
▸ ,worked 'up (about sth) *adj* (not used before a noun) (*informal*) very excited, upset or angry about sth: *What was Ben so worked up about?* ◇ *I can't get at all worked up about cars* (= I am not interested in or excited by cars). ◇ *She gets terribly worked up* (= nervous) *about exams.*

,work sth 'up **1** to gradually develop or increase sth until you have enough: *We jogged up the hill to work up an appetite.* ◇ *I can't work up much enthusiasm for this subject.* ◇ *She soon worked up a sweat.* **2** (into sth) to spend time and effort on a piece of work in order to improve or complete it: *The idea needs a lot of working up.* ◇ *You could*

work up this idea into a story. ◇ *Some of the sketches were worked up into paintings.*
♦ v + adv + n ♦ v + n/pron + adv

,work 'up to sth **1** to gradually prepare for and move towards sth that is more exciting or extreme: *He started slowly and worked up to running ten miles a day.* ◇ *The tension works up to a climax towards the end of the film.* **2** to prepare yourself to do sth difficult or unpleasant: *I haven't told him yet but I'm working up to it.* [SYN] **build up (to sth)**
♦ v + adv + prep

worm /wɜːm; *AmE* wɜːrm/

,worm your way/yourself 'into sth (*informal, disapproving*) to gradually make sb like or trust you, especially in order to gain an advantage for yourself: *Somehow he managed to* **worm his way into** *her confidence.*
[OBJ] **confidence, affections, heart**
♦ v + n/pron + prep

,worm sth 'out of sb (*informal*) to manage to obtain information from sb, often by asking them questions in a clever way for a long period of time: *It took me days to worm the truth out of my daughter.*
♦ v + n/pron + adv + prep

worry /'wʌri; *AmE* 'wɜːri/ (worries, worrying, worried)

'worry at sth (*often used in the progressive tenses*) **1** if an animal such as a dog **worries at sth**, it holds it in its teeth and shakes it about: *a dog worrying at a bone* ◇ (*figurative*) *She worried at the knot in the string* (= with her fingers). **2** to think or talk a lot about a problem and try to find a solution: *He lay awake all night worrying at the problem.*
♦ v + prep

wrap /ræp/ (-pp-)

,wrap sth a'round sb/sth (*BrE also* ,wrap sth 'round sb/sth) to put sth firmly around sth/sb: *He wrapped his arms tightly around my waist.* ◇ *A long scarf was wrapped round her neck.*
♦ v + n/pron + prep
▸ 'wrap-around *adj* [only before noun] going all or most of the way around sth: *The balcony has a wrap-around view of the sea* (= a very wide view). ◇ *wrap-around sunglasses* (= that fit closely and curve round the sides of the head) ◇ *a wrap-around skirt* (= that is closed by passing one part over another)

,wrap 'up; ,wrap it 'up (*slang*) used to tell sb rudely to stop talking and be quiet: *Oh wrap up and let somebody else say something!*
♦ v + adv ♦ v + it + adv

,wrap 'up (in sth), ,wrap sb 'up (in sth), ,wrap yourself 'up (in sth) to put warm clothes, etc. on yourself/sb: *Wrap up warm—it's really cold outside.* ◇ *I wrapped the twins up before letting* them go out. ◇ *We were all well wrapped up against the weather.* ◇ *I wrapped myself up against the cold.*

SYN **bundle up, bundle sb up (in sth)**
♦ v + adv ♦ v + n/pron + adv ♦ v + adv + n

wrap sth 'up 1 (in sth) to cover sth in paper or other material, to protect it or because you are giving it to sb as a present: *I wrapped the vase up in tissue paper.* ◇ *It took all the evening to wrap up the kids' presents.* ◇ (*figurative*) *There's a simple explanation wrapped up in all those long words.* **SYN** **do sth up (in sth)** **NOTE** Wrap sth is often used on its own with this meaning. **2** to complete sth in an acceptable way: *The discussions should be wrapped up by Friday.* ◇ *Well, I think that just about wraps it up for today.*
♦ v + n/pron + adv ♦ v + adv + n

▶ **'wrap-up** *n* (*especially AmE*) **1** a short summary of what has gone before, especially at the end of a news broadcast: *And to close, here is a wrap-up of today's developments.* **2** the final actions that complete sth: *the wrap-up of the campaign*

be ˌwrapped 'up in sb/sth to be so involved in a person or an activity that you do not notice other people or what is happening around you: *He was so wrapped up in his book that he didn't notice me leaving.* ◇ *Julia is completely wrapped up in her children.*
♦ be + v + adv + prep

wrench /rentʃ/

ˌwrench sth 'off; ˌwrench sth 'off sth to remove sth from sth by force with a strong twisting movement: *The tug of the rope nearly wrenched my arm off.* ◇ *He wrenched the picture off the wall and threw it to the ground.*
♦ v + n/pron + adv ♦ v + adv + n ♦ v + n/pron + prep

wrest /rest/

'wrest sth from sb/sth (*formal*) **1** to take sth such as power or control from sb/sth with great effort: *The rebels tried to wrest control of the town from government forces.* **2** to take sth from sb that they do not want to give, suddenly or violently: *The officer managed to wrest the gun from his grasp.*
♦ v + n/pron + prep

wrestle /'resl/

'wrestle with sth to struggle to deal with sth difficult: *Farmers are wrestling with the problem of the wet weather.* ◇ *He spent several more weeks wrestling with his conscience and then finally decided to resign.* ◇ *He wrestled with the reins as the horse galloped towards the cliff edge.*
SYN **grapple with sth**
♦ v + prep

wriggle /'rɪgl/

ˌwriggle 'out of sth; ˌwriggle 'out of doing sth (*informal*) to avoid doing sth unpleasant or sth that you do not want to do by making clever excuses: *to wriggle out of your responsibilities* ◇ *I've got an appointment I can't wriggle out of.* ◇ *Don't let Tom wriggle out of helping you.*
♦ v + adv + prep

wring /rɪŋ/ (wrung, wrung /rʌŋ/)

'wring sth from sb → WRING STH OUT OF/ FROM SB

ˌwring sth 'out to remove water or other liquid from a cloth, etc. by twisting it tightly and squeezing it: *Rinse the cloth and wring it out well.* ◇ *My clothes got so wet I could wring the water out!*
♦ v + n/pron + adv ♦ v + adv + n

be/get ˌwrung 'out (*AmE*) to feel extremely tired and in poor health: *David and I had had a big fight, and I was feeling completely wrung out.*
♦ be/get + v + adv

'wring sth out of/from sb to obtain sth from sb with difficulty, especially by putting pressure on them: *She eventually wrung an apology out of him.* ◇ *A few concessions were wrung from the government.*
♦ v + n/pron + prep

write /raɪt/ (wrote /rəʊt/, written /'rɪtn/)

ˌwrite a'way (to sb) (for sth) → WRITE OFF/ AWAY: *I wrote away to the company for a free sample.*

ˌwrite 'back (to sb) to write in reply to sb's letter: *I wrote and apologized, but he never wrote back.* ◇ *The school wrote back to me saying that all the courses were full.*
♦ v + adv

ˌwrite sth 'down (in/on sth) 1 to write sth on paper so that you do not forget it: *I wrote her address down in my notebook.* ◇ *There is a handout so you needn't write all this down.* **SYN** **take sth down 2** (*business*) to reduce the value of what a company owns when stating it in the company's accounts: *All stock over six months old was written down to 50%.*
♦ v + n/pron + adv ♦ v + adv + n

▶ **'write-down** *n* (*business*) a reduction in the value of a company owns, etc.

ˌwrite 'in (to sb/sth) to write a letter to an organization to state an opinion or to ask a question: *Write in to the programme and tell us your own opinion on this.* ◇ *500 viewers wrote in to complain about the advertisement.*
♦ v + adv

ˌwrite sb/sth 'in (*AmE*) to add an extra name to a list of candidates in an election so that you can vote for them: *She wrote Carrasco in on the ballot paper.* ◇ *Workers were handing out sample ballots with their candidate's name written in.*
♦ v + n/pron + adv ♦ v + adv + n

write

write sth down

note sth down ◆ **pencil sth in** ◆ **put sth down** ◆ **take sth down** ◆ **write sth down**

note sth down to write down sth important so that you do not forget it: *He carefully noted down all their names and addresses.*

pencil sth in to write down sb's name or details of an arrangement with them that you know might have to be changed later: *I'll pencil in the meeting for Friday.* NOTE **Pencil in** does not necessarily mean that a pencil is used.

put sth down to write sth on paper, especially in order to remember or record it: *The meeting's on the 22nd. Put it down in your diary.* ◇ *One day I'm going to put it all down in writing.*

take sth down to write sth down, especially what sb is saying, at the time that they are saying it: *Reporters were taking down every word he said.* NOTE **Take** can be used on its own when the object is **notes**: *Did you take notes at the lecture?*

write sth down to write sth on paper, especially to in order to remember or record it: *Write down the name and address before you forget it.*

PATTERNS AND COLLOCATIONS

- to write sth down/put sth down/note sth down/take sth down **in** sth/**with** sth
- to write sth down/put sth down/note sth down **on** sth
- to write down/put down your **name**
- to write down/put down/take (down) some **notes**

▶ **'write-in** *adj* (*AmE*) a vote for sb who is not an official candidate in an election, in which you write their name on your voting paper: *He qualified as a write-in in 15 states.* ◇ *a write-in candidate/vote*

,**write sb/sth 'in**; ,**write sb/sth 'into sth** to add a character or a scene to a play, a film/movie, a regular series, etc.: *Why did you write the plane crash in?* ◇ *It was the first time a disabled child had been written into a TV soap.* ◇ *He* **wrote** *himself* **into the history books** *by becoming the first player to win the championship five times.*
OPP ,**write sb/sth out, write sb/sth out of sth**
◆ v + n/pron + adv ◆ v + adv + n ◆ v + n/pron + prep

,**write sth 'in**; ,**write sth 'into sth** to include sth such as a special rule or a condition in a document, a contract, an agreement, etc.: *A get-out clause was written into the contract.*
◆ v + n/pron + adv ◆ v + adv + n ◆ v + n/pron + prep

,**write 'off/a'way (to sb) (for sth)** to write to an organization or a company, asking them to send you sth: *She wrote off to an agency for advice.*
SYN **send off (for sth), send away (for sth)**
◆ v + adv

,**write sb/sth 'off (as sth)** to consider that sb/sth is a failure or not important: *Don't write John off too soon—he may surprise you!* ◇ *I wrote off my symptoms as tiredness.*
◆ v + n/pron + adv ◆ v + adv + n

▶ **'write-off** *n* [sing.] (*informal*) a failure; a time when you do not achieve anything: *Today has been a write-off as far as work is concerned.*

,**write sth 'off 1** (*business*) to cancel a debt; to recognize that sth is a failure, has no value, etc.: *All outstanding Third World debts should now be written off.* **2** (*BrE*) to damage a vehicle so badly

that it is not worth spending money to repair it: *That's the third car he's written off this year.*
◆ v + n/pron + adv ◆ v + adv + n

▶ **'write-off** *n* **1** (*business*) an act of cancelling a debt and accepting that it will never be paid: *a £4.9 billion debt write-off* **2** (*BrE, informal*) a vehicle that is so badly damaged that it is not considered worth repairing: *They escaped with minor injuries but the van was a write-off.*

,**write sb/sth 'out**; ,**write sb/sth 'out of sth** to remove a character, a scene, etc. from a play, a film/movie, a regular series, etc.: *He got bored and asked to be written out of the series.* ◇ *The censor demanded that the scene be written out.*
OPP ,**write sb/sth in, write sb/sth into sth**
◆ v + n/pron + adv ◆ v + adv + n
◆ v + n/pron + adv + prep

,**write sth 'out** to write sth on paper clearly, including all the details: *Use symbols and abbreviations instead of writing things out in full.* ◇ *I wrote out the poem in my best hand-writing.* ◇ *I watched him write out a cheque for her.*
NOTE In informal spoken language **write sb out sth** is also used: *He wrote her out a cheque.*
◆ v + n/pron + adv ◆ v + n/pron + adv

,**write sb 'up** (*AmE*) to make an official report or complaint about sb in writing: *He wrote me up for illegal parking.* ◇ *The principal wrote him up for talking back to his teachers.*
◆ v + n/pron + adv ◆ v + adv + n

▶ **'write-up** *n* (*AmE*) an official report or complaint

,**write sth 'up 1** to write sth in a complete and final form, especially from notes that you have made: *She writes her lecture notes up every night before going out.* OBJ **notes, research, experi-**

ment **2** to write a review of a play, a concert, a book, etc. for a newspaper or magazine: *She wrote the movie up in glowing terms.*
◆ v + n/pron + adv ◆ v + adv + n
▶ **'write-up** *n* a review of a concert, a play, a book, etc. in a newspaper or magazine: *The concert got a good write-up in all the papers.*

X x

X /eks/ (**x's, x'ing, x'ed**)
,**x sth 'out** (*AmE, informal*) to put an 'x' through a written word, etc. to show that it is a mistake: *She x'ed out the final word in the sentence.*
SYN **cross sb/sth out**
◆ v + n/pron + adv ◆ v + adv + n

Y y

yank /jæŋk/
'yank at sth to pull at sth hard and quickly: *Someone yanked at my hair.*
◆ v + prep
,**yank sth 'off**; ,**yank sth 'off sth** to remove sth by pulling it quickly and hard: *He yanked off his shoes.* ◇ *She yanked the lid off the tin.*
◆ v + adv + n ◆ v + n/pron + adv ◆ v + n/pron + prep
,**yank sb/sth 'out**; ,**yank sb/sth 'out of sth** (*informal*) to remove sb/sth from somewhere by pulling hard and quickly: *He was yanked out of the house and bundled into a car.*
◆ v + n/pron + adv ◆ v + n/pron + adv + prep

yearn /jɜːn; *AmE* jɜːrn/
'yearn for sb/sth (*literary*) to want sb/sth very much, especially when this is difficult to get: *Mira yearned for a child.*
SYN **long for sb/sth**
◆ v + prep

yell /jel/
,**yell 'out**; ,**yell sth 'out** to suddenly shout sth in a loud voice: *She was yelling out in terror.* ◇ *He yelled out the names of the winners.*
◆ v + adv ◆ v + adv + n ◆ v + n/pron + adv
◆ v + adv + speech

yield /jiːld/
'yield to sth (*formal*) to be replaced by sth: *Barges yielded to road vehicles for transporting goods.*
◆ v + prep
'yield sth 'up (*formal*) **1** to allow sb else to take sth that you own and feel is very important for

you: *He swore he would never yield up the castle to the English.* **2** to reveal sth that has been hidden: *A thorough search of the site yielded up only a few ancient coins.*
◆ v + adv + n ◆ v + n/pron + adv

Z z

zero /'zɪərəʊ; *AmE* 'zɪroʊ, 'ziː-/ (**zeroes, zeroing, zeroed, zeroed**)
,**zero 'in on sb/sth 1** to aim weapons at sb/sth: *They zeroed in on the target.* ◇ (*figurative*) *Clare zeroed in on Craig* (= went to talk to him) *as soon as he entered the room.* **2** to fix all your attention on sb/sth: *Wasting no time, she zeroed in on the main topic.*
◆ v + adv + prep

zhoozh /ʒuːʒ/ (*also* **zhush** /ʒʊʃ/)
,**zhoozh sth 'up** (*informal*) to make sth more attractive or exciting: *Colin and Justin will be showing us some ideas to zhoozh up your Christmas decorations.* ◇ *Zhoozh up a salad with a little chilli oil.*
SYN **jazz sth up; juice sth up** (*especially AmE*); **liven sth up; spice sth up**
◆ v + adv + n ◆ v + n/pron + adv

zip /zɪp/ (**-pp-**)
NOTE A **zip** is a device consisting of two rows of metal or plastic teeth that you can pull together or pull apart.
,**zip 'through sth** to do, read, etc. sth very quickly: *Could you zip through my report and check it's OK?*
◆ v + prep
,**zip 'up**; ,**zip sb/sth 'up** to be fastened with a zip; to fasten sth with a zip: *The skirt zips up at the side.* ◇ *Will you zip me up* (= my dress), *please?* ◇ *I can't zip my jacket up!*
OPP **unzip sth**
◆ v + adv ◆ v + n/pron + adv ◆ v + adv + n
▶ **'zip-up** *adj* [only before noun] fastened with a zip: *a zip-up jacket*

zone /zəʊn; *AmE* zoʊn/
,**zone sth 'off** (**for sth**) to keep an area of land to be used for a particular purpose: *The city centre has been zoned off for pedestrians.*
◆ v + adv + n ◆ v + n/pron + adv
,**zone 'out** (*AmE, slang*) to fall asleep, become unconscious or stop paying attention: *Relax, take a deep breath, and zone out for a while.*
SYN **space out, space sb out** (*slang*)
◆ v + adv
▶ **'zone-out** *n* a time when you stop thinking or noticing what is going on around you

▶ ˌzoned 'out *adj* (*AmE, informal*) unable to think or to notice what is going on around you because of the effects of drugs or alcohol

zonk /zɒŋk; *AmE* zɑːŋk/

ˌzonk 'out; ˌzonk sb 'out (*slang, especially AmE*) to fall asleep, become unconscious or unable to think, either because you are very tired or because of the effects of drugs or alcohol; to make sb do this: *He zonked out after the big exam.* ◊ *I usually zonk out about 11 p.m.*
◆ v + adv ◆ v + n/pron + adv
▶ ˌzonked 'out *adj* (*slang, especially AmE*) sleeping, unconscious, or unable to think, especially from the effects of drugs or alcohol: *I feel totally zonked out after the day's work.*

zoom /zuːm/

NOTE A **zoom lens** is one that you use to make the thing that you are photographing appear nearer to you or further away from you than it really is.

ˌzoom 'in/'out (on sb/sth) if a camera **zooms in/out**, it shows the object that is being photographed from closer/further away, by using a zoom lens: *The camera zoomed in on her beautiful eyes.*
◆ v + adv
ˌzoom 'off (*informal*) to hurry away: *He jumped into his car and zoomed off.*
◆ v + adv

Guide to the particles

Introduction

This Guide deals with the main categories of meaning of the particles that occur most frequently in the verbs in this dictionary. Knowing something about the different meanings of particles can help you learn and understand how phrasal verbs are formed and help you understand new ones when you meet them. For a list of the particles used in phrasal verbs, see page ix.

When you look at verbs used with a particular particle, you can see that one particle can have several different meanings. The most obvious starting point is the basic or literal meaning of the particle, since this often combines with verbs to produce a meaning that you can easily recognize. For example, the basic meaning of the particle **down** involves 'movement from a higher position to a lower position'. It can be used in combination with a verb as a preposition: *He climbed down the mountain*; or as an adverb: *Come down at once!* This meaning

of **down** can help you to understand its more figurative use in other verbs. For example, **down** can also be used to express the related ideas of 'reducing something': *Turn down that radio*; 'keeping something low': *to keep down the rate of inflation*; or 'removing somebody from a powerful position': *to bring down the government*.

This shows that there is a system to the way phrasal verbs are formed. In other words, the combination of verbs and particles is not totally random. It also explains how new phrasal verbs come to be created, and how they can be understood even by people who have never heard them before.

The Guide lists the particles in alphabetical order, with their main meanings. After the explanation of the meaning, some verbs belonging to the group are given. For more information on how each verb in the lists is used, you should look the verb up in the dictionary.

ABOUT

About is often used to show the connection between the verb and its object, for example, *talk about something, worry about something*. In some of the meanings, the particles around and, especially in British English, round can be used instead.

Moving in different directions: *She got angry and started throwing things about.*

About can be used to indicate that you are moving in different directions or making rough or violent movements. The verb shows what kind of movement it is.

run about   crash about   throw about

Around and round can usually be used with the same meaning. About is used with a variety of other verbs to make a similar meaning, for example *jump about, scatter about*.

Doing nothing: *Groups of youths were hanging about with nothing to do.*

About is used with many verbs that suggest

you are spending your time in a lazy way. Other verbs refer to a silly way of behaving.

hang about   wander about   mess about

Around and round can usually be used with the same meaning. You can also add about to a variety of other verbs to make a similar meaning: for example, *faff about, muck about, potter about*.

Making something happen: *What has brought about this change in public opinion?*

About is used with some verbs to indicate something happening or somebody making something happen:

come about   bring about   set about

Surrounding and enclosing: *She threw her arms about me and hugged me.*

About can be used with some verbs to give the idea of something going around something and surrounding or enclosing it:

throw about   hedge about

Around and round are more common with this meaning.

AROUND

The basic meaning of around is of movement in a circle or curve to face in the opposite direction or to arrive at the other side of something, for example, *spin around, turn around, go around*. Round is often used instead of around, especially in British English. About is also sometimes used.

Moving in different directions: *The park was full of children running around.*

Around is used with some verbs to indicate movement in different directions or to many different places:

run around   bustle around
shop around

Round and about can be used in these verbs (*shop around* is an exception). Around can be used with many other verbs: *dance around, rush around, crash around,* etc.

Doing nothing: *Stop messing around and find something useful to do.*

Around can be used in verbs that suggest that you are spending your time in a lazy way. Other verbs refer to a silly way of behaving.

hang around   fool around

About can also be used with these verbs.

Surrounding and enclosing: *She threw her arms around his neck.*

Around can be used with some verbs to suggest surrounding someone or something:

crowd around   throw around
cluster around

Round can also be used with these verbs.

Being centred on something: *Their life revolves around going to parties.*

Around is used as a preposition with some verbs to suggest the idea of something having a particular idea, object, etc. as its centre or focus:

centre around   revolve around

Avoiding: *We'll have to find a way of getting around the problem.*

Around with verbs can be used to indicate that you are avoiding something:

skirt around   get around
skate around   work around

AT

At is a common word in English and is often used to show where something or somebody is in space or time.

Aiming and directing: *Stop staring at me!*

At is used with many verbs to give the idea of aiming or directing something at someone or something:

laugh at   look at   stare at
talk at   aim at   nag at

Attacking, striking and holding: *He struck at me several times with a knife.*

At can be used with verbs to give the idea of trying to attack, hit or hold someone or something:

strike at   fly at
grab at   get at

AWAY

The basic meaning of away indicates movement to a different place and it can be used with most verbs of movement, for example, *go away, run away, hurry away, drive away*. Off can be used instead of away with a similar meaning. Away often combines with another particle, particularly from, for example, *run away from, walk away from, do away with*.

Avoiding and not doing something: *Keep away from the edge of the water.*

Away is used with some verbs to show that somebody is avoiding a person, a place or a situation or is stopping being involved in something:

keep away   look away
back away   walk away from

Separating: *They broke away from the rest of the group.*

Away is used with some verbs giving the meaning of becoming separated from something or from a group of people or of making this happen:

come away   break away   call away
peel away   sheer away   strip away

Removing: *This is rubbish. Throw it away!*

Away is used with some verbs to give the idea of removing something from a particular place because you no longer want or need it, or of destroying something:

throw away   *frighten away*
do away with   *blast away*

Disappearing: *The shouts and cheers died away.*

Away is used with some verbs to give the idea of something disappearing gradually:

die away   *fade away*   *waste away*
wear away   *pass away*   *pine away*

Storing and hiding: *Put away your books now.*

Away can be used with some verbs to convey the idea of putting something in a place either to keep it safe or to stop people finding it:

put away   *file away*   *tidy away*
hide away   *clear away*   *lock away*

Working hard or continuously: *She spent hours working away at the problem.*

Away can be used to indicate that you are doing something, especially working hard or doing something difficult or boring, for a long period of time:

slog away   *work away*   *slave away*
bang away   *beaver away*   *plod away*

BACK

The basic meaning of back is returning to the place where you were before or to an earlier time. Many verbs of movement use back with this meaning, for example walk back, drive back.

Returning something: *I need to take the books back to the library.*

Back can be used to convey the idea of giving or taking something back to the place it came from. It can also mean reacting or replying to someone in a similar way to the way they have acted or spoken.

take back   *give back*   *write back*
call/ring back   *fight back*

Moving backwards; being behind or at a distance: *Stand back and let the ambulance through.*

Back can be used with verbs to give the idea of moving away from the front or edge of something or of being at a distance from something:

fall back   *stand back*   *keep back*
pull back   *push back*

Not making progress: *The fire has set the project back a few months.*

Back in some combinations suggests being kept or held in a position without making any progress:

hold back   *set back*   *keep back*

Repeating: *He wasn't there, so I phoned back later.*

Back can be used in verbs that express the idea of doing something again:

play back   *go back over*
read back   *call/phone back*

Regaining: *We hope to win the cup back next year.*

Back in combinations can be used with the idea of getting again something that was lost or of recovering from something:

win back   *get back*   *bounce back*
claw back   *ease back*   *grow back*

Being under control: *He tried to force back his tears.*

Back in combinations often means reducing something or keeping something such as an emotion under control:

cut back on   *force back*   *choke back*
bite back   *hold back*

Looking at the past: *This music takes me back to when I lived in Paris.*

Back can be used to talk about the past:

date back   *go back*   *take back*
look back   *think back*

DOWN

Down often has meanings that are the opposite of up. The literal meaning is movement in a downwards direction, moving from a higher to a lower position, for example, *climb down, bend down, fall down.* Many combinations of a verb and down refer to somebody putting something on a surface, for example, *bang down, lay down.* It is also used to express figurative ideas related to downward movement, such as decreasing, being reduced or failing.

Falling and destroying: *That old building should be knocked down.*

This use of the particle is most closely connected to the literal meaning of **down**, and suggests something or somebody falling to the ground and being destroyed or suffering damage:

pull down	*burn down*	*tear down*
knock down	*run down*	*beat down*

Reducing: *Please turn down the music.*

Down is used in many verbs that express the idea of something decreasing in amount, strength, speed, cost, importance, etc., or of somebody making something do this:

turn down	*bring down*	*calm down*
come down	*play down*	*cut down*

Suppressing: *The streets were sprayed to keep down disease.*

Down can be used with verbs to express the idea of keeping somebody or something under control or ending something, often using authority or force:

keep down	*clamp down*
come down on	*break down*

Defeating: *The scandal brought down the government.*

Down can be used to express the idea of defeating someone or something or being defeated in an argument, a competition, etc.:

bring down	*put down*	*vote down*
back down	*shout down*	*stare down*

Failing: *My car has broken down again.*

Down can be used to express the idea of something stopping, failing or not working properly:

break down	*close down*	*turn down*
let down	*wind down*	

Fixing: *We tied down the chairs to stop them from being blown away.*

Down can be used with the idea of fixing something firmly to something else:

tie down	*nail down*	*strap down*
batten down	*screw down*	*stick down*

Recording in writing: *I tried to write down all the relevant points.*

Down is used with verbs meaning writing or copying to give the idea of recording something in writing:

write down	*get down*	*note down*
jot down	*copy down*	*put down*

Eating: *He gulped down a sandwich between lessons.*

Down is used with some verbs to describe ways of eating or drinking:

gulp down	*gobble down*	*bolt down*
keep down	*stay down*	*wash down*

FOR

For is one of the most common words in English. It often combines with verbs to link the verb and its object, for example *ask for something, pay for something.*

Aims and goals: *It was sunny, so we headed for the coast.*

For can be used to refer to the aim or purpose of an action or to where you are going:

apply for	*press for*	*live for*
make for	*head for*	

Feelings towards other people: *After all these years, I still care for you.*

For can be used with some verbs to show how you feel about somebody or something, or to show how you are dealing with a person or a situation:

feel for	*fall for*	*fear for*
root for	*care for*	*stand up for*

IN

The basic meaning of in is 'contained inside something or somewhere', or 'movement from outside to inside'. It is often the opposite of out. The preposition into can also be used with verbs of movement.

Entering: *I would ask you in, but the house is a mess.*

In is used with many verbs with the literal meaning of entering somewhere, for example *go in, come in, walk in, invite in*:

break in	*get in*	*let in*
ask in	*breeze in*	*drop in*

Arriving: *What time did you get in last night?.*

In can be used in verb plus particle combinations that refer to a person, a vehicle, etc. arriving at a particular place:

get in	clock in	check in
pull in	draw in	flood in

Absorbing: *I couldn't take in so much information at one time.*

In can be used with certain verbs to give the idea of absorbing something:

take in	sink in	drink in
breathe in	soak in	

Including: *You can stir in some cream if you like.*

In can be used with some verbs that give the idea of adding or mixing something in something else, or of including something with something else:

add in	stir in	throw in
take in	blend in	fold in

Putting inside or between: *I put my hand in my pocket and took out some money.*

In can be used with some verbs, giving the idea of one thing being put into or going into another:

plug in	put in	key in
lay in	pump in	punch in

Beginning; introducing something new: *The government has brought in a new tax.*

In can be used in verbs that give the idea of something starting or of somebody introducing something new:

set in	bring in	phase in
creep in	usher in	

Collecting: *Can you get the chairs in before it starts raining?*

In can be used in combinations that refer to collecting things:

gather in	get in	pull in
fetch in	pack in	

Filling and completing: *Draw a circle, then colour it in.*

In is used in some combinations that refer to filling a drawing, a shape, a hole, etc. with something and completing it. Other similar verbs refer to writing something somewhere.

colour in	fill in	pencil in
block in	ink in	shade in

Taking part: *I started singing and everyone joined in.*

In is used with many verbs to suggest the idea of joining an activity and being involved in something. Sometimes the involvement of the person is not welcome:

join in	go in for	call in
interfere in	jump in	pitch in

Interrupting: *Don't barge in without knocking.*

In can be used with verbs to express the idea of someone interrupting a conversation or a meeting when the interruption is not wanted or welcome:

cut in	barge in	break in

Limiting: *My car was boxed in, so I couldn't drive away.*

In can be used in combinations that refer to somebody being prevented from leaving a place, or being free to do something:

snow in	block in	lock in
box in	fence in	hem in

Staying inside: *I'm tired – I think I'll stay in tonight.*

In can be used in combinations that mean remaining inside or at home instead of going out somewhere. The particle out can be used with the same verbs with the opposite meaning. In is also used with the meaning 'in bed'.

stay in	eat in	stop in
sleep in	lie in	

Damaging, destroying, falling: *The intruders tried to kick the door in.*

In is used in combinations that mean damaging or destroying things, especially by making them fall inwards. Other verbs refer to things falling inwards.

smash in	kick in	cave in

Stopping doing something: *I tried my best but in the end I gave in.*

In is used in combination with some verbs that mean stopping trying to resist something or giving up something such as your job:

give in	throw in
cave in	jack in

INTO

The literal meaning of **into** is movement from the outside of something to the inside, so it is used with many verbs that give the idea of entering something. It is often used in the same verbs and with the same meanings as the adverb **in**, for example, *burst in, burst into...* The particle can also be used in verbs that express metaphorical meanings, for example changing or being transformed.

Entering: *Thieves broke into the bank at night.*

Into is used in many combinations meaning to enter somewhere:

break into	get into	check into
crowd into	invite into	

Out of is often used with similar verbs as an opposite, for example, *get out of, check out of.*

Putting in, going in: *I dipped my spoon into the sauce.*

Into is used in many combinations referring to putting or going in or inside something:

plug into	tuck into	pay into
bore into	dip into	

Combining: *The houses blend into the background.*

Into is used in combinations that mean mixing one colour, substance, etc. into another so that they become one:

blend into	shade into	mix into
fade into	fold into	

Transforming and changing: *How can a child turn into such a monster?*

Into can be used to describe things that change or are transformed:

turn into	grow into
make into	change into

Persuading and forcing: *They pressed me into accepting the offer.*

Into is used with some verbs to convey the idea of persuading or making someone do something that they do not really want to

do. The verb describes the way you try to persuade somebody.

talk into	press into	frighten into
force into	shame into	starve into

Out of is often used with these verbs with the opposite meaning: *talk somebody out of something.*

Hitting and meeting: *I bumped into the table in the dark.*

Into can be used with verbs that describe objects hitting one another, and to describe people meeting by accident:

bang into	run into	bump into

Investigating: *Police are looking into the incident.*

Into can be used with some verbs that give the idea of investigating something in detail in order to discover the truth:

go into	look into
delve into	dig into

Starting: *The car burst into flames.*

Many combinations with into suggest starting doing something, often suddenly:

burst into	plunge into
rush into	get into

OF

When **of** is used in verb plus particle combinations it shows the relationship between the verb and somebody or something that is involved in the action.

Communicating and interpreting: *Do you know of a shop that sells Italian food?*

Of with some verbs shows that a particular piece of information or knowledge is being communicated to or interpreted by somebody:

hear of	know of	make of
remind of	speak of	

Characteristics and qualities: *This shampoo smells of apples.*

Of can be used with verbs to show the characteristics or qualities of someone or something, or what something contains:

smell of	remind of
make of	consist of

Removing, lacking: *The prince was stripped of his title.*

Of can be used with some verbs to indicate something is being removed from someone or something or that they do not have something:

rob of	starve of	deprive of
dispose of	strip of	

OFF

Off has a wide variety of meanings. It is often used with verbs of movement to indicate movement away from a place, for example, *run off, dash off, hurry off, march off,* where the verb shows how somebody departs. Off can sometimes be replaced by away in this meaning.

Departing: *We set off on our journey at dawn.*

The particle off can be used to give the idea of somebody starting a journey or leaving a place or of making somebody or something do this:

set off	take off	see off
make off	clear off	blast off

Starting: *OK, who wants to start off?*

Off in combinations can also suggest that something is beginning:

start off	spark off	kick off
lead off	touch off	

Ending; not happening: *The search was called off after 48 hours.*

Some verbs can be used with off to give the idea of something ending or being cancelled:

break off	ring off	put off
call off	cut off	log off

Finishing completely: *I have finally paid off all my debts.*

Off can be used with some verbs to emphasize that something is completely finished. Often these are verbs that can also be used on their own with a similar, but weaker, meaning:

finish off	pay off	sell off
go off	polish off	round off

Becoming less: *My headache is starting to wear off.*

Off can be used with some verbs to express the idea of something gradually decreasing in strength or effect:

wear off	level off	cool off
fall off	die off	ease off

Rejecting or dismissing: *He tried to brush me off, but I insisted on getting his name.*

Off is used with some verbs to suggest the idea of rejecting, dismissing or trying to ignore somebody or something:

write off	lay off	shrug off
laugh off	brush off	shake off

Resisting: *The home team fought off a strong challenge from the visitors.*

Some verbs using the particle off indicate that you are trying to stop something happening or trying to protect somebody or yourself from something harmful or unpleasant:

fight off	hold off	ward off
beat off	fend off	keep off

Removing: *Please cross my name off the list.*

Off is used with some verbs to give the idea of removing something from somewhere, for example by cutting or chopping. Some combinations of verbs have the idea of removing someone from your responsibility.

cut off	cross off	take off
palm off on	bump off	rub off

Dividing and separating: *Police have sealed off the city centre.*

In these combinations, off indicates that one area is divided or separated from another, for example with a barrier, to stop somebody or something going into it:

block off	fence off	seal off
curtain off	divide off	shut off

Being absent from work or school: *I'd like to take Thursday off, if that's OK.*

Off can be used with some verbs to talk about not going to work or school or leaving early:

take off	skive off
slip off	bunk off

Drawing attention: *He likes showing off his new sports car.*

Off occurs in combination with some verbs that indicate that someone is drawing attention to themselves or their opinions in some way. Other combinations describe how something draws attention to something else or makes it easy to see.

show off	set off
sound off	mouth off

Using: *The hairdryer can also work off batteries.*

Off can be used with some verbs to talk about things that are used, such as money, food, etc.:

live off	feed off
run off	work off

On can also be used with these verbs with a similar meaning.

Exploding: *The bomb went off before it could be made safe.*

This group of verbs is used for things such as weapons, that explode or are fired:

set off	blast off	go off
let off	fire off	

Cheating: *I've been ripped off lots of times by taxi drivers.*

Off is used with some verbs to indicate that something is done dishonestly or with the intention of cheating someone:

rip off	fob off
palm off	pass off as

ON

The basic meaning of on describes the position of one thing above or on top of another or resting on something. It is also used in combination with verbs of movement, where the preposition onto is also sometimes used. With some of these verbs it is the opposite of off (for example *get on the bus, get off the bus*).

Continuing: *I asked him to stop, but he carried on.*

The particle on can be used with many verbs to show that something continues and does not stop. It can also mean that you stop for a short time and then continue: *We spent a few days in Seattle and then flew on to L.A.* It can also be used in this way to express the idea of continuing to do something difficult or unpleasant, for example, *fight on, struggle on.* In other cases it suggests that something is continuing for too long, for example *drag on, drone on.*

keep on	stay on	go on
carry on	hurry on	move on

Developing and changing: *My French is coming on very well.*

On can be used with some verbs to talk about the way things are progressing or changing:

get on	come on	move on

Encouraging: *Come on, we're almost there!*

On in combination with some verbs gives the idea of supporting somebody or encouraging someone to do something:

urge on	come on
egg on	spur on

Starting: *I switched on my computer and started work.*

On can be used in verbs that talk about starting an activity or making a machine begin to work:

bring on	sign on	turn on
switch on	put on	

Off is often used with the some of these verbs with the opposite meaning (for example, *turn on the radio, turn off the radio*).

Holding and connecting: *I held on to stop myself from falling.*

On can be used in combinations to express the idea of holding something tightly. Other verbs describe how things are connected or attached to each other:

hang on	hold on	strap on
latch on	cling on	fasten on

Dressing: *Put on you coat before you go out.*

On can be used with different verbs to talk about ways of getting dressed:

put on	try on
pull on	slip on

Attacking: *They pick on people who are smaller than themselves.*

Some verbs with **on** indicate that someone is being attacked, either physically or with words:

| turn on | pick on | round on |
| jump on | set on | start on |

Thinking and commenting: *I haven't decided on the colour yet.*

On is used with some verbs of thinking or deciding to show what you are thinking or talking about:

| reflect on | decide on |
| touch on | sleep on |

Finding: *I suddenly hit on the solution.*

On is used with some verbs that mean finding something or someone suddenly or unexpectedly:

| hit on | stumble on | chance on |

Depending: *You can count on Gary to help you.*

On is often used with verbs to indicate that one thing is affected by or decided by something else. **On** can also indicate the person or thing that you trust or feel sure about.

| depend on | rely on |
| count on | hinge on |

OUT

The basic meaning of **out** is of movement from inside to outside, so it combines with many verbs of movement, for example, *storm out, rush out, go out.* Many verbs that combine with **out** also combine with the adverb plus preposition out of, for example, *storm out, storm out of the room.* **Out** and **in** can sometimes be used with the same verbs to express opposite meanings (for example, *go out, go in*).

Leaving: *We set out on our trip early in the morning.*

Out can be used in verbs that mean starting a journey or going away from a person or a place:

| set out | pop out |
| check out | start out |

Searching, observing, solving: *Can you find out if there's a train at that time?*

Out in some combinations gives the idea of searching for something such as a piece of information, the answer to a difficult problem, etc. and then finding it:

| find out | dig out | make out |
| turn out | hunt out | sort out |

Disappearing; using completely: *Why did the dinosaurs die out?*

Out can be used in phrasal verbs to suggest that something is gradually disappearing or has been used completely so that there is none left:

| die out | run out |
| go out | phase out |

Stopping an activity

Out is used in some verbs that describe an activity being stopped, often by using force or authority. Some verbs describe people or places being completely destroyed. Other verbs refer to a fire, etc. going out or being put out.

| stamp out | cut out | wipe out |
| burn out | beat out | blow out |

Stopping being involved: *The German runner has dropped out of the race.*

Out can be used in combinations that show that you are no longer involved in something or no longer want to be involved:

| fall out | pull out | bottle out |
| chicken out | drop out | opt out |

Producing: *We can turn out 200 cars a day.*

Out can used with verbs to talk about things being produced, especially when they are produced quickly and in large quantities:

| turn out | churn out |
| spill out | pour out |

Being outside: *They stayed out all night.*

Out can be used in combinations that express the idea of somebody going out of a place, such as their home, or doing something outside:

| get out | camp out | eat out |
| stay out | go out | lock out |

Speaking or shouting loudly: *I shouted out for help.*

Out can be used with some verbs that suggest that somebody is speaking loudly or angrily, perhaps to call for help or shout a warning:

bark out	*call out*	*scream out*
shout out	*snap out*	*yell out*

Sharing: *Can you help me to hand out the photocopies?*

Out can be used to convey the idea of something being distributed to or shared among people:

hand out	*give out*	*share out*
dish out	*dole out*	*serve out*

Finishing: *That walk has tired me out.*

Out can be used to convey the idea of something being completely finished or done:

hear out	*dry out*	*talk out*
tire out	*wear out*	

Out is often used to create new verbs that mean you have completely finished doing something and can do no more. For example: *I'm all partied out* (= I have been to so many parties that I can't go to any more).

Removing: *I'd like to throw out this old coat.*

Out is used with some verbs that mean removing something or somebody from somewhere, or removing yourself from somewhere:

take out	*knock out*	*pull out*
push out	*throw out*	*wash out*

Excluding: *If you can't answer a question, just leave it out.*

Out can be used in combinations that express the idea that someone or something is not included in an activity, a list, etc.:

leave out	*cross out*	*rule out*
filter out	*keep out*	*weed out*

Supporting: *Peter said he didn't mind helping out occasionally.*

Out is used with phrasal verbs that suggest helping or supporting somebody, especially by giving money, advice or encouragement:

help out	*bear out*	*bring out*
draw out	*reach out to*	

Choosing: *She asked me to pick out a present for myself.*

Out can be used to convey the idea of something being chosen from among many others:

pick out	*single out*	*pull out*
mark out	*separate out*	*sort out*

Lasting: *I don't think I can hold out much longer.*

Out can be used to convey the idea of resisting some kind of pressure or enduring a difficult situation:

hold out	*stick out*
last out	*ride out*

Attacking; reacting violently: *She lashed out at her attackers.*

Out can be used in verbs that show that someone is attacking somebody or reacting violently to something:

lash out	*strike out*	*fight out*
hit out	*kick out*	*shoot out*

Recording on paper: *We copied out the words of the song.*

Out can be used with verbs connected with writing or drawing to give the idea of something being recorded or written down on paper:

copy out	*sketch out*
map out	*write out*

Increasing: *You can spread out the map on the floor.*

Out is used with some verbs that show that something or somebody is increasing in size, shape, extent, etc.:

broaden out	*fill out*	*flesh out*
open out	*spread out*	

OVER

The basic meaning of over indicates movement from one side of something to the other, especially over the top of something (for example, *climb over a wall, fly over a city, cross over a road*). It can also indicate a position above something (*bend over something, lean over someone*).

Having a higher position: *My son towers over me.*

Over can be used to suggest that someone or something is taller or in a higher position than somebody or something else. It can also refer to somebody in a position of greater authority or responsibility.

tower over	*stand over*	*rule over*
preside over	*watch over*	

Covering: *The lake was completely frozen over.*

Over can be used in combination with verbs to show that something is completely covered with something such as ice or clouds. It is also used in a more figurative way to suggest that a difficulty or the truth is being hidden.

freeze over	*cloud over*	*gloss over*
paint over	*paper over*	

Moving to the side: *The driver pulled over to the side of the road to take a short break.*

A few verbs use over to indicate movement to the side of something:

pull over	*move over*

Visiting: *The neighbours have asked us over for tea.*

Over with some verbs suggests going from your house to somebody else's for a visit:

ask over	*drop over*	*come over*
invite over	*pop over*	

Considering, thinking about or examining: *I'd like to think over your offer.*

Over can be used with verbs that mean thinking about something carefully before you make a decision, or inspecting something to see if it is correct:

think over	*talk over*	*check over*
go over	*look over*	

Remaining: *She decided to stay over with her parents for a couple of days.*

Over can be used to convey the idea of something remaining in the same place or being kept to use at a later date:

stay over	*hold over*
be left over	*sleep over*

Changing position: *I drove first, then we changed over.*

Over can be used in combination with verbs suggesting the idea of two people or things changing places, jobs etc., or of a person changing their opinion or ideas:

take over	*swap over*	*win over*
change over	*hand over*	*swap over*

Falling: *I fell over and hurt my knee.*

Over can be used with verbs to express the idea of something falling to the ground, usually from an upright position:

fall over	*knock over*	*trip over*
keel over	*kick over*	*run over*

Finishing and recovering: *She's upset now, but she'll soon get over it.*

Over can be used in combinations that mean that something is temporary and will soon end:

blow over	*get over*	*get over with*

Communicating: *She is very good at putting over her ideas to an audience.*

Over can be used to convey the idea of giving somebody a message or a particular impression:

put over	*get over*	*come over*

Across can be used instead of over with these verbs with a very similar meaning.

Overflowing: *The crowd spilled over into the neighbouring streets.*

Over can be used in combinations that mean that something such as a liquid flows over the edge of a container. These verbs can also have a figurative meaning referring to very strong feelings.

boil over	*spill over*
brim over	*bubble over*

ROUND

The basic meaning of round is of movement in a circle or curve in order to face in the opposite direction or to arrive at the other side of something. It can sometimes be replaced by about and around with very little change of meaning.

Moving: *The kids ran round to keep warm.*
Round is used with some verbs to indicate movement in different directions:

move round	*run round*
hand round	*phone/call round*

Lack of activity and purpose: *We stood round, waiting for something to happen.*
Round can be used to suggest lack of activity or specific purpose:

stand round   *hang round*   *sit round*

Surrounding and enclosing: *He threw his arms round me.*
Round can be used to indicate that something is surrounded by something:

wrap round	*throw round*
go round	*gather round*

Being centred on something: *My whole life revolves round cooking and cleaning.*
Round can be used with a few verbs to indicate how something or somebody has a particular person or thing as the focus of their attention:

revolve round   *centre round*

Turning: *The car spun round several times and then hit a tree.*
Round is sometimes used in combinations with the idea of something turning in circles or turning to face the other way:

spin round   *swing round*   *wheel round*

Avoiding: *Politicians tend to skate round the issues.*
Round can be used with verbs to express the idea that you are avoiding something:

talk round   *skate round*

Persuading: *I managed to talk them round and they finally signed the contract.*
Round can be used with verbs to express the idea of persuading someone to change their minds about something:

talk round	*get round*
come round	*win round*

Visiting informally: *I'll drop round later and give you that book.*
Round is used with some verbs to indicate going to a particular place to visit a person briefly on an informal basis. Around is used with this meaning only in American English.

call round	*drop round*
pop round	*come round*

Sharing or distributing: *Could you hand round the sandwiches?*
Round in combinations can give the idea of sharing or distributing something between people:

hand round   *pass round*   *go round*

Recovering: *She came round a few hours after the operation.*
Round can be used with the idea of someone becoming conscious again or recovering from an illness:

come round   *bring round*   *pull round*

THROUGH

The basic meaning of through refers to passing from one side of something solid to the other side (for example, *go through a hole in a wall, see through a window*). It can be used with this meaning with many other verbs such as (*slice through, break through*).

Doing something thoroughly: *Can you look through this letter for me?*
Through can be used with verbs to give the idea of going from the beginning to the end of something and finishing it. The verb tells you what the activity is and how someone is doing it. It is often used to suggest doing something in a logical and thorough way and completing it.

look through	*rush through*
sit through	*read through*

Surviving, achieving: *She came through the operation and made a rapid recovery.*
Through can be used in combinations to express the idea of surviving a bad situation or getting past something difficult such as a test or a barrier:

live through	*come through*
get through	*pull through*

Communicating: *He won't listen to me. I can't get through to him.*

Through can be used in combinations that express the idea of communicating with somebody, for example by telephone:

put through   get through   fax through

Seeing clearly: *Her qualities shine through in everything she does.*

Through can be used with a few verbs to suggest that you can see or understand something or somebody very clearly:

see through   shine through   come through

TO

With verbs of movement, to expresses the idea of direction (for example walk to the office; fall to the ground).

Directing or aiming: *She devoted herself to her career.*

To used with verbs shows the direction that somebody or something is going or what is being aimed at:

gravitate to   devote to   gear to
pander to   point to

Showing relationships: *Who does this book belong to?*

To is used with verbs to indicate the relationship between people or things:

belong to   cling to   warm to
resort to   look up to   stick to

UP

The literal meaning of up is movement upwards, from a lower to a higher position, so it occurs with many verbs describing movement, such as *climb up, jump up, look up,* and *sit up.* It is also used with verbs of lifting to express the idea of raising something to a higher level (for example, *pick up, lift up, snatch up*). You will also find it used to express the related ideas of 'increase' and 'improvement'.

Increasing: *Gas is going up next week.*

Up is often used to give the idea of something increasing in volume, speed, price, strength, and reputation:

go up   speed up   turn up
grow up   build up   speak up

The opposite of the particle up is down, so these particles can be used in verbs that have opposite meanings. For example, the opposite of *turn up the heating* is *turn down the heating.*

Improving: *The year started badly but I think things are starting to look up.*

Up can be used to express the idea of things improving, such as the economy, your health or your knowledge:

look up   brush up   clear up
smarten up   cheer up   brighten up

Supporting: *I can back up what I said with figures.*

Up can be used to give the idea of providing support:

back up   shore up   speak up for
stand up for   bolster up   stick up for

Preparing: *You should warm up before exercising.*

Up is used with a group of verbs to give the idea of preparing for doing something:

draw up   set up   warm up
butter up   fix up   limber up

Creating and constructing: *She made up an excuse for being late.*

Up is also used to suggest creating, producing, inventing or constructing something, either physically or in your mind:

make up   dream up   build up
come up with   conjure up   put up

Completing and finishing: *We will have used up all our coal reserves by the end of the year.*

With some verbs that can be used on their own, up adds the idea of completing something:

end up   use up   wind up
dry up   dummy up   follow up

Damaging and destroying: *She tore up the letter and threw it in the bin.*

Up can be used to express the idea of something being damaged or spoilt in some way or not working well:

| tear up | blow up | mess up |
| beat up | play up | slip up |

Stopping, delaying and disrupting: *The police broke up the demonstration.*

Up can be used to give the idea of something stopping, being delayed or prevented from operating normally:

| break up | give up | pull up |
| hold up | slow up | |

Note that *slow up* and *slow down* have the same meaning.

Things happening: *A serious problem has come up.*

Up can be used to convey the idea of something happening or of something/somebody appearing, sometimes unexpectedly:

| turn up | come up | bring up |
| crop up | pop up | |

Approaching and getting closer for comfort: *I crept up behind her to surprise her.*

Up can be used to give the idea of something or somebody approaching or getting closer to somebody/something, sometimes in a rather secretive way, or for warmth and comfort:

| creep up | loom up | snuggle up |
| curl up | nuzzle up | sneak up |

Dividing and separating: *Slice up the tomatoes and add them to the mixture.*

Up can be used to give the idea of something being divided in some way, for example by being cut or chopped into small pieces. When it is used in connection with a group of people or a couple, it has the idea of separation.

| slice up | divide up | split up |
| break up | cut up | chop up |

Gathering and collecting: *Can you collect up the glasses?*

Up can be used with the idea of collecting things or people together:

| collect up | match up | stock up |
| team up | join up | meet up |

Fastening: *I tied up the parcel with string.*

Up can be used to talk about fastening things like clothes or objects. It can be used with the name of an object or a material to show how something is fastened, or with the name of a container to show where things are placed. Related to this is the idea of restricting the movement of somebody/something.

| do up | zip up | parcel up |
| tie up | brick up | lock up |

WITH

With is generally used to describe the connections and relationships between people, things, facts or situations.

Relationships between people: *My boyfriend wants to finish with me.*

With is used with verbs that describe relationships between people or the ending of a relationship:

| mess with | reason with | finish with |
| level with | trifle with | vie with |

Relationships between things

Verbs plus with often show connections between things, such as comparing, including, involving or separating:

| go with | crawl with | do away with |
| riddle with | square with | |

Relationships between people and things: *It's hard to deal with so many changes.*

With can be used to convey the idea of somebody taking action and getting involved in something, sometimes when they should not:

| deal with | wrestle with | juggle with |
| land with | lumber with | tamper with |

Giving support: *I don't agree with what you're saying.*

With is used with verbs that express the idea of agreeing with a person or an idea or providing support:

| agree with | side with |
| bear with | hold with |

Pronunciation

Phonetic symbols

Consonants

p	pen	h	how
b	bad	m	man
t	tea	n	no
d	did	ŋ	sing
k	cat	s	so
g	get	z	zoo
tʃ	chain	ʃ	she
dʒ	jam	ʒ	vision
f	fall	l	leg
v	van	r	red
θ	thin	j	yes
ð	this	w	wet

Vowels and diphthongs

iː	see	ɜː	fur
i	happy	ə	about
ɪ	sit	eɪ	say
e	ten	əʊ	go (*BrE*)
æ	cat	oʊ	go (*AmE*)
ɑː	father	aɪ	my
ɒ	got	ɔɪ	boy
ɔː	saw	aʊ	now
ʊ	put	ɪə	near
u	actual	eə	hair
uː	too	ʊə	pure
ʌ	cup		

The symbol /(r)/ indicates that British pronunciation will have /r/ only if a vowel sound follows directly at the beginning of the next word, as in **pore over**; otherwise /r/ is omitted. For Amercian English, all the /r/ sounds should be pronounced.

Stress in phrasal verbs

In speech it is important to use the correct stress patterns for phrasal verbs. To help with this, verbs are shown in this dictionary with stresses marked using the symbols / ' / (= a main stress) and / ˌ / (= a weaker secondary stress).

There are two patterns of stress in phrasal verbs. One type has a single stress, and it is always on the part of the phrase which is a verb. Examples are 'come to sth, 'go for sb, 'look at sth. The other type has two stresses; the first word is marked with a secondary stress, and a main stress is put on the particle. Examples are ˌget 'up, ˌput sth 'off, ˌgo 'off sth/sb.

One-stress verbs

One-stress phrasal verbs keep the single main stress on the verb in all situations. No stress is put on the particle or on any other words. Often the particle is a word such as **for** or **at** which has both strong and weak forms. Generally, the weak form of the word should be used, but if the particle comes at the end of a phrase, the strong form must be used, even though the word remains unstressed. For example: *The washing machine is broken. I'll have to get it 'looked at.* 'Look at is a one-stress verb so the main stress is on **looked** and there is no stress on **at**. But because **at** is at the end of a phrase it is pronounced in its strong form with vowel /æ/ and not /ə/.

Two-stress verbs

Two-stress phrasal verbs have the main stress on the particle, and this is the pattern that will be used when the verb as a whole is the last important item in a phrase.

What time are you ˌcoming 'back?
He ˌmade it 'up.
ˌFill them 'in.

But the speaker will put a strong stress on any other important word if it comes later than the verb. The stress on the particle is then weakened or lost, especially if it would otherwise be next to the other strong stress. For example in *I ˌcame back 'early*, the verb is ˌcome 'back , but in this sentence there is no main stress on **back** because it would clash with the stress on **early**.

In two-stress verbs with three words, such as ˌback a'way from, ˌaverage 'out at, the extra word helps to avoid a clash with a following stress and the weakening of the stress is optional. So you can say *It ˌaverages out at 'fifty*, with the stress on **out** weakened, or *It ˌaverages 'out at 'fifty*, in which the stress on **out** is kept. There is no difference of meaning between the two.

Stress on patterns with *doing*.

Some verbs are shown in the dictionary with forms that include **doing** (for example '*bank on sb/sth*, '*bank on doing sth*, '*bank on sb/sth doing sth*. Like **sb** and **sth**, the word **doing** is not part of the verb, but shows where another verb must be fitted into the pattern. For example: *He's banking on going to America.* The verbs with **doing** follow the same one-stress or two-stress patterns as other phrasal verbs. So the one-stress pattern '*bank on doing sth* shows that **on** never receives a stress. In a two-stress verb such as ˌput 'off doing sth, the stress on **off** will be lost if the -ing verb is important: *I'm ˌputting off 'writing to her.*

Key to the exercises

Recording phrasal verbs
(Suggested answer)
verb: mess around
meaning: to spend time and enjoy yourself with no particular purpose
example: We just messed around at home all day.

The position of objects
verb: head up sth
grammar code: v+adv+n, v+pron+adv
examples: She will head up the company/She will head it up.

Collocations
to find out information
to play down a problem
to work out a solution
to fill in a form
to phase in changes
to break off negotiations
to make up a story
to butt in on a conversation

Organizing by particles
entering: break into, get into, check into
changing: grow into, turn into, make into
persuading: talk into, pull into, draw into
investigating: look into, dig into, delve into

Organizing by topics
computers: log on; boot up; mouse over
feelings: get carried away; fall out; get on with
travel: take off; check in; touch down
crime: get away with; break into; track down

Organizing by opposites

pass out	come round
go away	come back
switch on	switch off
bring forward	put back
turn up	turn down
break up	get together

1 Up
1b Many people bring up their children to be well-mannered.
2c Students cheer up when their university exams are over.
3d Peter, hurry up or we'll miss the train.
4a Children grow up so fast and soon leave home.

1c Add up your expenses and give them to my secretary.
2a Hang up the phone – you've been talking for ages.
3d Give up chocolate if you want to get fit.
4b Wake up early if you want to get to work on time.

2 On
1c The professor carried on talking even though the seminar had finished.
2d The customer held on for several minutes then put the phone down.
3b My boss keeps on talking to me and interrupting my work.
4a The problem went on for months until we solved it.

3 Down
1 breaks
2 lets
3 turned
4 close

1 sit
2 keep
3 put
4 bend
5 lie

4 In
1 come in
2 check in
3 let in
4 breaks in

5 Off
1b Get off the bus at the next stop if you want the city centre.
2c Go off on holiday by yourself if you really want to relax.
3d Run off and play in the garden – you need some fresh air.
4a Set off early so you miss the traffic on the motorway.

6 Out
1 fall
2 getting
3 broken
4 came

7 Verbs with an adverb and a preposition
1 hang on to
2 looking forward to
3 run out of
4 put up with
5 get on with

Phrasal verb or single word?
1 set off
2 going up
3 got to
4 let us in
5 take our shoes off
6 went in
7 showed us round
8 came up
9 came back
10 laid on
11 asked for

Opposites
1c If we set off early, we'll get back before dark.
2e I decided to carry on with tennis and give up volleyball.
3d I put my bag down here. Did you pick it up by mistake?
4b You've been lying down all day. Get up and do something.
5a Take your jumper off and put a T-shirt on.

Multi-meaning verbs

1 catch up
2 fall out
3 takes off
4 give up
5 pick her up
6 come out
7 meet up

Page S10

Using the dictionary

formal	provide for sth
	attend to sb/sth
	dispense with sb/sth
	safeguard against sth
informal	boot sb out
	barge into sb
	bounce around
	hash sth over
neutral	turn up
	throw sth aside
	put sb up
	fade away

Page S11

Phrasal verbs in informal language

1 level with you
2 chickened out
3 check it out
4 rustle something up
5 whipped through
6 freak me out
7 cotton on
8 clammed up
9 cracks me up
10 thrown it together

Page S12

Phrasal verbs in emails

hear from
swot up
mess up
beaver away
veg out
breeze through
swanning around
muck around
look sb up
catch up with

1 beaver away
2 swot up
3 swan around
4 mess up
5 look sb up
6 catch up

7 muck around
8 breeze through (sth)
9 veg out

Page S13

Phrasal verbs in essays

1 These figures refer to the years 1960 to 1989.
2 The rise can be attributed to changes in living standards.
3 It should be pointed out that no action was ever taken.
4 I shall now sum up the main points we have examined.
5 I shall deal with each point individually.
6 How can we account for why this happened?
7 The statistics do not bear out the conclusion reached by others.

Phrasal verbs in business

1	b	5	b
2	c	6	c
3	a	7	c
4	a	8	a

Page S14

Phrasal verbs in reports

1 refers to
2 reported back
3 summed up
4 drawn up
5 gone through
6 puts forward
7 sets out
8 consists of
9 enlarges upon
10 accounts for
11 deals with

Page S15

Computers

Down
1 click on
2 pull-down
3 switch on
4 printout
6 shut down
7 scan in
9 back up
10 boot up
11 log in

Across
5 add-ons
8 hack into
12 go down
13 scroll down
14 type in
15 pop-up

Page S16

The environment
The greenhouse effect

1 Greenhouse gases are given off when fossil fuels are burned.
2 These greenhouse gases soak up heat that should escape into space.
3 This pushes up temperatures on earth.

Algae

1 Nitrates from fertilizers soak into the soil and end up in rivers and lakes.
2 Algae feed on the nitrates and multiply uncontrollably.
3 The algae use up the oxygen in the water, and fish die.

Deforestation

1 Humans burn or cut down too many trees.
2 Some areas turn into desert.
3 Some species die out because they have lost their habitat.

Page S17

Business

1888	catches on, take on
1902	teams up with, set up, sell off
1906	turning out
1945	takes over
1960	take off, bringing in
1969	buys up
1974	walk out, sparking off
1989	worn away, falling off, mount up, go under, bailed out
1999	takes over, caught out, shoots up, wind up
2000	laid off, closes down

Page S18

Sport

Football, and tonight's match in the European Cup ended in controversy after Italy came back from 2–0 down to beat Spain. At 2–2, the Italian goalkeeper Alberti appeared to bring down Rojas, the Spanish centre forward. As the Spanish players appealed for a penalty, the Italians played on and broke away to score. The Spanish captain Martín was then sent off for arguing with the referee. Italy ended up fortunate winners, but their goalkeeper Pollo picked up a hand injury and has been ruled out of the next two games.

The Tokyo marathon has been won by Takeshi Saito of Japan. Urged on by the home crowd, Saito forged ahead after just 5 kilometres and built up a 2-minute lead. The chasing runners did not give up, and gradually reduced the lead. The hot weather and the fast pace caused several leading athletes to drop out. Saito's recent training in the Sahara desert paid off as he held off the strong challenge of the Kenyan Daniel Nyanga, who caught up with 5 kilometres to go, then fell back in the final kilometre.

Tennis, and the unseeded Sofia Adamou of Greece has beaten Russia's Irena Markova in three sets to go through to the final of the French Open. Adamou said afterwards, "I've never come up against such a tough opponent. Before I came here I thought I'd get knocked out in the first round, but now I've got a chance of winning." Adamou, who only took up the sport four years ago, will pick up a cheque for $100 000. The loser will have to settle for just $50 000!

Pages S19-20

1 New verbs from nouns or adjectives.

1 flagged
2 ice
3 glam
4 tear
5 mouse

2 Modern life

Internet	click through
	dial-up
telecoms	charge sth up
	top-up
business	roll sth out
	spin-out
music	crossover
	lay sth down
military	armoured-up
	stand sb/sth down

3 Figurative meanings

1 chewed up
2 hauled in
3 buttoned up
4 landed on her
5 gave away
6 lock in

4 New particles

1 similar
2 similar
3 opposite
4 similar
5 opposite
6 similar
7 similar
8 opposite
9 similar
10 similar

Pages S21-22

Synonyms

A	B
invite sb out	ask sb out
fork out	shell out
egg sb on	urge sb on
think sth over	mull sth over
cheer sth up	liven sth up
pare sth down	cut sth back
knock sb down	run sb over

Opposites

	A	B
1	breathe in	breathe out
2	connect sth	disconnect sth
3	do sth up	undo sth
4	go out	stay in
5	let sth out	hold sth in

6 take sth   put sth
   apart   together
7 blow sth up   let sth down

1 I unplugged the DVD player.
2 The price of coffee has gone up again.
3 The scandal died down after the report came out.
4 I checked out of the clinic yesterday.
5 I need to take in this skirt a little.
6 She unbuttoned her jacket.

Pull through

1 healed up/healed
2 Get well
3 recover
4 pulled through
5 getting better

Look up to sb

1 respect
2 admired
3 looked up to
4 think highly of her

Choosing the best word

1 My olive tree has grown a lot since last year.
2 I got out of the car and started to walk.
3 I'll call you/phone you/ring you/telephone you/give you a call/give you a ring as soon as I arrive in Inverness.
4 Support for these proposals has waned/ebbed/ebbed away.
5 What time do you knock off work?
6 I'm sorry, I didn't catch/hear your name.
7 I watched a film, then went to bed.
8 I shuffled the cards then dealt seven to each player.